SPECIAL EDITION

# USING

Microsoft® Office

# Excel® 2007

*Bill Jelen, MrExcel*

800 East 96th Street
Indianapolis, Indiana 46240

# SPECIAL EDITION USING MICROSOFT® OFFICE EXCEL® 2007

International Standard Book Number: 0-7897-3611-X

CIP data available upon request

Printed in the United States of America

First Printing: December 2006

09  08  07  06        4  3  2  1

## Trademarks

## Warning and Disclaimer

## Bulk Sales

Que Publishing offers excellent discounts on this book when ordered in quantity for bulk purchases or special sales. For more information, please contact

**U.S. Corporate and Government Sales**
**1-800-382-3419**
**corpsales@pearsontechgroup.com**

For sales outside of the U.S., please contact

**International Sales**
**international@pearsoned.com**

**Associate Publisher**
Greg Wiegand

**Acquisitions Editor**
Loretta Yates

**Senior Development Editor**
Rick Kughen

**Managing Editor**
Gina Kanouse

**Project Editor**
Michael Thurston

**Copy Editor**
Kitty Jarrett

**Indexer**
Lisa Stumpf

**Proofreader**
Leslie Joseph

**Technical Editor**
Juan Pablo Gonzalez

**Publishing Coordinator**
Cindy Teeters

**Multimedia Developer**
Dan Scherf

**Interior Designer**
Anne Jones

**Cover Designer**
Anne Jones

**Page Layout**
Bronkella Publishing LLC
Nonie Ratcliff
TNT Design, Inc.

# CONTENTS

**III** Working in a Legacy Environment

**IV** Calculating with Excel

# About the Author

**Bill Jelen**, Excel MVP and MrExcel, has been using spreadsheets since 1985, and he launched the MrExcel.com website in 1998. His team provides custom Excel applications to clients around the world. You can see Bill as a regular guest on *Call for Help* with Leo Laporte in Australia, in Canada, and on Google Video. Bill produces a daily video podcast about Excel. He also enjoys taking his show on the road, doing a one- to four-hour power Excel seminar anywhere that a room full of accountants or Excellers will show up.

# DEDICATION

*To Mary Ellen Jelen*

# ACKNOWLEDGMENTS

Microsoft Excel 2007 is really an amazing new version. Thanks to Dave Gainer and his team for thinking outside the box and for 1.1 million rows. Both Dave Gainer and Jensen Harris were generous with their time, answering questions during the development of this book.

Thanks to Dan Bricklin and Bob Frankston for inventing the computer spreadsheet. Thanks to Mitch Kapor for Lotus 1-2-3. Like everyone else who uses computers to make a living, I owe a debt of gratitude to these three pioneers.

I've learned that when writing a 1,000-page book, there is not much time for anything else. Thanks to Lora White, Tracy Syrstad, and Barb Jelen for keeping MrExcel running while I wrote. As always, thanks to the hundreds of people answering 30,000 Excel questions a year at the MrExcel message board. Thanks to Duane Aubin, Wei Jiang, Suat Ozgur, Nate Oliver, and Jake Hildebrand for their programming expertise.

I am usually fairly involved in my community. For the past several months, I have shirked my responsibilities to the Lake Chamber of Commerce, the Relay for Life, and the Lake Rotary. Thanks to all the Rotarians for putting up with what had to be the worst presidency in the history of the club. Thanks to Bob Testa.

Several people pulled me out of a jam while writing this book. When no one at Microsoft could identify a single useful reason for DOUBLEFACT, Dwayne Kuemper pointed out that it could be used to calculate Texas Hold 'Em Probabilities. (And to whoever added DOUBLEFACT to some spreadsheet package 20 years ago, thanks for being prescient enough to know that Texas Hold 'Em would someday dominate one and half cable TV channels.) Gary Roderick gave me a great lesson on which financial functions really matter. Everything that Martin Quinn writes about using Excel for quantum chemistry is above my head, yet I thank him for explaining some of the higher-order math functions in a way I could understand. Mark Ospeck provided math assistance. My brother Bob Jelen provided Mark's phone number and humor during this process. Jerry Holloway is a constant friend who put up with statistical questions and musings.

This was a great year to be a part of the MVP program. Thanks to Michael Fosmire and Suzanna Moran for making this an excellent program for Excel MVPs. Jan Shanahan at Microsoft also takes great care of the authors and publishers.

At Pearson, Loretta Yates is an awesome acquisitions editor. She will go to bat for me on the important issues and tell me to deal with the ones I need to deal with. If you have ever written a book for any other publisher, you are missing out by not working with Loretta Yates. Greg Wiegand is probably the guy responsible for assigning my name to this book, and I appreciate the vote of confidence. Judi Taylor makes sure that you hear about the book. Thanks to Judi. Michael Thurston and Rick Kughen have been patient while shepherding the book through production. Copyeditor Kitty Jarrett, where were you during my high school English classes? Thanks to my agent, William Brown. Juan Pablo Gonzalez is the best technical editor anyone could ever want.

To everyone at Rogers Media and *Call for Help*, thanks for allowing me to continue to be the Excel correspondent. Thanks to Leo Laporte, Amber MacArthur, Katya Diakow, Mohit Rajans, Matt Harris, Steve Antal, Mike Lazazzera, Doug Robertson, Gregory Pilsworth, Sean Carruthers, Basil Coward, Aaren Perrier, Lorraine Quirk, Hayden Mindell, Kelly Colasanti, and Malcolm Dunlop. Thanks to Craig Crossman and everyone at the Computer America radio show.

Podcasting is the wave of the future. Thanks to Leo Laporte for suggesting the MrExcel podcast, and thanks to Lora White for actually making sure a podcast gets edited and posted five days a week.

Thanks to some early computing influences: Carl Bevington, Khalil Matta, Gary Kern, and Hector Guerrero. Thanks to my friend and client Jerry Kohl. Your ideas about how to make Excel sing are fantastic.

Thanks to Roy Bittan, Max Weinberg, Clarence Clemmons, Danny Federici, Garry Tallent, Steve Van Zandt, and Bruce Springsteen. iTunes indicates that it required 106 playings of *Born to Run* and 135 playings of the *Born to Run* 30th-anniversary podcast in order to complete this book. Maybe I should buy *Darkness on the Edge of Town* before writing *Special Edition Using Excel 14*....

Keeping the MrExcel name proud in Toronto are the 'Cellers softball team. Thanks to Matt, Doug, Denise, Rahul, Cat, Big Dog, The Rick, Michelle, Jono, Lori, Jeff, Scoop, Laurie, Jen, Johnny T, Andy, and Shari.

Finally, thanks to Josh Jelen, Zeke Jelen, and Mary Ellen Jelen. It is cool to work at home, but that means that I am always at work. There were weeks where "let me check on this chapter" turned into the entire evening. Thanks for your patience during 2006.

# WE WANT TO HEAR FROM YOU!

As the reader of this book, *you* are our most important critic and commentator. We value your opinion and want to know what we're doing right, what we could do better, what areas you'd like to see us publish in, and any other words of wisdom you're willing to pass our way.

As an associate publisher for Que Publishing, I welcome your comments. You can email or write me directly to let me know what you did or didn't like about this book—as well as what we can do to make our books better.

*Please note that I cannot help you with technical problems related to the topic of this book. We do have a User Services group, however, where I will forward specific technical questions related to the book.*

When you write, please be sure to include this book's title and author as well as your name, email address, and phone number. I will carefully review your comments and share them with the author and editors who worked on the book.

Email:      feedback@quepublishing.com

Mail:       Greg Wiegand
            Associate Publisher
            Que Publishing
            800 East 96th Street
            Indianapolis, IN 46240 USA

# READER SERVICES

Visit our website and register this book at www.quepublishing.com/register for convenient access to any updates, downloads, or errata that might be available for this book.

# INTRODUCTION

## In this introduction

I get to play the role of comic book superhero. As the "mighty man of macro," I take the stage and wow people with the amazing things they can do in Excel. In small teaching settings, I ask everyone to answer the most pointless question: "What version of Excel are you using?"

Why is this a pointless question? Because it simply does not matter. If the answer is any version of Excel that has come out in the past decade—going back to Excel 97—then every tip I have to share will work.

Microsoft has asked us to upgrade from Excel 97 to 2000, 2000 to XP, and XP to 2003, all without giving Excel fans much new content. Yes, they changed the PivotTable Wizard in Excel 2000, added function tips in XP, and began to support XML in 2003. But there was really nothing new.

I have long theorized that once Microsoft had driven a stake through the heart of Lotus 1-2-3, there was simply no need to innovate. Today, Microsoft is aware that Star Office is becoming a credible threat, and the Excel development team has responded with a vengeance.

# Jaw-Dropping New Excel Features

Excel 2007 is a complete rewrite of the program. The new feature set is amazing. You can now do far more with Excel and do it far faster than ever before. The following sections describe just a few of the new features of Excel 2007.

## The Massive Grid

For the past decade, we've dealt with 65,536 rows by 255 columns on a worksheet. 16.7 million cells sounds like a lot, but it is amazing how many times people encounter a dataset with 70,000 rows or 300 columns. Excel was almost big enough, but not quite. For many people, Access was only used as a product of desperation when they had more rows than Excel could accommodate.

A few years ago, I was able to spend a few hours with the Microsoft Excel project managers. They revealed that they were thinking of adding more rows and asked what I thought would be a reasonable figure. I remember telling them that if they didn't at least double the rows— going to at least 131,072—the increase would not be impressive. They also let on that many people wanted to have three years of daily dates plus totals stretching across the columns. I walked away from that meeting predicting a new grid of 131,000 rows by 1,024 columns.

At the MVP Summit in September 2005, Microsoft gave us the first look at the new version of Excel. I was blown away by the size of the grid: 1,048,576 rows by 16,384 columns. That is more than 17 billion cells on one worksheet! I was sitting next to Ken Wright, an Excel MVP from England. In his British accent, Ken dryly quipped, "...and if we fill that up, we could always just go to Sheet2."

The enormity of 17 billion cells is staggering. There is not a PC you could buy today that would hold 17 billion formulas. Microsoft has truly come out with a new file format that will last for the next 10 to 15 years. I am sure that by the time Excel 15 comes out, everyone will think it is commonplace to load up a half million records of transactional data.

To help you picture the situation, Figure I.1 contains an XY chart. The solid black rectangle in the upper-left corner is the relative size of Excel 2003. The large white square that makes up the rest of the chart is the relative size of Excel 2007. For a decade, you've been living in a tiny patch of real estate, and now the bounds are nearly endless.

To learn more about the Big Grid, see Chapter 7.

Relative size of Excel 2003          Relative size of Excel 2007

**Figure I.1**
The tiny black rectangle is the size of the old Excel compared to the new Excel.

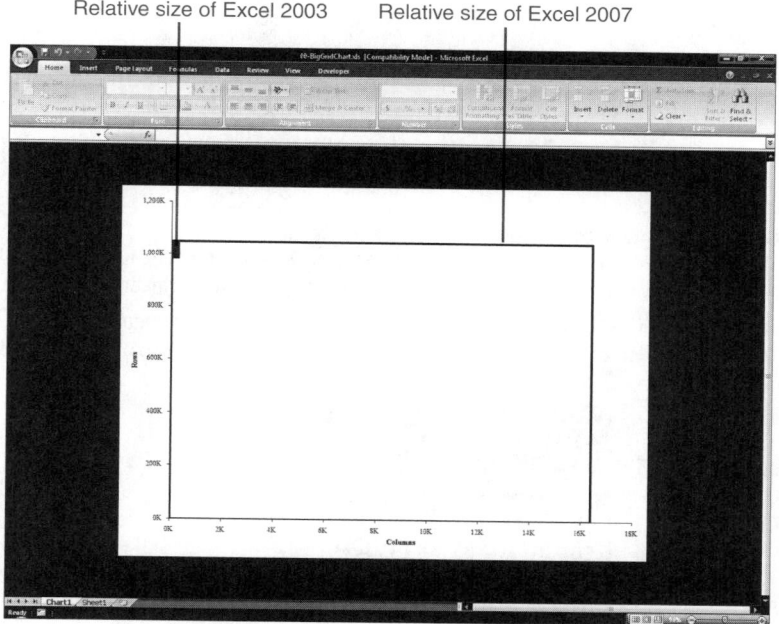

## FANTASTIC DATA VISUALIZATIONS

Excel 97 introduced conditional formatting. It was hard to use. A number of gotchas made it hard to figure out whether your conditional formatting was really working. When you figured out how to successfully set up conditional formatting, the feature was limited to three conditions. I eventually dropped this out of my power Excel seminar: It was too obscure, too hard, and not worth the effort to try to teach it.

Conditional formatting gets a complete makeover in Excel 2007. You now have one-click access to gradients, heat maps, and in-cell data bars. Managers' eyes tend to glaze over when they are presented with a table of numbers. Add a full-color data visualization, and the meaning of a table can spring to life, as shown in Figure I.2. For more about data visualization, see Chapter 9.

**Figure I.2**
Just a few clicks can create this heat map. While heat maps can measure any numeric range, this one ironically measures temperature.

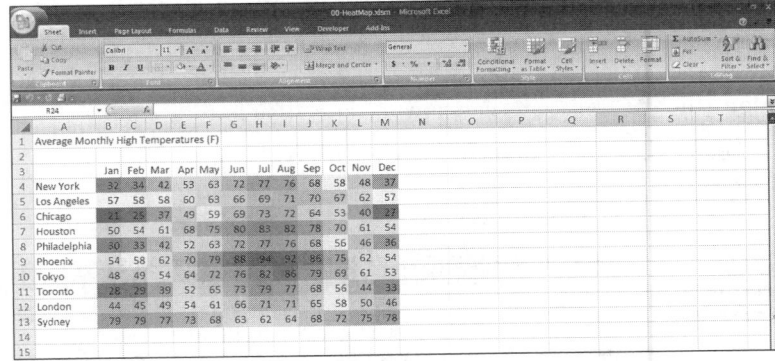

### Case Study: Backward Functionality Compatibility

The new data visualizations are designed to bring conditional formatting to the masses. What if you were one of the people who had taken the time to learn the old conditional formatting system?

Figure I.3 shows the Excel 2003 method for highlighting all rows that are above average in a range. Finding the Formula Is version of the conditional formatting dialog was beyond 99% of the Excel customers.

**Figure I.3**
Figuring out conditional formatting in Excel 2003 was difficult.

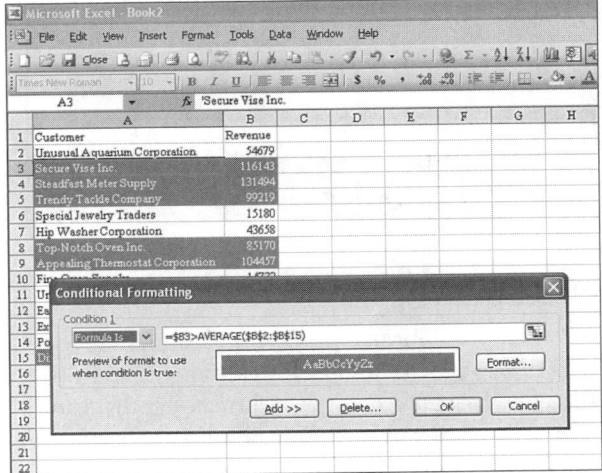

Excel 2007 provides options to highlight cells that are above average with just a few mouse clicks. A novice Excel customer could nearly duplicate Figure I.3 by selecting Home, Conditional Formatting, Top/Bottom Rules, Above Average, as shown in Figure I.4.

However, if you are a power user and still want to build conditional formatting the old way, you are more than welcome to. Near the bottom of each icon is a More Rules selection that takes you back to the familiar dialog boxes from prior versions of Excel. The new conditional formatting dialog, shown in Figure I.5, is not exactly like the old version shown in Figure I.3, but after you select the intuitive words Use a Formula to Determine Which Cells to Format, you are back in familiar territory.

**Figure I.4**
Conditional formatting is now just a few clicks away.

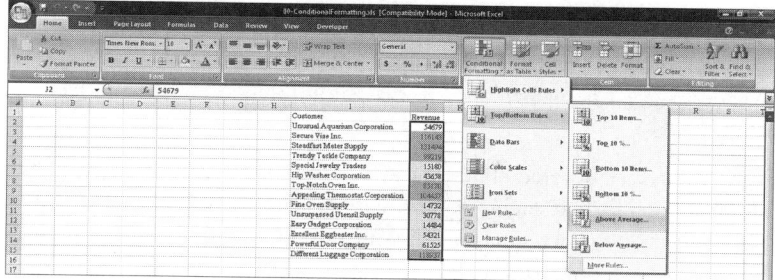

**Figure I.5**
You can do old-style conditional formatting in the new dialog.

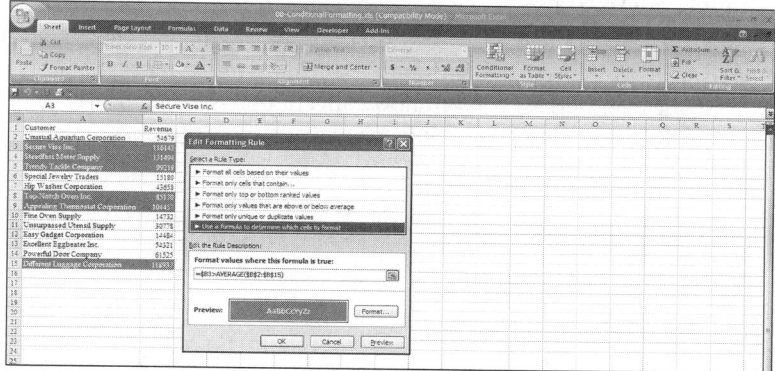

Power users should be relieved that they can easily get back to their familiar dialog boxes.

Look for the arrow icon in the bottom-right corner of many groups on the ribbon (you'll learn more about ribbons later in this Introduction). Clicking this icon is the fast shortcut back to the old-style dialog box, which is shown in Figure I.6.

**Figure I.6**
You can click the expand icon in the lower right corner of most groups' + sign in the triangle to access the old-style dialog boxes.

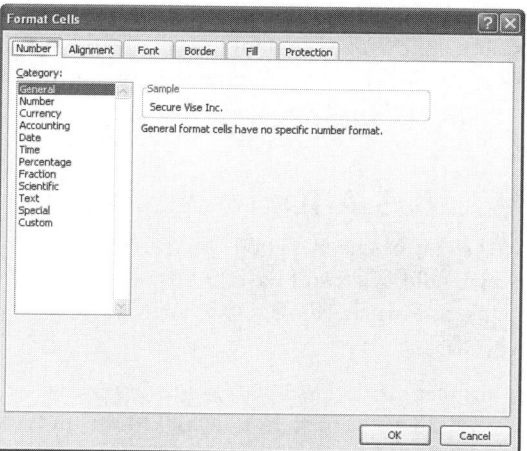

### TWENTY-FIRST CENTURY CHARTING

The charting in Excel 2003 is antique. It really had not changed in 15 years. Microsoft has provided a great new charting and diagramming engine and applied it to all Office 2007 components.

Features such as beveled edges, glow, and metallic bars are now just a click away. Rather than trying to format each element, you can simply hover over any of the 20 prepackaged themes to create charts that match your corporate color scheme and other designs. For more about charting, see Chapter 15.

### BUSINESS INTELLIGENCE

Excel 2007 has a new, easier-to-use interface for the pivot table engine. You can now quickly apply data visualizations to a pivot table. In addition, if you regularly build pivot tables from OLAP cube datasources, you can now convert a pivot table into a range of high-powered formulas that will query certain dimensions of the cube. For more about Business Intelligence, see Chapter 10.

### EASIER-TO-ENTER FORMULAS AND FUNCTIONS

Anyone who dabbled with the VBA programming language in Excel has enjoyed the AutoComplete functionality in VBA for several versions of Excel. This technology now comes to the user interface side of Excel, with AutoComplete technology guiding you through the entry of functions and formulas. For more about tables and easier formulas, see Chapter 8.

All the functions formerly housed in the Analysis ToolPack have now been promoted to full-fledged members of the Excel family. It was frustrating to find a cool function in the Analysis ToolPack but not know whether someone in your recipient list had failed to enable this add-in.

Excel 2007 replaces the Excel 2003 list functionality with new table functionality. This powerful option renders obsolete the need to double-click the fill handle to copy formulas. It also makes the concept of English-language formulas automatic for formulas next to a table.

## WHERE ARE MY MENUS AND TOOLBARS?

Everything we've discussed so far has been a good change. The grid size is amazing. The ease of use is amazing. So why did Microsoft have to drop the other shoe and remove the familiar File, Edit, View, Insert, Format, Tools, Data, Window, and Help menus from the top of the Excel window?

This is the single biggest problem with Excel 2007. I guarantee that by the time Excel 14 or Excel 15 rolls around, you will love it, but right now, right here, in the next two weeks, you will curse Microsoft more than you have ever cursed Microsoft.

The menu, toolbars, and task pane have been completely removed from Excel 2007.

Stop. Read that again.

The menu, toolbars, and task pane have been completely removed from Excel 2007.

If you are an intermediate Excel user, this change means that all the toolbar functionality you use everyday has been removed. This is a shocking change. It will take you a couple weeks to get used to it. Chapters 1 through 6 will cover this change in detail.

Although you won't like it at first, it might help to understand why Microsoft had to do away with the old system.

## WHY COULDN'T THEY LEAVE WELL ENOUGH ALONE?

Figure I.7 shows a screenshot of Word for Windows 1.0 from 1989. There were 2 toolbars, sporting a total of 26 icons.

**Figure I.7**
Word 1.0 featured 26 icons on two toolbars.

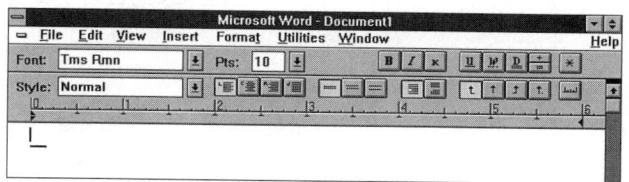

Word 2.0 in 1992 grew slightly, to 37 icons on 2 toolbars. By 1994, the common screen resolution had jumped from 640×480 to 800×600, and the number of toolbars had grown to eight. Context (right-click) menus were added. The icons were so confusing that Microsoft added ToolTips to each toolbar. Plus, Microsoft let you opt out of toolbars altogether with the new context menus.

Word 95 had nine toolbars. Word 97 had 18 toolbars and introduced cascading menus; there were too many commands to fit on a single list of menus, so you had to go searching through fly-out menus that populated each toolbar.

As new functionality was added, the number of toolbars continued to grow. A whole new feature called the task pane was introduced in Excel 2002. Microsoft was now using the top, bottom, and right edges of the screen to try to shoehorn in all the features.

Excel 2003 had 1,223 commands on 127 commandbars. If you tried to display them all at once, you would not be able to see the Excel grid at all, as shown in Figure I.8.

**Figure I.8**
By Excel 2003, the number of toolbars had grown out of control.

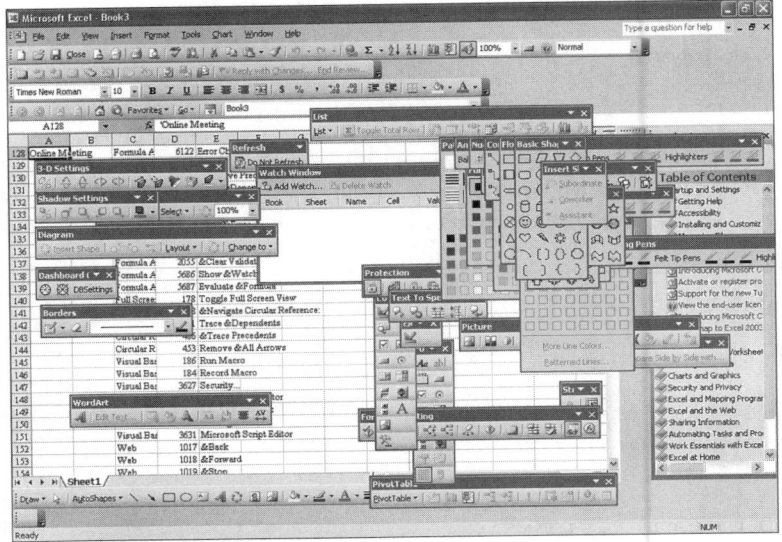

Furthermore, by Excel 2003, a lot of the toolbars were somewhat unpredictable. The Drawing toolbar was usually displayed at the bottom of the screen, but it could be moved anywhere on a particular computer. The List toolbar in Excel 2003 tended to come and go, without any rhyme or reason. Some toolbars would hang around long after they were needed (for example, there is no need to have the Picture toolbar displayed if there is not a picture on the worksheet, but Excel 2003 didn't seem to know that). Some crazy add-in on my computer kept disabling the PivotTable toolbar, which meant I wrote a couple lines of VBA to get it back every time I wanted to create a pivot table.

Microsoft figured that if it didn't make some sort of big change, this problem would only get worse in Excel 2007, Excel 14, Excel 15, and so on. Jensen Harris at Microsoft had predicted that there would be more than 100 different task panes shipping with Office 2007. Microsoft was, as always, intent on making the software more feature rich, but there was no real estate left in order to add these commands.

## THE MOST REQUESTED NEW FEATURES...

Microsoft conducts many usability studies. It visits companies, watches people use Office, and then asks them what new features would make their jobs easier. The common thread: People asked for features that had been added in Excel 97. But no one could find them.

Imagine how frustrated you would be if your boss walked in and asked you to produce the XYZ report. You would respond for the 400 millionth time, "I already gave you that report!" The boss would keep repeating this routine every day for 10 years. Very frustrating, indeed.

I can judge audience reaction in my seminars by the gasps. If I hear a gasp, it means that someone in the audience has been wasting hours each day and will be able to reduce that to a button click tomorrow at work. The "gasp" items—for example, automatic subtotals, the fill handle—were all added 10 years ago. The people in my seminars aren't stupid. There is clearly a problem when the average Joe can't find the features that are in Excel.

Microsoft would win big if it could allow people to actually find the powerful features that it added a decade ago. For a whole generation of beginning to intermediate users, all the power in Excel would suddenly be "new to you."

## A SCIENTIFIC APPROACH TO POPULAR FEATURES

Do you remember when Office introduced adaptive menus back in Excel 2000? The idea was that the menus had become too complex, so they would show you only the most popular menu items.

Do you have any idea how Microsoft decided what was most popular? It guessed. But it failed miserably.

A couple days after you installed Office 2003, an innocuous message would pop up, asking "Would You Like to Help Make Office Better?" If you chose Yes, Office collected information about how you selected commands—which toolbar buttons you pressed and in what order, whether you pasted by right-clicking or by pressing Ctrl+V? Since Office 2003 shipped, Microsoft has collected information on 1.3 billion sessions. Externally, this is called the Customer Experience Improvement Program. Internally, it is Service Quality Monitoring (SQM). The data from this program is SQM (pronounced "skwim") data. This is a fantastic amount of information about how real people use the software in real-life situations.

One interesting example is that power users had a hunch that everyone pasted by using Ctrl+V or by using the right-click context menu. There was a move to remove the Paste icon from the ribbon. In response to this hunch, someone pulled out the SQM data. Despite there being much faster ways to execute a paste, the toolbar button for paste was the most-used button in all of Office! Rather than rely on a hunch and remove the Paste button, Microsoft has vast amounts of statistical data and knew which were the most popular commands.

Here's another example: The Superscript button isn't even installed on the Formatting tool-bar in Word 2003. A person has to customize the toolbar to add the icon. However, this customized button is used more frequently than 30% of the default buttons on the Formatting toolbar.

When you understand that Microsoft wasn't just being capricious in selecting the toolbar icons to use, the removal of the well-known top-level menus starts to make a lot more sense.

Let's look at an example that affects Excel customers. Figure I.9 shows a typical dataset in Excel 2003. One column holds free-form text, so it ends up being too wide.

**Figure I.9**
Column D is too wide.

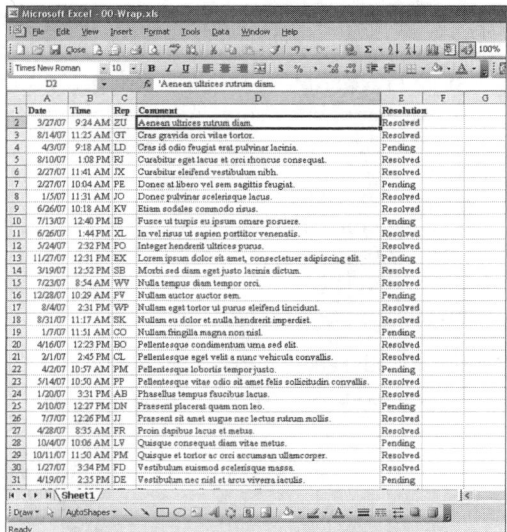

My usual tack in such a situation is to select Column D, turn on Word Wrap, and make the column narrower. As shown in Figure I.10, that fixes Column D, but then all the other columns have problems because I really want the words lined up with the top of each cell.

**Figure I.10**
Word Wrap is fine, but now all the other columns are bottom-justified, and they don't line up with the top of the paragraphs in Column D.

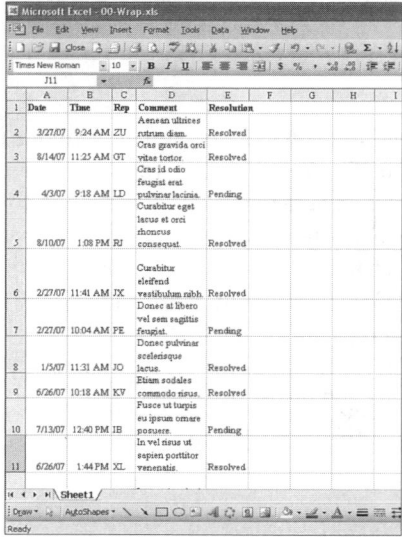

To fix the problems that now exist in this example, I could select all cells and then choose Format, Cells, Alignment; change the vertical alignment to Top; and then click OK. I know most of the keyboard shortcuts, so I can accomplish all this with 19 keystrokes and two trips to the Format Cells dialog box. I've never complained about this. It is just the way I had to do it in Excel 2003. I bet that you've repeated these steps a few times in your career.

Well, a lot of people sending SQM data to Microsoft must have been having exactly the same problem! As shown in Figure I.11, Excel 2007 now has a group on the ribbon that contains an icon for Wrap Text as well as an icon for top vertical alignment. On the face of it, this is not a big thing. But it means I can fix the problem described earlier with 2 clicks instead of 19 keystrokes. This type of change will really make me hate going back to Excel 2003 every time I have to handle data there.

**Figure I.11**
Excel 2007 lets you handle the text wrapping and alignment task without ever touching a dialog box.

Top Vertical Alignment          Wrap Text

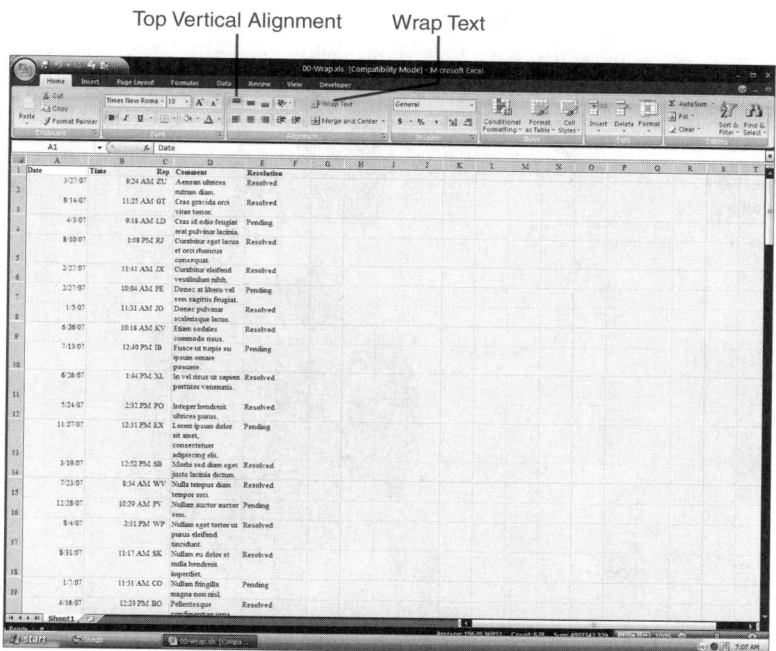

Clearly, enough people had SQM data turned on and had the same problem I had. Microsoft was able to detect that probably a million people were feeling the same pain on this issue, so it made life far easier for all Excel customers.

So although the initial reaction is to complain that Microsoft took away the old toolbars and menu, you need to stay calm and give the new design a chance. You will come to appreciate the thought (and data analysis) that was put into the decisions.

# INTRODUCING THE RIBBON

Instead of the menus and Standard and Formatting toolbars, Excel now has the ribbon. The ribbon is designed based on the thought that most people are using 1,280×1,024, or even 1,024×768, monitors. Instead of being a meaningless array of tiny icons, the ribbon uses lots of words and icons. Instead of being a single horizontal row of icons, the ribbon supports a two-dimensional layout of icons. Really popular features are large icons. Other functions can be grouped into related groups of icons.

The ribbon is tall, but it is no taller than the old setup, with the menus and the Standard and Formatting toolbars. Furthermore, you can completely hide the ribbon by pressing Ctrl+F1.

Although only one ribbon is visible at a time, there are actually seven ribbons available all the time: Home, Insert, Page Layout, Formulas, Data, Review and View. The most important stuff is on the left-most ribbon, so when you are looking for something, you should start there.

Depending on what is selected, more ribbon options appear. When you are adding a new business graphic (SmartArt), two new ribbons appear for SmartArt tools —Design and Format—as shown in Figure I.12. These ribbons appear only when the graphic is selected. When you go back to selecting a cell in your worksheet, the extra ribbons disappear.

**Figure I.12**
Two new ribbons appear anytime a SmartArt graphic is selected.

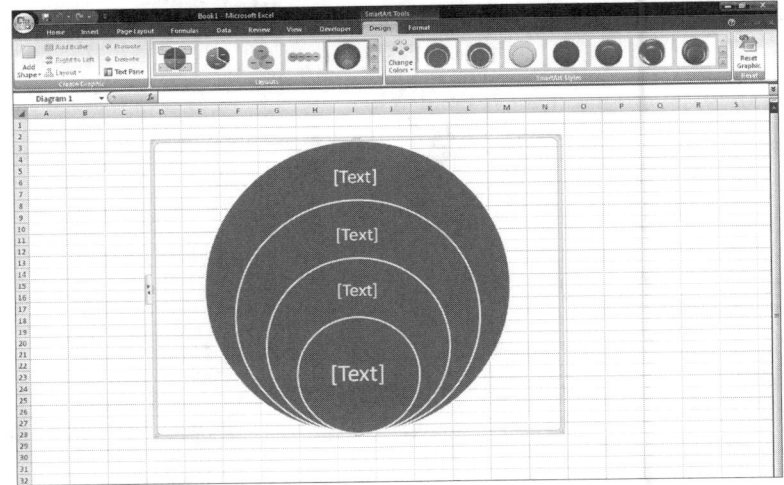

Extra ribbons appear for pivot tables, charts, pictures, and so on. In each case, the ribbon appears only as long as the pivot table, chart, picture, and so on is selected. As shown in Figure I.13, the Picture Tools ribbon offers functionality that is light-years ahead of previous versions of Excel, but it is not in the way until you actually insert a picture in your worksheet.

## RIBBON LIMITATIONS

The ribbon is always at the top. In recent versions of Excel, you could have toolbars docked at the bottom, the sides, or floating over your document. This functionality is no more. The ribbon is permanently at the top.

In previous versions of Excel, you could create a new custom toolbar with your favorite icons and have it floating over your document. This functionality is no more. There now is a Quick Access toolbar where you can add your favorite icons, but this toolbar is always at the top of the screen, either immediately below or immediately above the ribbon.

## RIBBON TRICKS

As you resize the Excel window, the ribbon becomes progressively more compact, but it does this intelligently. Figure I.14 shows the Home ribbon at a full 1,280 width. Figures I.15 and I.16 show the Home ribbon at progressively smaller window sizes. Even at a tiny window size, Excel still tries to intelligently group the major icons on the ribbon into a logical sequence, as shown in Figure I.17.

**Figure I.13**
The temporary ribbons often provide incredibly powerful tools.

**Figure I.14**
The Home ribbon at full size shows every icon.

**Figure I.15**
Initially, some groups become smaller. Notice that the Cells group now has three small icons.

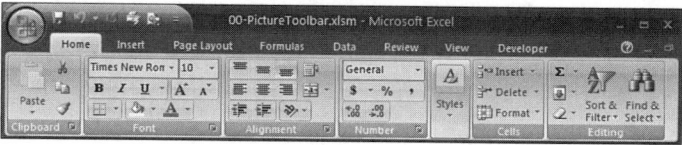

**Figure I.16**
The Quick Formatting and Cells groups now become drop-down icons to the entire toolsets.

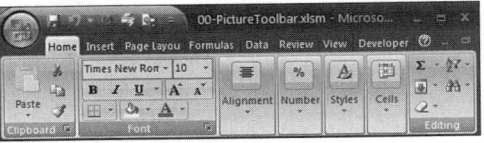

**Figure I.17**
Eventually, most groups become drop-down icons.

It is interesting to note that even as the icons get smaller, Microsoft opted to keep words and pictures for the icons. It has realized that people don't learn or remember the functionality based on a single 16×16 unlabeled icon. Learn more about the ribbon in Chapter 1.

## THE MINI TOOLBAR

If you were lucky enough to use Outlook 2003, you know that Microsoft added one really cool feature to that version. When a new email arrives in Outlook 2003, a small rectangle appears in the lower-right corner of your screen. The rectangle fades into view and lists the sender of the email and the first few sentences of the message. If you move your mouse toward the rectangle, it becomes solid and stays around. You can use quick icons to instantly delete or open the email. However, if you ignore the rectangle and just keep working in the other application, the rectangle quickly fades away.

Microsoft has added this feature to Excel 2007. It is sort of like popping up a context menu, except you don't have to right-click. The Mini Toolbar occasionally appears just above the active cell. If you move your mouse toward the Mini Toolbar, it solidifies and hangs around. Otherwise, the Mini Toolbar fades away. Learn more about the Mini Toolbar in Chapter 3.

## LIVE PREVIEW

Another amazing new feature in Excel 2007 is Live Preview. Say you are selecting fonts for a range. As you hover over each font in the list, the view of the spreadsheet instantly updates to show how the change would appear in the spreadsheet.

The Live Preview feature works for charts, images, and cells. It is amazing how fast the preview works. Learn more about Live Preview in Chapter 5.

# WHERE IS THE CLASSIC MODE?

Don't feel bad. Bill Gates asked this same question. Certainly, with changes this radical, there would be a way to switch back to a classic view, right?

There is not.

I am convinced that Microsoft took away the floating commandbar in order to prevent every Excel guru out there from bringing back the classic mode.

## CLASSIC MODE FOR KEYBOARD USERS

There is some relief for those who love keyboard shortcuts (also known as *hotkeys*). Consider the menus in Excel 2003. Notice that the *E* in Edit is underlined. If you hold down the Alt key while typing E, Excel opens the Edit menu. Within the Edit menu is the Fill command. The *i* in Fill is underlined. Typing Alt+I within the Edit menu brings up the Fill submenu. In the Fill submenu, the *J* in Justify is underlined. Typing Alt+J therefore invokes the Justify command.

Thus, without using the mouse, you can type Alt+EIJ to invoke the Edit, Fill, Justify command. I use these commands all the time, so I've memorized this keystroke combination.

If you have favorite keystroke combinations that you use all of the time, Microsoft will honor your knowledge. You can type Alt+EIJ to invoke Edit, Fill, Justify—or use your favorite hotkeys to invoke your favorite commands. A pop-up rectangle at the top of the screen shows the Office 2003 access key that you typed. You can continue typing access keys or press escape to cancel.

## THE JOURNEY

It is difficult to predict how the press will react to the ribbon. Will there be praise or ridicule of Microsoft's bold new user interface? That is a big question.

If you are reading this paragraph, I presume that you've made the leap and are at least trying out Excel 2007. This book will guide you on a journey through the new features in Excel 2007, hopefully easing the transition.

The book is organized into the following parts:

- **Part I, "Mastering the New User Interface"**—This first part of the book shows you in detail how best to deal with the ribbon.

- **Past II, "A Tour of What's New"**—This part walks you through the amazing new features in Excel 2007. There might be topics here that would generally be found later in an Excel book. For example, pivot tables are usually in the advanced chapters of a book. In this case, they are up front because they are new.

- **Part III, "Working in a Legacy Environment"**—In a perfect world, you, all your co-workers, and everyone you share files with will have switched to Excel 2007 at the same time. In reality, you are going to have to share files with people who don't have 1.1 million rows in their spreadsheets. This part of the book addresses how to enjoy the benefits of the new version while working with people who still use old ones.

- **Part IV, "Calculating with Excel"**—This part covers all the stuff that needs to be in an Excel book, from formulas to functions to linking.
- **Part V, "Formatting and Sharing Information"**—This part discusses how to make a workbook look good and how to share your workbooks by printing, creating PDFs, or publishing to the Web.
- **Part VI, "More Power"**—This part provides an introduction to VBA and information on customizing the ribbon, Excel Server, and more.

## CONVENTIONS USED IN THIS BOOK

The special conventions used throughout this book are designed to help you get the most from the book as well as Excel 2007.

### TEXT CONVENTIONS

Different typefaces are used to convey various things throughout the book. They include those shown in Table I.1.

| TABLE I.1—TYPEFACE CONVENTIONS | |
|---|---|
| **Typeface** | **Description** |
| Monospace | Screen messages and Web addresses appear in monospace. |
| *Italic* | New terminology appears in this italic. |
| **Bold** | References to text you should type appear in **bold**. |

Ribbon names, dialog box names, and dialog box elements are capitalized in this book (for example, Add Formatting Rule dialog, Sheet ribbon).

In this book, key combinations are represented with a plus sign. If the action you need to take is to press the Ctrl key and the T key simultaneously, the text tells you to press Ctrl+T.

### SPECIAL ELEMENTS

Throughout this book, you'll find tips, notes, cautions, cross-references, case studies, Excel in Practice boxes, sidebars, and Troubleshooting Tip boxes. These elements provide a variety of information, ranging from warnings you shouldn't miss to ancillary information that will enrich your Excel experience but isn't required reading.

**TIP FROM**

Tips point out special features, quirks, or software tricks that will help you increase your productivity with Excel 2007.

**NOTE**

Notes contain extra information or alternative techniques for performing tasks.

**CAUTION**

> Cautions call out potential gotchas.

## Cross References

→ See Chapter 99 for more information.

## Case Study: Other Elements

Sections such as Case Study, Excel in Practice, and Troubleshooting Tips are set off in boxes such as this one:

- Case studies walk you through the steps to complete a task.

- Excel in Practice boxes walk through real-life problems in Excel.

- Troubleshooting Tips boxes walk through steps to avoid certain problems or how to react when certain problems occur.

## Sidebars

Historical glimpses and other information that is not critical to your understanding appears as sidebars. I imagine that if the Cliff Claven character from *Cheers* knew a lot about Excel, these would be the kinds of things he would write.

# MASTERING THE NEW USER INTERFACE

# INTRODUCING THE RIBBON USER INTERFACE

**I**n this chapter

1

The Office 2007 user interface sports a complete makeover, and similar and extensive changes have been made to Excel, Word, PowerPoint, Access, and the Compose Mail portion of Outlook. With the new interface, Microsoft admits that it was wrong when it used the original menu and toolbars paradigm back in 1985. Microsoft admits that it was wrong to try adaptive menus in 2000. It admits that the task pane was wrong in Excel 2003. It admits that Clippy (the much-maligned Office Assistant) was the stupidest idea ever invented. Even if everyone agrees that these were bad ideas, it is shocking to have them taken away. (Except Clippy. I don't think anyone will miss Clippy). They may have been bad ideas, but we became familiar with them. Next week, when you are under pressure to close the books for the month, you will really wish those horrible menu items were back so you could get your work done.

I did not write this chapter first. I wanted to let the new Ribbon interface sink in for a while. I wanted to give it a chance. I can report, after several months of using Excel 2007, that I understand the Ribbon interface. I can almost always go directly to the correct ribbon. A few things are definitely easier with the Ribbon interface. My goal in this chapter is to give you a quick start to help you quickly get used to the Ribbon interface.

## THE EXCEL 2007 INTERFACE

Figure 1.1 shows the new Excel 2007 window. Note that the new interface has the following elements:

**Figure 1.1**
The Excel 2007 interface includes several new elements.

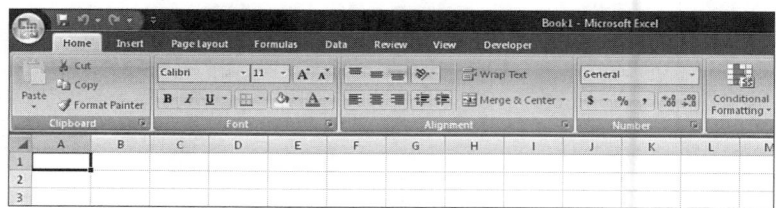

- **The Office icon menu**—This menu contains most items that used to be on the File menu. In the original beta versions of Excel, the Office icon menu was even called the File menu.

- **The Quick Access toolbar** —The Quick Access toolbar can be customized to include your favorite command icons. See Chapter 2 for information on customizing the Quick Access toolbar.

- **Tabs for Home, Insert, Page Layout, and other ribbons**—Each tab leads to a different ribbon. Figure 1.1 shows the Home ribbon.

- **Groups**—Each ribbon is divided into related commands. The name of each group appears at the bottom of the ribbon. In Figure 1.1, the groups shown are Clipboard, Font, Alignment, and Number. While you never specifically have to click on these names, they can assist you in finding a command on a busy ribbon. This book refers to them when directing you to a command.

- **Drop-down buttons**—With some buttons on the ribbon, a button for the most popular choice is attached to a drop-down icon. For example, the Paste icon on the left side of the Home ribbon is such a button. You can click the top half of the icon to initiate a paste, or you can click the drop-down arrow to display a menu of paste-related commands.

- **Dialog launchers**—You can click this icon in the lower-right corner of some groups to return to the familiar legacy version of the dialog box for that function.

NOTE

> The Excel 2007 interface has three available color schemes. You can select a blue scheme to match the Windows XP, a black scheme to match the Windows Vista theme, or a silver theme that provides higher contrast. Because the gray theme reproduces better in the printed pages of this book, most screen shots appear in the gray format. To change the color scheme, you select the Office icon and then choose Excel Options, Popular and choose a color scheme from the drop-down.

The following sections describe the various components of the Excel 2007 interface.

# USING THE OFFICE ICON MENU

The Office icon in the upper-left corner of the screen contains menu options for saving, printing, and sharing with others. You can click the Office icon to display its menu, as shown in Figure 1.2.

The Office icon menu contains menu items such as Save and Close that are straightforward choices. If you click one of those menu items, a command is performed. Other menu items, such as New, Open, and Print lead to dialog boxes where you can specify details about the command. With some commands, there is a right arrow next to the command. You can hover your mouse over this arrow to display a fly-out menu with more options, as shown in Figure 1.3.

**Figure 1.2**
The Office icon menu includes many items from the old File menu.

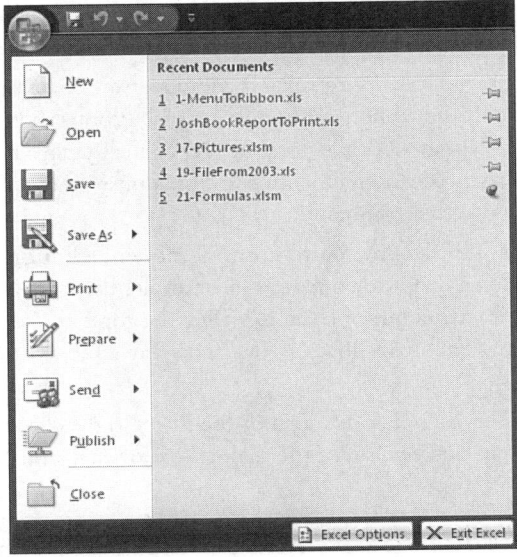

**Figure 1.3**
Some menu items lead to fly-out menus reminiscent of prior versions of Excel.

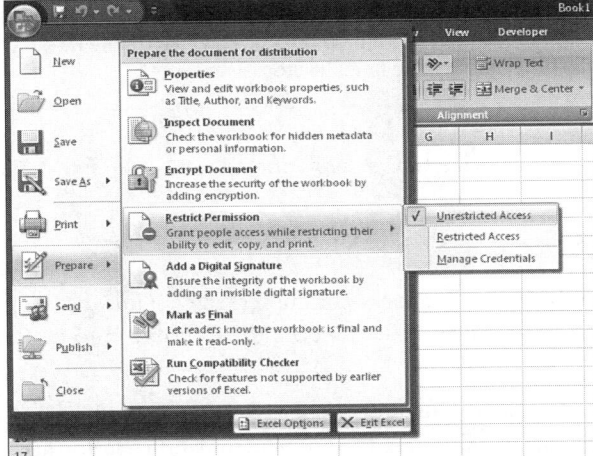

## Customizing the Recent Documents List

In prior versions of Excel, anywhere from four to nine of your recently used files would appear at the bottom of the File menu. This feature has been greatly improved and expanded in Excel 2007. You can now choose to display up to 50 recent documents. To change the limit, you choose the Office icon, Excel Options, Advanced, Display. Then you use the Show This Number Of Recent Documents spin button to increase the number to up to 50.

The Recent Documents list is more thorough in Excel 2007 than in previous versions. If you open a workbook by double-clicking the file in Windows Explorer, the workbook is logged to the Recent Documents list. This is an improvement over Excel 2003, where the recently used file list would routinely skip files that were not opened through the Excel File menu.

As shown in Figure 1.4, there is a gray thumbtack to the right of each file in the list. If you click the thumbtack, you pin that file to the list. Files that are pinned to the list appear in the Recent Documents list until you unpin them. To unpin an item, you click the thumbtack icon again. In the figure, the last file is pinned to the list.

**Figure 1.4**
Files can be pinned to permanently appear in the Recent Documents list.

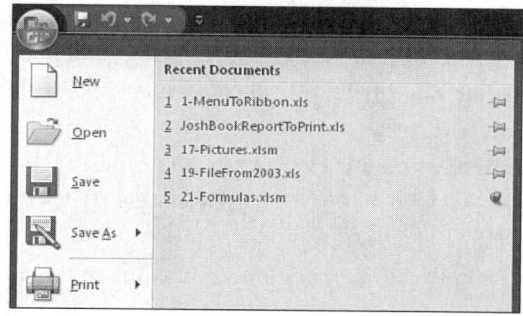

**TIP FROM**

If you share a computer and have privacy concerns, you might want to clear the recently used file list. In the Excel Options dialog, change the Recently Used File List setting in the Advanced Category to zero and close the dialog. This will delete the files from the list in Excel. If someone later resets the setting back to 50, Excel will begin building a new list of recently used files.

## USING THE EXCEL OPTIONS AND EXIT EXCEL BUTTONS

You can click the Exit Excel button to close Excel. When you do, Excel prompts you to save any unsaved documents.

Clicking the Excel Options button opens the Excel Options dialog, which allows you to set more than 100 settings in several categories. You can use this dialog to access Office Online, activate your installation of Office, and customize the Quick Access toolbar. (For details on customizing the Quick Access toolbar, see Chapter 2, "The Quick Access Toolbar." For details on the Excel Options dialog, see Chapter 6, "The Excel Options Dialog.")

# UNDERSTANDING THE RIBBON USER INTERFACE

The Ribbon user interface is the area at the top of the Excel window that contains all the features of the program. The Ribbon user interface is organized into a number of ribbons, such as Home, Insert, and Page Layout, that group features together.

Every ribbon is static. Items are not added to or removed from a ribbon in response to your actions in Excel. Unlike the adaptive menus introduced in Excel 2000, every person's Formulas ribbon looks identical to every other person's Formulas ribbon all the time (assuming that they have not been altered by a programmer, as described shortly).

It is possible for entire context-sensitive tabs to appear and disappear. For instance, the Picture Tools ribbon is visible only when there is a picture on your worksheet and the picture is selected. If you aren't working with the picture, the tab for Picture Tools is put away.

## MINIMIZING THE RIBBON

If you are working on a tablet PC or a laptop with a small screen, you might find that the Ribbon takes up too much space on your screen. You can choose to minimize the Ribbon. In this state, you will see only the Office icon, the Quick Access toolbar, and the ribbon tab names.

When the ribbon is minimized, you can click on a tab name and Excel will temporarily open that particular ribbon. After you have selected a command, the ribbon will automatically return to the minimized state.

To toggle into or out of having the Ribbon minimized, use one of these methods:

- Press Ctrl+F1
- Right-click the Ribbon and choose "Minimize the Ribbon"

## CHANGING THE RIBBON

The ribbons are always at the top of the screen. You cannot undock the ribbons and move them to a new location.

A programmer using XML can add new groups to an existing ribbon tab or can add new ribbon tabs. This is a disappointing change from the past 15 years of Excel. In any prior version, any person who could right-click and drag could customize a toolbar, create a new toolbar, or undock a toolbar so it could float in the work area. (All the Office MVP were vocal in their criticism of Microsoft for this decision.)

The bottom line is that if Microsoft allowed for customization of toolbars, anyone could basically design a toolbar to look like the old version of Excel. Because Microsoft is betting the ranch on the new user interface, it wants you to live with it and experience it. As Microsoft sees it, allowing you to go back to the way that you knew and loved would be counterproductive.

The ribbon tabs often expand to fill the space available depending on the resolution of your display. If you start to shrink the application, Excel replaces the large icons with smaller icons but keeps the groups in their original order.

NOTE

> Eventually, if the Excel window is less than 300 pixels wide, Excel puts away the ribbons completely. The theory is that if the application is that small, you have resized it to get it out of the way.

Although there are initially 7 ribbon tabs available, there are a total of 26 ribbon tabs in Excel 2007. The following sections describe the ribbons you are most likely to use.

## USING THE COMMON COMMANDS ON THE HOME RIBBON

Microsoft put the most common features on the Home ribbon. This ribbon includes cut, copy, and paste functions. Font formatting, cell alignment, and number formatting also appear on the Home ribbon. The new conditional formatting features have been placed to the Home ribbon, as have features related to tables, formatting, and editing.

Figure 1.5 shows the Home ribbon.

**Figure 1.5**
The most common commands are on the Home ribbon.

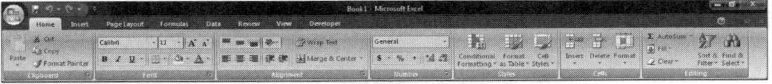

## USING THE ECLECTIC COMMANDS ON THE INSERT RIBBON

The Insert ribbon is the gateway to the fantastic new charting engine, with seven large icons dedicated to various chart types. You can also use this ribbon to insert shapes, pivot tables, illustrations, hyperlinks, and various text objects.

Figure 1.6 shows the Insert ribbon.

**Figure 1.6**
Charting and pivot tables are found on the Insert ribbon.

## CONTROLLING THEMES AND PAGE SETUP WITH THE PAGE LAYOUT RIBBON

Almost everything that used to be on the four-tab Page Setup dialog is now spread out across the Page Layout ribbon. The Scale to Fit options finally make sense after 15 years of being confusing.

Document themes, which are new to Excel 2007, allow you to quickly change a document to any of 20 built-in themes or custom themes that you design to match your corporate or some other color scheme. Word, PowerPoint, and Excel all offer the same 20 built-in themes, so all your Office creations can feature a consistent color scheme.

The Page Layout ribbon also includes custom views and various options for arranging objects on the worksheet (see Figure 1.7).

**Figure 1.7**
Most of the information from the old Page Setup dialog is now on Page Layout ribbon.

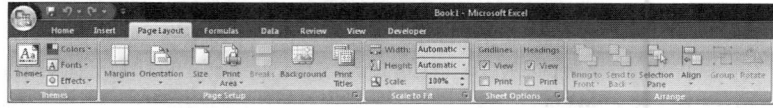

## CALCULATING WITH THE FORMULAS RIBBON

Excel 2007 introduces the AutoComplete feature, which you can use when building formulas in Excel. You begin building formulas graphically by using the function library icons on the Formulas ribbon. The improved Name Manager and other cell naming tools are in this ribbon.

If you frequently build complex formulas, you will love the Evaluate Formula and Watch Window options in the Formulas ribbon. Both features were added to Excel 2003, but they were so buried that most people never found them.

Finally, calculation options have been promoted from the Options dialog to a spot at the end of the Formulas ribbon, as shown in Figure 1.8.

**Figure 1.8**
You can build and audit formulas by using the Formulas ribbon.

## MANAGING DATA CONNECTIONS WITH THE DATA RIBBON

With the introduction of Excel Services for SharePoint, Microsoft realizes that Excel is often the presentation layer for data stored in corporate systems. Connections to external data, whether in Access, on the Web, or from SQL Server, can be managed from the Data ribbon, as shown in Figure 1.9.

**Figure 1.9**
You can manage external data connections by using the Data ribbon.

Several of the icons for sorting and filtering that appear in drop-downs on the Home ribbon are repeated on the Data ribbon. The gem on this ribbon is the Subtotals command. If you regularly have to insert totals after each customer or region, you should read Adding Automatic Subtotals in Chapter 35, "More Tips and Tricks for Excel 2007."

## REVIEWING DOCUMENTS WITH THE REVIEW RIBBON

All the reviewing tools, such as spellcheck, the thesaurus, and the new translation feature are on the Review ribbon, as shown in Figure 1.10. This ribbon also includes comment features from the old Reviewing toolbar, as well as protection and sharing options. The translation service is discussed in Chapter 35.

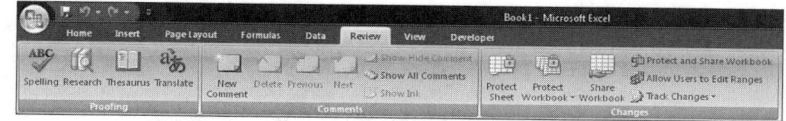

**Figure 1.10**
Spellcheck and thesaurus tools are on the Review ribbon.

## SEEING MORE WITH THE VIEW RIBBON

The Window menu was one of my most frequently visited menus in Excel 2003. Most of its options are now on the View ribbon in Excel 2007.

The new Page Layout view is a terrific addition to Excel 2007. Strangely, though, you can switch to this view by using the buttons near the right edge of the status bar. The large icons Normal, Page Break Preview, and Zoom are all duplicated and always visible in the status bar.

The icons in the Window group allow you to freeze titles at the top or left of the worksheet or switch to a different open workbook.

One feature available on the View ribbon is View Side by Side. If you have two workbooks open, you can scroll them simultaneously by using this feature that was introduced in Excel 2003. An old but often-overlooked feature allows you to see two worksheets from the same workbook simultaneously. To take advantage of this feature, you select New Window and then Arrange.

Figure 1.11 shows the View ribbon.

**Figure 1.11**
The old Window menu options are now on the View ribbon.

## MANAGING MACROS WITH THE DEVELOPER RIBBON

There is a ribbon just for those who regularly write VBA macros. Excel initially hides the Developer ribbon, but you can follow these steps to display it:

1. Click the Office icon menu.
2. Select Excel Options.
3. Select the Popular category.
4. In the Top Options For Working with Excel section, choose Show Developer Tab in the Ribbon.
5. Click OK.

As shown in Figure 1.12, the Developer ribbon offers one-click access to the Visual Basic Editor. The Macros button lists the available macros in the current workbook (similar to pressing Alt+F8 in Excel 2003).

Other options in the Developer tab include XML settings and the options from the old Control toolbox, which are now located under Controls, Insert.

**Figure 1.12**
Macro programmers will want to enable the Developer ribbon.

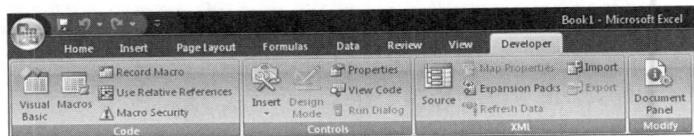

## ACCESSING THE CONTEXT-SENSITIVE RIBBONS

Excel 2007 has 18 additional ribbons that appear as necessary. All these ribbons are context sensitive. If you edit a page header in your worksheet, the Header & Footer Tools ribbon appears. When you click outside of the header, the Header & Footer Tools ribbon is put away.

Sometimes, there are more items than can fit on a single ribbon. For example, Chart Tools offers three ribbons: Design, Layout, and Format. In general, if a context menu includes multiple ribbons, the general options appear on the leftmost ribbon. The more specific items appear on additional ribbons to the right.

These are the context-sensitive ribbons:

- **Add-Ins**—This ribbon contains any menu items added through VBA macros or add-ins.

- **Chart Tools**—The Chart Tools ribbon includes three ribbons: Design, Layout, and Format. The Design ribbon provides features to change an entire chart. By the time you get to the Format ribbon, you are micromanaging small aspects of a chart.

- **Drawing Tools**—This ribbon includes a Format ribbon for working with shapes. To access the ribbon, you select Insert, Shapes.

- **Header & Footer**—This ribbon appears when you are editing the header or footer for a page in Page Layout view. To access the ribbon, you click View, Page Layout View and then click in either the header or footer zone.

- **Ink Tools**—This ribbon is for tablet PCs.

- **Picture Tools**—This ribbon is available after you insert clip art or an image and select the illustration.

- **Pivot Chart Tools**—After you insert a pivot chart, four new ribbons are available: Design, Layout, Format, and Analyze. The first three of these ribbons are similar to the ribbons on the Chart Tools ribbon. The fourth contains the pivot table features.

- **Pivot Table Tools**—This ribbon includes two ribbons: Options and Design. The major settings appear on the Options ribbon. Formatting options appear on the Design ribbon.

- **Print Preview Tools**—This small ribbon appears as the only ribbon when you are in Print Preview mode.

- **SmartArt Tools**—In Excel 2007, the former business diagrams has been renamed SmartArt. When you are working with organization charts or other SmartArt diagrams, two new ribbons are available: Design and Format.

- **Table Tools**—The Design ribbon allows for the formatting of a database in Excel after it has been converted to a table. In Excel 2007, tables replace Excel 2003 lists.

All these context ribbons come and go as you select and unselect certain items in Excel.

## FINDING OLD MENU ITEMS IN THE NEW INTERFACE

For the first few weeks that you use Excel, you will probably often try to figure out exactly where Microsoft decided to move a command. Table 1.1 shows each of the menu items in Excel 2003, followed by the current location of each command in Excel 2007.

Sometimes, a command is no longer offered in the Ribbon User Interface, but the icon is still available for you to add to the Quick Access toolbar. For these commands, the second column will say, "Office Icon, Excel Options (Add to Quick Access toolbar if you need it)." See Chapter 2 for information about customizing this toolbar.

In other cases, a command is no longer available in Excel 2007. In these cases, the second column will say, "(no equivalent)."

**TABLE 1.1   EXCEL 2003 MENU ITEMS AND THEIR LOCATIONS IN EXCEL 2007**

| Excel 2003 Command | Equivalent Excel 2007 command |
| --- | --- |
| File, New | Office icon, New |
| File, Open | Office icon, Open |
| File, Close | Office icon, Close |
| File, Save | Office icon, Save |
| File, Save As | Office icon, Save As |
| File, Save as Web Page | Office icon, Save As, Save As Web Page from Save As dialog |
| File, Save Workspace | View, Window, Save Workspace |
| File, File Search | (no equivalent) |
| File, Permission, Unrestricted Access | Office icon, Finish, Restrict Permission, Unrestricted Access |

*continues*

**TABLE 1.1** CONTINUED

| Excel 2003 Command | Equivalent Excel 2007 command |
|---|---|
| File, Permission, Do Not Distribute | Office icon, Finish, Restrict Permission, Do Not Distribute |
| File, Permission, Restrict Permission As | Office icon, Finish, Restrict Permission, Restrict Permission As |
| File, Web Page Preview | Office Icon, Excel Options (add to Quick Access toolbar if you need it) |
| File, Page Setup | Page Layout, Page Setup |
| File, Print Area, Set Print Area | Page Layout, Page Setup, Print Area, Set Print Area |
| File, Print Area, Clear Print Area | Page Layout, Page Setup, Print Area, Clear Print Area |
| File, Print Preview | Office icon, Print, Print Preview |
| File, Print | Office icon, Print, Print |
| File, Send To, Mail Recipient | Office Icon, Excel Options (add to Quick Access toolbar if you need it) |
| File, Send To, Mail Recipient (for Review) | Office Icon, Excel Options (add to Quick Access toolbar if you need it) |
| File, Send To, Mail Recipient (as Attachment) | Office icon, Send, E-Mail |
| File, Send To, Routing Recipient | (no equivalent) |
| File, Send To, Exchange Folder | Office Icon, Excel Options (add to Quick Access toolbar if you need it) |
| File, Send To, Online Meeting Participant | Office Icon, Excel Options (add to Quick Access toolbar if you need it) |
| File, Send To, Recipient using Internet Fax Service | Office icon, Send, Internet Fax |
| File, Properties | View, Show/Hide, Properties |
| File, 1 \aaProductFolders\SEU\ Macro to List MenuBars.xls | Office icon, 1 |
| File, Exit | Office icon, Exit Excel |
| Edit, Undo | Quick Access toolbar, Undo |
| Edit, Repeat | Quick Access toolbar, Repeat |
| Edit, Cut | Home, Clipboard, Cut |
| Edit, Copy | Home, Clipboard, Copy |
| Edit, Office Clipboard | Home, Clipboard |
| Edit, Paste | Home, Clipboard, Paste |

| Excel 2003 Command | Equivalent Excel 2007 command |
| --- | --- |
| Edit, Paste Special | Home, Clipboard, Paste, Paste Special |
| Edit, Paste as Hyperlink | Home, Clipboard, Paste, Paste as Hyperlink |
| Edit, Fill, Down | Home, Editing, Fill, Down |
| Edit, Fill, Right | Home, Editing, Fill, Right |
| Edit, Fill, Up | Home, Editing, Fill, Up |
| Edit, Fill, Left | Home, Editing, Fill, Left |
| Edit, Fill, Across Worksheets | Home, Editing, Fill, Across Worksheets |
| Edit, Fill, Series | Home, Editing, Fill, Series |
| Edit, Fill, Justify | Home, Editing, Fill, Justify |
| Edit, Clear, All | Home, Editing, Clear, Clear All |
| Edit, Clear, Formats | Home, Editing, Clear, Clear Formats |
| Edit, Clear, Contents | Home, Editing, Clear, Clear Contents |
| Edit, Clear, Comments | Home, Editing, Clear, Clear Comments |
| Edit, Delete | Home, Cells, Delete |
| Edit, Delete Sheet | Home, Cells, Delete, Delete Sheet |
| Edit, Move or Copy Sheet | Home, Cells , Format, Move or Copy Sheet |
| Edit, Find | Home, Editing, Find & Select, Find |
| Edit, Replace | Home, Editing, Find & Select, Replace |
| Edit, Go To | Home, Editing, Find & Select, Go To |
| Edit, Links | Office icon, Finish, Edit Links to Files |
| Edit, Object | Object-specific tabs in the menu bar when the object is selected |
| View, Normal | View, Workbook Views, Normal |
| View, Page Break Preview | View, Workbook Views, Page Break Preview |
| View, Task Pane | (no equivalent) |
| View, Toolbars, Standard | (no equivalent) |
| View, Toolbars, Customize | Office icon, Excel Options, Customization |
| View, Formula Bar | View, Show/Hide, Formula Bar |
| View, Status Bar | (no equivalent) |
| View, Header and Footer | Insert, Text, Header & Footer |
| View, Comments | Review, Comments, Show All Comments |
| View, Custom Views | Page Layout, Sheet Options, Custom Views |

*continues*

**TABLE 1.1    CONTINUED**

| Excel 2003 Command | Equivalent Excel 2007 command |
|---|---|
| View, Full Screen | View, Workbook Views, Full Screen |
| View, Zoom | View, Zoom, Zoom |
| Insert, Cells | Home, Cells, Insert, Insert Cells |
| Insert, Rows | Home, Cells, Insert, Insert Rows |
| Insert, Columns | Home, Cells, Insert, Insert Columns |
| Insert, Worksheet | Home, Cells, Insert, Insert Sheet |
| Insert, Chart | Insert, Charts |
| Insert, Symbol | Insert, Text, Symbol |
| Insert, Page Break | Page Layout, Page Setup, Breaks, Insert Page Break |
| Insert, Function | Formulas, Function Library, Function Wizard |
| Insert, Name, Define | Formulas, Named Cells, Name Manager |
| Insert, Name, Paste | Formulas, Named Cells, Use In Formula, Paste |
| Insert, Name, Create | Formulas, Named Cells, Create from Selection |
| Insert, Name, Apply | Formulas, Named Cells, Name a Range, Apply Names |
| Insert, Name, Label | Formulas, Named Cells, Name a Range |
| Insert, Comment | Review, Comments, New Comment |
| Insert, Picture, Clip Art | Insert, Illustrations, Clip Art |
| Insert, Picture, From File | Insert, Illustrations, Picture |
| Insert, Picture, From Scanner or Camera | Insert, Illustrations, Picture |
| Insert, Picture, AutoShapes | Insert, Shapes, Shapes |
| Insert, Picture, WordArt | Insert, Text, WordArt |
| Insert, Picture, Organization Chart | Insert, Illustrations, SmartArt |
| Insert, Diagram | Insert, Illustrations, SmartArt |
| Insert, Object | Insert, Text, Object |
| Insert, Hyperlink | Insert, Links, Hyperlink |
| Format, Cells | Home, Cells, Format, Cells |
| Format, Row, Height | Home, Cells, Format, Height |
| Format, Row, AutoFit | Home, Cells, Format, AutoFit |
| Format, Row, Hide | Home, Cells, Hide & Unhide, Hide Rows |
| Format, Row, Unhide | Home, Cells, Hide & Unhide, Unhide Rows |
| Format, Column, Width | Home, Cells, Format, Width |

| Excel 2003 Command | Equivalent Excel 2007 command |
|---|---|
| Format, Column, AutoFit Selection | Home, Cells, Format, AutoFit Selection |
| Format, Column, Hide | Home, Cells, Format, Hide & Unhide, Hide Columns |
| Format, Column, Unhide | Home, Cells, Format, Hide & Unhide, Unhide Columns |
| Format, Column, Standard Width | Home, Cells, Format, Standard Width |
| Format, Sheet, Rename | Home, Cells, Format, Rename Sheet |
| Format, Sheet, Hide | Home, Cells, Hide & Unhide, Hide Sheet |
| Format, Sheet, Unhide | Home, Cells, Hide & Unhide, Unhide Sheet |
| Format, Sheet, Background | Page Layout, Page Setup, Background |
| Format, Sheet, Tab Color | Home, Cells, Format, Tab Color |
| Format, AutoFormat | Home, Style, Format as Table |
| Format, Conditional Formatting | Home, Style, Conditional Formatting |
| Format, Style | Home, Style, Cell Styles |
| Tools, Spelling | Review, Proofing, Spelling |
| Tools, Research | Review, Proofing, Research |
| Tools, Error Checking | Formulas, Formula Auditing, Error Checking |
| Tools, Speech, Show Text To Speech Toolbar | (no equivalent) |
| Tools, Shared Workspace | Office Icon, Excel Options (add to Quick Access Toolbar if you need it) |
| Tools, Share Workbook | Review, Changes, Share Workbook |
| Tools, Track Changes, Highlight Changes | Review, Changes, Track Changes, Highlight Changes |
| Tools, Track Changes, Accept or Reject Changes | Review, Changes, Track Changes, Accept or Reject Changes |
| Tools, Protection, Protect Sheet | Home, Cells, Format, Protect Sheet |
| Tools, Protection, Allow Users to Edit Ranges | Review, Changes, Allow Users to Edit Ranges |
| Tools, Protection, Protect Workbook | Review, Changes, Protect Workbook |
| Tools, Protection, Protect and Share Workbook | Review, Changes, Protect Sharing |
| Tools, Online Collaboration, Meet Now | Office Icon, Excel Options (add to Quick Access toolbar if you need it) |
| Tools, Online Collaboration, Schedule Meeting | Office Icon, Excel Options (add to Quick Access toolbar if you need it) |
| Tools, Online Collaboration, Web Discussions | (no equivalent) |

*continues*

**TABLE 1.1** CONTINUED

| Excel 2003 Command | Equivalent Excel 2007 command |
|---|---|
| Tools, Goal Seek | Data, Data Tools, What-If Analysis, Goal Seek |
| Tools, Scenarios | Data, Data Tools, What-If Analysis, Scenario Manager |
| Tools, Formula Auditing, Trace Precedents | Formulas, Formula Auditing, Trace Precedents |
| Tools, Formula Auditing, Trace Dependents | Formulas, Formula Auditing, Trade Dependents |
| Tools, Formula Auditing, Trace Error | Formulas, Formula Auditing, Error Checking, Trace Error |
| Tools, Formula Auditing, Remove All Arrows | Formulas, Formula Auditing, Remove All Arrows |
| Tools, Formula Auditing, Evaluate Formula | Formulas, Formula Auditing, Evaluate Formula |
| Tools, Formula Auditing, Show Watch Window | Formulas, Formula Auditing, Show Watch Window |
| Tools, Formula Auditing, Formula Auditing Mode | Formulas, Formula Auditing, Show Formula |
| Tools, Formula Auditing, Show Formula Auditing Toolbar | (no equivalent) |
| Tools, Macro, Macros | Developer, Code, Macros |
| Tools, Macro, Record New Macro | Developer, Code, Record Macro |
| Tools, Macro, Security | Developer, Code, Macro Security |
| Tools, Macro, Visual Basic Editor | Developer, Code, Visual Basic |
| Tools, Macro, Microsoft Script Editor | (no equivalent) |
| Tools, Add-Ins | Office Icon, Excel Options (add to Quick Access toolbar if you need it) |
| Tools, AutoCorrect Options | Office Icon, Excel Options (add to Quick Access toolbar if you need it) |
| Tools, Customize | Office Icon, Excel Options (add to Quick Access toolbar if you need it) |
| Tools, Options | Office icon, Excel Options |
| Data, Sort | Home, Editing, Sort & Filter |
| Data, Filter, AutoFilter | Home, Editing, Sort & Filter, Filter |
| Data, Filter, Show All | Home, Editing, Sort & Filter, Clear |
| Data, Filter, Advanced Filter | Home, Editing, Sort & Filter, Advanced |
| Data, Form | Office Icon, Excel Options (add to Quick Access toolbar if you need it) |

| Excel 2003 Command | Equivalent Excel 2007 command |
| --- | --- |
| Data, Subtotals | Data, Outline, Subtotal |
| Data, Validation | Data, Data Tools, Data Validation |
| Data, Table | Data, Data Tools, What-If Analysis, Data Table |
| Data, Text to Columns | Data, Data Tools, Convert Text to a Table |
| Data, Consolidate | Data, Data Tools, Consolidate |
| Data, Group and Outline, Hide Detail | Data, Outline, Hide Detail |
| Data, Group and Outline, Show Detail | Data, Outline, Show Detail |
| Data, Group and Outline, Group | Data, Outline, Group |
| Data, Group and Outline, Ungroup | Data, Outline, Ungroup |
| Data, Group and Outline, Auto Outline | Data, Outline, Group, Auto Outline |
| Data, Group and Outline, Clear Outline | Data, Outline, Group, Clear Outline |
| Data, Group and Outline, Settings | Data, Outline, Settings |
| Data, PivotTable and PivotChart Report | Insert, Tables, Pivot Table |
| Data, Import External Data, Import Data | Office Icon, Excel Options (add to Quick Access toolbar if you need it) |
| Data, Import External Data, New Web Query | Data, Get External Data, From Web |
| Data, Import External Data, New Database Query | Office Icon, Excel Options (add to Quick Access toolbar if you need it) |
| Data, Import External Data, Edit Query | Office Icon, Excel Options (add to Quick Access toolbar if you need it) |
| Data, Import External Data, Data Range Properties | Data, Manage Connections, Properties |
| Data, Import External Data, Parameters | Office Icon, Excel Options (add to Quick Access toolbar if you need it) |
| Data, List, Create List | Data, List, Create List |
| Data, List, Resize List | Design, Properties, Resize Table |
| Data, List, Total Row | Design, Table Style Options, Total Row |
| Data, List, Convert to Range | Design, Tools, Convert to Range |
| Data, List, Publish List | Design, External Table Data, Export, Export to List |
| Data, List, View List on Server | Design, External Table Data, View on Server |
| Data, List, Unlink List | Design, External Table Data, Unlink List |
| Data, List, Synchronize List | Office Icon, Excel Options (add to Quick Access toolbar if you need it) |

*continues*

1

**TABLE 1.1   CONTINUED**

| Excel 2003 Command | Equivalent Excel 2007 command |
|---|---|
| Data, List, Discard Changes and Refresh | Office Icon, Excel Options (add to Quick Access toolbar if you need it) |
| Data, List, Hide Border of Inactive Lists | (no equivalent) |
| Data, XML, Import | Developer, XML, Import |
| Data, XML, Export | Developer, XML, Export |
| Data, XML, Refresh XML Data | Developer, XML, Refresh XML Data |
| Data, XML, XML Source | Developer, XML, XML Source |
| Data, XML, XML Map Properties | Developer, XML, Map Properties |
| Data, XML, Edit Query | Developer, XML, Edit Query |
| Data, XML, XML Expansion Packs | Developer, XML, Expansion Packs |
| Data, Refresh Data | Data, Manage Connections, Refresh |
| Chart, Chart Type | Design, Type, Chart Type |
| Chart, Source Data | Design, Data, Edit Data Source |
| Chart, Chart Options | Chart Tools Layout, Chart Elements |
| Chart, Locations | Chart Tools Design, Location, Move Chart |
| Chart, Add Data | Chart Tools Design, Data, Edit Data Source |
| Chart, Add Trendline | Chart Tools Layout, Chart Elements, Trendline |
| Chart, 3-D Views | Chart Tools Layout, 3-D Charts, 3-D View |
| Window, New Window | View, Window, New Window |
| Window, Arrange | View, Window, Arrange All |
| Window, Compare Side by Side with Macro | View, Window, View Side by Side to List MenuBars.xls |
| Window, Hide | View, Window, Hide |
| Window, Unhide | View, Window, Unhide |
| Window, Split | View, Window, Split |
| Window, Freeze Panes | View, Window, Freeze Panes |
| Window, 1 Book1 | View, Window, Switch Window |
| Help, Microsoft Excel Help | Question Mark icon at right side of ribbon |
| Help, Show the Office Assistant | (no equivalent) |
| Help, Microsoft Office Online | Office icon, Excel Options, Resources, Microsoft Office Online |
| Help, Contact Us | Office icon, Excel Options, Resources, Contact Us |

| Excel 2003 Command | Equivalent Excel 2007 command |
| --- | --- |
| Help, Check for Updates | Office icon, Excel Options, Resources, Check for Updates |
| Help, Detect and Repair | Office icon, Excel Options, Resources, Detect & Repair |
| Help, Activate Product | Office icon, Excel Options, Resources, Activate Product |
| Help, Customer Feedback Options | Office icon, Excel Options, Resources, Customer Feedback Options |
| Help, About Microsoft Office Excel | Office icon, Excel Options, Resources, About Microsoft Excel |

Table 1.2 shows all the icons in the default Standard toolbar in Excel 2003, along with their equivalent locations in Excel 2007.

**TABLE 1.2   EXCEL 2003 STANDARD TOOLBAR ICONS AND THEIR EXCEL 2007 EQUIVALENTS**

| Excel 2003 Standard Toolbar Icon | Equivalent Excel 2007 Command |
| --- | --- |
| New | Office icon, New |
| Open | Office icon, Open |
| Save | Office icon, Save |
| Permission | Office icon, Finish, Restrict Permission, Unrestricted Access |
| E-mail | Office icon, Send, Email |
| Print | Office icon, Print, Quick Print |
| Print Preview | Office icon, Print, Print Preview |
| Spelling | Review, Proofing, Spelling |
| Research | Review, Proofing, Research |
| Cut | Home, Clipboard, Cut |
| Copy | Home, Clipboard, Copy |
| Paste | Home, Clipboard, Paste |
| Format Painter | Home, Clipboard, Format Painter |
| Undo | Quick Access toolbar, Undo |
| Redo | Quick Access toolbar, Repeat |
| Insert Hyperlink | Insert, Links, Hyperlink |
| AutoSum | Home, Editing, Sum |
| Sort Ascending | Home, Editing, Sort & Filter, Sort Ascending |

*continues*

**TABLE 1.2 CONTINUED**

| Excel 2003 Standard Toolbar Icon | Equivalent Excel 2007 Command |
|---|---|
| Sort Descending | Home, Editing, Sort & Filter, Sort Descending |
| Chart Wizard | Insert, Charts |
| Drawing | (no equivalent) |
| Zoom | View, Zoom, Zoom |
| Help | Question Mark icon at right side of ribbon |

Table 1.3 shows the standard Formatting toolbar icons in Excel 2003, along with the locations of the equivalent commands in Excel 2007.

**TABLE 1.3 EXCEL 2003 FORMATTING TOOLBAR ICONS AND THEIR EXCEL 2007 EQUIVALENTS**

| Excel 2003 Formatting Toolbar Icon | Equivalent Excel 2007 Command |
|---|---|
| Font | Home, Font, Font |
| Font Size | Home, Font, Font Size |
| Bold | Home, Font, Bold |
| Italic | Home, Font, Italic |
| Underline | Home, Font, Underline |
| Align Left | Home, Alignment, Align Left |
| Align Center | Home, Alignment, Align Center |
| Align Right | Home, Alignment, Align Right |
| Merge & Center | Home, Alignment, Merge, Merge & Center |
| Currency Style | Home, Number, Accounting Number Format |
| Percent Style | Home, Number, Percent Style |
| Comma Style | Home, Number, Comma Style |
| Increase Decimal | Home, Number, Increase Decimal |
| Decrease Decimal | Home, Number, Decrease Decimal |
| Increase Indent | Home, Alignment, Increase Indent |
| Decrease Indent | Home, Alignment, Decrease Indent |
| Borders | Home, Font, Border |
| Fill Color | Home, Font, Fill Color |
| Font Color | Home, Font, Font Color |

# THE QUICK ACCESS TOOLBAR

**I**n this chapter

The Quick Access toolbar is a customizable toolbar. It remains visible, irrespective of which ribbon tab is currently displayed.

The ribbon offers big buttons with words, and when you learn where everything on the ribbon is, it is very easy to use. The ribbon has one permanent downside: Because there are seven or more ribbon tabs, you can see only a fraction of the available commands at any one time.

Because the Quick Access toolbar is always visible, you can store your most used commands and have them always visible.

There are probably a handful of toolbar buttons that you use constantly. For me, the list would be Sort Ascending, Print, Print Preview, Align Right, and Decrease Decimal. If I tried to locate these five commands, I would find that they are spread throughout the ribbon interface:

- Sort Ascending is hidden behind a drop-down on the Home ribbon, and it is also available as an icon on the Data ribbon.
- Print is now known as Quick Print. It does not appear on any ribbon. It is behind a drop-down on the Office Icon menu, and it also appears on the Quick Access toolbar.
- Print Preview has been relegated to a spot deep in the ribbon. You can find it by using the expand button on the Page Setup group in the Page Layout ribbon. It is also hidden behind the Print flyout on the Office Icon menu. I keep believing that it has to be an icon somewhere, but after months of using Excel 2007, I still can't find it.
- Align Right is on the Home ribbon, in the Alignment group.
- Decrease Decimal is in the Number group of the Home ribbon.

So, 40% of my top five icons are visible on the Home ribbon. One is always visible on the Quick Access toolbar, one is on the Data ribbon, and one is simply buried away. To access my top five favorite commands, it could require at least two clicks to change to the correct ribbon and then click the desired icon.

Luckily, the Quick Access toolbar comes to the rescue. The Quick Access toolbar holds up to 90 of your favorite icons. The Quick Access toolbar is always visible on the screen, so you can access its icons without needing to change to a different ribbon.

# CHANGING THE LOCATION OF THE QUICK ACCESS TOOLBAR

The Quick Access toolbar is initially displayed above the ribbon, just to the right of the Microsoft Office icon menu. Initially, the menu offers Save, Undo, Redo, and Quick Print icons. Figure 2.1 shows the initial location and configuration of the Quick Access toolbar.

The Quick Access toolbar

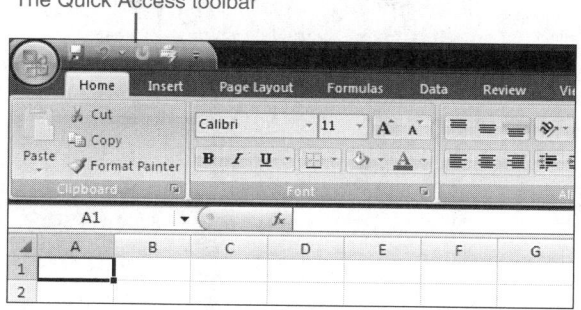

**Figure 2.1**
The default location of the Quick Access Toolbar is above the ribbon.

The other option is to display the Quick Access toolbar immediately below the ribbon. To do so, you click the drop-down arrow at the right edge of the Quick Access toolbar. Then you choose Place Quick Access Toolbar Below the Ribbon, as shown in Figure 2.2.

**Figure 2.2**
You can move the Quick Access toolbar below the ribbon.

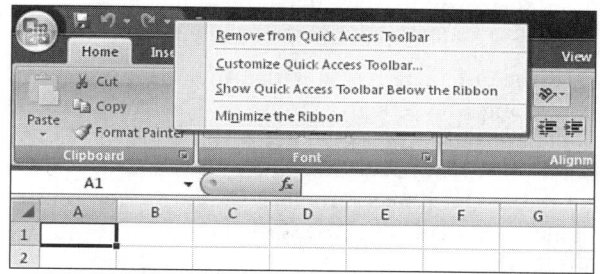

When the Quick Access toolbar is below the ribbon, you can use a similar method to move the Quick Access toolbar back above the ribbon: You click the drop-down on the right side of the Quick Access toolbar and choose Place Quick Access Toolbar Above the Ribbon.

# ADDING YOUR FAVORITE COMMANDS TO THE QUICK ACCESS TOOLBAR

When you find a command in the ribbon that you are likely to use often, you can add the command to the Quick Access toolbar. To do so, you simply right-click any command in the ribbon and choose Add to Quick Access Toolbar. For example, to add Print Preview to the Quick Access toolbar, you follow these steps:

1. Access the Office Icon menu.
2. Hover over the Print command's right-facing triangle to display the Print flyout menu.
3. Right-click on the Print Preview icon.
4. Choose Add to Quick Access Toolbar, as shown in Figure 2.3

Items added to the Quick Access toolbar using the right-click method are added to the right side of the Quick Access toolbar.

**Figure 2.3**
You can right-click any command to access the menu to add the command to the Quick Access toolbar.

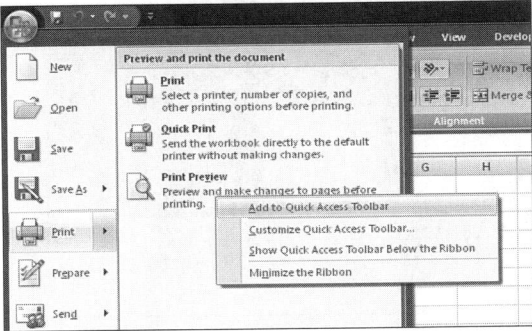

## KNOWING WHICH COMMANDS CAN BE ON THE QUICK ACCESS TOOLBAR

You can add commands to the Quick Access toolbar. You cannot add to the Quick Access toolbar the contents of many lists on the ribbon. Figuring out what you can and cannot add to the Quick Access toolbar requires a bit of experimentation.

For example, consider the Orientation icon in the Alignment group of the Home ribbon. You can use this icon to angle text counterclockwise. The icon also contains a drop-down that has a total of six commands: Angle Counterclockwise, Angle Clockwise, Vertical Text, Rotate Text Up, Rotate Text Down, and Alignment. If you right-click the Alignment icon and choose to add it to the Quick Access toolbar, the entire icon, along with the drop-down of six commands, is added to the Quick Access toolbar.

If you don't want to add the entire drop-down to the Quick Access toolbar, you can instead open the drop-down and then right-click one of the six items. Just this individual command is added to the Quick Access toolbar.

In Figure 2.4, the entire Alignment icon with the drop-down has already been added to the Quick Access toolbar. If you use the drop-down menu and the right-click menu, you can add one of the individual subcommands to the Quick Access toolbar as well.

**Figure 2.4**
You can add commands in this drop-down to the Quick Access toolbar.

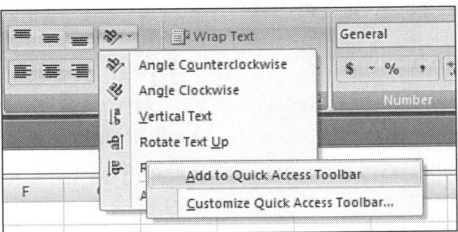

However, other drop-downs are not actually drop-downs of commands. Instead, they may lead to drop-downs with list boxes. For example, consider the font size drop-down shown in Figure 2.5. It is possible to add the entire font size drop-down as an icon on the Quick Access toolbar, but it is not possible to add to the Quick Access toolbar individual items from the list. You can add the drop-down itself, but you cannot, for example, add to the Quick Access toolbar an item that changes the font to 16 points.

**Figure 2.5**
You cannot add individual items from this list to the Quick Access toolbar. You can add the entire list.

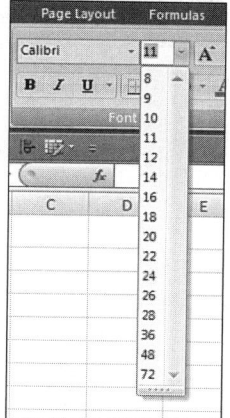

If you right-click an item in a list and the context menu doesn't offer the ability to add it to the Quick Access toolbar, then this is probably not a real command.

## REMOVING COMMANDS FROM THE QUICK ACCESS TOOLBAR

You can remove an icon from the Quick Access toolbar. You simply right-click the icon and choose Remove from Quick Access Toolbar.

You can also remove icons by using the Excel Options dialog, as discussed in the following section.

# CUSTOMIZING THE QUICK ACCESS TOOLBAR

You can make minor changes to the Quick Access toolbar by using the context menus, but you can have far more control over the Quick Access toolbar if you use the Customize command. You right-click the Quick Access toolbar and choose Customize Quick Access Toolbar in order to display the Customization section of the Excel Options dialog, as shown in Figure 2.6.

The Excel Options dialog offers many features for customizing the Quick Access toolbar:

- You can choose to customize the Quick Access toolbar for all documents on your computer or just for the current document.
- You can add separators between icons in order to group the icons logically.
- You can re-sequence the order of the icons on the toolbar.
- You can access 1,072 commands, including the commands from every ribbon and commands that are not available on any ribbon.
- You can reset the Quick Access toolbar to its original default state.
- You can move the ribbon to appear above or below the ribbon.

**Figure 2.6**
You can completely customize the Quick Access toolbar using the Excel Options dialog.

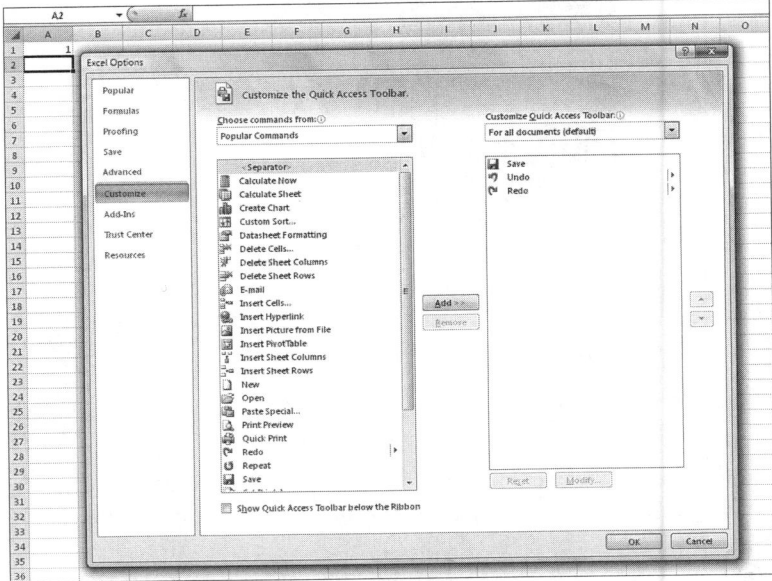

## USING THE EXCEL OPTIONS TO CUSTOMIZE THE QUICK ACCESS TOOLBAR FOR ALL WORKBOOKS

In the default state, the Customize Quick Access Toolbar drop-down in the Excel Options dialog is set to For All Documents (Default). This means that any changes you make to the Quick Access toolbar will apply to all Excel documents opened on this computer.

Initially, the Choose Commands From drop-down shows commands from the File section of the ribbon. These commands are associated with the Office Icon menu. The Choose Commands From drop-down lists commands every ribbon available in Excel—even ribbons that are available only temporarily. When you select a new ribbon from this drop-down, the Choose Commands From list box shows dozens of commands associated with that ribbon. Table 2.1 describes the categories available in the Choose Commands From drop-down.

| CATEGORIES AVAILABLE FOR CUSTOMIZING THE QUICK ACCESS TOOLBAR IN THE CHOOSE COMMANDS FROM DROP-DOWN | |
|---|---|
| **Category** | **Commands Available in the Category** |
| File | Commands associated with the Office Icon menu, such as new, open, save, print, send, and so on |
| Home | Formatting icons, conditional formatting, and so on |
| Insert | Charts, smart art, shapes, text boxes, and so on |
| Page Layout | Margins, orientation, page setup, and so on |
| Formulas | Function wizard, function library, names, and so on |
| Data | Sorting, filtering, consolidation, validation, and so on |

| Category | Commands Available in the Category |
|---|---|
| Review | Spellchecking, comments, protection, change tracking, and so on |
| View | Showing/hiding elements, zooming, arranging, workspaces, and so on |
| Developer | Macro recording, XML commands, and so on |
| Add-ins | Icons associated with installed add-ins |
| SmartArt Tools \| Design | SmartArt graphics elements |
| SmartArt Tools \| Format | Alignment, rotation, glows, effects, and so on |
| Chart Tools \| Design | Chart types, styles, layouts, quick styles, and so on |
| Chart Tools \| Layout | Formatting for chart elements |
| Chart Tools \| Format | Bevels, glows, gradients, and so on |
| Drawing Tools \| Format | Alignment, glows, shape changing, and so on |
| Picture Tools \| Format | Crop, contrast, bevel, presets, and so on |
| PivotTable Tools \| Options | Refreshes, sorts, formulas, collapsing, expanding, and so on |
| PivotTable Tools \| Design | Compacting, tabular and outline form, quick styles, totals, and so on |
| Header & Footer Tools \| Design | Custom header and footer text |
| Table Tools \| Design | Quick styles, removing duplicates, totals row, and so on |
| PivotChart Tools \| Design | Changing chart type, quick layout, and so on |
| PivotChart Tools \| Layout | Chart titles, walls, floors, legends, and so on |
| PivotChart Tools \| Format | Alignment, gradients, glows, and so on |
| PivotChart Tools \| Analyze | Expanding, collapsing, refreshing, and so on |
| Ink Tools \| Pens | Erasers, felt tips, ballpoints, ink colors, and so on |
| Print Preview | Next page, previous page, margins, and so on |
| Macros | Icons to run any VBA macros in an open workbook |
| Commands Not in the Ribbon | Autoformat, Camera Tool, Close All, Comma Format, Draw Border, Insert Page Break, Nudge, Paste Formats, Scenarios, Solitaire, Speak Cells, Strikethrough, Tilt, Zoom In, Zoom Out, and so on |

To add a new icon to the Quick Access toolbar for all workbooks, follow these steps:

1. Choose the proper command subset from the Choose Commands From drop-down.

2. Choose the icon in the Choose Commands From list box. You might have to scroll to see the complete list.

3. Click the Add button to add the command to the Customize Quick Access Toolbar.

The top choice in each category is a value called <Separator>. You can add this to the Customize Quick Access Toolbar list in order to create a vertical bar between icons on the

Quick Access toolbar. If you are going to use icons for all workbooks and additional icons for this workbook only, you might want to end the workbook icons with a separator to help identify where the icons for this workbook only begin.

## CUSTOMIZING ICONS FOR THE CURRENT WORKBOOK ONLY

Let's say you have 10 icons on your Quick Access toolbar for all workbooks. If you add additional icons for this workbook only, the icons will appear after the 10 icons for all workbooks. To add these additional icons, you follow these steps.

1. Right-click the Quick Access toolbar and choose Customize Quick Access Toolbar.

2. With the Customize Quick Access Toolbar drop-down set to For All Documents, choose the <Separator> icon at the top of the Choose Commands From list box. Click Add to add a vertical line at the end of the "all workbooks" section of the Quick Access toolbar.

3. From the Customize Quick Access Toolbar drop-down, choose For (This Workbook Name).

4. Use the Choose Commands From drop-down to find particular categories.

5. Select an icon in the Customize Quick Access Toolbar list.

6. Click the Add button.

7. Repeat steps 4–6 as needed.

8. Click OK to complete the operation.

When you are finished with this process, the Quick Access toolbar shows the icons that apply to all workbooks, a vertical separator, and then icons that apply only to the current workbook, as shown in Figure 2.7.

**Figure 2.7**
Icons for the current workbook appear after the usual Quick Access toolbar icons.

If you have the current workbook open and then switch to another open workbook, the icons assigned to the current workbook are hidden. If you arrange the windows so that you can see many workbooks at the same time, the icons for the current workbook stay visible as long as the workbook is visible. That particular workbook does not have to be the active workbook.

## FILLING UP THE QUICK ACCESS TOOLBAR

The Quick Access toolbar allows about 90 icons and/or separators. This is more than will fit across the screen on most monitors. If the monitor is not large enough to display all the icons, the first 54 of them are shown onscreen, and the rest are hidden behind a double arrow at the right edge of the Quick Access toolbar, as shown in Figure 2.8.

**Figure 2.8**
If you add too many icons to the Quick Access toolbar, they are hidden behind the double arrow at the right edge of the Quick Access toolbar.

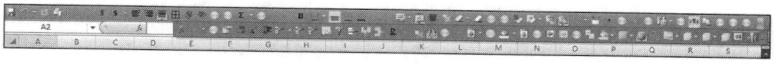

## REARRANGING ICONS ON THE QUICK ACCESS TOOLBAR

You can rearrange icons on the Quick Access toolbar by using the Excel Options dialog. You simply select any icon from the Customize Quick Access Toolbar list box and then use the up or down arrow buttons on the far right side of the dialog to move the icon up or down.

## RESETTING THE QUICK ACCESS TOOLBAR

If you start a new job and inherit someone else's computer, you might want to start with a fresh slate of icons on the Quick Access toolbar. To reset the Quick Access toolbar to the default configuration, follow these steps:

1. With the Customize Quick Access Toolbar drop-down set to For All Documents (Default), click the Reset button at the bottom of the Customize Quick Access Toolbar list box. A warning box asks if you want to reset the list for all workbooks.

2. Click OK, and the list returns to the four default icons (Save, Undo, Repeat, and Quick Print).

3. With the Customize Quick Access Toolbar drop-down set to For (This Workbook), click the Reset button at the bottom of the Customize Quick Access Toolbar list box. A warning box asks if you want to reset the list for this particular document.

4. Click OK, and the list clears.

## ASSIGNING VBA MACROS TO QUICK ACCESS TOOLBAR BUTTONS

Typically, a VBA macro is assigned to a shortcut key. In prior versions of Excel, it was easy to customize the menu system to add commands to invoke macros. In previous versions of Excel, there were more than 4,000 different icons available for the various custom menu items.

Excel 2007 offers a weak interface for adding custom macros to the Quick Access toolbar. In the Excel Options dialog, there is a drop-down called Macros. If you select this group, you will see all public macros in all open workbooks. You can select a macro and click Add to add that macro to the Quick Access toolbar.

Initially, every macro added to the Quick Access toolbar gets an identical icon. However, you can select an icon in the Customize Quick Access Toolbar list box and click the Modify button. The Modify Button dialog box that appears allows you to choose from 55 available icons for a macro. Most of these buttons are similar to icons that are already popular. For example, the Print icon is fairly well known and has a meaning. In addition to choosing from the 55 icons, you can type any text for a display name, as shown in Figure 2.9. The display name does not appear next to the button. But if you hover your mouse over the icon on the Quick Access toolbar, you can see the display name in a ToolTip.

NOTE

I am not sure why you would choose to use the Print icon for your macros. Considering that you used to have 4,096 choices and now have only 55 choices, this is another area where Excel 2007 does not live up to the prior version.

**Figure 2.9**
For macros, you can customize the button image and add a display name on the Quick Access toolbar.

**Troubleshooting Excel: The Downside of the Quick Access Toolbar**
Although the Quick Access toolbar is cool, it has a few drawbacks compared to the previous versions of Excel.

In prior versions of Excel, you could choose to display an icon, words, or words and an icon for items that you added to the custom toolbar. With Excel 2007, you are pretty much limited to just icons. When Microsoft explained the need for the ribbon, it was pretty confident that pictures and words were far superior to just pictures. It seems curious that they depreciated the ability to put words on the customizable Quick Access toolbar.

With prior versions of Excel, holding down Shift while clicking an icon usually invoked the reverse of the icon. For example, clicking Shift+Sort Ascending would perform Sort Descending. This functionality has been removed from Excel 2007.

With prior versions of Excel, you could easily have multiple custom toolbars. With Excel 2007, you can only customize the one Quick Access toolbar.

With previous versions of Excel, it was easy to drag and drop unused icons off the Standard toolbar. With Excel 2007, you have to learn XML in order to remove unused buttons or groups from the ribbon.

→ **See** "Customizing the Ribbon by Using CustomizeRibbon," on **page 1020**, in Chapter 38.

Finally, with prior versions of Excel, you could position custom toolbars anywhere. They could be docked on the top or bottom of the screen, or they could float anywhere over your screen. There were certainly instances when having a custom toolbar with a few icons right by your data was a huge benefit. Microsoft took a step backward by disallowing floating toolbars in Excel 2007.

**Excel in Practice: The Dream Quick Access Toolbar**

People upgrading from prior versions of Excel are used to accessing certain commands more than others. Including these icons on the Quick Access toolbar can help you work quickly and efficiently in Excel 2007. The following icons are my suggested dream team for the Quick Access toolbar:

| Icon | Group |
| --- | --- |
| New | File |
| Open | File |
| Save | File |
| Close | File |
| Quick Print | File |
| Print Preview | File |
| Check Spelling | Review |
| Undo | Home |
| Repeat | Home |
| AutoSum | Formula |
| Paste Values | Home |
| Sort Ascending | Data |
| Sort Descending | Data |
| Create Chart | Insert |
| Bold | Home |
| Italic | Home |
| Align Left | Home |
| Center | Home |
| Align Right | Home |
| Merge and Center | Home |
| Wrap Text | Home |
| Top Align | Home |
| Comma Style | Home |
| Increase Decimal | Home |
| Decrease Decimal | Home |
| Borders drop-down | Home |
| Fill Color | Home |
| Font Color | Home |

My Quick Access toolbar dream team is shown in Figure 2.10. Of course, these are my favorite icons, and this dream-team Quick Access toolbar is designed to replicate the popular icons from the old Standard and Formatting toolbars in Excel 2003, along with some new favorites. You will want to customize this list to add your favorite icons to the Quick Access toolbar.

**Figure 2.10**
This is the MrExcel dream team of favorite icons on the Quick Access toolbar.

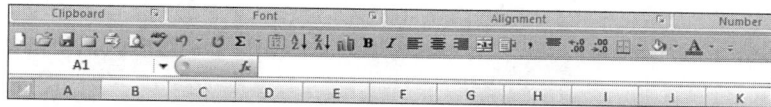

CHAPTER **3**

# THE MINI TOOLBAR AND OTHER U.I. IMPROVEMENTS

## In this chapter

Although the ribbon and Quick Access toolbar are likely to be the most talked-about features in the new Excel interface, several other features are worth mentioning:

- **Mini toolbar**—The mini toolbar appears whenever you select text. Although this may happen rarely when you're editing cells in Excel, it does happen frequently when you are working with charts, text boxes, and so on. The Mini toolbar offers quick access to font, size, bold, italics, alignment, color, indenting, and bullets.

- **Formula bar**—The formula bar includes the ability to expand or contract itself at your whim instead of the whim of Excel.

- **Zoom slider**—The Zoom slider allows you to quickly change from seeing one page to hundreds of pages at a time.

- **Status bar**—The status bar appears at the bottom of your worksheet window. Although you probably never noticed it, the status bar in previous versions of Excel reported the total of any selected cells. This information is now improved and expanded in Excel 2007.

- **View control**—The View control gives you one-click access to Page Break Preview mode, Normal mode, and the new Page Layout view.

- **New Sheet icon**—The New Sheet icon allows you to add new worksheets to a workbook with a single click.

# USING THE MINI TOOLBAR TO FORMAT SELECTED TEXT

The Mini toolbar is a shy attendant. When you select some text, almost imperceptibly, the Mini toolbar faintly appears above the text.

If you ignore the Mini toolbar, it fades away. However, if you move the mouse toward the Mini toolbar, the toolbar solidifies and offers you several text formatting options.

NOTE

> Microsoft began experimenting with fading toolbars in Outlook 2003. In that version, a new message toolbar would fade into view in the lower-right corner of your screen. You could glance down and read the first line of the email. You could ignore the toolbar, and the message would be waiting for you later in your inbox. Or you could move the mouse toward the notifier, and it would stay long enough for you to click Delete or Open. I enjoyed this feature of Outlook 2003. If my attention needed to stay on the task at hand, I could ignore the notifier, and it would unobtrusively fade away. However, if I was waiting for a message, I could handle it as it came in, avoiding a buildup of messages in my inbox.
>
> The new Mini toolbar is another feature that fades in if you move toward it and fades out if you ignore it. I expect to see more fade-in/fade-out features in future versions of Office.

In your initial use of Excel 2007, you might not see the Mini toolbar. Although you often select cells or ranges of cells, it is rare to select only a portion of a cell value in Cell Edit mode.

However, as you begin using charts, SmartArt diagrams, and text boxes, you will have the Mini toolbar appearing frequently.

To use the Mini toolbar, you follow these steps:

1. Select some text. If you are selecting text in a cell, you must select a portion of the text in the cell by using Cell Edit mode. In a chart, SmartArt diagram, or text box, you can select any text.

   The Mini toolbar appears faintly. On some computers and with some color schemes, "faintly" actually means "completely transparently."

2. Move the mouse pointer toward the Mini toolbar, and the toolbar solidifies. The Mini toolbar stays visible if your mouse is above it. After a period of inactivity, it disappears. If you move the mouse away from the Mini toolbar, it fades away.

3. Make changes in the Mini toolbar to affect the text you selected in step 1. The Mini toolbar always has the same icons, even though some of them may not apply in the current situation. In Figure 3.1, for example, it does not make sense to apply indenting to the chart axis title, but the icons are always there and in the same place.

**Figure 3.1**
You can barely make out the word *Magneto* above the number 2005. This is the Mini toolbar beginning to appear.

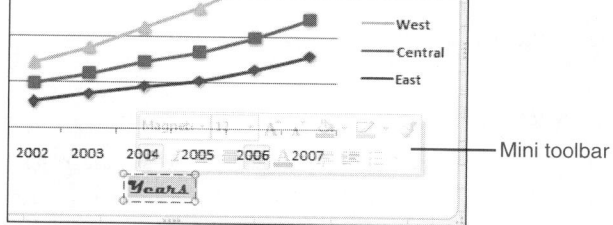

4. When you are done formatting the selected text, you can either move the mouse away from the Mini toolbar or use the Format Painter icon to apply the changes to additional text.

5. To use the Format Painter icon, click the paintbrush in the upper-right corner of the Mini toolbar. Then move toward other text in the document. The mouse pointer is a black-and-white paintbrush, to indicate that you are in Format Painter mode. When you click the other text, Excel applies the same formatting to the new text.

Initially, it is difficult to see the Mini toolbar. In Figure 3.1, look for the word Magneto just above the year 2005 on the x-axis. This word is the font name drop-down in the Mini toolbar. Plus, this is the second level of visibility; you actually have to have started moving your mouse toward the Mini toolbar in order to get it to appear this much.

If you continue moving the mouse toward the Mini toolbar, it solidifies a bit more. In Figure 3.2, the mouse pointer is just outside the border of the Mini toolbar. At this point, you can start to identify all the controls on it.

**Figure 3.2**
As you move the mouse closer to the Mini toolbar, it begins to solidify.

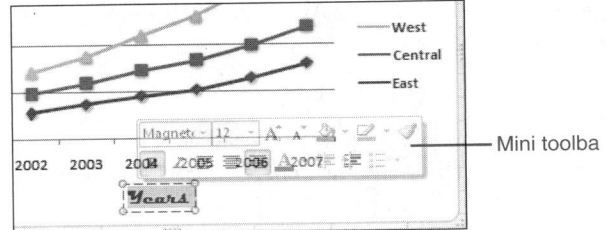

Mini toolba

In Figure 3.3, the Mini toolbar is completely visible. At this point, you can use any of its 14 controls in order to format the selected text.

**Figure 3.3**
In the fully visible state, the Mini toolbar offers a dozen controls for formatting text.

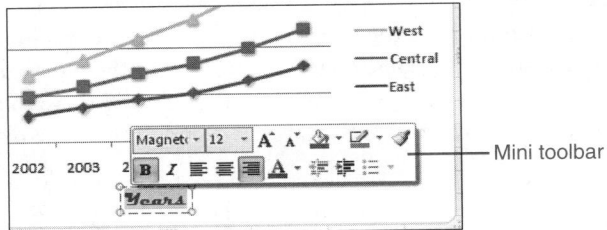

Mini toolbar

In the top row, the Mini toolbar offers five controls:

- **Font name drop-down**—You open this drop-down to choose a typeface. Each of the various font names is displayed in its own font so that you can select an appropriate font easily.
- **Font Size drop-down**—This drop-down offers font sizes from 8 to 96, in several increments.
- **Increase Font Size icon**—You click this icon to bump the font up to the next larger size.
- **Decrease Font Size icon**—You click this icon to make the font one size smaller.
- **Format Painter**—The format painter allows you to copy formatting from one place to another. (The format painter is discussed in detail in the following section.)

In the bottom row, the Mini toolbar offers nine controls:

- **Bold icon**—You use this to toggle bold on and off. If bold is already applied, the Bold icon has a glow effect around it.
- **Italics icon**—You use this to toggle italics on and off.
- **Align Left icon**—You click this control to left-align the text.
- **Center Align icon**—You click this control to center the text.
- **Right Align icon**—You click this control to right-align the text.
- **Font Color drop-down**—You use this drop-down to select a color. A menu item at the bottom of this drop-down allows you to display the Colors dialog box.
- **Decrease Indent icon**—You click this control to decrease the indent.

- **Increase Indent icon**—You click this control to increase the indent.
- **Bullet drop-down**—You can choose from seven styles of bullets or none. A menu item at the bottom of the drop-down allows you to open the Bullets and Numbering dialog box.

## USING THE FORMAT PAINTER TO COPY FORMATS

After you have formatted the selected text by using the Mini toolbar, you might want to apply the same formatting to other text. To do so, you follow these steps:

1. Click the Format Painter icon in the upper-right corner of the Mini toolbar.
2. Move your mouse away from the Mini toolbar, and it disappears. Your mouse pointer is now in the shape of a paintbrush, as shown in Figure 3.4.

**Figure 3.4**
The paintbrush icon indicates that the selected format will be applied to whatever you select next.

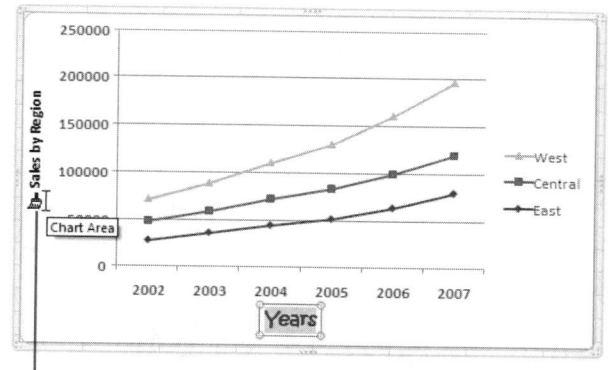

The Format Painter mouse pointer

3. Click the vertical axis title. The selected format is applied, as shown in Figure 3.5.

**Figure 3.5**
You can click another text element to apply the same formatting you have applied to other text.

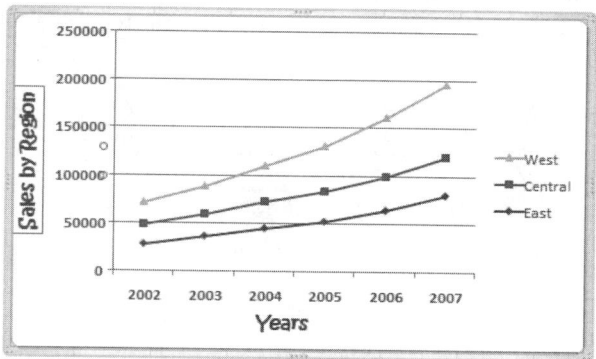

CAUTION

Using the Format Painter icon is difficult to master. You only get one click to apply the formatting. If you inadvertently click on a nontext element, you lose the Format Painter mouse pointer.

TIP FROM

*Bill Jelen*

The Format Painter command in the Clipboard group of the Home ribbon is a bit easier to use than the Format Painter icon. You can double-click this command to keep the application in Format Painter mode. You are then free to click multiple objects, applying the format to various elements.

## GETTING THE MINI TOOLBAR BACK

The shyness of the Mini toolbar might be the most frustrating part of using it. If you move the mouse away from the Mini toolbar, it fades away. If you immediately move back toward the Mini toolbar, it comes back. If you use the mouse for some other task, such as scrolling, the Mini toolbar permanently goes away. In this case, you might have to re-select the text in order to get the Mini toolbar to come back.

## DISABLING THE MINI TOOLBAR

If you are annoyed by the Mini toolbar, you can turn it off for all Excel workbooks. Here's what you do:

1. Select Office Icon, Excel Options.
2. In the Personalize category of the Excel Options dialog, clear the Show Mini Toolbar on Selection check box.

# EXPANDING THE FORMULA BAR

Formulas range from very simple to the very complex. As people began writing longer and longer formulas in Excel, an annoying problem began to appear: If the formula for a selected cell was longer than the formula bar, the formula bar would wrap and extend over the worksheet (see Figure 3.6). In many cases, the formula would obscure the first few rows of the worksheet. This was frustrating, especially if the selected cell was in the top few rows of the spreadsheet.

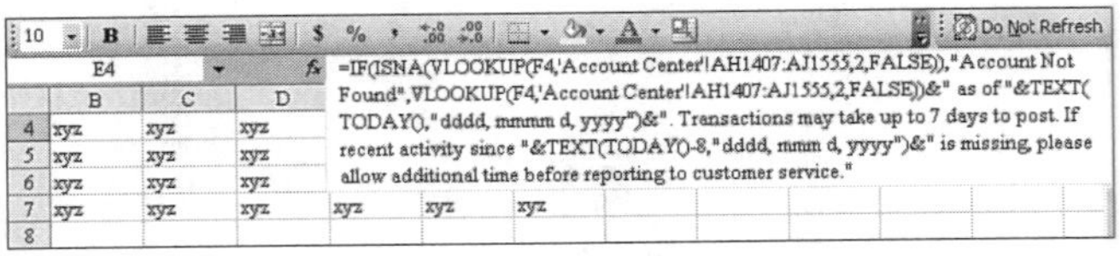

**Figure 3.6**
In prior versions of Excel, the formula bar could obscure cells on a worksheet. In this case, both the active cell, E4, and the dependent cell, F4, are hidden.

Excel 2007 features a new formula bar that prevents the formula from obscuring the spreadsheet. For example, in Figure 3.7, Cell E4 contains a formula that is longer than the formula bar. Notice the two new controls at the right end of the formula bar: a scrollbar and Expand Formula Bar icon (which looks like a down-pointing double arrow).

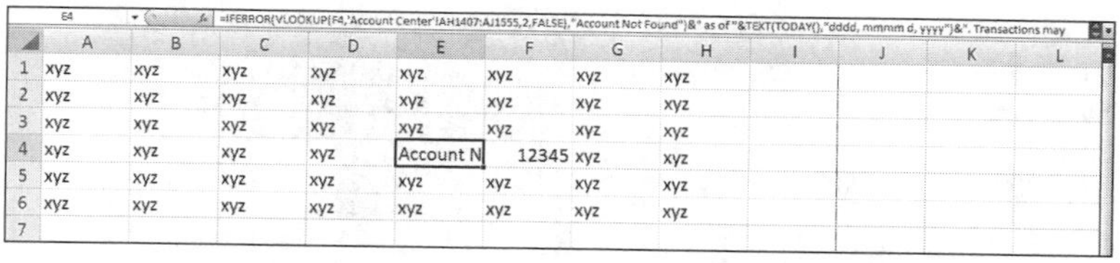

**Figure 3.7**
By default, Excel 2007 shows the initial portion of the formula.

You use the formula bar scrollbar to scroll through the formula, one line at a time. You use the Expand Formula Bar icon to expand the formula bar. As shown in Figure 3.8, expanding the formula bar actually moves the grid down. This way, you can see the formula bar and still see the cells in the grid, too. In expanded mode, the Expand Formula Bar icon is replaced by a double up-pointing arrow that you can use to contract the formula bar back to one line.

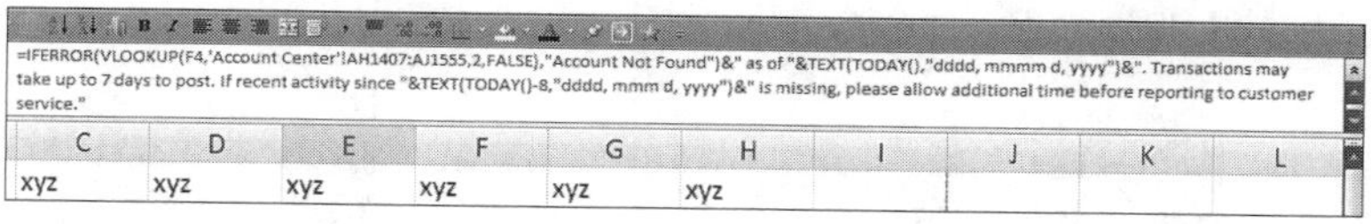

**Figure 3.8**
You can click a button to expand the formula bar.

After you collapse the formula bar, Excel has the annoying tendency to show only the last line of the formula. This could be confusing, especially if you look in the formula bar to learn whether a cell starts with an equals sign. For example, someone new to the spreadsheet shown in Figure 3.9 might not understand that Cell E4 contains a formula.

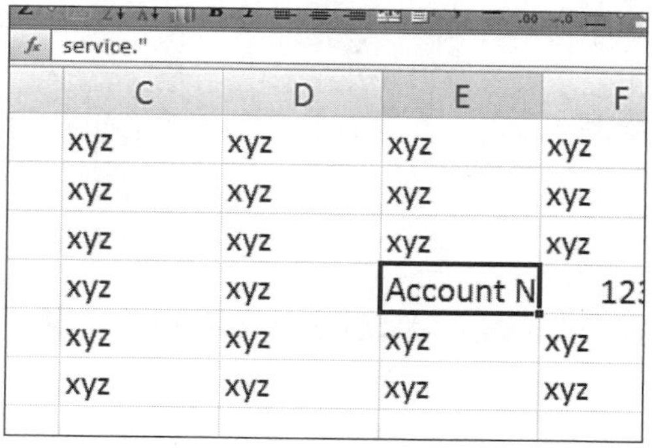

**Figure 3.9**
After you collapse the formula bar, it might show only the last line of the formula. This is a confusing view because it is not obvious how the cell value can result from this formula bar.

# ZOOMING IN AND OUT ON A WORKSHEET

In the lower-right corner of the Excel window, a new Zoom slider allows you to zoom from 400% to 10% with lightning speed. You simply drag the slider to the right to zoom in and to the left to zoom out. The Zoom Out and Zoom In buttons on either end of the slider allow you to adjust the zoom in 10% increments.

Figure 3.10 shows the zoom control set to the maximum zoom of 400%.

**Figure 3.10**
You can use the Zoom slider or the Zoom Out and Zoom In buttons to change the zoom.

| 189 | 474 | 473 | 478 |
| 190 | 474 | 473 | 473 |
| 191 | 471 | 471 | 475 |
| 192 | 475 | 479 | 477 |
| 193 | 475 | 477 | 479 |

Zoom controls

At the opposite end of the zoom spectrum, the 10% view shows an overview of 158 printed pages of the worksheet. As shown in Figure 3.11, you cannot make out any numbers at a 10% zoom. However, in the 40%–60% zoom range, you can see 3 to 10 pages and actually make out the numbers in the cells.

**Figure 3.11**
At 10% zoom, you can see 150+ pages at once.

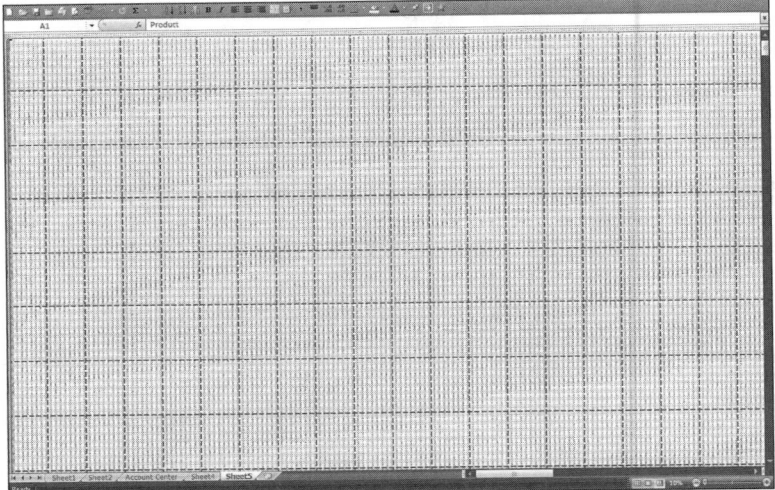

## USING THE STATUS BAR TO ADD NUMBERS

If you select several cells that contain numeric data and then look at the status bar, at the bottom of the Excel window, you can see that the status bar reports the average, count, and sum of the selected cells (see Figure 3.12).

If you need to quickly add the contents of several cells, you can simply select the cells and look for the total in the status bar. This feature has been in Excel for a decade, yet very few people realized it was there. In prior versions of Excel, only the sum would appear, but you could right-click the sum in order to see other values, such as the average, count, minimum, and maximum.

**Figure 3.12**
The status bar shows the sum, average, and count of the selected cells.

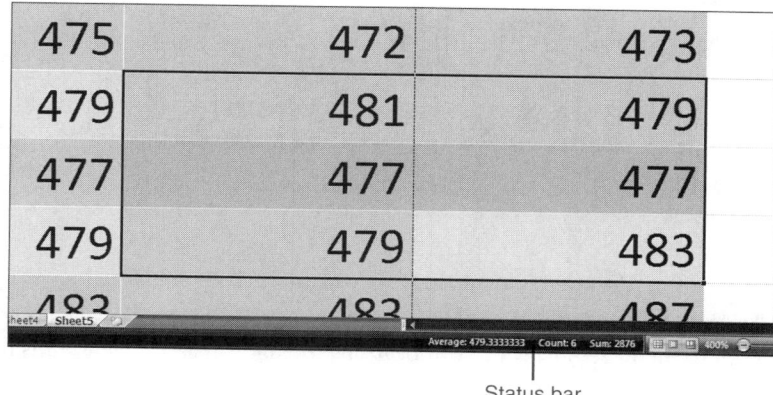

Status bar

As with past versions of Excel, in Excel 2007 you can customize which statistics are shown in the status bar. In Excel 2007, you can configure all of the status bar elements. To do so, you right-click the status bar to display the Status Bar Configuration panel. In this panel, you can see the current value of all status bar icons, whether they are hidden or not (see Figure 3.13).

**Figure 3.13**
You can configure the status bar to show or hide all these indicators.

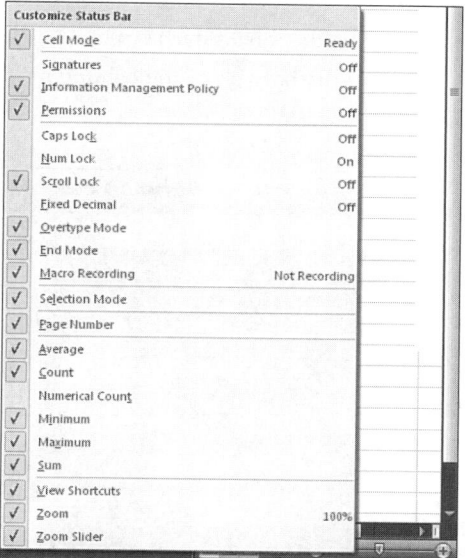

To add new items to the status bar, you click them in the Status Bar Configuration panel.

# SWITCHING BETWEEN NORMAL VIEW, PAGE BREAK PREVIEW, AND PAGE LAYOUT VIEW MODES

Three shortcut icons in the status bar allow you to quickly switch between three view modes as shown in Figure 3.14:

**Figure 3.14**
Three view short-
cuts appear in the
status bar.

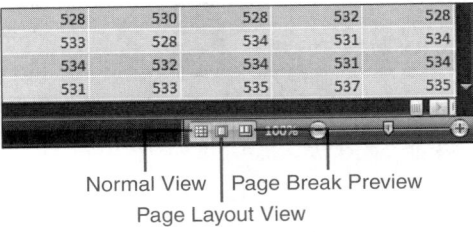

Normal View | Page Break Preview
Page Layout View

- **Normal View**—This mode shows worksheet cells as normal.
- **Page Break Preview**—This mode draws the page breaks with blue. You can actually drag the page breaks to new locations in Page Break preview. This mode has been available in several versions of Excel.
- **Page Layout View**—This is a new view in Excel 2007. It combines the best of Page Break Preview and Print Preview modes.

In Page Layout View mode, each page is shown, along with the margins, header, and footer. A ruler appears above the pages and to the left of the pages. You can make changes in this mode in the following ways:

- To change the margins, you drag the gray boxes in the ruler.
- To change column widths, you drag the borders of the column headers.
- To add a header, you click Click to Add Header.

**Figure 3.15**
The new Page Layout
View mode gives a
view of page breaks,
margins, headers, and
footers.

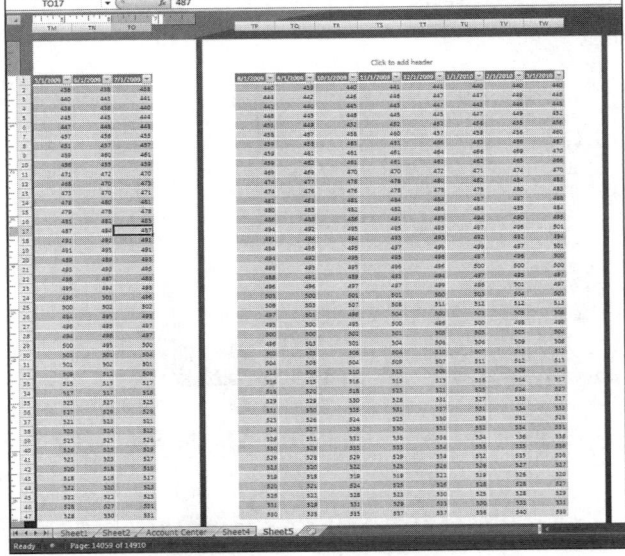

Because it is possible to navigate and enter formulas in any of the view modes, you might want to do actual worksheet editing in the new Page Layout View mode.

# USING THE NEW SHEET ICON TO ADD WORKSHEETS

The final new control in the Excel 2007 user interface is the Insert Worksheet icon. This icon appears as a small worksheet tab with a New icon. The tab appears to the right of the last worksheet tab, as shown in Figure 3.16.

**Figure 3.16**
Add a new worksheet to the end of your workbook by using the New Worksheet icon.

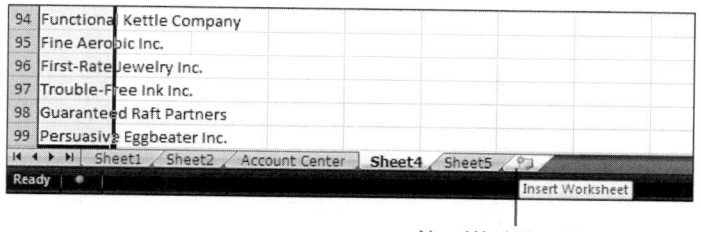

New Worksheet icon

You click the icon to add a new worksheet to the end of the workbook.

## DRAGGING A WORKSHEET TO A NEW LOCATION

After a worksheet has been added to the end of the workbook, you can drag the sheet to a new location in the middle of the workbook. Follow these steps to move a worksheet to a new location:

1. Click on the Worksheet tab.

2. Drag the mouse left or right. The mousepointer shows a sheet of paper under the mousepointer.

3. Watch for the insertion triangle just above the row of sheet names. In general, the insertion triangle will indicate that the sheet is dropped to the left of the sheet you are hovering above.

4. When the insertion triangle is in the correct location, release the mouse button.

The worksheet will be moved to the new location.

## INSERTING A WORKSHEET IN THE MIDDLE OF A WORKBOOK

Although using the New Worksheet icon and then dragging a worksheet to a new location is easier, you can also insert a worksheet in a particular location. To insert a worksheet to the left of the current worksheet, for example, you choose Home, Cells, Insert, Insert Sheet. The new sheet is added before the current sheet.

Alternatively, you can right-click any sheet and choose Insert. The Insert dialog appears, where you can choose to insert a worksheet or a variety of templates. The new sheet appears to the left of the selected tab.

# KEYBOARD SHORTCUTS

**I**n this chapter

If you are doing a lot of typing, being able to access commands from the keyboard is faster than moving your hand to the mouse. Excel 2007 introduces new keyboard accelerators, which are accessed using the Alt key, and many of the old Alt keyboard shortcuts still work. In addition, all the old Ctrl shortcut keys are still functional. For instance, Ctrl+C still copies a selection, Ctrl+X cuts a selection, and Ctrl+V pastes a selection.

In this chapter, I point out which of the old keyboard shortcuts still work, show you some new shortcuts, and introduce you to the new keyboard accelerators.

# USING THE NEW KEYBOARD ACCELERATORS

The goal of the new Excel 2007 keyboard accelerators is to allow you to access every command by using only the keyboard. In previous versions of Excel, many popular commands had keyboard accelerators, but many commands did not. Excel 2007 tries to ensure that every command can be invoked from the keyboard.

**CAUTION**

There is an arcane command in the Excel Options dialog that can cause the new keyboard accelerators not to work for you. It is possible that you turned on this setting in Excel 1995 and each successive upgrade of Excel has inherited the setting. You should check the setting before proceeding. To do so, you select the Office icon and then choose Excel Options. In the Advanced category, you scroll to near the bottom for Lotus Compatibility. If the setting for Microsoft Office Excel Menu Key has a slash (/), then you need to press the slash key rather than the Alt key for all the keyboard accelerators. If you prefer using the Alt key, you should clear the Menu Key setting. Just know that if you prefer using the slash key, you must use / in place of Alt with new keyboard accelerators.

To access the new accelerators, you press and release the Alt key. Notice that Excel places a ToolTip above each command, with an associated accelerator key.

Tiny letter ToolTips appear over each tab of the ribbon. In addition, number ToolTips appear over each icon in the Quick Access toolbar. Figure 4.1 shows the ToolTips.

**Figure 4.1**
Type the letters in the ToolTips along the top to open various ribbons. Typing the numbers in the numeric keytips access the Quick Access toolbar.

ToolTips with keyboard accelerators

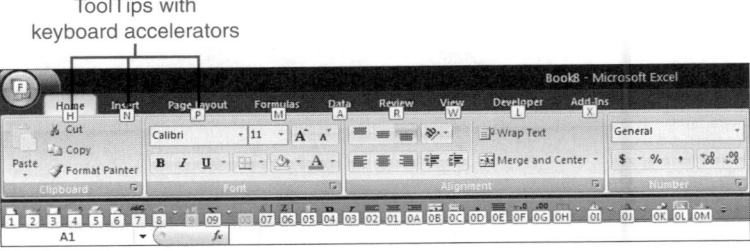

It is actually possible to memorize the keytips for the ribbon tabs.

Pressing Alt+F always accesses the Office icon menu in all Office 2007 applications.

**NOTE**

> Microsoft chose F as the accelerator for Office icon because in the original beta for Office 2007, the Office icon menu was the File menu.

Alt+H always accesses the Home ribbon in all Office 2007 applications. The accelerator definitions for each ribbon will remain constant even if new ribbon tabs are displayed. When you activate a pivot table, the original keytip letters (F, H, N, P, M, A, R, W, L, and X) remain, and two new keytips appear for the two new ribbons: JT for PivotTable Tools Options and JY for PivotTable Tools Design (see Figure 4.2).

**Figure 4.2**
New ribbon tabs get new letters, making sure the old letters remain constant.

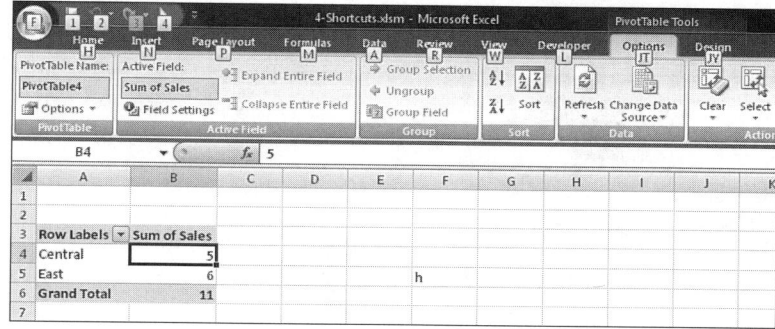

Unfortunately, the keytips for the Quick Access toolbar change every time you add new buttons or rearrange buttons on the Quick Access toolbar. If you want to memorize those keytips, you need to make sure you don't add a new Quick Access toolbar icon at the beginning of the list.

## SELECTING ICONS ON THE RIBBON

After you press the Alt key, you can press one of the keytip letters to bring up the appropriate ribbon. You now see that every icon on the ribbon has a keytip.

When you have chosen a ribbon, the keytips on the Quick Access toolbar disappear, so Microsoft is free to use the letters A through Z and the numbers 0 through 9.

On very busy ribbon tabs, some commands require two keystrokes (for example, A+C for Align Center in the Alignments Group of the Home ribbon, as shown in Figure 4.3). Note that once you have typed Alt to display the accelerators in the ToolTips, you do not have to continue holding down the Alt key.

**Figure 4.3**
After pressing the letter to switch to the ribbon, you type the letter or letters to invoke a particular command.

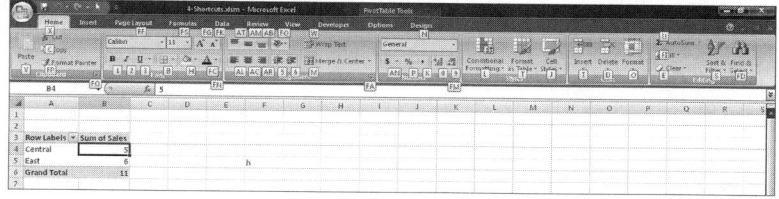

## SELECTING OPTIONS FROM A GALLERY

Figure 4.4 shows the results of pressing Alt+H+F+T, which is the equivalent of selecting Home, Format Table. This opens the gallery of possible table styles. As you can see in Figure 4.4, you can invoke the New Table Style and New Pivot Style commands at the bottom of the gallery by pressing N and P, respectively. However, there are no letters on the table style choices in the gallery.

In order to select a table style by using the keyboard, you need to use the arrow keys to move through the gallery. Because this gallery is two-dimensional, you can use the Up Arrow, Down Arrow, Right Arrow, Left Arrow, Page Down, Page Up, Home, and End keys to navigate through the gallery. When you have the desired table style highlighted, you press the Enter key to select it.

**Figure 4.4**
After opening a gallery, you use the arrow keys to navigate through the gallery and press Enter to select a style.

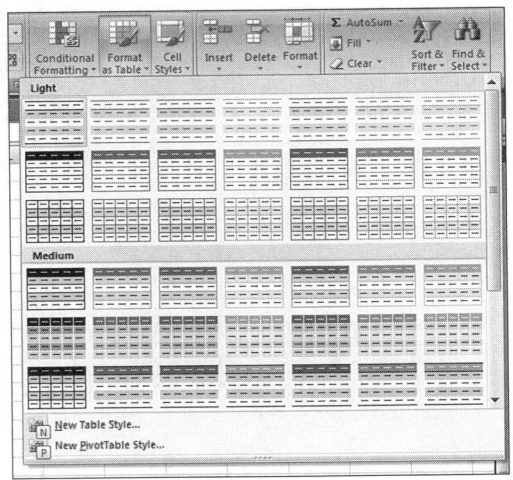

## NAVIGATING WITHIN DROP-DOWN LISTS

If you press Alt+H+F+S, which is the equivalent of selecting Home, Font Size, the font size in the drop-down is selected. You can either type a font size and press Enter or press the down arrow key to open the drop-down list. You can then use the Down Arrow, Up Arrow, Page Down, Page Up, Home, and End keys to navigate to a choice in the list. When you have the desired item highlighted, you press Enter to choose that item.

## BACKING UP ONE LEVEL THROUGH A MENU

Say that you press Alt+H to access the Home ribbon and then realize that you are in the wrong ribbon. You can press the Esc key to move back to display the ToolTips for the main menu choices.

If you want to clear the ToolTips completely, you can press Alt again.

## DEALING WITH KEYBOARD ACCELERATOR CONFUSION

If you want to select something on the Home ribbon in Figure 4.2, you may be frustrated because you can see the menu choices, but there are no ToolTips for most commands. For icons in the top of the ribbon, it appears that the main keytips apply to the menu items. For example, I keep thinking that the H keytip applies to Cut. Even though you are already on the Home ribbon, you need to press the H key to force Excel to show the ToolTips for the individual menu items on the Home ribbon.

> **NOTE**
>
> If you find the accelerator ToolTips to be confusing and unwieldy, you need to attack them one at a time. Find a task that you use regularly, such as sorting the current data set ascending by the selected column. Press the Alt key. Press A for the Data ribbon. You will see that A will sort ascending and D will sort desending. Those two should be easy enough to remember; Alt+A+A for sort ascending, and Alt+A+D for sort descending.

## SELECTING FROM LEGACY DIALOG BOXES

Some commands lead to legacy dialog boxes like the ones in previous editions of Excel. These dialog boxes do not display the Excel 2007 keytips. However, most of the dialog boxes do use the convention of having one letter of each command underlined (called a *hotkey*, in Microsoft parlance). In this case, you can press the underlined letter to select the command.

For example, you can press Alt+H+V+S instead of selecting Home, Paste, Paste Special. You are then presented with the Paste Special dialog box, as shown in Figure 4.5. In order to select Values and Transpose in this dialog, you press V for Values and E for Transpose (because those are the letters underlined in the dialog). You could then press Enter instead of clicking the default OK button.

**Figure 4.5**
In a legacy dialog box, you can type the underlined letters to select options.

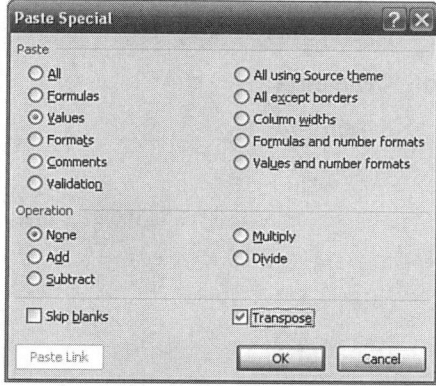

# USING THE SHORTCUT KEYS

Excel 2007 automatically recognizes all the Ctrl shortcut keys that were used in previous editions of Excel. In fact, many of these keys are consistent across all Windows applications. Table 4.1 lists the common Windows Ctrl shortcut keys.

**TABLE 4.1    WINDOWS SHORTCUT KEYS**

| Key Combination | Action |
| --- | --- |
| Ctrl+C | Copy |
| Ctrl+X | Cut |
| Ctrl+V | Paste |
| Ctrl+Z | Undo |
| Ctrl+Y | Redo |
| Ctrl+A | Select all |
| Ctrl+S | Save |
| Ctrl+O | Open |
| Ctrl+W or Ctrl+F4 | Close workbook |
| Ctrl+N | New workbook |
| Ctrl+P | Print |
| Ctrl+B | Bold |
| Ctrl+U | Underline |
| Ctrl+I | Italic |
| Ctrl+F | Find |

Table 4.2 illustrates the shortcut keys that you use to navigate.

**TABLE 4.2    SHORTCUT KEYS FOR NAVIGATION**

| Shortcut Key | Action |
| --- | --- |
| Ctrl+Home | Move to Cell A1 |
| Ctrl+End | Move to last active cell in the worksheet |
| Ctrl+Page Up | Move to previous worksheet |
| Ctrl+Page Down | Move to next worksheet |
| Shift+F11 | New Worksheet |
| Alt+Tab | Switch to next program |
| Alt+Shift+Tab | Switch to previous program |

| Shortcut Key | Action |
| --- | --- |
| Ctrl+Esc | Display Windows Start menu |
| Ctrl+F5 | Restore window size of current workbook |
| F6 | Switch to next pane in a window that has been split |
| Ctrl+F6 | When more than one workbook is open, switch to the next open workbook window |
| Ctrl+Shift+F6 | Switch to the previous workbook window |
| Ctrl+F9 | Minimize the window |
| Ctrl+F10 | Maximize the window |
| Ctrl+arrow key | Move to edge of current region |
| Home | Move to beginning of row |
| Ctrl+Backspace | Scroll to display the active cell |
| F5 | Display the GoTo dialog |
| Shift+F5 | Display the Find dialog |
| Shift+F4 | Find next |
| Ctrl+. (period) | Move to next corner of selected range |

Table 4.3 shows the shortcut keys you use to select data and cells.

## TABLE 4.3 SHORTCUT KEYS FOR SELECTING DATA AND CELLS

| Shortcut Key | Action |
| --- | --- |
| Ctrl+Spacebar | If used outside a table, select entire column; if used inside a table, toggle between selecting the data, data and headers, and the entire column |
| Shift+Spacebar | Select entire row |
| Shift+Backspace | With multiple cells selected, revert selection to only the active cell |
| Ctrl+Shift+* | Select the current region |
| Ctrl+/ | Select the array containing the active cell |
| Ctrl+Shift+O (letter O) | Select all cells that contain comments |
| Ctrl+\ | In a selected row, select the cells that don't match the value in the active cell |
| Ctrl+Shift+I | In a selected column, select the cells that don't match the value in the active cell |
| Ctrl+[ (opening square bracket) | Select all cells directly referenced by formulas in the selection |

*continues*

**TABLE 4.3 CONTINUED**

| Shortcut Key | Action |
|---|---|
| Ctrl+Shift+{ (opening brace) | Select all cells directly or indirectly referenced by formulas in the selection |
| Ctrl+] (closing square bracket) | Select cells that contain formulas that directly reference the active cell |
| Ctrl+Shift+} (closing brace) | Select cells that contain formulas that directly or indirectly reference the active cell |
| Alt+; (semicolon) | Select the visible cells in the current selection |

Table 4.4 shows the shortcut keys you use to extend a selection.

**TABLE 4.4 SHORTCUT KEYS FOR EXTENDING SELECTIONS**

| Shortcut Key | Action |
|---|---|
| F8 | Turn Extend mode on or off; in Extend mode, EXT appears in the status line, and the arrow keys extend the selection |
| Shift+F8 | Add another range of cells to the selection; or use the arrow keys to move to the start of the range you want to add and then press F8 and the arrow keys to select the next range |
| Shift+arrow key | Extend the selection by one cell |
| Ctrl+Shift+arrow key | Extend the selection to the last nonblank cell in the same column or row as the active cell |
| Shift+Home | Extend the selection to the beginning of the row |
| Ctrl+Shift+Home | Extend the selection to the beginning of the worksheet |
| Ctrl+Shift+End | Extend the selection to the last used cell on the worksheet (lower-right corner) |
| Shift+Page Down | Extend the selection down one screen |
| Shift+Page Up | Extend the selection up one screen |
| End+Shift+arrow key | Extend the selection to the last nonblank cell in the same column or row as the active cell |
| End+Shift+Home | Extend the selection to the last used cell on the worksheet (lower-right corner) |
| End+Shift+Enter | Extend the selection to the last cell in the current row |
| Scroll Lock+Shift+Home | Extend the selection to the cell in the upper-left corner of the window |
| Scroll Lock+Shift+End | Extend the selection to the cell in the lower-right corner of the window |

Table 4.5 shows the shortcut keys you use for entering, editing, formatting, and calculating data.

TABLE 4.5    SHORTCUT KEYS FOR DATA ENTRY, FORMATTING, AND CALCULATING DATA

| Shortcut Key | Action |
|---|---|
| Enter | Complete a cell entry and select the next cell below |
| Alt+Enter | Start a new line in the same cell |
| Ctrl+Enter | Fill the selected cell range with the current entry |
| Shift+Enter | Complete a cell entry and select the next cell above |
| Tab | Complete a cell entry and select the next cell to the right |
| Shift+Tab | Complete a cell entry and select the previous cell to the left |
| Esc | Cancel a cell entry |
| Arrow keys | Move one character up, down, left, or right |
| Home | Move to the beginning of the line |
| F4 or Ctrl+Y | Repeat the last action |
| Ctrl+Shift+F3 | Create names from row and column labels |
| Ctrl+D | Fill down |
| Ctrl+R | Fill to the right |
| Ctrl+F3 | Define a name |
| Ctrl+K | Insert a hyperlink |
| Ctrl+; (semicolon) | Enter the date |
| Ctrl+Shift+: (colon) | Enter the time |
| Alt+Down Arrow | Display a drop-down list of the values in the current column of a range |
| Ctrl+Z | Undo the last action |
| = (equal sign) | Start a formula |
| F2 | Move the insertion point into the formula bar when editing in a cell is turned off |
| Backspace | In the formula bar, delete one character to the left |
| Enter | Complete a cell entry from the cell or formula bar |
| Ctrl+Shift+Enter | Enter a formula as an array formula |
| Esc | Cancel an entry in the cell or formula bar |
| Shift+F3 | In a formula, display the Insert Function dialog box |
| Ctrl+A | When the insertion point is to the right of a function name in a formula, display the Function Arguments dialog box |

4

*continues*

**TABLE 4.5    SHORTCUT KEYS FOR DATA ENTRY, FORMATTING, AND CALCULATING DATA**

| Shortcut Key | Action |
| --- | --- |
| Ctrl+Shift+A | When the insertion point is to the right of a function name in a formula, insert the argument names and parentheses |
| F3 | Paste a defined name into a formula |
| Alt+= (equal sign) | Insert an AutoSum formula with the SUM function |
| Ctrl+Shift+" (quotation mark) | Copy the value from the cell above the active cell into the cell or the formula bar |
| Ctrl+' (apostrophe) | Copy a formula from the cell above the active cell into the cell or the formula bar |
| Ctrl+` (backtick) | Alternate between displaying cell values and displaying formulas |
| F9 | Calculate all worksheets in all open workbooks; when a portion of a formula is selected, calculate the selected portion and then press Enter or Ctrl+Shift+Enter (for array formulas) to replace the selected portion with the calculated value |
| Shift+F9 | Calculate the active worksheet |
| Ctrl+Alt+F9 | Calculate all worksheets in all open workbooks, regardless of whether they have changed since the last calculation |
| Ctrl+Alt+Shift+F9 | Recheck dependent formulas and then calculate all cells in all open workbooks, including cells not marked as needing to be calculated |
| F2 | Edit the active cell and position the insertion point at the end of the cell contents |
| Alt+Enter | Start a new line in the same cell |
| Backspace | Edit the active cell and then clear it or delete the preceding character in the active cell as you edit cell contents |
| Delete | Delete the character to the right of the insertion point or delete the selection |
| Ctrl+Delete | Delete text to the end of the line |
| F7 | Display the Spelling dialog box |
| Shift+F2 | Edit a cell comment |
| Enter | Complete a cell entry and select the next cell below |
| Ctrl+Z | Undo the last action |
| Esc | Cancel a cell entry |
| Ctrl+Shift+Z | When the AutoCorrect smart tag is displayed, undo or redo the last automatic correction |
| Delete | Clear the contents of the selected cells |

| Shortcut Key | Action |
|---|---|
| Ctrl+- (hyphen) | Delete the selected cells |
| Ctrl+Shift++ (plus sign) | Insert blank cells |
| Alt+' (apostrophe) | Display the Style dialog box |
| Ctrl+1 | Display the Format Cells dialog box |
| Ctrl+Shift+~ | Apply the General number format |
| Ctrl+Shift+$ | Apply the Currency format with two decimal places (negative numbers in parentheses) |
| Ctrl+Shift+% | Apply the Percentage format with no decimal places |
| Ctrl+Shift+^ | Apply the Exponential number format with two decimal places |
| Ctrl+Shift+# | Apply the Date format with the day, month, and year |
| Ctrl+Shift+@ | Apply the Time format with the hour and minute, and AM or PM |
| Ctrl+Shift+! | Apply the Number format with two decimal places, thousands separator, and minus sign (-) for negative values |
| Ctrl+B | Apply or remove bold formatting |
| Ctrl+I | Apply or remove italic formatting |
| Ctrl+U | Apply or remove underline |
| Ctrl+5 | Apply or remove strikethrough |
| Ctrl+9 | Hide the selected rows |
| Ctrl+Shift+( (opening parenthesis) | Unhide any hidden rows within the selection |
| Ctrl+0 (zero) | Hide the selected columns |
| Ctrl+Shift+) (closing parenthesis) | Unhide any hidden columns within the selection |
| Ctrl+Shift+& | Apply the outline border to the selected cells |
| Ctrl+Shift+_ (underscore) | Remove the outline border from the selected cells |

There are shortcut keys specifically for using the Border tab in the Format Cells dialog. You press Ctrl+1 to display the Format Cells dialog, and then you select the Border tab. Then you can use the shortcut keys shown in Table 4.6.

## TABLE 4.6 SHORTCUT KEYS FOR BORDERS

| Shortcut Key | Action |
|---|---|
| Alt+T | Apply or remove the top border |
| Alt+B | Apply or remove the bottom border |
| Alt+L | Apply or remove the left border |

*continues*

### TABLE 4.6   SHORTCUT KEYS FOR BORDERS

| Shortcut Key | Action |
| --- | --- |
| Alt+R | Apply or remove the right border |
| Alt+H | If cells in multiple rows are selected, apply or remove the horizontal divider |
| Alt+V | If cells in multiple columns are selected, apply or remove the vertical divider |
| Alt+D | Apply or remove the downward diagonal border |
| Alt+U | Apply or remove the upward diagonal border |

## USING EXCEL 2003 KEYBOARD ACCELERATORS

In previous versions of Excel, most menu items included one underlined letter. In those versions, you could hold down the Alt key while pressing the underlined letter to invoke the menu item. In the Excel 2003 screen shown in Figure 4.6, you can see that you can display the Edit menu by pressing Alt+E, and you can select Edit, Fill, Justify by pressing Alt+E+I+J.

**Figure 4.6**
Pressing Alt+E+I+J performs Edit, Fill, Justify.

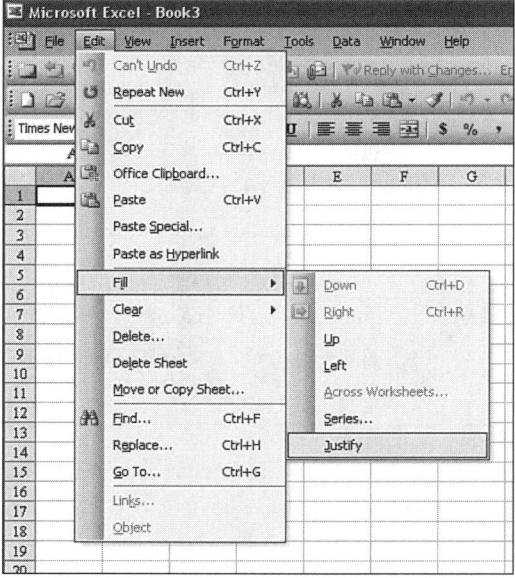

Instead of pressing Alt+E+I+J all at once, when the Edit menu is displayed, you can display the Fill fly-out menu by pressing I. Then, you can perform the Justify command by pressing J.

If you are a power Excel user, you probably have a few of these commands memorized. I always use Alt+E+I+J for Edit, Fill Justify; Alt+E+S+V for Edit, Paste Special, Values; and Alt+D+L for Data Validation. If you have some of these commands memorized, when you hear that the menu in Excel 2007 is completely gone, you might be worried that you have to relearn all the shortcut keys. But there is good news for the power Excel gurus who have favorite Alt shortcut keys burned into their minds: Most of them will continue to work as they did in Excel 2003.

If you were an intermediate Excel user who regularly used the Excel 2003 keyboard accelerators but had to look at the screen to use them, then you should start using the new keyboard accelerators discussed at the beginning of this chapter.

## INVOKING AN EXCEL 2003 ALT SHORTCUT

In Excel 2003, the main menus were File, Edit, View, Insert, Format, Tools, Data, Window, and Help, and the keyboard accelerator commands in Excel 2003 were Alt+F, Alt+E, Alt+V, Alt+I, Alt+O, Alt+T, Alt+D, Alt+W, and Alt+H.

If you are moving from Excel 2003 to Excel 2007, you will have the best success when trying to access commands on the Edit, View, Insert, Format, Tools, and Data menus. None of the keyboard accelerators associated with Window or Help work in Excel 2007. Alt+H takes you to the Home ribbon instead of the few commands on the Help menu, and Alt+W takes you to the View ribbon.

Some of the keyboard shortcuts associated with the File menu in Excel 2003 continue to work in Excel 2007. Pressing Alt+F opens the Office icon menu. In Excel 2003, pressing Alt+F+O would perform File, Open. It happens that O is the shortcut on the Office icon menu for open, so pressing Alt+F+O in Excel 2007 also performs File, Open.

For the shortcut keys Alt+E, Alt+V, Alt+I, Alt+O, Alt+T, and Alt+D, Excel switches into Office 2003 Access Key mode. In this mode, a ToolTip appears over the ribbon, indicating which letters you have typed so far (see Figure 4.7). When you have entered enough letters, the command is invoked. If you have forgotten the sequence, you can press Esc to exit the Excel 2003 Access Key mode.

**Figure 4.7**
The Office 2003 access key ToolTip shows which keys you have used so far while entering a legacy shortcut.

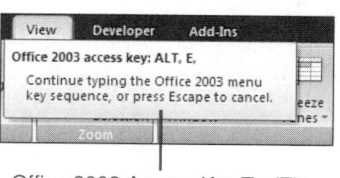

Office 2003 Access Key ToolTip

## DETERMINING WHICH COMMANDS WORK IN LEGACY MODE

If you try a command that no longer works in Excel 2007, nothing happens. Several commands don't make sense in the framework of Excel 2007, so they have been deprecated. For example View, Toolbars, Customize has no equivalent in Excel 2007 because the user interface does not allow for the customization of the ribbon; therefore, that command does not exist in Excel 2007.

Table 4.7 lists the legacy keyboard commands and shows which of them continue to work in Excel 2007.

**TABLE 4.7 EXCEL LEGACY KEYBOARD COMMANDS**

| Shortcut | Works in Excel 2007? | Command |
| --- | --- | --- |
| Alt+F+N | Yes | File, New |
| Alt+F+O | Yes | File, Open |
| Alt+F+C | Yes | File, Close |
| Alt+F+S | Yes | File, Save |
| Alt+F+A | Yes | File, Save As |
| Alt+F+G | No | File, Save as Web Page |
| Alt+F+W | No | File, Save Workspace |
| Alt+F+H | No | File, File Search |
| Alt+F+M | No | File, Permission |
| Alt+F+E | No | File, Check Out |
| Alt+F+E | No | File, Check In |
| Alt+F+R | No | File, Version History |
| Alt+F+B | No | File, Web Page Preview |
| Alt+F+U | No | File, Page Setup |
| Alt+F+T+S | No | File, Print Area, Set Print Area |
| Alt+F+T+C | No | File, Print Area, Clear Print Area |
| Alt+F+V | No | File, Print Preview |
| Alt+F+P | No | File, Print |
| Alt+F+D+M | No | File, Send To, Mail Recipient |
| Alt+F+D+S | No | File, Send To, Original Sender |
| Alt+F+D+C | No | File, Send To, Mail Recipient (for Review) |
| Alt+F+D+A | No | File, Send To, Mail Recipient (as Attachment) |
| Alt+F+D+R | No | File, Send To, Routing Recipient |
| Alt+F+D+E | No | File, Send To, Exchange Folder |
| Alt+F+D+O | No | File, Send To, Online Meeting Participant |
| Alt+F+D+X | No | File, Send To, Recipient Using Internet Fax Service |
| Alt+F+I | No | File, Properties |
| Alt+F+1 | Yes | File, 1 |

| Shortcut | Works in Excel 2007? | Command |
|---|---|---|
| Alt+F+2 | Yes | File, 2 |
| Alt+F+3 | Yes | File, 3 |
| Alt+F+4 | Yes | File, 4 |
| Alt+F+5 | Yes | File, 5 |
| Alt+F+6 | Yes | File, 6 |
| Alt+F+7 | Yes | File, 7 |
| Alt+F+8 | Yes | File, 8 |
| Alt+F+9 | Yes | File, 9 |
| Alt+F+T | No | File, Sign Out |
| Alt+F+X | Yes | File, Exit |
| Alt+E+U | Yes | Edit, Undo |
| Alt+E+R | Yes | Edit, Repeat |
| Alt+E+T | Yes | Edit, Cut |
| Alt+E+C | Yes | Edit, Copy |
| Alt+E+B | Yes | Edit, Office Clipboard |
| Alt+E+P | Yes | Edit, Paste |
| Alt+E+S | Yes | Edit, Paste Special |
| Alt+E+H | No | Edit, Paste as Hyperlink |
| Alt+E+I+D | Yes | Edit, Fill, Down |
| Alt+E+I+R | Yes | Edit, Fill, Right |
| Alt+E+I+U | Yes | Edit, Fill, Up |
| Alt+E+I+L | Yes | Edit, Fill, Left |
| Alt+E+I+A | Yes | Edit, Fill, Across Worksheets |
| Alt+E+I+S | Yes | Edit, Fill, Series |
| Alt+E+I+J | Yes | Edit, Fill, Justify |
| Alt+E+A+A | Yes | Edit, Clear, All |
| Alt+E+A+F | Yes | Edit, Clear, Formats |
| Alt+E+A+C | Yes | Edit, Clear, Contents |
| Alt+E+A+M | Yes | Edit, Clear, Comments |
| Alt+E+D | Yes | Edit, Delete |
| Alt+E+L | Yes | Edit, Delete Sheet |
| Alt+E+M | Yes | Edit, Move or Copy Sheet |

4

*continues*

**TABLE 4.7    CONTINUED**

| Shortcut | Works in Excel 2007? | Command |
|---|---|---|
| Alt+E+F | Yes | Edit, Find |
| Alt+E+E | Yes | Edit, Replace |
| Alt+E+G | Yes | Edit, Go To |
| Alt+E+K | Yes | Edit, Links |
| Alt+E+O | No | Edit, Object |
| Alt+E+O+V | No | Edit, Object, Convert |
| Alt+V+N | Yes | View, Normal |
| Alt+V+P | Yes | View, Page Break Preview |
| Alt+V+K | No | View, Task Pane |
| Alt+V+T+C | No | View, Toolbars, Customize |
| Alt+V+F | Yes | View, Formula Bar |
| Alt+V+S | No | View, Status Bar |
| Alt+V+H | Yes | View, Header and Footer |
| Alt+V+C | Yes | View, Comments |
| Alt+V+V | Yes | View, Custom Views |
| Alt+V+U | Yes | View, Full Screen (Caution: Use the Maximize button to return.) |
| Alt+V+Z | Yes | View, Zoom |
| Alt+I+E | Yes | Insert, Cells |
| Alt+I+R | Yes | Insert, Rows |
| Alt+I+C | Yes | Insert, Columns |
| Alt+I+W | Yes | Insert, Worksheet |
| Alt+I+H | Yes | Insert, Chart |
| Alt+I+S | Yes | Insert, Symbol |
| Alt+I+B | Yes | Insert, Page Break |
| Alt+I+A | Yes | Insert, Reset All Page Breaks |
| Alt+I+F | Yes | Insert, Function |
| Alt+I+N+D | Yes | Insert, Name, Define |
| Alt+I+N+P | Yes | Insert, Name, Paste |
| Alt+I+N+C | Yes | Insert, Name, Create |
| Alt+I+N+A | Yes | Insert, Name, Apply |

4

| Shortcut | Works in Excel 2007? | Command |
|---|---|---|
| Alt+I+N+L | Yes | Insert, Name, Label |
| Alt+I+M | Yes | Insert, Comment |
| Alt+I+A | Yes | Insert, Ink Annotations |
| Alt+I+P+C | Yes | Insert, Picture, Clip Art |
| Alt+I+P+F | Yes | Insert, Picture, From File |
| Alt+I+P+S | Yes | Insert, Picture, From Scanner or Camera |
| Alt+I+P+D | Yes | Insert, Picture, Ink Drawing and Writing |
| Alt+I+P+A | No | Insert, Picture, AutoShapes |
| Alt+I+P+W | No | Insert, Picture, WordArt |
| Alt+I+P+O | No | Insert, Picture, Organization Chart |
| Alt+I+G | No | Insert, Diagram |
| Alt+I+O | Yes | Insert, Object |
| Alt+I+I | Yes | Insert, Hyperlink |
| Alt+O+E | Yes | Format, Cells |
| Alt+O+R+E | Yes | Format, Row, Height |
| Alt+O+R+A | Yes | Format, Row, AutoFit |
| Alt+O+R+H | Yes | Format, Row, Hide |
| Alt+O+R+U | Yes | Format, Row, Unhide |
| Alt+O+C+W | Yes | Format, Column, Width |
| Alt+O+C+A | Yes | Format, Column, AutoFit Selection |
| Alt+O+C+H | Yes | Format, Column, Hide |
| Alt+O+C+U | Yes | Format, Column, Unhide |
| Alt+O+C+S | Yes | Format, Column, Standard Width |
| Alt+O+H+R | Yes | Format, Sheet, Rename |
| Alt+O+H+H | Yes | Format, Sheet, Hide |
| Alt+O+H+U | Yes | Format, Sheet, Unhide |
| Alt+O+H+B | Yes | Format, Sheet, Background |
| Alt+O+H+T | Yes | Format, Sheet, Tab Color |
| Alt+O+A | No | Format, AutoFormat |
| Alt+O+D | Yes | Format, Conditional Formatting |
| Alt+O+S | Yes | Format, Style |
| Alt+T+S | Yes | Tools, Spelling |

*continues*

4

**TABLE 4.7 CONTINUED**

| Shortcut | Works in Excel 2007? | Command |
|---|---|---|
| Alt+T+R | Yes | Tools, Research |
| Alt+T+K | Yes | Tools, Error Checking |
| Alt+T+H+H | No | Tools, Speech, Speech Recognition |
| Alt+T+H+T | No | Tools, Speech, Show Text to Speech Toolbar |
| Alt+T+D | Yes | Tools, Shared Workspace |
| Alt+T+B | Yes | Tools, Share Workbook |
| Alt+T+T+H | Yes | Tools, Track Changes, Highlight Changes |
| Alt+T+T+A | Yes | Tools, Track Changes, Accept or Reject Changes |
| Alt+T+W | Yes | Tools, Compare and Merge Workbooks |
| Alt+T+P+P | Yes | Tools, Protection, Protect Sheet |
| Alt+T+P+A | Yes | Tools, Protection, Allow Users to Edit Ranges |
| Alt+T+P+W | Yes | Tools, Protection, Protect Workbook |
| Alt+T+P+S | Yes | Tools, Protection, Protect and Share Workbook |
| Alt+T+N+M | Yes | Tools, Online Collaboration, Meet Now |
| Alt+T+N+S | Yes | Tools, Online Collaboration, Schedule Meeting |
| Alt+T+N+W | Yes | Tools, Online Collaboration, Web Discussions |
| Alt+T+N+N | Yes | Tools, Online Collaboration, End Review |
| Alt+T+G | Yes | Tools, Goal Seek |
| Alt+T+E | Yes | Tools, Scenarios |
| Alt+T+U+T | Yes | Tools, Formula Auditing, Trace Precedents |
| Alt+T+U+D | Yes | Tools, Formula Auditing, Trace Dependents |
| Alt+T+U+E | Yes | Tools, Formula Auditing, Trace Error |
| Alt+T+U+A | Yes | Tools, Formula Auditing, Remove All Arrows |
| Alt+T+U+F | Yes | Tools, Formula Auditing, Evaluate Formula |
| Alt+T+U+W | Yes | Tools, Formula Auditing, Show Watch Window |
| Alt+T+U+M | Yes | Tools, Formula Auditing, Formula Auditing Mode |
| Alt+T+U+S | No | Tools, Formula Auditing, Show Formula Auditing Toolbar |
| Alt+T+V | Yes | Tools, Solver |
| Alt+T+M+M | Yes | Tools, Macro, Macros |
| Alt+T+M+R | Yes | Tools, Macro, Record New Macro |
| Alt+T+M+S | Yes | Tools, Macro, Security |

4

| Shortcut | Works in Excel 2007? | Command |
|---|---|---|
| Alt+T+M+V | Yes | Tools, Macro, Visual Basic Editor |
| Alt+T+M+E | No | Tools, Macro, Microsoft Script Editor |
| Alt+T+I | Yes | Tools, Add-ins |
| Alt+T+C | No | Tools, COM Add-ins |
| Alt+T+A | Yes | Tools, AutoCorrect Options |
| Alt+T+C | No | Tools, Customize |
| Alt+T+O | No | Tools, Options |
| Alt+T+D | No | Tools, Data Analysis |
| Alt+D+S | Yes | Data, Sort |
| Alt+D+F+F | Yes | Data, Filter, AutoFilter |
| Alt+D+F+S | Yes | Data, Filter, Show All |
| Alt+D+F+A | Yes | Data, Filter, Advanced Filter |
| Alt+D+O | Yes | Data, Form |
| Alt+D+B | Yes | Data, Subtotals |
| Alt+D+L | Yes | Data, Validation |
| Alt+D+T | Yes | Data, Table |
| Alt+D+E | Yes | Data, Text to Columns |
| Alt+D+N | Yes | Data, Consolidate |
| Alt+D+G+H | Yes | Data, Group and Outline, Hide Detail |
| Alt+D+G+S | Yes | Data, Group and Outline, Show Detail |
| Alt+D+G+G | Yes | Data, Group and Outline, Group |
| Alt+D+G+U | Yes | Data, Group and Outline, Ungroup |
| Alt+D+G+A | Yes | Data, Group and Outline, Auto Outline |
| Alt+D+G+C | Yes | Data, Group and Outline, Clear Outline |
| Alt+D+G+E | Yes | Data, Group and Outline, Settings |
| Alt+D+P | Yes | Data, PivotTable and PivotChart Report |
| Alt+D+D+D | Yes | Data, Import External Data, Import Data |
| Alt+D+D+W | Yes | Data, Import External Data, New Web Query |
| Alt+D+D+N | Yes | Data, Import External Data, New Database Query |
| Alt+D+D+E | Yes | Data, Import External Data, Edit Query |
| Alt+D+D+A | Yes | Data, Import External Data, Data Range Properties |

*continues*

**TABLE 4.7   CONTINUED**

| Shortcut | Works in Excel 2007? | Command |
|---|---|---|
| Alt+D+D+M | Yes | Data, Import External Data, Parameters |
| Alt+D+I+C | Yes | Data, List, Create List |
| Alt+D+I+R | Yes | Data, List, Resize List |
| Alt+D+I+T | Yes | Data, List, Total Row |
| Alt+D+I+V | Yes | Data, List, Convert to Range |
| Alt+D+I+P | Yes | Data, List, Publish List |
| Alt+D+I+L | No | Data, List, View List on Server |
| Alt+D+I+U | No | Data, List, Unlink List |
| Alt+D+I+Y | No | Data, List, Synchronize List |
| Alt+D+I+D | No | Data, List, Discard Changes and Refresh |
| Alt+D+I+B | No | Data, List, Hide Border of Inactive Lists |
| Alt+D+X+I | Yes | Data, XML, Import |
| Alt+D+X+E | Yes | Data, XML, Export |
| Alt+D+X+R | Yes | Data, XML, Refresh XML Data |
| Alt+D+X+X | Yes | Data, XML, XML Source |
| Alt+D+X+P | Yes | Data, XML, XML Map Properties |
| Alt+D+X+Q | Yes | Data, XML, Edit Query |
| Alt+D+X+A | Yes | Data, XML, XML Expansion Packs |
| Alt+D+R | Yes | Data, Refresh Data |
| Alt+W+N | No | Window, New Window |
| Alt+W+A | No | Window, Arrange |
| Alt+W+B | No | Window, Compare Side by Side with `filename` |
| Alt+W+H | No | Window, Hide |
| Alt+W+U | No | Window, Unhide |
| Alt+W+S | No | Window, Split |
| Alt+W+F | No | Window, Freeze Panes |
| Alt+W+1 | No | Window, 1 |
| Alt+W+2 | No | Window, 2 |
| Alt+W+3 | No | Window, 3 |
| Alt+W+4 | No | Window, 4 |
| Alt+W+5 | No | Window, 5 |

| Shortcut | Works in Excel 2007? | Command |
|----------|----------------------|---------|
| Alt+W+6 | No | Window, 6 |
| Alt+W+7 | No | Window, 7 |
| Alt+W+8 | No | Window, 8 |
| Alt+W+9 | No | Window, 9 |
| Alt+W+M | No | Window, More Windows |
| Alt+H+H | No | Help, Microsoft Excel Help |
| Alt+H+O | No | Help, Show the Office Assistant |
| Alt+H+M | No | Help, Microsoft Office Online |
| Alt+H+C | No | Help, Contact Us |
| Alt+H+L | No | Help, Lotus 1-2-3 Help |
| Alt+H+K | No | Help, Check for Updates |
| Alt+H+R | No | Help, Detect and Repair |
| Alt+H+V | No | Help, Activate Product |
| Alt+H+F | No | Help, Customer Feedback Options |
| Alt+H+A | No | Help, About Microsoft Office Excel |

I am sure there are some people who liked using Alt+F+T+S in Excel 2003 for File, Print Area, Set Print Area. If you are one of those people, I'm sure you're unhappy that your favorite shortcut key is no longer supported. However, most of the powerful and common shortcut keys are still available, so there is a good chance that for most people who upgrade, their knowledge of past shortcut keys will help them in Excel 2007.

4

# GALLERIES, LIVE PREVIEW, AND THEMES

## In this chapter

A goal of Microsoft Excel 2007 is to make it easy to make great-looking documents. To this end, Microsoft has included 20 professionally designed themes. A *theme* is a combination of colors, fonts, and effects. If you change the theme, your whole document instantly gains a new look. Themes can be used across Excel, PowerPoint, and Word.

In addition to the 20 built-in themes, you can download new themes from Office Online, or create new custom themes (for example, to match your company's logo colors).

Galleries are new to Excel. Organized in rows and columns, a *gallery* is a drop-down that may contain 20 thumbnails of professionally designed choices. If you are formatting a table, creating a chart, or choosing an effect for an image, you can select built-in effects from a gallery. Many galleries allow you to customize new styles to be added to the gallery on your computer.

Live Preview is a testament to just how fast computers have become. If you would like to change a font style, you simply select the cells and then open the font name list box. As you hover over a font, the worksheet behind the list box instantly updates to show what the worksheet would look like if you chose the font.

The process of choosing a font or an effect often involves hovering here, hovering there, finding the appropriate font or effect, and clicking it.

# USING GALLERIES

A gallery is a new, super-sized selection box that appears from either a drop-down on a ribbon or from one of a number of icons on a ribbon.

The Format as Table icon on the Home ribbon is an example of a gallery that appears from a drop-down on the ribbon. When you select this drop-down, the first six rows of the gallery appear, as shown in Figure 5.1. Below the 42 choices shown, some menu items appear. These menu items usually take you to a More dialog box or to a dialog box to create a new style.

The gallery shown in Figure 5.1 has a scrollbar along the right side. You can scroll down to see the additional styles available in the gallery.

If you hover over any gallery thumbnail, a ToolTip appears, giving you information such as the name of the style.

Figure 5.2 shows the gallery after you scroll to the bottom. A ToolTip identifies one selection.

The Chart Styles gallery on the Chart Tools – Design ribbon is an example of a gallery that appears as several icons on the ribbon. As shown in Figure 5.3, the gallery initially shows six icons. There are three arrow icons to the right of the gallery. The first two arrows scroll one row at a time into view in the ribbon.

A more efficient method for viewing more items in the gallery is to use the More button to show all items in the gallery. The More button is the third button to the right of the gallery, as shown in Figure 5.4

**Figure 5.1**
Choose Format as Table, and a large gallery appears.

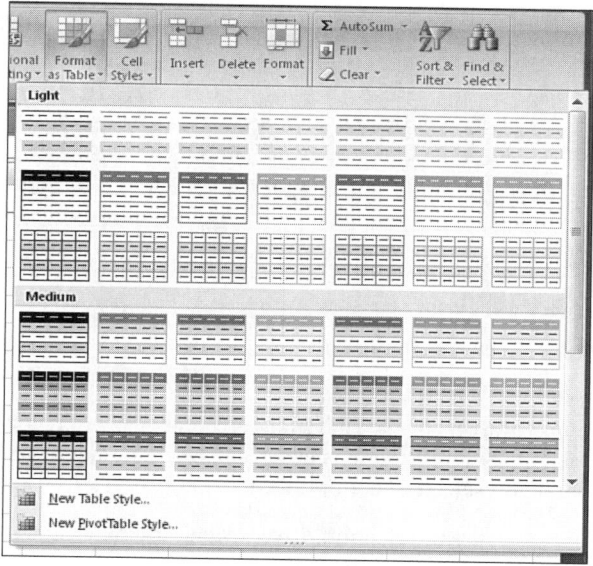

**Figure 5.2**
You have to scroll through some galleries to see the entire selection.

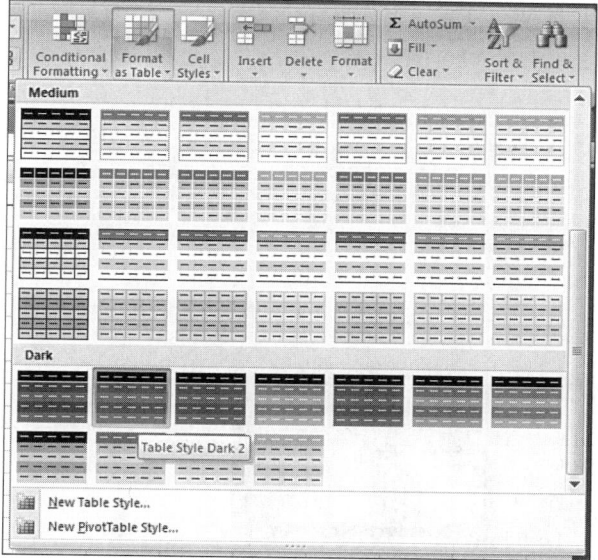

**Figure 5.3**
The up and down scroll buttons adjacent to the gallery in the ribbon enable you to scroll through one row at a time.

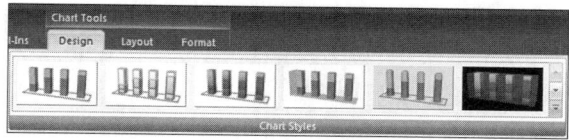

**Figure 5.4**
You use the More button to open the entire gallery.

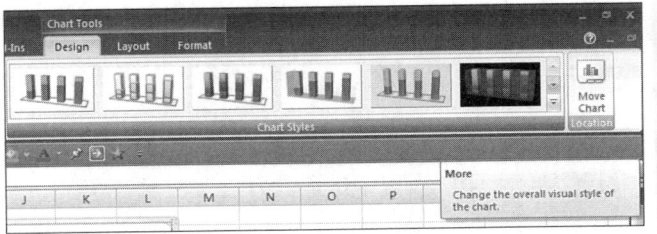

# USING LIVE PREVIEW

Live Preview provides an answer to the question, "What would this selection look like in the worksheet?"

If you open a drop-down list from the ribbon, Live Preview is often enabled. As you hover over various items in the list, the selected cells in the worksheet automatically preview what they would look like if you selected that option.

When you hover over a different selection, Live Preview quickly changes to reflect the new selection. Figure 5.5 shows a Live Preview of some text in the Parkway Resorthotel font.

**Figure 5.5**
If you hover for a second over one font, Excel shows a preview of the font in the selected cells.

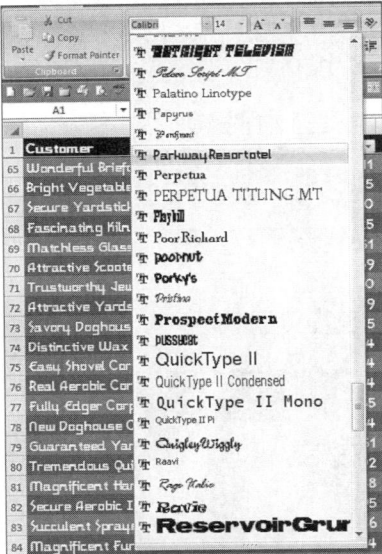

The preview shown with Live Preview is not permanent. If you hover over another item, the view of the workbook changes. In the process of scrolling up to the Cocktail Shaker font shown in Figure 5.6, for example, Excel flips through dozens of previews of the data.

If you close the list box without clicking an item, the workbook reverts to the original style.

The Live Preview feature works with items as mundane as the font size and font face drop-downs. It also works with many new features, such as table format and conditional formatting color scales.

**Figure 5.6**
If you move to a new font the preview changes.

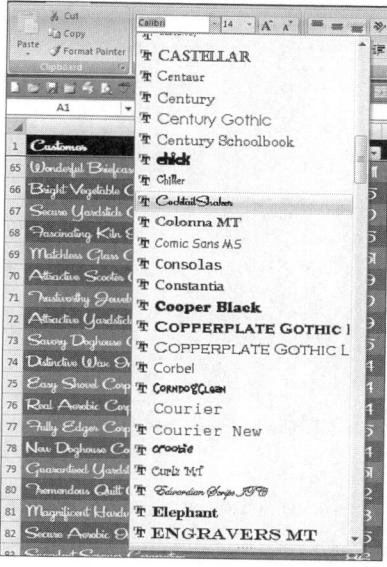

There are a few items with which Live Preview does not work. When you are trying to decide on a chart type, for example, Live Preview is not enabled. This is because Excel would actually have to add an object to the sheet in order to show you the preview. There are also a few drop-downs where Live Preview doesn't work. Microsoft figures you know what an underline or double underline would look like, so this drop-down does not allow Live Preview.

As with the Mini toolbar, you can choose to turn off Live Preview if it annoys you. From the Microsoft Office menu, you choose Excel Options. In the Personalize category of the Excel Options dialog, you can select the Enable Live Preview check box to enable Live Preview or clear it to disable Live Preview.

## UNDERSTANDING THEMES

A *theme* is a collection of colors, fonts, and effects. Office 2007 has 20 themes built in. You can also download new themes from Office online, and you can design your own themes, too.

Themes are shared in simple XML files, so they can easily be propagated throughout a company.

A theme has the following components:

- **Fonts**—A theme has two fonts: one for body text and one for titles. The fonts come into play a lot more in PowerPoint and Word, but there are styles in Excel that use them as well.

- **Colors**—There are 12 colors: 4 for text and backgrounds, 6 accent colors that are used in charts and table accents, and 2 for hyperlinks (1 for followed hyperlinks and 1 for unclicked hyperlinks). You see the 10 colors besides the hyperlink colors in the color chooser, as shown in Figure 5.7. The first 4 colors are for text and backgrounds. The next 6 colors are the accent colors. In each column, you then see various shades of these 10 colors.

- **Effects**—A theme includes a number of object effects, such as bevel and line style.

5

**Figure 5.7**
The color chooser shows 6 shades of each of the 10 theme colors.

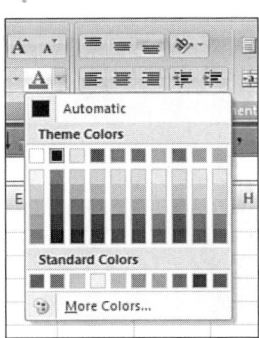

## CHOOSING A NEW THEME

You manage themes on the Page Layout ribbon. There are four drop-downs in the Themes group:

- **Themes**—This drop-down allows you to switch among the 20 built-in themes.
- **Colors**—This drop-down allows you to change the color scheme to use the colors from another theme.
- **Fonts**—This drop-down allows you to use the fonts from another theme.
- **Effects**—This drop-down allows you to use the effects from another theme.

Changing a theme affects charts, tables, SmartArt diagrams, and inserted objects. Note that you can use only one theme per workbook. If you are changing the theme on Sheet33, the same changes are made on all the other worksheets in the workbook.

To switch to another theme, you follow these steps:

1. Arrange your worksheet so that you can see any themed elements, such as tables or charts, on the right side of the screen.
2. From the Page Layout ribbon, choose the Themes drop-down from the Themes group.
3. Hover over the various themes. The worksheet updates to show the new colors, fonts, and effects.
4. When you have found a theme you like, click the theme to apply it to the workbook.

Figures 5.8 and 5.9 show the same worksheet with two different themes.

If you are strictly interested in the accent colors, you can select the Colors drop-down from the Themes group to get a great view of the accent colors used in each theme. Figure 5.10 shows the options in the Colors drop-down.

**Figure 5.8**
The Solstice theme features a sans serif font and bright colors.

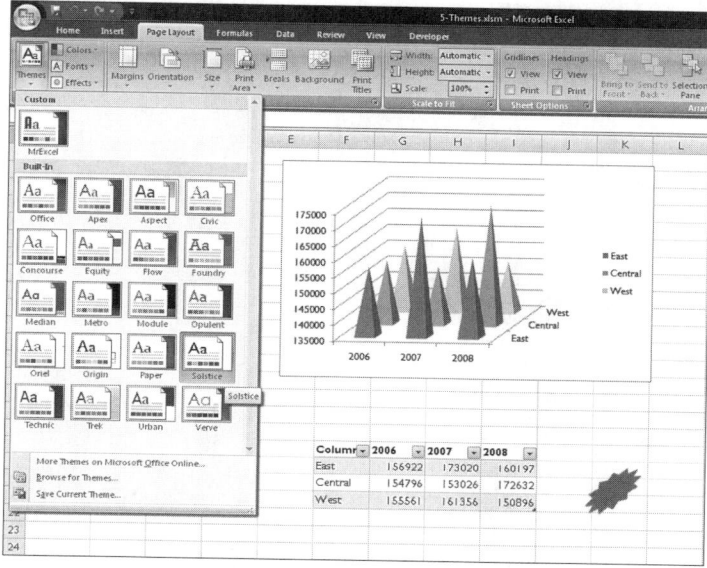

**Figure 5.9**
The Apex theme features a serif font, muted colors, and different effects.

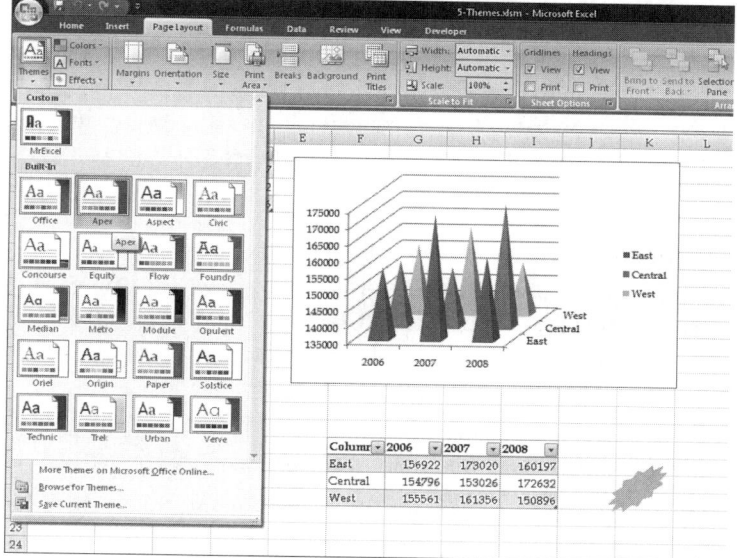

5

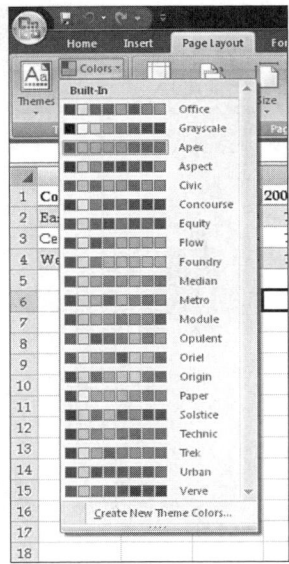

**Figure 5.10**
The Colors drop-down shows the accent colors for all 20 themes at once.

## CREATING A NEW THEME

You might want to develop a special theme. This is fairly easy to do: You basically need to select two fonts and six accent colors. For example, let's say you want to create a theme to match your company's color scheme. The hardest part is probably finding six colors to represent your company because most company logos have two or three colors. The following sections describe how to create a new theme and suggest resources for choosing complementary colors for your company colors.

### UNDERSTANDING RGB COLOR CODES

Colors on computer monitors are described as a mix of red (R), green (G), and blue (B). Each color channel is assigned a value from 0 to 255. For example, a color of R=255, G=0, B=0 is a bright red. As you add more blue, the red shifts toward a pink or violet color. A color of R=255, G=0, B=128 is a pinkish violet color.

A color of R=0, G=0, B=0 is black. A color of R=255, G=255, B=255 is white. You can create 16.7 million different colors by using combinations of red, green, and blue.

To discover the codes for your company's color scheme, follow these steps:

1. Open your company's home page in a browser.
2. In Internet Explorer, Select View, Source. In Firefox, choose View, Page Source. You now see the underlying HTML code.
3. Find the colors used in the page by searching for a pound sign (#). A webpage specifies colors by using a pound sign followed by six characters (for example, #4F81BD).

Although every webpage uses the #123456 notation for describing colors, Microsoft Excel's theme specification instead needs the RGB value for the color. Luckily, it is fairly easy to convert between the two.

TIP FROM

The color chooser in Photoshop shows the RGB value for any #123456 notation.

Hexadecimal is a numbering system that has digits 0 through 9 and A through F. Including 0, there are 16 digits in the hexadecimal numbering system. In the decimal system, a 2-digit number can represent 10×10 different combinations. There are 100 numbers, from 00 to 99. In a hex system, a 2-digit number can represent 16×16 different numbers—that is, 256 numbers, from 0 to 255.

In the #123456 nomenclature, the # sign indicates that the number is in hexadecimal. The first two digits are the hex representation of the red value. The next two digits are the hex representation of the green value. The next two digits are the hex representation of the blue value.

### CONVERTING FROM HEX TO DECIMAL

If you don't have Photoshop or another tool that converts from a hex color to an RGB value for you automatically, you can use functions in Excel to do the conversion. For example, the worksheet in Figure 5.11 converts from a hex color in Cell B1 to the RGB values in B7:B9:

- The formulas in B2:B4 use the MID function to extract each pair of numbers from the color code. The formula for Cell B2 is shown in Cell C2.
- The formulas in B7:B9 use the HEX2DEC function to convert the 2-digit hex number to decimal.

To represent the color #FF9108 in Excel, for example, you would use R=255, G=145, B=8.

**Figure 5.11**
This quick Excel worksheet can convert from a 6-digit hex color code to a decimal RGB value.

| | A | B | C | D |
|---|---|---|---|---|
| | B1 | ▼ | *fx* #FF9108 | |
| 1 | | #FF9108 | | |
| 2 | | FF | =MID(B1,2,2) | |
| 3 | | 91 | =MID(B1,4,2) | |
| 4 | | 08 | =MID(B1,6,2) | |
| 5 | | | | |
| 6 | | | | |
| 7 | R: | 255 | =HEX2DEC(B2) | |
| 8 | G: | 145 | =HEX2DEC(B3) | |
| 9 | B: | 8 | =HEX2DEC(B4) | |
| 10 | | | | |

### FINDING NEW COLORS

If you look at your company's logo and website, you can probably identify two or three colors to use in the theme. You need to come up with a total of six accent colors for a theme.

You can use the free web-based tool at http://wellstyled.com/tools/colorscheme2/index-en.html# to find colors that look good together.

To find complementary colors, you follow these steps:

1. Start with a hex representation of one of your logo colors.
2. Open http://wellstyled.com/tools/colorscheme2/index-en.html# in a browser.
3. In the lower-left corner, click the link for Enter RGB (rough conversion).
4. In the window that pops up, enter the portion of the color code after the pound sign (for example, FF9108).
5. Click each of the five icons under the color wheel on the left (for contrast, triad, tetrad, and analogic). In the Triad view, the website shows your original color, three others, and three variations of each, as shown in Figure 5.12. The right side of the website specifies the hex color codes for all the colors shown.

**Figure 5.12**
This webpage suggests colors that complement your logo colors.

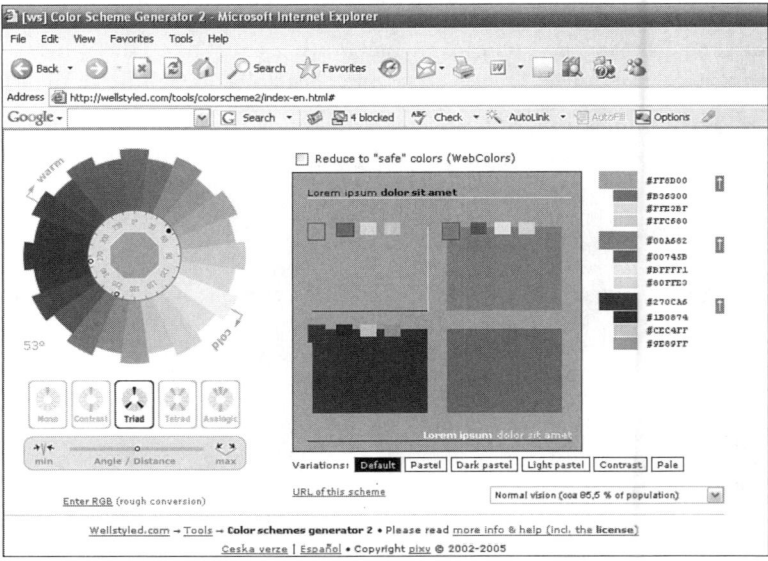

## SPECIFYING A THEME'S COLORS

To specify new theme colors, you follow these steps.

1. Select Page Layout, Themes, Colors, Create New Theme Colors. The Create New Theme Colors dialog appears. Remember that a theme is composed of 2 text colors, 2 background colors, 6 accent colors, and 2 hyperlink colors. These 12 colors are shown in the Create New Theme Colors dialog, as shown in Figure 5.13.

**Figure 5.13**
The 12 colors in the current theme are shown here.

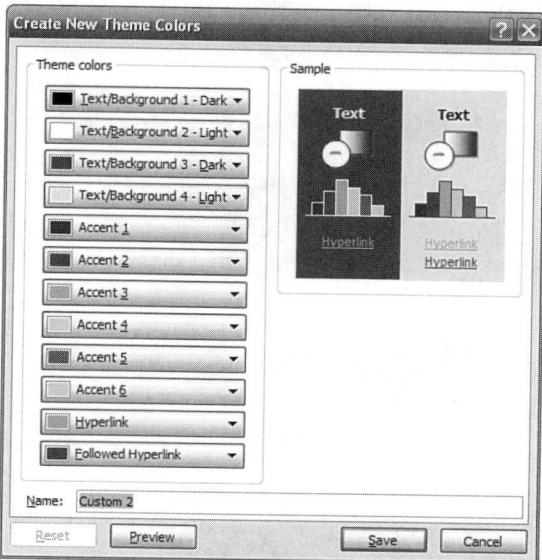

2. To change the first accent color, choose the drop-down next to Accent 1. The color chooser appears.

3. From the bottom of the color chooser drop-down, choose More Colors. The Colors dialog appears.

4. In the Custom tab of the Colors dialog, enter values for red, green, and blue, as shown in Figure 5.14. The New color block shows the color. Click OK to accept the color.

**Figure 5.14**
You specify the RGB values for the first color.

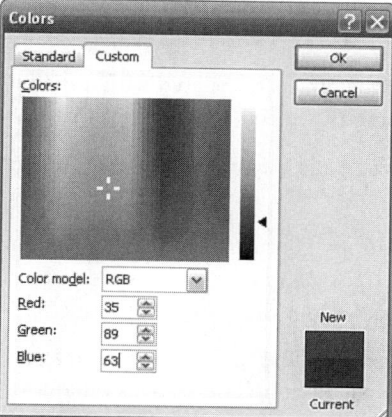

5. Repeat steps 2–4 for each of the accent colors.

6. If you want to change the colors for Hyperlink, Followed Hyperlink, and Text, repeat steps 2–4 for any of those.

7. In the Name box, give the theme a name, such as your company name.

8. Click Preview to see the theme applied to your workbook.

9. Click Save to accept the theme.

### SPECIFYING A THEME'S FONTS

To specify new theme fonts, you follow these steps:

1. Select Page Layout, Themes, Fonts, Create New Theme Fonts. The Create New Theme Fonts dialog appears, as shown in Figure 5.15. Remember that a font theme contains a heading font and a body font.

**Figure 5.15**
A theme is composed of two fonts.

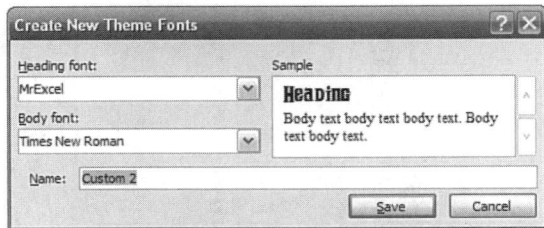

2. Select a font from the Heading Font drop-down. If a custom font is used in your company's logo, using it might be appropriate.

3. Select a font from the Body Font drop-down. This should be a font that is easy to read. Avoid stylized fonts for body copy.

4. Give the theme a name. It is okay to reuse the same name from the color theme.

5. Click Save to accept the theme changes.

### REUSING ANOTHER THEME'S EFFECTS

There is not a dialog box to choose the effects associated with a theme. Other than editing the XML by hand, you are stuck using the effects from one of the built-in themes.

To select effects for a theme, from the Page Layout, you select Themes, Effects and choose one of the existing themes.

The Effects dropdown is initially vexing. There are only subtle clues about the effects used in the theme, as shown in Figure 5.16. Each effects icon consists of a circle, an arrow, and a rectangle. These shapes give you clues about the effects in the theme.

When you insert a shape on a worksheet, there are six rows of Shape Styles available in the gallery on the Drawing Tools – Format ribbon. These styles range from simple (row 1) to moderate (row 4) to intense (row 6).

- The circle in the icon relates to simple shape styles.

- The arrow in the icon relates to moderate shape styles.

- The rectangle in the icon relates to intense shape styles.

**Figure 5.16**
The Effects dropdown offers subtle clues about the effects in a theme.

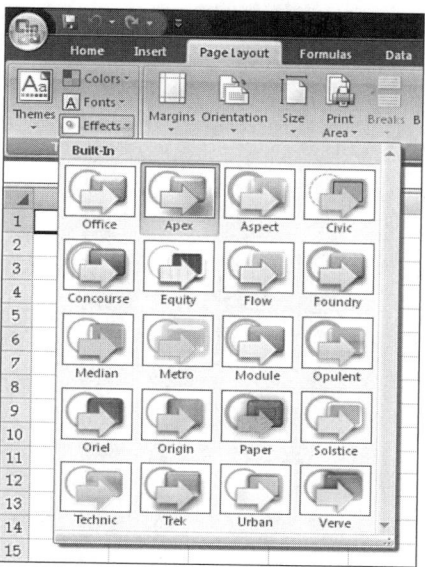

Examine the circle in the upper-left of each theme icon. Aspect, Concourse, Currency, and Opulent use a double line for the simple shape styles. Civic uses a broken line.

The effects used on the arrow indicate the shape effects used for moderate shape effects. For example, Equity uses a vertical pattern of lines in moderate styles. Currency applies a slight gradient. Trek uses more of a shadow than Technic.

The rectangle indicates the effects applied to intense styles. It is barely perceptible, but there is a bit of a reflection under the rectangle in Deluxe, and a glow around the rectangle in Metro.

These effects apply to various shape styles. In Figure 5.17, a dozen pairs of rounded rectangles are shown with 12 different Theme Effects. The top shape in each pair uses a moderate shape style. The bottom shape in each pair uses an intense shape style. The 12 pairs are arranged in the same order as effects in the theme box—Office, Apex, Aspect, and Civic in the first two rows; Concourse, Currency, Deluxe, and Equity in the next two rows; and Flow, Foundry, Median, and Metro in the last two rows.

These real examples show that Apex offers a more pronounced shadow than the other themes. Equity is darker. Metro has more of a glow. (For a color version of this figure, see http://www.mrexcel.com/05fig17.jpg).

NOTE

Figure 5.17 is a composite of 12 screenshots put together in Photoshop. There is not a way to represent more than one theme in a single Excel workbook.

**Figure 5.17**
These shapes illustrate changes introduced by the Theme Effects dropdown.

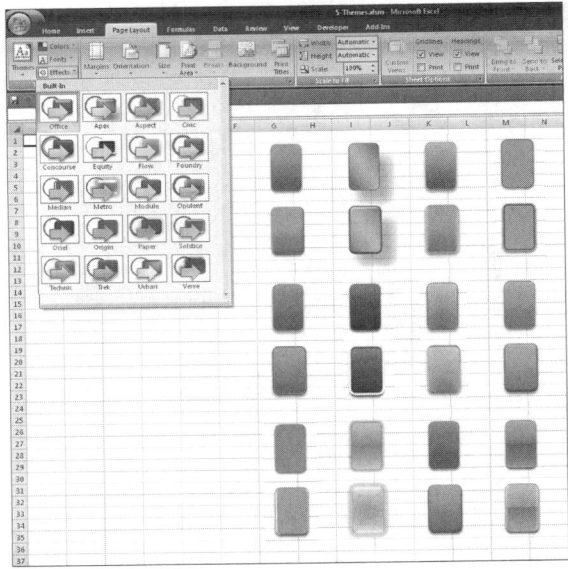

## SAVING A CUSTOM THEME

In order to reuse a theme, you must save it. From the Page Layout ribbon, you select Themes, Themes, Save Current Theme, as shown in Figure 5.18.

**Figure 5.18**
The option to save a theme is at the bottom of the Themes drop-down.

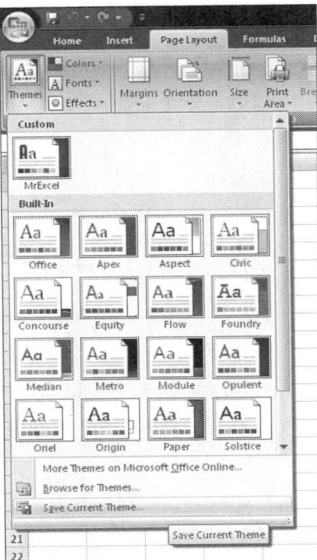

By default, themes are stored in the `Document Themes` folder. In Windows XP, this folder is in `C:\Documents and Settings\user name\Application Data\Microsoft\Templates\Document Themes\`. In Windows Vista, the folder is in `C:\Users\user name\AppData\Roaming\Microsoft\Templates\Document Themes`.

You need to give your theme a useful name and click Save.

## USING A THEME ON A NEW DOCUMENT

When you open a new document on the same computer, the Custom theme is in the Themes drop-down on the Page Layout ribbon. You can easily use this theme on all future documents.

## SHARING A THEME WITH OTHERS

If you want to share a theme with others, you need to send them the `.thmx` file from the theme folder.

The people you share the theme with can either copy the `.thmx` file to their equivalent folder or save the `.thmx` file to their desktop and use the Browse for Themes option, by choosing Page Layout, Themes, Themes, Browse for Themes.

5

CHAPTER **6**

# THE EXCEL OPTIONS DIALOG

**I**n this chapter

In previous versions of Excel, many options were controlled through either Tools, Options or Tools, Customize dialog. Tools, Customize was the important place to turn off the adaptive menus and to customize the toolbars. Tools, Options led to the busiest dialog box in Excel; the Options dialog has 173 settings on 14 tabs. In addition, the Options dialog had six buttons that would take you to further dialogs. It was a challenge to find something specific in the old Options dialog.

Fortunately, Microsoft has completely redesigned the Excel Options dialog for Excel 2007 (as it has the Options dialogs for the rest of Office 2007). Microsoft had the following goals for the Options dialogs for all the Office products:

- Show the most important settings earlier and more clearly so that they can be found. Most of the items you need to change are now found in the Popular, Formulas, Proofing, and Save categories.
- Move the arcane functions to an Advanced category.
- Add ToolTip icons next to many items so you can understand exactly what those settings do.
- Make it clear whether a setting affects all workbooks, the current workbook, or the current worksheet.

## INTRODUCING THE EXCEL OPTIONS DIALOG

This section shows you how to display Excel options and provides an overview of what you might find on each tab. Later sections of this chapter cover each tab in detail. The entry to the Excel Options dialog is at the bottom of the Office icon menu, near the Exit Excel button, as shown in Figure 6.1.

Instead of tabs, the Excel Options dialog uses nine categories of options along the left side, as shown in Figure 6.2. When you choose a category on the left, the settings for that category appear on the right.

6

**Figure 6.1**
The Excel Options button is on the Office icon menu.

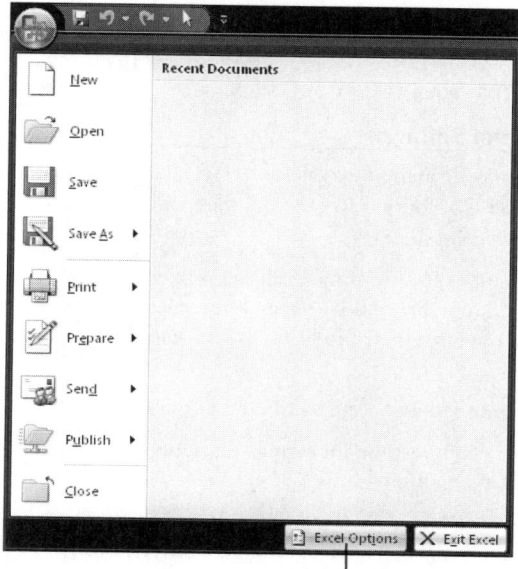

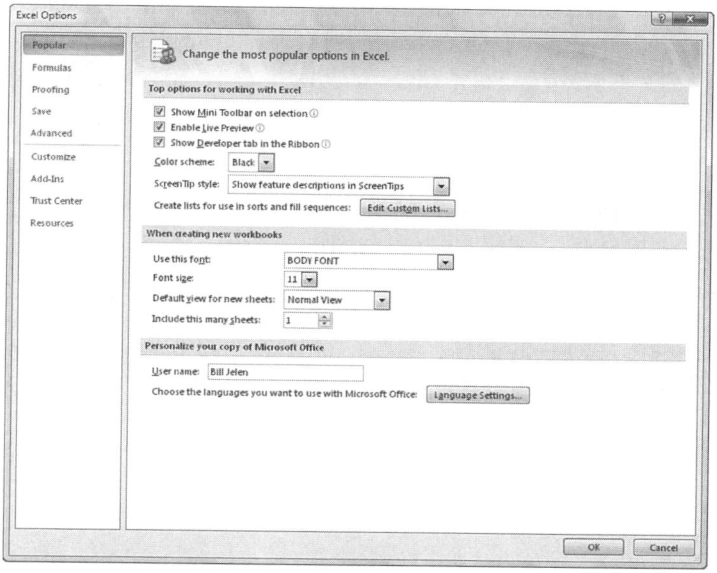

The Excel Options button

**Figure 6.2**
The Excel Options dialog has nine categories along the left side.

6

Table 6.1 shows the general types of settings you find in each category.

**TABLE 6.1    EXCEL OPTIONS DIALOG BOX SETTINGS**

| Category | Type of Settings |
| --- | --- |
| Personalize | The most commonly used settings, such as color schemes, custom lists, the default font for new workbooks, the number of sheets in a new workbook, and the customer name. |
| Formulas | All options for controlling calculation, error checking rules, and formula settings. Note that options for multithreaded calculation are currently considered obscure enough to be on the Advanced tab rather than on the Formulas tab. |
| Proofing | Spellcheck options and a link to the AutoCorrect dialog. |
| Save | The default method for saving, autorecovery settings, legacy colors, and webserver options. |
| Advanced | All previous options that Microsoft considers arcane, including editing, display, general, and Lotus compatibility settings. |
| Customize | Icons to customize the Quick Access toolbar. See Chapter 2, "The Quick Access Toolbar," for details on using this panel. |
| Add-Ins | A list of available and installed add-ins and smart tags. You can install new add-ins from the button at the bottom of this category. |
| Trust Center | Links to the Microsoft Trust Center, with eight additional categories. |
| Resources | Links to Office update, diagnostics, contact, and other information. |

## GETTING HELP WITH A SETTING

Many settings appear with a small *i* icon. If you hover the mouse near this icon, Excel displays a super ToolTip for the setting. The ToolTip explains what happens when you choose the setting and also provides some tips about what you need to be aware of when you turn on the setting. For example, the ToolTip in Figure 6.3 shows information about the calculation settings and also explains that you should use the F9 key to invoke a manual calculation.

**Figure 6.3**
You can see help on any setting by hovering over the *i* icon.

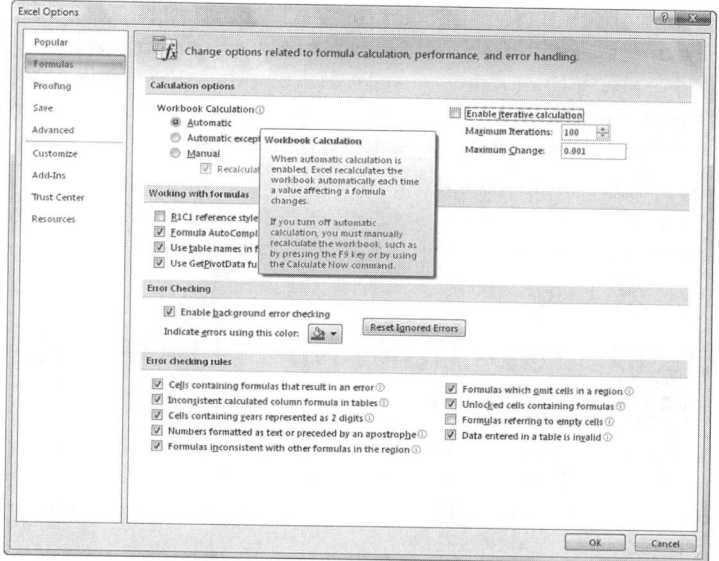

# TOGGLING THE NEW EXCEL 2007 FEATURES

Some of the features in Excel 2007 are memory intensive. If your computer is running sluggishly, you can turn off several of these memory-intensive features, which are found in the Popular category of the Excel Options dialog:

- **Show Mini Toolbar on Selection**—This feature is popular in Word, but it rarely appears in Excel. You actually have to select a few characters from a cell while the cell is in Edit mode. The mini toolbar provides quick access to text formatting tools.

- **Enable Live Preview**—When you hover over a gallery, the worksheet previews the change before you click the gallery item.

You can also turn off the following features, which are found in the Advanced category:

- **Alert the User When a Potentially Time-Consuming Operation Occurs**—When this option is set, Excel alerts you when a potentially time-consuming operation occurs. By default, Excel warns you when an operation will affect more than 35,554 cells. You can change the cell threshold, or simply turn this feature off. If you are about to do a subtotals command, you need to invoke the command whether it will take a long time or not.

6

- **Enable Multithreaded Calculations**—This option enables multithreaded calculation, which affects you only if your computer has multiple processors (commonly referred to as "dual core"). Excel can now make use of both processors in order to speed up calculation time. Note that the first recalculation of any workbook takes longer than normal because Excel has to build two calculation trees. Subsequent calculations are faster.

- **Group Dates in the AutoFilter Menu**—This setting causes daily dates to be grouped into months and years for easy selection in the AutoFilter drop-down. Autofilters are discussed in Chapter 13, "Removing Duplicates and Filtering."

# CONTROLLING THE LOOK AND FEEL OF THE WORKSHEET WINDOW

You might want to build a workbook that looks less like Excel because some people are intimidated by Excel. If you are building a workbook that must be distributed to many people who don't regularly use Excel, having it look less like Excel can improve acceptance of the workbook.

The Excel Options dialog allows you to turn off many screen elements. In the Advanced category, in the Display section, you can turn off the formula bar. This is an applicationwide setting; that is, when you disable this setting, the formula bar is disabled in all workbooks.

The following settings affect the entire workbook:

- **Show Horizontal Scroll Bar**—You can uncheck this option to hide the scroll bar at the bottom of the screen.

- **Show Vertical Scroll Bar**—You can uncheck this option to hide the scrollbar at the side of the screen.

- **Show Sheet Tabs**—You can uncheck this option to prevent someone from seeing all the tabs. You would usually provide a menu sheet with hyperlinks to allow the person to change from sheet to sheet. Note that if someone knows the Ctrl+Page Down and Ctrl+Page Up shortcuts, that person will still be able to navigate to other worksheets in your workbook.

The following items apply only to the current worksheet:

- **Show Row and Column Headers**—This turns off the A, B, C, and so on column headers and the 1, 2, 3, and so on row numbers.

- **Show Gridlines**—This turns off the lines between cells.

TIP FROM

To make the window look even less like Excel, you can hide the Ribbon by pressing Ctrl+F1 or remove the ribbon completely, as described in Chapter 38, "A Tour of the Best Add-ins for Excel."

Figure 6.4 shows the Display settings in the Excel Options dialog. Behind the dialog box, you can see the Excel window with all elements removed.

**Figure 6.4**
You can make Excel look less like Excel by using these options.

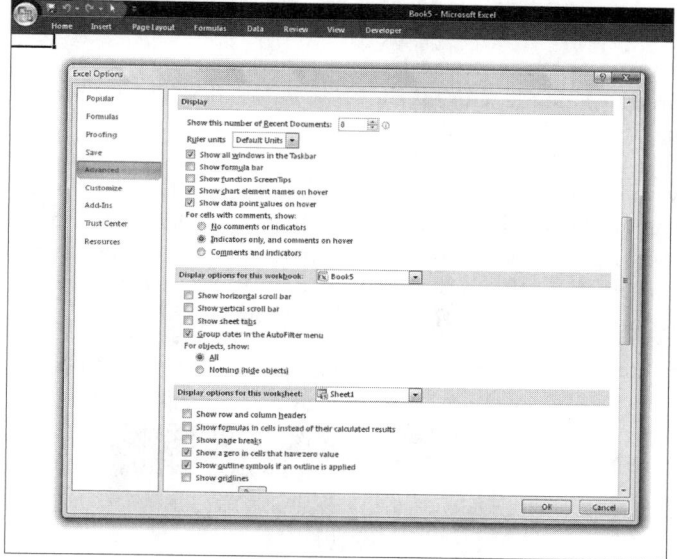

## INCREASING FILES IN THE RECENT DOCUMENTS LIST

The Office icon menu includes a list of your recently opened files. In previous versions of Excel, the default was to show four files in the list, and it could be increased to up to nine. In Excel 2007, the default is to show nine items in the list, and it can be increased to up to 50. If you increase this setting to 50 files, you can open any of the 50 recently used files simply by selecting it from the list.

To change the setting, you select the Office icon and then choose Excel Options, Advanced. In the Display section, you change Number of Documents in the Recent Documents List to the desired number of documents.

New in 2007: The Recent Documents list now includes files that you open directly from Windows Explorer. In previous versions of Excel, you had to use the Open or Save dialog to add a file to the recently used file list.

6

TIP FROM

*Bill Jelen*

If you share a computer and are concerned about the files in this list, you can spin the option down to 0 and then click OK. This will completely remove the 50 files from the list.

If you routinely open more than 50 documents, yet you have certain favorite documents, you can force those favorites to always be in the Recent Documents list. Here's how you do it:

1. If one of you favorite file is not currently in the list of recent documents, open the file.

2. Open the Office icon menu.

3. Locate the item in the Recent Documents section. Click the pushpin icon that appears to the right of the filename, as shown in Figure 6.5. The pushpin turns green to indicate that this item is pinned to the menu.

Any item with a pushpin will always appear in the Recent Documents list. Unfortunately, the pinned items do not always appear at the top of the list. The top spots are given to the files that you have had open most recently. If you pin several files to the list and then never open them again, those files will eventually move to the last spots on the list. However, because they are pinned, they will never fall off the end of the list.

To unpin an item from the Recent Documents list, you click the pushpin icon again.

**Figure 6.5**
You can pin your favorite files to the Recent Documents list.

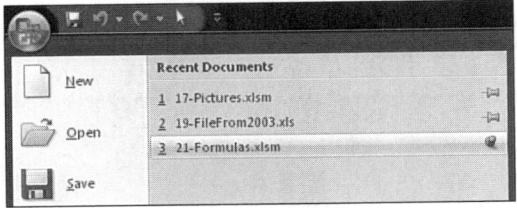

## CHANGING GRIDLINE COLOR

In previous versions of Excel, you had two choices for gridline color: gray and invisible. In Excel 2007, you can make the gridlines any of 56 colors. (It is not clear why Microsoft went back to a 56-color limit instead of 32-bit color scheme for this feature.)

To change the gridline color, you need to open the Excel Options dialog. Then you choose the Advanced category. Next, you scroll down to the Display Options for This Worksheet section. In the Gridline Color drop-down, you choose a color for the gridlines, as shown in Figure 6.6.

**Figure 6.6**
You can change the gridline color for the current worksheet.

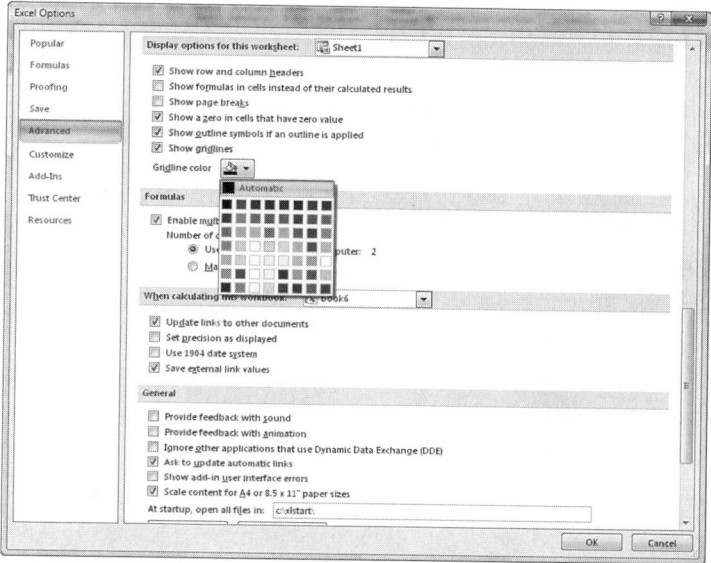

## EASING ENTRY OF NUMERIC DATA

A few options make it easier to enter a large range of numeric data. These functions are designed for people using the numeric keypad—which has the 10 digits, the four common operators, a decimal, and the Enter key—to enter numerals.

When you type a number in a cell and press the Enter key, Excel generally moves the cell pointer down one cell. This is fine if you are entering a column of numbers. However, if you would like to enter data in a row-by-row fashion, the default of moving the cell pointer down one row is frustrating.

You can specify that the cell pointer should move right, left, down, or up after pressing the Enter key. To do this, you choose the Office icon menu and then select Excel Options. In the Advanced section, you choose Editing Options. Then you change the setting for After Pressing Enter, Move Selection Direction, change the selection to Right. Note that if you uncheck the After Pressing Enter item, Excel keeps the cell pointer in the current cell when you press Enter.

Immediately below the After Pressing Enter setting, there is an option for automatically inserting a decimal point, assuming $n$ decimal places. If you need to enter a range of figures in dollars and cents, you can use this setting to prevent you from having to type the decimal point. If you enter 123, Excel converts it to 1.23.

6

# GUIDE TO EXCEL OPTIONS

Table 6.2 shows every Excel feature that you can change in the Excel Options dialog. The table shows the feature, the category where it can be modified, the section within the category, and the text of the option.

**TABLE 6.2    EXCEL OPTIONS, BY FEATURE**

| Feature | Category | Section | Text |
|---|---|---|---|
| Mini Toolbar | Popular | Top Options | Show Mini Toolbar on selection |
| Live Preview | Popular | Top Options | Enable Live Preview |
| Macros | Popular | Top Options | Show Developer Tab in the Ribbon |
| Skin | Popular | Top Options | Color Scheme |
| Screentips | Popular | Top Options | Screentip Style |
| Custom Lists | Popular | Top Options | Create Lists For Use In Sorts And Fill Seqences |
| Font | Popular | New Workbooks | Use This Font |
| Font Size | Popular | New Workbooks | Font Size |
| View | Popular | New Workbooks | Default View For New Sheets |
| Worksheets | Popular | New Workbooks | Include This Many Sheets |
| Name | Popular | Personalize | User Name |
| Languages | Popular | Personalize | Choose The Languages You Want To Use With Office |
| Calculation | Formulas | Calculation Options | Workbook Calculation Automatic |
| Calculation | Formulas | Calculation Options | Workbook Calculation Automatic Except For Data Tables |
| Calculation | Formulas | Calculation Options | Calculate Workbook Manual |
| Calculation Saving | Formulas | Calculation Options | Recalculate Workbook Before |
| Circular Reference Formulas | Formulas | Calculation Options | Enable Iterative Calculation |
| Circular Reference Formulas | Formulas | Calculation Options | Maximum Iterations |
| Circular Reference Formulas | Formulas | Calculation Options | Maximum Change |
| R1C1 Style | Formulas | Working With Formulas | R1C1 Reference Style |

6

| Feature | Category | Section | Text |
|---------|----------|---------|------|
| AutoComplete | Formulas | Working With Formulas | Formula AutoComplete |
| Formula Style | Formulas | Working With Formulas | Use Table Names In Formulas |
| GetPivotData | Formulas | Working With Formulas | Use GetPivotData Functions For PivotTable References |
| Error Checking | Formulas | Error Checking | Enable Background Error Checking |
| Error Indicators | Formulas | Error Checking | Indicate Errors Using This Color |
| Errors Ignored | Formulas | Error Checking | Reset Ignored Errors |
| Errors in Formulas | Formulas | Error Checking Rules | Error Checking Rules—Cells Containing Formulas That Result In An Error |
| Formulas—inconsistent in table | Formulas | Error Checking Rules | Error Checking Rules—Inconsistent Calculated Column Formulas In Tables |
| Dates as Text | Formulas | Error Checking Rules | Error Checking Rules—Cells Containing Years Represented As 2 Digits |
| Numbers as Text | Formulas | Error Checking Rules | Error Checking Rules—Numbers Formatted As Text Or Preceded By An Apostrophe |
| Formulas—inconsistent | Formulas | Error Checking Rules | Error Checking Rules—Formulas Inconsistent With Other Formulas In The Region |
| Formulas—omitted cells | Formulas | Error Checking Rules | Error Checking Rules—Formulas Which Omit Cells In A Region |
| Protected sheet with unlocked formulas | Formulas | Error Checking Rules | Error Checking Rules—Unlocked Cells Containing Formulas |
| Empty cells in formula | Formulas | Error Checking Rules | Error Checking Rules—Formulas Referring To Empty Cells |
| Table with invalid data | Formulas | Error Checking Rules | Error Checking Rules—Data Entered In A Table Is Invalid. |
| AutoCorrect | Proofing | Autocorrect Options | Autocorrect Options |
| Spelling | Proofing | When Correcting Spelling | Spelling—Ignore Words In Uppercase |
| Spelling | Proofing | When Correcting Spelling | Spelling—Ignore Words That Contain Numbers |

6

*continues*

**TABLE 6.2    CONTINUED**

| Feature | Category | Section | Text |
|---------|----------|---------|------|
| Spelling | Proofing | When Correcting Spelling | Spelling—Ignore Internet And File Addresses |
| Spelling | Proofing | When Correcting Spelling | Spelling—Flag Repeated Words |
| Spelling | Proofing | When Correcting Spelling | Spelling—Enforce Accented Uppercase In French |
| Spelling | Proofing | When Correcting Spelling | Spelling—Suggest From Main Dictionary Only |
| Spelling | Proofing | When Correcting Spelling | Spelling—Custom Dictionaries |
| Spelling | Proofing | When Correcting Spelling | Spelling—French Modes |
| Spelling | Proofing | When Correcting Spelling | Dictionary Language |
| File Format | Save | Save Workbooks | Save Files In This Format |
| AutoRecover | Save | Save Workbooks | Save AutoRecover Information Every n Minutes |
| AutoRecover Location | Save | Save Workbooks | AutoRecover File Location |
| Folder for Files | Save | Save Workbooks | Default File Location |
| AutoRecover—Disable | Save | Autorecover Exceptions For | Disable AutoRecover For This Workbook Only |
| Server | Save | Offline Editing Options For Document Management Server Files | Save Checked-Out Files To The Server Drafts Location On This Computer |
| Server | Save | Offline Editing Options For Document Management Server Files | Save Checked-Out Files To The Web Server |
| Server | Save | Offline Editing Options For Document Management Server Files | Server Drafts Location |
| Color | Save | Preserve Visual Appearance | Choose What Colors Will Be Seen In Previous Versions Of Excel |
| Direction after Enter | Advanced | Editing | After Pressing Enter, Move Selection Direction |
| Decimal places | Advanced | Editing | Automatically Insert A Decimal Point With N Places |

| Feature | Category | Section | Text |
|---|---|---|---|
| Fill Handle | Advanced | Editing | Enable Fill Handle And Cell Drag And Drop |
| Override alert | Advanced | Editing | Alert Before Overwriting Cells With Drag And Drop |
| In-cell editing | Advanced | Editing | Allow Editing Directly In Cell |
| Extend ranges | Advanced | Editing | Extend Data Range Formats And Formulas |
| Percentages | Advanced | Editing | Enable Automatic Percent Entry |
| AutoComplete | Advanced | Editing | Enable Autocomplete For Cell Values |
| Mouse Wheel | Advanced | Editing | Zoom On Roll With Intellimouse |
| Time Consuming Operation | Advanced | Editing | Alert The User When A Potentially Time Consuming Operation Occurs |
| Time Consuming Operation | Advanced | Editing | Time Consuming Is When This Number of Cells (In Thousands) Is Affected |
| Numeric separators | Advanced | Editing | Use System Separators |
| Numeric separators | Advanced | Editing | Decimal Separator |
| Numeric separators | Advanced | Editing | Thousands Separator |
| Paste | Advanced | Cut, Copy, And Paste | Show Paste Options Buttons |
| Insert | Advanced | Cut, Copy, And Paste | Show Insert Options Buttons |
| Images | Advanced | Cut, Copy, And Paste | Cut, Copy, And Sort Inserted Objects With Their Parent Cells |
| Recent File List | Advanced | Display | Show This Number of Recent Documents |
| Ruler | Advanced | Display | Ruler Units |
| Taskbar | Advanced | Display | Show All Windows In The Taskbar |
| Formula Bar | Advanced | Display | Show Formula Bar |
| Screentips | Advanced | Display | Show Function Screentips |
| Chart Elements | Advanced | Display | Show Chart Element Names On Hover |
| Chart Data Points | Advanced | Display | Show Data Point Values On Hover |

6

*continues*

**TABLE 6.2   CONTINUED**

| Feature | Category | Section | Text |
|---|---|---|---|
| Comment Display | Advanced | Display | For Cells With Comments, Show No Comments Or Indicators |
| Comment Display | Advanced | Display | For Cells With Comments, Show Indicators Only, And Comments On Hover |
| Comment Display | Advanced | Display | For Cells With Comments, Show Comment And Indicators |
| Scrollbars | Advanced | Display—Workbook | Show Horizontal Scroll Bar (Affects one workbook only) |
| Scrollbars | Advanced | Display—Workbook | Show Vertical Scroll Bar (Workbook only) |
| Tabs | Advanced | Display—Workbook | Show Sheet Tabs (Workbook only) |
| Dates in AutoFilter | Advanced | Display—Workbook | Group Dates In The AutoFilter Menu (Workbook only) |
| Images, hide | Advanced | Display—Workbook | For Objects, Show Or Hide (Workbook only) |
| Column & row headers | | Advanced | Display—Worksheets   Show Row And Column Headers (Affects one worksheet only) |
| Formulas, Show | Advanced | Display—Worksheets | Show Formulas In Cells Instead Of Their Calculated Results (Worksheet) |
| Page Breaks | Advanced | Display—Worksheets | Show Page Breaks (Worksheet) |
| Zero, Display | Advanced | Display—Worksheets | Show A Zero In Cells That Have Zero Value (Worksheet) |
| Outline Symbols | Advanced | Display—Worksheets | Show Outline Symbols If An Outline Is Applied (Worksheet) |
| Gridlines | Advanced | Display—Worksheets | Show Gridlines (Worksheet) |
| Gridline Color | Advanced | Display—Worksheets | Gridline Color (Worksheet) |
| Multi-Threaded Calculation | Advanced | Formulas | Enable Multi-Threaded Calculation |
| Multi-Threaded Calculation | Advanced | Formulas | Number of Calculation Threads |
| Links, update | Advanced | When Calculating Workbook | Update Links To Other Documents |

6

| Feature | Category | Section | Text |
|---|---|---|---|
| Precision as Displayed | Advanced | When Calculating Workbook | Set Precision As Displayed |
| Dates, 1904 system | Advanced | When Calculating Workbook | Use 1904 Date System |
| External Link Values | Advanced | When Calculating Workbook | Save External Link Values |
| Sound Feedback | Advanced | General | Provide Feedback With Sound |
| Animation Feedback | Advanced | General | Provide Feedback With Animation |
| DDE | Advanced | General | Ignore Other Applications That Use DDE |
| Links, update | Advanced | General | Ask To Update Automatic Links |
| Add-in errors | Advanced | General | Show Add-In User Interface Errors |
| Paper Size | Advanced | General | Scale Content for A4 or 8.5 x 11" Paper Sizes |
| Start-Up Folder | Advanced | General | At Start-Up, Open All Files In: |
| Web Options | Advanced | General | Web Options |
| Service Options | Advanced | General | Service Options |
| Menu Access Key | Advanced | Lotus Compatibility | Microsoft Office Excel Menu Key |
| Navigation Keys | Advanced | Lotus Compatibility | Transition Navigation Keys |
| Lotus Formula Evaluation | Advanced | Lotus For Worksheet | Lotus Transition Formula Evaluation |
| Lotus Formula Entry | Advanced | Lotus For Worksheet | Lotus Transition Formula Entry |
| QAT Location | Customization | N/A | Place Quick Access Toolbar Below The Ribbon |
| Add-Ins | Add-Ins | N/A | Manage Excel Add-Ins |
| Trust | Trust Center | N/A | Trust Center Settings |
| Updates | Resources | N/A | Check For Updates |
| Diagnose | Resources | N/A | Diagnose |
| Contact Microsoft | Resources | N/A | Contact Us |
| Activation | Resources | N/A | Activate |
| Registration | Resources | N/A | Register |
| About | Resources | N/A | About |

6

# A Tour of What's New

# THE BIG GRID

**I**n this chapter

The biggest fundamental change in Excel 2007 is the increased grid size. Microsoft is fond of calling this "the big grid." I would say that "big" is an understatement. When I heard rumors in 2004 that Microsoft would add rows to Excel, I thought perhaps they would double the 65,536 rows and Excel would have 130K rows. I even mentioned to Excel project manager Dave Gainer that if they didn't increase to at least 130K rows, it would be disappointing. For columns, I thought Microsoft would increase it to 1,024 columns, enough for three years of workday dates.

# EXCEL 2007 GRID LIMITS

The new grid in Excel offers 1,048,576 rows—that is, 2^20 rows—an increase from 65,536 rows in Excel 2003. It offers 16,384 columns—that is, 2^14 columns—an increase from 256 columns in Excel 2003. Overall, the new grid provides for 17.1 billion cells on each worksheet.

You will now be able to analyze more complex datasets. For example, if you regularly analyze 2,000 items, you can analyze 2.5 years of monthly data in one Excel worksheet. In Excel 2007, you can analyze 10 years of weekly data or 43 years of monthly data. Columnwise, previous versions of Excel could handle only nine months of daily data going across the worksheet. Excel 2007 can handle 45 years of daily dates or 63 years of weekdays.

It is interesting to compare the size increase in the history of spreadsheets. You will see that the size increase is unprecedented. Here is a brief history of spreadsheets:

- In October 1979, VisiCalc debuted, with 255 rows and 63 columns.
- In 1983, Lotus 1-2-3 debuted, with 8,192 rows and 256 columns. The 2 million cells per worksheet in this version was a 13,000% increase over VisiCalc.
- In 1987, early versions of Excel offered 16,384 rows by 255 columns. This 4 million cells was double the amount offered in Lotus 1-2-3 release 2.2.
- In Excel 97, Microsoft increased Excel to offer 65,536 rows by 255 columns. This 16.7 million cells per spreadsheet was quadruple the previous limit.
- In Excel 2007, the new grid size is 1,048,576 rows by 16,384 columns. This is 17.1 billion cells, which is a 102,300% increase over the previous limit.

The chart in Figure 7.1 shows the number of cells available in a single worksheet for various spreadsheet versions. Note that the y-axis is plotted using a logarithmic scale, which means that each gridline is 100 times larger than the previous gridline.

## WHO CAN USE 17 BILLION CELLS?

It is unlikely that many people will need 17 billion cells. In fact, most computers sold today do not have enough memory to fill the 17 billion cells on a single worksheet, let alone go to Sheet2. Another important question is, "Who needs more than 256 columns or more than 65,536 rows?" The answer: A lot of people.

**Figure 7.1**
Seventeen billion cells on a single worksheet is a bit more than "big."

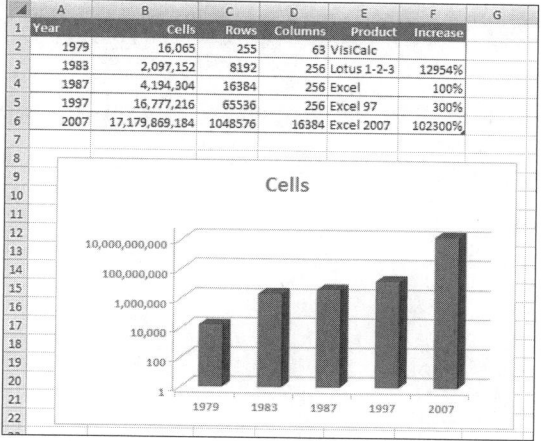

In previous versions of Excel, there has been no good way to organize a year's worth of daily dates going across a spreadsheet. In Excel 2007 you can now have labels in Column A and stretch 43+ years of daily dates across a column.

Small businesses that use QuickBooks often curse that software's desire to put blank columns between columns when exporting to Excel. With versions of Excel prior to Excel 2007, this imposed a limit of less than five years of weekly data across the columns. Even with QuickBooks wasting half the columns, with Excel 2007 you can now fit 157 years of weekly QuickBooks data across the columns. (If you have more than 157 years of QuickBooks data, you can probably archive some of that by now.)

The limit of 65,536 rows has been a problem for a while. I suspect that the 1.1 million row limit will continue to be a problem. One of my clients already has a dataset with 655,000 rows for his chain of retail stores. As that chain continues to open stores, I can foresee running out of rows in Excel 2007 in the next few years.

Many people resort to using Access only when their datasets have more than 65,536 rows. With Excel 2007, you'll be able to quickly summarize far more datasets, and casual use of Access should decrease.

## WHY ARE THERE ONLY 65,536 ROWS IN MY EXCEL 2007 SPREADSHEET?

When I initially installed Excel 2007, I loaded the largest Excel workbook I had. I pressed End+Down Arrow with anticipation. I was perplexed to see that there are only 65,536 rows in the spreadsheet, as shown in Figure 7.2.

Notice that the title bar for the workbook says that the file is 7-Ending.xls (Compatibility Mode). The key here is that the file is in Compatibility mode. In this mode, you cannot add features that were not available in Excel 2003. Compatibility mode is the default when you open a file created in Excel 97–2003.

To leave Compatibility mode, you click the Windows icon and then choose Convert, as shown in Figure 7.3.

7

**Figure 7.2**
What is all the hype?
There are still only
65,536 rows.

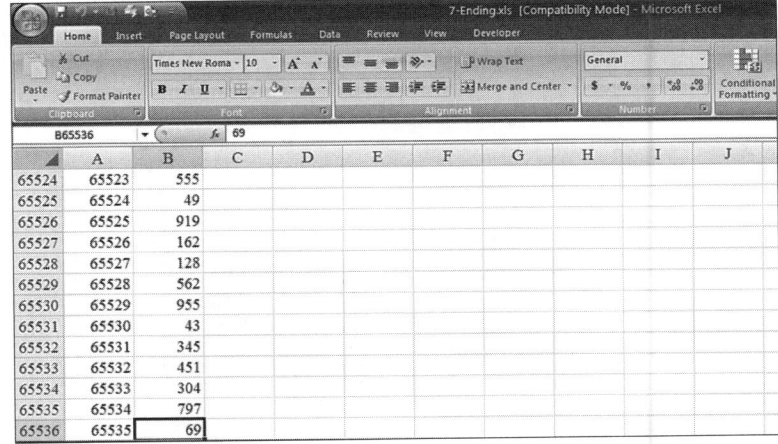

**Figure 7.3**
You choose Convert to
leave Compatibility
mode.

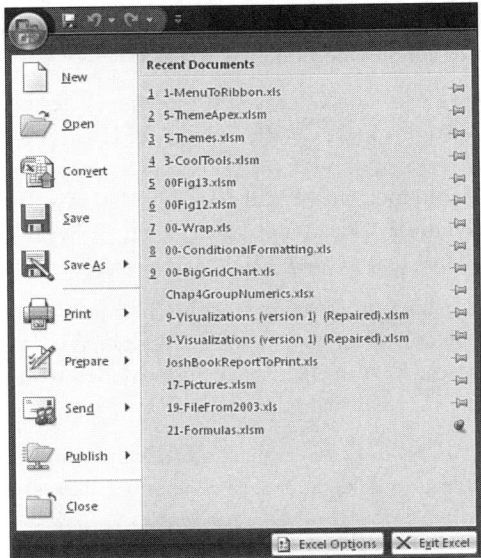

**CAUTION**

When you upgrade a file, Excel warns you that the original file will be replaced by the upgraded version, as shown in Figure 7.4. This behavior is a little annoying. In the process of saving the file as an XLSM file, Excel actually deletes the old XLS version of the file. To keep a version of the XLS file, either backup the file or use the following method described.

**Figure 7.4**
Converting actually deletes the original version of the file.

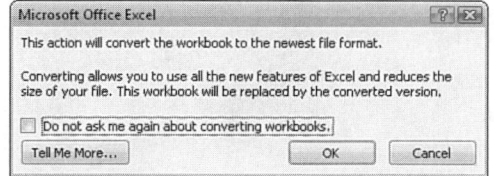

After you convert a file, the file still only shows 65,536 rows. You have to close the file and reopen it to access all the rows.

You might prefer this method instead of using the Convert option:

1. Open the Excel 2003 workbook.
2. Click the Office icon and then select Save As.
3. From the Save As Type dropdown, choose Excel Macro-Enabled Workbook (*.xlsm).
4. Choose Save.
5. Close the workbook.
6. Reopen the workbook.

When you follow these steps, the XLS version of the workbook remains on your hard drive.

With the bigger grid, it is far more likely that you will encounter larger files, formulas, and pivot tables. With a 102,300% increase in the file, many of the old limits in Excel 2003 no longer make sense. Because of the bigger grid, Microsoft provided relaxed limits in many areas. Limits are discussed in the next section.

There is also an unusual quirk with the big grid. Previously, columns were labeled from A to IV. Now, columns are labeled from A to XFD. This means that a lot of three-letter words are now valid column names. In previous versions of Excel, range names such as ROI2007 or TAX2004 would have been legal names. Now that these are actual cell addresses, those names can no longer be used in Excel 2007. The workaround is discussed in the section "Working with Excel 2003 Named Ranges in Excel 2007," later in this chapter.

# OTHER LIMITS IN EXCEL 2007

In addition to the grid size, a number of other aspects of Excel 2007 have new limits. Table 7.1 illustrates these new limits.

7

## TABLE 7.1—EXCEL 2007 LIMITS

| Item | Old Limit | New Limit |
|---|---|---|
| PC memory Excel can use | 1GB | Max allowed by Windows |
| Number of unique colors in a single workbook | 56 | 4.3 billion |
| Number of conditional format conditions on a cell | 3 | Limited by available memory |
| Number of levels of sorting | 3 | 64 |
| Number of items in the AutoFilter drop-down | 1,000 | 10,000 |
| Number of characters that can display in one cell | 1,024 | 32,768 |
| Number of characters in a cell that Excel can print | 1,024 | 32,768 |
| Number of unique cell styles in a workbook | 4,096 | 65,536 |
| Maximum length of formulas | 1,024 characters | 8,192 characters |
| Number of levels of nesting in formulas | 7 | 64 |
| Maximum number of arguments in a function | 30 | 255 |
| Number of characters that can be displayed in a cell formatted as text | 255 | 32K |
| Number of items that can be found with Find All | 65,536 | ~2 billion |
| Number of columns allowed in a pivot table | 255 | 16,384 |
| Number of unique items in a single pivot field | 32,768 | ~1 million |
| Number of fields in a pivot table | 255 | 16,384 |
| Number of cells that can depend on a single area before Excel must do full calculations instead of partial calculations (because it can no longer track the dependencies required to do partial calculations) | 8,102 | Limited by available memory |
| Number of different areas in a sheet that can have dependencies before Excel must do full calculations instead of partial calculations (because it can no longer track the dependencies required to do partial calculations) | 65,536 | Limited by available memory |
| Number of array formulas in a worksheet that can refer to another (given) worksheet | 65,536 | Limited by available memory |
| Number of categories that custom functions can be grouped into | 32 | 255 |
| Number of characters that can be updated in a nonresident external workbook reference | 255 | 32,768 |
| Number of rows of a column or columns that can be referred to in an array formula | 65,335 | Limitation removed (full-column references allowed) |

7

As you can see in Table 7.1, Excel 2007 has some excellent improvements. It also has some improvements that allow people to build worse spreadsheets.

Many people try to rely on nested IF functions when they should instead learn about VLOOKUP. Increasing from 7 to 64 nested functions allows people to put off learning about VLOOKUP for even longer. (If you've been avoiding VLOOKUP, read about it in Chapter 24, "Powerful Functions.")

With versions of Excel prior to Excel 2007, any pivot table that relied on daily dates almost always had to be built with the dates going down the side instead of across the rows. This was annoying, especially if you planned on rolling the dates up to months or quarters that would eventually fit in the 256 columns.

The number of Excel formats was a problem that was rarely encountered but that caused horrible frustration when it was hit. Now, the limit will be hit much less frequently.

Even with these new limits, some areas could still be improved. For example, there is still a limit of eight levels of indentation in outlining. However, for the most part, the new limits are incredible and allow much larger analyses to happen in Excel instead of elsewhere.

# Working with Excel 2003 Named Ranges in Excel 2007

The new columns in Excel go out to column XFD.

Many range names were valid in prior versions of Excel but are not valid in Excel 2007 because they are the same as Excel 2007 cell addresses. For example, TAX2006 might have been a range name in Excel 2003. This name is invalid in Excel 2007 because there is a cell called TAX2006.

Excel's solution is to prefix invalid range names with an underscore character when you upgrade the workbook. Excel gives you the warning "One or more names in this workbook conflict with a valid cell reference in Excel 2007." After you acknowledge the first message, Excel proceeds to tell you the complete list of names that it is changing, one at a time. You can either click OK to each name or skip the list by selecting OK to All.

However, despite Excel's solution, invalid range names can cause problems. If you have VBA macros that refer to the range name, you have to manually fix the VBA code. Furthermore, if you used the name in a text argument in a worksheet function, you have to manually update those formulas to use the new name.

This feature will not affect many people, but for those it does affect, it will be very annoying.

# Tips for Navigating the Big Grid

The navigation tips described in the following sections are not new to Excel 2007. However, with 16 billion cells, there is a better chance that you don't want to be scrolling around with the Page Up and Page Down keys.

## USING SHORTCUT KEYS TO MOVE AROUND

A variety of shortcuts enable you to quickly move around a worksheet:

| Shortcut | What It Does |
| --- | --- |
| Ctrl+Home | Move to Cell A1 |
| Home | Move to Column A of the current row |
| Ctrl+End | Move to the last used cell in a worksheet |
| Ctrl+any arrow key | Jump to the end of a contiguous range |
| Ctrl+Up Arrow | Move to the first row in the data if your data has no blank cells |
| Ctrl+Down Arrow | Move to the last row in the data if your data has no blank cells |

## USING THE END KEY TO NAVIGATE

The End key is one of the six keys above the arrow keys on a standard keyboard. When you press the End key, an indicator lights up in the status bar of the Excel window. When Excel is in End mode, you can press an arrow key or the Home key. Pressing an arrow key takes you to the edge of a contiguous range of cells. Pressing Home while in End mode will take you to the last used cell in the worksheet.

In Figure 7.5, pressing End and then the Down Arrow key causes the cell pointer to jump from D36 to D46. When the cell pointer is on the edge of a range, pressing End+Down Arrow again causes Excel to jump over a range of blank cells and land on the starting edge of the next range. For example, pressing End+Down Arrow from D46 causes the cell pointer to jump to D58.

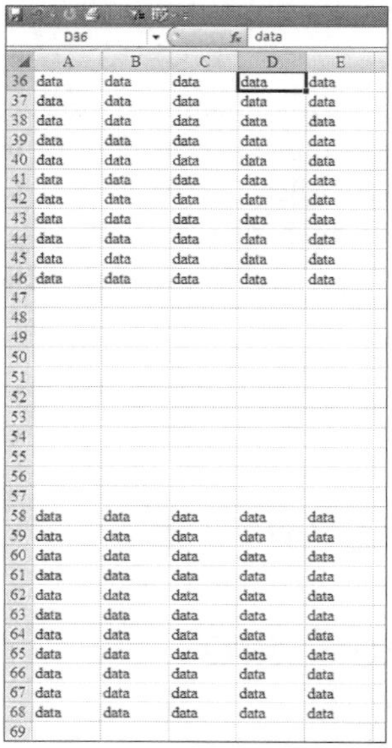

**Figure 7.5**
End+arrow key will cause Excel to jump over a range of blank cells or a contiguous range of cells.

If you press the End key to move right or down from the last cell that contains data, the cell pointer jumps to the last row or column in the spreadsheet. In a blank worksheet, you can press End+Down Arrow and End+Right Arrow to move to XFD1048576.

Pressing End and then Home causes the cell pointer to move to the last active cell in the worksheet.

## USING THE CURRENT RANGE TO NAVIGATE

If your data has many blank cells, using Ctrl+arrow keys or Ctrl+End key will lead to frustration.

You can press Ctrl+* to select the current region. A current region starts from the current nonblank cell and extends out in all directions until Excel encounters a completely blank row, a completely blank column, or the edge of the spreadsheet.

Then you can press Ctrl+. (that is, Ctrl plus the period key) to move the active cell to each corner of the selection. From the top-left cell of a region, you can press Ctrl+* and then press Ctrl+. twice to go to the last used cell in the current region.

## USING GO TO TO NAVIGATE

You can press the F5 key to display the Go To dialog. Then you can type a cell address and press OK to quickly jump to that cell.

You can also use the Name box the same way you use the Go To dialog. The Name box is the drop-down area immediately to the left of the formula bar. You click in the Name box, type a valid cell address, and press Enter. Excel then jumps to that cell.

7

# CHAPTER 8

# FABULOUS TABLE INTELLIGENCE

## In this chapter

A fundamental use of Excel is for analyzing two-dimensional tables of data. Most worksheets contain headings at the top and then rows of data. Most Excel customers spend a lot of time working with tables of data. Microsoft recognized this and added intelligent tables to Excel 2007. If you explicitly tell Excel 2007 that you are working on a table of data, it displays a custom Table ribbon that has a number of amazing features.

Some of the benefits of Excel's intelligent tables include the following:

- You can automatically add AutoFilter drop-downs to the headings in a table.
- You have one-click access to banded rows, banded columns, and other autoformats.
- You can toggle a total row on or off.
- You have one-click access to removing duplicates.
- You can automatically copy new formulas to all cells in a column.
- You can automatically extend a table when new data is typed below or to the right of the table. This feature also affects any charts, formulas, or pivot tables that pointed to the table, causing them to expand as well.
- You can extend conditional formatting to new rows in the table.
- You can automatically freeze panes to show the heading row as you scroll off the page.
- You can automatically set up range names for an entire table and each column within the table.

# DEFINING SUITABLE DATA FOR EXCEL TABLES

Many Excel spreadsheets contain data that is not suitable for Excel tables. For the purpose of this chapter, a *table* is a range of Excel data. Each row in the range is one record of data. Each row might describe, for example, an invoice or a customer or an inventory item. Each column in the table creates another field for each row. Fields might include invoice number, customer name, total sales, and so on. A table usually has headings in the first row.

The simple range in Figure 8.1 would make a suitable table because each row in this range is a record, and each column is a field.

**Figure 8.1**
This would make an ideal table in Excel.

| | A | B | C | D |
|---|---|---|---|---|
| 1 | Region | Customer | Revenue | Cost |
| 2 | East | Leading Camera Traders | 65073 | 31235 |
| 3 | Central | Magnificent Sandal Company | 23345 | 12840 |
| 4 | West | Special Edger Corporation | 98274 | 51102 |
| 5 | East | Cool Scooter Company | 20619 | 10310 |
| 6 | Central | Hip Calculator Corporation | 71626 | 34380 |
| 7 | West | Different Radio Inc. | 45541 | 20949 |
| 8 | East | Matchless Clipboard Company | 45521 | 24126 |
| 9 | Central | Top-Notch Kiln Inc. | 62009 | 29144 |

## DEFINING A TABLE

There are four ways to create a table in Excel 2007:

- Select a cell in the dataset and choose Insert, Tables, Table.
- Select a cell in the dataset and choose Home, Style, Format as Table. Choose a Style and then press OK.
- Select a cell in the dataset and press Ctrl+T.
- Select a cell in the dataset and press Ctrl+L. (In Excel 2003, tables were originally called lists. Ctrl+L was the shortcut for a list.)

When you use any of these methods, Excel uses IntelliSense to determine the edge of the table. Excel looks for a completely blank row and a completely blank column to define the edges of the table.

Excel shows the suspected table range in the Create Table dialog, as shown in Figure 8.2. You need to verify that this range is correct. If your table has headers, you leave the My Table Has Headers check box checked and press OK.

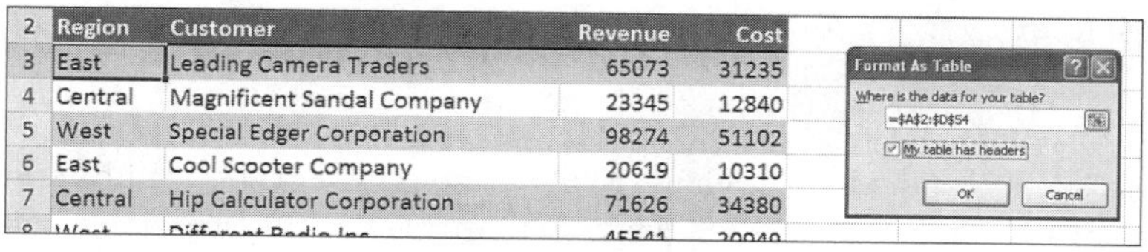

**Figure 8.2**
Excel's IntelliSense guesses the extent of the table.

As shown in Figure 8.3, Excel adds a default table format to your range. The headings gain autofilter drop-downs. A new ribbon called Table Tools—Design is displayed. Excel assigns a name similar to Table1 to the table. Don't worry; if any of this is annoying to you, you can turn off many of the features with a click of the mouse.

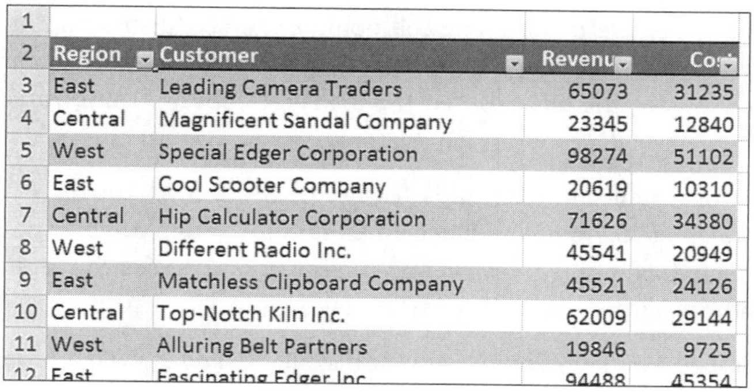

**Figure 8.3**
The table has an interesting autoformat, but there are many more features.

## KEEPING HEADERS IN VIEW

Notice that in Figure 8.3, the headings appear in Row 2 of the worksheet. As you scroll down through the table, you can eventually scroll to the point where Row 2 is no longer visible in the window. At this point, Excel moves the headings from Row 2 and shows them where column names A, B, C, D normally display. Figure 8.4 shows the headings as column names.

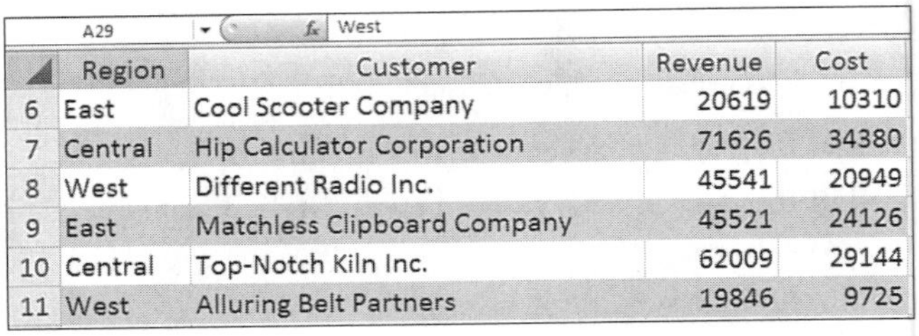

**Figure 8.4**
When you do not use the Freeze Panes command, Excel automatically moves the heading values up to the column names when you scroll the headings off the window.

| | A29 | | $f_x$ | West | | |
|---|---|---|---|---|---|---|
| | Region | Customer | | | Revenue | Cost |
| 6 | East | Cool Scooter Company | | | 20619 | 10310 |
| 7 | Central | Hip Calculator Corporation | | | 71626 | 34380 |
| 8 | West | Different Radio Inc. | | | 45541 | 20949 |
| 9 | East | Matchless Clipboard Company | | | 45521 | 24126 |
| 10 | Central | Top-Notch Kiln Inc. | | | 62009 | 29144 |
| 11 | West | Alluring Belt Partners | | | 19846 | 9725 |

These heading names stay as column names as long as all these are true:

- The cell pointer is inside the range of the table.

- The header row is not visible in the window.

- At least one row of the table is visible in the window. If you leave the cell pointer in the table and then use a scrollbar to scroll the table out of view, the column names revert to column letters.

Once any of the above conditions is no longer true, the headings disappear from the column name area.

## FREEZING WORKSHEET PANES

Excel 2007's automatic heading visibility feature is very cool. With earlier versions of Excel, many did not know there was a way to freeze panes. Whether you knew about that feature or not, it is a positive feature 90% of the time, though it's not perfect.

One problem with Excel 2007's automatic heading visibility feature is that the autofilter drop-downs disappear from the headings when they are scrolled up to the column names.

Second, it is a bit annoying that the headings disappear when you select a cell outside the table. I think that if I can see part of a table in the window, Excel should keep the headings up as part of the column names. The cell pointer can be a distraction in a dataset, and if, for example, you are showing your manager something on the screen, you might have a tendency to click outside the table so that the manager does not think you are trying to show him one particular cell.

Third, the automatic heading visibility feature does not work for the first column. In Figure 8.5, for example, a wide table has labels in Column A. After you choose First Column, Excel properly formats Column A. However, if you scroll over to see the month of December, Excel does not make the Column A values stay visible.

The old-style Freeze Panes command is still available and is even a bit easier to use in Excel 2007.

In prior versions of Excel, you were forced to put the cell pointer in the first cell that should not be frozen before invoking the Freeze Panes command. In Excel 2007, Microsoft has added two new commands that allow you to freeze the first row or the first column from anywhere. Here's how you freeze the first row:

**Figure 8.5**
The automatic heading visibility feature doesn't work for the first column.

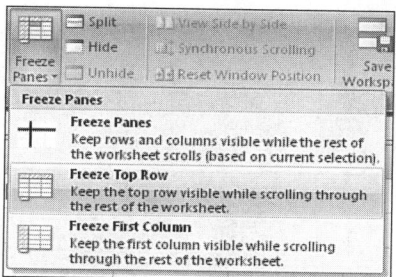

1. Make sure the row that you want to stay at the top of the window is the first visible row in the window.

2. From the Window group of the View ribbon, select Freeze Panes. The drop-down that appears is shown in Figure 8.6.

3. Select Freeze Top Row.

You can now scroll anywhere on the worksheet and always see the first row.

**Figure 8.6**
Excel 2007 adds two new commands to the Freeze Panes area.

It is annoying, but the Freeze First Column resets the Freeze First Row icon, and vice versa. If you need to freeze both the first column and first row, you will have to use the Freeze Panes command as described in the following sections.

## CLEARING FREEZE PANES

To turn off the Freeze Panes option, you again select the Freeze Panes icon in the View ribbon. The first option in the drop-down is now Unfreeze Panes. You can select this option to unlock the view; you can then scroll anywhere in the window.

## USING THE OLD VERSION OF FREEZE PANES FOR ABSOLUTE CONTROL

There may be times when you want several rows or columns to remain visible. Just as in previous versions of Excel, you can do this when you understand how Freeze Panes works.

8

Consider the worksheet in Figure 8.7. You would always want to see the data in Columns A:D at the left side of the window. There are several rows of title information that don't necessarily need to be visible at the top of the worksheet as you scroll, but it would be good to see Rows 5 and 6 at the top of the window as you scroll.

**Figure 8.7**
This worksheet is too complex for the new Freeze Top Row command to actually work as desired.

| | A | B | C | D | E | F | G | H | I | J | K |
|---|---|---|---|---|---|---|---|---|---|---|---|
| 1 | XYZ COMPANY | | | | | | | | | | |
| 2 | SALES REPORT | | | | | | | | | | |
| 3 | QUARTER 1, 2007 | | | | | | | | | | |
| 4 | | | | | | | | | | | |
| 5 | | | | | | Product Line A | | | Product Line B | | Pr |
| 6 | Country | Region | District | Sales Rep | Sales | Profit | GP% | Sales | Profit | GP% | Sales |
| 7 | USA | East | Northeast | Bauer | 9680 | 4743 | 49.0% | 4132 | 1694 | 41.0% | 11042 |
| 8 | USA | East | Northeast | Walker | 6406 | 2819 | 44.0% | 6544 | 2748 | 42.0% | 11601 |
| 9 | USA | East | Northeast | Strong | 4916 | 2163 | 44.0% | 20694 | 9105 | 44.0% | 7858 |
| 10 | USA | East | Northeast | Mosley | 10103 | 4142 | 41.0% | 14380 | 5752 | 40.0% | 19431 |
| 11 | USA | East | Northeast | Wilkins | 22590 | 10391 | 46.0% | 13835 | 6918 | 50.0% | 4898 |
| 12 | USA | East | Northeast | Walters | 3731 | 1679 | 45.0% | 1420 | 611 | 43.0% | 9059 |

You can set up the headings to stay visible by following these steps:

1. Click the arrow at the bottom of the vertical scrollbar four times to make Row 5 the first row visible in the window.

2. Select the first cell that will not be frozen in the window. Everything visible in the window above and to the left of this cell will be frozen. In Figure 8.8, this would be Cell E7. It is critical that you select this cell before moving on to step 3.

**Figure 8.8**
You select the first cell that won't be frozen.

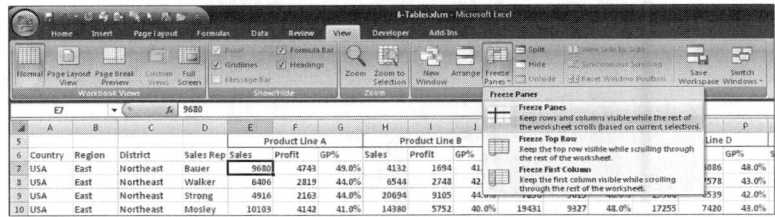

3. From the Window group of the View ribbon, select the Freeze Panes dropdown. Then select Freeze Panes again.

The result is that you can scroll down and right. Even out at Column V, Row 62, you can see the headings in Rows 5:6 and the values in Columns A:D, as shown in Figure 8.9.

The key to using the Freeze Panes command is that you must place the cell pointer before using the command. The command freezes everything that was above and to the left of the cell pointer location when the command was invoked.

To freeze only Columns A:B and no rows, you would invoke the command from Row 1 of Column C. Because there is nothing above the cell pointer, no rows are frozen.

**Figure 8.9**
After you use the original Freeze Panes command, you can have multiple rows and columns frozen at the top and left of the worksheet.

| | V62 | | | $f_x$ | =+U62/T62 | | | | | |
|---|---|---|---|---|---|---|---|---|---|---|
| | A | B | C | D | Q | R | S | T | U | V |
| 5 | | | | | | Product Line E | | | Total | |
| 6 | Country | Region | District | Sales Rep | Sales | Profit | GP% | Sales | Profit | GP% |
| 49 | USA | West | Texas | Wagner | 7919 | 3484 | 44.0% | 64198 | 28309 | 44.1% |
| 50 | USA | West | Texas | Herman | 21989 | 9235 | 42.0% | 67216 | 30802 | 45.8% |
| 51 | USA | West | Texas | Aguilar | 4198 | 2057 | 49.0% | 70391 | 29486 | 41.9% |
| 52 | USA | West | Southern CA | Jacobs | 12195 | 6098 | 50.0% | 50096 | 23583 | 47.1% |
| 53 | USA | West | Southern CA | Christian | 15485 | 6813 | 44.0% | 71579 | 30468 | 42.6% |
| 54 | USA | West | Southern CA | Robertson | 13196 | 5410 | 41.0% | 83251 | 36824 | 44.2% |
| 55 | USA | West | Southern CA | Duke | 6066 | 3033 | 50.0% | 66755 | 31176 | 46.7% |
| 56 | USA | West | Southern CA | Wilkins | 6179 | 3028 | 49.0% | 50730 | 23575 | 46.5% |
| 57 | USA | West | Southern CA | Harvey | 7569 | 3557 | 47.0% | 28716 | 13223 | 46.0% |
| 58 | USA | West | Southern CA | Ballard | 5361 | 2412 | 45.0% | 42453 | 18869 | 44.4% |
| 59 | USA | West | Northern CA | Gamble | 7906 | 3241 | 41.0% | 65368 | 28317 | 43.3% |
| 60 | USA | West | Northern CA | Jacobson | 20216 | 9299 | 46.0% | 97511 | 43316 | 44.4% |
| 61 | USA | West | Northern CA | Ortiz | 18270 | 7491 | 41.0% | 89676 | 39172 | 43.7% |
| 62 | USA | West | Northern CA | Welch | 9244 | 3698 | 40.0% | 45533 | 19588 | 43.0% |

# ADDING A TOTAL ROW TO A TABLE

There is a Totals Row checkbox in the Table Styles Options group of the Table Tools Design ribbon. When you select this box, Excel automatically adds a total to the bottom of your table.

By default, Excel adds the word Total to the first column of the table and adds a formula to the right-most column of the table to sum the column.

Figure 8.10 shows the default total row for a table. To add a sum formula to Column C, you select the cell for Column C in the total row. When a drop-down arrow appears, you select Sum from the list.

**Figure 8.10**
Clicking the Total Row check box in the ribbon adds a default total row. You use the drop-downs to change the function or add totals to other columns.

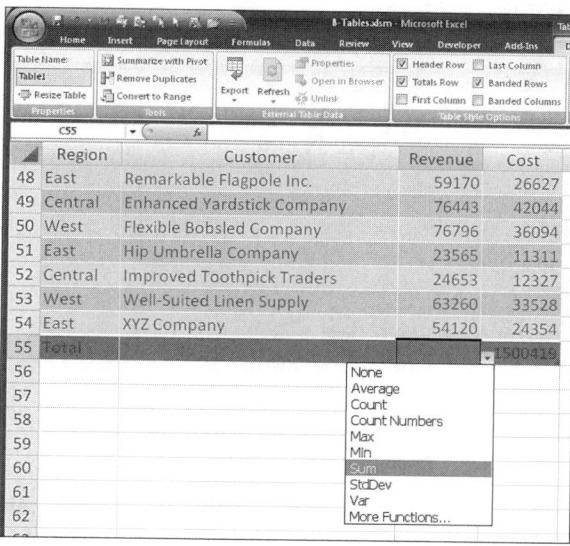

In Figure 8.10, instead of using the SUM formula, Excel uses the SUBTOTAL function, with a first argument of 109. The SUBTOTAL function is similar to the SUM function, with two exceptions. First, the function ignores other SUBTOTAL functions in the range. Second, with a first argument in the 101–109 range, Excel ignores any values that are hidden, including rows that are hidden by the autofilter drop-downs.

The total cost in Figure 8.10 is $1.4 million. In Figure 8.11, the Region column is filtered to only the Central region. Because the SUBTOTAL function ignores hidden rows, the total cost automatically updates to show $448,511.

**Figure 8.11**
You choose a region from the autofilter drop-down, and the SUBTOTALS function reflects the total of the visible rows.

| | Region | Customer | Revenue | Cost |
|---|---|---|---|---|
| 31 | Central | Sure Tackle Partners | 88095 | 46690 |
| 34 | Central | Fresh Radio Supply | 88460 | 45115 |
| 37 | Central | Handy Briefcase Company | 76463 | 34408 |
| 40 | Central | Supreme Notebook Traders | 11530 | 5650 |
| 43 | Central | Agile Marble Company | 55214 | 27607 |
| 46 | Central | Safe Raft Company | 61433 | 31331 |
| 49 | Central | Enhanced Yardstick Company | 76443 | 42044 |
| 52 | Central | Improved Toothpick Traders | 24653 | 12327 |
| 54 | Total | | 899216 | 448511 |

D54 — fx =SUBTOTAL(109,[Cost])

# TOGGLING TOTALS

When you use tables, you can toggle the total row on and off. You use the Total Row check box in the Table Tools Design ribbon to turn on or off the totals. In most cases, Excel remembers when you have customized the totals to provide totals for the last two columns. However, you might find that if you add new columns to a table, you will have to add these totals to the new columns using the dropdown in the total row.

# EXPANDING A TABLE

A common feature of tables is that they tend to grow and expand. Every day, you might add new records to a table or paste new records to the bottom of a table. Or, you might add a new column with a new calculation.

Excel can automatically expand a table, or you can choose to expand a table manually. When you expand a table, any references to the table automatically expand.

## ADDING ROWS TO A TABLE AUTOMATICALLY

The easiest way to add rows to a table is from the last row of the table. If you are in the last column of the last row and press the Tab key, Excel adds a new row to the table and moves the cell pointer to the first column in the new row. This behavior is similar to existing functionality in tables in Microsoft Word.

However, the simplest way to add a new row to a table is to click in the blank row under the table and type new data. As soon as you enter something in a cell just below the table, Excel expands the table formatting to include the new row. Excel also displays an AutoCorrect lightning bolt icon. If you don't want Excel to automatically expand the table, you can use the drop-down next to this icon to undo the table AutoExpansion, as shown in Figure 8.12.

**Figure 8.12**
If you type a new value below the table, Excel automatically extends the table to include the new row.

| | A | B | C | D | E | F | G |
|---|---|---|---|---|---|---|---|
| 43 | Central | Agile Marble Company | 55214 | 27607 | | | |
| 44 | West | Improved Briefcase Company | 57082 | 27399 | | | |
| 45 | East | Enhanced Bicycle Company | 13804 | 6902 | | | |
| 46 | Central | Safe Raft Company | 61433 | 31331 | | | |
| 47 | West | Tremendous Kettle Company | 16500 | 8250 | | | |
| 48 | East | Remarkable Flagpole Inc. | 59170 | 26627 | | | |
| 49 | Central | Enhanced Yardstick Company | 76443 | 42044 | | | |
| 50 | West | Flexible Bobsled Company | 76796 | 36094 | | | |
| 51 | East | Hip Umbrella Company | 23565 | 11311 | | | |
| 52 | Central | Improved Toothpick Traders | 24653 | 12327 | | | |
| 53 | West | Well-Suited Linen Supply | 63260 | 33528 | | | |
| 54 | East | XYZ Company | 54120 | 24354 | | | |
| 55 | | | | 45245 | | | |
| 56 | | | | | | | |
| 57 | | | | | | | |
| 58 | | | | | | | |
| 59 | | | | | | | |

## MANUALLY RESIZING A TABLE

The bottom-right cell of a table contains a small angle-bracket in the lower-right corner of the cell. You can use this angle-bracket to manually extend the table.

When you click the angle-bracket, you can either drag down to add more rows or drag right to add more columns to the table.

You can also select Table Tools, Design, Properties, Resize Table. The Resize Table dialog appears, allowing you to specify the new range for the table. There are a few limitations. For example, you cannot change the header row during this process.

## ADDING NEW COLUMNS TO A TABLE

To add a new column to a table, you go to the blank cell to the right of the last header and type a new header for the column. Excel automatically extends the table by another column and copies any table formatting to the new column. The AutoCorrect lightning bolt icon appears. If you don't want the new column to be part of the table, you use the drop-down next to the AutoCorrect icon to undo the table AutoExpansion.

# ADDING NEW FORMULAS TO TABLES

Way back in Excel 97, Microsoft added something called Natural Language Formulas to Excel. With Excel 2007, those old formulas are officially depreciated. However, the new-style table formulas are reminiscent of those formulas.

In Figure 8.13, a new column has been added to the table, with the heading Profit. To add a formula to that column, you follow these steps.

1. Select Cell E3.
2. Type an equals sign.

3. Using either the mouse or the arrow keys, select the first revenue cell in C3. Note that the formula is unlike any formula that you've seen before. It starts out with =[Revenue], as shown in Figure 8.13.

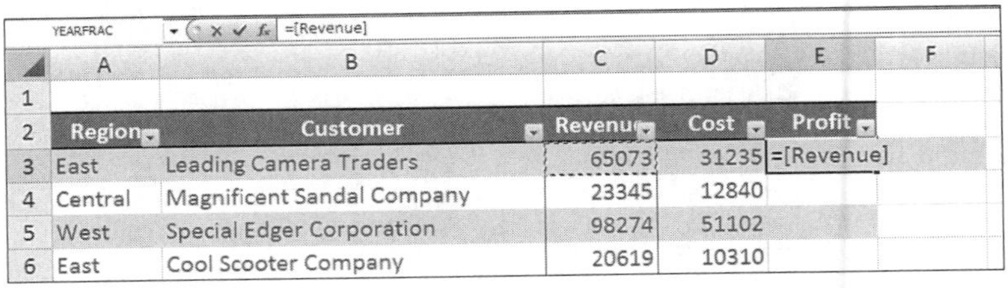

**Figure 8.13**
When you start entering a formula in a table, Excel uses table nomenclature for the formula references.

4. Type a minus sign.
5. Click Cell D3 for Cost. The formula now reads =[Revenue]-[Cost], as shown in Figure 8.14.

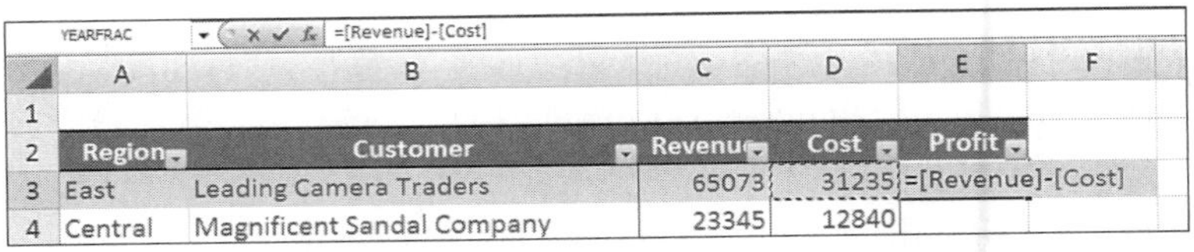

**Figure 8.14**
Without adding any named ranges, the formula =[Revenue] - [Cost] is easier to understand than D3–C3.

6. An amazing thing happens when you press the Enter key to accept the formula: Excel automatically copies the formula down to all rows in the table, as shown in Figure 8.15.

In prior versions of Excel, after adding a formula to a new column, you had to double-click the fill handle to copy the formula down to all rows of the table. This new functionality will save you time.

If you don't want to have the formula copied down to all rows, you can undo the behavior by selecting the AutoCorrect icon and then choosing the appropriate option.

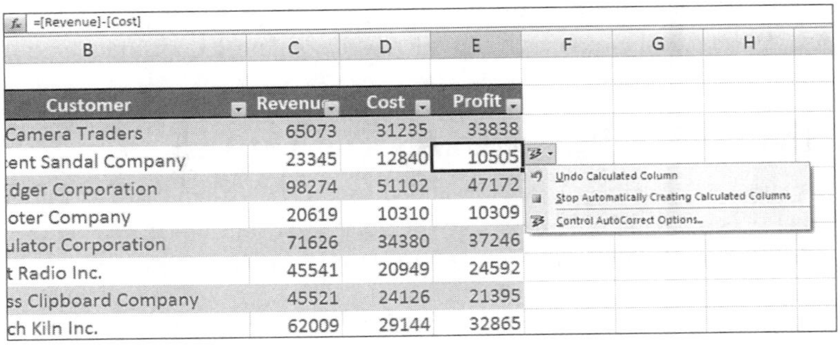

**Figure 8.15**
The new formula is automatically copied to all rows of the table.

## STOPPING THE AUTOMATIC COPYING OF FORMULAS

You might at some point have a column in a table and not want Excel to use the same formula everywhere in the column. Excel 2007 calls this a *calculated column exception*. Because any formula that you enter in the column is automatically copied to the entire column, you need to use special care to set up a calculated column exception.

Say that you already have a formula in a column and want to change to a different formula in just one cell. In this case, you follow these steps:

1. Enter the different formula in the one cell. Excel automatically copies the formula to the entire column.

2. Immediately click the Undo button in the Quick Access toolbar.

Excel marks this cell with a green triangle. If you hover your mouse over the green triangle, Excel tells you, "This cell is inconsistent with the column formula."

**TIP FROM**

*Bill Jelen*

> When you set up a single-cell column exception, Excel stops automatically copying formulas in that column.

There are other ways to set up a first column exception:

- Type data other than a formula in a calculated column cell.
- Delete a single formula from one or more cells in the calculated column.
- Move or delete a cell on another worksheet area that is referenced by one of the rows in the calculated column. This basically changes the formula in that one cell, creating a column exception. Excel then stops copying the calculation in that column.

## FORMATTING THE RESULTS OF A NEW FORMULA

The automatic copying of formulas includes one minor annoyance. In prior versions of Excel, you would add a new column by following these steps:

1. Type the heading.
2. Type the first formula.
3. Format the first formula.
4. Double-click the fill handle to copy the formula.

Now that Excel is, in essence, performing the last step for you, there is no chance to format the first cell before it gets copied. In Figure 8.16, the calculation for gross profit percentage was copied before the cell could be formatted as a percentage.

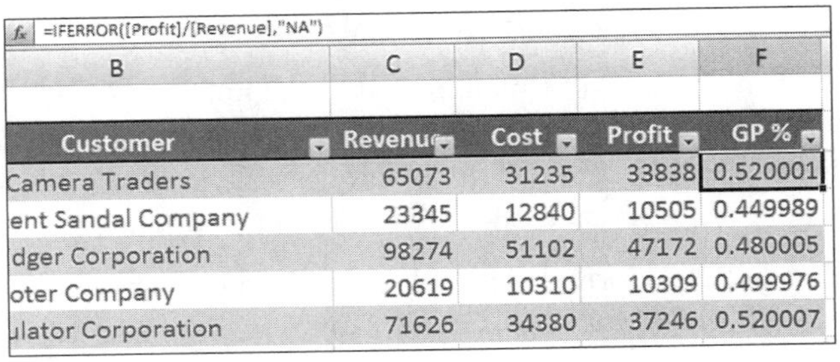

**Figure 8.16**
Excel copies a formula down to all rows before you have a chance to format the new column.

You can try formatting Cell F3 before entering the formula, but the table logic appears to overwrite this format when the formula is copied to the column. Thus, you have two options:

- Format the top cell as a percentage and then double-click the fill handle to copy the formatted cell down to all rows of the table.
- Select the table column first and then apply the percentage format to the entire column.

# SELECTING ONLY THE DATA IN THE COLUMN

There are several new options you can use when selecting data in a table. If you are going to format a table, you probably just want to format the numbers in the table and not the headings. Excel has added distinct methods for selecting the data portion of a column or selecting the entire table column with headings and totals.

## SELECTING BY RIGHT-CLICKING

One way to select the data in a column is to right-click on a cell in the table. From the context menu, you choose the Select option. The flyout menu offers three choices, as shown in Figure 8.17:

- **Table Column Data**—You select this option to select just the data rows of that column. This skips the heading row and the total row.
- **Entire Table Column**—You select this option to include the heading for the column and the cell in the total row.
- **Table Row**—You select this option to select an entire row of a table.

## SELECTING BY USING SHORTCUTS

You can also use the old Excel shortcuts to select rows or columns. These shortcut keys are modified when you are in a table:

- You can press Shift+Spacebar once to select an entire row in a table.
- You can press Shift+Spacebar a second time to select the entire worksheet row.
- You can press Ctrl+Spacebar once to select the table data in the current column of the table. This excludes the total row and the heading row. Figure 8.18 shows the selection after pressing Ctrl+Spacebar once from Cell C6.

**Figure 8.17**
You can right-click to select the data in the column.

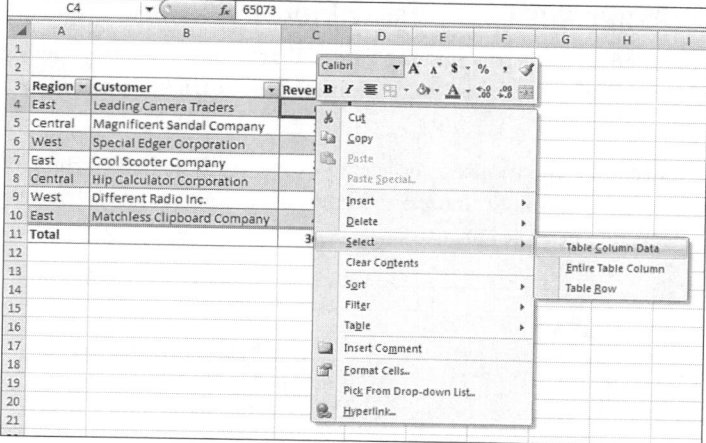

**Figure 8.18**
You can press Ctrl+Spacebar once to select the data portion of the current column.

| | A | B | C |
|---|---|---|---|
| 1 | | | |
| 2 | | | |
| 3 | Region ▾ | Customer ▾ | Revenue ▾ |
| 4 | East | Leading Camera Traders | 65073 |
| 5 | Central | Magnificent Sandal Company | 23345 |
| 6 | West | Special Edger Corporation | 98274 |
| 7 | East | Cool Scooter Company | 20619 |
| 8 | Central | Hip Calculator Corporation | 71626 |
| 9 | West | Different Radio Inc. | 45541 |
| 10 | East | Matchless Clipboard Company | 45521 |
| 11 | Total | | 369999 |

C8  fx 71626

- You can press Ctrl+Spacebar again to expand the selection to include the heading and total cell for that column, as shown in Figure 8.19.

**Figure 8.19**
You can press Ctrl+Spacebar a second time to expand the selection to include the heading and total cells.

C6  fx 98274

| | A | B | C |
|---|---|---|---|
| 1 | | | |
| 2 | | | |
| 3 | Region ▾ | Customer ▾ | Revenue ▾ |
| 4 | East | Leading Camera Traders | 65073 |
| 5 | Central | Magnificent Sandal Company | 23345 |
| 6 | West | Special Edger Corporation | 98274 |
| 7 | East | Cool Scooter Company | 20619 |
| 8 | Central | Hip Calculator Corporation | 71626 |
| 9 | West | Different Radio Inc. | 45541 |
| 10 | East | Matchless Clipboard Company | 45521 |
| 11 | Total | | 369999 |

- You can press Ctrl+Spacebar a third time to select the entire worksheet column.

## SELECTING BY USING THE NEW ARROW MOUSE POINTERS

Excel has added a new arrow mouse pointer that you can use in selecting table rows and table columns. The use of this mouse pointer is a bit tricky. The following figures show some examples:

■ In Figure 8.20, the mouse is hovering over the lower half of the Column A column letter. In this position, Column A is highlighted. You can click here any number of times to select the entire column.

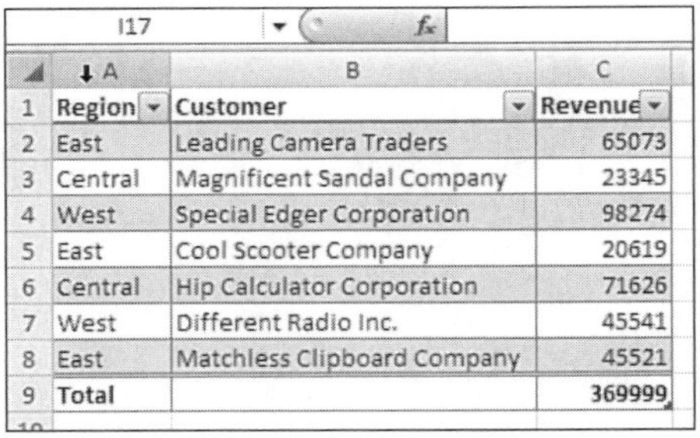

**Figure 8.20**
The traditional select column mouse pointer causes the row letter to be highlighted.

■ In Figure 8.21, the mouse is hovering over the top half of Cell A1. This is the first row of the table. The first click here selects A2:A8. The second click here selects A1:A9. Alternating clicks toggle between A2:A8 (the table data without headers and totals) and A1:A9 (the complete table column).

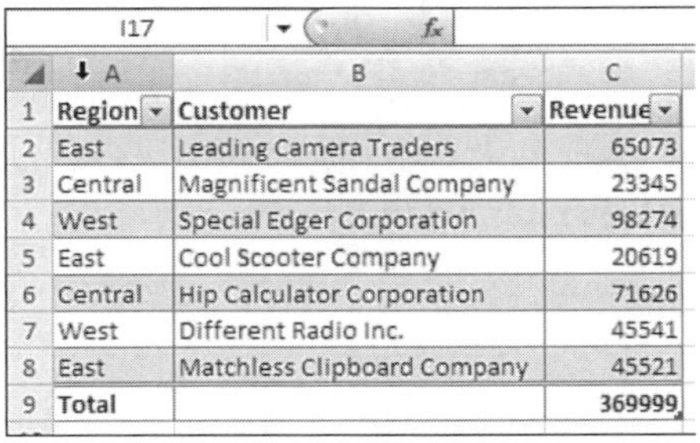

**Figure 8.21**
You can move just a bit into the table header, and the new (but identically appearing) mouse pointer takes over.

■ In Figure 8.22, the mouse is hovering over the top-left corner of Cell A1. The first click here selects A2:C8 (the table without headings and totals). The next click selects A1:A9 (the entire table). Additional clicks toggle between these two selections.

■ In Figure 8.23, the mouse is hovering near the left edge of Cell A2. Clicking here any number of times selects the entire table row (that is, A2:C2).

If you are a heavy-duty user of Excel, you will likely find yourself using these new table selection methods. The new conditional formatting options such as data bars and color scales require you to select the data in a column without the total row. Mastering the various selection methods will greatly enhance your ability to work with the new formatting.

**Figure 8.22**
You can move to the corner of the table to get the new table selection mouse pointer.

| | A | B | C |
|---|---|---|---|
| 1 | Region ▼ | Customer ▼ | Revenue ▼ |
| 2 | East | Leading Camera Traders | 65073 |
| 3 | Central | Magnificent Sandal Company | 23345 |
| 4 | West | Special Edger Corporation | 98274 |
| 5 | East | Cool Scooter Company | 20619 |
| 6 | Central | Hip Calculator Corporation | 71626 |
| 7 | West | Different Radio Inc. | 45541 |
| 8 | East | Matchless Clipboard Company | 45521 |
| 9 | Total | | 369999 |

Table3 ▼ ( ƒₓ East

**Figure 8.23**
At the left edge of a table row, the new table row selection pointer appears.

A12 ▼ (

| | A | |
|---|---|---|
| 1 | Region ▼ | Custome |
| 2 | East | Leading ( |
| 3 | Central | Magnific |
| 4 | West | Special E |

# USING TABLE DATA FOR CHARTS TO ENSURE STICKINESS

When you define a range as a table and expand the table, any references to the table also expand. If you routinely have to re-create new charts every month when you receive new data, you will love this feature.

Before creating a chart, you make a table out of the underlying data. In Figure 8.24, for example, the chart is based on the table in A1:D4. Currently, the chart has three months' worth of data.

**Figure 8.24**
This chart is based on the table in A1:D4.

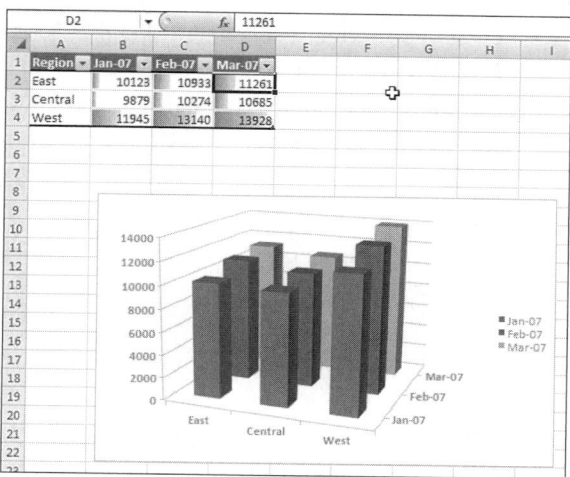

If you type a heading for the new month in Cell E1, immediately, the chart redraws to include data for April. You fill in the data for the new month, and you will not have to ever re-create a chart; the new data is added to the chart, preserving the old formatting, as shown in Figure 8.25.

8

**Figure 8.25**
You add new data to the table, and the chart automatically expands.

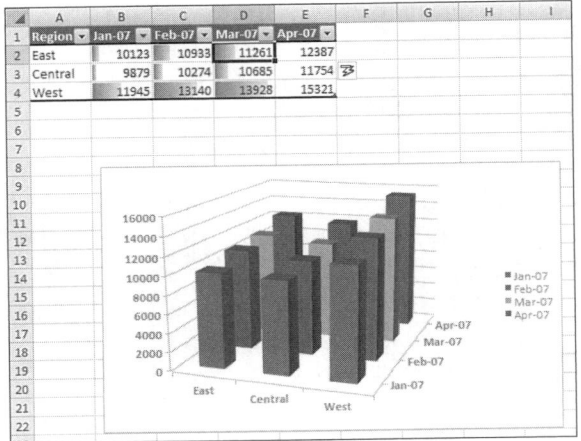

# REPLACING NAMED RANGES WITH TABLE REFERENCES

A benefit of using tables is that Excel understands a new reference style for formulas that point to data in a table. A new name is created automatically when a table is defined. The name includes the name of the table (something like Table1) and the name of the column.

The biggest benefit of this new referencing style is that the ranges that the names refer to are expanded automatically when the table expands. This new referencing style will eliminate many of the chances for error that existed with using named ranges.

## REFERENCING AN ENTIRE TABLE FROM OUTSIDE THE TABLE

When a table is defined, it becomes easier to reference the table from outside the table. Figure 8.26 shows a sales rep lookup table. Because this is the first table in the workbook, Excel has assigned the name Table1 to this table.

Figure 8.27 shows an invoice register located on another sheet in the workbook. Like many mainframe reports, this one includes the sales rep number, without the name and region information. To add a VLOOKUP function to Figure 8.27 that references Table1, follow these steps:

1. Start to type a VLOOKUP formula in Column D. When you get to the second argument, type the letter T, and the AutoComplete list scrolls down to the T entries. Among the function names are entries for Table1 and Table2, as shown in Figure 8.27.

2. Select Table1 from the list and press Tab.

3. Finish the formula so that it is =VLOOKUP($B2,Table1,COLUMN(B2),False).

4. Copy the formula to the rest of the range. Like chart references, table references are sticky. In Figure 8.28, there are a couple records for a new sales rep, S26. This rep is not yet in the original table.

5. Go back to the original table and add a new row with S25 data. All the formulas that reference Table1 automatically recalculate to include the new rows.

**Figure 8.26**
This sales rep lookup table is automatically assigned the name Table1.

| | A | B | C | D | E |
|---|---|---|---|---|---|
| | E25 | | fx | USA | |
| 1 | Rep | Name | District | Region | Country |
| 2 | S01 | JOHNS | N. Calif. | West | USA |
| 3 | S02 | COLE | Northeast | East | USA |
| 4 | S03 | STONE | Toronto | Canada | Canada |
| 5 | S04 | BEASLEY | MidAtlantic | East | USA |
| 6 | S05 | HUBER | N. Calif. | West | USA |
| 7 | S06 | ROSARIO | S. Calif. | West | USA |
| 8 | S07 | FROST | Detroit | Central | USA |
| 9 | S08 | GARRISON | Cleveland | Central | USA |
| 10 | S09 | HOLMAN | Chicago | Central | USA |
| 11 | S10 | BARR | Southeast | East | USA |
| 12 | S11 | HERRING | Chicago | Central | USA |
| 13 | S12 | WEBER | Quebec | Canada | Canada |
| 14 | S13 | GREEN | Chicago | Central | USA |
| 15 | S14 | BROCK | MidAtlantic | East | USA |
| 16 | S15 | BARRY | Southeast | East | USA |
| 17 | S16 | GONZALES | Chicago | Central | USA |
| 18 | S17 | FORBES | Detroit | Central | USA |
| 19 | S18 | CARTER | MidAtlantic | East | USA |
| 20 | S19 | MASON | N. Calif. | West | USA |
| 21 | S20 | DILLON | Northeast | East | USA |
| 22 | S21 | GARRETT | Cleveland | Central | USA |
| 23 | S22 | STEVENS | S. Calif. | West | USA |
| 24 | S23 | CRUZ | Northeast | East | USA |
| 25 | S24 | NOBLE | S. Calif. | West | USA |

**Figure 8.27**
Even though there are no defined names in the workbook, Excel understands the Table1 nomenclature.

| | A | B | C | D | E | F | G |
|---|---|---|---|---|---|---|---|
| | YEARFRAC | | X ✓ fx | =VLOOKUP($B2,T | | | |
| 1 | Invoice | Rep | Amount | Name | District | Region | Country |
| 2 | 1010 | S17 | 147 | =VLOOKUP($B2,T | | | |
| 3 | 1011 | S14 | 128 | VLOOKUP(lookup_value, table_array, col_index_num | | | |
| 4 | 1012 | S22 | 158 | | Table1 | | |
| 5 | 1013 | S15 | 172 | | Table2 | | |
| 6 | 1014 | S22 | 144 | | TAN | | |
| 7 | 1015 | S12 | 148 | | TANH | | |
| 8 | 1016 | S10 | 152 | | TBILLEQ | | |
| 9 | 1017 | S13 | 163 | | TBILLPRICE | | |
| 10 | 1018 | S13 | 145 | | TBILLYIELD | | |
| 11 | 1019 | S23 | 173 | | TDIST | | |
| 12 | 1020 | S25 | 138 | | TEXT | | |
| 13 | 1021 | S19 | 138 | | TIME | | |
| 14 | 1022 | S25 | 138 | | | | |

**Figure 8.28**
When you add the missing reps to Table1, the references here to Table1 expand as well.

| | A | B | C | D | E | F | G |
|---|---|---|---|---|---|---|---|
| 1 | Invoice | Rep | Amount | Name | District | Region | Country |
| 2 | 1010 | S17 | 147 | FORBES | Detroit | Central | USA |
| 3 | 1011 | S14 | 128 | BROCK | MidAtlant | East | USA |
| 4 | 1012 | S22 | 158 | STEVENS | S. Calif. | West | USA |
| 5 | 1013 | S15 | 172 | BARRY | Southeast | East | USA |
| 6 | 1014 | S22 | 144 | STEVENS | S. Calif. | West | USA |
| 7 | 1015 | S12 | 148 | WEBER | Quebec | Canada | Canada |
| 8 | 1016 | S10 | 152 | BARR | Southeast | East | USA |
| 9 | 1017 | S13 | 163 | GREEN | Chicago | Central | USA |
| 10 | 1018 | S13 | 145 | GREEN | Chicago | Central | USA |
| 11 | 1019 | S23 | 173 | CRUZ | Northeast | East | USA |
| 12 | 1020 | S26 | 138 | #N/A | #N/A | #N/A | #N/A |
| 13 | 1021 | S19 | 138 | MASON | N. Calif. | West | USA |
| 14 | 1022 | S26 | 138 | #N/A | #N/A | #N/A | #N/A |

## REFERENCING TABLE COLUMNS FROM OUTSIDE A TABLE

To reference an entire column from outside a table, you use the syntax `TableName[ColumnName]`. When you do this, Excel's AutoComplete feature provides a list of column names for you. After you type `Table1[`, the AutoComplete list shows all the columns in the table, plus additional keywords (which are discussed in the following section, "Using Structured References to Refer to Tables in Formulas"). The AutoComplete list is shown in Figure 8.29.

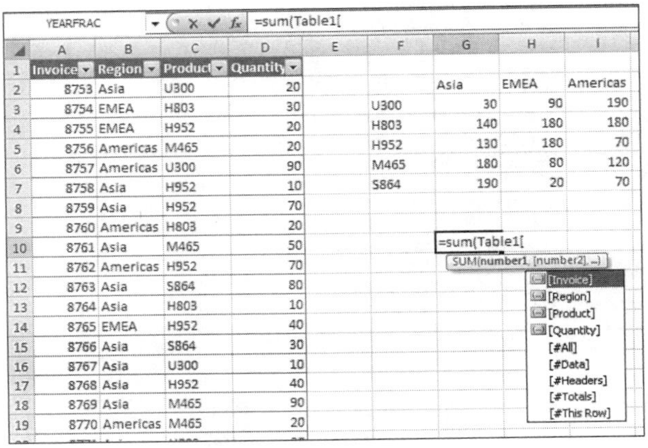

**Figure 8.29**
Excel offers AutoComplete entries from which you can choose the column name when entering a formula.

References to a table column do not include the header or total row. While this behavior is usually desired, there might be instances when you use a INDEX or OFFSET function that you expect Excel to include the heading as row 1 in the function.

The formula in Figure 8.30 uses three references to a table to find the sales for a particular product and a particular region. The nomenclature Quantity, Product, and Region is easier to understand than cell addresses such as D2:D87. This is the complete formula in Cell G3:

`=SUMIFS(Table1[Quantity],Table1[Product],$F3,Table1[Region],G$2)`

Table references are valid on any worksheet in the workbook. If you want to refer to a table that is seven worksheets away, you can still use the `Table1` nomenclature, without prefixing the worksheet name.

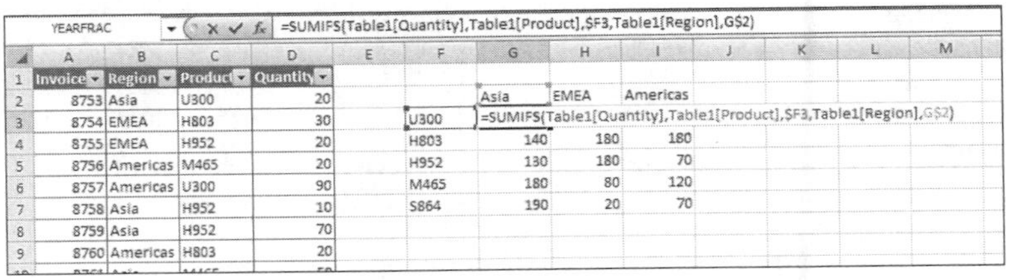

**Figure 8.30**
This formula is a fairly complex conditional sum. It relies on three columns from the table.

## USING STRUCTURED REFERENCES TO REFER TO TABLES IN FORMULAS

Microsoft has created a fairly comprehensive way to refer to various parts of tables. You've seen some of the table nomenclature syntax in the previous two sections. The following are complete details for writing formulas that refer to tables:

- The reference to a table starts with the table name. If you are creating the formula within the table itself, you can omit the table name.

- If no further qualifiers are entered, the table name refers to the data rows of the table. This excludes the headings and total rows.

- Further qualifiers should be enclosed in square brackets. If you are using one qualifier, only one set of square brackets is needed. You may specify *TableName[Qualifier]* or *TableName[[Qualifier]]*.

- If you are specifying multiple qualifiers, each qualifier must be surrounded by square brackets. The qualifiers must be separated by commas. The complete set of qualifiers must be surrounded by square brackets. The syntax follows this pattern: *TableName[[Qualifier1],[Qualifier2],Qualifier3]]*.

- For a table with a header row, each column heading is automatically added to the list of qualifiers.

- For a table without a header row, the list of qualifiers includes Column1, Column2, and so on.

- Every table also has these qualifiers: #All, #Data, #Headers, #Totals, #ThisRow.

- The #ThisRow qualifier must be used in conjunction with another qualifier.

This system allows you to select a wide variety of references without having to use cell references. To get the total of sales from Table1, you can either use =SUM(Table1[Sales]) or =Table1[[#Total],[Sales]]. The second syntax returns a #REF! error if someone turns off the Totals Row check box in the Table Tools Design ribbon.

Figure 8.31 shows various structured references.

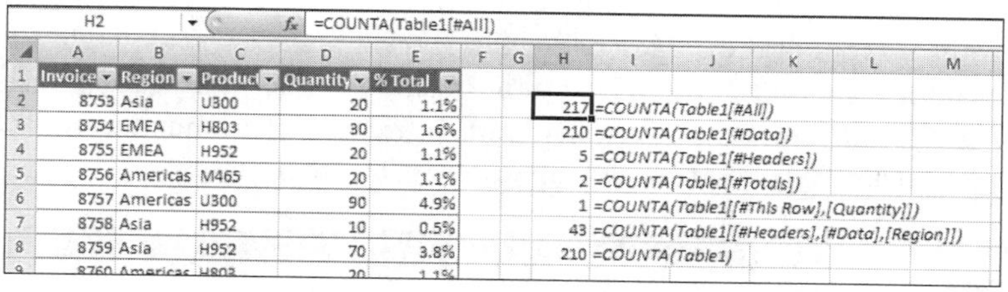

**Figure 8.31**
Structured references are shown in Column I.

## CREATING BANDED ROWS AND COLUMNS WITH TABLE STYLES

In previous versions of Excel, creating banded rows or columns required creative conditional formatting or tedious manual work. Creating banded rows or columns in a table is relatively simple in Excel 2007.

The fourth group on the Table Tools Design ribbon is Table Style Options. This group includes check boxes for Banded Rows and Banded Columns. These check boxes work only if the selected table style includes rules for banded columns and/or banded rows. If you have selected the plain white table style, turning on or off banded rows and columns will have no effect.

Figure 8.32 shows five tables. The first table contains banded rows. The second table has banded columns. The third table leaves banded rows and columns off, but the first column, last column, header row, and total row are checked. The top table in Column H contains both banded rows and banded columns. The last table contains a custom format to change the banding from one stripe to two stripes. The next section provides details on how to customize the table style.

**Figure 8.32**
These tables exhibit various combinations of the table style options. The fifth table requires a customization of the table style.

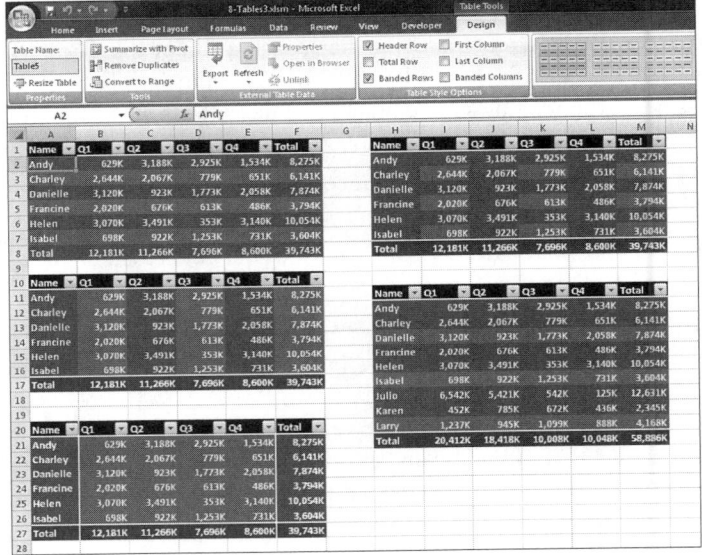

## CUSTOMIZING A TABLE STYLE: CREATING DOUBLE-HEIGHT BANDED ROWS

At the bottom of the Table Styles gallery, there is a New Table Style button. I would encourage you not to use this button! It can be rather intimidating to set up a completely new style. It is often easier to start with an existing style and modify it. To do this, you right-click a style and choose Duplicate, as shown in Figure 8.33.

**Figure 8.33**
Rather than choosing New Table Quick Style, you can choose to duplicate an existing style.

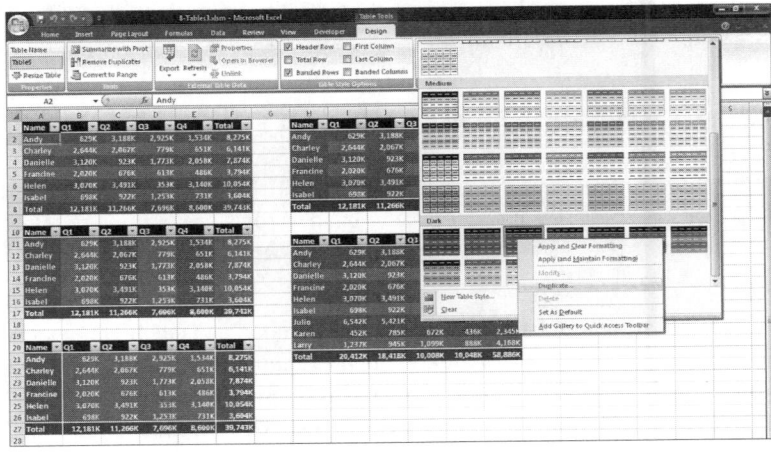

After you choose Duplicate, Excel displays the Modify Table Quick Style dialog box. Excel assigns a new name to the style, adding a 2 to the existing style name. You can rename the style if you like.

To create double-height banded rows, you follow these steps:

1. Choose First Row Stripe from the Table Element list. A Stripe Size drop-down appears.
2. Choose 2 from the Stripe Size drop-down.
3. Choose Second Row Stripe from the Table Element list. A Stripe Size drop-down appears.
4. Choose 2 from the Stripe Size drop-down.
5. If you would like your modified theme to be the default style for all new tables created in this document, choose the Set as Default Table Quick Style for This Document check box in the lower-left corner of the dialog.

**Figure 8.34**
For double-height row banding, you change the stripe size.

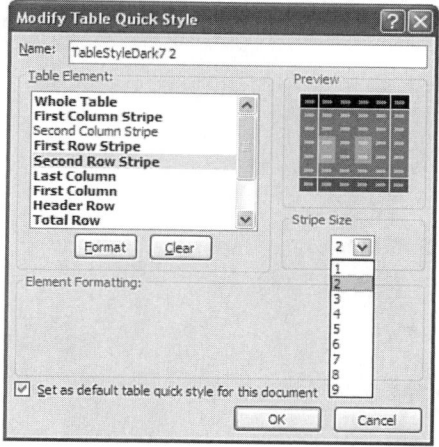

6. Click OK, and your custom style is saved to a new Custom section at the top of the Table Styles drop-down.

## CREATING BANDED ROWS OUTSIDE A TABLE

You might find some of the table behavior annoying. If you want banded columns but don't want to use a full-fledged table, you can temporarily create a table, apply a banded row format to the table, and then convert it back to a range in order to have a banded row format on the range. Here's how you do it:

1. Select a cell in the range to be formatted.
2. Press Ctrl+T to make the range a table.
3. If your default table style does not include banded rows, choose a new table style from the Table Styles gallery on the Table Tools Design ribbon.
4. In the Table Tools Design ribbon, choose Tools, Convert to Range. This removes the table properties but keeps the table formatting.

8

# DEALING WITH THE AUTOFILTER DROP-DOWNS

A common spreadsheet style rule says that you should right-justify the headings above numeric columns. If you regularly follow this convention, you will certainly be annoyed with the default choice that all tables are automatically created with the autofilter drop-downs applied.

In Figure 8.35, the first range contains data with the Q1 headings in the first row. If you apply a table to a range, the autofilter drop-downs completely cover the headings, making the table useless. The table in Rows 10:16 shows this.

One option, shown in Row 19, is to begin centering your headings instead of right-justifying them.

The final option, shown in Row 27, is to keep the table but turn off the autofilter for the table. Frustratingly, this option does not appear on the Table Tools Design ribbon. Instead, you need to go to Home, Editing, Sort & Filter, Filter to toggle away the drop-downs.

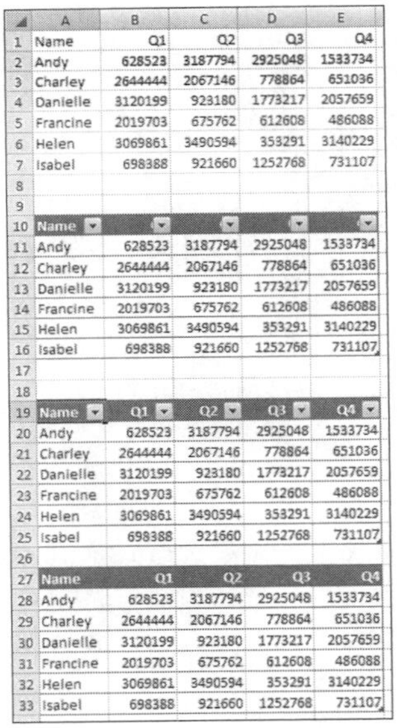

| | A | B | C | D | E |
|---|---|---|---|---|---|
| 1 | Name | Q1 | Q2 | Q3 | Q4 |
| 2 | Andy | 628523 | 3187794 | 2925048 | 1533734 |
| 3 | Charley | 2644444 | 2067146 | 778864 | 651036 |
| 4 | Danielle | 3120199 | 923180 | 1773217 | 2057659 |
| 5 | Francine | 2019703 | 675762 | 612608 | 486088 |
| 6 | Helen | 3069861 | 3490594 | 353291 | 3140229 |
| 7 | Isabel | 698388 | 921660 | 1252768 | 731107 |
| 8 | | | | | |
| 9 | | | | | |
| 10 | Name | | | | |
| 11 | Andy | 628523 | 3187794 | 2925048 | 1533734 |
| 12 | Charley | 2644444 | 2067146 | 778864 | 651036 |
| 13 | Danielle | 3120199 | 923180 | 1773217 | 2057659 |
| 14 | Francine | 2019703 | 675762 | 612608 | 486088 |
| 15 | Helen | 3069861 | 3490594 | 353291 | 3140229 |
| 16 | Isabel | 698388 | 921660 | 1252768 | 731107 |
| 17 | | | | | |
| 18 | | | | | |
| 19 | Name | Q1 | Q2 | Q3 | Q4 |
| 20 | Andy | 628523 | 3187794 | 2925048 | 1533734 |
| 21 | Charley | 2644444 | 2067146 | 778864 | 651036 |
| 22 | Danielle | 3120199 | 923180 | 1773217 | 2057659 |
| 23 | Francine | 2019703 | 675762 | 612608 | 486088 |
| 24 | Helen | 3069861 | 3490594 | 353291 | 3140229 |
| 25 | Isabel | 698388 | 921660 | 1252768 | 731107 |
| 26 | | | | | |
| 27 | Name | Q1 | Q2 | Q3 | Q4 |
| 28 | Andy | 628523 | 3187794 | 2925048 | 1533734 |
| 29 | Charley | 2644444 | 2067146 | 778864 | 651036 |
| 30 | Danielle | 3120199 | 923180 | 1773217 | 2057659 |
| 31 | Francine | 2019703 | 675762 | 612608 | 486088 |
| 32 | Helen | 3069861 | 3490594 | 353291 | 3140229 |
| 33 | Isabel | 698388 | 921660 | 1252768 | 731107 |

**Figure 8.35**
The headings in Row 1 become unusable when the range is converted to a table.

There are more tricks available for tables. See Chapter 13, "Removing Duplicates and Filtering," and Chapter 14, "Sorting," for more table tricks.

# CHAPTER 9

# VISUALIZING DATA IN EXCEL

**In this chapter**

Many people feel their eyes glaze over when they encounter a screen full of numbers. Fortunately, Microsoft has added terrific new data visualization features to Excel 2007 that make those screens full of numbers a little easier on the eyes.

Excel has had a weak conditional formatting feature for a decade. It was limited and tricky to use. Excel tipsters often showed the incredibly hard way to make conditional formatting just a bit more powerful.

In Excel 2007, Microsoft has made data visualization easy to use. You are just a few clicks away from features that would have required a Ph.D. in past versions of Excel. The following are some of the new possibilities in data visualization:

- Adding data bars (that is, tiny, in-cell bar charts) to cells based on the cell value.
- Adding color scales to cells based on the cell value. This is often called a *heat map*.
- Adding icon sets (think traffic lights) to cells based on the cell value.
- Adding color, bold, italics, patterns, and so on to cells based on the cell values.
- Quickly identifying cells that are above average. Quickly identifying the top *n* or bottom *n*% of cells.
- Quickly identifying duplicate values.
- Quickly identifying dates that are today or yesterday or last week.
- After you've added icons or color, sorting by color or by icon. This is a huge improvement, especially for VBA programmers who used to want to know which conditions were being met by a conditional format.

The following are some of the improved data visualization features in Excel 2007:

- A cell can meet more than one condition. If you have one rule that makes the cell bold and another rule that makes the cell red, for example, you can have some cells that are red, some that are red bold, some that are bold, and some that are normal.
- There is no longer a limit of only three rules per cell.
- You can easily manage rules. If you want to change the order in which rules are applied, it is easy to reorder the rules.
- It is now obvious that a cell's format can be based on other cell values. This was always the case in earlier versions of Excel, but most people using conditional format never discovered the secret. Further, a big improvement is that a formula can now refer to a cell on another worksheet in the current workbook.

When you use conditional formatting in a defined table, you have the option of highlighting the entire row if a cell in the row meets the condition.

Although it is very easy to set up basic conditional formatting, you need to know a few tricks, which I tell you about later in this chapter, for creating better conditional formatting than most people will figure out on their own.

# CREATING IN-CELL BAR CHARTS WITH DATA BARS

A *data bar* is a semitransparent swath of color that starts at the left edge of a cell. The smallest numbers in a formatted range have just a tiny bit of color in the cell. The largest numbers in the formatted range are 90% filled with color. This creates a visual effect that enables you to visually pick out the larger and smaller values.

Creating data bars requires just a few clicks. You follow these steps:

1. Select a range of numeric data (but do not include the total row in this selection). This range should be numbers of the same scale. For example, select a column of sales data or a column of profit data. If you attempted to format a column with number of vehicles sold in a month and a column of total dollars from those vehicles, none of the unit sold data would be large enough to warrant any color in the cell.

2. From the Home ribbon, in the Style group, select the Conditional Formatting icon.

3. Choose Data Bars from the drop-down. You can then choose one of six colors for the data bars: blue, green, red, orange, light blue, or purple. If you don't like these six basic colors, you can choose any color, as described in the next section.

The result is a swath of color in each cell in the selection, as shown in Figure 9.1.

**Figure 9.1**
It takes four clicks to create data bars in one of six basic colors.

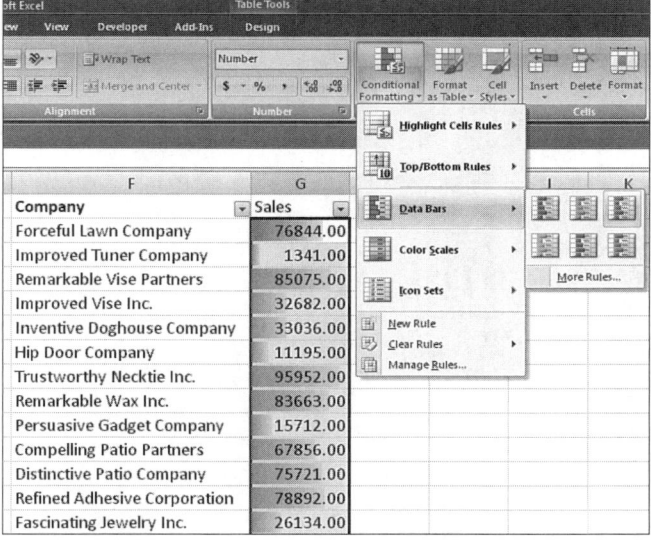

The data bar demonstrates a significant improvement over conditional formatting in Excel 2003. In prior versions, conditional formatting would assign a color based on a simple true/false test. In Excel 2007, the conditional formatting is a comparison between a set of cells.

## CUSTOMIZING DATA BARS

By default, Excel assigns the largest data bar to the cell with the largest value and the smallest data bar to the cell with the smallest value. You can customize this behavior by following these steps:

1. From the Conditional Formatting drop-down on the Home ribbon, choose Manage Rules.
2. From the Show Formatting Rules drop-down, choose This Worksheet. You now see a list of all rules applied to the sheet.
3. Click the Data Bar rule.
4. Click the Edit Rule button. You will see the Edit Formatting Rule dialog, as shown in Figure 9.2.

**Figure 9.2**
You can customize data bars by using this dialog.

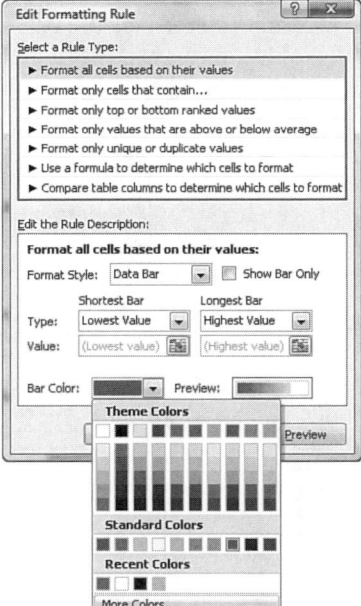

5. To change the color of the bar beyond the six basic colors, choose the Bar Color drop-down. You can choose from the theme colors or standard colors, or you can build any RGB value by choosing More Colors.
6. Select the Show Bar Only check box. Excel hides the numbers in the cells and shows only the data bars. This is an interesting variation, as shown in Figure 9.3.

There are two Type drop-downs: Shortest Bar and Longest Bar. These drop-downs offer choices for Lowest Value and Highest Value, Number, Percent, Formula, or Percentile. These are completely explained below.

**Figure 9.3**
Showing only the data bar is an interesting alternative.

| | A | B | C |
|---|---|---|---|
| 1 | Company ▾ | Sales ▾ | |
| 2 | Forceful Lawn Company | | |
| 3 | Improved Tuner Company | | |
| 4 | Remarkable Vise Partners | | |
| 5 | Improved Vise Inc. | | |
| 6 | Inventive Doghouse Company | | |
| 7 | Hip Door Company | | |
| 8 | Trustworthy Necktie Inc. | | |
| 9 | Remarkable Wax Inc. | | |
| 10 | Persuasive Gadget Company | | |
| 11 | Compelling Patio Partners | | |

## CONTROLLING THE SIZE OF THE SMALLEST/LARGEST DATA BAR

Sometimes, your data might have a few outliers. This happens with any dataset. Say that 99% of your customers are over $1,000 in sales, but a couple stray accounts have sales of just a few dollars. Microsoft gives you explicit control over the cell value that gets the smallest bar.

For example, consider Column A in Figure 9.4. The values are basically in the 1000 to 2000 range. However, one outlier value of 10 forces Excel to assign a medium-sized data bar to the 1000 value in Cell A1.

For the numbers in Column D, the steps in the preceding section were used to edit the rule. In this case, you can set the Shortest Bar Type drop-down to 1000. Excel then treats any value of 1000 as the value with the shortest bar. Any value less than 1000 is given the same size bar as the 1000 bar.

**Figure 9.4**
The default setting for D1:D7 assigns a value of 1000 as the shortest bar. The one outlier in Row 6 doesn't cause all the 1000–2000 values to appear the same.

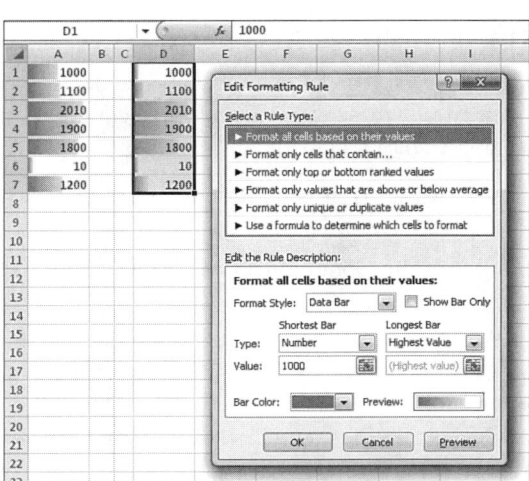

Here are the rules for each of the Type options:

■ For Lowest Value/Highest Value, Excel evaluates all the values in the range of cells and selects the lowest value as the shortest bar and the highest value as the longest bar. This is the default behavior.

■ For Number, you enter the values that should receive the shortest and/or longest bars. For numbers that are more or less than that value, Excel simply draws the shortest or longest bar, as appropriate.

■ For Percent, you enter a percentage to associate with the shortest and longest bars. For example, if the values in the selected cells range from 0 to 1000, then a minimum value associated with 10% would be 100. In this example, any cells having values equal to or less than 100 would have the shortest bar drawn in the cell.

■ Percentile examines the values in the range of cells, sorts them, and then uses their positions within the sorted list to determine their percentiles. In a set of 20 ordered cells, the 30th percentile would always be the sixth cell, regardless of the value contained within it. If you choose percentile and enter 10 for the shortest bar and 90 for the longest bar, any outliers outside the 10–90 range would get the shortest or longest bar assigned to them.

■ Formula allows you to enter a formula. The formula is evaluated to determine the value used for the shortest and longest bars. This is useful for developing conditional formats that aren't easily handled by the other four choices.

The one frustrating feature with data bars is that you cannot reverse the size of the data bars. Although in some scenarios such as top 100 rankings the lowest score might deserve the largest bar, there is no way to make this happen with a data bar. If you need to do this, you should consider using color scales instead.

# CREATING HEAT MAPS WITH COLOR SCALES

Color scales are similar to data bars. Instead of a variable-size bar in each cell, however, the color scale uses gradients of two or three different colors to communicate the relative size of each cell. Here's how you apply color scales:

1. Select a contiguous range within your data. Be sure not to include headings or total cells in the selection.

2. On the Home ribbon, select the Conditional Formatting drop-down, and then select Color Scales.

3. From the Color Scales fly-out, select one of the eight styles to apply the color scale to the range. Note that this fly-out offers subtle differences that you should pay attention to. The top four options are scales that use three colors. These are great onscreen or with color printers. The bottom four options are scales that use two colors. These are better with monochrome printers.

In a default color scale with a three-color scale, the smallest cells are assigned a value of red. The middle values are assigned a value of yellow. The largest cells are assigned a value of green. Even within the green values, the larger numbers are more green than the other numbers.

In Figure 9.5, values from 50 through 80 are various shades of green. Values such as 50 are a light yellow-green, and values of 80 are dark green.

**Figure 9.5**
Excel's new 32-bit color support provides a different shade for every value.

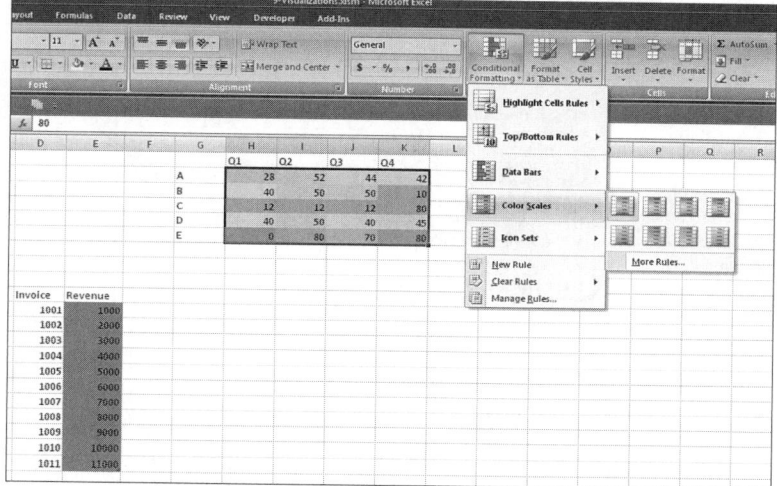

## CONVERTING TO MONOCHROMATIC DATA BAR

As you can see from the black-and-white screen images in this book, color scales with three colors do not look that good when printed on a monochromatic printer. When you know you'll be printing in black and white, one option is to convert the color scale to a monochromatic scale that will vary from white to a dark color. To do so, you follow these steps:

1. Select a single cell in your formatted range.

2. From the Insert ribbon, choose Conditional Formatting, Manage Rules. In the Conditional Formatting Rules Manager dialog that appears, the initial drop-down defaults to Current Selection. This will work fine, provided that your selection is part of the range that has conditional formatting. The dialog shows any conditional formatting rule(s) applied to the current selection, as shown in Figure 9.6.

3. Even if there is only one rule in the dialog, click the rule to select it and then click Edit Rule. Initially, the Edit Formatting Rule dialog shows the default three-color red-yellow-green scale, as shown in Figure 9.7. You might believe from this dialog that you can apply a color scale to only cells that are above or below average, but the dialog does not work that way. This common dialog is used to edit many types of conditional formatting, and color scales only apply to the top rule type, "Format all cells based on their values."

**Figure 9.6**
Manage rules in the
Conditional Formatting
Rules Manager dialog.

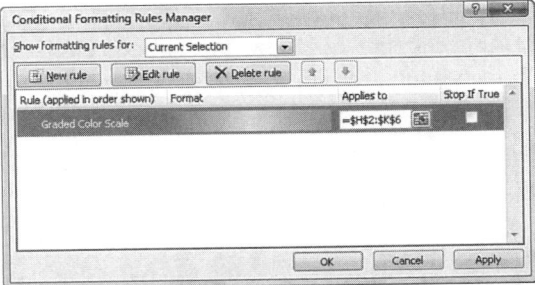

**Figure 9.7**
The Edit Formatting
Rule dialog box is
used throughout con-
ditional formatting.
Only the top rule type
is valid for color
scales.

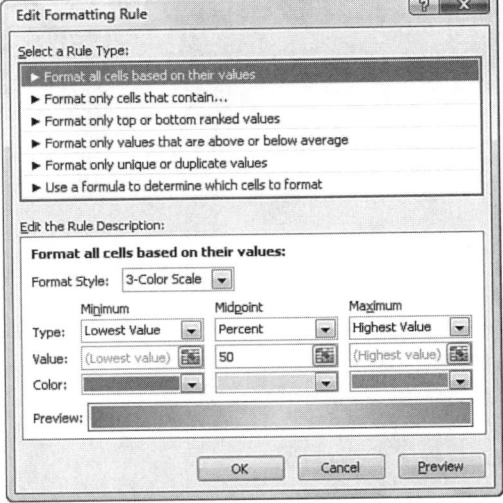

4. For color scales, change any of the settings in the lower half of the dialog box, in the Edit the Rule Description section. The Format Style drop-down includes the options 2-Color Scale, 3-Color Scale, Data Bar, and Icon Sets. Choose 2-Color Scale from the drop-down.

5. For the minimum, select the color drop-down and choose white. For the maximum, select the color drop-down and choose a dark color.

6. Choose Preview to apply the effect to the range. If it is acceptable, click OK to return to the Conditional Formatting Rules Manager dialog and then click OK again to complete the operation.

## TROUBLESHOOTING COLOR SCALES

Excel 2007 considers a three-color scale and a two-color scale to be completely different visualizations. This leads to some erratic behavior when you attempt to change the color scale pattern by using the Color Scale icon on the Conditional Formatting drop-down.

Say that you use the icon to apply a three-color red-yellow-green visualization. You decide to go back to the icon and instead apply a three-color blue-yellow-red visualization. Excel 2007 is smart enough to convert the red-yellow-green pattern to blue-yellow-red. This behavior is logical enough.

However, say that you decide to choose a visualization from the second row of color scales—perhaps the green-to-yellow visualization. Even though this is accessed on the same fly-out menu, Excel 2007 considers the two-color scale to be a different visualization. Instead of replacing the visualization, Excel adds a second rule. This can lead to muting of the colors from both rules.

To avoid this problem, when switching from two-color to three-color scales, be sure to use the Manage Rules choice at the bottom of the Conditional Formatting menu in order to convert from a three-color to a two-color scale.

## USING ICON SETS TO ADD ICONS BASED ON VALUE

The final type of new conditional formatting is called an *icon set*. Icon sets were popular with expensive management reporting software in the late 1990s. They've now been added to Excel. An icon set might include green, yellow, and red traffic lights, or another set of icons to show positive, neutral, and negative meanings. Excel can automatically apply an icon to a cell based on the relative size of the value in the cell compared to other values in the range.

Initially, icon sets look like they will be cool. However, there are a few limitations that will make them annoying in Excel 2007. I suspect that the implementation of icon sets will improve greatly in future versions of Excel.

Excel 2007 ships with icon sets that contain either three, four, or five different icons. The icons are always left-justified in the cell. Excel applies rules to add an icon to every cell in the range:

- For the three-icon sets, you have a choice between arrows, flags, two varieties of traffic lights, signs, and two varieties of what Excel calls "3 Symbols." This last group consists of a green check mark for the good cells, a yellow exclamation point for the middle cells, and a red X for the bad cells. You can either get the symbols in a circle (that is, 3 Symbols (Circled)) or alone on a white background (that is, 3 Symbols (Uncircled)). One version of the arrows is available in gray. All the other icon sets use red, yellow, and green.

- For the four-icon sets, there are two varieties of arrows, a red-to-black circleset, a series of cell-phone power indicators, and a set of four traffic lights. In the traffic light option, a black light appears indicates an option that is even worse than the red light. The ratings icons seem to have promise for working well on both a color display and a mono-chromatic printout.

- For the five-icon sets, there are two varieties of arrows, a set of five power bar icons, and an interesting set called *five quarters*. This last set is a monochrome circle. The circle is completely empty for the lowest values, 25% filled, 50% filled, 75% filled, and completely filled.

Samples of the 16 available icon sets are shown in Figure 9.8.

**Figure 9.8**
Excel 2007 offers 16 varieties of icon sets.

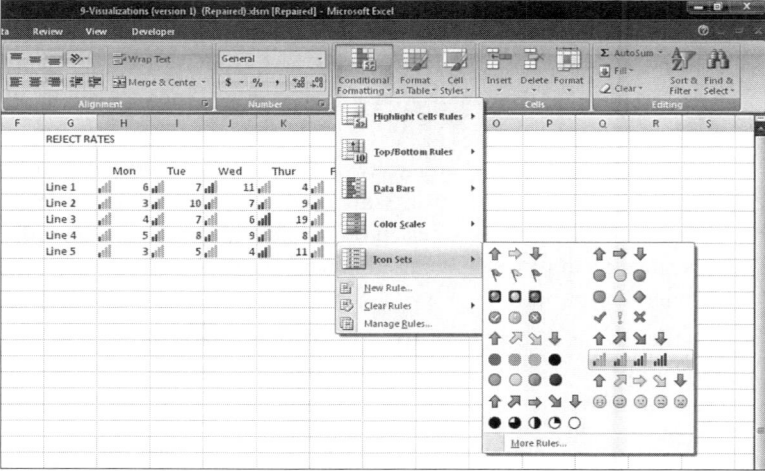

## SETTING UP AN ICON SET

Given that icon sets are in their first Excel incarnation, they require a bit more thought than the other data visualization offerings. Before you use icon sets, you should consider whether they will be printed in monochrome or displayed in color on the screen. Several of the 16 icon sets rely on color for differentiation and will look horrible in a black-and-white report.

After creating several reports with icon sets, I have started to favor the power bar indicators made popular by cell phones. They look good in both color and black and white. These icons are available in either four-icon or five-icon sets. To set up an icon set, you follow these steps:

1. Select a range of numeric data of a similar scale. Do not include the headers or total rows in this selection.

2. From the Home ribbon, in the Styles group, select the Conditional Formatting icon.

3. Choose Icon Sets from the drop-down. Select 1 of the 16 icon sets. In Figure 9.9, the "4 Ratings" choice is selected.

**Figure 9.9**
Initially, this icon set is horrible looking.

## MOVING NUMBERS CLOSER TO ICONS

In Figure 9.10, the icon set has been applied to a rectangular range of data. The icons are always left-justified. There is no way to center them. And there is no way to have an icon appear to the right of the value. This was an oversight on the part of the Excel team. In Figure 9.10, the icons for Column I appear to apply to the numbers in Column H.

One way to mitigate this problem is to center all the numbers in the range. This at least puts the value and the icon closer together. Rows 12 through 16 of Figure 9.10 show this solution.

Choosing left-justified is unsatisfactory. The numbers are completely hidden by the icon set, as shown in Rows 20 through 24 of Figure 9.10.

A better solution is to left-justify the numbers and then click the increase indent button twice. Rows 28 through 32 show this solution.

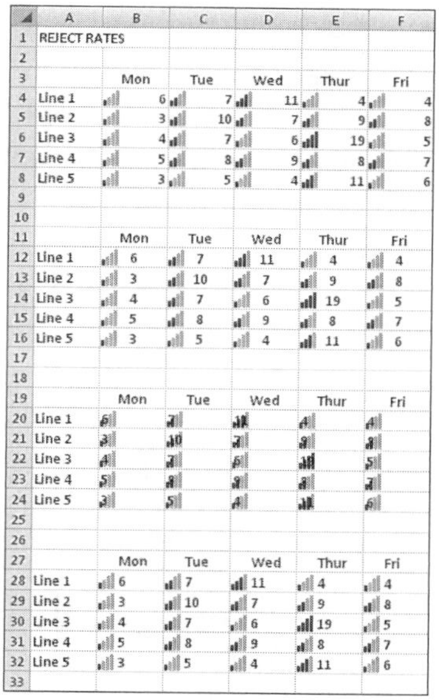

**Figure 9.10**
With a combination of justification and indenting, you can move the numbers closer to their icons.

## REVERSING THE SEQUENCE OF ICONS

In Figure 9.11, the values in the cells track reject rates for several manufacturing lines. The icon set offers green check marks, yellow exclamation points, and red X icons.

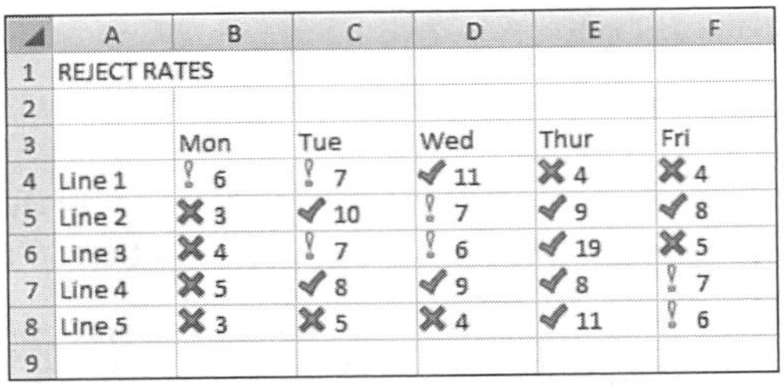

**Figure 9.11**
Excel gives green
check marks to the
highest reject rates.

| | A | B | C | D | E | F |
|---|---|---|---|---|---|---|
| 1 | REJECT RATES | | | | | |
| 2 | | | | | | |
| 3 | | Mon | Tue | Wed | Thur | Fri |
| 4 | Line 1 | ! 6 | ! 7 | ✓ 11 | ✗ 4 | ✗ 4 |
| 5 | Line 2 | ✗ 3 | ✓ 10 | ! 7 | ✓ 9 | ✓ 8 |
| 6 | Line 3 | ✗ 4 | ! 7 | ! 6 | ✓ 19 | ✗ 5 |
| 7 | Line 4 | ✗ 5 | ✓ 8 | ✓ 9 | ✓ 8 | ! 7 |
| 8 | Line 5 | ✗ 3 | ✗ 5 | ✗ 4 | ✓ 11 | ! 6 |
| 9 | | | | | | |

In the default view of the data, Excel always assumes that higher numbers are better. This is not the case in this situation, where higher reject rates are bad.

Unlike with color scales or data bars, with icon sets, you can reverse the order. To do so, you follow these steps:

1. Select one cell in your data.
2. From the Conditional Formatting icon, select Manage Rules.
3. Choose the Icon Set rule by clicking Icon Set. The rule color changes from gray to blue.
4. Click the Edit Rule button. The Edit Formatting Rule dialog appears.
5. In the Edit Formatting Rule dialog, choose the Reverse Icon Order check box. Click OK twice to close both open dialog boxes.

The icon order is reversed, as shown in Figure 9.12.

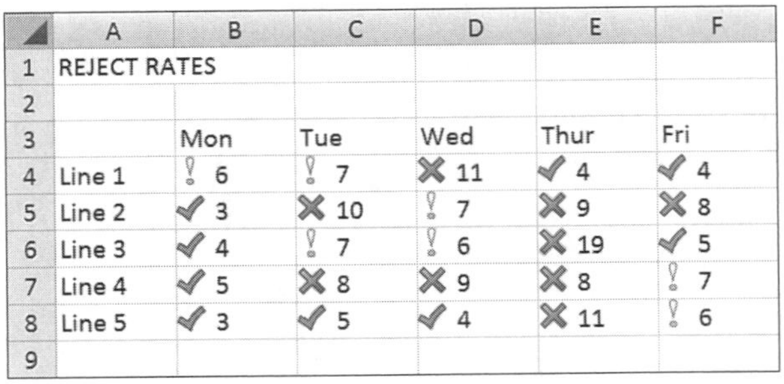

**Figure 9.12**
The bad cells now get
the red X icons.

| | A | B | C | D | E | F |
|---|---|---|---|---|---|---|
| 1 | REJECT RATES | | | | | |
| 2 | | | | | | |
| 3 | | Mon | Tue | Wed | Thur | Fri |
| 4 | Line 1 | ! 6 | ! 7 | ✗ 11 | ✓ 4 | ✓ 4 |
| 5 | Line 2 | ✓ 3 | ✗ 10 | ! 7 | ✗ 9 | ✗ 8 |
| 6 | Line 3 | ✓ 4 | ! 7 | ! 6 | ✗ 19 | ✓ 5 |
| 7 | Line 4 | ✓ 5 | ✗ 8 | ✗ 9 | ✗ 8 | ! 7 |
| 8 | Line 5 | ✓ 3 | ✓ 5 | ✓ 4 | ✗ 11 | ! 6 |
| 9 | | | | | | |

# USING STOP IF TRUE TO IMPROVE ALL CONDITIONAL FORMATTING

The data visualizations described so far in this chapter cause every cell in the range to receive color, icons, or data bars. This is somewhat limiting. What if you just want an icon on the really bad cells? What if you only want a color scale on the top 20% of records? How can you do this? The process is unintuitive, but it is easy to set up. Basically, you apply the icon set or color scale to the entire range. Then, you add a new conditional format—a very boring format—to all the cells that you don't want to have the icon. For example, you might tell Excel to use a white background on all cells with values less than 5. The final important step is to manage the rules and tell Excel to stop processing more rules if the first rule is met. This requires a bit of cleverness. If you want to apply icons to cells with values over 10, you first tell Excel to make all the cells under 10 look like every other cell in Excel. Turning on Stop if True is the key to getting Excel to not apply icons to cells with values under 10.

Figure 9.13 shows a useful visualization in which only reject rates of 10% or above receive a red icon. All the other cells have no icons.

**Figure 9.13**
Using Stop if True on an invisible rule for the cells that are okay is the key to having icons appear on the really bad cells.

| | A | B | C | D | E | F | G |
|---|---|---|---|---|---|---|---|
| 1 | REJECT RATES | | | | | | |
| 2 | | | | | | | |
| 3 | | | Mon | Tue | Wed | Thur | Fri |
| 4 | Line 1 | 6 | | 7 | ✖ 11 | 4 | 4 |
| 5 | Line 2 | 3 | ✖ 10 | | 7 | 9 | 8 |
| 6 | Line 3 | 4 | | 7 | 6 | ✖ 19 | 5 |
| 7 | Line 4 | 5 | | 8 | 9 | 8 | 7 |
| 8 | Line 5 | 3 | | 5 | 4 | ✖ 11 | 6 |
| 9 | | | | | | | |

In Figure 9.13, the goal is to have a red X appear on any cell that contains a value of 10 or above. You can use the following steps to create an analysis similar to this:

1. Select the range of numeric data.

2. Choose Conditional Formatting, Icon Sets, 3 Symbols (Uncircled).

3. Choose Conditional Formatting, Highlight Cell Rules, Less Than. The Less Than dialog appears.

4. In the Less Than dialog, enter the first number that should have the icon (10 in this example). Everything less than this number will have alternate formatting.

5. The With drop-down initially shows Light Red Fill with Dark Red Text. Change this to Custom Format. Excel displays the Format Cells dialog, expecting you to choose a font color, border, fill, or number format.

6. You want cells meeting this condition to stay as white cells, so simply click OK to close the Format Cells dialog.

7. Click OK to close the Less Than dialog. It may appear that steps 3 through 6 had no impact. Don't be concerned that nothing appears to be working yet!

8. Choose Conditional Formatting, Manage Rules. The Conditional Formatting Rules Manager dialog appears, showing two rules. The rule that you added most recently is on top, ready to be evaluated first.

9. The rightmost column contains a check box called Stop if True. Check this box for the Cell Value < 10 rule. Checking this box prevents the Icon Set rule from being run when the value is under 10.

9

10. While still in the Conditional Formatting Rules Manager dialog, click the Icon Set rule to select it and then click Edit Rule. The Edit Formatting Rule dialog appears.

11. In the Edit Formatting Rule dialog, click the Reverse Icon Order check box at the bottom of the dialog.

12. The default values for the icon set now have the dialog box showing "X when value is >= 67 percentile." Change the first Type drop-down from Percentile to Number.

13. In this example, every cell with a reject rate of 10 or above needs an icon, so change the first Value text box to a value of 10.

14. Although you really don't care about the other two icon ranges, Excel presents an error message that the icon ranges overlap. You therefore have to fix the settings for the second range. Change the second Type drop-down from Percentile to Number. Change the second Value drop-down to anything that won't interfere with the first icon.

15. Click OK to close the Edit Formatting Rule dialog. Click OK to close the Conditional Formatting Rules Manager dialog. You have now achieved the desired effect.

Although this seems like an intimidating set of instructions, the Conditional Formatting Rules Manager dialog and the Edit Formatting Rule dialog are intuitive to navigate, and you can complete this process quickly.

# USING THE TOP/BOTTOM RULES

The top/bottom rules are a mix of the old- and new-style conditional formatting. They are similar to the old conditional formatting because you must select one formatting scheme to apply to all the cells that meet the rule. However, they are new because rather than specifying a particular number limit, you can ask for any of these conditions:

- **Top 10 Items**—You can ask for the top 10, top 20, or any number of items.

- **Top 10 %**—If 20% of your records account for 80% of your revenue, you can highlight the top 20% or any other percentage.

- **Bottom 10 Items**—To highlight the lowest-performing records, you choose Bottom 10.

- **Bottom 10 %**—To highlight the records in the lowest 5%, you choose Bottom 10%.

- **Above Average**—You can highlight the records that are above the average. As with all the other rules, the average is recalculated as the numbers in the range change.

- **Below Average**—You can highlight the records that are below the average.

To set up any of these conditional formatting rules, you follow these steps:

1. From the Home ribbon, select Conditional Formatting, Top/Bottom Rules, and then choose one of the six rule types shown in Figure 9.14.

**Figure 9.14**
You can choose one of these six rule types.

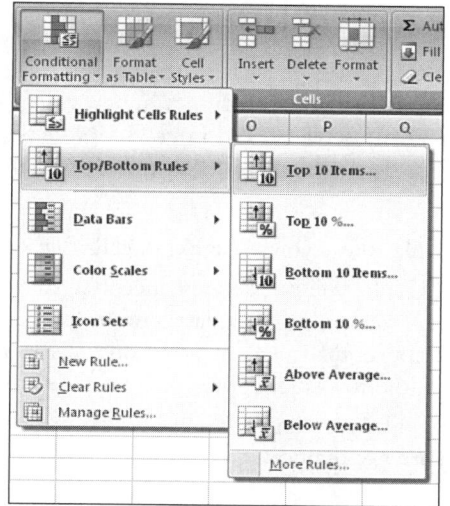

The dialog for above/below average does not require you to select a threshold value, but for the other four rule types, Excel asks you to enter the value for $N$. As you change the spin button, the Live Preview feature keeps updating the selection with the appropriate number of highlighted cells.

2. The drop-down portion of the dialog initially shows Light Red Fill with Dark Red Text. When you choose the drop-down, you have the six default styles shown in Figure 9.15 and the powerful Custom Format option. If one of the six styles is suitable, choose it. Otherwise, proceed to step 3.

**Figure 9.15**
There are six canned format styles available for any rule. If you don't like these, you can choose Custom Format.

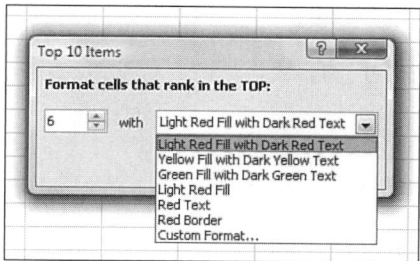

3. If you choose Custom Format, you are taken to a special version of the Format Cells dialog box. This version has Number, Font, Border, and Fill tabs. You can choose settings on one or more of these tabs. Click OK to close the Format Cells dialog.

4. Click OK to close the dialog box for your particular rule.

Excel adds the rule to the list of rules. By default, rules added most recently are applied first.

# USING THE HIGHLIGHT CELLS RULES

The traditional conditional formatting rules appear in the Highlight Cells Rules menu item of the Conditional Formatting drop-down, along with several new rules. The traditional rules include Greater Than, Less Than, Between, and Equal To. Note that slightly obscure rules such as Greater Than or Equal To are hidden behind the More Rules option. The following are the new rules:

- **Text That Contains**—This rule allows you to highlight cells that contain certain text.

- **A Date Occurring**—With this rule, you can define conceptual rules such as yesterday, today, tomorrow, last week, this week, next week, last month, this month, next month, or in the last seven days. The conceptual rules are based on the system clock, so if you open the workbook next week, the rows highlighted change, based on the system clock.

- **Duplicate Values**—With this rule, you can highlight both records of a duplicate or highlight all the records that are not duplicated.

The options for Highlight Cell Rules are shown in Figure 9.16.

**Figure 9.16**
Many powerful and easy conditions are available in the Highlight Cell Rules menu.

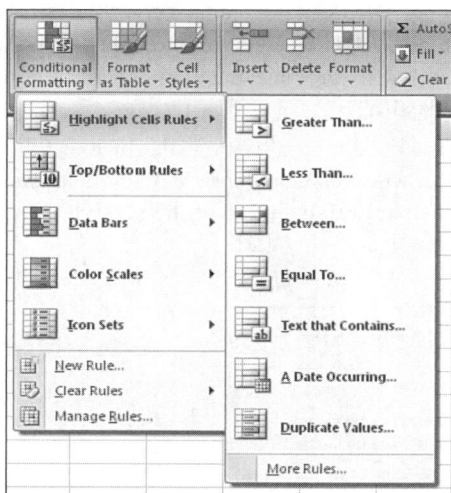

## HIGHLIGHTING CELLS BY USING GREATER THAN AND SIMILAR RULES

You might think that Greater Than and the similar rules for Less Than, Equal To, or Not Equal To are some of the less powerful conditional formatting rules. In fact, these are the first rules described in this chapter that you can use to base the conditional format threshold on a particular cell or cells. This allows you to build some fairly complex rules without having to resort to the formula option of conditional formatting.

To set up a rule to highlight values greater than a threshold, you follow these steps:

1. Select a range of data. Unlike with the other rules, you might choose to include totals in this selection.

2. Select Home, Styles, Conditional Formatting, Highlight Cell Rules, Greater Than to display the Greater Than dialog box.

3. Enter a threshold value in the Greater Than dialog.

4. Choose one of the six formats from the With drop-down. Or, choose Custom Format from the With drop-down to have complete control over the number format, font, borders, and fill.

5. Click OK to apply the format.

By way of example, let's look at several options for filling in the threshold value in the Greater Than dialog box. Figure 9.17 shows the conditional formatting rule for all cells greater than 700. This is a simple threshold value.

**Figure 9.17**
You can format all cells greater than a certain value, such as 700.

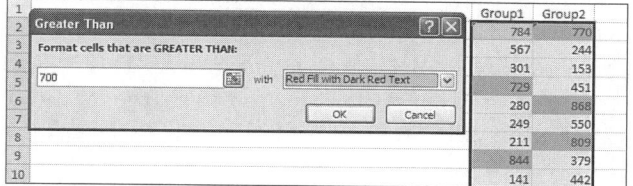

If you use the reference icon at the right side of the threshold box, you can select a particular cell. In Figure 9.18, Cell B2 was selected using the reference box. Note that Excel filled in the correct format of =$B$2.

**Figure 9.18**
You can format all cells greater than a certain cell. You use an equals sign and an absolute reference with both dollar signs.

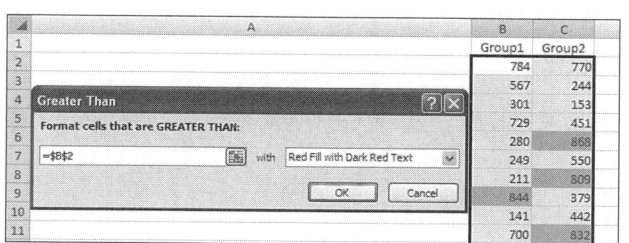

The fact that Excel used an equals sign is a good indication that you can fill in any formula in the Greater Than box. Furthermore, you can achieve some interesting effects by using cell references that are not absolute references.

The trick here is to pay attention to which cell is the active cell in the name box. To select the range B2:C22, you might click in C22 and drag up to B2. This would leave the active cell as C22. Or, you might click in B2 and drag down to C22. This would leave the active cell as B2. Conditional formatting formulas should always be built assuming that the top-left cell of the selection is the active cell.

You can use the following steps to create a conditional formatting rule to highlight any cell in Column C where the value is greater than 110% of the corresponding value in Column B:

1. Click in Cell C2 and drag down to the end of the data. Make sure that the name box indicates that C2 is the active cell.

2. Select Home, Styles, Conditional Formatting, Highlight Cell Rules, Greater Than. The Greater Than dialog appears.

3. In the Greater Than dialog box, click in the Refers To box and then click on B2. Excel enters the formula =$B$2.

4. Press the F4 key twice to change the reference to =$B2. This allows Excel to compare each cell to the value in B, but it allows the row to change for each cell. The key point here is that your active cell is in Row 2 of Column C, so the cell referred to must also be in Row 2.

5. The insertion point will be at the end of =$B2. Notice that in the lower-left corner of your screen, the indicator says Point. This is a very frustrating state. If you start to type and make a mistake, using any arrow key will insert new cell addresses instead of backspacing. Before you start typing the rest of the formula, press the F2 key until the status changes from Point to Edit.

6. Type the rest of the formula, *1.1, as shown in Figure 9.19.

7. Click OK to accept the formula.

Excel highlights all the cells in Column C that are 110% of Column B or greater.

**Figure 9.19**
Although the greater-than concept seems simplistic, you can build some fairly complex formulas in this quick format dialog.

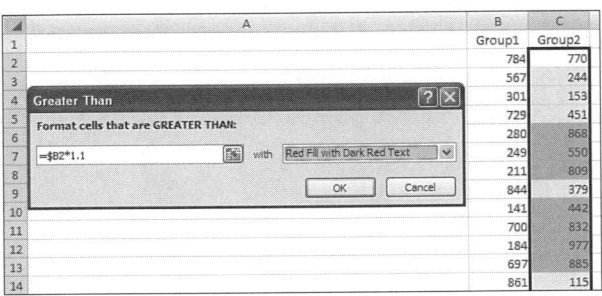

The greater-than concepts discussed here apply equally well to the Less Than, Equal to, and Between rules. If you need to access other rules, such as Greater Than or Equal To, you can follow these steps:

1. Set up the rule by using Greater Than.
2. From the Conditional Formatting icon, choose Manage Rules.
3. Select the Greater Than rule and click Edit Rule.
4. Use the drop-down shown in Figure 9.20 to select Greater Than or Equal To.

**Figure 9.20**
After using a quick format with Greater Than, you can go to the Manage Rules option to change from Greater Than to Greater Than or Equal To.

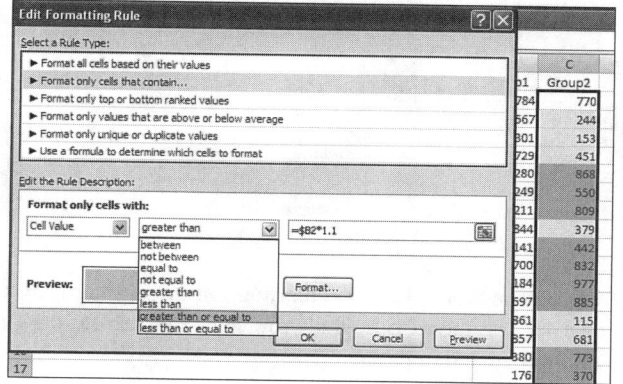

## COMPARING DATES BY USING CONDITIONAL FORMATTING

The date feature is new in Excel 2007. If you are familiar with the reporting engine in Quicken or QuickBooks, the list of available dates will seem similar. A nice feature is that Excel understands the dates conceptually. If you define a feature to highlight dates from last week, the rule automatically updates based on the system clock. If you open the workbook a month from now, new dates are formatted, based on the conditional formatting.

Some of the date selections are self-explanatory, such as Yesterday, Today, and Tomorrow. Other items need some explanation:

- A week is defined as the seven days from Sunday through Saturday. Choosing This Week highlights all days from Sunday through Saturday, including the current date.
- In the Last 7 Days includes today and the six days before today.
- This Month corresponds to all days in this calendar month. Last Month is all days in the previous calendar month. For example, if today is May 1 or May 31, the period Last Month applies to April 1 through April 30.

Figure 9.21 shows the various formatting options, with a system date of May 14, 2007.

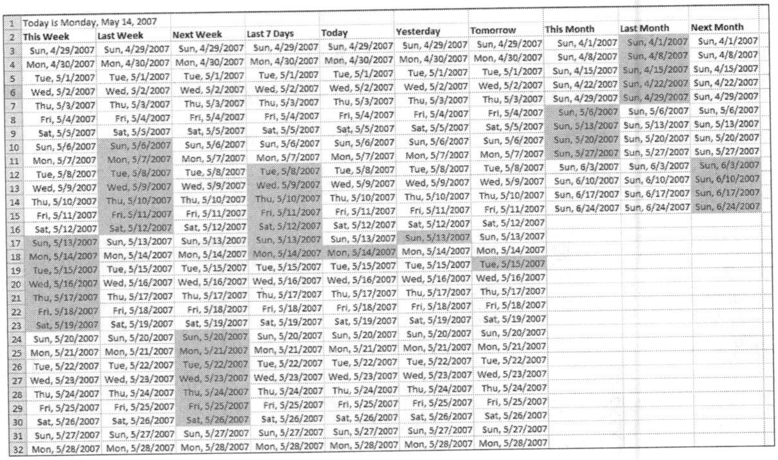

**Figure 9.21**
In the Last 7 days is the odd option among the date formatting options.

| | Today is Monday, May 14, 2007 | | | | | | | | | |
|---|---|---|---|---|---|---|---|---|---|---|
| | This Week | Last Week | Next Week | Last 7 Days | Today | Yesterday | Tomorrow | This Month | Last Month | Next Month |
| 3 | Sun, 4/29/2007 | Sun, 4/29/2007 | Sun, 4/29/2007 | Sun, 4/29/2007 | Sun, 4/29/2007 | Sun, 4/29/2007 | Sun, 4/29/2007 | Sun, 4/1/2007 | Sun, 4/1/2007 | Sun, 4/1/2007 |
| 4 | Mon, 4/30/2007 | Mon, 4/30/2007 | Mon, 4/30/2007 | Mon, 4/30/2007 | Mon, 4/30/2007 | Mon, 4/30/2007 | Mon, 4/30/2007 | Sun, 4/8/2007 | Sun, 4/8/2007 | Sun, 4/8/2007 |
| 5 | Tue, 5/1/2007 | Tue, 5/1/2007 | Tue, 5/1/2007 | Tue, 5/1/2007 | Tue, 5/1/2007 | Tue, 5/1/2007 | Tue, 5/1/2007 | Sun, 4/15/2007 | Sun, 4/15/2007 | Sun, 4/15/2007 |
| 6 | Wed, 5/2/2007 | Wed, 5/2/2007 | Wed, 5/2/2007 | Wed, 5/2/2007 | Wed, 5/2/2007 | Wed, 5/2/2007 | Wed, 5/2/2007 | Sun, 4/22/2007 | Sun, 4/22/2007 | Sun, 4/22/2007 |
| 7 | Thu, 5/3/2007 | Thu, 5/3/2007 | Thu, 5/3/2007 | Thu, 5/3/2007 | Thu, 5/3/2007 | Thu, 5/3/2007 | Thu, 5/3/2007 | Sun, 4/29/2007 | Sun, 4/29/2007 | Sun, 4/29/2007 |
| 8 | Fri, 5/4/2007 | Fri, 5/4/2007 | Fri, 5/4/2007 | Fri, 5/4/2007 | Fri, 5/4/2007 | Fri, 5/4/2007 | Fri, 5/4/2007 | Sun, 5/6/2007 | Sun, 5/6/2007 | Sun, 5/6/2007 |
| 9 | Sat, 5/5/2007 | Sat, 5/5/2007 | Sat, 5/5/2007 | Sat, 5/5/2007 | Sat, 5/5/2007 | Sat, 5/5/2007 | Sat, 5/5/2007 | Sun, 5/13/2007 | Sun, 5/13/2007 | Sun, 5/13/2007 |
| 10 | Sun, 5/6/2007 | Sun, 5/6/2007 | Sun, 5/6/2007 | Sun, 5/6/2007 | Sun, 5/6/2007 | Sun, 5/6/2007 | Sun, 5/6/2007 | Sun, 5/20/2007 | Sun, 5/20/2007 | Sun, 5/20/2007 |
| 11 | Mon, 5/7/2007 | Mon, 5/7/2007 | Mon, 5/7/2007 | Mon, 5/7/2007 | Mon, 5/7/2007 | Mon, 5/7/2007 | Mon, 5/7/2007 | Sun, 5/27/2007 | Sun, 5/27/2007 | Sun, 5/27/2007 |
| 12 | Tue, 5/8/2007 | Tue, 5/8/2007 | Tue, 5/8/2007 | Tue, 5/8/2007 | Tue, 5/8/2007 | Tue, 5/8/2007 | Tue, 5/8/2007 | Sun, 6/3/2007 | Sun, 6/3/2007 | Sun, 6/3/2007 |
| 13 | Wed, 5/9/2007 | Wed, 5/9/2007 | Wed, 5/9/2007 | Wed, 5/9/2007 | Wed, 5/9/2007 | Wed, 5/9/2007 | Wed, 5/9/2007 | Sun, 6/10/2007 | Sun, 6/10/2007 | Sun, 6/10/2007 |
| 14 | Thu, 5/10/2007 | Thu, 5/10/2007 | Thu, 5/10/2007 | Thu, 5/10/2007 | Thu, 5/10/2007 | Thu, 5/10/2007 | Thu, 5/10/2007 | Sun, 6/17/2007 | Sun, 6/17/2007 | Sun, 6/17/2007 |
| 15 | Fri, 5/11/2007 | Fri, 5/11/2007 | Fri, 5/11/2007 | Fri, 5/11/2007 | Fri, 5/11/2007 | Fri, 5/11/2007 | Fri, 5/11/2007 | Sun, 6/24/2007 | Sun, 6/24/2007 | Sun, 6/24/2007 |
| 16 | Sat, 5/12/2007 | Sat, 5/12/2007 | Sat, 5/12/2007 | Sat, 5/12/2007 | Sat, 5/12/2007 | Sat, 5/12/2007 | Sat, 5/12/2007 | | | |
| 17 | Sun, 5/13/2007 | Sun, 5/13/2007 | Sun, 5/13/2007 | Sun, 5/13/2007 | Sun, 5/13/2007 | Sun, 5/13/2007 | Sun, 5/13/2007 | | | |
| 18 | Mon, 5/14/2007 | Mon, 5/14/2007 | Mon, 5/14/2007 | Mon, 5/14/2007 | Mon, 5/14/2007 | Mon, 5/14/2007 | Mon, 5/14/2007 | | | |
| 19 | Tue, 5/15/2007 | Tue, 5/15/2007 | Tue, 5/15/2007 | Tue, 5/15/2007 | Tue, 5/15/2007 | Tue, 5/15/2007 | Tue, 5/15/2007 | | | |
| 20 | Wed, 5/16/2007 | Wed, 5/16/2007 | Wed, 5/16/2007 | Wed, 5/16/2007 | Wed, 5/16/2007 | Wed, 5/16/2007 | Wed, 5/16/2007 | | | |
| 21 | Thu, 5/17/2007 | Thu, 5/17/2007 | Thu, 5/17/2007 | Thu, 5/17/2007 | Thu, 5/17/2007 | Thu, 5/17/2007 | Thu, 5/17/2007 | | | |
| 22 | Fri, 5/18/2007 | Fri, 5/18/2007 | Fri, 5/18/2007 | Fri, 5/18/2007 | Fri, 5/18/2007 | Fri, 5/18/2007 | Fri, 5/18/2007 | | | |
| 23 | Sat, 5/19/2007 | Sat, 5/19/2007 | Sat, 5/19/2007 | Sat, 5/19/2007 | Sat, 5/19/2007 | Sat, 5/19/2007 | Sat, 5/19/2007 | | | |
| 24 | Sun, 5/20/2007 | Sun, 5/20/2007 | Sun, 5/20/2007 | Sun, 5/20/2007 | Sun, 5/20/2007 | Sun, 5/20/2007 | Sun, 5/20/2007 | | | |
| 25 | Mon, 5/21/2007 | Mon, 5/21/2007 | Mon, 5/21/2007 | Mon, 5/21/2007 | Mon, 5/21/2007 | Mon, 5/21/2007 | Mon, 5/21/2007 | | | |
| 26 | Tue, 5/22/2007 | Tue, 5/22/2007 | Tue, 5/22/2007 | Tue, 5/22/2007 | Tue, 5/22/2007 | Tue, 5/22/2007 | Tue, 5/22/2007 | | | |
| 27 | Wed, 5/23/2007 | Wed, 5/23/2007 | Wed, 5/23/2007 | Wed, 5/23/2007 | Wed, 5/23/2007 | Wed, 5/23/2007 | Wed, 5/23/2007 | | | |
| 28 | Thu, 5/24/2007 | Thu, 5/24/2007 | Thu, 5/24/2007 | Thu, 5/24/2007 | Thu, 5/24/2007 | Thu, 5/24/2007 | Thu, 5/24/2007 | | | |
| 29 | Fri, 5/25/2007 | Fri, 5/25/2007 | Fri, 5/25/2007 | Fri, 5/25/2007 | Fri, 5/25/2007 | Fri, 5/25/2007 | Fri, 5/25/2007 | | | |
| 30 | Sat, 5/26/2007 | Sat, 5/26/2007 | Sat, 5/26/2007 | Sat, 5/26/2007 | Sat, 5/26/2007 | Sat, 5/26/2007 | Sat, 5/26/2007 | | | |
| 31 | Sun, 5/27/2007 | Sun, 5/27/2007 | Sun, 5/27/2007 | Sun, 5/27/2007 | Sun, 5/27/2007 | Sun, 5/27/2007 | Sun, 5/27/2007 | | | |
| 32 | Mon, 5/28/2007 | Mon, 5/28/2007 | Mon, 5/28/2007 | Mon, 5/28/2007 | Mon, 5/28/2007 | Mon, 5/28/2007 | Mon, 5/28/2007 | | | |

The date formatting option would be particularly good for highlighting the items in a to-do list that are due, overdue, or about to be due. You can follow these steps to set up a conditional format for maintenance due dates:

1. Select a range of cells that contain dates.
2. From the Home ribbon, choose Conditional Formatting, Highlight Cell Rules, A Date Occurring. Choose This Week from the drop-down and a yellow font on a yellow background.
3. From the Home ribbon, choose Conditional Formatting, Highlight Cell Rules, A Date Occurring. Choose Last 7 Days from the drop-down. Leave the format as a red font on a red background.
4. Choose Conditional Formatting, Manage Rules. Click New Rule.
5. In Select a Rule Type, choose Format Only Cells That Contain.
6. In the bottom drop-down, select Dates Occurring. In the right drop-down, choose Today.
7. Click the Format button. Choose a white font and a green background.
8. Click the OK button to return to the Conditional Formatting Rules Manager dialog. If you followed steps 1 through 7, the Today rule should be first, followed by the Last 7 Days rule, followed by the This Week rule. Click the Stop if True check mark for each of the three rules. Click OK to apply the rules.

This set of rules highlights items due today in green. Anything that is past due in the past 6 days is highlighted in red. Future items from this week are highlighted in yellow.

## IDENTIFYING DUPLICATE OR UNIQUE VALUES BY USING CONDITIONAL FORMATTING

Conditional formatting can mark either duplicate or unique values in a list of values. It seems that Microsoft missed an opportunity to include a different version of unique values than the one that it included. It would be very useful if they had included an option to mark only the first occurrence of each unique item.

In Column A of Figure 9.22, Excel has marked the duplicate values. Both Adam and Bill appear twice in the list, and Excel has marked both occurrences of the values. You might be tempted to sort by color to bring the red-fonted cells to the top, but you will still have to carefully go through to delete one of each pair.

**Figure 9.22**
Marking duplicates or unique values with conditional formatting requires additional work to decide which of the duplicates to keep in order to produce a unique list.

| | A | B | C | D |
|---|---|---|---|---|
| 1 | Duplicates | | Unique | |
| 2 | | | | |
| 3 | Adam | | Adam | |
| 4 | Bill | | Bill | |
| 5 | Charley | | Charley | |
| 6 | Adam | | Adam | |
| 7 | Bill | | Bill | |
| 8 | Dan | | Dan | |
| 9 | | | | |

In Column C of Figure 9.22, Excel has applied a conditional format to the unique values in the list. In Excel parlance, this means that Excel marks the items that appear only once in a list. If you would keep just the marked cells as a list of the unique names in the list, you would effectively miss any name that was duplicated.

In a perfect world, this feature would have the logic to include one of each name in the conditional format. You would end up with C3, C4, C5, and C8 highlighted. In the current implementation, you have to write a complex COUNTIF equation to mark the unique values.

## USING CONDITIONAL FORMATTING FOR TEXT CONTAINING A VALUE

The Text That Contains formatting rule is designed to search text cells for cells that contain a certain value.

Figure 9.23 contains a column of cells. Each cell in the column contains a complete address, with street, city, state, and zip. It would normally be fairly difficult to find all the records for a particular state. However, this is easy to do with conditional formatting. You simply follow these steps:

**Figure 9.23**
Without having to use a wildcard character, the new Text That Contains dialog allows you to mark cells based on a partial value.

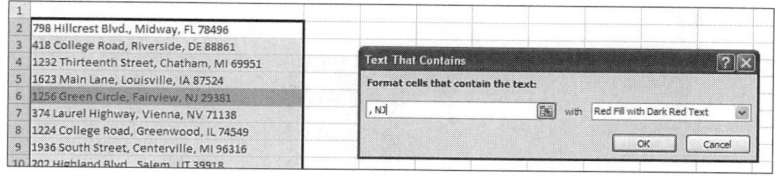

1. Select a range of cells that contain text.
2. From the Home ribbon, choose Conditional Formatting, Highlight Cell Rules, Text That Contains.
3. In the Refers To box, enter a comma, a space, and the state that you want to find. Note that this test is not case-sensitive (for example, searching for ", nj" is the same as searching for ", NJ").
4. Choose an appropriate color from the drop-down.
5. Click OK to apply the format.

As with the Find dialog box, you are allowed to use wildcard characters. You can use an asterisk (*) to indicate any number of characters, and you can use a question mark (?) to indicate a single character.

# TWEAKING RULES WITH ADVANCED FORMATTING

All the formats available from icons on the Conditional Formatting group are referred to as *quick formatting*. According to legend, the Excel team bought a number of Excel books, and if the author spent a page trying to explain a convoluted way to format something using formulas in conditional formatting, then that option became a quick formatting icon.

Every quick formatting item has an option at the bottom called More Rules. When you click this option and get to the New Formatting Rule dialog, you find that there are options available that didn't make it as quick formatting icons.

The next section of this chapter discusses using the formula option for conditional formatting. Almost anything is possible by using the formula option, but it is harder to use than the quick formatting icons. If Excel offers a built-in, advanced option, you should certainly use it instead of trying to build a formula to do the same thing.

The lists shown in Tables 9.1 and 9.2 are organized to show all the options for specific rule types. The six rule types are in the top of the New Formatting Rule dialog. Items listed in the right column are advanced options that are only available by clicking More Rules.

**TABLE 9.1—OPTIONS FOR FORMATTING CELLS BASED ON CONTENT**

| Option | Advanced Options Available Using More Rules |
|---|---|
| Cell value between x and y. | Cell value not between x and y. |
| Cell value equal to x. | Cell value not equal to x. |
| Cell value greater than x. | Cell value less than x. |
| Cell value greater than or equal to x. | Cell value less than or equal to x. |
| Specific text containing x. | Specific text not containing x. <br> Specific text beginning with x. <br> Specific text ending with x. |

| Option | Advanced Options Available Using More Rules |
|---|---|
| Dates occurring yesterday. | |
| Dates occurring today. | |
| Dates occurring tomorrow. | |
| Dates occurring in the last 7 days. | |
| Dates occurring last week. | |
| Dates occurring next week. | |
| Dates occurring last month. | |
| Dates occurring this month. | |
| Dates occurring next month. | |
| More Rules | Blanks. |
| | No Blanks. |
| | Errors. |
| | No Errors. |

### TABLE 9.2—OPTIONS FOR FORMATTING VALUES THAT ARE ABOVE OR BELOW AVERAGE

| Option | Advanced Options Available Using More Rules |
|---|---|
| Above the average for the selected range. | 1 standard deviation above the average for the selected range.<br>2 standard deviations above the average for the selected range.<br>3 standard deviations above the average for the selected range. |
| Below the average for the selected range. | 1 standard deviation below the average for the selected range.<br>2 standard deviations below the average for the selected range.<br>3 standard deviations below the average for the selected range. |

## USING A FORMULA FOR RULES

Excel has three dozen quick conditional formatting rules and twice as many advanced conditional formatting rules. What if you need to build a conditional format that is not covered in the quick or advanced rules? As long as you can build a logical formula to describe the condition, you can build your own conditional formatting rule based on a formula.

Some basic tips can help you successfully use formulas in conditional formatting rules. When you understand these rules, you can build just about any rule you can imagine.

One new feature in Excel 2007 is that a formula is allowed to refer to cells on another worksheet. This allows you to compare cells on one worksheet to a worksheet from a previous month or to use a VLOOKUP table on another worksheet.

### GETTING TO THE FORMULA BOX

To set up a conditional format based on a rule, you follow these steps:

1. Select a range of cells.

2. In the Style group of the Home ribbon, choose Conditional Formatting, Add New Rule.

3. In the New Formatting Rule dialog, choose the rule type "Use a formula to determine which cells to format." You now see the New Formatting Rule dialog box, which is shown in Figure 9.24.

The following section give you some tips for building a successful formula.

**Figure 9.24**
The New Formatting Rule dialog is the gateway to many powerful custom formatting rules.

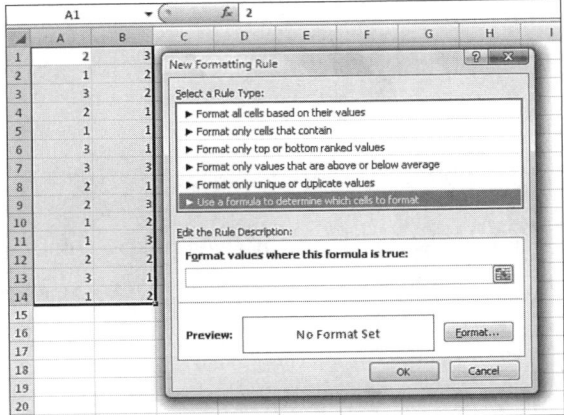

### WORKING WITH THE FORMULA BOX

Following are the key concepts involved in writing a successful formula:

- The formula must start with an equals sign.

- The formula must evaluate to a logical value of TRUE or FALSE. The numeric equivalents of 1 and 0 are also acceptable results.

- When you use the mouse to select a cell or cells on a worksheet, Excel inserts an absolute reference to the cell. This is rarely what you need for a successful conditional formatting rule. You can immediately press the F4 key three times to toggle away the dollar signs in the formula.

- You probably have many cells selected before starting the conditional formatting rule. You need to look at the left of the formula bar to see which cell in the selection is the active cell. If you write a relative formula, you should write the formula that would appear in the active cell. Excel applies the formula appropriately to all cells. This is a key point. If you look in Figure 9.24, you'll see that the name box indicates that the active cell is A1. Any conditional formatting rule needs to be written as if you were writing for cell A1.

- If the dialog box is in the way of cells you need to select, you can drag the dialog box out of the way by dragging the blue title bar. If you absolutely need to get the dialog box out of the way, you can use the Collapse Dialog button at the right side of the formula box. This collapses the dialog to a tiny area. To return it to full size, you click the Expand Dialog button at the right side of the collapsed dialog.

- The formula box is one of the evil set of controls that have three possible statuses: Enter, Point, and Edit. Look in the lower-left corner of the Excel screen. The status initially says that you are in Enter mode. This means that Excel is expecting you to type characters such as the equals sign. If, instead, you use the mouse to select a cell, Excel changes to Point mode. In Point mode, the selected cell's address is added to the formula box. The annoying thing is that from Enter mode, if you use any of the navigation keys (that is, Page Down, Page Up, Left Arrow, Right Arrow, Down Arrow, Up Arrow), Excel also changes to Point mode. This can be very frustrating if you are using the Left Arrow key to edit a portion of the formula.

- The solution to working with the formula bar is to use the F2 key. You can press the F2 key to toggle between Enter, Edit, and Point mode. Before using the Left Arrow key or Right Arrow key to move within a formula, you must press F2 until the status bar indicates that you are in Edit mode.

The following sections describe several useful conditional formatting rules. This list only scratches the surface of the possible rules you can build. It is designed to generate ideas of what you can accomplish by using conditional formatting.

## FINDING CELLS CONTAINING DATA FROM YESTERDAY, TODAY, OR TOMORROW

The quick formatting feature offers to highlight yesterday or today or tomorrow, but what if you need to find any cells that are either yesterday, today, or tomorrow?

There are a couple ways to approach this formula. Each way uses the TODAY() function, which returns the date from the system clock.

The first formula is to write several tests to see if the selected cell is equal to various values, as follows:

- `=TODAY()=B4` highlights values from today.
- `=B4=(TODAY()-1)` highlights values from yesterday.
- `=B4=(TODAY()+1)` highlights values from tomorrow.

To write a formula that highlights cells that have any of these three, you have to combine the three things in the OR() function, like this:

`=OR(TODAY()=B4, B4=(TODAY()-1), B4=(TODAY()+1))`

Instead of using this formula, you could instead write a formula that subtracts the cell from the TODAY() function. In the preceding three scenarios, the result of TODAY()-B4 would be either -1, 0, or 1.

To simplify the formula, you could use the ABS() absolute value function to convert the result to a positive number and then see if the result is less than two.

In Figure 9.25, the formula =ABS(TODAY()-B4)<2 highlights the dates that are within one day of today. Note in this figure that the active cell is B4; hence, the use of B4 in the formula. You can generalize this formula by changing the 2. If you used 8 instead of 2, you would highlight everything within plus or minus one week of today.

**Figure 9.25**
This formula highlights everything within one day of today.

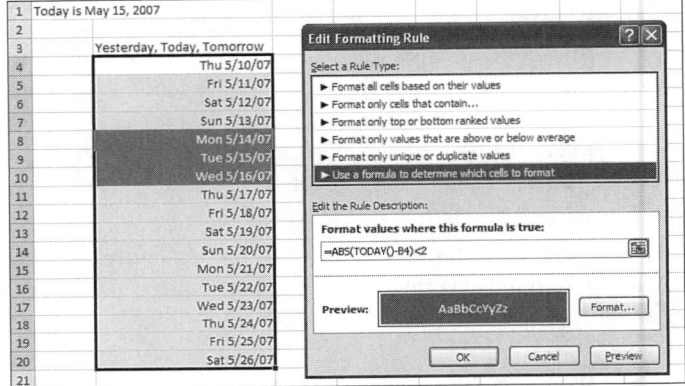

## FINDING CELLS CONTAINING DATA FROM THE NEXT SEVEN DAYS

In the A Date Occurring dialog, there is an option to display the last seven days. There is no corresponding feature to display the next seven days.

In Figure 9.26, the active cell is D4. The following would be the formula to find everything in the next seven days:

=D4-TODAY()<=7

**Figure 9.26**
This formula is a bit complex, but it gives you the equivalent of Next 7 Days. Clearly, the quick format option Last 7 Days is far easier, but because Microsoft did not give you a Next 7 Days option, you can create this on your own.

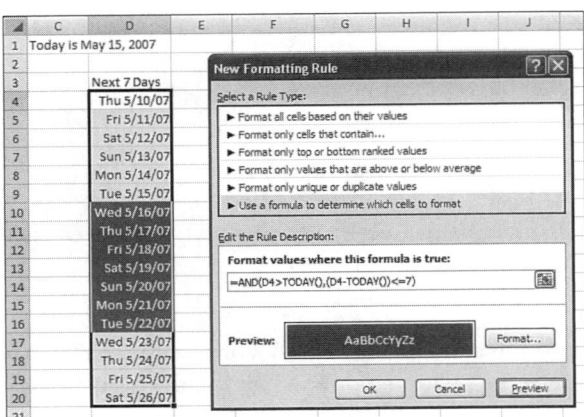

However, this would highlight everything in the past as well as items in the next week. To limit the rule to only items that are after today, you would use the following:

```
=D4>TODAY()
```

To combine these two rules into a single formula, you would use this:

```
=AND(D4>TODAY(),(D4-TODAY())<=7)
```

To generalize this formula, you could change the 7 to any number of days.

## FINDING CELLS CONTAINING DATA FROM THE PAST 30 DAYS

The Excel quick formatting option offers to highlight this month or last month. However, highlighting this month or last month can mean a number of vastly different things. Highlighting this month on the second of the month shows a lot of the future and only 1 day of the past. The same rule on the 29th of the month highlights a lot of the past and only a few days of the future. It would be more predictable to write a rule that shows the past 30 days.

You create this rule similarly to the way you created the Next Seven Days rule in the preceding section. You first compare the date in the cell by using TODAY() to make sure the date in the cell is less than today. Because the active cell in Figure 9.27 is F4, you use the following formula:

```
=F4<TODAY()
```

**Figure 9.27**
For completeness, this conditional formatting formula can show you the last *n* days. If *n* were 7, you would use the quick formatting option. For all other values of *n*, you use this formula.

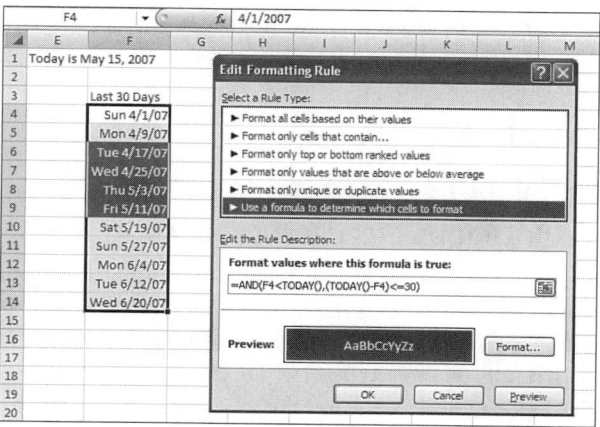

You then can subtract F4 from TODAY() to see if it is less than or equal to 30. This portion of the formula is as follows:

```
=(TODAY()-F4)<=30
```

To combine these into a single formula, you use the AND() function:

```
=AND(F4<TODAY(),(TODAY()-F4)<=30)
```

To generalize this formula for other periods, such as the past 15 days or the past 45 days, you change the 30 to a different number.

## HIGHLIGHTING DATA FROM SPECIFIC DAYS OF THE WEEK

The WEEKDAY() function converts a date to a number from 1 through 7. When used without any additional arguments, the value of WEEKDAY(*date*) for a Sunday is 0 and Saturday is 7.

In Figure 9.28, the active cell is H4. If you needed to highlight all the Wednesdays, you could check to see if WEEKDAY(H4)=4. To find all the Fridays, you would check to see if WEEKDAY(H4)=6. To find either date, you would use =OR(WEEKDAY(H4)=4,WEEKDAY(H4)=6).

**Figure 9.28**
Highlighting a particular day of the week is easy with WEEKDAY(). This formula is a bit complex to highlight dates that are either Wednesday or Friday.

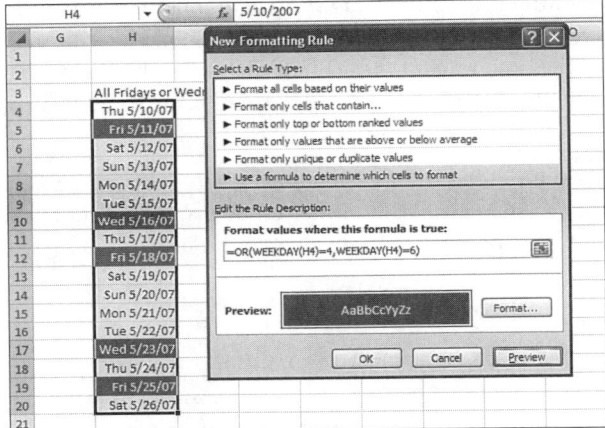

To generalize this formula, you could substitute any number from 1 through 7 to highlight Sundays, Mondays, and so on.

## HIGHLIGHTING THE FIRST UNIQUE OCCURRENCE OF AN ITEM

Excel offers two quick conditions for highlighting either duplicates or unique items. However, neither of them do what you really need. Ideally, you would want a rule that highlights the first unique item in a list. Then, all the highlighted items would make up the unique items in the list. Or, you might want a rule that highlights the second, third, and fourth instance of a duplicated item but not the first item.

You can use the COUNTIF function coupled with a very strange range argument to solve this problem: =COUNTIF(A2:A10,A2) counts how many times A2 occurs in the range A2:A10. You want Excel to count the occurrence of each cell in all the cells above and including the current cell. In Cell A10, this formula would be =COUNTIF(A$2:A10,A10). If the value is 1, then you know this is the first occurrence of the value in A10. If the value is greater than 1, then this value is a duplicate of a value already in the list.

It is easier to picture the formula for the 10th row of the range than for the 1st row of the range. However, the formula remains relatively the same.

In Figure 9.29, the active cell is A2. To highlight the first unique value and not highlight the duplicates, the formula in the conditional formatting formula needs to be `=COUNTIF(A$2:A2,A2)=1`. The really important element of this formula is the one single dollar sign before one portion of A2 in the first argument of the formula.

**Figure 9.29**
Unlike the quick formatting for unique values, this rule creates a true list in which every unique value is highlighted once. The unhighlighted cells are duplicates.

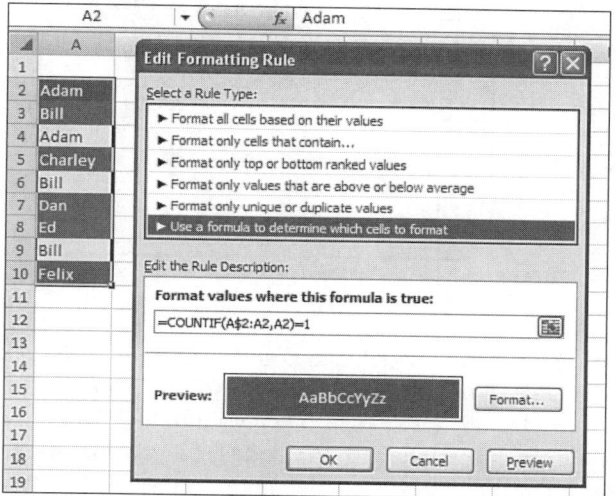

## HIGHLIGHTING TRUE DUPLICATES

The Excel quick conditional formatting rule for duplicates highlights all cells that are duplicated. This is great if you need to manually inspect each pair of duplicates and decide which record to keep. However, if you just want to blindly keep the first occurrence from each duplicate, you need a way to highlight the second and subsequent duplicates in the range.

This example is nearly identical to the previous example: You can edit that formula to check whether COUNTIF is greater than 1 instead of equal to 1.

In Figure 9.30, the active cell is A2. The conditional formatting formula needs to be `=COUNTIF(A$2:A2,A2)>1`.

## HIGHLIGHTING A SPECIFIC ROW

If you use the new table feature in Excel 2007, highlighting an entire row is simple: The Edit Rule dialog offers an option to highlight the entire row.

However, if you do not want to use the table feature in Excel, you can still highlight the entire row, based on the value in one column of the row.

**Figure 9.30**
You can delete all the highlighted cells and still have a unique list of values.

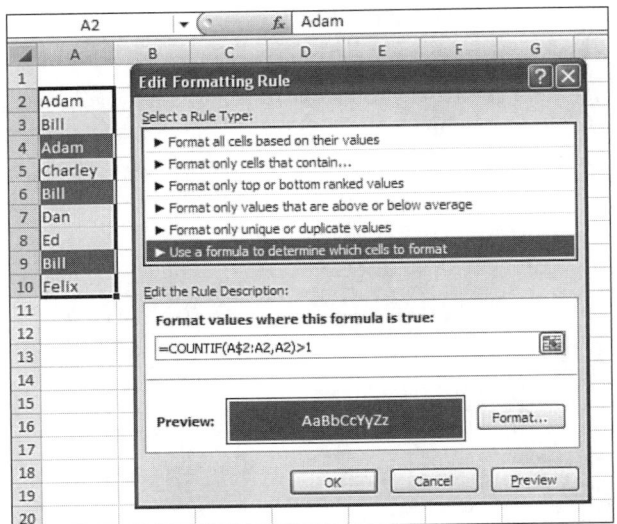

In Figure 9.31, cell A2 is the active cell. You need to select the entire range of A2:G14. Your goal is to write a rule for all of those cells that will look at Column D for the same row as the cell. In this case and in any case in which you want to highlight the entire row based on one column, you use the mixed reference with a dollar sign before the column letter. You want to see if =$D2 is equal to the largest value in the range.

**Figure 9.31**
The combination of a mixed reference and the absolute reference allows you to highlight an entire row.

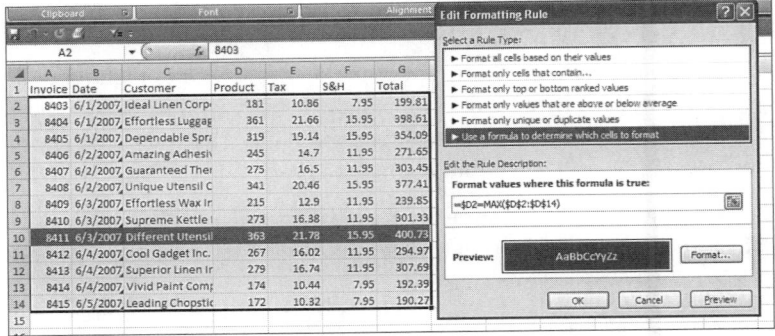

To find the largest value in Column D, you use an absolute reference to D2:D14—that is, =MAX($D$2:$D$14). The conditional formatting formula for this specific case is =$D2=MAX($D$2:$D$14).

To change this rule to highlight the smallest value in Column D, you change MAX to MIN.

To base the test on another column, you simply change D to the other column in three places in the formula.

Clearly, using the Excel 2007 table feature and the Format Entire Row check box is easier than using the formula. The formula is shown here for cases in which you are prevented from using or don't want to use the table feature.

## HIGHLIGHTING EVERY OTHER ROW WITHOUT USING A TABLE

You might find yourself using the Format as Table feature only to add alternating bands of color to a table. If you don't need the other table features, using a conditional format can achieve the same effect.

Do you remember when you were first learning to do division? You would express the quotient as an integer and then a remainder. For example, 9 divided by 2 is 4 with a remainder of 1, sometimes written as 4R1.

The trick to formatting every other row is to check the remainder of the row number after dividing by 2. Excel has functions that make this easy. First, =ROW(A2) returns the row number of the given cell. Next, =MOD(ROW(A2),2) divides the row number by 2 and tells you the remainder. The task is then simply to highlight the rows where the remainder is equal to 1.

In Figure 9.32, the active cell is A2. The formula to achieve the banding effect is =MOD(ROW(A2),2)=0.

To generalize this formula for your particular dataset, you could change A2 to be the active cell's address.

**Figure 9.32**
It is possible to create a row banding effect without using the Excel 2007 table formatting.

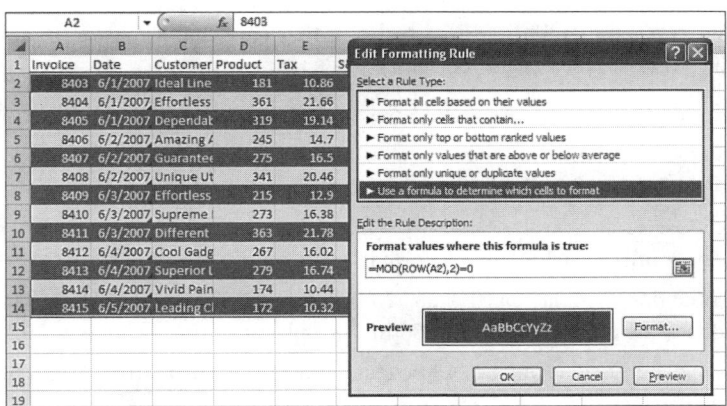

9

The Excel 2007 table formatting allows you to create alternate formatting where every other two rows are formatted. To duplicate this with conditional formatting, you have to divide the row number by 4 and examine the remainder. There are four possible remainders; 0, 1, 2, and 3. You can either look for results greater than 1 or less than 2 to be formatted. To do this, you change the preceding formula to =MOD(ROW(A2),4)<2, as shown in Figure 9.33.

**Figure 9.33**
By changing the divisor in the MOD function, you can create different banding effects.

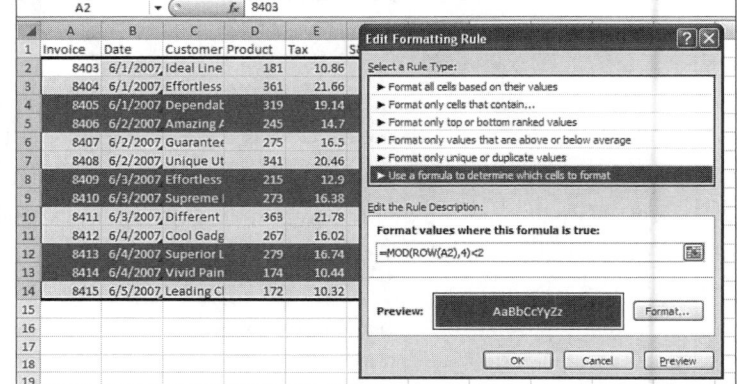

## COMPARING ONE WORKSHEET TO ANOTHER

A new feature in Excel 2007 is the ability to build a conditional formatting formula that references cells on another worksheet in the same workbook.

In Figure 9.34, the workbook has worksheets, JAN and FEB. The structure of the worksheets is identical: Sales data for each state and product starts in Cell B6.

Say that you want to highlight any sales in February that are lower than the corresponding sales in January. Here's what you do:

1. Highlight the entire range of your sales data on the FEB worksheet.

2. Note in the name box which cell is the active cell. You will be writing the conditional formula for this cell. In Figure 9.34, the active cell is B6.

3. Choose Home, Styles, Conditional Formatting, Add New Rule, Use a Formula to Determine Which Cells to Format.

4. Enter the formula =JAN!B6>B6. To generalize for your workbook, you can substitute the address of the active cell for B6 in both places in the formula.

5. Click the Format button. Choose an appropriate formatting pattern.

6. Click OK until you've closed all the dialogs.

The result, as shown in Figure 9.34, is to highlight any products for which the sales are trending down.

**Figure 9.34**
This formula finds whether the value in the current worksheet is smaller than the value in last month's worksheet.

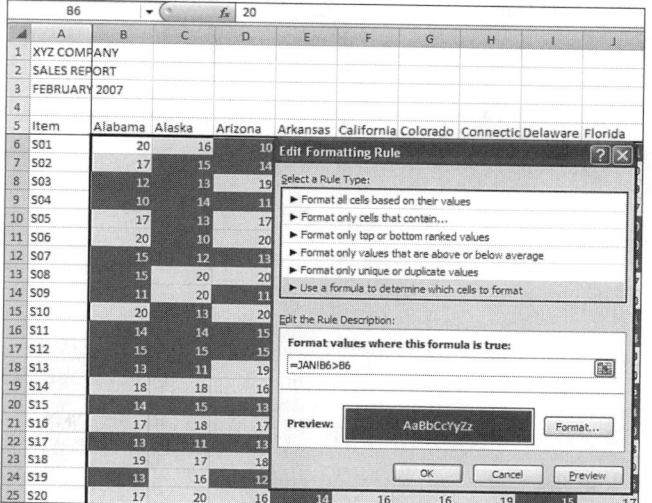

9

## COMBINING RULES

A major improvement in conditional formatting in Excel 2007 is the ability to have multiple conditions evaluate to TRUE. In prior versions of Excel, when a condition was met, Excel quit evaluating additional conditions. For each rule in Excel 2007, you can decide whether Excel should stop evaluating additional rules or whether Excel can continue evaluating rules.

For example, one rule might set the font color to blue. Another rule might set the font style to bold. Cells meeting both rules can be formatted in blue bold. Cells meeting one rule can be either blue or bold. Cells meeting neither rule will be in normal font style.

If two rules attempt to create conflicting formatting, Excel uses the first rule in the list. For example, if Rule 1 turns the font red and Rule 7 turns the font blue, the font is red.

There are 10 types of formatting that can be changed in each cell. Naturally, each type conflicts with others of the same type. Only the first rule that evaluates to TRUE can change the fill color.

Very few formatting styles conflict with each other. Only the cell fill and the color scale are mutually exclusive. Otherwise, you can have up to nine rules evaluate to true for any given cell. Table 9.3 illustrates the interplay between the 10 formatting styles.

### TABLE 9.3 CELL FORMATTING STYLES

| Style | Effect |
| --- | --- |
| Font color | Changes the font color for cells meeting a condition. |
| Font style | Applies normal, bold, italic, or bold italic to cells meeting a condition. |
| Underline | Adds or removes single or double underlining for cells meeting a condition. |

*continues*

| TABLE 9.3 | CONTINUED |
| --- | --- |
| **Style** | **Effect** |
| Strikethrough | Applies strikethrough for cells meeting a condition. |
| Number format | Changes the number format for cells meeting a condition. This is new in Excel 2007. Keep in mind that the custom number format ; ; ; prevents any characters from being displayed in the cell. |
| Border | Alters the borders for cells meeting a condition. You might think that you could combine two rules that both affect the border. For example, you might want to make the top border blue for cells that meet Rule 1 and the right border red for cells that meet Rule 2. Even though this conceptually makes sense, Excel allows only the first true rule to change the borders. |
| Cell fill | Changes the cell background for cells meeting a condition. Amazingly, this works fine in combination with data bars. (The cell fill appears to the right of the data bar.) It also works fine with icon sets, and it works fine with all the options above. However, cell fill and color scales cannot coexist. Only the first true rule appears in the cell. |
| Color scale | Changes the cell background for all cells in the range, with the color being determined by the value of one cell in relation to the other cells in the range. This rule can coexist with everything but itself and the cell fill formatting. |
| Data bar | Adds an in-cell bar chart in each cell. This rule can coexist with any other type of rule. |
| Icon set | Adds an icon in the left side of the cell. This rule can coexist with any other type of rule. |

# CLEARING CONDITIONAL FORMATS

There are a number of ways to clear conditional formats. A few quick options are available from the ribbon:

- You can highlight the entire range with conditional formatting and then use Home, Styles, Conditional Formatting, Clear, Selected Cells. This removes all conditions from the current selection.

- To clear all the conditional formats from the current worksheet, you can use Home, Styles, Conditional Formatting, Clear, Entire Sheet. This is handy if you have only one set of rules set up on the sheet. You can delete all the rules without having to select the entire range.

- If you have rules assigned to a pivot table or a table, you can select one cell in the pivot table or table. This enables new options for Home, Styles, , Conditional Formatting, Clear, This Table or Home, Styles, Conditional Formatting, Clear, This PivotTable.

NOTE

Deleting columns or deleting rows deletes the rules associated with those columns or rows. Using the Delete key on the keyboard or selecting Home, Editing, Clear, All or Home, Editing, Clear, Formats removes the rules.

If you have multiple rules assigned to a range and you need to delete just a portion of those rules, you can use Home, Styles, Conditional Formatting, Manage Rules. In the Conditional Formatting Rules Manager dialog, you should use the top drop-down to display rules in the current selection, this worksheet, or any other worksheet. You can then highlight a specific rule and click the Delete Rule button.

# EXTENDING THE REACH OF CONDITIONAL FORMATS

In every example in this chapter, you have been advised to highlight the entire range before setting up the conditional format. It is also possible to assign a conditional format to one cell and then extend the rule to other cells. There are two ways to copy a conditional format:

- You can select a cell with the appropriate rule and then Ctrl+C to copy it. Then you select the new range and select Home, Clipboard, Paste, Paste Special, Formats, OK to copy the conditional formatting from the one cell to the entire range.

- You can select Home, Styles, Conditional Formatting, Manage Rules. Then you select a rule. In the Applies To column you see the list of cells that have this rule. You can type a new range there or use the collapse button to make the dialog smaller so that you can highlight the new range.

When you are using conditional formats that compare one cell to the entire range, using the second method is safer to ensure that Excel understands your intention.

# SPECIAL CONSIDERATIONS FOR TABLES

If you use conditional formatting on a range that has been converted to an Excel 2007 table, the dialog box includes the check box Apply to Entire Row. This setting is great for highlighting an entire row based on the conditions for one row. In Excel 2003, this formatting required you to use the more difficult Formula version of conditional formatting. Now, in Excel 2007, you can easily apply it to any quick conditional formatting, provided that you set up the range as a table first.

For example, you can format the entire record for the records that have the three largest values in the sales column. To do so, you follow these steps:

1. Select the entire range to be formatted as a table.

2. From the Home ribbon, select Style, Format as a Table and then choose one of the light styles.

3. On the Table Design ribbon, uncheck Banded Rows.

4. Change your selection to include only the numbers in the product sales column. In Figure 9.35, this would be C2:C14.

5. On the Home ribbon, select Style, Conditional Formatting, T. The Top N dialog appears.

6. In the Top N dialog, click the Format Entire Row check box.

7. Click OK to apply the formatting.

The keys to making this work are that the entire range in A:F must be formatted as a table. Then, you need to apply the conditional formatting only to the one column that matters—in this case, the product sales column. After you displayed the Top N dialog box, Excel adds a Format Entire Row check box.

**Figure 9.35**
Excel adds Format Entire Row if your entire conditional formatting area is inside an Excel 2007 table.

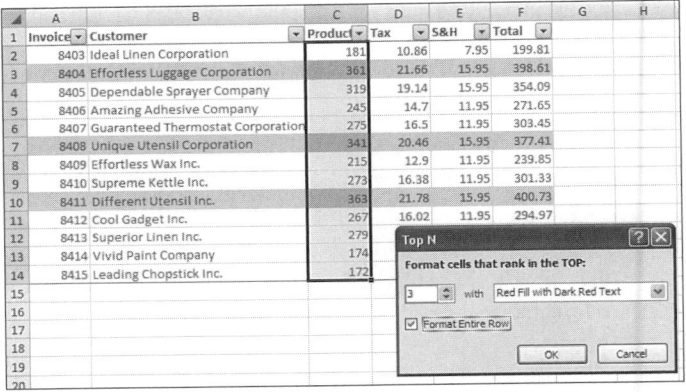

For more information on defining a range as a table, see Chapter 8, "Fabulous Table Intelligence."

## SPECIAL CONSIDERATIONS FOR PIVOT TABLES

The next three chapters discuss pivot tables in detail. This section talks about the special conditional formatting options that are available for pivot tables.

A typical pivot table contains two or more levels of summary data. In the pivot table in Figure 9.36, for example, Cells G4:I22 contain sales data. However, data in Column I contains the sum of sales for two different products. If you tried to create a data bar for this entire range, the values in Column I would make the data bars in the G:H range look too small. Similarly, the totals in Rows 4, 10, 16, and 22 would cause the data bars in the detail rows to appear too small.

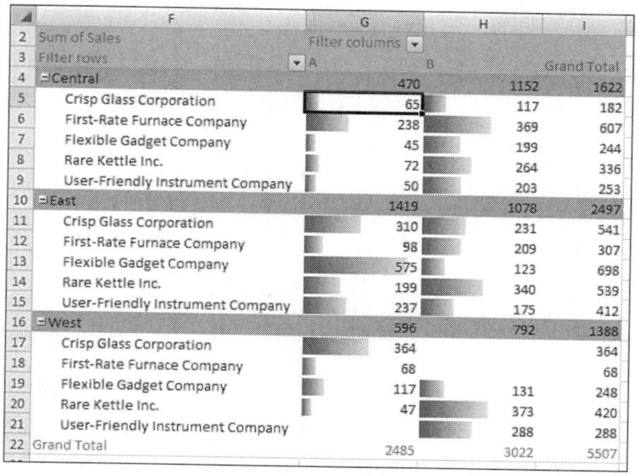

**Figure 9.36**
The trick to a successful conditional format in a pivot table is to apply the format only to items at the same detail level.

To set up a data bar for the detail items in a pivot table, you follow these steps:

1. Select a detail cell in the pivot table. In Figure 9.36, any cell in G5:H9, G11:H15, or C17:H21 would qualify as a detail cell. All these cells include sales figures, and none of them contain total rows or total columns.

2. From the Home ribbon, choose Conditional Formatting, New Rule. The New Formatting Rule dialog appears.

3. Because your selection is inside a pivot table, you have new options at the top of the New Formatting Rule dialog:

    - **Selected Cells**—You can apply the rule to just the one cell. This is not what you want in this case.

    - **All cells showing "Sum of Sales" values**—You can apply the rule to cells including the total column, grand total row, and all the subtotal rows. Remember that the size of the grand total causes all the detail items to have data bars that are too small.

    - **All cells showing "Sum of Sales" values for "Customer" and "Product"**—This is the option you use most of the time. The meaning of this option is dependent on careful selection of a detail cell in step 1. If you selected a subtotal row instead, this option would apply the data bars only to the subtotal rows.

    Your actual words in the second and third options vary, depending on the fields displayed in your pivot table. For successful pivot table formatting, choose the third option.

4. Define the data bar as usual in the New Formatting Rule dialog, as shown in Figure 9.37.

9

**Figure 9.37**
New options are available in the top section of the New Formatting Rule dialog for a pivot table.

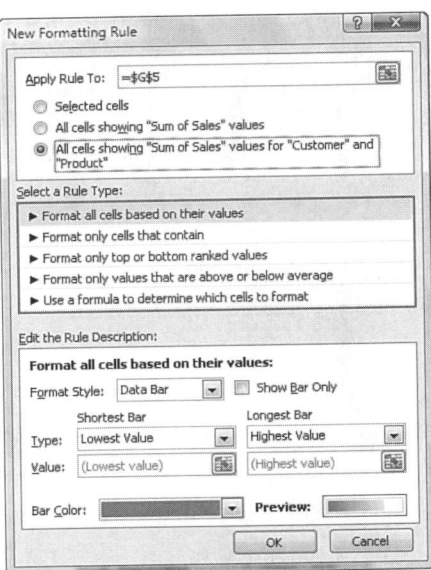

For more details about pivot tables, see Chapters 10, "Using Pivot Tables to Analyze Data," through 12, "Using Pivot Tables in Practice."

### Excel in Practice: Showing Data Bars in Two Colors

Any software package is a work in progress. You can bet that some new features in Excel 2007 will be even better in Excel 14. An obscure trick has been posted in David Gainer's blog. (Dave is the lead Excel project manager at Microsoft.)

It turns out that every conditional formatting rule has a formula value that determines whether the rule is shown. Microsoft exposed this rule in the user interface for some conditional formatting rules but not for the data bars. You can, however, access it in the VBA editor!

Say that your goal is to add a data bar to a range of cells. If the value is 90 or above, you would like the bars to be green. If the value is 89 or below, you would like the bars to be red. Here's how you accomplish this:

1. Select the range of cells to be formatted.
2. Use the conditional formatting quick options to add to the range a data bar that is red.
3. Select Conditional Formatting, Add New Rule to add a second rule that applies a green data bar. You see only the most recent rule, so all the data bars are green.
4. Note in the Name box which cell is the active cell. You will need this information in step 7.
5. Press Alt+F11 to switch to the VBA editor.
6. Press Ctrl+G to display the Immediate pane.
7. Type `Selection.FormatConditions(1).Formula = "=if(A2>89, TRUE, FALSE)"` and then press Enter. Cell A2 should be changed to the name of the active cell from step 4.

The result is that the green bars are visible only when the value is 90 or above. In all other cases, the bars appear red.

CHAPTER **10**

# USING PIVOT TABLES TO ANALYZE DATA

## In this chapter

For 12 years, pivot tables have been the most powerful feature in Excel. However, Microsoft estimates that fewer than 10% of people use pivot tables. To make this helpful feature less intimidating in Excel 2007, Microsoft rewrote the pivot table interface to make it vastly simpler to use.

# What Is Possible with Pivot Tables

NOTE

Although I loved the drag-and-drop functionality in pivot tables, it was a source of frustration for people new to pivot tables. With the drag-and-drop interface, it is possible to accidentally drop a field in the wrong place, essentially destroying the pivot table. When this happened to a pivot table rookie, the person was often frustrated enough to quit using pivot tables.

At the end of this chapter, I show pivot table veterans how to get back to the old interface.

Say that you have 400,000 records of transactional data. It is really easy for some people to figure out that this represents $x million. But to really learn some things about the data, you need to do some more analysis to spot trends in the data. A pivot table lets you analyze trends in data without having to worry about formulas. Your focus is more on finding trends than on worrying about writing formulas in Excel.

By using a pivot table, it is possible to create a number of views of your data, including the following:

- Breakdown of sales, by product
- Sales by month, this year versus last year
- Percentage of sales, by customer
- Customers who bought xyz in the east
- Sales by product, by month
- Top five customers, with products

Of course, these are just examples. You can use pivot tables to slice and dice your data in almost any imaginable way.

# Preparing Your Data for Pivot Table Analysis

Pivot tables are best created from transactional data—that is, raw data files directly from your company's IS department. You don't want any totals in the data. You don't want blank lines, blank columns, or formatting.

The data shown in Figure 10.1 is perfect for pivot tables. Every row in the table represents the sale of one product to one customer on one date. A pivot table could summarize one or more of the numeric fields in this data.

**Figure 10.1**
A transactional dataset is great for pivot tables.

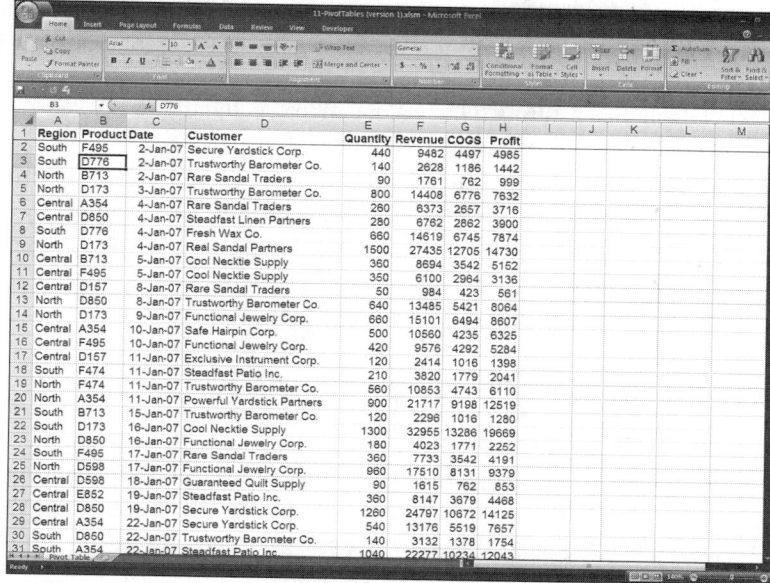

The data shown in Figure 10.2 is a typical Excel worksheet, but it has a number of problems that make it unsuitable for use in a pivot table:

**Figure 10.2**
This dataset is not suitable for pivot table analysis.

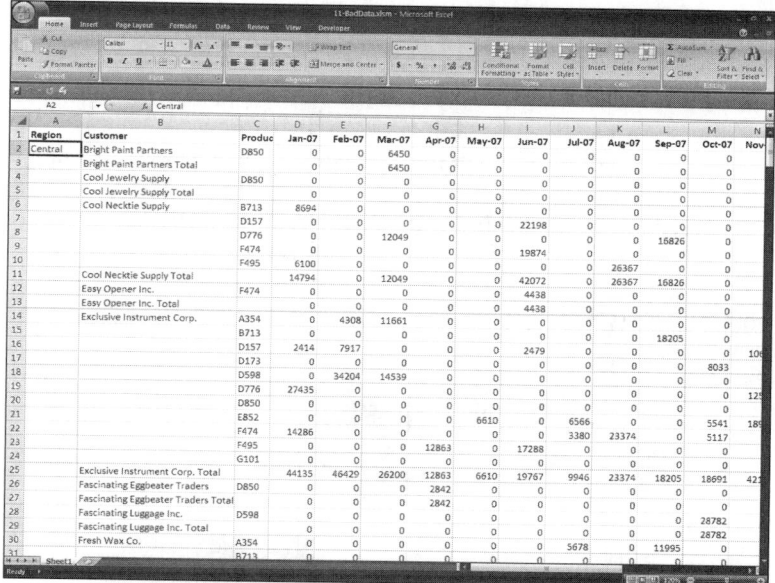

■ The date field is going across the columns. This makes it very difficult to create a pivot table. If your data is in this format, you really need to reorganize it with the month field going down the rows. If you have 12 months going across the worksheet, you need to copy Columns A through C plus one month column to a new worksheet—possibly increasing your record count by a factor of 12.

■ Totals are already built in to the data. Row 3 and Row 11 contain totals by customers. The data for use in a pivot table should contain no extra subtotal rows.

■ There are many blank cells in the dataset. Cell A2 contains the word *Central*, and then the next 137 cells in Column A are blank. While a human can understand that all these cells belong to the central region, a computer cannot.

If you have a dataset like the one shown in Figure 10.2, go back to the source of the data. If you are in a corporate environment, you can explore with your IT department where this summary came from. If the summary came from Quickbooks or another software package, try running a trial balance report that is at the detail level. Someone must have started with transactional data in order to create this summary. If it will take six months for IT to get to your project, you might want to follow the steps outlined in the following section to make the data suitable for use in a pivot table.

## MAKING DATA SUITABLE FOR PIVOT TABLES

As noted in the preceding section, there are problems with the dataset shown in Figure 10.2. Many common datasets from software packages like Peachtree or Quicken or even from Oracle or SAP will have similar problems to this dataset. By using your Excel skills, you can convert the data into a suitable format. It isn't easy. It isn't something you should do everyday. But it is possible. Here's what you do:

1. Make a copy of the dataset. It is easy to make a mistake in this sequence of events, so you should not do all these steps on your original dataset. To copy the dataset, right-click the sheet tab and choose Move or Copy. In the Move or Copy dialog that appears, choose Create a Copy. In the To Book drop-down, choose (New Book), as shown in Figure 10.3.

**Figure 10.3**
You need to make a copy of the dataset.

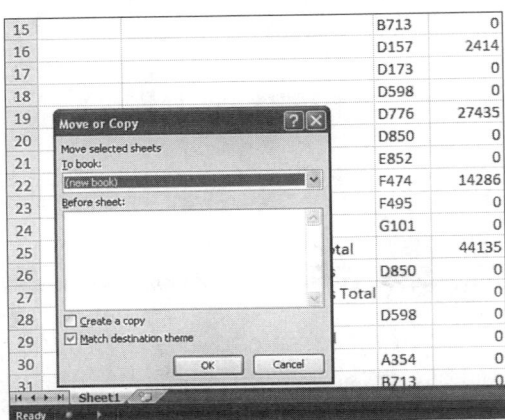

2. Ensure that there are no formulas in the data. You will later be sorting this data, and you want to make sure that you freeze all the current values. Above and to the left of cell A1, click on the light gray triangle to select all cells. Press Ctrl+C to copy them. On the Home ribbon, use the Paste drop-down to choose Paste Values, as shown in Figure 10.4.

**Figure 10.4**
You need to convert any formulas to values.

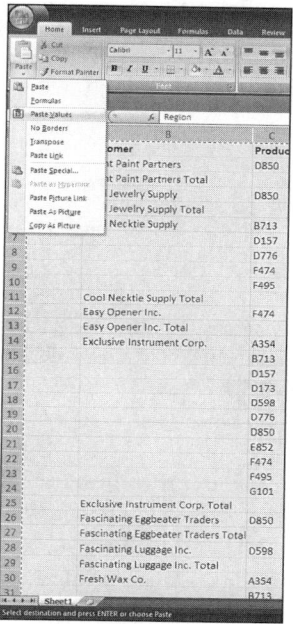

3. Examine the data. Look for patterns in your dataset similar to the patterns in this dataset. In this dataset, the total rows happen to have a blank cell in column C. See if you can find a similar rule in your dataset. A blank cell in Column C is a total record that you do not want in the final dataset. It would be tempting to sort by Column C right now, but see if the problems in step 4 apply to you first.

4. In this dataset, the region and customer information in the left columns are not repeated on every row. If your dataset has this same problem, then you will want to fill in those columns before sorting the total rows to the bottom of the data. You need to fill in those empty cells in Columns A and B first. Scroll down until you find the last row with data. Place the cell pointer in Column B of the last row. Press Ctrl+Shift+Home to select from the final row up to Cell A1.

5. You want to select only the blank cells within this selection. Press the F5 key to display the Go To dialog. In the lower-left corner of the Go To dialog, click the Special button. In the Go to Special dialog that appears, choose Blanks, as shown in Figure 10.5. Click OK. You are taken to the first blank cell in Column B, and the selection includes all blank cells in the original selection.

**Figure 10.5**
After selecting a range in Columns A and B, use the Go to Special dialog to select only the blank cells.

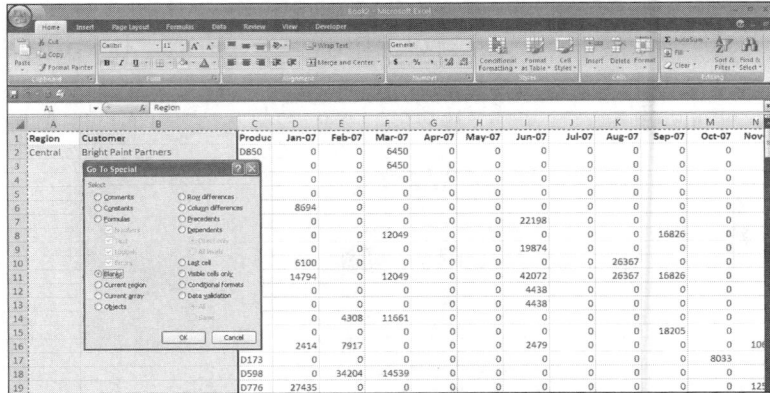

**CAUTION**

Resist the urge to press an arrow key because you still have a bunch of cells selected. Pressing an arrow key to navigate would unselect all these cells, and you would have to go back to step 3. Instead, you can use the scrollbars to scroll up.

6. Use the three-keystroke arrow key method to enter this formula. It is best to not even look at the screen while you do this because your cell addresses will probably be different from the ones shown in the book. Press the =, the up-arrow key, and Ctrl+Enter (see Figure 10.6). All the blank cells in your selection are instantly filled with a formula that points to the cell above the current cell.

**Figure 10.6**
Using Ctrl+Enter fills the formula in all cells of the selection.

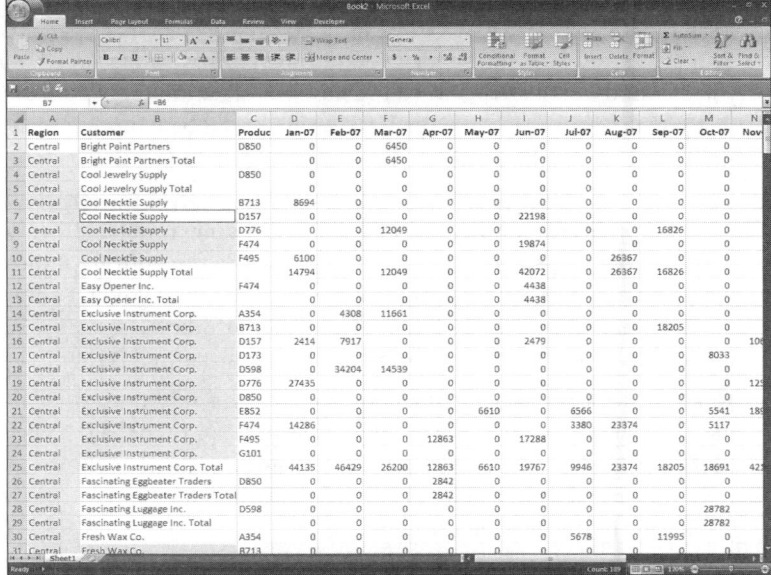

7. Convert all the formulas in Columns A and B to values. Unfortunately, you cannot use Copy and Paste on the current selection. You need to reselect the data as you did in step 4. Select a single cell in Column B. Press the End key and then press the down-arrow key to move to the last data cell in Column B. Hold down Ctrl+Shift+Home to select up to cell A1. On the Sheet ribbon, click the Copy icon. From the Paste drop-down, choose Paste Values.

8. Because you determined in step 3 that any blank cells in Column C are total records that need to be deleted, select Cell C1. From the Sort & Filter drop-down, choose Sort A-Z. In an ascending sort, any blank cells are moved to the end of the range.

9. With the cell pointer still in Cell C1, press the End key and then press the down-arrow key twice. You are now in the first row without any data in Column C. Scroll down to visually verify that all these rows have the word *Total* in Column B, as shown in Figure 10.7. These are rows that you want to delete.

**Figure 10.7**
All the extra total rows are now at the bottom.

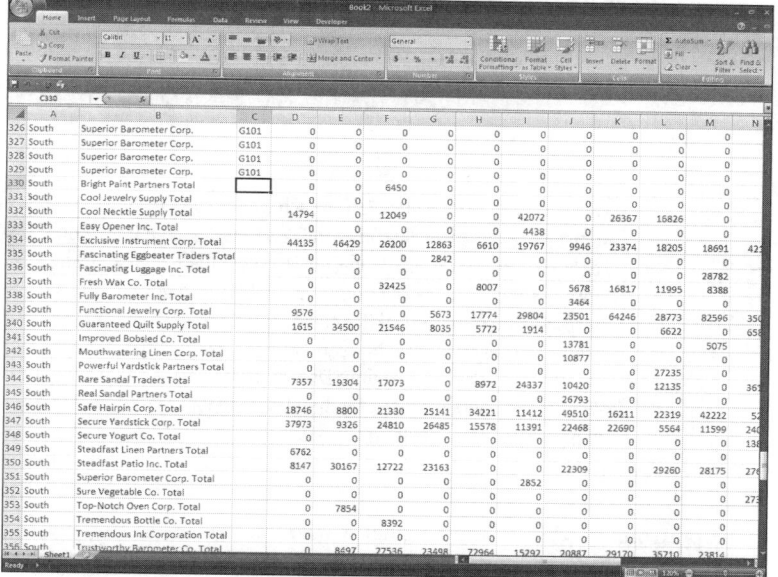

10. Move to Column B. While holding down the Shift key, press End and then the down-arrow key to select the rest of the rows. Right-click in the selection and choose Delete. In the Delete dialog that appears, choose Entire Row. At this point, you have solved two of the problems described earlier. The final problem is to turn the monthly data that is spread across the columns into row-oriented data.

11. To prepare to fix the final problem, insert a new column with the heading Month. In this dataset, Column D would be appropriate.

12. Open a new workbook. Copy Cells A1:E1 from the original workbook to the new workbook. Change Cell E1 to Revenue.

13. In the original workbook, copy Cell E1 to all the cells from D2 down to the end of your data, as shown in Figure 10.8.

**Figure 10.8**
Columns A:E in the original dataset can be copied to the new workbook.

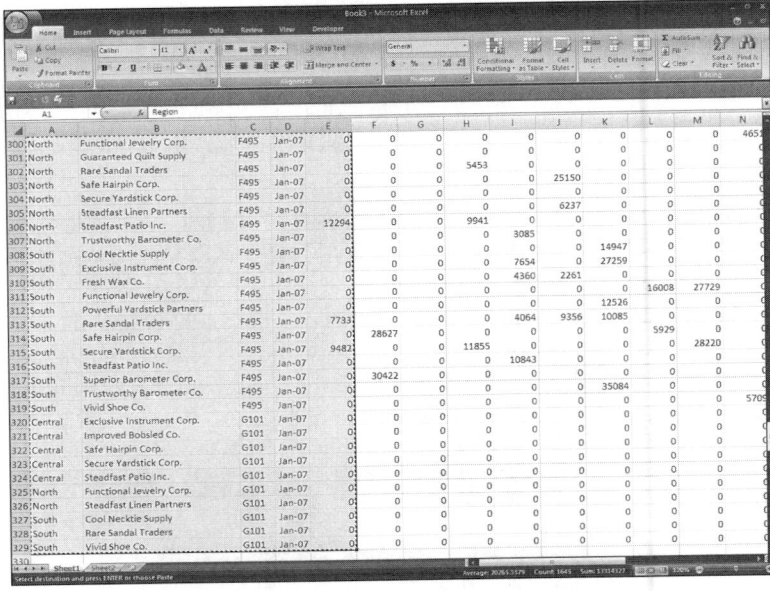

**TIP FROM**

Instead of repeating step 13 for each month, you could set up a set of formulas once. To do so, you put the cell pointer in D2. Using Name a Range on the Formulas ribbon, define `UpRight` as `=!E1`. In Cell D2, enter the formula `=UpRight`. In Cell D3, enter the formula `=D2`. Put the cell pointer in Cell D3 and double-click the fill handle to copy this formula down the rest of the column. Note that when you use this method, you can skip step 12 for each month, but you have to change the paste operation to a paste values operation in step 13. Caution: Do not use this trick if you have VBA code in your workbook! Calculations caused by the VBA code will return a value from the active sheet at the time of the calculation.

14. Copy Columns A:E of the original workbook. Switch to the new workbook. Paste the cells to the next blank row, in Column A. For the first month, this will be Cell A2, as shown in Figure 10.9.

15. Switch back to the workbook that contains all your data. At this point, you have copied all of the January 2007 sales to the new workbook. Remember that you are working on a copy of the data. Thus, it is safe to delete the entire Column E in this workbook. The next month then moves over to Column E.

16. Repeat steps 13–15 for each month column. This is the most tedious part of the process. If you have 12 months of data, you must complete these steps 12 times. If you have data for 60 months, it would almost be better to skip ahead to Chapter 36, "Automating Repetitive Functions Using VBA Macros," to learn how to write a macro to do this step.

17. The initial dataset contained 328 rows of data. At the end, you will end up with 3,936 rows of data (328×12) in the new workbook, as shown in Figure 10.10.

**Figure 10.9**
Columns A:E in the original dataset can be copied to the new workbook.

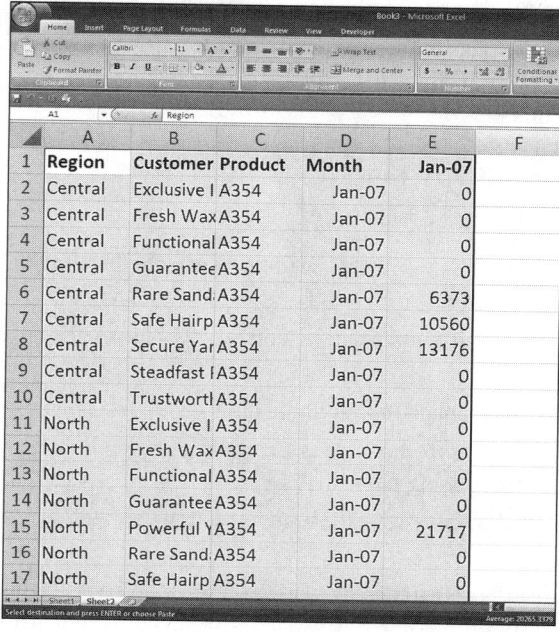

**Figure 10.10**
If all goes well, you should have 12 times more records in the new dataset as in the original.

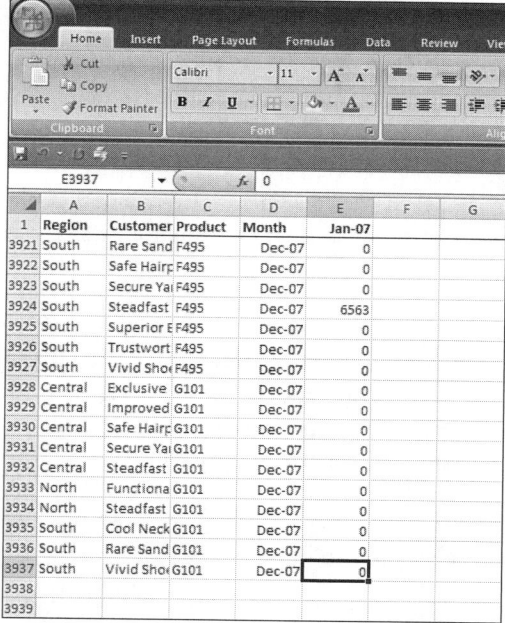

18. Because there are many datapoints where the revenue was zero, you can sort the new dataset in descending order by Column E and then delete all the rows with zero in Column E. You end up with a compact dataset of 531 rows by 5 columns.

You can complete the process described here in less than 15 minutes. It is not a particularly pleasant process. But if the data came from an inflexible software package, or your IT department tells you that you cannot have the new dataview for the next month or year, you know you can rely on this process.

## RECAPPING THE RULES FOR PIVOT TABLE DATA

To create pivot tables, follow these rules:

- Make sure each column has a one-cell heading. Keep the headings unique; don't use the same heading for two columns.
- If a column should contain numeric data, don't allow blank cells in the column. Use zeros instead of blanks.
- Do not use blank rows or blank columns.
- If summary data is missing from the detail rows, use the techniques described in steps 4–7 above to fill in the missing data.
- If totals are embedded in your report, remove them using techniques similar to step 8–10 above.
- If your data has months spread across many columns, go back to the source software program to see if a different view of the data is available. If this is not an option, use techniques similar to steps 11-16 to solve the problem.

# CREATING YOUR FIRST PIVOT TABLE

When you have your data in the correct format, creating and manipulating a pivot table is very easy.

Let's say that your manager has asked you to summarize some data to show revenue by region and product. To create a pivot table to do this, you follow these steps:

1. Select one cell in your data.
2. From the Insert ribbon, click the PivotTable icon in the Tables group.
3. Excel displays the Create PivotTable dialog, shown in Figure 10.11. In the top portion of the dialog, confirm that Excel's IntelliSense chose the right range for your data. In the lower portion of the dialog, you can choose to create your pivot table on a new worksheet or in a blank portion of the existing worksheet.

You are now just two clicks away from the answer you need. But first, let's take a quick look around the new look of pivot tables, shown in Figure 10.12:

- Two Pivot Table ribbons are grouped under PivotTable Tools. The Options ribbon contains most of the powerful pivot table features. The Design ribbon contains formatting icons.

**Figure 10.11**
Most of the time, you can simply click OK to get through this dialog.

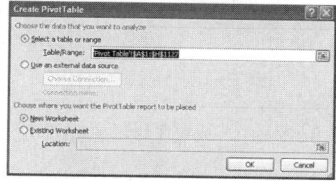

**Figure 10.12**
The new look of pivot tables is actually far simpler than the previous three- or four-step wizard.

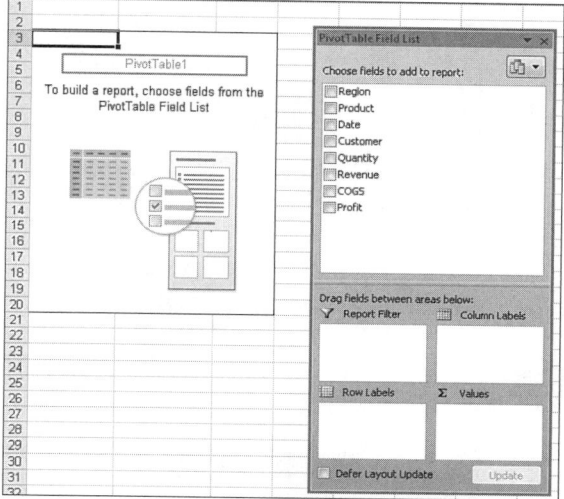

10

- The PivotTable Field List box, which looks like a task pane, appears in the right side of the screen. You can toggle it on and off by using the PivotTable Tools – Options – Show/Hide – Field List icon in the ribbon.

- There is a drop-down icon at the top of the Field List box. This drop-down offers five different views of the Field List box. You can experiment with these. Although each view is different, you may find that you don't have a favorite and they all seem basically equivalent.

- The old red exclamation point you used to refresh a table in earlier versions of Excel has been replaced by a large Refresh icon like the one you are familiar with in Internet Explorer. This icon is located in PivotTable Tools – Options – Data group. If your underlying dataset changed, you could click the Refresh icon to recalculate the pivot table.

- Many powerful items such as Table Options, Group, and Change Data Source are now easily available on the Options ribbon. These items were buried in previous versions of Excel.

- Before you add your first field to a pivot table, a graphic appears in Column A, directing you to choose fields from the PivotTable Field List box.

To create a pivot table, you simply use the PivotTable Field List box to check which fields to include in the table. Excel makes fairly intelligent guesses based on the field type. In the current example, Excel builds a passable table using the default guesses. You have to make one adjustment to perfect the table.

In the PivotTable Field List box, you choose Region, Product, and Revenue. When you choose the Revenue field, Excel adds a new field called Sum of Revenue to the Σ Values section of the PivotTable Field List box. Excel decides that this belongs in the Σ Values section because the field is basically numeric. When you choose Region and Product, Excel moves those to the Row Labels section of the PivotTable Field List box.

At this point, the default pivot table looks as shown in Figure 10.13. In Cell B4, you can see that the central region sold $4.67 million. In Cells B5:B15, you can see the revenue for each product in the central region.

**Figure 10.13**
The default pivot table after five clicks. It would be easier to understand if regions went across Columns B, C, and D.

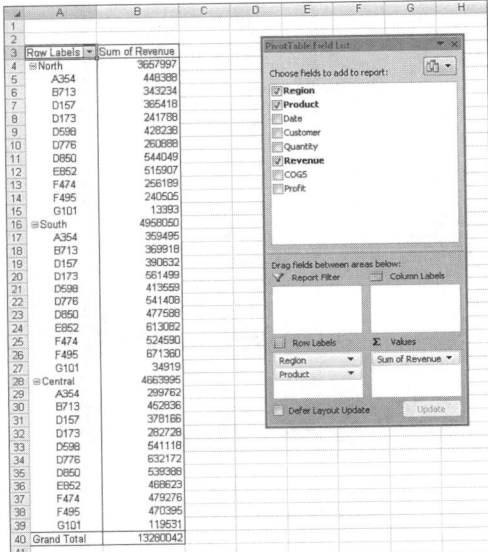

# CHANGING THE DEFAULT LAYOUT OF A PIVOT TABLE

The annoying thing about the table in Figure 10.13 is that it would be easier to read the table if the Region field went across Columns B, C, and D, with a total for the three regions in Column E.

When you use the checkmark method for building a pivot table, Excel can't read your mind about which fields would look better when used as column labels. Luckily, it is very easy to move fields in a pivot table, as described in the following sections.

## A QUICK LOOK AROUND THE PIVOTTABLE FIELD LIST BOX

In Figure 10.13, the PivotTable Field List box is composed of a list of fields at the top and then four distinct areas below (Report Filter, Column Labels, Row Labels, and Σ Values).

The drop-down at the top offers five different views of the Field List box. As shown in Figure 10.14, the name for the default view is Fields and Drop Zones Stacked. This view could have shortcomings if you had more than 16 fields in the field list. You can also see in Figure 10.14 that there is not quite room for the text *Sum of Revenue* to appear in the Σ Values section.

**Figure 10.14**
This drop-down offers five views of the PivotTable Field List box.

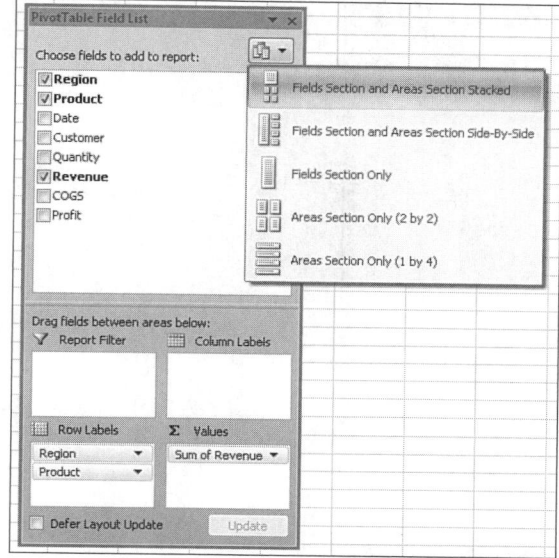

Figure 10.15 shows the Fields and Drop Zones Side by Side view. This view would allow up to 28 fields to be visible in the Field List box. It still has the problem that you can't see the entire name *Sum of Revenue* in the Σ Values section.

**Figure 10.15**
The Fields and Drop Zones Side by Side view offers more room, for a longer list of fields.

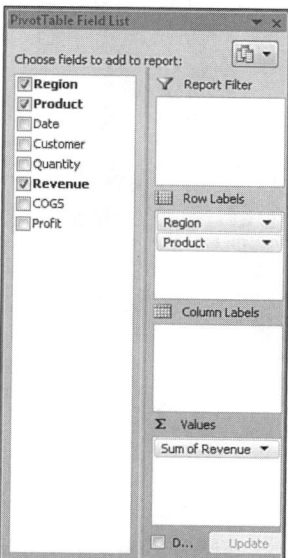

10

Figure 10.16 shows the Field List box in Fields Only view. You can use this view if you can trust Excel to put the fields in the right place.

**Figure 10.16**
The Fields Only view can accommodate a long list of fields or fields with really long names.

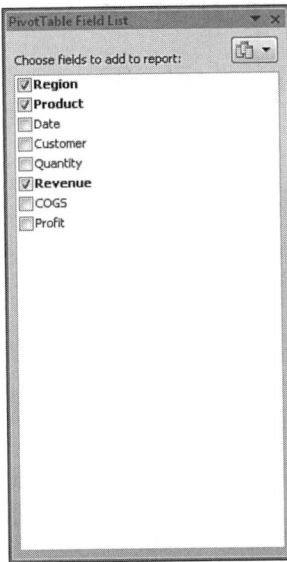

Figure 10.17 shows Drop Zones Only (2 by 2) view, with the layout fields arranged in a 2×2 grid. Figure 10.18 shows Drop Zones Only (1 by 4) view, with the sections arranged in a 1×4 grid.

**Figure 10.17**
After the fields have been added to the layout sections, you can hide the list to concentrate on layout.

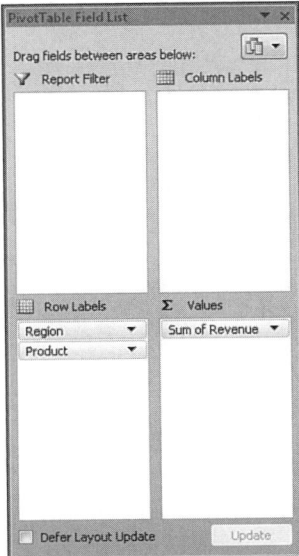

**Figure 10.18**
This view would be best for long field names.

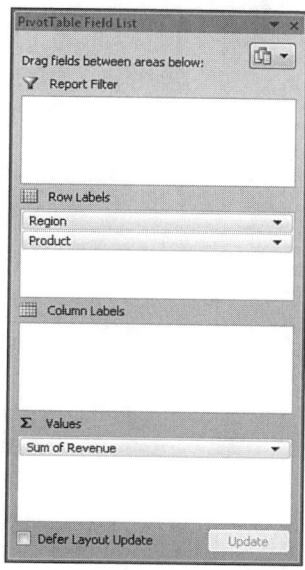

The drop zone sections of the PivotTable Field List Box are as follows:

- **Report Filter**—You use this section to limit the report to only certain criteria. This section is analogous to the PageField section in the old pivot table model.

- **Row Labels** —This section is for fields that will appear on the left side of the table. If you have more than one field in the Row Labels section, they will appear in a hierarchical view, with the second field arranged under the first field.

- **Column Labels**—This section is for fields that will stretch along the top rows of columns of your table.

- **Σ Values**—This section is for all the numeric fields that are summarized in the table. By default, most fields are automatically summed, but you can change the default calculation to an average, minimum, maximum, or other calculations, as described in "Finishing Touches: Numeric Formatting in a Pivot Table."

## REARRANGING A PIVOT TABLE

Four of the five views of the PivotTable Field List box include the four drop zones described in the preceding section. These areas are the keys for rearranging the look of a pivot table.

The Row Labels section from our earlier example has Region and Product fields. In your pivot table, you will have different field names. Each of these fields has a drop-down. If you choose the Product drop-down, you see the list of options shown in Figure 10.19.

**Figure 10.19**
Many arrangement options are available in the drop-down for each field in the layout area.

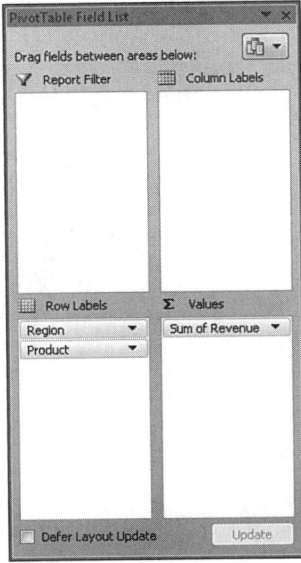

From the drop-down list in 10.19, if you choose Move to Column Labels, the data is arranged in what is called a crosstab analysis, as shown in Figure 10.20.

**Figure 10.20**
This crosstab analysis presents the data clearly. Creating it required six mouse clicks.

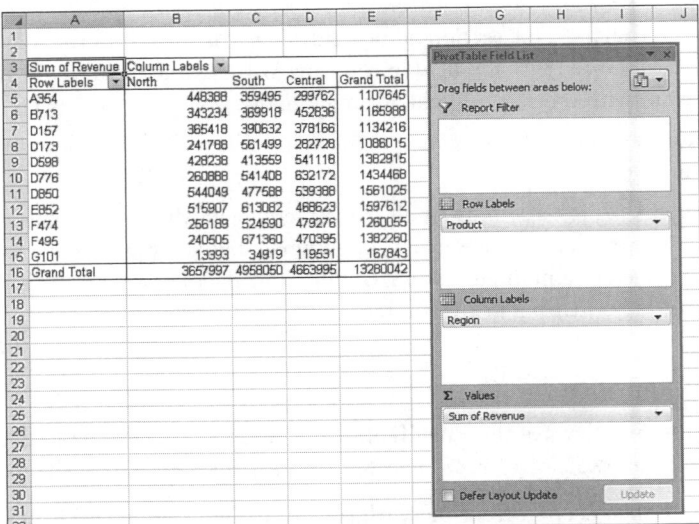

| Row Labels | North | South | Central | Grand Total |
|---|---|---|---|---|
| A354 | 448388 | 359495 | 299762 | 1107645 |
| B713 | 343234 | 369918 | 452836 | 1165988 |
| D157 | 365418 | 390632 | 378166 | 1134216 |
| D173 | 241788 | 561499 | 282728 | 1086015 |
| D598 | 428238 | 413559 | 541118 | 1382915 |
| D776 | 260888 | 541408 | 632172 | 1434468 |
| D850 | 544049 | 477588 | 539388 | 1561025 |
| E852 | 515907 | 613082 | 468623 | 1597612 |
| F474 | 256189 | 524590 | 479276 | 1260055 |
| F495 | 240505 | 671360 | 470395 | 1382260 |
| G101 | 13393 | 34919 | 119531 | 167843 |
| Grand Total | 3657997 | 4958050 | 4663995 | 13280042 |

In this example, you used the drop-down shown in Figure 10.19 to move a field from one section to another. You can instead drag a field within the Field List box drop zones. To do this, in Figure 10.19, you click the Region field and drop it in the Column Labels section.

## FINISHING TOUCHES: NUMERIC FORMATTING IN A PIVOT TABLE

Once you have arranged your data in the report, you will want to consider formatting the numeric fields. For example, in Figure 10.21, it would be helpful if the numbers were formatted with commas as thousands separators.

There is a temptation to format a pivot table just like you format any other range in a worksheet. However, as you will see later in this chapter, a pivot table is very fluid. Although the numbers in the figure currently occupy Cells B5:E16, with a couple mouse clicks, they could soon occupy Cells B4:B48 or even Cells B4:B539. Because any pivot table might be changing shape, it is best to do all formatting through the pivot table interface.

If you tell Excel that a particular field should always have the format $#,##0, then no matter how you change the pivot table, Excel will remember the format.

For example, in the PivotTable Field List box, you should click the Sum of Revenue drop-down in the Σ Values section. Be careful. Revenue appears twice in the PivotTable Field List box. There is a Revenue field with a checkbox in the Fields section. There is a Sum of Revenue button in the Σ Values section. Both Revenue and Sum of Revenue have drop-down arrows when selected. You are specifically looking for the Sum of Revenue button in the Σ Values layout section of the PivotTable Field List box.

When you choose the Sum of Revenue drop-down arrow in the Σ Values section, you should choose Field Settings, as shown in Figure 10.21.

**Figure 10.21**
You choose Sum of Revenue, Choose Field Settings.

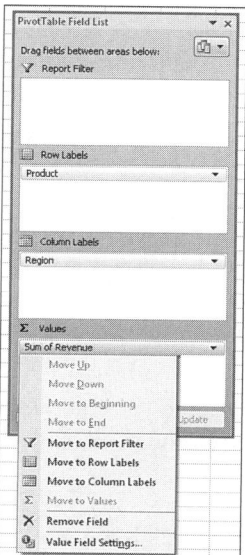

10

The Summarize By tab of the Data Field Settings dialog allows you to change the summary function from Sum to Count, Average, Min, Max, etc. In the lower-left corner of this dialog, click the Number Format button, as shown in Figure 10.22. You can then choose a numeric format from a special version of the Format Cells dialog.

**Figure 10.22**
Numeric formats are behind the button in the lower-left corner of this dialog.

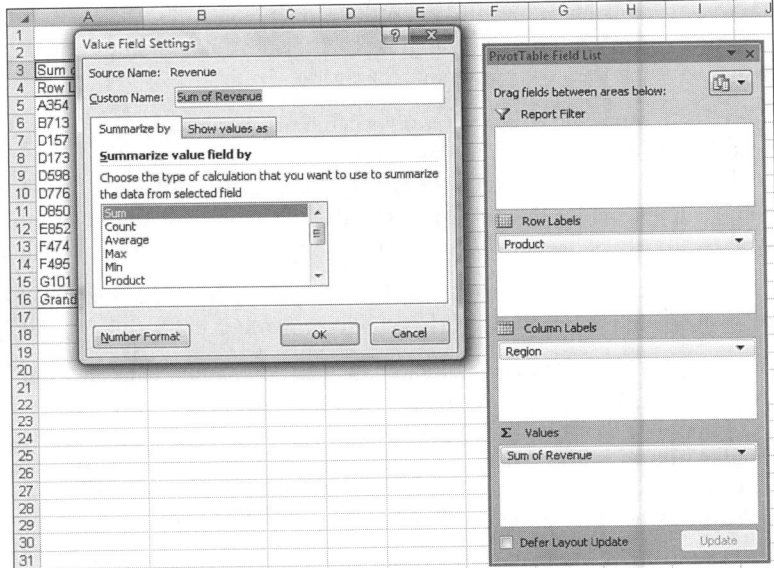

When you have a pivot table, it is easy to further customize it. For example, in the Below the Field List box, you can drag Product from the Row Labels section to the Column Labels section. Then you can choose Customer, which by default moves to the Row Labels section. In two more clicks, you have created a completely different summary of the data.

# ADDING NEW FIELDS TO A PIVOT TABLE

The first pivot table you created in this chapter gives a great view of sales by product by region. The fantastic thing about pivot tables is that they allow you to drill in and get more detail from your data. Once you have created your first pivot table, think about ways that you can add more data to the report in order to further explain the values you see in the summary.

As an example, say that you want to add customer data to your product/region summary report. This would be a good report to produce for a product line manager. It is incredibly easy to transform your first pivot table into a report that shows such customer detail. You have two choices. In the PivotTable Field List box, you can drag the Customer field over to be the second field in the Row Labels section. Alternatively, you can simply choose the check box next to Customer in the field list. By default, this adds the field as the last field in the Row Labels area. In your dataset, follow the same step to add the new field to the layout.

After you make either of these changes, within a second, Excel redraws the pivot table to show the customers who purchased each product, as shown in Figure 10.23.

**Figure 10.23**
You can choose the Customer field in the field list to add customers to a pivot table.

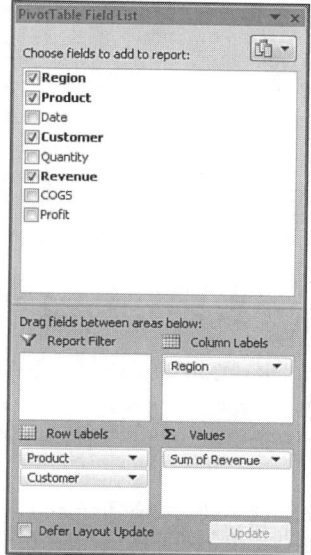

# ELIMINATING BLANK CELLS FROM A PIVOT TABLE

Once you produce a report with two or more fields, you might be frustrated by a problem common to most pivot tables. Look at Row 9 in Figure 10.23. This customer made purchases from the central and north regions of your company but did not make any purchases from the south region. By default, a pivot table shows a blank in this cell to indicate that there were no records matching for this customer in that particular region.

Many people would rather see a zero in this cell than see it blank. To override the blank setting, on the PivotTable Tools - Options ribbon, in the PivotTable Options group, choose the Options icon. As shown in Figure 10.24, there are five tabs in the PivotTable Options dialog that appears. The first tab, Layout & Format, has a setting called For Empty Cells Show. You should change this setting from a blank to a zero.

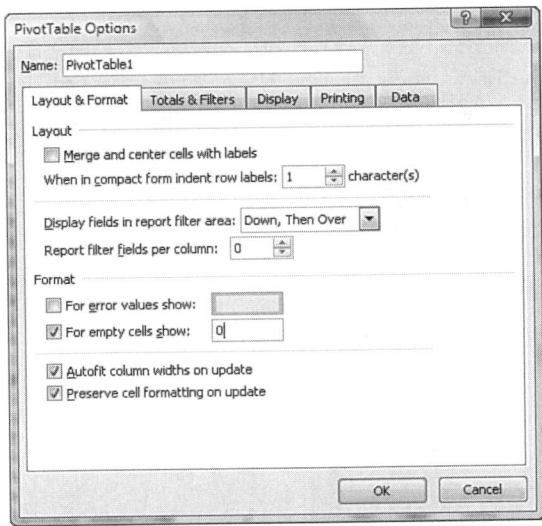

**Figure 10.24**
You can use For Empty Cells Show 0 to force Excel to fill in the empty cells in the data section of a pivot table.

# USING PIVOT TABLE LEGACY MODE

If you are an expert in creating pivot tables in Excel 2003, you might be distraught that the pivot table interface has changed considerably. While the new interface will allow people new to pivot tables to create pivot tables flawlessly, you might wish to use the legacy pivot table functionality to create your pivot tables.

The Excel 95 - Excel 2003 pivot table interface allowed you to drag and drop fields right onto the pivot table. Many people did not notice the subtle visual clues that allowed you to know where the dropped field would appear. Many people would try to drop a new column field between the column area and the data area, resulting in disaster if Excel interpreted the field as a data field. Microsoft changed the interface to protect these new people from themselves.

However, if you have previously mastered the drag and drop method, you might want a way back to that mode. Microsoft provides a way, but it is fairly hidden.

1. Create a new pivot table.
2. On the PivotTable Tools - Options ribbon, choose the Options icon from the PivotTable Options group.
3. In the Pivot Table Options dialog that appears, go to the Display tab and choose Classic PivotTable Layout (Enables Dragging of Fields in the Grid), as shown in Figure 10.25. With this option selected, you can continue to build pivot tables using the old Excel 2003 interface, as shown in Figure 10.26.

**Figure 10.25**
You can go back to the old drag-and-drop layout.

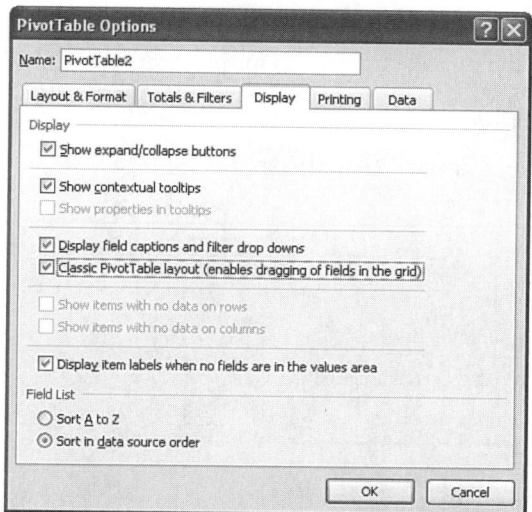

**Figure 10.26**
When you get back to the old layout, don't accidentally drop Revenue in the Row Fields section.

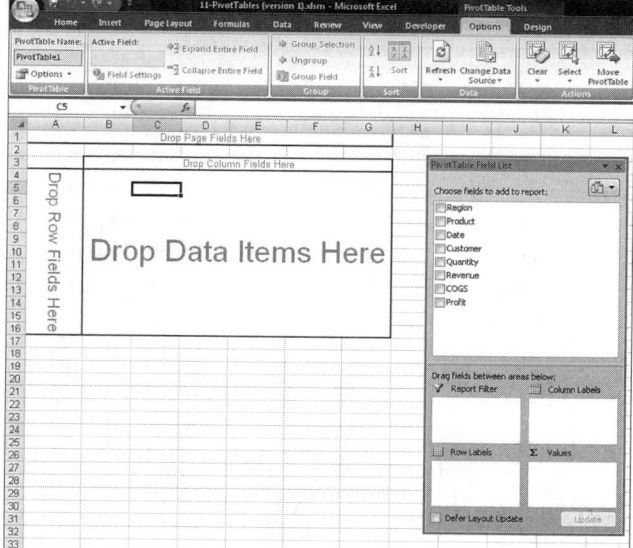

# PIVOT TABLE LIMITATIONS

Pivot tables are the greatest invention in spreadsheets, but they do have a few limitations. However, as described in the following sections, many of their limitations have been significantly improved in Excel 2007.

## CAPACITY LIMITATIONS

As shown in Table 10.1, the capacity limitations for pivot tables have been greatly improved in Excel 2007.

### TABLE 10.1   PIVOT TABLE CAPACITY LIMITATIONS

| Item | Old Limit | Excel 2007 Limit |
|------|-----------|------------------|
| Number of rows allowed | 64,000 | 1 million |
| Number of columns allowed | 256 | 16,000 |
| Maximum number of unique items in one field | 32,000 | 1 million |
| The length at which fields' labels are truncated | 255 | 32,000 |
| Number of fields in the field list | 255 | 16,000 |

## INABILITY TO COMBINE FEATURES

There are some limitations when it comes to combining features within pivot tables:

- If any field is grouped, you cannot add a calculated item to that field or any other field in the table.
- If you have grouped a field by $x$ number of days, you can no longer group that same field by months, quarters, or years.
- If your are querying a huge underlying dataset, you may experience a delay after you make a change to the pivot table. In these cases, you can go to the bottom of the field list and select the option Defer Layout Update. This allows you to rearrange fields in the layout section and then click the Update button to implement all the changes at once. The limitation is that if you uncheck the Defer Layout Update without clicking the Update button, your changes are lost.

## CHANGES TO UNDERLYING DATA NOT APPEARING IN A PIVOT TABLE

Most people are shocked to learn that changes to underlying data do not appear in a pivot table. After all, you change a cell in Excel, and all the formulas derived from the cell automatically change. You would think that the same should hold true for pivot tables, but it does not.

Pivot tables are fast because the data from the worksheet is loaded into a special cache in memory. If you build a pivot table and then change the underlying data, you must click the Refresh icon in the Data group of the PivotTable Tools - Options ribbon in order to have the change appear in the pivot table.

10

## THE DISAPPEARANCE OF THE PIVOTTABLE FIELD LIST BOX

Sometimes the PivotTable Field List box seems to disappear randomly. It is not actually randomly, but it seems like it. Say you have data on Sheet1. You build a new pivot table on Sheet2. My argument is that as long as you are on Sheet2, you are clearly working with or looking at the pivot table. Microsoft disagrees with me. Microsoft's rule is that as soon as you click in any cell outside the confines of the pivot table, Excel should put away the PivotTable Field List box and switch to a ribbon other than one of the pivot table ribbons. To solve this problem, you can select a cell within the pivot table again to redisplay the PivotTable Field List box.

The pivot table ribbons exhibit strange behavior. If you are on the PivotTable Tools - Options ribbon, you can click one cell outside the pivot table and then immediately select a cell back inside the pivot table, and Excel redisplays the PivotTable Tools - Options ribbon. However, if you are at the right edge of the pivot table and click the right-arrow key twice and then the left-arrow key twice, you have now touched two cells outside the pivot table, so the PivotTable ribbon does not redisplay until you click on the Options tab in the ribbon.

## HAVING A BLANK CELL IN THE UNDERLYING DATA CONFUSE EXCEL

Say your dataset has thousands of rows of data. For any reason, if one of the revenue cells happens to be blank, this completely confuses Excel. There can be 999,999 cells with numbers and 1 blank cell, but Excel will no longer realize that the Revenue column is a numeric column.

Two things tip you off to this problem. First, if you attempt to simply check the box for Revenue in the field list, Excel moves it to the Row Labels section instead of the Σ Values section. Second, if you are in the habit of dragging the Revenue field to the Σ Values section, you see numbers that are too low. If you are an $11 million company and your pivot table shows your revenue as $1,124, you can assume that you probably have one or more blank cells in the underlying revenue data. In Figure 10.27, the blank Cell F4 causes Excel to assume that Revenue is a label field. If you build the pivot table anyway, Excel counts the revenue records instead of summing them.

You need to be aware of this limitation. To correct the problem, you have two choices. The better solution is to fill in the underlying blank cells with zeros. But the easier solution is to double-click the Sum of Revenue heading and then change Data Field Settings to Sum from Count.

10

**Figure 10.27**
A single blank cell in the Revenue column makes Excel count instead of sum revenue.

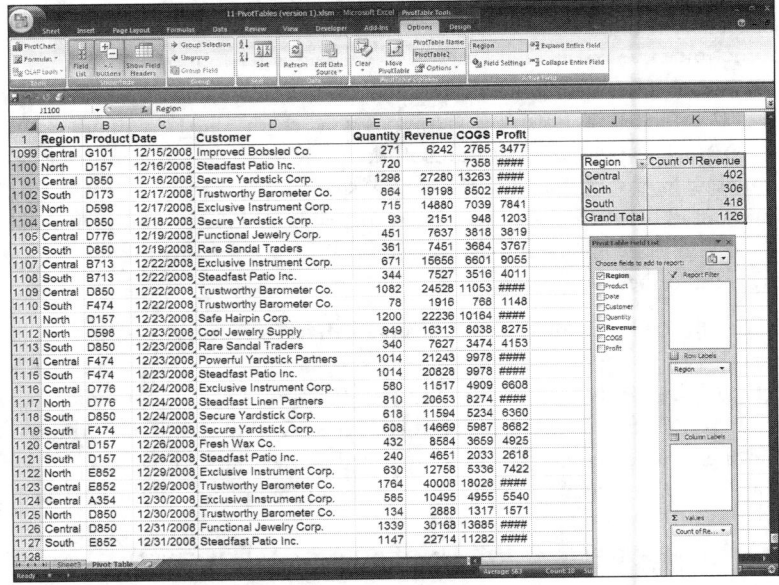

### Troubleshooting Tip: You Cannot Change, Move a Part of, or Insert Cells

Many times, pivot tables get you very close to the final report you want, and you just want to insert a row or move one bit of the table. You cannot do this. If you try, you will be greeted with the message shown in Figure 10.28. This is a fair limitation. After all, Excel needs to figure out how to redraw the table when you move something in the field list.

**Figure 10.28**
You should not try to insert a column in the middle of a pivot table.

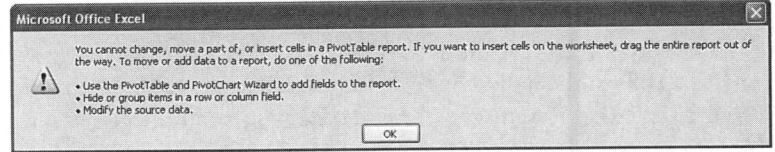

The solution is to copy the pivot table and use Paste Special Values. You can either put this on a new worksheet or simply paste the entire table back over itself. If you go to a new worksheet, you can continue to modify the original pivot table. If you paste values over the original worksheet, the pivot table converts to a range, and you cannot pivot it further.

# FORMATTING PIVOT TABLES

## In this chapter

As shown in Chapter 10, pivot tables are very fast at creating summary reports from thousands of rows of data. Once you've developed the summary information, you might need to spend some time improving the format of the pivot table. Excel 2007 offers some exciting new options in pivot table formatting. Unfortunately, Excel 2007 still offers some annoying problems that have plagued pivot table fans for a decade.

# THE NEW COMPACT VIEW

In the pivot table shown in Figure 11.1, Column A contains three different fields: Region, Product, and Customer. This is a new view in Excel 2007, and it is called the compact form of the pivot table. Microsoft thinks so much of this new view that it is the default view for any pivot table that has two or more fields in the Row Labels section of the layout area.

## COLLAPSING AND EXPANDING ITEMS

In Figure 11.1, Customer is the innermost field. The outer fields are Product and Region. Note that each product listed in Column A is preceded by a tiny minus button. You could use the individual minus buttons to collapse the details for a given product. For example, in Figure 11.1, A354 is collapsed to a single line in row 7.

**Figure 11.1**
You can use the minus and plus buttons to collapse and expand various sections of a report.

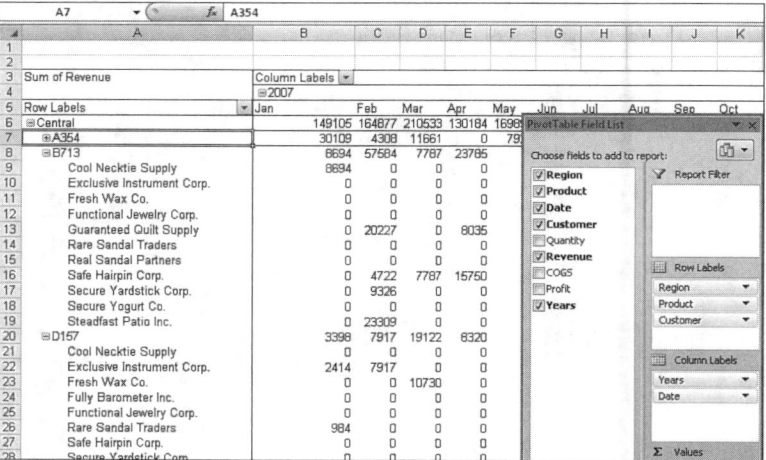

## COLLAPSING AND EXPANDING ACTIVE FIELDS

Rather than clicking a dozen minus signs to collapse individual sections of a pivot table, you can use the icons Expand Entire Field and Collapse Entire Field. These buttons, which appear in the Active Field group of the Options ribbon, are a little tricky to use successfully.

In Figure 11.2, the cell pointer is on Cell A6. This cell contains the central region. As you can see, the active field indicator shows that the active field is Region.

**Figure 11.2**
The active field indicator changes to a different field based on the location of the cell pointer.

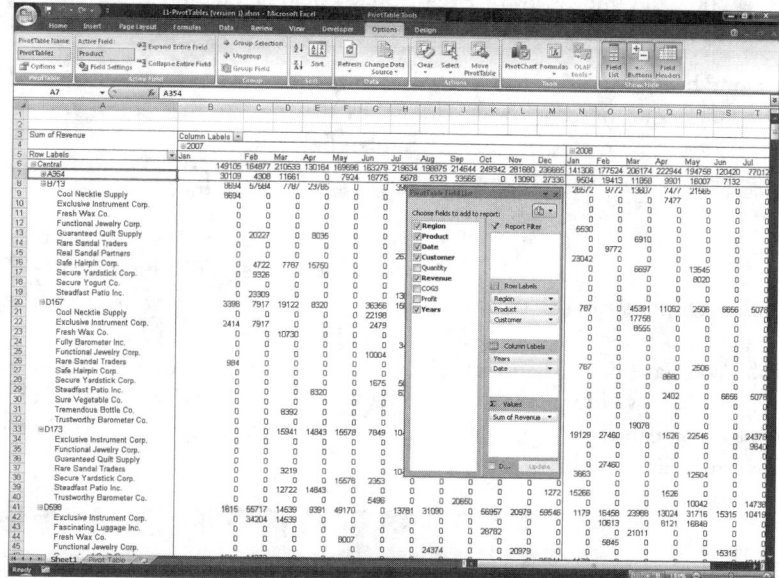

Before you can make effective use of the buttons in the Active Field group of the Options ribbon, you need to figure out how to make your desired field become the active field.

The logic of which field is the active field is frustrating. Many powerful buttons in the ribbon act upon the active field, so being able to quickly make a certain field the active field is a good skill to learn. This explanation might help to clarify the bizarre rules used by Excel 2007.

It seems like there should be a drop-down in the Active Field text box to allow you to select the active field. It seems like there should be a way to touch a field in the field list to choose an active field. But neither of these methods works. Instead, you have to move the cell pointer around in order to make the ribbon realize which field is the active one.

- If you move the cell pointer to Cell A7, the active field changes to be the Product field. Moving the cell pointer to A17, A29, A42, and so on also causes the Product field to be the active field.

- If you move the cell pointer to any of Cells A8:A16, the active field changes to be Customer.

- If you move the cell pointer to any of Cells B5:Z5, the active field changes to be Date.

- If you move the cell pointer to any of Cells B4:Z5, the active field changes to be Years.

- Cells A6 and A5 are also considered to be Region fields. Not shown in the screenshot, but the other two region fields in A126 and A244 are also region cells.

- If you move the cell pointer to any of Cells B6:Z370, the active field is Revenue. Cell A3 and, surprisingly, Cell A4 are both considered to be Revenue.

## COLLAPSING FIELDS OFFERS IMPROVED FUNCTIONALITY

The expand/collapse functions were cryptic in Excel 2003. They have been promoted in Excel 2007 and improved. In Excel 2007, a field can be in a pivot table and completely hidden through the collapse button.

Imagine being in a sales meeting with one report shown on the screen. When the attendees start asking questions, without adding any new data to the report, you could click the expand buttons to show the details for the hidden field.

Here is one example to illustrate the powerful possibilites.

Putting the cell pointer in Cell A7, as shown in Figure 11.3, causes Product to be the active field. Now, if you click Collapse Entire Field in the Active Field group of the PivotTable Tools - Options ribbon, you end up with a nicely compact view of just Regions and Products, as shown in Figure 11.3. Without removing the Customer field from the pivot table, you have made the pivot table more summarized. You can imagine projecting this image on the wall in a sales meeting. When someone asks about sales of B713 in the north region, you can expand just that one group by using the plus button in Cell A18. This is a powerful feature of pivot tables.

**Figure 11.3**
After selecting a product cell, you can choose Collapse Entire Field to hide the detail inside a product level.

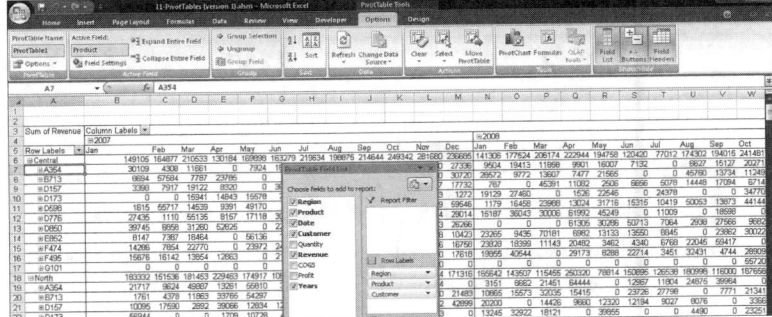

It is possible to collapse multiple fields. For example, in Figure 11.3, you can select Cell A6 and choose Collapse Entire Field to produce a summary of just the three regions and a grand total.

The collapse function also works for multiple fields in the column label area. For example, you can select Cell B4 and then choose Collapse Entire Field in order to hide the months and just show the years and a total. Figure 11.4 shows the pivot table collapsed down to regions and years.

**Figure 11.4**
A pivot table provides a tight summary when you group by regions and years.

| Sum of Revenue | Filter columns | | |
|---|---|---|---|
| | ⊞ 2007 | ⊞ 2008 | Grand Total |
| Filter rows | | | |
| ⊞ Central | 2388736 | 2275259 | 4663995 |
| ⊞ North | 1870922 | 1780075 | 3650997 |
| ⊞ South | 2499338 | 2458712 | 4958050 |
| Grand Total | 6758996 | 6514046 | 13273042 |

## USING THE EXPAND ENTIRE FIELD BUTTON

The Expand Entire Field button has some surprising features. First, the button appears to have a bit of memory because it acts differently depending on how you collapsed a field. Second, when you attempt to expand a field at the lowest level of detail, Excel offers to add more fields to the table. Finally, expanding a value cell produces a cool filter report.

Say that you start with the pivot table shown in Figure 11.2. You collapse the products as shown in Figure 11.3. Then you collapse the regions as shown in Figure 11.4. If you select Cell A6 and choose Expand Entire Field, Excel expands the regions to include products, making Column A similar to the Column A shown in Figure 11.3.

On the other hand, say that you start with Figure 11.4 and collapse the Region field so you can see only the three regions. If you then expand the Region field, Excel expands the regions and the products in order to go back to the Column A shown in Figure 11.2.

In Figure 11.5, Customer is the innermost row field. Notice that Cell A8 does not contain a plus button, so there is really no way to expand the Customer field. However, if you choose a customer and then select Expand Entire Field, Excel figures that you must be trying to drill down. The Show Detail dialog appears, with a list of the database fields that are not yet in the row area of the pivot table. You can choose any of them to add it as the innermost row field. In previous versions of Excel, if you tried to expand a field that had no additional detail, you would be out of luck. In Excel 2007, Microsoft nicely assumes that someone must be asking you questions and wonderfully offers to help.

**Figure 11.5**
If you try to expand the innermost row or column field, Excel tries to oblige by allowing you to add another field to the pivot table.

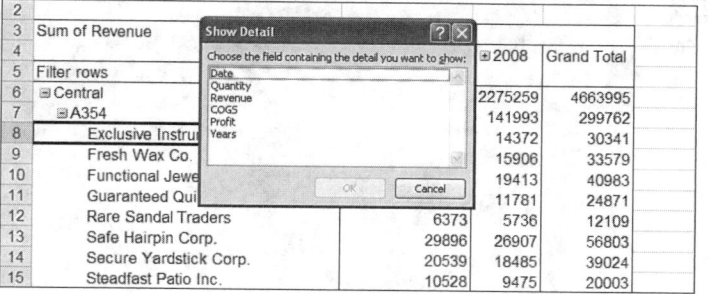

## EXPANDING A VALUE CELL

A pivot table helps you to notice things in your data. If you look at 100,000 rows of transactional data, it is hard to spot any errors. However, if you summarize that data down to a 20-row pivot table, you are more likely to notice if there are problems with the data.

When you look at a pivot table, you might say, for example, "Wait a second, this particular customer never buys that particular product. What is going on?" A pivot table makes this question easy to answer. You can select the revenue cell for that customer. In the figure, Cell B14 is the value cell showing sales to Secure Yardstick in January 2007. At this point, you can either double-click B14 or select B14 and click the Expand Entire Field button. In response to either action, Excel goes back to the original dataset and extracts the records that comprise the sales. Excel then writes the records to a new worksheet to the left of your pivot table sheet. This trick works for any value cell in the pivot table. In Figure 11.6, choosing Expand Entire Field causes Excel to extract all the records for the central region sales of product D173 in 2008.

**Figure 11.6**
To query the records behind the selected number, you can double-click the cell or click Expand Entire Field.

| | | | | | |
|---|---|---|---|---|---|
| 3 | Sum of Revenue | Filter columns | | | |
| 4 | | | ⊞2007 | ⊞2008 | Grand Total |
| 5 | Filter rows | | | | |
| 6 | ⊟Central | | 2388736 | 2275259 | 4663995 |
| 7 | ⊞A354 | | 157769 | 141993 | 299762 |
| 8 | ⊞B713 | | 243460 | 209376 | 452836 |
| 9 | ⊞D157 | | 210093 | 168073 | 378166 |
| 10 | ⊞D173 | | 128512 | 154216 | 282728 |
| 11 | ⊞D598 | | 312785 | 22 Sum of Revenue | 118 |
| 12 | ⊞D776 | | 329257 | 30 Value: 154216 | 172 |
| 13 | ⊞D850 | | 265707 | 27 Row: Central - D173 | 888 |
| 14 | ⊞E852 | | 207355 | 261268 Column: 2008 | 468623 |
| 15 | ⊟E474 | | 260256 | 210020 | 470276 |

The results of expanding Cell C10 in Figure 11.6 are shown in Figure 11.7. Excel always adds a new sheet to the left of the pivot table. Also, if you discover a problem with this data, remember that you need to go back to the original dataset to make corrections.

**Figure 11.7**
Excel quickly extracts just the 2008 records for D173 for the central region.

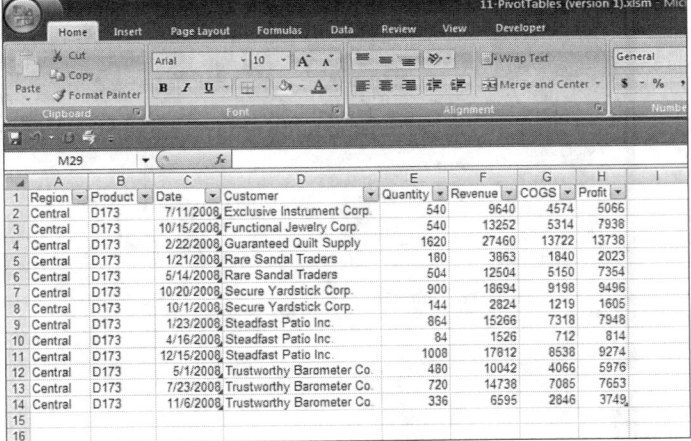

## REPORT LAYOUT OPTIONS

All the figures so far in this chapter have shown Excel's new default compact form of the pivot table. If you prefer the Excel 2003 style of pivot tables, you can switch back to those styles. To do so, you need to access the Layout group on the Design ribbon in order to revert to the old style.

Figure 11.8 shows the outline form of the pivot table from the preceding example. In this view, each field in the row area takes another column in the table. Whereas the compact form puts Region, Product, and Customer all in Column A, the outline form uses Columns A, B, and C for these three fields. Note that by default the outline form shows the total for each group at the top of the group.

**Figure 11.8**
The outline form of a pivot table.

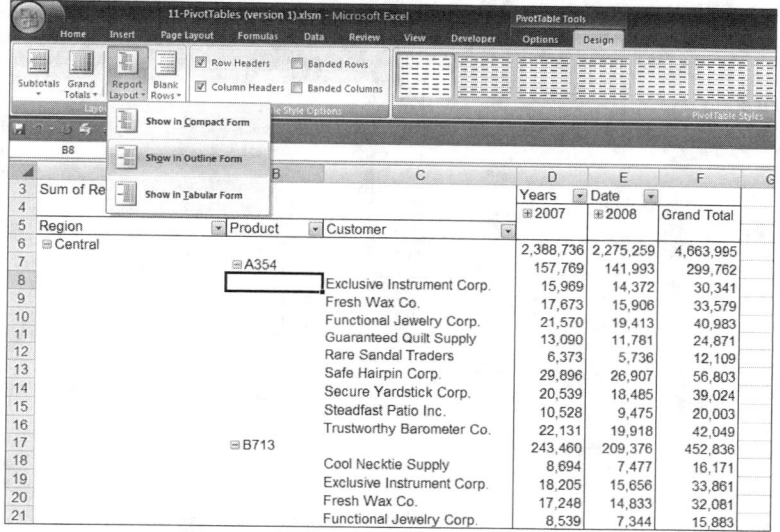

Figure 11.9 shows the tabular form of the same pivot table. This is the style of pivot tables that has been around since pivot tables were introduced in 1993. As you can see, a total appears at the bottom of each group.

**Figure 11.9**
The tabular form of a pivot table.

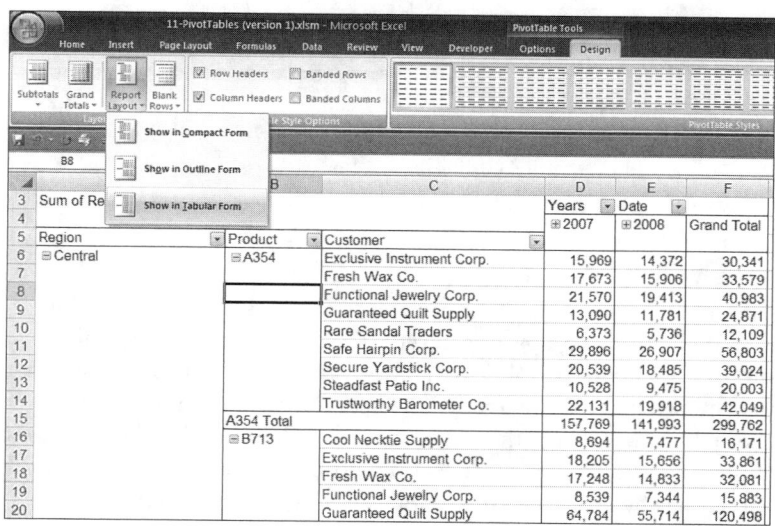

In addition to the three report layout options, you can choose to move the subtotals to the bottom of each group in either the compact or outline forms of the pivot table. You can choose this option from the Subtotals icon of the Layout group of the Design ribbon. Figure 11.10 shows the compact form with a subtotal at the bottom of each group.

**Figure 11.10**
Subtotals can move to the bottom of any layout style.

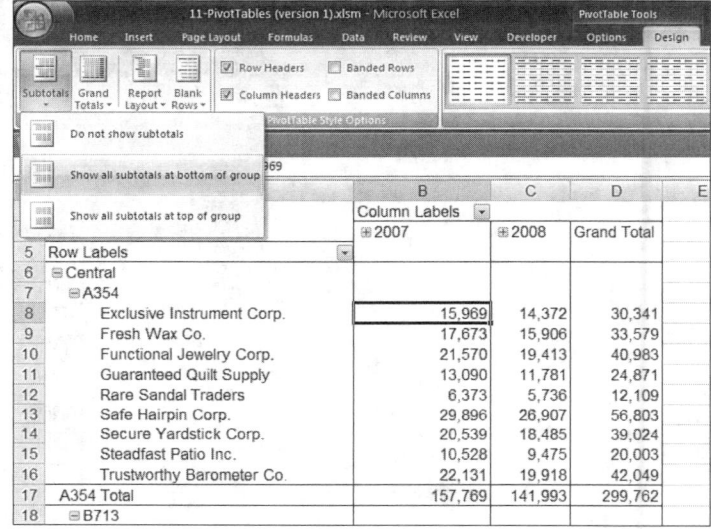

| | A | B | C | D | E |
|---|---|---|---|---|---|
| | | Column Labels | | | |
| | | ⊞ 2007 | ⊞ 2008 | Grand Total | |
| 5 | Row Labels | | | | |
| 6 | ⊟ Central | | | | |
| 7 | ⊟ A354 | | | | |
| 8 | Exclusive Instrument Corp. | 15,969 | 14,372 | 30,341 | |
| 9 | Fresh Wax Co. | 17,673 | 15,906 | 33,579 | |
| 10 | Functional Jewelry Corp. | 21,570 | 19,413 | 40,983 | |
| 11 | Guaranteed Quilt Supply | 13,090 | 11,781 | 24,871 | |
| 12 | Rare Sandal Traders | 6,373 | 5,736 | 12,109 | |
| 13 | Safe Hairpin Corp. | 29,896 | 26,907 | 56,803 | |
| 14 | Secure Yardstick Corp. | 20,539 | 18,485 | 39,024 | |
| 15 | Steadfast Patio Inc. | 10,528 | 9,475 | 20,003 | |
| 16 | Trustworthy Barometer Co. | 22,131 | 19,918 | 42,049 | |
| 17 | A354 Total | 157,769 | 141,993 | 299,762 | |
| 18 | ⊟ B713 | | | | |

**NOTE**

You cannot move the subtotals to the top of each group for the tabular form.

## ADDING BLANK ROWS

A new feature in Excel 2007 is that you can toggle on and off a blank row between groups in a pivot table. You do this in a drop-down below the Blank Rows icon in the Layout group of the Design ribbon. Adding a blank row between groups makes the presentation easier to read, as shown in Figure 11.11.

## TURNING OFF TOTALS

Sometimes a pivot table is just an intermediate result. Perhaps you need to use the totals presented by a pivot table as a new database. In that case, you really would want just one row for each unique combination of region, product, and customer. The subtotal rows between products and regions would actually get in the way. In such a case, you can use the Subtotals drop-down in the Layout group of the Design ribbon to turn off the subtotals. This produces a tight table of data, as shown in Figure 11.12. You can also turn off the grand totals by using the Grand Totals drop-down in the same group.

**Figure 11.11**
Blank rows between groups improve the readability of the data.

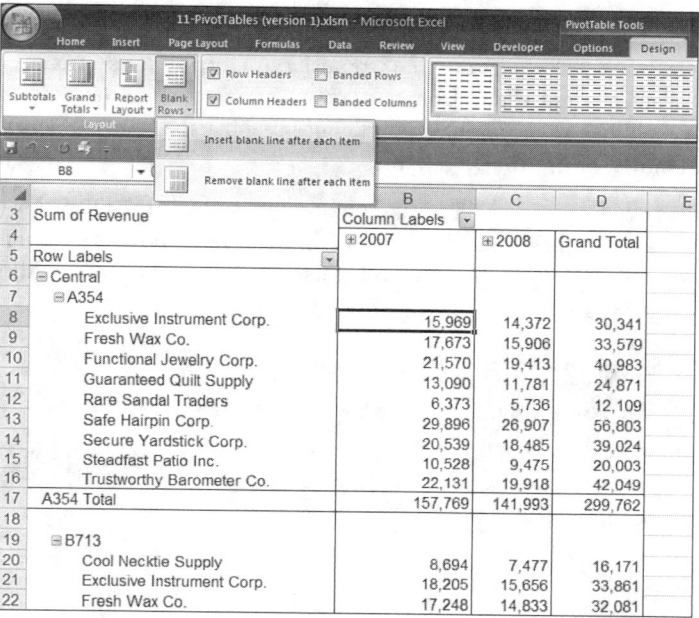

**Figure 11.12**
You can turn off the subtotals to produce a dataset with one row for each unique combination of the row fields.

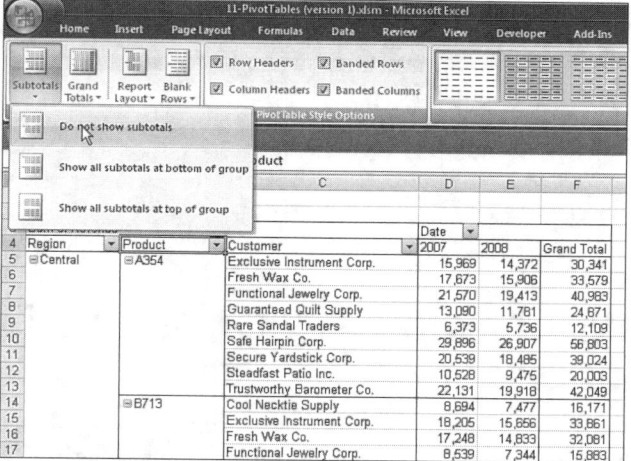

Despite years of requests, Microsoft still cannot provide a view of this data where the regions and products are repeated in the blank cells in Columns A and B. To solve that problem, see the section "Excel in Practice," later in this chapter.

11

## REMOVING A FIELD FROM A PIVOT TABLE

To remove a field from a pivot table, you use the Drop zones section of the PivotTable Field List box. You can drag a field from the layout section back to the field list. When you are above the field list, the mouse cursor changes to a black X. At this point, you release the field to remove it from the pivot table.

Another way to remove a field from a pivot table is to use the drop-down associated with the field in the Drop zones area of the PivotTable Field List box, as shown in Figure 11.13. This drop-down includes the option Remove Field, which removes the field from the drop zones but leaves it available in the Field List box for future use.

**Figure 11.13**
To remove a field, you can either drag it from this area or use the drop-down.

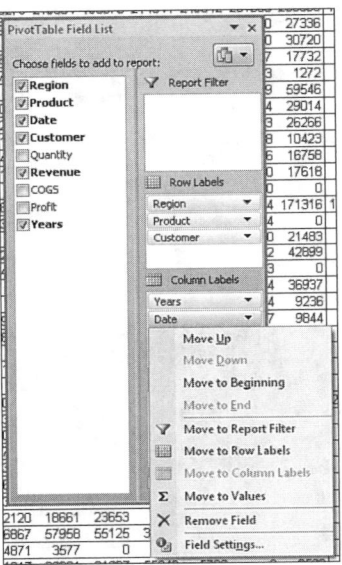

## SPECIAL CONSIDERATIONS WHEN ADDING DATA FIELDS TO THE VALUE SECTION

Pivot tables take on a strange quality when you attempt to report more than one value field combined with two or more label fields. Figure 11.14 shows a fairly nice-looking pivot table that summarizes revenue by product and year.

In real life, your manager would look at this table and ask if you could add a profit field to the analysis. This seems simple enough: You could drag the Product field from the field list and drop it in the Σ Values layout section of the PivotTable Field List box. When you do this, though, Excel produces the horrible-looking table shown in Figure 11.15. Revenue is reported in Columns B, D, and F. Profit is interspersed between the revenue numbers. The label Total Sum of Revenue is incredibly redundant.

**Figure 11.14**

Like most of the other examples in this chapter, this pivot table looks good because there is only one value field.

| Sum of Revenue | Years | | |
|---|---|---|---|
| Product | 2007 | 2008 | Grand Total |
| A354 | 582970 | 524675 | 1107645 |
| B713 | 626876 | 539112 | 1165988 |
| D157 | 630121 | 497095 | 1127216 |
| D173 | 493643 | 592372 | 1086015 |
| D598 | 799375 | 583540 | 1382915 |
| D776 | 747119 | 687349 | 1434468 |
| D850 | 768976 | 792049 | 1561025 |
| E852 | 706907 | 890705 | 1597612 |
| F474 | 707896 | 552159 | 1260055 |
| F495 | 695113 | 687147 | 1382260 |
| G101 | 0 | 167843 | 167843 |
| Grand Total | 6758996 | 6514046 | 13273042 |

**Figure 11.15**

Excel's default view with two value fields is horrible.

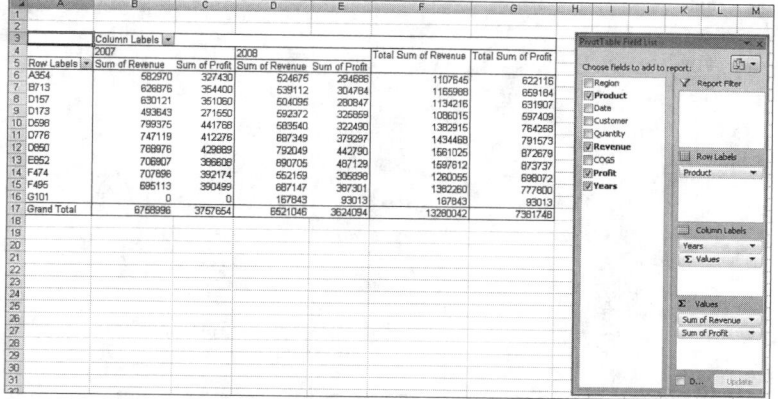

Notice in the Column Labels drop zone section of the PivotTable Field List box that a new button has been added. You can move this Σ Values button to one of three other locations in an attempt to make the table look better.

If you move the button to be the first column label, you rearrange the revenue columns to appear in Columns B, C, and F, as shown in Figure 11.16. This table still feels disjointed, with the Total Sum of Revenue column separated from the Sum of Revenue column.

If you move the Σ Values button to be the first row label, the resulting view (shown in Figure 11.17) actually looks fairly good, except that the Total Sum of Revenue row that should appear as Row 16 actually appears as Row 27.

**Figure 11.16**
Revenue and total revenue are still disjointed.

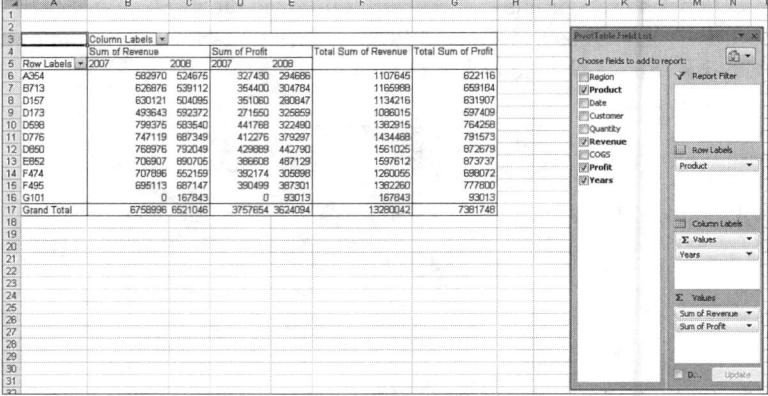

**Figure 11.17**
If Microsoft would move Row 27 to Row 16, this view would look good.

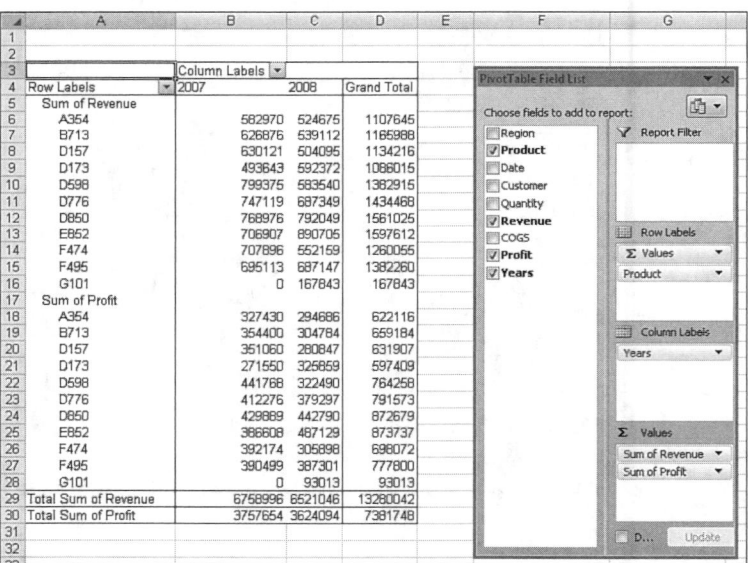

The final option is to move the Σ Values button so that it is the second row label. As you can see in Figure 11.18, this is a noisy view of the data.

**TIP FROM**

> The Excel team could solve this problem by adding a new option to the Totals & Filters tab of the PivotTable Options dialog. The option could be called Multiple Value Fields: Keep Grand Total with Each Value Field. There is even space for this option. If Microsoft would add this one option, pivot tables would reach a state of perfection.

**Figure 11.18**
Unfortunately, this is the final option. It is difficult to decide which of the four views is the least annoying.

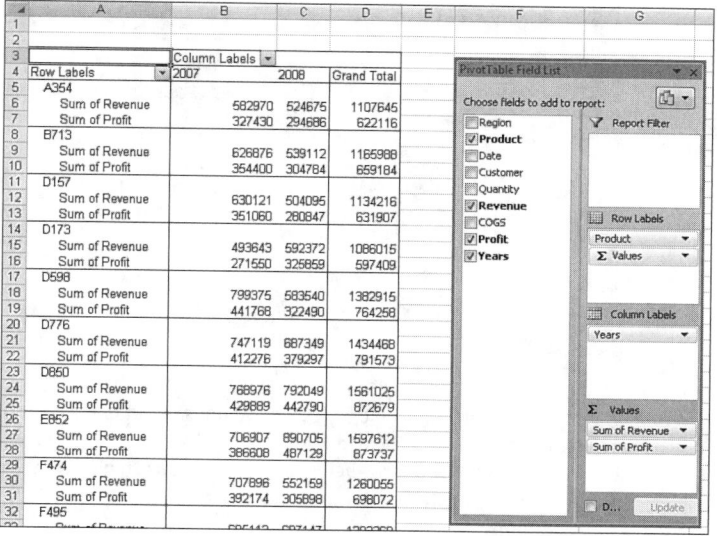

# FORMATTING A PIVOT TABLE

Excel offers many PivotTable Styles formatting galleries on the Design ribbon and many conditional formatting choices on the Home ribbon. You can safely use either of these options to format a pivot table.

If you instead try to format individual cells in a pivot table, you will experience frustration. After you rearrange the pivot table, your manual formatting will be lost or damaged.

## USING THE PIVOTTABLE STYLES

The PivotTable Styles group on the Design ribbon contains many built-in styles for a pivot table. These styles differ significantly from the built-in styles available in Excel 2003. Whereas the AutoFormat styles in Excel 2003 would actually change the shape of a pivot table, the formatting styles in Excel 2007 simply apply a style to the table, without changing the structure.

To start formatting a pivot table, you select a style from the PivotTable Styles group. Figure 11.19 shows a style with banded columns.

11

**Figure 11.19**
The first step in formatting should be to select a master style from the PivotTable Quick Styles group on the Styles ribbon.

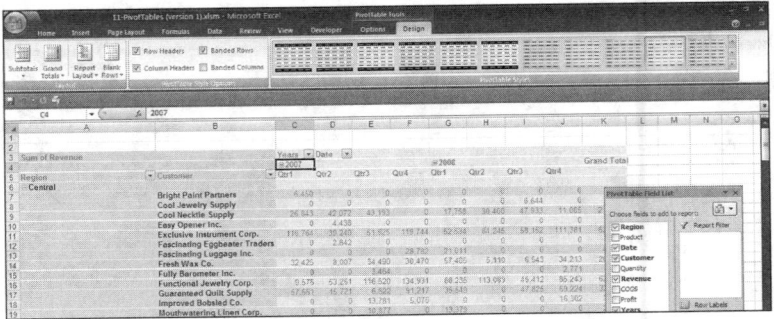

**CAUTION**

There are some PivotTable Styles that do not support banded rows or banded columns. If you find that clicking Banded Rows has no effect, try selecting a different style. Hint: If you turn on Banded Rows before selecting the PivotTable Styles dropdown, the gallery will show which styles allow for banded rows.

## MODIFYING THE PIVOTTABLE STYLES GROUP WITH THE PIVOTTABLE STYLE OPTIONS

After choosing a style, you can fine-tune the gallery options.

All the icons in the Layout group turn on and off various elements of the style chosen in the Styles group. In Figure 11.20, the banded columns have been turned off to remove the alternate column formatting. Row headers have also been turned off, so the bold font has been removed from Column A.

**Figure 11.20**
Turning off row headers only turns off the bold formatting applied to Column A. It does not affect the row headers.

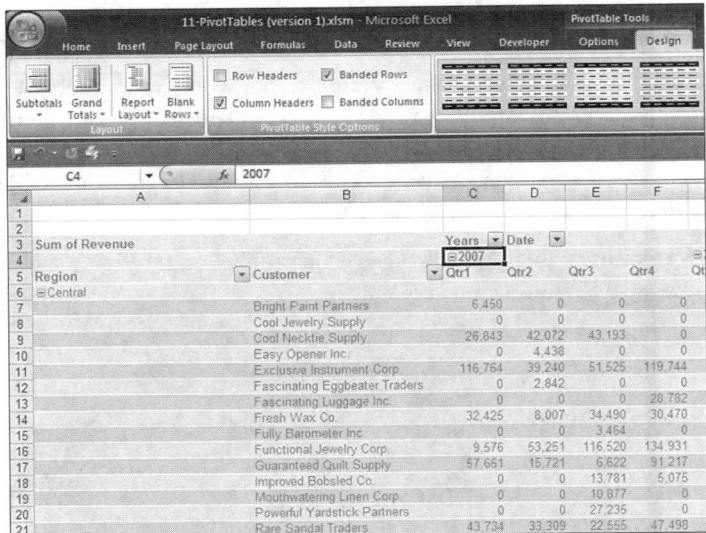

In Figure 11.21, the banded columns and row headers have been turned back on. Banded columns provide the lighter shading in Columns C, E, G, and I. Row headers make Column A appear in bold font. The column headers in this table have been turned off, which means the dark shading has been removed from Rows 3 through 5. Note that turning banded rows on or off has no effect because the selected style does not support banded rows.

**Figure 11.21**
The four icons in the PivotTable Style Options group turn on and off various elements of the built-in style.

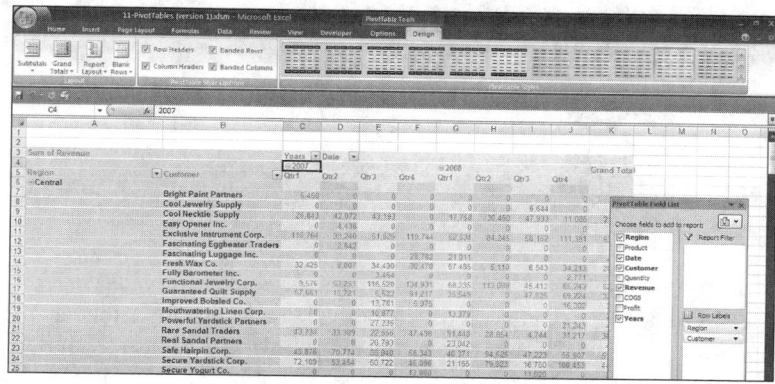

## MODIFYING THE PIVOTTABLE STYLES GROUP WITH THE THEMES ICONS

On the Page Layout ribbon, you can use the Themes group to further modify the style selected in the PivotTable Styles group. The style you selected in the PivotTable Styles group in the previous section features banded columns. By using the Themes drop-down or the Colors drop-down, you can change the color scheme applied to the table. This increases the visual appeal of the pivot table immensely.

**Figure 11.22**
You can change the look of a pivot table by applying a new theme or color to it.

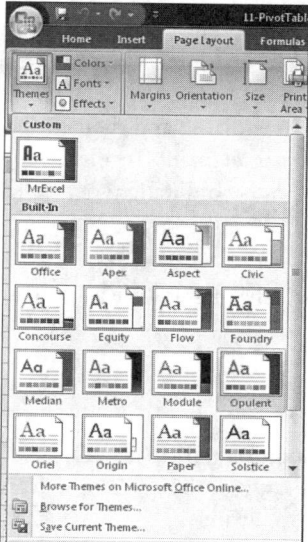

11

## MODIFYING THE PIVOTTABLE STYLES GROUP BY CUSTOMIZING A STYLE

You can create new styles, but it is usually easier to modify an existing style. To do this, in the PivotTable Styles group of the Design ribbon, you can right-click a style and choose Duplicate, as shown in Figure 11.23.

**Figure 11.23**
Rather than build a style from scratch, you can duplicate one that is similar.

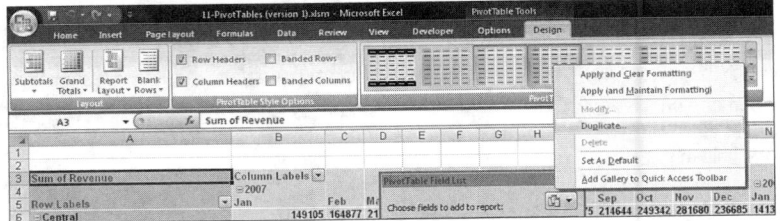

If you modify Table Style 3, Excel offers the new name Table Style 3 2. You can give the style a new descriptive name in the Modify Table Quick Style dialog. You can customize numerous elements. Without even touching the Format button, you can do some cool modifications. For example, you can use banded rows. In the Table Element list box, you choose First Row Stripe. A new setting called Stripe Size appears on the right side of the table. If you change the Stripe Size setting from 1 to 2, the color banding for the dark rows will comprise two rows. You can change Second Row Stripe so that it also has a stripe size of 2. The banded rows then use alternate stripes that are each two rows high. (Note that you have to click OK to see the change in your worksheet.) Figure 11.24 shows how the worksheet looks after you apply the setting and then redisplay the Modify Table Quick Style dialog.

After duplicating a style, the duplicated style will appear at the top of the PivotTable Styles gallery. Select the duplicated style in order to apply it to your pivot table.

After you specify a new style, it appears in the PivotTable Styles group in the Design ribbon. You can right-click the new style and choose Modify if you want to further refine the style. To modify a particular portion of a table, you can choose the element from the Table Element list box in the Modify Table Quick Style dialog and then click Format. You can modify the alignment, font, border, and fill for an element. In Figure 11.25, the First Header Cell setting is modified to have a 14-point bold italic typeface.

> **NOTE** Any changes applied to a pivot table style are available only in the current document.

## USING CONDITIONAL FORMATTING

Doing so is a little tricky, but you can get conditional formatting to work properly for a pivot table. Before using conditional formatting, you should choose from the Styles group of the Styles ribbon a group that has minimal formatting.

**Figure 11.24**
Stripe Size controls
how many rows or
columns are in each
color band.

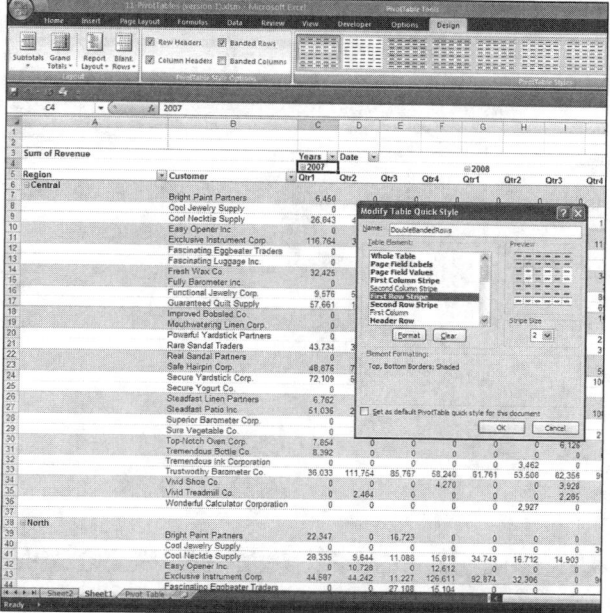

**Figure 11.25**
You can apply differ-
ent formatting to any
element of a pivot
table.

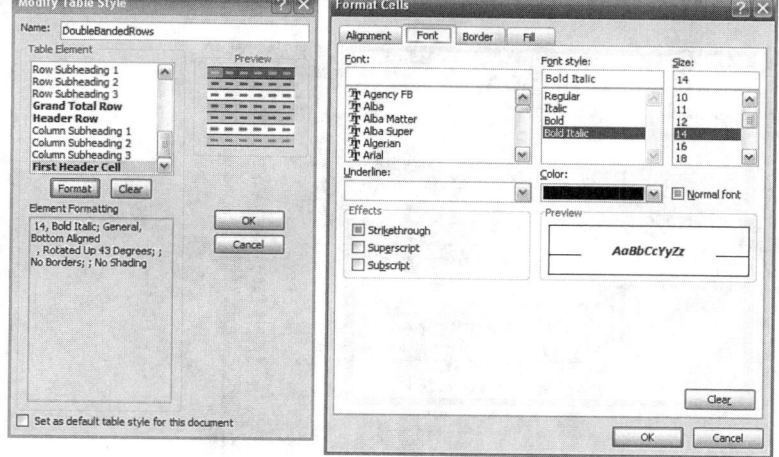

To try using conditional formatting, select Cells B5:C34, as shown in Figure 11.26. This
comprises the complete Sum of Revenue section, except for the grand totals. On the Home
ribbon, you choose the Conditional Formatting drop-down and then choose Data Bars. If
you choose one of the six styles shown, it automatically applies to just the 60 cells selected.
Instead, you want to select More Rules.

**Figure 11.26**
The key to successfully applying a conditional format to a pivot table is to select More Rules instead of a default style.

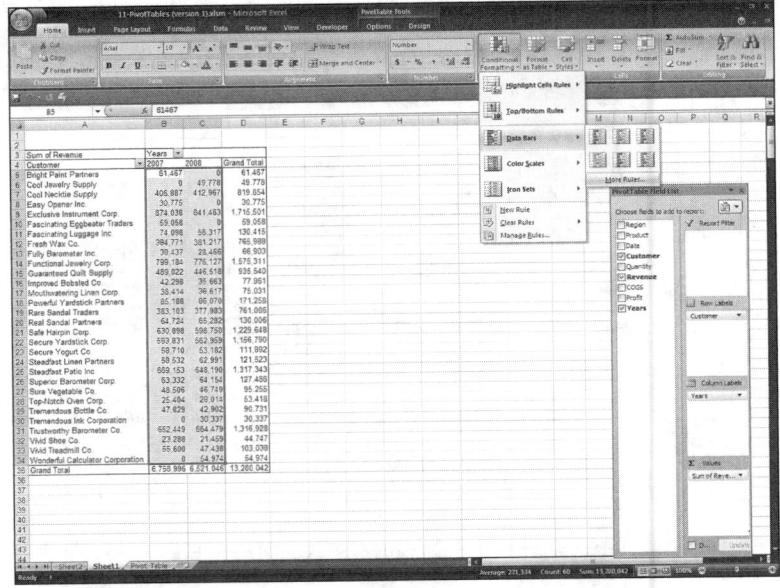

When you select More Rules, the New Formatting Rule dialog appears. You can see in Figure 11.27 that Excel was planning to apply the rule to the selected cells. This is the default.

**Figure 11.27**
Even though a pivot table is selected, Excel defaults to the selected cells.

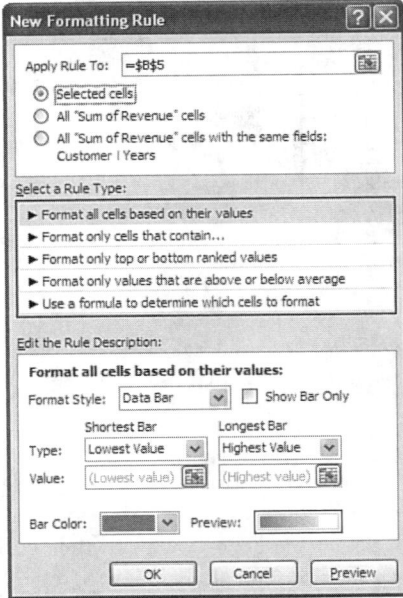

There are two additional options in the dialog. If you select the All "Sum of Revenue" Cells option button, Excel applies the formatting to the selected cells plus the grand total row and the grand total column. This will not give the right effect because the total row, with totals for 30 customers, will far and away get the largest bar. All the other customers will be relegated to short bars.

Instead, you want to choose the option button All "Sum of Revenue" Cells with the Same Fields: Customer | Years. The result is that the data bars are applied just to the interior of the pivot table, as shown in Figure 11.28.

**Figure 11.28**

If you limit the data bars to the customer rows of the Sum of Revenue section, the data bars scale intelligently.

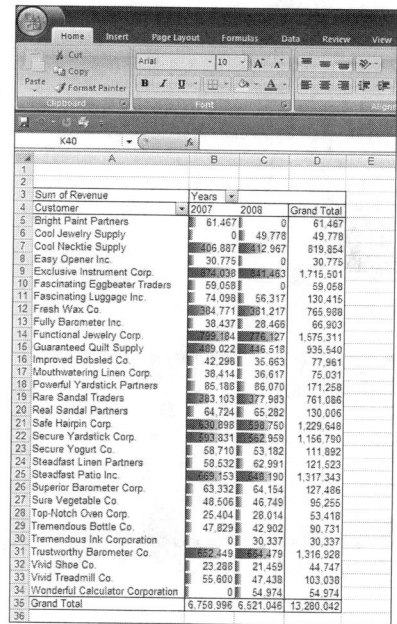

By following these steps, you can pivot any other single field into the Row Labels section of the layout and still maintain an intelligent data bar. Figure 11.29 shows a pivot table showing products. Figure 11.30 shows a pivot table showing regions. Figure 11.31 shows a pivot table showing quarters. In each case, the data bars scale appropriately.

**Figure 11.29**
The data bars work fine as the table is changed to show products.

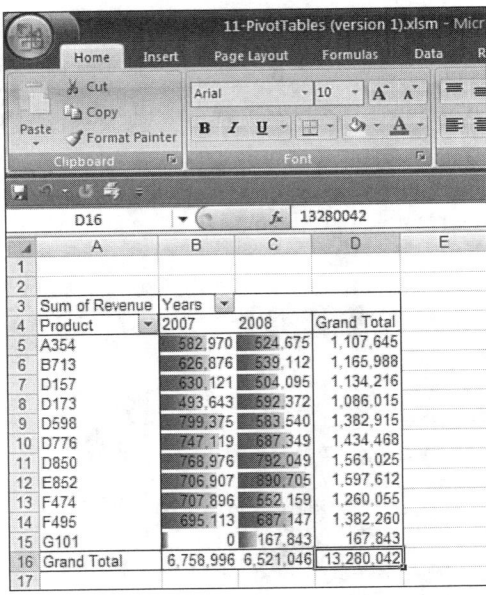

**Figure 11.30**
The data bars also work fine as the table is changed to show regions.

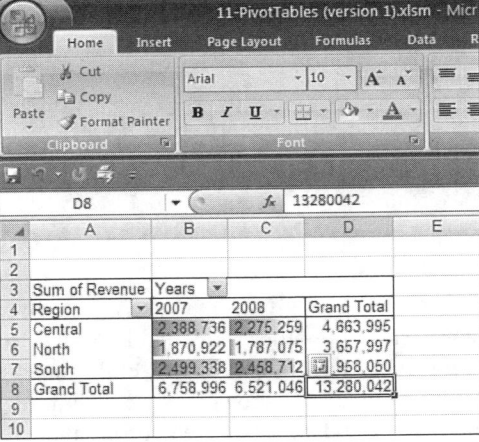

**Figure 11.31**
The data bars also work fine as the table is changed to show quarters.

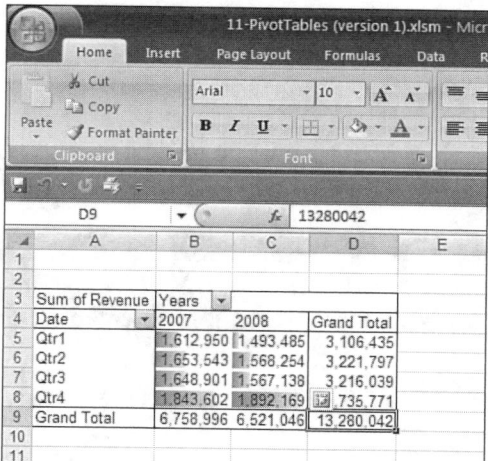

The data bars somewhat fail when you add two fields to the Row Labels section. In Figure 11.32, the subtotals in Rows 5, 17, and 29 overshadow the individual product totals in the other rows. This causes the data bars for the individual products to all look relatively similar, which dampens the impact.

**Figure 11.32**
The conditional formatting is not as effective when the Row Labels section has two fields.

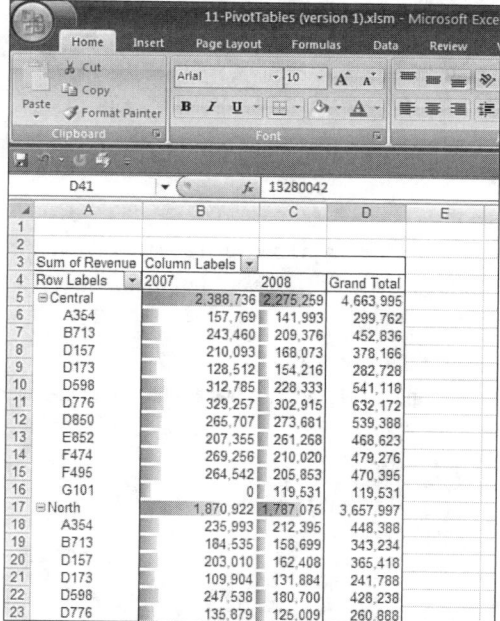

11

## Excel in Practice: Fixing the Blank Cell Dilemma

In this chapter you have built a pivot table to find the revenue for each unique combination of region, product, and customer. Say that you now need to produce a CSV (comma-separated values) file to be imported into another system.

Using the tools in Excel, you remove the grand totals and the subtotals. You also switched to a tabular layout. The result, as shown in Figure 11.33, is nearly perfect.

**Figure 11.33**
Pivot tables get you 90% of the way to the final goal.

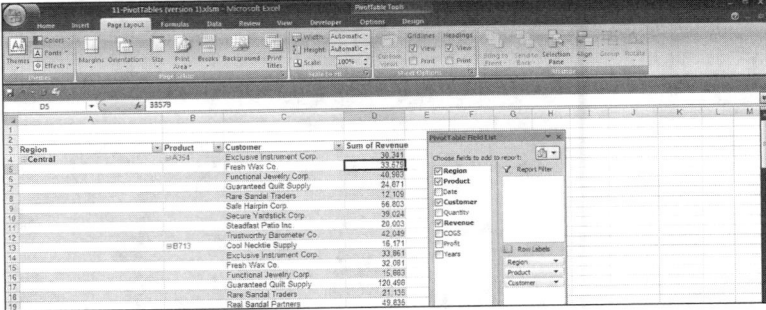

The problem with this pivot table is that Excel does not fill in the blank cells in Columns A and B. But every computer system in the world expects those cells to be filled in. Even Excel could not deal with this worksheet as the input for any data analysis tools.

To solve this problem, you follow these steps:

1. Create a new blank workbook.
2. Switch back to the original workbook.
3. Select the entire pivot table.
4. Press Ctrl+C to copy the pivot table.
5. Switch to the new workbook.
6. Use Home, Paste, Paste Values to paste the values to Cell A1.
7. Select all the cells in Columns A and B, starting in Row 3 and extending down to the end of the data.
8. Press F5 to display the Go To dialog.
9. Click the Special button in the Go To dialog.
10. Choose the Blanks selection in the Go to Special dialog.
11. Press the = key, the up-arrow key, and Ctrl+Enter. Each blank is filled with the value from above it.
12. Reselect the data in Columns A and B.
13. Press Ctrl+C to copy.
14. Choose Home, Paste, Paste Values to change the formulas to values.
15. Use File, Save As to save this workbook for another system.

CHAPTER **12**

# PIVOT TABLE DATA CRUNCHING FOR EXCEL 2007

## In this chapter

Pivot tables in Excel 2007 offer far more options than what have been discussed in the previous two chapters. This chapter will show you how to expand the possibilities of analyses available with pivot tables. This is a great sampling of the most common analyses you might want to perform. If you want to see every possible feature in a pivot table, check out the Pivot Table Data Crunching book that Mike Alexander and I wrote. It is available from the Que Business Solutions series.

# GROUPING DAILY DATES TO MONTHS AND YEARS

In Chapter 10, I encouraged you to go back to your source software and ask for a report of data at the detail level. This data will undoubtedly report data at the daily level instead of the monthly level.

People in manufacturing plants care about the productivity from every day. However, people in accounting tend to care about performance of each month.

Pivot tables make it incredibly easy to roll data up from daily dates to weekly, monthly, quarterly, or yearly analyses, depending on your requirements.

The best way to teach you this technique is to walk through a real example. Of course, in your data, fields might be slightly different. Let's assume, though, that you have some sort of field with data at the daily level.

The pivot table in Figure 12.1 has three fields in the Row Labels section, and it has the Date field in the Column Labels section. Because the original data on which this pivot table is based had information by day, the pivot table has 471 columns, which is not very useful.

NOTE

> Any prior book would have to contain a paragraph about the hazards of building this report with dates going across the columns since the 471 dates would overflow the 255 available columns. The fact that Excel can now accommodate 43 years of daily data across the 16,384 columns makes this a moot point.

**Figure 12.1**
Because the underlying transactional date had daily dates, a summary pivot table by date starts out showing daily dates.

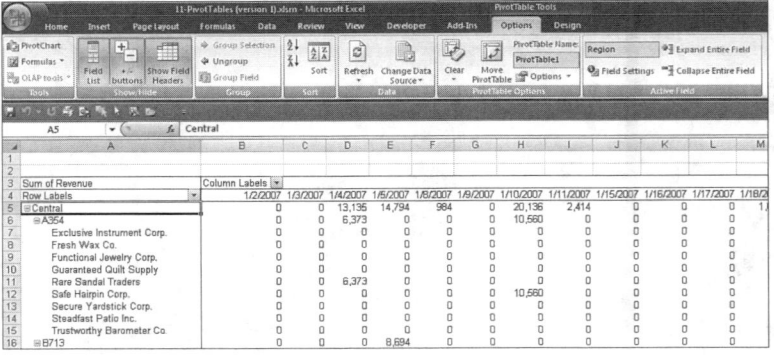

Notice in the Group section of the Options ribbon that Group Field is grayed out. Now look to the right, in the Active Field section. Currently, the active field is the Region field, probably because the cell pointer is currently on a Region field in Cell A5.

If you use the cell pointer to select a date in Cell B4, the Active Field section changes to show that Date is the active field. The Group Field icon becomes active. You can click the Group Field icon to display the Grouping dialog box, which is shown in Figure 12.2.

**Figure 12.2**
Choose to group by
Months and Years

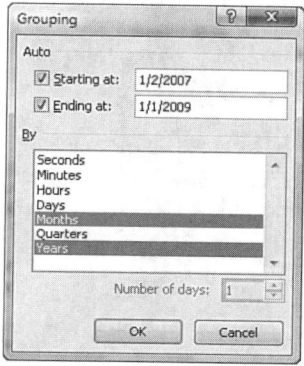

CAUTION

Initially, the Grouping dialog box offers to group by months. Selecting the Months setting causes Excel to group records from January 2007 and January 2008 into a single column called January. Although this is interesting for a special type of analysis called seasonality analysis, it is rarely what you want.

In the Grouping dialog, be sure to choose both Months and Years, as shown in Figure 12.2. You can also group by quarters.

After you select Months and Years, the daily dates along the top of the pivot table are replaced with months. In the PivotTable Field List box, there are now two fields in the Column Labels layout section: The Date field now contains your monthly data, and a new virtual field called Years is added to the list.

# SORTING AND FILTERING

The ability to filter data has improved dramatically in Excel 2007. Few people were able to locate the Top 10 AutoShow settings in previous versions of Excel, but they are now much easier to access—right from the PivotTable Field List box.

In case you never encountered the Top 10 AutoShow in previous versions of Excel, it would allow you to limit a report to show the top 15 customers or the bottom 5 products.

My general rule is that the higher the manager, the less they can deal with detailed data. The new Filtering features in Excel 2007 pivot tables will let you limit the report to just the top *n* records.

In Excel 2007, this feature is easier to access from the PivotTable Field List box. Being able to produce a report of the top *n* items makes pivot tables even more powerful.

The following examples walk through a sample dataset. In your dataset, you can easily extrapolate to achieve a similar result for any field.

Figure 12.3 shows a pivot table that lists revenue by customer for two years. There are 30 different customers in the list. Customers are listed down the row area, and the Years field goes across the column area. Revenue for the two years totals $13.3 million.

**Figure 12.3**
This pivot table showing revenue by customer is unfiltered and unsorted.

| Sum of Revenue | Years | | |
|---|---|---|---|
| Customer | 2007 | 2008 | Grand Total |
| Bright Paint Partners | $61,467 | $0 | $61,467 |
| Cool Jewelry Supply | $0 | $49,778 | $49,778 |
| Cool Necktie Supply | $406,887 | $412,967 | $819,854 |
| Easy Opener Inc. | $30,775 | $0 | $30,775 |
| Exclusive Instrument Corp. | $874,038 | $841,463 | $1,715,501 |
| Fascinating Eggbeater Traders | $59,058 | $0 | $59,058 |
| Fascinating Luggage Inc. | $74,098 | $56,317 | $130,415 |
| Fresh Wax Co. | $384,771 | $381,217 | $765,988 |
| Fully Barometer Inc. | $38,437 | $28,466 | $66,903 |
| Functional Jewelry Corp. | $799,184 | $776,127 | $1,575,311 |
| Guaranteed Quilt Supply | $489,022 | $446,518 | $935,540 |
| Improved Bobsled Co. | $42,298 | $35,663 | $77,961 |
| Mouthwatering Linen Corp. | $38,414 | $36,617 | $75,031 |
| Powerful Yardstick Partners | $85,188 | $86,070 | $171,258 |
| Rare Sandal Traders | $383,103 | $377,983 | $761,086 |
| Real Sandal Partners | $64,724 | $65,282 | $130,006 |
| Safe Hairpin Corp. | $630,898 | $598,750 | $1,229,648 |
| Secure Yardstick Corp. | $593,831 | $562,959 | $1,156,790 |
| Secure Yogurt Co. | $58,710 | $53,182 | $111,892 |
| Steadfast Linen Partners | $58,532 | $62,991 | $121,523 |
| Steadfast Patio Inc. | $669,153 | $648,190 | $1,317,343 |
| Superior Barometer Corp. | $63,332 | $64,154 | $127,486 |
| Sure Vegetable Co. | $48,506 | $46,749 | $95,255 |
| Top-Notch Oven Corp. | $25,404 | $28,014 | $53,418 |
| Tremendous Bottle Co. | $47,829 | $42,902 | $90,731 |
| Tremendous Ink Corporation | $0 | $30,337 | $30,337 |
| Trustworthy Barometer Corp. | $652,449 | $664,479 | $1,316,928 |
| Vivid Shoe Co. | $23,288 | $21,459 | $44,747 |
| Vivid Treadmill Co. | $55,600 | $47,438 | $103,038 |
| Wonderful Calculator Corporation | $0 | $54,974 | $54,974 |
| Grand Total | $6,758,996 | $6,521,046 | $13,280,042 |

You can access Excel's powerful filtering and sorting features for any field in the field list portion of the PivotTable Field List box. In Figure 12.4, Customer appears twice in the PivotTable Field List box. The Customer field visible in the Row Labels layout section already has a drop-down visible. This is not the field you want to use. You therefore need to hover over the Customer field that appears in the top portion of Figure 12.4. When you hover over any field in the field list, a drop-down appears near the field, as shown in Figure 12.4.

**NOTE**

A drop-down in Cell A4 of Figure 12.3 offers functionality for the Customer field that is similar to that of the drop-down in Figure 12.4. However, similar drop-downs are not available for other fields in the pivot table. Filters for all fields are readily available in the field list.

## LIMITING A REPORT TO THE TOP SEVEN CUSTOMERS

Sales managers often like to see reports of the top customers. Pivot tables enable you to easily create such reports.

**Figure 12.4**
You hover over any field in the field list and then choose the drop-down arrow that appears.

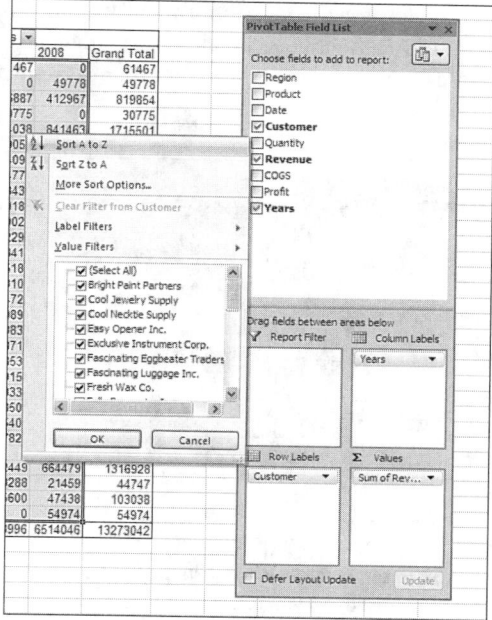

To create a report of a company's top customers, you hover over the Customer field in the field list portion of the PivotTable Field List box. When a drop-down appears near the list, you should choose it. You want to filter the list based on a value in the table, so you should choose the Value Filters selection. As shown in Figure 12.5, the final choice in the Value Filters is Top 10. You should choose this option.

**Figure 12.5**
To find the customers with top revenue, you can filter on customer.

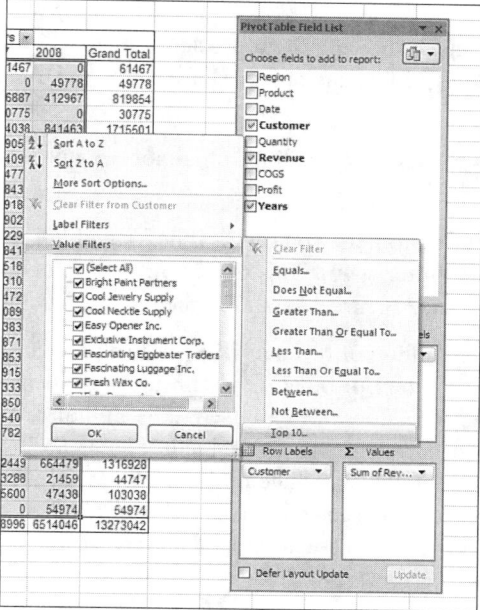

Excel displays the Top 10 Filter dialog for the Customer field. Initially, this dialog offers to display the top 10 items, by sum of revenue. You can change the dialog to show the top or bottom customers, and you can change it to display any number of items. Figure 12.6 shows a report of the top seven customers.

**Figure 12.6**
A company's top seven customers, determined using the Top 10 Filter on the Customer field.

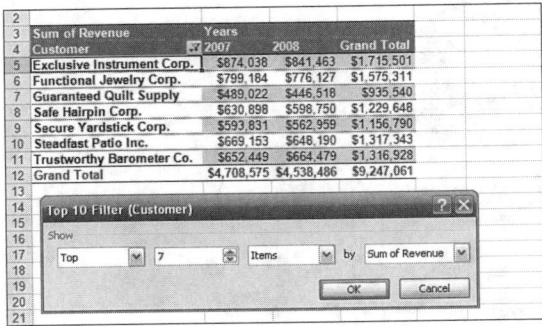

You have to click OK to see the filter applied. In the figures in this chapter, I have redisplayed the Top 10 Filter dialog so you can see the selections.

## SHOWING THE BOTTOM 25% OF CUSTOMERS

In the previous example, you asked for a specific number of customers or products or items. Although this feature is often called the top 10 feature, it can be used to show either the top or bottom of the dataset. It can be used to show $n$ items, or the items that make up $n$% of the dataset.

If your company has 12 customers, showing the top 10 customers will not be that interesting. Futher, if your company has 12,000 customers, showing the top 10 might miss a lot of customers.

The following example walks through how to limit the report to a percentage of the customers.

To show the bottom quarter of customers, you can use the Value filter in the Customer drop-down to select the Top 10 filter again. This time, however, you choose Bottom 25 Percent based on Sum of Revenue. Figure 12.7 shows the result of doing this.

The original dataset had $13.3 million of revenue. Twenty-five percent of $13.3 million is $3.3 million. Curiously, applying the Bottom 25 Percent filter results in 23 customers and $4 million of revenue. This initially does not make sense: $4 million is 30% of the revenue coming from 77% of your customers. The largest value in Figure 12.7 is Cool Necktie Supply, at $819,000. If Excel would have excluded this customer, the report would have contained only $3.2 million of revenue. Because that is just short of 25%, Excel includes the next smallest customer to make sure you see at least 25% of the revenue.

**Figure 12.7**
These 23 customers comprise the bottom 25% of a company's revenue.

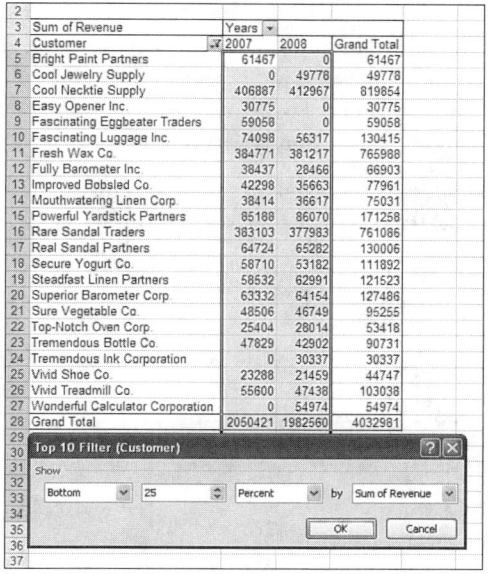

## SHOWING THE TOP OR BOTTOM CUSTOMERS WHO MAKE UP A SPECIFIC DOLLAR AMOUNT

The Top 10 Filter dialog offers a new and interesting third option. Instead of asking for items or a percentage, you can ask for a particular sum, as shown in Figure 12.8.

**Figure 12.8**
The Sum function is new in the Top 10 Filter dialog.

| Sum of Revenue | Years | | |
|---|---|---|---|
| Customer | 2007 | 2008 | Grand Total |
| Bright Paint Partners | 61467 | 0 | 61467 |
| Cool Jewelry Supply | 0 | 49778 | 49778 |
| Cool Necktie Supply | 406887 | 412967 | 819854 |
| Easy Opener Inc. | 30775 | 0 | 30775 |
| Fascinating Eggbeater Traders | 59058 | 0 | 59058 |
| Fascinating Luggage Inc. | 74098 | 56317 | 130415 |
| Fresh Wax Co. | 384771 | 381217 | 765988 |
| Fully Barometer Inc. | 38437 | 28466 | 66903 |
| Improved Bobsled Co. | 42298 | 35663 | 77961 |
| Mouthwatering Linen Corp. | 38414 | 36617 | 75031 |
| Powerful Yardstick Partners | 85188 | 86070 | 171258 |
| Rare Sandal Traders | 383103 | 377983 | 761086 |
| Real Sandal Partners | 64724 | 65282 | 130006 |
| Secure Yogurt Co. | 58710 | 53182 | 111892 |
| Steadfast Linen Partners | 58532 | 62991 | 121523 |
| Superior Barometer Corp. | 63332 | 64154 | 127486 |
| Sure Vegetable Co. | 48506 | 46749 | 95255 |
| Top-Notch Oven Corp. | 25404 | 28014 | 53418 |
| Tremendous Bottle Co. | 47829 | 42902 | 90731 |
| Tremendous Ink Corporation | 0 | 30337 | 30337 |
| Vivid Shoe Co. | 23288 | 21459 | 44747 |
| Vivid Treadmill Co. | 55600 | 47438 | 103038 |
| Wonderful Calculator Corporation | 0 | 54974 | 54974 |
| Grand Total | 2050421 | 1982560 | 4032981 |

Top 10 Filter (Customer) — Show: Bottom 30 Sum by Sum of Revenue — Items/Percent/Sum — OK Cancel

12

You can ask to see the customers who make up the bottom $1.5 million. However, the spin button paradigm clearly does not work here. It would literally take 1,499,989 clicks on the up spin button. You could attempt to use the spin button in Figure 12.8 to dial up to 1,500,000, but it would take forever. When you want to use the Sum function, you can actually click into the second field in the dialog and type a number such as 1500000.

The result shown in Figure 12.9 includes enough customers so that the total exceeds $1.5 million. Fascinating Luggage in Row 9 pushes the total over $1.5 million, to end at $1,514,795.

**Figure 12.9**
The third option in the Top 10 Filter dialog locates the customers who account for a specific amount of revenue.

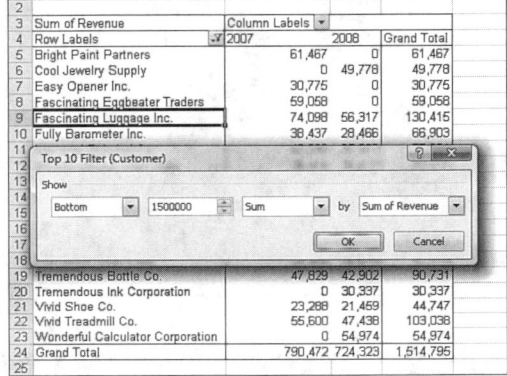

## SORTING A FIELD

In Figures 12.3 through 12.9, the filtered pivot table report is presented in alphabetical order. In each case, the report would be more interesting if it were presented sorted by revenue instead of by customer name.

The Customer drop-down offers choices to sort a field in ascending or descending order, as shown in Figure 12.10. However, you can find more powerful options by selecting More Sort Options from this drop-down.

When you choose More Sort Options from the Customer drop-down, the Sort dialog appears. This dialog initially offers to sort in ascending order, based on customer. If you choose Descending and then use the drop-down, you can choose to sort the report based on sum of revenue. This produces the report shown in Figure 12.11.

Take a look at the report in Figure 12.11. Note that it is sorted based on grand total revenue. What if you wanted to sort the report based on 2007 revenue? Excel 2007 now gives you the capability to do this. After choosing More Sort Options, you click the More Options button in the Sort dialog to open the More Sort Options dialog.

As shown in Figure 12.12, the More Sort Options dialog includes a section to sort by the grand total. If you change this option to Sort by Values in Selected Row, you can then specify that the customer sort should be based on either Column B or Column C. In Figure 12.12, Values in Selected Row is set to $B$5 to indicate that the report should be sorted by 2007 revenue. The left side of Figure 12.12 shows the result of this sort.

**Figure 12.10**
The Customer drop-down shows choices to sort alphabetically, but the real power is behind the More Sort Options choice.

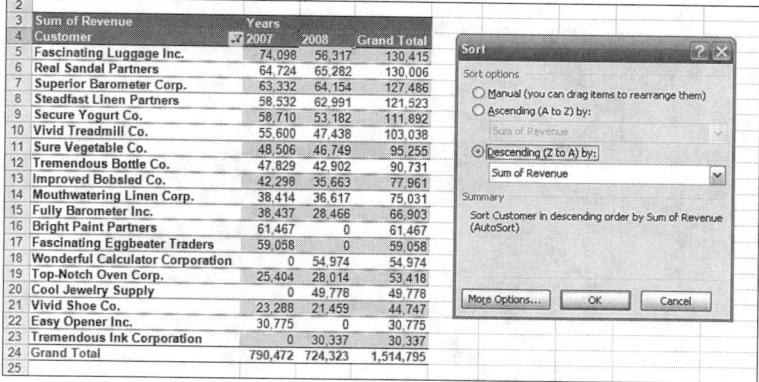

**Figure 12.11**
To create a report sorted from high to low by revenue, choose to sort the customer field based on sum of revenue.

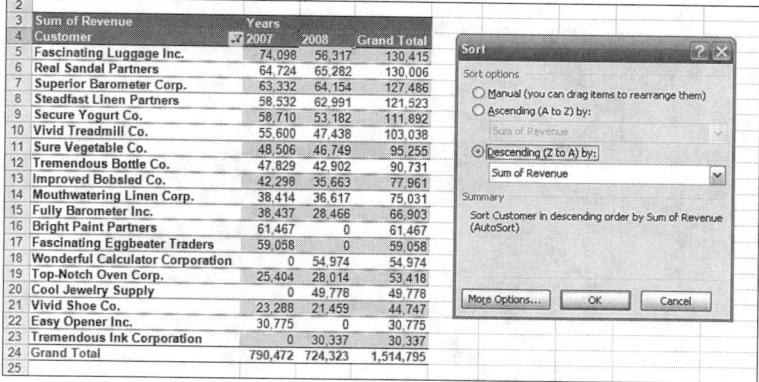

**Figure 12.12**
Perhaps this dialog should be called Even More Sort Options or Double Super Secret Sort Options.

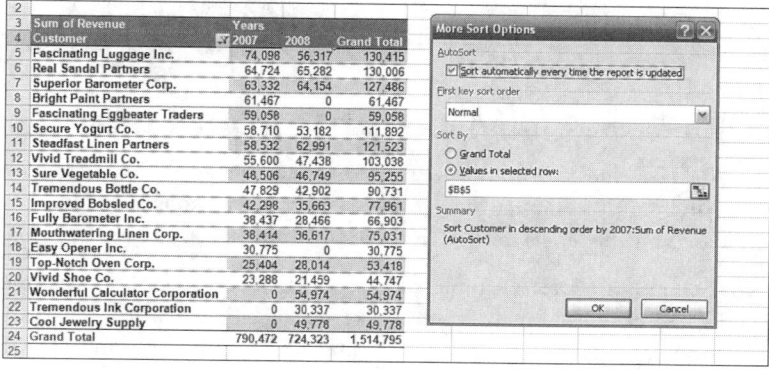

12

## WHY NOT SORT WITH THE DATA RIBBON?

You might be wondering why you should go to the hassle of using the Sort and More Sort Options dialogs. Wouldn't it be easier to select Cell B5 and use the Sort Descending button on the Data ribbon? Yes. It would be easier to sort by clicking this button for this one view of the pivot table. However, as you continue to pivot the table into other configurations, Excel does not remember that you always want the data sorted into this particular sort. If you use the sort options in the PivotTable Field List box, you are telling Excel to always sort this pivot table in a certain way. Any sort property you set here will remain in effect as you add and remove fields.

Figure 12.13 shows the same table from Figure 12.12, with the Customer filter removed. Because the report is sorted based on the Customer field, Excel continues to sort the report in descending revenue order from 2007.

**Figure 12.13**

This interesting view makes you wonder why you lost Bright Paint as a customer in 2008.

| Sum of Revenue | Years | | |
|---|---|---|---|
| Customer | 2007 | 2008 | Grand Total |
| Exclusive Instrument Corp. | 874,038 | 841,463 | 1,715,501 |
| Functional Jewelry Corp. | 799,184 | 776,127 | 1,575,311 |
| Steadfast Patio Inc. | 669,153 | 648,190 | 1,317,343 |
| Trustworthy Barometer Co. | 652,449 | 664,479 | 1,316,928 |
| Safe Hairpin Corp. | 630,898 | 598,750 | 1,229,648 |
| Secure Yardstick Corp. | 593,831 | 562,959 | 1,156,790 |
| Guaranteed Quilt Supply | 489,022 | 446,518 | 935,540 |
| Cool Necktie Supply | 406,887 | 412,967 | 819,854 |
| Fresh Wax Co. | 384,771 | 381,217 | 765,988 |
| Rare Sandal Traders | 383,103 | 377,983 | 761,086 |
| Powerful Yardstick Partners | 85,188 | 86,070 | 171,258 |
| Fascinating Luggage Inc. | 74,098 | 56,317 | 130,415 |
| Real Sandal Partners | 64,724 | 65,282 | 130,006 |
| Superior Barometer Corp. | 63,332 | 64,154 | 127,486 |
| Bright Paint Partners | 61,467 | 0 | 61,467 |
| Fascinating Eggbeater Traders | 59,058 | 0 | 59,058 |
| Secure Yogurt Co. | 58,710 | 53,182 | 111,892 |
| Steadfast Linen Partners | 58,532 | 62,991 | 121,523 |
| Vivid Treadmill Co. | 55,600 | 47,438 | 103,038 |
| Sure Vegetable Co. | 48,506 | 46,749 | 95,255 |
| Tremendous Bottle Co. | 47,829 | 42,902 | 90,731 |
| Improved Bobsled Co. | 42,298 | 35,663 | 77,961 |
| Fully Barometer Inc. | 38,437 | 28,466 | 66,903 |
| Mouthwatering Linen Corp. | 38,414 | 36,617 | 75,031 |
| Easy Opener Inc. | 30,775 | 0 | 30,775 |
| Top-Notch Oven Corp. | 25,404 | 28,014 | 53,418 |
| Vivid Shoe Co. | 23,288 | 21,459 | 44,747 |
| Wonderful Calculator Corporation | 0 | 54,974 | 54,974 |
| Tremendous Ink Corporation | 0 | 30,337 | 30,337 |
| Cool Jewelry Supply | 0 | 49,778 | 49,778 |
| Grand Total | 6,758,996 | 6,521,046 | 13,280,042 |

# EXPLORING EVEN MORE FILTERING OPTIONS

The Top 10 Value filter has been around for years. Excel 2007 introduces all sorts of interesting filters. For example, Figure 12.14 shows the options available to filter the Customer field based on the labels in the Customer column.

If your team is assigned customers alphabetically, you can ask for just the customers between A and E. You can ask for just customers with a particular word in their name. You can ask for customers that end in *Inc*. You can filter based on literally anything. Figure 12.15 shows the Label Filter dialog, where you can select numerous filters.

**Figure 12.14**
This list shows the ways to filter the Customer field based on the labels in the customer column.

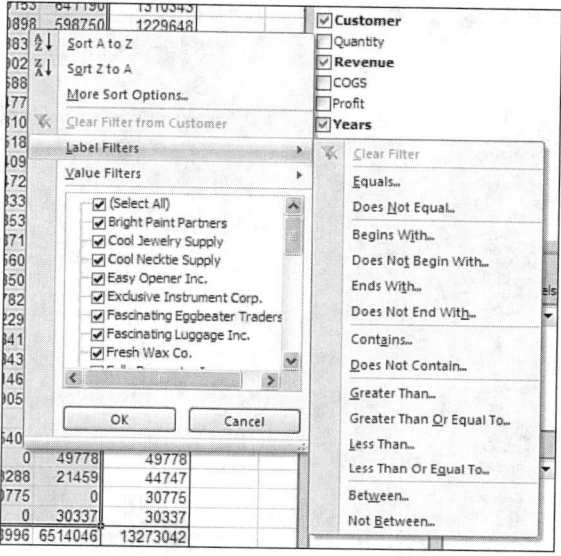

**Figure 12.15**
One of the myriad label filters available.

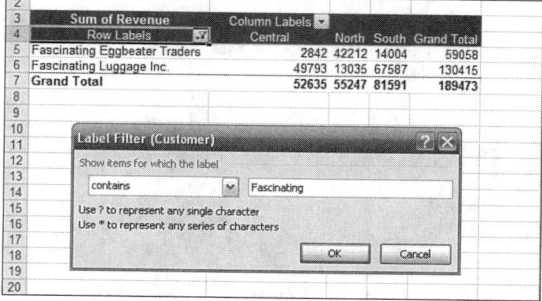

## FILTERING USING CHECK BOXES

The Customer drop-down includes a list of all the customers in the database. If you needed to exclude a few specific customers, you could simply uncheck their boxes in the filter list, as shown in Figure 12.16.

Because it is easier to select 3 customers than to unselect 27, if you need to remove most of the items from the list of customers, you can follow these steps:

1. Choose Select All to reselect all customers.
2. Choose Select All to uncheck all customers.
3. Select the particular customers you want to view.

**Figure 12.16**
Based on Figure 12.14, you know that three customers had no revenue in 2008. The filter shown here removes those three customers from the analysis.

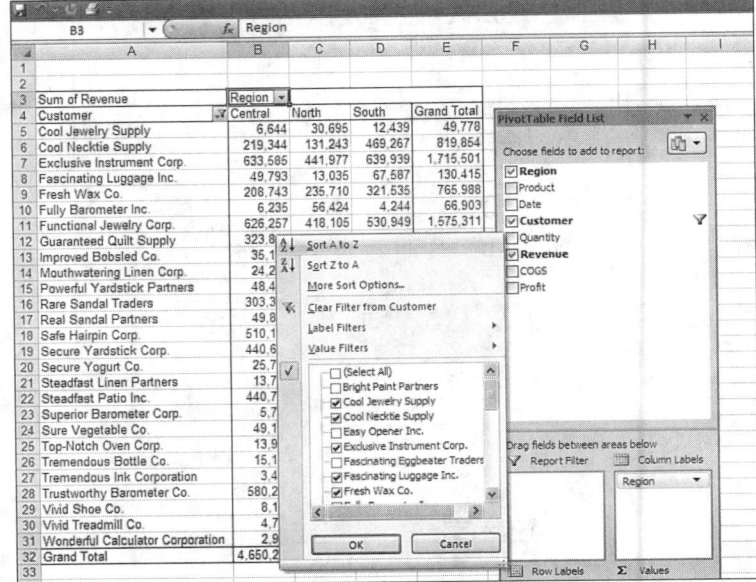

The results are shown in Figure 12.17.

**Figure 12.17**
You can turn Select All on and then off to unselect all customers.

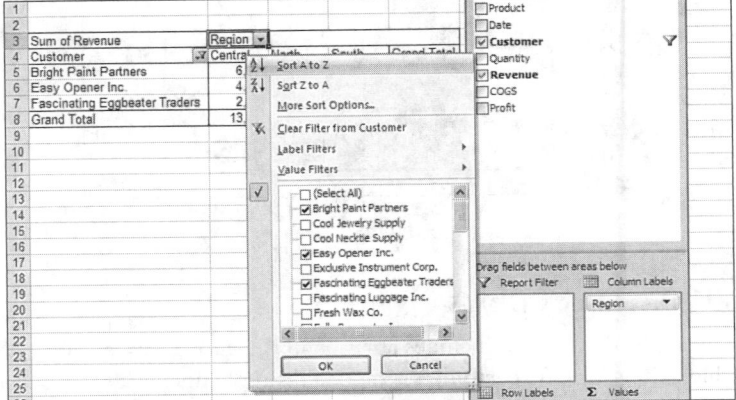

## USING DATE FILTERS

It is possible to sort by fields that are not currently displayed in a pivot table. Figure 12.18 shows a variety of date filters that are available for the Date field. In addition to the standard filters, such as This Year, Next Year, and Last Year, the report offers powerful filters such as Year to Date.

As an example of using a date filter, Figure 12.19 shows all dates in the period Quarter 4.

**Figure 12.18**
Excel offers a number of canned date filters. Users of QuickBooks will recognize this list.

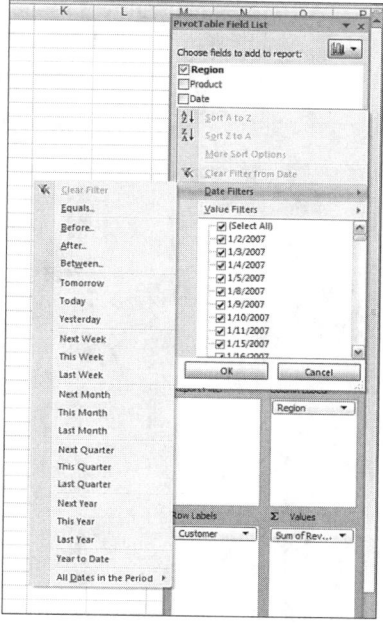

**Figure 12.19**
All dates in Quarter 4.

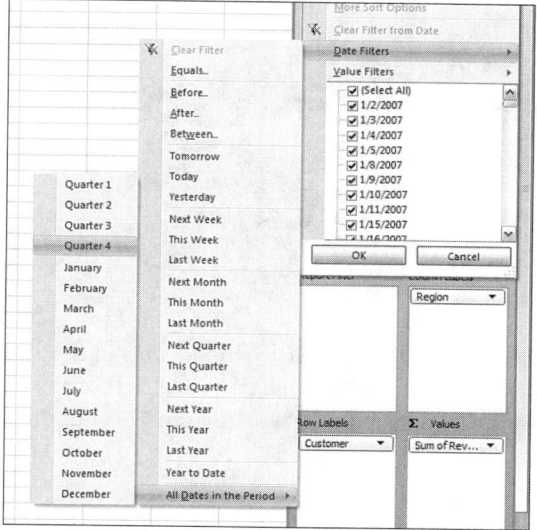

## FILTERING BY USING THE REPORT FILTER

Those who are familiar with pivot tables in previous versions of Excel know the report filter as the Page Field area of the layout. Although the new field filtering tools described in the preceding sections offer far more powerful filtering, you can use the report filter drop zone to add filter cells to a pivot table in order to do basic ad hoc analysis.

To add a filter dropdown to the top of the pivot table, you drag the Product field to the Report Filter section of the PivotTable Field List box, as shown in Figure 12.20. This adds a new heading called Product in Cell A1. Cell A2 then contains a drop-down that is initially set to (All).

**Figure 12.20**
The Product field is added as a report filter.

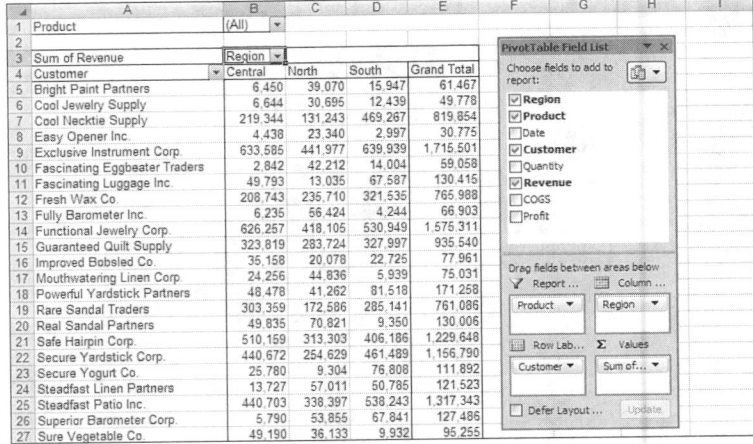

Next, from the drop-down in Cell A2, you need to select a product from the list. The pivot table then redraws, showing only totals for that product (see Figure 12.21). This is a great report to give to a marketing manager for product G101.

**Figure 12.21**
A report for a single product.

| Product | G101 | | | |
|---|---|---|---|---|
| Sum of Revenue | Region | | | |
| Customer | Central | North | South | Grand Total |
| Cool Necktie Supply | 0 | 0 | 18,385 | 18,385 |
| Exclusive Instrument Corp. | 37,085 | 0 | 0 | 37,085 |
| Functional Jewelry Corp. | 0 | 5,721 | 0 | 5,721 |
| Improved Bobsled Co. | 6,242 | 0 | 0 | 6,242 |
| Rare Sandal Traders | 0 | 0 | 9,512 | 9,512 |
| Safe Hairpin Corp. | 23,423 | 0 | 0 | 23,423 |
| Secure Yardstick Corp. | 20,484 | 0 | 0 | 20,484 |
| Steadfast Linen Partners | 0 | 7,672 | 0 | 7,672 |
| Steadfast Patio Inc. | 32,297 | 0 | 0 | 32,297 |
| Vivid Shoe Co. | 0 | 0 | 7,022 | 7,022 |
| Grand Total | 119,531 | 13,393 | 34,919 | 167,843 |

Excel 2007 now gives you the ability to choose multiple items in the report filter. The Product drop-down contains the Select Multiple Items check box. If you choose this option, each product in the list is prefixed by a check box. You can select multiple items for the filter, as shown in Figure 12.22.

**Figure 12.22**
You can now select multiple items from the filter drop-down.

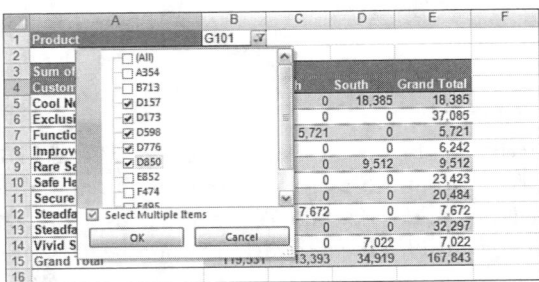

**CAUTION**

When you select multiple items from the report filter, Cell B1 no longer lists the products. Instead, it takes on the not-so-useful heading (Multiple Items).

## LOOPING THROUGH EACH VALUE IN A REPORT FILTER

With the report filter, it is easy to print a report for one specific product or region or any field.

After you print a report for the manager interested in that one specific item, word will spread, and all the other managers will want the similar report. Selecting each value one at a time can get tedious. Creating a tiny Excel VBA macro can simplify the process. The following macro will print the pivot table for each value found in the product report filter:

```
Sub PrintAll()
    Dim Pi as PivotItem
    With ActiveSheet.PivotTables(1)
    For Each Pi In .PivotFields("Product").PivotItems
        .PivotFields("Product").CurrentPage = Pi.Value
        ActiveSheet.PrintOut
    Next Pi
    End With
End Sub
```

For more information on macros, see Chapter 36, "Automating Repetitive Functions Using VBA Macros."

## USING SHOW PAGES TO REPLICATE A PIVOT TABLE

While this previous macro will print many versions of one pivot table, there is an alternate solution to the problem. This technique actually makes many copies of the pivot table, with a different Report Filter value in each copy. If your pivot table contains at least one Report Filter field, select the Options dropdown from the Options ribbon. Choose Show Pages from the dropdown menu. Confirm which field should be used. Excel will add worksheets to your workbook. Each worksheet will contain the original pivot table, with a different value chosen for the selected filter field.

## BUILDING THE ULTIMATE AD HOC REPORTING TOOL

The report filter is a great ad hoc answer tool. You could, in theory, give a pivot table with multiple report filters to your VP and allow him to answer many questions that might arise. This type of report allows for ad-hoc querying of the underlying data.

To build an ad-hoc query report, you move all your label fields to the report filter area. You also move all the value fields to the Σ Values area, as shown in Figure 12.23.

**Figure 12.23**
An ad hoc reporting tool.

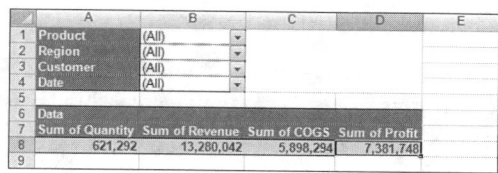

If someone calls with a question, such as these, you can quickly find the answer by using the various drop-downs:

- How much did we sell in the north region? (Figure 12.24 shows how to answer this question.)
- How much did the Fresh Wax customer buy? (Figure 12.25 shows how to answer this question.)
- How many of product A354 did the south region sell in January 2007? (Figure 12.26 shows how to answer this question.)

**Figure 12.24**
North region sales.

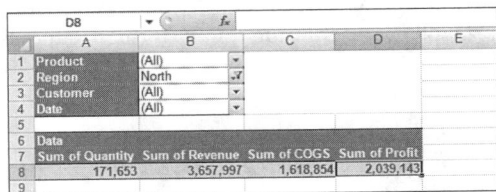

**Figure 12.25**
Sales to Fresh Wax.

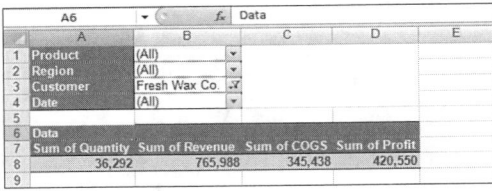

**Figure 12.26**
Sales of A354 in the south region.

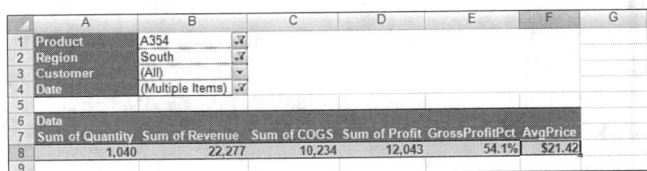

## USING A FORMULA TO ADD A FIELD TO A PIVOT TABLE

In the examples shown in the preceding sections, the pivot table shows all the value fields from the original dataset. In some cases, however, you might want to add new fields, such as Average Price or Gross Profit Percent. You can add new fields by using the Calculated Field tool.

Select PivotTable Tools, Options, Tools, Formulas, Calculated Field.... This will display the Insert Calculated Field dialog, as shown in Figure 12.27.

To add a field to the pivot table, you follow these steps:

1. In the Insert Calculated Field dialog, first type a name for the field. The field name should not contain spaces. In this particular example, a name such as **GPPct** (for Gross Profit Percent) would work.

**Figure 12.27**
You use this dialog to define a calculated field.

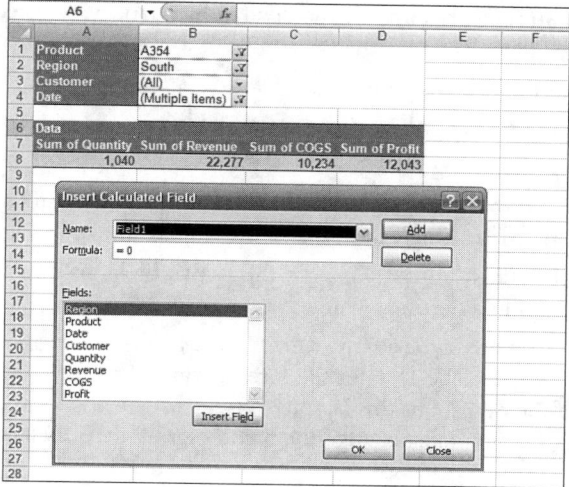

2. Build your formula using the field names in the Fields listbox and the Insert Field button. In this example, the formula for determining gross profit percent is profit divided by revenue, so click Profit in the Fields list and then click Insert Field.

3. Type a slash (/) to indicate division.

4. Click Revenue in the Fields list and then click Insert Field. The dialog now looks as shown in Figure 12.28.

**Figure 12.28**
Defining a Gross Profit Percent calculated field.

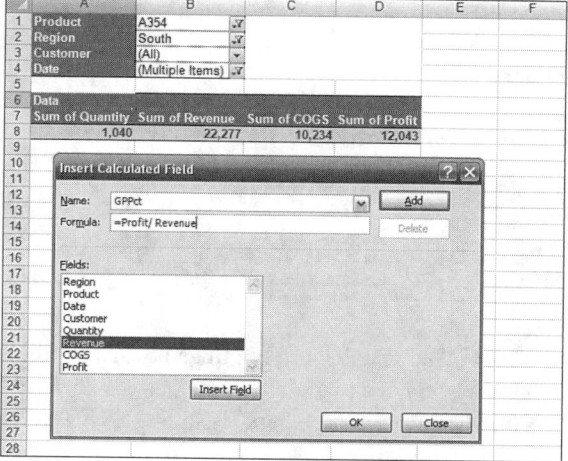

5. Click the Add button to accept the GPPct field.

6. You can define additional fields as needed. For example, enter **AveragePrice** in the Name text box to add another field.

7. The formula for average price is revenue divided by quantity, so select the Revenue field and then click Insert Field.

8. Type a slash (/) to indicate division.

9. Select the Quantity field and then click Insert Field.

10. Click OK to close the dialog.

11. The fields are added to the pivot table as Sum of GPPct and Sum of AveragePrice. Both fields have numeric formatting that is inappropriate, as shown in Figure 12.29.

12. Select Sum of GPPct in Cell E7. Then, in the Active Field group, choose Field Settings to display the Data Field Settings dialog for the field.

13. In the Custom Name box, type a new name for the field. The current name of Sum of GPPct is not correct. Excel calculates the formula on the totals, so it is really a Gross Profit Percent of the Sums, but this is not a very good name. You might be tempted to use GPPct again, but you must change the name slightly here, as shown in Figure 12.30.

**Figure 12.29**
The calculations are correct, but the numeric formatting is wrong.

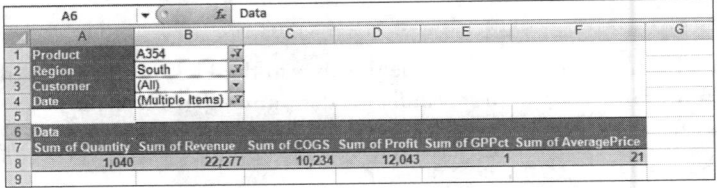

**Figure 12.30**
Adjust the name and numeric formatting in the Data Field Settings dialog.

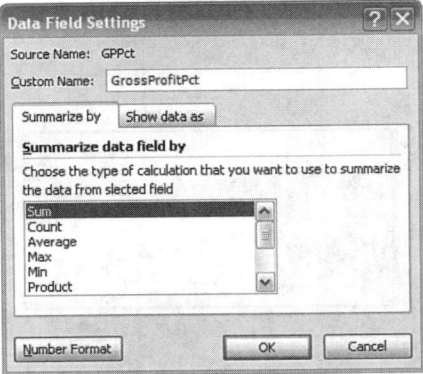

14. In the Data Field Settings dialog, click the Number Format button. Assign a numeric format of Percentage with one decimal place.

15. Repeat steps 12–14 for the AveragePrice field, assigning to it a numeric format of Currency with two decimal places.

After you correctly define the fields, they are correctly calculated for any variation of the pivot table. Figure 12.31 shows details for sales of Item A354 by month. This report shows a fair amount of variability in pricing from month to month.

**Figure 12.31**
The calculated fields apply to any combination of label fields.

| Years | Date | Sum of Quantity | Sum of Revenue | Sum of COGS | Sum of Profit | GrossProfitPct | AvgPrice |
|-------|------|-----------------|----------------|-------------|---------------|----------------|----------|
| ⊟ 2007 | Jan | 3,240 | 74,103 | 31,843 | 42,260 | 57.0% | $22.87 |
|  | Feb | 900 | 17,543 | 8,281 | 9,262 | 52.8% | $19.49 |
|  | Mar | 2,860 | 61,548 | 26,272 | 35,276 | 57.3% | $21.52 |
|  | Apr | 1,760 | 41,989 | 17,987 | 24,002 | 57.2% | $23.86 |
|  | May | 3,880 | 84,190 | 37,373 | 46,817 | 55.6% | $21.70 |
|  | Jun | 1,950 | 46,052 | 19,376 | 26,676 | 57.9% | $23.62 |
|  | Jul | 270 | 5,678 | 2,287 | 3,391 | 59.7% | $21.03 |
|  | Aug | 2,060 | 47,625 | 20,249 | 27,376 | 57.5% | $23.12 |
|  | Sep | 1,610 | 33,565 | 14,979 | 18,586 | 55.4% | $20.85 |
|  | Oct | 2,260 | 48,075 | 21,978 | 26,097 | 54.3% | $21.27 |
|  | Nov | 3,830 | 81,632 | 37,230 | 44,402 | 54.4% | $21.31 |
|  | Dec | 2,020 | 40,970 | 17,685 | 23,285 | 56.8% | $20.28 |
| ⊟ 2008 | Jan | 1,548 | 34,972 | 15,034 | 19,938 | 57.0% | $22.59 |
|  | Feb | 3,114 | 67,187 | 30,545 | 36,642 | 54.5% | $21.58 |
|  | Mar | 1,566 | 33,309 | 14,997 | 18,312 | 55.0% | $21.27 |
|  | Apr | 3,780 | 85,344 | 35,831 | 49,513 | 58.0% | $22.58 |
|  | May | 891 | 20,426 | 8,561 | 11,865 | 58.1% | $22.92 |
|  | Jun | 954 | 20,099 | 9,467 | 10,632 | 52.9% | $21.07 |
|  | Jul | 540 | 11,804 | 5,519 | 6,285 | 53.2% | $21.86 |
|  | Aug | 1,926 | 43,477 | 19,061 | 24,416 | 56.2% | $22.57 |
|  | Sep | 2,736 | 59,519 | 25,832 | 33,687 | 56.6% | $21.75 |
|  | Oct | 2,214 | 44,527 | 19,540 | 24,987 | 56.1% | $20.11 |
|  | Nov | 4,122 | 93,516 | 40,647 | 52,869 | 56.5% | $22.69 |
|  | Dec | 585 | 10,495 | 4,955 | 5,540 | 52.8% | $17.94 |
| Grand Total |  | 50,616 | 1,107,645 | 485,529 | 622,116 | 56.2% | $21.88 |

# ADDING NEW ITEMS ALONG A DIMENSION

Figure 12.32 is a report that shows the quantity of items sold, by product. This report compares sales for various regions. It is an example of a report that is often produced from transactional data.

**Figure 12.32**
You need to customize the reporting hierarchy for the product lines.

| Sum of Quantity | Region | | | |
|-----------------|---------|-------|-------|-------------|
| Product | Central | North | South | Grand Total |
| A354 | 14,402 | 20,140 | 16,074 | 50,616 |
| B713 | 20,107 | 15,847 | 17,334 | 53,288 |
| D157 | 17,118 | 17,712 | 18,126 | 52,956 |
| D173 | 14,520 | 11,946 | 25,630 | 52,096 |
| D598 | 26,091 | 20,484 | 19,429 | 66,004 |
| D776 | 29,512 | 12,442 | 25,862 | 67,816 |
| D850 | 24,585 | 23,954 | 22,533 | 71,072 |
| E852 | 22,356 | 24,429 | 28,906 | 75,691 |
| F474 | 22,588 | 12,388 | 24,654 | 59,630 |
| F495 | 21,918 | 11,585 | 30,770 | 64,273 |
| G101 | 5,401 | 726 | 1,723 | 7,850 |
| Grand Total | 218,598 | 171,653 | 231,041 | 621,292 |

Most companies probably group the items shown in this report in some logical manner. Perhaps one functional group is responsible for the A*xx* and B*xx* series products. Another functional group might handle the D*xx* line, and the final group might handle the E*xx*, F*xx*, and G*xx* lines.

Excel offers two methods for this reporting: You can either define calculated items or use grouping. As discussed in the following section, if you decide to use calculated items, you need to be incredibly careful that you do not report the wrong numbers.

12

## USING CALCULATED ITEMS

A calculated item adds a new data item to one field in the pivot table. This new data item is calculated from values in other data items along the same dimension.

Consider the data in Figure 12.32. You can define a new calculated item that is the total of Products A354 and B713. Before you do this, however, note that the total quantity shown in Figure 12.32 is 621,292.

Because the new item will be added to the product dimension, you have to select a cell that has a product name. In this example, Cell A4 through A15 would work. You need to choose PivotTable Tools, Options, Tools, Formulas, Calculated Item to access the Insert Calculated Item dialog (which is similar to the Insert Calculated Field dialog). You define a name for the item, such as ABGroup, and then use the Insert Item button to add items to the formula. Figure 12.33 shows the definition of the grouping of the A*xx* and B*xx* items.

You need to add additional definitions for DGroup and EFGGroup. When you finish, these items are added to the end of the product list. The calculations work. As shown in Figure 12.34, the 103,904 reported for the ABGroup total is really the result of adding 50,616 and 53,288. However, the grand total shown in Row 19 has increased from 621,292 to 1,242,584. It is very easy to report the wrong numbers when you use calculated items.

**Figure 12.33**
Defining a new item along the Product dimension.

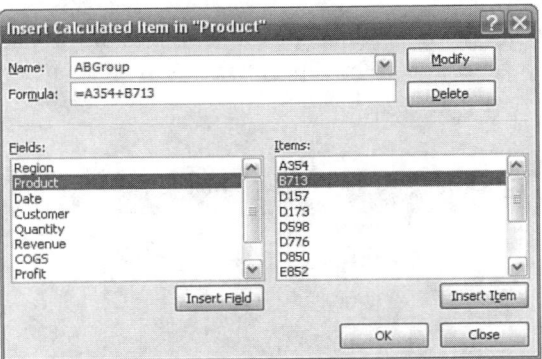

**Figure 12.34**
Using calculated items causes the grand total in Row 19 to be wrong.

| | Product | Central | North | South | Grand Total |
|---|---|---|---|---|---|
| 2 | | | | | |
| 3 | Sum of Quantity | Region | | | |
| 4 | Product | Central | North | South | Grand Total |
| 5 | A354 | 14,402 | 20,140 | 16,074 | 50,616 |
| 6 | B713 | 20,107 | 15,847 | 17,334 | 53,288 |
| 7 | D157 | 17,118 | 17,712 | 18,126 | 52,956 |
| 8 | D173 | 14,520 | 11,946 | 25,630 | 52,096 |
| 9 | D598 | 26,091 | 20,484 | 19,429 | 66,004 |
| 10 | D776 | 29,512 | 12,442 | 25,862 | 67,816 |
| 11 | D850 | 24,585 | 23,954 | 22,533 | 71,072 |
| 12 | E852 | 22,356 | 24,429 | 28,906 | 75,691 |
| 13 | F474 | 22,588 | 12,388 | 24,654 | 59,630 |
| 14 | F495 | 21,918 | 11,585 | 30,770 | 64,273 |
| 15 | G101 | 5,401 | 726 | 1,723 | 7,850 |
| 16 | ABGroup | 34,509 | 35,987 | 33,408 | 103,904 |
| 17 | DGroup | 111,826 | 86,538 | 111,580 | 309,944 |
| 18 | EFGGroup | 72,263 | 49,128 | 86,053 | 207,444 |
| 19 | Grand Total | 437,196 | 343,306 | 462,082 | 1,242,584 |
| 20 | | | | | |

The only way that grouping items would make sense is if you used the Product filter to hide all the detail items and show only the calculated items, as shown in Figure 12.35.

**Figure 12.35**

Using calculated items makes sense only if you hide the items that make up the calculated items or remove the grand totals.

| Sum of Quantity | Region | | | |
|---|---|---|---|---|
| Product | Central | North | South | Grand Total |
| ABGroup | 34,509 | 35,987 | 33,408 | 103,904 |
| DGroup | 111,826 | 86,538 | 111,580 | 309,944 |
| EFGGroup | 72,263 | 49,128 | 86,053 | 207,444 |
| Grand Total | 218,598 | 171,653 | 231,041 | 621,292 |

Instead of using calculated items, you should consider using the grouping functionality, as discussed in the following section.

## ORGANIZING A HIERARCHY BY USING GROUPING

As shown in the previous section, using Calculated Items can lead to wrong results in the pivot table totals. You should consider defining subtotals along a dimension by using the Grouping feature instead.

For effective grouping, you will select item labels that make up a group and then click on the Group Selection icon.

For example, consider the pivot table shown in Figure 12.32. Select the products that make up the first group (that is, Cells A5:A6). On the Options ribbon, you click the Group Selection icon to group these products into a group. As shown in Figure 12.36, after you group the first items, a new Column A is added, called Product2. The first items are grouped into a new value called Group1. All the other items are in their own groups. This is okay; you can fix it with a few more clicks.

**Figure 12.36**

After you group the first few items, the remaining items fall into their own individual groups.

| Sum of Quantity | | Region | | | |
|---|---|---|---|---|---|
| Product2 | Product | Central | North | South | Grand Total |
| Group1 | A354 | 14,402 | 20,140 | 16,074 | 50,616 |
| | B713 | 20,107 | 15,847 | 17,334 | 53,288 |
| D157 | D157 | 17,118 | 17,712 | 18,126 | 52,956 |
| D173 | D173 | 14,520 | 11,946 | 25,630 | 52,096 |
| D598 | D598 | 26,091 | 20,484 | 19,429 | 66,004 |
| D776 | D776 | 29,512 | 12,442 | 25,862 | 67,816 |
| D850 | D850 | 24,585 | 23,954 | 22,533 | 71,072 |
| E852 | E852 | 22,356 | 24,429 | 28,906 | 75,691 |
| F474 | F474 | 22,588 | 12,388 | 24,654 | 59,630 |
| F495 | F495 | 21,918 | 11,585 | 30,770 | 64,273 |
| G101 | G101 | 5,401 | 726 | 1,723 | 7,850 |
| Grand Total | | 218,598 | 171,653 | 231,041 | 621,292 |

To build the D group, you select Cells B7 through B11. Then you click Group Selection to form a group of these items. Next, you select cells B12:B16 and click Group Selection to make the final group. The pivot table now has a completely new field, which you can easily expand or collapse, as shown in Figure 12.37.

At this point, you have defined groups along a dimension. Excel shows the items in their various groups, but there are no totals for each group. To add subtotals to the analysis, follow these steps:

1. From the Styles ribbon choose Subtotals and then Show Subtotals.

2. Select Field Settings and give the grouped field a meaningful name. In the current example, something like Product Line would be appropriate.

3. At this point, the various groups will have generic names like Group1, Group2, etc. Select a cell with a group name. Right in the cell, type the new name **AB Group**.

4. Select the remaining group name cells and rename them.

The final report is shown in Figure 12.38.

**Figure 12.37**
You group the remaining items.

| Sum of Quantity | | Region | | | |
|---|---|---|---|---|---|
| Product2 | Product | Central | North | South | Grand Total |
| Group1 | A354 | 14,402 | 20,140 | 16,074 | 50,616 |
| | B713 | 20,107 | 15,847 | 17,334 | 53,288 |
| Group2 | D157 | 17,118 | 17,712 | 18,126 | 52,956 |
| | D173 | 14,520 | 11,946 | 25,630 | 52,096 |
| | D598 | 26,091 | 20,484 | 19,429 | 66,004 |
| | D776 | 29,512 | 12,442 | 25,862 | 67,816 |
| | D850 | 24,585 | 23,954 | 22,533 | 71,072 |
| Group3 | E852 | 22,356 | 24,429 | 28,906 | 75,691 |
| | F474 | 22,588 | 12,388 | 24,654 | 59,630 |
| | F495 | 21,918 | 11,585 | 30,770 | 64,273 |
| | G101 | 5,401 | 726 | 1,723 | 7,850 |
| Grand Total | | 218,598 | 171,653 | 231,041 | 621,292 |

**Figure 12.38**
Using the group selection and a few modifications, you can add a new dimension for the product line managers.

| Sum of Quantity | | Region | | | |
|---|---|---|---|---|---|
| ProductLine | Product | Central | North | South | Grand Total |
| AB Group | A354 | 14,402 | 20,140 | 16,074 | 50,616 |
| | B713 | 20,107 | 15,847 | 17,334 | 53,288 |
| AB Group Total | | 34,509 | 35,987 | 33,408 | 103,904 |
| Dgroup | D157 | 17,118 | 17,712 | 18,126 | 52,956 |
| | D173 | 14,520 | 11,946 | 25,630 | 52,096 |
| | D598 | 26,091 | 20,484 | 19,429 | 66,004 |
| | D776 | 29,512 | 12,442 | 25,862 | 67,816 |
| | D850 | 24,585 | 23,954 | 22,533 | 71,072 |
| Dgroup Total | | 111,826 | 86,538 | 111,580 | 309,944 |
| EFGGroup | E852 | 22,356 | 24,429 | 28,906 | 75,691 |
| | F474 | 22,588 | 12,388 | 24,654 | 59,630 |
| | F495 | 21,918 | 11,585 | 30,770 | 64,273 |
| | G101 | 5,401 | 726 | 1,723 | 7,850 |
| EFGGroup Total | | 72,263 | 49,128 | 86,053 | 207,444 |
| Grand Total | | 218,598 | 171,653 | 231,041 | 621,292 |

# SHOWING PERCENTAGES INSTEAD OF VALUES

Figure 12.39 shows a report of profit by product and region. This report shows revenue in what is known as Normal view. Excel provides many additional views that can show any value field as a percentage of a total.

**Figure 12.39**
The Normal view of profit shows actual dollars in each cell.

| Sum of Profit | Filter columns | | | |
|---|---|---|---|---|
| Filter rows | Central | North | South | Grand Total |
| A354 | 169,029 | 251,043 | 202,044 | 622,116 |
| B713 | 259,469 | 196,281 | 203,434 | 659,184 |
| D157 | 211,216 | 202,339 | 218,352 | 631,907 |
| D173 | 151,495 | 133,544 | 312,370 | 597,409 |
| D598 | 298,715 | 234,579 | 230,964 | 764,258 |
| D776 | 351,218 | 143,569 | 296,786 | 791,573 |
| D850 | 299,466 | 311,004 | 262,209 | 872,679 |
| E852 | 252,562 | 285,562 | 335,613 | 873,737 |
| F474 | 267,574 | 139,281 | 291,217 | 698,072 |
| F495 | 262,516 | 134,695 | 380,589 | 777,800 |
| G101 | 67,588 | 7,246 | 18,179 | 93,013 |
| Grand Total | 2,590,848 | 2,039,143 | 2,751,757 | 7,381,748 |

To select a different view, you first select any value cell and then choose Field Settings from the Active Field group of the Options ribbon.

The Data Field Settings dialog appears. Its Show Data As tab stores all the percentage options. You can select any of the following options from the Show Data As tab without specifying additional information:

- **Normal**—Shows actual numbers.
- **% of Row**—Calculates the percentage of the row.
- **% of Column**—Calculates the percentage of the column.
- **% of Total**—Calculates the percentage of the grand total.
- **Index**—Assigns a relative importance of each cell in the pivot table.

The following option from the Show Data As tab requires that you specify a base field:

- **Running Total In**—Calculates a cumulative total as you go down the column.

The other three options on the Show Data As tab allow you to choose a base field and a base item:

- **Difference From**—Calculates a change from a base item.
- **% Of**—Calculates a percentage of a base item.
- **% Difference From**—Calculates a percentage difference from a base item.

Figure 12.40 shows a report that displays revenue as the percentage of the row. Each row adds up to a grand total of 100%. This type of report is useful for spotting trends by region. For example, you can see in Figure 12.40 that for some reason, Product D776 does much better in the central than most other products.

**Figure 12.40**
You can use this report to see how each product does by region.

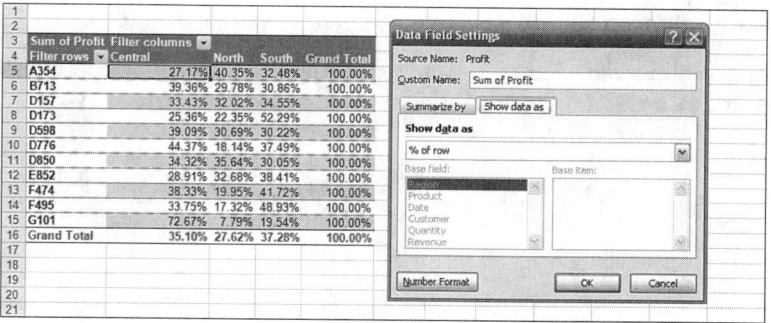

Figure 12.41 shows revenue as a percentage of the column. Each column adds up to 100%. This is useful for comparing products within a region. You can see in this figure that Product D850 is the most important product in the north, whereas F495 seems to be a major component of southern sales.

**Figure 12.41**
You can use this report to see which products are important in each region.

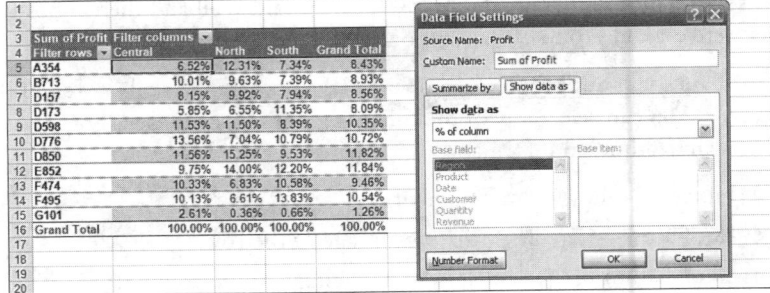

The final percentage option is to take a percentage of the total. In this case, each cell in B5:E15 would represent a percentage of the grand total in E16.

## CALCULATING THE DIFFERENCE FROM ONE DAY TO ANOTHER USING THE DIFFERENCE FROM FIELDS

The last type of setting for Show Data As are the Difference settings. These settings are the most complex. They allow you to compare all of the values along a dimension to another value along the same dimension.

The settings can be absolute, where every day's sales is compared to the sales on the first day of the dataset. Or, the settings can be relative, where every day's sales are compared to the previous day.

These final settings—the difference settings—round out a diverse group of powerful Show Data As options. The options provide nearly unlimited flexibility.

Consider the report in Figure 12.42. Each column from B through F shows off a different type of Show Data As setting. Column B shows the data as normal. Column C shows a running total. Column D shows a percentage of total. Column E uses the tricky Difference from Yesterday. Column F uses the difference from the first day in the period.

This section walks you through how to set up the report shown in Figure 12.42. In this report, each column shows a different view of revenue for January 2007.

**Figure 12.42**
This report shows five views of revenue.

| Filter rows | Sum of Revenue | RunningTotal | PctTotal | DifferenceFromYesterday | % Difference from Jan2 |
|---|---|---|---|---|---|
| 1/2/2007 | 13,871 | 13,871 | 3.04% | | |
| 1/3/2007 | 14,408 | 28,279 | 3.16% | 537 | 3.87% |
| 1/4/2007 | 55,189 | 83,468 | 12.10% | 40781 | 297.87% |
| 1/5/2007 | 14,794 | 98,262 | 3.24% | -40395 | 6.65% |
| 1/8/2007 | 14,469 | 112,731 | 3.17% | -325 | 4.31% |
| 1/9/2007 | 15,101 | 127,832 | 3.31% | 632 | 8.87% |
| 1/10/2007 | 20,136 | 147,968 | 4.42% | 5035 | 45.17% |
| 1/11/2007 | 38,804 | 186,772 | 8.51% | 18668 | 179.75% |
| 1/15/2007 | 2,296 | 189,068 | 0.50% | -36508 | -83.45% |
| 1/16/2007 | 36,978 | 226,046 | 8.11% | 34682 | 166.58% |
| 1/17/2007 | 25,243 | 251,289 | 5.54% | -11735 | 81.98% |
| 1/18/2007 | 1,615 | 252,904 | 0.35% | -23628 | -88.36% |
| 1/19/2007 | 32,944 | 285,848 | 7.22% | 31329 | 137.50% |
| 1/22/2007 | 38,585 | 324,433 | 8.46% | 5641 | 178.17% |
| 1/23/2007 | 31,001 | 355,434 | 6.80% | -7584 | 123.50% |
| 1/25/2007 | 27,448 | 382,882 | 6.02% | -3553 | 97.88% |
| 1/26/2007 | 8,186 | 391,068 | 1.80% | -19262 | -40.98% |
| 1/29/2007 | 22,389 | 413,457 | 4.91% | 14203 | 61.41% |
| 1/30/2007 | 39,155 | 452,612 | 8.59% | 16766 | 182.28% |
| 1/31/2007 | 3,408 | 456,020 | 0.75% | -35747 | -75.43% |
| Grand Total | 456,020 | | 100.00% | | |

If you wished to build a report similar to the one in Figure 12.42, you actually have to drag the same field to the Σ Values section several times. Each copy of the value field will have a different setting in the Show Data As area.

The following steps illustrate how each of the five columns in Figure 12.42 were defined:

1. Build a pivot table with Date in the Row Labels section and Revenue in the Σ Values section.

2. Filter the dates to include values in January 2007.

3. Drag the Revenue field to the Σ Values section four additional times.

4. Select Cell C5 (the first cell in the Revenue2 field) and then click Data Field Settings. Change the field name to **RunningTotal**. In the Show Data As drop-down, select Running Total In and then specify that you want to see the running total in the Date field. Finally, choose Date as the base field, as shown in Figure 12.43.

**Figure 12.43**
A running total requires you to specify a base field.

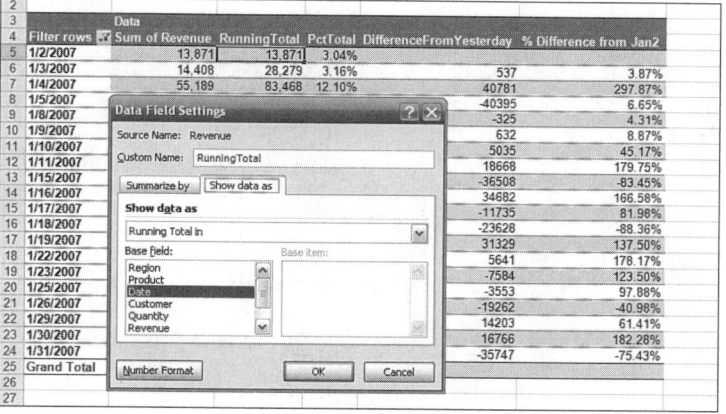

5. Select Cell D5 (the first cell in the Revenue3 field) and then click Data Field Settings. Name the field **PctTotal**. Click the Show Values As tab. In the dropdown for Show Values As, choose "% of column".

6. Select Cell E5 (the Revenue4 field) and then click Data Field Settings. Change Custom Name to **DifferenceFromYesterday** and set the Show Data As value to **Difference From**. Specify both a base field and a base item. The base field is the date item. For the Base item, choose (Previous), as shown in Figure 12.44, to compare each day's sales to the previous day's sales.

7. Select Cell F5 (the Revenue5 field) and then click Data Field Settings. In this case, choose % Difference From. The base field is still the Date field, but you want the base item to be the first day of the month, so choose 1/2/2007, as shown in Figure 12.45. Each value in this column then compares the day's sales to the sales on the first day of the month.

12

**Figure 12.44**
Each of the Difference From settings requires a base field and a base item.

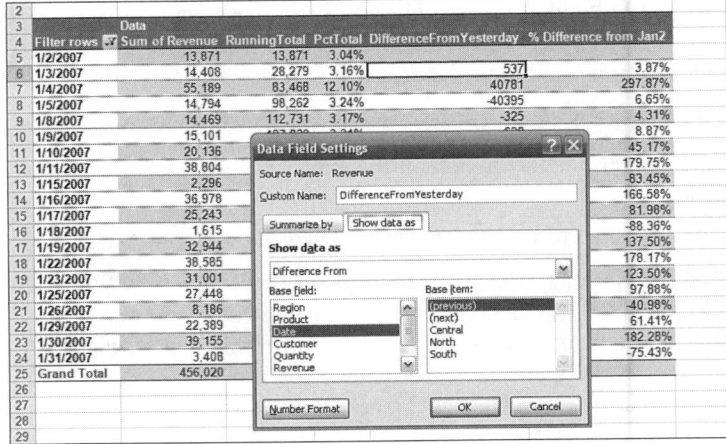

**Figure 12.45**
In this case, each cell compares the current day's sales to the sales on a specific day.

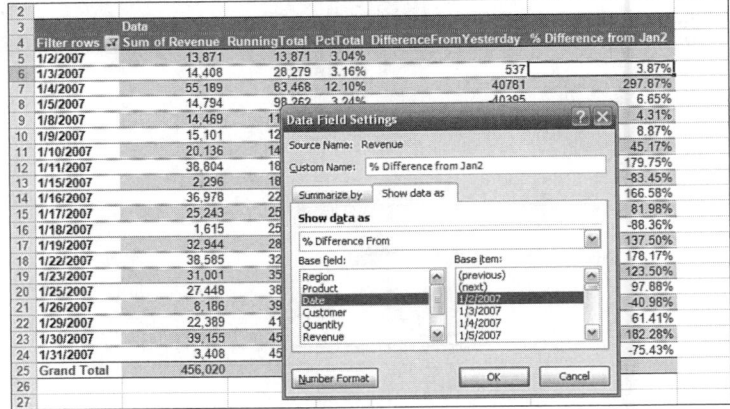

**CAUTION**

Some of these settings cannot survive subsequent pivot operations. For example, Figure 12.46 shows the table with Date grouped up to months and years. In this case, the running total had to be defined again, with a base field of Dates. The difference fields in column E & F had to be redefined after grouping. Notice that the running total starts over in January 2008. However, the % Of column in D is a percentage of the grand total in Row 31.

**Figure 12.46**
You need to redefine many of the Difference Of calculations after pivoting a table.

| Filter rows | Sum of Revenue | RunningTotal | PctTotal | DifferenceFromYesterday | % Difference from Jan2 |
|---|---|---|---|---|---|
| 1/2/2007 | 13,871 | 13,871 | 0.10% | | |
| 1/3/2007 | 14,408 | 28,279 | 0.11% | 537 | 3.87% |
| 1/4/2007 | 55,189 | 83,468 | 0.42% | 40781 | 297.87% |
| 1/5/2007 | 14,794 | 98,262 | 0.11% | -40395 | 6.65% |
| 1/8/2007 | 14,469 | 112,731 | 0.11% | -325 | 4.31% |
| 1/9/2007 | 15,101 | 127,832 | 0.11% | 632 | 8.87% |
| 1/10/2007 | 20,136 | 147,968 | 0.15% | 5035 | 45.17% |
| 1/11/2007 | 38,804 | 186,772 | 0.29% | 18668 | 179.75% |
| 1/15/2007 | 2,296 | 189,068 | 0.02% | -36508 | -83.45% |
| 1/16/2007 | 36,978 | 226,046 | 0.28% | 34682 | 166.58% |
| 1/17/2007 | 25,243 | 251,289 | 0.19% | -11735 | 81.98% |

NOTE

> The Field Settings dialog allows you to define a calculation that makes no sense. For example, you could ask to see each date as a percentage of the Bright Paint customer. Although Excel accepts this as a setting, the result is all #N/A values.

# EXPLORING INTERESTING USES FOR PIVOT TABLES

So far in this chapter, you have used pivot tables to perform various summary analyses, which is the reason pivot tables were invented. However, pivot tables are so easy to create and use that they often provide the quickest way to accomplish a task. The following sections describe some other uses for pivot tables.

## GENERTING A UNIQUE LIST

One quirky use of pivot tables is to generate a unique list of values in any field. For example, say you have a dataset that has 1,126 rows of transactional data. You need to quickly produce a unique list of the customers in the dataset. Although you could click the new Remove Duplicates icon on the Data ribbon to destructively find the unique customers, you can instead use a pivot table to do this in three clicks of the mouse:

1. Select a cell in your dataset and click the PivotTable icon on the Insert ribbon.
2. Click OK to accept the defaults on the Create PivotTable dialog.
3. Select Customer in the PivotTable Field List box.

You end up with a unique list of customers, as shown in Figure 12.47. You can copy this list and use Paste Special Values to move the list wherever you might need it to be.

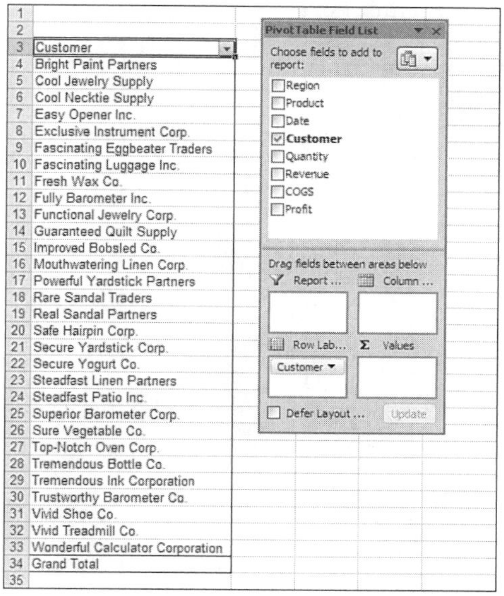

**Figure 12.47**
Using pivot tables has always been the fastest way to get a unique list, and it is even faster in Excel 2007.

## COUNTING RECORDS

Another unusual use for pivot tables is to count how many records meet certain criteria. These datasets may contain columns of text without a single number anywhere in the range. You can still use a pivot table to analyze the data.

For example, Figure 12.48 shows a dataset that has no numeric data at all. It is a log of all the quality errors on a manufacturing line. Even though there is nothing to add up, you can analyze this data by using a pivot table. Follow these steps:

**Figure 12.48**
This dataset has no numeric data, but will be great in a pivot table.

| 1700 | 8/21/2007 | A | Emissions failure |
| 1701 | 8/25/2007 | D | Dome Light Failure |
| 1702 | 8/28/2007 | B | Fit & Finish - Roof |
| 1703 | 8/28/2007 | B | Fit & Finish - Roof |
| 1704 | 8/14/2007 | D | Power Window Failure |
| 1705 | 8/15/2007 | C | Fan Belt Failure |
| 1706 | 8/1/2007 | A | Cruise Control Failure |
| 1707 | 8/22/2007 | D | Fuel Injection Failure |
| 1708 | 8/3/2007 | B | Radio Failure |
| 1709 | 8/28/2007 | B | Fit & Finish - Roof |
| 1710 | 8/22/2007 | D | Heater Failure |
| 1711 | 8/17/2007 | B | Heater Failure |
| 1712 | 8/29/2007 | D | Sunroof Leaking |

1. Choose Insert, PivotTable and accept the default location.

2. Choose the Defect field to see a unique list of defects. Then drag the Defect field to the Σ Values section of the table. Because the field contains text, Excel automatically chooses to count the field instead of sum it.

3. Move the Line field to the Column Labels section of the table.

Figure 12.49 shows the completed pivot table with a data bar added to the grand total. It looks like the biggest problem is in Fit & Finish – Roof.

**Figure 12.49**
By counting the defects, you see that there is a problem in the Roof department.

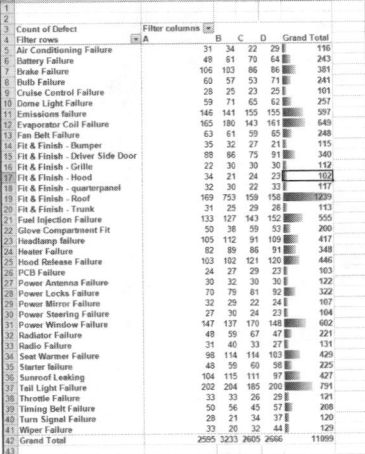

Once you have produced one view of your data with a pivot table, you can use the flexibility of a pivot table to further analyze the data.

In the previous example, the pivot table indicated that there might be a problem with one particular step of a manufacturing process. However, there are additional fields in the underlying dataset that are not part of the analysis.

If you use the Report Filter to limit the report to just data for the one problematic manufacturing step, you can add additional fields to the pivot table to analyze if the problem started on a certain date, or is limited to a certain line or a certain shift.

To further analyze the table, follow these steps:

1. Move Defect from Row Labels to Report Filter and select the Roof item.
2. Move the Date field to the Row Labels section, as shown in Figure 12.50.

In the finished pivot table, shown in Figure 12.50, you can see that something happened on the 28th of the month that started causing a problem on the B line. By the 30th of the month, the problem had spread to the A, C, and D lines. You can guess that some new shipment of defective material probably arrived in the plant around this time frame.

This is just one example of the analysis that can be done by filtering a pivot table. The initial pivot table identified that the problem was in one area of the plant. Subsequent versions of the pivot table focused on that one area and brought more data to the table to locate the source of the problem.

**Figure 12.50**
Pivot a few more fields, and you have a picture that the problem started on the B line toward the end of the month.

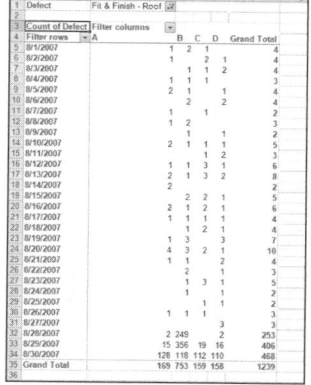

**TIP FROM**

*Bill Jelen*

Analyses like these make pivot tables powerful and make them my favorite tool. For even more examples of pivot tables, check out *Pivot Tables for Excel 2007*, co-written by Michael Alexander and me.

12

## COMPARING TWO LISTS

One common hurdle in Excel is comparing data in two lists. You might have a snapshot of data from last week or last month and a new snapshot from today. How can you figure out what changed from the first list to the second list?

In the real world, some items from the first list will be deleted. Some items in the first list will get new values. Some items will appear on the second list that were never on the first list.

Most people attack this problem manually, comparing the two printed lists with a high-lighter, trying to find the items that stayed the same and finding the items that changed.

A clever way to compare the lists is to use a pivot table. The data from both lists is copied into a new consolidated list. The records from each list are identified as being from either the original or latest list.

When you create a pivot table with the item key as the Row Label, the identifier as the column label, and the values, you can quickly see which items changed from list to list.

Specifically, say that you have two lists. List 1 is the sales forecast from last week. List 2 is the sales forecast from today. Both lists happen to have 33 records, but they are not the same 33 records!

Some customers are new, some were deleted, and some were changed. How can you quickly find out what changed between the two forecasts? To figure it out, follow these steps:

**Figure 12.51**
What changed between forecasts?

1. Add a new field called WhichForecast. In this field, use the value First for all the original forecasts.

2. Copy the new forecast beneath the original forecast and add the value Now for the new field.

3. Create a pivot table with Customer in the Row Labels section, WhichForecast in the Column Labels section, and Forecast in the Σ Value area.

4. Select the First header. Then select Options, Tools, Pivot Formulas, Insert Calculated Item to define the calculation Change = Now – First.

The result is the pivot table shown in Figure 12.52. In this view, you can quickly see that the forecasts for Astonishing Paint, Trustworthy Utensil, and Unsurpassed Sprayer were lost in the past week. New forecasts for First-Rate Sprayer, Magnificent Ink, and Trouble-Free Shoe appeared. Forceful Chopstick and Paramount Bobsled recorded minor changes.

**Figure 12.52**
You combine the two lists into a single list with a new field and then generate a pivot table to compare.

| | First | Now | Change |
|---|---|---|---|
| **Sum of Forecast** | **Filter columns** | | |
| **Filter rows** | | | |
| Agile Utensil Corporation | 14014 | 14014 | 0 |
| Astonishing Paint Corporation | 10615 | | -10615 |
| Astonishing Shingle Inc. | 24618 | 24618 | 0 |
| Crisp Utensil Corporation | 14133 | 14133 | 0 |
| Dependable Juicer Corporation | 21786 | 21786 | 0 |
| Different Yardstick Supply | 18009 | 18009 | 0 |
| Distinctive Electronics Inc. | 22043 | 22043 | 0 |
| Effortless Vise Company | 21628 | 21628 | 0 |
| Excellent Eggbeater Inc. | 28646 | 28646 | 0 |
| Fine Oven Corporation | 23137 | 23137 | 0 |
| First-Rate Sprayer Corporation | | 18524 | 18524 |
| Forceful Chopstick Company | 12633 | 2000 | -10633 |
| Functional Briefcase Corporation | 26351 | 26351 | 0 |
| Guarded Sandal Inc. | 25026 | 25026 | 0 |
| Magnificent Furnace Supply | 21249 | 21249 | 0 |
| Magnificent Ink Inc. | | 19654 | 19654 |
| Matchless Flagpole Supply | 29066 | 29066 | 0 |
| New Gadget Company | 28414 | 28414 | 0 |
| New Scooter Company | 10690 | 10690 | 0 |
| Paramount Bobsled Inc. | 23537 | 28000 | 4463 |
| Paramount Clipboard Company | 23104 | 23104 | 0 |
| Powerful Aquarium Inc. | 27778 | 27778 | 0 |
| Rare Juicer Inc. | 18458 | 18458 | 0 |
| Remarkable Flagpole Company | 14303 | 14303 | 0 |
| Savory Gadget Corporation | 11584 | 11584 | 0 |
| Stunning Calculator Company | 17250 | 17250 | 0 |
| Supreme Kiln Supply | 25387 | 25387 | 0 |
| Sure Shoe Company | 20738 | 20738 | 0 |
| Trouble-Free Juicer Inc. | 17275 | 17275 | 0 |
| Trouble-Free Shoe Corporation | | 29845 | 29845 |
| Trustworthy Linen Corporation | 20376 | 19000 | -1376 |
| Trustworthy Utensil Inc. | 28184 | | -28184 |
| Unsurpassed Sprayer Partners | 14142 | | -14142 |
| User-Friendly Opener Corporation | 29890 | 29890 | 0 |
| Vibrant Lawn Corporation | 11446 | 11446 | 0 |
| Vivid Bobsled Company | 12183 | 12183 | 0 |
| **Grand Total** | 667693 | 678229 | 7536 |

**CAUTION**

There is a "feature" of pivot tables that many consider to be a bug. If you go outside of the pivot table and use a mouse to build a formula that points inside the pivot table, you will get a bizarre formula that cannot be copied. For example, in Figure 12.52, it might be tempting to use a formula in the worksheet to calculate the change column. To do this, you go to Cell H3 and type an equals sign. Then, using the mouse or arrow keys, you select G3, type a minus sign, and then press F3.

When you use this method to enter a formula, Excel builds a complex formula using GetPivotData functions. The problem is that when you copy this formula down to the other cells, the formula continues to look to cells G3 and F3, as shown in Figure 12.53. This is rarely what you want. To overcome this problem, you need to actually **type** the formula **=G3-F3**. To turn off this behavior, you select Excel Options, Formulas and then uncheck the option Generate GetPivotData Functions.

12

**Figure 12.53**
When you use the mouse to build a formula that contains cells in a pivot table, Excel substitutes GetPivotData functions for the cell address.

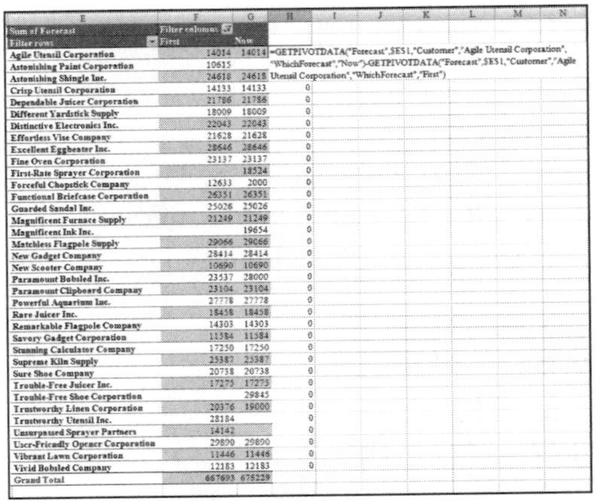

## GROUPING BY WEEK

A previous example showed how to group daily dates up to months, quarters, or years. Occassionally, someone will have a need to group daily dates up to weeks. Even though the Grouping dialog doesn't offer grouping by week, you can achieve this effect by doing the following:

1. Select a date field and click the Group Field icon on the Options ribbon.

2. In the Grouping dialog, choose to group only by days. This enables the Number of Days spin button in the lower-right corner.

3. Dial the Number of Days spin button up to 7 days. Because this dataset starts on January 2, 2007 (a Tuesday), your default weeks would run Tuesday through Monday.

4. If you want your weeks to run Monday through Sunday, change the Starting At value to **1/1/2007**. If you want your weeks to run Sunday through Saturday, change the Starting At value to **12/31/2006**.

Figure 12.54 shows the Grouping dialog box and the result of following these steps.

**Figure 12.54**
Even though weeks are not an option, you can group by them by using the Number of Days option.

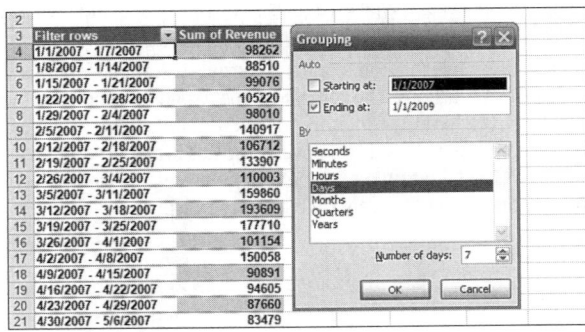

CAUTION

> When you group a field by week, you cannot group that field by any other time measures, such as month, quarter, or year.

## Excel In Practice: Comparing Months from One Year to the Next

If you have a dataset that contains two or more years of data, you can build an interesting year-over-year view of the data. To do this, you build a pivot table with dates running down the Row Labels area. Then you click Group Field and specify that you want to group by months and years, as shown in Figure 12.55.

**Figure 12.55**
You can group dates by up to months and years.

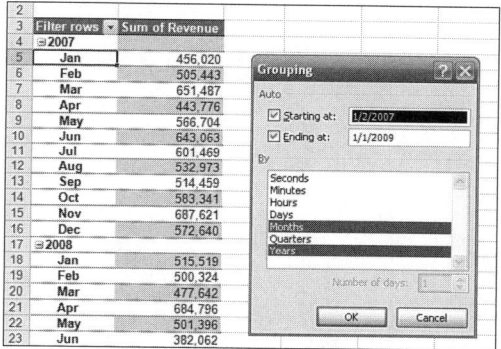

Although the default view of the data is with the years and months along the Row Labels dimension, you can easily move the newly created Years field to the column labels in order to create a comparison that shows one year compared to the next year (see Figure 12.56).

**Figure 12.56**
You can move the Years field to the column area to crosstab years and months.

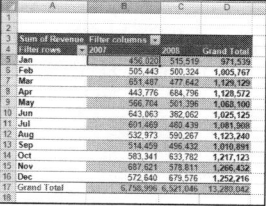

# FINDING MORE INFORMATION ON PIVOT TABLES

A number of aspects of pivot tables are not covered in this and the previous two chapters. Other parts of this book provide further information on pivot tables:

- If you want to know how to create a pivot table from Access data, see Chapter 41, "Connecting with Word, Access, PowerPoint, and OneNote."

12

- If you want to know how to create pivot charts from pivot tables, see Chapter 15, "Charting."
- Pivot tables figure prominently in the new Office Services for Sharepoint. See Chapter 39 for more details.
- Pivot table source data can automatically expand if your data is set up as a table. For information on using tables in Excel 2007, see Chapter 8, "Fabulous Table Intelligence."

**12**

CHAPTER **13**

# REMOVING DUPLICATES AND FILTERING

## In this chapter

Duplicate data is a common problem in Excel. Microsoft has provided new tools in Excel 2007 to make finding and eliminating duplicates easier.

Autofiltering has been in Excel for a decade, but it has received a makeover in Excel 2007. The autofilter drop-downs now allow you to multiselect values and offer new smart filters.

The Advanced Filter command continues to be available, still as complicated as ever. The hope is that with the excellent improvements to autofiltering and the addition of duplicate handling, you will never have to turn to Advanced Filter. In previous versions of Excel, I almost always had to resort to using Advanced Filter to find a list of unique values. The new Remove Duplicates command allows you to find unique values with a couple mouse clicks.

# USING REMOVE DUPLICATES TO FIND UNIQUE VALUES

By its nature, transactional data has a lot of detail. You end up with transactional data in Excel because it is often the easiest to obtain. As you start to analyze transactional data, you often want to find the number of customers or number of products or number of something in the dataset.

Transactional data can tell you, for example, that there were 34 invoices issued last month, but that doesn't mean there were 34 customers. Some of those customers might have bought from you repeatedly, so that 20 customers could account for 34 invoices. To find the number of unique customers, you need to find a way to eliminate the duplicate records in a dataset. In the past, this usually meant using Advanced Filter or possibly a pivot table. In Excel 2007, there is a new data tool to remove duplicates, called Remove Duplicates, and it is much easier to use.

The first thing to realize is that the Remove Duplicates tool is destructive. It really removes the duplicate records. If you want to keep the original transactional data intact, you should make a copy of the customer column in a blank section of the workbook (or make a backup copy of the workbook).

To find the unique values in a dataset, you follow these steps:

1. Copy the dataset to a blank section of the worksheet. Make sure to leave a blank column between your real data and the copy of the data.
2. Select a single cell within the dataset.
3. On the Data ribbon, in the Data Tools group, choose Remove Duplicates. Excel expands the selection to include the entire range. In the Remove Duplicates dialog, Excel predicts whether your data has headers. This dialog also shows a list of the fields in the dataset. In Figure 13.1, for example, the goal is to find a unique list of customers.
4. You don't care about the invoice numbers, so uncheck Invoice from the Columns list.
5. Click OK to perform the action. Excel tells you how many duplicate values were found and removed, and it also tells you how many unique values remain.

**Figure 13.1**
You choose which columns should be considered when analyzing duplicates.

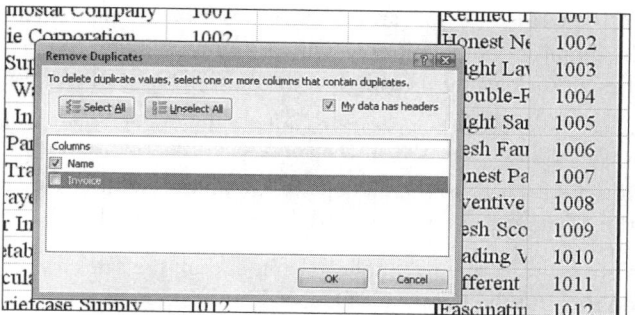

## REMOVING DUPLICATES BASED ON SEVERAL COLUMNS

In the previous set of steps, you analyzed only a single column when looking for duplicates. Sometimes, you need to find each unique combination of two fields (for example, a list of each unique combination of customer and product).

In this case, you follow these steps:

1. Copy the dataset to a blank section of the worksheet. Make sure to leave a blank column between your real data and the copy of the data.
2. Select a single cell within the dataset.
3. On the Data ribbon, in the Data Tools group, choose Remove Duplicates.
4. In the Remove Duplicates dialog, leave the boxes for both the Name and Product columns checked, as shown in Figure 13.2.

**Figure 13.2**
To find each unique combination of customer and product, you choose both fields.

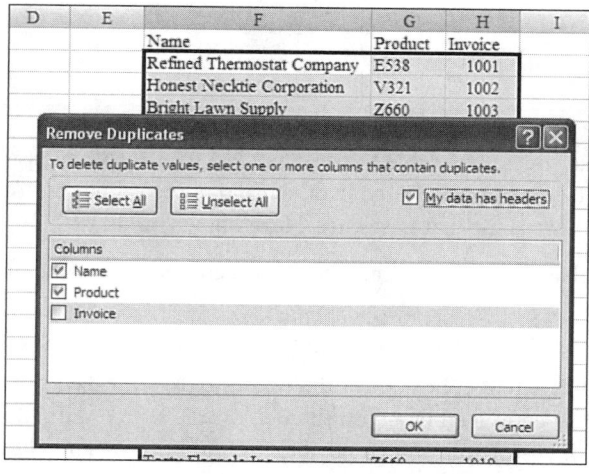

In this case, the result is a list of all products ordered by each customer.

## HANDLING DUPLICATES OTHER WAYS

The Remove Duplicates command is also available in Table Tools, Design ribbon. If you have defined a table as a range, you can remove duplicates from that ribbon.

Remember that the Remove Duplicates command is destructive. Sometimes, you might want to find the duplicates and choose which version to remove. In that case, you choose Home, Conditional Formatting, Highlight Cell Rules, Duplicate Values.

→ To learn more about choosing which duplicates to remove, **see** "Identifying Duplicate or Unique Values Using Conditional Formatting," **page 173**, in Chapter 9.

Other times, you might want to send a copy of the unique values to a new location. In that case, you use the Advanced Filter command discussed later in this chapter.

Finally, you might want to remove duplicates but add up the sales for all the removed records and add them to the Customer field. While this can be achieved with pivot tables, it can also be achieved by using the Consolidate feature, which is discussed in the next section.

## COMBINING DUPLICATES AND ADDING VALUES

In Figure 13.3, each customer appears one or more times in the list with a sales value. In addition to finding a unique list of customers, you would like to know the total sales for each customer.

**Figure 13.3**
You start at a blank section of the workbook before invoking the Consolidate feature.

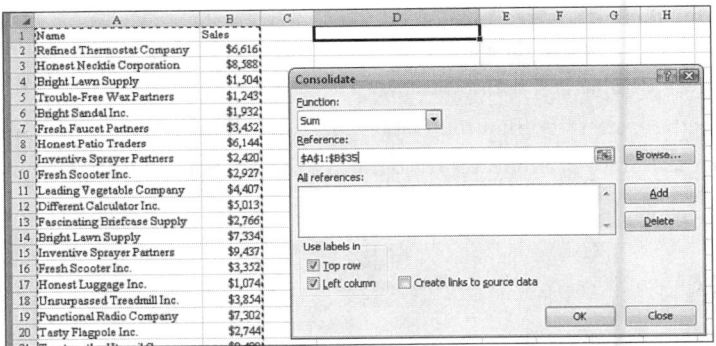

Although you could use a pivot table to find the total sales for each customer, you can also use the data tools to consolidate the table down to one record per customer, with the total sales from all the records for that customer. Here's how you do it:

1. Do not pre-select the data. Instead, move the cell pointer to a blank section of the worksheet.

2. Select Data, Data Tools, Consolidate. The Consolidate dialog box appears.

3. In the Consolidate dialog box, enter the reference to your data in the Reference box. The data will be combined based on the field in the left column of the range. If you had multiple lists of customers, you could click the Add button and enter additional ranges.

4. Make sure to check the Top Row and Left Column check boxes in the Use Labels in section.

5. Click OK.

Excel creates a new table. Each customer appears in the table just once. The sales associated with all the records of the customer appear in the new total, as shown in Figure 13.4.

Two annoyances remain with this command. First, the heading for the leftmost column is never filled in. Second, the command leaves the results in the same sequence in which they originally appeared. In this example, you will probably want to add the heading to Cell D2 and also sort the data.

**Figure 13.4**
The total sales in Columns B and E are the same.

D1

| | A | B | C | D | E | F |
|---|---|---|---|---|---|---|
| 1 | Name | Sales | | | Sales | |
| 2 | Refined Thermostat Company | $6,616 | | Refined Thermostat Company | $12,923 | |
| 3 | Honest Necktie Corporation | $8,588 | | Honest Necktie Corporation | $8,588 | |
| 4 | Bright Lawn Supply | $1,504 | | Bright Lawn Supply | $8,838 | |
| 5 | Trouble-Free Wax Partners | $1,243 | | Trouble-Free Wax Partners | $2,459 | |
| 6 | Bright Sandal Inc. | $1,932 | | Bright Sandal Inc. | $5,301 | |
| 7 | Fresh Faucet Partners | $3,452 | | Fresh Faucet Partners | $11,005 | |
| 8 | Honest Patio Traders | $6,144 | | Honest Patio Traders | $10,917 | |
| 9 | Inventive Sprayer Partners | $2,420 | | Inventive Sprayer Partners | $11,857 | |
| 10 | Fresh Scooter Inc. | $2,927 | | Fresh Scooter Inc. | $6,279 | |
| 11 | Leading Vegetable Company | $4,407 | | Leading Vegetable Company | $4,407 | |
| 12 | Different Calculator Inc. | $5,013 | | Different Calculator Inc. | $5,013 | |
| 13 | Fascinating Briefcase Supply | $2,766 | | Fascinating Briefcase Supply | $2,766 | |
| 14 | Bright Lawn Supply | $7,334 | | Honest Luggage Inc. | $1,074 | |
| 15 | Inventive Sprayer Partners | $9,437 | | Unsurpassed Treadmill Inc. | $5,959 | |
| 16 | Fresh Scooter Inc. | $3,352 | | Functional Radio Company | $7,302 | |
| 17 | Honest Luggage Inc. | $1,074 | | Tasty Flagpole Inc. | $2,744 | |
| 18 | Unsurpassed Treadmill Inc. | $3,854 | | Trustworthy Utensil Company | $8,490 | |
| 19 | Functional Radio Company | $7,302 | | Real Washer Corporation | $1,367 | |
| 20 | Tasty Flagpole Inc. | $2,744 | | Hip Shoe Company | $4,440 | |
| 21 | Trustworthy Utensil Company | $8,490 | | Best Bottle Corporation | $9,919 | |
| 22 | Trouble-Free Wax Partners | $1,216 | | Forceful Ink Inc. | $2,099 | |
| 23 | Real Washer Corporation | $1,367 | | Different Lawn Company | $3,362 | |
| 24 | Hip Shoe Company | $4,440 | | Unique Belt Partners | $5,413 | |
| 25 | Best Bottle Corporation | $6,561 | | | | |
| 26 | Unsurpassed Treadmill Inc. | $2,105 | | | | |
| 27 | Bright Sandal Inc. | $3,369 | | | | |
| 28 | Best Bottle Corporation | $3,358 | | | | |
| 29 | Forceful Ink Inc. | $2,099 | | | | |
| 30 | Honest Patio Traders | $4,773 | | | | |
| 31 | Fresh Faucet Partners | $7,553 | | | | |
| 32 | Refined Thermostat Company | $6,307 | | | | |
| 33 | Different Lawn Company | $3,362 | | | | |
| 34 | Unique Belt Partners | $3,432 | | | | |
| 35 | Unique Belt Partners | $1,981 | | | | |
| 36 | | | | | | |

# Filtering Records

Microsoft added powerful new features to the Filter command in Excel 2007. (This feature was formerly called AutoFilter, but it has been renamed simply as a Filter in Excel 2007.) Filtering works on any range of data with headings in the first row of the range. It works with ranges that have been defined as tables as well as regular ranges.

The following are some new features in Excel 2007 filtering:

- Multiselection is available in the filter drop-down. If you want to select rows that meet one of two values or rows for all but one particular value, this is now possible, using the regular filter.
- You can filter by color or icon set.
- You can filter text columns based on cells that begin with a value, end with a value, or contain a value.
- You can filter number columns based on cells that are greater than, less than, or between values. You can choose Top 10, Above Average, or Below Average.
- You can filter date values by year or month. You can filter to conceptual values such as this month, last quarter, or year to date.
- You can filter by selection. Rather than choosing from the filter drop-down, you can right-click any value and choose to filter based on the selected cell's value, color, font color, or icon.

The various features work great when one column contains values of the same type. For example, Excel expects that if you have dates in a column, all the cells except the header will be dates. Excel offers special text, number, or date formats based on what it sees in the column. These special formats are mutually exclusive: If you have a column with a mix of dates, numbers, and text, Excel offers only the special filtering type for the value type that occurs most frequently in the column. If you happen to have exactly 150 values with text, 150 values with numbers, and 150 values with dates, Excel offers the text filters. With a tie between dates and values, Excel offers the value filters.

## USING A FILTER

The icon to turn on the filter drop-downs toggles the feature on and off. To turn on the feature, you click the icon once. To turn off the feature, you click the icon again.

You need to select one cell in your data range before clicking the filter. You should have no blank rows or blank columns in the range to be filtered.

You can turn on the filter drop-downs by using any of these methods:

- From the Home ribbon, choose Editing, Sort & Filter, Filter.
- From the Data ribbon, choose Sort & Filter, Filter.
- Apply a table format to a range.
- Right-click any cell, choose Filter, and then select one of the options under Filter. In addition to performing the filter, this will turn on the filter feature if it was not previously turned on.

When the filter is turned on, a drop-down arrow is added to each heading in the range.

Figure 13.5 shows the menu available for one drop-down. This particular column includes text values, so the special filter flyout menu includes various special text filters.

**Figure 13.5**
The filter drop-down now features a multi-select list as well as new special filters.

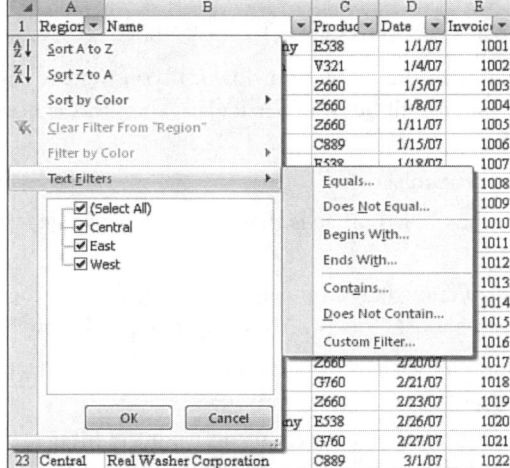

## SELECTING ONE OR MULTIPLE ITEMS FROM THE FILTER DROP-DOWN

In previous versions of Excel, the filter drop-down included a simple list of items in the column, and you would select one of the values. The multiselect nature of filters in 2007 offers far more power, but you have to exercise special care in using the drop-down.

Follow these steps to select a single item:

1. When you initially select the drop-down, all the items that appear in the column are selected with a check mark, as shown in Figure 13.6.

**Figure 13.6**
By default, all the values in the column are selected.

2. To select a single value, first click Select All. This unchecks all the items in the list, as shown in Figure 13.7.

**Figure 13.7**
Click Select All to remove the check mark from all items.

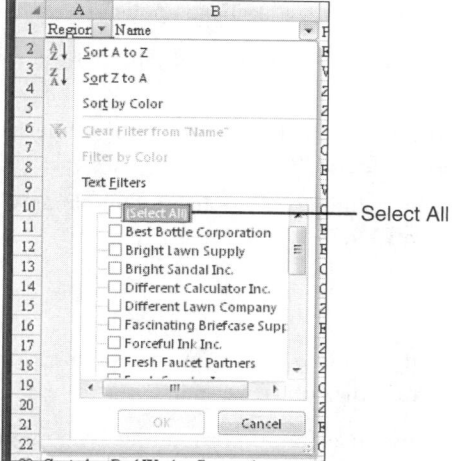

Select All

13

3. Click the value you want to filter on, as shown in Figure 13.8.

**Figure 13.8**
When the checkmarks have been removed, you select the one value of interest and click OK.

4. Click OK at the bottom of the drop-down to apply the filter.

The process you use to filter to multiple values is similar. You first click Select All to remove the check marks from all items. You can then select the items that should be included in the filter.

The multiselection ability provides a vast improvement for filtering. You could argue that it now requires four clicks where the old autofilter required only two clicks, but the improvements are worth this hassle.

In the case where you need to select everything except one certain value, the new feature is set up perfectly. You select the drop-down, uncheck the undesired value, and click OK.

## IDENTIFYING WHICH COLUMNS HAVE FILTERS

Visual clues in Excel 2007 indicate that a filter has been applied to a dataset:

- The row numbers in the range appear in blue to indicate that the rows have a filter applied.
- The message area of the status bar in the lower-left corner of the screen shows a message similar to "22 of 34 records found."
- The drop-down for the filtered column changes from a simple drop-down arrow to a Filter icon, as shown in Figure 13.9.

## COMBINING FILTERS

Filters are additive. For example, if you place a filter on one column, you can then apply a filter to another column in order to show even fewer rows.

You cannot apply two filters to the same column. For example, you might want to select all the West region cells that are red. This is not allowed. Each column's drop-down includes the list of values, a Filter by Color option, and a Special Filter option. From this complete list of filters for the one column, you can select only one filter.

**Figure 13.9**
After you filter Column A to two values, the icon on the filter drop-down changes.

| ⊿ | A | B | C |
|---|---|---|---|
| 1 | Region ▾ | Name ▾ | Produc |
| 2 | West | Refined Thermostat Company | E538 |
| 4 | Central | Bright Lawn Supply | Z660 |
| 6 | West | Bright Sandal Inc. | Z660 |
| 7 | Central | Fresh Faucet Partners | C889 |
| 8 | Central | Honest Patio Traders | E538 |
| 9 | West | Inventive Sprayer Partners | V321 |

## CLEARING FILTERS

After a filter has been applied, you have several options for clearing the filter:

- From the filter drop-down, select Clear Filter from Column. This leaves filters on in other columns.

- From the filter drop-down, choose a different filter.

- From the Data ribbon, choose Sort & Filter, Clear. This clears selected filters from any column but leaves the drop-downs in place so that you can continue to select other filters.

- Choose the Filter icon from the Data ribbon or the Home ribbon to clear all filters and turn off the filter feature.

## REFRESHING FILTERS

If data in a range changes, the filters do not automatically update. This could happen if you add new rows. It could happen if you edit data. It could also happen if your data range has formulas that point to lookup tables in other parts of the workbook.

In such a case, you need to have Excel calculate the filter again. Excel calls this feature Reapply. There are several ways you can reapply a filter:

- On the Data ribbon, select the Sort & Filter group and then click Reapply.

- On the Home ribbon, select Editing Group, Sort & Filter, Reapply.

- Right-click a cell and then choose Filter, Reapply.

## RESIZING THE FILTER DROP-DOWN

The filter drop-down always starts fairly small. If you have a long list of items, you might want the drop-down to be larger. To make this happen, you hover your mouse over the lower-right corner of the drop-down. When the mouse pointer changes to a two-headed diagonal arrow, you click and drag down or to the right.

## FILTERING BY SELECTION

You can filter without using the filter drop-downs. Microsoft Access has offered a Filter by Selection icon in the toolbar for over a decade. Excel has finally added this functionality, but it is still hidden in an obscure place.

To access the feature, you right-click any cell and then choose Filter from the context menu. You then have an opportunity to filter based on the cell's value, color, font color, or icon, as shown in Figure 13.10.

13

**Figure 13.10**
Although it is hidden, the Filter by Selection command provides a quick way to see all the other rows that match a single cell.

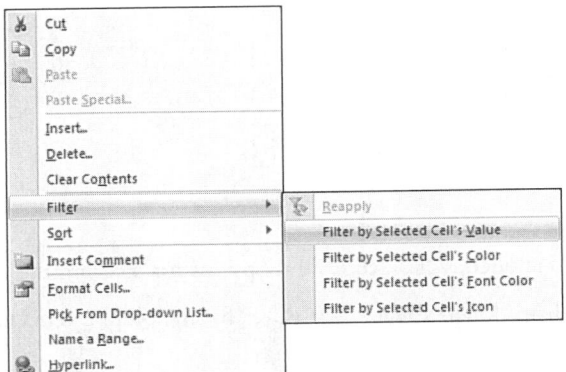

This feature works even if the filter drop-downs have not been activated previously. Using this feature turns on the filter drop-downs for the dataset.

It would be really cool if you could use this feature to multiselect values (for example, if you selected a cell that said East and then Ctrl+clicked on a cell for West). You might think that filtering by selection would filter to both East and West, but that does not work in Excel 2007. It would be excellent if Microsoft would add the ability to multiselect using this feature and would promote the feature to an icon on the ribbon in Excel 2009.

## FILTERING BY COLOR OR ICON

Cell colors are more prevalent in Excel 2007 than in prior versions, given the greatly improved conditional formatting tools. However, this feature also works with cells to which you have manually applied fill color.

Imagine that you are tracking numerous projects in Excel. You manually highlight certain projects in red if you are missing key elements of the project information. You can use Filter by Color to show only the rows that have red fill.

Filter by Color works for the cell color, the font color, or the icon in the cell. (Icons are available only from conditional formatting.)

→ For more information on icon sets, **see** "Setting Up an Icon Set," on page **162**, in Chapter 9.

As shown in Figure 13.11, the Filter by Color flyout menu offers to filter based on fill color, font color, or icon. Note that the sections of the flyout menu appear only if you have used color or icons in the range. If all your cells contain black text, Filter by Font Color will not appear in the flyout menu. If your range contains all black text on white background, without icons, the Filter by Color menu will be disabled.

## HANDLING DATE FILTERS

The default method for filtering a column of dates has changed dramatically in Excel 2007. In previous versions, the drop-down list contained a list of the dates in the column. In Excel 2007, Excel automatically groups the dates into hierarchical groups.

In Figure 13.12, the underlying data contains daily dates. However, the default drop-down shows options for the years found in the dataset.

**Figure 13.11**
The Filter by Color flyout menu offers to filter by icon, cell color, or font color.

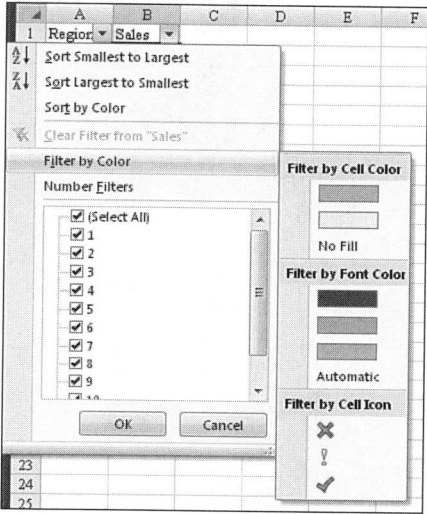

**Figure 13.12**
Excel automatically groups dates up to years in the filter drop-down.

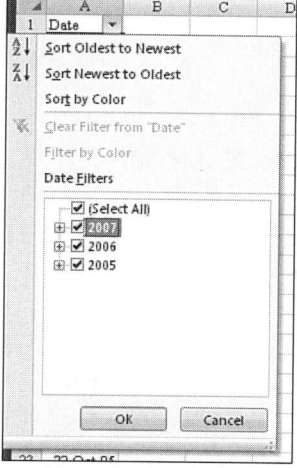

You click the plus sign next to any year to expand the list to show months within the year, as shown in Figure 13.13.

You can then click the plus sign next to a month in order to see the days within the month.

TIP FROM

You can turn off the hierarchical grouping of dates in the filter drop-down. To do so, you click the Microsoft Office button and then select Excel Options, Advanced. Under Display for This Workbook, you select a workbook and then clear the check box for Group Dates in the AutoFilter Menu.

**Figure 13.13**
You can expand the hierarchical view to see months within the years.

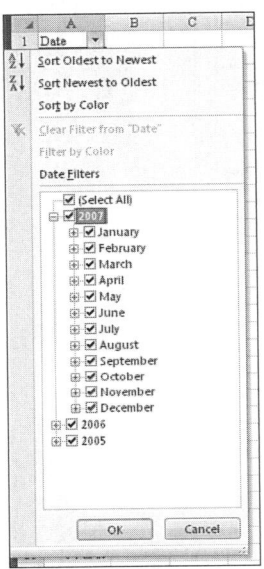

## USING SPECIAL FILTERS FOR DATES, TEXT, AND NUMBERS

Excel examines the data in a column to determine whether it contains mostly text, mostly dates, or mostly numeric values. Depending on which data type appears most often, Excel offers special filters designed for that data type.

For columns that contain text, Excel has the filters Begins With, Ends With, Contains, Does Not Contain, Equals, and Does Not Equal. You are allowed to use wildcard characters in these filters. You can use an asterisk (*) for any number of characters or a question mark (?) to represent a single character.

For columns with numeric values, the special filters include Top 10, Above Average, Below Average, Between, Less Than, Greater Than, Does Not Equal, and Equals, as shown in Figure 13.14.

For the filter named Top 10, you can specify the top or bottom values. You can specify whether the results are based on the top 10 items or the top 10% of items. Finally, you can change the number 10 to any number. Thus, you can use this filter to show the bottom 20% or the top 3 items.

For columns with dates, the special filters include Before, After, or Between a particular day, week, month, quarter, or year; Year to Date; or All Dates in a particular period, as shown in Figure 13.15.

All the special filters offer a pathway to the Custom AutoFilter dialog. This filter allows you to combine two conditions by using an AND or OR clause. This feature solves your problems some of the time, but there are still complex conditions in which you need to resort to using the advanced filter.

**Figure 13.14**
The special filters for numeric values give you the ability to find the above-average records or the top and bottom percentages, among other things.

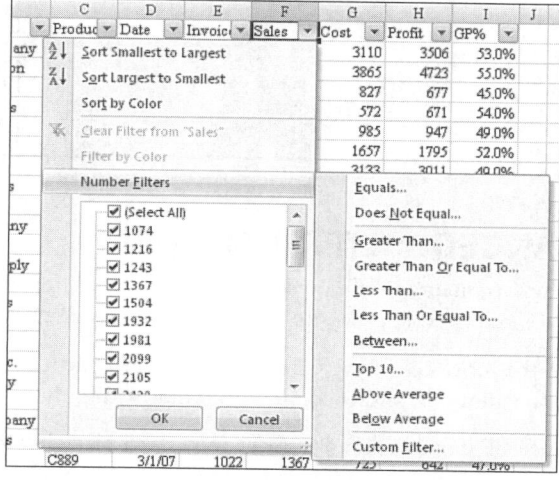

**Figure 13.15**
Excel offers a myriad of date filters.

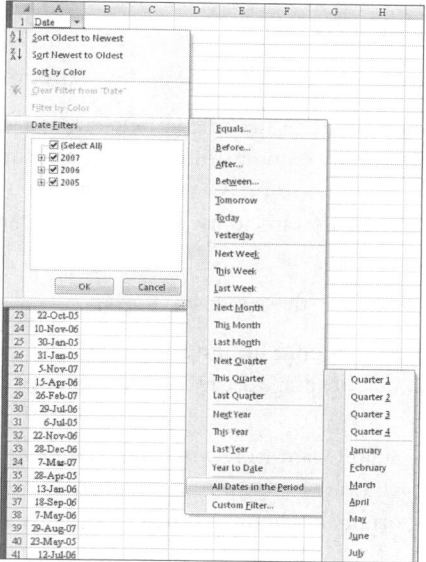

In Excel 2007, the Custom AutoFilter dialog has been nominally improved, adding a calendar control for selecting dates when you are filtering a date column.

You can use the dialog shown in Figure 13.16 to select dates that are within a certain range of dates.

**Figure 13.16**
The custom filters allow you to build simple combinations of two conditions for filtering.

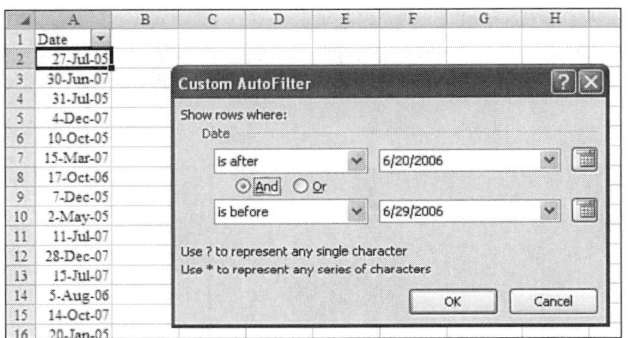

# USING THE ADVANCED FILTER COMMAND

The old Advanced Filter command is still present in Excel 2007. Microsoft should give this feature a new name. It is remarkably powerful and does much more than filtering.

It is admittedly one of the more confusing commands in Excel, particularly because there are eight different ways you can use it, and each method requires slightly different steps.

You can use the Advanced Filter command to filter records in place like the filter command, or you can use it to copy matching records to a new location. If you choose to copy records to a new location, you can copy all the input columns in order, or you can specify a subset of columns and/or a new sequence of columns.

You can ask Excel to only give you a unique list of items in the output range.

You can build a simple filter for one column. You can combine any number of filters for multiple columns. You can build incredibly complex filters, using any formula imaginable. Or you can use no criteria at all. Using no criteria is common when you are using Advanced Filter to extract unique values or when you want to use Advanced Filter to reorder the sequence of columns.

To use Advanced Filter on a dataset, follow these steps:

1. If you are using criteria, copy one or more headings from your dataset to a blank section of the worksheet. Under each heading, list the value(s) that you want to be included.

2. If you are using an output range and want to reorder the columns or include a subset of the columns, copy the headings into the appropriate order in a blank section of the worksheet. If you want all the original columns in their original sequence, the output range can be any blank cell.

3. Select a cell in your data range.

4. Choose Data, Sort & Filter, Advanced.

5. If Excel nags you with the Large Operation dialog, click OK.

6. Verify that the list range contains your original dataset.

7. If you are using criteria, enter the criteria range.

8. If you want to copy the matching records to a new location, choose Copy to Another Location. This enables the reference box for Copy to. Fill in the output range.

9. If you want the output range to contain only unique values, click Unique Records Only. If your output range contained a single field, you get a list of the values in that field which match the criteria. If your output range contains two or more fields, you get every unique combination of those two or more fields.

10. Click OK to perform the filter.

---

**Troubleshooting Excel: Advanced Filter Criteria**

It is not obvious from the instructions for using Advanced Filter, but you can build advanced filter criteria that can ask for a range of values. If you are using an advanced filter, it is unlikely that you will want to filter to the customer with exactly $7,553 in sales, but you might want to filter to invoices that are over $5,000 in sales. To set this up, you enter `Sales` in Cell K1. In Cell K2, you enter the text `>5000`. Excel then returns all invoices in excess of $5,000.

---

In Figure 13.17, the Advanced Filter operation will extract all west region sales of product E538. Four fields from the matching records will be copied to columns N:Q.

**Figure 13.17**
Advanced Filter is a powerful tool that can do much more than filter.

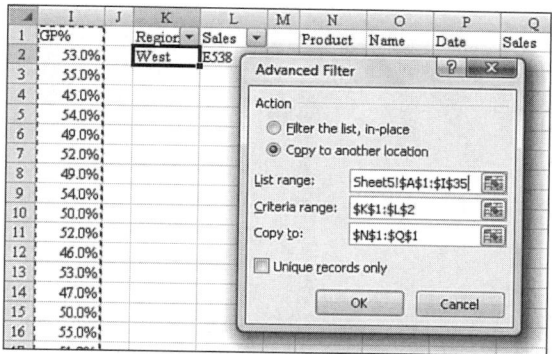

**Excel in Practice: Using Formulas for Advanced Filter Criteria**

Sometimes, you might need to filter based on criteria that are too complex for any of Excel's built-in rules.

For example, say that you want to create an advanced filter to find all records where one of 30 customers bought one of 20 products. The necessary criteria range would cover 601 rows and would take you hours to build.

There is one obscure syntax of advanced filter criteria that allows you to filter to anything for which you can build a TRUE/FALSE formula. You use the following specifics to set up a filter that contains formulas:

- This criteria range is two cells tall by one column wide.
- The top cell is blank.
- The second cell contains a formula. This formula should have relative references that point to the first data row of the input range.

13

- The formula should evaluate to TRUE or FALSE. For example, to select all the West records where the invoice is above average for the West, you would use this:

```
=AND(A2="West",F2>AVERAGEIF($A$2:$A$35,"West",$F$2:$F$35))
```

When Excel sees that the first row of the criteria range is blank, it takes the formula in the second cell and applies it to all rows in the range. Any rows that would evaluate to TRUE are returned in the filter.

# SORTING DATA

## In this chapter

Sorting data is one of the key capabilities of a spreadsheet program such as Excel. With a click of the mouse, you can rearrange data so that it is presented in an alphabetical sequence or in a sequence with the largest numbers at the top or bottom of a list of data.

One of the considerations when sorting is what happens when there are ties in the column upon which the sort is based. If you have a database of product sales and sort the data by the product field, it is likely you will have many rows with identical products. In that case, you can specify a secondary sort criteria. You might want to have Excel sort the records so that sales date is to be used to sequence records where there is a tie in the product field. In this case, you might say you want to sort by sales date within product. Excel makes this task easy.

In the past, Excel could only handle three key fields in a sort. You could specify that you wanted to sort by date within product within region. But in a large company it is very likely you would sell the same product on the same date in the same region. With only three sort levels, there would still be ties in the data.

In Excel 2007, you can now specify up to 64 sort criteria.

Excel 2007 offers powerful sorting capabilities. You are no longer limited to three sorting levels. Options are available to do case-sensitive sorting. In addition, you can now sort data by color. This sounds like a silly feature, but it is very handy for finding all the cells you marked in red or to bring together the results of conditional formatting. Methods for sorting by a custom list and sorting from left to right are still available in Excel 2007, and now they're a bit more accessible.

# INTRODUCING THE NEW SORT DIALOG

Sorting in Excel 2007 is handled with the redesigned Sort dialog or using the AZ or ZA buttons on the Home ribbon. In all, there are five entry points for sorting:

- Select the Home ribbon and then select Editing, Sort & Filter, Sort.
- Right-click any cell and choose Sort.
- Select Sort from any autofilter drop-down.
- Select the Data ribbon and then select Sort & Filter, AZ or Sort & Filter, ZA.
- Open the new custom Sort dialog box by selecting Sort & Filter, Sort on the Data ribbon.

The Sort dialog in Excel 2007 offers up to 64 different sorting levels. If you get into sorting by color, you often have to specify several rules for one column, so the theoretical number of columns you can sort by is probably fewer than 64. However, compared to the previous limit of three sort levels, this is a fantastic improvement.

To sort a dataset by the values in four columns, for example, you follow these steps:

1. Ensure that each column has a one-row heading above the data.
2. Select a cell within the data.
3. Select the Home ribbon and then select Editing, Sort & Filter, Custom Sort or choose the Data ribbon and then select Sort & Filter, Sort. The Sort dialog appears.

4. If your data is not in a defined table, make sure that the My Data Has Headers box is checked.

5. In the Sort By drop-down, choose the Major Sort field. If you want to sort by region and then customer with region, for example, select the Region field as the First Sort field.

6. To sort by values, leave the Sort On drop-down set to Values.

7. In the Order drop-down, choose either A to Z or Z to A. If your column contains dates, this drop-down offers Oldest to Newest and Newest to Oldest. If your column contains mostly numbers, this drop-down offers Smallest to Largest and Largest to Smallest.

8. Click the button Add Level.

9. Repeat steps 5 through 8 for each additional sort field.

10. Review your sort choices, which should look similar to the ones shown in Figure 14.1. If you see that you have added one of the fields in the wrong order, you can select that field and use the up or down arrow button at the top of the Sort dialog to reorder the fields in the sort.

**Figure 14.1**
Performing a four-field sort based on values.

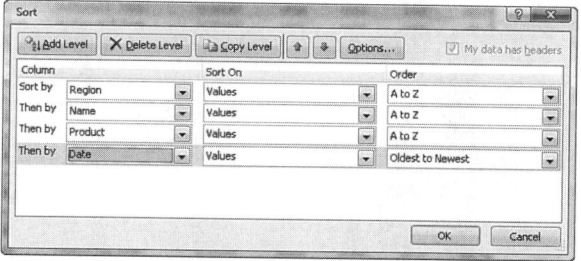

11. When you are ready to perform the sort, click OK.

If you have multiple records with identical values in all four fields, the sort retains the previous sequence for the tied records. If you ever have to sort by more than 64 columns, this feature allows you to sort by the minor columns first and then by the major columns.

# USING SPECIALIZED SORTING

While the process shown in Figure 14.1 is the typical use for sorting, there are specialized options that are available.

In certain cases you might wish to sort by color, sort by case, sort into a custom sequence, or even sort data in a left-to-right fashion.

Excel 2007 offers methods to solve all of these needs.

## SORTING BY COLOR OR ICON

Excel can sort data by fill color, font color, or icon sets. This also works with color applied through conditional formatting or color that you applied by using the cell format icons.

Because color is subjective, there is not a default color sequence. If one column contains 17 different colors, you will have to set up 17 rules in the Sort dialog just to sort by that one column.

To sort by color, you follow these steps:

1. Select a cell within your data.

2. Select the Home ribbon and then select Editing, Sort & Filter, Custom Sort or select the Data ribbon and then select Sort & Filter, Sort. The Sort dialog appears.

3. Select the desired field from the Sort By drop-down.

4. Change the Sort On drop-down to Cell Color.

5. In the Order drop-down, choose the color that should appear first.

6. In the final drop-down, choose On Top.

7. To specify the next color, click the Copy Level button at the top of the Sort dialog.

8. Choose the next color in the Order drop-down for the copied rule.

9. Repeat steps 7 and 8 for each additional color. The Sort dialog should look as shown in Figure 14.2.

**Figure 14.2**
When you sort by color, you have to explicitly specify the order of the colors.

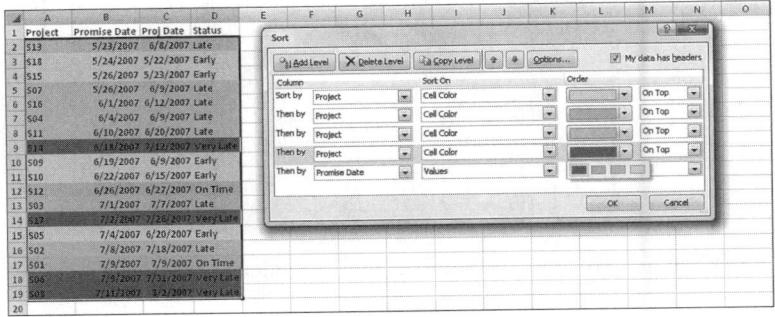

10. If you want to specify that values in another column should be used to break ties in the color column, choose the Add Level button and specify the additional columns.

11. Click OK to sort the data.

## FACTORING CASE INTO A SORT

Typically, an Excel sort ignores the case of the text. Values that are lowercase, uppercase, or any combination of the two are treated equally in a sort. In Figure 14.3, for example, all the values in A2:A9 would be considered a tie.

In Excel 2007, a case-sensitive sort sorts lowercase values before uppercase values. For example, abc will sort before ABC. Similarly, ABc will sort before ABC.

If you want Excel to consider case when sorting, you use the Options button on the Sort dialog. Follow these steps to factor case into a sort:

14

1. Select a cell within your data.
2. Select the Data ribbon and then select Sort & Filter, Sort or select the Home ribbon and then select Editing, Sort & Filter, Custom Sort. The Sort dialog appears.
3. Choose the column from the Sort By drop-down.
4. Click the Options button. The Sort Options dialog appears.
5. Choose the Case Sensitive check box, as shown in Figure 14.3.

**Figure 14.3**
Using Sort Options when you need Excel to factor uppercase and lowercase into a sort.

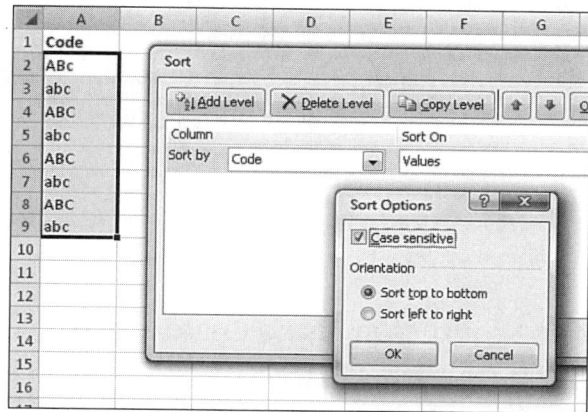

6. Click OK to close the Sort Options dialog.
7. Click OK to sort.

## REORDERING COLUMNS WITH A LEFT-TO-RIGHT SORT

If you receive a dataset from a colleague and the columns are in the wrong sequence, you could cut and paste them into the right sequence, or you could fix them all in one pass by using a left-to-right sort. To do this, you follow these steps:

1. Insert a new blank row above the headings.
2. In the new row, type numbers corresponding to the correct sequence of the columns.
3. Make sure that one cell in the range is selected.
4. Select the Data ribbon and then select Sort & Filter, Sort or select the Home ribbon and then select Editing, Sort & Filter, Custom Sort. The Sort dialog appears.
5. Click the Options button. The Sort Options dialog appears.
6. Choose Sort Left to Right. Click OK to close the Sort Options dialog.
7. The Sort By drop-down now contains a list of row numbers. Choose the first row. The remaining drop-downs should already include Values and A to Z, as shown in Figure 14.4.

14

**Figure 14.4**
You can add an extra row to specify the correct sequence of the columns and then sort from left to right.

8. Click OK to perform the sort.

9. Delete your temporary extra row at the top of the dataset. The columns are then resequenced into the desired order.

## SORTING INTO A UNIQUE SEQUENCE BY USING CUSTOM LISTS

Sometimes, company tradition dictates that regions or products should be presented in an order that is not alphabetic. For example, the sequence East, Central, West makes more sense geographically than the alphabetic sequence Central, East, West.

It is possible to set up a custom list to tell Excel that the region sequence is East, Central, West. You can then sort your data based on this sequence. You only need to set up the custom list once per computer. Follow these steps to do so.

1. Go to a blank section of any worksheet. Type the correct sequence for the values in a column.

2. Select this range.

3. Click the Office icon. At the bottom of the menu, choose Excel Options. The Options dialog appears.

4. Click the Personalize group. In the top section, choose Edit Custom Lists. The Custom Lists dialog appears.

5. In the Custom Lists dialog, the bottom section shows the range of cells that you selected in step 2 (see Figure 14.5). If it is correct, click the Import button. Your new list, with the correct sequence, is added to the default custom lists.

6. Click OK to close the Custom Lists dialog. Click OK to close the Options dialog.

7. Clear your temporary data range from step 1.

After you set up a custom list, it is available for more than just custom sorting. The custom list can be used when dragging the fill handle in order to extend a list. Here are the steps to use the new custom list with the fill handle:

1. Type **East** in a cell and then select the cell.

2. Drag the square dot from the lower-right corner to the right. Excel automatically types additional values from your custom list.

**Figure 14.5**
By preselecting the range with your correct list sequence, you only have to click Import and OK in this dialog.

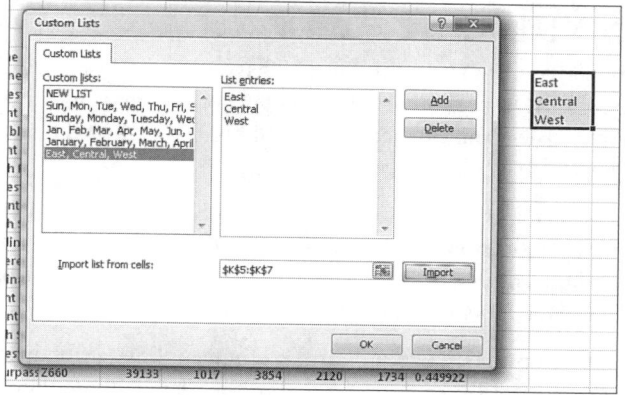

To use the list with custom sorting, you follow these steps:

1. Select one cell in your data.
2. Select the Data ribbon and then select Sort & Filter, Sort or select the Home ribbon and then select Editing, Sort & Filter, Custom Sort. The Sort dialog appears.
3. In the Sort By drop-down, choose the region with the custom sort sequence.
4. From the Order drop-down, choose Custom List. You should now be back in the Custom Lists dialog shown in Figure 14.5.
5. Click your custom list and then click OK. The Sort dialog shows that the order is based on your custom list (see Figure 14.6).

**Figure 14.6**
Excel indicates that the Region field will be sorted into East, Central, West sequence.

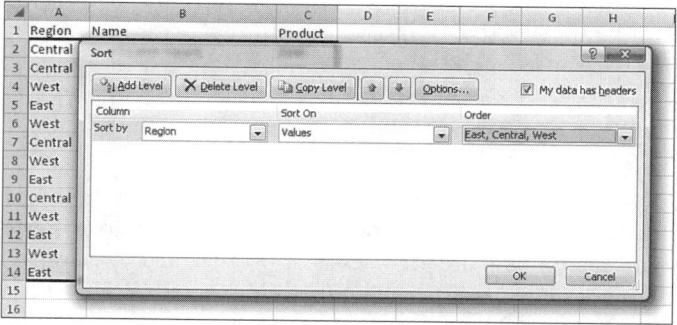

**NOTE**

In previous versions of Excel, you could not combine a custom list sort with other custom list sorts. When you use Excel 2007, you could sort every column by additional custom lists. You could also optionally add additional columns to the sort.

6. Click OK to sort into the custom sequence.

# ONE-CLICK SORTING

All the examples discussed so far in this chapter have used the Sort dialog box. The Sort dialog box is required for left-to-right sorting, custom sorting, and case-sensitive sorting. It also makes color sorting easier. You can accomplish all other sorts by using the AZ buttons on the various ribbons.

It is important to select a single cell in the column to be sorted. When you select a single cell, Excel extends the selection to encompass the entire current region. If you select two cells or even the whole column, Excel warns you that it is about to sort part of your data and ignore the adjacent data. This is rarely what you want.

The one-click sorting options are found on the Home and Data ribbons. On the Home ribbon, they are in the Sort & Filter drop-down. On the Data ribbon, they are clearly visible as AZ and ZA buttons.

You can also find sorting options by right-clicking a cell in the column you want to sort and choosing Sort. As shown in Figure 14.7, options in this menu allow you to sort in ascending or descending order, as well as to put the cell color, font color, or icon on top.

**Figure 14.7**
By using the context menu, you can do rudimentary quick sorts by color.

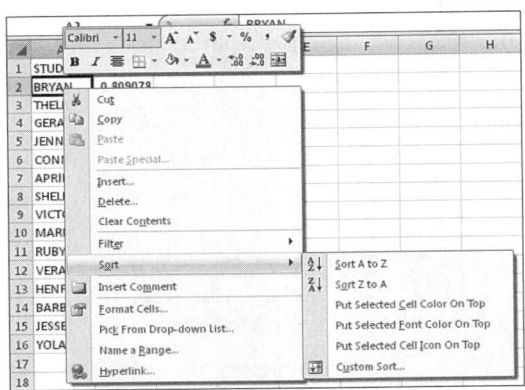

Additional quick sorting options are located in the autofilter drop-downs. You can use these options to sort in ascending order, in descending order, and by color, as shown in Figure 14.8. For tips on setting up the autofilter drop-downs, see Chapter 13, "Removing Duplicates and Filtering."

**Figure 14.8**
By using the context menu, you can do rudimentary quick sorts by color.

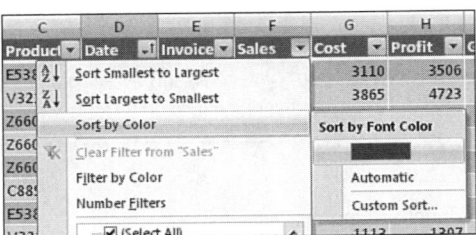

Whereas Excel 2003 used the phrase Sort Ascending, Excel 2007 now uses one of several phrases—Sort A to Z, Sort Oldest to Newest, and Sort Smallest to Largest—all of which are equivalent to Sort Ascending. Excel selects the phrase based on whether the selected column contains mostly text, dates, or numbers.

## SORTING BY SEVERAL COLUMNS BY USING ONE-CLICK SORTING

Even though the AZ button sorts by one column at a time, you can also sort a list by several columns by using the AZ button.

Remember that when Excel encounters a tie in the Sort column, the previous order remains intact. Because of this rule, you can perform quick sorts in reverse order. For example, if you wanted to sort by product within region, you would follow these steps:

1. Select one cell in the Product column.
2. Click the AZ button in the Data ribbon.
3. Select one cell in the Region column.
4. Click the AZ button in the Data ribbon.

As shown in Figure 14.9, several rows have a tie with the Central region in Column A. These rows are sequenced as the result of the sort on the Product column.

**Figure 14.9**
After two quick sorts using icons on the Data ribbon, you have sorted by product within region.

| | A | B | C | D | E | F | G | H | I |
|---|---|---|---|---|---|---|---|---|---|
| 1 | Region | Name | Product | Date | Invoice | Sales | Cost | Profit | GP% |
| 2 | Central | Fresh Faucet Partners | C889 | 1/15/07 | 1006 | 3452 | 1657 | 1795 | 52.0% |
| 3 | Central | Bright Lawn Supply | C889 | 2/7/07 | 1013 | 7334 | 3887 | 3447 | 47.0% |
| 4 | Central | Real Washer Corporation | C889 | 3/1/07 | 1022 | 1367 | 725 | 642 | 47.0% |
| 5 | Central | Honest Patio Traders | E538 | 1/18/07 | 1007 | 6144 | 3133 | 3011 | 49.0% |
| 6 | Central | Trustworthy Utensil Company | E538 | 2/26/07 | 1020 | 8490 | 3821 | 4669 | 55.0% |
| 7 | Central | Honest Patio Traders | E538 | 3/22/07 | 1029 | 4773 | 2196 | 2577 | 54.0% |
| 8 | Central | Hip Shoe Company | G760 | 3/6/07 | 1023 | 4440 | 2353 | 2087 | 47.0% |
| 9 | Central | Bright Lawn Supply | Z660 | 1/5/07 | 1003 | 1504 | 827 | 677 | 45.0% |
| 10 | Central | Different Lawn Company | Z660 | 3/30/07 | 1032 | 3362 | 1547 | 1815 | 54.0% |
| 11 | Central | Fresh Faucet Partners | | 3/26/07 | 1030 | 7553 | 4154 | 3399 | 45.0% |
| 12 | East | Leading Vegetable Company | E538 | 1/31/07 | 1010 | 4407 | 2115 | 2292 | 52.0% |
| 13 | East | Different Calculator Inc. | E538 | 2/1/07 | 1011 | 5013 | 2707 | 2306 | 46.0% |
| 14 | East | Unsurpassed Treadmill Inc. | E538 | 3/12/07 | 1025 | 2105 | 1158 | 947 | 45.0% |
| 15 | East | Best Bottle Corporation | E538 | 3/15/07 | 1027 | 3358 | 1645 | 1713 | 51.0% |
| 16 | East | Functional Radio Company | G760 | 2/21/07 | 1018 | 7302 | 3286 | 4016 | 55.0% |
| 17 | East | Trouble-Free Wax Partners | G760 | 2/27/07 | 1021 | 1216 | 584 | 632 | 52.0% |
| 18 | East | Honest Necktie Corporation | V321 | 1/4/07 | 1002 | 8588 | 3865 | 4723 | 55.0% |

# SORTING RANDOMLY

Say that you have a list of students, and you need to select the sequence in which they should present their science projects. Rather than always allowing Amber and Andy to go first, you can sort the class into a random sequence. To do so, you follow these steps.

1. Add a new column to the right of your list. Give the column a heading such as Sequence or Random or anything else.
2. In the first data cell of the new column, type =RAND() and then press Ctrl+Enter. The formula will calculate a random decimal value between 0 and 1.

14

3. Double-click the fill handle in the lower-right corner of this cell to copy the formula to all rows of your data.

4. Select the heading in the new column.

5. From the Data ribbon, select Sort & Filter, AZ. The list will be sorted into a random sequence.

6. Delete the data in the temporary new column.

> **NOTE**
>
> When you perform a random sort, it is important to note that the data is sorted into a new sequence. However, the numbers in the =RAND column do not appear to be in sequence. This is because the random numbers are recalculated after the sort is completed.

### Excel Troubleshooting: Fixing Sort Problems

If it appears that a sort did not work correctly, check this list of troubleshooting tips:

■ If the headers were sorted into the data, it usually means that one or more columns had a blank heading. Every column should have a nonblank heading. If you want the heading to appear blank, use an underscore in a white font to fool Excel. If you cannot insert a heading, you will have to use the Short Dialog.

■ Unhide rows and columns before sorting. Hidden rows are not resequenced in a sort.

■ Use only one row for headings. If you need the headings to appear as if they are taking up several rows, put the headings in one row and wrap the text. To have control over where the text wraps, type the first line, press Alt+Enter, and then type the second line.

■ Data in a column should be a similar type. If you have a column of zip codes, you might have numeric cells for zip codes of 10001 through 99999 and text cells for zip codes of 00001 through 09999. Because text cells get sorted sequentially after numeric cells, sorting the zip codes in this case will appear not to work. To fix this problem, you convert the entire column to one data type to achieve the expected results.

■ If your data has volatile formulas or formulas that point to cells outside the sort range, Excel calculates the range after sorting. If your sort sequence is based on this column, Excel accurately sorts the data, based on the information before the recalculation. If the values change after calculation, it will appear that the sort did not work. For an example, see Figure 14.10.

**Figure 14.10**
After you randomly sort, the RAND( ) function recalculates, giving the appearance that the sort did not work.

| | A | B | C | D | E |
|---|---|---|---|---|---|
| | | B2 | | fx | =RAND() |
| 1 | STUDENT | Sequence | | | |
| 2 | VERA | 0.685007 | | | |
| 3 | YOLANDA | 0.980332 | | | |
| 4 | JESSE | 0.785948 | | | |
| 5 | RUBY | 0.769471 | | | |
| 6 | APRIL | 0.229694 | | | |
| 7 | SHELLEY | 0.941594 | | | |
| 8 | BRYAN | 0.873112 | | | |
| 9 | GERALD | 0.681781 | | | |
| 10 | CONNIE | 0.632655 | | | |
| 11 | JENNY | 0.486557 | | | |
| 12 | VICTORIA | 0.278906 | | | |
| 13 | MARILYN | 0.203279 | | | |
| 14 | HENRY | 0.58145 | | | |
| 15 | THELMA | 0.012183 | | | |
| 16 | BARBARA | 0.137912 | | | |

■ If your data must have blank columns or rows, follow the steps in the sidebar "Excel in Practice: Sorting with Blank Columns."

## Excel in Practice: Sorting with Blank Columns

In a perfect world, you will never have datasets with completely blank columns. However, this is not always possible. I've worked for managers who demanded a blank column between each data column in order to have a small break between the bottom cell borders in the headings. Also, QuickBooks is notorious for exporting data to Excel with blank columns between data columns.

You cannot successfully sort a dataset that contains blank columns by using the quick sort buttons. Therefore, you need to follow these steps to sort the data by using the Sort dialog:

1. Examine the data. Even if there are multiple rows of headings, include only the last row of headings, directly above your data row.

2. Select a range that includes all columns and the one heading row.

3. From the Data ribbon, click the Sort button. The Sort dialog appears.

4. In the Sort dialog, select the check box My Data Has Headers.

5. As shown in Figure 14.11, the Sort By column contains a mix of column headings and placeholders for blank headings, such as (Column G). Choose the proper heading from the drop-down.

**Figure 14.11**
To sort data with blank columns, you must first preselect the entire range to be sorted.

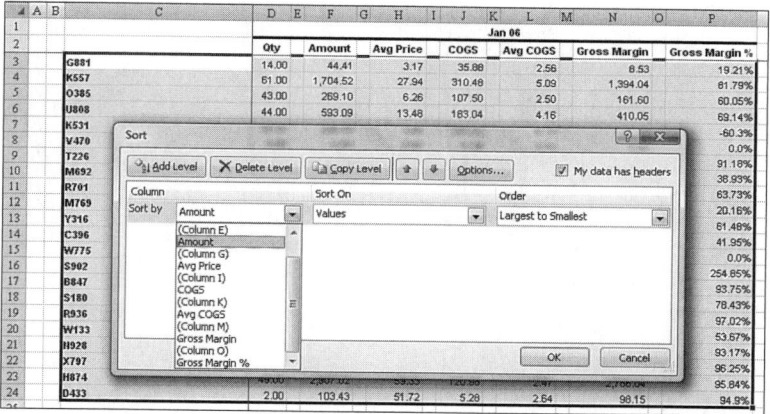

Click OK, and the entire dataset is properly sorted.

# CHAPTER 15

# USING EXCEL CHARTS

## In this chapter

The charting engine in previous versions of Excel was antique. Nothing had changed in the past 15 years. Microsoft took a giant step forward with the charting engine for Office 2007. People who use Word, PowerPoint, and Excel will all be using the new charting engine in Office 2007.

Although the eye-candy appeal of the charts is fabulous, there are no new chart types in Excel 2007. It seems that the charting team spent all its resources and time rewriting the chart engine and ran out of time to honor the many customer requests for new charting types. I expect that those new chart types will be addressed in Excel 14.

It is easy to create a great-looking chart in Excel 2007. You choose a chart type, and you can customize it with a chart layout. You can change colors by selecting a built-in chart style or a theme. After you make these three or four choices, you will have one of thousands of styles of professional charts. In case one of the thousands of variations is not exactly right for you, Excel provides settings to adjust most chart elements.

If you are a fan of visual information, I recommend that you buy every book available from Edward Tufte. Most charting books recommend his book *The Visual Display of Quantitative Information* as the source for ideas about how to graphically display information. I recommend buying the complete suite: *Envisioning Information*, *Beautiful Evidence*, and *Visual Explanations: Images and Quantities, Evidence and Narrative*.

# UNDERSTANDING THE COMPONENTS OF A CHART

A chart graphically represents numerical data. For every chart, there is underlying data. In Excel, the data is usually in a range of worksheet. This range is called the Source Data.

A simple chart would have one series of data. A series might be monthly sales for the East region for each month from January through June. Typically, a series will include the following components:

- **Series Name**—This is one cell that contains the name of the series. An example might be a cell with the value "East Region."
- **Series Values**—This is a row or column of cells that contain the individual sales for each time period.
- **Category Labels**—This is a row or column of cells that contains the name for each time period. The Category Labels typically have the same size and shape as the Series Values.

You will often include multiple series on one chart. For example, you might include additional series for Central and West regions. This allows you to compare sales for the East, Central, and West regions at a glance. Each additional series requires another cell for a Series Name and cells for Series Values. There is no need to repeat the Category Labels.

As the data is translated to a chart, look for these elements.

The Category Labels appear along the Category Axis. This is typically the axis along the bottom of the chart. Mathemeticians will call this the X-axis.

Each Series is plotted with a slightly different color. A legend will typically appear on the right side of the chart to identify the color for each series.

The Value Axis indicates the scale for the data points. In Figure 15.1, the scale is from 0 to 30,000.

**Figure 15.1**
Components of source data and a chart.

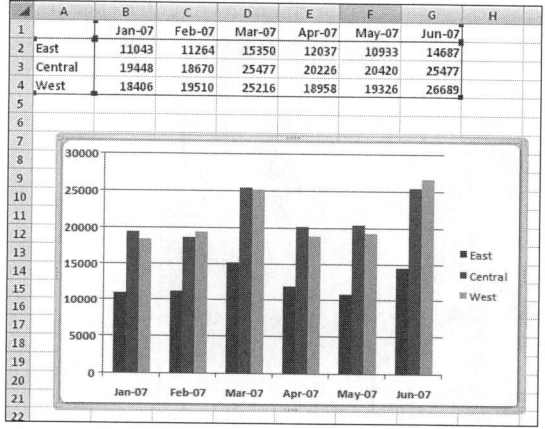

# SETTING UP YOUR DATA FOR CHARTING

The first step in creating a chart is to set up your data. There are a number of things you should do before you start charting:

- Ensure that your chart data is in a contiguous block.
- Ensure that headings along the left column and top row identify each series.
- If either your row or column headings contain dates or numerals, take care to leave the upper-left corner of the chart range blank (see cell A1 in Figure 15.2). Leaving this cell blank allows Excel's IntelliSense to work correctly. Following the discussion about chart components, there are series values in B2:G4 and series labels in A2:A4. The category labels are in B2:G7. There is no need to have a label in A1 for the category labels. When Excel sees text in A1 and numbers in B1:B7, it will assume that there are no category labels, and your chart will rarely appear as you want.

If your data follows these rules, you will be able to create charts with just a few mouse clicks.

If your data can not follow these rules, you can still chart the data, but you will have to manually enter the address for each data series value, the data series label, and the category labels.

**Figure 15.2**
If your data has numeric or date headings, leave the upper-left corner cell blank.

| | G4 | | fx | 26689 | | |
|---|---|---|---|---|---|---|
| | A | B | C | D | E | F | G |
| 1 | | Jan-07 | Feb-07 | Mar-07 | Apr-07 | May-07 | Jun-07 |
| 2 | East | 11043 | 11264 | 15350 | 12037 | 10933 | 14687 |
| 3 | Central | 19448 | 18670 | 25477 | 20226 | 20420 | 25477 |
| 4 | West | 18406 | 19510 | 25216 | 18958 | 19326 | 26689 |
| 5 | | | | | | | |

# INSERTING A CHART BY CHOOSING A CHART TYPE

For the most popular chart types, creating a chart in Excel 2007 takes just three clicks. Microsoft makes available 73 basic chart types from seven drop-down icons on the Insert ribbon.

The Charting group on the Insert ribbon includes seven drop-downs, as shown in Figure 15.3. The first six of these drop-downs hold the most popular charting types, and the Other Charts drop-down contains the remaining charting types. These are the available Charting group drop-downs:

**Figure 15.3**
Each of the seven charting drop-downs includes various chart styles. In this figure, the drop-down for Column charts is displayed.

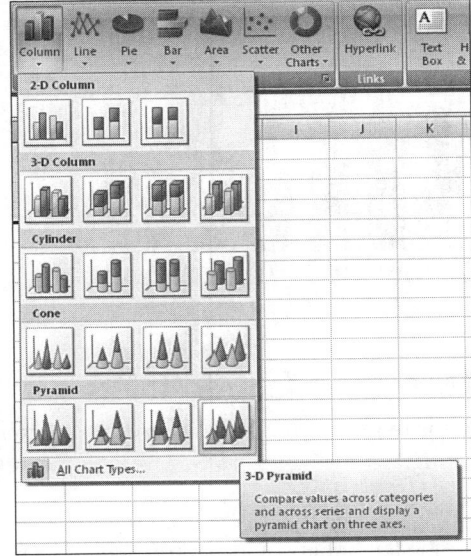

- **Column**—This drop-down includes 2-D Column, 3-D Column, Cylinder, Cone, and Pyramid chart types. All column chart types feature markers that relate the vertical height to size.
- **Line**—This drop-down includes 2-D Line and 3-D Line chart types.
- **Pie**—This drop-down includes 2-D Pie and 3-D Pie chart types. A pie chart is suitable for a dataset that has only one series of information.
- **Bar**—This drop-down includes 2-D Bar, 3-D Bar, Cylinder, Cone, and Pyramid chart types. All bar chart types feature markers that relate the horizontal width to size.
- **Area**—This drop-down includes 2-D area and 3-D area chart types. Area charts are similar to line charts except that the area underneath the line is filled with color.
- **Scatter**—This drop-down is used to plot data on x and y axes.
- **Other Charts**—This drop-down includes stock, surface, doughnut, bubble, and radar charts.

To create a chart by using the ribbon drop-downs, you follow these steps:

1. Select your data in the worksheet. Include headings in the top row and left column.

2. From the Charts group of the Insert ribbon, select the drop-down for a chart type.

3. From the gallery that appears, choose a chart type. A default chart of a default size is added to the worksheet, as shown in Figure 15.4.

**Figure 15.4**
This is a default chart at a default size. You can easily customize the chart.

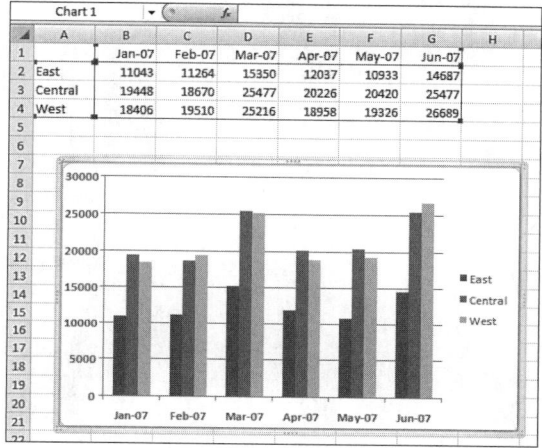

## USING THE CREATE CHART DIALOG

At the bottom of each charting drop-down is the link All Chart Types. After a chart is created, you can either click All Chart Types or select Chart Tools Design, Change Chart Type. Clicking either button leads to the Change Chart Type dialog box, which shows the 73 available chart types (see Figure 15.5).

**Figure 15.5**
The 73 chart types seem like a dizzying array of choices.

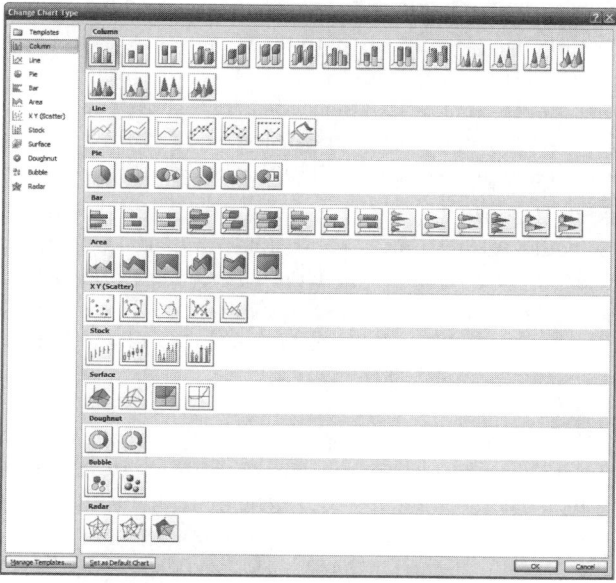

Although there are 73 chart types, there are three basic patterns that run through most chart types (see Figure 15.6):

**Figure 15.6**
Clustered, stacked, and 100% stacked chart choices pervade most of the chart types.

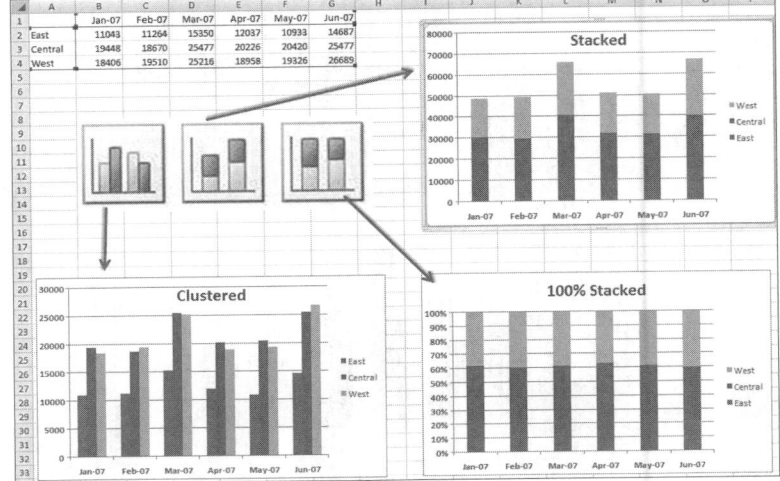

- **Clustered**—In a clustered chart, bars from each series are plotted side-by-side. This type of chart allows you to compare each element to the next. The drawback to this type of chart is that you cannot easily tell if the sum of the data is increasing or decreasing. A clustered chart is shown in the lower-left corner of Figure 15.6. In the Change Chart Type dialog, clustered chart types show a light blue and dark blue marker next to each other.

- **Stacked**—In a stacked chart, bars from each series are plotted on top of each other. With this type of chart, it is very easy to tell if the total of all series is increasing or decreasing, but it is difficult to tell if a particular series (other than the first series) increases from month to month. A stacked chart is shown in the upper-right corner of Figure 15.6. In the Change Chart Type dialog, stacked chart types show a dark blue marker on top of a light blue marker. The markers shown are of different heights.

- **100% Stacked**—In a 100% stacked chart, bars from each series are plotted on top of each other, and all bars are scaled to have a height of 100%. This chart type allows you to tell which data points make up the largest percentage of each bar. A 100% stacked chart appears in the lower-right corner of Figure 15.6. In the Change Chart Type dialog, a 100% stacked type has a dark marker on top of a light marker, and the heights of the two markers are identical.

When you look through the 3-D chart types, you usually see the three types described here, plus a fourth type, 3-D column, where the markers for each series are placed in front of each other. This chart type has problems if some of the markers for the last series are shorter than the markers for the earlier series. The 3-D column type of chart is shown in the upper-right corner of Figure 15.7. In the Change Chart Type dialog, this type of chart shows the short light-blue markers in front of the tall dark-blue markers.

**Figure 15.7**
If you are choosing from 3-D chart types, a fourth option appears, with the markers for each series one in front of the other.

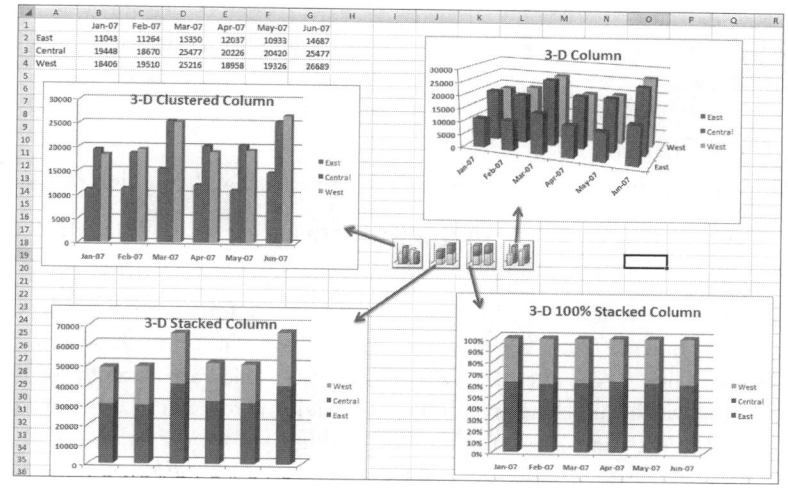

15

As you look through the 73 chart types in the Change Chart Type dialog, you see that the column, line, bar, and area charts have multiple groups that repeat these three or four chart styles. For the most part, the various groups switch between rectangles, cubes, cylinders, cones, pyramids, lines showing markers, and lines without markers.

Figure 15.8 shows logical chart groupings of the icons that appear in the Insert Chart dialog box.

**Figure 15.8**
Column, line, bar, and area charts comprise several logical groups of the basic chart types.

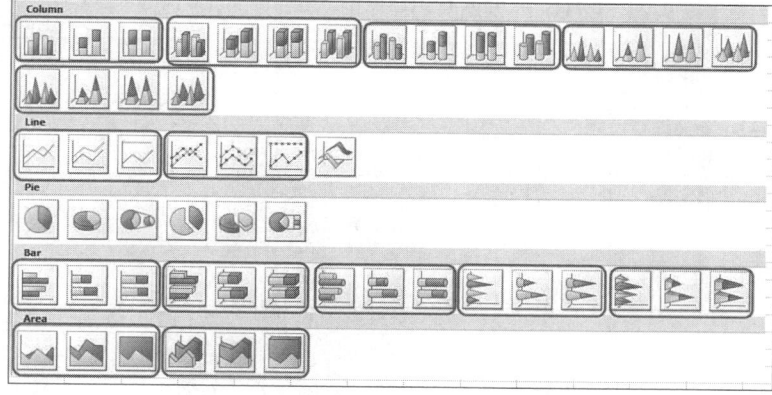

## CHANGING A CHART'S TYPE

On the Chart Tools Design ribbon, the leftmost icon is the Change Chart Type icon. You click this to access the Change Chart Type dialog. You can then select from among the 73 chart types.

For some reason, Microsoft does not include the Live Preview ability in the Change Chart Type dialog. You might find yourself clicking a chart type and then clicking OK and repeating this several times until you find the right chart. (When you consider your annoyance with the lack of Live Preview on this dialog, it is amazing how quickly you've grown used to the concept of Live Preview everywhere else in Excel 2007!)

## MOVING OR RESIZING A CHART

Move a chart by clicking on the border of the chart and dragging to a new location.

You face a subtle challenge when you want to move a chart. I initially found myself clicking in the wrong place when trying to move a chart.

You are conditioned that when you hover and see a four-headed arrow, you can click and move the object. There are many spots inside of a chart that show a four-headed arrow when you hover over them. However, the four-headed arrow might be offering to move the plot area within the chart area. The four-headed arrow might be offering to move the legend within the chart area. It might be offering to move the chart area within the chart container. If you are trying to move the chart to a new location, you need to click on white space somewhere outside the plot area. For example, click on the white space between the axis values or white space above the legend.

For trouble-free moving, make sure to hover the mouse over the border of the chart object. You can then click and drag to a new location.

**TIP FROM**

*Bill Jelen*

> If you hover just inside the border, Excel will show a four-headed arrow and then display a Chart Area tooltip. Move the mouse to over the border surrounding the chart object. You will see the same four headed arrow but there will be no tooltip. For trouble-free moves, you should not see a Chart Area tooltip before clicking.

**Figure 15.9**
Click on the border of the chart object to move the chart.

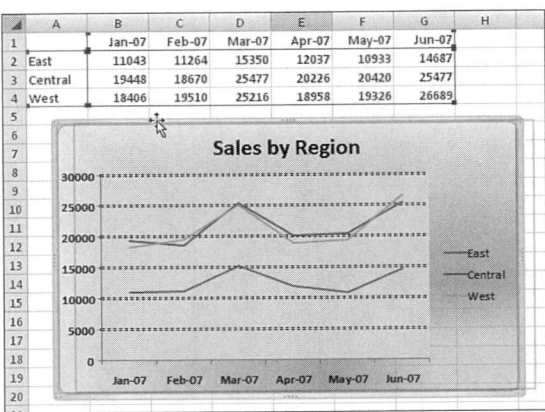

To resize a chart, click on the dots in the border of the chart and drag. There are eight sets of dots in the border. If you you click on the dots in any of the four corners, you can resize the chart in two directions. If you click on the dots in the center of each of the four edges, you can resize the chart in one direction.

# CHOOSING A CHART LAYOUT TO FURTHER CUSTOMIZE THE CHART TYPE

Your first choice in creating a chart was to choose a chart type. Your next choice is to choose a chart layout.

In previous versions of Excel, there were many settings for legends, data tables, titles, and so on. They were scattered across a wide variety of dialog boxes and were often difficult to find. For each type of chart, Excel 2007 offers a dozen predefined combinations of chart elements. Each combination is known as a *chart layout*. The Chart Layouts gallery is on the Chart Tools Design ribbon. This should be your second stop when creating a chart.

> **NOTE**
>
> The charting team at Microsoft studied numerous chart examples in magazines, books, and customer spreadsheets to find popular ways of organizing charts. The canned layouts shipped with Excel 2007 reflect the most popular layouts the team found. For example, the Layout 11 in Figure 15.10 is a sparkline chart from Tufte. In my opinion, if Microsoft is reading Tufte, it is heading in the right direction.

The chart layouts vary, depending on the chart type selected. Figure 15.10 shows the 12 layouts available for a line chart.

**Figure 15.10**
There are 12 layouts available for line charts.

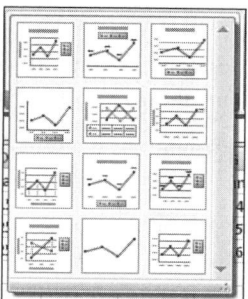

Figure 15.11 shows the 11 chart styles available for 2-D clustered columns charts. In Gerry Verschuuren's book *Excel for Scientists and Engineers*, he spends two pages discussing the steps required to make a staple of scientific analysis—the histogram chart. Note that Microsoft now includes the histogram as Layout 8 in Figure 15.11.

As you change the chart type to each of the 73 different layouts, you find that the number and organization of available chart layouts changes. Unfortunately, there is no way to add new layouts to the gallery. If you want to create a new layout, you need to use a template, as discussed later in this chapter.

15

**Figure 15.11**
The 11 layouts for column charts are different from layouts for line charts.

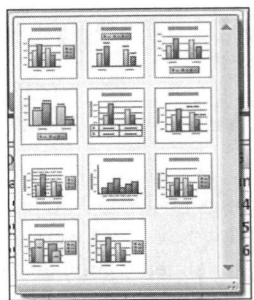

# CUSTOMIZING A CHART BY USING A CHART STYLE OR THEME

So far in this chapter, we've covered the first two steps in creating a chart: selecting a chart type and selecting a chart layout. Next, you can customize the colors in the chart.

To customize the colors on a chart, from the Chart Tools Design ribbon, you open the Chart Styles gallery. There are 48 styles in this gallery, and they are all designed to make a chart that looks good. (Microsoft hired professional designers to design the themes in this and other galleries).

Each theme in Office has six defined accent colors. The 48 styles represent various combinations of these six colors.

Six styles use a mix of accent colors. Six styles are designed in grayscale for monochrome printers. Thirty-six styles use a single accent color but show it in different hues.

The left column contains grayscale styles. The next column uses a different accent color for each series.

The next six columns of styles offer varying hues of one accent color. Each row offers a slightly different mix of effects applied to the data points. The last row of icons has dark backgrounds that match many slide layouts in PowerPoint. (For information on copying charts to PowerPoint, see Chapter 37, "Interacting with Other Office Applications.")

Figure 15.12 shows the Chart Styles gallery.

If you don't like the 48 chart styles, you can change to a new theme. On the Page Layout ribbon, you choose the Colors icon from the Themes group to see the various color themes that can be applied to the chart, as shown in Figure 15.13. The Colors drop-down shows the six fill colors for each theme and is a good place to start if you are preparing a color presentation.

For a well-balanced design, it is best to note the color scheme from the Colors drop-down and then select that theme from the Themes drop-down. When you do this, you apply the matching font and effects from the theme.

**Figure 15.12**
You can choose new colors from the 20 built-in themes.

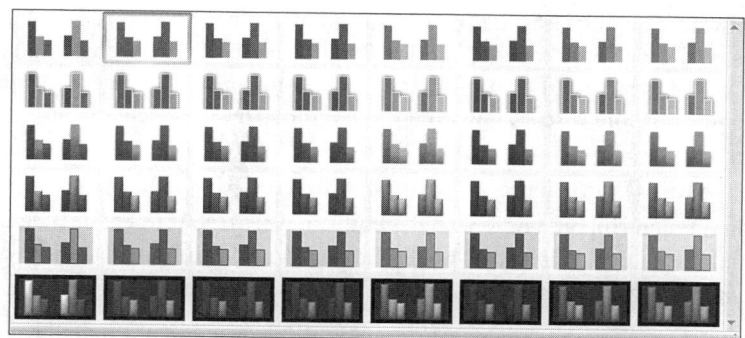

**Figure 15.13**
The 54 chart styles use colors from the current theme.

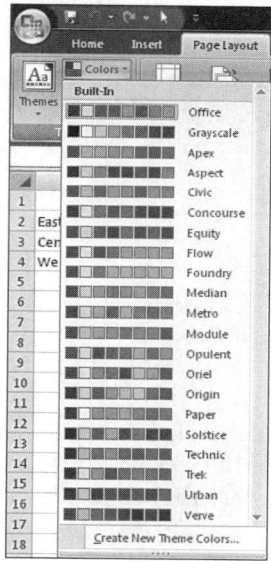

**NOTE**

There are 20-built in themes. Each theme has an associated font theme, color theme, and effects theme. You could actually choose one theme from the font area, a different theme from the color area, and a different theme from the effects area. When combined with the 54 chart styles, approximately 10 chart layouts, and 73 chart types, you have 5.8 million chart variations within six clicks of the mouse.

**CAUTION**

Changes to chart styles affect only the current chart. Changes to document themes affect all charts in the workbook, so be careful when changing themes.

With what you have learned so far, you can easily make millions of different chart combinations, and we've only touched on the Design ribbon. There are two additional charting ribbons—Layout and Format—that allow you to control various elements of a chart. The following sections discuss how to use the options on these ribbons.

## CHANGING CHART SETTINGS BY USING THE LAYOUT RIBBON

In the Design ribbon, you selected a built-in chart layout to create a certain combination of titles, legend, data labels, data table, axes, gridlines, and background. By using the Layout ribbon, you can customize the settings for those elements.

The Layout ribbon is shown in Figure 15.14. Each of the elements, from Chart Title through Chart Floor, offers several simple-to-understand options. There was always an arcane way to achieve these results in Excel 2003, but Excel 2007 makes it far easier and obvious to discover the possibilities.

**Figure 15.14**
The Layout ribbon offers easy-to-find drop-downs to control the major elements of a chart.

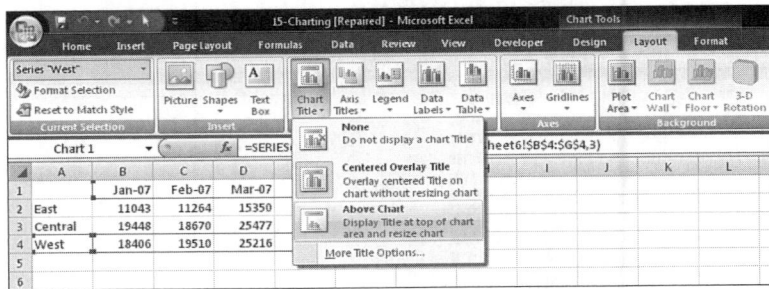

In each drop-down for the chart elements, Excel offers built-in options to handle the most popular choices. In Figure 15.15, the built-in chart title choices make sense: Either you have no title, a title above the chart, or an overlay on the chart with a title.

**Figure 15.15**
Logical built-in choices allow you to customize each element.

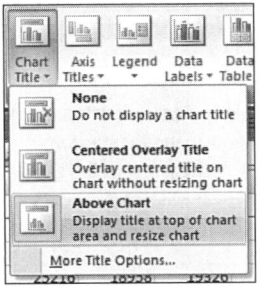

If you need more control, you can choose the More Options choice at the bottom of each element to reach a six-category Format dialog.

## MICROMANAGING BY USING THE FORMAT RIBBON

The Format ribbon provides absolute control over every aspect of a chart. To successfully use it, you need to understand the importance of the Current Selection group in the ribbon.

Initially, the drop-down at the top of the Current Selection group contains the values for Chart Area, as shown in Figure 15.16. Any changes you make to the settings in the remaining four groups affect the element selected in the drop-down in the Current Selection group.

**Figure 15.16**
The four groups on the right of the Format ribbon affect the item chosen in the Current Selection group.

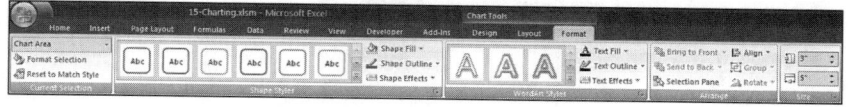

Clicking the Format Selection button in the Current Selection group takes you to a Format dialog box that affects the item in the Current Selection drop-down. In Figure 15.17, for example, a rectangular gradient has been applied to 82% of the chart area, and the rest of the chart area has been set to 72% transparency.

**Figure 15.17**
In addition to the presets in the ribbon groups, the Format Selection button leads to this dialog, which has far more settings.

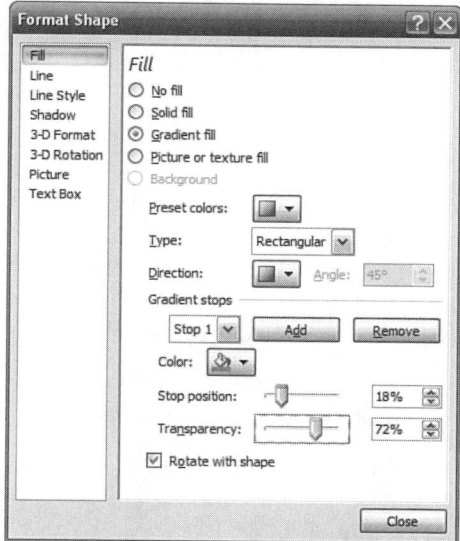

The Format ribbon provides more than 500 settings that affect the chart area. You can use the drop-down in the Current Selection group to select other elements. Figure 15.18 shows the various elements you can select by using the Current Selection group. You can adjust more than 500 settings under Back Wall, Chart Area, Chart Title, Floor, Category Axis, Legend, Plot Area, Side Wall, Value Axis, Gridlines, Walls, and each series.

15

**Figure 15.18**
You can select another chart element from this drop-down to have the remaining groups apply to a new element.

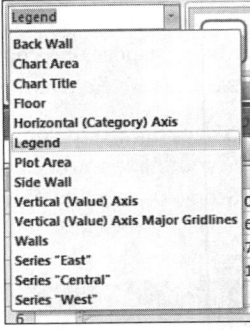

In all, this single ribbon allows you to adjust 7,500 settings for a chart.

NOTE

You can format any element by right-clicking the element and then choosing Format from the context menu that appears.

# CHARTING TRICKS AND TECHNIQUES

Although Excel 2007 offers millions of nice-looking charts, there are still secret tips and tricks that will allow people who take the time to read this book to do what is not obvious to others. Read on to learn them.

## MIXING CHART TYPES ON ONE CHART

Sometimes you want to use more than one chart type on a single chart. For example, Figure 15.19 shows a chart in which two series are measuring different measures. The first series shows sales in millions, and the second series shows a customer satisfaction scale. In order to denote that these are different measures, you might want to show the sales numbers as a column chart and the satisfaction as a line chart. To do so, you follow these steps:

1. Right-click the second data series. From the context menu that appears, choose Change Series Chart Type. The Change Chart Type dialog appears.

**Figure 15.19**
You right-click the series that should have a new chart type.

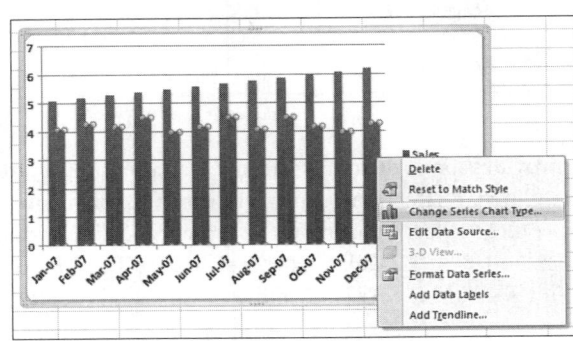

2. From the Change Chart Type dialog, choose a line style.

3. Click OK. The chart now offers a mix of chart types on the same chart, as shown in Figure 15.20.

**Figure 15.20**
A combination chart shows one or more series with a different chart types.

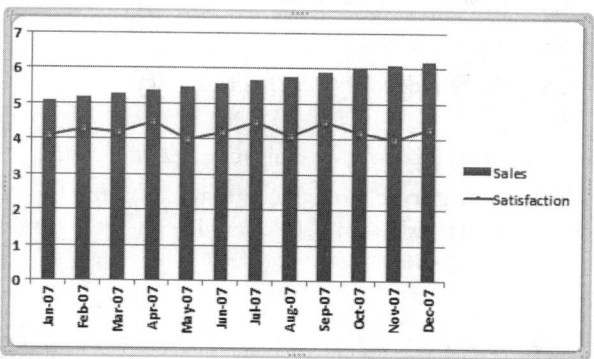

N O T E

The procedure described here works because the scale of the numbers in millions and the satisfaction are of the same order of magnitude. In many cases, however, your series will be of different orders of magnitude. If the orders of magnitude are different, you have to follow the steps in the next section, "Showing Numbers of Different Scale on a Chart," instead of these.

## SHOWING NUMBERS OF DIFFERENT SCALE ON A CHART

Say your data series contains numbers of vastly different scales. In Figure 15.21, for example, a sales chart shows total dollars and unit sales for one particular product line. Because sales are in the thousands, and the units are less than 10, there is no chance to even see the second series in order to right-click it, as in the example described in the previous section.

**Figure 15.21**
The order-of-magnitude difference between the series makes it impossible to see Series 2.

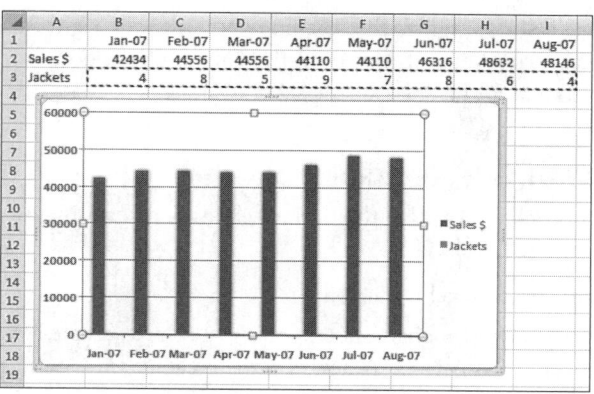

15

In this case, you would want the first series plotted against one axis and the second series plotted against a second axis. Each chart can have two scales, corresponding to the left and right vertical axes.

To enable the second axis, you follow these steps:

1. Choose Chart Tools Format ribbon.

2. From the Current Selection drop-down, choose the second series. In this example, it is called Series Jackets.

3. Click the Format Selection icon in the Current Selection group.

4. In the Series Options category, choose Secondary Axis in the Plot Series On frame. This adds a second vertical axis with a scale suitable for the second series, as shown in Figure 15.22.

**Figure 15.22**
One series is plotted on a second vertical axis with a different scale. This allows series with differing orders of magnitude to coexist on the chart.

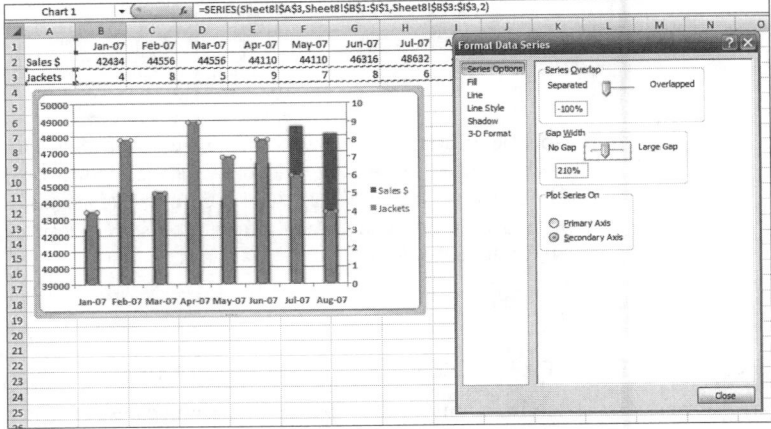

5. Optionally, right-click the second series and choose Change Series Chart Type. Then select a line chart.

6. Optionally, use color to signify that the line applies to the right axis. To format the right axis, select Secondary Vertical Axis from the Current Selection drop-down. Choose a text fill color to match the color of the second series.

## CREATING A CHART WITH ONE KEYSTROKE

One of my favorite tricks in Excel is the trick of creating a chart by using one keystroke. Here's how you do it in Excel 2007:

1. Select the range of data to be charted.

2. To create a chart on a new chart sheet, press F11. Or, to create a chart embedded on the current sheet, press Alt+F1. A new chart is created.

The new chart reflects the default chart style. In the default installation of Excel 2007, the default chart type is a clustered 2-D column chart. You can change the default chart type by following these steps:

1. Build a chart of the desired chart type.
2. Select the chart.
3. From the Chart Tools Design ribbon, choose Change Chart Type. The Change Chart Type dialog appears.
4. In the lower-left corner of the Change Chart Type dialog, click the button Set As Default Chart.

After you follow these steps, all future charts created with F11 or Alt+F1 will use this chart type.

## Adding New Data to a Chart by Pasting

A cool trick—adding new data to a chart by pasting—has existed in Excel since 1997, although not many people knew about it. Say that you have a chart showing data for several months. You have nicely formatted and customized the chart. You now have new data available. It is not necessary to re-create the chart. Instead, you can paste the new data to the existing chart.

You follow these steps to expand the chart by pasting new data on the chart:

1. Make sure the new data has a heading consistent with the old data. Note that if you accidentally enter the heading as Text instead of Date or vice versa, the trick will have unexpected results.
2. Select the new data, including the heading.
3. Press Ctrl+C to copy the new data.
4. Select the chart.
5. Press Ctrl+V to paste the new data on the chart.

**NOTE**

> In previous versions of Excel, you could drag and drop new data on the chart. Microsoft has removed this feature from Excel 2007.

## Adding New Data to a Chart by Using a Table

If you use Excel's new table functionality, charts are automatically updated when new data is added. This method works even if the chart is based on data that is not currently in a table. You follow these steps to make the data into a table and extend the chart:

1. Select a cell in the source data for the chart.
2. Type Ctrl+T to make the range into a table.

15

3. Confirm the location for the table.

4. Note that even though you had left the top-left corner cell blank, the table functionality now must assign a column name, such as Column1, to this column (see Figure 15.23).

**Figure 15.23**
Converting the source data into a table.

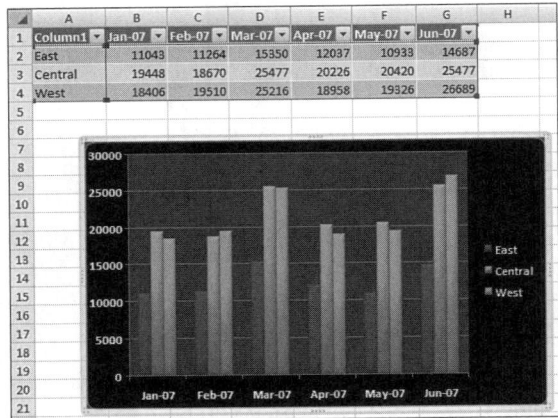

5. In the blank column next to the table, type the heading for the next month. Excel automatically extends the table and adds the new month to the chart, as shown in Figure 15.24.

**Figure 15.24**
When you type a new column heading, Excel extends the table and consequently the chart.

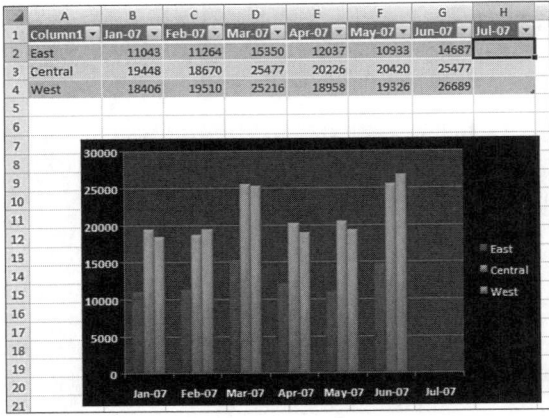

6. Type the values for the new column. Excel extends both the table and the chart.

## ADDING DROP LINES TO A SURFACE CHART

Surface charts can be hard to read. Excel draws a smooth line between adjacent data points. It is difficult for your eye to follow the label on the x-axis up to the point on the surface chart. For example, Figure 15.25 shows a surface chart. Can you tell if the point for June 2002 is above or below 70%?

**Figure 15.25**
Surface charts can be difficult to read.

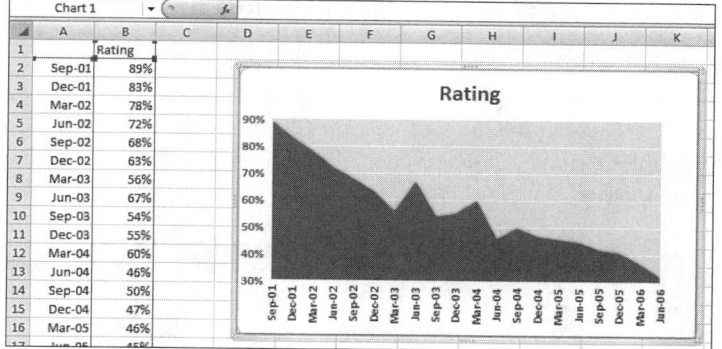

To make surface charts easier to read, you can add drop lines from each point on the surface chart in Excel 2007. Here's how you do it:

1. Select the chart.

2. From the Chart Tools Layout ribbon, in the Analysis group, choose Lines, Drop Lines. Excel draws a vertical line from the x-axis to the surface of the chart, as shown in Figure 15.26.

**Figure 15.26**
Vertical drop lines make it easier to figure out where each data point crosses the chart.

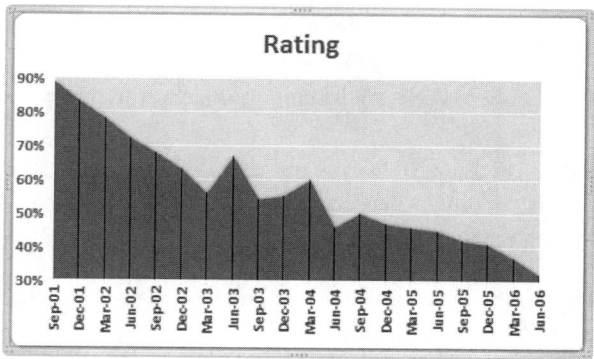

## PREDICTING THE FUTURE BY USING A TRENDLINE

Chapter 27, "Using Trig, Matrix, and Engineering Functions," presents some fairly complicated functions for calculating linear regression lines. Rather than use those functions, it is far simpler to plot the data on a chart and ask Excel to add a trendline.

In Figure 15.27, a line chart shows progress toward a goal for the first eight days of a month. Excel can add a trendline to the chart and extend the trendline to predict the final goal. You can consider the trendline to be a predictor of what will happen if things continue to progress at the same pace. If the trendline after 30 days does not meet the goal, you need to start working harder.

You follow these steps to add a trendline to a chart:

1. Select a chart that contains data of past actuals.

2. From the Chart Tools Layout ribbon, in the Analysis group, choose the Trendline drop-down. Although Excel offers four canned trendlines, you need to choose More Trendline Options to force the trendline to predict the future. The Format Trendline dialog appears.

**Figure 15.27**
You select the chart and then choose More Trendline Options from the Trendline drop-down.

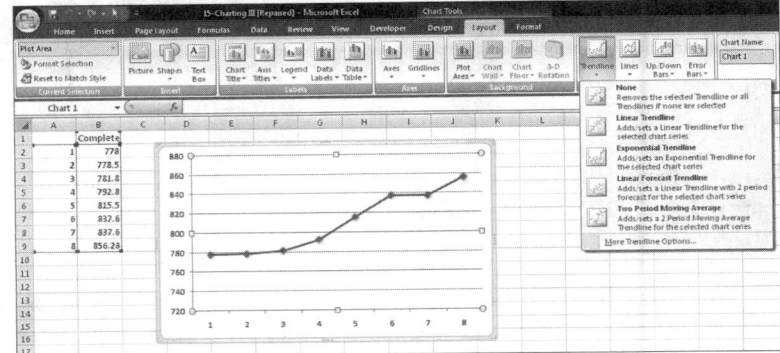

3. In the Format Trendline dialog, enter a positive value in the Forecast Forward section. In this case, 22 days would be appropriate.

4. Optionally, if you want to display a legend on the chart, type a custom name for the Trendline name.

5. Optionally, choose the Line Style category and change the line style to a dashed line. This helps indicate that the projection is not real data but is a simple mathematical projection of what could happen.

A new series is added to the chart, as shown in Figure 15.28. The series uses straight-line regression to calculate future data points.

## CREATING STOCK CHARTS

Excel offers four varieties of stock market charts to track historical stock performance. Each variety requires a slightly different organization for the data. The order of the data must exactly match the following requirements:

- **High-Low-Close**—These charts require four columns of data: date, high, low, and close.

- **Open-High-Low-Close**—These charts require five columns of data: date, open, high, low, and close.

**Figure 15.28**
The projection line predicts that this book will have 1,000+ pages. Turn to the last page to see if it is correct.

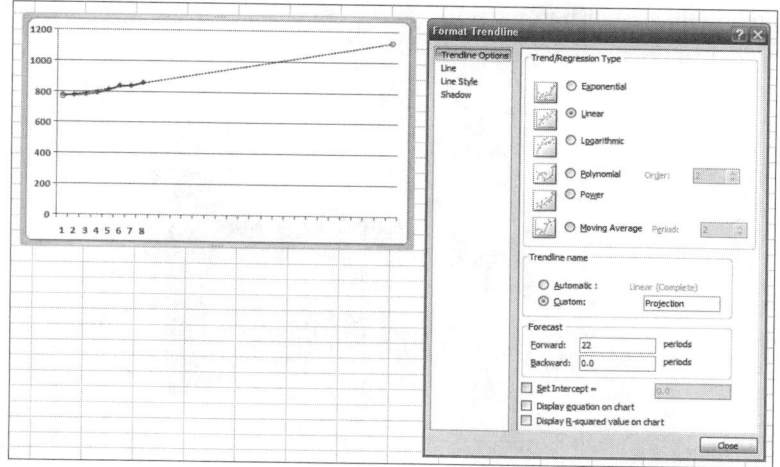

- **Volume-High-Low-Close**—These charts require five columns of data: date, volume, high, low, and close.

- **Volume-Open-High-Low-Close**—These charts require six columns of data: date, volume, open, high, low, and close.

To create a stock chart, you follow these steps:

1. Import your data from http://finance.yahoo.com or another data source.

2. If necessary, cut and paste the columns into the proper sequence to match your desired chart type.

3. Sort the data by date, oldest to newest.

4. Select the data, including the headings.

5. From the Insert ribbon, choose Charts, Other Charts, Stock. Select the appropriate chart type to match your data, as shown in Figure 15.29.

**Figure 15.29**
Your data must match the sequence specified in the ToolTip.

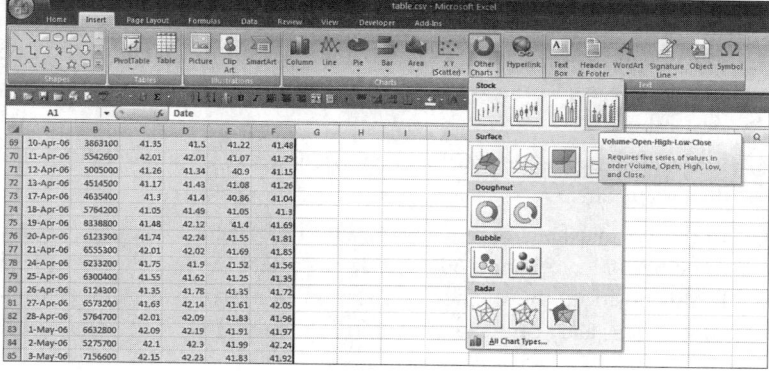

6. Optionally, choose a new color scheme from the Chart Styles gallery.

15

The result, as shown in Figure 15.30, is a stock chart good enough to print in the *Wall Street Journal*.

**Figure 15.30**
Excel creates this stock chart.

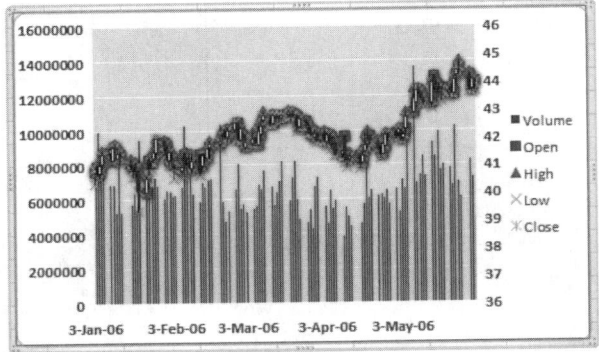

## DEALING WITH SMALL PIE SLICES

In many data series, a few pie slices take up 80% of the pie, and many tiny slices account for the rest of the pie. Typically, these last pie slices end up at the back of the pie, where it is impossible to fit the labels, so no one can make out what they are.

One solution is to rotate the pie so that the smaller pie slices are near the front. Here's how you do it:

1. Enter one series of data. Sort the values from high to low.

2. Create a pie chart by using the 3D Pie type.

3. On the Labels group of the Chart Tools Layout ribbon, turn off the legend.

4. In the same group, select the Data Labels drop-down and then choose More Data Label Options. Turn off the value and turn on Category Name and Percentage. Choose Best Fit.

5. Right-click in the pie chart and choose Format Data Series. The Format Data Series dialog appears.

6. In the Format Data Series dialog, the first category is Angle of First Slice. Move this up to be between 150 and 160, in order to rotate the last slices to the right-front position. In this position, the smaller slices are in front, so there is more room for many labels to appear near each other, as shown in Figure 15.31.

**Figure 15.31**
Adjusting the Angle of First Slice setting to around 150 moves the smaller final slices toward the right front of the pie.

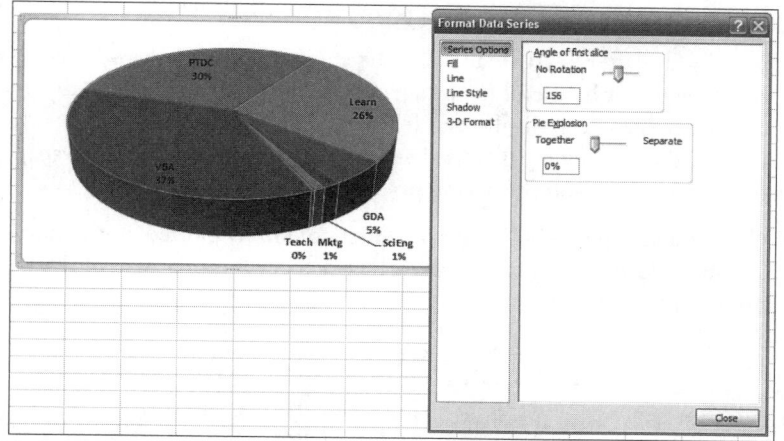

When you have several small data points at the end of a pie chart series, and you need to be able to see all the smaller segments, you can change the chart type to a special type called bar of pie. In this type, the smallest few categories are exploded out and shown as a bar chart next to the pie.

To change an existing pie chart to a bar of pie chart, you follow these steps:

1. Select the chart.

2. From the Type group of the Chart Tools Design ribbon, choose Change Chart Type. The Change Chart Type dialog appears.

3. In the Change Chart Type dialog, choose the last option for pie charts: Bar of Pie.

4. Click OK to close the dialog.

5. Right-click the chart and choose Format Data Series. The Format Data Series dialog appears.

6. In the Format Data Series dialog, you have control over the number of values in the bar chart. In Figure 15.32, for example, the settings call for the last four items to be in the other bar chart. Note that the total of 285 for those four items is shown on the chart as Other 285. The bar chart breaks down the 285 by category.

**Figure 15.32**
In a bar of pie chart, the tiny slices are exploded so it's easy to see the details.

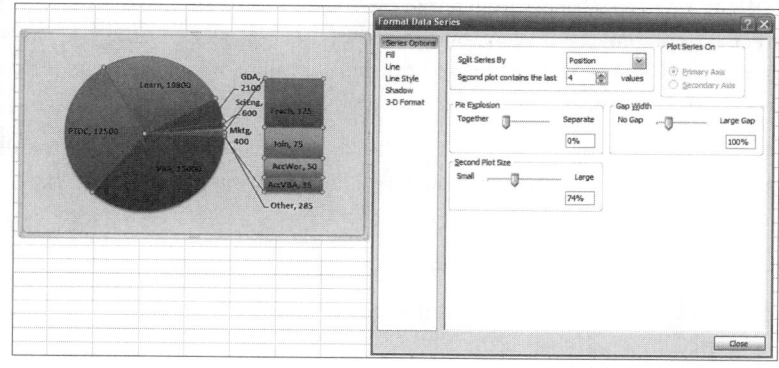

15

## DISPLAYING THREE VARIABLES BY USING A BUBBLE CHART

Typically, a scatter chart or an XY chart shows points in a two-dimensional x,y-coordinate grid. This might be useful for exploring the relationship between two measures. By using a bubble chart, you can display the relationship between *three* variables. In Figure 15.33, for example, the chart compares used vehicle prices from the local newspaper. The table shows age in year, miles, and the asking price.

When you set up a bubble chart, the first column is plotted along the x-axis. The second column is plotted along the y-axis. The price becomes the size of the bubble at the intersection of each x,y coordinate.

**Figure 15.33**
The size of the sphere at each intersection communicates the information about a third dimension. In this example, the bubble size represents relative price.

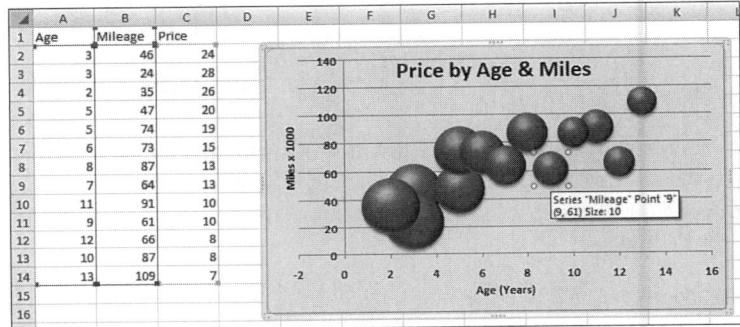

## CHANGING THE LOCATION OF A CHART

Charts can be embedded on a worksheet, or they can exist on their own sheets. To move a chart from one place to another, you follow these steps:

1. Select the Chart Tools Design ribbon and then select Location, Move Chart. Excel displays the Move Chart dialog.

2. You can either choose to place the object in an existing sheet or to move the chart to a new sheet.

## SAVING A FAVORITE CHART STYLE AS A TEMPLATE

Although Microsoft has provided great-looking built-in charts, you will likely design some great-looking charts of your own. After you have designed one, you can save it as a template. When you build new charts based on that template, all the settings for colors, fonts, effects, and chart elements are applied to the new data.

For all the power and glitz of Excel's built-in chart styles, the chart templates feature will save you massive amounts of time if you routinely customize your charts, for example, to meet a company standard.

You follow these steps to create a template:

1. Build a chart and customize it as necessary.

2. Select the chart. In the Type group of the Chart Tools Design ribbon, select Save Template. Give the chart template a name. Excel saves the template with a .crtx file extension.

To create a chart by using your template, you follow these steps:

1. Select the data you want to chart.
2. From the Insert ribbon, choose any of the Chart drop-downs and then select All Chart Types. The Create Chart dialog appears.
3. In the Create Chart dialog, choose the Templates category.
4. Click the desired Template, if there is more than one.
5. Click OK. Excel creates the chart with all the custom formatting from the saved template.

If you like your template so much that you want all future charts to be based on the template, you can follow these steps to make it the default style:

1. Select a chart based on the desired template.
2. From the Chart Tools Design ribbon, select Change Chart Type. The Create Chart dialog appears.
3. In the Create Chart dialog, choose the Templates category.
4. Select the desired template.
5. In the lower-left corner of the Change Chart Type dialog, choose Set as Default Chart.

Then, in the future, you can quickly create a chart that uses this template by following these steps:

1. Select the data you want to chart.
2. Press Alt+F1.

> **NOTE**
>
> The process of creating and customizing charts every month used to be a time-consuming process. The ability to save every nuance of desired formatting as a template and then make the template the default for all future charts is something that would have made my job as a financial analyst far easier.

# USING PIVOT CHARTS

Pivot tables are discussed in detail in Chapters 10, "Using Pivot Tables to Analyze Data," 11, "Formatting Pivot Tables," and 12, "Using Pivot Tables in Practice." Pivot charts have been an underused component of pivot tables for several versions of Excel.

A pivot chart is a chart based on an underlying pivot table. As you sort, filter, and change the field layout of the pivot table, the associated chart will automatically update.

15

In Excel 2007, the pivot chart engine shares the same charting engine with the rest of Office. Style changes made to a pivot chart persist after you add new fields to the pivot chart. In addition, in Excel 2007, Microsoft has added the PivotChart Filter Pane dialog to allow you to filter various aspects of a pivot chart.

To create a pivot chart, you follow these steps:

1. Select a single cell in your data.
2. From the Insert ribbon, choose Tables, PivotTable, PivotChart. The Create PivotTable with PivotChart dialog appears.
3. Click OK to create a pivot chart on a new worksheet. A blank pivot chart is created and the PivotTable Field List appears.
4. Drop your primary chart field on the Axis Fields drop zone.

NOTE

> The PivotTable field list is similar to the one used in pivot tables, with two exceptions:
> - The Row Labels drop zone is called Axis Fields.
> - The Columns Labels drop zone is called Legend Fields.

5. If you drop a field on the Legend Fields drop zone, it is treated as an additional data series in the chart, so drop a secondary chart field here.
6. Drag a summable field such as Revenue, to the Sum Values drop zone.
7. Select the chart. From the PivotChart Tools Design ribbon, click Chart Type. Choose either a clustered or stacked bar or column chart.
8. Optionally, move any filter fields to the Report Filter drop zone.
9. Optionally, apply a style to the chart by selecting Chart Styles from the PivotChart Tools Design ribbon.

As shown in Figure 15.34, Excel create a chart for the selected fields. You can use the new PivotChart Filter Pane dialog to filter the chart to any specific subset of values.

**Figure 15.34**
In Excel 2007, you can pivot a pivot chart, and it retains its formatting and styles.

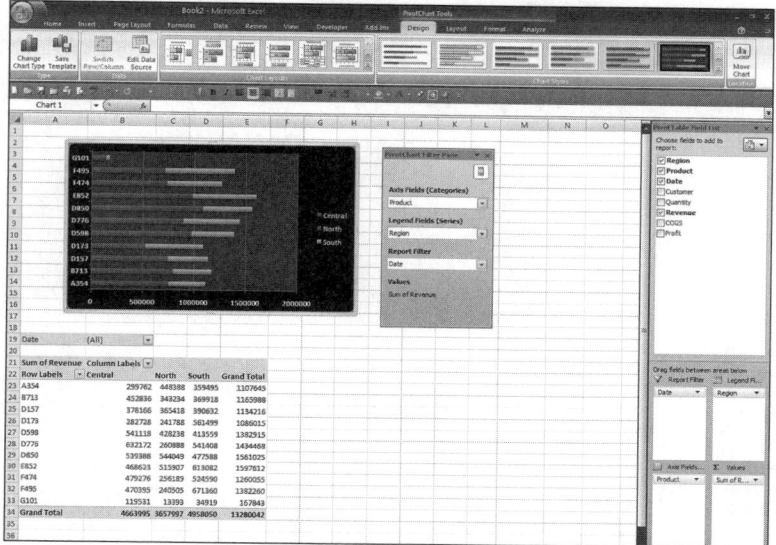

CHAPTER **16**

# USING SMARTART, SHAPES, WORDART, AND TEXT BOXES

## In this chapter

Images and artwork provide an interesting visual break from tables of numbers. Office 2007 provides four elements that can be used to illustrate a workbook:

- **SmartArt**—SmartArt is a collection of similar shapes, arranged to imply a process, groups, or a hierarchy. In former versions of Excel, SmartArt was known as Diagrams. As in the past, it is easy to add new shapes, reverse the order of shapes, and change the color of shapes. Office 2007 includes a text editor that allows for Level 1 and Level 2 text for each shape in a diagram. Many styles of SmartArt include the capability to add a small picture or logo to each shape.

- **Shapes**—You can add interesting shapes to a document. A shape can contain words; it is the only art object in which the words can come from a cell on the worksheet. You can add glow, bevel, and 3-D effects to shapes. In previous versions of Excel, shapes were known as AutoShapes. Microsoft has added some new shapes as well as several formatting properties.

- **WordArt**—You use WordArt to present ordinary text it in a stylized manner. You can use it to bend, rotate, and twist the characters in text. In Excel 2007, you can add glow, bevel, and material effects. WordArt has been completely redesigned from previous versions of Excel.

- **Text boxes**—You use a text box to allow text to flow in a defined area. This feature is excellent if you need to include paragraphs of body copy in a worksheet. A new feature in Excel 2007 is the ability to have text flow through multiple columns in a single text box.

# USING SMARTART

You use SmartArt to show a series of similar shapes, where each shape represents a related step, concept, idea, or grouping.

SmartArt in Excel 2007 is an enhanced version of business diagrams from previous versions of Excel. In Excel 2007, Microsoft has addressed many of the shortcomings of business diagrams, including the following:

- Each shape has an associated text editor.
- Shapes can contain Level 1 text for headlines and Level 2 text for body copy.
- Some styles now allow shapes to include an image.
- Automatic settings in SmartArt can automatically resize the text in all shapes to allow the longest text to fit.
- Quick Styles allows you to apply glow and bevels to an entire SmartArt diagram.

The goal of SmartArt is to allow you to create a great-looking graphic with a minimum of effort. After you define a SmartArt image, you can quickly change to any of the other 84 styles by choosing the desired style from the gallery. Text is carried from one style to the next. Figure 16.1 shows four different SmartArt styles:

- **Basic Process**—In this style, all text is typed as Level 1.
- **Accent Process**—This style puts the Level 1 text in the background and highlights the Level 2 text in the foreground boxes.
- **Picture Accent Process**—This style gives equal weight to the Level 1 and Level 2 text. Pictures are added behind each shape.
- **Picture Accent List**—Unlike the process charts, a list chart does not include arrows to indicate a process.

**Figure 16.1**
Subtle differences in 4 of the 84 possible SmartArt styles give more weight to either Level 1 or Level 2 text.

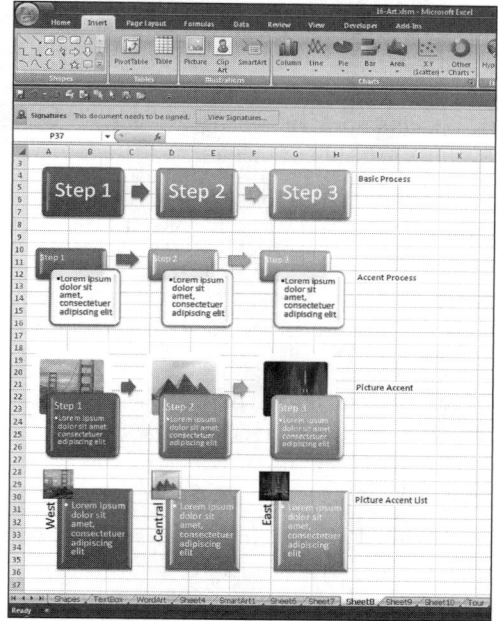

If you want to fine-tune the text in a particular box, you can select SmartArt Tools from the Format ribbon to micromanage any element in the SmartArt. Use caution, as adjusting the built-in properties is a great way to very quickly ruin the look of the SmartArt.

## ELEMENTS COMMON ACROSS MOST SMARTART

A SmartArt style is a collection of two or more related shapes. In most styles, you can add additional shapes in order to illustrate a longer process. A few styles are limited to only *n* items. Each shape can contain a headline (Level 1 text), body copy (Level 2 text), and a graphic. Some of the 84 styles show only Level 1 text. If you switch to a style that does not display Level 2 text and then back, the shape remembers the Level 2 text it originally had.

Some of the 84 SmartArt styles can include pictures. You should add pictures after you have selected your final style. Changing layout styles always causes pictures to be lost, so you should finalize a layout before adding the images. Some styles include arrows between shapes to illustrate a process.

While you're editing SmartArt, a text pane that is slightly reminiscent of PowerPoint appears. You can type some bullet points in the text pane. If you demote a bullet point, the text changes from Level 1 text to Level 2 text. If you add a new bullet point, Excel adds a new shape to the SmartArt.

## A TOUR OF THE SMARTART CATEGORIES

The SmartArt gallery groups the 84 SmartArt layouts into seven broad categories:

- **List**—This category is designed to show a nonsequential list of information. Variations include horizontal, vertical, and bending lists. Some lists include chevrons, and some include pictures. In general, these styles do not include arrows between shapes.

- **Process**—This category is designed to show a sequential list of steps. Variations include horizontal, vertical, bending, equations, funnels, gears, and several varieties of arrows. Some process charts allow the inclusion of images. Most styles include arrows or other connectors in order to convey a sequence.

- **Cycle**—This category is designed to show a series of steps that repeat. It includes cycle charts, radial charts, a gear chart, and a pie chart.

- **Hierarchy**—This category is designed to show organization charts, decision trees, and other hierarchical relationships. Variations include horizontal, vertical, and with and without connecting lines.

- **Relationship**—This category is designed to show a relationship between items. Many of these layouts in this category are duplicated from the other six categories. The category includes one to five examples each of arrow, chart, cycle, equation, funnel, gear, hierarchy, list, process, pyramid, radial, target, and Venn chart layouts.

- **Matrix**—This category is designed to show four quadrants of a list. Only two options exist: either four quadrants and a central element or four quadrants.

- **Pyramid**—This category is designed to show containment, overlapping, proportional, or interconnected relationships.

Figure 16.2 shows one version of each of the seven categories.

## INSERTING SMARTART

Although there are 84 different layouts of SmartArt, you follow the same basic steps to insert any SmartArt layout:

1. Select a cell in a blank section of the workbook.

2. From the Insert ribbon, choose SmartArt from the Illustrations group. The Choose a SmartArt Graphic dialog appears.

3. In the left side of the Choose a SmartArt Graphic dialog, select a category.

4. Click a SmartArt type in the center of the Choose a SmartArt Graphic dialog.

5. Read the description on the right side. This description tells you whether the layout is good for Level 1 text, Level 2 text, or both. In Figure 16.3, the Vertical Chevron List layout is good for large amounts of Level 2 text.

List     Hierarchical     Pyramid

**Figure 16.2**
SmartArt diagrams
exist in seven broad
categories.

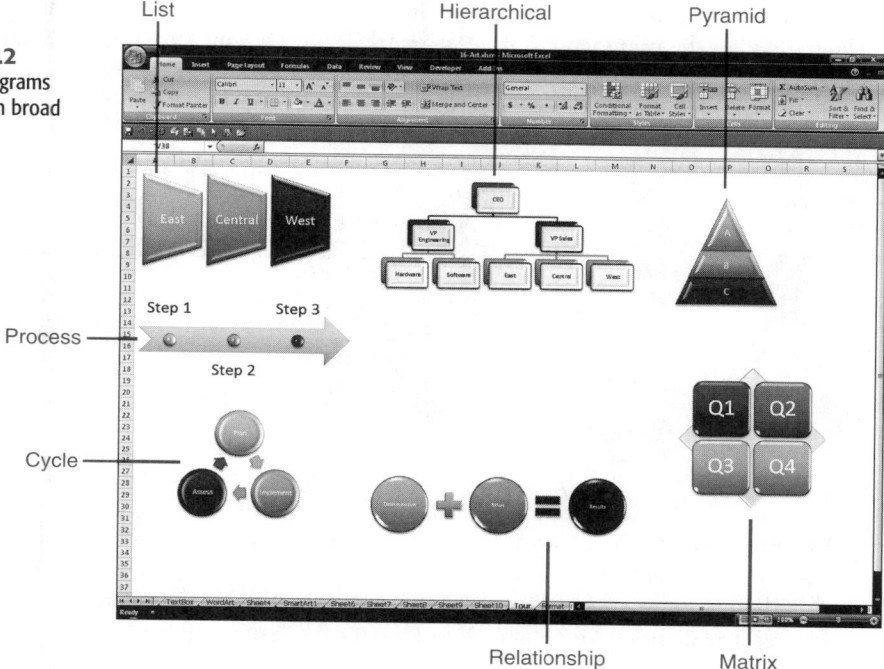

Process

Cycle

Relationship     Matrix

16

**Figure 16.3**
The description for
each style provides
information about
whether a particular
style is appropriate for
more Level 1 or Level
2 text.

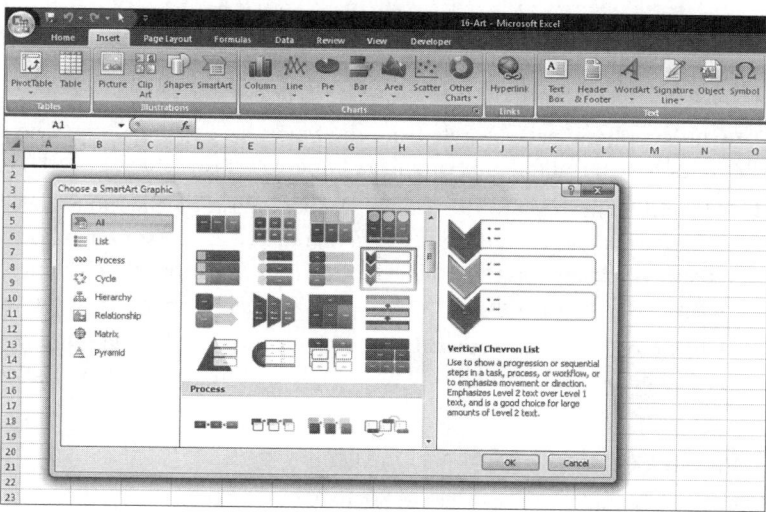

6. Repeat steps 4 and 5 until you find a style suitable for your content. Then click OK. As shown in Figure 16.4, an outline of the SmartArt is drawn on the worksheet. The flashing insertion cursor is in the first item of the text pane. One element of the SmartArt is selected. When you type text at the flashing insertion point, it is added to the selected shape.

7. Fill in the text pane with text for your SmartArt. You can add, delete, promote, or demote items by using icons in the SmartArt Tools, Design, Create Graphic group. The SmartArt updates as you type more text. In many cases, adding a new Level 1 item adds a new shape element to the SmartArt.

**Figure 16.4**
When you type in the text pane, the text is added to the selected element of the SmartArt.

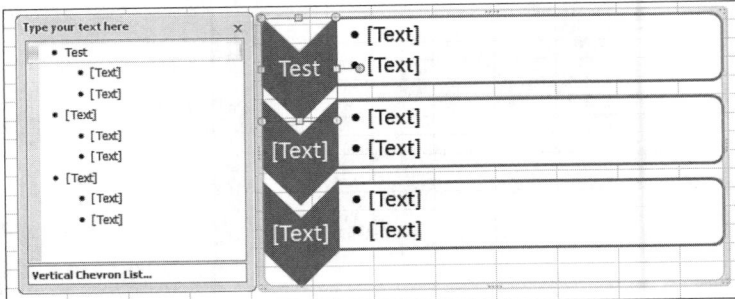

8. Add longer text to the SmartArt, and Excel shrinks the font size of all the elements in order to make the text fit. You can make the entire SmartArt graphic larger at any time by grabbing the resize handles in the corners of the SmartArt and dragging to a new size. After you resize the graphic, Excel resizes the text to make it fit in the SmartArt at the largest size possible.

9. If you like, change the color scheme of the SmartArt, which initially appears in one color. To do so, select SmartArt Tools Design, SmartArt Styles, Change Colors. Excel offers several versions of monochrome styles and five styles of color variations for each shape.

10. Choose a basic or 3-D style from the SmartArt Styles gallery. The Inset or Cartoon styles have a suitable mix of effects but are still readable.

11. Move the SmartArt to the proper location. Position the mouse over the border of the SmartArt, avoiding the eight Resize handles. The cursor changes to a four-headed arrow. Click and drag the SmartArt to a new location. If you drag the SmartArt to the left side of the worksheet, the text pane moves to the right of the SmartArt.

12. Click outside the SmartArt. Excel embeds the SmartArt graphic in the worksheet and hides the SmartArt ribbons. The completed SmartArt is shown in Figure 16.5.

### CHANGING EXISTING SMARTART TO A NEW STYLE

There are a couple ways to change SmartArt to a new style:

■ You can left-click the SmartArt and then choose the SmartArt Tools, Layouts from the Design ribbon to choose a new layout. As shown in Figure 16.6, the Layouts drop-down initially shows only the styles that Excel thinks are a close fit to the current style. If you want to access the complete list of styles, you have to select More Layouts. The advantage of this method is that Live Preview shows you the changes before you commit to a style. Figures 16.7 through 16.9 show other styles in Live Preview.

**Figure 16.5**
You click outside the SmartArt boundary to embed the completed SmartArt.

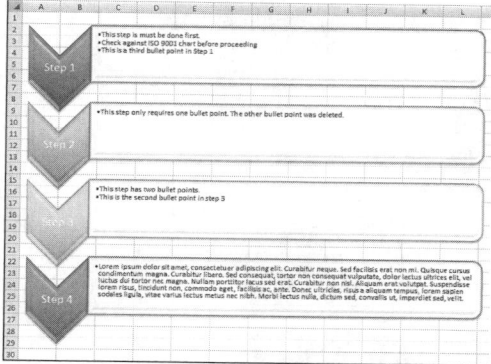

**Figure 16.6**
List Process 2 provides a new shape for each bullet point in Level 2.

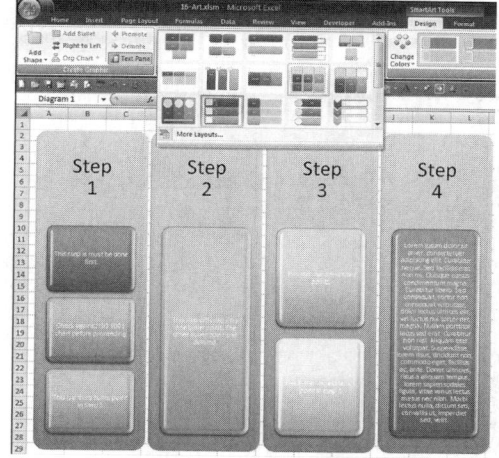

**Figure 16.7**
Picture List 1 allocates a lot of space for images and minimal space for text.

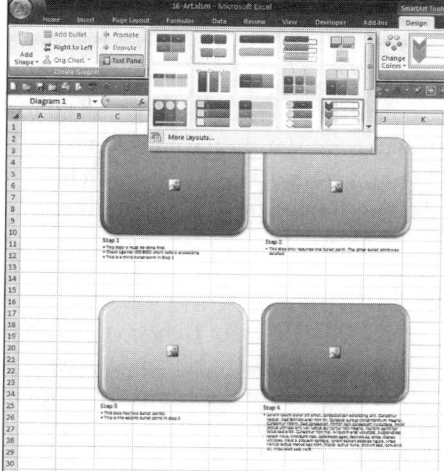

**16**

**Figure 16.8**
Vertical List 1 is good for large amounts of Level 2 text.

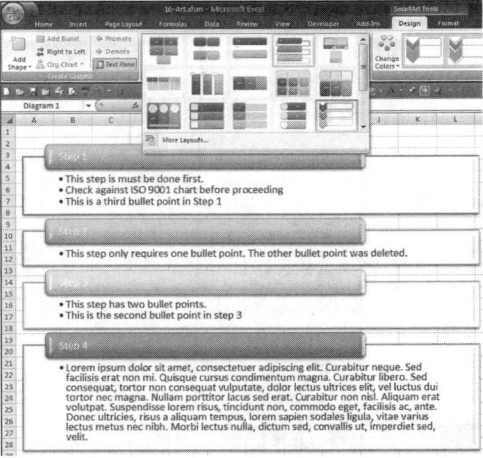

**Figure 16.9**
Picture List 2 can handle a balance of text and pictures.

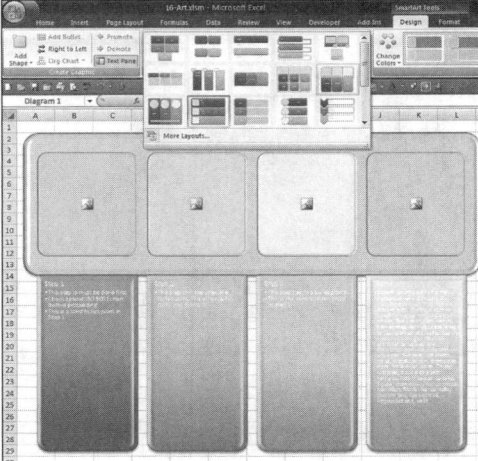

■ A faster way to access the complete list of styles is to right-click between two shapes in the SmartArt and choose Change Layout from the context menu. This step is a little tricky because you cannot click an existing shape; you must click inside the SmartArt border, but on a section of the SmartArt that contains nothing.

## MICROMANAGING SMARTART ELEMENTS

The are two ribbons for SmartArt tools. The Design ribbon allows you to change the overall design of the SmartArt. If you stay on the Design ribbon, Microsoft makes sure that your SmartArt looks good. It keeps the font for all Level 2 text consistent for all shapes. It keeps all the shapes proportional. If you have a particular need to override some aspect of one shape, however, you can do so on the Format ribbon.

CAUTION

When you change any setting on the Format ribbon, Microsoft turns off the automatic formatting for the other elements. Changing a setting on the Format ribbon is a great way to make horrible-looking SmartArt. If you absolutely have to use the Format ribbon, you should first get your SmartArt as close as possible to the final version by using the Design ribbon.

## CHANGING TEXT FORMATTING IN ONE ELEMENT

In Automatic mode, Excel chooses a font size that is small enough to show the longest text completely. This can cause problems if you have one shape with long text and short text everywhere else. In this case, Excel chooses a small font size for the long text and then forces all the other items to have tiny text as well. In such a situation, you might want to override the text size for the shape that has the longest text. Excel then automatically resizes the font size in the remaining automatic shapes to be larger.

The mini toolbar is useful for making these changes. You select the text either directly in the shape or in the text pane. Immediately after you complete the selection, you should watch for an almost-transparent formatting box to appear. Then you immediately move the mouse to the box to prevent it from disappearing. You can then change the font size by using the drop-down in the mini toolbar. If you allow the mini toolbar to disappear, you can use the formatting tools on the Home ribbon to change the font size.

In Figure 16.10, the long Level 2 text in step 4 was resized. Excel then calculated the proper text size for steps 1 through 3, resulting in the text in the top three shapes automatically growing to a larger font size.

**Figure 16.10**
When you manually override the font size in the fourth shape, the text in the remaining three shapes automatically becomes larger.

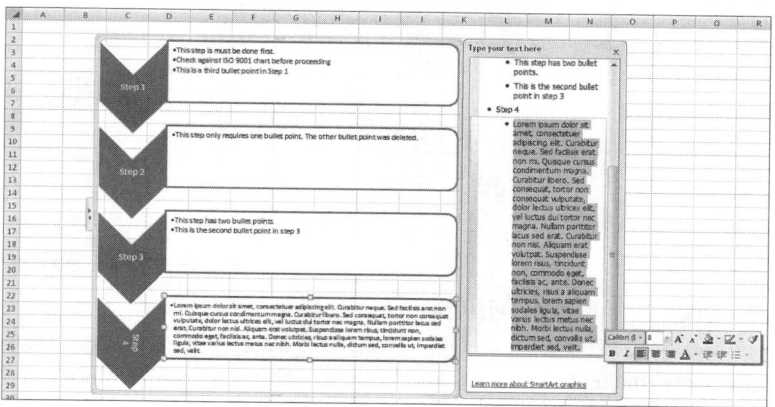

### CHANGING ONE SHAPE

There are many items you can edit for a SmartArt shape. To see how this works, click any shape in the SmartArt and then try the following:

- You can use the green handle to rotate the shape.
- You can use the resize handles to resize the shape.
- You can use the move handle to nudge the shape.
- You can choose Shapes, Change Shape from the SmartArt Tools Format ribbon to completely change the shape.
- You can choose settings from the Shape Styles group to change fill, outline, and effects for the shape.
- You can choose settings from the WordArt Styles group to change the text inside the shape.
- You can right-click the shape and choose Format Shape to have complete control over the shape.

In general, SmartArt created on the Design ribbon looks uniform and neat. When you move to the Format ribbon, the possibility for chaos arises. For example, the SmartArt in Figure 16.11 contains mixed effects, font sizes, and rotation; it was created in the Format ribbon.

**Figure 16.11**
After experimenting with the Format ribbon, you can choose Reset Graphic on the Design ribbon to turn the SmartArt back into something more uniform.

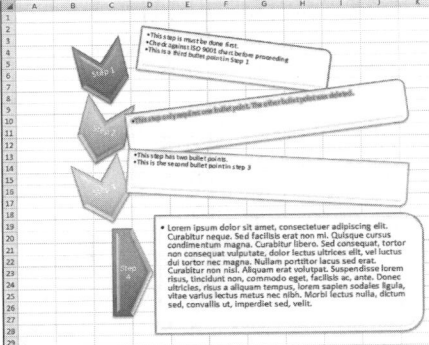

## CONTROLLING SMARTART SHAPES FROM THE TEXT PANE

The text pane represents a fantastic improvement over business diagrams in Excel 2003. By using only the keyboard, you can add or delete shapes and promote or demote items. Further, the text pane has proofing tools such as spell check. Using the text pane is similar to creating bullet points in a PowerPoint slide.

Figure 16.12 shows a newly inserted pyramid SmartArt in Excel. By default, most new SmartArt diagrams have three shapes, but you can change that number by using the text pane.

**Figure 16.12**
A default SmartArt includes three shapes. You can edit the number of shapes by using the text pane.

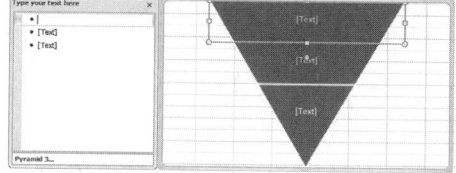

The following rules apply to the text pane for SmartArt:

- You press Up Arrow or Down Arrow keys to move from one line to another.
- You press the Enter key to insert a new line below the current line. The new line will be at the same level as the current line. Adding a new Level 1 line inserts a new shape in the SmartArt.
- You press the Tab key to demote Level 1 text to Level 2 text.
- You press Shift+Tab to promote Level 2 text to Level 1 text.
- You press the Backspace key on an empty line to delete the line.
- You press Delete at the end of any line to combine text from the next line with this line.
- You press End to move to the end of the current line.
- You press Home to move to the beginning of the current line.

As you add shapes, Excel continues to attempt to squeeze them into the default size. You can resize an entire piece of SmartArt by using the resize handles around the SmartArt.

Strictly as an example of how the text pane works, you can use the following steps to customize Figure 16.12 into Figure 16.13. This example illustrates how quickly and simply you can change from the default SmartArt with three shapes to any number of shapes:

1. Type **Shape 1** and then press Enter.
2. Type **Subtext** and then press Tab to demote the item. Then press the Down Arrow key to move to Text 2.
3. Type **Shape 2** and then press Enter.
4. Type **Point 1** and then press Tab and Enter.
5. Type **Point 2** and then press Tab and the Down Arrow key.
6. Type **Shape 3** and then press Enter.

7. Type **Point 3** and then press Tab and Enter.

8. Excel wants the next item to be Level 2 text, so press Shift+Tab to promote this item.

9. Type **Shape 4** and then press Enter, type **Shape 5** and then press Enter, type **Shape 6** and then press Enter, and type **Shape 7** and then press Enter.

9. Type **Point 4** and then press Tab, Enter, and Shift+Tab, and then type **8**.

10. Using the mouse, resize the SmartArt so it is larger.

11. From the Quick Styles gallery on the Design ribbon, choose a color scheme.

The result is shown in Figure 16.13. As this example shows, by using only the keyboard and the text pane, you can quickly expand SmartArt and add Level 2 subpoints.

**Figure 16.13**
You can add additional shapes and subpoints simply by using the text pane.

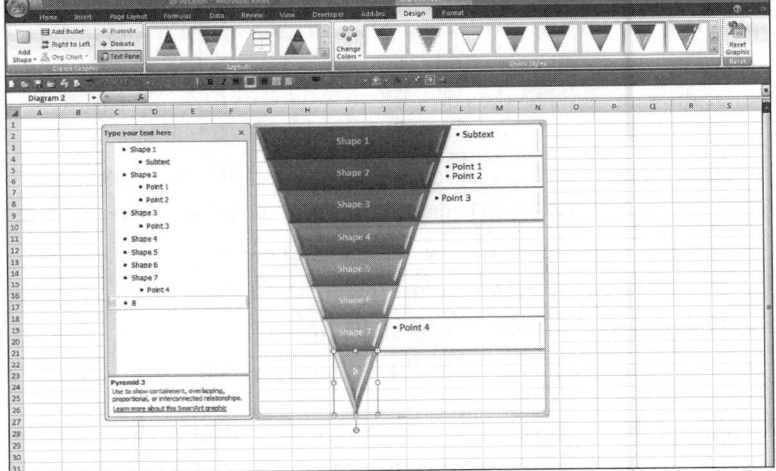

## ADDING IMAGES TO SMARTART

Seven SmartArt layouts in the List category are designed to hold small images in addition to the text. In some of these styles, the picture is emphasized; in others, the focus shifts to the text, and the picture is an accent:

- **Picture Caption List**—This style includes a large picture and is designed to emphasize the picture.

- **Horizontal Picture List**—This style includes a large picture and a large space for text. It is good for a balance of pictures and text.

- **Continuous Picture List**—This style includes a large picture and minimal text.

- **Vertical Picture List** —This style contains a small square picture and text.

- **Vertical Picture Accent List**—This style contains a small round picture on the left and text.

- **Bending Picture Accent List**—This style contains a small circular picture.

- **Picture Accent List**—This style contains a small square picture in the upper right of each block.

When you select one of these styles, you first build the text and then add shapes as necessary. The SmartArt shows a picture icon in each shape, as shown in Figure 16.14.

**Figure 16.14**
In the SmartArt styles that include pictures, you should arrange the shapes before trying to add pictures.

You can click a picture icon to display the Insert Picture dialog. Then you can choose a picture and click Insert. You repeat this process to add each additional picture. The pictures are automatically resized to fit the allotted area, as shown in Figure 16.15.

**Figure 16.15**
Pictures have been added to each shape. Only seven SmartArt styles are prebuilt with placeholders for pictures.

**CAUTION**

If you change the layout of SmartArt after adding pictures, the picture information is lost. This is particularly frustrating when you switch from a picture style to another picture style.

## SPECIAL CONSIDERATIONS FOR ORGANIZATIONAL CHARTS AND HIERARCHICAL SMARTART

Hierarchical SmartArt can contain more than two text levels. As you add more levels to the SmartArt, Excel continues to intelligently add boxes and resize them to fit.

Figure 16.16 shows a diagram created in the Hierarchy 1 style. In this style, each level is assigned a different color.

**Figure 16.16**
Hierarchical SmartArt can contain more than two levels.

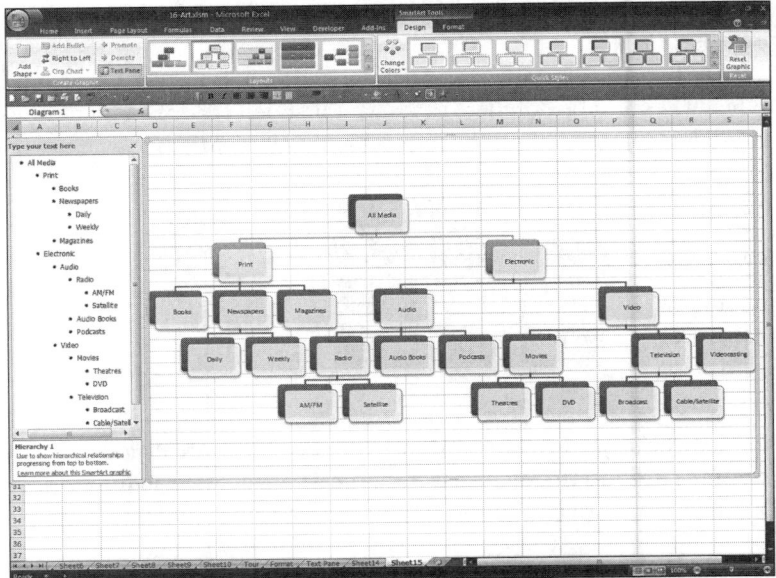

The first style available in the Hierarchical category is the Organization Chart style. This style is used to describe reporting relationships in an organization. There are a few extra options in the ribbon for organization charts. For example, if you select the SmartArt Tools Design ribbon, the Add Shape drop-down includes the option Add Assistant, as shown in Figure 16.17. You can select this option to add an extra shape immediately below the selected level.

**Figure 16.17**
The Add Assistant selection adds a box for an administrative assistant below the selected shape.

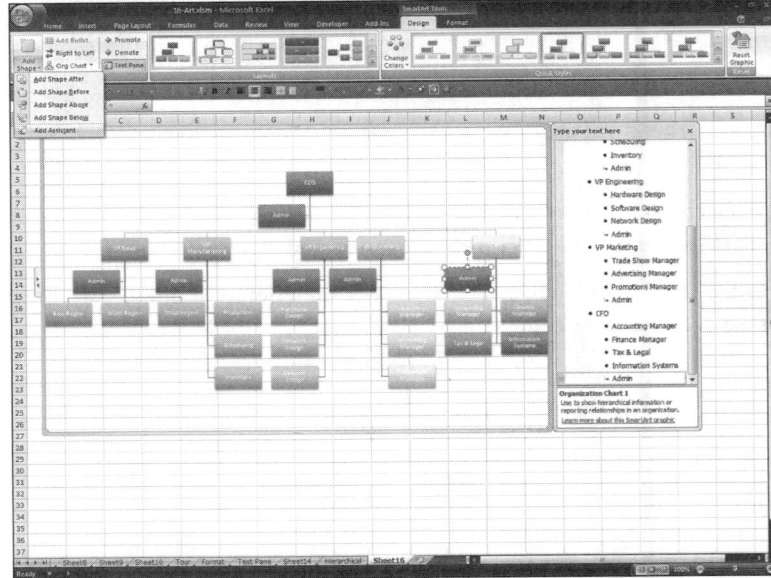

In the Create Graphic group of the Design ribbon, the Org Chart drop-down offers four options for showing the boxes within a group. First, you select the manager for the group. Then you select the appropriate type from the drop-down to affect all direct reports for the manager. Figure 16.18 illustrates the four options for Org Chart:

- **VP of Sales**—This option shows a standard organization chart. The regions are arranged side-by-side.
- **VP of Manufacturing**—This option has a Right Hanging group. The departments are arranged vertically to the right of the line.
- **VP of Engineering**—This option has a Left Hanging group. The departments are arranged vertically to the left of the line.
- **CFO**—This option has a Both group. The direct reports are listed in two columns under the manager, on both sides of the vertical line.

In each group, the assistant box is keyed a different color and is set off from the other boxes.

**Figure 16.18**
Organization charts include additional options to control the arrangement of direct reports.

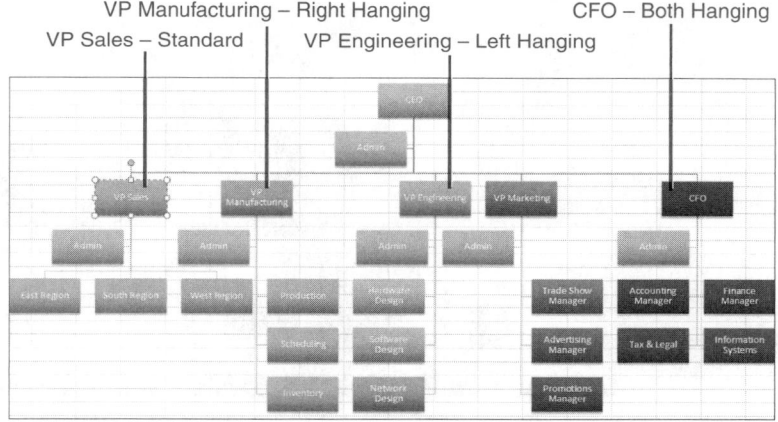

## USING LIMITED SMARTART

Most of the SmartArt examples in the previous section are expandable: As you add Level 1 text, new shapes are added to the SmartArt. However, some SmartArt styles cannot be expanded:

- The top-left image in Figure 16.19 shows a gear chart. Both the gear and funnel charts are limited to three items. If you add additional items to the text pane, each appears with a red x. These items do not display in the SmartArt, but they are stored in case you later change to another SmartArt layout.

- Many of the arrow layouts in the Relationship category are limited to two shapes.

- The Matrix layouts are limited to four quadrants. Grid Matrix offers four quadrants plus a title, as shown in the center of Figure 16.19.

- The Segmented Pyramid style can be expanded, but it must contain 1, 4, 9, or 16 shapes. As soon as you add a fifth style to the SmartArt in the upper-left corner of the display, an entire row is added to the bottom of the pyramid, resulting in the SmartArt shown in the lower right of Figure 16.19.

- The Equation style can be expanded, but the answer is always the last Level 1 item in the text pane.

**Figure 16.19**
Arrows, gears, funnels, and matrix shapes have certain limitations on the number of shapes they can contain.

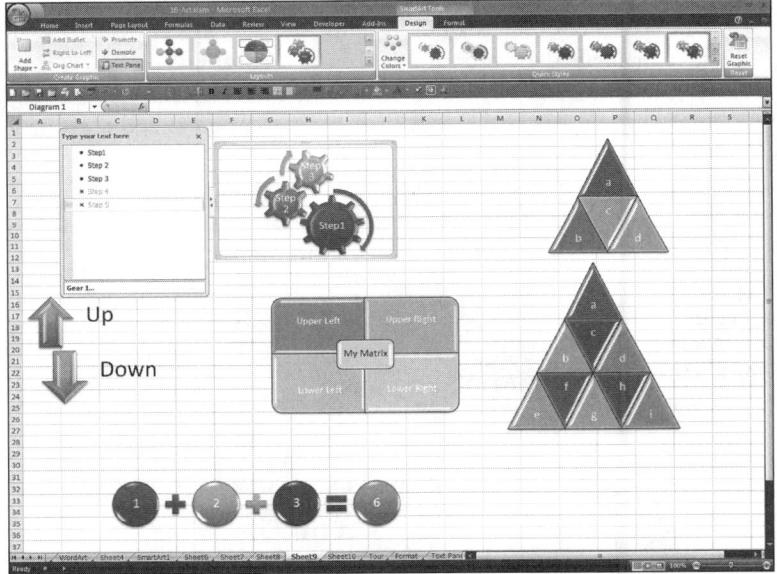

All in all, SmartArt is a great addition to the Office family. The one real drawback related to SmartArt in Excel 2007 is the inability to link cell content to the text in SmartArt. To do that, you have to use shapes, as described in the following section.

# USING SHAPES TO DISPLAY CELL CONTENTS

Shapes were known in previous versions of Excel as AutoShapes. Microsoft has added new shapes to the already long list of shapes available in AutoShapes. In addition, Excel 2007 shapes have some new formatting options, such as shadow, glow, and bevel.

Perhaps the best part of shapes is that you can tie the text on a shape to a worksheet cell. In Figure 16.20, for example, the shape is set to display the current value of cell B26. Every time the worksheet is calculated, the text on the shape is updated.

**Figure 16.20**
Shapes can be set to
display the current
value of a cell.

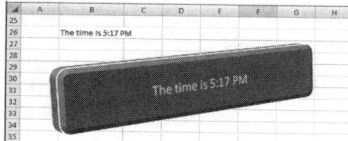

You follow these steps to insert a shape into a worksheet:

1. Select a blank area of the worksheet.
2. From the Insert ribbon, open the Shapes drop-down.
3. Select 1 of the 160 basic shapes, as shown in Figure 16.21.

**Figure 16.21**
Choose from these
shapes.

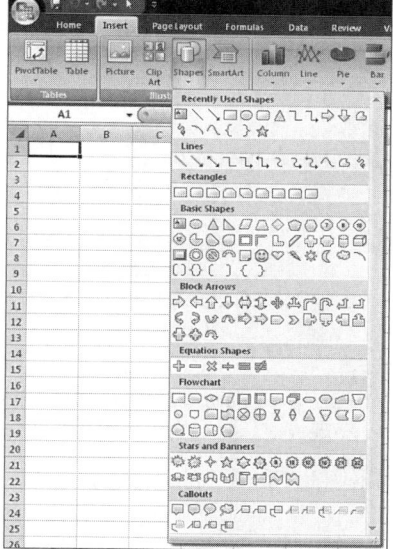

4. The mouse pointer changes to a small crosshair. Click and drag in the worksheet to draw the shape.
5. Choose a color scheme from the Shapes Styles drop-down.
6. Select Shape Effects, Preset and select an effect.
7. Look for a yellow diamond on the shape. It allows you to change the inflection point for the shape. On the rounded rectangle, for example, sliding the yellow diamond controls how wide the rounded corners are.

16

8. Look for a green circle on the outside of the shape. Drag this circle to rotate the shape, if necessary.

9. To include static text in the shape, click in the middle of the shape and type the text. You can control the style by using the WordArt Styles drop-down. You can control text size and color by using the formatting buttons on the Home ribbon. The shape can include text from any cell, but it cannot perform a calculation. If you want the shape to include a calculated value, skip this step and follow steps 10 through 12.

10. If desired, add a new cell that will format a message for the WordArt. As shown in Figure 16.22, add the formula `="We are at "&TEXT(B13,"0%")&" of our goal!"` to an empty cell to convert the calculation in Cell B13 to a suitable message.

11. Click in the middle of the text box as if you were about to type some text.

12. Click in the formula bar and type `=B14` and then press Enter. As shown in Figure 16.22, the shape displays the results from the selected cell.

**Figure 16.22**
This shape picks up the formula from Cell B14 to show a message that changes with the worksheet.

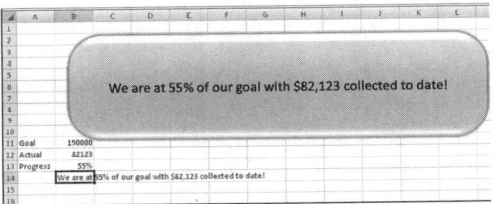

## WORKING WITH SHAPES

The Drawing Tools section of the Format ribbon contains sections to change the shape style, fill, outline, effects, and WordArt effects.

In the Insert Shapes dialog, you use the Edit Shape, Change Shape command to choose another shape style.

If you right-click a shape and choose Format Shape, Excel displays the Format Shape dialog, with the fine-tuning settings Fill, Line, Line Style, Shadow, 3D Format, 3D Rotation, and Text Placement.

## USING THE FREEFORM SHAPE TO CREATE A CUSTOM SHAPE

Despite my friendly relationship with Microsoft, I have not convinced them to add the MrExcel logo to the Shapes gallery (yet). However, you can build any shape by using the Freeform line tools in the Shapes gallery.

After you create a shape, you can add 3-D effects, glow, and so on to make a cool-looking version of your company logo, as shown in Figure 16.23.

**Figure 16.23**
This shape was created with the freeform shape tool and then enhanced using the Drawing Tools section of the Format ribbon.

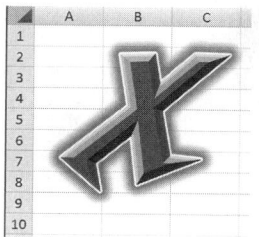

To create a custom shape, you follow these steps:

1. Insert a picture of the shape that you can use as a guide to trace.

2. From the Insert ribbon, choose the Shapes drop-down. In the Lines section, the last two shapes are Freeform and Scribble. Select the FreeForm shape.

3. Click one corner of your logo.

4. Move the mouse to the adjacent corner of the logo and click again.

5. Repeat step 4 for each corner. If your logo has a curve, click several times around the perimeter of the curve. The more often you click, the better the curve will be.

6. When you arrive back at the original corner, click one final time to close the shape and complete the drawing.

7. Use the effect and fill settings to color and stylize the logo.

# Using WordArt for Interesting Titles and Headlines

WordArt has been rewritten in Excel 2007. As in previous versions, WordArt is best used sparingly—possibly for a headline or title at the top of a page. It is best used for impressive display fonts to add interest to a report. You would probably not want to create an entire 20-page document in WordArt.

To use WordArt, you follow these steps:

1. Select a blank section of the worksheet.

2. From the Insert ribbon, choose the WordArt drop-down.

3. As shown in Figure 16.24, choose from the 30 WordArt presets in the drop-down. Don't worry that these presets seem less exciting than the WordArt in prior versions of Excel. You will be able to customize the WordArt later.

4. Excel adds the generic text *Your Text Here* in the preset WordArt you chose. Select this default text and then type your own text.

5. Select the text. Choose a new font style by using either the mini toolbar that appears or the Home ribbon.

16

**Figure 16.24**
Excel offers 25
WordArt presets.

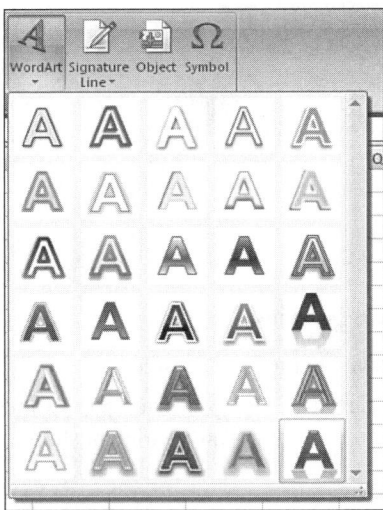

6. Use the WordArt Styles group on the Drawing Tools Format ribbon to color the WordArt. To the right of the Styles drop-down are icons for text color and line color and a drop-down for effects. The Effects drop-down includes the fly-out menus Shadow, Reflection, Glow, Soft Edges, Bevel, and 3D Rotation.

7. To achieve the old-style WordArt effects, from the Format ribbon, select Drawing Tools, WordArt Styles, Text Effects, Transform and then select a shape for the text. Figure 16.25 shows the WordArt with a Wave 1 transformation.

**Figure 16.25**
WordArt includes the
Transform menu to
bend and twist type.

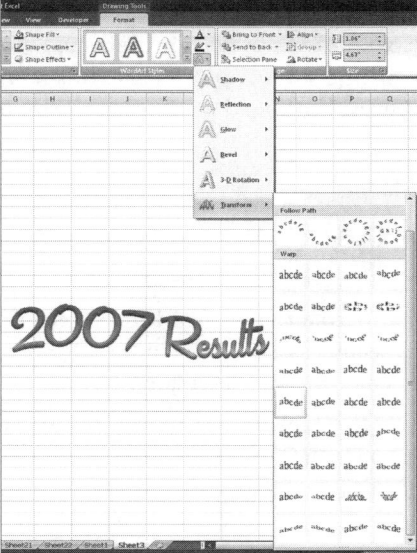

# USING TEXT BOXES TO FLOW LONG TEXT PASSAGES

WordArt is perfect for short titles. However, it is not suitable for long text passages that you want to fit in a range. Figure 16.26 shows a series of sentences in a column. The sentences are of different lengths. You would like to have them fit in a range from Column A through Column D.

**Figure 16.26**
There are times when you need Excel to act like a word processor.

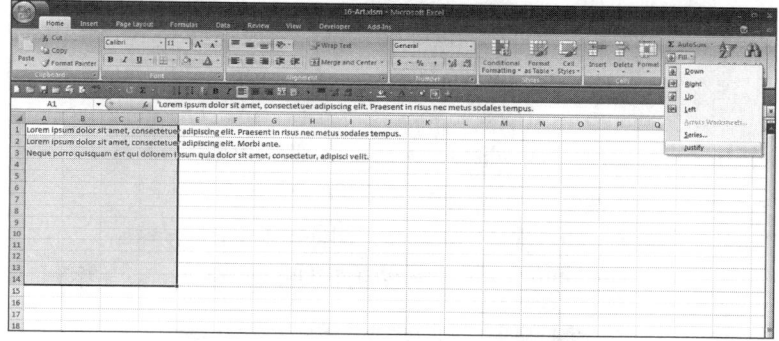

16

You can solve this particular problem by following these steps:

1. Select a range to include the sentences and extend the range out to Column D.
2. Select the Home ribbon and then select Editing, Fill, Justify. Excel word wraps the sentences to fit the current widths of Columns A:D, as shown in Figure 16.27.

**Figure 16.27**
The Justify command wraps the text to the width of the range that was selected before the command was invoked.

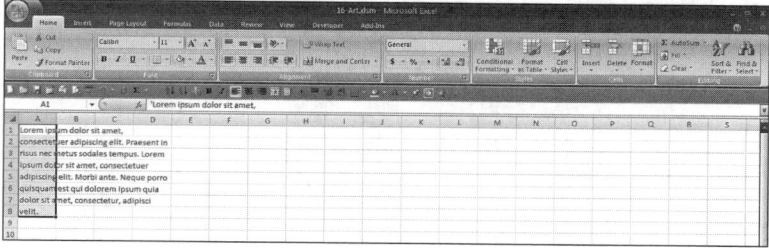

This solution is not perfect. It was written over a decade ago, when a cell could not contain more than 255 characters.

If you subsequently resize Column A, the text does not reflow. You have to use the Justify command again. In addition, if you change the font size of the text in Column A, you have to use the Justify command again.

If any cell in the input range contains more than 255 characters, the cell is truncated. This is the fatal flaw that causes Justify to fail most often. To solve this problem, you use a Text Box object. This object has been improved in Excel 2007 to easily allow multiple columns in the text box.

To use a Text Box object to create two columns of text, you follow these steps:

1. Select a blank section of the worksheet.
2. From the Insert ribbon, choose Text, Text Box.
3. Drag in your document to draw a large text box on the worksheet.
4. Either type your text here or switch to Word, copy the text, and then switch back to Excel and paste the text.
5. Right-click the text box and choose Exit Edit Mode.
6. Use the Font group on the Home ribbon to adjust the font size and face.
7. Right-click the text box. Choose Format Shape. The Format Shape dialog appears.
8. In the Format Shape dialog, choose the Text Box category.
9. Adjust the margins and alignment, if desired.
10. Click the Columns button. The Columns dialog appears.
11. Choose two columns with nonzero spacing between them, as shown in Figure 16.28.

**Figure 16.28**
You can change the number of columns.

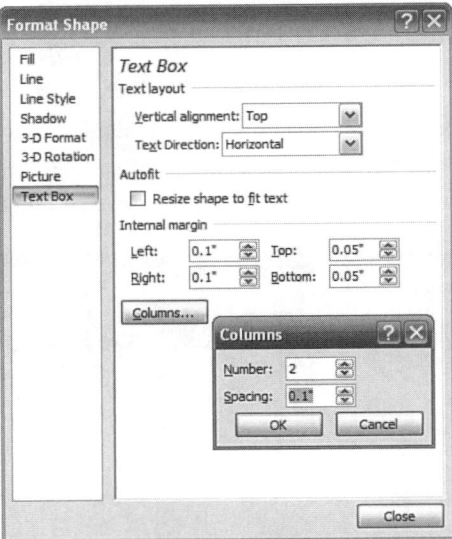

12. Click OK to close the Columns dialog. Click Close to close the Format Shape dialog.

The result, as shown in Figure 16.29, is a text box that has two columns of text. As you change the size of the text, it automatically reflows to fit the desired columns.

**Figure 16.29**
A text box can hold
long passages of text.

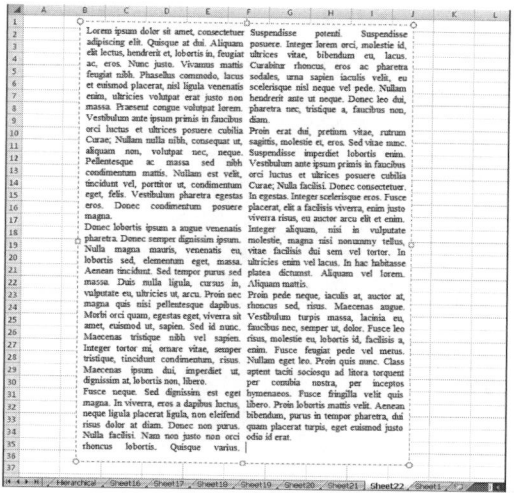

The SmartArt, WordArt, and Shapes tools in Excel 2007 allow you to add visual interest to your workbooks. In Chapter 17, "Using Pictures and Clip Art," you will learn about Excel's picture-handling abilities.

**Excel Troubleshooting: Eliminating Stray Drawing Objects**

All the drawing tools are new in Excel 2007. As you add multiple objects to one screen in an Excel workbook, you find stray ghost objects left behind. It seems that when the selection box for the second shape overwrites the first shape, part of the shape is lost.

To solve this problem, you scroll down the worksheet so that the shapes are not visible. When you scroll back up, Excel redraws the shapes correctly.

# USING PICTURES AND CLIP ART

## In this chapter

Excel worksheets have a tendency to be dominated by numbers. A picture can liven up a spreadsheet and add interest. The picture functionality in Excel 2007 is vastly improved over that in previous versions of Excel.

Excel 2007 offers 28 quick picture styles, plus the tools to create thousands of additional effects.

When the spreadsheet was invented in 1979, accountants were amazed and thrilled with the simple black-and-white, numbers-only spreadsheets. The new image processing tools available in Excel 2007 elevate spreadsheets from simple tables of numbers to beautiful marketing showpieces.

# USING PICTURES ON WORKSHEETS

The first step in creating a great-looking picture is to insert a picture on a worksheet. To do so, you follow these steps:

1. Select the cell where you would like the upper-left corner of the picture to be positioned.
2. From the Insert ribbon, select Illustrations, Picture.
3. Browse to the folder that contains your pictures.
4. Choose the picture you want. (Valid types include JPG, GIF, PNG, BMP, and many others.) Click Insert.

When the picture is inserted, a new Picture Tools Format tab appears on the ribbon, as shown in Figure 17.1.

**Figure 17.1**
When a picture is selected, the new Picture Tools Format ribbon is available.

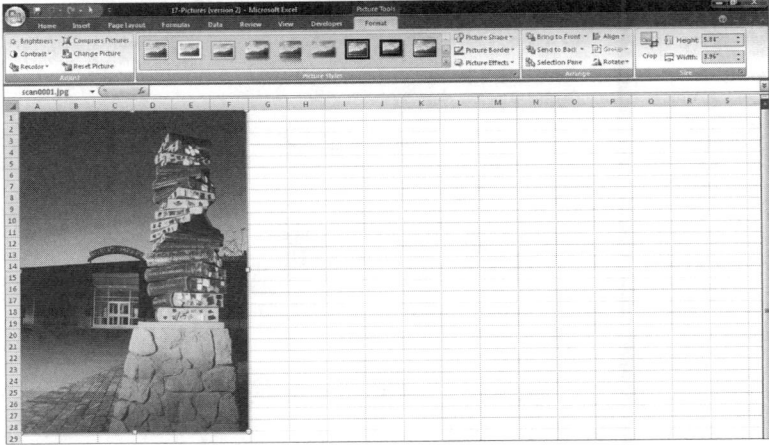

## FORMATTING WITH PICTURE STYLES

For a quick way to make a picture look interesting, you can use one of the 28 presets in the Picture Styles gallery. These presets include various combinations of rotation, shadow, frame, and shape. Here's how you use them:

1. Select a picture. The Picture Tools ribbon appears.
2. To the right of the Picture Styles icon, choose the drop-down arrow.
3. Hover over the 28 built-in styles until you find one that is suitable.
4. To apply the style, click the style in the gallery.

Figure 17.2 shows the gallery and several varieties of built-in picture styles.

**Figure 17.2**
The Picture Styles gallery offers many quick alternatives for formatting pictures.

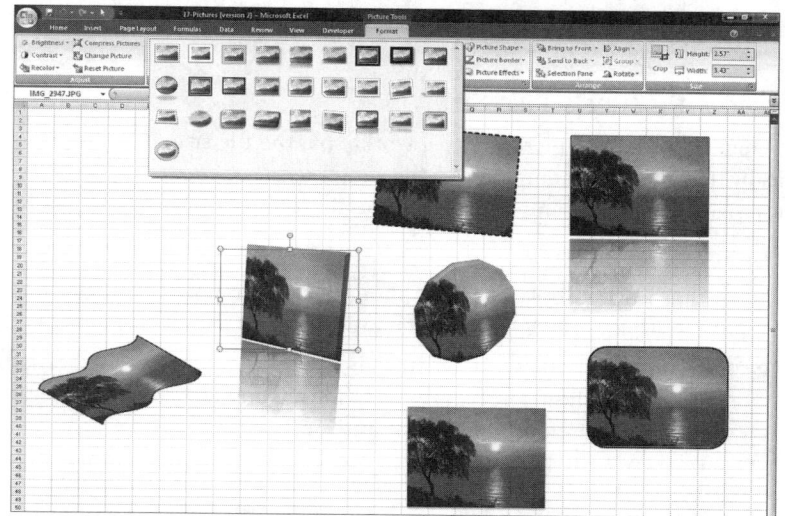

## Resizing and Cropping Pictures

One problem you might have when using a picture on a worksheet is that the image may be too large. As digital cameras improve, it is becoming increasingly common for digital images to be 4, 5, 6, or more megapixels. These images are very large, For example, an image from a 3 megapixel camera occupies from A1 through Q41.

You can use the Zoom slider in the lower-right corner of the window to zoom out so that you can see the complete image. Then you can resize the picture. It is important that you resize the picture so that it remains proportional. The tools in the Format ribbon allow you to do this.

In the Picture Tools section of the Format ribbon, there are Height and Width spin buttons in the Size group. You can use either of them to resize an image. Any change you make to either spin button results in a proportional change to the other spin button as well.

You can also resize a picture by dragging one of the corner handles inward or outward.

Cropping a picture involves removing extraneous parts of the picture while in Crop mode. To crop a picture, you follow these steps:

1. Select a picture.
2. Click the Crop icon in the Size group of the Picture Tools section of the Format ribbon. Eight crop handles appear on the edges and corner of the picture. Use the handles as follows:

- To crop out one side of a picture, drag the center handle on that side inward toward the middle of the picture.
- To crop both sides equally, hold down Ctrl while you drag the center handle on either side inward.
- To crop equally on all four sides, hold down Ctrl while dragging one of the corner handles inward.

3. When the picture is cropped appropriately, click the Crop icon in the Picture Tools Format ribbon to exit Crop mode.

## REDUCING A PICTURE'S FILE SIZE

When you import a picture into a workbook, the file size of the workbook can grow dramatically. If you are planning on only viewing the image onscreen, you can dramatically reduce the size of the picture to also reduce the size of the workbook. Here's how you do it:

1. Select the picture.
2. In the Picture Tools Format ribbon, select Compress Pictures from the Adjust group. Excel displays the Compress Pictures dialog as shown in Figure 17.3.
3. If desired, click the Options button. Excel will allow you to choose from three compression rates, as shown in Figure 17.3. This dialog estimates the file size reduction that you can accomplish by applying compression.

**Figure 17.3**
You use the Compress Pictures dialog to reduce file size.

4. To reduce the file size even more, click the Options button in the Compress Pictures dialog. The Compression Settings dialog appears.

5. Select a compression setting in the Compression Settings dialog. By default, Excel compresses the picture to 220 dpi, which is suitable for printing. If you will only be showing the workbook in a presentation, however, the 150 dpi setting will be fine. To minimize the file size as much as possible, use the 96 dpi setting, as shown in Figure 17.4.

**Figure 17.4**
The Compression Settings dialog allows you to change compression settings based on the planned use of the workbook.

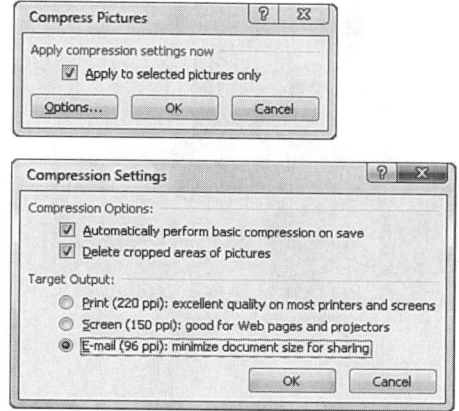

## APPLYING A COLOR TO A PICTURE

For an old-time look, you can apply a sepia tone to a photograph. Using Excel 2007, you can now convert photographs to appear in any color. Here's how:

1. Select the image.

2. From the Adjust group of the Format ribbon, choose Recolor from the Picture Tools group. Then choose one of the four color mode options: grayscale, sepia, washed out, or black and white. Or choose grayscale colored by one of the six accent colors in the current theme.

3. If you choose More Dark Variations, you can choose to color the image in any of 16 million colors.

Because of the physical limitations of this book, any of the color options shown here would look like grayscale. Therefore, Figure 17.5 shows the stark contrast of the black-and-white color mode.

## CHANGING BRIGHTNESS AND CONTRAST

You can use the Brightness and Contrast drop-downs in the Adjust group to make a picture darker or lighter. These drop-downs offer choices from +40% to -40%, in 10 percentage-point increments. For more control, choose Picture Corrections Options from the bottom of the menu. The Format Shape dialog offers a range of -100% to +100% in 1% intervals.

**Figure 17.5**
By selecting the recolor option, you can washout a photo, present it in one of 16 million colors, or produce a stark black-and-white image, as shown here.

Increasing the brightness makes an image lighter. Increasing the contrast makes the blacks blacker and the whites whiter. Both of these adjustments cause the photograph to lose some detail. If the image you're working with is going to be printed in a glossy annual report, it would be better to use an image editing tool such as Photoshop. For the department staff meeting, though, Excel's options are good enough.

## ADDING BORDERS

The Border menu on the Picture Tools Format ribbon lets you add a border around an image. You can choose any color, various line thicknesses, and dashed-line effects, as shown in Figure 17.6.

## ADDING EFFECTS

The Picture Effects dropdown is where most of the powerful new image toys are located. You can use the tools from this menu, for example to apply a glow effect, a preset bevel effect, and a 3-D effect, as shown in Figure 17.7. The bevel effect is found under the Preset fly out menu. This definitely runs circles around anything that was possible in prior versions of Excel.

The Shadow flyout menu under the Picture Effects dropdown allows for nine different types of shadows behind the picture, called outer shadows. There are also nine different types of shadows you can use within the picture, making it look as though the picture is actually set into a window behind the spreadsheet. There are five types of perspective shadows. Figure 17.8 shows the various shadow options.

**Figure 17.6**
The Border group allows you to add a border around an image.

**Figure 17.7**
You can add a soft glow, 3-D, and bevel effects to make this cool picture in three clicks.

The Preset flyout menu contains 12 versions of bevels that you can apply to the photograph, as shown in Figure 17.9.

As shown in Figure 17.10, the 3-D Rotation flyout menu offers 25 various types of 3-D rotation. After you choose one of these 25 presets, you can drag the green handle to adjust the angle of rotation.

17

**Figure 17.8**
The Shadow drop-down offers 23 shadow presets and the link More Shadows, which gives you absolute control over shadows.

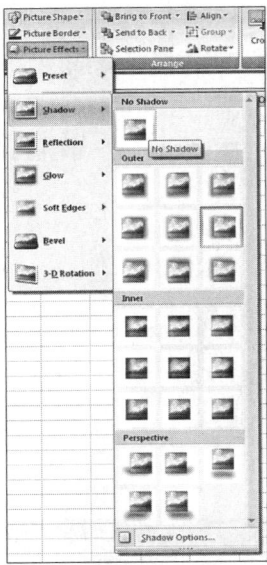

**Figure 17.9**
Adding beveled edges to a workbook takes on a new dimension in Excel 2007.

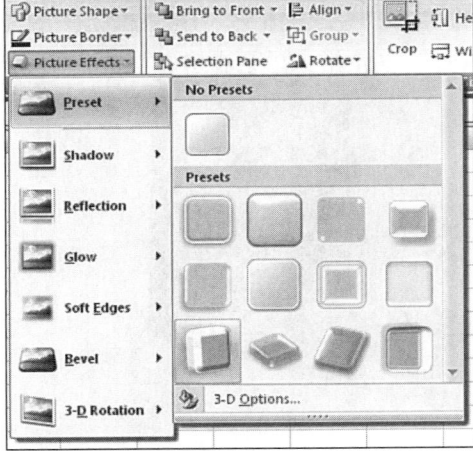

The Glow menu enables you to add a glow in one of four thicknesses in each of the six colors of the current theme. You can choose More Glow Colors to choose from any of 16 million colors.

The Soft Edges drop-down enables you to feather the edges of the workbook in 1-, 2.5-, 5-, 10-, 25-, and 50-point settings.

The Reflection drop-down offers reflections in light, half, and full, with an offset of 1, 4, or 8 points.

**Figure 17.10**
Twenty-five varieties
of 3-D Rotation are
available.

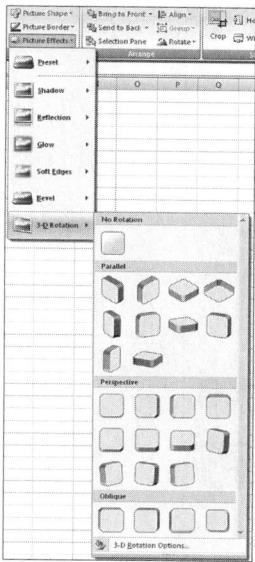

17

If you want even more control over picture effects, look for a More option in most effects'
drop-down menus. When you click this option, the Format Object dialog appears, offering
you complete control over fill, line, line style, shadow, 3-D format, and 3-D rotation.

## ARRANGING PICTURES

The Arrange group on the Picture Tools Format ribbon offers a rotation tool. You can use
this tool to flip a portrait picture to landscape or vice versa. You can use the Bring to Back
and Send to Back options to determine which of two overlapping pictures is displayed
on top.

The Align option allows you to snap the pictures to a grid or to make sure that several
images line up. To use the latter feature, you need to select the image that was placed last.
Try this example:

1. Select Image3.
2. Ctrl+click Image2 and then Ctrl+click Image1.
3. Choose Align, Align Left. The left edges of Image2 and Image3 move so they line up
   with the left edge of Image1.

All the available alignment options are shown in Figure 17.11. One interesting option here
is View Gridlines, which was formerly tucked away on an obscure tab in the Options dialog.

17

**Figure 17.11**
The Align drop-down
allows you to line up
multiple images with
each other.

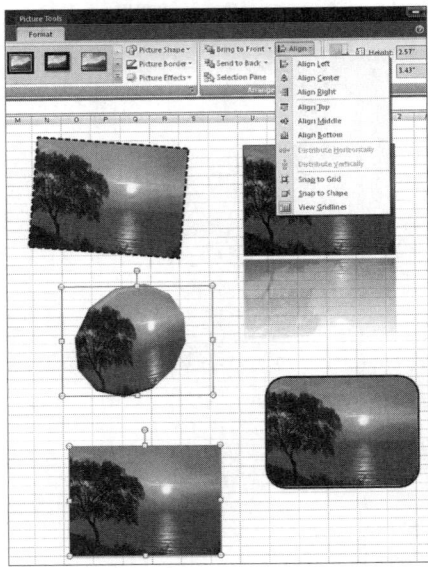

If you select multiple images and group them together by using the Group drop-down, you can then move the images, and their location relative to each other remain the same.

### DISPLAYING THE SELECTION PANE

The selection and visibility pane is new in Excel 2007. It lists all the images on the worksheet and allows you to make certain images invisible. To display the pane, you select the Picture Tools Format ribbon and then select Arrange, Selection Pane.

There is a check box to the right of each image name. You can select this check box to toggle the visibility. The buttons Show All and Hide All allow you to quickly show and hide all images.

# USING CLIP ART

Clip art has gotten a makeover in Excel 2007. Clips from Office Online are now automatically incorporated in the results when you are connected to the Internet.

To add clip art to a worksheet, you follow these steps:

1. Position the cell pointer near where you want the clip art to be inserted.
2. Choose Insert, Illustrations, Clip Art.
3. Type a keyword for the clip art in the Search For box. Then press Go. A gallery of matching clip art is displayed in the Clip Art pane.

4. Every clip art thumbnail has a drop-down available on the right side. Choose a drop-down to display a context menu, as shown in Figure 17.12. Choose Insert to add the clip art at the active cell.

5. Resize the clip art as needed to fit the desired space.

**Figure 17.12**
You can choose Insert to add clip art at the desired location.

The Clip Art context menu also includes the following options:

- **Copy**—You use this option to copy the clip art to the clipboard
- **Delete from Clip Organizer**—You use this option to delete any local copy of the clip art.
- **Make Available Offline**—You use this option to copy the clip art from Clips Online to your computer.
- **Move to Collection**—You use this option to organize clip art on your computer.
- **Edit Keywords**—You use this option to add your own keywords to clip art. This is like tagging in Flickr.com.
- **Find similar style**—You use this option to narrow the results to similar images.
- **Preview/Properties**—You use this option to display the exact size of the clip art before you import it.

After you add clip art, you can resize it by dragging any of the resize handles around the selected clip art.

# Working in a Legacy Environment

# FILE FORMAT DIFFERENCES

**I**n this chapter

Microsoft does not introduce file format changes lightly. File sharing becomes a nightmare when someone using Excel 2007 tries to share files with someone using Excel 2003.

Excel 2007 offers three new file formats. This chapter discusses these three file formats. Chapter 19, "Compatibility Mode," discusses how you can continue to share files with people using older versions of Excel.

**NOTE**

A fourth file format, the .XLAM file type, can be used by developers to distribute add-ins to extend the functionality of Excel. This file type is beyond the scope of this book.

# A BRIEF HISTORY OF FILE FORMATS

Excel has traditionally stored workbooks in Binary Interchange File Format (BIFF). The BIFF specification has changed occasionally over time.

In 1993, when Excel expanded to 16,384 rows, Microsoft began using BIFF5 format. In 1993, most companies did not have corporate local area networks (LANs); a file format conversion therefore usually affected just one person on one computer. If you had upgraded from Excel 4 to Excel 5, as long as you had a way to convert your Excel 4 files to Excel's new BIFF5 format, everything was fine.

In 1997, Microsoft introduced a major file change, BIFF8. This version of BIFF allowed 65,536 rows. The rise of the Internet and email meant that far more people were now sharing files. Excel 97 offered a way to save files in the old format in case you needed to share files with a person using prior versions of Excel.

All BIFF versions are proprietary formats. Figure 18.1 shows a simple Excel 2003 spreadsheet and the corresponding BIFF, as viewed in Notepad. You would certainly never be able to open a Notepad window and begin typing a new spreadsheet. Similarly, it would be very difficult for other applications to extract data from the BIFF format.

**Figure 18.1**
BIFF files are difficult for other applications to read.

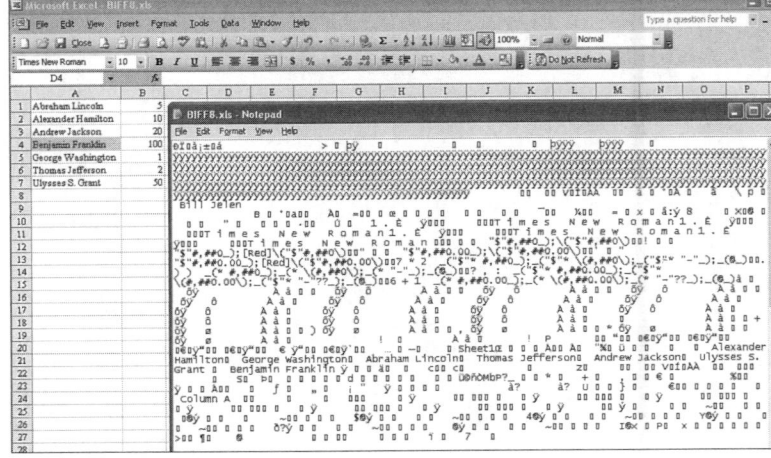

In Excel 2000, Microsoft flirted with a new HTML file format. By default, files were stored as XLS files in BIFF8 format. However, you could save a file as an HTML file and later open that HTML file in Excel 2000. With some limitations, most contents of the file and formatting could be successfully round-tripped from Excel to HTML and back to Excel.

This produced an interesting new paradigm: It would be possible for any program that could read or write text files to extract data from the Excel HTML file. Figure 18.2 shows the Figure 18.1 spreadsheet saved in HTML format. A program other than Excel could easily read or produce this format.

**Figure 18.2**
Starting in Excel 2000, you could choose to save your Excel files as HTML.

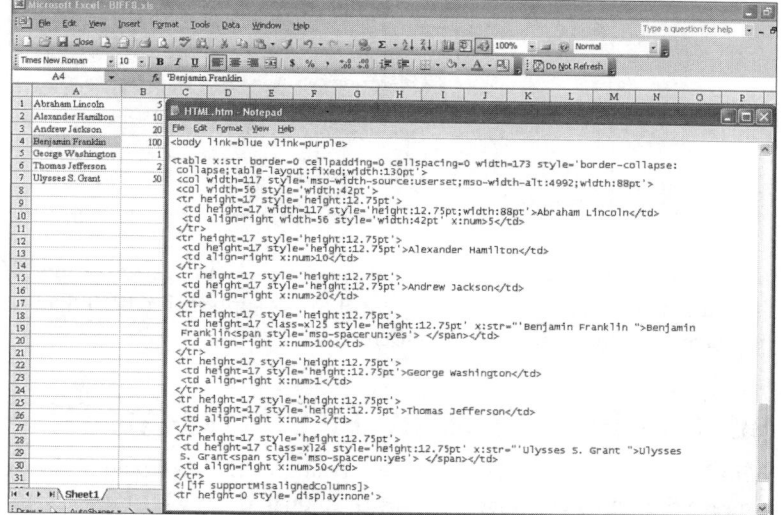

Using HTML made sense in 1998–2000. The rise of the Internet made HTML a very popular format. However, although HTML is a great language for the display of information, it is not necessarily a smart language.

In 1998, the World Wide Web Consortium published the first 1.0 specification for a new language called Extensible Markup Language (XML), which presents data that any platform or application can read. Like HTML, XML is a simple text file that can be read or created with Notepad. Excel 2002 offered a way to export data in XML. Excel 2003 continued to use BIFF8 as the standard file format, but you could choose to save a workbook in XML format. When you later opened the XML file in Excel, all the formulas and formatting would be successfully round-tripped. XML in Excel 2003 did not support VBA or charts.

Figure 18.3 shows the spreadsheet from Figures 18.1 and 18.2, saved as XML in Excel 2003.

There are a number of advantages to XML. Because an XML file is a simple text file, any program can easily read data from it. This file format is also less prone to corruption than BIFF. If you randomly wipe out several bytes of a BIFF file, it is likely that the file will be corrupt and no longer open in Excel. If you truncate or corrupt several bytes of an XML file, the rest of the data is still readable in Excel.

**Figure 18.3**
Excel 2003 offered support for XML formats.

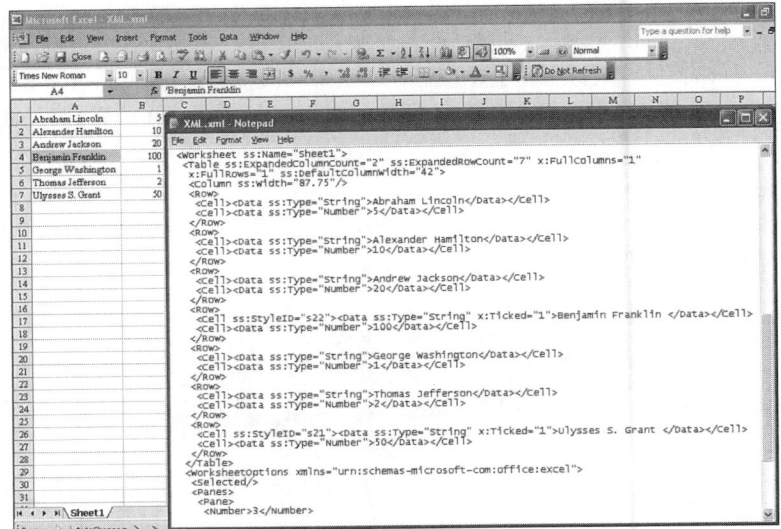

Excel 2007 offers three new official file formats—BIFF12, XLSX, and XLSM—described in the following sections. In addition, Excel offers support for BIFF8 and even BIFF5, in case you have files floating around from Excel 95.

# USING THE NEW BINARY FILE FORMAT: BIFF12

With Excel 2007's increase in rows and columns, BIFF8 would no longer work. Excel 2007 can save files in a new binary file format known as BIFF12. Files stored in BIFF12 have an .xlsb file extension. The Save As dialog box calls this type of file Excel Binary Workbook. For the first time, the binary workbook is not the default method for saving in Excel.

BIFF12 suffers from the same problems as all previous BIFF versions: It is difficult for other applications to read from or write to BIFF formats, and if parts of the BIFF12 file become corrupted or truncated, Excel has a difficult time successfully loading the file.

If you are extremely concerned with performance issues, you might want to use BIFF12 because a large BIFF12 file loads more quickly and saves more quickly than the new XML formats.

# USING THE NEW XML FILE FORMATS: XLSX AND XLSM

XML in Excel 2003 was almost an ideal solution: Files could be round-tripped from Excel to XML and back to Excel, provided that the files did not include VBA macros, charts, or other embedded images.

Excel 2007 now offers complete 100% support for every feature in the new XML file formats. Workbooks can contain charts, tables, WordArt, SmartArt, shapes, and images. For security purposes, Excel supports XML file formats that are macro free and file formats that are macro-enabled. These are the two XML file formats that Excel 2007 supports:

- **XLSX**—Files stored with the .xlsx extension are the default file type in Excel 2007. This XML file format does not allow macros.

- **XLSM**—Files stored with the .xlsm extension are XML files that allow for the inclusion of VBA macros.

The new XLSX and XLSM file formats are actually zip files, which makes it easy to look inside the file formats.

Figure 18.4 shows a worksheet that has a number of elements. It has a table in Row 21, WordArt, SmartArt, a chart, a shape with a glow effect, and clip art with a reflection.

**Figure 18.4**
This workbook is saved in XLSM, one of the new XML formats.

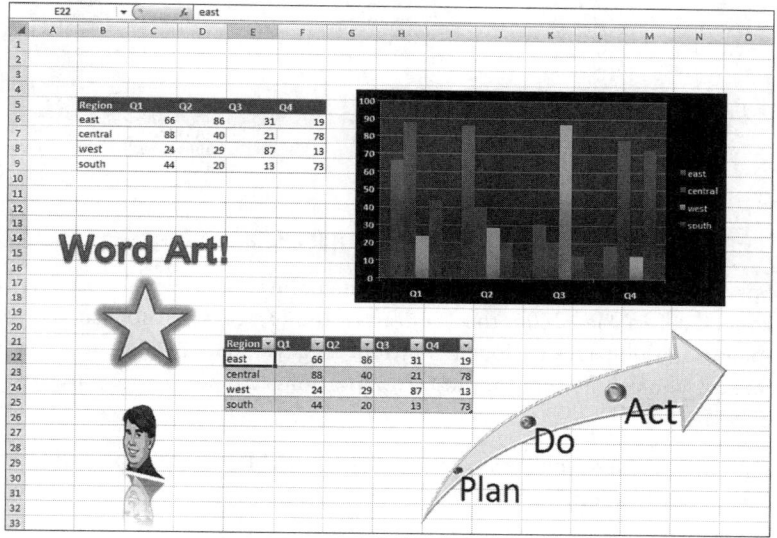

To look inside any Excel 2007 document, you follow these steps:

1. In Windows Explorer, right-click the document name, which is in the format as *filename*.xlsm, and choose Rename.

2. Change the file extension to .zip. Windows warns you that if you change a file extension, the file may become unusable.

3. Click Yes to confirm the change.

4. Open the ZIP file with WinZip or any other zip utility.

As shown in Figure 18.5, inside the ZIP file, you can see several XML components. The embedded image is included in the ZIP file. All the settings and styles, drawings, and data are stored as separate XML files within the ZIP file. Unzipped, these components would take up 159KB. Because they are zipped files, the data is stored in 29KB.

**Figure 18.5**
The components of the workbook are stored as XML files, zipped, and then renamed with an `.xlsx` or `.xlsm` extension.

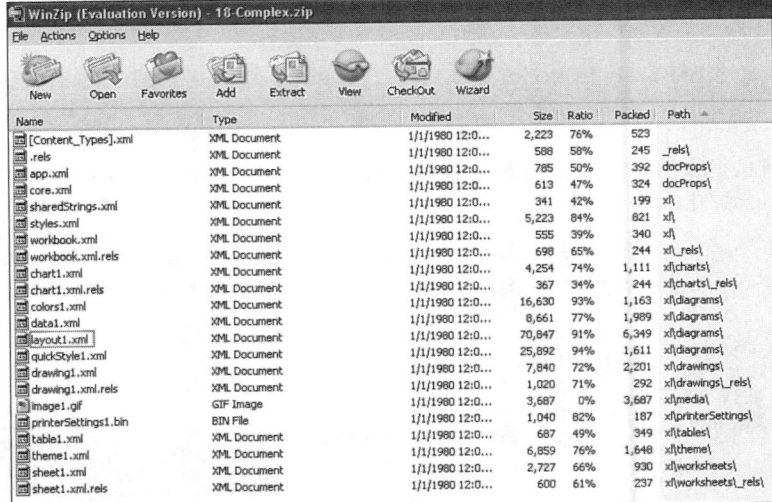

| Name | Type | Modified | Size | Ratio | Packed | Path |
|------|------|----------|------|-------|--------|------|
| [Content_Types].xml | XML Document | 1/1/1980 12:0... | 2,223 | 76% | 523 | |
| .rels | XML Document | 1/1/1980 12:0... | 588 | 58% | 245 | _rels\ |
| app.xml | XML Document | 1/1/1980 12:0... | 785 | 50% | 392 | docProps\ |
| core.xml | XML Document | 1/1/1980 12:0... | 613 | 47% | 324 | docProps\ |
| sharedStrings.xml | XML Document | 1/1/1980 12:0... | 341 | 42% | 199 | xl\ |
| styles.xml | XML Document | 1/1/1980 12:0... | 5,223 | 84% | 821 | xl\ |
| workbook.xml | XML Document | 1/1/1980 12:0... | 555 | 39% | 340 | xl\ |
| workbook.xml.rels | XML Document | 1/1/1980 12:0... | 698 | 65% | 244 | xl\_rels\ |
| chart1.xml | XML Document | 1/1/1980 12:0... | 4,254 | 74% | 1,111 | xl\charts\ |
| chart1.xml.rels | XML Document | 1/1/1980 12:0... | 367 | 34% | 244 | xl\charts\_rels\ |
| colors1.xml | XML Document | 1/1/1980 12:0... | 16,630 | 93% | 1,163 | xl\diagrams\ |
| data1.xml | XML Document | 1/1/1980 12:0... | 8,661 | 77% | 1,989 | xl\diagrams\ |
| layout1.xml | XML Document | 1/1/1980 12:0... | 70,847 | 91% | 6,349 | xl\diagrams\ |
| quickStyle1.xml | XML Document | 1/1/1980 12:0... | 25,892 | 94% | 1,611 | xl\diagrams\ |
| drawing1.xml | XML Document | 1/1/1980 12:0... | 7,840 | 72% | 2,201 | xl\drawings\ |
| drawing1.xml.rels | XML Document | 1/1/1980 12:0... | 1,020 | 71% | 292 | xl\drawings\_rels\ |
| image1.gif | GIF Image | 1/1/1980 12:0... | 3,687 | 0% | 3,687 | xl\media\ |
| printerSettings1.bin | BIN File | 1/1/1980 12:0... | 1,040 | 82% | 187 | xl\printerSettings\ |
| table1.xml | XML Document | 1/1/1980 12:0... | 687 | 49% | 349 | xl\tables\ |
| theme1.xml | XML Document | 1/1/1980 12:0... | 6,859 | 76% | 1,648 | xl\theme\ |
| sheet1.xml | XML Document | 1/1/1980 12:0... | 2,727 | 66% | 930 | xl\worksheets\ |
| sheet1.xml.rels | XML Document | 1/1/1980 12:0... | 600 | 61% | 237 | xl\worksheets\_rels\ |

# THE FUTURE OF FILE FORMATS

Spreadsheet XML will dramatically change the way other applications can interact with Excel data. In May 2006, the 1.3 draft of the Office XML format specifications already spanned 4,000 pages of documentation. As developers become more familiar with the format, you can be sure that more applications will be able to consume Excel spreadsheets in XML.

For the current specification on Spreadsheet XML, use Google to search for "spreadsheet XML specification."

18

# CHAPTER 19

# WORKING WITH PRIOR VERSIONS OF EXCEL

## In this chapter

With not just one new file format but three file formats in Excel 2007, you will face a number of problems as you try to share files with people who use previous versions of Excel.

If you are using Excel 2007 and want to open a file created in Excel 5 through Excel 2007, your copy of Excel will gladly open the file, but the file will be in a special Compatibility mode. In this mode, you cannot use more than 65,536 rows, and you cannot use more than 256 columns. When you attempt to save the file, the Compatibility Checker will tell you what functionality will be lost.

In order to unlock the larger grid in Excel 2007 for a file created in an earlier version of Excel, you need to upgrade the file.

If you start with a new spreadsheet in Excel 2007 and want to share the file with someone using Excel 5, 95, 97, or 2000, you have to use the Compatibility Checker and save the file in a previous version of Excel.

If you start with a new spreadsheet in Excel 2007 and want to share the file with someone using Excel 2002 or Excel 2003, you can encourage that person to download the Compatibility Pack for the Microsoft Office 2007 system. This converter allows Excel 2002 and Excel 2003 to open files stored in the new XLSB, XLSM, and XLSX formats.

# OPENING EXCEL 2007 FILES IN PREVIOUS VERSIONS OF EXCEL

If you attempt to open an Excel 2007 file in Excel 2002 or Excel 2003, you will see a message that the file was created in a newer version of Excel. Excel offers to allow you to download a converter so that you can open the file, as shown in Figure 19.1.

**Figure 19.1**
Your coworkers using Excel 2003 or Excel 2002 will be greeted with this message when they attempt to open one of your files.

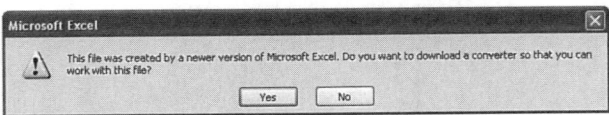

You follow these steps to download and install the converter:

1. Click Yes on the dialog box shown in Figure 19.1. A browser window launches, showing the home page of the Microsoft Office Compatibility Pack.

2. The converter requires that you be running Windows Vista, Windows XP, or Windows 2000. If you are using Windows XP, you need to be using Service Pack 2. If you are using Windows 2000, you need to be using Service Pack 4. If you are not at these levels, follow the links on the browser page.

3. The converter requires Office 2003 to be upgraded to Service Pack 2 or Excel 2002 to be upgraded to Service Pack 3. Select Help, About in Excel to determine your current service pack level. If you do not have the required service pack, follow the links on the browser page to download the upgrade.

4. Close all Office programs, including Excel. (Keep your browser open.)

5. Download and install the appropriate Office 2007 File Format Awareness Update by following the link on the browser page. The download is approximately 18MB, and the installation takes an unusually long time, often appearing to stop between steps. Eventually, the process starts the Office Installer and installs several items.

6. Return to the Compatibility Pack webpage. Choose the link to download the Compatibility Pack. The download is approximately 54MB. Run `o2007cnv.exe` after you download it. At the end of the installation, if you are prompted to restart your computer, do so.

After you install the Compatibility Pack, you can directly open XLSM, XLSX, and XLSB files in Excel 2003 or Excel 2002.

## OPENING A BASIC EXCEL 2007 FILE IN EXCEL 2003

Figure 19.2 shows a simple workbook in Excel 2007. Figure 19.3 shows the same workbook opened in Excel 2003. There are minor changes in the workbook. For example, the custom color in Cell B12 is converted to the closest color in the standard Excel 2003 pallet of 56 colors.

**Figure 19.2**
This basic worksheet in Excel 2007 converts nicely to Excel 2003.

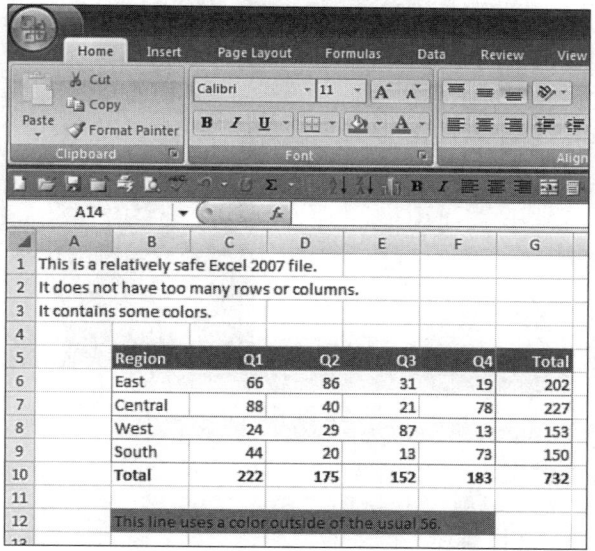

You can edit this workbook in Excel 2003, save it as an Excel 2007 file format, and successfully open it in Excel 2007.

## OPENING AN ADVANCED EXCEL 2007 FILE IN EXCEL 2003

The Excel 2007 workbook shown in Figure 19.4 contains several elements that seem to be incompatible with Excel 2003. For example, the range in E21:I25 is an Excel 2007 table. The function in Cell F27 uses the new SUMIFS function. An image in Cell C27 has a reflection effect applied to it. The shape in Cell C18 is a shape that was not available in Excel

2003. The WordArt in Cell B14 is a different style than the styles available in Excel 2003. The chart uses Excel 2007 formatting. The SmartArt uses a shape that is not available in Excel 2003 diagrams.

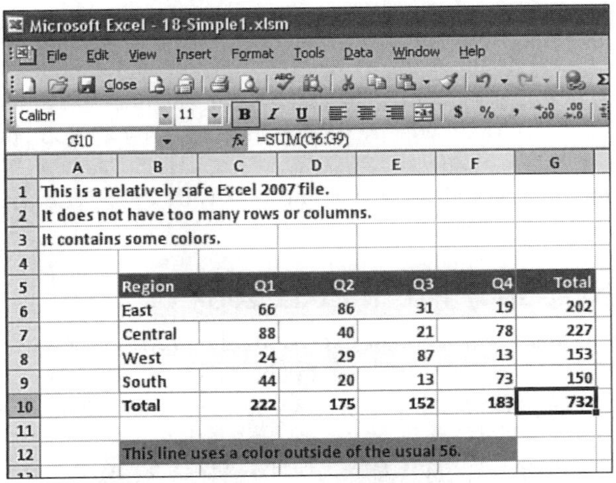

**Figure 19.3**
Some minor formatting changes occur, but everything else translates perfectly.

**Figure 19.4**
This file in Excel 2007 purposely uses many features that would seem to be incompatible with Excel 2003.

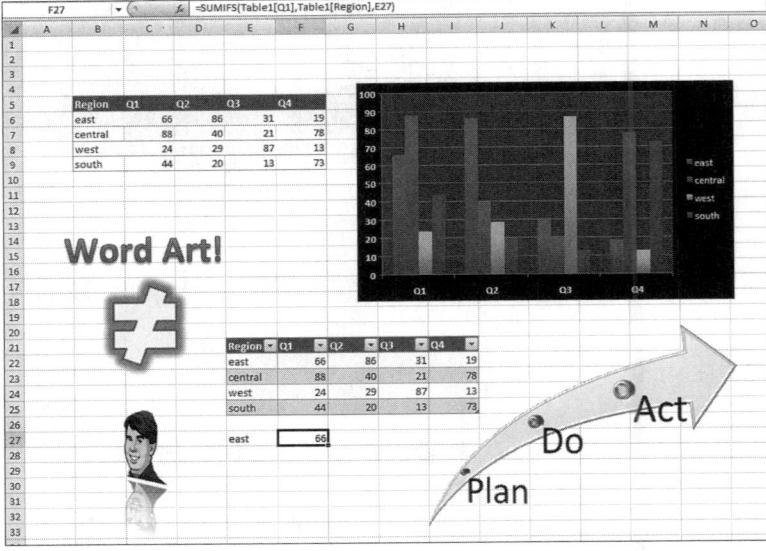

When you attempt to open this workbook in Excel 2003, Excel warns you that there is significant loss of functionality. Because of the loss of functionality, Excel forces the document to be opened as read-only. You have to use File, Save As to save the file with a new name. This prevents the original document from losing fidelity.

**Figure 19.5**
If too much functionality will be lost, Excel 2003 forces the file to be opened as read-only.

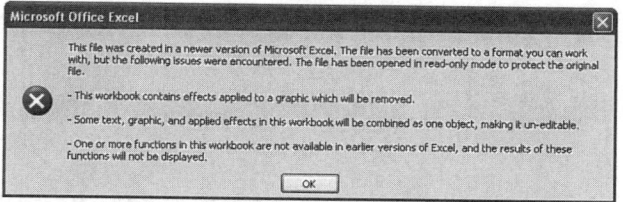

Excel 2003 does its best to deal with the incompatible features. As shown in Figure 19.6, the chart formatting comes across amazingly well. The SmartArt looks fine, but it is no longer editable. The table in E21:I25 has been converted to an Excel 2003 list. The formula in Cell F27 has been converted from table nomenclature to actually refer to the correct cells. However, because the formula uses a function that is new in Excel 2007, the function returns a #NAME? error. The WordArt converts horribly. The shape converts, but the glow is lost.

**Figure 19.6**
Various elements are converted okay, while others, such as the WordArt and Excel 2007 functions, fail miserably.

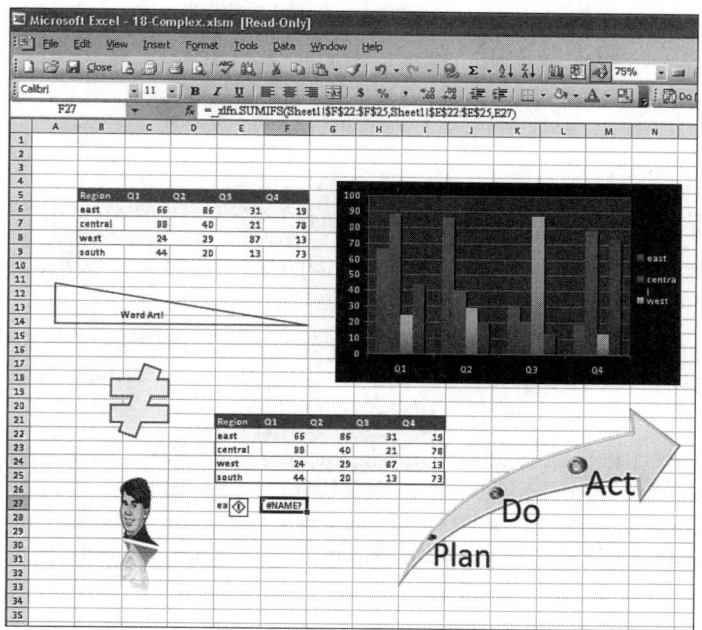

On the machine running Excel 2003, you have to save the file with a new name. If you then attempt to open that file in Excel 2007, much of the formatting returns. Figure 19.7 shows the file after it is saved in Excel 2003 and then opened in Excel 2007. The glow on the object returns. The WordArt looks good again. The SmartArt is again editable. The chart has some problems, although this varies by chart. The one real loss of fidelity is the table function in Cell F27. In the original document, shown in Figure 19.4, this formula used table nomenclature. In Excel 2003, the table nomenclature was replaced with actual cell references, and when the file is brought back to Excel 2007, those cell references remain.

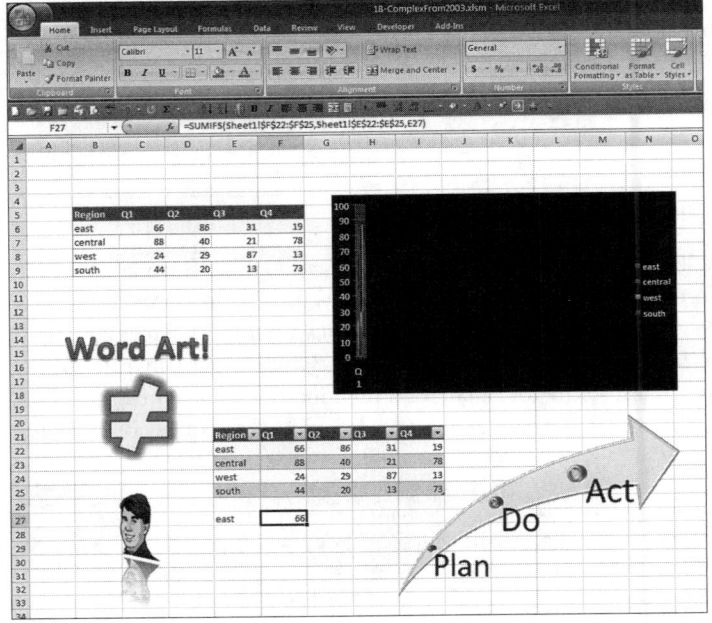

## OPENING WORKSHEETS BY USING THE LARGE GRID IN EXCEL 2003

The one situation that Excel 2003 absolutely cannot deal with is data in rows 65,537 and below and data in Columns IW and beyond.

When you attempt to open a file that has data outside the Excel 2003 grid, data outside the bounds of the original grid is not converted. Further, any formulas inside the grid that point to cells in the big grid return a #REF! error.

Excel opens the file in read-only mode, encouraging you to save it with a new name, so as not to destroy the original file with data beyond Column IV, Row 65,536. When you save the file in Excel 2003, this data is permanently lost. Even if you save the file in Excel 2003 and reopen it in Excel 2007, everything beyond row 65,536 has been truncated.

# CREATING EXCEL 2007 FILE FORMATS IN EXCEL 2003

After you install the Office 2007 Compatibility Pack on a machine running Excel 2002 or Excel 2003, you will be able to save files from Excel 2003 or Excel 2002 in one of the new Excel 2007 file formats. The advantage is that when the file is later opened on a machine running Excel 2007, the file will not be forced into the compatibility mode.

After you have the Compatibility Pack installed, you follow these steps to save files in an Excel 2007 format:

1. Open or create a workbook in Excel 2002 or Excel 2003.

2. Select File, Save As. The Save As dialog box appears.

3. Open the Save as Type drop-down and scroll to the bottom of the list. Choose one of the Excel "12" file types, as shown in Figure 19.8.

4. Type a filename

5. Click Save. Excel runs a converter to convert the workbook to the chosen Excel 2007 format.

**Figure 19.8**
After you install the converter in Excel 2003, you can save files in any of the Excel 2007 formats.

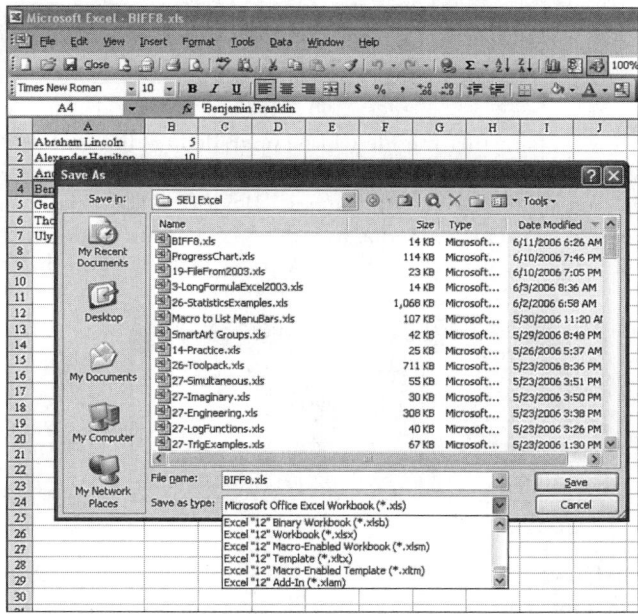

# OPENING EXCEL 2003 FILES IN EXCEL 2007

The easiest way to get your old Excel files into Excel 2007 is to open them directly in Excel 2007. Excel 2007 will be able to import files saved in any version from Excel 5 through Excel 2003. However, files opened in this manner open in a bizarre Compatibility mode.

When a legacy Excel file is opened in Excel 2007, the title bar isays [Compatibility Mode]. In this mode, Excel 2007 allows only 65,536 rows and 256 columns. It is impossible to insert more columns or rows in the file. If you add additional sheets, the sheets will have only 65,536 rows and 256 columns.

You can add new features while the file is in Compatibility mode. For example, you can use the AVERAGEIFS function and use colors beyond the 56-color palette. However, when you attempt to save the file, the Compatibility Checker warns you about the fidelity that will be lost. When a file is in the hampered Compatibility mode state, you cannot access any cells in the expanded grid area of the worksheet. In order to access the additional rows, you have to upgrade the file

To upgrade the file, you follow these steps:

19

1. From the Office icon menu, select Convert. As shown in Figure 19.9, this icon features a green up arrow, indicating that you will be upgrading the file.

**Figure 19.9**
The Convert icon is available only when the active workbook is in Compatibility mode.

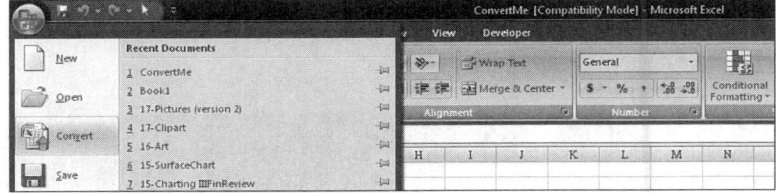

A dialog box explains that the file will be upgraded to the newest file format, as shown in Figure 19.10. The most important part of this dialog is that your original XLS file will be deleted and replaced with the new XLSX or XLSM file. I suppose this is to prevent anyone from accidentally opening the XLS version of the file. However, taking this action will break any existing Excel workspaces that relied on the old version of the file.

**Figure 19.10**
Note that the conversion process will replace the original file with an Excel 2007 file.

2. Press End+Down Arrow. Frustratingly, the file still has only 65,536 rows.
3. Choose the Office icon menu and then select Close to close the file.
4. Choose the Office icon menu and then select 1 to reopen the converted file. Your file now has 1.1 million rows.

# PREPARING TO SAVE EXCEL 2007 FILES FOR EXCEL 97 THROUGH EXCEL 2003

You are likely to need to send your Excel 2007 workbooks to someone who is using an older, unsupported version of Excel, such as Excel 97 or Excel 2000. There is no Compatibility Pack available for those versions. You may also run into people using Excel 2003 who for some reason are not able to download the Compatibility Pack. In these cases, you will have the possibly frustrating situation of needing to downgrade a file in order to save it as an XLS format that the other person can open.

Your first stop should be the Compatibility Checker. This utility analyzes which Excel 2007 features you have used that will not be available in prior versions of Excel. In some cases, this is only a minor problem. For example, if you have used a color outside the palette of 56 colors, Excel simply substitutes another color. Excel considers this a minor loss of fidelity. In other cases, your workbook will extend beyond either Row 65,536 or Column IV, and some of your data will be truncated if you downgrade the file.

To run the Compatibility Checker, you follow these steps:

1. From the Office icon, select Finish, Compatibility Checker. Excel displays a list of problems with the workbook. Note that the Compatibility Checker dialog is a bit too small and displays only two items at a time. You might need to scroll through several screens of problems. If the workbook has no compatibility problems, the message "No Compatibility Issues Were Found" is displayed. To the right of each problem, Excel displays the number of cells affected by the problem. Some simple problems have a Fix hyperlink. Other problems cannot be automatically fixed. If you click the Find hyperlink next to the problem, Excel closes the dialog and changes the active cell to the first cell that has the problem.

2. To fix a problem cell, take the required action. In many cases, you don't have to fix the problem. For example, if it is merely a formatting issue, you can take your chances in trusting that Excel will apply the closest available format.

3. Repeat steps 1 and 2 for additional problems.

The Compatibility Checker dialog, shown in Figure 19.11, classifies problems in two groups. Major problems appear first, in a section called Significant Loss of Functionality. Minor problems appear later, in a section called Minor Loss of Fidelity.

**Figure 19.11**
A list of problems appears in the dialog box.

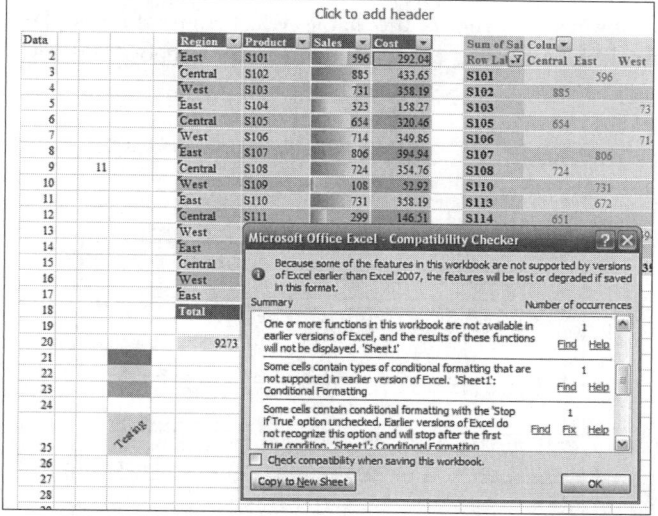

The following are examples of some problems that might appear in the Significant Loss of Functionality section:

- "This workbook contains data in cells outside of the row and column limit of the selected format. Data beyond 256 (IV) columns by 65,536 rows will not be saved. Formula references to data in this region will return a #REF! error."

- "Some formulas contain references to tables that are not supported in the selected file format. These references will be converted to cell references."

- "One or more functions in the workbook are not available in earlier versions of Excel and the results of these functions will not be displayed."

- "Some cells contain types of conditional formatting that are not supported in earlier versions of Excel."

- "Some cells contain conditional formatting with the 'Stop if True' option unchecked. Earlier versions of Excel do not recognize this option and will stop after the first true condition."

- "Some cells contain conditional formatting with cell references to other worksheets. These conditions will not be evaluated in earlier versions of Excel."

The following are examples of some of the problems that might appear in the Minor Loss of Fidelity section:

- "This workbook contains a table with table style applied. Table style formatting will not be displayed in previous versions of Excel."

- "Some cells or styles contain formatting that is not supported in the selected file format. These formats will be converted to the closest format available."

If you are attempting to fix all the problems listed, it can be frustrating bouncing between the Compatibility Checker dialog and the worksheet. If you click the Copy to New Sheet button in the lower-left corner of the dialog, Excel copies the complete report, along with hyperlinks to all the offending cells, to a compatibility report in the workbook, as shown in Figure 19.12.

**Figure 19.12**
You can click Copy to New Sheet to produce the compatibility report on a new worksheet.

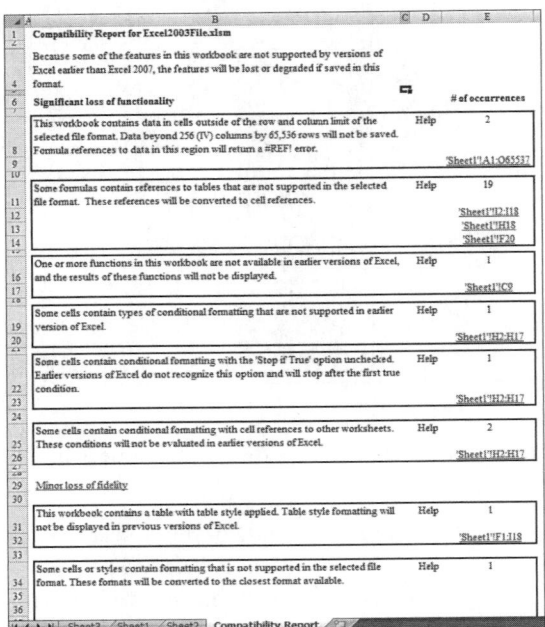

## SAVING EXCEL 2007 FILES FOR EXCEL 97 THROUGH EXCEL 2003

After checking for compatibility problems, you follow these steps to save a file as an XLS file:

1. From the Office icon, choose Save As. The Save As dialog appears.
2. In the Save as Type drop-down, select Excel 97-2003 Workbook (*.xls).
3. If necessary, type a new filename.
4. Click the Save button. Excel displays the Compatibility Checker one more time.
5. In the Compatibility Checker, click the Continue button. If you have unresolved formula problems, Excel asks "Do you want to recalculate all formulas when this workbook is opened?" If you want the recipient of the workbook to see the current values, choose No.

# THE DIGITAL DIVIDE

Compatibility problems are frustrating. If you are reading this book, you are presumably the owner of Excel 2007. As you send files to others, you will hear the excuse, "I received an email, but the file was in some bizarre format that my copy of Excel couldn't open." As I consider the fantastic new features in Excel 2007, my main concern is the compatibility of the file formats with those people who don't upgrade. Although the Compatibility Checker can handle many problems, it simply cannot deal with situations in which the workbook contains more than 65,536 rows. Although there are 40 billion workbooks with fewer than 65,536 rows in use today, people will quickly start moving datasets to Excel instead of Access, and the rift between the Excel 2007 customers and everyone else will be the digital divide of 2007 and 2008.

19

# CALCULATING WITH EXCEL

CHAPTER **20**

# UNDERSTANDING FORMULAS

## In this chapter

Excel's forte is performing calculations. When you use Excel, you typically use a combination of cells with numbers and cells with formulas. After you design a spreadsheet to calculate something, you can easily change the numbers used in the assumption cells and then watch Excel instantly calculate new results.

# GETTING THE MOST FROM THIS CHAPTER

Don't skip this entire chapter, because one particular trick in this chapter will save you daily frustration.

I regularly entertain accountants and auditors with my Power Excel program. While this program is a fun, laughter-filled tour through the inside tricks of Microsoft Excel, I do know that people are learning new things along the way.

I call them "gasp moments."

Imagine this setting: I am in front of 200 managerial accountants—these are people who have Excel open 40 hours a week. You can generally figure that these folks are super-efficient with Excel. For any trick that I show, it might be already in the arsenal of half to three-quarters of the room. I will see a lot people nodding their heads and see an expression of surprise on a portion of the attendees.

Universally, though, there are a few tricks that get a universal gasp—perhaps 90% of the people never knew the trick and realize just how powerful it is. I thrive on the gasp moments.

I understand that everyone reading this book believes that they know Excel formulas. And, to a certain extent, this chapter is mostly a primer for the person who is new to Excel. However, even the most astute person using Excel should check out these sections of the chapter:

- Everyone should read "Copying a Formula by Double-Clicking the Fill Handle." Somehow, most people have learned to drag the fill handle to copy a formula. This leads to horrible frustration on long data sets, as you go flying past the end of the data. This simple but powerful trick is the one that universally amazes attendees of my seminar.

- Honestly answer this question: Do you really understand the difference between cell H1 and cell $H$1? If you think the latter has anything to do with currency, you need to thoroughly review "Overriding Relative Behavior—Absolute Cell References." This isn't a trick, but one of the fundamental building blocks to building Excel worksheets. I would say that 5% of the people in a Power Excel seminar did not understand this, and perhaps 30% of the people in a community computer club presentation did not understand this. If you don't know when and why to use the dollar signs, you are in good company with 20 million other people using Excel. It is worth your time to learn this essential technique.

- Finally, I can predict someone's age by how they enter formulas. There are three ways, and I believe that my preferred way is the best. I probably won't convince you to change, but if you understood my way, you would be able to enter formulas far faster than the other two ways. To get a good understanding of the alternatives, read "Three Methods of Entering Formulas."

# INTRODUCTION TO FORMULAS

In Chapter 7, Table 7.1 shows a list of changed limits in Excel. A few of these limits relate specifically to formulas. For example, the number of characters in a formula increased from 1,024 to 8,192. The number of levels of nesting for IF functions increased from 7 to 64. Thanks to Excel 2007's improved limits, you can calculate almost anything with a formula in Excel.

This chapter and Chapter 21, "Doing Cool Tricks with Formulas," deal with formula basics. Chapters 22, "Understanding Functions," through 27, "Using Math and Engineering Functions," introduce adding functions to your formulas. Chapter 28, "Connecting Worksheets, Workbooks, and External Data," introduces formulas that calculate data found on other worksheets or in other workbooks. Chapter 29, "Using Super Formulas in Excel," provides interesting examples, such as 3D formulas and the all-powerful array formulas.

**NOTE**

The need to recalculate case studies at M.I.T. led Dan Bricklin to invent the first spreadsheet program, VisiCalc.

Because of the record-oriented nature of spreadsheets, you can generally build a formula once and then copy that formula to hundreds or thousands of cells without changing anything in the formula.

**TIP FROM**

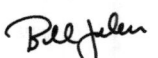

Designing a formula that can be written once and then copied to a rectangular range of data is a fantastic way to make your use of Excel more efficient.

## FORMULAS VERSUS VALUES

When looking at an Excel grid, you can't tell the difference between a cell with a formula and one that contains numbers. To see if a cell contains a number or a formula, you select the cell. Look in the formula bar. If the formula bar contains a number, as shown in Figure 20.1, you know that it is a static value. As shown in Figure 20.2, if the formula bar contains a formula (most formulas start with =), you know that the number shown in the grid is the result of a formula calculation.

**20**

**Figure 20.1**
The formula bar reveals whether a value is a static number or a calculation. In this case, Cell B2 contains a static number.

|   | A | B | C | D |
|---|---|---|---|---|
| 1 | SKU | Mfg Cost | | |
| 2 | J41 | 16.4 | | |
| 3 | J20 | 14.47 | | |
| 4 | I51 | 16.14 | | |
| 5 | F69 | 14.31 | | |
| 6 | G61 | 14.81 | | |

B2    $f_x$  16.4

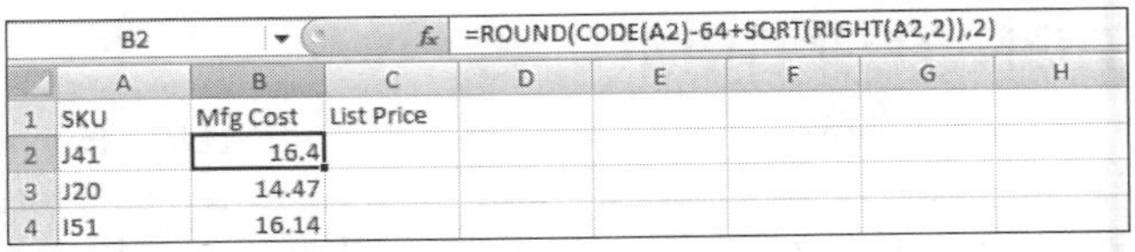

**Figure 20.2**
In this case, Cell B2 contains the result of a formula calculation. A formula usually starts with an equals sign.

| B2 | | | $f_x$ | =ROUND(CODE(A2)-64+SQRT(RIGHT(A2,2)),2) | | | |
| --- | --- | --- | --- | --- | --- | --- | --- |
| | A | B | C | D | E | F | G | H |
| 1 | SKU | Mfg Cost | List Price | | | | | |
| 2 | J41 | 16.4 | | | | | | |
| 3 | J20 | 14.47 | | | | | | |
| 4 | I51 | 16.14 | | | | | | |

# ENTERING YOUR FIRST FORMULA

Your first formula was probably a SUM function, entered with the AutoSum button. However, for this discussion, I am talking about a pure mathematic formula that uses a value in a cell, added, subtracted, divided, or multiplied by a number or another cell.

There are billions of variations of formulas that can be used. Everyday life throws situations at you that can be solved with this type of formula. Keep these important points in mind as you start tinkering with your own formulas:

- Every formula starts with an equal sign.
- Entering formulas is then just like typing an equation in a calculator with one exception (see the next point).
- If one of the terms in your formula is already stored in a cell in Excel, you can point to that cell's address instead of typing in the number in that cell. Using this method will allow you to change the value in one cell and then watch all of the formulas recalculate.

To illustrate these points, watch the steps to building a basic formula for a specific example.

In Figure 20.3, you want to enter a formula to calculate a target sales price. Cell B2 shows the product cost. In Column C, you want to calculate list price as two times the cost plus $3.

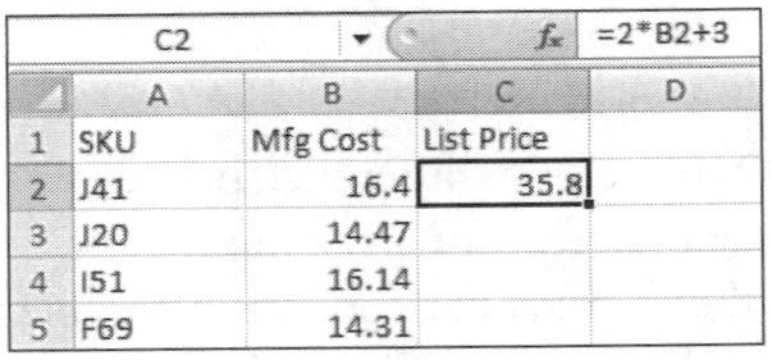

**Figure 20.3**
The formula in Cell C2 recalculates if the value in Cell B2 changes.

| C2 | | | $f_x$ | =2*B2+3 |
| --- | --- | --- | --- | --- |
| | A | B | C | D |
| 1 | SKU | Mfg Cost | List Price | |
| 2 | J41 | 16.4 | 35.8 | |
| 3 | J20 | 14.47 | | |
| 4 | I51 | 16.14 | | |
| 5 | F69 | 14.31 | | |

20

To enter a formula, follow these steps:

1. Put the cell pointer in Cell C2.
2. Type an equal sign. The equal sign tells Excel that you are starting a formula.
3. Type 2*B2. This indicates that you want to multiply two times the value in cell B2.
4. Type +3 to add three to the result. There should be no spaces in the formula. If your formula reads =2*B2+3, proceed to step 5. Otherwise, use the backspace key to correct the formula.
5. Press Enter. Excel calculates the formula in Cell C2.

By default Excel usually moves the cell pointer down or to the right after you finish entering a formula. You should move the cell pointer back to Cell C2 to inspect the formula, as shown in Figure 20.3. Note that Excel shows a number in the grid, but the formula bar reveals the formula behind the number.

## THE RELATIVE NATURE OF FORMULAS

The formula =2*B2+3 really says "multiply two by the cell immediately to the left of me and add three." If you need to put this formula in Cells C3 to C999, you do not need to re-enter the formula 996 times. You can simply copy the formula and paste it to all the cells. As you copy, Excel copies the essence of the formula: "Multiply two by the cell to the left of me and add three." As you copy the formula to Cell C3, the formula becomes =2*B3+3. Excel handles all this automatically.

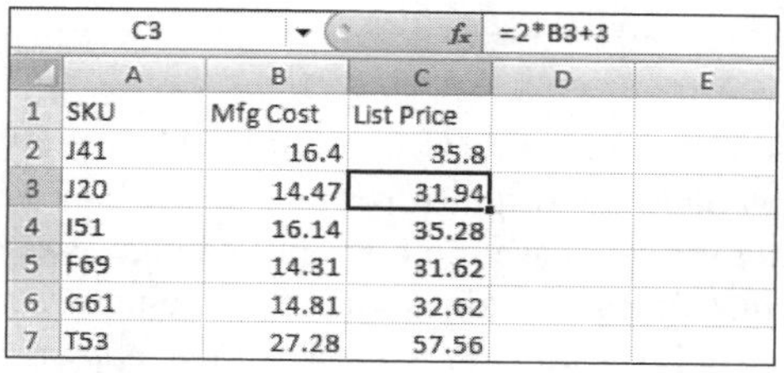

**Figure 20.4**
After you paste the formula, Excel automatically updates the cell reference to point to the current row.

| | A | B | C | D | E |
|---|---|---|---|---|---|
| 1 | SKU | Mfg Cost | List Price | | |
| 2 | J41 | 16.4 | 35.8 | | |
| 3 | J20 | 14.47 | 31.94 | | |
| 4 | I51 | 16.14 | 35.28 | | |
| 5 | F69 | 14.31 | 31.62 | | |
| 6 | G61 | 14.81 | 32.62 | | |
| 7 | T53 | 27.28 | 57.56 | | |

C3    $f_x$ =2*B3+3

Excel's ability to change *B2* to *B3* in the formula is called *relative referencing*. This is the default behavior of a reference. Sometimes, you do not want Excel to change a reference as the formula is copied, as explained in the next section.

## OVERRIDING RELATIVE BEHAVIOR: ABSOLUTE CELL REFERENCES

Excel's ability to change a formula as it is copied is what makes spreadsheets so useful. However, there are times when you need part of a formula to always point at one particular cell. This happens a lot when you have a setting at the top of the worksheet, such as a growth rate or a tax rate. It would be nice to change this cell once and have all of the formulas use the new rate.

The following example sets up a sample worksheet that exhibits this problem and shows you how to use an arcane notation style to easily solve the problem. When you see a reference with two dollar signs, for example $G$1, this indicates an absolute reference to G1.

Say that you have a sales tax factor in a single cell at the top of a worksheet. After you enter the formula =C2*G1, it accurately calculates the tax in Cell D2, as shown in Figure 20.5.

However, when you copy the same formula to Cell C3, you get a zero as the result. As you can see in Figure 20.6, Excel correctly changed Cell C2 to C3 in the copied formula. However, Excel also changed G1 to G2. Because there is nothing in G2, the calculation predicts a zero.

20

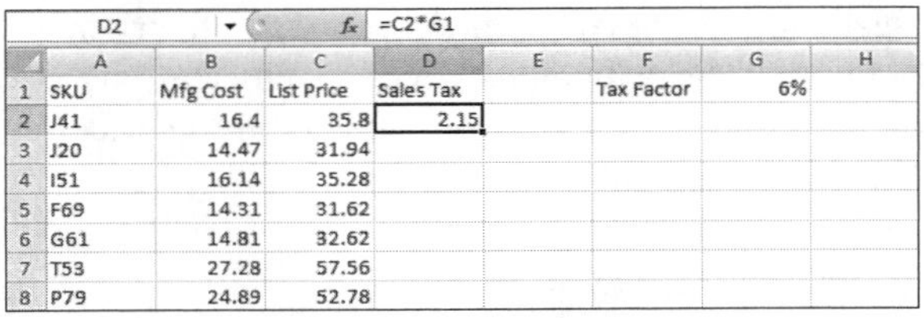

**Figure 20.5**
This formula works fine in Row 2.

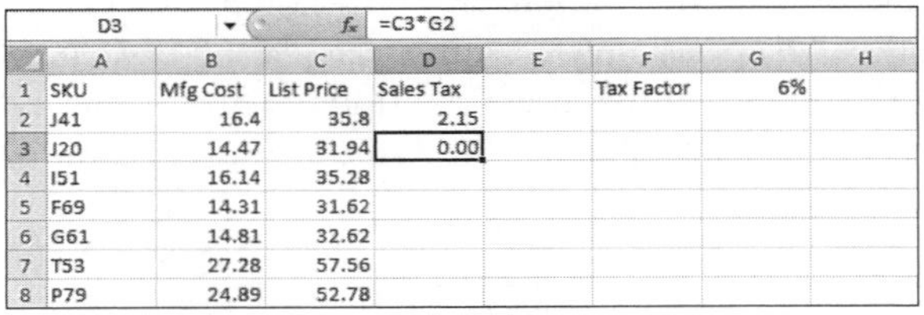

| | D2 | | $f_x$ =C2*G1 | | | | | |
|---|---|---|---|---|---|---|---|---|
| | A | B | C | D | E | F | G | H |
| 1 | SKU | Mfg Cost | List Price | Sales Tax | | Tax Factor | 6% | |
| 2 | J41 | 16.4 | 35.8 | 2.15 | | | | |
| 3 | J20 | 14.47 | 31.94 | | | | | |
| 4 | I51 | 16.14 | 35.28 | | | | | |
| 5 | F69 | 14.31 | 31.62 | | | | | |
| 6 | G61 | 14.81 | 32.62 | | | | | |
| 7 | T53 | 27.28 | 57.56 | | | | | |
| 8 | P79 | 24.89 | 52.78 | | | | | |

**Figure 20.6**
This formula fails in Row 3.

| | D3 | | $f_x$ =C3*G2 | | | | | |
|---|---|---|---|---|---|---|---|---|
| | A | B | C | D | E | F | G | H |
| 1 | SKU | Mfg Cost | List Price | Sales Tax | | Tax Factor | 6% | |
| 2 | J41 | 16.4 | 35.8 | 2.15 | | | | |
| 3 | J20 | 14.47 | 31.94 | 0.00 | | | | |
| 4 | I51 | 16.14 | 35.28 | | | | | |
| 5 | F69 | 14.31 | 31.62 | | | | | |
| 6 | G61 | 14.81 | 32.62 | | | | | |
| 7 | T53 | 27.28 | 57.56 | | | | | |
| 8 | P79 | 24.89 | 52.78 | | | | | |

Because the sales tax factor is only in G1, you really want Excel to always point to G1. To make this happen, you need to build the original formula as =C2*$G$1. The two dollar signs tell Excel that you do not want to have the reference change as the formula is copied. The $ before the G freezes the reference to always point to Column G. The $ before the 1 freezes the reference to always point to Row 1. Now, when you copy this formula from Cell D2 to other cells in Column D, Excel changes the formula to =C3*$G$1.

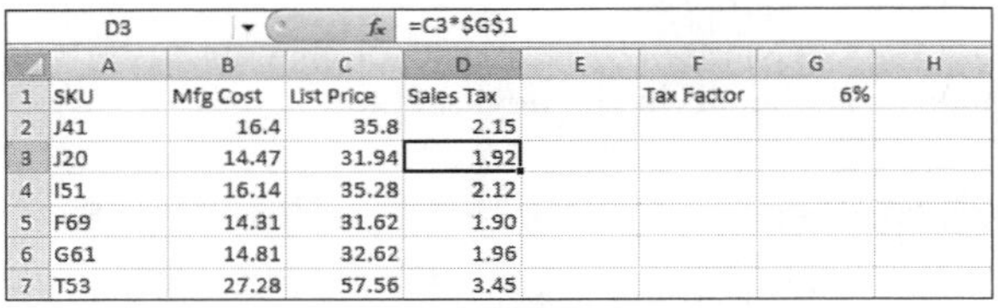

**Figure 20.7**
The dollar signs in the formula make sure that the copied formula always points to Cell G1.

| | D3 | | $f_x$ =C3*$G$1 | | | | | |
|---|---|---|---|---|---|---|---|---|
| | A | B | C | D | E | F | G | H |
| 1 | SKU | Mfg Cost | List Price | Sales Tax | | Tax Factor | 6% | |
| 2 | J41 | 16.4 | 35.8 | 2.15 | | | | |
| 3 | J20 | 14.47 | 31.94 | 1.92 | | | | |
| 4 | I51 | 16.14 | 35.28 | 2.12 | | | | |
| 5 | F69 | 14.31 | 31.62 | 1.90 | | | | |
| 6 | G61 | 14.81 | 32.62 | 1.96 | | | | |
| 7 | T53 | 27.28 | 57.56 | 3.45 | | | | |

To recap, a reference with two dollars signs is called an *absolute reference*.

## USING MIXED REFERENCES TO COMBINE THE FEATURES OF RELATIVE AND ABSOLUTE REFERENCES

In a number of situations, you might want to build a reference that has only one dollar sign. For example, in Figure 20.8, you want to use the monthly bonus rate in Row 3, but you want to allow the column to change. The formula for Cell C19 would be =C6*C$3.

When you copy this formula, it always points to the bonus amount in Row 3, but the remaining elements of the formula are relative. For example, the formula in D21 is =D8*D$3, which multiplies Jessica's February sales by the February bonus rate.

There are two kinds of mixed references. One mixed reference freezes the row number and allows the column letter to change. The other mixed reference freezes the column letter, but allows the row number to change. No one has thought up clever names to distinguish between these references—they are both simply called mixed references.

**Figure 20.8**
By having the dollar sign before the 3 in C$3, you lock the reference to Row 3 but allow the formula to point to Columns D, E, and so on as you copy the formula.

| | C19 | | | $f_x$ | =C6*C$3 | | | |
|---|---|---|---|---|---|---|---|---|
| | B | C | D | E | F | G | H | I |
| 1 | Plasma Sales Bonus Calculation | | | | | | | |
| 2 | | | | | | | | |
| 3 | Bonus % | $3 | $2 | $0 | $2 | $3 | $1 | |
| 4 | | | | | | | | |
| 5 | Units Sold | Jan | Feb | Mar | Apr | May | Jun | |
| 6 | CAROLYN | 81 | 82 | 83 | 77 | 63 | 55 | |
| 7 | LINDSAY | 61 | 94 | 51 | 93 | 68 | 50 | |
| 8 | JESSICA | 64 | 85 | 76 | 65 | 89 | 95 | |
| 9 | SHELLY | 94 | 89 | 65 | 62 | 62 | 54 | |
| 10 | JENNY | 52 | 84 | 67 | 51 | 87 | 88 | |
| 11 | JEFF | 79 | 64 | 75 | 82 | 79 | 48 | |
| 12 | MARCIA | 77 | 55 | 81 | 96 | 59 | 72 | |
| 13 | GREGORY | 58 | 83 | 93 | 81 | 56 | 60 | |
| 14 | LUIS | 94 | 62 | 73 | 53 | 88 | 66 | |
| 15 | DENNIS | 53 | 59 | 80 | 92 | 75 | 71 | |
| 16 | | | | | | | | |
| 17 | | | | | | | | |
| 18 | Bonus | Jan | Feb | Mar | Apr | May | Jun | |
| 19 | CAROLYN | $243 | $164 | $0 | $154 | $189 | $55 | |
| 20 | LINDSAY | $183 | $188 | $0 | $186 | $204 | $50 | |
| 21 | JESSICA | $192 | $170 | $0 | $130 | $267 | $95 | |

As another example of the other kind of mixed reference, in Figure 20.9, you want a single formula to multiply the daily rate from Column A by the number of days in Row 4. This formula requires both kinds of mixed references.

**Figure 20.9**
You can create a formula by using a combination of dollar signs to allow Cell C6 to be copied to all cells in the table.

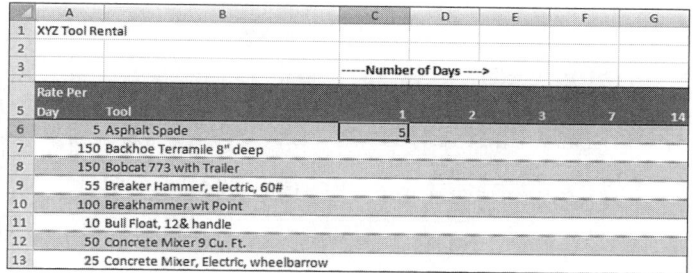

In this case, you want the Cell A6 reference to always point to Column A, even as the formula is copied to the right. The A6 portion of the formula should therefore be entered as $A6. You also want the C5 portion of the formula to always point to Row 5, even as the formula is copied down the rows. The C5 portion of the formula should therefore be entered as C$5.

## USING THE F4 KEY TO SIMPLIFY DOLLAR SIGN ENTRY

In the preceding section, you had to enter quite a few dollar signs in formulas. But you do not have to type the dollar signs! Immediately after entering a reference, you can press the F4 key to toggle the reference from a relative reference to an absolute reference that automatically has the dollar signs before the row and column. If you continue pressing F4, the reference toggles to a mixed reference with a dollar sign before the row number and then to a mixed reference with a dollar sign before the column letter. Pressing F4 again returns the reference to a relative reference. I find that it is easier to choose the right reference by looking at the various reference options offered by the F4 key.

20

The following sequence walks through how the F4 key works while you are entering a formula. This particular example was chosen because it requires two different types of mixed references.

The important concept is that you start pressing F4 after typing a cell reference but before you type a mathematical operator.

1. Type **=A6** (see Figure 20.10).

**Figure 20.10**
This is a relative reference: A6 without any dollar signs.

| | A | B | C | D | E | F | G | H |
|---|---|---|---|---|---|---|---|---|
| 1 | XYZ Tool Rental | | | | | | | |
| 2 | | | | | | | | |
| 3 | | | -----Number of Days ----> | | | | | |
| | Rate Per | | | | | | | |
| 5 | Day | Tool | 1 | 2 | 3 | 7 | 14 | 21 |
| 6 | 5 | Asphalt Spade | =A6 | | | | | |
| 7 | 150 | Backhoe Terramile 8" deep | | | | | | |
| 8 | 150 | Bobcat 773 with Trailer | | | | | | |
| 9 | 55 | Breaker Hammer, electric, 60# | | | | | | |

PV    × ✓ ƒₓ  =A6

2. Before typing the asterisk to indicate multiplication, press the F4 key. On the first press of F4, the reference changes to =$A$6, as shown in Figure 20.11.

**Figure 20.11**
After you press F4 once, the reference changes to an absolute reference, with two dollar signs.

PV    × ✓ ƒₓ  =$A$6

| | A | B | C | D | E |
|---|---|---|---|---|---|
| 1 | XYZ Tool Rental | | | | |
| 2 | | | | | |
| 3 | | | -----Number of Days ----> | | |
| | Rate Per | | | | |
| 5 | Day | Tool | 1 | 2 | 3 |
| 6 | 5 | Asphalt Spade | =$A$6 | | |
| 7 | 150 | Backhoe Terramile 8" deep | | | |
| 8 | 150 | Bobcat 773 with Trailer | | | |
| 9 | 55 | Breaker Hammer, electric, 60# | | | |

3. Press the F4 key again. The reference changes to A$6 to freeze the reference to Row 6, as shown in Figure 20.12.

**Figure 20.12**
You press F4 again to switch to a mixed reference with the row number locked.

PV    × ✓ ƒₓ  =A$6

| | A | B | C | D | E |
|---|---|---|---|---|---|
| 1 | XYZ Tool Rental | | | | |
| 2 | | | | | |
| 3 | | | -----Number of Days ----> | | |
| | Rate Per | | | | |
| 5 | Day | Tool | 1 | 2 | 3 |
| 6 | 5 | Asphalt Spade | =A$6 | | |
| 7 | 150 | Backhoe Terramile 8" deep | | | |
| 8 | 150 | Bobcat 773 with Trailer | | | |
| 9 | 55 | Breaker Hammer, electric, 60# | | | |

**TIP FROM**

If you're having a difficult time remembering whether you want the dollar signs before the row or column or both, you can press F4 and then look at the formula to figure out if you are freezing the correct element—either the row or column.

4. Press F4 one more time. Excel locks just the column, changing the reference to =$A6, as shown in Figure 20.13. This is the version of the reference that you want.

**Figure 20.13**
You can press F4 again to switch to a mixed reference with the column letter locked.

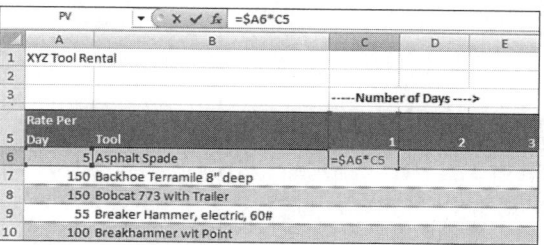

**NOTE**

After you press F4 again, Excel returns the reference to the relative state A6. As you continue to press F4, Excel toggles between the four modes. It is fine to toggle between them all and then choose the correct one. If you accidentally toggle past the $A6 version, you can just keep pressing F4 until the correct mode comes up again.

5. To continue the formula, type an asterisk to indicate multiplication and then click Cell C5 with the mouse. At the point shown in Figure 20.14, you would have to press F4 twice to change C5 to a reference that locks only the row (that is, C$5).

**Figure 20.14**
After clicking C5 with the mouse, you need to press F4 twice to change this reference.

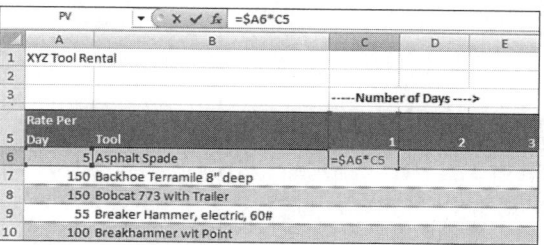

6. Press Enter to accept the formula.
7. When you copy the formula from Cell C6 to the range C6:H36, the formula automatically multiplies the rate in Column A by the number of days in Row 5. Figure 20.15 shows the copied formula in Cell E9. The formula correctly multiplies the 55-dollar rate in Cell A9 by the three days figure in Cell E5.

**Figure 20.15**
By using the correct combination of row and column mixed references, you can enter this formula once and successfully copy it to the entire rectangular range.

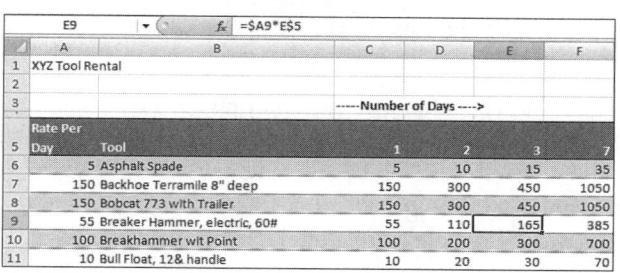

20

### USING F4 AFTER A FORMULA IS ENTERED

The F4 trick described in the preceding section works immediately after you enter a reference. If you try to change Cell A6 after you type the asterisk, pressing the F4 key has no effect.

You can still use F4 in this case, however. You simply click somewhere in the formula bar adjacent to the characters A6. Pressing F4 now adds dollar signs to that reference.

### USING F4 ON A RECTANGULAR RANGE

Some functions allow you to specify a rectangular range. For example, in Figure 20.16, you would like to enter a formula to calculate month-to-date sales. One formula in Cell C29 is =SUM(B2:B29). To be able to copy this formula, you need to change the formula to be =SUM(B$2:B29).

**Figure 20.16**
Using F4 at this point will never produce the desired result.

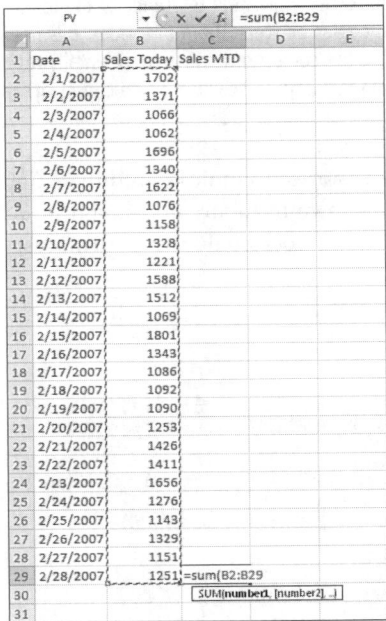

At the point in the figure, you might be tempted to press the F4 key. However, pressing F4 at this point would convert the reference to the fully absolute range $B$2:$B$29. Continuing to press F4 would toggle to B$2:B$29, then $B2:$B29, then B2:B29. Excel does not even attempt to go through the other 12 possible combinations of dollar signs in order to eventually offer B$2:B29.

In this case, you need to click the insertion point just before, just after, or in the middle of the characters *B2* in the formula bar. If you then press F4, you toggle through the various dollar sign combinations, just on the B2 reference. Pressing F4 twice results in the proper combination, as shown in Figure 20.17.

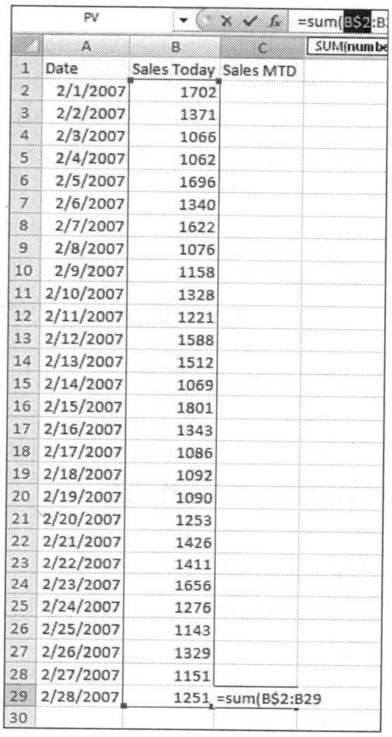

**Figure 20.17**
Using F4 is tricky when your reference is a rectangular range—you must click in to the formula.

| | A | B | C |
|---|---|---|---|
| 1 | Date | Sales Today | Sales MTD |
| 2 | 2/1/2007 | 1702 | |
| 3 | 2/2/2007 | 1371 | |
| 4 | 2/3/2007 | 1066 | |
| 5 | 2/4/2007 | 1062 | |
| 6 | 2/5/2007 | 1696 | |
| 7 | 2/6/2007 | 1340 | |
| 8 | 2/7/2007 | 1622 | |
| 9 | 2/8/2007 | 1076 | |
| 10 | 2/9/2007 | 1158 | |
| 11 | 2/10/2007 | 1328 | |
| 12 | 2/11/2007 | 1221 | |
| 13 | 2/12/2007 | 1588 | |
| 14 | 2/13/2007 | 1512 | |
| 15 | 2/14/2007 | 1069 | |
| 16 | 2/15/2007 | 1801 | |
| 17 | 2/16/2007 | 1343 | |
| 18 | 2/17/2007 | 1086 | |
| 19 | 2/18/2007 | 1092 | |
| 20 | 2/19/2007 | 1090 | |
| 21 | 2/20/2007 | 1253 | |
| 22 | 2/21/2007 | 1426 | |
| 23 | 2/22/2007 | 1411 | |
| 24 | 2/23/2007 | 1656 | |
| 25 | 2/24/2007 | 1276 | |
| 26 | 2/25/2007 | 1143 | |
| 27 | 2/26/2007 | 1329 | |
| 28 | 2/27/2007 | 1151 | |
| 29 | 2/28/2007 | 1251 | =sum(B$2:B29 |
| 30 | | | |

The formula bar shows: =sum(B$2:B

# THREE METHODS OF ENTERING FORMULAS

In the examples in the previous sections, you entered a formula by typing it. Although you generally need to start a formula by typing the equals sign (or the plus sign), after that point, you have three options:

- Type the complete formula as described above.
- Type operator keys, but use the mouse to touch cell references. I will call this the mouse method.
- Type the operator keys, and use the arrow keys to specify the cell references by navigating to the cells. I will call this the arrow key method.

Assume that in Figure 20.18, you would like to multiply the merchandise total in Cell B2 by the sales tax rate in Cell F1.

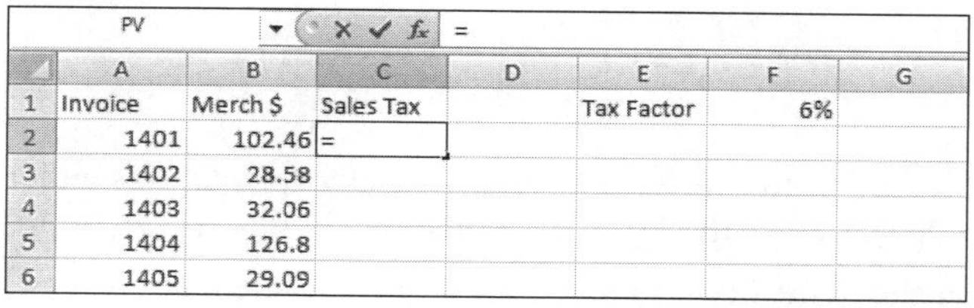

**Figure 20.18**
There are three methods for entering the formula =B2*$F$1.

| | A | B | C | D | E | F | G |
|---|---|---|---|---|---|---|---|
| 1 | Invoice | Merch $ | Sales Tax | | Tax Factor | 6% | |
| 2 | 1401 | 102.46 | = | | | | |
| 3 | 1402 | 28.58 | | | | | |
| 4 | 1403 | 32.06 | | | | | |
| 5 | 1404 | 126.8 | | | | | |
| 6 | 1405 | 29.09 | | | | | |

20

## MOUSE METHOD FOR ENTERING FORMULAS

If you started using computers after the advent of Microsoft Windows 3.1, it is likely that you use the mouse method for entering formulas. This method is intuitive, but it requires you to move your hand between the keyboard to the mouse several times, as in this example:

1. Type =.
2. Click in Cell B2.
3. Type *. (If you have a desktop keyboard, you can use the asterisk key on the numeric keypad to avoid pressing the Shift key.)
4. Click in Cell C1.
5. Press F4 to add the dollar signs.
6. Press Enter. This usually moves the cell pointer to Cell C3.

This method requires only four keystrokes, but it requires you to move to the mouse twice. Moving to the mouse is the slowest part of entering formulas, but this method is easier than typing the entire formula if you are not a touch typist.

## ENTERING FORMULAS USING THE ARROW KEY METHOD

The arrow key method is popular with people who started using spreadsheets in the days of Lotus 1-2-3 release 2.2. It is worthwhile to learn this method because it is incredibly fast. Almost all the formula entry can be accomplishing using keys on the right side of the keyboard. Here's how it works:

1. In Cell C2 type +. (If you have a desktop keyboard, you can use the plus key on the numeric keypad to avoid pressing the Shift key.)
2. Press the left-arrow key to move the flashing cell border to Cell B2. Note that the active cell (that is, with a solid border) is still Cell C2. The flashing border is like a second cell pointer that you can use to point to the correct cell for the formula. As shown in Figure 20.19, the temporary formula in the formula bar reads +B2.

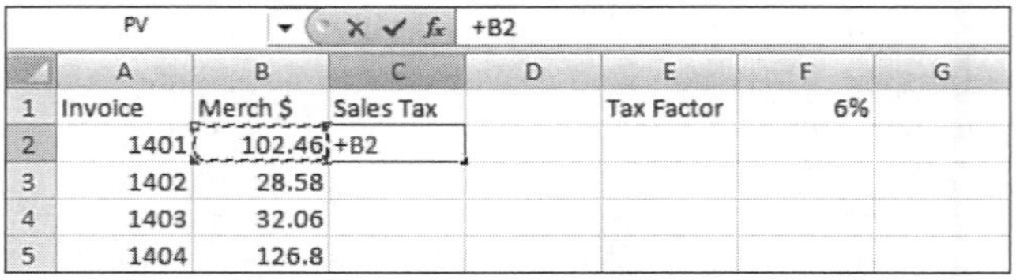

**Figure 20.19**
By using the arrow keys during formula entry, you create a flashing border that you can use to navigate to a cell reference.

3. To add Cell B2 as the correct reference in the formula, press either an operator key (for example, *, +), a parenthesis, or the Enter key. In this case, type *.
4. Note that the dashed cell pointer disappears, and the focus is now back to the original cell, C2.

5. Press the right-arrow key three times. The flashing cell border moves to D2, E2, and then F2. With each keypress, the temporary formula in the formula bar shows an incorrect formula (+B2*D2, +B2*E2, and +B2*F2). Figure 20.20 shows what the screen looks like after you press the right-arrow key three times.

**NOTE** As you are moving the flashing cell border with the mouse, ignore the formula bar and watch just the flashing cell border.

**Figure 20.20**
After step 4, the focus moves to the original cell. Thus, you only have to press the right-arrow key three times instead of four times to arrive at Cell F2.

| PV | | ▼ | × ✓ fx | +B2*F2 | | |
|---|---|---|---|---|---|---|
| | A | B | C | D | E | F | G |
| 1 | Invoice | Merch $ | Sales Tax | | Tax Factor | 6% | |
| 2 | 1401 | 102.46 | +B2*F2 | | | | |
| 3 | 1402 | 28.58 | | | | | |
| 4 | 1403 | 32.06 | | | | | |
| 5 | 1404 | 126.8 | | | | | |

6. Type the up-arrow key to move the flashing cell border to the correct location, Cell F1. The temporary formula in the formula bar now shows +B2*F1.

7. Press the F4 key to add dollar signs to the F1 reference.

8. Press Ctrl+Enter to accept the formula and keep the cell pointer in Cell C2.

Using this method requires 10 keystrokes, with no trips to the mouse. You can enter formulas that have no absolute references, mixed references, parentheses, or exponents by using just the arrow keys and the keys on the numeric keypad.

**TIP FROM**

Even if you are mouse-centric, you should try this method for half a day. When you get the feel for navigating by using the arrow keys, you can enter formulas much faster by using this method.

**NOTE** Officially, every formula must start with an equals sign. However, to make former Lotus 1-2-3 users comfortable, Excel allows you to start a formula with a plus sign. Power Excel users have discovered that using a plus sign allows you to start a formula by typing on the numeric keypad. Because I routinely start formulas with the plus sign, I am often asked why I start with =+ instead of just =. Even though the formulas appear that way onscreen, I don't actually enter the =. When a formula starts with a plus sign, Excel adds an equals sign and does not remove the plus sign, so you end up with a formula that looks like =+B2*$F$1.

20

# ENTERING THE SAME FORMULA IN MANY CELLS

So far in this chapter, you've entered a formula in one cell and then copied and pasted to get the formula in many cells. There are three alternate strategies:

- Preselect the entire range where the formulas need to go. Enter the formula for the first cell and press Ctrl+Enter to simultaneously enter the formula in the entire selection.
- Enter the formula in the first cell and then use the fill handle to copy the formula.
- The new method in Excel 2007 is to define the range as a table. New formulas will be copied automatically.

## COPYING A FORMULA BY USING CTRL+ENTER

This strategy works when you are entering formulas for a screen full or two of data:

1. If you have just a few cells, select them before entering the formula.
2. Click in the first cell and drag down to the last cell, as shown in Figure 20.21. Notice from the name box that the active cell is the first cell.

**Figure 20.21**
You click in the first cell and drag down to the last cell to select a range with the first cell as the active cell.

| | C2 | | | $f_x$ | | | |
|---|---|---|---|---|---|---|---|
| | A | B | C | D | E | F | G |
| 1 | Invoice | Merch $ | Sales Tax | | Tax Factor | 6% | |
| 2 | 1401 | 102.46 | | | | | |
| 3 | 1402 | 28.58 | | | | | |
| 4 | 1403 | 32.06 | | | | | |
| 5 | 1404 | 126.8 | | | | | |
| 6 | 1405 | 29.09 | | | | | |
| 7 | 1406 | 122.67 | | | | | |
| 8 | 1407 | 67.67 | | | | | |
| 9 | 1408 | 56.77 | | | | | |
| 10 | 1409 | 112.61 | | | | | |
| 11 | 1410 | 145.55 | | | | | |
| 12 | 1411 | 125.39 | | | | | |
| 13 | 1412 | 49.02 | | | | | |
| 14 | 1413 | 41.14 | | | | | |
| 15 | 1414 | 75.03 | | | | | |
| 16 | 1415 | 87.67 | | | | | |
| 17 | 1416 | 139.04 | | | | | |
| 18 | 1417 | 106.18 | | | | | |
| 19 | 1418 | 57.38 | | | | | |
| 20 | 1419 | 96.58 | | | | | |
| 21 | | | | | | | |
| 22 | | | | | | | |

3. Enter the formula by using any of the three methods described earlier in this chapter. Even if you use the arrow key method, Excel keeps the entire range selected. Figure 20.22 shows the formula after you press F4 to convert the F1 reference to $F$1.
4. At this point, you would normally press Enter to complete the formula. Instead, press Ctrl+Enter to enter this formula in the entire selected range. Note that Excel does not enter =B2*$F$20 in each cell. Instead, it converts the formula as if it were copied to each cell. Figure 20.23 shows the formula in Cell C20.

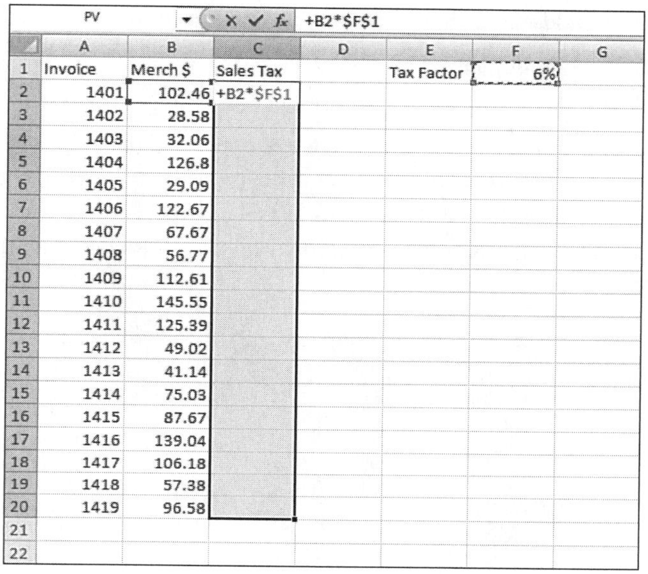

**Figure 20.22**
Even with a large range selected, the formula is built only in the active cell.

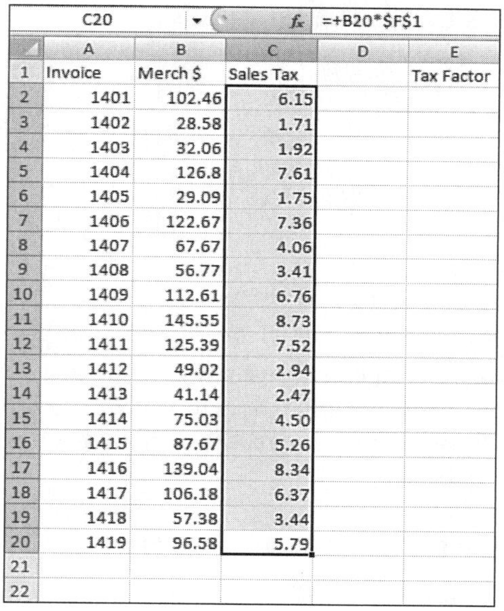

| | A | B | C | D | E | F | G |
|---|---|---|---|---|---|---|---|
| | PV | | | fx | +B2*$F$1 | | |
| 1 | Invoice | Merch $ | Sales Tax | | Tax Factor | 6% | |
| 2 | 1401 | 102.46 | +B2*$F$1 | | | | |
| 3 | 1402 | 28.58 | | | | | |
| 4 | 1403 | 32.06 | | | | | |
| 5 | 1404 | 126.8 | | | | | |
| 6 | 1405 | 29.09 | | | | | |
| 7 | 1406 | 122.67 | | | | | |
| 8 | 1407 | 67.67 | | | | | |
| 9 | 1408 | 56.77 | | | | | |
| 10 | 1409 | 112.61 | | | | | |
| 11 | 1410 | 145.55 | | | | | |
| 12 | 1411 | 125.39 | | | | | |
| 13 | 1412 | 49.02 | | | | | |
| 14 | 1413 | 41.14 | | | | | |
| 15 | 1414 | 75.03 | | | | | |
| 16 | 1415 | 87.67 | | | | | |
| 17 | 1416 | 139.04 | | | | | |
| 18 | 1417 | 106.18 | | | | | |
| 19 | 1418 | 57.38 | | | | | |
| 20 | 1419 | 96.58 | | | | | |
| 21 | | | | | | | |
| 22 | | | | | | | |

**Figure 20.23**
Pressing Ctrl+Enter tells Excel to enter the formula in the active cell and to also copy it to the rest of the selection.

| | A | B | C | D | E |
|---|---|---|---|---|---|
| | C20 | | | fx | =+B20*$F$1 |
| 1 | Invoice | Merch $ | Sales Tax | | Tax Factor |
| 2 | 1401 | 102.46 | 6.15 | | |
| 3 | 1402 | 28.58 | 1.71 | | |
| 4 | 1403 | 32.06 | 1.92 | | |
| 5 | 1404 | 126.8 | 7.61 | | |
| 6 | 1405 | 29.09 | 1.75 | | |
| 7 | 1406 | 122.67 | 7.36 | | |
| 8 | 1407 | 67.67 | 4.06 | | |
| 9 | 1408 | 56.77 | 3.41 | | |
| 10 | 1409 | 112.61 | 6.76 | | |
| 11 | 1410 | 145.55 | 8.73 | | |
| 12 | 1411 | 125.39 | 7.52 | | |
| 13 | 1412 | 49.02 | 2.94 | | |
| 14 | 1413 | 41.14 | 2.47 | | |
| 15 | 1414 | 75.03 | 4.50 | | |
| 16 | 1415 | 87.67 | 5.26 | | |
| 17 | 1416 | 139.04 | 8.34 | | |
| 18 | 1417 | 106.18 | 6.37 | | |
| 19 | 1418 | 57.38 | 3.44 | | |
| 20 | 1419 | 96.58 | 5.79 | | |
| 21 | | | | | |
| 22 | | | | | |

20

## COPYING A FORMULA BY DRAGGING THE FILL HANDLE

If you want to enter a formula in one cell and then copy it to the other cells in a range, you can use the fill handle (that is, the square dot in the lower-right corner of the cell pointer). There are two ways to use the fill handle:

- Drag the fill handle.
- Double-click the fill handle.

The dragging method works fine when you have less than one screen full of data:

1. Enter the formula in Cell B2.

2. Press Ctrl+Enter to accept the formula and keep the cell pointer in Cell B2.

3. Click the fill handle. You know that you are above the fill handle when the mouse pointer changes to a thick plus sign, as shown in Figure 20.24. Drag the mouse down to the last row of data (in this case, Cell C20).

4. When you release the mouse button, the original cell is copied to all the cells in the selected range.

**Figure 20.24**
You can copy a formula by clicking and dragging the fill handle.

| | C2 | | | $f_x$ | =+B2*$F$1 | |
|---|---|---|---|---|---|---|
| | A | B | C | D | | E |
| 1 | Invoice | Merch $ | Sales Tax | | | Tax Factor |
| 2 | 1401 | 102.46 | 6.15 | | | |
| 3 | 1402 | 28.58 | | | | |
| 4 | 1403 | 32.06 | | | | |
| 5 | 1404 | 126.8 | | | | |
| 6 | 1405 | 29.09 | | | | |
| 7 | 1406 | 122.67 | | | | |
| 8 | 1407 | 67.67 | | | | |
| 9 | 1408 | 56.77 | | | | |
| 10 | 1409 | 112.61 | | | | |
| 11 | 1410 | 145.55 | | | | |
| 12 | 1411 | 125.39 | | | | |
| 13 | 1412 | 49.02 | | | | |
| 14 | 1413 | 41.14 | | | | |
| 15 | 1414 | 75.03 | | | | |
| 16 | 1415 | 87.67 | | | | |
| 17 | 1416 | 139.04 | | | | |
| 18 | 1417 | 106.18 | | | | |
| 19 | 1418 | 57.38 | | | | |
| 20 | 1419 | 96.58 | | | | |
| 21 | | | | | | |
| 22 | | | | | | |

This method is fine for copying a formula to a few cells. However, if you have thousands or hundreds of thousands of cells, it is annoying to drag to the last row. Invariably, as the scroll effect speeds up, you end up flying past the last row. In such a case, it is easier to copy a formula by double-clicking the fill handle.

## COPYING A FORMULA BY DOUBLE-CLICKING THE FILL HANDLE

In most datasets, double-clicking the fill handle is the fastest way to copy the formula. While you will love this method, you need to understand a few shortcomings that can hamper the method when an adjacent column has blank cells amongst the data.

Figure 20.25 shows a table that has hundreds of rows of data. You want to copy the formula from Cell C2 down to all the rows of data in Column B.

**Figure 20.25**
Dragging the fill handle is frustrating in a table that has hundreds of rows. The double-click method will end that frustration.

| | C2 | | fx | =+B2*$F$1 | | |
|---|---|---|---|---|---|---|
| | A | B | C | D | E | F | G |
| 1 | Invoice | Merch $ | Sales Tax | | Tax Factor | 6% | |
| 2 | 1401 | 102.46 | 6.15 | | | | |
| 3 | 1402 | 28.58 | | | | | |
| 4 | 1403 | 32.06 | | | | | |
| 5 | 1404 | 126.8 | | | | | |
| 6 | 1405 | 29.09 | | | | | |

In this particular case, Cell B2 is nonblank, and Column B contains a value in every row down to the end of the data. This is the perfect condition for using the technique of double-clicking the fill handle. Follow these steps:

1. Enter the formula in Cell B2.
2. Press Ctrl+Enter to accept the formula and keep the cell pointer in Cell B2.
3. Double-click the fill handle.

The active cell is copied down to the last row of your data, as shown in Figure 20.26.

**Figure 20.26**
You can double-click the fill handle to copy to the last row of your data.

| | C2 | | fx | =+B2*$F$1 | | |
|---|---|---|---|---|---|---|
| | A | B | C | D | E | F | G |
| 1 | Invoice | Merch $ | Sales Tax | | Tax Factor | 6% | |
| 2 | 1401 | 102.46 | 6.15 | | | | |
| 3 | 1402 | 28.58 | 1.71 | | | | |
| 4 | 1403 | 32.06 | 1.92 | | | | |
| 5 | 1404 | 126.8 | 7.61 | | | | |
| 6 | 1405 | 29.09 | 1.75 | | | | |
| 7 | 1406 | 122.67 | 7.36 | | | | |
| 8 | 1407 | 67.67 | 4.06 | | | | |
| 9 | 1408 | 56.77 | 3.41 | | | | |
| 10 | 1409 | 112.61 | 6.76 | | | | |
| 11 | 1410 | 145.55 | 8.73 | | | | |
| 12 | 1411 | 125.39 | 7.52 | | | | |
| 13 | 1412 | 49.02 | 2.94 | | | | |
| 14 | 1413 | 41.14 | 2.47 | | | | |
| 15 | 1414 | 75.03 | 4.50 | | | | |
| 16 | 1415 | 87.67 | 5.26 | | | | |
| 17 | 1416 | 139.04 | 8.34 | | | | |
| 18 | 1417 | 106.18 | 6.37 | | | | |
| 19 | 1418 | 57.38 | 3.44 | | | | |
| 20 | 1419 | 96.58 | 5.79 | | | | |
| 21 | 1420 | 30.33 | 1.82 | | | | |
| 22 | 1421 | 99.69 | 5.98 | | | | |
| 23 | 1422 | 51.05 | 3.06 | | | | |
| 24 | 1423 | 101.02 | 6.06 | | | | |
| 25 | 1424 | 68.76 | 4.13 | | | | |
| 26 | 1425 | 103.46 | 6.21 | | | | |
| 27 | 1426 | 55.24 | 3.31 | | | | |
| 28 | 1427 | 148.7 | 8.92 | | | | |
| 29 | 1428 | 116.47 | 6.99 | | | | |
| 30 | 1429 | 134.67 | 8.08 | | | | |
| 31 | 1430 | 54.63 | 3.28 | | | | |
| 32 | 1431 | 40.43 | 2.43 | | | | |
| 33 | 1432 | 38.34 | 2.30 | | | | |
| 34 | 1433 | 129.93 | 7.80 | | | | |
| 35 | 1434 | 32.49 | 1.95 | | | | |
| 36 | 1435 | 36.68 | 2.20 | | | | |
| 37 | 1436 | 71.3 | 4.28 | | | | |

The fill handle double-click method is fast. There are several arcane rules that can trip up the data, particularly if the column to the left contains a blank cell before the end of the data. Excel will be tricked into stopping the copy early because of this blank cell.

There are other rules. The fill handle can copy based on data in the adjacent column to the right or even data in the current column.

20

You should always type End and then the down arrow to make sure that the formula was copied far enough.

For a complete discussion of the arcane rules, see the Excel Troubleshooting section at the end of this chapter.

# COPYING A FORMULA BY USING THE TABLE TOOL

The table tool is a new feature in Excel 2007. When you use this tool, if you tell Excel that your current dataset is a table, Excel automatically copies new formulas down to the rest of the cells in the table.

Figure 20.27 shows an Excel worksheet that has headings at the top and many rows of data below the headings. Notice the blank Cell C15, which would normally trip up the fill handle double-click method.

**Figure 20.27**
This is a typical work-sheet in Excel.

| | A | B | C | D | E | F | G | H | I |
|---|---|---|---|---|---|---|---|---|---|
| | | | | | | | A2 | | fx  J41 |

| | A | B | C | D | E | F | G | H | I |
|---|---|---|---|---|---|---|---|---|---|
| 1 | SKU | Mfg Cost | List Price | Sales Tax | | | Tax Factor | 6% | |
| 2 | J41 | 16.4 | 35.8 | | | | | | |
| 3 | J20 | 14.47 | 31.94 | | | | | | |
| 4 | I51 | 16.14 | 35.28 | | | | | | |
| 5 | F69 | 14.31 | 31.62 | | | | | | |
| 6 | G61 | 14.81 | 32.62 | | | | | | |
| 7 | T53 | 27.28 | 57.56 | | | | | | |
| 8 | P79 | 24.89 | 52.78 | | | | | | |
| 9 | I20 | 13.47 | 29.94 | | | | | | |
| 10 | K41 | 17.4 | 37.8 | | | | | | |
| 11 | X93 | 33.64 | 70.28 | | | | | | |
| 12 | K11 | 14.32 | 31.64 | | | | | | |
| 13 | P54 | 23.35 | 49.7 | | | | | | |
| 14 | B20 | 6.47 | 15.94 | | | | | | |
| 15 | J37 | 16.08 | | | | | | | |
| 16 | B46 | 8.78 | 20.56 | | | | | | |
| 17 | H66 | 16.12 | 35.24 | | | | | | |
| 18 | W75 | 31.66 | 66.32 | | | | | | |
| 19 | P27 | 21.2 | 45.4 | | | | | | |
| 20 | K22 | 15.69 | 34.38 | | | | | | |

To define a range as a table, select a cell within the dataset and type Ctrl+T or Ctrl+L. Excel uses its IntelliSense to guess the edges of the table. If its guess is correct, click OK in the Create Table dialog, as shown in Figure 20.28.

**Figure 20.28**
The Create Table dialog.

As shown in Figure 20.29, after Excel recognizes the range as a table, several changes occur:

**Figure 20.29**
Defining a range as a table provides formatting and powerful features such as autofilters and natural language formulas.

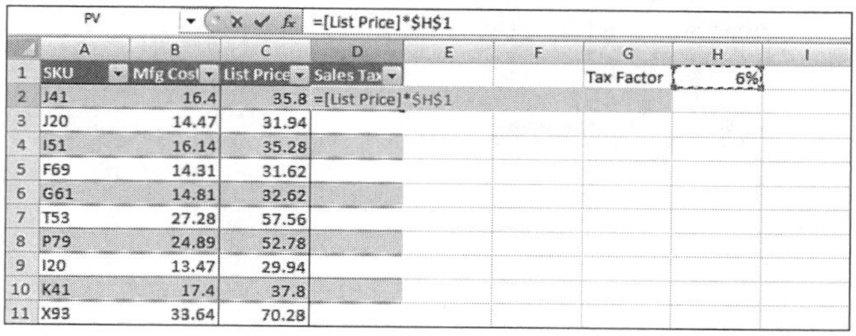

- The table is formatted with the default formatting. Depending on your preferences, this might include banded rows or columns.
- AutoFilter drop-downs are added to the headings.
- Any formulas that you enter use the headings to refer to cells within the table.

If you now enter a formula in the table, Excel automatically copies that formula down to all rows of the table. The entire range, starting at D3 and extending downward, flashes black momentarily. This copy works even better than the fill handle double-click method because the copy is able to go past the blank cell in Row 15.

> **NOTE**
>
> As shown in Figure 20.30, there is a lightning bolt drop-down to the right of Cell D3. This drop-down offers you the opportunity to stop Excel from automatically copying the formula down.

**Figure 20.30**
Thanks to the new table tool in Excel 2007, a new formula entered anywhere in Column D is automatically copied to all the cells in Column D.

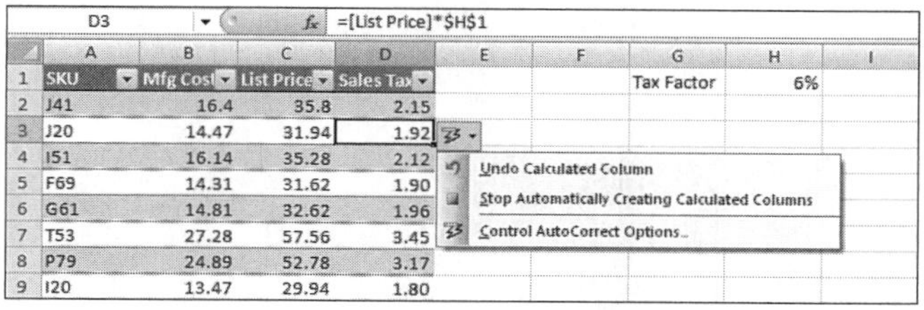

**Troubleshooting Tip: Overcoming the Arcane Rules for Fill Handle Double-Clicking**
The fill handle double-click trick is one of the best and least-known tricks. (I get a bunch of gasps whenever I show this trick in an Excel seminar.)

The problem with this method is that there are some fairly arcane rules that govern how this works. Three cells govern whether or how the double-click trick will work: the cell immediately to the left of the active cell, the cell immediately below the active cell, and the cell immediately to the right of the active cell.

In Figure 20.31, the active cell is B4. When you double-click the fill handle, Excel first looks at the three cells highlighted in blue. If all three of them are blank, Excel ignores the double-click.

If the cell immediately below the active cell is nonblank, Excel copies the active cell down until it discovers a blank cell in the current column. In the example in the figure, this causes the formula to be copied down and overwrite the existing cell values in B4:B19, as shown in Figure 20.32.

20

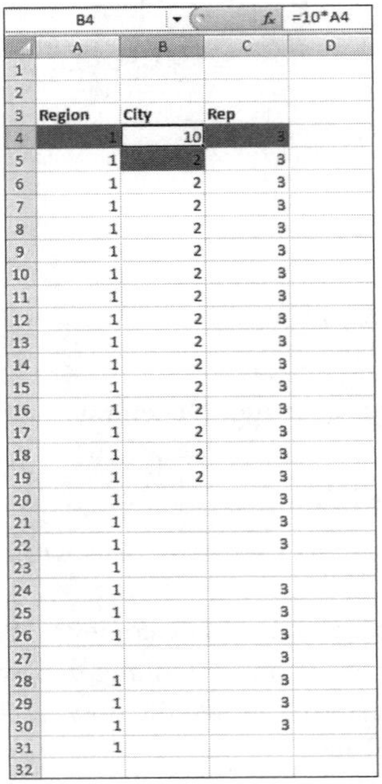

**Figure 20.31**
Excel looks at the three cells immediately to the bottom, left, and right of the active cell.

| | B4 | ▼ | *fx* | =10*A4 |
|---|---|---|---|---|
| | A | B | C | D |
| 1 | | | | |
| 2 | | | | |
| 3 | Region | City | Rep | |
| 4 | 1 | 10 | 3 | |
| 5 | 1 | 2 | 3 | |
| 6 | 1 | 2 | 3 | |
| 7 | 1 | 2 | 3 | |
| 8 | 1 | 2 | 3 | |
| 9 | 1 | 2 | 3 | |
| 10 | 1 | 2 | 3 | |
| 11 | 1 | 2 | 3 | |
| 12 | 1 | 2 | 3 | |
| 13 | 1 | 2 | 3 | |
| 14 | 1 | 2 | 3 | |
| 15 | 1 | 2 | 3 | |
| 16 | 1 | 2 | 3 | |
| 17 | 1 | 2 | 3 | |
| 18 | 1 | 2 | 3 | |
| 19 | 1 | 2 | 3 | |
| 20 | 1 | | 3 | |
| 21 | 1 | | 3 | |
| 22 | 1 | | 3 | |
| 23 | 1 | | | |
| 24 | 1 | | 3 | |
| 25 | 1 | | 3 | |
| 26 | 1 | | 3 | |
| 27 | | | 3 | |
| 28 | 1 | | 3 | |
| 29 | 1 | | 3 | |
| 30 | 1 | | 3 | |
| 31 | 1 | | | |
| 32 | | | | |

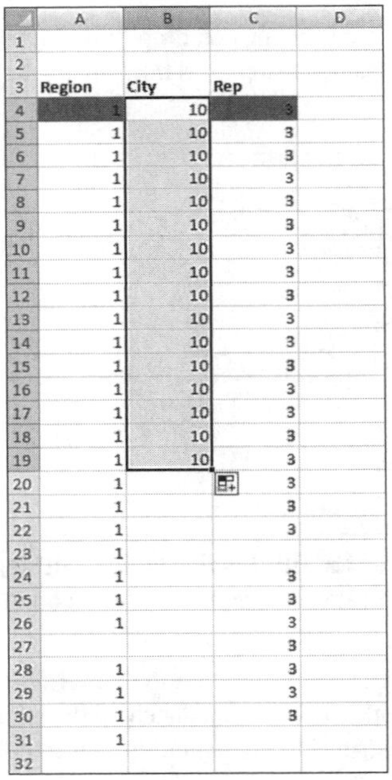

**Figure 20.32**
If the cell below the active cell is nonblank, Excel copies the cell until it encounters a blank cell in the current column.

| | A | B | C | D |
|---|---|---|---|---|
| 1 | | | | |
| 2 | | | | |
| 3 | Region | City | Rep | |
| 4 | 1 | 10 | 3 | |
| 5 | 1 | 10 | 3 | |
| 6 | 1 | 10 | 3 | |
| 7 | 1 | 10 | 3 | |
| 8 | 1 | 10 | 3 | |
| 9 | 1 | 10 | 3 | |
| 10 | 1 | 10 | 3 | |
| 11 | 1 | 10 | 3 | |
| 12 | 1 | 10 | 3 | |
| 13 | 1 | 10 | 3 | |
| 14 | 1 | 10 | 3 | |
| 15 | 1 | 10 | 3 | |
| 16 | 1 | 10 | 3 | |
| 17 | 1 | 10 | 3 | |
| 18 | 1 | 10 | 3 | |
| 19 | 1 | 10 | 3 | |
| 20 | 1 | | 3 | |
| 21 | 1 | | 3 | |
| 22 | 1 | | 3 | |
| 23 | 1 | | | |
| 24 | 1 | | 3 | |
| 25 | 1 | | 3 | |
| 26 | 1 | | 3 | |
| 27 | | | 3 | |
| 28 | 1 | | 3 | |
| 29 | 1 | | 3 | |
| 30 | 1 | | 3 | |
| 31 | 1 | | | |
| 32 | | | | |

If the cell below the active cell is blank, Excel next looks to see whether the cell to the left of the cell is nonblank. In Figure 20.33, there are cells to the left and right of the active cell. Although the data in Column C is filled in to the end, there is a blank cell in the middle of the Column A data. However, because cell A5 is nonblank, Column A becomes the column that governs the action of the fill handle double-click. Excel copies the formula only until it encounters a blank cell in Column A.

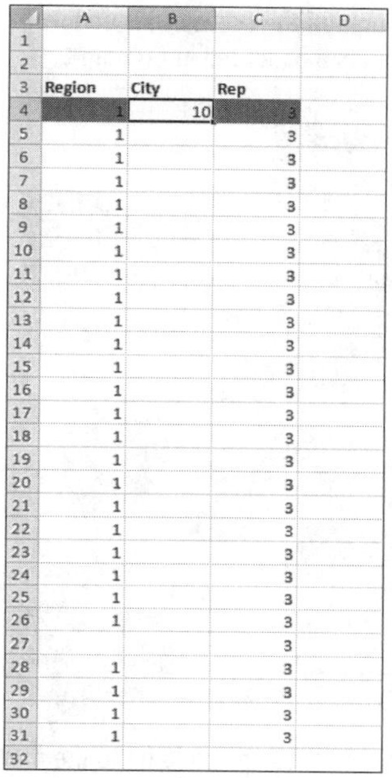

**Figure 20.33**
Even though the data is "better" in Column C, the fact that Cell A5 is nonblank causes Excel to copy only until it encounters a blank cell in Column A.

| | A | B | C | D |
|---|---|---|---|---|
| 1 | | | | |
| 2 | | | | |
| 3 | Region | City | Rep | |
| 4 | 1 | 10 | 3 | |
| 5 | 1 | | 3 | |
| 6 | 1 | | 3 | |
| 7 | 1 | | 3 | |
| 8 | 1 | | 3 | |
| 9 | 1 | | 3 | |
| 10 | 1 | | 3 | |
| 11 | 1 | | 3 | |
| 12 | 1 | | 3 | |
| 13 | 1 | | 3 | |
| 14 | 1 | | 3 | |
| 15 | 1 | | 3 | |
| 16 | 1 | | 3 | |
| 17 | 1 | | 3 | |
| 18 | 1 | | 3 | |
| 19 | 1 | | 3 | |
| 20 | 1 | | 3 | |
| 21 | 1 | | 3 | |
| 22 | 1 | | 3 | |
| 23 | 1 | | 3 | |
| 24 | 1 | | 3 | |
| 25 | 1 | | 3 | |
| 26 | 1 | | 3 | |
| 27 | | | 3 | |
| 28 | 1 | | 3 | |
| 29 | 1 | | 3 | |
| 30 | 1 | | 3 | |
| 31 | 1 | | 3 | |
| 32 | | | | |

This situation happens quite frequently: You want to copy a formula based on the adjacent column, but the column to the left has one blank cell in the midst of the data. This blank cells fools Excel, causing the copy to stop prematurely. In this situation, you can double-click the fill handle in Cell B4, and the formula in that cell is copied to B5:B26, as shown in Figure 20.34.

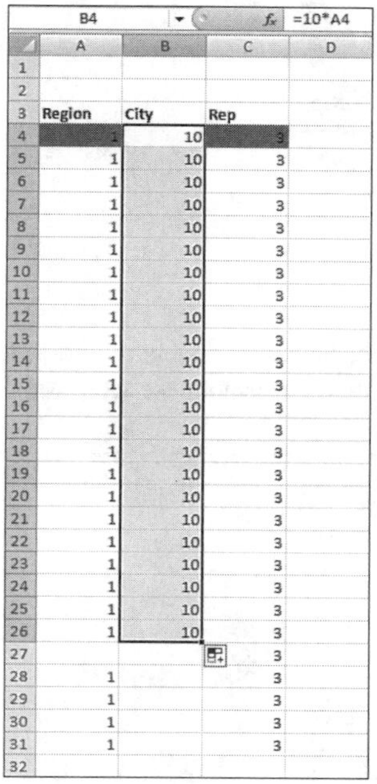

**Figure 20.34**
The fill handle double-click stops prematurely because of the blank Cell A27.

|  | B4 | | $f_x$ | =10*A4 | |
|---|---|---|---|---|---|
| | A | B | C | D | |
| 1 | | | | | |
| 2 | | | | | |
| 3 | Region | City | Rep | | |
| 4 | 1 | 10 | 3 | | |
| 5 | 1 | 10 | 3 | | |
| 6 | 1 | 10 | 3 | | |
| 7 | 1 | 10 | 3 | | |
| 8 | 1 | 10 | 3 | | |
| 9 | 1 | 10 | 3 | | |
| 10 | 1 | 10 | 3 | | |
| 11 | 1 | 10 | 3 | | |
| 12 | 1 | 10 | 3 | | |
| 13 | 1 | 10 | 3 | | |
| 14 | 1 | 10 | 3 | | |
| 15 | 1 | 10 | 3 | | |
| 16 | 1 | 10 | 3 | | |
| 17 | 1 | 10 | 3 | | |
| 18 | 1 | 10 | 3 | | |
| 19 | 1 | 10 | 3 | | |
| 20 | 1 | 10 | 3 | | |
| 21 | 1 | 10 | 3 | | |
| 22 | 1 | 10 | 3 | | |
| 23 | 1 | 10 | 3 | | |
| 24 | 1 | 10 | 3 | | |
| 25 | 1 | 10 | 3 | | |
| 26 | 1 | 10 | 3 | | |
| 27 | | | 3 | | |
| 28 | 1 | | 3 | | |
| 29 | 1 | | 3 | | |
| 30 | 1 | | 3 | | |
| 31 | 1 | | 3 | | |
| 32 | | | | | |

The final situation happens when only the cell to the right of the active cell is nonblank, as shown in Figure 20.35. In this case, Excel copies the cell until it encounters a blank cell in Column C.

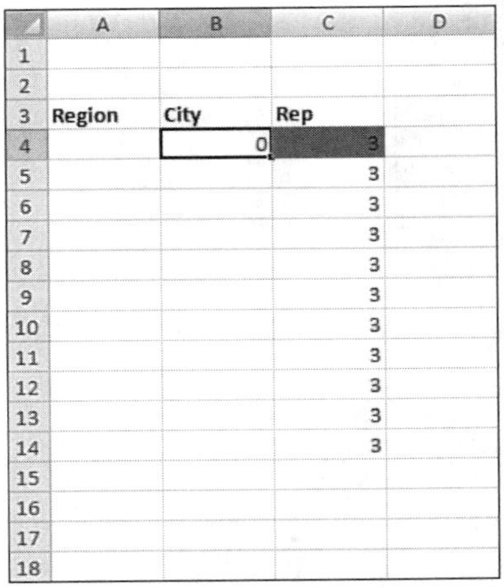

**Figure 20.35**
When only the cell to the right of the active cell is nonblank, Excel copies data down until it encounters a blank cell in the column to the right of the active cell.

| | A | B | C | D |
|---|---|---|---|---|
| 1 | | | | |
| 2 | | | | |
| 3 | Region | City | Rep | |
| 4 | | | 0 | 3 |
| 5 | | | | 3 |
| 6 | | | | 3 |
| 7 | | | | 3 |
| 8 | | | | 3 |
| 9 | | | | 3 |
| 10 | | | | 3 |
| 11 | | | | 3 |
| 12 | | | | 3 |
| 13 | | | | 3 |
| 14 | | | | 3 |
| 15 | | | | |
| 16 | | | | |
| 17 | | | | |
| 18 | | | | |

The ability to have the fill handle double-click trick work based on a column to the right of the active cell is useful. In this case, the cell is copied correctly to B5:B14, as shown in Figure 20.36.

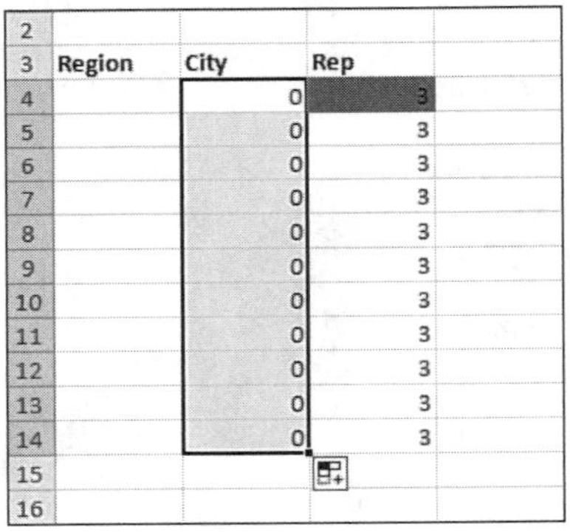

**Figure 20.36**
The fill handle double-click method works for adjacent data—even data to the right of the active cell.

| | | | |
|---|---|---|---|
| 2 | | | |
| 3 | Region | City | Rep |
| 4 | | 0 | 3 |
| 5 | | 0 | 3 |
| 6 | | 0 | 3 |
| 7 | | 0 | 3 |
| 8 | | 0 | 3 |
| 9 | | 0 | 3 |
| 10 | | 0 | 3 |
| 11 | | 0 | 3 |
| 12 | | 0 | 3 |
| 13 | | 0 | 3 |
| 14 | | 0 | 3 |
| 15 | | | |
| 16 | | | |

It is good to understand the arcane rules involved in the fill handle double-click trick. After you use this method, you can press the End key and then the down-arrow key to make sure Excel copied the cell to the real end of your data set.

## Excel in Practice: Using the Fill Handle Double-Click Method

Blank cells in adjacent cells cause problems for the fill handle double-click method. There are situations where you need to copy a formula down a column. The column to the right is perfectly filled in without any blanks and the column to the left has many blanks.

In this case, you would prefer that Excel looks to the adjacent column on the right. However, if the first few cells to the left of the formula are nonblank, Excel will always base the copy on the column to the left.

In this case, you can solve the problem by temporarily inserting a blank column to the left of your formula. This will prevent Excel from basing the copy on the blank-ridden left column.

Here is a specific example.

Say you have a file that contains name and address information, as shown in Figure 20.37. Before you import this information to your label printing program, you need to combine the city, state, and zip code columns into a single column.

**Figure 20.37**
You need to convert this data to only four columns before importing to your label printing program.

| | A | B | C | D | E | F | G |
|---|---|---|---|---|---|---|---|
| 1 | NAME | ADDR1 | ADDR2 | CITY | ST | ZIP | |
| 2 | STEVEN BARRETT | 722 Willow Blvd. | Apt. 9 | Fairview | CT | 69939 | |
| 3 | WILLIE HENSON | 1388 Cedar Avenue | | Louisville | WV | 31345 | |
| 4 | OPAL ANTHONY | 425 Jackson Blvd. | | Franklin | IA | 46767 | |
| 5 | AARON FOWLER | 1672 Fourth Road | | Andover | SC | 10017 | |
| 6 | JAN MCGUIRE | 317 Walnut Lane | | City | NJ | 39510 | |
| 7 | DENISE BUCKNER | 1470 Miller Avenue | | Rochester | DC | 60149 | |
| 8 | JOE NICHOLSON | 566 Sixth Lane | | Akron | NM | 28609 | |
| 9 | KIMBERLY SOSA | 899 Lakeview Circle | | Midway | AZ | 66378 | |
| 10 | PEARL YATES | 469 River Street | Suite 1 | Greenwood | CA | 62809 | |
| 11 | VERONICA WALLACE | 1309 Fifteenth Street | | Louisville | TN | 56407 | |
| 12 | STANLEY RAYMOND | 163 Sycamore Highway | | Midway | AR | 97976 | |

To combine City, State, and Zip into a single field, insert a blank Column D and enter the formula =E2&" "&F2&", "&G2 in cell D2, as shown in Figure 20.38.

**Figure 20.38**
You would like to copy this formula by double-clicking the fill handle.

| D2 | | fx | =E2&" "&F2&" "&G2 | | | | |

| | A | B | C | D | E | F | G | H |
|---|---|---|---|---|---|---|---|---|
| 1 | NAME | ADDR1 | ADDR2 | | CITY | ST | ZIP | |
| 2 | STEVEN BARRETT | 722 Willow Blvd. | Apt. 9 | Fairview CT 69939 | Fairview | CT | 69939 | |
| 3 | WILLIE HENSON | 1388 Cedar Avenue | | | Louisville | WV | 31345 | |
| 4 | OPAL ANTHONY | 425 Jackson Blvd. | | | Franklin | IA | 46767 | |
| 5 | AARON FOWLER | 1672 Fourth Road | | | Andover | SC | 10017 | |
| 6 | JAN MCGUIRE | 317 Walnut Lane | | | City | NJ | 39510 | |
| 7 | DENISE BUCKNER | 1470 Miller Avenue | | | Rochester | DC | 60149 | |
| 8 | JOE NICHOLSON | 566 Sixth Lane | | | Akron | NM | 28609 | |

Remember the rules for the fill handle double-click method: Excel first looks in Cell D3. Because that cell is blank, Excel then looks at Cell C2.

It happens that Column C is very sparse. It is nonblank only when the person lives in an apartment. However, because Cell C2 is non-blank, Excel allows Column C to govern how far the fill handle double-click method works. Because the first blank cell in Column C is C3, Excel actually does not copy D2 at all when you double-click. However, if you remember the action shown in Figure 20.32, you realize that you could use the fill handle double-click trick if Cell C2 were blank.

To force Excel to base the copy on the data to the right, insert another temporary blank Column D. Now when you double-click the formula in Cell E2, it uses the city in Column F as the guide and successfully copies the formula to the end of the database, as shown in Figure 20.39.

20

**Figure 20.39**
Because the cell to the left of Cell E2 is blank, the double-click trick works successfully.

`=F2&" "&G2&" "&H2`

| B | C | D | E | F | G |
|---|---|---|---|---|---|
|  | ADDR2 |  |  | CITY | ST |
| ow Blvd. | Apt. 9 |  | Fairview CT 69939 | Fairview | CT |
| dar Avenue |  |  | Louisville WV 3134 | Louisville | WV |
| son Blvd. |  |  | Franklin IA 46767 | Franklin | IA |
| urth Road |  |  | Andover SC 10017 | Andover | SC |
| nut Lane |  |  | City NJ 39510 | City | NJ |
| ller Avenue |  |  | Rochester DC 6014 | Rochester | DC |
| h Lane |  |  | Akron NM 28609 | Akron | NM |
| eview Circle |  |  | Midway AZ 66378 | Midway | AZ |
| r Street | Suite 1 |  | Greenwood CA 628 | Greenwood | CA |
| teenth Street |  |  | Louisville TN 56407 | Louisville | TN |
| amore Highway |  |  | Midway AR 97976 | Midway | AR |
| dge Highway |  |  | Barrington CA 4160 | Barrington | CA |
| eventh Blvd. |  |  | Rosemount NJ 392 | Rosemount | NJ |
| nset Lane |  |  | Vienna NE 21922 | Vienna | NE |
| tory Highway |  |  | Oak Grove SC 7260 | Oak Grove | SC |
| th Avenue |  |  | Andover NE 92284 | Andover | NE |
| is Avenue | Apt. 2 |  | Centerville NV 174 | Centerville | NV |
| ow Avenue |  |  | Oak Grove SD 7035 | Oak Grove | SD |
| ylor Lane |  |  | Salem AL 85790 | Salem | AL |
| hington Avenue |  |  | Rochester ST 6433 | Rochester | ST |

You can now delete the temporary Column D.

# CONTROLLING FORMULAS

## In this chapter

While you can go a long way with simple formulas, it is also possible to build extremely powerful formulas. The topics in this chapter will explain the finer points of formula operators, date math, and how Excel distinguishes between cutting and copying cells referenced in formulas.

# FORMULA OPERATORS

Excel offers the mathematical operators shown in Table 21.1.

TABLE 21.1 MATHEMATICAL OPERATORS

| Operator | Description |
| --- | --- |
| + | Addition |
| - | Subtraction |
| * | Multiplication |
| / | Division or fractions |
| ^ | Exponents |
| ( ) | Overriding the order of operations |
| - | Unary minus (for negative numbers) |
| & | Joining text (concatenation) |
| > | Greater than |
| < | Less than |
| >= | Greater than or equal to |
| <= | Less than or equal to |
| <> | Not equal to |
| = | Equal to |
| , | Union operator as in SUM(A1,B2) |
| : | Range operator as in SUM(A1:B2) |

## THE ORDER OF OPERATIONS

When a formula contains many calculations, Excel will evaluate the formula in a certain order. Rather than calculating from left to right as a calculator might, Excel will perform certain types of calculations such as multiplication before calculations such as addition.

You can override the default order of operations with parentheses. If you don't use parentheses, Excel uses the following order of operations:

1. Unary minus is evaluated first.
2. Exponents are evaluated next.
3. Multiplication and division are handled next, in a left-to-right manner.
4. Addition and subtraction are handled next, in a left-to-right manner.

21

The following sections provide some examples of order of operations.

### UNARY MINUS EXAMPLE

The unary minus is always evaluated first. Think about when you use exponents to raise a number to a power. If you raise -2 to the second power, Excel calculates -2 × -2, which is +4. So the formula =-2^2 evaluates to 4.

If you raise -2 to the third power, Excel calculates (-2) × (-2) × (-2). Multiplying -2 by -2 results in +4, and multiplying +4 four by -2 results in -8. So the simple formula =-2^3 generates -8.

You need to understand a subtle but important distinction. When Excel encounters the formula =-2^3, it evaluates the unary minus first. If you want the exponent to happen first and then have the unary minus applied, you have to write the formula as =-(2^3). However, in a formula such as =100-2^3, the minus sign is considered to be a subtraction operator and not a unary minus sign. In this case, 2^3 is evaluated as 8, and then 8 is subtracted from 100.

Figure 21.1 shows the results of three formulas involving raising -2 to various powers.

**Figure 21.1**
Beware the unary minus. Three very similar formulas have different results, depending on where the minus sign occurs.

| | A | B | C | D | E |
|---|---|---|---|---|---|
| | | B2 | | $f_x$ =-2^A2 | |
| 1 | Power | -2^___ | -(2^___) | 100-2^___ | |
| 2 | 1 | -2 | -2 | 98 | |
| 3 | 2 | 4 | -4 | 96 | |
| 4 | 3 | -8 | -8 | 92 | |
| 5 | 4 | 16 | -16 | 84 | |
| 6 | 5 | -32 | -32 | 68 | |
| 7 | 6 | 64 | -64 | 36 | |
| 8 | | | | | |

### ADDITION AND MULTIPLICATION EXAMPLE

The order of operations is important when you are mixing addition/subtraction with multiplication/division. For example, if you want to add 20 to 30 and then multiply by 1.06 to calculate a total with tax, the following formula leads to the wrong result:

=20+30*1.06

NOTE

To see how Excel calculates the formulas you enter, you simply enter a formula in a cell. From the Formulas ribbon, you choose Formulas, Formula Auditing, Evaluate Formula to open the Evaluate Formula dialog and watch the formula calculate in slow motion.

The result you are looking for is 53. However, the Evaluate Formula dialog shows that Excel calculates the formula =20+30*1.06 like so (see Figure 21.2):

1.06 × 30 = 31.8

31.8 + 20 = 51.8

**Figure 21.2**
The underline indicates that Excel does the multiplication first.

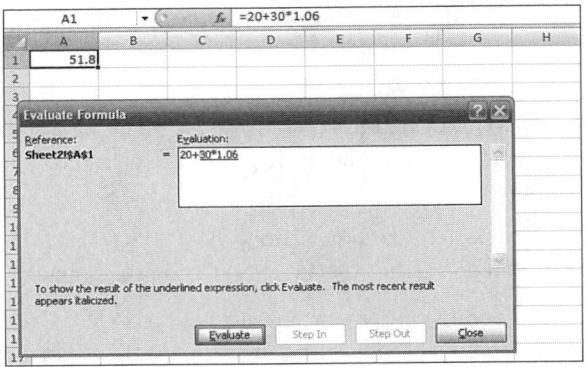

Excel's answer is $1.20 less than expected because the formula is not written with the default order of operations in mind.

To force Excel to do the addition first, you enclose the addition in parentheses:

=(20+30)*1.06

Figure 21.3 shows the second step in the Evaluate Formula dialog for this formula. The addition in parentheses is done first, and then 50 is multiplied by 1.06 to get the correct answer of $53.

**Figure 21.3**
Excel evaluates the operation in parentheses first.

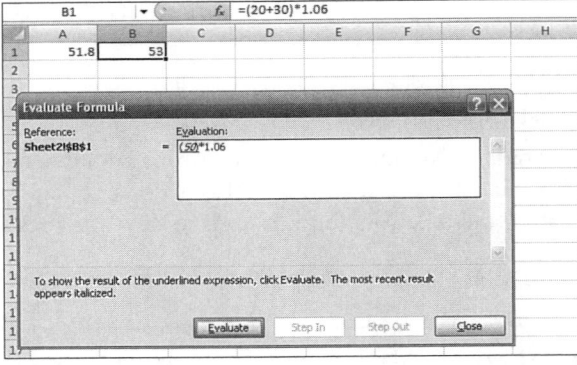

## STACKING MULTIPLE PARENTHESES

If you need to use multiple sets of parentheses when doing math by hand, you might write math formulas with square brackets and curly braces, like this:

{3-[6*4*3-(3-6)+2]/27}*14

In Excel, you simply use multiple sets of parentheses, as follows:

=(3-(6*4*3-(3-6)+2)/27)*14

Formulas with multiple parentheses in Excel are therefore very confusing. Excel does two things to try to improve this situation:

- First, as you are typing a formula, Excel colors the parentheses in a set order: black, dark green, purple, brown, light green, orange, magenta, blue, medium green, purple, brown, light green, and so on. If you bump the zoom up on your screen to 400%, you might actually be able to make out the color differences in the parentheses. However, at the normal zoom, the colors black, green, purple, and brown are all dark, and it is difficult to tell one from the other.

- When you type a closing parenthesis, Excel shows the opening parenthesis in bold for a fraction of a second. This would be more helpful if Excel kept the opening parenthesis in bold for 5 seconds or 20 seconds. But at about half a second, it is nothing more than a frustrating reminder that your reflexes are not fast enough. Figure 21.4 attempts to show the bolded condition at a ridiculously high zoom.

**Figure 21.4**
This screen shot shows that after you type the fifth closing parenthesis, the eighth opening parenthesis is briefly shown in bold.

| | A | B | C |
|---|---|---|---|
| 1 | 51.8 | 53 | 2.0740741 |
| 2 | | | |
| 3 | | | |
| 4 | =(((((((((1))))) | | |
| 5 | | | |

Matching parentheses in bold

TIP FROM

*Bill Jelen*

Out of frustration with Excel's inability to actually highlight the matching parenthesis, I usually resort to using Notepad to make understanding complicated formulas easier. To do this, you select the cell. In the formula bar, you drag to select the entire formula and then press Ctrl+C to copy it. Next, you open a new Notepad window and paste to Notepad. As shown in Figure 21.5, you can add line breaks and spaces in Notepad to visualize the formula.

**Figure 21.5**
You copy the formula from the formula bar and paste to a text editor, where you can actually break the formula into components.

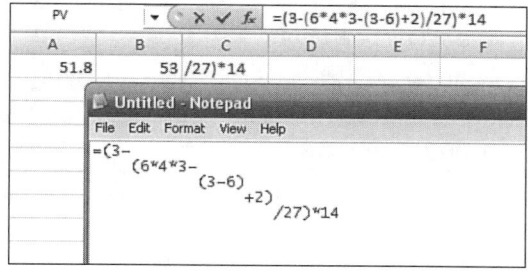

# UNDERSTANDING ERROR MESSAGES IN FORMULAS

Don't be frustrated when a formula returns an error result. These eventually happen to everyone. The key is to understand the difference between the various error values so that you can begin to troubleshoot the problem.

As you enter formulas, you might encounter a number of errors, including these:

- **#VALUE!**—This error indicates that you are trying to do math with nonnumeric data. For example, the formula =4+apple will return a #VALUE! error. This error also occurs if you try to enter an array formula and fail to use Ctrl+Shift+Enter, as described in Chapter 29, "Using Super Formulas in Excel."

- **#DIV/0!**—This error occurs when a number is divided by zero—that is, when a fraction's denominator evaluates to zero.

- **#REF!**—This error occurs when a cell reference is not valid. It can occur when one of the cells referenced in the formula has been deleted. It can also occur if you cut and paste another cell over a cell referenced in this formula. If you are using Dynamic Data Exchange (DDE) formulas to link to external systems and those systems are not running, you may also get this error.

- **#N/A!**—This error occurs when a value is not available to a function or a formula. #N/A! errors most often occur as a result of key values not being found during lookup functions. They can occur as a result of HLOOKUP, LOOKUP, MATCH, or VLOOKUP. They can also result when an array formula has one argument that is not the same shape as the other arguments or when a function omits one or more required arguments. Interestingly, when an #N/A! error enters a range, all subsequent calculations that refer to the range have a value of #N/A!.

- **######**—This is not really an error. It simply means that the result is too wide to display in the current column width, so you need to make the column wider to see the actual result.

**CAUTION**

> While ###### usually means the column is not wide enough, Excel also uses this symbol to indicate that you are subtracting a later date from an earlier date.

In Figure 21.6, cell E17 is a simple SUM function. It is returning an #N/A! error because Cell E11 contains the same error. Cell E11 contains the formula =D11*C11. The root cause of the problem is the VLOOKUP function in Cell D11. Because Dill cannot be found in the product table in G7:H9, the VLOOKUP function returns #N/A!.

Figure 21.6 shows only a small table, so it is relatively easy to find the earlier #N/A! errors. If you were totaling 100,000 rows, however, it could be difficult to find the one offending cell. To track errors down, you follow these steps:

1. Select the cell that shows the final error. To the left of that cell, you should see an exclamation point in a yellow diamond.

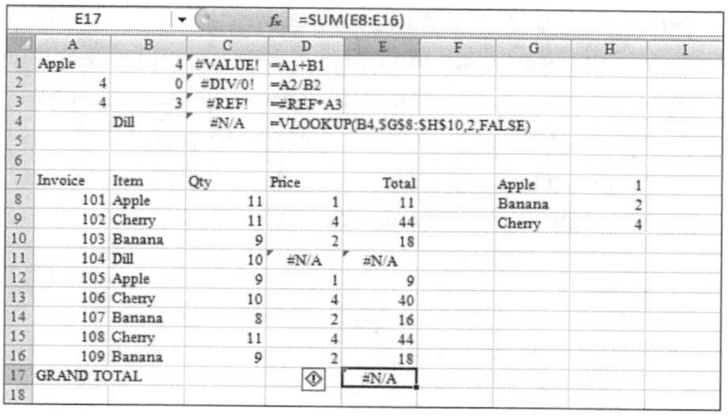

**Figure 21.6**
The error in E17 is actually caused by an error two calculations earlier.

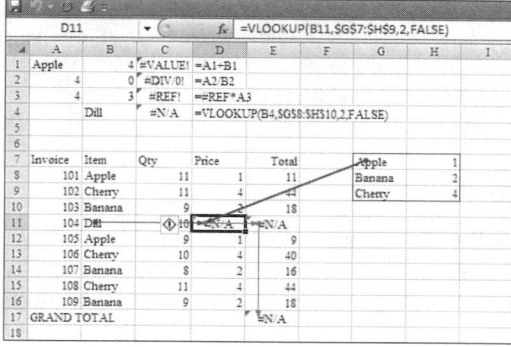

2. Hover the cursor over the yellow diamond to reveal a drop-down arrow.

3. From the drop-down menu, choose Trace Error. Excel draws in red arrows pointing back to the source of the error, as shown in Figure 21.7. From the original #N/A! error in Cell D11, for example, blue arrows demonstrate what cells were causing the error.

4. Repeat steps 1-3 for the cell causing the error in order to trace the original root cause of the problem.

**Figure 21.7**
Choosing Trace Error reveals the cells leading to the error.

# USING FORMULAS TO JOIN TEXT

You use the ampersand (&) operator when you need to join text. Officially, it is known as the concatenation operator.

For example, the formula =A2&B2 joins the text values shown in the two cells A2 and B2, as shown in Figure 21.8.

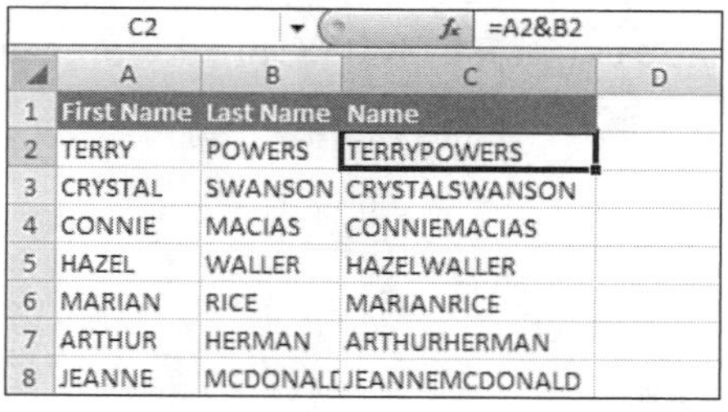

**Figure 21.8**
The & operator is used to join two text cells.

When using the & operator, you might want to include a space between the two items that are combined to improve the appearance of the output. For example, if the cells contain first name and last name, you might want to have a space between the names. To include a space between cells, you follow the & with a space enclosed in quotes (that is, &" "). As shown in Figure 21.9, the formula =A2&" "&B2 generates a better-looking result than =A2&B2. (Instead of using a space, you can also use any other text between the cells, by enclosing that text in quotes.)

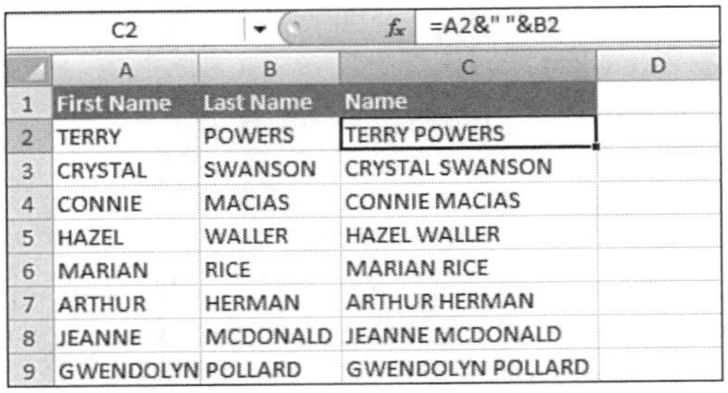

**Figure 21.9**
You can join cells with any text in quotation marks.

| | A | B | C | D |
|---|---|---|---|---|
| | | | C2 | fx =A2&" "&B2 |
| 1 | First Name | Last Name | Name | |
| 2 | TERRY | POWERS | TERRY POWERS | |
| 3 | CRYSTAL | SWANSON | CRYSTAL SWANSON | |
| 4 | CONNIE | MACIAS | CONNIE MACIAS | |
| 5 | HAZEL | WALLER | HAZEL WALLER | |
| 6 | MARIAN | RICE | MARIAN RICE | |
| 7 | ARTHUR | HERMAN | ARTHUR HERMAN | |
| 8 | JEANNE | MCDONALD | JEANNE MCDONALD | |
| 9 | GWENDOLYN | POLLARD | GWENDOLYN POLLARD | |

**CAUTION**

When you enter the formula in Figure 21.9, you have to hold down the Shift key to enter the quotation marks in " ". Many Excel users accidentally hold down the Shift key while pressing the spacebar. However, Shift+Spacebar is the Excel shortcut for selecting an entire row. If your formula changes to =A2&"A:A because you pressed Shift+Spacebar, you can type the Esc key and start over.

## JOINING TEXT AND A NUMBER

In many cases, you can use the & operator to join text with a number. In Figure 21.10, the formula in Cell C2 joins the words "The Answer is " with the result of the calculation in Cell B2. Because Cell B2 contains an integer with no special formatting, the answer appears correctly.

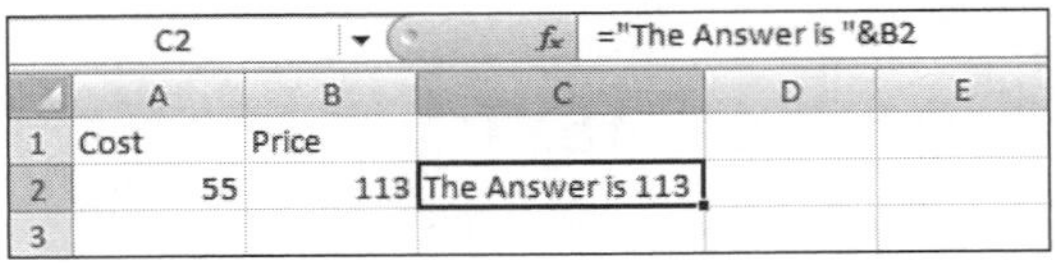

**Figure 21.10**
Joining text with a number works if the number is formatted with general formatting.

| | A | B | C | D | E |
|---|---|---|---|---|---|
| | | | C2 | fx ="The Answer is "&B2 | |
| 1 | Cost | Price | | | |
| 2 | 55 | 113 | The Answer is 113 | | |
| 3 | | | | | |

In Figure 21.11, Cell B2 is formatted to display a currency symbol and two decimal places. When you join this value to text in Cell C2, Excel ignores the formatting in Cell B2 and shows the result with all the decimal places. A similar problem exists when you want to join text with a date. Excel ignores the fact that the text in Cell B4 is formatted as a date and shows the underlying value in Cell C4.

**Figure 21.11**
Joining text with a date or with formatted numbers rarely works well.

| | C4 | | | $f_x$ | ="His birthday is "&B4 |
|---|---|---|---|---|---|
| | A | B | C | | D |
| 1 | Cost | Price | | | |
| 2 | 47.22 | $97.91 | The Answer is 97.9122 | | |
| 3 | | | | | |
| 4 | | 2/17/1965 | His birthday is 23790 | | |
| 5 | | | | | |
| 6 | | | | | |
| 7 | | | | | |

In this case, you need to discover the numeric formatting code associated with the original cell. To do so, you follow these steps:

1. Select Cell B2.

2. Press Ctrl+1 to display the Format Cells dialog.

3. On the Number tab, choose the Custom category. This reveals the actual formatting codes for the cell.

As shown in Figure 21.12, the actual formatting code for B2 is $#,##0.00. If you repeat these steps for Cell B4, you learn that the actual formatting code is m/d/yyyy.

→ For a complete discussion of numeric formatting codes, **see** Chapter 32, "Formatting Worksheets," **page 891**.

**Figure 21.12**
If you choose the Custom category, you learn the actual codes used to produce the numeric format.

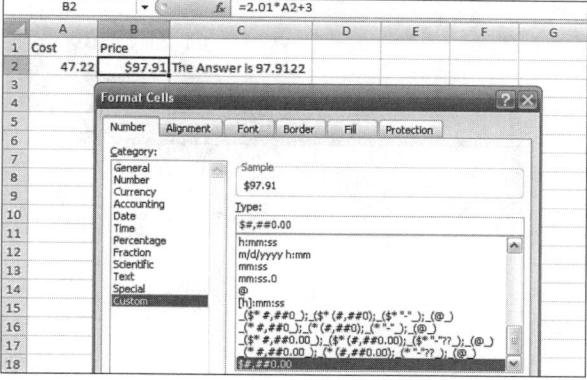

When you know the numeric formatting codes, you can achieve the desired effect by using those codes, enclosed in quotation marks, as the second argument of the TEXT function. In Figure 21.13, the formula in Cell C2 is ="The Answer is "&Text(B2, "$#,##0.00"). You can use a knowledge of custom numeric formatting codes to actually change the look of the joined value. In Cell C4, the new formula is ="His birthday is "&TEXT(B4, "dddd mmmm d, yyyy").

**Figure 21.13**
You can use the **TEXT** function to replicate formatting, as in Cell C2, or to change the formatting, as in Cell C4.

| | C2 | | | $f_x$ | ="The Answer is "&TEXT(B2,"$#,##0.00") |
|---|---|---|---|---|---|
| | A | B | C | D | E | F |
| 1 | Cost | Price | | | | |
| 2 | 47.22 | $97.91 | The Answer is $97.91 | | | |
| 3 | | | | | | |
| 4 | | 2/17/1965 | His birthday is Wednesday February 17, 1965 | | | |
| 5 | | | | | | |

21

# COPYING VERSUS CUTTING A FORMULA

In Figure 21.14, the formula in Cell C7 references A7+B7. Because there are no dollar signs within the formula, those are relative references.

→ To learn more about relative versus absolute references, **see** "Overriding Relative Behavior: Absolute Cell References," **page 389**, in Chapter 20

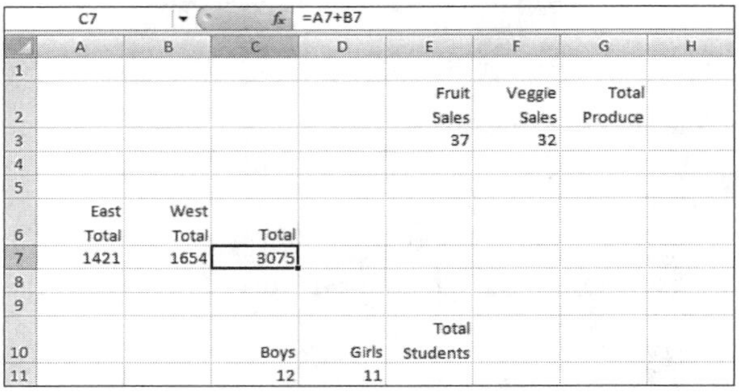

**Figure 21.14**
The formula in Cell C7 adds the two numbers to the left of the formula.

If you copy Cell C7 and paste it to Cell G3, the formula works perfectly, as shown in Figure 21.15.

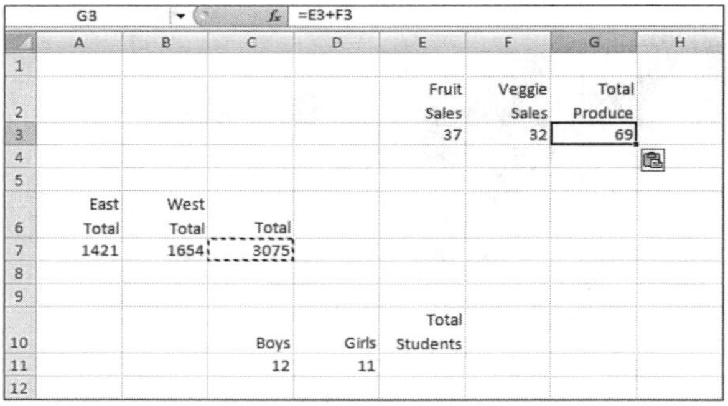

**Figure 21.15**
When Cell C7 is copied to Cell G3, the formula still adds the two numbers to the left of the formula.

However, if you cut Cell C7 and paste it to a new location, the formula continues to point to Cells A7+B7, as shown in Figure 21.16. While cutting and copying are relatively similar in applications such as Word, they are very different in Excel. It is important to understand the effect of cutting a formula in Excel as opposed to copying the formula.

When you cut a formula, the formula continues to point to the original precedents, no matter where you paste it.

A similar rule applies to the references mentioned in a formula. The formula in Cell C7 points to A7 and B7. As long as you copy Cell A7 and/or Cell B7, you can paste them anywhere without changing the formula in C7. Figure 21.17 shows the result of copying A7:B7 for 20 rows: Nothing changes in the formula.

**Figure 21.16**
Using cut and paste on a formula forces the formula to continue to point to the original cells.

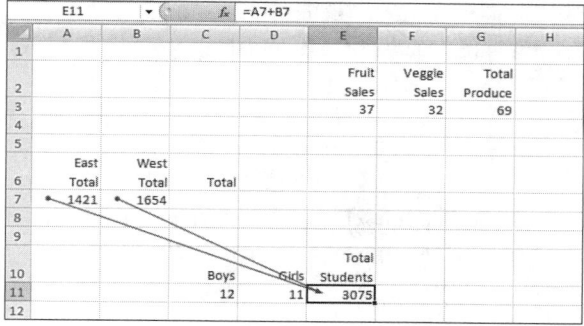

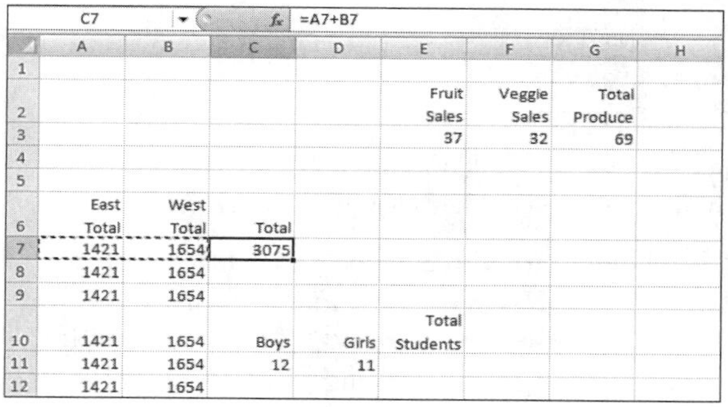

**Figure 21.17**
Copying the precedent cells from Cell C7 does not have any effect on Cell C7.

However, if you cut and paste A7:B7 to a new location, such as E5:F5, the formula in Cell C7 changes. After the paste, the formula points to the new location of the pasted cells, as shown in Figure 21.18

**Figure 21.18**
Cutting the precedent cells from Cell C7 causes the formula in C7 to change to reflect the new location.

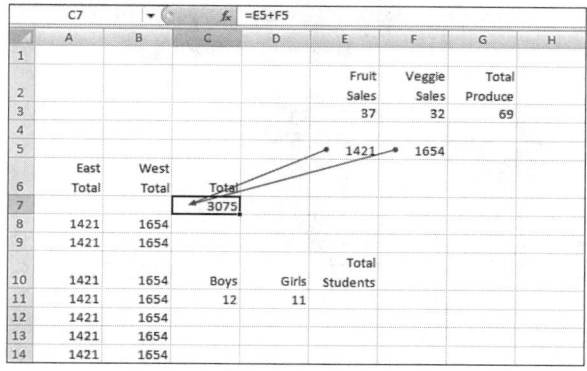

# AUTOMATICALLY FORMATTING FORMULA CELLS

The rules for formatting the result of a formula seem to be inconsistent. Say that you have $1.23 in Cell A1, as shown in Figure 21.19.

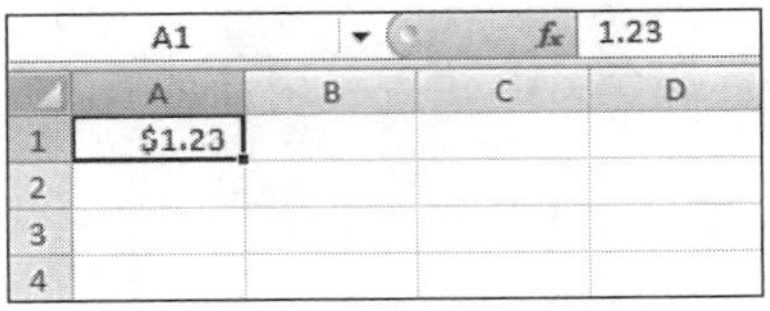

**Figure 21.19**
In this case, all cells are in general format, except Cell A1.

| A1 | | $f_x$ | 1.23 | |
|---|---|---|---|---|
| | A | B | C | D |
| 1 | $1.23 | | | |
| 2 | | | | |
| 3 | | | | |
| 4 | | | | |

If you enter =A1+3 in an another cell with general format, the result automatically inherits the currency format of Cell A1, as shown in Figure 21.20.

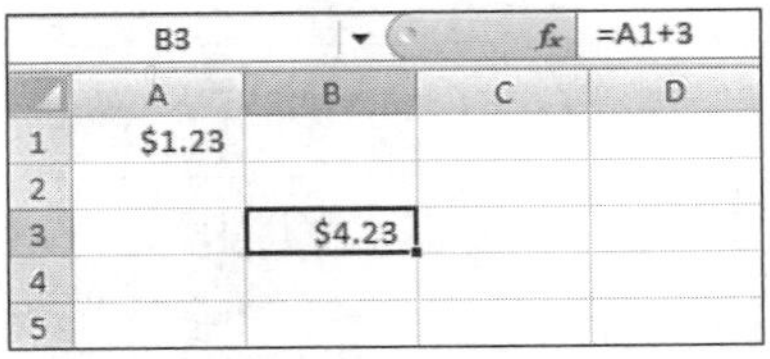

**Figure 21.20**
No formatting is applied to B3. Excel copies the format from Cell A1 automatically.

| B3 | | $f_x$ | =A1+3 | |
|---|---|---|---|---|
| | A | B | C | D |
| 1 | $1.23 | | | |
| 2 | | | | |
| 3 | | $4.23 | | |
| 4 | | | | |
| 5 | | | | |

Note that the formatting is copied whether you use =A1+3 or =3+A1.

While Excel formulas should start with an equals sign, many desktop computer owners will start their formulas with the plus sign on the numeric keypad. This trick works to provide compatibility for people formerly using Lotus 1-2-3. If you regularly use the plus sign to start a formula, the rules for automatically formatting a cell are different. In Figure 21.21, Cell A1 has a currency format, and Cell A3 has a number format with zero decimal places. The formula in Cell C3 is +A1+A3. This result mysteriously loses the currency symbol but is formatted as a number with two decimal places. In Cell C5, the formula is reversed: +A3+A1. Here, the formula picks up the format of the last cell mentioned—the currency from Cell A1.

If you enter your formulas starting with a plus sign, you can control the format by referencing a cell with similar formatting second. If you enter your formulas with an equals sign, it is best to reference the cell with similar formatting first.

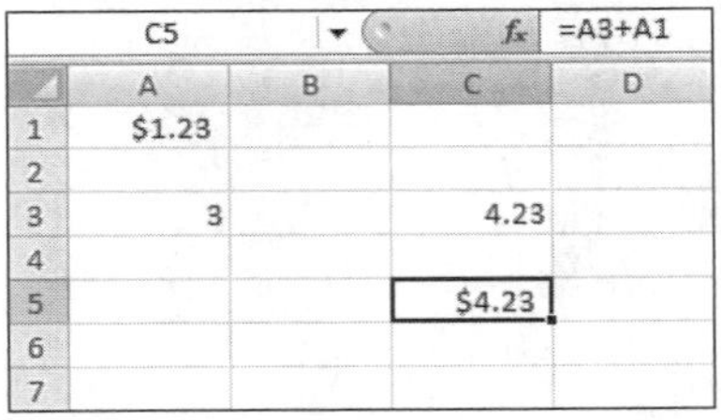

**Figure 21.21**
When starting formulas with a plus sign, the automatic formatting of cells C3 and C5 is different, depending on which cell was mentioned last.

| C5 | | $f_x$ | =A3+A1 | |
|---|---|---|---|---|
| | A | B | C | D |
| 1 | $1.23 | | | |
| 2 | | | | |
| 3 | 3 | | 4.23 | |
| 4 | | | | |
| 5 | | | $4.23 | |
| 6 | | | | |
| 7 | | | | |

Figure 21.22 compares the automatic formatting derived from entering the formula in various ways. Cell A1 is formatted as currency, A3 as number, A5 as percentage. The formulas in Column D of the left window were entered using equal signs. The formulas in Column D of

the right window were entered using plus signs. In each group, a different cell was mentioned first and last in the formula. Excel automatically assigned all the formats in Column C. The formula for each Column C cell is shown to the right, in Column D.

**Figure 21.22**
The automatic formatting of cells C3 and C5 is different, depending on if you use = or + to start a formula.

C3 =+A3+A5+A1

21-Formulas.xlsm:2

| | A | B | C | D |
|---|---|---|---|---|
| 1 | $1.23 | | 369.00% | +A1+A3+A5 |
| 2 | | | | |
| 3 | 1.23 | | 3.69 | +A3+A5+A1 |
| 4 | | | | |
| 5 | 123% | | $3.69 | +A5+A1+A3 |

21-Formulas.xlsm:1

| | A | B | C | D |
|---|---|---|---|---|
| 1 | $1.23 | | 369.00% | +A1+A3+A5 |
| 2 | | | | |
| 3 | 1.23 | | 3.69 | +A3+A5+A1 |
| 4 | | | | |
| 5 | 123% | | $3.69 | +A5+A1+A3 |

# Using Date Math

Dates in Excel are stored as the number of days since January 1, 1900. For example, Excel store the date Feb-17-2007 as 39130. In Figure 21.23, Cell A1 contains the date. Cell A2 contains the formula =A1 and has been formatted to show a number.

**Figure 21.23**
Although Cell A1 is formatted as a date, it really contains the number of days since January 1, 1900.

A2 =A1

| | A | B | C | D |
|---|---|---|---|---|
| 1 | 2/17/2007 | | | |
| 2 | 39130 | | | |
| 3 | | | | |
| 4 | | | | |

This convenient system allows you to do some pretty simple math. For example, Figure 21.24 shows a range of invoice dates in Column B. The terms for the invoice are in Column D. You can calculate the due date by adding Cells B2 and D2. Here is what actually happens in Excel's calculation engine:

1. The date in Cell B2—2/1/2007—is stored as 39114.
2. Excel adds 10 to that number to get the answer 39124.
3. Excel formats this number as a date, to yield 2/11/2007.

**Figure 21.24**
When the answer is formatted correctly, Excel's date math is very cool.

E2 =B2+D2

| | A | B | C | D | E | F |
|---|---|---|---|---|---|---|
| 1 | Invoice | Date | Amount | Terms | Due Date | |
| 2 | 1101 | 2/1/2007 | 172.54 | 10 | 2/11/2007 | |
| 3 | 1102 | 2/1/2007 | 189.22 | 15 | 2/16/2007 | |
| 4 | 1103 | 2/1/2007 | 233.52 | 30 | 3/3/2007 | |
| 5 | 1104 | 2/1/2007 | 132 | 30 | 3/3/2007 | |

However, a frustrating problem can occur if the cell containing the formula has the wrong numeric format. For example, in Figure 21.25, you can see that Column E inherited the numeric formatting of Column D after a blank Column E was inserted. Cell E2 has exactly the same formula as Figure 21.24, but the answer here is incorrect. It's important to recognize that dates in 2006–2009 fall in the range of 38,718 to 40,178. So if you are expecting a date answer as the result of a formula and get a number in this range, the answer probably needs to have a date format applied.

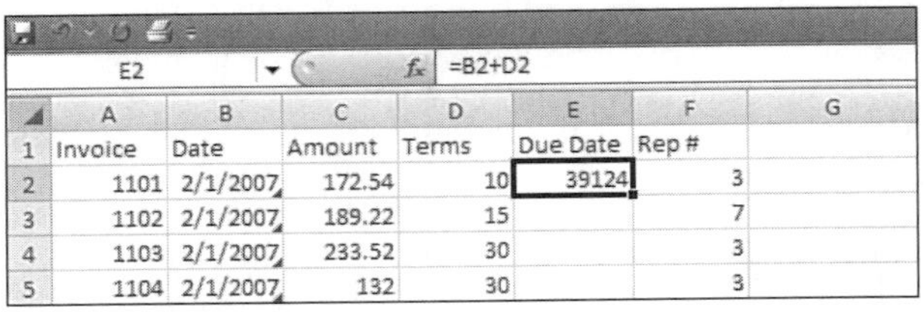

**Figure 21.25**

Here, the same formula as before appears to give the wrong answer. However, it is a formatting problem.

To apply a date format, on the Home Ribbon, you use the Number drop-down to choose the Date format. The answer in Cell E2 now appears correctly, as shown in Figure 21.26.

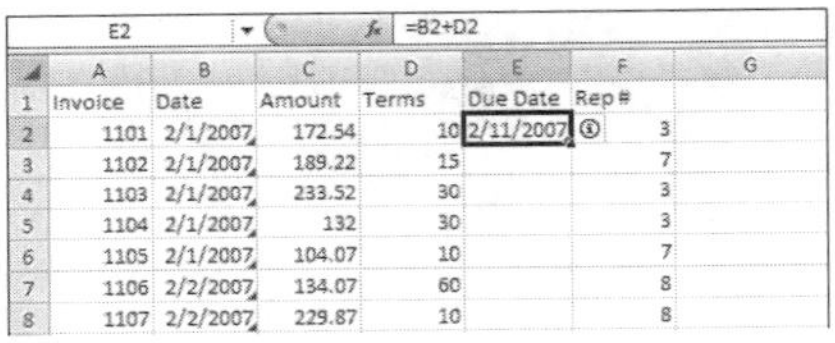

**Figure 21.26**

After you apply the Date format, the answer is displayed correctly.

Why doesn't Excel automatically format all results as dates? It's because in many cases you want to calculate the number of days between two dates. In Figure 21.27, for example, the formula in Cell C4 should correctly calculate the number of days from today until the next milestone. Although the result should be 14 days, the result in the spreadsheet is shown as the date 1/14/1900.

You need to apply a numeric format to the range containing the formula. When you choose Number from the Number drop-down on the Home Ribbon, the formula appears with the correct result (see Figure 21.28).

Any time you are doing math between two dates, you should plan on needing to change the format of the result to be either Number or Date, depending on the situation.

→ To learn about many other useful date functions in Excel, **see** "Examples of Date and Time Functions," **page 490** in Chapter 23.

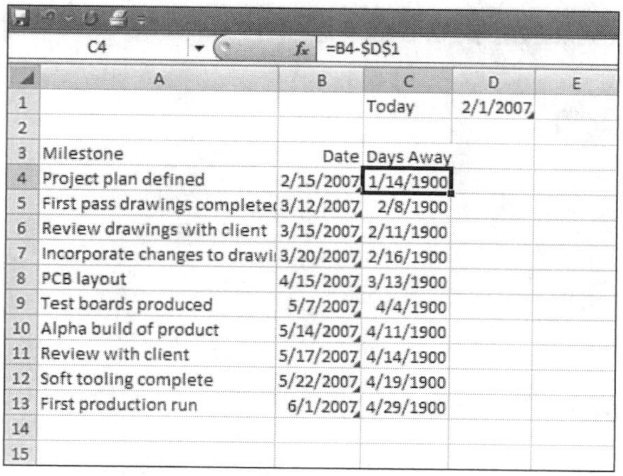

**Figure 21.27**
Here, you want the answer to be formatted as a number instead of a date.

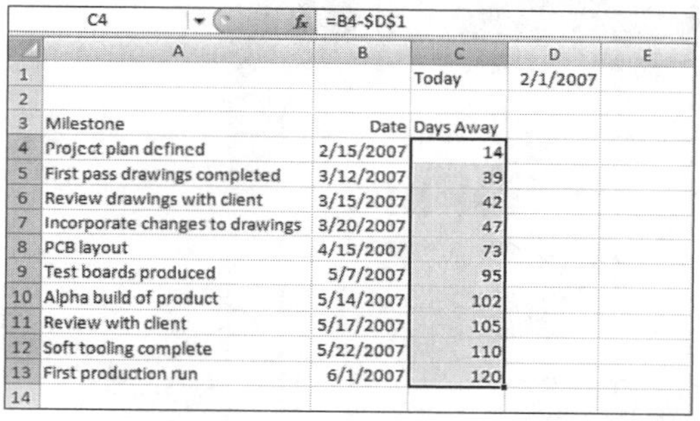

**Figure 21.28**
When you apply a numeric format, the answers are correct.

# TROUBLESHOOTING FORMULAS

It is difficult to figure out worksheets set up by other people. When you receive a worksheet from a co-worker, use the information in the following sections to find and examine the formulas.

## HIGHLIGHTING ALL FORMULA CELLS

The first technique when examing a new worksheet is to find all of the cells that contain formulas. The following steps will identify all of the formula cells in the worksheet:

1. Press F5 to display the Go To dialog.
2. In the lower-left corner of the Go To dialog, click the Special button to display the Go To Special dialog.
3. In the Go To Special dialog, choose the Formulas option button, as shown in Figure 21.29.
4. Click OK to select all formula cells.
5. To quickly highlight all the cells that contain formulas, use the paint bucket icon in the Home Ribbon to mark all the formula cells as shown in Figure 21.30.

**Figure 21.29**
The Go To Special dialog has many incredibly powerful features.

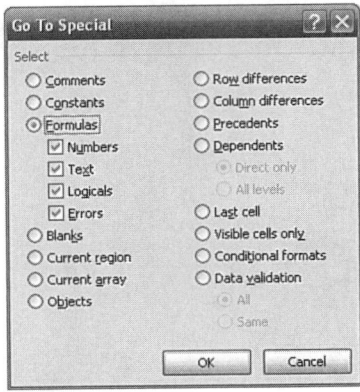

Cells containing formulas

**Figure 21.30**
Immediately after selecting all formulas, you choose the paint bucket icon to color the formula cells.

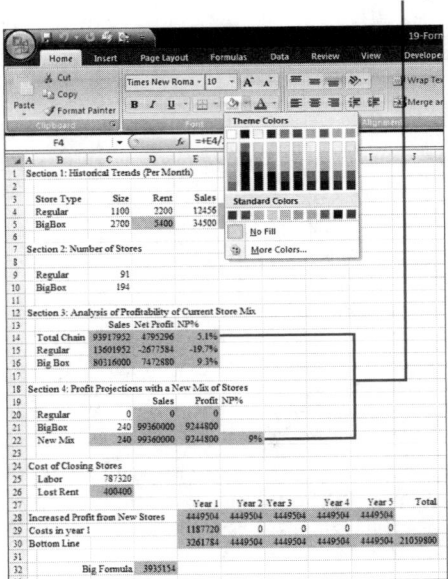

## SEEING ALL FORMULAS

For a long time, Excel has given users the ability to see all the formulas in a worksheet. The mode that provides this functionality is called Show Formulas mode.

On most U.S. keyboards, the key just below the Esc key in the upper-left corner of the keyboard contains a tilde (~) and also a backtick (`). In previous versions of Excel, you had to press Ctrl+~ or Ctrl+` in order to toggle into and out of Show Formulas mode, in which each column is a little wider. Instead of showing the results of the formula, in Show Formulas mode, each cell shows the formula itself (see Figure 21.31). You had to press this keystroke again to return to Regular mode.

In addition to recognizing Ctrl+`, Excel 2007 has added an icon in the Formula Auditing section of the Formulas ribbon that enables you to toggle into and out of Show Formulas mode.

**Figure 21.31**

Show Formulas mode shows the formulas in the cells instead of the results. This is handy for quick formula auditing.

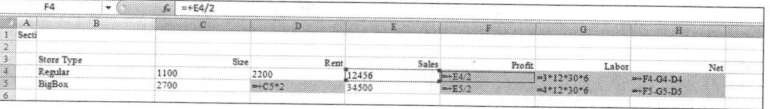

## EDITING A SINGLE FORMULA TO SHOW DIRECT PRECEDENTS

It is helpful to identify cells that are used to calculate a formula. These cells are called the precedents of the cell.

A cell can have several levels of precedents. In a formula such as =D5+D7, there are two direct precedents: D5 and D7. However, all of the direct precedents of D5 & D7 are second-level precedents of the original formula.

If you are interested in visually examing the direct precedents of a cell, follow these steps:

1. Select a cell that has a formula.

2. Press F2 to put the cell in Edit mode. In this mode, each reference of the formula is displayed in a different color. For example, the formula in Cell H5 refers to three cells. The characters F5 in the formula appear in blue and correspond to the blue box around Cell F5 in Figure 21.32.

3. Visually check the formula to ensure that it is correct.

**Figure 21.32**

Editing a single formula lights up the direct precedent cells.

| A | B | C | D | E | F | G | H | I |
|---|---|---|---|---|---|---|---|---|
| 1 | Section 1: Historical Trends (Per Month) | | | | | | | |
| 2 | | | | | | | | |
| 3 | Store Type | Size | Rent | Sales | Profit | Labor | Net | |
| 4 | Regular | 1100 | 2200 | 12456 | 6228 | 6480 | -2452 | |
| 5 | BigBox | 2700 | 5400 | 34500 | 17250 | 8640 | =+F5-G5-D5 | |
| 6 | | | | | | | | |

PV ✕ ✓ fx =+F5-G5-D5

## USING FORMULA AUDITING ARROWS

If you have a complicated formula, you might wish to identify direct precedents and then possibly second- or third-level precedents. You can have Excel draw arrows from the current cells to all cells that make up the precedents for the current cell. Here's what you do:

1. From the Formula Auditing group on the Formulas ribbon, click Trace Precedents. Excel draws arrows from the current cell to all the cells that are directly referenced in the formula. In Figure 21.33, for example, an arrow is drawn to a worksheet icon near Cell B30. This indicates that at least one of the precedents for this cell is on another worksheet.

21

**Figure 21.33**
The results of trace precedents for Cell D32.

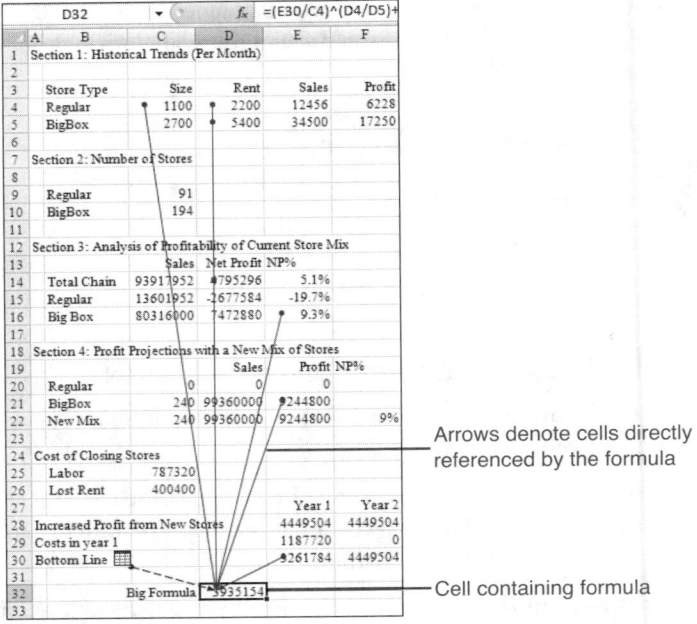

Arrows denote cells directly referenced by the formula

Cell containing formula

2. Click Trace Precedents again. Excel draws arrows from the precedent cells to the precedents of those cells. These are the second-level precedents of the original cell. Figure 21.34 shows the results of clicking Trace Precedents five times. Practically every cell on the worksheet is a precedent of Cell D32.

**Figure 21.34**
Precedents traced five times to find every precedent of the formula.

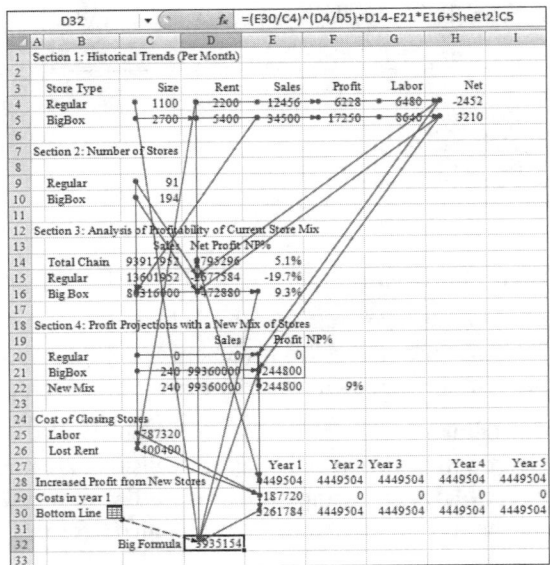

3. To remove the arrows, use the Remove Arrows icon in the Formula Auditing group.

While it may be impossible to actually follow the lines for all five levels of precedents, the diagram does indicate that the formula in D32 is vastly more complex than the six cells mentioned in the formula. To truly understand what your coworker has built in this worksheet, you will have to follow the logic through two dozen cells. Or, more simply, you know that you should not delete any of those cells if you want the formula to continue to calculate a correct result.

## TRACING DEPENDENTS

The Formula Auditing section provides another interesting option besides the ones discussed so far in this chapter: You can use it to trace dependents so that you can find all the cells on the current worksheet that depend on the active cell. Before deleting a cell, you might consider clicking Trace Dependents in order to determine whether any cells on the current sheet refer to this cell. This will prevent many #REF! errors from occurring.

CAUTION

Even if tracing dependents does not show any cells dependent on the current cell, there still might be other cells on other worksheets or on other workbooks that rely on this cell.

TIP FROM

Third-party vendors have developed an add-in that will trace dependents and precedents on other worksheets. See http://www.mrexcel.com/tracedependents.shtml for more information.

## USING THE WATCH WINDOW

If you have a large spreadsheet, you might want to watch the results of some distant cells. You can use the Watch Window icon in the Formula Auditing section of the Formulas ribbon to open a floating box called the Watch Window screen. Here's what you do:

1. Click the Add Watch icon. The Add Watch dialog appears.

2. In the Add Watch dialog, specify a cell to watch, as shown in Figure 21.35.

   After you add several cells, the Watch Window screen floats above your worksheet, showing the current value of each cell that was added to it. The Watch Window identifies the current value and the current formula of each watched cell.

In theory, you would use this feature to watch a value in a far-off section of the worksheet.

TIP FROM

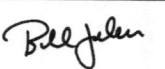

To quickly jump to a watched cell, you can double-click the cell in the Watch Window screen.

21

**Figure 21.35**
Adding a watch to the Watch Window screen.

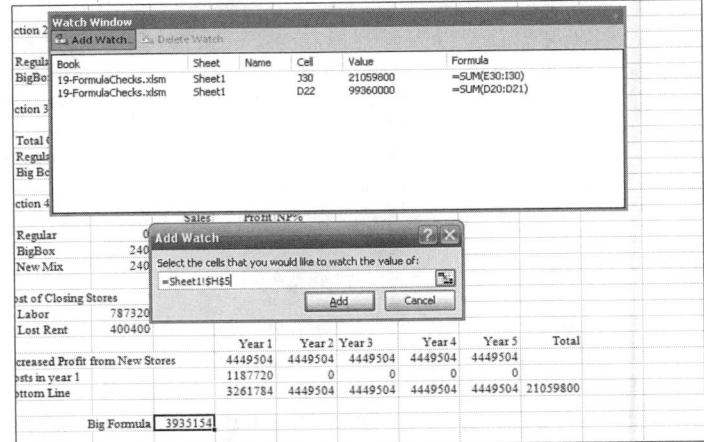

## EVALUATING A FORMULA SLOWLY

Most of the time, Excel calculates formulas in an instant. It will help your understanding of the formula if you could watch it being calculated in slow motion. If you need to see exactly how a formula is calculated, you can follow these steps:

1. Select the cell that contains the formula you're interested in.

2. On the Formulas ribbon, in the Formula Auditing group, choose Evaluate Formula. The Evaluate Formula dialog appears, showing the formula. One component of the formula is highlighted: It is the next section of the formula to be calculated.

3. If desired, click Evaluate to calculate the highlighted portion of the formula.

4. Click Step In to begin a new Evaluate section for the cell references in the underlined portion of the formula. Figure 21.36 shows the Evaluate Formula dialog after stepping in to the E30 portion of the formula.

**Figure 21.36**
The Evaluate Formula dialog allows you to calculate a formula in slow motion.

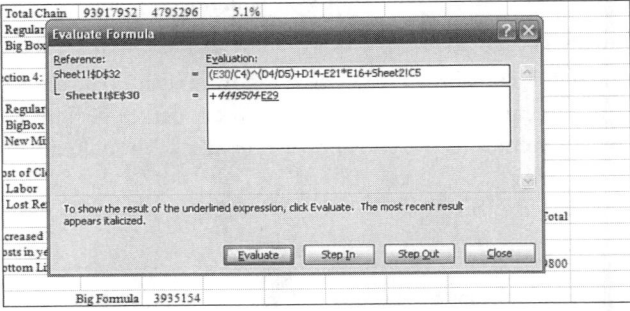

## EVALUATING PART OF A FORMULA

Sometimes you do not need to evaluate an entire formula by using the Evaluate Formula feature. In such a case, you can follow these steps:

1. Use the mouse to select just the desired portion of the formula in the formula bar, as shown in Figure 21.37.

**Figure 21.37**
You can select a portion of the formula in the formula bar.

2. Press F9. Excel calculates just the highlighted portion of the formula, as shown in Figure 21.38.

**Figure 21.38**
You can press F9 to calculate just the highlighted portion of the formula.

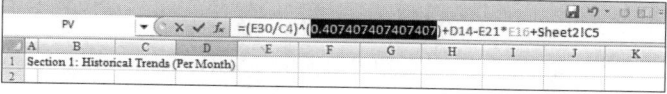

**CAUTION**

Be sure to press the Esc key to exit the formula after you use this method. If you instead press Enter to accept the formula, that portion of the formula permanently stays in its calculated form (for example, 0.407407).

21

# UNDERSTANDING FUNCTIONS

## In this chapter

**22**

Excel is used on 400 million desktops around the world. People from all careers use Excel, as do many home users who use Excel's powerful features to track their finances, investments, and more. Part of Excel's versatility is its wide range of built-in functions.

Excel 2003 offered 255 built-in functions. Another 89 functions shipped with Excel but were available only to people who installed the Analysis Toolpack (ATP). Excel 2007 offers 356 functions. It also includes the following:

- 89 ATP functions, which are now part of the default Excel installation

- 5 new general-purpose functions

- 7 new cube functions that are useful to people who are connecting to a multidimensional database, such as SQL Server Analysis Services

The functions available in Excel 2007 are applicable to a wide range of industries. There are financial functions to help investors, bankers, and bond traders. There are math and statistical functions to help scientists. There are engineering functions for engineers. There are general-purpose functions for everyone. No matter what you are trying to do in Excel, there are functions for you. If there is not a built-in function, there is a good chance that a third-party vendor sells an add-in program to Excel that adds new customized functions to Excel to assist in your particular industry. If not, you can pick up a book on programming VBA to learn how to write your own custom functions in Excel. (For example, Chapter 4 of *VBA and Macros for Microsoft Excel* by Jelen and Syrstad, offers 30 cool functions you can add to Excel.)

Although it would be impractical to cover each of the 356 functions in great detail in a single chapter, this chapter covers a number of the most commonly used functions in Exce 2007.

# WORKING WITH FUNCTIONS

To successfully use functions in a worksheet, you need to follow the function syntax. Keep in mind that a formula that makes use of a function needs to start with an equals sign. You type the function name, an opening parenthesis, function arguments (separated by commas), and the closing parenthesis.

The general syntax of a function looks like this:

```
=FunctionName(Argument1,Argument2,Argument3)
```

In general, there should be no spaces anywhere in a function. Specifically, there should never be a space between the function name and the opening parenthesis. Some people like to add a space after each comma in a function, like this:

```
=FunctionName(Argument1, Argument2, Argument3)
```

Although this is not required, it does increase the readability of the final function. For what it's worth, Excel correctly calculates a formula with or without these spaces, so it's a personal choice as to whether you include them.

Parentheses are needed with every function, including functions that require no arguments. For example, these functions still require the parentheses:

```
=NOW()
=DATE()
```

The arguments for a function should be entered in the correct order, as specified in this book or Excel Help. For example, the PMT() function expects the arguments to have the interest rate first, followed by the number of periods, followed by the present value. If you attempt to send the arguments in the wrong order, Excel will happily calculate the wrong result.

In many cases, you can enter arguments as numbers or as cell references. For example, all these formulas are valid:

```
=SUM(1,2,3^2,4/5,6*7)
=SUM(A1:A9,C1,D2,Sheet2!E3:M10)
=SUM(A1:A9,100,200,B3*5)
```

Excel functions can return a number of errors. This happens most frequently when one of the arguments passed to the function is outside the range of what the function expects. When you receive a #NUM!, #VALUE!, or #N/A! error, you should look in Excel Help for the function. The Remarks section usually indicates exactly what problems can causes each type of error.

## THE FORMULAS RIBBON IN EXCEL 2007

One way to find functions in Excel 2007 is on the Formulas ribbon. The ribbon offers Function Wizard, AutoSum, Recently Used, Financial, Logical, Text, Date & Time, Lookup & Reference, Math & Trig, and More Functions icons.

As shown in Figure 22.1, when you click the More Functions icon, a drop-down with four additional function groups—Statistical, Engineering, Cube, and Information—appears.

**Figure 22.1**
The Formulas ribbon contains icons for finding functions.

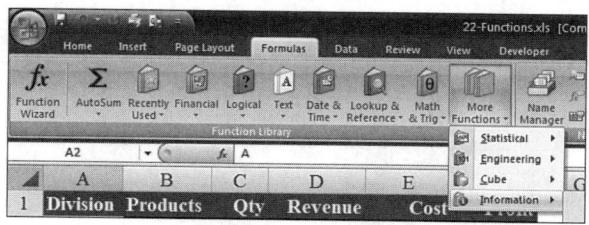

The Formulas ribbon is designed to make it easier to find the right function. You simply select an icon from the ribbon, and an alphabetical list of functions in that group appears. If you hover your mouse over a function in the list, Excel displays a description of what the function does, as shown in Figure 22.2.

**Figure 22.2**
Hover over a function, and Excel displays a tip, explaining what the function does.

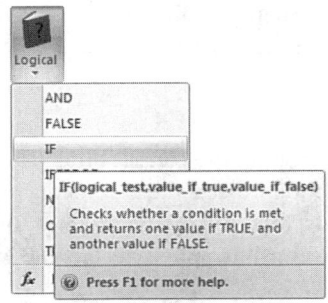

## FINDING THE FUNCTION YOU NEED

The inherent problem with the Formulas ribbon is that you often have to guess where your desired function might be hiding. The function categories have been established in Excel for a decade, and in some cases, functions are tucked away in strange places.

For example, the SUM() function is a Math & Trig function. This makes sense because adding numbers is clearly a mathematical process. However, the AVERAGE() function is not available in the Math & Trig icon. (It is under More Functions, Statistical.) The COUNT() function could be math, reference, or information, but it is found under More Functions, Statistical.

By dividing the list of functions up into categories, Microsoft has made it rather difficult to find certain functions. Fortunately, as described in the following sections, there are some tricks you can use to make this process simpler.

## USING AUTOCOMPLETE TO FIND FUNCTIONS

One new feature in Excel 2007 is Formula AutoComplete. Sometimes you might be able to remember the first letter of a function but not all the rest of the letters. For example, there are five varieties of the function you use to do averages, and they all start with A. Rather than trying to figure out whether the averaging function you need is in the Math or Statistical icon, you can just start typing =A in a cell. Excel displays a pop-up window with all the functions that begin with *A*, as shown in Figure 22.3.

**Figure 22.3**
Rather than use the icons on the Formulas ribbon, you can type =A to display an alphabetical list of the *A* functions.

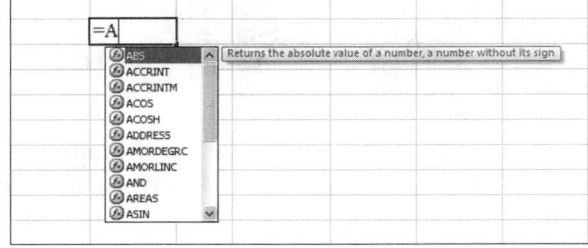

As you continue to type, the pop-up list of functions narrows to a shorter list. After you type =AV, you see a short list of the five averaging functions. You can use the up-arrow and down-arrow keys or the mouse to select a function and read the ToolTip to learn what the function does, as shown in Figure 22.4.

**Figure 22.4**
As you type a second letter of the function name, you see a shorter list of matching functions. You can use the arrow keys to see a description of what a function does.

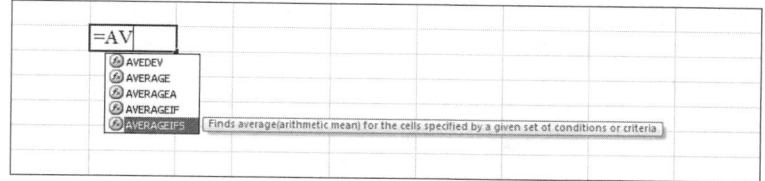

To accept a function name from the list, you can either double-click the function name or choose the name and press Tab.

## USING THE FUNCTION WIZARD TO FIND FUNCTIONS

At the bottom of every list of functions is an icon for the Function Wizard. To access the Function Wizard, you can also use the small fx button to the left of the formula bar, or the More Functions option at the bottom of the AutoSum drop-down, or the large Function Wizard button on the Formulas ribbon. Figure 22.5 shows just 3 of the 14 ways you can access the Function Wizard. With 14 different ways to access the Function Wizard, you can guess that this is the best way to find functions.

These icons lead to the Function Wizard

**Figure 22.5**
You can access the Function Wizard by using any of these icons.

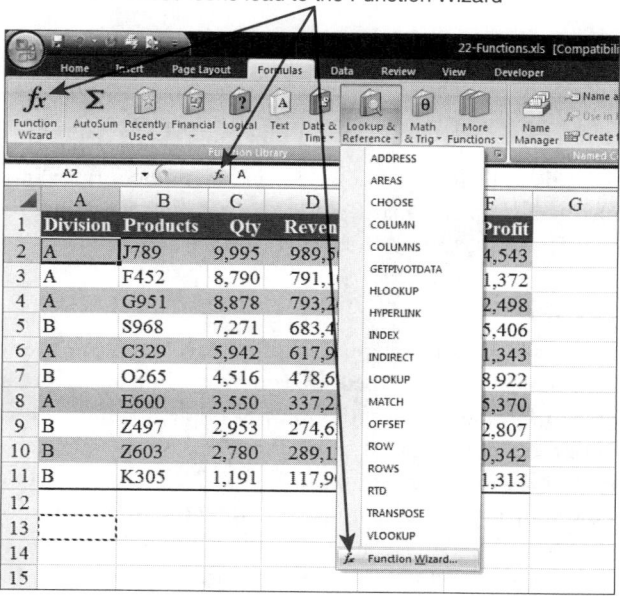

Choosing any of these options to open the Function Wizard causes the Insert Function dialog to appear.

In the Excel 2003 version of the Function Wizard, Microsoft added a handy search utility. For example, if you typed **Car Payment** and then clicked Go, Excel would suggest PMT (the correct function) as well as NPER, ISPMT, PV, PPMT, and IPMT. The search functionality was a fantastic addition to Excel 2003 and should be your first stop when trying to find a function in Excel 2007.

When you choose a function in the Insert Function dialog, the dialog displays the syntax for the function, as well as a one-sentence description of the function, as shown in Figure 22.6. If you need more details, you can click the Help on This Function hyperlink in the lower-left corner of the Insert Function dialog.

**Figure 22.6**
The Insert Function dialog allows you to browse the syntax and descriptions. The Help on This Function hyperlink leads to more help.

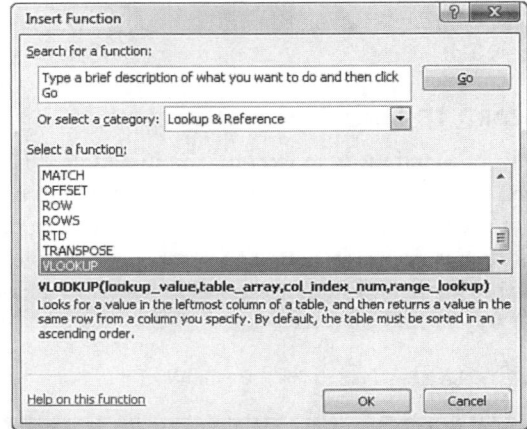

# GETTING HELP WITH EXCEL FUNCTIONS

There are three levels of help available for every Excel function: an in-cell ToolTip, the Function Arguments dialog, and Excel Help. You will find the Function Arguments dialog to be one of the best ways of getting help.

## USING IN-CELL TOOLTIPS

In any cell, you can type an equals sign, a function name, and the opening parenthesis. Excel displays a ToolTip that shows the expected arguments. In many cases, this ToolTip is enough to guide you through the function. For example, I can usually remember that the function for figuring out a car loan payment is =PMT(), but I can never remember the order of the arguments. The ToolTip, as shown in Figure 22.7, is enough to remind me that rate comes first, followed by number of periods, and then the principal amount or present value. Any function names displayed in square brackets are optional, so in the example shown in Figure 22.7, you know that you may not have to enter anything for *fv* or *type*.

**Figure 22.7**
The ToolTip will assist you in remembering the proper order for the arguments.

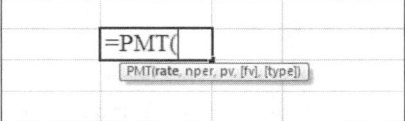

As you type each comma in the function, the next argument in the ToolTip lights up in boldface. This way, you always know which argument you are entering.

## USING THE FUNCTION ARGUMENTS DIALOG

When you access a function through the Function Wizard or a drop-down list, Excel displays the Function Arguments dialog. This dialog is one of the best features in Excel.

**TIP FROM**

*Bill Jelen*

> If you type =FunctionName( in a cell, you can press Ctrl+A anytime after the opening parenthesis to display the Function Arguments dialog.

As shown in Figure 22.8, the Function Arguments dialog has many elements:

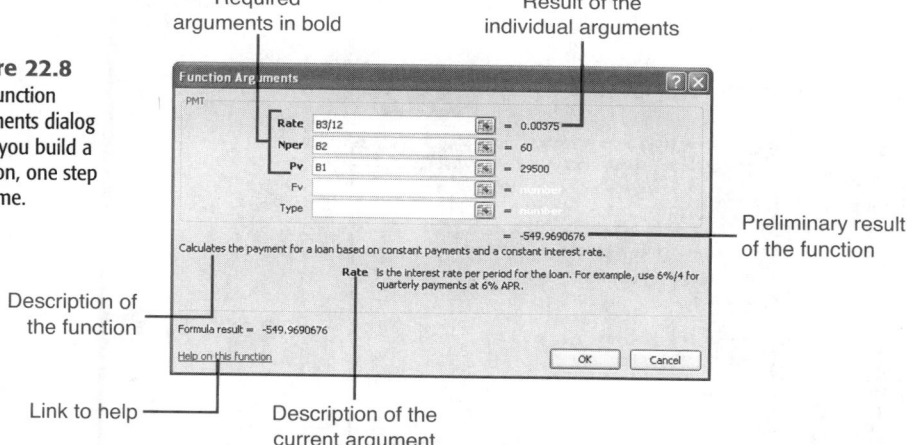

**Figure 22.8**
The Function Arguments dialog helps you build a function, one step at a time.

- The one-sentence description of the function appears in the center of the dialog.
- As you tab into the text box for each argument, the description of the argument is shown in the dialog. This description guides you as to what Excel is expecting. For example, in the dialog shown in Figure 22.8, Excel reminds you that the interest rate needs to be divided by four for quarterly payments. This reminds you to divide the APR in Cell B3 by 12.
- To the right of each argument in the dialog is a reference button. You can click this button to collapse the dialog so you can point to the cells for that argument.
- To the right of each text box is a label that shows the result of the entry for that argument.
- Any arguments in bold are required. Arguments not in bold are optional.
- After you enter the required arguments, the dialog shows the preliminary result of the formula. This is on the right side, just below the last argument text box. It appears again in the lower-left corner, just above the Help on This Function hyperlink.
- A Help on This Function hyperlink to the Help topic for the function appears in the lower-left corner of the dialog.

## USING EXCEL HELP

The Excel Help topics for the functions are incredibly complete. You will find the following sections in each function's Help topic:

- The function syntax appears at the top of the topic. This includes a description of each function that may be more complete than the description in the Function Arguments dialog.

- The Remarks section helps troubleshoot possible problems with the function. It discusses specific limits for each argument and describes the meaning of each possible error that could be returned from the function.

- Each function has an example section. You can copy an example to a blank worksheet to see the function actually working.

- The See Also section at the bottom of a Help topic allows you to discover related functions. The logical groupings suggested by See Also is far more useful than the category groupings in the Formulas ribbon.

Figure 22.9 shows the example and See Also sections of a help topic.

**Figure 22.9**
Excel Help is particularly useful for the Excel functions.

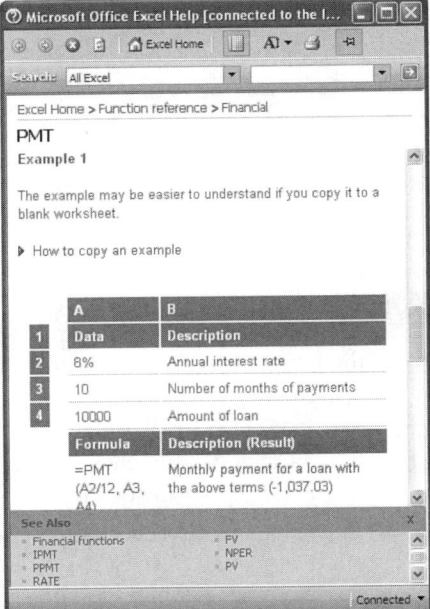

## USING AUTOSUM

Microsoft realizes that the most common function is the SUM() function. It is so popular that Excel provides one-click access to the AutoSum feature.

The AutoSum icon is the large Greek letter sigma that is second icon on the Formulas ribbon. You can click this icon to use AutoSum, or you can use the drop-down at the bottom of the icon to access AutoSum versions of Average, Count Numbers, Max, and Min, as shown in Figure 22.10.

**Figure 22.10**
The AutoSum drop-down offers the ability to average and more.

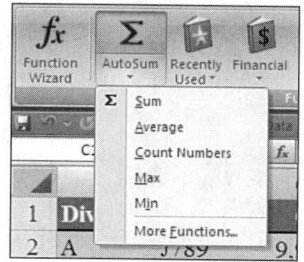

When you click the AutoSum button, Excel seeks to add up the numbers that are above or to the left of the current cell. In general, when you click the AutoSum icon, Excel guesses which cells you are trying to sum. Excel automatically types the SUM() formula. You should review Excel's guess to make sure that Excel chose the correct range to sum. In Figure 22.11, for example, Excel correctly guesses that you want to sum the column of revenue above the cell.

**Figure 22.11**
The AutoSum feature is proposing a formula to sum D2:D11.

| | A | B | C | D | E |
|---|---|---|---|---|---|
| 1 | **Division** | **Products** | **Qty** | **Revenue** | **Cost** |
| 2 | A | J789 | 9,995 | 989,505 | 474,962 |
| 3 | A | F452 | 8,790 | 791,100 | 379,728 |
| 4 | A | G951 | 8,178 | 793,266 | 380,768 |
| 5 | B | S968 | 7,271 | 683,474 | 328,068 |
| 6 | A | C329 | 5,942 | 617,968 | 296,625 |
| 7 | B | O265 | 4,516 | 478,696 | 229,774 |
| 8 | A | E600 | 3,550 | 337,250 | 161,880 |
| 9 | B | Z497 | 2,953 | 274,629 | 131,822 |
| 10 | B | Z603 | 2,780 | 289,120 | 138,778 |
| 11 | B | K305 | 1,191 | 117,909 | 56,596 |
| 12 | | | | =SUM(D2:D11) | |
| 13 | | | | SUM(number1, [number2], …) | |
| 14 | | | | | |

**TIP FROM**

*Bill Jelen*

Pressing Alt+= is equivalent to clicking the AutoSum icon.

## POTENTIAL PROBLEMS WITH AUTOSUM

While you should always check the range proposed by the AutoSum feature, there are some cases in which you should be especially wary. If your headings above the data are numeric, for example, this will fool AutoSum. In Figure 22.12, the 2003 heading in C1 is numeric. This causes Excel to incorrectly include the heading in the total for Column C.

**Figure 22.12**
Numeric headings
confuse AutoSum.

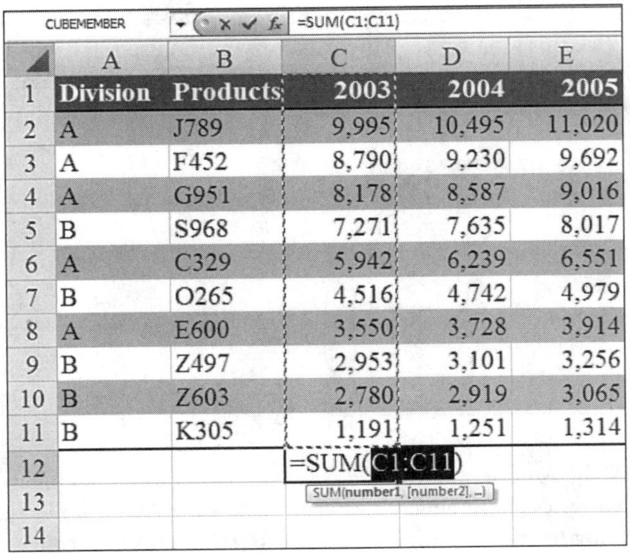

| | A | B | C | D | E |
|---|---|---|---|---|---|
| | | | | CUBEMEMBER ▾ ⊗ ✕ ✓ ƒ× =SUM(C1:C11) | |
| 1 | **Division** | **Products** | **2003** | **2004** | **2005** |
| 2 | A | J789 | 9,995 | 10,495 | 11,020 |
| 3 | A | F452 | 8,790 | 9,230 | 9,692 |
| 4 | A | G951 | 8,178 | 8,587 | 9,016 |
| 5 | B | S968 | 7,271 | 7,635 | 8,017 |
| 6 | A | C329 | 5,942 | 6,239 | 6,551 |
| 7 | B | O265 | 4,516 | 4,742 | 4,979 |
| 8 | A | E600 | 3,550 | 3,728 | 3,914 |
| 9 | B | Z497 | 2,953 | 3,101 | 3,256 |
| 10 | B | Z603 | 2,780 | 2,919 | 3,065 |
| 11 | B | K305 | 1,191 | 1,251 | 1,314 |
| 12 | | | =SUM(C1:C11) | | |
| 13 | | | SUM(number1, [number2], ...) | | |
| 14 | | | | | |

When Excel proposes the wrong range for a sum, you use your mouse to highlight the correct range before pressing Enter.

Excel avoids including other SUM() functions in an AutoSum range. If a range contains a SUM() function that references other cells, Excel prematurely stops just before the SUM() function. In Figure 22.13, Cell C4 contains the formula =SUM(H3:H4). Using AutoSum in Cell C12 causes Excel to propose summing C5:C11. This problem happens only when the SUM() function references other cells. If Cell C4 contained =7000+1878 or =H3+H4 or =SUM(7000,1878), AutoSum would include the cell.

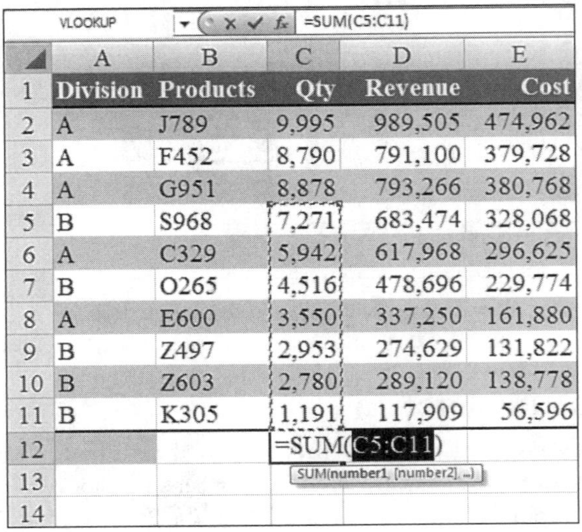

**Figure 22.13**
A SUM() function like
the one in Cell C4
causes AutoSum to
stop prematurely.

| | A | B | C | D | E |
|---|---|---|---|---|---|
| | | | | VLOOKUP ▾ ⊗ ✕ ✓ ƒ× =SUM(C5:C11) | |
| 1 | **Division** | **Products** | **Qty** | **Revenue** | **Cost** |
| 2 | A | J789 | 9,995 | 989,505 | 474,962 |
| 3 | A | F452 | 8,790 | 791,100 | 379,728 |
| 4 | A | G951 | 8,878 | 793,266 | 380,768 |
| 5 | B | S968 | 7,271 | 683,474 | 328,068 |
| 6 | A | C329 | 5,942 | 617,968 | 296,625 |
| 7 | B | O265 | 4,516 | 478,696 | 229,774 |
| 8 | A | E600 | 3,550 | 337,250 | 161,880 |
| 9 | B | Z497 | 2,953 | 274,629 | 131,822 |
| 10 | B | Z603 | 2,780 | 289,120 | 138,778 |
| 11 | B | K305 | 1,191 | 117,909 | 56,596 |
| 12 | | | =SUM(C5:C11) | | |
| 13 | | | SUM(number1, [number2], ...) | | |
| 14 | | | | | |

Excel prefers to sum a column of numbers instead of a row of numbers. Figure 22.14 shows a strange anomaly. If you place the cell pointer in Cell G2 and click AutoSum, Excel correctly guesses that you want to total C2:F2. Cell G3 works fine. However, when you get to Cell G4, Excel has a choice. There are two numbers above G4 and four numbers to the left of G4. Because there are two numbers directly above, Excel tries to total those two numbers. This problem only seems to happen in the third row of the dataset. After that, Excel sees that the three cells above are all summing across the rows, and AutoSum works perfectly in G5:G11.

**Figure 22.14**

Excel can choose between summing two numbers above or four numbers to the left. Excel chooses incorrectly.

## SPECIAL TRICKS WITH AUTOSUM

There is an amazing trick you can use with AutoSum. If you select a range of cells before clicking the AutoSum button, Excel does a much better job of predicting what to sum.

In Figure 23.13, for example, you could select G2:G11 before clicking the AutoSum button, and Excel would know to sum each row. Be careful, though, because Excel does not preview its guess before entering the formula. You should always check a formula after using AutoSum to make sure the correct range was selected.

If your selection contains a mix of blank cells and nonblank cells, Excel adds the AutoSum to only the blank cells. In Figure 22.14, for example, you select the range C1:G12 before clicking the AutoSum button.

**Figure 22.15**

If your selection contains a mix of blank and nonblank cells, AutoSum only writes to the blank cells.

22

After you click the AutoSum button, Excel correctly filled in totals for all the rows and columns, as shown in Figure 22.16.

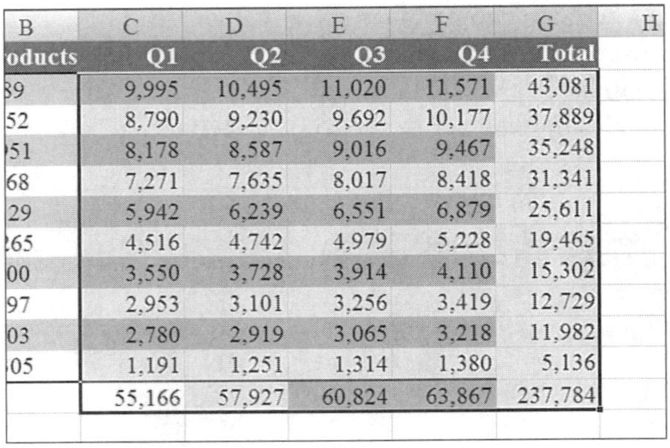

**Figure 22.16**
By using AutoSum, you can add 15 SUM( ) formulas with one click.

| B | C | D | E | F | G | H |
|---|---|---|---|---|---|---|
| oducts | Q1 | Q2 | Q3 | Q4 | Total | |
| 89 | 9,995 | 10,495 | 11,020 | 11,571 | 43,081 | |
| 52 | 8,790 | 9,230 | 9,692 | 10,177 | 37,889 | |
| 51 | 8,178 | 8,587 | 9,016 | 9,467 | 35,248 | |
| 68 | 7,271 | 7,635 | 8,017 | 8,418 | 31,341 | |
| 29 | 5,942 | 6,239 | 6,551 | 6,879 | 25,611 | |
| 65 | 4,516 | 4,742 | 4,979 | 5,228 | 19,465 | |
| 00 | 3,550 | 3,728 | 3,914 | 4,110 | 15,302 | |
| 97 | 2,953 | 3,101 | 3,256 | 3,419 | 12,729 | |
| 03 | 2,780 | 2,919 | 3,065 | 3,218 | 11,982 | |
| 05 | 1,191 | 1,251 | 1,314 | 1,380 | 5,136 | |
| | 55,166 | 57,927 | 60,824 | 63,867 | 237,784 | |

## USING THE AUTOSUM DROP-DOWN

In prior versions of Excel, the AutoSum button was flanked by a small drop-down arrow that allowed you to use the AutoAverage, AutoMin, AutoMax, and AutoCount features. In Excel 2007, you can still click an arrow to access these features, and the drop-down arrow on the icon is more prominent than it used to be.

To see how this works, you can select a cell or range of cells. From the AutoSum drop-down, you choose another function. Excel uses the same guessing logic as with AutoSum, but it instead enters a formula for Average, Min, Max, or Count, as shown in Figure 22.17.

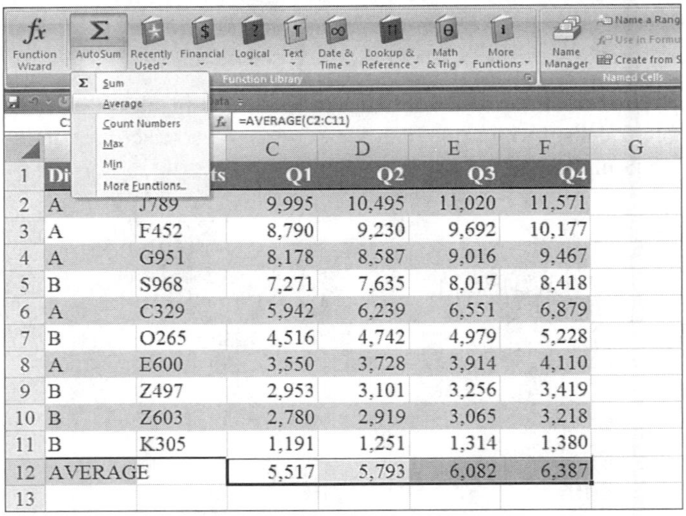

**Figure 22.17**
You can use the drop-down on the AutoSum icon to access the features AutoAverage, AutoMin, AutoMax, and AutoCount.

| | | | | C | D | E | F | G |
|---|---|---|---|---|---|---|---|---|
| 1 | Di | | ts | Q1 | Q2 | Q3 | Q4 | |
| 2 | A | J789 | | 9,995 | 10,495 | 11,020 | 11,571 | |
| 3 | A | F452 | | 8,790 | 9,230 | 9,692 | 10,177 | |
| 4 | A | G951 | | 8,178 | 8,587 | 9,016 | 9,467 | |
| 5 | B | S968 | | 7,271 | 7,635 | 8,017 | 8,418 | |
| 6 | A | C329 | | 5,942 | 6,239 | 6,551 | 6,879 | |
| 7 | B | O265 | | 4,516 | 4,742 | 4,979 | 5,228 | |
| 8 | A | E600 | | 3,550 | 3,728 | 3,914 | 4,110 | |
| 9 | B | Z497 | | 2,953 | 3,101 | 3,256 | 3,419 | |
| 10 | B | Z603 | | 2,780 | 2,919 | 3,065 | 3,218 | |
| 11 | B | K305 | | 1,191 | 1,251 | 1,314 | 1,380 | |
| 12 | AVERAGE | | | 5,517 | 5,793 | 6,082 | 6,387 | |
| 13 | | | | | | | | |

=AVERAGE(C2:C11)

# USING THE NEW GENERAL-PURPOSE FUNCTIONS IN EXCEL 2007

Excel 2007 has five new functions that were added at the request of customers: IFERROR(), AVERAGEIF(), SUMIFS(), AVERAGEIFS(), and COUNTIFS(). As described in the following sections, they are a great addition to the Excel function set.

## THE BEST NEW ADDITION: IFERROR()

Excel errors are not the friendliest things. No one really understands the screaming #VALUE! or #N/A! errors. With the all-capital letters and the exclamation point, they are scary looking. Furthermore, the default performance is that one single #N/A error in a column of one million good values causes the total for the column to calculate as #N/A.

In Chapter 24, "Using Powerful Functions: Logical, Lookup, and Database Functions," you will learn about the VLOOKUP() function. The VLOOKUP() function is great, for example, for converting a number to a name. Say that your company hires a new employee and you encounter data for the employee before anyone has updated the lookup table. This results in an #N/A! error.

You might want the table to include something friendlier than the #N/A! error. Perhaps you would like the text New Rep to appear instead of the unfriendly #N/A!. There was not an easy way to do this in prior versions of Excel. You had to use a formula such as =IF(ISNA(VLOOKUP(A2,$AA$1:$AB$99,2,FALSE)),"New Rep", VLOOKUP(A2,$AA$1:$AB$99, 2,FALSE)). This formula forces Excel to use the VLOOKUP() function once, determine if it is an #N/A error, and then calculate the VLOOKUP() function again. This is a pain for anyone using Excel. If they have to change the VLOOKUP(), they have to change it twice in the formula. Also, it takes Excel longer to calculate because it potentially has to do each good VLOOKUP() twice.

Microsoft corrected this problem in Excel 2007 by adding the IFERROR() function. With the IFERROR() function, you can use VLOOKUP() function once and then provide an alternate value or formula in case the VLOOKUP() function returns an error.

The following section describes using IFERROR().

### SYNTAX: IFERROR(*value*,*value_if_error*)

This function returns a value you specify if a formula evaluates to an error; otherwise, it returns the result of the formula. You use the IFERROR() function to trap and handle errors in a formula.

NOTE

> A formula is a sequence of values, cell references, names, functions, or operators in a cell that together produce a new value.

Note the following in this syntax:

- `value` is the value, cell reference, or formula that is checked for an error.
- `value_if_error` is the value to return if the formula evaluates to an error.
- The following error types are evaluated: `#N/A`, `#VALUE!`, `#REF!`, `#DIV/0!`, `#NUM!`, `#NAME?`, and `#NULL!`.
- If `value` or `value_if_error` is an empty cell, `IFERROR()` treats it as an empty string value (that is, `""`).
- If `value` is an array formula, `IFERROR()` returns an array of results for each cell in the range specified in `value`.
- In this example, the long formula with two `VLOOKUP()` functions is shortened to `=IFERROR(VLOOKUP(A2,$AA$1:$AB$99,2,FALSE), "New Rep")`. As you can see, using the `IFERROR()` function is much easier and faster.

Figure 22.18 shows the `IFERROR()` function.

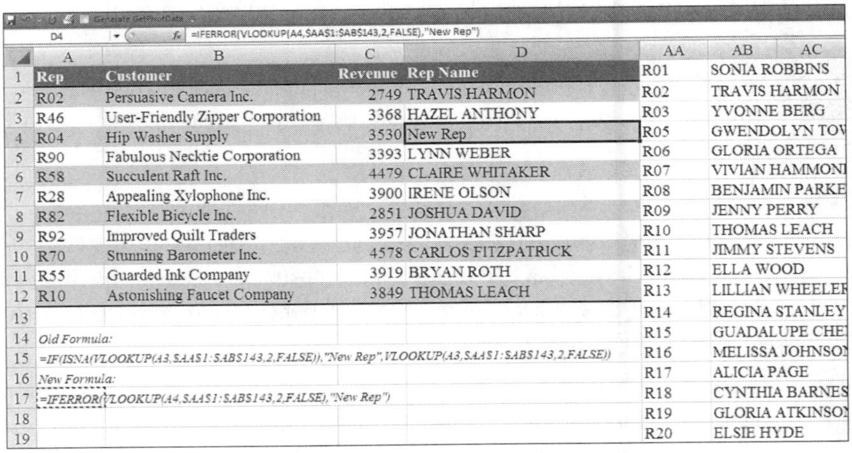


| | A | B | C | D | AA | AB |
|---|---|---|---|---|---|---|
| 1 | Rep | Customer | Revenue | Rep Name | R01 | SONIA ROBBINS |
| 2 | R02 | Persuasive Camera Inc. | 2749 | TRAVIS HARMON | R02 | TRAVIS HARMON |
| 3 | R46 | User-Friendly Zipper Corporation | 3368 | HAZEL ANTHONY | R03 | YVONNE BERG |
| 4 | R04 | Hip Washer Supply | 3530 | New Rep | R05 | GWENDOLYN TOV |
| 5 | R90 | Fabulous Necktie Corporation | 3393 | LYNN WEBER | R06 | GLORIA ORTEGA |
| 6 | R58 | Succulent Raft Inc. | 4479 | CLAIRE WHITAKER | R07 | VIVIAN HAMMONI |
| 7 | R28 | Appealing Xylophone Inc. | 3900 | IRENE OLSON | R08 | BENJAMIN PARKE |
| 8 | R82 | Flexible Bicycle Inc. | 2851 | JOSHUA DAVID | R09 | JENNY PERRY |
| 9 | R92 | Improved Quilt Traders | 3957 | JONATHAN SHARP | R10 | THOMAS LEACH |
| 10 | R70 | Stunning Barometer Inc. | 4578 | CARLOS FITZPATRICK | R11 | JIMMY STEVENS |
| 11 | R55 | Guarded Ink Company | 3919 | BRYAN ROTH | R12 | ELLA WOOD |
| 12 | R10 | Astonishing Faucet Company | 3849 | THOMAS LEACH | R13 | LILLIAN WHEELER |
| 13 | | | | | R14 | REGINA STANLEY |
| 14 | Old Formula: | | | | R15 | GUADALUPE CHE |
| 15 | =IF(ISNA(VLOOKUP(A3,$AA$1:$AB$143,2,FALSE)),"New Rep",VLOOKUP(A3,$AA$1:$AB$143,2,FALSE)) | | | | R16 | MELISSA JOHNSO |
| 16 | New Formula: | | | | R17 | ALICIA PAGE |
| 17 | =IFERROR(VLOOKUP(A4,$AA$1:$AB$143,2,FALSE),"New Rep") | | | | R18 | CYNTHIA BARNES |
| 18 | | | | | R19 | GLORIA ATKINSO |
| 19 | | | | | R20 | ELSIE HYDE |

**Figure 22.18**
You can use the `IFERROR()` function to capture `#N/A!` errors in `VLOOKUP()` errors, divide-by-zero errors, or any other errors you can foresee.

## ADDING AVERAGEIF() TO CONDITIONAL FORMULAS

`COUNTIF()` and `SUMIF()` have been a part of Excel for several years. These functions allow you to calculate a total for records in a range that match one particular condition. Although you could always do this with an array formula, people have found `SUMIF()` and `COUNTIF()` to be easier to use.

Microsoft has added `AVERAGEIF()` to the function list. This function, which is similar to `SUMIF()`, is described in the following section.

### SYNTAX: `AVERAGEIF(range,criteria,[average_range])`

This function returns the average (arithmetic mean) of all the cells in a range that meet a given criterion.

Note the following in this syntax:

- *range* is one or more cells to average.
- *criteria* is the criteria in the form of a number, an expression, a cell reference, or text that defines which cells are averaged. For example, *criteria* can be expressed as 32, "32", ">32", "apples", or B4.
- *average_range* is the set of cells to average. If this is omitted, *range* is used.
- Cells in *range* that contain TRUE or FALSE are ignored. If a cell in *range* or *average_range* is an empty cell, AVERAGEIF() ignores it. If a cell in *criteria* is empty, AVERAGEIF() treats it as a 0 value. If no cells in the range meet *criteria*, AVERAGEIF() returns the #DIV/0! error value.
- You can use the wildcard characters question mark (?) and asterisk (*) in *criteria*. A question mark matches any single character; an asterisk matches any sequence of characters. If you want to find an actual question mark or asterisk, you need to type a tilde (~) before the character.
- *average_range* does not have to be the same size and shape as *range*. Which cells are averaged is determined by using the top-left cell in *average_range* as the beginning cell and then including cells that correspond in size and shape to *range*.

In Figure 22.19, the formulas in D15:D16 use the AVERAGEIF() formula to average only the records that match the divisions in A15:A16.

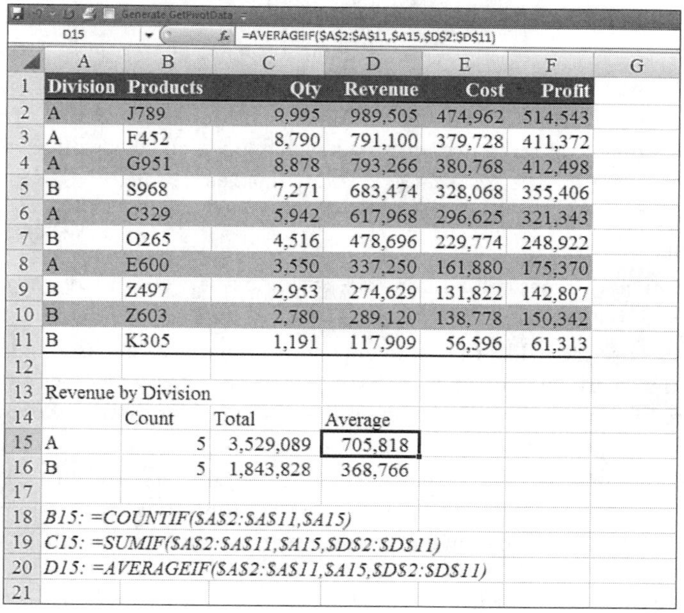

D15 =AVERAGEIF($A$2:$A$11,$A15,$D$2:$D$11)

| | A | B | C | D | E | F | G |
|---|---|---|---|---|---|---|---|
| 1 | Division | Products | Qty | Revenue | Cost | Profit | |
| 2 | A | J789 | 9,995 | 989,505 | 474,962 | 514,543 | |
| 3 | A | F452 | 8,790 | 791,100 | 379,728 | 411,372 | |
| 4 | A | G951 | 8,878 | 793,266 | 380,768 | 412,498 | |
| 5 | B | S968 | 7,271 | 683,474 | 328,068 | 355,406 | |
| 6 | A | C329 | 5,942 | 617,968 | 296,625 | 321,343 | |
| 7 | B | O265 | 4,516 | 478,696 | 229,774 | 248,922 | |
| 8 | A | E600 | 3,550 | 337,250 | 161,880 | 175,370 | |
| 9 | B | Z497 | 2,953 | 274,629 | 131,822 | 142,807 | |
| 10 | B | Z603 | 2,780 | 289,120 | 138,778 | 150,342 | |
| 11 | B | K305 | 1,191 | 117,909 | 56,596 | 61,313 | |
| 12 | | | | | | | |
| 13 | Revenue by Division | | | | | | |
| 14 | | Count | Total | Average | | | |
| 15 | A | 5 | 3,529,089 | 705,818 | | | |
| 16 | B | 5 | 1,843,828 | 368,766 | | | |
| 17 | | | | | | | |
| 18 | *B15: =COUNTIF($A$2:$A$11,$A15)* | | | | | | |
| 19 | *C15: =SUMIF($A$2:$A$11,$A15,$D$2:$D$11)* | | | | | | |
| 20 | *D15: =AVERAGEIF($A$2:$A$11,$A15,$D$2:$D$11)* | | | | | | |
| 21 | | | | | | | |

**Figure 22.19**
Like SUMIF() and COUNTIF(), the new AVERAGEIF() function can filter records based on one criterion.

## USING CONDITIONAL FORMULAS WITH MULTIPLE CONDITIONS: SUMIFS(), AVERAGEIFS(), AND COUNTIFS()

When someone sees how easy using SUMIF() is, and they invariably want the function to do more. One of the most frequent questions at the MrExcel message board is along the lines of this: "I am using SUMIF() to get a total by region. How can I put two conditions in there to only get the total for a certain region and product?" In versions of Excel prior to Excel 2007, there were ways to do this, but they were difficult. You had to use either SUMPRODUCT() or an array formula. There is a lot of complexity in going from a simple SUMIF() to the complex Boolean logic required to understand SUMPRODUCT().

Thankfully, in Excel 2007, Microsoft implemented new versions of SUMIF(), COUNTIF(), and AVERAGEIF() that can handle not just two conditions, but unlimited conditions. The three new functions add the letter S to the end of the function name (that is, SUMIFS(), COUNTIFS(), and AVERAGEIFS()), to signify that multiple IFs are being considered. With SUMIFS() and AVERAGEIFS(), you first specify the range to be summed or averaged. You then specify pairs of arguments. In each pair, you first specify the range to check and then the value to match in that range. The following sections describe these three functions.

SYNTAX: SUMIFS(*sum_range,criteria_range1,criteria1[,criteria_range2,*
*criteria2...]* )

The SUMIFS() function adds the cells in a range that meet multiple criteria.

Note the following in this syntax:

- *sum_range* is the range to sum.
- *criteria_range1, criteria_range2,* and so on are one or more ranges in which to evaluate the associated criteria.
- *criteria1, criteria2,* and so on are one or more criteria in the form of a number, an expression, a cell reference, or text that define which cells will be added. For example, they can be expressed as 32, "32", ">32", "apples", or B4.
- Each cell in *sum_range* is summed only if all the corresponding criteria specified are true for that cell.
- Cells in *sum_range* that contain TRUE evaluate to 1; cells in *sum_range* that contain FALSE evaluate to 0.
- You can use the wildcard characters question mark (?) and asterisk (*) in *criteria*. A question mark matches any single character; an asterisk matches any sequence of characters. If you want to find an actual question mark or asterisk, you need to type a tilde (~) before the character.
- Each *criteria_range* does not have to be the same size and shape as *sum_range*. Which cells are averaged is determined by using the top-left cell in that *criteria_range* as the beginning cell and then including cells that correspond in size and shape to *sum_range*.

In Figure 22.20, you want to build a table that shows the total by region and product. *sum_range* is the revenue in E7:E26. The first criteria pair consists of the regions in $C$7:$C$26 being compared to the word East in B$1. The second criteria pair consists of the divisions in $A$7:$A$26 being compared to the letter A in $A2. The formula in B2 is =SUMIFS($E$7:$E$26,$C$7:$C$26,B$1,$A$7:$A$26,$A2). You can copy this formula to B2:C3.

**Figure 22.20**
The new SUMIFS() function is used to create this summary by region and product.

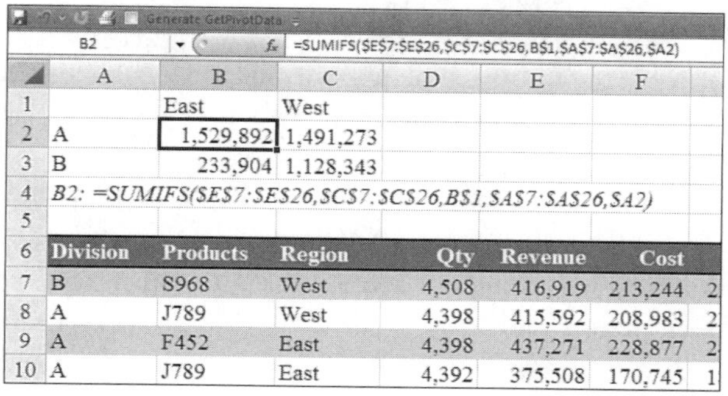

| | A | B | C | D | E | F |
|---|---|---|---|---|---|---|
| | | East | West | | | |
| 1 | | | | | | |
| 2 | A | 1,529,892 | 1,491,273 | | | |
| 3 | B | 233,904 | 1,128,343 | | | |
| 4 | B2: =SUMIFS($E$7:$E$26,$C$7:$C$26,B$1,$A$7:$A$26,$A2) | | | | | |
| 5 | | | | | | |
| 6 | Division | Products | Region | Qty | Revenue | Cost |
| 7 | B | S968 | West | 4,508 | 416,919 | 213,244 | 2 |
| 8 | A | J789 | West | 4,398 | 415,592 | 208,983 | 2 |
| 9 | A | F452 | East | 4,398 | 437,271 | 228,877 | 2 |
| 10 | A | J789 | East | 4,392 | 375,508 | 170,745 | 1 |

B2 =SUMIFS($E$7:$E$26,$C$7:$C$26,B$1,$A$7:$A$26,$A2)

SYNTAX: AVERAGEIFS(*average_range*,*criteria_range1*,*criteria1*[,*criteria_range2*, *criteria2*...])

The AVERAGEIFS() function is similar to SUMIFS(). It returns the average (arithmetic mean) of all cells that meet multiple criteria. The arguments are the same as for SUMIFS().

SYNTAX: COUNTIFS(*range1*,*criteria1*[,*range2*, *criteria2*...])

COUNTIFS() counts the number of cells in a range that meet multiple criteria. The COUNTIFS() syntax is a bit different from the syntax of the other new functions. With COUNTIFS(), there is no need to specify *sum_range*. The arguments in *COUNTIFS()* consist of pairs specifying criteria. The first argument in each pair specifies a criteria region. The second argument in each pair specifies the criteria value to match.

# USING THE NEW CUBE FUNCTIONS IN EXCEL 2007

Several high-end analysis tools store data in a multidimensional format. Examples of these services are Essbase and SQL Server Analysis Services.

With Microsoft's increased focus on business intelligence, they are encouraging more large businesses to purchase SQL Server Analysis Services from Microsoft. To assist those customers, the new CUBE functions help these customers extract data from their databases.

In most cases, you will never actually enter these functions. They are created for you automatically after you (1) build a pivot table based on an OLAP data source and (2) choose Pivot Table Tools, Options, OLAP Tools, Convert to Formulas to convert the pivot table to live formulas. In response, Excel will automatically enter the proper cube functions.

Excel automatically creates formulas for you, using the seven new cube functions. Most of the time, you encounter these formulas after they have been created for you by Excel.

While 99% of Excel customers will never need these formulas, and 99% of the remaining 1% will have Excel create the formulas automatically, it is possible to write the formulas manually. You have to specify the connection string to identify the OLAP source.

The following sections provide a brief overview of the cube functions. If you need to create these formulas manually, consult Excel help for more details.

**SYNTAX:** CUBEMEMBER(*connection*,*member_expression*[,*caption*])

The CUBEMEMBER() function returns a member or tuple in a cube hierarchy. You can use it to validate that the member or tuple exists in the cube.

**SYNTAX:** CUBEMEMBERPROPERTY(*connection*,*member_expression*,*property*)

The CUBEMEMBERPROPERTY() function returns the value of a member property in the cube. You can use it to validate that a member name exists within the cube and to return the specified property for that member.

**SYNTAX:** CUBERANKEDMEMBER(*connection*,*set_expression*,*rank*[,*caption*])

The CUBERANKEDMEMBER() function returns the $n$th, or ranked, member in a set. You can use it to return one or more elements in a set, such as the top sales performer or top 10 students.

**SYNTAX:** CUBESET(*connection*,*set_expression*[,*caption*][,*sort_order*][,*sort_by*])

The CUBESET() function defines a calculated set of members or tuples by sending a set expression to the cube on the server, which creates the set. The function then returns that set to Excel. You can use CUBESET() to build dynamic reports that aggregate and filter data, by using the return value as a slicer in the CUBEVALUE() function, the CUBERANKEDMEMBER() function to choose specific members from the calculated set, and the CUBESETCOUNT() function to control the size of the set.

**SYNTAX:** CUBESETCOUNT(*set*)

The CUBESETCOUNT() function returns the number of items in a set.

**SYNTAX:** CUBEVALUE(*connection*,*member_expression1*[,*member_expression2*...])

The CUBEVALUE() function returns an aggregated value from a cube.

**SYNTAX:** CUBEKPIMEMBER(*connection*,*kpi_name*,*kpi_property*[,*caption*])

The CUBEKPIMEMBER() function returns a key performance indicator (KPI) name, property, and measure, and it displays the name and property in the cell. A KPI is a quantifiable measurement, such as monthly gross profit or quarterly employee turnover, used to monitor an organization's performance. (To use this function, you must have SQL Server Analysis Services 2005 or later.)

# USING THE FORMER ATP FUNCTIONS

In versions of Excel prior to Excel 2007, a wide variety of functions were known as the ATP functions. These functions were available only on computers that had enabled the Analysis Toolpack (ATP) add-in.

Even if you had enabled the ATP, there was a danger that you could send a workbook to a co-worker who had not enabled the ATP. If this happened, all the formulas that used any of the 89 ATP functions would change to NAME! errors.

Although it was easy to enable the ATP (by selecting Tools, Add-ins, Check Analysis Toolpack and then clicking OK), there was a great deal of paranoia about using these functions, sending the workbook out, and having others obtain the wrong results. For this reason, some companies instituted policies against using the ATP functions. People would write elaborate formulas to duplicate what could easily be done with the ATP.

In a smart move, Microsoft has promoted the 89 ATP functions to be part of the standard Excel package starting with Excel 2007. This means that you can safely share an Excel 2007 workbook with any other person using Excel 2007, and all the functions will continue to work. However, you need to be aware that if you are sharing a workbook with a person who is using a legacy version of Excel, the functions in the ATP may change to NAME! errors on the other computer.

The individual functions are covered in the next five chapters. However, the following alphabetical list is provided as a guide to which functions are potentially problems when sharing with people using prior versions of Excel.

The following are the functions that used to be included in the ATP but are now a default part of Excel 2007: ACCRINT(), ACCRINTM(), AMORDEGRC(), AMORLINC(), BESSELI(), BESSELJ(), BESSELK(), BESSELY(), BIN2DEC(), BIN2HEX(), BIN2OCT(), COMPLEX(), CONVERT(), COUPDAYBS(), COUPDAYS(), COUPDAYSNC(), COUPNCD(), COUPNUM(), COUPPCD(), CUMIPMT(), CUMPRINC(), DEC2BIN(), DEC2HEX(), DEC2OCT(), DELTA(), DISC(), DOLLARDE(), DOLLARFR(), DURATION(), EDATE(), EFFECT(), EOMONTH(), ERF(), ERFC(), ERROR.TYPE(), FACTDOUBLE(), FVSCHEDULE(), GCD(), GESTEP(), HEX2BIN(), HEX2DEC(), HEX2OCT(), IMABS(), IMAGINARY(), IMARGUMENT(), IMCONJUGATE(), IMCOS(), IMDIV(), IMEXP(), IMLN(), IMLOG10(), IMLOG2(), IMPOWER(), IMPRODUCT(), IMREAL(), IMSIN(), IMSQRT(), IMSUB(), IMSUM(), INTRATE(), ISEVEN(), ISODD(), LCM(), MDURATION(), MROUND(), MULTINOMIAL(), NETWORKDAYS(), NOMINAL(), OCT2BIN(), OCT2DEC(), ODDFPRICE(), ODDFYIELD(), ODDLPRICE(), ODDLYIELD(), PRICE(), PRICEDISC(), PRICEMAT(), QUOTIENT(), RANDBETWEEN(), RECEIVED(), SERIESSUM(), SQL.REQUEST(), SQRTPI(), TBILLEQ(), TBILLPRICE(), TBILLYIELD(), WEEKNUM(), WORKDAY(), XIRR(), XNPV(), YEARFRAC(), YIELD(), YIELDDISC(), YIELDMAT().

# THE FUNCTION REFERENCE CHAPTERS

The next five chapters provide a fairly comprehensive reference for most of the 356 functions in Excel 2007. At the beginning of each of these chapters is an alphabetical list of the functions described, along with arguments and a short description of each function. Following the alphabetical list are examples of how to use the functions. These examples describe all the required arguments. The examples are designed to give you ideas of how to use the functions in real life.

Function coverage is broken out as follows:

■ Chapter 23, "Using Everyday Functions: Basic Math and Date Functions," describes functions that many people encounter in their everyday life: some of the math functions, date functions, and text functions.

22

- Chapter 24, "Using Powerful Functions: Logical, Lookup, and Info Functions," describes functions that are a bit more difficult but that should be a part of your everyday arsenal. These include a series of functions for making decisions in a formula. They include the IF function and are known collectively as the *logical functions*. Chapter 24 also describes the information, lookup, and database functions.

- Chapter 25, "Using Financial Functions," describes the financial functions. The first section of the chapter includes functions that anyone can use to calculate a car loan or to plan for retirement. The later sections of the chapter include functions for depreciation, business valuation, and bond investing.

- Chapter 26, "Using Statistical Functions," describes statistical functions. Many of these functions are functions that are useful everyday (for example, AVERAGE(), MAX(), MIN(), RANK()). The chapter also describes many highly specialized functions that are useful to scientists and engineers.

- Chapter 27, "Using Math and Engineering Functions," describes trigonometry and engineering functions. The trigonometry functions are grouped along with the other math functions in the Math Functions icon, but they are described separately in this book because they are more specialized. The engineering functions are highly specialized.

# CHAPTER 23

# USING EVERYDAY FUNCTIONS: MATH, DATE AND TIME, AND TEXT FUNCTIONS

**I**n this chapter

Excel offers many functions for dealing with basic math, dates and times, and text. This chapter describes the functions found under the Date & Time icon and the Math & Trig icon on the Formulas ribbon.

Table 23.1 provides an alphabetical list of all of Excel 2007's math functions. Detailed examples of these functions are provided later in this chapter.

**TABLE 23.1    ALPHABETICAL LIST OF MATH FUNCTIONS**

| Function | Description |
| --- | --- |
| ABS(*number*) | Returns the absolute value of a number. The absolute value of a number is the number without its sign. |
| CEILING(*number*,*significance*) | Returns the number rounded up, away from zero, to the nearest multiple of significance. For example, if you want to avoid using pennies in your prices and your product is priced at $4.42, you can use the formula =CEILING(4.42,0.05) to round prices up to the nearest nickel. |
| COMBIN(*number*,*number_chosen*) | Returns the number of combinations for a given number of items. You use COMBIN to determine the total possible number of groups for a given number of items. |
| COUNTIF(*range*,*criteria*) | Counts the number of cells within a range that meet the given criteria. |
| EVEN(*number*) | Returns number rounded up to the nearest even integer. You can use this function for processing items that come in twos. For example, say a packing crate accepts rows of one or two items. The crate is full when the number of items, rounded up to the nearest two, matches the crate's capacity. |
| EXP(*number*) | Returns e raised to the power of *number*. The constant e equals 2.71828182845904, the base of the natural logarithm. |
| FACT(*number*) | Returns the factorial of a number. The factorial of a number is equal to $1 \times 2 \times 3 \times \ldots \times number$. |
| FACTDOUBLE(*number*) | Returns the double factorial of a number. |
| FLOOR(*number*,*significance*) | Rounds the number down, toward zero, to the nearest multiple of significance. |
| GCD(*number1*,*number2*,...) | Returns the greatest common divisor of two or more integers. The greatest common divisor is the largest integer that divides both *number1* and *number2* without a remainder. |
| INT(*number*) | Rounds a number down to the nearest integer. |
| LCM(*number1*,*number2*,...) | Returns the least common multiple of integers. The least common multiple is the smallest positive integer that is a multiple of all integer arguments *number1*, *number2*, and so on. You use LCM to add fractions that have different denominators. |

| Function | Description |
|----------|-------------|
| MOD(*number*,*divisor*) | Returns the remainder after *number* is divided by *divisor*. The result has the same sign as *divisor*. |
| MROUND(*number*,*multiple*) | Returns a number rounded to the desired multiple. |
| ODD(*number*) | Returns number rounded up to the nearest odd integer. |
| PI() | Returns the number 3.14159265358979, the mathematical constant pi, accurate to 15 digits. |
| POWER(*number*,*power*) | Returns the result of a number raised to a power. |
| PRODUCT(*number1*,*number2*,...) | Multiplies all the numbers given as arguments and returns the product. |
| QUOTIENT(*numerator*,*denominator*) | Returns the integer portion of a division operation. You use this function when you want to discard the remainder of a division. |
| RAND() | Returns an evenly distributed random number greater than or equal to 0 and less than 1. A new random number is returned every time the worksheet is calculated. |
| RANDBETWEEN(*bottom*,*top*) | Returns a random number between the numbers specified. A new random number is returned every time the worksheet is calculated. |
| ROMAN(*number*,*form*) | Converts an Arabic numeral to Roman, as text. |
| ROUND(*number*,*num_digits*) | Rounds a number to a specified number of digits. |
| ROUNDDOWN(*number*,*num_digits*) | Rounds a number down, toward zero. |
| ROUNDUP(*number*,*num_digits*) | Rounds a number up, away from zero. |
| SIGN(*number*) | Determines the sign of a number. Returns 1 if the number is positive, 0 if the number is 0, and -1 if the number is negative. |
| SQRT(*number*) | Returns a positive square root. |
| SQRTPI(*number*) | Returns the square root of (*number* × pi). |
| SUBTOTAL(*function_num*, *ref1*,*ref2*,...) | Returns a subtotal in a list or database. It is generally easier to create a list with subtotals by using the Subtotals command (from the Data menu). After the subtotal list is created, you can modify it by editing the SUBTOTAL function. |
| SUM(*number1*,*number2*,...) | Adds all the numbers in a range of cells. |
| SUMIF(*range*,*criteria*,*sum_range*) | Adds the cells specified by the given criteria. |
| SUMPRODUCT(*array1*,*array2*, *array3*,...) | Multiplies corresponding components in the given arrays and returns the sum of those products. |
| TRUNC(*number*,*num_digits*) | Truncates a number to an integer by removing the fractional part of the number. |

23

Table 23.2 provides an alphabetical list of all of Excel 2007's date and time functions. Detailed examples of these functions are provided later in this chapter.

### TABLE 23.2 ALPHABETICAL LIST OF DATE AND TIME FUNCTIONS

| Function | Description |
|---|---|
| DATE(*year*,*month*,*day*) | Returns the serial number that represents a particular date. |
| DATEDIF(*start_date*,*end_date*,*unit*) | Calculates the number of days, months, or years between two dates. This function is provided for compatibility with Lotus 1-2-3. |
| DATEVALUE(*date_text*) | Returns the serial number of the date represented by *date_text*. You use DATEVALUE to convert a date represented by text to a serial number. |
| DAY(*serial_number*) | Returns the day of a date, represented by a serial number. The day is given as an integer ranging from 1 to 31. |
| DAYS360(*start_date*,*end_date*,*method*) | Returns the number of days between two dates, based on a 360-day year (that is, 12 30-day months), which is used in some accounting calculations. You use this function to help compute payments if your accounting system is based on 12 30-day months. |
| EDATE(*start_date*,*months*) | Returns the serial number that represents the date that is the indicated number of months before or after a specified date (that is, the *start_date*). You use EDATE to calculate maturity dates or due dates that fall on the same day of the month as the date of issue. |
| EOMONTH(*start_date*,*months*) | Returns the serial number for the last day of the month that is the indicated number of months before or after *start_date*. You use EOMONTH to calculate maturity dates or due dates that fall on the last day of the month. |
| HOUR(*serial_number*) | Returns the hour of a time value. The hour is given as an integer, ranging from 0 (12:00 a.m.) to 23 (11:00 p.m.). |
| MINUTE(*serial_number*) | Returns the minutes of a time value. The minutes are given as an integer, ranging from 0 to 59. |
| MONTH(*serial_number*) | Returns the month of a date represented by a serial number. The month is given as an integer, ranging from 1 (for January) to 12 (for December). |

| Function | Description |
|---|---|
| NETWORKDAYS(*start_date*,*end_date*,*holidays*) | Returns the number of whole working days between *start_date* and *end_date*. Working days exclude weekends and any dates identified in holidays. You use NETWORKDAYS to calculate employee benefits that accrue based on the number of days worked during a specific term. |
| NOW() | Returns the serial number of the current date and time. |
| SECOND(*serial_number*) | Returns the seconds of a time value. The seconds are given as an integer in the range 0 to 59. |
| TIME(*hour*,*minute*,*second*) | Returns the decimal number for a particular time. The decimal number returned by TIME is a value ranging from 0 to 0.99999999, representing the times from 0:00:00 (12:00:00 a.m.) to 23:59:59 (11:59:59 p.m.). |
| TIMEVALUE(*time_text*) | Returns the decimal number of the time represented by a text string. The decimal number is a value ranging from 0 to 0.99999999, representing the times from 0:00:00 (12:00:00 a.m.) to 23:59:59 (11:59:59 p.m.). |
| TODAY() | Returns the serial number of the current date. The serial number is the date/time code that Microsoft Excel uses for date and time calculations. |
| WEEKDAY(*serial_number*,*return_type*) | Returns the day of the week corresponding to a date. The day is given as an integer, ranging from 1 (for Sunday) to 7 (for Saturday), by default. |
| WEEKNUM(*serial_num*,*return_type*) | Returns a number that indicates where the week falls numerically within a year. |
| WORKDAY(*start_date*,*days*,*holidays*) | Returns a number that represents a date that is the indicated number of working days before or after a date (the starting date). Working days exclude weekends and any dates identified as holidays. You use WORKDAY to exclude weekends or holidays when you calculate invoice due dates, expected delivery times, or the number of days of work performed. To view the number as a date, you select Format, Cells, click Date in the Category box, and then click a date format in the Type box. |
| YEAR(*serial_number*) | Returns the year corresponding to a date. The year is returned as an integer in the range 1900 through 9999. |
| YEARFRAC(*start_date*,*end_date*,*basis*) | Calculates the fraction of the year represented by the number of whole days between two dates (*start_date* and *end_date*). You use the YEARFRAC worksheet function to identify the proportion of a whole year's benefits or obligations to assign to a specific term. |

23

Table 23.3 provides an alphabetical list of all of Excel 2007's text functions. Detailed examples of these functions are provided later in this chapter.

**TABLE 23.3 ALPHABETICAL LIST OF TEXT FUNCTIONS**

| Function | Description |
| --- | --- |
| ASC(*text*) | Changes full-width (double-byte) English letters or katakana within a character string to half-width (single-byte) characters. |
| BAHTTEXT(*number*) | Converts a number to Thai text and adds the suffix Baht. This function was new in Excel XP. |
| CHAR(*number*) | Returns the character specified by *number*. You use CHAR to translate code page numbers you might get from files on other types of computers into characters. |
| CLEAN(*text*) | Removes all nonprintable characters from text. You use CLEAN on text imported from other applications that contains characters that may not print with your operating system. For example, you can use CLEAN to remove some low-level computer code that is frequently at the beginning and end of data files and cannot be printed. |
| CODE(*text*) | Returns a numeric code for the first character in a text string. The returned code corresponds to the character set used by your computer. |
| CONCATENATE(*text1*,*text2*,...) | Joins several text strings into one text string. |
| DOLLAR(*number*,*decimals*) | Converts a number to text using currency format, with the decimals rounded to the specified place. The format used is $#,##0.00_);($#,##0.00). |
| EXACT(*text1*,*text2*) | Compares two text strings and returns TRUE if they are exactly the same, and FALSE otherwise. EXACT is case-sensitive but ignores formatting differences. You use EXACT to test text being entered into a document. |
| FIND(*find_text*,*within_text*, *start_num*) | Finds one text string (*find_text*) within another text string (*within_text*) and returns the number of the starting position of *find_text*, from the first character of *within_text*. You can also use SEARCH to find one text string within another, but unlike SEARCH, FIND is case-sensitive and doesn't allow wildcard characters. |
| FINDB(*find_text*,*within_text*, *start_num*) | Finds one text string (*find_text*) within another text string (*within_text*) and returns the number of the starting position of *find_text*, based on the number of bytes each character uses, from the first character of *within_text*. You use FINDB with double-byte characters. You can also use SEARCHB to find one text string within another. |

| Function | Description |
|---|---|
| FIXED(*number*,*decimals*,*no_commas*) | Rounds a number to the specified number of decimals, formats the number in decimal format using a period and commas, and returns the result as text. |
| JIS(*text*) | Changes half-width (single-byte) English letters or katakana within a character string to full-width (double-byte) characters. |
| LEFT(*text*,*num_chars*) | Returns the first character or characters in a text string, based on the number of characters specified. |
| LEFTB(*text*,*num_bytes*) | Returns the first character or characters in a text string, based on the number of bytes specified. You use LEFTB with double-byte characters. |
| LEN(*text*) | Returns the number of characters in a text string. |
| LENB(*text*) | Returns the number of bytes used to represent the characters in a text string. You use LENB with double-byte characters. |
| LOWER(*text*) | Converts all uppercase letters in a text string to lowercase. |
| MID(*text*,*start_num*,*num_chars*) | Returns a specific number of characters from a text string, starting at the position specified, based on the number of characters specified. |
| MIDB(*text*,*start_num*,*num_bytes*) | Returns a specific number of characters from a text string, starting at the position specified, based on the number of bytes specified. You use MIDB with double-byte characters. |
| PHONETIC(*reference*) | Extracts the phonetic (furigana) characters from a text string. Furigana are a Japanese reading aid. They consist of smaller kana printed next to a kanji to indicate its pronunciation. |
| PROPER(*text*) | Capitalizes the first letter in a text string and any other letters in text that follow any character other than a letter. Converts all other letters to lowercase. |
| REPLACE(*old_text*,*start_num*, *num_chars*,*new_text*) | Replaces part of a text string, based on the number of characters specified, with a different text string. |
| REPLACEB(*old_text*,*start_num*, *num_bytes*,*new_text*) | Replaces part of a text string, based on the number of bytes specified, with a different text string. You use REPLACEB with double-byte characters. |
| REPT(*text*,*number_times*) | Repeats text a given number of times. You use REPT to fill a cell with a number of instances of a text string. |
| RIGHT(*text*,*num_chars*) | Returns the last character or characters in a text string, based on the number of characters specified. |

*continues*

23

**TABLE 23.3 CONTINUED**

| Function | Description |
|---|---|
| RIGHTB(*text*,*num_bytes*) | Returns the last character or characters in a text string, based on the number of bytes specified. You use RIGHTB with double-byte characters. |
| SEARCH(*find_text*,*within_text*, *start_num*) | Returns the number of the character at which a specific character or text string is first found, beginning with *start_num*. You use SEARCH to determine the location of a character or text string within another text string so that you can use the MID or REPLACE functions to change the text. |
| SEARCHB(*find_text*,*within_text*, *start_num*) | Finds one text string (*find_text*) within another text string (*within_text*) and returns the number of the starting position of *find_text*. The result is based on the number of bytes each character uses, beginning with *start_num*. You use SEARCHB with double-byte characters You can also use FINDB to find one text string within another. |
| SUBSTITUTE(*text*,*old_text*, *new_text*,*instance_num*) | Substitutes *new_text* for *old_text* in a text string. You use SUBSTITUTE when you want to replace specific text in a text string; you use REPLACE when you want to replace any text that occurs in a specific location in a text string. |
| T(*value*) | Returns the text referred to by *value*. |
| TEXT(*value*,*format_text*) | Converts a value to text in a specific number format. |
| TRIM(*text*) | Removes all spaces from text except for single spaces between words. You use TRIM on text that you have received from another application that may have irregular spacing. |
| UPPER(*text*) | Converts text to uppercase. |
| VALUE(*text*) | Converts a text string that represents a number to a number. |
| YEN(*number*,*decimals*) | Converts a number to text, using the Japanese yen currency format, with the number rounded to a specified place. |

# EXAMPLES OF MATH FUNCTIONS

The most common formula in Excel is a formula to add a column of numbers. In addition to SUM, Excel offers a wide variety of mathematical functions.

## Using SUM to Add Numbers

The SUM function is by far the most commonly used function in Excel. This function can add numbers from one or more ranges of data.

Syntax: `=SUM(number1,number2,...)`

The SUM function adds all the numbers in a range of cells. The arguments *number1*, *number2*,... are 1 to 255 arguments for which you want the total value or sum.

A typical use of this function is `=SUM(B4:B12)`. It is also possible to use `=SUM(1,2,3)`. In the latter example, you cannot specify more than 255 individual values. In the former example, you can specify up to 255 ranges, each of which can include thousands of cells.

In Figure 23.1, cell B25 contains a formula to sum three individual cells: `=SUM(B17,B19,B23)`.

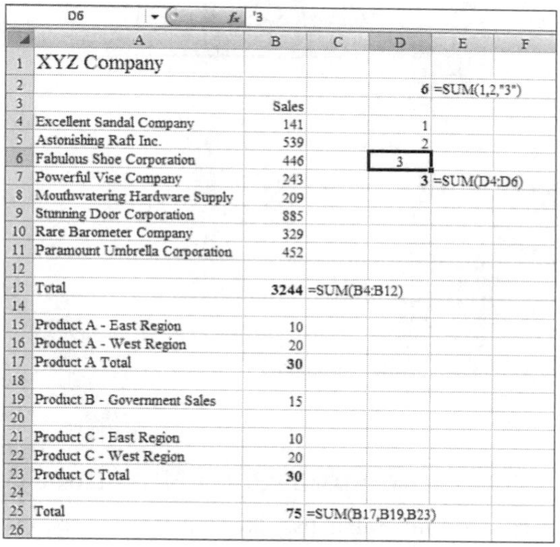

D6 | '3

| | A | B | C | D | E | F |
|---|---|---|---|---|---|---|
| 1 | XYZ Company | | | | | |
| 2 | | | | 6 | =SUM(1,2,"3") | |
| 3 | | Sales | | | | |
| 4 | Excellent Sandal Company | 141 | | 1 | | |
| 5 | Astonishing Raft Inc. | 539 | | 2 | | |
| 6 | Fabulous Shoe Corporation | 446 | | 3 | | |
| 7 | Powerful Vise Company | 243 | | 3 | =SUM(D4:D6) | |
| 8 | Mouthwatering Hardware Supply | 209 | | | | |
| 9 | Stunning Door Corporation | 885 | | | | |
| 10 | Rare Barometer Company | 329 | | | | |
| 11 | Paramount Umbrella Corporation | 452 | | | | |
| 12 | | | | | | |
| 13 | Total | 3244 | =SUM(B4:B12) | | | |
| 14 | | | | | | |
| 15 | Product A - East Region | 10 | | | | |
| 16 | Product A - West Region | 20 | | | | |
| 17 | Product A Total | 30 | | | | |
| 18 | | | | | | |
| 19 | Product B - Government Sales | 15 | | | | |
| 20 | | | | | | |
| 21 | Product C - East Region | 10 | | | | |
| 22 | Product C - West Region | 20 | | | | |
| 23 | Product C Total | 30 | | | | |
| 24 | | | | | | |
| 25 | Total | 75 | =SUM(B17,B19,B23) | | | |
| 26 | | | | | | |

**Figure 23.1**
A variety of SUM formulas

It is unlikely that you will need more than 255 arguments in this function, but if you do, you can group arguments in parentheses. For example, `=SUM((A10,A12),(A14,16))` would count as only 2 of the 255 allowed arguments.

If a text value that looks like a number is included in a range, the text value is not included in the result of the sum. Strangely enough, if you specify the text value directly as an argument in the function, Excel does add it to the result. For example, `=SUM(1,2,"3")` will be `6`, yet `=SUM(D4:D6)` in Figure 23.1 will result in `3`.

If one cell in a referenced range contains an error, the result of the SUM function is an error.

It is valid to create a spearing formula. This type of formula adds the identical cell from many worksheets. For example, `=SUM(Jan:Dec!B20)` would add Cell B20 on all 12 sheets between January and December.

To quickly enter a SUM formula, you can press Alt+= or click the AutoSum icon on the Formulas ribbon. In Figure 23.2, pressing the AutoSum icon will add totals to the 13 selected blank cells all at once (see Figure 23.3).

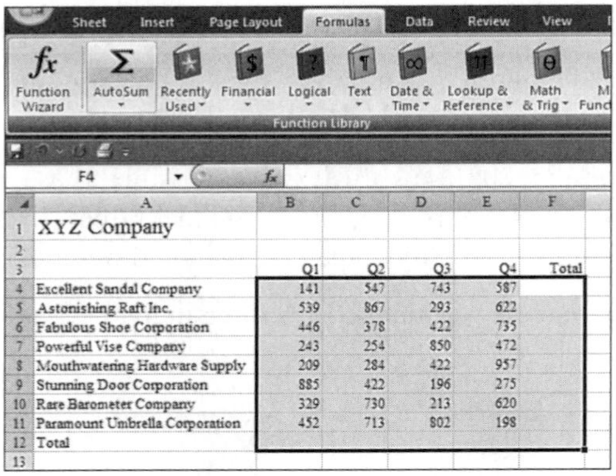

**Figure 23.2**
The AutoSum icon (the Greek letter sigma) adds sum formulas to all the selected cells at once.

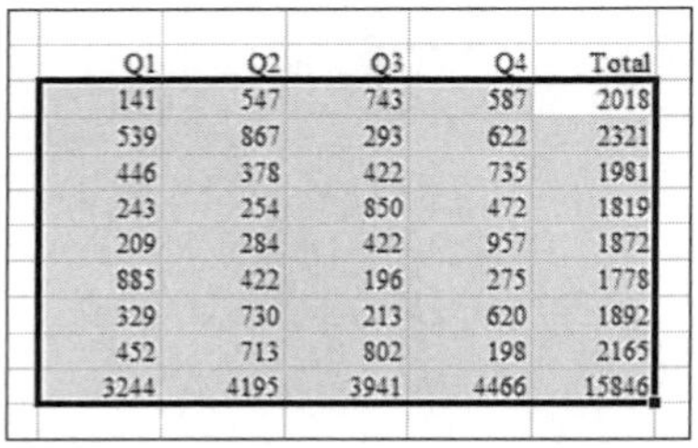

**Figure 23.3**
After clicking AutoSum, the total formulas are automatically entered.

## USING COUNT OR COUNTA TO COUNT NUMBERS OR NONBLANK CELLS

A number of functions process nonblank cells. =COUNT counts all the numeric or date cells in a range. =COUNTA counts all the nonblank cells in a range.

CAUTION

> COUNT and COUNTA are found in the Statistical drop-down under the More Functions icon of the Formulas ribbon.

SYNTAX: =COUNT(*value1*,*value2*,...)

The COUNT function counts the number of cells that contain numbers and also numbers within the list of arguments. You use COUNT to get the number of numeric entries in a range or array.

The arguments *value1*, *value2*,... are 1 to 255 arguments that can contain or refer to a variety of different types of data, but only numbers are counted.

Note that while a single error cell in a range causes the SUM function to return an error, the same condition is ignored in the COUNT function.

=COUNT(1,2,"3") results in the text entry being counted. If you refer to a range that contains text that looks like a number, the text is not included in the count.

SYNTAX: =COUNTA(*value1*,*value2*,...)

COUNTA counts the number of cells that are not empty and the values within the list of arguments. You use COUNTA to count the number of cells that contain data in a range or an array.

The arguments *value1*, *value2*,... are 1 to 255 arguments representing the values you want to count. In this case, a value is any type of information, including empty text ("") but not including empty cells. If an argument is an array or a reference, empty cells within the array or reference are ignored. If you do not need to count logical values, text, or error values, you should use the COUNT function.

Note that error cells are included in the results from COUNTA.

CHOOSING BETWEEN COUNT AND COUNTA

The key to choosing between COUNT and COUNTA is to analyze the data that you want to count. In Figure 23.4, someone has used X's in Column B to indicate that training has been started. In this case, you would use COUNTA to get an accurate count. Column C contains dates (which are treated as numeric). In Column C, either COUNT or COUNTA returns the correct result. Column D has a mix of text and numeric entries. If you want to count how many people took the test, you use COUNTA. If you want to count how many people received a numeric score, you use COUNT.

**Figure 23.4**
Whether you use COUNT or COUNTA depends on whether your data is numeric. COUNT counts only dates and numeric entries. COUNTA counts anything that is nonblank.

| D18 | | $f_x$ =COUNTA(D2:D15) | | |
|---|---|---|---|---|
| | A | B | C | D |
| | | Training Started | Training Complete | Test Score |
| 1 | NAME | | | |
| 2 | TERRY LEBLANC | | | |
| 3 | LUIS CHRISTENSEN | X | 3/1/2007 | 97 |
| 4 | JENNIFER GALLOWAY | X | | |
| 5 | ROSEMARY ATKINS | X | 3/15/2007 | 85 |
| 6 | GLORIA DUNLAP | X | | |
| 7 | PATSY WARD | | | |
| 8 | CLAIRE RUSH | X | 3/7/2007 | Incomplete |
| 9 | MARIE HOFFMAN | X | | |
| 10 | JEANNE CLEMONS | | | |
| 11 | MARJORIE LOPEZ | X | 3/5/2007 | 92 |
| 12 | JACOB INGRAM | X | | |
| 13 | EDWARD HOOD | | | |
| 14 | MARTIN HAYES | X | 3/9/2007 | 45 |
| 15 | CHARLENE BURKE | X | | |
| 16 | | | | |
| 17 | COUNT: | 0 | 5 | 4 |
| 18 | COUNTA: | 10 | 5 | 5 |
| 19 | | | | |

CAUTION

> Using more than 30 arguments in COUNT or COUNTA causes backward compatibility problems with Excel 2003 and earlier.

## USING ROUND, ROUNDDOWN, ROUNDUP, INT, TRUNC, FLOOR, CEILING, EVEN, ODD, OR MROUND TO REMOVE DECIMALS OR ROUND NUMBERS

A wide variety of functions—including ROUND, ROUNDDOWN, ROUNDUP, INT, TRUNC, FLOOR, CEILING, EVEN, ODD, and MROUND—can be used to round a result or to remove decimals from a result.

SYNTAX: =TRUNC(*number*), =INT(*number*), =EVEN(*number*), and =ODD(*number*)

The TRUNC, INT, EVEN, and ODD functions always change a number to an integer. The syntax in each case is similar: The function accepts a single number or a single cell containing a number.

To remove the decimals from a result, you use the =TRUNC function. This truncates a number to the integer portion of the number. For example, =TRUNC(1.9) is 1, and =TRUNC(-1.9) is -1.

To remove the decimals from a result and always round down to the next lowest integer, you use =INT. For positive numbers, TRUNC and INT return identical values. There is a subtle difference between TRUNC and INT. When you have a negative number, INT rounds away from zero to produce the next lowest integer. Thus, =INT(-1.1) is -2.

EVEN rounds a number away from zero to the next even integer. For example, =EVEN(3) is 4, and =EVEN(-3) is -4. If the number is already an even integer, no adjustment is made; for example, =EVEN(6) is 6. This function is ideal for ordering products packed two to a case.

ODD rounds a number away from zero to the next odd integer. For example, =ODD(1.1) is 3, and =ODD(-3.1) is -5. If the number is already an odd integer, no adjustment is made.

Figure 23.5 compares the results of TRUNC, INT, EVEN, and ODD.

**Figure 23.5**
TRUNC and INT are nearly identical, except when the numbers become negative.

| B2 | | $f_x$ =INT(A2) | | |
|---|---|---|---|---|
| | A | B | C | D | E |
| | | INT | TRUNC | EVEN | ODD |
| 1 | | INT | TRUNC | EVEN | ODD |
| 2 | 2.5 | 2 | 2 | 4 | 3 |
| 3 | 2 | 2 | 2 | 2 | 3 |
| 4 | 1.5 | 1 | 1 | 2 | 3 |
| 5 | 1 | 1 | 1 | 2 | 1 |
| 6 | 0.5 | 0 | 0 | 2 | 1 |
| 7 | 0 | 0 | 0 | 0 | 1 |
| 8 | -0.5 | -1 | 0 | -2 | -1 |
| 9 | -1 | -1 | -1 | -2 | -1 |
| 10 | -1.5 | -2 | -1 | -2 | -3 |
| 11 | -2 | -2 | -2 | -2 | -3 |
| 12 | -2.5 | -3 | -2 | -4 | -3 |

SYNTAX: =ROUND(*number*,*num_digits*), ROUNDUP(*number*,*num_digits*), and ROUNDDOWN(*number*,*num_digits*)

Three more functions—ROUND, ROUNDUP, and ROUNDDOWN—round a number to a specified number of decimal places. They all take the following arguments:

- *number*—This is the number you want to round.
- *num_digits*—This specifies the number of digits to which you want to round number.

With ROUND, if the number of digits is zero, the number is rounded to the nearest integer, following these rules:

- Values up to 0.49 are rounded toward zero. For example, ROUND(1.49,0) results in 1, and ROUND(-1.49,0) results in -1.
- Values of 0.5 and above are rounded away from zero. For example, ROUND(1.5,0) results in 2, and ROUND(-1.5,0) results in -2.

If the num_digits is positive, the number is rounded to have the specified number of decimal places. If the number of digits is negative, the number is rounded to the left of the decimal point. For example, ROUND(117,-1) is rounded to the nearest 10, or a value of 120.

To override the rounding rules, you can use ROUNDDOWN or ROUNDUP:

- The ROUNDDOWN function always rounds toward zero. For example, =ROUNDDOWN(1.999,0) rounds to 1, and =ROUNDDOWN(-19.999,0) rounds to -19. You might use this function when judging a contest in which if the entrant does not completely finish a task, he or she does not get credit for the unfinished portion of the task.
- The result of the ROUNDUP function always rounds away from zero. For example, =ROUNDUP(1.01,0) rounds up to 2, and =ROUNDUP(-1.01,0) rounds to -2. You might use this function when calculating prices because if the customer uses any fractional portion of a product, he or she is charged for the complete product.

Using a negative number for the number of digits provides an interesting result. If you need to round a number to the nearest thousand, you can indicate that it should be rounded to -3 decimal places. For example, ROUND(1,234,567,-3) would be 1,235,000.

Figure 23.6 compares ROUND, ROUNDUP, and ROUNDDOWN.

**Figure 23.6**
These three functions always round to a power of 10.

| | A | B | C | D | E |
|---|---|---|---|---|---|
| 1 | Number | # Digits | Round | Round Up | Round Down |
| 2 | 314159.265359 | 5 | 314159.265360 | 314159.265360 | 314159.265350 |
| 3 | 314159.265359 | 4 | 314159.265400 | 314159.265400 | 314159.265300 |
| 4 | 314159.265359 | 3 | 314159.265 | 314159.266 | 314159.265 |
| 5 | 314159.265359 | 2 | 314159.27 | 314159.27 | 314159.26 |
| 6 | 314159.265359 | 1 | 314159.3 | 314159.3 | 314159.2 |
| 7 | 314159.265359 | 0 | 314159 | 314160 | 314159 |
| 8 | 314159.265359 | -1 | 314160 | 314160 | 314150 |
| 9 | 314159.265359 | -2 | 314200 | 314200 | 314100 |
| 10 | 314159.265359 | -3 | 314000 | 315000 | 314000 |
| 11 | 314159.265359 | -4 | 310000 | 320000 | 310000 |
| 12 | 314159.265359 | -5 | 300000 | 400000 | 300000 |
| 13 | 1.500000 | 0 | 2 | 2 | 1 |
| 14 | -1.500000 | 0 | -2 | -2 | -1 |
| 15 | 1.490000 | 0 | 1 | 2 | 1 |
| 16 | -1.490000 | 0 | -1 | -2 | -1 |
| 17 | | | | | |

C2 — fx =ROUND(A2,B2)

SYNTAX: =MROUND(*number*,*multiple*), =CEILING(*number*,*signifigance*), and =FLOOR(*number*,*significance*)

The last three functions in this group—MROUND, CEILING, and FLOOR—round a number to a certain multiple. They require you to enter the number and the multiple to which to round. They all take the following arguments:

- *number*—This is the number you want to round.

- *multiple* or *significance*—This is the nearest multiple that you want to round toward. Note that if *number* is negative, *multiple* or *significance* must also be negative.

Say that you handle pricing for a line of products. Your general rule is to mark up the product cost, which results in a series of strange prices, such as $185.9375, as shown in Figure 23.7. To round each price to the nearest increment of $5, you would use =MROUND(C2,5). You could also use MROUND to round to the nearest quarter: =MROUND(C2,0.25).

**Figure 23.7**
MROUND rounds a price to a certain multiple. Here, Column D is the calculated prices rounded to the nearest $5.

| | A | B | C | D | E |
|---|---|---|---|---|---|
| 1 | SKU | COST | LIST | PRICE | |
| 2 | D194 | 87.81 | 185.938 | 185 | |
| 3 | A274 | 14.94 | 34.125 | 35 | |
| 4 | B274 | 21.31 | 47.3958 | 45 | |
| 5 | A164 | 12.75 | 29.5625 | 30 | |
| 6 | F229 | 86.55 | 183.313 | 185 | |

D2 — fx =MROUND(C2,5)

The *multiple* argument in MROUND is allowed to be negative.

CAUTION

> There is one strange behavior to look out for with MROUND, FLOOR, and CEILING. If the number is negative, you must ensure that the second argument for the function is also negative. There certainly could be situations in which you don't know in advance whether your numbers will be negative. If you think that your numbers might be a mix of positive and negative values, you should use =MROUND(C2,5*SIGN(C2)). This will ensure that the second parameter matches the sign of the first parameter.

In other situations, you may want to round a number up to a certain multiple. Figure 23.8 shows a requisition list. Column A shows the quantity needed, and Column B shows the item. The purchasing agent discovered a vendor who offers a significant discount, but only if you buy in complete case quantities. Column C shows the size of the case for each product. To calculate the total number to order, you need to round a number in Column A up to the nearest multiple of the case size found in Column C. You use =CEILING(A4,C4) to achieve this effect.

**Figure 23.8**
CEILING rounds a number up to the next multiple.

| D4 | | | fx | =CEILING(A4,C4) | |
|---|---|---|---|---|---|
| | A | B | C | D | E |
| 1 | Orders for full cases receive a 25% discount | | | | |
| 2 | | | | | |
| 3 | Quantity Needed | Product | Case Pack | Optimal Order | |
| 4 | 121 | A108 | 8 | 128 | |
| 5 | 110 | A116 | 16 | 112 | |
| 6 | 108 | B108 | 8 | 112 | |
| 7 | 172 | C108 | 8 | 176 | |
| 8 | 176 | D108 | 8 | 176 | |
| 9 | 12 | E124 | 24 | 24 | |

CEILING rounds away from zero. If you use =CEILING(-9,-6), the function rounds -9 to -12.

The FLOOR function rounds a number to the next lowest multiple. Say that you employ several student workers who do piece work. They assemble products and then pack them six to a case. Your contract with the workers says that you only pay for complete cases. Column B in Figure 23.9 shows the total number of units assembled. You use =FLOOR(B6,6) to round this quantity down to the nearest multiple of six. Note that if the value is already a multiple of six, as in Cell B10, FLOOR does not change the number.

All the functions for rounding can actually be replaced with a clever combination of INT and ROUND functions. If you receive a spreadsheet from an old-time Lotus 1-2-3 user, you may see formulas like the ones in Figure 23.10:

■ Cell B13 is equivalent to using MROUND with a multiple of 20. The formula divides 135 by 20, giving 6.75. ROUND rounds this to 7. Finally, outside the parentheses, the formula multiplies by 20 to arrive at the answer of 140.

- Cell C13 is equivalent to using FLOOR with a significance of 20. The formula divides 135 by 20, giving 6.75. The INT removes the decimal places, leaving the integer 6. The formula then multiplies this result by 20 to arrive at 120.

- Cell D13 is equivalent to using CEILING with a significance of 20. The formula divides 135 by 20, giving 6.75. Next, the formula adds just less than 0.5 to make sure that any value greater than 6 is rounded up to 7. Finally, the result is multiplied by 20 to arrive at 140.

**Figure 23.9**
FLOOR rounds a number down to the next multiple.

| | D6 | | | $f_x$ | =FLOOR(B6,C6) | |
|---|---|---|---|---|---|---|
| | A | B | C | D | E | |
| 1 | Piece Work Supply | | | | | |
| 2 | Productivity Report | | | | | |
| 3 | Workers are Paid for Complete Cases only | | | | | |
| 4 | | | | | | |
| 5 | NAME | Quantity Complete | Per Case | Complete Case Quantity | | |
| 6 | LAURIE | 846 | 6 | 846 | | |
| 7 | JOE | 658 | 6 | 654 | | |
| 8 | BRUCE | 1186 | 6 | 1182 | | |
| 9 | MELVIN | 968 | 6 | 966 | | |
| 10 | OLIVIA | 942 | 6 | 942 | | |

**Figure 23.10**
A combination of ROUND and INT can replace any of the eight other functions used for rounding.

| | D13 | | | $f_x$ | =ROUND((A13/20)+0.49,0)*20 | |
|---|---|---|---|---|---|---|
| | A | B | C | D | E | F |
| 1 | | Nearest 20 | Prev 20 | Next 20 | | |
| 2 | 348 | 340 | 340 | 360 | | |
| 3 | 780 | 780 | 780 | 780 | | |
| 4 | 82 | 80 | 80 | 100 | | |
| 5 | 480 | 480 | 480 | 480 | | |
| 6 | 644 | 640 | 640 | 660 | | |
| 7 | 300 | 300 | 300 | 300 | | |
| 8 | 630 | 640 | 620 | 640 | | |
| 9 | 454 | 460 | 440 | 460 | | |
| 10 | 658 | 660 | 640 | 660 | | |
| 11 | 521 | 520 | 520 | 540 | | |
| 12 | 87 | 80 | 80 | 100 | | |
| 13 | 135 | 140 | 120 | 140 | | |
| 14 | B13: =ROUND((A13/20),0)*20 | | | | | |
| 15 | C13: =INT(A13/20)*20 | | | | | |
| 16 | D13: =ROUND((A13/20)+0.49,0)*20 | | | | | |
| 17 | | | | | | |
| 18 | | | | | | |

In previous versions of Excel, functions such as MROUND were not part of the core Excel. They were enabled when someone installed the Analysis Toolpack. Because new Excel users might never have installed the Analysis Toolpack, some people would avoid using MROUND and would instead write the formulas as shown in Figure 23.10. Now that Microsoft has elevated all the Analysis Toolpack functions to be part of the core Excel 2007 product, it is safe to use those functions.

## USING SUBTOTAL INSTEAD OF SUM WITH MULTIPLE LEVELS OF TOTALS

Consider the dataset shown in Figure 23.11. This report shows a list of invoices for each customer. Someone has manually inserted rows and used the SUM function to total each customer. Cells C5, C10, C15, and so on contain a SUM function.

**Figure 23.11**
Whoever manually summed these rows doesn't know about the Subtotal command on the Data ribbon.

| | A | B | C |
|---|---|---|---|
| | C5 | | $f_x$ =SUM(C2:C4) |
| 1 | Customer | Invoice | Revenue |
| 2 | Amazing Flagpole Corporation | 1158 | 114.93 |
| 3 | Amazing Flagpole Corporation | 1127 | 622.12 |
| 4 | Amazing Flagpole Corporation | 1118 | 736.38 |
| 5 | Amazing Flagpole Corporation | Total | 1473.43 |
| 6 | | | |
| 7 | Brilliant Washer Partners | 1139 | 430.33 |
| 8 | Brilliant Washer Partners | 1129 | 614.59 |
| 9 | Brilliant Washer Partners | 1146 | 346.09 |
| 10 | Brilliant Washer Partners | Total | 1391.01 |
| 11 | | | |
| 12 | Compelling Shovel Company | 1123 | 670.62 |

It would be very difficult to enter a grand total at the bottom of this dataset. You might have to enter a long formula that only points at the summary rows. In this particular case, the formula to provide a grand total for 15 customers would be possible, as shown in Figure 23.12. If you had 500 customers, however, the formula would be nearly impossible to enter.

**Figure 23.12**
It is difficult to enter the grand total formula.

| | A | B | C | D | E | F | G | H |
|---|---|---|---|---|---|---|---|---|
| | C77 | | $f_x$ =C5+C10+C15+C20+C25+C30+C35+C40+C45+C50+C55+C60+C65+C70+C75 | | | | | |
| 1 | Customer | Invoice | Revenue | | | | | |
| 69 | Supreme Washer Supply | 1148 | 341.13 | | | | | |
| 70 | Supreme Washer Supply | Total | 1533.86 | | | | | |
| 71 | | | | | | | | |
| 72 | Well-Suited Utensil Corporation | 1120 | 709.41 | | | | | |
| 73 | Well-Suited Utensil Corporation | 1153 | 224.07 | | | | | |
| 74 | Well-Suited Utensil Corporation | 1122 | 690.03 | | | | | |
| 75 | Well-Suited Utensil Corporation | Total | 1623.51 | | | | | |
| 76 | | | | | | | | |
| 77 | GRAND TOTAL | | 20598.01 | | | | | |
| 78 | | | | | | | | |
| 79 | | | | | | | | |
| 80 | | | | | | | | |

Many accountants can teach you the old accounting trick that you can actually total the entire column and divide by two in order to get the grand total. This is based on the assumption that every dollar is in the column twice: once on the detail row and once on the summary row. As shown in Figure 23.13, this trick does work, but it is hard to explain to your manager why it works.

The solution is to use the SUBTOTAL function. This powerful function is relatively new; it was introduced in Excel 97.

**Figure 23.13**
The old accounting trick of adding an entire column and dividing by two works but is hard to explain.

| | A | B | C |
|---|---|---|---|
| | C77 | fx | =SUM(C2:C75)/2 |
| 1 | Customer | Invoice | Revenue |
| 63 | Secure Adhesive Supply | 1117 | 757.14 |
| 64 | Secure Adhesive Supply | 1130 | 605.52 |
| 65 | **Secure Adhesive Supply** | **Total** | **1864.11** |
| 66 | | | |
| 67 | Supreme Washer Supply | 1133 | 562.94 |
| 68 | Supreme Washer Supply | 1126 | 629.79 |
| 69 | Supreme Washer Supply | 1148 | 341.13 |
| 70 | **Supreme Washer Supply** | **Total** | **1533.86** |
| 71 | | | |
| 72 | Well-Suited Utensil Corporation | 1120 | 709.41 |
| 73 | Well-Suited Utensil Corporation | 1153 | 224.07 |
| 74 | Well-Suited Utensil Corporation | 1122 | 690.03 |
| 75 | **Well-Suited Utensil Corporation** | **Total** | **1623.51** |
| 76 | | | |
| 77 | **GRAND TOTAL** | | **20598.01** |
| 78 | | | |

**TIP FROM**

*Bill Jelen*

The best way to insert the SUBTOTAL function is to use the Subtotals icon on the Data ribbon, as described in Chapter 35, "More Tips and Tricks for Excel 2007." However, you can set up these functions manually.

SYNTAX: =SUBTOTAL(*function_num,ref1,ref2,...*)

In its default use, SUBTOTAL works just like the SUM function, except it throws out other instances of the SUBTOTAL function within the range being summed. The SUBTOTAL function takes the following arguments:

- *function_num*—This is a number from 1 to 11. The most common function number is the number 9, which (for no logical reason) is used to sum. When Microsoft introduced the SUBTOTAL function, it offered 11 options: AVERAGE, COUNT, COUNTA, MAX, MIN, PRODUCT, STDEV, STDEVP, SUM, VAR, and VARP. It just happens that SUM is the ninth item in this list when these functions are arranged alphabetically in the English language, so 9 became the function number for SUM.

- *ref1,ref2,...* —These are up to 29 ranges or references that you want to subtotal. Unlike with SUM, the references in a SUBTOTAL function cannot be 3D references.

Any other nested subtotals in the range are ignored to prevent double counting.

The SUBTOTAL function always ignores rows hidden as the result of a filter. This makes the SUBTOTAL function great in combination with autofilter, as you'll see later in this chapter, in Figure 23.15.

A feature added in Excel 2002 is that you can add 100 to the function number in order to prevent Excel from including rows hidden by using the Hide command. Note that this functionality works only with hidden rows. If you hide columns and attempt to subtotal in a horizontal fashion, the hidden columns are not ignored.

TABLE 23.4—FUNCTION ARGUMENTS FOR SUBTOTAL

| function_num (Includes Hidden Values) | function_num (Ignores Hidden Values) | Function |
|---|---|---|
| 1 | 101 | AVERAGE |
| 2 | 102 | COUNT |
| 3 | 103 | COUNTA |
| 4 | 104 | MAX |
| 5 | 105 | MIN |
| 6 | 106 | PRODUCT |
| 7 | 107 | STDEV |
| 8 | 108 | STDEVP |
| 9 | 109 | SUM |
| 10 | 110 | VAR |
| 11 | 111 | VARP |

In Figure 23.14, the customer summary rows were built with the SUBTOTAL function, allowing the grand total row to be calculated with the simple formula =SUBTOTAL(9,C2:C76).

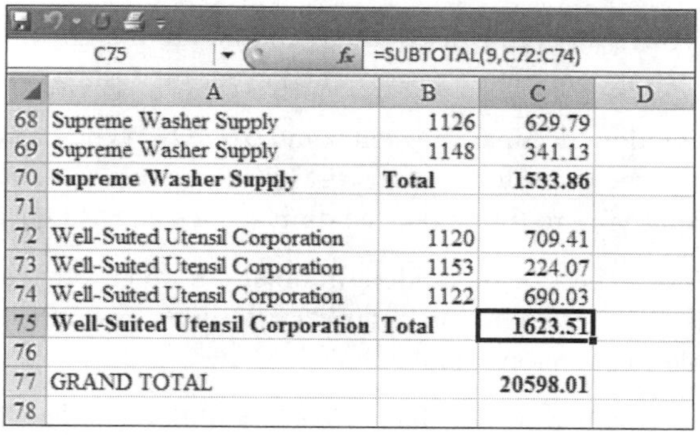

**Figure 23.14**
When you use SUBTOTAL instead of SUM for the customer totals, the problem of creating a grand total becomes simple.

USING SUBTOTAL INSTEAD OF SUM TO IGNORE ROWS HIDDEN BY A FILTER

If you are using autofilter to query a dataset, you can use the SUBTOTAL function instead of the SUM function in order to show the total of the visible rows. In Figure 23.15, Cell E1 contains a SUM function, which totals rows whether they are visible or not. Cell E2 contains a SUBTOTAL function. As you use the autofilter drop-downs to show just rows for sales of J730 by Jamie, the SUBTOTAL function updates to reflect the total of the visible rows. This makes the SUBTOTAL function a great tool for ad hoc reporting.

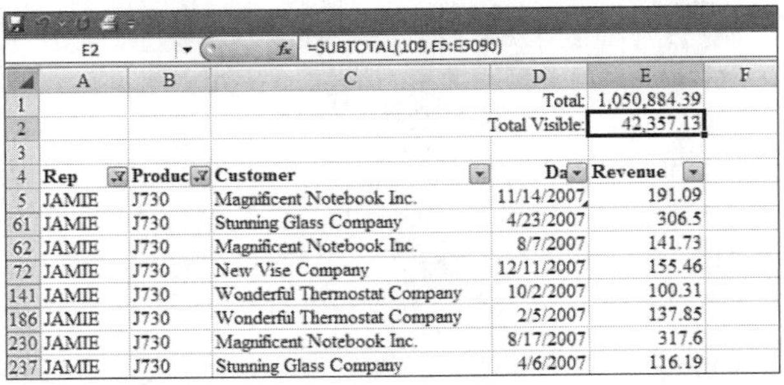
E2 =SUBTOTAL(109,E5:E5090)

| | A | B | C | D | E | F |
|---|---|---|---|---|---|---|
| 1 | | | | Total: | 1,050,884.39 | |
| 2 | | | | Total Visible: | 42,357.13 | |
| 3 | | | | | | |
| 4 | Rep | Produc | Customer | Da | Revenue | |
| 5 | JAMIE | J730 | Magnificent Notebook Inc. | 11/14/2007 | 191.09 | |
| 61 | JAMIE | J730 | Stunning Glass Company | 4/23/2007 | 306.5 | |
| 62 | JAMIE | J730 | Magnificent Notebook Inc. | 8/7/2007 | 141.73 | |
| 72 | JAMIE | J730 | New Vise Company | 12/11/2007 | 155.46 | |
| 141 | JAMIE | J730 | Wonderful Thermostat Company | 10/2/2007 | 100.31 | |
| 186 | JAMIE | J730 | Wonderful Thermostat Company | 2/5/2007 | 137.85 | |
| 230 | JAMIE | J730 | Magnificent Notebook Inc. | 8/17/2007 | 317.6 | |
| 237 | JAMIE | J730 | Stunning Glass Company | 4/6/2007 | 116.19 | |

**Figure 23.15**
The SUBTOTAL function in Cell E2 ignores rows hidden as the result of a filter.

**NOTE**

> Although the function in Figure 23.15 uses the function number 109, the Subtotal command always ignores rows hidden as the result of a filter. =SUBTOTAL(9,E5:E5090) would return an identical result.

## USING RAND AND RANDBETWEEN TO GENERATE RANDOM NUMBERS AND DATA

There are a number of situations in which you might want to generate random numbers. Excel offers two functions to assist with this process: RAND and RANDBETWEEN.

### SYNTAX: =RAND()

The RAND function returns an evenly distributed random number greater than or equal to 0 and less than 1. A new random number is returned every time the worksheet is calculated.

=RAND() generates a random decimal between 0 and 0.99999. Whether you are a teacher trying to randomly assign the order for book report presentations, or the commissioner of a fantasy football league trying to figure out the draft sequence, =RAND() can help.

If you want to use RAND to generate a random number but don't want the numbers to change every time the cell is calculated, you can enter =RAND() in the formula bar and then press F9 to change the formula to a random number.

To generate a random number greater than or equal to 0 but less than 100, you can use RAND()*100.

To generate a random sequence for a list, you select a blank column next to your data and enter =RAND() in the column. Every time you press the F9 key, the column generates a new set of random numbers. You might want to agree up front with the draft participants that you will press F9 three times to randomize the list and then convert the formulas to values. To do so, you follow these steps:

1. Enter the heading `Random` in Row 1 next to your data.
2. Enter `=RAND()` in Cell B2.
3. Move the cell pointer to Cell B2 and double-click the fill handle.
4. Turn off automatic calculation. From the Office icon in the upper-left corner, choose Excel Options, Formulas and then choose Manually in the Calculation options section. Click OK to return to the worksheet.
5. Press the F9 key three times.
6. Choose one cell in Column B.
7. From the Home ribbon, choose Sort & Filter, Sort Smallest to Largest. The new sequence of items in Column A is a random sequence (see Figure 23.16).



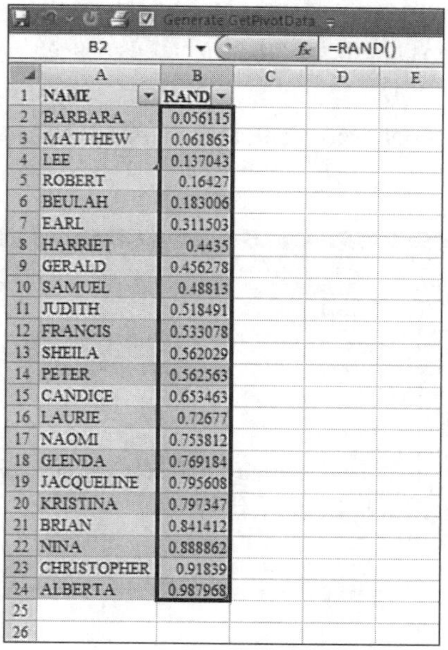

| | A | B | C | D | E |
|---|---|---|---|---|---|
| 1 | NAME | RAND | | | |
| 2 | BARBARA | 0.056115 | | | |
| 3 | MATTHEW | 0.061863 | | | |
| 4 | LEE | 0.137043 | | | |
| 5 | ROBERT | 0.16427 | | | |
| 6 | BEULAH | 0.183006 | | | |
| 7 | EARL | 0.311503 | | | |
| 8 | HARRIET | 0.4435 | | | |
| 9 | GERALD | 0.456278 | | | |
| 10 | SAMUEL | 0.48813 | | | |
| 11 | JUDITH | 0.518491 | | | |
| 12 | FRANCIS | 0.533078 | | | |
| 13 | SHEILA | 0.562029 | | | |
| 14 | PETER | 0.562563 | | | |
| 15 | CANDICE | 0.653463 | | | |
| 16 | LAURIE | 0.72677 | | | |
| 17 | NAOMI | 0.753812 | | | |
| 18 | GLENDA | 0.769184 | | | |
| 19 | JACQUELINE | 0.795608 | | | |
| 20 | KRISTINA | 0.797347 | | | |
| 21 | BRIAN | 0.841412 | | | |
| 22 | NINA | 0.888862 | | | |
| 23 | CHRISTOPHER | 0.91839 | | | |
| 24 | ALBERTA | 0.987968 | | | |
| 25 | | | | | |
| 26 | | | | | |

**Figure 23.16**
Barbara gets to draft first in this season's fantasy football league, thanks to the `RAND` function.

You can also use this technique to select a random subset from a dataset. If your manager wants you to contact every 20th customer, you can select all the customers where `=RAND()` is 0.05 or less.

SYNTAX: `=RANDBETWEEN(bottom,top)`

Whereas `=RAND()` returns a random decimal, `=RANDBETWEEN` generates an integer between two integers.

The `RANDBETWEEN` function returns a random number between the numbers you specify. A new random number is returned every time the worksheet is calculated. This function takes the following arguments:

- *`bottom`*—This is the smallest integer `RANDBETWEEN` can return.
- *`top`*—This is the largest integer `RANDBETWEEN` can return.

23

To generate random numbers between 50 and 59, inclusive, you use `=RANDBETWEEN(50,59)`. `RANDBETWEEN` is easier to use than `=RAND` to achieve random integers; with `=RAND`, you would have to use `=INT(RAND()*10)+50` to generate this same range of data.

Even though `RANDBETWEEN` generates integers, you can use it to generate sales prices or even letters. `=RANDBETWEEN(5000,9900)/100` generates random prices between $50.00 and $99.00.

The capital letter A is also known as character 65 in the ASCII character set. B is 66, C is 67, and so on up through Z, which is character 90. You can use `=CHAR(RANDBETWEEN(65,90))` to generate random capital letters.

Many of the product SKUs in this book were generated using `=CHAR(RANDBETWEEN(65,90))& RANDBETWEEN(101,199)`.

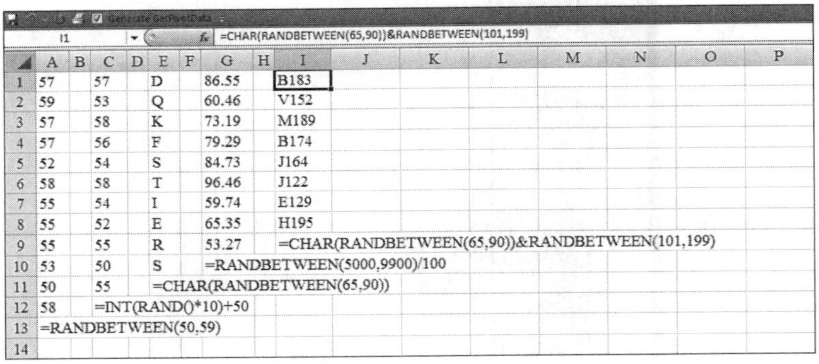

I1 =CHAR(RANDBETWEEN(65,90))&RANDBETWEEN(101,199)

| | A | B | C | D | E | F | G | H | I | J | K | L | M | N | O | P |
|---|---|---|---|---|---|---|---|---|---|---|---|---|---|---|---|---|
| 1 | 57 | | 57 | | D | | 86.55 | | B183 | | | | | | | |
| 2 | 59 | | 53 | | Q | | 60.46 | | V152 | | | | | | | |
| 3 | 57 | | 58 | | K | | 73.19 | | M189 | | | | | | | |
| 4 | 57 | | 56 | | F | | 79.29 | | B174 | | | | | | | |
| 5 | 52 | | 54 | | S | | 84.73 | | J164 | | | | | | | |
| 6 | 58 | | 58 | | T | | 96.46 | | J122 | | | | | | | |
| 7 | 55 | | 54 | | I | | 59.74 | | E129 | | | | | | | |
| 8 | 55 | | 52 | | E | | 65.35 | | H195 | | | | | | | |
| 9 | 55 | | 55 | | R | | 53.27 | | =CHAR(RANDBETWEEN(65,90))&RANDBETWEEN(101,199) | | | | | | | |
| 10 | 53 | | 50 | | S | | =RANDBETWEEN(5000,9900)/100 | | | | | | | | | |
| 11 | 50 | | 55 | | =CHAR(RANDBETWEEN(65,90)) | | | | | | | | | | | |
| 12 | 58 | | =INT(RAND()*10)+50 | | | | | | | | | | | | | |
| 13 | =RANDBETWEEN(50,59) | | | | | | | | | | | | | | | |
| 14 | | | | | | | | | | | | | | | | |

**Figure 23.17**
`RANDBETWEEN` can generate integers, or, with a little creativity, prices or letters.

### CHOOSING A RANDOM ITEM FROM A LIST

In Figure 23.18, you want to randomly assign employees to certain projects. The list of projects is in Column A. The list of employees is in E2:E6. As shown in Figure 23.18, the function for B2:B11 is `=INDEX($E$2:$E$6,RANDBETWEEN(1,5))`.

## USING =ROMAN() TO FINISH MOVIE CREDITS

Excel can convert numbers to Roman numerals. If you stay in the theater after a movie until the very end of movie credits, you will see that the copyright date is always expressed in Roman numerals. If you are the next Steven Spielberg, you can use `=ROMAN(2007)` or `=ROMAN(YEAR(Now()))` to generate such a numeral.

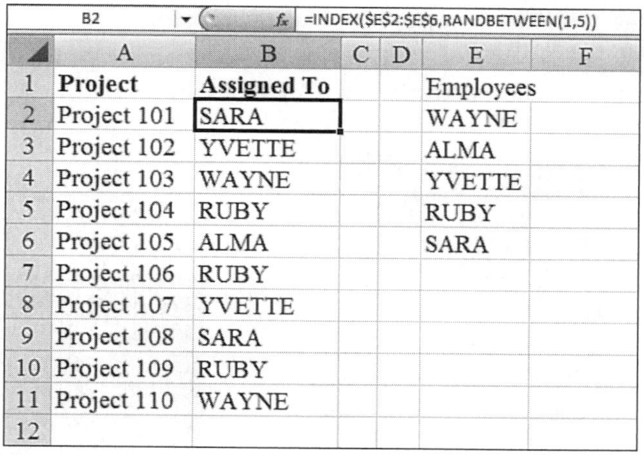

**Figure 23.18**
I wonder if Dilbert's pointy-haired boss assigns projects this way.

| | A | B | C | D | E | F |
|---|---|---|---|---|---|---|
| | B2 | ▼ | | *fx* | =INDEX($E$2:$E$6,RANDBETWEEN(1,5)) | |
| 1 | **Project** | **Assigned To** | | | Employees | |
| 2 | Project 101 | SARA | | | WAYNE | |
| 3 | Project 102 | YVETTE | | | ALMA | |
| 4 | Project 103 | WAYNE | | | YVETTE | |
| 5 | Project 104 | RUBY | | | RUBY | |
| 6 | Project 105 | ALMA | | | SARA | |
| 7 | Project 106 | RUBY | | | | |
| 8 | Project 107 | YVETTE | | | | |
| 9 | Project 108 | SARA | | | | |
| 10 | Project 109 | RUBY | | | | |
| 11 | Project 110 | WAYNE | | | | |
| 12 | | | | | | |

**CAUTION**

In a previous book, I joked that if you had bad financial news to share with stockholders, you might try converting your financial statement to Roman numerals. However, you can use the ROMAN function only in limited circumstances. Negative numbers, 0, and numbers over 3,999 cannot be represented with the ROMAN function.

SYNTAX: =ROMAN(*number*,*form*)

The ROMAN function converts an Arabic numeral to Roman, as text. This function takes the following arguments:

- *number*—This is the Arabic numeral you want converted.
- *form*—This is a number that specifies the type of Roman numeral you want. The Roman numeral style ranges from Classic to Simplified, becoming more concise as the value of *form* increases.

There are some arcane rules with Roman numerals. In classic Roman numbers, an I before a V is used to indicate the number 4. In classic Roman numbers, it is valid to use an I before a V or an X, but it is not valid to use an I before an L, a C, a D, or an M.

As shown in Figure 23.19, the *form* argument allows Excel to bend these rules progressively more:

- ROMAN(1999,0) results in MCMXCIX. The M is 1000, the CM is 900, the XC is 90, and the IX is 9; 1000 + 900 + 90 + 9 = 1999
- ROMAN(1999,1) results in MLMVLIV. The M is 1000, the LM is 950, the VL is 45, and the IV is 4; 1000 + 950 + 45 + 4 = 1999.
- ROMAN(1999,2) results in MXMIX. The M is 1000, the XM is 990, and the IX is 9; 1000 + 990 + 9 = 1999.

- ROMAN(1999,3) results in MVMIV. The M is 1000, the VM is 995, and the IV is 4; 1000 + 995 + 4 = 1999.

- ROMAN(1999,4) results in MIM. The M is 1000 and the IM is 999; 1000+999 = 1999.

**Figure 23.19**
You can create movie credit dates with Cell A3 or present bad news with F1:G13. Compare the various forms of Roman numerals in A7:A11.

| | A3 | ▾ | fx | =ROMAN(2007) | | |
|---|---|---|---|---|---|---|
| ▲ | A | B | C | D | E | F | G |
| 1 | NextSpielberg Productions, Inc. | | | | | VNIFORM FAVCET SVPPLY | |
| 2 | Movie Credit Assistant | | | | | INCOME STATEMENT | |
| 3 | MMVII | =ROMAN(2007) | | | | | |
| 4 | MMVII | =ROMAN(YEAR(NOW())) | | | | REVENUE | MMMCMXCIX |
| 5 | | | | | | COST OF GOOD SOLD | MMCCXXXIX |
| 6 | MCMXCIX | =ROMAN(1999) | | | | GROSS PROFIT | MDCCLX |
| 7 | MCMXCIX | =ROMAN(1999,0) | | | | | |
| 8 | MLMVLIV | =ROMAN(1999,1) | | | | SALES EXPENSE | DCXCIX |
| 9 | MXMIX | =ROMAN(1999,2) | | | | MARKETING EXPENSE | CDXXI |
| 10 | MVMIV | =ROMAN(1999,3) | | | | R&D EXPENSE | DCI |
| 11 | MIM | =ROMAN(1999,4) | | | | TOTAL EXPENSES | MDCCXXI |
| 12 | | | | | | | |
| 13 | | | | | | NET INCOME | XXXIX |
| 14 | | | | | | | |

## USING ABS() TO FIGURE OUT THE MAGNITUDE OF ERROR

Say that you work for a local TV station, and you want to prove that your forecaster is more accurate than those at the other stations in town. The forecaster at the rival station in town is horrible—some days he misses high, and other days he misses low. The rival station uses Figure 23.20 to say that his average forecast is 99% accurate. All those negative and positive errors cancel each other out in the average.

**Figure 23.20**
ABS measures the size of an error, ignoring the sign.

| | I4 | ▾ | fx | =ABS(G4-H4) | | | | | |
|---|---|---|---|---|---|---|---|---|---|---|
| ▲ | A | B | C | D | E | F | G | H | I | J |
| 1 | Weather Forecast Accuracy - Action News | | | | | Weather Forecast Accuracy Using ABS() | | | | |
| 2 | | | | | | | | | | |
| 3 | Date | Forecast | Actual | Error | | Date | Forecast | Actual | Error | |
| 4 | 6/1/2007 | 87 | 67 | 20 | | 6/1/2007 | 87 | 67 | 20 | |
| 5 | 6/2/2007 | 52 | 72 | -20 | | 6/2/2007 | 52 | 72 | 20 | |
| 6 | 6/3/2007 | 93 | 73 | 20 | | 6/3/2007 | 93 | 73 | 20 | |
| 7 | 6/4/2007 | 55 | 75 | -20 | | 6/4/2007 | 55 | 75 | 20 | |
| 8 | 6/5/2007 | 94 | 74 | 20 | | 6/5/2007 | 94 | 74 | 20 | |
| 9 | 6/6/2007 | 54 | 74 | -20 | | 6/6/2007 | 54 | 74 | 20 | |
| 10 | 6/7/2007 | 89 | 69 | 20 | | 6/7/2007 | 89 | 69 | 20 | |
| 11 | 6/8/2007 | 49 | 69 | -20 | | 6/8/2007 | 49 | 69 | 20 | |
| 12 | 6/9/2007 | 93 | 73 | 20 | | 6/9/2007 | 93 | 73 | 20 | |
| 13 | 6/10/2007 | 48 | 68 | -20 | | 6/10/2007 | 48 | 68 | 20 | |
| 14 | 6/11/2007 | 88 | 68 | 20 | | 6/11/2007 | 88 | 68 | 20 | |
| 15 | 6/12/2007 | 53 | 73 | -20 | | 6/12/2007 | 53 | 73 | 20 | |
| 16 | 6/13/2007 | 98 | 78 | 20 | | 6/13/2007 | 98 | 78 | 20 | |
| 17 | 6/14/2007 | 56 | 76 | -20 | | 6/14/2007 | 56 | 76 | 20 | |
| 18 | 6/15/2007 | 100 | 80 | 20 | | 6/15/2007 | 100 | 80 | 20 | |
| 19 | 6/16/2007 | 62 | 82 | -20 | | 6/16/2007 | 62 | 82 | 20 | |
| 20 | TOTAL | 1171 | 1171 | 0 | | TOTAL | 1171 | 1171 | 320 | |
| 21 | | | | | | | | | 27.3% | |
| 22 | Claim: Our forecast is 100% accurate! | | | | | Reality: The forecast averages 27% wrong | | | | |
| 23 | | | | | | | | | | |

The ABS function measures the size of the error. Positive errors are reported as positive, and negative errors are reported as positive as well. You can use `=ABS(A2-B2)` to demonstrate that the other station's forecaster is off by 20 degrees on average.

SYNTAX: `=ABS(number)`

The ABS function returns the absolute value of a number—that is, the number without its sign. With this function, the argument *`number`* is the real number of which you want the absolute number.



## Using PI to Calculate Cake or Pizza Pricing

How many more ingredients are in a 16-inch pizza than an 8-inch pizza? Be careful—it is not double!

The formula for the area of a circle is $\pi \times r^2$. The radius of a circle is half the diameter. The function `=PI()`returns the constant for PI. You use `=PI()*(B7/2)^2` to calculate the number of square inches in a 16-inch pizza. As shown in Figure 23.21, the 16-inch size contains nearly four times the area of an 8-inch circle.

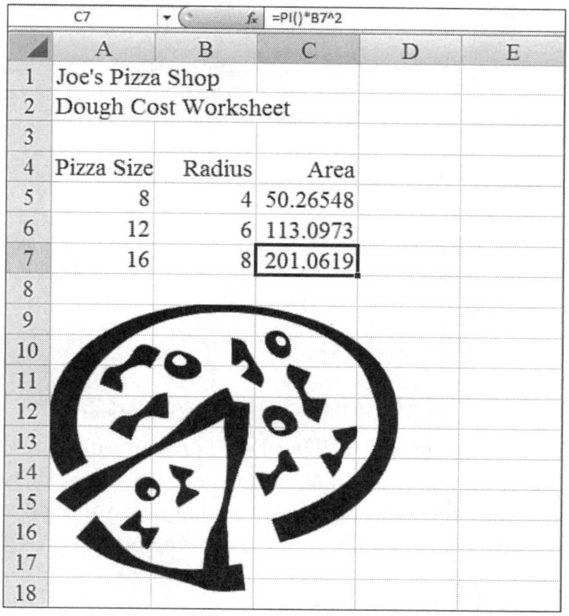

C7 =PI()*B7^2

| | A | B | C | D | E |
|---|---|---|---|---|---|
| 1 | Joe's Pizza Shop | | | | |
| 2 | Dough Cost Worksheet | | | | |
| 3 | | | | | |
| 4 | Pizza Size | Radius | Area | | |
| 5 | 8 | 4 | 50.26548 | | |
| 6 | 12 | 6 | 113.0973 | | |
| 7 | 16 | 8 | 201.0619 | | |

**Figure 23.21**
Most pizza shops don't have a dedicated cost accountant.

If your company makes anything round—drink coasters, drum heads, wedding cakes, pizzas, or Frisbees—you want to use `=PI()` when calculating your product cost.

SYNTAX: `=PI()`

The PI function returns the number 3.14159265358979, the mathematical constant $\pi$, accurate to 15 digits.

## USING =COMBIN TO FIGURE OUT LOTTERY PROBABILITY

Your office lottery pool may agree to bet $1 on the lottery each week but to double the bet when the jackpot is a higher payout than the odds against winning.

The COMBIN function can figure out the number of combinations for most lottery systems. If you have to correctly select 6 numbers out of a pool of 48 numbers, you can use =COMBIN(48,6) to find that there are 11.1 million combinations.

Figure 23.22 shows a variety of lottery odds.

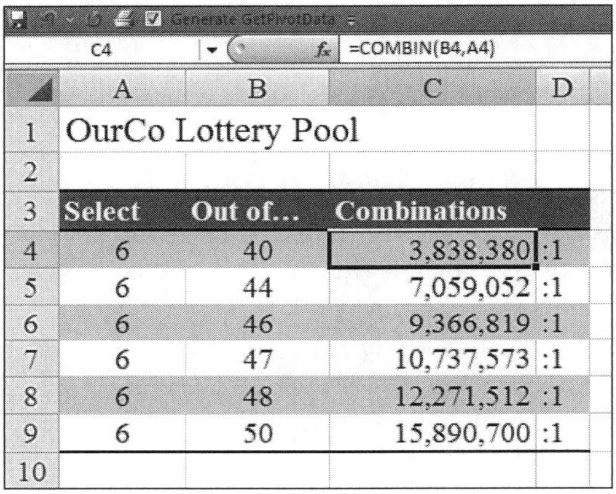

**Figure 23.22**
The odds of winning the lottery in a 44-number games are twice as good as in a 50-number game.

|  | C4 | | $f_x$ | =COMBIN(B4,A4) | |
|---|---|---|---|---|---|
|  | A | B | C | D |
| 1 | OurCo Lottery Pool | | | |
| 2 | | | | |
| 3 | Select | Out of... | Combinations | |
| 4 | 6 | 40 | 3,838,380 :1 | |
| 5 | 6 | 44 | 7,059,052 :1 | |
| 6 | 6 | 46 | 9,366,819 :1 | |
| 7 | 6 | 47 | 10,737,573 :1 | |
| 8 | 6 | 48 | 12,271,512 :1 | |
| 9 | 6 | 50 | 15,890,700 :1 | |
| 10 | | | | |

NOTE

The COMBIN function assumes that you don't care about the sequence of the numbers chosen. If you have to worry about the sequence, you should use =PERMUT, as described in Chapter 26, "Using Statistical Functions."

## USING FACT TO CALCULATE THE PERMUTATION OF A NUMBER

Let's say that you have seven slides in a PowerPoint presentation. Furthermore, say you want to find the number of unique sequences in which the slides can be arranged; this is called the *factorial* of seven. You calculated this by using $7 \times 6 \times 5 \times 4 \times 3 \times 2 \times 1$. To find the factorial of any positive integer, you use the FACT function.

SYNTAX: =FACT(*number*)

The FACT function returns the factorial of a number. The factorial of a number is equal to $1 \times 2 \times 3 \times ... \times number$. *number* is the nonnegative number of which you want the factorial. If *number* is not an integer, it is truncated.

By definition, FACT(0) is 1.

There is a similar function called `FACTDOUBLE`. A double factorial multiplies every other number. For even numbers, this is a calculation such as

`FACTDOUBLE(8) = 8*6*4*2`. For odd numbers, the calculation is `FACTDOUBLE(9) = 9*7*5*3*1`.

Various factorials are shown in Figure 23.23.

**Figure 23.23**
Excel calculates the `FACT` and `DOUBLEFACT` of various numbers.

B11 =FACT(A11)

| | A | B | C | D | E | F |
|---|---|---|---|---|---|---|
| 1 | Number | Factorial | Equivalent to | | Double Factorial | Equivalent to |
| 2 | 0 | 1 | | | 1 | |
| 3 | 1 | 1 | =1 | | 1 | =1 |
| 4 | 2 | 2 | =1*2 | | 2 | =2 |
| 5 | 3 | 6 | =1*2*3 | | 3 | =1*3 |
| 6 | 4 | 24 | =1*2*3*4 | | 8 | =2*4 |
| 7 | 5 | 120 | =1*2*3*4*5 | | 15 | =1*3*5 |
| 8 | 6 | 720 | =1*2*3*4*5*6 | | 48 | =2*4*6 |
| 9 | 7 | 5040 | =1*2*3*4*5*6*7 | | 105 | =1*3*5*7 |
| 10 | 8 | 40320 | =1*2*3*4*5*6*7*8 | | 384 | =2*4*6*8 |
| 11 | 9 | 362880 | =1*2*3*4*5*6*7*8*9 | | 945 | =1*3*5*7*9 |
| 12 | 99 | 9.3E+155 | =1*2*3*...*98*99 | | 2.72539E+78 | =1*3*5*...*97*99 |
| 13 | | | | | | |

**NOTE**

> It is difficult to find real-world uses for `DOUBLEFACT`. MathWorld.com notes some interesting uses for `DOUBLEFACT(N)` where N is less than zero, but Excel does not calculate `DOUBLEFACT` for negative numbers. Fans of the poker game Texas Hold'Em will be delighted to know that `DOUBLEFACT` is useful in calculating Texas Hold'Em probabilities. For complete details, look up Poker Probabilities (Texas Hold'Em) in Wikipedia.

## USING GCD AND LCM TO PERFORM SEVENTH-GRADE MATH

My seventh-grade math teacher, Mr. Irwin, taught me about greatest common denominators and least common multiples. (For example, the least common multiple of 24 and 36 is 72. The greatest common denominator of 24 and 36 is 12.) I have to admit that I never saw these concepts again until my son Josh was in seventh grade. This must be permanently part of the seventh-grade curriculum.

If you are in seventh grade or you are assisting a seventh grader with his or her math lesson, you will be happy to know that Excel can calculate these values for you.

### SYNTAX: `=GCD(number1,number2,...)`

The `GCD` function returns the greatest common divisor of two or more integers. The greatest common divisor is the largest integer that divides both *`number1`* and *`number2`* without a remainder.

The arguments *`number1, number2,...`* are 1 to 29 values. If any value is not an integer, it is truncated. If any argument is nonnumeric, `GCD` returns a `#VALUE!` error. If any argument is less than zero, `GCD` returns a `#NUM!` error. The number 1 divides any value evenly. A prime number has only itself and 1 as even divisors.

SYNTAX: =LCM(number1,number2,...)

The LCM function returns the least common multiple of integers. The least common multiple is the smallest positive integer that is a multiple of all integer arguments—number1, number2, and so on. You use LCM to add fractions with different denominators.

The arguments number1, number2,... are 1 to 29 values for which you want the least common multiple. If the value is not an integer, it is truncated. If any argument is nonnumeric, LCM returns a #VALUE! error. If any argument is less than one, LCM returns a #NUM! error.

## USING MULTINOMIAL TO SOLVE A COIN PROBLEM

While the multinomial distribution is a fairly complex mathematical concept, the example below illustrates a fun puzzle that can be solved with the function.

SYNTAX: =MULTINOMIAL(number1,number2,...)

The MULTINOMIAL function returns the ratio of the factorial of a sum of values to the product of factorials. The arguments number1, number2,... are 1 to 29 values for which you want the multinomial. For example, MULTINOMIAL(a,b,c,d) is (a+b+c+d)! / a!b!c!d!.

Say that you have a huge jar that contains hundreds of pennies, nickels, dimes, and quarters. You reach into the jar and pull out six coins. How many possible arrangements of the coins can there be? To picture this problem, you should sort the six types of coins from low to high. You can use three movable dividers to group the coins into denominations. In the left side of Figure 23.24, for example, you've arranged the dividers to indicate one penny, one nickel, three dimes, and one quarter. It is possible to pull out none of a particular coin. In the image on the right, you've pulled out five pennies and one dime. In this case, the dividers are adjacent for nickels and pennies. In every case, the quarter divider must always be at the bottom, so how many ways are there to arrange the other three dividers among six coins?

Someone figured out that the answer to this problem is the factorial of (Dividers + Coins) ÷ Factorial of Coins × Factorial of Dividers. In math terms, this is (3+6)! / 3!6!. Remarkably, Excel has a function for solving the coin problem. =MULTINOMIAL(3,6) performs the calculation (3+6)!/3!6!.

## USING MOD TO FIND THE REMAINDER PORTION OF A DIVISION PROBLEM

The MOD function is one of the obscure math functions that I find myself using quite frequently. Have you ever been in a group activity where everyone in the group was to count off by sixes? This is a great way to break up a group into six subgroups. It makes sure that friends who were sitting together get put into disparate groups.

Using the MOD function is a great way to perform this concept with records in a database. Perhaps for auditing, you need to check every eighth invoice. Or you need to break up a list of employees into four groups. You can solve these types of problems by using the MOD function.

Think way back to when you were first learning division. If you had to divide 43 by 4, you would have written that the answer was 10 with a remainder of 3. If you divide 40 by 4, the answer is 10 with a remainder of 0.

**Figure 23.24**
Solving this problem with MULTINOMIAL will amuse Boy Scout groups and middle school math students.

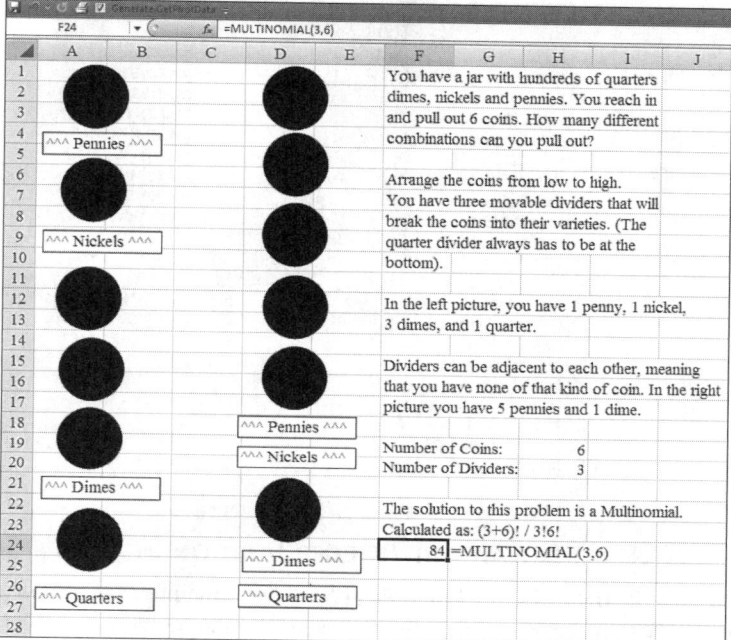

23

**NOTE**

MOD is short for *modulo*, the mathematical term for this operation. You would normally say that 17 modulo 3 is 2.

The MOD function divides one number by another and reports back just the remainder portion of the result. You end up with an even distribution of remainders. If you convert the formulas into values and sort, your data is broken into similar-size groups.

**SYNTAX:** =MOD(*number*,*divisor*)

The MOD function returns the remainder after *number* is divided by divisor. The result has the same sign as divisor. This function takes the following arguments:

- *number*—This is the number for which you want to find the remainder.
- *divisor*—This is the number by which you want to divide number. If *divisor* is 0, MOD returns a #DIV/0! error.

The MOD function is good for classifying records that follow a certain order. For example, the SmartArt gallery contains 84 icons arranged with 4 icons per row. To find the column for the 38th icon, use =MOD(38,4).

The example in figure 23.25 assigns all employees to one of four groups.

**Figure 23.25**
To organize these employees into four groups, you use =MOD(ROW(),4). Then you paste the values and sort by the remainders.

23

| | A | B | C | D | E | F |
|---|---|---|---|---|---|---|
| | NAME | MOD 4 | | | NAME | MOD 4 |
| 1 | NAME | MOD 4 | | | NAME | MOD 4 |
| 2 | DELORES REYNOLDS | 2 | | | MAXINE HILL | 0 |
| 3 | ALLISON CAREY | 3 | | | SANDY DILLARD | 0 |
| 4 | MAXINE HILL | 0 | | | VINCENT CANNON | 0 |
| 5 | THERESA VAUGHN | 1 | | | MAXINE ROMAN | 0 |
| 6 | EUNICE GILLIAM | 2 | | | RALPH FRANKLIN | 0 |
| 7 | CLAIRE SOLOMON | 3 | Paste | | MISTY HUFF | 0 |
| 8 | SANDY DILLARD | 0 | Values | | RANDY DECKER | 0 |
| 9 | ERIC DANIEL | 1 | and | | BARBARA ACOSTA | 0 |
| 10 | NORA OCHOA | 2 | Sort | | ANN MEJIA | 0 |
| 11 | LORI WILEY | 3 | | | DELORES HINES | 0 |
| 12 | VINCENT CANNON | 0 | | | CATHERINE CASEY | 0 |
| 13 | TINA KINNEY | 1 | | | MARIE MASSEY | 0 |
| 14 | CARLOS HOLMAN | 2 | | | CANDICE VASQUEZ | 0 |
| 15 | BRANDI ACOSTA | 3 | | | KEVIN DELGADO | 0 |
| 16 | MAXINE ROMAN | 0 | | | LYNN JIMENEZ | 0 |
| 17 | SAMUEL ROJAS | 1 | | | HARRIET CLARKE | 0 |
| 18 | DANNY HINTON | 2 | | | THERESA VAUGHN | 1 |
| 19 | JEREMY HESTER | 3 | | | ERIC DANIEL | 1 |
| 20 | RALPH FRANKLIN | 0 | | | TINA KINNEY | 1 |
| 21 | BILLIE TURNER | 1 | | | SAMUEL ROJAS | 1 |

B2 =MOD(ROW(),4)

## USING QUOTIENT TO ISOLATE THE INTEGER PORTION IN A DIVISION PROBLEM

As you just learned, the MOD function isolates the remainder portion in a division problem. The QUOTIENT function isolates the integer portion in a division problem.

If you divide 43 by 4, the answer is 10 with a remainder of 3. The QUOTIENT function returns just the whole number 10 and ignores the remainder.

This function is great for calculating full cases of products. Say that you pay a worker for assembling products. You pay the worker each complete case of 4 items produced. If he produces 43 items in his shift, this is 10 complete cases. =QUOTIENT(43,4) would provide an answer of 10.

SYNTAX: =QUOTIENT(*numerator*,*denominator*)

The QUOTIENT function returns the integer portion in a division problem. You use this function when you want to discard the remainder in a division problem. This function takes the following arguments:

- *numerator*—This is the dividend.
- *denominator*—This is the divisor.

If either argument is nonnumeric, QUOTIENT returns a #VALUE! error.

Many people simulate the QUOTIENT function by using the INT function. To keep the integer portion of a division, you could use =INT(43/4). However, QUOTIENT and INT differ when the result is negative. Whereas QUOTIENT(5,-4) returns -1, INT(5/-4) actually goes down to -2. Thus, using QUOTIENT is more accurate than using INT if the results might be negative. Figure 23.26 shows the differences between INT and QUOTIENT.

**Figure 23.26**
QUOTIENT is more accurate than INT when the result is negative.

| H6 | | $f_x$ | =QUOTIENT(F6,G6) | | | | | |
| --- | --- | --- | --- | --- | --- | --- | --- | --- |
| | A | B | C | D | E | F | G | H | I |
| 1 | Number | Divisor | Quotient | INT(a/b) | | Number | Divisor | Quotient | INT(f/g) |
| 2 | 1 | 4 | 0 | 0 | | 1 | -4 | -0 | -1 |
| 3 | 2 | 4 | 0 | 0 | | 2 | -4 | -0 | -1 |
| 4 | 3 | 4 | 0 | 0 | | 3 | -4 | -0 | -1 |
| 5 | 4 | 4 | 1 | 1 | | 4 | -4 | -1 | -1 |
| 6 | 5 | 4 | 1 | 1 | | 5 | -4 | -1 | -2 |
| 7 | 6 | 4 | 1 | 1 | | 6 | -4 | -1 | -2 |
| 8 | 7 | 4 | 1 | 1 | | 7 | -4 | -1 | -2 |
| 9 | 8 | 4 | 2 | 2 | | 8 | -4 | -2 | -2 |
| 10 | 9 | 4 | 2 | 2 | | 9 | -4 | -2 | -3 |
| 11 | 10 | 4 | 2 | 2 | | 10 | -4 | -2 | -3 |
| 12 | 11 | 4 | 2 | 2 | | 11 | -4 | -2 | -3 |
| 13 | 12 | 4 | 3 | 3 | | 12 | -4 | -3 | -3 |
| 14 | 13 | 4 | 3 | 3 | | 13 | -4 | -3 | -4 |
| 15 | 14 | 4 | 3 | 3 | | 14 | -4 | -3 | -4 |
| 16 | 15 | 4 | 3 | 3 | | 15 | -4 | -3 | -4 |
| 17 | 16 | 4 | 4 | 4 | | 16 | -4 | -4 | -4 |
| 18 | 17 | 4 | 4 | 4 | | 17 | -4 | -4 | -5 |

## USING PRODUCT TO MULTIPLY NUMBERS

The PRODUCT function multiplies a range of numbers by each other. Although you could calculate =PRODUCT(2,2), the PRODUCT function is designed to multiply all numbers in a range, such as =PRODUCT(A2:A50).

SYNTAX: =PRODUCT(number1,number2,...)

The PRODUCT function multiplies all the numbers given as arguments and returns the product. The arguments number1, number2,... are 1 to 30 numbers that you want to multiply. If you pass a single-cell argument that contains a text representation of a number, it is used in the multiplication. However, if one of the arguments is a multicell range, then any text entry in that range is ignored.

## USING SQRT AND POWER TO CALCULATE SQUARE ROOTS AND EXPONENTS

Most calculators offer a square root button, so it seems natural that Excel would offer a SQRT function to do the same thing. To square a number, you multiply the number by itself, ending up with a square. For example, $5 \times 5 = 25$.

A square root is a number that, when multiplied by itself, leads to a square. For example, the square root of 25 is 5, and the square root of 49 is 7. Some square roots are more difficult to calculate. The square root of 8 is a number between 2 and 3—somewhere close to 2.828. You can calculate the number with =SQRT(8).

A related function is the POWER function. If you want to write the shorthand for $6 \times 6 \times 6 \times 6 \times 6$, you would say "six to the fifth power," or $6^5$. Excel can calculate this with =POWER(6,5).

SYNTAX: =SQRT(number)

The SQRT function returns a positive square root. The argument number is the number for which you want the square root. If number is negative, SQRT returns a #NUM! error.

SYNTAX: =POWER(*number*,*power*)

The POWER function returns the result of a number raised to a power. This function takes the following arguments:

■ *number*—This is the base number. It can be any real number.

■ *power*—This is the exponent to which the base number is raised.

The POWER function works with all sorts of irrational numbers, such as 98.2 raised to the 3.4 power.

### FIGURING OUT OTHER ROOTS AND POWERS

The SQRT function is provided because some math people expect it to be there. There are no equivalent functions to figure out other roots.

If you multiply $5 \times 5 \times 5$ to get 125, then the third root of 125 is 5. The fourth root of 625 is 5. Even a $30 calculator offers a key to generate various roots beyond a square root. Excel does not offer a cube root function. In reality, even the POWER and the SQRT functions are not necessary. Chapter 20, "Understanding Formulas," explains how the carat operator can be used to calculate powers and roots:

■ =6^3 is 6 raised to the third power, which is $6 \times 6 \times 6$, or 216

■ =2^8 is 2 to the eighth power, which is $2 \times 2 \times 2 \times 2 \times 2 \times 2 \times 2 \times 2$, or 256

For roots, you can raise a number to a fractional power:

■ =256^(1/8) is the eighth root of 256. This is 2.

■ =125^(1/3) is the third root of 125. This is 5.

Thus, instead of using =SQRT(25), you could just as easily use =25^(1/2). However, people reading your worksheets are more likely to understand =SQRT(25) than =25^(1/2).

NOTE

> There is a specialized version of SQRT, SQRTPI, which is discussed in Chapter 27, "Using Trig, Matrix, and Engineering Functions." This function first multiplies a number by PI and then takes the square root of the result. You can win a real pizza pie if you can think of a useful reason to do this. See Chapter 27.

## USING SIGN TO DETERMINE THE SIGN OF A NUMBER

Although the SIGN function really belongs with the information functions, Microsoft groups it with the math functions. You can see it used in the MROUND function example shown previously in this chapter to prevent an error. Simply, =SIGN(*number*) reports whether *number* is negative, zero, or positive.

SYNTAX: =SIGN(*number*)

SIGN determines the sign of a number. It returns 1 if the number is positive, 0 if the number is 0, and -1 if the number is negative. The argument *number* is any real number.

## USING COUNTIF AND SUMIF TO CONDITIONALLY COUNT OR SUM DATA

The COUNTIF and SUMIF functions are young and popular. As opposed to most functions that have been around since the 1980s, these functions were added in Excel 97. Math purists may point out that you could perform equivalent calculations by using DSUM or SUMPRODUCT or even an array formula long before Microsoft added these functions. However, it is far easier to grasp doing calculations with COUNTIF and SUMIF.

Figure 23.27 shows a database that contains thousands of records. Your goal is to find out how many records came from each region. One way to write the formula for the east region is =COUNTIF($C$11:$C$5011,"East"). However, it is far more interesting to write the formula as shown in Cell B2: =COUNTIF($C$11:$C$5011,A2). After this formula is entered, you can build a table of the unique regions in Column A, copy the formula down Column B, and quickly have a summary table built with the help of COUNTIF.

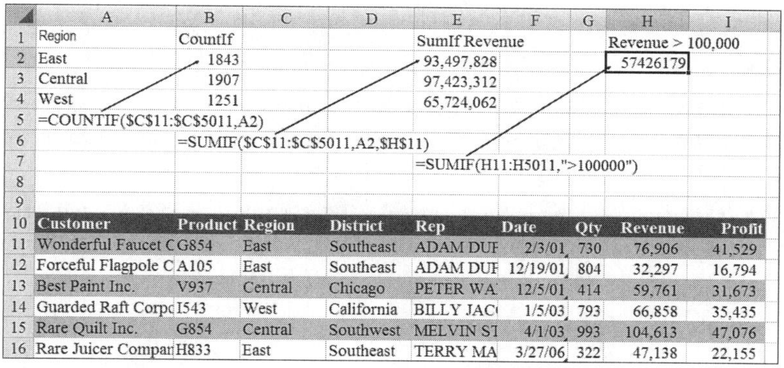

**Figure 23.27**

COUNTIF and SUMIF are simpler to use than DSUM, SUMPRODUCT, or array formulas.

SYNTAX: =COUNTIF(*range*,*criteria*)

The COUNTIF function counts the number of cells within a range that meet the given criteria. This function takes the following arguments:

- *range*—This is the range of cells from which you want to count cells.
- *criteria*—This is the criteria in the form of a number, an expression, or text that defines which cells will be counted. For example, criteria can be expressed as 32, "32", ">32", or "apples".

After you have mastered COUNTIF, it is easy to master SUMIF. In most cases, the SUMIF function adds one new argument. Whereas COUNTIF would ask for a range of data and then the value to look for in that range, SUMIF usually needs three arguments: SUMIF asks for a range of data, the value to look for in that range, and then another range of data to be summed when a match is found.

In Figure 23.27, B11:B5011 contains the range to search. Cell A2 contains the value for which to search. When Excel finds a matching value in Column B, you want Excel to return the corresponding cell from the revenue column in H11:H5011. Most people would write =SUMIF($C$11:$C$5011,A2,$H$11:H$5011) to do this. It turns out that Excel forces the third argument to have the same shape as the first argument. If you would happen to accidentally specify H11:H4011, Excel would ignore your range and use H11:H5011 because this is the same shape as the first argument. Thus, it is sufficient to write the formula as =SUMIF($C$11:$C$5011,A2,$H$11).

SYNTAX: =SUMIF(*range*,*criteria*,*sum_range*)

The SUMIF function adds the cells specified by a given criteria. Occasionally, the range you want to search is also the range to sum. For example, perhaps your criteria is to look for rows where the revenue is greater than 100,000. In this case, because your range to add is the same as your range to search, you can leave off the third argument, as shown in Cell H2 of Figure 23.27.

The SUMIF function takes the following arguments:

- *range*—This is the range of cells you want evaluated.
- *criteria*—This is the criteria in the form of a number, an expression, or text that defines which cells will be counted. For example, criteria can be expressed as 32, "32", ">32", or "apples".
- *sum_range*—This is the range of cells to sum. The cells in *sum_range* are summed only if their corresponding cells in *range* match the criteria. If *sum_range* is omitted, the cells in *range* are summed.

**NOTE**

An interesting variation on the SUMIF and COUNTIF functions is worth mentioning. It is possible to build the *criteria* argument on-the-fly. To count records that are above *average*, you can use =COUNTIF(H11:H5011,">"&AVERAGE(H11:H5011)).

Mastering the SUMIF and COUNTIF functions invariably leads to more questions about doing more powerful versions. If you need to sum based on more than one condition, you should study DSUM in Chapter 24, "Using Powerful Functions: Logical, Lookup, and Database Functions," SUMPRODUCT in Chapter 27, array formulas in Chapter 30, "Using Names in Excel," or the new COUNTIFS and SUMIFS functions in Chapter 22, "Understanding Functions."

# DATES AND TIMES IN EXCEL

Date calculations can drive people crazy in Excel. If you gain a certain confidence with dates in Excel, you will be able to quickly resolve formatting issues that come up.

Here is why dates are a problem. First, Excel stores dates as the number of days since January 1, 1900. For example, March 16, 2007, is 39157 days after 1/1/1900. When you enter 3/16/2007 in a cell, Excel secretly converts this entry to 39157 and formats the cell to display a date instead of the value. So far, so good. The problem arises when you try to calculate something based on the date.

When you try to perform a calculation on two cells when the first cell is formatted as currency and the second cell is formatted as fixed numeric with three decimals. Excel has to decide if the new cell inherits the currency format or the fixed with three decimals format. These rules are hard to figure out. In any given instance, you might get the currency format or the fixed with three decimals format, or you might get the format previously assigned to the cell with the new formula. With numbers, a result of $80.52 or 80.521 look about the same. You can probably understand either format.

However, imagine that one of the cells is formatted as a date. Another cell contains the number 30. If you add the 30 to the date, which format does Excel use? If the cell containing the new formula happened to be previously assigned a numeric format, the answer suddenly switches from a date format to the numeric equivalent. This is frustrating. It is confusing. You start with March 16, 2007, add 30 days, and get an answer of 39187. This makes no sense to an Excel novice. It forces many people to give up on dates and start storing dates as text that look like dates. This is unfortunate because you can't easily do calculations on text cells that look like dates.

Here is a general guideline to remember: If you are working with dates in the range of the years 2000 to 2015, those numeric equivalents are from 36,526 through 42,369. If you do some date math and get a strange answer in the 35,000–45,000 range, Excel probably has the right answer, but the numeric format of the answer cell is simply wrong. You need to select Home, Number, Date to correct the format.

The Excel method for storing dates is simple when you understand it. If you have a date cell and need to add 15 days to it, you simply add the number 15 to the cell. Every day is equivalent to the number 1, and every week is equivalent to the number 7. This is very simple to understand.

When you see 39157 instead of March 16, 2007, Excel calls the 39157 a *serial number*. Some of the Excel functions discussed here convert from a serial number to text that looks like a date or vice versa. For time, Excel simply adds a decimal to the serial number. There are 24 hours in a day. The serial number for 6 a.m. is 0.25. The serial number for noon is 0.5. The serial number for 6 p.m. is 0.75. The serial number for 3 p.m. on March 16, 2007, is 39157.625. To see how this works, try this out:

1. Open a blank Excel workbook.
2. In any cell, enter a number in the range of 35,000 to 45,000.
3. Add a decimal point and any random digits after the decimal.
4. Select that cell.

5. From the Home ribbon, choose the plus sign in the lower-right corner of the Number group.

6. In the Date category, scroll down and choose the format 3/14/01 1:30 PM. Excel displays your random number as a date and time. If the decimal portion of your number is greater than 0.5, the result will be in the p.m. portion of the day.

7. Go to another cell and enter the day you were born, using a four-digit year. (This doesn't work if you are older than 107).

8. Again select the cell and format it as a number. Excel converts to show how many days after the start of the last century you were born. This is great trivia, but not necessarily useful.

The point is that Excel dates are nothing to be afraid of. You need to understand that behind the scenes, Excel is storing your dates as serial numbers and your times as decimal serial numbers. Occasionally, circumstances cause a date to be displayed as a serial number. While this freaks some people out, it is easy to fix using the Format Cells dialog. Other times, when you want the serial number (for example, to calculate elapsed days between two dates), Excel converts the serial number to a date, indicating, for example, that an the invoice is past due by "February 15 1900" days. When you get these types of non sequiturs, you can just visit the Format Cells dialog.

**CAUTION**

Although most Excel date issues can be resolved with formatting, there are some real date problems that you should be aware of:

- On a Macintosh, Excel dates are stored since January 1, 1904. If you are using a Mac, your serial number for a date in 2007 will be different from that on a Windows PC. Excel handles this conversion when files are moved from one platform to another.

- Excel dates cannot handle dates in the 1800s or before. This really hacks off all my friends who do genealogy. If your Great-Great-Great Uncle Silas was born on February 17, 1895, you are going to have to store that as text.

- Excel dates from January 1, 1900, through March 1, 1900, are generally wrong. See Figure 23.28 and the following sidebar for more details.

- Around Y2K, someone decided that 1930 is the dividing line for two digit years. If you enter a date with a two-digit year, the result is in the range of 1930 through 2029. If you enter 12/31/29, this will be interpreted as 2029. If you enter 1/1/30, it will be interpreted as 1930. If you need to enter a mortgage ending date of 2037, for example, just be sure to use the four digit year, 6/15/2037.

**Blame It on Sisogenes**

The programmer who designed Lotus 1-2-3 was not a date fanatic.

Back in 45BC, an astronomer named Sisogenes calculated that the earth took 365 days, 5 hours, 48 minutes, and 46 seconds to travel around the sun. He advised Julius Caesar that this was "close enough" to 365.25 days, and the leap year was born.

This worked through Caesar's lifetime. But those missing 11 minutes and 14 seconds began to add up. By 1582, things were out of whack by about 11 days. The spring equinox was falling on March 10 instead of March 21.

Pope Gregory mandated that the calendar jump by 11 days. In Catholic countries, they went from October 4, 1582, to October 15, 1582. Other countries, though, resisted the change. England finally added the 11 days in 1752. Russia added them in 1918. Historians note that there was rioting over the change (possibly from all the people who lost out on their birthday cake?).

To prevent further rioting, Gregory proposed that we skip three leap years out of every 400 years. This led to some arcane rules for leap years:

- Leap years happen in years divisible by 4.
- Leap years are skipped if the year is divisible by 100.
- Leap years are not skipped if the year is divisible by 400.

The date February 29, 2000, was actually an exception to an exception to an exception to an exception. But everyone thought it was just another leap year.

23

**Figure 23.28**
A team of astronomers probably worked for hours to calculate what now takes seconds in Excel.

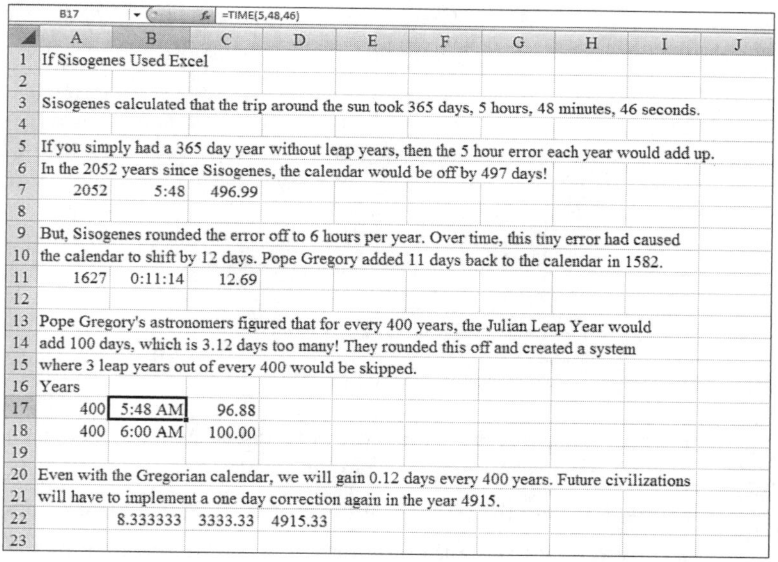

The problem is that there was no leap year in 1900. The programmer working on Lotus 1-2-3 in Mitch Kapor's Cambridge basement didn't know this rule and programmed a 2/29/1900 into Lotus 1-2-3.

By the late 1980s, there were millions of Lotus spreadsheets created that had dates in them. Any competitor to Lotus had to ensure that its program would come up with the exact same result as the industry-standard Lotus 1-2-3. This forced Excel, Quattro, and others to program the same error into their packages. Now, there are billions of spreadsheets with dates in them. If Microsoft would ever correct this problem, there would again be rioting in the streets.

The odds of this problem actually affecting you are slim. You would need to be calculating a date span from before February 28, 1900, to after March 1, 1900. Because Excel can only handle dates going back to January 1, 1900, there are only 49 possible starting dates that cause problems.

## UNDERSTANDING EXCEL DATE AND TIME FORMATS

It is worthwhile to learn the various Excel custom codes for date and time formats. Figure 23.29 shows a table of how March 5 would be displayed in various numeric formats. The codes in A4:A13 show the possible codes for displaying just date, month, or year. Most people know the classic mm/dd/yyyy format, but there are far more formats available. You can cause Excel to spell out the month and weekday by using codes such as dddd, mmmm d, yyyy. These are the possibilities:

**Figure 23.29**
Any of these custom date format codes can be typed in the Custom Numeric Format box.

|   | A | B | C |
|---|---|---|---|
| 1 | 3/5/2007 | | |
| 2 | | | |
| 3 | FORMAT | DISPLAYS AS | NOTE |
| 4 | m | 3 | 1 or 2 digit month as needed |
| 5 | mm | 03 | Always 2 digits for month |
| 6 | mmm | Mar | 3 letter month abbreviation |
| 7 | mmmm | March | Spell out the month |
| 8 | mmmmm | M | 1st text - for JFMAMJJASOND |
| 9 | d | 5 | 1 or 2 digit day as needed |
| 10 | dd | 05 | Always 2 digits for day |
| 11 | ddd | Mon | 3 letter day abbreviation |
| 12 | dddd | Monday | Spell out the weekday |
| 13 | yy | 07 | 2 digits for year |
| 14 | yyyy | 2007 | 4 digits for year |
| 15 | mm/dd/yyyy | 03/05/2007 | |
| 16 | mmm d, yy | Mar 5, 07 | |
| 17 | d-mmmm-yyyy | 5-March-2007 | |
| 18 | | | |

- **mm**—Displays the month with two digits. Months before October are displayed with a leading zero (for example, January is 01).
- **m**—Displays the month with one or two digits, as necessary.
- **mmm**—Displays a three-letter abbreviation for the month (for example, Jan, Feb).
- **mmmm**—Spells out the month (for example, January, February).
- **mmmmm**—First letter of the month, useful for creating "JFMAMJJASOND" chart labels.
- **dd**—Displays the day of the month with two digits. Dates earlier than the 10th of the month are displayed with a leading zero (for example, the 1st is 01).
- **d**—Displays the day of the month with one or two digits, as needed.
- **ddd**—Displays a three-letter abbreviation for the name of the weekday (for example, Mon, Tue).
- **dddd**—Spells out the name of the weekday (for example, Monday, Tuesday).
- **yy or y**—Uses two digits for the year (for example, 07).
- **yyyy or yyy**—Uses four digits for the year (for example, 2007).

You are allowed to string together any combination of these codes with a space, comma, slash, or dash. It is valid to repeat a portion of the date format. For example, the format dddd, mmmm d, yyyy shows the day portion twice in the date and would display as Monday, March 5, 2007.

> Custom number formats are entered in the Format Cells dialog. There are three ways to display this dialog:
>
> - Press Ctrl+1.
> - From the Home ribbon, in the Number group, choose the drop-down and select More from the bottom of the drop-down.
> - Click the expand icon in the lower-right corner of the Number group on the Home ribbon.
>
> When the Format Cells dialog is displayed, you choose the Number tab. In the Category list, you choose Custom. In the Type box, you enter your custom format. The Sample box displays the active cell with the format applied.

**23**

Although the date formats are mostly intuitive, there are several difficulties in the time formats. The first problem is the M code. Excel has already used M to mean month. In a time format, you cannot use M alone to mean minutes. The M code must either be preceded or followed by a colon.

There is another difficulty: When you are dealing with years, months, and days, it is often perfectly valid to mention only one of the portions of the date without the other two. It is common to hear any of these statements:

"I was born in 1965."

"I am going on vacation in July."

"I will be back on the 27th."

If you have a date such as March 5, 2007, and use the proper formatting code, Excel happily tells you that this date is March or 2007 or the 5th. Technically, Excel is leaving out some really important information—the 5th of what? As humans, we can often figure out that this probably means the 5th of the next month. Thus, we aren't shocked that Excel is leaving off the fact that it is March 2007.

Imagine how strange it would be if Excel would do this with regular numbers. Say you have the number 352. Would Excel ever offer a numeric format that would display just the tens portion of the number? If you put 352 in a cell, would Excel display 5 or 50? It would make no sense.

Excel treats time as an extension of dates and is happy to show you only a portion of the time. This can cause great confusion. To Excel, 40 hours really means 1 day and 16 hours. If you create a timesheet in Excel and format the total hours for the week as H:MM, Excel thinks that you are purposefully leaving off the day portion of the format! Excel presents 45 hours as just 21 hours because it assumes you can figure out there is 1 day from the context. But our brains don't work that way. 21 hours means 21 hours, not 1 day and 21 hours.

To overcome this problem in Excel, you use square brackets. Surrounding any time element with square brackets tells Excel to include all greater time/date elements in that one element, as in the following examples:

- 5 days and 10 hours in [H] format would be 130.
- 5 days and 10 hours in [M] format would be 7,800, to represent that many minutes.
- 5 days and 10 hours in [S] format would be 468,000, to represent that many seconds.

As shown in Figure 23.30, the time formatting codes include h, hh, s, ss, :mm, and mm:, all of which can be modified with square brackets.

**Figure 23.30**
Custom time format codes.

| | A | B | C | D | E |
|---|---|---|---|---|---|
| 1 | 20:05:07 | | | | |
| 2 | | | | | |
| 3 | FORMAT | DISPLAYS AS | NOTE | | |
| 4 | h | 20 | *1 or 2 digit hour as needed* | | |
| 5 | hh | 20 | *Always 2 digits for hour* | | |
| 6 | h:mm | 20:05 | *1 or 2 digit hour as needed* | | |
| 7 | hh:mm | 20:05 | *Always 2 digits for hour* | | |
| 8 | h:mm:ss | 20:05:07 | *Hours, minutes, seconds in military time* | | |
| 9 | h:m:s | 20:5:7 | *Strange looking, but a valid code* | | |
| 10 | s | 7 | *Seconds, using 1 or 2 digits* | | |
| 11 | ss | 07 | *Seconds, using 2 digits* | | |
| 12 | h:mm AM/PM | 8:05 PM | *Hours and minutes with AM or PM* | | |
| 13 | [h]:mm | 44:05 | *Include any full days as hours* | | |
| 14 | [m] | 2645 | *Include any hours or days as minutes* | | |
| 15 | [s] | 158707 | *Include any days, hours or minutes as seconds* | | |
| 16 | | | | | |

To display date and time, you enter the custom date format code, a space, and then the time format code.

# EXAMPLES OF DATE AND TIME FUNCTIONS

In all the examples in the following sections, you should use care to ensure that the resulting cell is formatted using the proper format, as discussed in the preceding section.

## USING NOW AND TODAY TO CALCULATE THE CURRENT DATA AND TIME OR CURRENT DATE

There are a couple keyboard shortcuts for entering date and time. Pressing Ctrl+; enters the current date in a cell. Pressing Ctrl+: enters the current time in a cell. However, both of these hotkeys create a static value; that is, the date or time reflects the instant that you typed the hotkey and never changes in the future.

Excel offers two functions for calculating the current date: NOW and TODAY. These functions are excellent for figuring out the number of days until a deadline or how late an open receivable might be.

## SYNTAX: =NOW() AND TODAY()

NOW returns the serial number of the current date and time. TODAY returns the serial number of the current date. The TODAY function returns today's date, without any time attached. The NOW function returns the current date and time.

Both of these functions can be made to display the current date, but there is an important distinction when you are performing calculations with the functions.

In Figure 23.31, Column A contains NOW functions, and Column C contains TODAY functions. Row 2 is formatted as a date and time. Row 3 is formatted as a date. Row 4 is formatted as numeric. Cell A3 and C3 look the same. If you simply need to display the date without using it in a calculation, then NOW or TODAY work fine.

**Figure 23.31**
NOW and TODAY can be made to look alike, but you need to choose the proper one if you are going to be using the result in a later calculation.

| | A | B | C | D |
|---|---|---|---|---|
| 1 | NOW() | | TODAY() | Comment |
| 2 | 4/14/07 11:49 AM | | 4/14/07 12:00 AM | Formatted as Date/Time |
| 3 | 4/14/07 | | 4/14/07 | Formatted as Date |
| 4 | 39186.4925 | | 39186.0000 | Formatted as Serial Number |
| 5 | | | | |
| 6 | | | | |
| 7 | 12/25/2007 | | 12/25/2007 | Deadline |
| 8 | 254.5075 | | 255.0000 | Days Until Deadline |
| 9 | | | | |

Row 8 calculates the number of days until a deadline approaches. While most people would say that tomorrow is 1 day away, the formula in A8 would tend to say that the deadline is 0.5141 days away. This can be deceiving. If you are going to use the result of NOW or TODAY in a date calculation, you should use TODAY to prevent Excel from reporting fractional days. The formula in A8 is =A7-A3, formatted as numeric instead of a date.

**CAUTION**

> It would be nice if NOW() would function like a real-time clock, constantly updating in Excel. However, the result is calculated when the file is opened, with each press of the F9 key and when an entry is made elsewhere in the worksheet.

## USING YEAR, MONTH, DAY, HOUR, MINUTE, AND SECOND TO BREAK A DATE/TIME APART

If you have a column of dates in April 2007, you can easily make them all look the same by using the MMM-YY format. However, the dates in the actual cells are still different. The April 2007 records are not sorted as if they were a tie. Excel offers six functions that you can use to extract a single portion of the date: YEAR, MONTH, DAY, HOUR, MINUTE, and SECOND.

In Figure 23.32, cell A1 contains a date and time. Functions in A3 through A8 break out the date into components:

- =YEAR(date) returns the year portion as a four-digit year.
- =MONTH(date) returns the month number, from 1 through 12.
- =DAY(date) returns the day of the month, from 1 through 31.
- =HOUR(date) returns the hour, from 1 to 24.
- =MINUTE(date) returns the minute, from 1 to 60.
- =SECOND(date) returns the second, from 1 to 60.

In each case, *date* must contain a valid Excel serial number for a date. The cell containing the *date* serial number may be formatted as a date or as a number.

**Figure 23.32**
These six functions allow you to isolate any portion of a date or time.

| | A | B | C |
|---|---|---|---|
| | A3 | ▾ | *f*ₓ =YEAR(A1) |
| 1 | 4/5/06 7:18:29 PM | | |
| 2 | | | |
| 3 | 2006 | =YEAR(A1) | |
| 4 | 4 | =MONTH(A1) | |
| 5 | 5 | =DAY(A1) | |
| 6 | 19 | =HOUR(A1) | |
| 7 | 18 | =MINUTE(A1) | |
| 8 | 29 | =SECOND(A1) | |
| 9 | | | |

## USING DATE TO CALCULATE A DATE FROM YEAR, MONTH, AND DAY

The DATE function is one of the most amazing functions in Excel. Microsoft implemented this function excellently, allowing you to do amazing date calculations.

**SYNTAX:** =DATE(*year*,*month*,*day*)

The DATE function returns the serial number that represents a particular date. This function takes the following arguments:

- *year*—This argument can be one to four digits. If *year* is between 0 and 1899 (inclusive), Excel adds that value to 1900 to calculate the year. For example, =DATE(100,1,2) returns January 2, 2000 (1900+100). If year is between 1900 and 9999 (inclusive), Excel uses that value as the year. For example, =DATE(2000,1,2) returns January 2, 2000. If *year* is less than 0 or is 10000 or greater, Excel returns a #NUM! error.

- *month*—This is a number representing the month of the year. If month is greater than 12, month adds that number of months to the first month in the year specified. For example, =DATE(1998,14,2) returns the serial number representing February 2, 1999.

- *day*—This is a number representing the day of the month. If *day* is greater than the number of days in the month specified, *day* adds that number of days to the first day in the month. For example, =DATE(1998,1,35) returns the serial number representing February 4, 1998. In a trivial example, =DATE(2007,3,5) returns March 5, 2007.

The true power in the DATE function occurs when one or more of the year, month, or day are calculated values. Here are some examples:

- If Cell A2 contains an invoice date and you want to calculate the day one month later, you use =DATE(Year(A2),Month(A2)+1,Day(A2)).
- To calculate the beginning of the month, you use =DATE(Year(A2),Month(A2),1).
- To calculate the end of the month, you use =DATE(Year(A2),Month(A2)+1,1)-1.

The DATE function is amazing because it enables Excel to deal perfectly with invalid dates. If your calculations for *month* causes it to exceed 12, this is no problem. For example, if you ask Excel to calculate =DATE(2006,16,45), Excel considers the 16th month of 2006 to be April 2007. To find the 45th day of April 2007, Excel moves ahead to May 15, 2007.

Figure 23.33 shows various results of the DATE and TIME functions.

**Figure 23.33**
The formulas in Column D use DATE or TIME functions to calculate an Excel serial number from three arguments.

| | A | B | C | D | E |
|---|---|---|---|---|---|
| | | | | D2 =DATE(A2,B2,C2) | |
| 1 | Year | Month | Day | DATE | |
| 2 | 2006 | 16 | 45 | 5/15/2007 | |
| 3 | 2008 | 1 | 60 | 2/29/2008 | |
| 4 | 2009 | 1 | 60 | 3/1/2009 | |
| 5 | 2007 | 3 | 5 | 3/5/2007 | |
| 6 | | | | | |
| 7 | | | | | |
| 8 | Hour | Minute | Second | TIME | |
| 9 | 1 | 12 | 23 | 1:12:23 AM | |
| 10 | 13 | 12 | 23 | 1:12:23 PM | |
| 11 | 12 | 72 | 23 | 1:12:23 PM | |
| 12 | 37 | 12 | 23 | 1:12:23 PM | |
| 13 | | | | | |

## USING TIME TO CALCULATE A TIME

The TIME function is similar to the DATE function. It calculates a time serial number given a specific hour, minute, and second.

SYNTAX: =TIME(*hour*,*minute*,*second*)

The TIME function returns the decimal number for a particular time. The decimal number returned by TIME is a value ranging from 0 to 0.99999999, representing the times from 0:00:00 (12:00:00 a.m.) to 23:59:59 (11:59:59 p.m.). This function takes the following arguments:

- *hour*—This is a number from 0 to 23, representing the hour.
- *minute*—This is a number from 0 to 59, representing the minute.
- *second*—This is a number from 0 to 59, representing the second.

As with the DATE function, Excel can handle situations in which the *minute* or *second* argument calculates to more than 60. For example, =TIME(12,72,120) evaluates to 1:14 PM.

Additional examples of TIME are shown in the bottom half of Figure 23.33 in the preceding section.

## USING DATEVALUE TO CONVERT TEXT DATES TO REAL DATES

It is easy to end up with a worksheet full of text dates. Sometimes this is due to importing data from another system. Sometimes it is caused by someone not understanding how dates work.

If your dates are in many conceivable formats, you can use the DATEVALUE function to convert the text dates to serial numbers, which can then be formatted as dates.

SYNTAX: =DATEVALUE(*date_text*)

The DATEVALUE function returns the serial number of the date represented by *date_text*. You use DATEVALUE to convert a date represented by text to a serial number. The argument *date_text* is text that represents a date in an Excel date format. For example, "1/30/1998" and "30-Jan-1998" are text strings within quotation marks that represent dates. Using the default date system in Excel for Windows, *date_text* must represent a date from January 1, 1900, to December 31, 9999. DATEVALUE returns a #VALUE! error if *date_text* is out of this range. If the year portion of *date_text* is omitted, DATEVALUE uses the current year from your computer's built-in clock. Time information in *date_text* is ignored.

Any of the text values in Column A of Figure 23.34 are successfully translated to a date serial number. In this instance, Excel should have been smart enough to automatically format the resulting cells as dates. By default, the cells are formatted as numeric. This leads many people to believe that DATEVALUE doesn't work. You have to apply a date format in order to achieve the desired result.

**CAUTION**

The DATEVALUE function *must* be used with text dates. If you have a column of values in which some values are text and some are actual dates, using DATEVALUE on the actual dates will cause a #VALUE error.

**Figure 23.34**
The formulas in Column B use DATEVALUE to convert the text entries in Column A to date serial numbers.

| B2 | ▼ | *fx* =DATEVALUE(A2) |
|---|---|---|

| ◢ | A | B |
|---|---|---|
| 1 | **TEXT** | **DATEVALUE** |
| 2 | 03/05/07 | 39146 |
| 3 | 03/05/2007 | 39146 |
| 4 | 3/5/2007 | 39146 |
| 5 | 5-Mar-07 | 39146 |
| 6 | Mar 5, 2007 | 39146 |
| 7 | March 05, 2007 | 39146 |
| 8 | 03-05-2007 | 39146 |
| 9 | 3-5-2007 | 39146 |
| 10 | | |

**23**

## USING TIMEVALUE TO CONVERT TEXT TIMES TO REAL TIMES

It is easy to end up with a column of text values that look like times. Similarly to DATEVALUE, you can use the TIMEVALUE function to convert these to real times.

SYNTAX: =TIMEVALUE(*time_text*)

The TIMEVALUE function returns the decimal number of the time represented by a text string. The decimal number is a value ranging from 0 to 0.99999999, representing the times from 0:00:00 (12:00:00 a.m.) to 23:59:59 (11:59:59 p.m.). The argument *time_text* is a text string that represents a time in any one of the Microsoft Excel time formats. For example, "6:45 PM" and "18:45" are text strings within quotation marks that represent time. Date information in *time_text* is ignored.

The TIMEVALUE function is difficult to use because it is easy for a person to enter the wrong formats. In Figure 23.35, many people would interpret Cell A8 as meaning 45 minutes and 30 seconds. Excel, however, treats this as 45 hours and 30 minutes. This misinterpretation makes TIMEVALUE almost useless for a column of cells that contain a text representation of minute and seconds. (The "Excel Troubleshooting" section later in this chapter discusses how to solve this.)

Frustratingly, Excel does not automatically format the results of this function as a time. Column B shows the result as Excel presents it. Column C shows the same result after a time format has been applied.

**Figure 23.35**
The formulas in Column B use TIMEVALUE to convert the text entries in Column A to times. If there is not a leading zero before entries with minutes and seconds, the formula produces an unexpected result.

| | B2 | ▼ | *fx* | =TIMEVALUE(A2) | |
|---|---|---|---|---|---|
| | A | B | C | | |
| 1 | TEXT | TIMEVALUE | FORMATTED | | |
| 2 | 1:10 | 0.048611111 | 1:10:00 AM | | |
| 3 | 1:10 AM | 0.048611111 | 1:10:00 AM | | |
| 4 | 1:10 PM | 0.548611111 | 1:10:00 PM | | |
| 5 | 13:10 | 0.548611111 | 1:10:00 PM | | |
| 6 | 1:10:30 | 0.048958333 | 1:10:30 AM | | |
| 7 | 1:45:30 | 0.073263889 | 1:45:30 AM | | |
| 8 | 45:30 | 0.895833333 | 9:30:00 PM | | |
| 9 | 0:45:30 | 0.031597222 | 12:45:30 AM | | |
| 10 | | | | | |

## USING WEEKDAY TO GROUP DATES BY DAY OF THE WEEK

The WEEKDAY function would not be so intimidating if people could just agree how to number the days. This one function can give three different results.

SYNTAX: =WEEKDAY(*serial_number*,*return_type*)

The WEEKDAY function returns the day of the week corresponding to a date. The day is given as an integer, ranging from 1 (Sunday) to 7 (Saturday), by default. This function takes the following arguments:

- *serial_number*—This is a sequential number that represents the date of the day you are trying to find. Dates may be entered as text strings within quotation marks (for example, "1/30/1998", "1998/01/30"), as serial numbers (for example, 35825, which represents January 30, 1998), or as results of other formulas or functions (for example, DATE-VALUE("1/30/1998")).

- *return_type*—This is a number that determines the type of return value:

  - If *return_type* is 1 or omitted, WEEKDAY works like the calendar on your wall. Typically, calendars are printed with Sunday on the left and Saturday on the right. The default version of WEEKDAY numbers these columns from 1 through 7.

  - If *return_type* is 2, you are using the biblical version of WEEKDAY. In the biblical version, Sunday is the seventh day. Working backward, Monday must occupy the 1 position.

  - If *return_type* is 3, you are using the accounting version of WEEKDAY. In this version, Monday is assigned a value of 0, followed by 1 for Tuesday, and so on. This version makes it very easy to group records by week. If Cell A2 contains a date, then A2-WEEKDAY(A2,3) converts the date to the Monday that starts the week.

Figure 23.36 shows the results of WEEKDAY for all three return types.

**Figure 23.36**
Columns B, C, and D compare the `WEEKDAY` function for the three different `return_type` values shown in Row 3.

B4 =WEEKDAY($A4,B$3)

| | A | B | C | D |
|---|---|---|---|---|
| 1 | | *Return_Type ----->* | | |
| 3 | Date | 1 | 2 | 3 |
| 4 | Sunday, April 01, 2007 | 1 | 7 | 6 |
| 5 | Monday, April 02, 2007 | 2 | 1 | 0 |
| 6 | Tuesday, April 03, 2007 | 3 | 2 | 1 |
| 7 | Wednesday, April 04, 2007 | 4 | 3 | 2 |
| 8 | Thursday, April 05, 2007 | 5 | 4 | 3 |
| 9 | Friday, April 06, 2007 | 6 | 5 | 4 |
| 10 | Saturday, April 07, 2007 | 7 | 6 | 5 |
| 11 | Sunday, April 08, 2007 | 1 | 7 | 6 |
| 12 | | | | |



## USING WEEKNUM TO GROUP DATES INTO WEEKS

`WEEKNUM` is a disappointing function. It is disappointing because Microsoft does not perform the function correctly. Microsoft is probably keeping the calculation consistent with some earlier spreadsheets that started doing this incorrectly. However, it would be really easy for Microsoft to add a new pair or *`return_type`* arguments that would calculate `WEEKNUM` correctly.

SYNTAX: `=WEEKNUM(`*`serial_num`*`,`*`return_type`*`)`

The `WEEKNUM` function returns a number that indicates where the week falls numerically within a year. This function takes the following arguments:

- *`serial_num`*—This is a date within the week.
- *`return_type`*—This is a number that determines on what day the week begins. The default is `1`. If *`return_type`* is `1` or omitted, the week begins on Sunday. If *`return_type`* is `2`, the week begins on Monday.

Figure 23.37 shows `WEEKNUM` for the first eight days of each year of the next eight years. Rows 13 through 20 show `WEEKNUM` with a *`return_type`* of `1`, so the week starts on Sunday.

Look at Column F. The first day of the year is a Sunday. This works; Cells F13:F19 report the first seven days as Week 1, and Cell F20 reports Sunday, January 8, 2012, as the first "day of the" week for Week 2.

However, look at E13:E20. In this case, the year 2011 starts on a Saturday. The first day of the year is treated as Week 1. Excel says that Week 2 starts on January 2, 2010. It is horrible to have a one-day week starting your year. It guarantees that you will have a significant Week 53 at the end of the year.

There is an ANSI standard for week numbering. This system says that your Week 1 must have at least four days. In the ANSI system, Saturday, January 1, 2011, would be called Week 0. In this system, whichever week contains January 4 is considered Week 1.

## ALTERNATE CALENDAR SYSTEMS AND DAYS360

There are many alternate calendar systems that you might have to work with in Excel. Here are some examples:

**Figure 23.37**
Excel calculates week numbers, but they are out of sync with the rest of the world.

| | A | B | C | D | E | F | G | H |
|---|---|---|---|---|---|---|---|---|
| | A13 | | fx | =WEEKNUM(A2,1) | | | | |
| 1 | | | | | | | | |
| 2 | Mon 1/1/07 | Tue 1/1/08 | Thu 1/1/09 | Fri 1/1/10 | Sat 1/1/11 | Sun 1/1/12 | Tue 1/1/13 | Wed 1/1/14 |
| 3 | Tue 1/2/07 | Wed 1/2/08 | Fri 1/2/09 | Sat 1/2/10 | Sun 1/2/11 | Mon 1/2/12 | Wed 1/2/13 | Thu 1/2/14 |
| 4 | Wed 1/3/07 | Thu 1/3/08 | Sat 1/3/09 | Sun 1/3/10 | Mon 1/3/11 | Tue 1/3/12 | Thu 1/3/13 | Fri 1/3/14 |
| 5 | Thu 1/4/07 | Fri 1/4/08 | Sun 1/4/09 | Mon 1/4/10 | Tue 1/4/11 | Wed 1/4/12 | Fri 1/4/13 | Sat 1/4/14 |
| 6 | Fri 1/5/07 | Sat 1/5/08 | Mon 1/5/09 | Tue 1/5/10 | Wed 1/5/11 | Thu 1/5/12 | Sat 1/5/13 | Sun 1/5/14 |
| 7 | Sat 1/6/07 | Sun 1/6/08 | Tue 1/6/09 | Wed 1/6/10 | Thu 1/6/11 | Fri 1/6/12 | Sun 1/6/13 | Mon 1/6/14 |
| 8 | Sun 1/7/07 | Mon 1/7/08 | Wed 1/7/09 | Thu 1/7/10 | Fri 1/7/11 | Sat 1/7/12 | Mon 1/7/13 | Tue 1/7/14 |
| 9 | Mon 1/8/07 | Tue 1/8/08 | Thu 1/8/09 | Fri 1/8/10 | Sat 1/8/11 | Sun 1/8/12 | Tue 1/8/13 | Wed 1/8/14 |
| 10 | | | | | | | | |
| 11 | | | | | | | | |
| 12 | WEEKNUM WITH RETURN_TYPE OF 1 (Week begins on Sunday) | | | | | | | |
| 13 | 1 | 1 | 1 | 1 | 1 | 1 | 1 | 1 |
| 14 | 1 | 1 | 1 | 1 | 1 | 1 | 1 | 1 |
| 15 | 1 | 1 | 1 | 2 | 2 | 1 | 1 | 1 |
| 16 | 1 | 1 | 2 | 2 | 2 | 1 | 1 | 1 |
| 17 | 1 | 1 | 2 | 2 | 2 | 1 | 1 | 2 |
| 18 | 1 | 2 | 2 | 2 | 2 | 1 | 2 | 2 |
| 19 | 2 | 2 | 2 | 2 | 2 | 1 | 2 | 2 |
| 20 | 2 | 2 | 2 | 2 | 2 | 2 | 2 | 2 |
| 21 | | | | | | | | |
| 22 | | | | | | | | |
| 23 | WEEKNUM WITH RETURN_TYPE OF 2 (Week begins on Monday) | | | | | | | |
| 24 | 1 | 1 | 1 | 1 | 1 | 1 | 1 | 1 |
| 25 | 1 | 1 | 1 | 1 | 1 | 2 | 1 | 1 |
| 26 | 1 | 1 | 1 | 1 | 2 | 2 | 1 | 1 |
| 27 | 1 | 1 | 1 | 2 | 2 | 2 | 1 | 1 |
| 28 | 1 | 1 | 2 | 2 | 2 | 2 | 1 | 1 |
| 29 | 1 | 1 | 2 | 2 | 2 | 2 | 1 | 2 |
| 30 | 1 | 2 | 2 | 2 | 2 | 2 | 2 | 2 |
| 31 | 2 | 2 | 2 | 2 | 2 | 2 | 2 | 2 |
| 32 | | | | | | | | |

- Manufacturers often redefine a quarter as being composed of 13 workweeks, with the first 4 weeks being called Month 1, the next 4 weeks being Month 2, and the final 5 weeks being Month 3. This is known as a 4-4-5 calendar.

- Retailers use a special retail calendar composed of 52 7-day weeks. Each week ends on a Sunday. If you compare Week 7, Day 6 of one year to Week 7, Day 6 of another year, you are assured that you are comparing a Saturday to a Saturday and can have a like comparison.

- Some accounting systems use a 360-day calendar. In this type of system, the year is divided into 12 months of 30 days. There is special handling for months with 31 days. Unfortunately, U.S. and European accounting boards disagree on the special handling, so there are two sets of rules.

Out of these three alternate calendar systems, Excel handles only the 360-day calendar. Excel provides the DAYS360 function and the YEARFRAC function to deal with the date system.

SYNTAX: =DAYS360(*start_date*,*end_date*,*method*)

The DAYS360 function returns the number of days between two dates, based on a 360-day year (12 30-day months), which is used in some accounting calculations. You use this function to help compute payments if your accounting system is based on 12 30-day months. This function takes the following arguments:

- *start_date* and *end_date*—These are the two dates between which you want to know the number of days. If *start_date* occurs after *end_date*, DAYS360 returns a negative number. Dates may be entered as text strings within quotation marks (for example, "1/30/1998",

"1998/01/30"), as serial numbers (for example, 35825, which represents January 30, 1998, if you're using the 1900 date system), or as results of other formulas or functions (for example, DATEVALUE("1/30/1998")).

- *method*—This is a logical value that specifies whether to use the U.S. or European method in the calculation:
  - FALSE or omitted is a U.S. (National Association of Securities Dealers) method. If the starting date is the 31st of a month, it becomes equal to the 30th of the same month. If the ending date is the 31st of a month and the starting date is earlier than the 30th of a month, the ending date becomes equal to the 1st of the next month; otherwise, the ending date becomes equal to the 30th of the same month.
  - TRUE is a European method. Starting dates or ending dates that occur on the 31st of a month become equal to the 30th of the same month.

## USING YEARFRAC OR DATEDIF TO CALCULATE ELAPSED TIME

If you work in a human resources department, you might be concerned with years of service in order to calculate a certain benefit. Excel provides one function, YEARFRAC, that can calculate decimal years of service in five different ways. An old function, DATEDIF, has been hanging around since Lotus 1-2-3; it can calculate the difference between two dates in complete years, months, or days.

SYNTAX: =YEARFRAC(*start_date,end_date,basis*)

The YEARFRAC function calculates the fraction of the year represented by the number of whole days between two dates (*start_date* and *end_date*). You use the YEARFRAC worksheet function to identify the proportion of a whole year's benefits or obligations to assign to a specific term.

This function takes the following arguments:

- *start_date*—This is a date that represents the start date. Dates may be entered as text strings within quotation marks (for example, "1/30/1998", "1998/01/30"), as serial numbers (for example, 35825, which represents January 30, 1998, if you're using the 1900 date system), or as results of other formulas or functions (for example, DATE-VALUE("1/30/1998")).
- *end_date*—This is a date that represents the end date.
- *basis*—This is the type of day count basis to use. Figure 23.38 compares the five types of basis available:
  - If *basis* is 0 or omitted, Excel uses a 30/360 plan, modified for American use. In this plan, the employee earns 1/360 of a year's credit on most days. The employee earns no service on the day after any 31st of the month. In a leap year, the employee earns 2/360 of a year for showing up on March 1. In a non–leap year, the employee earns 3/360 of a year for showing up on March 1.
  - If *basis* is 1, the actual number of elapsed days is divided by the actual number of days in the year. This method works well and ensures that the year fraction ends up being 1 on the anniversary date, whether it is a leap year or not.

23

- If *basis* is 2, the actual number of elapsed days is divided by 360. If someone would show up and work for 30 years straight for one employer, this method would give that person an extra 0.4528 years of credit. Sisogenes would be spinning in his grave.

- If *basis* is 3, the actual number of elapsed days is divided by 365. This works great for three out of every four years. It is slightly wrong in leap years.

- If *basis* is 4, Excel uses a 30/360 plan, modified for European use. This is similar to the default *basis* of 0. In this plan, the employee gets no credit for working any 31st of the month. The employee still gets triple credit for working March 1 (to make up for the 29th and 30th of February). In a leap year, March 1 is worth only double credit.

SYNTAX: =DATEDIF(*start_date*,*end_date*,*unit*)

In contrast to YEARFRAC, the DATEDIF function calculates complete years, months, or days. This function calculates the number of days, months, or years between two dates. It is provided for compatibility with Lotus 1-2-3. This function takes the following arguments:

- *start_date*—This is a date that represents the first, or starting, date of the period. Dates may be entered as text strings within quotation marks (for example, "2001/1/30"), as serial numbers, or as the results of other formulas or functions (for example, DATEVALUE("2001/1/30")).

- *end_date*—This is a date that represents the last, or ending, date of the period.

- *unit*—This is the type of information you want returned. The various values for *unit* are shown in Table 23.5.

**TABLE 23.5  *unit* VALUES USED BY THE DATEDIF FUNCTION**

| unit Value | Description |
| --- | --- |
| Y | The number of complete years in the period. A complete year is earned on the anniversary date of the employee's start date. |
| M | The number of complete months in the period. This number is incremented on the anniversary date. If the employee was hired on January 18, that person has earned one month of service on the 18th of February. If an employee is hired on January 31, then she earns credit for the month when she shows up for work on the 1st after any month with fewer than 31 days. |
| D | The number of days in the period. This could be figured out by simply subtracting the two dates. |
| MD | The number of days, ignoring months and years. You could use a combination of two DATEDIF functions—one using M and one using MD—to calculate days. |
| YM | The number of months, ignoring years. You could use a combination of two DATEDIF functions—one using Y and one using YM— to calculate months. |
| YD | The number of days, ignoring complete years. |

Figure 23.38 compares the five types of *basis* of YEARFRAC with the six *unit* values of DATEDIF. Each cell uses $A$1 as the start date and that row's Column A as the end date.

**Figure 23.38**
If your benefits package includes information about complete months, then YEARFRAC with a *basis* value of 0 works best. Otherwise, a *basis* value of 1 is the most accurate.

| | A | B | C | D | E | F | G | H | I | J | K | L | M |
|---|---|---|---|---|---|---|---|---|---|---|---|---|---|
| | | B372 | | fx | =YEARFRAC($A$1,$A372,B$5) | | | | | | | | |
| 1 | 1/1/2008 | Basis - for YEARFRAC ----> | | | | | Unit - for DATEDIF ----> | | | | | | |
| 2 | | 30/360 | /Actual | /360 | /365 | 30/360 | | (years) | (months) | (days) | (days) | (months) | (days) |
| 3 | | (Amer.) | | | | (Euro) | | | | | | | |
| 5 | DATE | 0 | 1 | 2 | 3 | 4 | | Y | M | D | MD | YM | YD |
| 366 | 12/26/2008 | 0.98611 | 0.98361 | 1. | 0.9863 | 0.98611 | | 0 | 11 | 360 | 25 | 11 | 360 |
| 367 | 12/27/2008 | 0.98889 | 0.98634 | 1.00278 | 0.98904 | 0.98889 | | 0 | 11 | 361 | 26 | 11 | 361 |
| 368 | 12/28/2008 | 0.99167 | 0.98907 | 1.00556 | 0.99178 | 0.99167 | | 0 | 11 | 362 | 27 | 11 | 362 |
| 369 | 12/29/2008 | 0.99444 | 0.9918 | 1.00833 | 0.99452 | 0.99444 | | 0 | 11 | 363 | 28 | 11 | 363 |
| 370 | 12/30/2008 | 0.99722 | 0.99454 | 1.01111 | 0.99726 | 0.99722 | | 0 | 11 | 364 | 29 | 11 | 364 |
| 371 | 12/31/2008 | 1. | 0.99727 | 1.01389 | 1. | 0.99722 | | 0 | 11 | 365 | 30 | 11 | 365 |
| 372 | 1/1/2009 | 1. | 1. | 1.01667 | 1.00274 | 1. | | 1 | 12 | 366 | 0 | 0 | 0 |
| 373 | | | | | | | | | | | | | |

## USING EDATE TO CALCULATE LOAN OR INVESTMENT MATURITY DATES

If someone invests in a six-month CD on the 17th of the month, the maturity date is on the 17th of another month. This would be a fairly straightforward calculation if no one invested on the 31st of a month.

The maturity rules work such that if you invest on the 31st of a month, and the CD would be scheduled to mature on the 31st of June, the CD maturity actually happens on the last day of June, which is June 30.

If a CD is to mature on the 31st, 30th, or 29th day of February, the CD matures on the last day of February.

SYNTAX: =EDATE(*start_date*,*months*)

The EDATE function returns the serial number that represents the date that is the indicated number of months before or after a specified date (that is, *start_date*). You use EDATE to calculate maturity dates or due dates that fall on the same day of the month as the date of issue. This function takes the following arguments:

- *start_date*—This is a date that represents the start date. Dates may be entered as text strings within quotation marks (for example, "1/30/1998", "1998/01/30"), as serial numbers (for example, 35825, which represents January 30, 1998, if you're using the 1900 date system), or as results of other formulas or functions (for example, DATE-VALUE("1/30/1998")). If the start_date is not valid, EDATE returns a #NUM! error.

- *months*—This is the number of months before or after *start_date*. A positive value for *months* yields a future date; a negative value yields a past date. If *months* is not an integer, it is truncated.

Figure 23.39 shows several examples of EDATE. Note that in Column B, the function is a no-brainer. You could easily calculate it by using the DATE function. The only interesting cases occur on the 29th, 30th, and 31st of the month.

23

**Figure 23.39**
You can use EDATE to calculate the maturity date for a security.

| B4 | | fx | =EDATE(B$3,$A4) | |
| --- | --- | --- | --- | --- |
| | A | B | C | D | E |
| 1 | MATURITY DATES | | | | |
| 2 | | | | | |
| 3 | Months | 1/1/08 | 1/29/08 | 1/30/08 | 1/31/08 |
| 4 | 6 | 7/1/08 | 7/29/08 | 7/30/08 | 7/31/08 |
| 5 | 5 | 6/1/08 | 6/29/08 | 6/30/08 | 6/30/08 |
| 6 | 4 | 5/1/08 | 5/29/08 | 5/30/08 | 5/31/08 |
| 7 | 3 | 4/1/08 | 4/29/08 | 4/30/08 | 4/30/08 |
| 8 | 2 | 3/1/08 | 3/29/08 | 3/30/08 | 3/31/08 |
| 9 | 1 | 2/1/08 | 2/29/08 | 2/29/08 | 2/29/08 |
| 10 | 0 | 1/1/08 | 1/29/08 | 1/30/08 | 1/31/08 |
| 11 | -1 | 12/1/07 | 12/29/07 | 12/30/07 | 12/31/07 |
| 12 | -2 | 11/1/07 | 11/29/07 | 11/30/07 | 11/30/07 |
| 13 | -3 | 10/1/07 | 10/29/07 | 10/30/07 | 10/31/07 |
| 14 | -4 | 9/1/07 | 9/29/07 | 9/30/07 | 9/30/07 |
| 15 | -5 | 8/1/07 | 8/29/07 | 8/30/07 | 8/31/07 |
| 16 | -6 | 7/1/07 | 7/29/07 | 7/30/07 | 7/31/07 |
| 17 | | | | | |

Note that EDATE can be used to back into an investment date from a maturity date. For example, the records in Rows 11 through 16 pass a negative number for the *months* parameter.

**CAUTION**

> You have to format the result of the EDATE formula to be a date to see the expected results.

## USING EOMONTH TO CALCULATE THE END OF THE MONTH

Before Excel 2007, about 89 functions were available only in the Analysis Toolpack. Some companies had rules that you were not allowed to build spreadsheets using the functions in the Analysis Toolpack. This rule was probably created by some corporate executive who didn't know how to turn on the Analysis Toolpack!

One of my favorite puzzles at MrExcel.com came from someone who worked at such a company. How can you calculate the end of the month without using EOMONTH? This is a hard question; the end of the month is the 31st if the month number is 1, 3, 5, 7, 8, 10, or 12. It is the 30th if the month number is 4, 6, 9, or 11. If the month number is 2, then you have to look at the year to figure out if it is a leap year for 29 days or not a leap year for 28 days. The formula to solve this was horrible:

```
=DATE(YEAR(A2),MONTH(A2),CHOOSE(MONTH(A2),31,28,31,30,31,30,31,31,30,31,30,31)
    +IF(MOD(YEAR(A2),4)=0,1,0))
```

Well-known Excel guru Aladin Akyurek weighed in with the great answer and ended the entire discussion. Aladin suggested using the DATE function to move up to the first of the next month and then simply subtract one day, using this formula:

```
=DATE(YEAR(A2),MONTH(A2)+1,1)-1
```

The sheer simplicity of this is beautiful. However, the whole question becomes immaterial now that EOMONTH has been promoted to be part of the actual Excel function set.

SYNTAX: =EOMONTH(*start_date*,*months*)

The EOMONTH function returns the serial number for the last day of the month that is the indicated number of months before or after *start_date*. You use EOMONTH to calculate maturity dates or due dates that fall on the last day of the month. This function takes the following arguments:

- *start_date*—This is a date that represents the starting date. Dates may be entered as text strings within quotation marks (for example, "1/30/1998", "1998/01/30"), as serial numbers, or as results of other formulas or functions (for example, DATE-VALUE("1/30/1998")). If *start_date* is not a valid date, EOMONTH returns a #NUM! error.

- *months*—This is the number of months before or after *start_date*. A positive value for *months* yields a future date; a negative value yields a past date. If *months* is not an integer, it is truncated. If *start_date* plus *months* yields an invalid date, EOMONTH returns a #NUM! error.

=EOMONTH(A2,0) converts any date to the end of the month.

**CAUTION**

> You have to format the result of the EOMONTH formula to be a date to see the expected results.

## USING WORKDAY OR NETWORKDAYS TO CALCULATE WORKDAYS

If you work in a service industry, allow me to apologize to you on behalf of Microsoft. If you work in retail, this section won't work for you. If you are in one of the countries where you have every Thursday off, this will not work. The workday functions work only for those people who still work in a traditional Monday-through-Friday work environment.

If you happen to be in a Monday-through-Friday environment, the functions WORKDAY and NETWORKDAYS are pretty cool. For example, they are great for calculating shipping days when you ship with FedEx or UPS. It takes a little work to get the holidays set up with these functions. Here's how you do it:

1. In an out-of-the-way section of a spreadsheet, enter any holidays that will fall during the workweek. This might be federal holidays, floating holidays, company holidays, and so on. The list of holidays can either be entered down a column or across a row. In the top portion of Figure 23.40, the holidays are in E2:E7.

2. Enter a starting date in a cell, such as B1.

3. Enter the number of workdays that the project is expected to take in another cell, such as B2.

4. Enter the ending date formula as =WORKDAY(B1,B2,E2:E7).

23

**Figure 23.40**

WORKDAY and NETWORKDAY can calculate the number of Monday-through-Friday days, exclusive of a range of holidays.

| | B3 | ▼ | $f_x$ =WORKDAY(B1,B2,E2:E7) | | | |
|---|---|---|---|---|---|---|
| ◢ | A | B | | C | D | E |
| 1 | Start Date: | Wednesday, April 18, 2007 | | | | Holidays |
| 2 | # Work Days | 65 | | | | 1/1/2006 |
| 3 | End Date: | Wednesday, July 18, 2007 | | | | 5/29/2006 |
| 4 | | =WORKDAY(B1,B2,E2:E7) | | | | 7/4/2006 |
| 5 | | | | | | 11/23/2006 |
| 6 | Start Date: | Saturday, April 14, 2007 | | | | 12/24/2006 |
| 7 | End Date: | Monday, June 18, 2007 | | | | 12/25/2006 |
| 8 | # Work Days | 46 | | | | |
| 9 | | =NETWORKDAYS(B6,B7,E2:E7) | | | | |
| 10 | | | | | | |

The NETWORKDAYS function takes two dates and figures out the number of workdays between them. For example, you might have a project that is due on June 18, 2007. If today is April 14, 2007, NETWORKDAYS can calculate how many workdays there are until the project is due.

SYNTAX: =NETWORKDAYS(*start_date,end_date,holidays*)

The NETWORKDAYS function returns the number of whole workdays between *start_date* and *end_date*. Workdays exclude weekends and any dates identified in holidays. You use NETWORKDAYS to calculate employee benefits that accrue based on the number of days worked during a specific term. This function takes the following arguments:

- *start_date*—This is a date that represents the start date. Dates may be entered as text strings within quotation marks (for example, "1/30/1998", "1998/01/30"), as serial numbers, or as results of other formulas or functions (for example, DATEVALUE("1/30/1998")).

- *end_date*—This is a date that represents the end date.

- *holidays*—This is an optional range of one or more dates to exclude from the working calendar, such as state and federal holidays and floating holidays. The list can be either a range of cells that contain the dates or an array constant of the serial numbers that represent the dates. If any argument is not a valid date, NETWORKDAYS returns a #NUM! error.

In Figure 23.40, the current date is entered in Cell B6. The project due date is entered in Cell B7. The holidays range is in E2:E7, as in the previous example. The formula in Cell B8 to calculate workdays is =NETWORKDAYS(B6,B7,E2:E7).

---

**Excel in Practice: Converting a Holiday Range to an Array**

The problem with putting the list of holidays in a range on a worksheet is that someone might accidentally overwrite or change the range of holidays.

The syntax for the workdays functions mentions that the holiday range can be converted to an array of serial numbers. To embed the holidays inside a function, you follow these steps:

1. In Figure 23.40, select cell B3.

2. In the Formula Bar, use the mouse to select the characters E2:E7.

3. Press the F9 key. Excel will replace the selected characters with the calculated version of those characters. In this case, the calculation is the array {38718,38866,etc.} as shown in Figure 23.41.

4. Press Enter to accept the new formula.

5. You can now delete the holidays in column E.

**Figure 23.41**
You can remove the holiday cells from the worksheet after embedding the array in the formula.

| | B3 | | | fx | =WORKDAY(B1,B2,{38718;38866;38902;39044;39075;39076}) | | | |
|---|---|---|---|---|---|---|---|---|
| | A | B | C | D | E | F | G |
| 1 | Start Date: | Wednesday, April 18, 2007 | | | | | |
| 2 | # Work Days | 65 | | | | | |
| 3 | End Date: | Wednesday, July 18, 2007 | | | | | |
| 4 | | =WORKDAY(B1,B2,{38718;38866;38902;39044;39075;39076}) | | | | | |
| 5 | | | | | | | |

# EXAMPLES OF TEXT FUNCTIONS

When they think of Excel, most people think of numbers. Excel is great at dealing with numbers, and it lets you write formulas to produce new numbers. Excel offers a whole cadre of formulas for dealing with text.

You might sometimes be frustrated because you receive data from other users and the text is not in the format you need. Or, the mainframe might send customer names in uppercase, or the employee in the next department might put a whole address in a single cell. Excel provides text functions to deal with all these situations and more.

## JOINING TEXT WITH THE AMPERSAND (&) OPERATOR

Chapter 20, "Formula Basics," mentions the ampersand (&) operator, but it is worth mentioning again here because it is the most important tool for dealing with text. The & is an operator that you use to join text.

Say that you have a worksheet with first name in Column A and last name in Column B, as shown in Figure 23.42. You need to put these names together in a single cell. If you use the formula =A2&B2 in Cell C2, Excel smashes the names together (for example, STEVENWOODWARD). Instead, you have to join three elements. In between A2 and B2, you need to join a single space in double quotes. The formula to do this is =A2&" "&B2.

**Figure 23.42**
The & character can be used to join text in cells or text enclosed in quotes.

| | C2 | | fx | =A2&" "&B2 | |
|---|---|---|---|---|---|
| | A | B | C |
| 1 | FIRST NAME | LAST NAME | NAME |
| 2 | STEVEN | WOODWARD | STEVEN WOODWARD |
| 3 | LINDSAY | RHODES | LINDSAY RHODES |
| 4 | VIVIAN | WALKER | VIVIAN WALKER |
| 5 | WALTER | SHAW | WALTER SHAW |
| 6 | MATTIE | PIERCE | MATTIE PIERCE |
| 7 | ELLEN | ATKINS | ELLEN ATKINS |
| 8 | MADELINE | MARTINEZ | MADELINE MARTINEZ |

23

**NOTE**

If you only want to keep the data in Column C, you have to convert the formulas to values before deleting Columns A and B. To do this, you select the data in Column C and then press Ctrl+C to copy. Then you select Home, Paste, Paste Values to convert the formulas to values.

Some people prefer to use the CONCATENATE function instead of the &. This function does not perform the way that I want it to perform, and I generally avoid it, but it is described in the following section.

SYNTAX: =CONCATENATE (*text1,text2,...*)

The CONCATENATE function joins several text strings into one text string. The arguments *text1, text2,...* are 1 to 30 text items to be joined into a single text item. The text items can be text strings, numbers, or single-cell references.

The problem with this function is that it can only select single cell references. An attempt to use =CONCATENATE(A2:B2) returns a #VALUE! error. If you have to enter =CONCATENATE(A2, " ",B2), it is easier to use =A2&" "&B2. Further, the function can handle only 30 references. If you are joining cells with spaces in between, you will run out of terms after just 15 cells. With the &, you can join more than 30 items.

## USING LOWER, UPPER, OR PROPER TO CONVERT TEXT CASE

Three functions—LOWER, UPPER, and PROPER—convert text to or from capital letters. In Figure 23.43, the products in Column A were entered in a haphazard fashion. Some products used lowercase, and some products used uppercase. Column B uses =UPPER(A2) to make all the products a uniform uppercase.

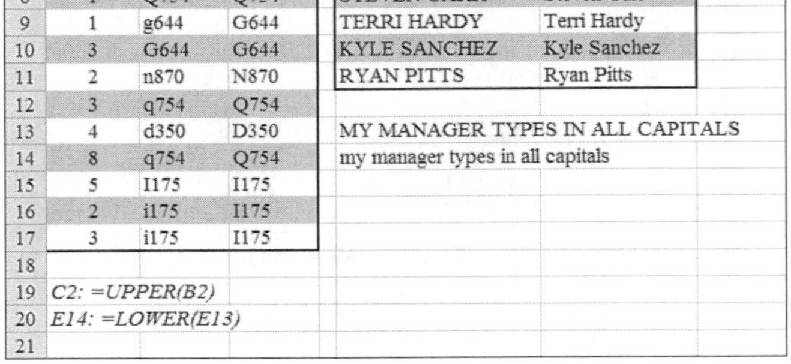

**Figure 23.43**
UPPER, LOWER, and PROPER can convert text to and from capital letters.

In Cell E13, text was entered by someone who never turns off Caps Lock. You can convert this uppercase to lowercase with =LOWER(E13).

> **N O T E**
>
> It would be great if Microsoft would add a function to convert to sentence case. We can hope that they add such a function in future versions of Excel.

In Column E, you see a range of names in uppercase. You can use =PROPER(E2) to convert the name to proper case, which capitalizes just the first letter of each word. The PROPER function is mostly fantastic, but there are a few cells that you have to manually correct. PROPER does correctly capitalize names with apostrophes, such as O'Rasi in Cell F3. It does not, however, correctly capitalize the interior c in McCartney in Cell F4. The function is also notorious for creating company names such as Ibm, 3m, and Aep.

**Syntax: =LOWER(*text*)**

The LOWER function converts all uppercase letters in a text string to lowercase. The argument *text* is the text you want to convert to lowercase. LOWER does not change characters in text that are not letters.

**Syntax: =PROPER(*text*)**

The PROPER function capitalizes the first letter in a text string and any other letters in text that follow any character other than a letter. It converts all other letters to lowercase letters.

The argument *text* is text enclosed in quotation marks, a formula that returns text, or a reference to a cell containing the text you want to partially capitalize.

**Syntax: =UPPER(*text*)**

The UPPER function converts text to uppercase. The argument *text* is the text you want converted to uppercase. *text* can be a reference or text string.

## Using TRIM to Remove Trailing Spaces

If you frequently import data, you might be plagued with a couple of annoying situations. This section and the next one deal with those situations.

You may have trailing spaces at the end of text cells. Although "ABC" and "ABC    " might look alike when viewed in Excel, they cause functions such as MATCH and VLOOKUP to fail. TRIM removes leading and trailing spaces.

In Figure 23.44, you have a simple VLOOKUP in Column B. The formula in Cell B2 is =VLOOKUP(A2,$F$2:$G$5,2,FALSE). Even though you can clearly see that M40498 is in the lookup table, VLOOKUP returns an #N/A! error, indicating that the product ID is missing from the lookup table.

**Figure 23.44**
This VLOOKUP should work, but in this instance, it fails.

| | A | B | C | D | E | F | G |
|---|---|---|---|---|---|---|---|
| | B2 | | | | fx | =VLOOKUP(A2,$F$2:$G$5,2,FALSE) | |
| 1 | ITEM | VLOOKUP | | | | Item | Description |
| 2 | M40498 | #N/A | | | | M40498 | 10" GOLD WEAVE |
| 3 | M40583 | #N/A | | | | M40583 | 12" GOLD WEAVE |
| 4 | M40485 | #N/A | | | | M40584 | 14" GOLD FLORENTINE |
| 5 | | | | | | M40485 | 16" SILVER WEAVE |
| 6 | | | | | | | |

To diagnose and correct this problem, you follow these steps:

1. Select one of the data cells in Column F. Press the F2 key to put the cell in Edit mode. A flashing insertion character appears at the end of the cell. Check to see if the flashing cursor is immediately after the last character.

2. Select one of the data cells in Column A. Press the F2 key to put the cell in Edit mode. Note whether the flashing insertion character is immediately after the last character. Figure 23.45 shows that the products in Column A have several trailing spaces after them. The products in the lookup table do not have any trailing spaces.

**Figure 23.45**
Spaces are padding the right side of the products in Column A.

| | A | B | C | D | E | F | G |
|---|---|---|---|---|---|---|---|
| | A2 | | | x ✓ fx | M40498 | | |
| 1 | ITEM | VLOOKUP | | | | Item | Description |
| 2 | M40498 | #N/A | | | | M40498 | 10" GOLD WEAVE |
| 3 | M40583 | #N/A | | | | M40583 | 12" GOLD WEAVE |
| 4 | M40485 | #N/A | | | | M40584 | 14" GOLD FLORENTINE |
| 5 | | | | | | M40485 | 16" SILVER WEAVE |
| 6 | | | | | | | |

3. If the problem is occurring in the values being looked up, you could simply modify the formula in Cell B2 to use the TRIM function. The new formula would be =VLOOKUP(TRIM(A2),$F$2:$G$5,2,FALSE). Figure 23.46 shows how this solves the problem.

**Figure 23.46**
Using TRIM to remove leading spaces allows VLOOKUP to work.

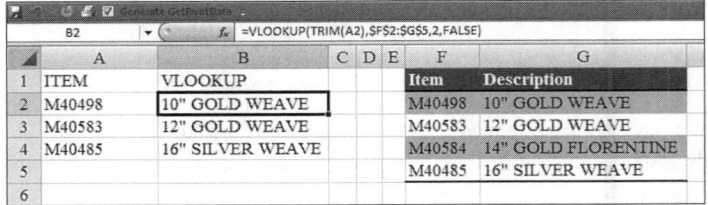

| | A | B | C | D | E | F | G |
|---|---|---|---|---|---|---|---|
| | B2 | | | | fx | =VLOOKUP(TRIM(A2),$F$2:$G$5,2,FALSE) | |
| 1 | ITEM | VLOOKUP | | | | Item | Description |
| 2 | M40498 | 10" GOLD WEAVE | | | | M40498 | 10" GOLD WEAVE |
| 3 | M40583 | 12" GOLD WEAVE | | | | M40583 | 12" GOLD WEAVE |
| 4 | M40485 | 16" SILVER WEAVE | | | | M40584 | 14" GOLD FLORENTINE |
| 5 | | | | | | M40485 | 16" SILVER WEAVE |
| 6 | | | | | | | |

4. If the problem is occurring in the first column of the lookup table, insert a new temporary column. Enter the function =TRIM(F2) in the temporary column. Copy this formula down to all rows of the lookup table. Copy the new formulas and select Home,

Paste, Values to paste the new values. Although the old and new values look the same, the TRIM function has removed the trailing spaces and now the products match.

### SYNTAX: =TRIM(*text*)

The TRIM function removes all spaces from text except for single spaces between words. You use TRIM on text that you have received from another application that may have irregular spacing. The argument *text* is the text from which you want spaces removed.

In Figure 23.47, Cell C1 contains six letters: ABC DEF. You might assume that the cell is set to be centered. However, the formula in Cell C2 appends an asterisk to each end of the value in Cell C1. This formula shows that there are several leading and trailing spaces in the value.

Using =LEN(C1) shows that the text actually contains 15 characters instead of 6 characters. The TRIM(C1) formula removes any leading spaces, any trailing spaces, and any extra interior spaces. The function still leaves one space between ABC and DEF because you want to continue to have words separated by a single space.

The formulas in Cells C5 and C6 confirm that the leading and trailing spaces are removed and that the length of the new value is only seven characters.

**Figure 23.47**
TRIM removes leading spaces and extra interior spaces.

| | A | B | C |
|---|---|---|---|
| | | | C5 ▾ *fx* ="*"&C4&"*" |
| 1 | | Original Value: | ABC   DEF |
| 2 | | ="*"&C1&"*" | *  ABC   DEF  * |
| 3 | | Length(C1) | 15 |
| 4 | | TRIM(C1) | ABC DEF |
| 5 | | ="*"&C4&"*" | *ABC DEF* |
| 6 | | LENGTH(C3) | 7 |
| 7 | | | |

## USING CLEAN TO REMOVE NONPRINTABLE CHARACTERS FROM TEXT

Although TRIM works great, the CLEAN function no longer works as advertised. CLEAN is designed to remove nonprintable characters from text.

Besides extra spaces, another annoying problem with data from other systems is that it may contain nonprintable characters. Excel offers a function that is supposed to remove nonprintable characters, but Microsoft's definition of a nonprintable character is far too narrow. The function was clearly written before the proliferation of web queries, Oracle, and SAP.

### SYNTAX: =CLEAN(*text*)

The CLEAN function removes all nonprintable characters from text. You use CLEAN on text imported from other applications that contains characters that may not print with your operating system. For example, you can use `CLEAN` to remove some low-level computer code that is frequently at the beginning and end of data files and cannot be printed.

The argument *text* is any worksheet information from which you want to remove nonprintable characters.

Unfortunately, Microsoft's definition of nonprintable characters is limited to the "old-time" bad characters. Today, you are likely to encounter far more bad characters than those.



Figure 23.48 shows data in Column A with characters that I routinely find in imported data. You might expect the `CLEAN` function in Column B to fix all these problems. If so, you will be highly disappointed. In the first pass, `CLEAN` did not clean any of the bad characters. After I edited Cell A2 to use a traditional nonprintable character, Cell B2 was able to clean that one character.

**Figure 23.48**
`CLEAN` removes a short list of nonprintable characters. Unfortunately, today's data is littered with a new crop of nonprintable characters.

B2 fx =CLEAN(A2)

| | A | B | C | D |
|---|---|---|---|---|
| 1 | M40498Š | M40498Š | | |
| 2 | M40583□ | M40583 | | |
| 3 | M40585 | M40585 | | |
| 4 | M70193Š | M70193Š | | |
| 5 | M70208Š | M70208Š | | |
| 6 | E91310Š | E91310Š | | |
| 7 | E91131Š | E91131Š | | |
| 8 | | | | |

To figure out exactly how `CLEAN` works, you need the `CHAR` function, which is conveniently scheduled to be discussed next. Read on for more of the `CLEAN` saga.

## USING THE CHAR FUNCTION TO GENERATE ANY CHARACTER

Computers have the ability to display 255 different characters in any given font. For the past 20 years, this set of 255 characters has been known as the ASCII (pronounced "ask-key") character set. My U.S. keyboard gives me the ability to type 96 of those characters. The keyboard in another country may offer several more or fewer characters, but the point is that you cannot access all 255 characters by using your keyboard.

You might have ventured into Start, All Programs, Accessories, System Tools, Character Map in order to find a particular character in the Wingdings character set. Also, if you have a favorite symbol, you might have memorized that you can insert the symbol by using a hotkey. For example, if you hold down Alt, type 0169 on the numeric keypad, and then release Alt, an Office program inserts the copyright symbol (©).

In Excel, rather than use hotkeys and the character map, you can use the `CHAR` function to generate a specific character.

SYNTAX: =CHAR(*number*)

The CHAR function returns the character specified by a number. You use CHAR to translate code page numbers you might get from files on other types of computers into characters.

The argument *number* is a number between 1 and 255 that specifies which character you want. The character is from the character set used by your computer.

Although I know a few characters off the top of my head, I usually take a look at all characters in a set by entering =CODE(ROW()) in Cells A1:A255. This returns Character 65 in Row 65, and so on.

To figure out which characters were actually removed by the CLEAN function (refer to the preceding section), I built a table with the numbers from 1 through 255. In Figure 23.49, Column A contains the character number. Column B has the function =CHAR(A2) to display that character in the Times New Roman font. Column C has a formula to reveal whether CLEAN removes that character: =IF(LEN(CLEAN(B2))=0,"YES","NOT"). After you copy these formulas to all 255 rows, you will learn that CLEAN removes characters numbered 1 through 31, 129, 141, 144, and 157.

To fit in one screen of cells, Figure 23.49 shows all the codes arranged on one page.

If you see a strange character in your data, you can learn the character number by using the CODE function, as described in the following section.

## USING THE CODE FUNCTION TO LEARN THE CHARACTER NUMBER FOR ANY CHARACTER

Each font set offers 255 different characters, numbered from 1 through 255. Old-time computer folks might know some of the popular codes off the top of their heads. For example, a capital A is 65. The capital letters run from 65 to 90, a space is 32, a lowercase letter a is 97, and the other lowercase letters run from 97 through 122.

In the early days of personal computers, every computer was packed with a list of the ASCII codes for each character. Today, with the character map, no one has to memorize character codes. However, in some instances, you might want to learn exactly what character you are seeing in a cell. The CODE function returns the character code for one character at a time.

SYNTAX: =CODE(*text*)

The CODE function returns a numeric code for the first character in a text string. The returned code corresponds to the character set used by your computer. The argument *text* is the text for which you want the code of the first character. This is an important distinction. CODE returns the code for only the first character in a cell. =CODE("A") and =CODE("ABC") return only 65 to indicate the capital letter A.

A new problem began happening in Excel in the past few years. People started encountering values with which TRIM would not remove the spaces from the text. For example, Figure 23.50 shows a value in Column A that very clearly contains several spaces in between the letters A and B.

AI29    *fx* =IF(LEN(CLEAN(AH29))=0,"Yes","Not")

| C# | Status | C# | Status | C# | Status | C# | Status | C# | Status | C# | Status | C# | Status | C# | Status | C# | Status |
|---|---|---|---|---|---|---|---|---|---|---|---|---|---|---|---|---|---|
| 1 □ | Yes | 30 □ | Yes | 59 ; | Not | 88 X | Not | 116 t | Not | 144 □ | Yes | 172 ¬ | Not | 200 È | Not | 228 ä | Not |
| 2 □ | Yes | 31 □ | Yes | 60 < | Not | 89 Y | Not | 117 u | Not | 145 ' | Not | 173 | Not | 201 É | Not | 229 å | Not |
| 3 □ | Yes | 32 | Not | 61 = | Not | 90 Z | Not | 118 v | Not | 146 ' | Not | 174 ® | Not | 202 Ê | Not | 230 æ | Not |
| 4 □ | Yes | 33 ! | Not | 62 > | Not | 91 [ | Not | 119 w | Not | 147 " | Not | 175 ¯ | Not | 203 Ë | Not | 231 ç | Not |
| 5 □ | Yes | 34 " | Not | 63 ? | Not | 92 \ | Not | 120 x | Not | 148 " | Not | 176 ° | Not | 204 Ì | Not | 232 è | Not |
| 6 □ | Yes | 35 # | Not | 64 @ | Not | 93 ] | Not | 121 y | Not | 149 • | Not | 177 ± | Not | 205 Í | Not | 233 é | Not |
| 7 □ | Yes | 36 $ | Not | 65 A | Not | 94 ^ | Not | 122 z | Not | 150 – | Not | 178 ² | Not | 206 Î | Not | 234 ê | Not |
| 8 □ | Yes | 37 % | Not | 66 B | Not | 95 _ | Not | 123 { | Not | 151 — | Not | 179 ³ | Not | 207 Ï | Not | 235 ë | Not |
| 9 □ | Yes | 38 & | Not | 67 C | Not | 96 ` | Not | 124 \| | Not | 152 ˜ | Not | 180 ´ | Not | 208 Ð | Not | 236 ì | Not |
| 10 □ | Yes | 39 ' | Not | 68 D | Not | 97 a | Not | 125 } | Not | 153 ™ | Not | 181 µ | Not | 209 Ñ | Not | 237 í | Not |
| 11 □ | Yes | 40 ( | Not | 69 E | Not | 98 b | Not | 126 ~ | Not | 154 š | Not | 182 ¶ | Not | 210 Ò | Not | 238 î | Not |
| 12 □ | Yes | 41 ) | Not | 70 F | Not | 99 c | Not | 127 □ | Not | 155 › | Not | 183 · | Not | 211 Ó | Not | 239 ï | Not |
| 13 □ | Yes | 42 * | Not | 71 G | Not | 100 d | Not | 128 € | Not | 156 œ | Not | 184 ¸ | Not | 212 Ô | Not | 240 ð | Not |
| 14 □ | Yes | 43 + | Not | 72 H | Not | 101 e | Not | 129 □ | Yes | 157 □ | Yes | 185 ¹ | Not | 213 Õ | Not | 241 ñ | Not |
| 15 □ | Yes | 44 , | Not | 73 I | Not | 102 f | Not | 130 ‚ | Not | 158 ž | Not | 186 º | Not | 214 Ö | Not | 242 ò | Not |
| 16 □ | Yes | 45 - | Not | 74 J | Not | 103 g | Not | 131 ƒ | Not | 159 Ÿ | Not | 187 » | Not | 215 × | Not | 243 ó | Not |
| 17 □ | Yes | 46 . | Not | 75 K | Not | 104 h | Not | 132 „ | Not | 160 | Not | 188 ¼ | Not | 216 Ø | Not | 244 ô | Not |
| 18 □ | Yes | 47 / | Not | 76 L | Not | 105 i | Not | 133 … | Not | 161 ¡ | Not | 189 ½ | Not | 217 Ù | Not | 245 õ | Not |
| 19 □ | Yes | 48 0 | Not | 77 M | Not | 106 j | Not | 134 † | Not | 162 ¢ | Not | 190 ¾ | Not | 218 Ú | Not | 246 ö | Not |
| 20 □ | Yes | 49 1 | Not | 78 N | Not | 107 k | Not | 135 ‡ | Not | 163 £ | Not | 191 ¿ | Not | 219 Û | Not | 247 ÷ | Not |
| 21 □ | Yes | 50 2 | Not | 79 O | Not | 108 l | Not | 136 ˆ | Not | 164 ¤ | Not | 192 À | Not | 220 Ü | Not | 248 ø | Not |
| 22 □ | Yes | 51 3 | Not | 80 P | Not | 109 m | Not | 137 ‰ | Not | 165 ¥ | Not | 193 Á | Not | 221 Ý | Not | 249 ù | Not |
| 23 □ | Yes | 52 4 | Not | 81 Q | Not | 110 n | Not | 138 Š | Not | 166 ¦ | Not | 194 Â | Not | 222 Þ | Not | 250 ú | Not |
| 24 □ | Yes | 53 5 | Not | 82 R | Not | 111 o | Not | 139 ‹ | Not | 167 § | Not | 195 Ã | Not | 223 ß | Not | 251 û | Not |
| 25 □ | Yes | 54 6 | Not | 83 S | Not | 112 p | Not | 140 Œ | Not | 168 ¨ | Not | 196 Ä | Not | 224 à | Not | 252 ü | Not |
| 26 □ | Yes | 55 7 | Not | 84 T | Not | 113 q | Not | 141 □ | Yes | 169 © | Not | 197 Å | Not | 225 á | Not | 253 ý | Not |
| 27 □ | Yes | 56 8 | Not | 85 U | Not | 114 r | Not | 142 Ž | Not | 170 ª | Not | 198 Æ | Not | 226 â | Not | 254 þ | Not |
| 28 □ | Yes | 57 9 | Not | 86 V | Not | 115 s | Not | 143 □ | Yes | 171 « | Not | 199 Ç | Not | 227 ã | Not | 255 ÿ | Not |

**Figure 23.49**
This figure shows all CHAR values in the Times New Roman dataset. Only the characters highlighted in black are removed by CLEAN.

**Figure 23.50**
CODE is instrumental in learning why the TRIM function won't work on the data in Column A.

| | A | B | C | D | E |
|---|---|---|---|---|---|
| | | | E3 | | $f_x$ =CODE(MID(A3,C3,1)) |
| | A | B | C | D | E |
| 1 | TEXT | TRIM | START | MID | CODE |
| 2 | A    B | A    B | 1 | A | 65 |
| 3 | A    B | A    B | 2 | | 160 |
| 4 | A    B | A    B | 3 | | 160 |
| 5 | A    B | A    B | 4 | | 160 |
| 6 | A    B | A    B | 5 | | 160 |
| 7 | A    B | A    B | 6 | | 160 |
| 8 | A    B | A    B | 7 | | 160 |
| 9 | A    B | A    B | 8 | B | 66 |
| 10 | | | | | |

Excel pros know that they could remove the extra interior spaces by using =TRIM(A2). But if you look at the formula in Cell B2, you see that TRIM is not removing the interior spaces. This requires some additional investigation, and CODE is the key to solving the problem. Because CODE can work on only the first character in a cell, formulas in Columns C and D isolate each character in the text. (For details on this, see the section "Syntax: MID(text,start_num,num_chars)," later in this chapter).

The CODE(D2) formula in Column E shows the character number for each character in the text. Things start out well enough, with a character 65 being returned for the A. They also end up okay, with a character 66 being returned for the B at the end in Row 9. However, all the middle characters are returning a character 160 instead of a typical space—character 32.

If you've ever created a small webpage, you might have learned that browsers ignore consecutive spaces. If you really want to keep two words separated by four spaces, you need to use Word1    Word2. I learned this trick somewhere on the Web and never really thought about what   means. It turns out that it is a nonbreaking space. And, you guessed it, a nonbreaking space occupies character position 160, so it looks just like a space. Web designers use it all the time to format webpages. Consequently, it is ending up in data that people paste into Excel from the Web, and it is making it appear that TRIM does not always work.

**NOTE**

To actually remove nonbreaking space characters, you have to use the SUBSTITUTE function, discussed in the section "Using SUBSTITUTE and REPLACE to Replace Characters," later in this chapter.

## USING LEFT, MID, OR RIGHT TO BREAK TEXT

One of the newer rules in information processing is that each field in a database should contain exactly one piece of information. Throughout the history of computers, there have been millions of examples of people trying to cram many pieces of information into a single field.

Although this works great for humans, it is pretty difficult to have Excel to sort a column by everything in the second half of a cell.

Column A in Figure 23.51 contains part numbers. As you might guess, the Part Number field really contains two pieces of information: a three-character vendor code, a dash, and a five-digit part number.

23

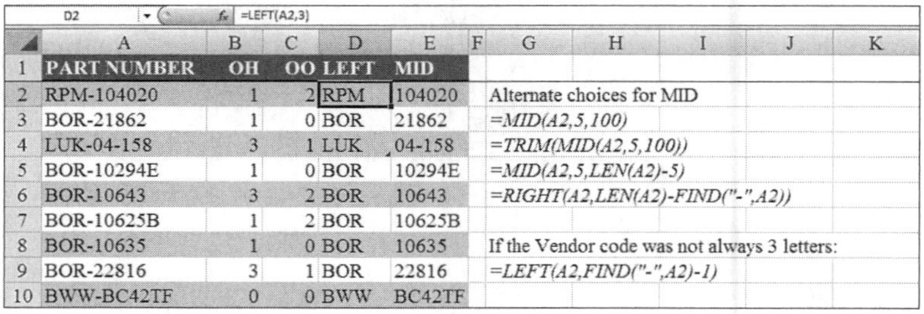
D2 =LEFT(A2,3)

| | A | B | C | D | E | F | G |
|---|---|---|---|---|---|---|---|
| 1 | PART NUMBER | OH | OO | LEFT | MID | | |
| 2 | RPM-104020 | 1 | 2 | RPM | 104020 | | Alternate choices for MID |
| 3 | BOR-21862 | 1 | 0 | BOR | 21862 | | =MID(A2,5,100) |
| 4 | LUK-04-158 | 3 | 1 | LUK | 04-158 | | =TRIM(MID(A2,5,100)) |
| 5 | BOR-10294E | 1 | 0 | BOR | 10294E | | =MID(A2,5,LEN(A2)-5) |
| 6 | BOR-10643 | 3 | 2 | BOR | 10643 | | =RIGHT(A2,LEN(A2)-FIND("-",A2)) |
| 7 | BOR-10625B | 1 | 2 | BOR | 10625B | | |
| 8 | BOR-10635 | 1 | 0 | BOR | 10635 | | If the Vendor code was not always 3 letters: |
| 9 | BOR-22816 | 3 | 1 | BOR | 22816 | | =LEFT(A2,FIND("-",A2)-1) |
| 10 | BWW-BC42TF | 0 | 0 | BWW | BC42TF | | |

**Figure 23.51**
`LEFT` makes quick work of extracting the vendor code. Several varieties of `MID` or `RIGHT` extract the part number.

When a customer comes in to buy a part, he probably doesn't care about the vendor. So the real question is "Do you have anything in stock that can fix my problem?"

Excel offers three functions—`LEFT`, `MID`, and `RIGHT`—that allow you to isolate just the first or just the last characters, or even just the middle characters, from a column.

Syntax: =`LEFT(`*`text`*`,`*`num_chars`*`)`

The `LEFT` function returns the first character or characters in a text string, based on the number of characters specified. This function takes the following arguments:

- *`text`*—This is the text string that contains the characters you want to extract.
- *`num_chars`*—This specifies the number of characters you want `LEFT` to extract. *`num_chars`* must be greater than or equal to zero. If *`num_chars`* is greater than the length of text, `LEFT` returns all of *`text`*. If *`num_chars`* is omitted, it is assumed to be `1`.

Syntax: =`RIGHT(`*`text`*`,`*`num_chars`*`)`

The `RIGHT` function returns the last character or characters in a text string, based on the number of characters specified. This function takes the following arguments:

- *`text`*—This is the text string that contains the characters you want to extract.
- *`num_chars`*—This specifies the number of characters you want `RIGHT` to extract. *`num_chars`* must be greater than or equal to zero. If *`num_chars`* is greater than the length of text, `RIGHT` returns all of *`text`*. If *`num_chars`* is omitted, it is assumed to be `1`.

Syntax: =`MID(`*`text`*`,`*`start_num`*`,`*`num_chars`*`)`

`MID` returns a specific number of characters from a text string, starting at the position specified, based on the number of characters specified. This function takes the following arguments:

- *text*—This is the text string that contains the characters you want to extract.
- *start_num*—This is the position of the first character you want to extract in text. The first character in text has *start_num* 1, and so on. If *start_num* is greater than the length of text, MID returns "" (that is, empty text). If *start_num* is less than the length of text, but *start_num* plus *num_chars* exceeds the length of text, MID returns the characters up to the end of text. If *start_num* is less than 1, MID returns a #VALUE! error.
- *num_chars*—This specifies the number of characters you want MID to return from text. If *num_chars* is negative, MID returns a #VALUE! error.

In Figure 23.51, it is easy to extract the three-digit vendor code by using =LEFT(A2,3). It is a bit more difficult to extract the part number. As you scan through the values in Column A, it is clear that the vendor code is consistently three letters. With the dash in the fourth character of the text, that means that the part number starts in the fifth position. If you are using MID, you therefore use 5 as the *start_num* argument.

However, there are a few thousand part numbers in the dataset. Right up front, in Cell A4, is a part number that breaks the rule. LUK-04-158 contains six characters after the dash. This might seem to be an isolated incident, but in Row 10, BWW-BC42TW also contains six characters after the dash. Because this type of thing happens in real life, two errors in the first nine records are enough to warrant a little extra attention. The four possible strategies for extracting the part number are listed in G2:G6. They are:

- Ask MID to start at the fifth character and return a large enough number of characters to handle any possible length (that is, =MID(A2,5,100)).
- Ask MID to start at the fifth character but use TRIM around the whole function to prevent any trailing spaces from being included (that is, =TRIM(MID(A2,5,100))).
- Ask MID to start at the fifth character, but calculate the exact number of characters by using the LEN function (that is, =MID(A2,5,LEN(A2)-4)).
- Skip MID altogether and ask RIGHT to return all the characters after the first dash. This requires you to use the FIND function to locate the first dash (that is, =RIGHT(A2,LEN(A2)-FIND("-",A2))).

## USING LEN TO FIND THE NUMBER OF CHARACTERS IN A TEXT CELL

It seems pretty obscure, but you will find the LEN function amazingly useful. The LEN function determines the length of characters in a cell, including any leading or trailing spaces.

SYNTAX: =LEN(*text*)

The LEN function returns the number of characters in a text string. The argument *text* is the text whose length you want to find. Spaces count as characters.

There are instances in which LEN can be used in conjunction with LEFT, MID, or RIGHT to isolate a portion of text. (Refer to the example in the previous section.)

LEN can also be used to find records that are longer than a certain limit. Say you are about to order nameplates for company employees. Each nameplate can accommodate 15 characters. In Figure 23.52, you add the LEN function next to the names and sort by the length, in descending order. Any problem names appear at the top of the list.

**Figure 23.52**
LEN identifies the number of characters in a cell.

## USING SEARCH OR FIND TO LOCATE CHARACTERS IN A PARTICULAR CELL

Two nearly identical functions can scan through a text cell, looking for a particular character or word. Many times, you just want to know if the word appears in the text. These functions go further than telling you if the character exists in the text; they tell you at exactly which character position the character or word is found. The character position can be useful in subsequent formulas with LEFT, RIGHT, or REPLACE.

First, let's look at an example of using FIND to determine whether a word exists in another cell. Figure 23.53 shows a database of customers. The database was created by someone who doesn't know Excel and jammed every field into a single cell.

**Figure 23.53**
When the manager asked an employee to type this in Excel, she didn't realize that the employee had never used Excel before.

NOTE

Like all the other datasets in this book, these names and addresses are randomly generated from lists of the most popular first name, last name, street name, and city names. Don't try to send Christmas cards to these people as none of the addresses actually exist. And don't think that the zip codes are real; everything here is completely random.

Here is how to make this work properly:

1. To find all the customers in California, in Cell B2, enter =FIND(", CA",A2). When you enter the formula, you get a #VALUE! error. This is okay. In fact, it is useful information: It tells you that CA is not found in the first record.

2. Copy the formula down to all rows.

3. Sort low to high by Column B. 98% of the records have a #VALUE! error and sort to the bottom of the list. The few California records have a valid result for the formula in Column B and sort to the top of the list, as shown in Figure 23.54.

**23**

**Figure 23.54**
You don't care where FIND found the text; you simply want to divide the list into records with valid values versus errors.

| | A | B | C |
|---|---|---|---|
| | B2 | ▼ | *fx* =FIND(", CA",A2) |
| 1 | Name & Address | California? | |
| 2 | Marilyn Atkins, 1581 Twelfth Avenue, Oak Grove, CA 69942 | 47 | |
| 3 | Joshua Moreno, 1469 Hickory Street, Mill Valley, CA 41204 | 48 | |
| 4 | Kayla Zimmerman, 265 Hickory Street, Rochester, IN 40154 | #VALUE! | |
| 5 | Cynthia Kemp, 264 Ash Lane, Naperville, MS 81585 | #VALUE! | |
| 6 | Jacqueline Bradshaw, 561 Forest Road, St Joseph, CT 65131 | #VALUE! | |
| 7 | Bobby Salazar, 1774 Laurel Street, Bloomingdale, VI 73546 | #VALUE! | |

**CAUTION**

The trick with this application of FIND is to look for something that is only likely to be found in California records. If you had customers in Cairo, Illinois, they would have also been found by the FIND command you just used. The theory with this sort of search is that you can quickly check through the few matching records to find false positives.

FIND and SEARCH are similar to one another. The FIND function does not distinguish between uppercase and lowercase letters. FIND identifies CA, ca, Ca, and cA as matches for CA. If you need to find a cell with exactly AbCdEf, you need to use the SEARCH command instead of FIND. Also, SEARCH allows for wildcard characters in *find_text*. A question mark (?) finds a single character, and an asterisk (*) finds any number of characters.

The FIND function makes it easy to find the first instance of a particular character in a cell. However, if your text values contain two instances of a character, your task is a bit more difficult. In Figure 23.55, the part numbers in Column A really contain three segments, each separated by a dash:

1. To find the first dash, enter =FIND("-",A2) in Column B.

2. To find the second dash, use the optional *start_num* parameter to the FIND function. The *start_num* parameter is a character position. You want the function to start looking after the first instance of a dash. This can be calculated as the result of the first FIND in Column B plus one. Thus, the formula in cell C2 is =FIND("-",A2,B2+1).

3. After you find the character positions of the dashes, isolate the various portions of the part number. In Column D, for the first part of the number, enter =LEFT(A2,B2-1). This

basically asks for the left characters from the part number, stopping at one fewer than the first dash.

4. In Column E, for the middle part of the number, enter =MID(A2,B2+1,C2-B2-1). This asks Excel to start at the character position one after the first dash and then continue for a length that is one fewer than the first dash subtracted from the second dash.

5. In Column F, for the final part of the number, enter =RIGHT(A2,LEN(A2)-C2). This calculates the total length of the part number, subtracts the position of the second dash, and returns those right characters.

**Figure 23.55**
Formulaically isolating data between the first and second dashes can be done, but it helps to break each number down into small parts.

| | A | B | C | D | E | F | G | H |
|---|---|---|---|---|---|---|---|---|
| | | First Dash | Second Dash | First Part | 2nd Part | 3rd Part | | Formulas: |
| 1 | Part Number | | | | | | | |
| 2 | 37767-33-385568 | 6 | 9 | 37767 | 33 | 385568 | | B2: =FIND("-",A2) |
| 3 | 632-6-43 | 4 | 6 | 632 | 6 | 43 | | C2: =FIND("-",A2,B2+1) |
| 4 | 10-13-5656 | 3 | 6 | 10 | 13 | 5656 | | D2: =LEFT(A2,B2-1) |
| 5 | 9-671672-119067 | 2 | 9 | 9 | 671672 | 119067 | | E2: =MID(A2,B2+1,C2-B2-1) |
| 6 | 41-50555-51 | 3 | 9 | 41 | 50555 | 51 | | F2: =RIGHT(A2,LEN(A2)-C2) |
| 7 | 568-536-177914 | 4 | 8 | 568 | 536 | 177914 | | |
| 8 | 1596-9-25472 | 5 | 7 | 1596 | 9 | 25472 | | |
| 9 | 4-4421-2 | 2 | 7 | 4 | 4421 | 2 | | |

C2 | fx =FIND("-",A2,B2+1)

SYNTAX: =FIND(*find_text*,*within_text*,*start_num*)

FIND finds one text string (*find_text*) within another text string (*within_text*) and returns the number of the starting position of *find_text* from the first character of *within_text*. You can also use SEARCH to find one text string within another, but unlike SEARCH, FIND is case-sensitive and doesn't allow wildcard characters.

The FIND function takes the following arguments:

- *find_text*—This is the text you want to find. If *find_text* is " " (that is, empty text), FIND matches the first character in the search string (that is, the character numbered start_num or 1). *find_text* cannot contain any wildcard characters.

- *within_text*—This is the text that contains the text you want to find.

- *start_num*—This specifies the character at which to start the search. The first character in *within_text* is character number 1. If you omit *start_num*, it is assumed to be 1.

If *find_text* does not appear in *within_text*, FIND return a #VALUE! error. If *start_num* is not greater than zero, FIND returns a #VALUE! error. If *start_num* is greater than the length of *within_text*, FIND return a #VALUE! error.

SYNTAX: =SEARCH(*find_text*,*within_text*,*start_num*)

SEARCH returns the number of the character at which a specific character or text string is first found, beginning with *start_num*. You use SEARCH to determine the location of a character or text string within another text string so that you can use the MID or REPLACE functions to change the text.

The SEARCH function takes the following arguments:

- *find_text*—This is the text you want to find. You can use the wildcard characters question mark (?) and asterisk (*) in *find_text*. A question mark matches any single character; an asterisk matches any sequence of characters. If you want to find an actual question mark or asterisk, you type a tilde (~) before the character. If *find_text* is not found, a #VALUE! error is returned.

- *within_text*—This is the text in which you want to search for *find_text*.

- *start_num*—This is the character number in *within_text* at which you want to start searching. If *start_num* is omitted, it is assumed to be 1. If *start_num* is not greater than zero or is greater than the length of *within_text*, a #VALUE! error is returned.

## USING SUBSTITUTE AND REPLACE TO REPLACE CHARACTERS

When you have the ability to find text, you might want to replace text. Excel offers two functions for this: SUBSTITUTE and REPLACE. The SUBSTITUTE function is easier to use and should be your first approach.

SYNTAX: =SUBSTITUTE(*text*,*old_text*,*new_text*,*instance_num*)

The SUBSTITUTE function substitutes *new_text* for *old_text* in a text string. You use SUBSTITUTE when you want to replace specific text in a text string; you use REPLACE when you want to replace any text that occurs in a specific location in a text string.

The SUBSTITUTE function takes the following arguments:

- *text*—This is the text or the reference to a cell that contains text for which you want to substitute characters.

- *old_text*—This is the text you want to replace.

- *new_text*—This is the text you want to replace *old_text* with.

- *instance_num*—This specifies which occurrence of *old_text* you want to replace with *new_text*. If you specify *instance_num*, only that instance of *old_text* is replaced. Otherwise, every occurrence of *old_text* in *text* is changed to *new_text*.

For example, =SUBSTITUTE("Sales Data","Sales","Cost") would generate "Cost Data".

The SUBSTITUTE function works similarly to a traditional find and replace command. Compared to the SUBSTITUTE function, the REPLACE function is difficult enough to make even an old programmer's head spin.

SYNTAX: =REPLACE(*old_text*,*start_num*,*num_chars*,*new_text*)

REPLACE replaces part of a text string, based on the number of characters specified, with a different text string. This function takes the following arguments:

- *old_text* —This is text in which you want to replace some characters.

- *start_num*—This is the position of the character in *old_text* that you want to replace with *new_text*.

- *num_chars*—This is the number of characters in *old_text* that you want REPLACE to replace with new_text.

- *new_text*—This is the text that will replace characters in *old_text*.

In order to successfully use REPLACE, you have to use functions to determine the location and number of characters to replace. In most circumstances, SUBSTITUTE is easier to use.

## USING REPT TO REPEAT TEXT MULTIPLE TIMES

A little-known trick has been around for 20-plus years and still works today. Go to a blank cell. Enter a backslash (\) and any one character. Excel fills the cell with that character! Enter \*, and the cell is filled with asterisks. Make the column wider or less narrow, and the number of asterisks changes to fill the cell.

In Excel, if you use \ -, Excel repeats the two characters over and over until the cell is filled. Cells in Rows 8 through 11 of Figure 23.56 show various cells that use the backslash trick.

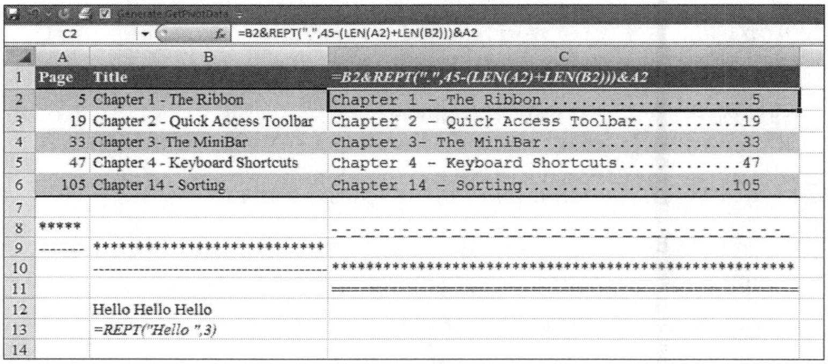

**Figure 23.56**
The REPT function can be used to calculate a certain number of repeated entries.

There is an Excel function, REPT, that formalizes this repetition a bit.

SYNTAX: =REPT(*text*,*number_times*)

The REPT function repeats text a given number of times. You use REPT to fill a cell with a number of instances of a text string. This function takes the following arguments:

- *text*—This is the text you want to repeat.

- *number_times*—This is a positive number that specifies the number of times to repeat text. If *number_times* is 0, REPT returns "" (that is, empty text). If *number_times* is not an integer, it is truncated. The result of the REPT function cannot be longer than 32,767 characters.

In Microsoft Word, it is easy to create a row of periods between text and a page number. In Excel, you have to resort to clever use of the REPT function to do this.

In Figure 23.56, Column A contains a page number. Column B contains a chapter title. The goal in Column C is to join enough periods between Columns B and A to make all the page numbers line up.

The number of periods to print is the total desired length, less the length of Columns A and B. The formula for Cell C2 is =B2&REPT(".",45-(LEN(A2)+LEN(B2)))&A2.

**NOTE**

In order to make this work, you have to change the font in Column C to be a fixed-width font such as Courier New.

23

## USING EXACT TO TEST CASE

For the most part, Excel isn't concerned about case. To Excel, ABC and abc are the same thing. In Figure 23.57, Cells A1 and B1 contain the same letters, but the capitalization is different.

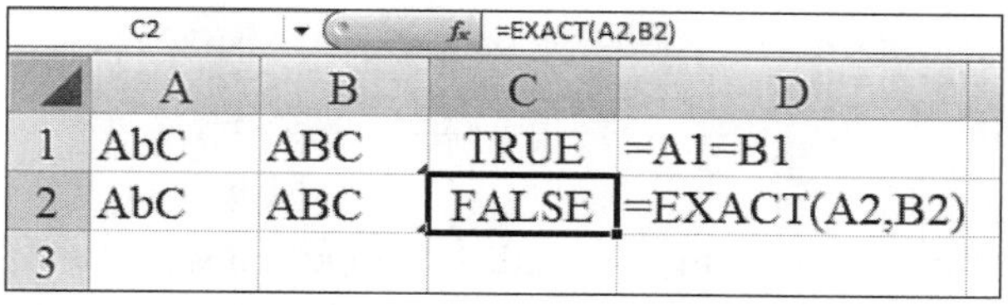

**Figure 23.57**
Excel usually over-looks differences in capitalization when deciding whether two values are equal. You can use EXACT to find out whether they are equal and the same case.

| | A | B | C | D |
|---|---|---|---|---|
| | C2 | | fx | =EXACT(A2,B2) |
| 1 | AbC | ABC | TRUE | =A1=B1 |
| 2 | AbC | ABC | FALSE | =EXACT(A2,B2) |
| 3 | | | | |

The formula in Cell C1 tests whether these values are equal. In the rules of Excel, AbC and ABC are equivalent. The formula in Cell C1 indicates that the values are equal. To some people, these two text cells may not really be equivalent. If you work in a store that sells the big plastic letters that go on theatre marquees, your order for 20 letter a figures should not be filled with an order for 20 letter A figures.

Excel forces you to use the EXACT function to compare these two cells to learn that they are not exactly the same.

SYNTAX: =EXACT(*text1*,*text2*)

The EXACT function compares two text strings and returns TRUE if they are exactly the same and FALSE otherwise. EXACT is case-sensitive but ignores formatting differences. You use EXACT to test text being entered into a document. This function takes the following arguments:

- *text1*—This is the first text string.
- *text2*—This is the second text string

### USING TEXT, DOLLAR, AND FIXED TO FORMAT A NUMBER AS TEXT

Excel is great at numbers. Put a number in a cell, and you can format it in a variety of ways. However, when you join a cell containing text with a cell containing a number or a date, Excel falls apart.

Consider Figure 23.58. Cell A11 contains a date and is formatted as a date. When you join the name in Cell B11 with the date in Cell A11, Excel automatically converts the date back to a numeric serial number. This is frustrating.



**Figure 23.58**
`TEXT`, `DOLLAR`, and `FIXED` can be used to format a number as text.

C12 | =B12&" was born on "&TEXT(A12,"m/d/y")

| | A | B | C | D | E | F | G | H |
|---|---|---|---|---|---|---|---|---|
| 1 | 1234.56 | $1,234.56 | *=DOLLAR(A1)* | | | | | |
| 2 | 1234.56 | $1,235 | *=DOLLAR(A2,0)* | | | | | |
| 3 | 1234.56 | $1,234.56 | *=DOLLAR(A3,2)* | | | | | |
| 4 | | | | | | | | |
| 5 | 1234.56 | 1,234.56 | *=FIXED(A5)* | | | | | |
| 6 | 1234.56 | 1,235 | *=FIXED(A6,0)* | | | | | |
| 7 | 1234.56 | 1235 | *=FIXED(A7,0,TRUE)* | | | | | |
| 8 | | | | | | | | |
| 9 | 3/5/2006 | Sunday, March 5, 2006 | | | | | | |
| 10 | | | | | | | | |
| 11 | 12/1/1989 | Joe | Joe was born on 32843 | =B11&" was born on "&A11 | | | | |
| 12 | 12/1/1989 | Joe | Joe was born on 12/1/89 | =B12&" was born on "&TEXT(A12,"m/d/y") | | | | |
| 13 | | | | | | | | |

Today, the `TEXT` function is the most versatile solution to this problem. If you understand the basics of custom numeric formatting codes, you can easily use `TEXT` to format a date or a number in any conceivable format. For example, the formula in Cell C12 uses `=TEXT(A12,"m/d/y")` to force the date to display as a date.

The `TEXT` function gives you a lot of versatility. To learn the custom formatting codes for a cell, you can select the cell, display the Format Cells dialog (by pressing Ctrl+1), and choose the Custom category on the Number tab. Excel shows you the codes used to create that format.

If you don't care to learn the number formatting codes, you can use either the `DOLLAR` or `FIXED` function to return a number as text, with a few choices regarding number of decimals and whether Excel should use the thousands separator. The formulas shown in C2:C7 in Figure 23.58 return the formatted text values shown in Column B.

### SYNTAX: =`TEXT(`*`value`*`,`*`format_text`*`)`

The `TEXT` function converts a value to text in a specific number format. Formatting a cell with an option on the Number tab of the Format Cells dialog changes only the format, not the value. Using the `TEXT` function converts a value to formatted text, and the result is no longer calculated as a number.

The `TEXT` function takes the following arguments:

- *`value`*—This is a numeric value, a formula that evaluates to a numeric value, or a reference to a cell that contains a numeric value.

- *format_text*—This is a number format in text form from the Category box on the Number tab in the Format Cells dialog box. *format_text* cannot contain an asterisk (*) and cannot be the general number format.

### SYNTAX: =DOLLAR(*number,decimals*)

The DOLLAR function converts a number to text using currency format, with the decimals rounded to the specified place. The format used is $#,##0.00_);($#,##0.00). The major difference between formatting a cell that contains a number with the Format Cells dialog and formatting a number directly with the DOLLAR function is that DOLLAR converts its result to text. A number formatted with the Cells command is still a number. You can continue to use numbers formatted with DOLLAR in formulas because Microsoft Excel converts numbers entered as text values to numbers when it calculates.

The DOLLAR function takes the following arguments:

- *number*—This is a number, a reference to a cell that contains a number, or a formula that evaluates to a number.
- *decimals*—This is the number of digits to the right of the decimal point. If *decimals* is negative, *number* is rounded to the left of the decimal point. If you omit *decimals*, it is assumed to be 2.

### SYNTAX: =FIXED(*number,decimals,no_commas*)

The FIXED function rounds a number to the specified number of decimals, formats the number in decimal format using a period and commas, and returns the result as text. The major difference between formatting a cell that contains a number with the Format Cells dialog and formatting a number directly with the FIXED function is that FIXED converts its result to text. A number formatted with the Format Cells dialog is still a number. This function takes the following arguments:

- *number*—This is the number you want to round and convert to text.
- *decimals*—This is the number of digits to the right of the decimal point. Numbers in Microsoft Excel can never have more than 15 significant digits, but *decimals* can be as large as 127. If *decimals* is negative, *number* is rounded to the left of the decimal point. If you omit *decimals*, it is assumed to be 2.
- *no_commas*—This is a logical value that, if TRUE, prevents FIXED from including commas in the returned text. If *no_commas* is FALSE or omitted, the returned text includes commas as usual.

## USING THE T AND VALUE FUNCTIONS

The T and VALUE functions are left over from Lotus days.

=T("*text*") returns the original text. If Cell B1 contains the number 123, =T(B1) would return an empty text. Basically, T() returns the value in the cell only if it is *text*.

=VALUE() converts text that looks like a number or a date to the number or the date.

## Using Functions for Non-English Character Sets

There are 11 more functions that have not been covered in this section. These functions deal with text in character systems where each character takes up more than 1 byte. This is true in many Asian languages. The following functions are beyond the scope of this edition: ASC, BAHTTEXT, FINDB, JIS, LEFTB, MIDB, PHONETIC, REPLACEB, RIGHTB, SEARCHB, YEN but are described earlier in this chapter, in Table 23.3.

---

**Excel Troubleshooting: Text Times Entered as** M:SS **Instead of** H:MM:SS

In Figure 23.59, Column B contains a series of time trial results. When you total the column in Cell B12, you realize that all the times were entered as text.

**Figure 23.59**
You can use the LEFT and RIGHT text functions to provide the arguments for the TIME function.

| | A | B | C | D | E | F |
|---|---|---|---|---|---|---|
| | | | | fx =TIME(0,LEFT(B2,1),RIGHT(B2,2)) | | |
| 1 | NAME | TIME | TIMEVALUE | TIME2 | TIMEVALUE-2 | |
| 2 | CHARLOTTE | 2:50 | 2:50:00 | 0:02:50 | 0:02:50 | |
| 3 | HARRIET | 1:38 | 1:38:00 | 0:01:38 | 0:01:38 | |
| 4 | JUAN | 1:25 | 1:25:00 | 0:01:25 | 0:01:25 | |
| 5 | KARLA | 1:23 | 1:23:00 | 0:01:23 | 0:01:23 | |
| 6 | JERRY | 2:44 | 2:44:00 | 0:02:44 | 0:02:44 | |
| 7 | ROSEMARY | 2:39 | 2:39:00 | 0:02:39 | 0:02:39 | |
| 8 | TERRI | 1:42 | 1:42:00 | 0:01:42 | 0:01:42 | |
| 9 | FRED | 1:17 | 1:17:00 | 0:01:17 | 0:01:17 | |
| 10 | JESSE | 1:10 | 1:10:00 | 0:01:10 | 0:01:10 | |
| 11 | ADA | 1:34 | 1:34:00 | 0:01:34 | 0:01:34 | |
| 12 | TOTAL | 0:00:00 | 18:22:00 | 0:18:22 | 0:18:22 | |
| 13 | | | | | | |

The formulas in Column C use =TIMEVALUE(B2). However, a time such as 2 minutes 50 seconds is converted in the function to 2 hours 50 minutes. In this case, TIMEVALUE does not work.

There are two alternative strategies:

- One solution is to use the TIME function. In Column D, the text times are converted to real times by using the TIME function. In each case, the hours should be zero. The minutes are =LEFT(B2,1). The seconds are =RIGHT(B2,0). The formula in Cell D2 is =TIME(0,LEFT(B2,1),RIGHT(B2,2)). You copy this formula down and format the range as a time.

- The other solution is to use the concatenation operator to pad the left of Column B with 0:0. This allows the text to work in the TIMEVALUE function. The formula in Cell E2 is =TIMEVALUE("0:0"&B2). Again, you need to copy this formula down and format the range as a time.

---

# CHAPTER 24

# USING POWERFUL FUNCTIONS: LOGICAL, LOOKUP, AND DATABASE FUNCTIONS

**I**n this chapter

This chapter covers four groups of workhorse functions. If you are processing spreadsheets of medium complexity, you will find yourself turning to logical and lookup functions regularly.

- The logical functions, including the ubiquitous IF function, help you make decisions.
- The information functions might be less important than they once were, now that Microsoft has added the IFERROR function, but INFO, CELL, and TYPE still come in handy.
- The lookup functions include the powerful VLOOKUP, MATCH, and INDIRECT functions, which are invaluable when you are doing something in Excel that really should be done in Access. And, let's face it, with 1.1 million rows in Excel 2007, we will all be doing more things in Excel that should be done in Access.
- Finally, the database functions provide the DSUM functions. Although these functions fell out of favor when pivot tables were introduced, they are a very powerful set of functions that are worthwhile to master.

Table 24.1 provides an alphabetical list of all of Excel 2007's logical functions. Detailed examples of these functions are provided later in this chapter.

**TABLE 24.1    ALPHABETICAL LIST OF LOGICAL FUNCTIONS**

| Function | Description |
|---|---|
| AND(*logical1,logical2,...*) | Returns TRUE if all its arguments are TRUE; returns FALSE if one or more arguments is FALSE. |
| FALSE() | Returns the logical value FALSE. |
| IF(*logical_test,value_if_true, value_if_false*) | Returns one value if a condition specified evaluates to TRUE and another value if it evaluates to FALSE. |
| IFERROR(*value,value_if_error*) | Returns value_if_error if expression is an error and the value itself if otherwise. |
| NOT(*logical*) | Reverses the value of its argument. You use NOT when you want to make sure a value is not equal to another particular value. |
| OR(*logical1,logical2,...*) | Returns TRUE if any argument is TRUE; returns FALSE if all arguments are FALSE. |
| TRUE() | Returns the logical value TRUE. |

Table 24.2 provides an alphabetical list of all of Excel 2007's information functions. Detailed examples of these functions are provided in the remainder of the chapter.

**TABLE 24.2  ALPHABETICAL LIST OF INFORMATION FUNCTIONS**

| Function | Description |
|---|---|
| CELL(*info_type*,*reference*) | Returns information about the formatting, location, or contents of the upper-left cell in a reference. |
| ERROR.TYPE(*error_val*) | Returns a number corresponding to one of the error values in Microsoft Excel or returns an #N/A error if no error exists. You can use ERROR.TYPE in an IF function to test for an error value and return a text string, such as a message, instead of the error value. |
| INFO(*type_text*) | Returns information about the current operating environment. |
| ISBLANK(*value*) | Returns TRUE if *value* refers to an empty cell. |
| ISERROR(*value*) | Returns TRUE if *value* refers to any error value (that is, #N/A, #VALUE!, #REF!, #DIV/0!, #NUM!, #NAME?, or #NULL!). |
| ISERR(*value*) | Returns TRUE if *value* refers to any error value except #N/A. |
| ISEVEN(*number*) | Returns TRUE if *number* is even and FALSE if *number* is odd. |
| ISLOGICAL(*value*) | Returns TRUE if *value* refers to a logical value. |
| ISNA(*value*) | Returns TRUE if *value* refers to the #N/A (value not available) error value. |
| ISNONTEXT(*value*) | Returns TRUE if *value* refers to any item that is not text. (Note that this function returns TRUE if *value* refers to a blank cell.) |
| ISNUMBER(*value*) | Returns TRUE if *value* refers to a number. |
| ISODD(*number*) | Returns TRUE if *number* is odd and FALSE if *number* is even. |
| ISREF(*value*) | Returns TRUE if *value* refers to a reference. |
| ISTEXT(*value*) | Returns TRUE if *value* refers to text. |
| N(*value*) | Returns a value converted to a number. |
| NA() | Returns the error value #N/A, which means "no value is available." You use NA to mark empty cells. By entering #N/A in cells where you are missing information, you can avoid the problem of unintentionally including empty cells in your calculations. (When a formula refers to a cell containing #N/A, the formula returns the #N/A error value.) |
| TYPE(*value*) | Returns the type of *value*. You use TYPE when the behavior of another function depends on the type of value in a particular cell. |

24

Table 24.3 provides an alphabetical list of all of Excel 2007's lookup functions. Detailed examples of these functions are provided later in this chapter.

**TABLE 24.3 ALPHABETICAL LIST OF LOOKUP FUNCTIONS**

| Function | Description |
|---|---|
| ADDRESS(row_num,column_num, abs_num,a1,sheet_text) | Creates a cell address as text, given specified row and column numbers. |
| AREAS(reference) | Returns the number of areas in a reference. An area is a range of contiguous cells or a single cell. |
| CHOOSE(index_num,value1, value2,...) | Uses index_num to return a value from the list of value arguments. You use CHOOSE to select one of up to 29 values, based on the index number. For example, if value1 through value7 are the days of the week, CHOOSE returns one of the days when a number between 1 and 7 is used as index_num. |
| COLUMN(reference) | Returns the column number of the given reference. |
| COLUMNS(array) | Returns the number of columns in an array or a reference. |
| GETPIVOTDATA(pivot_table,name) | Returns data stored in a pivot table report. You can use GETPIVOTDATA to retrieve summary data from a pivot table report, provided that the summary data is visible in the report. |
| HLOOKUP(lookup_value, table_array,row_index_num, range_lookup) | Searches for a value in the top row of a table or an array of values and then returns a value in the same column from a row you specify in the table or array. You use HLOOKUP when your comparison values are located in a row across the top of a table of data and you want to look down a specified number of rows. You use VLOOKUP when your comparison values are located in a column to the left of the data you want to find. |
| HYPERLINK(link_location, friendly_name) | Creates a shortcut or jump that opens a document stored on a network server, an intranet, or the Internet. When you click the cell that contains the HYPERLINK function, Excel opens the file stored at link_location. |
| INDEX(array,row_num, column_num) | Returns the value of a specified cell or array of cells within array. |
| INDEX(reference,row_num, column_num,area_num) | Returns a reference to a specified cell or cells within reference. |
| INDIRECT(ref_text,a1) | Returns the reference specified by a text string. References are immediately evaluated to display their contents. You use INDIRECT when you want to change the reference to a cell within a formula without changing the formula itself. |
| LOOKUP(lookup_value, lookup_vector,result_vector) | Returns a value either from a one-row or one-column range. This vector form of LOOKUP looks in a one-row or one-column range (known as a vector) for a value and returns a value from the same position in a second one-row or one-column range. This function is included for compatibility with other worksheets. You should use VLOOKUP instead. |

24

| Function | Description |
|---|---|
| LOOKUP(*lookup_value*,*array*) | Returns a value from an array. The array form of LOOKUP looks in the first row or column of an array for the specified value and returns a value from the same position in the last row or column of the array. This function is included for compatibility with other spreadsheet programs. You should use VLOOKUP instead. |
| MATCH(*lookup_value*, *lookup_array*,*match_type*) | Returns the relative position of an item in an array that matches a specified value in a specified order. You use MATCH instead of one of the LOOKUP functions when you need the position of an item in a range instead of the item itself. |
| OFFSET(*reference*,*rows*, *cols*,*height*,*width*) | Returns a reference to a range that is a specified number of rows and columns from a cell or range of cells. The reference that is returned can be a single cell or a range of cells. You can specify the number of rows and the number of columns to be returned. |
| ROW(*reference*) | Returns the row number of a reference. |
| ROWS(*array*) | Returns the number of rows in a reference or an array. |
| RTD(*progid*,*server*,*topic*, [*topic2*],…) | Retrieves real-time data from a program that supports COM automation. This function was new in Excel XP. |
| TRANSPOSE(*array*) | Returns a vertical range of cells as a horizontal range or vice versa. TRANSPOSE must be entered as an array formula in a range that has the same number of rows and columns, respectively, as array has columns and rows. You use TRANSPOSE to shift the vertical and horizontal orientation of an array on a worksheet. For example, some functions, such as LINEST, return horizontal arrays. LINEST returns a horizontal array of the slope and y-intercept for a line. Use TRANSPOSE to convert the LINEST result to a vertical array. |
| VLOOKUP(*lookup_value*, *table_array*,*col_index_num*, *range_lookup*) | Searches for a value in the leftmost column of a table and then returns a value in the same row from a column you specify in the table. You use VLOOKUP instead of HLOOKUP when your comparison values are located in a column to the left of the data you want to find. |
| YEN(*number*,*decimals*) | Converts a number to text, using the Japanese yen currency format, with the number rounded to a specified place. |

Table 24.4 provides an alphabetical list of all of Excel 2007's database functions. Detailed examples of these functions are provided later in this chapter.

24

**TABLE 24.4 ALPHABETICAL LIST OF DATABASE FUNCTIONS**

| Function | Description |
|---|---|
| DAVERAGE(*database*,*field*,*criteria*) | Averages the values in a column in a list or database that match the conditions specified. |
| DCOUNT(*database*,*field*,*criteria*) | Counts the cells that contain numbers in a column in a list or database that match the conditions specified. |
| DCOUNTA(*database*,*field*,*criteria*) | Counts all the nonblank cells in a column in a list or database that match the conditions specified. |
| DGET(*database*,*field*,*criteria*) | Extracts a single value from a column in a list or database that matches the conditions specified. |
| DMAX(*database*,*field*,*criteria*) | Returns the largest number in a column in a list or database that matches the conditions specified. |
| DMIN(*database*,*field*,*criteria*) | Returns the smallest number in a column in a list or database that matches the conditions specified. |
| DPRODUCT(*database*,*field*,*criteria*) | Multiplies the values in a column in a list or database that match the conditions specified. |
| DSTDEV(*database*,*field*,*criteria*) | Estimates the standard deviation of a population based on a sample, using the numbers in a column in a list or database that match the conditions specified. |
| DSTDEVP(*database*,*field*,*criteria*) | Calculates the standard deviation of a population based on the entire population, using the numbers in a column in a list or database that match the conditions specified. |
| DSUM(*database*,*field*,*criteria*) | Adds the numbers in a column in a list or database that match the conditions specified. |
| DVAR(*database*,*field*,*criteria*) | Estimates the variance of a population based on a sample, using the numbers in a column in a list or database that match the conditions specified. |
| DVARP(*database*,*field*,*criteria*) | Calculates the variance of a population based on the entire population, using the numbers in a column in a list or database that match the conditions specified. |

Table 24.5 provides an alphabetical list of all of Excel 2007's external functions. Detailed examples of these functions are provided later in this chapter.

## TABLE 24.5  ALPHABETICAL LIST OF EXTERNAL FUNCTIONS

| Function | Description |
| --- | --- |
| CALL(register_id,argument1,...) | Calls a procedure in a dynamic link library (DLL) or code resource. You use this syntax only with a previously registered code resource that uses arguments from the REGISTER function. |
| CALL(file_text,resource, type_text,argument1,...) | Calls a procedure in a DLL or code resource. You use this syntax to simultaneously register and call a code resource for the Macintosh. |
| CALL(module_text,procedure, type_text,argument1,...) | Calls a procedure in a DLL or code resource. You use this syntax to simultaneously register and call a code resource for Windows machines. |
| EUROCONVERT(number,source, target,full_precision, triangulation_precision) | Converts a number to euros, converts a number from euros to a euro member currency, or converts a number from one euro member currency to another by using the euro as an intermediary (that is, triangulation). The currencies available for conversion are those of the European Union (EU) members that have adopted the euro. |
| REGISTER.ID(file_text,resource, type_text) | Returns the register ID of the specified DLL or code resource that has been previously registered. If the DLL or code resource has not been registered, this function registers the DLL or code resource and then returns the register ID for the Macintosh. |
| REGISTER.ID(module_text, procedure,type_text) | Returns the register ID of the specified DLL or code resource that has been previously registered. If the DLL or code resource has not been registered, this function registers the DLL or code resource and then returns the register ID for Windows. |
| SQL.REQUEST(connection_string, output_ref,driver_prompt, query_text,col_names_logical) | Connects with an external data source and runs a query from a worksheet. SQL.REQUEST then returns the result as an array, without the need for macro programming. If this function is not already available, you should install the Microsoft Excel ODBC add-in (XLODBC.XLA). |

24

# EXAMPLES OF LOGICAL FUNCTIONS

With only seven functions, the logical function group is one of the smallest in Excel. Its IF function is an easy-to-understand function that allows you to solve a wide variety of problems.

## USING THE IF FUNCTION TO MAKE A DECISION

Many calculations in our lives are not straightforward. Say that a manager offers a bonus program if her team meets its goals. Or perhaps a commission plan offers a bonus if a certain profit goal is met. These types of calculations can be solved by using the IF function.

SYNTAX: IF(*logical_test*,*value_if_true*,*value_if_false*)

There are three arguments in the IF function. The first argument is any logical test that will result in a TRUE or FALSE. For example, you might have logical tests such as these:

```
A2>100
B5="West"
C99<=D99
```

All logical tests involve one of the comparison operators shown in Table 24.6.

TABLE 24.6    COMPARISON OPERATORS

| Comparison Operator | Meaning | Example |
|---|---|---|
| = | Equal to | C1=D1 |
| > | Greater than | A1>B1 |
| < | Less than | A1<B1 |
| >= | Greater than or equal to | A1>=0 |
| <= | Less than or equal to | A1<=99 |
| <> | Not equal to | A2<>B2 |

The remaining two arguments are the formula or value to use if the logical test is true and the formula or value to use if the logical test is false.

When you read an IF function, you should think of the first comma as the word *then* and the second comma as the word *otherwise*. For example, =IF(A2>10,25,0) would be read as "If A2>10, then 25; otherwise, 0."

Figure 24.1 calculates a sales commission. The commission rate is 1.5% of revenue. However, if the gross profit percentage is 50% or higher, the commission rate is 2.5% of revenue.

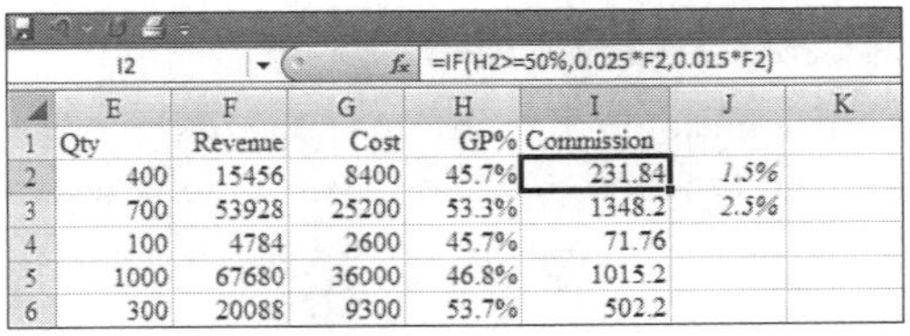

**Figure 24.1**
In Rows 2, 4, and 5, the commission is 1.5%. In rows 3 and 6, the commission is 2.5%.

| | E | F | G | H | I | J | K |
|---|---|---|---|---|---|---|---|
| | | | | I2 | | fx =IF(H2>=50%,0.025*F2,0.015*F2) | |
| 1 | Qty | Revenue | Cost | GP% | Commission | | |
| 2 | 400 | 15456 | 8400 | 45.7% | 231.84 | 1.5% | |
| 3 | 700 | 53928 | 25200 | 53.3% | 1348.2 | 2.5% | |
| 4 | 100 | 4784 | 2600 | 45.7% | 71.76 | | |
| 5 | 1000 | 67680 | 36000 | 46.8% | 1015.2 | | |
| 6 | 300 | 20088 | 9300 | 53.7% | 502.2 | | |

In this case, the logical test is `H2>=50%`. The formula if that test is true is `0.025*F2`. Otherwise, the formula is `0.015*F2`. You could build the formula as `=IF(H2>=50%,0.025*F2, 0.015*F2)`.

> **NOTE**
>
> Mathematicians would correctly note that in both the second and third arguments of the formula `=IF(H2>=50%,0.025*F2,0.015*F2)`, you are multiplying by F2. You could therefore simplify the formula by using `=IF(H2>=50%,0.025,0.015)*F2`.

## USING THE AND FUNCTION TO CHECK FOR TWO OR MORE CONDITIONS

The previous example had one simple condition: If the value in Column H was greater than or equal to 50%, the commission rate changed.



There are many cases in which you might need to test for two or more conditions. Say that a retail store manager offers a $25 bonus for every leather jacket sold on Fridays this month. In this case, the logical test requires you to determine whether both conditions are true. You can do this with the `AND` function.

SYNTAX: `AND(`*`logical1,logical2,...`*`)`

The arguments *`logical1,logical2,...`* are from 1 to 255 expressions that evaluate to either `TRUE` or `FALSE`. The function returns `TRUE` only if all arguments are `TRUE`.

In Figure 24.2, the function in Cell F2 checks whether Cell E2 is a jacket and whether the date in Cell D2 falls on a Friday:

```
=AND(E2="Jacket",WEEKDAY(D2,2)=5)
```

**Figure 24.2**
The `AND` function is `TRUE` only when every condition is met.

F2 — =AND(E2="Jacket",WEEKDAY(D2,2)=5)

| | A | B | C | D | E | F | G | H |
|---|---|---|---|---|---|---|---|---|
| 1 | Store | Cust | Associate | Date | Item | Bonus? | | |
| 2 | S18 | C422 | Jenny | 4/13/2007 | Handbag | FALSE | | |
| 3 | S5 | C244 | Bill | 4/9/2007 | Jacket | FALSE | | |
| 4 | S13 | C668 | Diana | 4/26/2007 | Hat | FALSE | | |
| 5 | S19 | C825 | Bill | 4/13/2007 | Jacket | TRUE | | |
| 6 | S15 | C590 | Bill | 4/23/2007 | Coaster | FALSE | | |
| 7 | S5 | C857 | Bill | 4/9/2007 | Handbag | FALSE | | |
| 8 | S16 | C179 | Bill | 4/9/2007 | Jacket | FALSE | | |
| 9 | S8 | C510 | Diana | 4/24/2007 | Jacket | FALSE | | |
| 10 | S17 | C676 | Bill | 4/24/2007 | Hat | FALSE | | |
| 11 | S17 | C594 | Diana | 4/1/2007 | Handbag | FALSE | | |
| 12 | S15 | C196 | Diana | 4/1/2007 | Jacket | FALSE | | |
| 13 | S18 | C678 | Jenny | 4/21/2007 | Hat | FALSE | | |
| 14 | S18 | C468 | Jenny | 4/3/2007 | Jacket | FALSE | | |
| 15 | S12 | C533 | Bill | 4/27/2007 | Jacket | TRUE | | |

### USING THE AND FUNCTION TO COMPARE TWO LISTS

The `AND` function can handle up to 255 expressions. Each expression can contain a range that might contain many instances of `TRUE` or `FALSE`.

A common issue is figuring out whether two worksheets are identical. In Figure 24.3, Columns A:E contain the original worksheet. This worksheet was passed among several co-workers and ended back at your desk. You follow these steps to compare the two worksheets:

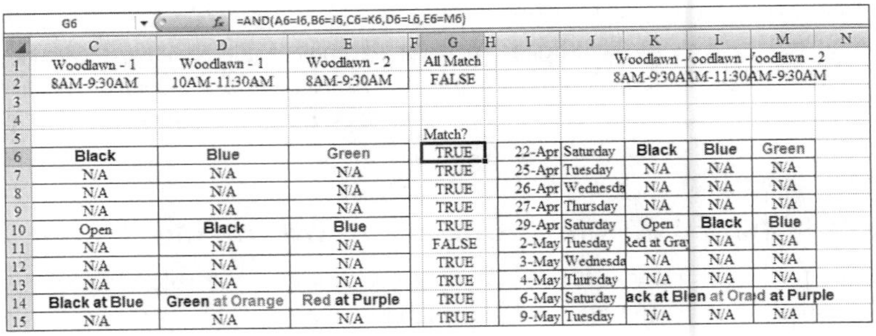

G6 =AND(A6=I6,B6=J6,C6=K6,D6=L6,E6=M6)

| | C | D | E | F | G | H | I | J | K | L | M | N |
|---|---|---|---|---|---|---|---|---|---|---|---|---|
| 1 | Woodlawn - 1 | Woodlawn - 1 | Woodlawn - 2 | | All Match | | | | Woodlawn - | oodlawn - | oodlawn - 2 | |
| 2 | 8AM-9:30AM | 10AM-11:30AM | 8AM-9:30AM | | FALSE | | | | 8AM-9:30A | AM-11:30 | AM-9:30AM | |
| 3 | | | | | | | | | | | | |
| 4 | | | | | | | | | | | | |
| 5 | | | | | Match? | | | | | | | |
| 6 | Black | Blue | Green | | TRUE | | 22-Apr | Saturday | Black | Blue | Green | |
| 7 | N/A | N/A | N/A | | TRUE | | 25-Apr | Tuesday | N/A | N/A | N/A | |
| 8 | N/A | N/A | N/A | | TRUE | | 26-Apr | Wednesda | N/A | N/A | N/A | |
| 9 | N/A | N/A | N/A | | TRUE | | 27-Apr | Thursday | N/A | N/A | N/A | |
| 10 | Open | Black | Blue | | TRUE | | 29-Apr | Saturday | Open | Black | Blue | |
| 11 | N/A | N/A | N/A | | FALSE | | 2-May | Tuesday | Red at Gra | N/A | N/A | |
| 12 | N/A | N/A | N/A | | TRUE | | 3-May | Wednesda | N/A | N/A | N/A | |
| 13 | N/A | N/A | N/A | | TRUE | | 4-May | Thursday | N/A | N/A | N/A | |
| 14 | Black at Blue | Green at Orange | Red at Purple | | TRUE | | 6-May | Saturday | ack at Bl | en at Ora | d at Purple | |
| 15 | N/A | N/A | N/A | | TRUE | | 9-May | Tuesday | N/A | N/A | N/A | |

**Figure 24.3**
AND can test whether a large range of logical tests are all TRUE.

1. Leave three blank columns—Columns F, G, and H—to the right of your original data.
2. Copy the data range of the returned worksheet. Paste this copy, starting in Column I of the original worksheet.
3. Add the heading Match? in Column G.
4. Add a formula in Column G to compare whether each of the cells in the original dataset match the cells in the returned dataset. Add the formula `=AND(A6=I6,B6=J6,C6=K6,D6=L6,E6=M6)` in Cell G6 to compare all five cells in the dataset.
5. Copy the formula down Column G from Cell G6 to match the number of rows in the dataset.
6. In Cell G2, enter an `AND` formula to test whether all the formulas in Column G are `TRUE`. Even though this range contains more than 255 cells, it is still valid to use it as one of the expressions in the `AND` function. The formula in G2 is `=SUM(G6:G999)`. This is a quick way to find out whether every row is identical without having to scroll through pages of data, looking for a single `FALSE` result. If Cell G2 returns `TRUE`, you know that the original and returned worksheets are identical. If Cell G2 returns `FALSE`, one or more of the rows have been changed.
7. Select G6:G99. From the Sheet ribbon, select Find & Select, Find. The Find and Replace dialog appears.
8. In the Find and Replace dialog, type `FALSE` in the Find What box. You must click the Options button and change the Look In drop-down from Formulas to Values in order to find formulas that result in a value of `FALSE`.

## Using OR to Check Whether Any Conditions Are Met

You might have a situation in which a certain formula is based on meeting one of several conditions. A sales manager may want to reward big orders and new customers' orders. The manager may offer a commission bonus if the order is over $50,000 or if the customer is a new customer this year.

To test whether a particular sale meets either condition, you use the OR function. The OR function returns TRUE if any condition is TRUE and returns FALSE if none of the conditions are TRUE.

SYNTAX: OR(*logical1*,*logical2*,...)

The OR function checks whether any of the arguments are TRUE. It returns a FALSE only if all of the arguments are FALSE. If any argument is TRUE, the function returns TRUE.

The arguments *logical1*,*logical2*,... are 1 to 255 conditions that can evaluate to TRUE or FALSE.

In Figure 24.4, the logical test to see if revenue is over $50,000 is E2>50000. The logical test to see if the customer is new this year is D2=2007. The structure of this OR function is =OR(D2=2007,E2>50000).

You can use the OR function as the first argument to the IF function to produce the formula shown in Cell F2: =IF(OR(D2=2007,E2>50000),0.025*E2,0.015*E2).

**Figure 24.4**
OR checks whether a record meets at least one of several criteria.

| | B | C | D | E | F | G |
|---|---|---|---|---|---|---|
| 1 | Customer | Associate | Cust Since | Revenue | Commission | |
| 2 | First-Rate Sandal Company | GERALD | 2007 | 15456 | 386.4 | |
| 3 | Fascinating Linen Company | JOSEPH | 2006 | 53928 | 1348.2 | |
| 4 | Flexible Hairpin Corporation | SHELLY | 2003 | 4784 | 71.76 | |
| 5 | Attractive Yogurt Corporation | JOY | 2007 | 67680 | 1692 | |
| 6 | Dependable Vise Traders | JOY | 2003 | 20088 | 301.32 | |
| 7 | Wonderful Kettle Inc. | FANNIE | 2003 | 32760 | 491.4 | |
| 8 | Unsurpassed Thermostat Inc. | JOSEPH | 2003 | 34768 | 521.52 | |
| 9 | First-Rate Instrument Inc. | JOY | 2002 | 7704 | 115.56 | |
| 10 | Forceful Juicer Company | GERALD | 2005 | 52152 | 1303.8 | |
| 11 | Guarded Tuner Inc. | GERALD | 2006 | 34224 | 513.36 | |
| 12 | Leading Utensil Supply | FANNIE | 2007 | 14544 | 363.6 | |
| 13 | Rare Shoe Company | SHELLY | 2004 | 26208 | 393.12 | |
| 14 | Flexible Calculator Corporation | JOSEPH | 2007 | 13824 | 345.6 | |
| 15 | Steadfast Shovel Traders | JOSEPH | 2004 | 49400 | 741 | |
| 16 | Unsurpassed Washer Inc. | JOSEPH | 2001 | 31620 | 474.3 | |
| 17 | Excellent Freezer Company | SHELLY | 2004 | 52416 | 1310.4 | |
| 18 | Guarded Bicycle Corporation | SHELLY | 2004 | 17160 | 257.4 | |
| 19 | Well-Suited Doghouse Company | SHELLY | 2002 | 39900 | 598.5 | |
| 20 | Savory Freezer Corporation | GERALD | 2001 | 8148 | 122.22 | |
| 21 | Dependable Utensil Company | GERALD | 2005 | 6912 | 103.68 | |
| 22 | Wonderful Jewelry Inc. | FANNIE | 2005 | 44940 | 674.1 | |
| 23 | Unusual Vegetable Supply | FANNIE | 2005 | 42640 | 639.6 | |
| 24 | Savory Oven Traders | JOSEPH | 2001 | 20800 | 312 | |
| 25 | Vibrant Clipboard Corporation | GERALD | 2007 | 51088 | 1277.2 | |
| 26 | Improved Adhesive Inc. | FANNIE | 2006 | 49104 | 736.56 | |
| 27 | Effortless Quilt Corporation | FANNIE | 2001 | 67568 | 1689.2 | |
| 28 | User-Friendly Bottle Corporation | JOSEPH | 2004 | 11844 | 177.66 | |
| 29 | Tremendous Saddle Corporation | JOY | 2007 | 40352 | 1008.8 | |
| 30 | Trouble-Free Banister Supply | SHELLY | 2006 | 45360 | 680.4 | |
| 31 | Forceful Oven Inc. | FANNIE | 2003 | 36000 | 540 | |

F2: =IF(OR(D2=2007,E2>50000),0.025*E2,0.015*E2)

## NESTING IF FUNCTIONS

The IF function offers only two possible formulas. Either the logical test is TRUE and the first formula is used or the logical test is FALSE and the second formula is used.

Many situations have a series of choices. In a human resources department, for example, annual merit raises may be given out based on the employee's numeric rating in an annual review. Employees are ranked on a 5-point scale. The rules for setting the raise are as follows:

- 4.5 or higher: 5% raise

- 4 or higher: 4.5% raise

- 3.25 or higher: 3% raise

- 2.5 or higher: 1% raise

- Under 2.5: no raise

You would build the IF statement by following these steps.

1. Test for the highest condition first. Excel stops testing when the first condition is met. If your first test were to see if an employee had a rating of higher than 2.5, then anyone from 2.5 to 5 would get a 1% raise. In this case, you want to give a 5% raise to anyone with a rating of 4.5 or greater, so the formula starts out as =IF(B2>=4.5,5%,. There is only one argument left in the current IF function—the argument for *value_if_false*.

2. Instead of using a value as the third argument, start a second IF function to be used if the first test is FALSE. This IF function starts out IF(B2>=4,4.5%,. Combine this start of an IF function with the first IF function: =IF(B2>=4.5,5%,IF(B2>=4,4.5%,. There are still three possible raise levels and only one argument left in the second IF function.

3. Start a third IF function to be used as the *value_if_false* argument for the second IF function: IF(B2>=3.25,3%,. At this point, if the employee was not ranked above 3.25, there are only two possibilities left. Either the employee was 2.5 and above for a 1% raise, or he or she gets no raise.

4. Create the fourth IF function: IF(B2>=2.5,1%,0).

5. With the four IF functions, be careful to provide four closing parentheses at the end of the function: =IF(B2>=4.5,5%,IF(B2>=4,4.5%,IF(B2>=3.25,3%,IF(B2>=2.5,1%,0%)))) (see Figure 24.5).

**Figure 24.5**
This formula contains four nested IF functions.

| | C2 | | | fx | =IF(B2>=4.5,5%,IF(B2>=4,4.5%,IF(B2>=3.25,3%,IF(B2>=2.5,1%,0%)))) | | | | | |
|---|---|---|---|---|---|---|---|---|---|---|
| | A | B | C | D | E | F | G | H | I | J |
| 1 | EMPLOYEE | RANK | RAISE | | | | | | | |
| 2 | JIMMY CAMPBELL | 1.6 | 0.00% | | | | | | | |
| 3 | DENNIS PENA | 3.4 | 3.00% | | | | | | | |
| 4 | MARK LANCASTER | 4.8 | 5.00% | | | | | | | |
| 5 | KEITH AGUIRRE | 4.3 | 4.50% | | | | | | | |
| 6 | MARIAN SUAREZ | 3.8 | 3.00% | | | | | | | |
| 7 | SAMUEL WOODWARD | 3 | 1.00% | | | | | | | |
| 8 | PHILLIP MULLINS | 2.4 | 0.00% | | | | | | | |
| 9 | JOHNNY KNOX | 1.3 | 0.00% | | | | | | | |

CAUTION

These IF formulas are hard to read. There is a temptation to use them for situations with very long lists of conditions. Excel prevents you from nesting more than seven levels of IF functions. Beyond that point, you should use VLOOKUP, which is explained later in this chapter.

## USING THE TRUE AND FALSE FUNCTIONS

There are two remaining functions in the logical group. You should not need to use either of them. If you encounter a function with either the TRUE or FALSE function, you can simply replace the function with the value TRUE or FALSE. Microsoft added TRUE and FALSE to provide compatibility with other vendors' spreadsheet programs.

A formula such as =IF(OR(A2>5,B2=0),TRUE(),FALSE()) can be rewritten as =IF(OR(A2>5,B2=0),TRUE,FALSE).

## USING THE NOT FUNCTION TO SIMPLIFY THE USE OF AND AND OR

In the language of Boolean logic, there are typically NAND, NOR, and XOR functions, which stand for Not And, Not Or, and Exclusive Or. To simplify matters, Excel offers the NOT function.

SYNTAX: NOT(*logical*)

Quite simply, NOT reverses a logical value. TRUE becomes FALSE, and FALSE becomes TRUE when processed through a NOT function.

Say that you need to find all flights landing outside of Oklahoma. You could build a massive OR statement to find every airport code in the U.S., or you could simply build an OR function to find Tulsa and Oklahoma City and then use a NOT function to reverse the result:
=NOT(OR(A2="Tulsa",A2="Oklahoma City")).

## USING THE IFERROR FUNCTION TO SIMPLIFY ERROR CHECKING

The IFERROR function, which is new in Excel 2007, was added at the request of many customers. To help understand the IFERROR function, it would be good to understand how error checking was performed during the 22 years before Excel 2007 was released.

Figure 24.6 shows a typical spreadsheet that calculates a ratio of sales to hours. Even though this formula works most of the time, in occasional records, the divisor is zero, and the formula returns an #DIV/0 error.

**Figure 24.6**
The zero in the divisor in Row 5 causes a division-by-zero error.

| | A | B | C | D | E |
|---|---|---|---|---|---|
| | D2 | | | fx =B2/C2 | |
| 1 | Name | Sales | Hours | Sales Per Hour | |
| 2 | TERRI | 15 | 7 | 2.14 | |
| 3 | MYRTLE | 13 | 5 | 2.60 | |
| 4 | PAUL | 6 | 8 | 0.75 | |
| 5 | VERA | 0 | 0 | #DIV/0! | |
| 6 | ALICIA | 3 | 7 | 0.43 | |
| 7 | VICTORIA | 13 | 4 | 3.25 | |
| 8 | RYAN | 13 | 6 | 2.17 | |

The typical way to deal with this in Excel 2003 and earlier was to set up an IF function to check whether the divisor was zero: =IF(C5=0,0,B5/C5). If the divisor was zero, the formula would simply return a zero as the result; otherwise, the formula would perform the calculation.

It was typical in earlier versions of Excel to use this type of IF formula on thousands of rows of data. The formula is more complex and takes longer to calculate than the new IFERROR function. However, this particular formula is tame compared to some of the formulas needed to check for errors.

A very common error occurs when you use the VLOOKUP function to retrieve a value from a lookup table. In Figure 24.7, the VLOOKUP function in Cell D2 asks Excel to look for the rep number S07 from Cell B2 and find the corresponding name in the lookup table of F2:G9. This works great, returning JESSE from the table. However, a problem arises when the sales rep is not found in the table. In Row 7, rep S09 is new and has not yet been added to the table, so Excel returns the #N/A result.

**Figure 24.7**
An #N/A error means that the value is not in the lookup table.

| | D2 | ▾ | fx | =VLOOKUP(B2,$F$2:$G$9,2,FALSE) | | |
|---|---|---|---|---|---|---|
| ▲ | A | B | C | D | E | F | G |
| 1 | Invoice | Rep | Amount | Name | | Rep | Name |
| 2 | 15100 | S07 | 128.59 | JESSE | | S01 | GRACE |
| 3 | 15101 | S06 | 144.67 | ERIN | | S02 | JULIE |
| 4 | 15102 | S05 | 121 | JEREMY | | S03 | CHRISTY |
| 5 | 15103 | S04 | 169.47 | THELMA | | S04 | THELMA |
| 6 | 15104 | S04 | 169.62 | THELMA | | S05 | JEREMY |
| 7 | 15105 | S09 | 172.55 | #N/A | | S06 | ERIN |
| 8 | 15106 | S08 | 112.68 | MARION | | S07 | JESSE |
| 9 | 15107 | S02 | 145.44 | JULIE | | S08 | MARION |
| 10 | 15108 | S01 | 101.05 | GRACE | | | |
| 11 | 15109 | S05 | 197.68 | JEREMY | | | |

If you wanted to avoid #N/A errors, the generally accepted workaround through Excel 2003 was to write this horrible formula:

```
=IF(ISNA(VLOOKUP(B7,$F$2:$G$9,2,FALSE)),"New Rep", VLOOKUP(B7,$F$2:$G$9,2,FALSE))
```

In English, this formula basically says to first find the rep name in the lookup table. If the rep is not found and returns the #N/A error, then use some other text—in this case, the words New Rep. If the rep is found, then perform the lookup again and use that result.

Because VLOOKUP was one of the most time-intensive functions, it was horrible to have Excel perform every VLOOKUP twice in this formula. In a dataset with 50,000 records, it could take minutes for the VLOOKUP to complete. Microsoft wisely added the new IFERROR function to handle all these error-checking situations.

SYNTAX: IFERROR(value,value_if_error)

The advantage of the IFERROR function is that the calculation is evaluated only once. If the calculation results in any type of an error value (such as #N/A, #VALUE!, #REF!, #DIV/0!, #NUM!, #NAME?, or #NULL!), Excel returns the alternate value. If the calculation results in any other valid value (whether it is numeric, logical, or text), Excel returns the calculated value.

The formula from the preceding section can be rewritten as =IFERROR(VLOOKUP(B7, $F$2:$G$9,2,FALSE),"New Rep"), as shown in Figure 24.7. This calculation is easier to write and calculates much more quickly than the method required in Excel 2003 and earlier.

**CAUTION**

> If you are going to be sharing your workbook with people who use previous versions of Excel, you should avoid using IFERROR. Instead, you should test for the various error conditions as described in the next section.

# EXAMPLES OF INFORMATION FUNCTIONS

Found under the More Function icon, the 17 information functions return eclectic information about any cell. Ten of the 17 functions are called the IS functions because they test for various conditions.

## USING THE IS FUNCTIONS TO TEST FOR ERRORS

Figure 24.8 shows the results of four functions for testing error values:

**Figure 24.8**
The results of IS functions for detecting errors.

| B2 | =ERROR.TYPE(A2) | | | |
|---|---|---|---|---|
| A | B | C | D | E |
| 1 | Value | Error.Type | IsErr | IsError | IsNA |
| 2 | #NULL! | 1 | TRUE | TRUE | FALSE |
| 3 | #DIV/0! | 2 | TRUE | TRUE | FALSE |
| 4 | #VALUE! | 3 | TRUE | TRUE | FALSE |
| 5 | #REF! | 4 | TRUE | TRUE | FALSE |
| 6 | #NAME? | 5 | TRUE | TRUE | FALSE |
| 7 | #NUM! | 6 | TRUE | TRUE | FALSE |
| 8 | #N/A | 7 | FALSE | TRUE | TRUE |
| 9 | | | | | |

24

- ISERROR—This function evaluates whether a calculation or value results in any type of error. If your workbooks will only be used by people using Excel 2007 or newer, you should use the IFERROR function instead of ISERROR. However, if you need to share your workbook with people using Excel 2003, you should use ISERROR, usually in combination with an IF function. Here is an example: =IF(ISERROR(A2),"Unknown",A2).

- ISERR—This function is similar to ISERROR, except it does not report #N/A errors.

- ISNA—This function specifically tests whether a result returns an #N/A error.

- ERROR.TYPE—This function lets you know specifically what error is being returned. This function returns a value from 1 through 7 to indicate #NULL!, #DIV/0!, #VALUE!, #REF!, #NAME?, #NUM!, and #N/A, respectively. It is possible to write a lengthy formula such as the following to decode these values and provide a friendlier error message.:

```
=IF(NOT(ISERROR(A2)),A2,CHOOSE(ERROR.TYPE(A2),"Null Value Found",
"Division by Zero","Invalid Value","Missing Reference","Undefined Name",
"Numeric Error","Value Not Available"))
```

## USING IS FUNCTIONS TO TEST FOR TYPES OF VALUES

Figure 24.9 shows the results for the seven remaining IS functions, each of which reveals whether a value contains a particular type of value:

**Figure 24.9**
The results of IS functions for detecting certain types of values.

| | A | B | C | D | E | F | G | H |
|---|---|---|---|---|---|---|---|---|
| | K20 | ▼ | fx | | | | | |
| 1 | Value | IsBlank | IsEven | IsOdd | IsLogical | IsText | IsNonText | IsNumber |
| 2 | 1 | FALSE | FALSE | TRUE | FALSE | FALSE | TRUE | TRUE |
| 3 | 2 | FALSE | TRUE | FALSE | FALSE | FALSE | TRUE | TRUE |
| 4 | TRUE | FALSE | #VALUE! | #VALUE! | TRUE | FALSE | TRUE | FALSE |
| 5 | FALSE | FALSE | #VALUE! | #VALUE! | TRUE | FALSE | TRUE | FALSE |
| 6 | 7/1/2006 | FALSE | FALSE | TRUE | FALSE | FALSE | TRUE | TRUE |
| 7 | ABC | FALSE | #VALUE! | #VALUE! | FALSE | TRUE | FALSE | FALSE |
| 8 | | TRUE | TRUE | FALSE | FALSE | FALSE | TRUE | FALSE |
| 9 | #N/A | FALSE | #N/A | #N/A | FALSE | FALSE | TRUE | FALSE |
| 10 | | | | | | | | |

- ISBLANK—This function returns TRUE only if a cell is completely empty. A cell that contains several spaces is not considered to be blank. Even a cell that contains a single apostrophe and no spaces is not considered to be blank by the ISBLANK function. It would have been more appropriate if the folks at Lotus 1-2-3 would have called this the @IsEmpty function, but you are stuck with the bad name now that it has been in use forever.

- ISEVEN—This function indicates whether a number is evenly divisible by 2. Note in Cell C8 that an empty cell is considered to be zero and reports as even. Using a date as the value in ISEVEN returns a value, but that value does not make sense. Using text or logical values in the ISEVEN function causes a #VALUE! error. Mathematicians in the audience may suggest that you could just as easily use =MOD(A2,2)=0 to figure out whether a number is even. Unless you are a mathematician, however, it is far easier to remember =ISEVEN().

- ISODD—This function indicates whether a number is not evenly divisible by 2. An empty cell is considered zero and returns FALSE to ISODD. The same limitations listed for ISEVEN apply to ISODD. Also, if your value contains decimal places, they are ignored by both the ISEVEN and ISODD functions. Numbers such as 1.02, 1.2, 1.5, 1.9, 1.99999999 all return TRUE for the ISODD function.

- ISLOGICAL—This function indicates whether the value is either TRUE, FALSE, or an expression that results in TRUE or FALSE. Note that there is a very important distinction here. ISLOGICAL does not tell you whether a value is FALSE. It merely indicates that the expression results in one of the valid logical values of TRUE or FALSE.

- ISTEXT—This function returns TRUE if the value contains text. This is good for finding values such as ABC in Cell A16 and also for finding cells that look like numbers but are actually stored as text.

- ISNONTEXT—This returns TRUE for anything that is nontext. Numbers, logicals, dates, empty cells, and even error cells return TRUE for ISNONTEXT.

- ISNUMBER—This function returns TRUE for numeric cells and dates. Note that although the empty Cell A8 can be calculated as even in Cell C8, it returns FALSE to ISNUMBER in Cell H8.

The functions in this section are almost always used in conjunction with an IF function. For example, zip codes in the United States should always be five digits. This causes problems when someone is keying in a zip code for certain eastern cities that start with a zero. In Cell C6 of Figure 24.10, for example, the proper way to key a zip code for Portland, Maine, is to type an apostrophe and then 04123. Most people forget the apostrophe, and Excel drops the leading zero, as shown in Cell C5.

**Figure 24.10**
The formula in Column D detects nontext zip codes and converts to text with five digits.

| | D5 | ▼ | | *fx* | =IF(ISNONTEXT(C5),RIGHT("0000"&C5,5),C5) | |
|---|---|---|---|---|---|---|
| | A | B | C | D | E | F |
| 1 | City | ST | Zip Code | Zip Fixed | | |
| 2 | Salem | OH | 44460 | 44460 | | |
| 3 | Uniontown | OH | 44685 | 44685 | | |
| 4 | Schenectady | NY | 12345 | 12345 | | |
| 5 | Portland | ME | 4123 | 04123 | | |
| 6 | Portland | ME | 04123 | 04123 | | |
| 7 | St Thomas | VI | 801 | 00801 | | |
| 8 | St Thomas | VI | 00801 | 00801 | | |
| 9 | | | | | | |

The formula in Column D, =IF(ISNONTEXT(C5),RIGHT("0000"&C5,5),C5), fixes errant zip codes in Column C. If the value in Column C in nontext, the program pads the left side of the zip code with zeros and then takes the five right-most digits.

Another use of the IS functions is in the formulas for a conditional formatting rule. In Figure 24.11, a few cells have been erroneously entered as text instead of numbers. Setting up a rule to mark any cells where the formula =ISTEXT(B2) is true quickly reveals the cells that need to be updated.

**Figure 24.11**
An ISTEXT function is used in conditional formatting to mark any numbers erroneously entered as text.

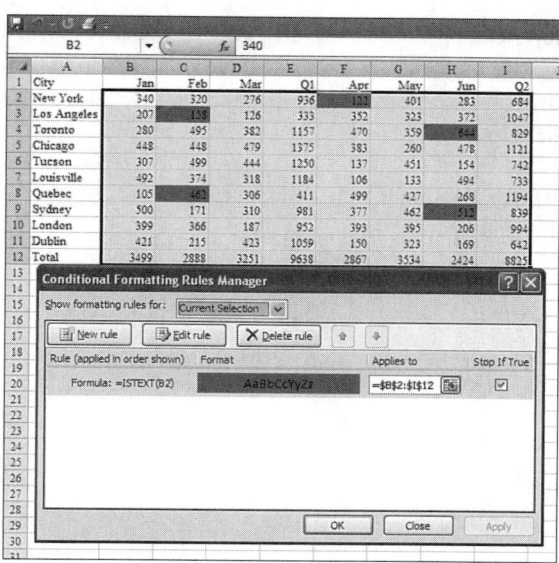

**NOTE**

For more information on using formulas as rules for conditional formatting, see Chapter 9, "Visualizing Data in Excel."

## USING THE ISREF FUNCTION

The ISREF function tests whether a value is a reference.

SYNTAX: ISREF(*value*)

ISREF returns TRUE if the value is a valid reference. Initially, this function may seem to be useless. After all, you would inherently know that A2 is a valid reference—you would not have to use a function to test it.

The following formulas return TRUE: =ISREF(A2), =ISREF(XFD1048576), and =ISREF(A2:Z99). The following formulas return FALSE: =ISREF("A2"), =ISREF(99), and =ISREF(2+2).

There are two special circumstances in which ISREF is actually useful. Say that you have designed a spreadsheet with the named range "ExpenseTotal". If you are worried that someone might have deleted this particular row, you can check whether ExpenseTotal is still a valid name by using =ISREF(ExpenseTotal). Here's an example:

=IF(ISREF(ExpenseTotal),ExpenseTotal*2,"Named Range Has Been Deleted")

### USING THE ISREF FUNCTION TO CHECK A REFERENCE

The lookup function Indirect allows you to build a cell reference by using a formula. In Figure 24.12, the cell address in Cell D14 is built using a formula to concatenate a column letter with a row number. Cell D15 then uses the Indirect function to return the value stored in the cell referenced by the formula in Cell D14. As you can imagine, this process is subject to error. Someone might enter a negative number, as shown in Cell D18. Before using the Indirect function, you can check whether the reference in Cell D14 is a valid reference by using =ISREF(Indirect(D14)).

## USING THE N FUNCTION TO ADD A COMMENT TO A FORMULA

You can call Excel's N function a creative use for an obsolete function. Lotus 1-2-3 used to offer an N() function that would convert a value as follows:

- N(any number) would return that number.
- N(a date) would return the serial number of the date.
- N(True) would return 1.
- N(False) would return 0.
- N(any error) would return the error.
- N(any text) would return 0.

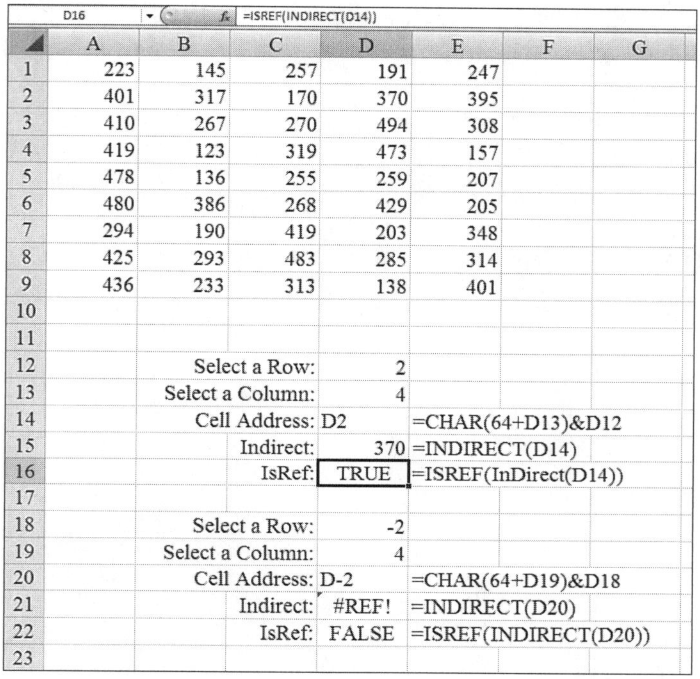

**Figure 24.12**
You can prevent problems with Indirect by checking ISREF(Indirect()) first.

| | D16 | ▾ | fx | =ISREF(INDIRECT(D14)) | | | |
|---|---|---|---|---|---|---|---|
| | A | B | C | D | E | F | G |
| 1 | 223 | 145 | 257 | 191 | 247 | | |
| 2 | 401 | 317 | 170 | 370 | 395 | | |
| 3 | 410 | 267 | 270 | 494 | 308 | | |
| 4 | 419 | 123 | 319 | 473 | 157 | | |
| 5 | 478 | 136 | 255 | 259 | 207 | | |
| 6 | 480 | 386 | 268 | 429 | 205 | | |
| 7 | 294 | 190 | 419 | 203 | 348 | | |
| 8 | 425 | 293 | 483 | 285 | 314 | | |
| 9 | 436 | 233 | 313 | 138 | 401 | | |
| 10 | | | | | | | |
| 11 | | | | | | | |
| 12 | | | Select a Row: | 2 | | | |
| 13 | | | Select a Column: | 4 | | | |
| 14 | | | Cell Address: | D2 | =CHAR(64+D13)&D12 | | |
| 15 | | | Indirect: | 370 | =INDIRECT(D14) | | |
| 16 | | | IsRef: | TRUE | =ISREF(InDirect(D14)) | | |
| 17 | | | | | | | |
| 18 | | | Select a Row: | -2 | | | |
| 19 | | | Select a Column: | 4 | | | |
| 20 | | | Cell Address: | D-2 | =CHAR(64+D19)&D18 | | |
| 21 | | | Indirect: | #REF! | =INDIRECT(D20) | | |
| 22 | | | IsRef: | FALSE | =ISREF(INDIRECT(D20)) | | |
| 23 | | | | | | | |

None of these are terribly interesting functions. Basically, you could replicate just about any of them by referring to the value and changing the cell format.

An interesting unintended use of the function is that N(*any text*) always returns 0. A cool trick is to leave yourself a comment about a long formula by adding the N function to the end of the formula. You just need to make sure that your comment contains text. Because N(*text*) is 0, the outcome of the function does not change. When you come back to the formula several months later, you can see your comment in the formula bar, as shown in Figure 24.13.

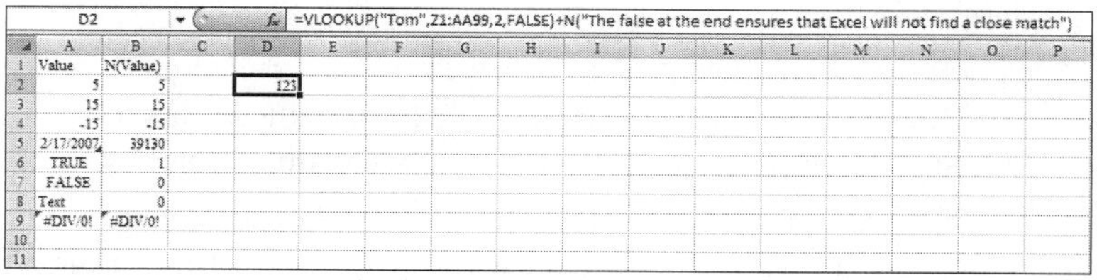

**Figure 24.13**
Because N of *text* is 0, you can store a comment in the N function.

| | D2 | ▾ | fx | =VLOOKUP("Tom",Z1:AA99,2,FALSE)+N("The false at the end ensures that Excel will not find a close match") |
|---|---|---|---|---|
| | A | B | C | D ... |
| 1 | Value | N(Value) | | |
| 2 | 5 | 5 | | 123 |
| 3 | 15 | 15 | | |
| 4 | -15 | -15 | | |
| 5 | 2/17/2007 | 39130 | | |
| 6 | TRUE | 1 | | |
| 7 | FALSE | 0 | | |
| 8 | Text | 0 | | |
| 9 | #DIV/0! | #DIV/0! | | |
| 10 | | | | |
| 11 | | | | |

## USING THE NA FUNCTION TO FORCE CHARTS TO NOT PLOT MISSING DATA

Say that you are in charge of a school's annual fund drive. Each day, you mark the fundraising total on a worksheet by following these steps:

1. In Column A (see Figure 24.14) you enter the results of each day's collection, through nine days of the fund drive.

**Figure 24.14**
Using NA in the chart on the right allows the trendline to ignore future missing data points and project a reasonable ending result.

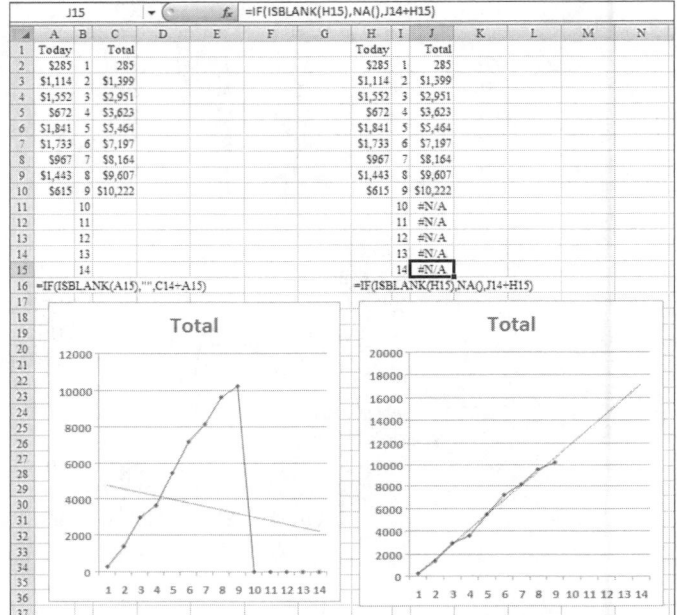

2. Enter a formula in Column C to keep track of the total collected throughout the fund drive.

3. To avoid making it look like the fund drive collected nothing in Days 10 through 14, enter a formula in Column C to checks whether Column A is blank. If it is, the IF function inserts a null cell in Column C. For example, the formula in Cell C15 is `=IF(ISBLANK(A15),"",A15+C14)`.

4. Build a line chart based on B1:C15. Add a trendline to the chart to predict future fundraising totals.

5. As shown in Columns A:G of Figure 24.14, this technique fails. Even though the totals for Days 10 through 14 are blank, Excel charts those days as zero. The linear trendline predicts that your fundraising will go down, with a projected total of just over $2,000.

6. Try the exact same chart again, but this time use the NA function instead of " " in the IF statement in step 3. The formula is shown in Cell H16, and the results are in Cell J15. Excel understands that NA values should not be plotted. The trendline is calculated based on only the data points available and projects a total just under $18,000.

In many cases, you are trying to avoid #N/A! errors. However, in the case of charting a calculated column, you might want to have #N/A! to produce the correct look to the chart.

## USING THE INFO FUNCTION TO PRINT INFORMATION ABOUT A COMPUTER

The remaining information functions tell you some piece of information about a particular cell or about the computer. The INFO function is left over from Lotus 1-2-3. Some of the information it provides would be useful only in Lotus. However, a few of the options may be useful to display in an Excel spreadsheet.

SYNTAX: =INFO(*type_text*)

The INFO function returns information about the current operating environment.

The following are valid values for the *type_text* argument:

- Directory—Returns the folder where the current workbook is saved. If the file is not yet saved, returns #N/A.

- NumFile—Returns the number of open files. This is not just open workbooks, but all files open on the system.

- MemAvail—Returns the available memory. This appears to be some old DOS version of the memory available. Even on a system with 128MB of RAM, the total memory reported is about 4MB, so it might be the memory assigned to the partition running Excel.

- MemUsed—Specifies the memory in use by Excel.

- TotMem—Returns the total of the previous two results.

- Origin—Returns the text "$A:" and the absolute cell address of the upper-left cell visible in the current window. The "$A:" prefix is a notation used by Lotus 1-2-3 release 3.0. You might start to think that there could be uses for this result. For example, = INDIRECT(TRIM(MID(INFO("Origin"),2,50))) would return the value shown in the upper-left corner of the visible window. Note, however, that in Excel 2007, you can use the scrollbars to change the upper-left cell, and Excel does not recalculate, leaving the Origin result incorrect until you change a cell in Excel.

- OSVersion—Returns the version number of your operating system.

- Recalc—Returns either Manual or Automatic to indicate the current recalculation status. You might provide a hint to the spreadsheet reader with =IF(INFO("Recalc")="Manual","Press F9 to calculate",""). 

- Release—Specifies the release number of Excel. For Excel 2007, this is 12.0. You might be able to use this information in combination with IF and INDIRECT to correctly build a reference to the entire worksheet.

- System—Returns either mac or pcdos, to indicate Macintosh or Windows.

24

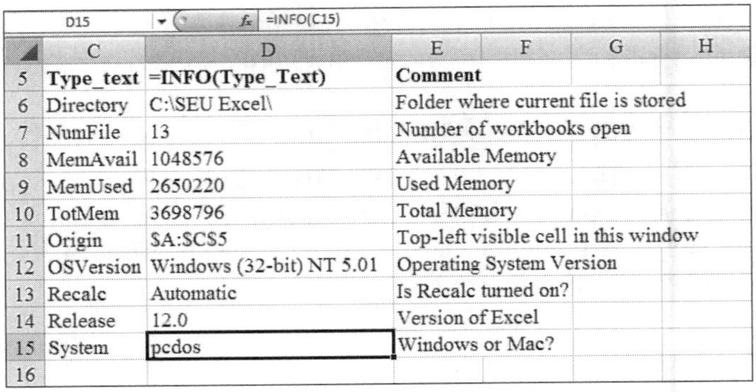

**Figure 24.15**
A few of the argument values for INFO() still return useful results.

| | C | D | E | F | G | H |
|---|---|---|---|---|---|---|
| | | D15 ▾ ( fx =INFO(C15) | | | | |
| 5 | Type_text | =INFO(Type_Text) | Comment | | | |
| 6 | Directory | C:\SEU Excel\ | Folder where current file is stored | | | |
| 7 | NumFile | 13 | Number of workbooks open | | | |
| 8 | MemAvail | 1048576 | Available Memory | | | |
| 9 | MemUsed | 2650220 | Used Memory | | | |
| 10 | TotMem | 3698796 | Total Memory | | | |
| 11 | Origin | $A:$C$5 | Top-left visible cell in this window | | | |
| 12 | OSVersion | Windows (32-bit) NT 5.01 | Operating System Version | | | |
| 13 | Recalc | Automatic | Is Recalc turned on? | | | |
| 14 | Release | 12.0 | Version of Excel | | | |
| 15 | System | pcdos | Windows or Mac? | | | |
| 16 | | | | | | |

Figure 24.15 shows the results of several variations of the INFO function.

## USING THE CELL FUNCTION

The CELL function can tell you specific information about a specific cell, or it can tell you specific information about the last cell changed in the worksheet.

Again, some of the types of information are a bit dated. For example, the Color argument was written in the day when a cell was either black or possibly red if the value was negative. The Prefix argument is based on when cells could be left-justified, centered, or right-justified. Even though Excel has offered several levels of indenting for a decade, the Prefix version of the CELL function does not reveal anything about the indentation level.

SYNTAX: CELL(info_type,reference)

To use the CELL function, you specify the type of information and optionally a cell reference. If you specify a cell reference, Excel provides information about the cell in the reference. If you leave off the reference, Excel returns information about the last cell changed in the workbook.

The argument info_type is a text value that specifies what type of cell information you want. The following are the possible values of info_type and the corresponding results:

- contents—Returns the value in the upper-left cell in reference.
- address—Returns the address of the first cell in reference, as text. As shown in Cell B5 of Figure 24.16, this is always returned in absolute reference style.
- row—Returns the row number of the cell in reference.
- col—Returns the column number of the cell in reference.
- filename—Returns the filename (including the full path) of the file that contains reference, as text. Returns empty text ("") if the worksheet that contains reference has not yet been saved. Interestingly, this argument now also returns the worksheet name if the workbook contains multiple worksheets.

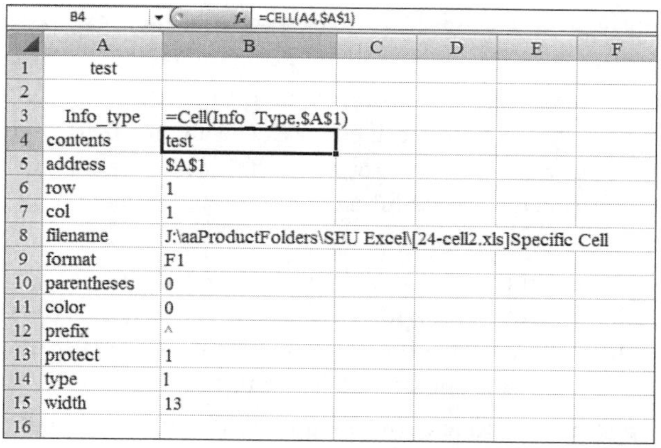

**Figure 24.16**
The CELL function returns information about a specific cell, in this case, Cell A1.

| | B4 | ▼ | fx | =CELL(A4,$A$1) | | | |
|---|---|---|---|---|---|---|---|
| | A | B | C | D | E | F |
| 1 | test | | | | | |
| 2 | | | | | | |
| 3 | Info_type | =Cell(Info_Type,$A$1) | | | | |
| 4 | contents | test | | | | |
| 5 | address | $A$1 | | | | |
| 6 | row | 1 | | | | |
| 7 | col | 1 | | | | |
| 8 | filename | J:\aaProductFolders\SEU Excel\[24-cell2.xls]Specific Cell | | | | |
| 9 | format | F1 | | | | |
| 10 | parentheses | 0 | | | | |
| 11 | color | 0 | | | | |
| 12 | prefix | ^ | | | | |
| 13 | protect | 1 | | | | |
| 14 | type | 1 | | | | |
| 15 | width | 13 | | | | |
| 16 | | | | | | |

- **format**—Returns the text value corresponding to the number format of the cell. Returns - at the end of the text value if the cell is formatted in color for negative values. Returns () at the end of the text value if the cell is formatted with parentheses for positive or all values. The values reported as a format reflect old Lotus 1-2-3 codes. When you format, Excel attempts to convert the current numeric format to an old-style Lotus 1-2-3 formatting code. Table 24.7 shows some examples.

**TABLE 24.7—CUSTOM CODES IN EXCEL AND LOTUS 1-2-3**

| Excel Format | Excel Custom Code | Lotus Format Code |
|---|---|---|
| General | General | G |
| Numeric, no Decimal | 0 | F0 |
| Numeric, 2 Decimals | 0.00 | F2 |
| Comma, 2 Decimals | #,##0.00 | ,2 |
| Currency, 2 Decimals | $#,##0.00_) | C2 |
| Percent, 1 Decimal | 0.0% | P1 |
| Scientific Notation | 0.00E+00 | S2 |
| Fractions | # ?/? | G |
| Date | m/d/yy | D4 |
| Date | d-mmm-y | D1 |
| Date | d-mmm | D2 |
| Date | mmm-yy | D3 |
| Time | H:mm AM/PM | D7 |

- **parentheses**—Returns 1 if the cell is formatted with parentheses for positive or all values; otherwise, returns 0.

- color—Returns 1 if the cell is formatted in color for negative values; otherwise, returns 0.

- prefix—Returns the text value corresponding to the "label prefix" of the cell. Returns a single quotation mark (') if the cell contains left-aligned text, double quotation mark (") if the cell contains right-aligned text, a caret (^) if the cell contains centered text, a backslash (\) if the cell contains fill-aligned text, and empty text ("") if the cell contains anything else.

- protect—Returns 0 if the cell is not locked and 1 if the cell is locked. Remember that by default, all Excel cells start with their locked property set to TRUE. The locked property is taken into account only if protection is enabled. This argument for the CELL function reports a 1 even if protection is not turned on.

- type—Returns the text value corresponding to the type of data in the cell. Returns b for blank if the cell is empty, l for label if the cell contains a text constant, and v for value if the cell contains anything else.

- width—Returns the column width of the cell, rounded to an integer. Each unit of column width is equal to the width of one character in the default font size. Be careful with this: It is now possible to change column widths without causing Excel to calculate. You might have to press F9 to have the result of this formula change.

- reference—Is an optional cell reference. If reference is omitted, CELL returns the information about the last changed cell.

Figure 24.16 shows every CELL option for a specific cell: Cell A1.

For additional examples, see Excel Help for the CELL function.

## USING CELL TO TRACK THE LAST CELL CHANGED

If you leave off the second argument of the CELL function, Excel returns the information about the last cell changed in the workbook.

You follow these steps to create an interesting watch window of the last cells changed:

1. In an out-of-the-way spot, enter the formula =CELL("address").
2. Just below this formula, enter the formula =CELL("Contents").
3. Just below that formula, enter the formula =CELL("filename").
4. Select all three of these cells.
5. From the Formulas ribbon, choose the Watch Window icon. The Watch Window dialog appears.
6. Click the Add Watch button in the Watch Window dialog.

**7.** Because initially, the default file widths are not wide enough to show the complete value, drag the vertical bars between the headings in the watch window so that you can see the complete Value and Formula columns. The other columns for Book, Sheet, and Cell can be made smaller.

The result, as shown in Figure 24.17, is a floating window that always reveals the last changed cell address and contents.

**Figure 24.17**
The watch window always shows the last cell changed and the value of that cell.

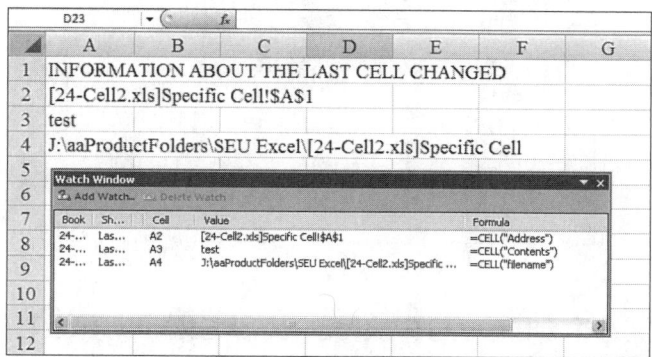

## USING TYPE TO DETERMINE TYPE OF CELL VALUE

The final information function is the TYPE function. You use =TYPE(*value*) to determine whether a value is a number, text, logical, an error value, or an array. Note that dates are treated as numbers.

SYNTAX: =TYPE(*value*)

The TYPE function returns a numeric code that tells you about the type of value.

The TYPE function returns the following values:

- 1—for a numeric or date type
- 2—for a text type
- 4—for a logical type
- 16—for an error type
- 64—for an array type

Figure 24.18 shows the results for various values in the TYPE function.

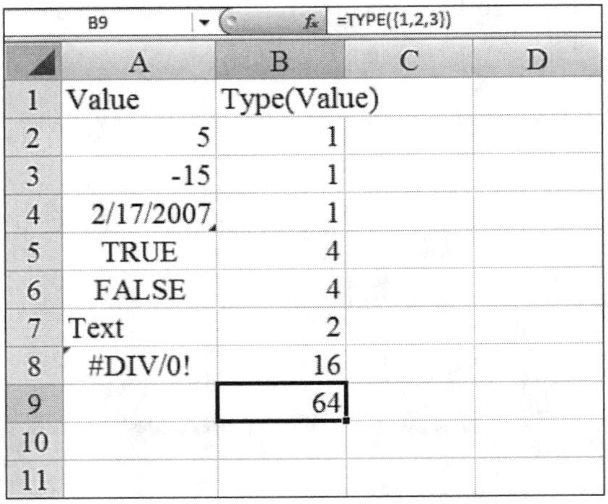

**Figure 24.18**
The TYPE function returns what type of value is specified as an argument.

| | A | B | C | D |
|---|---|---|---|---|
| | Value | Type(Value) | | |
| 1 | Value | Type(Value) | | |
| 2 | 5 | 1 | | |
| 3 | -15 | 1 | | |
| 4 | 2/17/2007 | 1 | | |
| 5 | TRUE | 4 | | |
| 6 | FALSE | 4 | | |
| 7 | Text | 2 | | |
| 8 | #DIV/0! | 16 | | |
| 9 | | 64 | | |
| 10 | | | | |
| 11 | | | | |

B9    *fx* =TYPE({1,2,3})

# EXAMPLES OF LOOKUP AND REFERENCE FUNCTIONS

The Lookup & Reference icon contains 18 functions. The all-star of this group is the venerable VLOOKUP function—one of the most powerful and most used functions in Excel. As database people point out, a lot of work done in Excel should probably be done in Access. The VLOOKUP function allows you to perform the equivalent of a join operation in a database.

This lookup and reference group also includes several functions that seem useless when considered alone. However, when combined, they allow for some very powerful manipulations of data. The examples in the following sections reveal details on how to use the lookup functions and how to combine them to create powerful results.

## USING THE CHOOSE FUNCTION FOR SIMPLE LOOKUPS

Most lookup functions require you to set up a lookup table in a range on the worksheet. However, the CHOOSE function allows you to specify up to 254 choices right in the syntax of the function. The formula that requires the lookup should be able to calculate an integer from 1 to 29 in order to use the CHOOSE function.

SYNTAX: CHOOSE(*index_num*,*value1*,*value2*,...)

The CHOOSE value will choose a value from a list of values, based on an index number.

The CHOOSE function takes the following arguments:

- index_num—This specifies which value argument is selected. index_num must be a number between 1 and 254 or a formula or reference to a cell containing a number between 1 and 254:
  - If index_num is 1, CHOOSE returns value1; if it is 2, CHOOSE returns value2; and so on.

- If `index_num` is a decimal, it is rounded down to the next lowest integer before being used.
- If `index_num` is less than 1 or greater than the number of the last value in the list, `CHOOSE` returns a `#VALUE!` error.

- `value1,value2,...`—These are 1 to 254 value arguments from which `CHOOSE` selects a value or an action to perform based on *`index_num`*. The arguments can be numbers, cell references, defined names, formulas, functions, or text.

The example in Figure 24.19 shows survey data from a number of respondents. Columns B:F indicate their responses on five measures of your service. Column G calculates an average that ranges from 1 to 5. Say that you want to add words to Column H to characterize the overall rating from the respondent. The following formula is used in Cell H4:

```
=CHOOSE(G4,"Strongly Disagree","Disagree","Neutral","Agree","Strongly Agree")
```

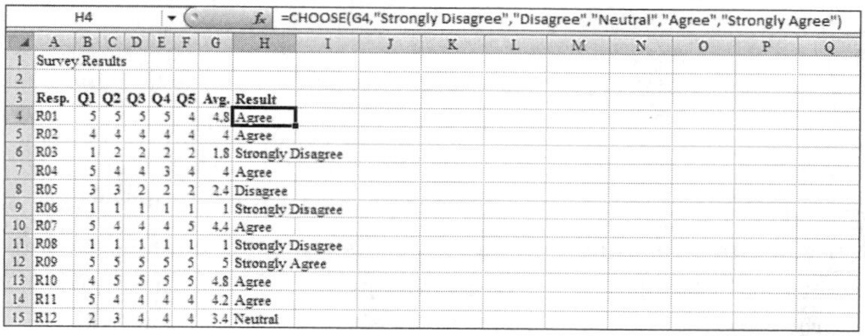
H4 =CHOOSE(G4,"Strongly Disagree","Disagree","Neutral","Agree","Strongly Agree")

| | A | B | C | D | E | F | G | H |
|---|---|---|---|---|---|---|---|---|
| 1 | Survey Results | | | | | | | |
| 2 | | | | | | | | |
| 3 | Resp. | Q1 | Q2 | Q3 | Q4 | Q5 | Avg. | Result |
| 4 | R01 | 5 | 5 | 5 | 5 | 4 | 4.8 | Agree |
| 5 | R02 | 4 | 4 | 4 | 4 | 4 | 4 | Agree |
| 6 | R03 | 1 | 2 | 2 | 2 | 2 | 1.8 | Strongly Disagree |
| 7 | R04 | 5 | 4 | 4 | 3 | 4 | 4 | Agree |
| 8 | R05 | 3 | 3 | 2 | 2 | 2 | 2.4 | Disagree |
| 9 | R06 | 1 | 1 | 1 | 1 | 1 | 1 | Strongly Disagree |
| 10 | R07 | 5 | 4 | 4 | 4 | 5 | 4.4 | Agree |
| 11 | R08 | 1 | 1 | 1 | 1 | 1 | 1 | Strongly Disagree |
| 12 | R09 | 5 | 5 | 5 | 5 | 5 | 5 | Strongly Agree |
| 13 | R10 | 4 | 5 | 5 | 5 | 5 | 4.8 | Agree |
| 14 | R11 | 5 | 4 | 4 | 4 | 4 | 4.2 | Agree |
| 15 | R12 | 2 | 3 | 4 | 4 | 4 | 3.4 | Neutral |

**Figure 24.19**
`CHOOSE` is great for simple choices where the index number is between 1 and 29.

## Using VLOOKUP with TRUE to Find a Value Based on a Range

`VLOOKUP` stands for *vertical lookup*. This function behaves differently, depending on the fourth parameter. This section describes using `VLOOKUP` where you need to choose a value based on a table that contains ranges.

Say that you have a list of students and their scores on a test. The school grading scale is based on these ranges:

- 92–100 is an A.
- 85–91 is a B.
- 70–85 is a C.
- 65–69 is a D.
- Below 65 is an F.

You follow these steps to set up a `VLOOKUP` for this scenario:

1. Because in this version of `VLOOKUP` you do not have to list every possible grade, build a table showing the scores where the grading scale changes from one grade to the next.

2. Although the published grading scale starts with the higher values, your lookup table must be sorted in ascending sequence. This requires a bit of translation as you set up the table. While the grading scale says below 65 is an F, you need to set up the table to show that an F corresponds to any grade at 0 or above. Therefore, in Cell E2 enter 0, and in Cell F2, enter F.

3. Continue building the grading scale in successive rows of Columns E and F. Anything above a 65 is given a D. Anything above 70 is given a C. Note that this is somewhat counterintuitive and is the opposite order that you would use if you were building a grading scale using nested IF functions.

4. Ensure that the numeric values are the leftmost column in your lookup table. In Figure 24.20, the lookup table range is E2:F6. When you use VLOOKUP, Excel searches the first column of the lookup table for the appropriate score.

5. When using this version of VLOOKUP with ranges, sort the list in ascending order. If you are not sure of the proper order, use the Sort command from the Sheet ribbon to sort the table.

6. Because the first argument in the VLOOKUP function is the student's score, in Cell C2, enter =VLOOKUP(B2,.

7. Because the next argument is the range of the lookup table, be sure to press the F4 key after typing E2:F6 in order to change to an absolute reference of $E$2:$F$6.

8. Ensure that the third argument specifies which column of the lookup table should be returned. Because the letter grade is in the second column of E2:F6, use 2 for the third argument.

9. Ensure that the final argument is either TRUE or simply omitted. This tells Excel that you are using the sorted range variety of lookup.

10. After you enter the formula in Cell C2, again select Cell C2 and double-click the fill handle to copy the formula down to all students.

**Figure 24.20**
The VLOOKUP formula in Column C finds the correct grade from the table in Columns E and F.

| | C2 | | ƒx | =VLOOKUP(B2,$E$2:$F$6,2,TRUE) | | | | |
|---|---|---|---|---|---|---|---|---|
| | A | B | C | D | E | F | G |
| 1 | Student | Score | Grade | | | | |
| 2 | CECILIA ALBERT | 96 | A | | 0 | F | |
| 3 | KRISTEN FOREMAN | 88 | B | | 65 | D | |
| 4 | DOROTHY MARTINEZ | 76 | C | | 70 | C | |
| 5 | LUIS FISCHER | 93 | A | | 85 | B | |
| 6 | TERRY SKINNER | 89 | B | | 92 | A | |
| 7 | SHELLEY OSBORN | 69 | D | | | | |
| 8 | MARVIN SCHULTZ | 77 | C | | | | |
| 9 | JOE TRUJILLO | 93 | A | | | | |
| 10 | WILLIAM SKINNER | 92 | A | | | | |

### USING VLOOKUP WITH FALSE TO FIND AN EXACT VALUE

In some situations, you do not want VLOOKUP to return a value based on a close match. Instead, you want Excel to find the exact match in the lookup table.

Figure 24.21 shows a table of sales. The original table had just Columns A through C: Rep #, Date, and Sale Amount. Although a data analyst might have all the rep numbers memorized, the manager who is going to see the report prefers to have the rep names on the report.

To fill in the rep names from a lookup table, you follow these steps:

1. In Columns F and G, paste a table of rep numbers and rep names. Note that it is not important that this table be sorted by the rep number field. It is fine that the table is alphabetical.
2. Use `FALSE` as the fourth parameter in `VLOOKUP`. You need to do this because close matches are not acceptable here. If something was sold by a new rep with number R9, you do not want to give credit to the name associated with R8 just because it is a close match. Either Excel finds an exact match and returns the result, or Excel doesn't give you a result.
3. For Cell D2, you want Excel to use the rep number in A2, so in Cell D2, enter `=VLOOKUP(A2,`.
4. The lookup table is in F2:G7, so type `F2:G7` and then press the F4 key to make the reference absolute. This allows you to copy the formula in step 7. After pressing F4, type a comma.
5. In the lookup table, the rep name is in Column 2 of the table, so type `2` to specify that you want to return the second column of the lookup table.
6. Finish the function with `FALSE)`. Press Ctrl+Enter to accept the formula and keep the cursor in Cell D2.
7. Double-click the fill handle to copy the formula down to all the rows.
8. `VLOOKUP` is a very time-intensive calculation. Having thousands of `VLOOKUP` formulas significantly affects your recalculation times. In this particular case, you've successfully added rep names. It would be appropriate to convert these live formulas to their current values. Therefore, press Ctrl+C to copy. Then, from the Sheet ribbon, choose Paste, Paste Values to convert the formulas to values.
9. Look through the results. If a sale was credited to a new rep who is not in the table, the name appears as `#N/A`. Manually fix these records, if needed.

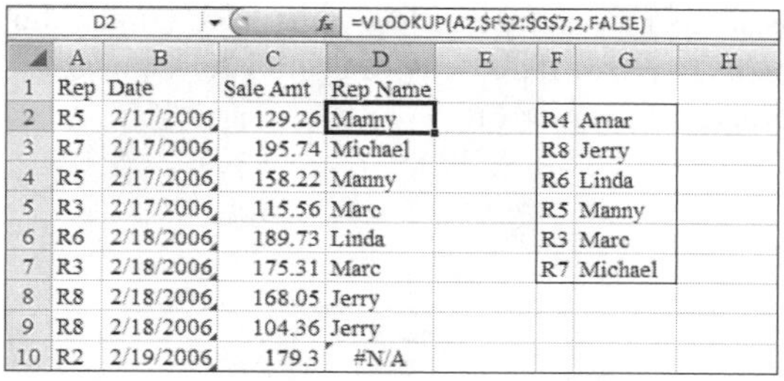

D2 =VLOOKUP(A2,$F$2:$G$7,2,FALSE)

| | A | B | C | D | E | F | G | H |
|---|---|---|---|---|---|---|---|---|
| 1 | Rep | Date | Sale Amt | Rep Name | | | | |
| 2 | R5 | 2/17/2006 | 129.26 | Manny | | R4 | Amar | |
| 3 | R7 | 2/17/2006 | 195.74 | Michael | | R8 | Jerry | |
| 4 | R5 | 2/17/2006 | 158.22 | Manny | | R6 | Linda | |
| 5 | R3 | 2/17/2006 | 115.56 | Marc | | R5 | Manny | |
| 6 | R6 | 2/18/2006 | 189.73 | Linda | | R3 | Marc | |
| 7 | R3 | 2/18/2006 | 175.31 | Marc | | R7 | Michael | |
| 8 | R8 | 2/18/2006 | 168.05 | Jerry | | | | |
| 9 | R8 | 2/18/2006 | 104.36 | Jerry | | | | |
| 10 | R2 | 2/19/2006 | 179.3 | #N/A | | | | |

**Figure 24.21**
In this case, VLOOKUP needs to find the exact rep number from the table in Columns E and F.

To recap, there are two versions of the `VLOOKUP` formula that behave very differently: `VLOOKUP` with `FALSE` as the fourth parameter looks for an exact match, and `VLOOKUP` with `TRUE` as the fourth parameter looks for the closest (lower) match. In the TRUE version, the lookup table must be sorted. In the FALSE version, the table can be in any sequence. In every case, the key field must be in the left column of the lookup table.

NOTE

> If your lookup table is arranged with the key field in Row 1, you should use HLOOKUP (described later in this chapter). If your data is vertical but the key field is not the leftmost column, you can use a combination of INDEX and MATCH, also explained later in this chapter.

Syntax: VLOOKUP(*lookup_value*,*table_array*,*col_index_num*,*range_lookup*)

VLOOKUP searches for a value in the leftmost column of a table and then returns a value in the same row from a column you specify in the table. The VLOOKUP function takes the following arguments:

- lookup_value—This is the value to be found in the first column of the table. lookup_value can be a value, a reference, or a text string.

- table_array—This is the table of information in which data is looked up. You can use a reference to a range (for example, E2:F9) or a range name, such as RepTable.

- col_index_num—This is the column number in table_array from which the matching value must be returned. A col_index_num value of 1 returns the value in the first column in table_array; a col_index_num value of 2 returns the value in the second column in table_array, and so on. If col_index_num is less than 1, VLOOKUP returns the #VALUE! error value; if col_index_num is greater than the number of columns in table_array, VLOOKUP returns the #REF! error value.

- range_lookup—This is a logical value that specifies whether VLOOKUP should find an exact match or an approximate match. If it is TRUE or omitted, an approximate match is returned. In other words, if an exact match is not found, the next largest value that is less than *lookup_value* is returned. If it is FALSE, VLOOKUP finds an exact match. If one is not found, the error value #N/A is returned. If VLOOKUP can't find *lookup_value* and if *range_lookup* is TRUE, it uses the largest value that is less than or equal to lookup_value. If lookup_value is smaller than the smallest value in the first column of *table_array*, VLOOKUP returns an #N/A error. If VLOOKUP can't find *lookup_value*, and *range_lookup* is FALSE, VLOOKUP returns an #N/A error.

### USING VLOOKUP TO MATCH TWO LISTS

If Excel is used throughout your company, you undoubtedly have many lists in Excel. People use Excel to track everything. How many times are you faced with a situation in which you have two versions of a list and you need to match them up?

In Figure 24.22, the worksheet has two simple lists. Column A shows last week's version of who was coming to an event. Column C shows this week's version of who is coming to an event. You want to quickly find out if anyone is new. You need to follow these steps:

1. Add the heading There? to Cell D2.
2. Because the formula in Cell D3 should look at the value in Cell C3 to see if that person is in the original list in Column A, start the formula with `=VLOOKUP(C3,$A$3:$A$15,`.
3. Because your only choice for the column number is to return the first column from the original list, finish the function with `1,FALSE)`. Then press Ctrl+Enter to accept the formula and stay in Cell C3.
4. Double-click the fill handle to copy the formula down to all rows.



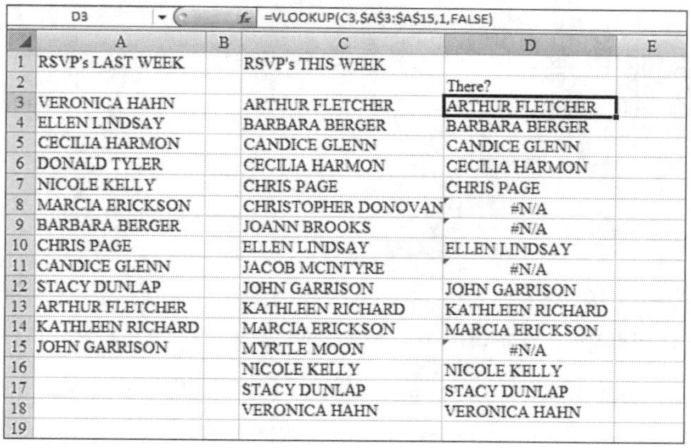

D3 =VLOOKUP(C3,$A$3:$A$15,1,FALSE)

| | A | B | C | D | E |
|---|---|---|---|---|---|
| 1 | RSVP's LAST WEEK | | RSVP's THIS WEEK | | |
| 2 | | | | There? | |
| 3 | VERONICA HAHN | | ARTHUR FLETCHER | ARTHUR FLETCHER | |
| 4 | ELLEN LINDSAY | | BARBARA BERGER | BARBARA BERGER | |
| 5 | CECILIA HARMON | | CANDICE GLENN | CANDICE GLENN | |
| 6 | DONALD TYLER | | CECILIA HARMON | CECILIA HARMON | |
| 7 | NICOLE KELLY | | CHRIS PAGE | CHRIS PAGE | |
| 8 | MARCIA ERICKSON | | CHRISTOPHER DONOVAN | #N/A | |
| 9 | BARBARA BERGER | | JOANN BROOKS | #N/A | |
| 10 | CHRIS PAGE | | ELLEN LINDSAY | ELLEN LINDSAY | |
| 11 | CANDICE GLENN | | JACOB MCINTYRE | #N/A | |
| 12 | STACY DUNLAP | | JOHN GARRISON | JOHN GARRISON | |
| 13 | ARTHUR FLETCHER | | KATHLEEN RICHARD | KATHLEEN RICHARD | |
| 14 | KATHLEEN RICHARD | | MARCIA ERICKSON | MARCIA ERICKSON | |
| 15 | JOHN GARRISON | | MYRTLE MOON | #N/A | |
| 16 | | | NICOLE KELLY | NICOLE KELLY | |
| 17 | | | STACY DUNLAP | STACY DUNLAP | |
| 18 | | | VERONICA HAHN | VERONICA HAHN | |
| 19 | | | | | |

**Figure 24.22**
An #N/A error as the result of VLOOKUP tells you that the person is new to the list.

For any cells where Column D contains a name, it means that the person was on the RSVP list from last week. If the result of the VLOOKUP is #N/A, you know that this person is new since the previous week.

**TIP FROM**

If you study the data in Figure 24.22, you see that there are three more names in the Column C list than in the Column A list, yet four people were reported as being new this week. This means that one of the people from last week has dropped off the list. To quickly find who dropped off the list, you can use the formula `=VLOOKUP(A3,$C$3:$C$18,1,FALSE)` in B3:B15 to find that Donald Tyler has dropped off the list.

Note that you can also use MATCH to solve this problem.

## USING COLUMN TO ASSIST WITH VLOOKUP WHEN FILLING A WIDE TABLE

You have to keep in mind some special considerations when you have to retrieve many columns from a table. If you carefully think about the first formula, you can quickly copy the first formula to the entire table.

Figure 24.23 shows a table of several hundred SKUs, starting in Row 21. For each SKU, the table contains the inventory of that product on hand in the 12 regional warehouses. Range A6:B13 contains a customer order for various SKUs. You would like to build a table to help visualize which warehouse has most of the items in stock. If you can find one warehouse that has all the inventory, you can minimize order shipping costs by shipping the entire order from that particular warehouse.

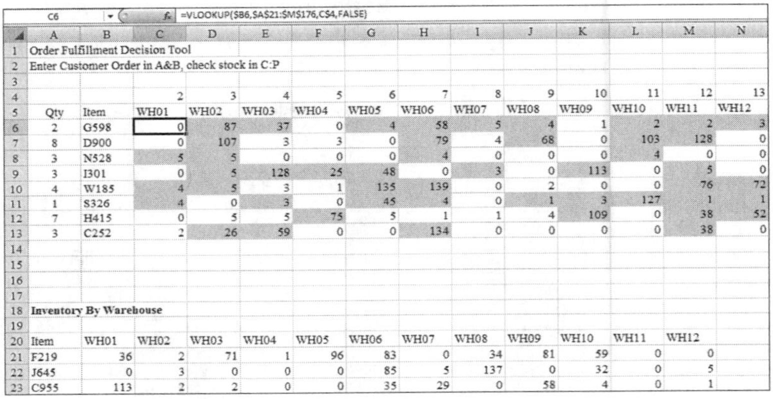

C6 =VLOOKUP($B6,$A$21:$M$176,C$4,FALSE)

| | A | B | C | D | E | F | G | H | I | J | K | L | M | N |
|---|---|---|---|---|---|---|---|---|---|---|---|---|---|---|
| 1 | Order Fulfillment Decision Tool | | | | | | | | | | | | | |
| 2 | Enter Customer Order in A&B, check stock in C:P | | | | | | | | | | | | | |
| 3 | | | | | | | | | | | | | | |
| 4 | | | 2 | 3 | 4 | 5 | 6 | 7 | 8 | 9 | 10 | 11 | 12 | 13 |
| 5 | Qty | Item | WH01 | WH02 | WH03 | WH04 | WH05 | WH06 | WH07 | WH08 | WH09 | WH10 | WH11 | WH12 |
| 6 | 2 | G598 | 0 | 87 | 37 | 0 | 4 | 58 | 5 | 4 | 1 | 2 | 2 | 3 |
| 7 | 8 | D900 | 0 | 107 | 3 | 3 | 0 | 79 | 4 | 68 | 0 | 103 | 128 | 0 |
| 8 | 3 | N528 | 5 | 5 | 0 | 0 | 0 | 4 | 0 | 0 | 0 | 4 | 0 | 0 |
| 9 | 3 | I301 | 0 | 5 | 128 | 25 | 48 | 0 | 3 | 0 | 113 | 0 | 5 | 0 |
| 10 | 4 | W185 | 4 | 5 | 3 | 1 | 135 | 139 | 0 | 2 | 0 | 0 | 76 | 72 |
| 11 | 1 | S326 | 4 | 0 | 3 | 0 | 45 | 4 | 0 | 1 | 3 | 127 | 1 | 1 |
| 12 | 7 | H415 | 0 | 5 | 5 | 75 | 5 | 1 | 1 | 4 | 109 | 0 | 38 | 52 |
| 13 | 3 | C252 | 2 | 26 | 59 | 0 | 0 | 134 | 0 | 0 | 0 | 0 | 38 | 0 |
| 14 | | | | | | | | | | | | | | |
| 15 | | | | | | | | | | | | | | |
| 16 | | | | | | | | | | | | | | |
| 17 | | | | | | | | | | | | | | |
| 18 | **Inventory By Warehouse** | | | | | | | | | | | | | |
| 19 | | | | | | | | | | | | | | |
| 20 | Item | WH01 | WH02 | WH03 | WH04 | WH05 | WH06 | WH07 | WH08 | WH09 | WH10 | WH11 | WH12 | |
| 21 | F219 | 36 | 2 | 71 | 1 | 96 | 83 | 0 | 34 | 81 | 59 | 0 | 0 | |
| 22 | J645 | 0 | 3 | 0 | 0 | 0 | 85 | 5 | 137 | 0 | 32 | 0 | 5 | |
| 23 | C955 | 113 | 2 | 2 | 0 | 0 | 35 | 29 | 0 | 58 | 4 | 0 | 1 | |

**Figure 24.23**
The COLUMN function in Row 4 ensures that you can enter the VLOOKUP formula once and copy it to the entire rectangular range.

To solve this problem, you follow these steps:

1. Copy the range of warehouse names from B20:M20 to C5:N5.
2. Think about the third argument in the VLOOKUP function. For the formula in Column C, you want to return the second column from the table. For the formula in Column D, you want to return the third column. If you actually enter the 2 in the formula in Column C, then after copying the formula over to D:N, you have to edit the third argument repeatedly.
3. Create a range above your table, perhaps in Row 4, that contains the numbers 2 through 13. You can then use cells in this row when building the third argument in the formula. In Cell C4, enter the function =COLUMN(B2). Because Column B is the second column, this formula returns 2.
4. Select Cell C4. Drag the fill handle to the right to copy the formula over through Column N. The Cell B2 reference is relative, resulting in the formula returning the numbers 2, 3, 4, and so on.
5. In Cell C6, enter =VLOOKUP(B6. When you later copy this formula, you always want the formula to point to Column B, but you want to allow the formula to point to Rows 7, 8,

and so on. If you press the F4 key three times, the reference changes to $B6. Type a comma.

6. Type A21:M176. Press F4 to change this reference to $A$21:$M$176. Type a comma.

7. For the third argument, you want to point to the number 2 in Cell C4. You always want this part of the formula to point to Row 4, and you want to allow the column letter to change as the formula is copied to the right. Press the F4 key twice in order to change the reference to C$4.

8. Finish the formula with ,FALSE). Press Ctrl+Enter to accept the formula and stay in Cell C4.

9. Optionally, add a conditional format to Cell C4 to highlight the cell if this formula is true: =C6>=$A6.

10. Double-click the fill handle to copy the formula to C4:C13.

11. Drag the fill handle from the corner of C13 to the right until you have filled in the formula in the range of C:N.

The result is a table that shows the current inventory for each item, by warehouse. If you added the conditional formatting in step 9, you can quickly see which warehouses can fulfill most of the order.

Although having the COLUMN function in Row 4 allows you to visually understand the example better, you could easily eliminate Row 4 and rewrite the formula in Cell C6 as
=VLOOKUP($B6,$A$21:$M$176,COLUMN(B1),FALSE).

SYNTAX: COLUMN(*reference*)

The COLUMN function returns the column number of a given reference. This function takes the argument *reference*, which is the cell or range of cells for which you want the column number. If *reference* is omitted, it is assumed to be the reference of the cell in which the COLUMN function appears.

If *reference* is a range of cells, and if COLUMN is entered as a horizontal array, COLUMN returns the column numbers of *reference* as a horizontal array. In this case, *reference* cannot refer to multiple areas.

## USING HLOOKUP FOR HORIZONTAL LOOKUP TABLES

HLOOKUP stands for *horizontal lookup*. This function is similar to VLOOKUP.

HLOOKUP operates in two distinct manners, based on the fourth parameter. If the fourth parameter is the value FALSE, then HLOOKUP is looking for an exact match in the top row of the table. This is great when you're looking up product codes, customer numbers, or any other discrete bits of information.

If the fourth parameter is the value TRUE (or is omitted), then HLOOKUP is treating the first row of the table as a sorted range of values. Excel looks for the closest lower value than the one you specified. This is great when you're trying to determine in which range a value belongs.

24

**Syntax:** HLOOKUP(*lookup_value*,*table_array*,*row_index_num*,*range_lookup*)

The HLOOKUP function searches for a value in the top row of a table. When the value is found, HLOOKUP returns a value from a particular row in the column. This function takes the following arguments:

- lookup_value—This is a value to be found in the first row of the table. lookup_value can be a value, a reference, or a text string.
- table_array—This is a table of information in which data is looked up. You use a reference to a range or a range name. The values in the first row of *table_array* can be text, numbers, or logical values. If *range_lookup* is TRUE, the values in the first row of *table_array* must be placed in ascending order such as ..., -2, -1, 0, 1, 2,...; A–Z; or FALSE, TRUE. Otherwise, HLOOKUP may not give the correct value. If *range_lookup* is FALSE, *table_array* does not need to be sorted. The search is not case-sensitive: Uppercase and lowercase text are equivalent.
- row_index_num—This is the row number in table_array from which the matching value is returned. A row_index_num of 1 returns the first row value in table_array, a row_index_num of 2 returns the second row value in table_array, and so on. If row_index_num is less than 1, HLOOKUP returns a #VALUE! error; if row_index_num is greater than the number of rows in table_array, HLOOKUP returns a #REF! error.
- range_lookup—This is a logical value that specifies whether you want HLOOKUP to find an exact match or an approximate match. If it is TRUE or omitted, an approximate match is returned. In other words, if an exact match is not found, the next largest value that is less than *lookup_value* is returned. If it is FALSE, HLOOKUP finds an exact match. If one is not found, the error #N/A is returned.

Although you are probably familiar with sorting a list from top to bottom, most people rarely sort a list from left to right. If you are using the TRUE version of HLOOKUP, you have to make sure that your table is sorted from left to right by the top row. To sort data from left to right, you follow these steps:

1. Select your range of data. In Figure 24.24, this would be G3:L8.

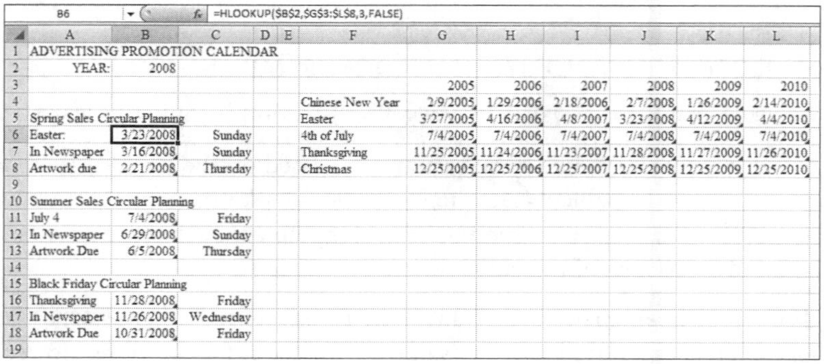

B6 =HLOOKUP($B$2,$G$3:$L$8,3,FALSE)

| | A | B | C | D | E | F | G | H | I | J | K | L |
|---|---|---|---|---|---|---|---|---|---|---|---|---|
| 1 | ADVERTISING PROMOTION CALENDAR | | | | | | | | | | | |
| 2 | YEAR: | 2008 | | | | | | | | | | |
| 3 | | | | | | | 2005 | 2006 | 2007 | 2008 | 2009 | 2010 |
| 4 | | | | | | Chinese New Year | 2/9/2005 | 1/29/2006 | 2/18/2006 | 2/7/2008 | 1/26/2009 | 2/14/2010 |
| 5 | Spring Sales Circular Planning | | | | | Easter | 3/27/2005 | 4/16/2006 | 4/8/2007 | 3/23/2008 | 4/12/2009 | 4/4/2010 |
| 6 | Easter: | 3/23/2008 | Sunday | | | 4th of July | 7/4/2005 | 7/4/2006 | 7/4/2007 | 7/4/2008 | 7/4/2009 | 7/4/2010 |
| 7 | In Newspaper | 3/16/2008 | Sunday | | | Thanksgiving | 11/25/2005 | 11/24/2006 | 11/23/2007 | 11/28/2008 | 11/27/2009 | 11/26/2010 |
| 8 | Artwork due | 2/21/2008 | Thursday | | | Christmas | 12/25/2005 | 12/25/2006 | 12/25/2007 | 12/25/2008 | 12/25/2009 | 12/25/2010 |
| 9 | | | | | | | | | | | | |
| 10 | Summer Sales Circular Planning | | | | | | | | | | | |
| 11 | July 4 | 7/4/2008 | Friday | | | | | | | | | |
| 12 | In Newspaper | 6/29/2008 | Sunday | | | | | | | | | |
| 13 | Artwork Due | 6/5/2008 | Thursday | | | | | | | | | |
| 14 | | | | | | | | | | | | |
| 15 | Black Friday Circular Planning | | | | | | | | | | | |
| 16 | Thanksgiving | 11/28/2008 | Friday | | | | | | | | | |
| 17 | In Newspaper | 11/26/2008 | Wednesday | | | | | | | | | |
| 18 | Artwork Due | 10/31/2008 | Friday | | | | | | | | | |
| 19 | | | | | | | | | | | | |

**Figure 24.24**
The table in F:L is horizontal, so you use the HLOOKUP function.

2. From the Sheet ribbon, select the Sort & Filter drop-down. The Sort dialog appears.

3. In the Sort dialog, click the Options button. The Sort Options dialog appears.

4. In the Sort Options dialog, choose Sort Left to Right. Click OK to close the Sort Options dialog.

5. In the Sort dialog, choose to sort by Row 3. Click OK to sort.

Figure 24.24 shows a tool used by the advertising department of a retail store. The store runs annual promotions for certain holidays. The table in F3:L8 tells the days for holidays in each of several years.

The advertising manager knows that the store wants to run a sale circular the Sunday before the holiday and that the art department needs the material 24 days before the ad is to run. By changing the year in Cell B2, the advertising manager can create a new schedule for each year. To help the advertising manager, you would follow these steps:

1. Ensure that the formula for each holiday starts as =HLOOKUP($B$2,. This tells Excel to use the year found in Cell B2 as the value to look up.

2. Ensure that the lookup table is in $G$3:$L$8. Excel looks through the first row of this table to find the matching year.

3. When the matching column is found, you want Excel to return the date for Easter. Although this is in Row 5 of the worksheet, it is in the third row of the table, so ensure that the third parameter for the function is 3.

4. Your years are already sorted left to right, but if you use a value of TRUE for the fourth parameter, this would cause problems in the year 2011, so make the fourth parameter FALSE. Ensure that the formula in Cell B6 is =HLOOKUP($B$2,$G$3:$L$8,3,FALSE).

5. Copy this formula to Cell B11 and edit the formula to change the third parameter from 3 to 4.

## USING THE MATCH FUNCTION TO LOCATE THE POSITION OF A MATCHING VALUE

At first glance, MATCH seems like a function that would rarely be useful. MATCH returns the relative position of an item in a range that matches a specified value in a specified order. You use MATCH instead of one of the lookup functions when you need the position of an item in a range instead of the item itself.

Have you ever had a manager call and ask, "Can you tell me on which row I would find this value?" The manager wants to know the value or some piece of data on that record but rarely wants to know that XYZ is found on the 111th relative row within the range A99:11432.

There are several instances in which MATCH comes in very handy. In the first instance, consider a situation in which you are merely using VLOOKUP to find whether an item is in a list. In that case, you really don't care what value is returned. You are either interested in seeing if a valid value is returned (meaning that the entry is in the old list) or if an #N/A is returned (meaning that the entry is new). In this case, using MATCH is a slightly faster way to achieve the same result.

Another use of MATCH is when it is used in conjunction with the INDEX function. MATCH has two features that make it more versatile than VLOOKUP. MATCH allows for wildcard matches. MATCH also allows for a search based on an exact match, based on the number just below the value, or based on a value greater than or equal to the lookup value. This third option is not available in the VLOOKUP or HLOOKUP functions.

**SYNTAX:** MATCH(*lookup_value*,*lookup_array*,*match_type*)

The MATCH function returns the relative position of an item in a column of values. It is useful for determining if a certain value exists in a list.

The MATCH function takes the following arguments:

- lookup_value—This is the value you use to find the value you want in a table. lookup_value can be a value (that is, number, text, or logical value) or a cell reference to a number, text, or logical value.

- lookup_array—This is a contiguous range of cells that contains possible lookup values. lookup_array can be an array or an array reference.

- match_type—This is the number -1, 0, or 1. *match_type* specifies how Microsoft Excel matches *lookup_value* with values in *lookup_array*. If *match_type* is 1, MATCH finds the largest value that is less than or equal to *lookup_value*. *lookup_array* must be placed in ascending order, such as ... -2, -1, 0, 1, 2,...; A–Z; or FALSE, TRUE. If *match_type* is 0, MATCH finds the first value that is exactly equal to *lookup_value*. *lookup_array* can be in any order. If *match_type* is -1, MATCH finds the smallest value that is greater than or equal to *lookup_value*. *lookup_array* must be placed in descending order, such as TRUE, FALSE; Z–A; or ...2, 1, 0, -1, -2,.... If *match_type* is omitted, it is assumed to be 1.

MATCH returns the position of the matched value within *lookup_array*, not the value itself. For example, MATCH("b",{"a","b","c"},0) returns 2, the relative position of "b" within the array {"a","b","c"}.

MATCH does not distinguish between uppercase and lowercase letters when matching text values.

If MATCH is unsuccessful in finding a match, it returns an #N/A error.

If *match_type* is 0 and *lookup_value* is text, *lookup_value* can contain the wildcard characters asterisk (*) and question mark (?). An asterisk matches any sequence of characters; a question mark matches any single character.

## USING MATCH TO COMPARE TWO LISTS

You may face situations in which you have two versions of a list, and you need to match them up.

In Figure 24.25, the worksheet has two simple lists. Column A shows last week's list. Column C shows this week's version of the list. You want to quickly find out which items are new. Here's how you do it:

**Figure 24.25**

MATCH operates slightly more quickly than VLOOKUP and achieves the same result in this special case where you are trying to figure out whether a value is in another list.

| | D3 | ▾ | fx | =MATCH(C3,$A$3:$A$11,0) | | |
|---|---|---|---|---|---|---|
| | A | B | C | D | E |
| 1 | ENTRIES LAST WEEK | | ENTRIES THIS WEEK | | |
| 2 | | | | There? | |
| 3 | PILGRIM | | COLUMBIA | 2 | |
| 4 | COLUMBIA | | CONSTELLATION | 8 | |
| 5 | MAYFLOWER | | COURAGEOUS | #N/A | |
| 6 | VOLUNTEER | | DEFENDER | 5 | |
| 7 | DEFENDER | | FREEDOM | #N/A | |
| 8 | RELIANCE | | INTREPID | 9 | |
| 9 | RANGER | | MAYFLOWER | 3 | |
| 10 | CONSTELLATION | | PILGRIM | 1 | |
| 11 | INTREPID | | RANGER | 7 | |
| 12 | | | RELIANCE | 6 | |
| 13 | | | STARS AND STRIPES | #N/A | |
| 14 | | | VOLUNTEER | 4 | |
| 15 | | | WEATHERLY | #N/A | |
| 16 | | | YOUNG AMERICA | #N/A | |
| 17 | | | | | |

1. Add the heading There? to Cell D2.

2. Because the formula in Cell D3 looks at the value in Cell C3 to see if that value is in the original list in Column A, start the formula with =MATCH(C3,$A$3:$A$11,.

3. Because you want an exact match, use 0 as the third parameter. Finish the function with a ). Press Ctrl+Enter to accept the formula and stay in Cell C3.

4. Double-click the fill handle to copy the formula down to all rows.

For any cells where Column D contains a number, it means that the entry was on the original list from last week. If the result of MATCH is #N/A, you know that this item is new since the previous week.

## USING INDEX AND MATCH FOR A LEFT LOOKUP

INDEX is another function that doesn't immediately seem to have many great uses. In its basic form, INDEX returns the cell from a particular row and column of a rectangular range.

As shown in Figure 24.26, using =INDEX(B5:D9,3,2) seems like a needlessly complicated way to refer to Cell C7.

However, in the previous section, you learned about a function that searches through a range and tells you the position of the match within the range. Finding the position of a match is not very useful. However, finding the position of a match is very useful when used inside of the INDEX function.

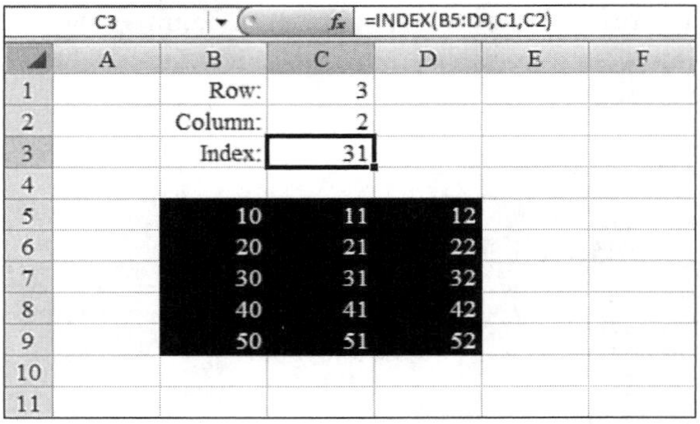

C3 =INDEX(B5:D9,C1,C2)

| | A | B | C | D | E | F |
|---|---|---|---|---|---|---|
| 1 | | Row: | 3 | | | |
| 2 | | Column: | 2 | | | |
| 3 | | Index: | 31 | | | |
| 4 | | | | | | |
| 5 | | 10 | 11 | 12 | | |
| 6 | | 20 | 21 | 22 | | |
| 7 | | 30 | 31 | 32 | | |
| 8 | | 40 | 41 | 42 | | |
| 9 | | 50 | 51 | 52 | | |
| 10 | | | | | | |
| 11 | | | | | | |

**Figure 24.26**
On its own, `INDEX` is not a particularly useful function.

In Figure 24.27, a customer number is entered in Cell A1. The customer lookup table appears in Columns F, G, and H. The main problem is that the customer table does not have the customer number on the left side.

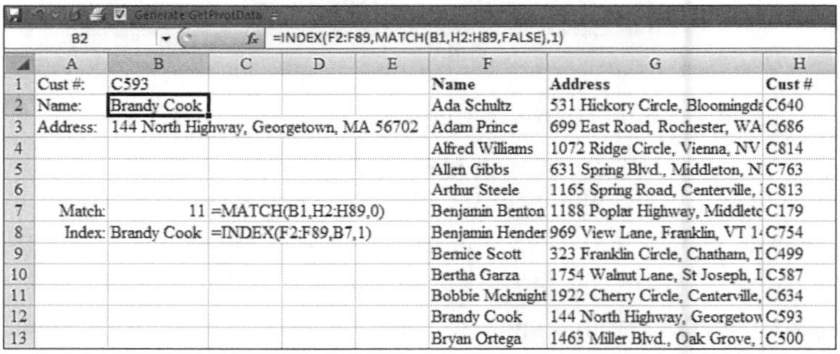

B2 =INDEX(F2:F89,MATCH(B1,H2:H89,FALSE),1)

| | A | B | C | D | E | F | G | H |
|---|---|---|---|---|---|---|---|---|
| 1 | Cust #: | C593 | | | | Name | Address | Cust # |
| 2 | Name: | Brandy Cook | | | | Ada Schultz | 531 Hickory Circle, Bloomingd | C640 |
| 3 | Address: | 144 North Highway, Georgetown, MA 56702 | | | | Adam Prince | 699 East Road, Rochester, WA | C686 |
| 4 | | | | | | Alfred Williams | 1072 Ridge Circle, Vienna, NV | C814 |
| 5 | | | | | | Allen Gibbs | 631 Spring Blvd., Middleton, N | C763 |
| 6 | | | | | | Arthur Steele | 1165 Spring Road, Centerville, | C813 |
| 7 | Match: | 11 | =MATCH(B1,H2:H89,0) | | | Benjamin Benton | 1188 Poplar Highway, Middletc | C179 |
| 8 | Index: | Brandy Cook | =INDEX(F2:F89,B7,1) | | | Benjamin Hender | 969 View Lane, Franklin, VT 1 | C754 |
| 9 | | | | | | Bernice Scott | 323 Franklin Circle, Chatham, I | C499 |
| 10 | | | | | | Bertha Garza | 1754 Walnut Lane, St Joseph, I | C587 |
| 11 | | | | | | Bobbie Mcknight | 1922 Cherry Circle, Centerville, | C634 |
| 12 | | | | | | Brandy Cook | 144 North Highway, Georgetow | C593 |
| 13 | | | | | | Bryan Ortega | 1463 Miller Blvd., Oak Grove, | C500 |

**Figure 24.27**
This combination of `INDEX` and `MATCH` allows you to look up data that is to the left of a key field.

In many cases, you would simply copy Column H to Column E and use Column E as the key of the table. However, the table in F:H is likely to be repopulated every day from a web query or an OLAP query, and it might become monotonous to move the data after every refresh. The solution is to use a combination of `INDEX` and `MATCH`. Here's what you do:

1. Use the formula `=MATCH(B1,H2:H89,0)` to search through Column H to find the row with the customer number that matches the one in Cell B1. In this case, C593 is in Row 12, which is the 11th row of the table.
2. Be sure to use exactly the same shape range as the first argument in the `INDEX` function: `=INDEX(F2:F89,WhichRow,WhichColumn)` searches through the customer names in Column F.
3. For the second parameter of the `INDEX` function, specify the relative row number. This information was provided by the `MATCH` function in step 1.
4. Ensure that the third parameter of the `INDEX` function is the relative column number. Because the range F2:F89 has only one column, this is either `1` or can simply be omitted.

5. Putting the formula together, the formula in Cell B2 is =INDEX(F2:F89,MATCH(B1, H2:H89,FALSE),1).

SYNTAX: INDEX(*array*,*row_num*,*column_num*)

The INDEX function will return the value at the intersection of a particular row and column within a range.

The INDEX function takes the following arguments:

- array—This is a range of cells or an array constant. If array contains only one row or column, the corresponding row_num or column_num argument is optional. If array has more than one row and more than one column, and if only row_num or column_num is used, INDEX returns an array of the entire row or column in array.
- row_num—This selects the row in array from which to return a value. If row_num is omitted, column_num is required.
- column_num—This selects the column in array from which to return a value. If *column_num* is omitted, *row_num* is required.

If both the *row_num* and *column_num* arguments are used, INDEX returns the value in the cell at the intersection of *row_num* and *column_num*.

If you set *row_num* or *column_num* to 0, INDEX returns the array of values for the entire column or row, respectively. To use values returned as an array, you use the INDEX function as an array formula in a horizontal range of cells for a row and in a vertical range of cells for a column. To enter an array formula, you press Ctrl+Shift+Enter.

*row_num* and *column_num* must point to a cell within *array*; otherwise, INDEX returns a #REF! error.

## USING MATCH AND INDEX TO FILL A WIDE TABLE

The lookup functions VLOOKUP, HLOOKUP, and MATCH can be very processor intensive when the lookup table contains hundreds of thousands of rows.

Back in Figure 24.23, Excel had to do 96 VLOOKUP functions. However, after Excel figured out the position of Item G598 in the lookup table for Cell C6, it had to go back through exactly the same steps for Cell D6, E6, F6, G6, and so on. You made Excel find exactly the same item 12 times, and that is a very slow process.

If the recalculation times are taking too long, you should consider using one MATCH per row to find the relative row number and then using 12 speedy INDEX functions to fill in the values in that row. Figure 24.28 illustrates a problem where you can use this trick. In this case, the list of inventory items is 14,000 rows. Here's what you do:

1. Copy the range of warehouse names from B20:M20 to D5:O5.

2. In Cell C6, enter =MATCH(B6,$A$21:$A$14060,0). This formula finds an exact match for C529. The answer 8005 means that product C529 is on the 8,005th relative row of the lookup range.

3. Copy the formula in Cell C6 to C6:C13.

4. As you build the INDEX function, be careful that the array range encompasses the same rows used in the MATCH function. Start the formula in Cell D6 as =INDEX($B$21:$M$14060. Make sure to press F4 to make this reference be absolute.

5. Make the next argument the relative row number within the lookup range. This is the value from Column C, so use $C6. If you type C6 and then press the F4 key three times, Excel adds the dollar sign before the C in C6.

6. Add the final argument, the column number. For the first warehouse, this would be Column 1. However, rather than type a 1 for the formula, use COLUMN(A1). This allows you to copy the formula to the rest of the range. Finish the formula with a parenthesis. The final formula is =INDEX($B$21:$M$14060,$C6,COLUMN(A4)).

7. Optionally, add a conditional format to Cell D6 to highlight the cell if this formula evaluates to TRUE: =D6>=$A6.

8. Copy the formula from Cell D6 to D6:O13.

**Figure 24.28**
This performs eight relatively slow MATCH functions and then 96 relatively fast INDEX functions.

| | A | B | C | D | E | F | G | |
|---|---|---|---|---|---|---|---|---|
| | | | | | | | | |
| 1 | Order Fulfillment Decision Tool | | | | | | | |
| 2 | Enter Customer Order in A&B, check stock in C:P | | | | | | | |
| 3 | | | | | | | | |
| 4 | | | | | | | | |
| 5 | Qty | Item | Match | WH01 | WH02 | WH03 | WH04 | W |
| 6 | 2 | C529 | 8005 | 0 | 5 | 0 | 81 | |
| 7 | 10 | F708 | 3635 | 1 | 2 | 0 | 88 | |
| 8 | 9 | X291 | 452 | 0 | 80 | 0 | 0 | |
| 9 | 1 | E890 | 6335 | 2 | 87 | 0 | 1 | |
| 10 | 5 | C299 | 12192 | 0 | 2 | 4 | 0 | |
| 11 | 4 | S323 | 7450 | 4 | 5 | 3 | 69 | |
| 12 | 1 | V600 | 9038 | 131 | 48 | 129 | 1 | |
| 13 | 9 | P765 | 8596 | 3 | 0 | 70 | 2 | |
| 14 | | | | | | | | |

D6 = =INDEX($B$21:$M$14060,$C6,COLUMN(A4))

## AVOIDING THE LOOKUP FUNCTION

The LOOKUP function is still in Excel because some other spreadsheet program had invented this poorly thought-out function. The LOOKUP function can arbitrarily switch from acting like an HLOOKUP to acting like a VLOOKUP, depending on the shape of the lookup table. If the table contains more rows than columns, the function performed a VLOOKUP. If the function contained more columns than rows, it performed an HLOOKUP. You should stay away from this function. If you encounter it in an old spreadsheet, you should consider switching it to VLOOKUP or HLOOKUP.

## USING FUNCTIONS TO DESCRIBE THE SHAPE OF A CONTIGUOUS REFERENCE

Four functions can be used to identify the location and shape of a contiguous range:

- COLUMN(reference)—This returns the column number of the upper-left corner of a reference, using numbers from 1 to 16,384. If reference is omitted, the function returns the column number of the cell where the formula is entered.

- `ROW(reference)`—This returns the row number of the upper-left corner of the reference, using numbers from 1 to 1,045,876. If `reference` is omitted, the function returns the column number of the cell where the formula is entered.
- `COLUMNS(reference)`—This returns the number of columns in a reference. In this case, `reference` must be a single contiguous range.
- `ROWS(reference)`—This returns the number of rows in a reference. Again, `reference` must be a single contiguous range.

Figure 24.29 displays the `ROW`, `COLUMN`, `ROWS`, and `COLUMNS` functions of a named range. The range occupies the black cells in B7:D11.

**Figure 24.29**
These functions describe the location and shape of a range.

B1 | fx =COLUMN(MyRange)

| | A | B | C | D | E |
|---|---|---|---|---|---|
| 1 | Column | 2 | =COLUMN(MyRange) | | |
| 2 | Row | 7 | =ROW(MyRange) | | |
| 3 | Columns | 3 | =COLUMNS(MyRange) | | |
| 4 | Rows | 5 | =ROWS(MyRange) | | |
| 5 | Areas | 1 | =AREAS(MyRange) | | |
| 6 | | | | | |
| 7 | | 1 | 2 | 4 | |
| 8 | | 8 | 16 | 32 | |
| 9 | | 64 | 128 | 256 | |
| 10 | | 512 | 1024 | 2048 | |
| 11 | | 4096 | 8192 | 16384 | |
| 12 | | | | | |



## USING AREAS AND INDEX TO DESCRIBE A RANGE WITH MORE THAN ONE AREA

All the functions listed in the preceding section fail if *`reference`* describes a range that is noncontiguous. You can check for that condition by using the `AREAS` function.

### SYNTAX: AREAS(REFERENCE)

This function returns the number of contiguous ranges in a reference. The argument *`reference`* usually refers to a named range.

In Figure 24.30, `MyAreas` is a defined name that describes the cells in black. In Rows 1 through 4, all the traditional functions fail, with `#REF!` errors, because the reference contains more than one contiguous range.

### SYNTAX: `INDEX(`*`reference,row_num,column_num,area_num`*`)`

If you need to determine the location and shape of each contiguous range, you have to do so one area at a time. There is a second syntax of the `INDEX` function that returns a reference to one specific area of a reference. This syntax includes the following arguments:

- `reference`—This is a reference to one or more cell ranges. If you are entering a nonadjacent range for the reference, you need to enclose `reference` in parentheses. If each area in `reference` contains only one row or column, the `row_num` or `column_num` argument, respectively, is optional. For example, for a single row reference, you use `INDEX(reference,column_num)`.
- `row_num`—This is the number of the row in `reference` from which to return a reference.
- `column_num`—This is the number of the column in `reference` from which to return a reference.
- `area_num`—This selects a range in `reference` from which to return the intersection of `row_num` and `column_num`. The first area selected or entered is numbered 1, the second is 2, and so on. If *`area_num`* is omitted, `INDEX` uses area 1. For example, if *`reference`* describes the cells (A1:B4,D1:E4,G1:H4), then *`area_num`* 1 is the range A1:B4, *`area_num`* 2 is the range D1:E4, and *`area_num`* 3 is the range G1:H4.

**Figure 24.30**
To describe a reference with multiple contiguous ranges, you have to use the reference form of the INDEX function.

B16 =COLUMN(INDEX(MyAreas,,,B$15))

| | A | B | C | D | E | F |
|---|---|---|---|---|---|---|
| 1 | Column | #REF! | =COLUMN(MyAreas) | | | |
| 2 | Row | #REF! | =ROW(MyAreas) | | | |
| 3 | Columns | #REF! | =COLUMNS(MyAreas) | | | |
| 4 | Rows | #REF! | =ROWS(MyAreas) | | | |
| 5 | Areas | 4 | =AREAS(MyAreas) | | | |
| 6 | | | | | | |
| 7 | | 1 | 2 | 4 | | |
| 8 | | | | | | |
| 9 | | | 8 | 16 | 32 | |
| 10 | | | | | | |
| 11 | | 64 | 128 | 256 | | |
| 12 | | | | | | |
| 13 | 512 | 1024 | 2048 | | | |
| 14 | | | | | | |
| 15 | *Area:* | *1* | *2* | *3* | *4* | |
| 16 | Column | 2 | 3 | 2 | 1 | |
| 17 | Row | 7 | 9 | 11 | 13 | |
| 18 | Columns | 3 | 3 | 3 | 3 | |
| 19 | Rows | 1 | 1 | 1 | 1 | |
| 20 | Areas | 1 | 1 | 1 | 1 | |
| 21 | | | | | | |

After *`reference`* and *`area_num`* have selected a particular range, *`row_num`* and *`column_num`* select a particular cell: *`row_num`* 1 is the first row in the range, *`column_num`* 1 is the first column, and so on. The reference returned by `INDEX` is the intersection of *`row_num`* and *`column_num`*.

If you set *`row_num`* or *`column_num`* to `0`, `INDEX` returns the reference for the entire column or row, respectively.

*row_num*, *column_num*, and *area_num* must point to a cell within *reference*; otherwise, INDEX returns a #REF! error. If *row_num* and *column_num* are omitted, INDEX returns the area in *reference* specified by *area_num*.

The result of the INDEX function is a reference, and it is interpreted as such by other formulas. Depending on the formula, the return value of INDEX may be used as a reference or as a value. For example, the formula CELL("width",INDEX(A1:B2,1,2)) is equivalent to CELL("width",B1). The CELL function uses the return value of INDEX as a cell reference. On the other hand, a formula such as 2*INDEX(A1:B2,1,2) translates the return value of INDEX into the number in Cell B1.

Using this version of INDEX, you can build formulas that work on one particular area in a named range. Here's how you do it:

1. In B15:E15, enter the numbers 1 through 4. These correspond to the four areas in MyAreas.

2. When you build the INDEX function, you want Excel to return a reference to the entire rows and columns of the first area of the range, so use =INDEX(MyAreas,,,1) to return such a reference.

3. Instead of using 1 for the *areas* argument of INDEX, use =INDEX(MyAreas,,,B$15).

4. Enter the formula =COLUMN(INDEX(MyAreas,,,B$15)) in Cell B16 to define the starting column of area 1 of MyAreas.

5. Copy the formula from step 4 to B17:B20. Edit each function to change COLUMN to ROW, COLUMNS, ROWS, and AREAS.

6. Copy B17:B20 to Columns C, D, and E.

The result, as shown in Figure 24.30, includes four sets of formulas in B16:E20 that completely describe the four areas of the named range MyAreas.

## USING NUMBERS WITH OFFSET TO DESCRIBE A RANGE

The language of Excel is numbers. There are functions that can count the number of entries in a range. There are functions that can tell you the numeric position of a looked-up value. When you know that a particular value is found in Row 20, what if you then want to do calculations on other cells in Row 20?

The OFFSET function handles this very situation. You can use OFFSET to describe a range using mostly numbers. OFFSET is very flexible: It can be used to describe a single cell, or it can be used to describe a rectangular range.

Although INDEX can return a single cell from a rectangular range, it has limitations. If you specify C5:Z99 as the range for an INDEX function, you can select only cells that are below and/or to the right of C5. The OFFSET function can move up or down and left or right from the starting cell, C5.

SYNTAX: `OFFSET(reference,rows,cols,height,width)`

The `OFFSET` function returns a reference to a range that is a given number of rows and columns from a given reference.

The `OFFSET` function takes the following arguments:

- `reference`—This is the reference from which you want to base the offset. `reference` must be a reference to a cell or range of adjacent cells; otherwise, `OFFSET` returns a `#VALUE!` error.
- `rows`—This is the number of rows, up or down, that you want the upper-left cell to refer to. Using `5` as the `rows` argument, for example, specifies that the upper-left cell in the reference is five rows below reference. `rows` can be positive (which means below the starting reference) or negative (which means above the starting reference).
- `cols`—This is the number of columns, to the left or right, that you want the upper-left cell of the result to refer to. Using `5` as the *`cols`* argument, for example, specifies that the upper-left cell in the reference is five columns to the right of reference. *`cols`* can be positive (which means to the right of the starting reference) or negative (which means to the left of the starting reference). If *`rows`* and *`cols`* offset *`reference`* over the edge of the worksheet, `OFFSET` returns a `#REF!` error. Figure 24.31 demonstrates various combinations of *`rows`* and *`cols`* from a starting cell of Cell C5.

**Figure 24.31**
These `OFFSET` functions return a single cell that is a certain number of rows and columns away from Cell C5.

C10 | fx =OFFSET($C$5,A10,B10,1,1)

| | A | B | C | D | E | F | G |
|---|---|---|---|---|---|---|---|
| 1 | Examples of 1-cell ranges returned by Offset | | | | | | |
| 2 | | | | | | | |
| 3 | 1 | 2 | 4 | 8 | 16 | | |
| 4 | 32 | 64 | 128 | 256 | 512 | | |
| 5 | 1024 | 2048 | 4096 | 8192 | 16384 | | |
| 6 | 32768 | 65536 | 131072 | 262144 | 524288 | | |
| 7 | 1048576 | 2097152 | 4194304 | 8388608 | 16777216 | | |
| 8 | | | | | | | |
| 9 | Row | Column | Offset | | | | |
| 10 | -2 | 0 | 4 | =OFFSET($C$5,A10,B10,1,1) | | | |
| 11 | 0 | -2 | 1024 | | | | |
| 12 | 0 | 2 | 16384 | | | | |
| 13 | 2 | 0 | 4194304 | | | | |
| 14 | -2 | -2 | 1 | | | | |
| 15 | 2 | 2 | 16777216 | | | | |
| 16 | | | | | | | |

- `height`—This is the height, in number of rows, that you want the returned reference to be. `height` must be a positive number.
- `width`—This is the width, in number of columns, that you want the returned reference to be. `width` must be a positive number. If `height` or `width` is omitted, it is assumed to be the same height or width as `reference`.

OFFSET allows you to specify a reference. It doesn't move any cell. It doesn't change the selection. It is just a numeric way to describe a reference. OFFSET can be used in any function that is expecting a reference argument.

Excel Help provides a trivial example of =SUM(OFFSET(C2,1,2,3,1)), which sums E3:E5. However, this example is silly. No one would ever actually write such a formula! If you were to write such a formula, you would just write =SUM(E3:E5) instead. The power of OFFSET comes when at least one of the four numeric arguments is calculated by the COUNT function or a lookup function.

In Figure 24.32, you can use COUNT(A5:A99) to count how many entries are in Column A. If you assume that there are no blanks in the range of data, you can use the COUNT result as the *height* argument in OFFSET to describe the range of numbers. Here's what you do:

**Figure 24.32**

Every argument except *height* is hard-coded in these functions. The *height* argument comes from a COUNT function to allow the range to expand as more entries are added.

| | A | B | C | D | E | F | G | H | I | J | K | L |
|---|---|---|---|---|---|---|---|---|---|---|---|---|
| | A3 | | | | $f_x$ | =SUM(OFFSET(A5,0,0,COUNT(A5:A999),1)) | | | | | | |
| 1 | Example of Dynamic Range Generated by Offset | | | | | | | | | | | |
| 2 | =SUM(OFFSET(A5,0,0,COUNT(A5:A999),1)) | | | | | | | | | | | |
| 3 | 3 | | 15 | | 31 | | 63 | | 255 | | 1023 | |
| 4 | | | | | | | | | | | | |
| 5 | 1 | | 1 | | 1 | | 1 | | 1 | | 1 | |
| 6 | 2 | | 2 | | 2 | | 2 | | 2 | | 2 | |
| 7 | | | 4 | | 4 | | 4 | | 4 | | 4 | |
| 8 | | | 8 | | 8 | | 8 | | 8 | | 8 | |
| 9 | | | | | 16 | | 16 | | 16 | | 16 | |
| 10 | | | | | | | 32 | | 32 | | 32 | |
| 11 | | | | | | | | | 64 | | 64 | |
| 12 | | | | | | | | | 128 | | 128 | |
| 13 | | | | | | | | | | | 256 | |
| 14 | | | | | | | | | | | 512 | |
| 15 | | | | | | | | | | | | |

1. There is nothing magic about the reference, so write it as =OFFSET(A5,.

2. Don't move the starting position any rows or columns from Cell A5. The starting position is A5, so you always use 0 and 0 for rows and columns. Therefore, the formula is now =OFFSET(A5,0,0,.

3. If you only want to include the number of entries in the list, use COUNT(A5:A999) as the height of the range. The formula is now =OFFSET(A5,0,0,COUNT(A5:A999),.

4. The width is one column, so make the function =OFFSET(A5,0,0,COUNT(A5:A999),1).

5. Use your OFFSET function anywhere that you would normally specify a reference. You can use =SUM(OFFSET(A5,0,0,COUNT(A5:A999),1)) or specify that formula as the series in a chart. This creates a dynamic chart that grows or shrinks as the number of entries changes.

For a more complex example of OFFSET, examine Figure 24.33, which shows several yearly tables, starting in Cell C8. Each month of the table contains from one to five entries. The person using this spreadsheet would select a year and a month from Cells E1 and E2. The goal is to find information about the entries for that particular month and year. Here's how you do it:

**Figure 24.33**
Even with a poorly designed database spreadsheet, various combinations of OFFSET can locate and total cells for a specific month.

| | C | D | E | F | G | H | I | J | K | L | M | N | O |
|---|---|---|---|---|---|---|---|---|---|---|---|---|---|
| 1 | Select a Year: | 2002 | | | Row for Year: | | 9 | =MATCH(E1,C1:C96,0) | | | | | |
| 2 | Select a month: | May | | | Column for Month: | | 8 | =MATCH(E2,$A$8:$O$8,0) | | | | | |
| 3 | | | | | # of Entries: | | 4 | =COUNT(OFFSET(A1,I1-1,I2-1,5,1)) | | | | | |
| 4 | | | | | Min Entry: | | 2165 | =MIN(OFFSET(A1,I1-1,I2-1,I$3,1)) | | | | | |
| 5 | | | | | Max Entry: | | 4817 | =MAX(OFFSET(A1,I1-1,I2-1,I$3,1)) | | | | | |
| 6 | | | | | Sum for Month: | | 13843 | =SUM(OFFSET(A1,I1-1,I2-1,I$3,1)) | | | | | |
| 7 | | | | | | | | | | | | | |
| 8 | | Jan | Feb | Mar | Apr | May | Jun | Jul | Aug | Sep | Oct | Nov | Dec |
| 9 | 2002 | 2050 | 2820 | 1485 | 1576 | 4647 | 3451 | 1361 | 1066 | 2078 | 3565 | 3455 | 1359 |
| 10 | | 1160 | | 1633 | | 2165 | | 3135 | | 2750 | | 3679 | 3884 |
| 11 | | 1864 | | | | 2214 | | | | 4437 | | 3122 | |
| 12 | | 1217 | | | | 4817 | | | | | | 4166 | |
| 13 | | | | | | | | | | | | 3950 | |
| 14 | | Jan | Feb | Mar | Apr | May | Jun | Jul | Aug | Sep | Oct | Nov | Dec |
| 15 | 2003 | 2422 | 2292 | 1641 | 1270 | 4110 | 1012 | 3071 | 3783 | 4400 | 3966 | 2629 | 3077 |
| 16 | | 1248 | | 1031 | | 2708 | | 2830 | | 3290 | | 4307 | 3666 |
| 17 | | 1313 | | | | 2590 | | 1095 | | 1134 | | 1399 | |
| 18 | | 2531 | | | | 3575 | | | | | | 1956 | |
| 19 | | | | | | 4524 | | | | | | | |
| 20 | | Jan | Feb | Mar | Apr | May | Jun | Jul | Aug | Sep | Oct | Nov | Dec |
| 21 | 2004 | 1011 | 1902 | 1567 | 3474 | 2184 | 4663 | 3841 | 1087 | 3229 | 4640 | 4353 | 1420 |
| 22 | | 1963 | 3230 | | 2894 | 3662 | 4167 | 2821 | | 1824 | | 4293 | 3935 |
| 23 | | 1245 | 2379 | | | 4964 | | 4049 | | 1718 | | 1150 | |
| 24 | | | | | | 4078 | | | | | | 1986 | |
| 25 | | | | | | | | | | | | 1024 | |
| 26 | | | | | | | | | | | | | |

Formula bar: I4 =MIN(OFFSET(A1,I1-1,I2-1,I$3,1))

1. Have the formula in Cell I1 find the starting row for the particular year, using the MATCH function shown in Cell J1.

2. Have the formula in Cell I2 find the column for the chosen month, using the MATCH function shown in Cell J2.

3. Build the OFFSET function to describe the range for that month and year. You know that it starts in the *row* in I1 and the *column* in I2. If you make the *reference* Cell A1, then Row 15 is 14 rows below A1. Therefore, use =OFFSET(A1,I1-1,.

4. The starting column is in Cell I2. Column 8 is seven columns to the right of A1. Therefore, you now use =OFFSET(A1,I1-1,I2-1.

5. The structure of the worksheet allows for up to five entries per month, arranged down a row. Thus, *height* is 5 and *width* is 1. Use the following formula to describe the possible range for the month: =OFFSET(A1,I1-1,I2-1,5,1). This would be good enough to use for MIN, MAX, SUM, and so on.

6. To chart the data, figure out the exact height. Use the =COUNT(OFFSET(A1,I1-1,I2-1,5,1)) formula in Cell I3 to count the number of entries for the month.

7. Use the formula =OFFSET(A1,I1-1,I2-1,I3,1) to describe the exact month. Add additional formulas in I4:I6 to figure out the minimum, maximum, and sum of those cells.

The OFFSET function initially seems intimidating, especially in light of the example you just walked through. Remember that for useful results from OFFSET, you usually replace one or more of the final four arguments with a calculation.

## USING ADDRESS TO FIND THE ADDRESS FOR ANY CELL

If someone asked you for the cell address for the cell in Row 5, Column 5, you could probably come up with E5 pretty quickly. How about if someone asked you for the 26th row of the 26th column? This is Z26. Again, it is pretty easy to come up with this if you know that there are 26 letters in the alphabet.

If someone asks you to calculate the address of Row 2 and Column 30, you have to divide 30 by 26 to learn that the product is 1 with a remainder of 4. This could lead you to conclude the cell address is the first letter of the alphabet—A—and the fourth letter of the alphabet—D—to come up with AD2. This type of calculation becomes far more complex with 16,384 columns. For example, how would you calculate the address for Row 2 of Column 14123?

Luckily, Excel provides the ADDRESS function to convert any intersection of row and column number to an address. =ADDRESS(2,14123) returns the text of $TWE$2.

SYNTAX: ADDRESS(*row_num,column_num,abs_num,a1,sheet_text*)

The default version of ADDRESS returns the cell address as an absolute address with both dollar signs. There are optional parameters to control this behavior:

- row_num—This is the row number to use in the cell reference.
- column_num—This is the column number to use in the cell reference.
- abs_num—This specifies the type of reference to return. If it is 1 or omitted, the returned address has both dollar signs and is absolute. If it is 2, the row is held absolute, but the column is relative. If it is 3, the row is relative and the column is absolute. If it is 4, the address is relative, with no dollar signs.
- a1—This is a logical value that specifies the A1 or R1C1 reference style. If a1 is TRUE or omitted, ADDRESS returns an A1-style reference; if it is FALSE, ADDRESS returns an R1C1-style reference.
- sheet_text—This is text that specifies the name of the worksheet to be used as the external reference. If sheet_text is omitted, no sheet name is used.

Figure 24.34 shows eight ways to describe one cell, depending on the various combinations of absolute and A1 arguments.

The *sheet_text* argument is interesting. It is difficult to remember the arcane rules for when to use apostrophes and where the exclamation point needs to go in an address. If you specify *sheet_text* as the name of a worksheet or use the style [*book_name*]*SheetName*, Excel builds the proper reference. Cell B12 in Figure 24.34 shows the result from an ADDRESS function that builds a reference to another workbook.

**TIP FROM**

> To find the value of a cell described by ADDRESS, you use the INDIRECT function.

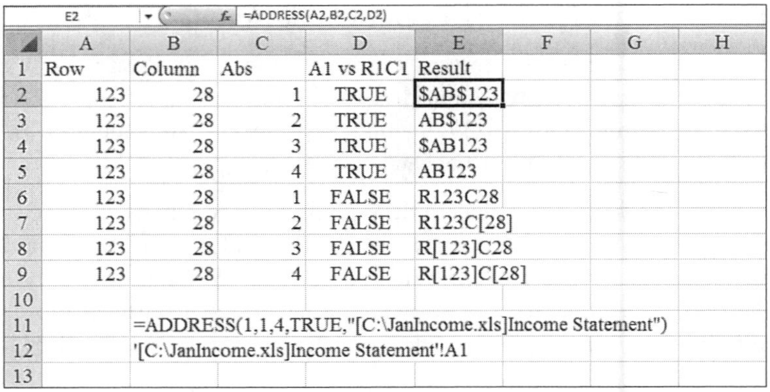

**Figure 24.34**

ADDRESS can return a cell address in A1 or R1C1 style.

| | A | B | C | D | E | F | G | H |
|---|---|---|---|---|---|---|---|---|
| | E2 | | fx | =ADDRESS(A2,B2,C2,D2) | | | | |
| 1 | Row | Column | Abs | A1 vs R1C1 | Result | | | |
| 2 | 123 | 28 | 1 | TRUE | $AB$123 | | | |
| 3 | 123 | 28 | 2 | TRUE | AB$123 | | | |
| 4 | 123 | 28 | 3 | TRUE | $AB123 | | | |
| 5 | 123 | 28 | 4 | TRUE | AB123 | | | |
| 6 | 123 | 28 | 1 | FALSE | R123C28 | | | |
| 7 | 123 | 28 | 2 | FALSE | R123C[28] | | | |
| 8 | 123 | 28 | 3 | FALSE | R[123]C28 | | | |
| 9 | 123 | 28 | 4 | FALSE | R[123]C[28] | | | |
| 10 | | | | | | | | |
| 11 | | =ADDRESS(1,1,4,TRUE,"[C:\JanIncome.xls]Income Statement") | | | | | | |
| 12 | | '[C:\JanIncome.xls]Income Statement'!A1 | | | | | | |
| 13 | | | | | | | | |

## USING INDIRECT TO BUILD AND EVALUATE CELL REFERENCES ON-THE-FLY

The INDIRECT function is deceivingly powerful. Consider this trivial example: In Cell A1, enter the text B2. In Cell B2, enter a number. =INDIRECT(A1)

The reference text can be any text that you can string together using various text functions. This allows you to create complex references that dynamically point to other sheets or to other open workbooks.

The reference text can also be a range name. You could have a validation list box where someone selects a value from a list. If you have predefined a named range that corresponds to each possible entry on the list, INDIRECT can point to the various named ranges on-the-fly.

When you use traditional formulas, even absolute formulas, there is a chance that someone could insert rows or columns that would move the reference. If you need a formula to always point to Cell J10, no matter how someone rearranges the worksheet, you can use =INDIRECT("J10") to handle this.

SYNTAX: INDIRECT(*ref_text,a1*)

The INDIRECT function returns the reference specified by a text string.

The INDIRECT function takes the following arguments:

- ref_text—This is a reference to a cell that contains an A1-style reference, an R1C1-style reference, a name defined as a reference, or a reference to a cell as a text string. If ref_text is not a valid cell reference, INDIRECT returns a #REF! error. If ref_text refers to an external workbook, the other workbook must be open. If the source workbook is not open, INDIRECT returns a #REF! error.

- a1—This is a logical value that specifies what type of reference is contained in the cell ref_text. If a1 is TRUE or omitted, *ref_text* is interpreted as an A1-style reference. If *a1* is FALSE, *ref_text* is interpreted as an R1C1-style reference.

Figure 24.35 is a monthly worksheet in a workbook that has 12 similar sheets. In each worksheet, the data headings are in Row 6, and the invoices appear for some number of rows, starting in Row 7. Each worksheet has a total for the month in Cell D2.

**Figure 24.35**
You can add a year-to-date formula to all sheets.

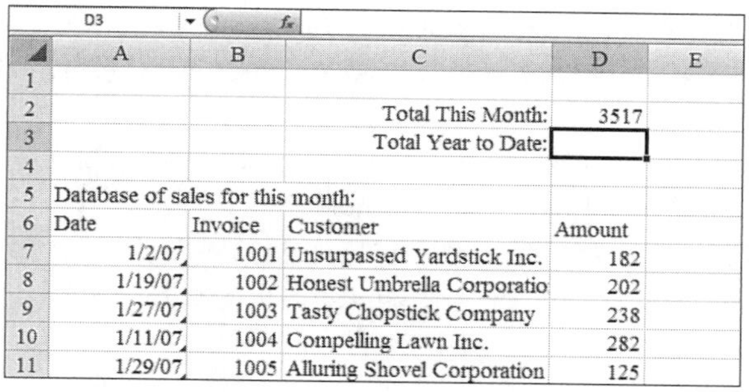

| | A | B | C | D | E |
|---|---|---|---|---|---|
| 1 | | | | | |
| 2 | | | Total This Month: | 3517 | |
| 3 | | | Total Year to Date: | | |
| 4 | | | | | |
| 5 | Database of sales for this month: | | | | |
| 6 | Date | Invoice | Customer | Amount | |
| 7 | 1/2/07 | 1001 | Unsurpassed Yardstick Inc. | 182 | |
| 8 | 1/19/07 | 1002 | Honest Umbrella Corporatio | 202 | |
| 9 | 1/27/07 | 1003 | Tasty Chopstick Company | 238 | |
| 10 | 1/11/07 | 1004 | Compelling Lawn Inc. | 282 | |
| 11 | 1/29/07 | 1005 | Alluring Shovel Corporation | 125 | |

In this example, you would like to add a year-to-date total in Cell D3 on each worksheet. This is fairly difficult to do without VBA. Many VBA books include a user-defined function to describe the previous sheet in a workbook. However, this function would fail if you sent the workbook to someone who disables macros on his or her computer. Instead, you could solve this problem with clever use of text functions and the `INDIRECT` function. To do so, you follow these steps:

1. Select the Jan worksheet.
2. Shift+click the Dec worksheet to put all 12 sheets in Group mode.
3. In Cell A1, enter the formula `=A7`. This adds the first date as a title for the worksheet.
4. Format Cell A1 with the custom format *mmmm, yyyy*. This causes the date to appear as January, 2007.
5. Right-click the Jan tab name and choose Ungroup Sheets.
6. Enter `=D2` as the year-to-date formula in Cell D3 of the Jan tab.
7. On the Feb worksheet, build a text formula that returns the name of the previous month. The quest becomes how to build a formula that looks like `=Jan!D3`.
8. Jan is a three-letter abbreviation for any date in the month of January. Therefore, enter a January date in a cell and format the cell with the custom number format *mmm*, so that the result is the word `Jan`.
9. The `TEXT` function takes a number or date and displays it using a specific custom number format, so on the February sheet, use `=TEXT(A1,"mmm")`, which results in the value `Feb`. This is close. If you could find a way to get the name of the previous month, the problem would be solved.
10. The value in Cell A1 is a live date. You can use date math to calculate a different date, such as the date one month earlier. Use the `DATE(`*`year,month,day`*`)` function to return a date in the previous month. For the year parameter, use `YEAR(A1)`. For the month

parameter, use `MONTH(A1)-1`. For the day parameter, use `DAY(A1)`. The formula `=DATE(YEAR(A1),MONTH(A1)-1,1)` returns a date that is the first of the previous month.

11. Combining steps 9 and 10 into a single formula, use `=TEXT(DATE(YEAR(A1), MONTH(A1)-1,1),"MMM")` to return the value of `Jan` on the Feb worksheet, `Feb` on the March worksheet, and so on.

12. Use the generic formula `=TEXT(DATE(YEAR(A1),MONTH(A1)-1,1),"MMM")&"!D3"` to build the reference.

13. Select the Feb worksheet. Shift+click the Dec worksheet to place these 11 worksheets in Group mode. In Cell D3, enter this formula:
`=INDIRECT(TEXT(DATE(YEAR(A1),MONTH(A1)-1,1),"mmm")&"!D3")+D2`.

14. Right-click any sheet tab and choose Ungroup to take the workbook out of Group mode.

The result, as shown in Figure 24.36, is a formula on the last 11 worksheets that automatically pulls the year-to-date total from the previous worksheet and adds it to the current worksheet total.

**Figure 24.36**
Cell D4 dynamically builds a text formula to reference the previous sheet, and then `INDIRECT` evaluates the formula.

| | A | B | C | D | E | F |
|---|---|---|---|---|---|---|
| | | | D3 ▾ | *fx* =INDIRECT(TEXT(DATE(YEAR(A1),MONTH(A1)-1,1),"mmm")&"!D3")+D2 | | |
| 1 | October, 2007 | | | | | |
| 2 | | | Total This Month: | 3614 | | |
| 3 | | | Total Year to Date: | 34772 | | |
| 4 | | | | | | |
| 5 | Database of sales for this month: | | | | | |
| 6 | Date | Invoice | Customer | Amount | | |
| 7 | 10/7/07 | 1001 | Stunning Shoe Corporation | 239 | | |
| 8 | 10/9/07 | 1002 | Forceful Lawn Corporation | 161 | | |
| 9 | 10/8/07 | 1003 | Vibrant Flagpole Corporatio | 169 | | |
| 10 | 10/4/07 | 1004 | Rare Saddle Corporation | 225 | | |
| 11 | 10/13/07 | 1005 | Tremendous Xylophone Inc. | 110 | | |
| 12 | 10/29/07 | 1006 | Real Electronics Traders | 297 | | |
| 13 | 10/15/07 | 1007 | Tasty Chopstick Company | 140 | | |

## USING THE HYPERLINK FUNCTION TO QUICKLY ADD HYPERLINKS

Excel enables you to add a hyperlink by using the user interface. On the Insert ribbon, you choose the Hyperlink icon. Then you specify text to appear in the cell and the underlying address. Building links in this way is easy, but it is tedious to build them one at a time. If you have hundreds of links to add, you can add them quickly by using the HYPERLINK function.

**SYNTAX:** HYPERLINK(*link_location,friendly_name*)

The HYPERLINK function creates a shortcut that opens a document stored on your hard drive, a network server, or on the Internet.

The HYPERLINK function takes the following arguments:

- `link_location`—This is the URL address on the Internet. It could also be a path, filename, and location in another file. For example, you could link to

`"[C:\files\Jan2007.xls]!Sheet1!A15"`. Note that `link_location` can be a text string enclosed in quotes or a cell that contains the link.

- `friendly_name`—This is the underlined text or numeric value that is displayed in the cell. `friendly_name` is displayed in blue and is underlined. If `friendly_name` is omitted, the cell displays the `link_location` value as the jump text. *friendly_name* can be a value, a text string, a name, or a cell that contains the jump text or value. If *friendly_name* returns an error (for example, #VALUE!), the cell displays the error instead of the jump text.

**NOTE**

Note that Excel does not check whether the link location is valid at the time you create the link. If the link is not valid when someone clicks it, the person encounters an error.

**TIP FROM**

It is difficult to select a cell that contains a HYPERLINK function. If you click the cell, Excel attempts to follow the hyperlink. Instead, you should click a cell near the cell and then use the arrow keys to move into the cell.

24

Figure 24.37 shows a list of web pages in Column A. Column B contains the titles of those web pages. To quickly build a table of hyperlinks, you use =HYPERLINK(A2,B2) in Cell C2 and copy the formula down the column. After the hyperlinks are created, you can copy Column C and use Paste Values on Column C. You are then free to delete Columns A and B.

**Figure 24.37**
The formulas in Column C allow you to create hundreds of hyperlinks in seconds.

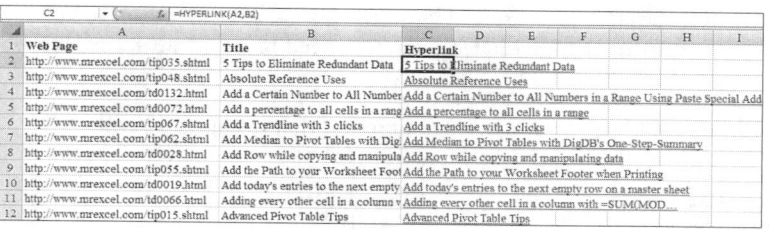

## USING THE TRANSPOSE FUNCTION TO FORMULAICALLY TURN DATA

With many people using Excel in a company, there are bound to be different usage styles from person to person. Some people build their worksheets horizontally, and other people build their worksheets vertically. In Figure 24.38, for example, the monthly totals stretch horizontally across row 80. However, for some reason, you need these figures to be arranged going vertically down from Cell B84.

The typical method is to copy C80:N80 and then use Sheet, Paste, Transpose. This copies a snapshot of the totals in Row 80 to a column of data.

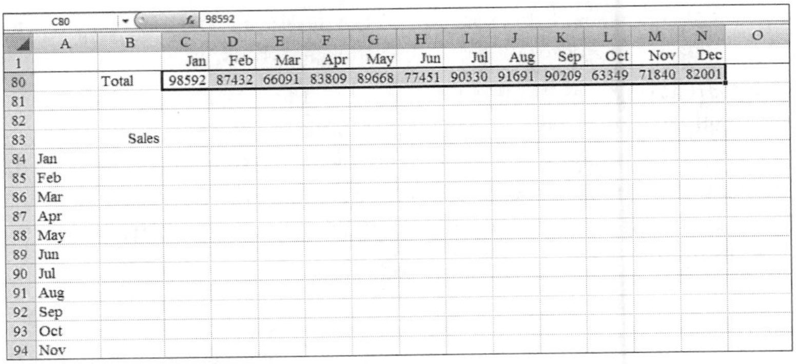

**Figure 24.38**
Turning C80:N80 into
a vertical range is
called *transposing*
the data.

This is fine if you only need a snapshot of the totals. But what if you want to see the totals continually updated in Column B? Excel provides the TRANSPOSE function for such situations. However, because the function returns several answers, you need to use special care when entering the formula. Here's how:

1. Note that C80:N80 contains 12 cells.

2. Select an identical number of cells starting in B84. Select B84:B95.

3. Even though you have 12 cells selected, type the formula =TRANSPOSE(C80:N80) just as if you only had 1 cell selected.

4. To tell Excel that this is a special type of formula called an *array formula*, hold down Ctrl+Shift while you press Enter.

Excel shows the formula surrounded by curly braces in the formula bar. This is one single formula entered in 12 cells. Therefore, you cannot delete or change one cell in the range. If you want to change the formula, you need to delete all 12 cells in B84:B95 in a single command.

Figure 24.39 shows a TRANSPOSE function that occupies 12 cells.

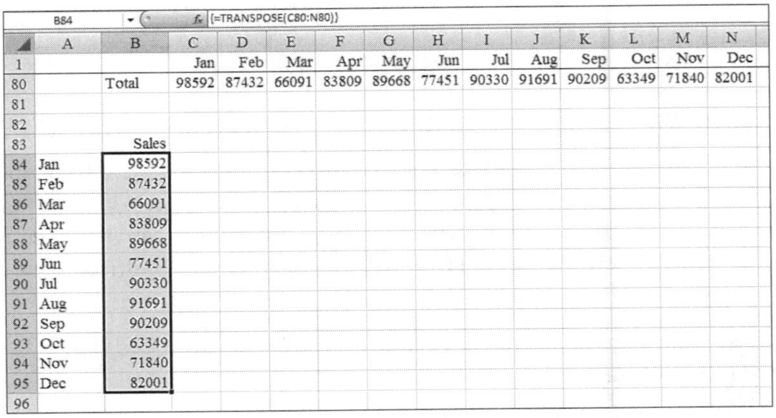

**Figure 24.39**
One TRANSPOSE func-
tion occupies 12 cells,
from B84:B95.

> **NOTE**
>
> You can also use TRANSPOSE to turn a vertical range into a horizontal range.

SYNTAX: TRANSPOSE(*array*)

The TRANSPOSE function will transpose a vertical range into a horizontal array or vice versa.

The argument *array* is an array or a range of cells on a worksheet that you want to transpose. The transposition of an array is accomplished by using the first row of the array as the first column of the new array, the second row of the array as the second column of the new array, and so on.

## USING THE RTD FUNCTION AND COM ADD-INS TO RETRIEVE REAL-TIME DATA

Third-party applications are available to send streaming real-time data to an Excel spreadsheet. They became very popular with stock day traders back in the late 1990s. If you have one of these COM add-ins installed on your system, you can set up a formula to retrieve real-time data from the COM add-in by using the RTD function. If you have such a COM add-in installed, the vendor of the add-in should provide sample workbooks with RTD functions already in place.

Syntax: RTD(*progid*,*server*,*topic1*,[*topic2*],...)

The RTD function returns real time data from a program that supports COM automation.

The RTD function takes the following arguments:

- progid—This is the name of the Program ID of a registered COM automation add-in that has been installed on the local computer. You need to enclose the name in quotation marks.
- server—This is name of the server where the add-in should be run. If there is no server and the program is run locally, you leave this argument blank.
- topic1, topic2,...—These are 1 to 28 parameters that together represent a unique piece of real-time data.

## USING GETPIVOTDATA TO RETRIEVE ONE CELL FROM A PIVOT TABLE

You might turn to this book in order to find out how to use most of the functions. For the GETPIVOTDATA function, however, you are likely to turn to this book to find out *why* the function is being automatically generated for them.

Say that you have a pivot table on a worksheet. You should click outside the pivot table. Next, you type an equals sign and then with the mouse, click one of the cells in the data area of the pivot table. Although you might expect this to generate a formula such as =E9, instead, Excel puts in the formula =GETPIVOTDATA("Sales",$B$5,"Customer","Astonishing Glass Company","Region","West"), as shown in Figure 24.40.

**Figure 24.40**
Excel inserts this strange function in the worksheet.

| | B | C | D | E | F | G | H | I |
|---|---|---|---|---|---|---|---|---|
| | | | | | =GETPIVOTDATA("Sales",$B$5,"Customer","Astonishing Glass Company","Region","West") | | | |
| 5 | Sum of Sales | Region | | | | | | |
| 6 | Customer | East | Central | West | Grand Total | | | |
| 7 | Alluring Ink Company | 0 | 170 | 0 | 170 | | | |
| 8 | Alluring Quilt Company | 289 | 0 | 0 | 289 | | | |
| 9 | Astonishing Glass Company | 0 | 0 | 314 | 314 | | 314 | |
| 10 | Astonishing Shovel Inc. | 190 | 0 | 0 | 190 | | | |
| 11 | Bright Shoe Company | 0 | 246 | 0 | 246 | | | |
| 12 | Brilliant Luggage Inc. | 0 | 307 | 0 | 307 | | | |
| 13 | Different Belt Corporation | 0 | 0 | 249 | 249 | | | |

This function is very annoying. As you copy the formula down to more rows, the function keeps retrieving sales to Astonishing Glass in the West region. By default, Excel is generating this function instead of a simple formula such as =E9. This happens whether you use the mouse or the arrow keys to specify the cell in the formula.

To avoid this behavior, you can type the entire formula by manually typing it on the keyboard. Typing =E9 in a cell forces Excel to create a relative reference to Cell E9. You are then free to copy the formula to other cells.

There is also a way to turn off this behavior permanently:

1. Select a cell inside an active pivot table.

2. The Pivot Table Tools ribbons appears. Choose the Options ribbon. From the PivotTable group, select the Options drop-down and then select the Generate GetPivotData icon (see Figure 24.41). The behavior turns off.

**Figure 24.41**
You can disable the GETPIVOTDATA function option.

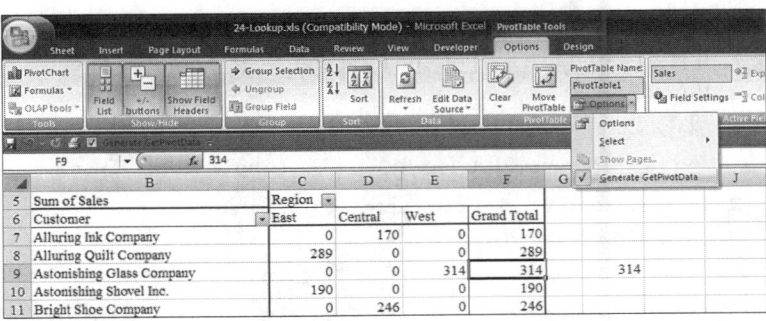

3. Enter formulas by using the mouse, arrow keys, or keyboard without generating the GETPIVOTDATA function.

Microsoft made GETPIVOTDATA the default behavior because the function is pretty cool. Now that you've learned how to turn off the behavior, you might want to understand exactly how it works in case you ever need to use the function.

SYNTAX: GETPIVOTDATA(*data_field*,*pivot_table*,*field1*,*item1*,*field2*,*item2*,...)

The GETPIVOTDATA function returns data stored in a pivot table report. You can use GETPIVOTDATA to retrieve summary data from a pivot table report, provided that the summary data is visible in the report. This function takes the following arguments:

- data_field—This is the name, enclosed in quotation marks, for the data field that contains the data you want to retrieve.

- pivot_table—This is a reference to any cell, range of cells, or named range of cells in a pivot table report. This information is used to determine which pivot table report contains the data you want to retrieve.

- field1, item1, field2, item2,...—These are 1 to 14 pairs of field names and item names that describe the data you want to retrieve. The pairs can be in any order. Field names and names for items other than dates and numbers are enclosed in quotation marks. For OLAP pivot table reports, items can contain the source name of the dimension as well as the source name of the item.

Calculated fields or items and custom calculations are included in GETPIVOTDATA calculations.

If *pivot_table* is a range that includes two or more pivot table reports, data is retrieved from whichever report was created in the range most recently.

If the *field* and *item* arguments describe a single cell, the value of that cell is returned, regardless of whether it is a string, a number, an error, and so on.

If an item contains a date, the value must be expressed as a serial number or populated by using the DATE function so that the value is retained if the spreadsheet is opened in a different locale. For example, an item referring to the date March 5, 1999, could be entered as 36224 or DATE(1999,3,5). Times can be entered as decimal values or by using the TIME function.

If *pivot_table* is not a range in which a pivot table report is found, GETPIVOTDATA returns #REF!. If the arguments do not describe a visible field, or if they include a page field that is not displayed, GETPIVOTDATA returns #REF!.

# EXAMPLES OF DATABASE FUNCTIONS

If you were a serious data analyst in the 1980s and the early 1990s, you would have been enamored with the database functions. I personally used @DSUM every hour of my work life for many years. It was one of the most powerful weapons in any spreadsheet arsenal. Combined with a data table, the DSUM, DMIN, DMAX, and DAVERAGE functions got a serious workout when users performed data analysis in a spreadsheet.

Then, in 1993, Microsoft Excel added the pivot table to the Data menu in Excel. Pivot tables changed everything. Those powerful database functions seemed tired and worn out. Since that day in 1993, I had never used DSUM again until I created the example described in the following section. As far as I knew, the database functions had been living in a cave in South Carolina.

Maybe it is like the nostalgia of finding a box of photos of an old girlfriend, but I realize that the database functions are still pretty powerful. Customers whined enough to have Microsoft add AVERAGEIF to the COUNTIF and SUMIF arsenal. This was unnecessary: Customers could have done this easily by setting up a small criteria range and using DAVERAGE.

Eleven of the 12 database functions are similar. DSUM, DAVERAGE, DCOUNT, DCOUNTA, DMAX, DMIN, DPRODUCT, DSTDEV, DSTDEVP, DVAR, and DVARP all perform the equivalent operation of their non-D equivalents, but they allow for complex criteria to include records that meet certain criteria.

To save you the hassle of looking up the confusing few, DCOUNT counts numeric cells, and DCOUNTA counts nonblank cells. DSTDEV and DVAR calculate the standard deviation and variance of a sample of a population. DSTDEVP and DVARP calculate the standard deviation and variance of the entire population. The 12th database function, DGET, has the same arguments, but it acts a bit differently, as explained later in this chapter.

## USING DSUM TO CONDITIONALLY SUM RECORDS FROM A DATABASE

There are three arguments to every database function. It is very easy to get your first DSUM working. The *criteria* argument is the one that offers vast flexibility. The following section explains the syntax for DSUM. The syntax for the other 11 database functions is identical to this.

SYNTAX: DSUM(*database*,*field*,*criteria*)

The DSUM function will add records from one field in a dataset, provided that the records meet some criteria that you specify.

The DSUM function takes the following arguments:

- database—This is the range of cells that make up the list or database, including the heading row. A *database* is a list of related data in which rows of related information are records and columns of data are fields. In Figure 24.42, the database is the 5,000 rows of data located at A23:I5024.

**Figure 24.42**
A simple criteria range specifies to limit DSUM to only records for Best Paint Inc. as a customer.

| | A | B | C | D | E | F | G | H | I |
|---|---|---|---|---|---|---|---|---|---|
| | | B1 | | fx | =DSUM($A$23:$I$5024,H$23,$A$17:$I$18) | | | | |
| 1 | DSUM | 657,028 | | | | | | | |
| 2 | DAVERAGE | 59,730 | | | | | | | |
| 3 | DCOUNT | 11 | | | | | | | |
| 4 | DCOUNTA | 11 | | | | | | | |
| 5 | DMAX | 89,898 | | | | | | | |
| 6 | DMIN | 26,058 | | | | | | | |
| 7 | DPRODUCT | 2.05.E+52 | | | | | | | |
| 8 | DSTDEV | 17,960 | | | | | | | |
| 9 | DSTDEVP | 17,124 | | | | | | | |
| 10 | DVAR | 322,545,029 | | | | | | | |
| 11 | DVARP | 293,222,753 | | | | | | | |
| 13 | | | | | | | | | |
| 17 | Customer | Product | Region | District | Rep | Date | Qty | Revenue | Profit |
| 18 | Best Paint Inc. | | | | | | | | |
| 19 | | | | | | | | | |
| 23 | Customer | Product | Region | District | Rep | Date | Qty | Revenue | Profit |
| 24 | Wonderful Faucet Co | G854 | East | Southeast | ADAM DUFFY | 2/3/01 | 730 | 76,906 | 41,529 |
| 25 | Forceful Flagpole Co | A105 | East | Southeast | ADAM DUFFY | 12/19/01 | 804 | 32,297 | 16,794 |
| 26 | Best Paint Inc. | V937 | Central | Chicago | PETER WARD | 12/5/01 | 414 | 59,761 | 31,673 |

- field—This indicates which column is used in the function. You have three options when specifying a field: You can point to the cell with the field name, such as H23 for Revenue; you can include the word Revenue as the *field* argument; or you can use the number 8 to indicate that Revenue is the eighth field in the database.

- criteria—This is the range of cells that contains the conditions specified. You can use any range for the criteria argument, as long as it includes at least one column label and at least one cell below the column label for specifying a condition for the column. Learning how to create powerful criteria ranges allows you to unlock the powerful potential of the database functions. Several examples are provided in the following sections.

## CREATING A SIMPLE CRITERIA RANGE FOR DATABASE FUNCTIONS

While a criteria range needs only one field heading from the database, it is just as easy to copy the entire set of headings to a blank section of the worksheet. In Figure 24.42, for example, the headings in A17:I17, along with at least one additional row, create a criteria range.

In Figure 24.42, you see results of the 11 database functions for a simple criteria where the customer is Best Paint Inc. Each formula specifies a database of $A$23:$I$5024. The field is H23, which is the heading for Revenue. The criteria range is A17:I18. In this example, the criteria range could have easily been A17:A18, but the A17:I18 form allows you to enter future criteria without respecifying the criteria range.

NOTE

To conserve space, the remaining examples in the following sections show only the DSUM result. You can compare the various results to the $657,000 of revenue for the current example.

## USING A BLANK CRITERIA RANGE TO RETURN ALL RECORDS

This is a trivial example, but if the second row of the criteria range is completely blank, the database function returns the total of all rows in the dataset. As shown in Figure 24.43, this is $256 million. This is equivalent to using the SUM function.

**Figure 24.43**
If the second row of the criteria is blank, the result reflects all rows.

| | A | B | C | D | E | F | G | H | I |
|---|---|---|---|---|---|---|---|---|---|
| | B1 | ▼ ( fx =DSUM($A$23:$I$5024,H$23,$A$17:$I$18) | | | | | | | |
| 1 | DSUM | 256,645,202 | | | | | | | |
| 13 | | | | | | | | | |
| 17 | Customer | Product | | Region | District | Rep | | Date | Qty | Revenue | Profit |
| 18 | | | | | | | | | |
| 19 | | | | | | | | | |
| 23 | **Customer** | **Product** | | **Region** | **District** | **Rep** | | **Date** | **Qty** | **Revenue** | **Profit** |
| 24 | Wonderful Faucet Cc | G854 | | East | Southeast | ADAM DUFFY | | 2/3/01, | 730 | 76,906 | 41,529 |
| 25 | Forceful Flagpole Cc | A105 | | East | Southeast | ADAM DUFFY | | 12/19/01, | 804 | 32,294 | 16,794 |
| 26 | Best Paint Inc. | V937 | | Central | Chicago | PETER WARD | | 12/5/01, | 414 | 59,761 | 31,673 |
| 27 | Guarded Raft Corpor | I543 | | West | California | BILLY JACOBS | | 1/5/03, | 793 | 66,858 | 35,435 |
| 28 | Rare Quilt Inc. | G854 | | Central | Southwest | MELVIN STAFFO | | 4/1/03, | 993 | 104,613 | 47,076 |

## USING AND TO JOIN CRITERIA

Many people using SUMIF in Excel 2003 and before are likely to want to know how to conditionally sum based on two conditions. This is simple to do with DSUM. If two criteria are placed on the same row of the criteria range, they are joined by an AND. In Figure 24.44, for example, the $123,000 is the sum of records where the customer is Best Paint and the product is V937.

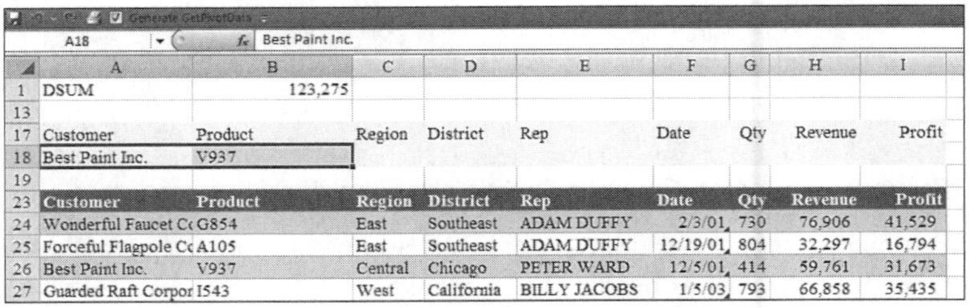

**Figure 24.44**
When two criterion are on the same line, they are joined by an AND function; rows must meet both criteria to be included in the DSUM.

## USING OR TO JOIN CRITERIA

When two criteria are placed on separate rows of the criteria range, they are joined by an OR function. In Figure 24.45, the $2.1 million represents records for either Improved Radio Traders or Best Paint.

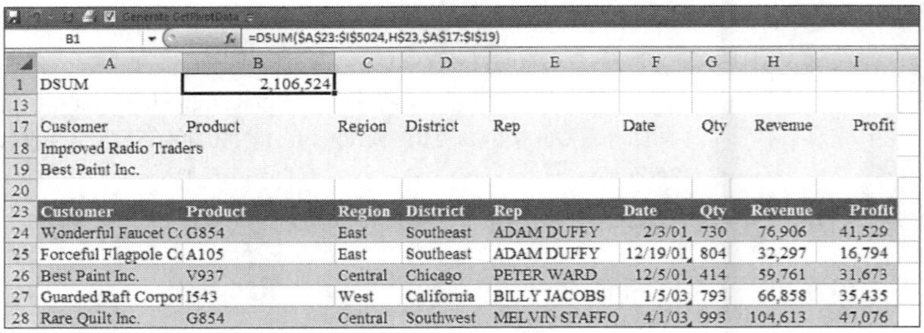

**Figure 24.45**
When two criteria are on different rows, they are joined by an OR function; rows can meet either criteria to be included in the DSUM.

You can use OR to join criteria from different fields. The criteria range in Figure 24.46 shows a Region value of West joined by an OR with a District value of Texas. This pulls a superset of all the West records plus just the Texas records from the central region.

## USING DATES OR NUMBERS AS CRITERIA

The example in Figure 24.47 finds records with a date in 2006 and with revenue under $50,000. The criteria in F18 for the date could have used any of these formats:

```
>12/31/2005
>=12/31/2005
>=31-Dec-2005
```

**Figure 24.46**
The criteria to be joined with OR can be in separate columns.

| | A | B | C | D | E | F | G | H | I |
|---|---|---|---|---|---|---|---|---|---|
| | | B1 | ▾ | fx =DSUM($A$23:$I$5024,H$23,$A$17:$I$19) | | | | | |
| 1 | DSUM | 65,724,062 | | | | | | | |
| 13 | | | | | | | | | |
| 17 | Customer | Product | Region | District | Rep | | Date | Qty | Revenue | Profit |
| 18 | | | West | | | | | | | |
| 19 | | | | Texas | | | | | | |
| 20 | | | | | | | | | | |
| 23 | Customer | Product | Region | District | Rep | | Date | Qty | Revenue | Profit |
| 24 | Wonderful Faucet Cc | G854 | East | Southeast | ADAM DUFFY | | 2/3/01 | 730 | 76,906 | 41,529 |
| 25 | Forceful Flagpole Cc | A105 | East | Southeast | ADAM DUFFY | | 12/19/01 | 804 | 32,297 | 16,794 |
| 26 | Best Paint Inc. | V937 | Central | Chicago | PETER WARD | | 12/5/01 | 414 | 59,761 | 31,673 |
| 27 | Guarded Raft Corpor | I543 | West | California | BILLY JACOBS | | 1/5/03 | 793 | 66,858 | 35,435 |
| 28 | Rare Quilt Inc. | G854 | Central | Southwest | MELVIN STAFFO | | 4/1/03 | 993 | 104,613 | 47,076 |

**Figure 24.47**
Using dates or numbers in criteria.

| | A | B | C | D | E | F | G | H | I |
|---|---|---|---|---|---|---|---|---|---|
| | | B1 | ▾ | fx =DSUM($A$23:$I$5024,H$23,$A$17:$I$18) | | | | | |
| 1 | DSUM | 11,478,140 | | | | | | | |
| 13 | | | | | | | | | |
| 17 | Customer | Product | Region | District | Rep | | Date | Qty | Revenue | Profit |
| 18 | | | | | | | >1/1/2006 | <50000 | | |
| 20 | | | | | | | | | | |
| 23 | Customer | Product | Region | District | Rep | | Date | Qty | Revenue | Profit |
| 24 | Wonderful Faucet Cc | G854 | East | Southeast | ADAM DUFFY | | 2/3/01 | 730 | 76,906 | 41,529 |
| 25 | Forceful Flagpole Cc | A105 | East | Southeast | ADAM DUFFY | | 12/19/01 | 804 | 32,297 | 16,794 |
| 26 | Best Paint Inc. | V937 | Central | Chicago | PETER WARD | | 12/5/01 | 414 | 59,761 | 31,673 |
| 27 | Guarded Raft Corpor | I543 | | West | California | BILLY JACOBS | | 1/5/03 | 793 | 66,858 | 35,435 |

24

### USING THE MIRACLE VERSION OF A CRITERIA RANGE

Using the criteria ranges in the preceding examples, you could easily build any complex criteria with multiple AND or OR operators.

However, this could get complex. Imagine if you wanted to pull all the records for five specific customers and five specific products. You would have to build a criteria range that is 26 rows tall. Basically, the 1st row would be the headings for customer and product. The 2nd row would indicate that you wanted to see records for Customer1 and Product1. The 3rd row would indicate that you wanted to see records for Customer1 and Product2. The 4th row would indicate that you wanted to see records for Customer1 and Product3. The seventh row would indicate Customer2 and Product1. The 26th row would indicate Customer5 and Product5.

If you needed to pull seven customers and seven products from five districts, your criteria range would grow to be 246 rows tall and would probably never finish calculating.

There is a miraculous version of the criteria range that completely avoids this problem. Here's how it works:

- The criteria range consists of a range that is two cells tall and one or more cells wide.

- Contrary to instructions in Excel help, the top cell of the criteria range cannot contain a field heading. The top cell must be blank.

- The second row in the criteria range can contain any formula that evaluates to TRUE or FALSE. This formula must point to cells in the first data row of the database. The formula can be as complex as you wish, with AND, OR, VLOOKUP, NOT, and MATCH; it can contain any combination of functions.

For a simple example, say that you wanted to find records that match 1 of 15 customers. You would copy the customers to K24:K38. In the second row of the criteria field, you would write the formula =NOT(ISNA(MATCH(A24,$K$24:$K$38,0))). This formula does a MATCH on the first customer in the database to see if it is in the list in K. The ISNA and NOT functions make sure that the criteria cell returns a TRUE when the customer is 1 of the 15 customers.

Very quickly and without complaint, Excel compares the 5,000 rows of your database with this complex formula, and the DSUM produces the correct value, as shown in Figure 24.48

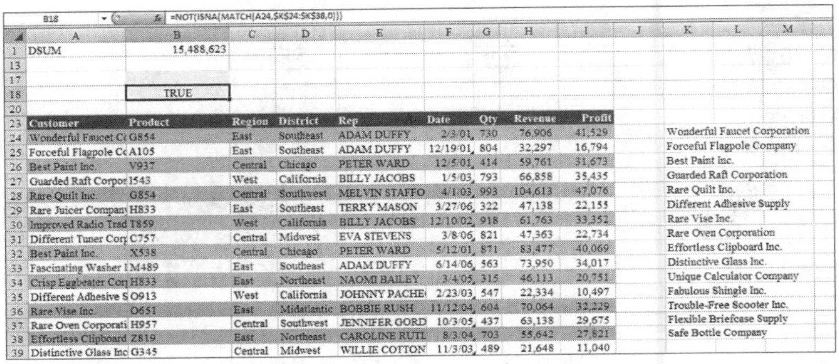

**Figure 24.48**
The formula version of the criteria range is rare but incredibly powerful.

## USING THE DGET FUNCTION

The DGET function returns a single cell from a database. The problem is that this function is incredibly picky. If your criteria range matches zero records, DGET returns a #VALUE error. If your criteria range returns more than one row, DGET returns a #NUM! error.

In order to have DGET work, you need to be able to write a criteria record that causes one and only one row to be evaluated as TRUE.

SYNTAX: DGET(database,field,criteria)

The DGET function will return a single cell matching criteria from a dataset.

The DGET function takes the following arguments:

- database—This is the range of cells that make up the list or database. A *database* is a list of related data in which rows of related information are records and columns of data are fields. The first row of the list contains labels for each column.

- field—This indicates which column is used in the function. Field can be given as text, with the column label enclosed between double quotation marks, such as "Age" or "Yield", or as a number that represents the position of the column within the list (for example, 1 for the first column, 2 for the second column, and so on).

■ criteria—This is the range of cells that contains the conditions you specify. You can use any range for the *criteria* argument, as long as it includes at least one column label and at least one cell below the column label for specifying a condition for the column.

---

### Excel in Practice: Using DSUM with a Data Table

If you don't want to use a pivot table, you can do a crosstab analysis by using a combination of the DSUM function and the Data Table command. The Data Table command works best when a problem is set up with two variables. In the DSUM function, you might have two variables defined in the criteria range.

To set up a two-variable table using the DSUM function, follow these steps:

1. Ensure that the upper-left corner of the table is a formula that relies on at least two variables. In Figure 24.49, Cell B1 contains a DSUM that relies on the criteria ranges in A17:I18.

**Figure 24.49**
The Data Table dialog requires two cells.

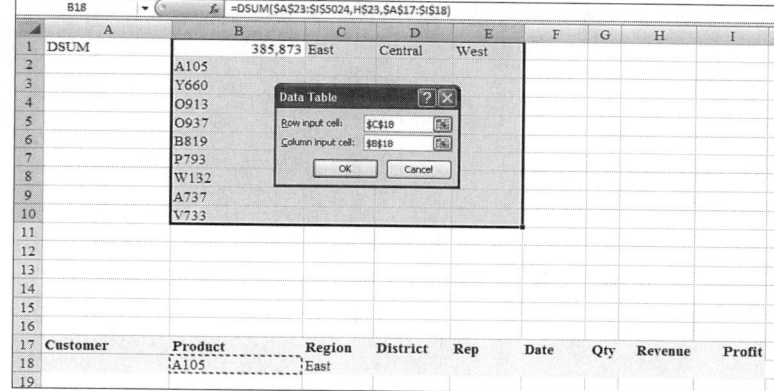

2. Down the left side of the table, arrange a list of values that should be substituted for one variable. In this example, the column contains a list of products that will eventually be substituted into Cell B18.

3. Across the top row of the table, arrange a list of values that should be substituted for the other variable. In this example, the row contains a list of regions that will eventually be substituted into Cell C18.

4. Select the range for the table. This selection should include the formula as the upper-left corner cell. It should also include the column and row of headings.

5. From the Data ribbon, choose What-if Analysis, Data Table. The Data Table dialog appears, asking for two cells.

6. For the row input cell, enter the cell where the regions should be substituted. In this case, it is cell C18 in the criteria range.

7. For the Column input cell, enter the cell where the values down the left column will be substituted. In this case, it is Cell B18 in the criteria range. The complete dialog box should look as shown in Figure 24.49.

The result is a crosstab analysis that shows the DSUM for every combination of product and region. Excel actually creates a TABLE array function to produce the answers. This is a live formula: If you change the product names or regions, the cells inside the table recalculate.

**Figure 24.50**

The resulting table provides a crosstab analysis similar to that in a pivot table.

| C2 | fx {=TABLE(C18,B18)} | | | |
|---|---|---|---|---|
| | A | B | C | D | E |
| 1 | DSUM | 385,873 | East | Central | West |
| 2 | | A105 | 385,873 | 601,184 | 259,097 |
| 3 | | Y660 | 1,152,227 | 1,422,736 | 1,111,337 |
| 4 | | O913 | 533,199 | 420,141 | 250,002 |
| 5 | | O937 | 1,562,404 | 1,498,932 | 1,146,197 |
| 6 | | B819 | 939,941 | 887,263 | 744,571 |
| 7 | | P793 | 553,087 | 690,740 | 146,925 |
| 8 | | W132 | 831,363 | 612,993 | 409,939 |
| 9 | | A737 | 1,609,888 | 952,950 | 919,978 |
| 10 | | V733 | 781,398 | 1,034,379 | 617,554 |
| 11 | | | | | |

# USING FINANCIAL FUNCTIONS

While the bulk of Excel's financial functions are for professional financiers and investors, there are a few functions that are useful for anyone planning to use a loan to purchase a car or house. The examples in this chapter represent a small subset of the calculations possible with Excel's financial functions.

Table 25.1 provides an alphabetical list of all of Excel 2007's financial functions. Detailed examples of the functions are provided in the remainder of the chapter.

**TABLE 25.1    ALPHABETICAL LIST OF FINANCIAL FUNCTIONS**

| Function | Description |
|---|---|
| `ACCRINT(issue,first_interest, settlement,rate,par, frequency,basis)` | Returns the accrued interest for a security that pays periodic interest. |
| `ACCRINTM(issue,maturity,rate, par,basis)` | Returns the accrued interest for a security that pays interest at maturity. |
| `AMORDEGRC(cost,date_purchased, first_period,salvage,period, rate,basis)` | Returns the depreciation for each accounting period. This function is provided for the French accounting system. If an asset is purchased in the middle of the accounting period, the prorated depreciation is taken into account. The function is similar to `AMORLINC`, except that a depreciation coefficient is applied in the calculation, depending on the life of the assets. |
| `AMORLINC(cost,date_purchased, first_period,salvage,period, rate,basis)` | Returns the depreciation for each accounting period. This function is provided for the French accounting system. If an asset is purchased in the middle of the accounting period, the prorated depreciation is taken into account. |
| `COUPDAYBS(settlement,maturity, frequency,basis)` | Returns the number of days from the beginning of the coupon period to the settlement date. |
| `COUPDAYS(settlement,maturity, frequency,basis)` | Returns the number of days in the coupon period that contains the settlement date. |
| `COUPDAYSNC(settlement,maturity, frequency,basis)` | Returns the number of days from the settlement date to the next coupon date. |
| `COUPNCD(settlement,maturity, frequency,basis)` | Returns a number that represents the next coupon date after the settlement date. To view the number as a date, you select Format, Cells and then click Date in the Category box. Then you click a date format in the Type box. |
| `COUPNUM(settlement,maturity, frequency,basis)` | Returns the number of coupons payable between the settlement date and maturity date, rounded up to the nearest whole coupon. |

25

| Function | Description |
|---|---|
| COUPPCD(settlement,maturity, frequency,basis) | Returns a number that represents the previous coupon date before the settlement date. To view the number as a date, you select Format, Cells and then click Date in the Category box. Then you click a date format in the Type box. |
| CUMIPMT(rate,nper,pv, start_period,end_period,type) | Returns the cumulative interest paid on a loan between start_period and end_period. |
| CUMPRINC(rate,nper,pv, start_period,end_period,type) | Returns the cumulative principal paid on a loan between start_period and end_period. |
| DB(cost,salvage,life, period,month) | Returns the depreciation of an asset for a specified period, using the fixed-declining-balance method. |
| DDB(cost,salvage,life, period,factor) | Returns the depreciation of an asset for a specified period using the double-declining-balance method or some other specified method. |
| DISC(settlement,maturity,pr, redemption,basis) | Returns the discount rate for a security. |
| DOLLARDE(fractional_dollar, fraction) | Converts a dollar price expressed as a fraction into a dollar price expressed as a decimal number. You use DOLLARDE to convert fractional dollar numbers, such as securities prices, to decimal numbers. |
| DOLLARFR(decimal_dollar, fraction) | Converts a dollar price expressed as a decimal number into a dollar price expressed as a fraction. You use DOLLARFR to convert decimal numbers to fractional dollar numbers, such as securities prices. |
| DURATION(settlement,maturity, coupon yld,frequency,basis) | Returns the Macaulay duration for an assumed par value of $100. The duration is defined as the weighted average of the present value of the cash flows and is used as a measure of a bond price's response to changes in yield. |
| EFFECT(nominal_rate,npery) | Returns the effective annual interest rate, given the nominal annual interest rate and the number of compounding periods per year. |
| FV(rate,nper,pmt,pv,type) | Returns the future value of an investment, based on periodic, constant payments and a constant interest rate. |
| FVSCHEDULE(principal,schedule) | Returns the future value of an initial principal after applying a series of compound interest rates. You use FVSCHEDULE to calculate future value of an investment with a variable or adjustable rate. |
| INTRATE(settlement,maturity, investment,redemption,basis) | Returns the interest rate for a fully invested security. |

25

*continues*

**TABLE 25.1 CONTINUED**

| Function | Description |
|---|---|
| IPMT(*rate*,*per*,*nper*,*pv*,*fv*,*type*) | Returns the interest payment for a given period for an investment, based on periodic, constant payments and a constant interest rate. For a more complete description of the arguments in IPMT and for more information about annuity functions, see PV. |
| IRR(*values*,*guess*) | Returns the internal rate of return for a series of cash flows represented by the numbers in *values*. These cash flows do not have to be even, as they would be for an annuity. However, the cash flows must occur at regular intervals, such as monthly or annually. The internal rate of return is the interest rate received for an investment consisting of payments (negative values) and income (positive values) that occur at regular periods. |
| ISPMT(*rate*,*per*,*nper*,*pv*) | Calculates the interest paid during a specific period of an investment. This function is provided for compatibility with Lotus 1-2-3. |
| MDURATION(*settlement*,*maturity*, *coupon*,*yld*,*frequency*,*basis*) | Returns the modified duration for a security with an assumed par value of $100. |
| MIRR(*values*,*finance_rate*, *reinvest_rate*) | Returns the modified internal rate of return for a series of periodic cash flows. MIRR considers both the cost of the investment and the interest received on reinvestment of cash. |
| NOMINAL(*effect_rate*,*npery*) | Returns the nominal annual interest rate, given the effective rate and the number of compounding periods per year. |
| NPER(*rate*,*pmt*,*pv*,*fv*,*type*) | Returns the number of periods for an investment, based on periodic, constant payments and a constant interest rate. |
| NPV(*rate*,*value1*,*value2*,...) | Calculates the net present value of an investment by using a discount rate and a series of future payments (negative values) and income (positive values). |
| ODDFPRICE(*settlement*,*maturity*, *issue*,*first_coupon*,*rate*,*yld*, *redemption*,*frequency*,*basis*) | Returns the price per $100 face value of a security having an odd (short or long) first period. |
| ODDFYIELD(*settlement*,*maturity*, *issue*,*first_coupon*,*rate*,*pr*, *redemption*,*frequency*,*basis*) | Returns the yield of a security that has an odd (short or long) first period. |
| ODDLPRICE(*settlement*,*maturity*, *last_interest*,*rate*,*yld*, *redemption*,*frequency*,*basis*) | Returns the price per $100 face value of a security having an odd (short or long) last coupon period. |

| Function | Description |
|---|---|
| ODDLYIELD(*settlement*,*maturity*, *last_interest*,*rate*,*pr*, *redemption*,*frequency*,*basis*) | Returns the yield of a security that has an odd (short or long) last period. |
| PMT(*rate*,*nper*,*pv*,*fv*,*type*) | Calculates the payment for a loan based on constant payments and a constant interest rate. |
| PPMT(*rate*,*per*,*nper*,*pv*,*fv*,*type*) | Returns the payment on the principal for a given period for an investment based on periodic, constant payments and a constant interest rate. |
| PRICE(*settlement*,*maturity*,*rate*, *yld*,*redemption*,*frequency*,*basis*) | Returns the price per $100 face value of a security that pays periodic interest. |
| PRICEDISC(*settlement*,*maturity*, *discount*,*redemption*,*basis*) | Returns the price per $100 face value of a discounted security. |
| PRICEMAT(*settlement*,*maturity*, *issue*,*rate*,*yld*,*basis*) | Returns the price per $100 face value of a security that pays interest at maturity. |
| PV(*rate*,*nper*,*pmt*,*fv*,*type*) | Returns the present value of an investment. The present value is the total amount that a series of future payments is worth now. For example, when you borrow money, the loan amount is the present value to the lender. |
| RATE(*nper*,*pmt*,*pv*,*fv*,*type*,*guess*) | Returns the interest rate per period of an annuity. RATE is calculated by iteration and can have zero or more solutions. If the successive results of RATE do not converge to within 0.0000001 after 20 iterations, RATE returns a #NUM! error. |
| RECEIVED(*settlement*,*maturity*, *investment*,*discount*,*basis*) | Returns the amount received at maturity for a fully invested security. |
| SLN(*cost*,*salvage*,*life*) | Returns the straight-line depreciation of an asset for one period. |
| SYD(*cost*,*salvage*,*life*,*per*) | Returns the sum-of-years'-digits depreciation of an asset for a specified period. |
| TBILLEQ(*settlement*,*maturity*, *discount*) | Returns the bond-equivalent yield for a Treasury bill (T-bill). |
| TBILLPRICE(*settlement*,*maturity*, *discount*) | Returns the price per $100 face value for a T-bill. |
| TBILLYIELD(*settlement*,*maturity*,*pr*) | Returns the yield for a T-bill. |
| VDB(*cost*,*salvage*,*life*,*start_period*, *end_period*,*factor*,*no_switch*) | Returns the depreciation of an asset for any specified period, including partial periods, using the double-declining-balance method or some other specified method. VDB stands for variable declining balance. |

25

*continues*

**TABLE 25.1 CONTINUED**

| Function | Description |
|---|---|
| XIRR(*values,dates,guess*) | Returns the internal rate of return for a schedule of cash flows that is not necessarily periodic. To calculate the internal rate of return for a series of periodic cash flows, you use the IRR function. |
| XNPV(*rate,values,dates*) | Returns the net present value for a schedule of cash flows that is not necessarily periodic. To calculate the net present value for a series of cash flows that is periodic, you use the NPV function. |
| YIELD(*settlement,maturity,rate, pr,redemption,frequency,basis*) | Returns the yield on a security that pays periodic interest. You use YIELD to calculate bond yield. |
| YIELDDISC(*settlement,maturity, pr,redemption,basis*) | Returns the annual yield for a discounted security. |
| YIELDMAT(*settlement,maturity, issue,rate,pr,basis*) | Returns the annual yield of a security that pays interest at maturity. |

## EXAMPLES OF COMMON HOUSEHOLD LOAN AND INVESTMENT FUNCTIONS

While Excel is popular with banking and investment professionals, it is handy for just about anyone who deals with financial transactions. This first section of this chapter applies to anyone who is planning on buying a car or a house. With a little preplanning with Excel, you can build very simple worksheets that allow you to calculate various monthly payments for various loan amounts.

You need to keep in mind two universal rules when dealing with all financial functions:

- Make sure your time units are consistent. If you are calculating a monthly loan payment, the interest rate argument should be expressed as a monthly figure. Most interest rates are quoted as an annual figure, such as 5.5%. To convert, you divide 5.5% by 12.

- When money is changing hands, consider the direction in which money is flowing. In any transaction, some cash will be flowing toward you (positive), and some cash will be flowing away from you (negative). If you try to enter all terms as positive, you will end up with a result that is not meaningful. For example, say you want a car loan where the bank gives $20,000 at the beginning and then gives you another $377 per month. NPER(5%/12,377,20000) would come up with an incorrect result for your problem because one of the cash flows needs to be negative. If you are considering the loan from the point of view of the customer, the formula would be NPER(5%/12,-377,20000). If you are considering the loan from the point of view of the bank, the formula would be NPER(5%/12,377,-20000).

## USING PMT TO CALCULATE THE MONTHLY PAYMENT ON AN AUTOMOBILE LOAN

Buying a car is one of the most exciting purchases. Whether the car is brand-new or just new to you, nothing attracts attention in your neighborhood like a new car pulling into the driveway.

Before shopping for a car, you should take a five-minute spin through Excel to calculate potential car payments. Knowing the price that will get you to the desired car payment will allow you to haggle with the sales rep from a position of knowledge.

### SYNTAX: PMT(rate,nper,pv,fv,type)

The PMT function calculates the payment for a loan based on constant payments and a constant interest rate. This function takes the following arguments:

- *rate*—This is the interest rate for the loan. Note that interest rate is often expressed as an annual rate. If you are calculating a monthly payment, you have to divide that rate by 12.
- *nper*—This is the term, or the total number of payments for the loan.
- *pv*—This is the present value, or the loan amount; it is also known as the principal.
- *fv*—This is an optional future value, or a cash balance you want to attain after the last payment is made. For a car payment calculation, this should be 0. If fv is omitted, it is assumed to be 0, that is, the future value of a loan is zero.
- *type*—This is the number 0 or 1 and indicates when payments are due. The default value of 0 assumes that the first payment is due after a month has elapsed. If you have to make the first payment on the day the loan is issued, you should set this value to 1.

> **NOTE**
>
> The payment returned by PMT includes principal and interest but not taxes, insurance, escrow, or fees sometimes associated with loans.

For a reality check, try multiplying the calculated payment by *nper*. This way, you can calculate the total of all payments over the life of the loan. In Figure 25.1, you see that a $29,000 car actually costs $32,835 in principal and interest.

**Figure 25.1**
PMT calculates a monthly loan payment.

| | B5 | ▾ | *fx* =PMT(B2/12,B3,B1) | | | |
|---|---|---|---|---|---|---|
| | A | B | C | D | E | F |
| 1 | Loan Amount | -29000 | Negative, as the money is leaving the bank | | | |
| 2 | Rate | 5% | Annual rate; divide by 12 in the function | | | |
| 3 | Term | 60 | Months | | | |
| 4 | | | | | | |
| 5 | **PMT** | $547.27 | =PMT(B2/12,B3,B1) | | | |
| 6 | | | | | | |
| 7 | Total Paid | $32,835.95 | | | | |
| 8 | | =B3*B5 | | | | |
| 9 | | | | | | |

## USING RATE TO DETERMINE AN INTEREST RATE

The PMT function is useful when you are considering a new loan. If you are analyzing a loan that you've been paying for a while, you might know the monthly payment but forget the interest rate. The RATE function can help you determine the rate.

SYNTAX: RATE(*nper*,*pmt*,*pv*,*fv*,*type*,*guess*)

The RATE function returns the interest rate per period of an annuity. RATE is calculated by iteration and can have zero or more solutions. If the successive results of RATE do not converge to within 0.0000001 after 20 iterations, RATE returns a #NUM! error. This function takes the following arguments:

- *nper*—This is the total number of payment periods in an annuity.
- *pmt*—This is the payment made each period and cannot change over the life of the annuity. Typically, *pmt* includes principal and interest but no other fees or taxes. If *pmt* is omitted, you must include the *fv* argument.
- *pv*—This is the present value—the total amount that a series of future payments is worth now.
- *fv*—This is the future value, or a cash balance you want to attain after the last payment is made. If *fv* is omitted, it is assumed to be 0 (the future value of a loan, for example, is zero).
- *type*—This is the number 0 or 1 to indicate when payments are due. The default value of 0 assumes that payments are due at the end of the period. A value of 1 means the payments are due at beginning of each period.
- *guess*—This is your guess for what the rate will be. If you omit *guess*, it is assumed to be 10%. If RATE does not converge, you can try different values for *guess*. RATE usually converges if *guess* is between 0 and 1.

Make sure you are consistent about the units you use for specifying *guess* and *nper*. If you make monthly payments on a four-year loan at 12% annual interest, you use 12% / 12 for *guess* and 4 × 12 for *nper*. If you make annual payments on the same loan, you use 12% for *guess* and 4 for *nper*.

Figure 25.2 shows how to calculate an interest rate.

**Figure 25.2**
Given the other terms for a loan, back into the interest rate with RATE.

| | A | B | C | D | E |
|---|---|---|---|---|---|
| | B6 | | *fx* =RATE(B1, B2, B3)*12 | | |
| 1 | Term | 60 | Months of the loan | | |
| 2 | Payment | 377 | Monthly payment | | |
| 3 | Loan Amount | -20000 | Amount of the loan | | |
| 4 | | | | | |
| 5 | Annual rate of the loan with the above terms | | | | |
| 6 | **Rate** | **4.95%** | =RATE(B1, B2, B3)*12 | | |
| 7 | | | | | |

## USING PV TO FIGURE OUT HOW MUCH HOUSE YOU CAN AFFORD

If you are looking for a monthly house payment of $1,500 with a 15-year loan at 6% annual interest rate, you can back into the loan amount by using the PV function.

**Figure 25.3**
You use PV to calculate how much you can borrow to meet a monthly payment budget.

| | B5 | ▼ | *fx* =PV(B2/12,B3,B1) | | | |
|---|---|---|---|---|---|---|
| ◢ | A | B | C | D | E | F |
| 1 | Desired Payment | -1500 | Negative, as it is money leaving your wallet | | | |
| 2 | Rate | 6% | Annual rate; divide by 12 in the function | | | |
| 3 | Term | 180 | Months; =15*12 | | | |
| 4 | | | | | | |
| 5 | PV | $177,755.27 | =PV(B2/12,B3,B1) | | | |
| 6 | | | | | | |
| 7 | Don't forget that taxes, insurance, and escrow will be added to the | | | | | |
| 8 | desired payment in B1 | | | | | |
| 9 | | | | | | |

SYNTAX: PV(*rate*,*nper*,*pmt*,*fv*,*type*)

The PV function returns the present value of an investment. The present value is the total amount that a series of future payments is worth now. For example, when you borrow money, the loan amount is the present value to the lender. This function takes the following arguments:

- *rate*—This is the interest rate per period. For example, if you obtain an automobile loan at a 10% annual interest rate and make monthly payments, your interest rate per month is 10%/12, or 0.83%. You would therefore enter 10% / 12, or 0.83%, or 0.0083, into the formula as *rate*.

- *nper*—This is the total number of payment periods in an annuity. For example, if you get a four-year car loan and make monthly payments, your loan has 4 × 12 (or 48) periods. You would enter 48 into the formula for *nper*.

- *pmt*—This is the payment made each period and cannot change over the life of the annuity. Typically, *pmt* includes principal and interest but no other fees or taxes. For example, the monthly payments on a $10,000, four-year car loan at 12% are $263.33. You would enter -263.33 into the formula for *pmt*. If *pmt* is omitted, you must include the *fv* argument.

- *fv*—This is the future value, or a cash balance you want to attain after the last payment is made. If *fv* is omitted, it is assumed to be 0 (the future value of a loan, for example, is zero). For example, if you want to save $50,000 to pay for a special project in 18 years, then $50,000 is the future value. You could then make a conservative guess at an interest rate and determine how much you must save each month. If *fv* is omitted, you must include the *pmt* argument.

- *type*—This is the number 0 or 1 to indicate when payments are due. The default value of 0 assumes that payments are due at the end of the period. A value of 1 means the payments are due at beginning of each period.

25

In Figure 25.3, Cell B5 calculates the loan principal amount that would result in the desired payment, including principal and interest. You also need to budget for monthly insurance, taxes, and fees that might be a part of your monthly payment to the bank.

## USING NPER TO ESTIMATE HOW LONG A NEST EGG WILL LAST

NPER stands for number of periods. If you have a 401(k) retirement account and are trying to calculate how long you can withdraw fixed monthly payments from the account, use NPER.

SYNTAX: NPER(*rate, pmt, pv, fv, type*)

The NPER function returns the number of periods for an investment, based on periodic, constant payments and a constant interest rate. This function takes the following arguments:

- *rate*—This is the interest rate per period.
- *pmt*—This is the payment made each period; it cannot change over the life of the annuity. Typically, *pmt* contains principal and interest but no other fees or taxes.
- *pv*—This is the present value, or the lump-sum amount that a series of future payments is worth right now.
- *fv*—This is the future value, or a cash balance you want to attain after the last payment is made. If *fv* is omitted, it is assumed to be 0 (the future value of a loan, for example, is zero). If you want to leave an inheritance to your kids, you use that amount as the FV.
- *type*—This is the number 0 or 1 to indicate when payments are due. The default value of 0 assumes that payments are due at the end of the period. A value of 1 means the payments are due at beginning of each period.

In Figure 25.4, the NPER function in Cell B5 estimates how many months you can withdraw the amount in Cell B2. Note that the monthly withdrawal is negative from the point of view of the retirement account.

**Figure 25.4**
You use NPER to figure out how long an annuity can pay out before it ends in a zero balance.

| | A | B | C |
|---|---|---|---|
| | B5 | ▾ | *fx* =NPER(B3/12,B2,B1) |
| 1 | Nest Egg Today | 457124 | Value of retirement account |
| 2 | Monthly Withdrawal | -2800 | Desired monthly withdrawal |
| 3 | Interest Rate | 3.5% | Assumed interest rate |
| 4 | | | |
| 5 | **Months** | **222.01** | =NPER(B3/12,B2,B1) |
| 6 | Years | 18.5 | =B5/12 |
| 7 | | | |

## USING FV TO ESTIMATE THE FUTURE VALUE OF A REGULAR SAVINGS PLAN

The future value calculation assumes that you will make regular monthly payments to a savings plan every month. It also assumes that the interest rate does not change throughout the life of the savings plan. If you are young, it is likely that you will be able to save more as your income grows later. However, using the savings calculator in Figure 25.5 helps you to realize the value of regular savings.

**Figure 25.5**
You can estimate the future value of a regular savings plan.

| B8 | | $f_x$ =FV(B5/12,B3,-B4,-B6) | |
|---|---|---|---|
| | A | B | C |
| 1 | Age Now | 25 | |
| 2 | Retirement Age | 65 | |
| 3 | Number of Months | 480 | =(B2-B1)*12 |
| 4 | Monthly Savings | 125 | |
| 5 | Interest Rate | 6% | |
| 6 | Savings Balance Now | 542 | |
| 7 | | | |
| 8 | **Future Value** | **$254,875.28** | =FV(B5/12,B3,-B4,-B6) |
| 9 | | | |

SYNTAX: FV(rate,nper,pmt,pv,type)

The FV function returns the future value of an investment, based on periodic, constant payments and a constant interest rate. This function takes the following arguments:

- rate—This is the interest rate per period.
- nper—This is the total number of payment periods in an annuity.
- pmt—This is the payment made each period; it cannot change over the life of the annuity. Typically, pmt contains principal and interest but no other fees or taxes. If pmt is omitted, you must include the pv argument.
- pv—This is the present value, or the lump-sum amount that a series of future payments is worth right now. If pv is omitted, it is assumed to be 0, and you must include the pmt argument.
- type—This is the number 0 or 1 to indicate when payments are due. The default value of 0 assumes that payments are due at the end of the period. A value of 1 means the payments are due at beginning of each period.

For all the arguments, cash you pay out, such as deposits to savings, is represented by negative numbers; cash you receive, such as dividend checks, is represented by positive numbers.

Figure 25.5 shows how to use FV for a simple savings calculator. The formula in Cell B8 assumes that you continue making the deposit each month from Cell B4 until you retire and that interest rates remain constant. If you already have some amount in savings, you enter that in Cell B6.

Note that the FV formula uses a negative version of Cells B4 and B6. This is because these are amounts that leave your wallet and go to the bank or mutual fund.

# Examples of Functions for Financial Professionals

Whereas the typical consumer is interested in the amount of his or her monthly car payment, a loan maker is interested in the month-by-month breakdown of principal and interest. Excel offers a complete cadre of functions to do these calculations.

## Using PPMT to Calculate the Principal Payment for Any Month

After a bank writes a car loan, the consumer makes monthly payments. To calculate the principal portion of the payment for any period in the loan, you use PPMT. Of course, you can use a range of these formulas—one for each month—to build an amortization table.

Syntax: PPMT(*rate,per,nper,pv,fv,type*)

The PPMT function returns the payment on the principal for a given period for an investment, based on periodic, constant payments and a constant interest rate. This function takes the following arguments:

- *rate*—This is the interest rate per period.
- *per*—This specifies for which period the principal payment will be returned. It must be in the range 1 to *nper*.
- *nper*—This is the total number of payment periods in an annuity.
- *pv*—This is the present value—the total amount that a series of future payments is worth now.
- *fv*—This is the future value, or a cash balance you want to attain after the last payment is made. If *fv* is omitted, it is assumed to be 0—that is, the future value of a loan is zero.
- *type*—This is the number 0 or 1 to indicate when payments are due. The default value of 0 assumes that payments are due at the end of the period. A value of 1 means the payments are due at beginning of each period.

In Figure 25.6, Cell B9 calculates the principal payment for Period 1. The *per* argument comes from the month number in Column A. Copying the formula down for all months produces an amortization table.

NOTE

In this example, the interest component could either be calculated with PMT-PPMT or using the IPMT function. IPMT is discussed in the next section.

## Using IPMT to Calculate the Interest Portion of a Loan Payment for Any Month

Whereas the PPMT function calculates the principal payment for any month of a loan, the IPMT function calculates the interest portion of the payment. The results of IPMT are shown in Column C of Figure 25.6.

**Figure 25.6**
Similar PPMT functions in B9:B56 calculate the monthly principal portion of the loan payment.

| | A | B | C | D | E |
|---|---|---|---|---|---|
| | | B9 ▾ | $f_x$ =PPMT($B$2/12,A9,$B$3,$B$1) | | |
| 1 | Loan Amt | -22000 | | | |
| 2 | Rate | 5% | | | |
| 3 | Term | 48 | | | |
| 4 | PMT | 506.6445 | | | |
| 5 | | | | | |
| 6 | | B9: | =PPMT($B$2/12,A9,$B$3,$B$1) | | |
| 7 | | C9: | =IPMT($B$2/12,A9,$B$3,$B$1) | | |
| 8 | Month | Principal | Interest | | |
| 9 | 1 | $414.98 | $91.67 | | |
| 10 | 2 | $416.71 | $89.94 | | |
| 11 | 3 | $418.44 | $88.20 | | |
| 12 | 4 | $420.19 | $86.46 | | |
| 13 | 5 | $421.94 | $84.71 | | |
| 14 | 6 | $423.70 | $82.95 | | |

SYNTAX: IPMT(*rate*,*per*,*nper*,*pv*,*fv*,*type*)

The IPMT function returns the interest payment for a given period for an investment, based on periodic, constant payments and a constant interest rate. This function takes the following arguments:

- *rate*—This is the interest rate per period.
- *per*—This is the period for which you want to find the interest and must be in the range 1 to *nper*.
- *nper*—This is the total number of payment periods in an annuity.
- *pv*—This is the present value, or the lump-sum amount that a series of future payments is worth right now.
- *fv*—This is the future value, or a cash balance you want to attain after the last payment is made.
- *type*—This is the number 0 or 1 to indicate when payments are due. The default value of 0 assumes that payments are due at the end of the period. A value of 1 means the payments are due at beginning of each period.

The IPMT function is similar to the PPMT function. Combined, they can create a simple amortization table (refer to Figure 25.6).

NOTE

You may encounter an old worksheet that uses ISPMT, which is the Lotus 1-2-3 version of IPMT. For details on ISPMT, see Excel Help. For new worksheets, you should use IPMT instead of ISPMT.

25

## USING CUMIPMT TO CALCULATE TOTAL INTEREST PAYMENTS DURING A TIME FRAME

The CUMIPMT function is great for figuring out your yearly tax deduction for your mortgage interest. After specifying the typical components of a loan (that is, rate, term, amount), you specify that you want to calculate the interest for particular periods, such as Periods 6 through 18.

SYNTAX: CUMIPMT(*rate*,*nper*,*pv*,*start_period*,*end_period*,*type*)

The CUMIPMT function returns the cumulative interest paid on a loan between *start_period* and *end_period*. This function takes the following arguments:

- *rate*—This is the interest rate.
- *nper*—This is the total number of payment periods.
- *pv*—This is the present value.
- *start_period*—This is the first period in the calculation. Payment periods are numbered beginning with 1.
- *end_period*—This is the last period in the calculation.
- *type*—This is the number 0 or 1 to indicate when payments are due. The default value of 0 assumes that payments are due at the end of the period. A value of 1 means the payments are due at beginning of each period.

*nper*, *start_period*, *end_period*, and *type* are truncated to integers. If *rate* is less than or equal to 0, *nper* is less than or equal to 0, or *pv* is less than or equal to 0, CUMIPMT returns a #NUM! error. If *start_period* is less than 1, *end_period* is less than 1, or *start_period* is greater than *end_period*, CUMIPMT returns a #NUM! error. If *type* is any number other than 0 or 1, CUMIPMT returns a #NUM! error.

Figure 25.7 calculates the total interest paid during each year of the loan. The mildly difficult portion of the sample spreadsheet is that the number of months in the first year will likely be less than 12. Cell D12 uses =13-MONTH(B5). Cell C13 uses =D12+1. Cell D13 uses =C12+11 to calculate the last period for each year.

Column F of this spreadsheet uses CUMPRINC, which is discussed in the next section.

## USING CUMPRINC TO CALCULATE TOTAL PRINCIPAL PAID IN ANY RANGE OF PERIODS

The corollary to CUMIPMT is a function to calculate the total principal paid during any range of periods of a loan: CUMPRINC.

SYNTAX: CUMPRINC(*rate*,*nper*,*pv*,*start_period*,*end_period*,*type*)

The CUMPRINC function returns the cumulative principal paid on a loan between *start_period* and *end_period*. This function takes the following arguments:

- *rate*—This is the interest rate.
- *nper*—This is the total number of payment periods.

- *pv*—This is the present value.

- *start_period*—This is the first period in the calculation. Payment periods are numbered beginning with 1.

- *end_period*—This is the last period in the calculation.

- *type*— This is the number 0 or 1 to indicate when payments are due. The default value of 0 assumes that payments are due at the end of the period. A value of 1 means the payments are due at beginning of each period.

**Figure 25.7**
You use Column E to plan your tax deductions by year.

| | E12 | ▾ | fx | =CUMIPMT($B$2/12,$B$3,$B$1,$C12,$D12,0) | | |
|---|---|---|---|---|---|---|
| | A | B | C | D | E | F | G |
| 1 | Mortage Amt. | 225000 | | | | | |
| 2 | Rate | 6% | | | | | |
| 3 | Term | 180 | | | | | |
| 4 | PMT | -1898.7 | Not necessary for the calculation, here FYI | | | | |
| 5 | First Payment | Aug-01 | Cell D12 uses this in =13-MONTH(B5) | | | | |
| 6 | | | | | | | |
| 7 | | E12 | =CUMIPMT($B$2/12,$B$3,$B$1,$C12,$D12,0) | | | | |
| 8 | | F12 | =CUMPRINC($B$2/12,$B$3,$B$1,$C12,$D12,0) | | | | |
| 9 | | | Payment Numbers | | | | |
| 11 | | Year | From | Through | Interest | Principal | |
| 12 | | 2001 | 1 | 5 | -5,586.12 | -3,907.27 | |
| 13 | | 2002 | 6 | 17 | -12,999.39 | -9,784.74 | |
| 14 | | 2003 | 18 | 29 | -12,395.89 | -10,388.24 | |
| 15 | | 2004 | 30 | 41 | -11,755.17 | -11,028.97 | |
| 16 | | 2005 | 42 | 53 | -11,074.92 | -11,709.21 | |

*nper*, *start_period*, *end_period*, and *type* are truncated to integers. If *rate* is less than or equal to 0, *nper* is less than or equal to 0, or *pv* is less than or equal to 0, CUMPRINC returns a #NUM! error. If *start_period* is less than 1, *end_period* is less than 1, or *start_period* is greater than *end_period*, CUMPRINC returns a #NUM! error. If *type* is any number other than 0 or 1, CUMPRINC returns a #NUM! error.

Figure 25.7 shows an example of CUMPRINC.

## USING EFFECT TO CALCULATE THE EFFECT OF COMPOUNDING PERIOD ON INTEREST RATES

Does it really matter if your bank compounds interest daily, monthly, or quarterly? If the numbers are big enough, it can matter. The EFFECT function converts an interest rate to an effective rate, depending on how frequently the bank compounds the interest.

SYNTAX: EFFECT(*nominal_rate*,*npery*)

The EFFECT function returns the effective annual interest rate, given the nominal annual interest rate and the number of compounding periods per year. This function takes the following arguments:

25

- *nominal_rate*—This is the nominal interest rate.
- *npery*—This is the number of compounding periods per year. *npery* is truncated to an integer.

If either argument is nonnumeric, EFFECT returns a #VALUE! error. If *nominal_rate* is less than or equal to 0 or if *npery* is less than 1, EFFECT returns a #NUM! error.

In Figure 25.8, the nominal interest rate is 6%. If the bank compounds interest once per year, the effective interest rate is still 6%, as shown in Cell A5. If interest is compounded monthly, the effective rate increases to 6.17%. Row 9 compares the monthly mortgage payment at the various effective rates. Daily compounding adds about $23 per month to a typical mortgage payment.

**Figure 25.8**
Row 5 shows the effective interest rates for various compounding periods. Row 9 shows the monthly payment difference.

| | D5 | ▾ | $f_x$ =EFFECT($B$1,D4) | | |
|---|---|---|---|---|---|
| | A | B | C | D | E |
| 1 | Interest Rate | 6% | | | |
| 2 | | | | | |
| 3 | Compounding Periods ----> | | | | |
| 4 | 1 | 4 | 12 | 365 | |
| 5 | 0.06 | 0.061364 | 0.061678 | 0.061831 | |
| 6 | | | | =EFFECT($B$1,D4) | |
| 7 | | | | | |
| 8 | Mortgage Payment on 200K loan, 30 years | | | | |
| 9 | $1,199.10 | $1,216.69 | $1,220.76 | $1,222.75 | |
| 10 | | | | | |

## USING NOMINAL TO CONVERT THE EFFECTIVE INTEREST RATE TO A NOMINAL RATE

If you need to compare two investments, one quoting a nominal rate and one quoting an effective rate, you can convert the effective rate to a nominal rate by using NOMINAL

SYNTAX: NOMINAL(*effect_rate*,*npery*)

The NOMINAL function returns the nominal annual interest rate, given the effective rate and the number of compounding periods per year. This function takes the following arguments:

- *effect_rate*—This is the effective interest rate.
- *npery*—This is the number of compounding periods per year.

*npery* is truncated to an integer. If either argument is nonnumeric, NOMINAL returns a #VALUE! error. If *effect_rate* is less than or equal to 0 or if *npery* is less than 1, NOMINAL returns a #NUM! error.

# EXAMPLES OF DEPRECIATION FUNCTIONS

When a company buys a large asset, such as a piece of machinery, accounting rules specify how the asset should be expensed each year. This is called *depreciation*. Excel offers four common methods for calculating depreciation: straight-line, declining-balance, double-declining-balance, and sum-of-years'-digits methods.

The following terms are common to all the depreciation methods:

- **Cost**—This is the initial cost of the asset. For example, the machinery might cost $120,000.

- **Useful life**—This is how long you expect to use the asset. If you think the machinery will be used for 10 years before being replaced, the life is 10 years.

- **Salvage value**—This is the value of the asset at the end of the useful life. Perhaps after 10 years, you can sell the machine to a scrap dealer for $1,000 or to a trade school for $5,000. This is the salvage value.

Figure 25.9 compares the four depreciation methods.

**Figure 25.9**
Columns B through E compare four methods of depreciation.

| | A | B | C | D | E | F | G |
|---|---|---|---|---|---|---|---|
| | | | | | | D6 | =DDB($B$1,$B$2,$B$3,A6) |
| 1 | Cost | 120000 | | | | | |
| 2 | Salvage Value | 20000 | | | | | |
| 3 | Useful Life | 10 years | | | | | |
| 4 | | | | | | | |
| 5 | Year | Straight Line | Declining Balance | Double Declining | Sum of Years Digits | VDB | VDB |
| 6 | 1 | $10,000.00 | $19,680.00 | $24,000.00 | $18,181.82 | $24,000.00 | $24,000.00 |
| 7 | 2 | $10,000.00 | $16,452.48 | $19,200.00 | $16,363.64 | $19,200.00 | $19,200.00 |
| 8 | 3 | $10,000.00 | $13,754.27 | $15,360.00 | $14,545.45 | $15,360.00 | $15,360.00 |
| 9 | 4 | $10,000.00 | $11,498.57 | $12,288.00 | $12,727.27 | $12,288.00 | $12,288.00 |
| 10 | 5 | $10,000.00 | $9,612.81 | $9,830.40 | $10,909.09 | $9,830.40 | $9,830.40 |
| 11 | 6 | $10,000.00 | $8,036.31 | $7,864.32 | $9,090.91 | $7,864.32 | $7,864.32 |
| 12 | 7 | $10,000.00 | $6,718.35 | $6,291.46 | $7,272.73 | $6,291.46 | $6,291.46 |
| 13 | 8 | $10,000.00 | $5,616.54 | $5,033.16 | $5,454.55 | $5,033.16 | $5,033.16 |
| 14 | 9 | $10,000.00 | $4,695.43 | $132.66 | $3,636.36 | $132.66 | $132.66 |
| 15 | 10 | $10,000.00 | $3,925.38 | $0.00 | $1,818.18 | $0.00 | $0.00 |
| 16 | | | | | | | |
| 17 | | B6: =SLN($B$1,$B$2,$B$3) | | | | | |
| 18 | | C6: =DB($B$1,$B$2,$B$3,A6) | | | | | |
| 19 | | D6: =DDB($B$1,$B$2,$B$3,A6) | | | | | |
| 20 | | E6: =SYD($B$1,$B$2,$B$3,A6) | | | | | |
| 21 | | | | | | | |

25

## USING SLN TO CALCULATE STRAIGHT-LINE DEPRECIATION

The straight-line method is the simplest depreciation method. Using this method, the value of the asset is depreciated evenly over the asset's useful life. At the end of the useful life, the item is depreciated on the company's books to the salvage value level.

Syntax: SLN(*cost*,*salvage*,*life*)

The SLN function returns the straight-line depreciation of an asset for one period. This function takes the following arguments:

- *cost*—This is the initial cost of the asset.
- *salvage*—This is the asset's value at the end of the depreciation period (sometimes called the salvage value of the asset).
- *life*—This is the number of periods over which the asset is being depreciated (sometimes called the useful life of the asset).

## Using DB to Calculate Declining-Balance Depreciation

In the declining-balance method, depreciation happens at a constant rate. The advantage of this method is that more depreciation happens in the earlier years, providing a better tax benefit in early years.

Let's look at a simple example. Say that a $100,000 asset is depreciated 20% in Year 1. This results in a $20,000 depreciation expense. After Year 1, the asset would be have a value of $80,000 on the books. In Year 2, the remaining balance of $80,000 is multiplied by the same 20% rate to yield a depreciation of $16,000. The depreciation in Year 3 is 20% of the remaining $64,000, or $12,800.

The trick to this method is figuring out the correct percentage to use for each year. This involves fractional exponents and a little algebra. If you use the DB function, however, you don't have to worry about any of that. Excel calculates this rate, rounded to three decimal places, as the first step in the process. This rounding to three decimal places causes the calculation to be off by a few dollars at the end of the useful life.

For details on special handling of Year 1 and the last year, as well as the algebra behind the rate formula, see Excel Help for this function.

Syntax: DB(*cost*,*salvage*,*life*,*period*,*month*)

The DB function returns the depreciation of an asset for a specified period, using the fixed-declining-balance method. This function takes the following arguments:

- *cost*—This is the initial cost of the asset.
- *salvage*—This is the value at the end of the depreciation period (sometimes called the salvage value of the asset).
- *life*—This is the number of periods over which the asset is being depreciated (sometimes called the useful life of the asset).
- *period*—This is the period for which you want to calculate the depreciation. *period* must use the same units as *life*.
- *month*—This is the number of months in the first year. If *month* is omitted, it is assumed to be 12.

## USING DDB TO CALCULATE DOUBLE-DECLINING-BALANCE DEPRECIATION

The double-declining-balance method is a very aggressive (and legal) method for calculating depreciation. Assume that you purchased a computer. In the first year, the item might be state-of-the-art. By Year 2, it is worth far less because technology would have passed the computer by.

The name of this method reflects the fact that the depreciation rate is double the normal rate but also that the depreciation rate is applied to the declining balance of the asset's value.

If the asset is to be depreciated over five years, the normal straight-line rate would be 20%. In the double-declining-balance method, you get to use 40% in each year. For example, the first year, depreciation on a $100,000 asset would be 40%. But in Year 2, the 40% is multiplied by the remaining asset value of $60,000. This method generates much higher depreciation in the first few years of the asset life than the other methods.

Although the name of this method contains the world *double*, Microsoft covered the possibility of other multipliers. There is a 150DB method that multiplies the rate by 1.5 instead of 2. To calculate 150DB, you use 1.5 as the fourth argument. If no fourth argument is supplied, the fourth argument is assumed to be 2, resulting in DDB.

**NOTE**

> In many depreciation systems, you are allowed to switch from double-declining-balance to the straight-line method when the straight-line method produces a higher depreciation. To do this, you use the VDB function, which is described shortly.

25

SYNTAX: DDB(*cost,salvage,life,period,factor*)

The DDB function returns the depreciation of an asset for a specified period using the double-declining-balance method or some other specified method. This function takes the following arguments:

- *cost*—This is the initial cost of the asset.
- *salvage*—This is the value at the end of the depreciation period.
- *life*—This is the number of periods over which the asset is being depreciated.
- *period*—This is the period for which you want to calculate the depreciation. *period* must use the same units as life.
- *factor*—This is the rate at which the balance declines. If *factor* is omitted, it is assumed to be 2 (the double-declining-balance method).

All five of these arguments must be positive numbers.

In order to allow DDB to work, you need to abandon the method at some point and switch to a straight-line method for the remaining asset value. If you attempt to use DDB for the entire life of the asset, you will not write off enough of the value.

Figure 25.10 illustrates how DDB fails to accumulate $500,000 of depreciation.

**Figure 25.10**
The DDB method fails to accumulate enough depreciation. You might want to use the newer VDB method, which automatically switches for you. Column D shows this method.

| | D6 | ▾ | $f_x$ =VDB($B$1,$B$2,$B$3,$A6-1,$A6,2,FALSE) | | | |
|---|---|---|---|---|---|---|
| ◢ | A | B | C | D | E | F |
| 1 | Cost | 500000 | | | | |
| 2 | Salvage Value | 0 | | | | |
| 3 | Useful Life | 10 | | | | |
| 4 | | | | | | |
| 5 | Year | Straight Line | Double Declining | VDB NoSwitch= FALSE | VDB NoSwitch= TRUE | |
| 6 | 1 | $50,000.00 | $100,000.00 | $100,000.00 | $100,000.00 | |
| 7 | 2 | $50,000.00 | $80,000.00 | $80,000.00 | $80,000.00 | |
| 8 | 3 | $50,000.00 | $64,000.00 | $64,000.00 | $64,000.00 | |
| 9 | 4 | $50,000.00 | $51,200.00 | $51,200.00 | $51,200.00 | |
| 10 | 5 | $50,000.00 | $40,960.00 | $40,960.00 | $40,960.00 | |
| 11 | 6 | $50,000.00 | $32,768.00 | $32,768.00 | $32,768.00 | |
| 12 | 7 | $50,000.00 | $26,214.40 | $32,768.00 | $26,214.40 | |
| 13 | 8 | $50,000.00 | $20,971.52 | $32,768.00 | $20,971.52 | |
| 14 | 9 | $50,000.00 | $16,777.22 | $32,768.00 | $16,777.22 | |
| 15 | 10 | $50,000.00 | $13,421.77 | $32,768.00 | $13,421.77 | |
| 16 | TOTAL | $500,000.00 | $446,312.91 | $500,000.00 | $446,312.91 | |
| 17 | | | | | | |
| 18 | | | B6: =DDB($B$1,$B$2,$B$3,A6) | | | |
| 19 | | | C6: =VDB($B$1,$B$2,$B$3,$A6-1,$A6,2,FALSE) | | | |
| 20 | | | C6 Alt: =VDB($B$1,$B$2,$B$3,$A6-1,$A6) | | | |
| 21 | | | D6: =VDB($B$1,$B$2,$B$3,$A6-1,$A6,2,TRUE) | | | |

To overcome this problem with DDB, you can use the VDB method. The VDB function is a far more powerful function. Using VDB to calculate a double-declining-balance problem correctly is somewhat like using a sledgehammer to push in a thumbtack. VDB is covered in detail later in this chapter, but you can follow these steps to solve the current problem:

1. Change the function name from DDB to VDB.

2. Because both DDB and VDB take the same first three arguments—*cost*, *salvage*, and *life*—leave those three arguments alone.

3. Give DDB a period number. Cell C6 uses the year number from Cell A6 for the period. VDB needs a start period and an end period. For VDB, change A6 to A6-1,A6. This is a bit strange; you are asking VDB to calculate the depreciation from the end of Year 0 to the end of Year 1.

4. Determine whether the DDB function is done. *factor* is assumed to be 2. *factor* is usually left off the function. If DDB has no fourth argument, then VDB does not need a fifth argument.

5. To allow VDB to switch to the straight-line method, ensure that the sixth argument is FALSE. The name of this argument is *no_switch*, so by specifying FALSE, you are

invoking a double negative to ask VDB to switch to the straight-line method when appropriate. Because FALSE is the default, you can often leave off the fifth and sixth arguments with VDB.

Complete details on the more powerful uses of VDB are provided later in this chapter.

## USING SYD TO CALCULATE SUM-OF-YEARS'-DIGITS DEPRECIATION

The sum-of-years'-digits method is another accelerated depreciation system. It ensures that the value of the asset drops more in the earlier years of the asset's life than in later years.

Say that you have an asset with a useful life of seven years. You need to add all the years from seven to one: 7 + 6 + 5 + 4 + 3 + 2 + 1 = 28. In the first year, you can write off 7 / 28 of the value. In the next year, you can write off 6 / 28. In successive years, you can write off 5 / 28, 4 / 28, 3 / 28, 2 / 28, and 1 / 28 of the depreciable value.

SYNTAX: SYD(cost,salvage,life,per)

The SYD function returns the sum-of-years'-digits depreciation of an asset for a specified period. This function takes the following arguments:

- cost—This is the initial cost of the asset.
- salvage—This is the value at the end of the depreciation period (sometimes called the salvage value of the asset).
- life—This is the number of periods over which the asset is being depreciated (sometimes called the useful life of the asset).
- per—This is the period and must use the same units as life.

## USING VDB TO CALCULATE DEPRECIATION FOR ANY PERIOD

As mentioned in the discussion of the DDB function, the VDB function is newer and far more powerful than the other depreciation functions.

It is interesting for tax purposes to know the annual depreciation amounts. However, if you work for a public company, you have to report depreciation at least quarterly. Figure 25.11 shows an example that calculates the exact depreciation to be booked each quarter.

SYNTAX: VDB(cost,salvage,life,start_period,end_period,factor,no_switch)

The VDB function returns the depreciation of an asset for any specified period, including partial periods, using the double-declining-balance method or some other specified method. VDB stands for *variable declining balance*.

The VDB function takes the following arguments:

- cost—This is the initial cost of the asset.
- salvage—This is the value at the end of the depreciation period.

- *life*—This is the number of periods over which the asset is being depreciated. To calculate depreciation for periods smaller than a year, you multiply the number of years by 12 or even 365.

- *start_period*—This is the starting period for which you want to calculate the depreciation. *start_period* must use the same units as *life*.

- *end_period*—This is the ending period for which you want to calculate the depreciation. *end_period* must use the same units as *life*.

- *factor*—This is the rate at which the balance declines. If *factor* is omitted, it is assumed to be 2 (the double-declining-balance method). You change *factor* if you do not want to use the double-declining-balance method.

- *no_switch*—This is a logical value that specifies whether to switch to straight-line depreciation when depreciation is greater than with the declining-balance calculation. If this is FALSE or omitted, Excel switches to the straight-line method when it becomes more beneficial to do so. If this value is TRUE, Excel holds on to the DDB method until the end of *life*.

All these arguments except *no_switch* must be positive numbers.

**Figure 25.11**
VDB allows you to calculate depreciation for each month or quarter.

| | C7 | | $f_x$ =VDB($B$1,$B$2,$B$3*365,$A7-$B$4,$B7-$B$4,2,FALSE) | | | |
|---|---|---|---|---|---|---|
| | A | B | C | D | E | F |
| 1 | Cost | 50000 | | | | |
| 2 | Salvage Value | 5000 | | | | |
| 3 | Useful Life | 7 | | | | |
| 4 | Start Date | 5/1/2007 | | | | |
| 5 | | | | | | |
| 6 | Start Date | End Date | VDB | | | |
| 7 | 5/1/2007 | 6/30/2007 | $2,294.92 | | | |
| 8 | 7/1/2007 | 9/30/2007 | $3,278.63 | | | |
| 9 | 10/1/2007 | 12/31/2007 | $3,050.74 | | | |
| 10 | 1/1/2008 | 3/31/2008 | $2,808.57 | | | |
| 11 | 4/1/2008 | 6/30/2008 | $2,615.40 | | | |
| 12 | 7/1/2008 | 9/30/2008 | $2,461.61 | | | |
| 13 | | | | | | |
| 14 | A7: =B4 | | | | | |
| 15 | B7: =VDB($B$1,$B$2,$B$3*365,$A7-$B$4,$B7-$B$4,2,FALSE) | | | | | |
| 16 | A8: =B7+1 | | | | | |
| 17 | B8: =EOMONTH(A8,2) | | | | | |
| 18 | | | | | | |

To set up a schedule that shows depreciation for each quarter, you follow these steps:

1. Enter the cost, salvage value, and useful life at the top of the worksheet.

2. Enter the date on which the equipment is placed in service in Cell B4.

3. Enter dates for the first quarter in Cells A7 and B7. The value in Cell A7 is the date the unit is placed in service. Manually figure out the last date of the quarter for Cell B7.

4. Ensure that the formula for Columns A and B in each subsequent row is the same. In Cell A8, enter =B7+1. In Cell B8, enter is =EOMONTH(A8,2). The EOMONTH function reports the end of the month that falls two months after what is shown in Cell A8. Copy these formulas down as far as necessary.

5. To build the VDB function, use the normal values for cost and salvage value. Instead of 7 for *life*, use $7 \times 365$ to have the function calculate a daily depreciation rate.

6. For *start_period*, use the date in Column A minus the date in *service*.

7. For *end_period*, use the date in Column B minus the date in *service*.

8. If you are using the double-declining-balance method, omit the fifth and sixth arguments.

9. Copy the VDB function down to all your rows.

The table shown in Figure 25.11 shows the depreciation to be booked each quarter for this particular piece of machinery.

**NOTE**

> If you happen to work for a French-owned company, you need to keep in mind special considerations when calculating depreciation. Read the Help topics for AMORDEGRC and AMORLINC to understand these methods that have been added to Excel to accommodate the French accounting rules.

25

# FUNCTIONS FOR INVESTMENT ANALYSIS

The invention of the computer spreadsheet in 1979 enabled the rapid growth of the mergers and acquisitions business in the 1980s. Business plans can be modeled in Excel, with the resulting series of net income values discounted to determine the current value of a business. Excel offers a wide array of functions that can be used to analyze a business investment

## USING THE NPV FUNCTION TO DETERMINE NET PRESENT VALUE

Let's say that you have a pile of cash. You have the opportunity to invest that cash in a long-term CD that earns 4% interest. You also have the opportunity to use that cash to buy a business. The 4% is called the *hurdle rate*. If the business cannot return more than the 4% hurdle rate, you should probably look for another business.

You've analyzed the business plan and projected that the business will generate a certain series of net income over each of the next five years. You can analyze the net present value of the investment by using the NPV function.

SYNTAX: NPV(*rate,value1,value2,...*)

The NPV function calculates the net present value of an investment by using a discount rate and a series of future payments (negative values) and income (positive values). This function takes the following arguments:

■ *rate*—This is the rate of discount over the length of one period.

■ *value1,value2,...*—These are 1 to 254 arguments representing the payments and income. Instead, you can refer to a range of values. *value1*, *value2*,... must be equally spaced in time and occur at the end of each period. The function uses the order of *value1*, *value2*,... to interpret the order of cash flows. You need to be sure to enter your payment and income values in the correct sequence.

The NPV investment begins one period before the date of the *value1* cash flow and ends with the last cash flow in the list.

Arguments of *value1*, *value2*,... are cash flows at the end of Year 1, Year 2, and so on.

In this example, if you buy a business for $50,000, this amount should not be entered as a value in the function. Instead, you should subtract the $50,000 from the result of NPV.

NPV is similar to the PV function. The primary difference between PV and NPV is that PV allows cash flows to begin either at the end or at the beginning of the period. Unlike the variable NPV cash flow values, PV cash flows must be constant throughout the investment.

NPV is also related to the IRR function. IRR is the rate for which NPV equals zero: NPV(IRR(...), ...) = 0.

In Figure 25.12, the business will cost $50,000. The business will lose $5,000 in Year 1 and then generate $61,000 over the next four years. Based on these cash flows, NPV is negative, meaning that a CD at 4% would provide a better return.

**Figure 25.12**
NPV can analyze a periodic series of cash flows.

| | A | B | C | D | E |
|---|---|---|---|---|---|
| | | B9 | $f_x$ =NPV(B1,B3:B7)+B2 | | |
| 1 | Discount Rate | 4% | | | |
| 2 | Cost of Business: | -50,000 | | | |
| 3 | Return from year 1: | -5,000 | | | |
| 4 | Return from year 2: | 5,000 | | | |
| 5 | Return from year 3: | 12,000 | | | |
| 6 | Return from year 4: | 19,000 | | | |
| 7 | Return from year 5: | 25,000 | | | |
| 8 | | | | | |
| 9 | NPV | -2,727 | | | |
| 10 | | | | | |
| 11 | B9: =NPV(B1,B3:B7)+B2 | | | | |
| 12 | | | | | |
| 13 | Internal Rates of Return: | | | | |
| 14 | After 2 years: | -72.98% | =IRR(B$2:B4,-0.5) | | |
| 15 | After 3 years: | -35.93% | =IRR(B$2:B5,0.01) | | |
| 16 | After 4 years: | -11.97% | =IRR(B$2:B6) | | |
| 17 | After 5 years: | 2.66% | =IRR(B$2:B7) | | |
| 18 | | | | | |

N O T E

> NPV requires the cash flows to occur at a regular rate. If you instead have a series of projected cash flows on varying dates, you should use XNPV instead. See the section "Using XNPV to Calculate the Net Present Value When the Payments Are Not Periodic," later in this chapter.

## USING IRR TO CALCULATE THE RETURN OF A SERIES OF CASH FLOWS

In the previous section, you used the NPV function to determine whether a business investment met or did not meet a certain desired rate of return. In Figure 25.12, NPV is negative, indicating that the business was not able to produce a 4% return after five years. If you actually want to figure out the internal rate of return, you use the IRR function.

There is one critical difference between IRR and NPV: In the NPV function, the initial investment in the business is *not* included in the list of arguments. In the IRR function, the initial investment in the business needs to be included as the first cash flow. Because this is money paid for the business, it should be negative.

SYNTAX: IRR(*values*,*guess*)

The IRR function returns the internal rate of return for a series of cash flows, represented by the numbers in *values*. These cash flows do not have to be even, as they would be for an annuity. However, the cash flows must occur at regular intervals, such as monthly or annually. The internal rate of return is the interest rate received for an investment, consisting of payments (negative values) and income (positive values) that occur at regular periods.

The IRR function takes the following arguments:

- *values*—This is an array or a reference to cells that contain numbers for which you want to calculate the internal rate of return. *values* must contain at least one positive value and one negative value to calculate the internal rate of return. IRR uses the order of *values* to interpret the order of cash flows. You need to be sure to enter your payment and income values in the sequence you want. If an array or a reference argument contains text, logical values, or empty cells, those values are ignored.

- *guess*—This is a number that you guess is close to the result of IRR. Microsoft Excel uses an iterative technique for calculating IRR. Starting with guess, IRR cycles through the calculation until the result is accurate within 0.00001%. If IRR can't find a result that works after 20 tries, a #NUM! error is returned. In most cases, you do not need to provide guess for the IRR calculation. If guess is omitted, it is assumed to be 0.1 (that is, 10%). If IRR gives a #NUM! error, or if the result is not close to what you expected, you can try again with a different value for guess.

IRR is closely related to NPV, the net present value function. The rate of return calculated by IRR is the interest rate corresponding to a net present value of zero. The following formula demonstrates how NPV and IRR are related: Enter = NPV(IRR(B1:B6),B1:B6) in a cell. This equals 3.60E-08 Within the accuracy of the IRR calculation, the value 3.60E-08 is effectively zero.

25

In Figure 25.12, the formula in Cell B17 shows that the business investment would generate a rate of return of 2.7% if analyzed over a five-year period. The arguments for this function include the initial $50,000 investment in the business as well as the net incomes from the next five years.

Similar formulas in Cells B14 and B15 return a #NUM! error. The formulas were edited to add a *guess* value. Based on the –12% return through four years, *guess* for three years was –10%.

NOTE

> IRR fails to take into account that the money earned in Year 1 could start generating interest if invested in a CD. To calculate a rate of return including the reinvestment of profits, you use MIRR, which is described in the following section.

## USING MIRR TO CALCULATE INTERNAL RATE OF RETURN, INCLUDING INTEREST RATES

MIRR calculates a modified internal rate of return. This function assumes that cash flows from the business are reinvested at some interest rate. It also offers an argument to specify the initial interest rate of the business loan used to purchase the business.

SYNTAX: MIRR(*values*,*finance_rate*,*reinvest_rate*)

The MIRR function returns the modified internal rate of return for a series of periodic cash flows. MIRR considers both the cost of the investment and the interest received on reinvestment of cash. This function takes the following arguments:

- *values*—This is an array or a reference to cells that contain numbers. These numbers represent a series of payments (negative values) and income (positive values) occurring at regular periods. *values* must contain at least one positive value and one negative value to calculate the modified internal rate of return. Otherwise, MIRR returns a #DIV/0! error. If an array or a reference argument contains text, logical values, or empty cells, those values are ignored; however, cells with the value 0 are included.
- *finance_rate*—This is the interest rate you pay on the money used in the cash flows.
- *reinvest_rate*—This is the interest rate you receive on the cash flows as you reinvest them.

MIRR uses the order of values to interpret the order of cash flows. You need to be sure to enter your payment and income values in the sequence you want and with the correct signs (that is, positive values for cash received, negative values for cash paid).

In Figure 25.13, you are analyzing a business that was started five years ago with a $120,000 loan. The business has generated profits of $17,000, $34,000, $38,000, $5,000, and $32,000. The original loan had an interest rate of 5%, and the profits were reinvested at 6%. The MIRR in Cell B10 is 3.4%. For comparison, the IRR of the same cash flows would be only 1.64%.

**Figure 25.13**
You can determine a modified rate of return, figuring in a financing rate and the interest rate for reinvested profits.

| | A | B | C | D |
|---|---|---|---|---|
| B10 | ▼ | *fx* =MIRR(B1:B6,B7,B8) | | |
| 1 | Cost of Business: | ($120,000) | | |
| 2 | Return first year | 17,000 | | |
| 3 | Return second year | 34,000 | | |
| 4 | Return third year | 38,000 | | |
| 5 | Return fourth year | 5,000 | | |
| 6 | Return fifth year | 32,000 | | |
| 7 | Int. rate for $120K Loan | 5.00% | | |
| 8 | Int. rate for reinvested profits | 6.00% | | |
| 9 | | | | |
| 10 | **MIRR** | **3.4%** =MIRR(B1:B6,B7,B8) | | |
| 11 | | | | |

## USING XNPV TO CALCULATE THE NET PRESENT VALUE WHEN THE PAYMENTS ARE NOT PERIODIC

The previous examples assume that everything happens on the last day of each year. In reality, the business purchase date and the business sales date might occur on other days. In such a case, you use XNPV.

SYNTAX: XNPV(*rate*,*values*,*dates*)

The XNPV function returns the net present value for a schedule of cash flows that is not necessarily periodic. To calculate the net present value for a series of cash flows that is periodic, you use the NPV function. The XNPV function takes the following arguments:

- *rate*—This is the discount rate to apply to the cash flows.
- *values*—This is a series of cash flows that corresponds to a schedule of payments in *dates*. The first payment is optional and corresponds to a cost or payment that occurs at the beginning of the investment. If the first value is a cost or payment, it must be a negative value. All succeeding payments are discounted based on a 365-day year. The series of values must contain at least one positive value and one negative value.
- *dates*—This is a schedule of payment dates that corresponds to the cash flow payments. The first payment date indicates the beginning of the schedule of payments. All other dates must be later than this date, but they may occur in any order. Only dates are considered; any times appended to the dates are truncated.

If any argument is nonnumeric, XNPV returns a #VALUE! error. If any number in *dates* is not a valid date, XNPV returns a #NUM! error. If any number in *dates* precedes the starting date, XNPV returns a #NUM! error. If *values* and *dates* contain different numbers of values, XNPV returns a #NUM! error.

In Figure 25.14, the company was bought on March 15, 2001. The company posted no net profit in 2002. The company was sold in February 2006. The XNPV function in Row 9 shows that this deal clearly beat the 4% hurdle rate.

25

**Figure 25.14**
XNPV takes into account a series of cash flows on a series of dates. The dates don't have to have identical periods, as in NPV.

| | B9 | ▼ | $f_x$ =XNPV(B1,B2:B7,A2:A7) | | | |
|---|---|---|---|---|---|---|
| | A | | B | C | D | E |
| 1 | Discount Rate | | 4% | | | |
| 2 | | 3/15/2001 | -50,000 | Buy the business | | |
| 3 | | 12/31/2001 | -5,000 | Loss in year 1 | | |
| 4 | | 12/31/2003 | 5,000 | profit in year 3 | | |
| 5 | | 12/31/2004 | 12,000 | more profit in year 4 | | |
| 6 | | 12/31/2005 | 19,000 | profit in year 5 | | |
| 7 | | 2/17/2006 | 242,000 | sell the business | | |
| 8 | | | | | | |
| 9 | XNPV | | 175,154 | =XNPV(B1,B2:B7,A2:A7) | | |
| 10 | | | | | | |
| 11 | XIRR | | 40.71% | =XIRR(B2:B7,A2:A7) | | |
| 12 | | | | | | |

## USING XIRR TO CALCULATE A RETURN RATE WHEN CASH FLOW DATES ARE NOT PERIODIC

As in the XNPV example, you can calculate an internal rate of return for a business deal where the dates don't necessarily fall on the last day of the year. To do so, you use XIRR, an example of which is shown at the bottom of Figure 25.14.

SYNTAX: XIRR(*values*,*dates*,*guess*)

The XIRR function returns the internal rate of return for a schedule of cash flows that is not necessarily periodic. To calculate the internal rate of return for a series of periodic cash flows, you use the IRR function. This function takes the following arguments:

- *values*—This is a series of cash flows that corresponds to a schedule of payments in *dates*. The first payment is optional and corresponds to a cost or payment that occurs at the beginning of the investment. If the first value is a cost or payment, it must be a negative value. All succeeding payments are discounted based on a 365-day year. The series of values must contain at least one positive and one negative value.

- *dates*—This is a schedule of payment dates that corresponds to the cash flow payments. The first payment date indicates the beginning of the schedule of payments. All other dates must be later than this date, but they may occur in any order.

- *guess*—This is a number that you guess is close to the result of XIRR.

Numbers in *dates* are truncated to integers. XIRR expects at least one positive cash flow and one negative cash flow; otherwise, XIRR returns a #NUM! error. If any number in *dates* is not a valid date, XIRR returns a #NUM! error. If any number in *dates* precedes the starting date, XIRR returns a #NUM! error. If *values* and *dates* contain different numbers of values, XIRR returns a #NUM! error. In most cases, you do not need to provide *guess* for the XIRR calculation. If it is omitted, *guess* is assumed to be 0.1 (that is, 10%).

XIRR is closely related to XNPV, the net present value function. The rate of return calculated by XIRR is the interest rate corresponding to XNPV = 0.

# EXAMPLES OF FUNCTIONS FOR BOND INVESTORS

A bond is an I.O.U. You lend an amount to the issuer. The issuer pays you periodic interest payments and at the maturity date of the bond returns your money. Various governments issue many bonds. Bond maturities can extend anywhere from 1 day to 30 years. Many concepts and terms apply to the bond functions.

For the following discussion, let's assume that a city issues a 30-year municipal bond. The bond is issued on July 1, 2007. The bond's maturity date is June 30, 2037. The city agrees to pay 5% interest semiannually.

Here is what makes bonds interesting: They can be bought and sold after the issue date. Say that 14 months have gone past. Interest rates have now risen. The bond is going to keep paying 5% interest for the next 30 years. If interest rates have moved above 5%, then a potential buyer of the bond will not want to pay $1,000 for the bond. Instead, they buyer might pay $950. Thus, there is a price paid for the bond, and there is a value of the bond at maturity.

Many bond functions ask for these arguments:

- *settlement*—This is the day that the buyer purchases the bond. It might be the issue date but is usually after the issue date. In the preceding example, the settlement date is September 1, 2008.

- *maturity*—This is the day that the issuer will pay the face value of the bond. In the preceding example, the maturity date is June 30, 2037.

- *rate*—This is the published coupon rate for the bond. In the preceding example, it is 5%.

- *pr*—This is the price that the current buyer paid for the bond. If the bond was purchased on the issue date, the price matches the face value of the bond. If it was purchased on a later date, the price is higher or lower than the face value, depending on whether interest rates go up or down. (If interest rates go up, bond prices go down. If interest rates go down, bond prices go up). *pr* is expressed as the price per $100 of face value. If you buy a $1,000 face-value bond for $950, the price is $95 per $100, so you enter 95 for the *price* argument.

- *redemtion*—This is the value of the bond on the maturity date. It is the amount the issuer will pay back to the holder of the bond. The price is expressed as the price per $100 of face value. If you buy a $1,000 face-value bond that will pay $1,000 at maturity, you enter 100 for the *redemption* argument.

- *frequency*—This is the number of interest payments per year. For semiannual interest payments, you enter 2. For quarterly payments, you enter 4. For annual payments, you enter 1. In Excel, these are the only three *frequency* values allowed.

- *basis*—This is a code used to identify the number of days in a year. The values are the same as those available in the YEARFRAC function. See the discussion of YEARFRAC in Chapter 23, "Using Everyday Functions: Math, Date and Time, and Text Functions." For most U.S. bonds, *basis* is 0 to indicate a 30/360 NASD calendar. For European bonds, consult Excel Help for the YIELD function.

25

## USING YIELD TO CALCULATE A BOND'S YIELD

A $1,000 bond might promise to pay 5% interest. However, if you buy the bond on the secondary market for $95, the actual yield will not be 5%. As you are trying to compare various investments, comparing the yield is one way to decide between multiple investment opportunities. To do this, you can use Excel's YIELD function.

**Figure 25.15**
You use YIELD to calculate the yield rate for a bond. In these examples, the price in Row 4 changes.

| | B9 | ▾ | ƒx =YIELD(B1,B2,B3,B4,B5,B6,B7) | | |
|---|---|---|---|---|---|
| ◢ | A | B | C | D | E |
| 1 | Settlement date | 1-Sep-08 | 1-Sep-08 | 1-Sep-08 | |
| 2 | Maturity date | 30-Jun-37 | 30-Jun-37 | 30-Jun-37 | |
| 3 | Percent coupon | 5.00% | 5.00% | 5.00% | |
| 4 | Price | $95 | $93 | $105 | |
| 5 | Redemption value | $100 | $100 | $100 | |
| 6 | Frequency | 2 | 2 | 2 | |
| 7 | 30/360 basis | 0 | 0 | 0 | |
| 8 | | | | | |
| 9 | **Yield** | **5.34%** | **5.49%** | **4.68%** | |
| 10 | | | | | |

SYNTAX: YIELD(*settlement*,*maturity*,*rate*,*pr*,*redemption*,*frequency*,*basis*)

The YIELD function returns the yield on a security that pays periodic interest. You use YIELD to calculate bond yield. This function takes the following arguments:

- *settlement*—This is the security's settlement date. The security settlement date is the date after the issue date when the security is traded to the buyer. Dates may be entered as text strings within quotation marks (for example, "1/30/1998", "1998/01/30"), as serial numbers (for example, 39156, which represents March 15, 2007), or as results of other formulas or functions (for example, DATE(2007,3,15)).

- *maturity*—This is the security's maturity date. The maturity date is the date when the security expires.

- *rate*—This is the security's annual coupon rate.

- *pr*—This is the security's price per $100 face value.

- *redemption*—This is the security's redemption value per $100 face value.

- *frequency*—This is the number of coupon payments per year. For annual payments, *frequency* is 1; for semiannual, *frequency* is 2; and for quarterly, *frequency* is 4.

- *basis*—This is the type of day count basis to use. It defaults to 0, which is appropriate for U.S. bonds.

*settlement*, *maturity*, *frequency*, and *basis* are truncated to integers. If *settlement* or *maturity* is not a valid date, YIELD returns a #NUM! error. If *rate* is less than 0, YIELD returns a #NUM! error. If *pr* is less than or equal to 0 or if *redemption* is less than or equal to 0, YIELD returns a #NUM! error. If *frequency* is any number other than 1, 2, or 4, YIELD returns a #NUM!

error. If *basis* is less than 0 or if *basis* is greater than 4, YIELD returns a #NUM! error. If *settlement* is greater than or equal to *maturity*, YIELD returns a #NUM! error.

Figure 25.15 shows an example of YIELD.

## USING PRICE TO BACK INTO A BOND PRICE

If you know the yield for a bond, you can use PRICE to calculate the price per $100 of face value.

SYNTAX: PRICE(*settlement*,*maturity*,*rate*,*yld*,*redemption*,*frequency*,*basis*)

The PRICE function returns the price per $100 face value of a security that pays periodic interest. This function takes the following arguments:

- *settlement*—This is the security's settlement date. This is the date on which you purchased the bond.
- *maturity*—This is the security's maturity date. The maturity date is the date when the security expires.
- *rate*—This is the security's annual coupon rate.
- *yld*—This is the security's annual yield.
- *redemption*—This is the security's redemption value per $100 face value.
- *frequency*—This is the number of coupon payments per year. You use 2 for semiannual.
- *basis*—This is the type of day count basis to use. You use 0 for U.S. bonds.

*settlement*, *maturity*, *frequency*, and *basis* are truncated to integers. If *settlement* or *maturity* is not a valid date, PRICE returns a #NUM! error. If *yld* is less than 0 or if *rate* is less than 0, PRICE returns a #NUM! error. If *redemption* is less than or equal to 0, PRICE returns a #NUM! error. If *frequency* is any number other than 1, 2, or 4, PRICE returns a #NUM! error. If *basis* is less than 0 or if *basis* is greater than 4, PRICE returns a #NUM! error. If *settlement* is greater than or equal to *maturity*, PRICE returns a #NUM! error.

In Figure 25.16, the yield for the bond exceeds the coupon rate. This indicates that the price will be less than $100.

When a bond is sold on the secondary market, it is often sold in between interest payments. Each interest payment date is called a *coupon date*. You analyze days until the next coupon date by using the COUP functions.

A whole series of COUP functions analyze the coupon period. The functions can tell you the previous coupon date, the next coupon date, how many days since the previous coupon date, and how many days until the next coupon date:

- COUPDAYS—This returns the number of days in this coupon period.
- COUPDAYBS—This returns the number of days from the beginning of the coupon period until the settlement date. The BS in the function name stands for from *beginning to settlement*.

25

- COUPDAYSNC—This returns the number of days from the settlement until the next coupon date. NC stands for *next coupon*.
- COUPPCD—This returns the date of the previous coupon date.
- COUPNCD—This returns the date of the next coupon date.
- COUPNUM—This returns the number of coupon dates left until maturity.

**Figure 25.16**
If you know the yield, you can back into the price by using the PRICE function.

| | A | B | C |
|---|---|---|---|
| | B9 | =PRICE(B1,B2,B3,B4,B5,B6,B7) | |
| 1 | Settlement date | 1-Sep-08 | |
| 2 | Maturity date | 30-Jun-37 | |
| 3 | Percent coupon | 5.00% | |
| 4 | Percent Yield | 5.34% | |
| 5 | Redemption value | $100 | |
| 6 | Frequency | 2 | |
| 7 | 30/360 basis | 0 | |
| 8 | | | |
| 9 | Price | $ 95.02 | |
| 10 | | | |

All the COUP functions require the same four arguments: settlement, maturity, frequency, and basis. For an explanation of these arguments, see the sections on YIELD and PRICE.

Figure 25.17 shows these coupon functions for a particular security.

**Figure 25.17**
You can analyze what portion of a coupon period has gone past at the settlement date for the bond.

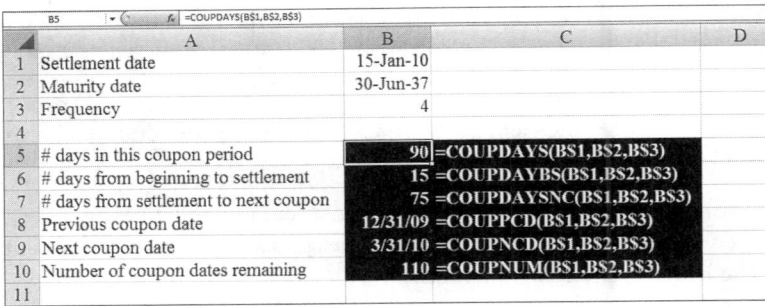

| | A | B | C | D |
|---|---|---|---|---|
| | B5 | =COUPDAYS(B$1,B$2,B$3) | | |
| 1 | Settlement date | 15-Jan-10 | | |
| 2 | Maturity date | 30-Jun-37 | | |
| 3 | Frequency | 4 | | |
| 4 | | | | |
| 5 | # days in this coupon period | 90 | =COUPDAYS(B$1,B$2,B$3) | |
| 6 | # days from beginning to settlement | 15 | =COUPDAYBS(B$1,B$2,B$3) | |
| 7 | # days from settlement to next coupon | 75 | =COUPDAYSNC(B$1,B$2,B$3) | |
| 8 | Previous coupon date | 12/31/09 | =COUPPCD(B$1,B$2,B$3) | |
| 9 | Next coupon date | 3/31/10 | =COUPNCD(B$1,B$2,B$3) | |
| 10 | Number of coupon dates remaining | 110 | =COUPNUM(B$1,B$2,B$3) | |
| 11 | | | | |

## USING RECEIVED TO CALCULATE TOTAL CASH GENERATED FROM A BOND INVESTMENT

When you buy a bond, your settlement date is probably between two coupon dates. Unless you are buying the bond on the issue date, you receive less than the complete number of interest payments. To calculate the total future cash flows from a bond from the day you buy it until the maturity date, you use the RECEIVED function.

SYNTAX: RECEIVED(*settlement*,*maturity*,*investment*,*discount*,*basis*)

The RECEIVED function returns the amount received at maturity for a fully invested security. This function takes the following arguments:

- *settlement*—This is the security's settlement date. This is the date on which you purchased the security.

- *maturity*—This is the security's maturity date. The maturity date is the date when the security expires.

- *investment*—This is the amount invested in the security.

- *discount*—This is the security's discount rate.

- *basis*—This is the type of day count basis to use. You use 0 for U.S. bonds.

*settlement*, *maturity*, and *basis* are truncated to integers. If *settlement* or *maturity* is not a valid date, RECEIVED returns a #NUM! error. If *investment* is less than or equal to 0 or if *discount* is less than or equal to 0, RECEIVED returns a #NUM! error. If *basis* is less than 0 or if *basis* is greater than or equal to 4, RECEIVED returns a #NUM! error. If *settlement* is greater than or equal to *maturity*, RECEIVED returns a #NUM! error.

In Figure 25.18, Columns B, C, and D show the total received for a bond purchased on various dates. The function takes into account the days to the next coupon date.

**Figure 25.18**
In the 15 days between Cells B1 and C1, you lose $4 in interest.

| | B7 | ▾ | *f*x | =RECEIVED(B1,B2,B3,B4,B5) | |
|---|---|---|---|---|---|
| | A | B | C | D | E |
| 1 | Settlement Date | 1-Mar-07 | 15-Mar-07 | 18-Jul-07 | |
| 2 | Maturity Date | 15-Jun-15 | 15-Jun-15 | 15-Jun-15 | |
| 3 | Investment | 1,000 | 1,000 | 1,000 | |
| 4 | Discount Rate | 4.50% | 4.50% | 4.50% | |
| 5 | Actual/360 basis | 0 | 0 | 0 | |
| 6 | | | | | |
| 7 | RECEIVED | $ 1,594.90 | $ 1,590.46 | $ 1,552.49 | |
| 8 | | | | | |

## USING INTRATE TO BACK INTO THE COUPON INTEREST RATE

If you have a fully invested bond and know what it will pay on maturity, you can use Excel's INTRATE function to back into the interest rate.

SYNTAX: INTRATE(*settlement*,*maturity*,*investment*,*redemption*,*basis*)

The INTRATE function returns the interest rate for a fully invested security. This function takes the following arguments:

- *settlement*—This is the security's settlement date.

- *maturity*—This is the security's maturity date.

- *investment*—This is the amount invested in the security.
- *redemption*—This is the amount to be received at maturity.
- *basis*—This is the type of day count basis to use. You use 0 for U.S. bonds.

*settlement*, *maturity*, and *basis* are truncated to integers. If *settlement* or *maturity* is not a valid date, INTRATE returns a #NUM! error. If *investment* is less than or equal to 0 or if *redemption* is less than or equal to 0, INTRATE returns a #NUM! error. If *basis* is less than 0 or if *basis* is greater than 4, INTRATE returns a #NUM! error. If *settlement* is greater than or equal to *maturity*, INTRATE returns a #NUM! error.

INTRATE calculates (Redemption value – Investment) / Investment and multiplies this by (Number of days in year / Days from settlement to maturity).

In Figure 25.19, Excel uses INTRATE to back into the interest rate that the bond is paying.

**Figure 25.19**
The INTRATE function can be used to derive the underlying interest rate for the bond.

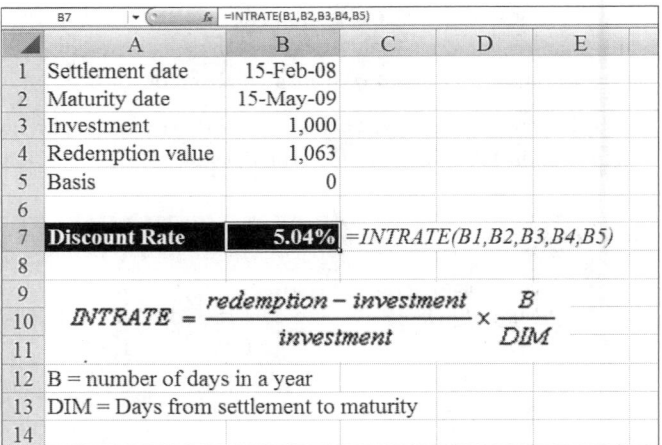

## USING DISC TO BACK INTO THE DISCOUNT RATE

If you have a security and know the price, you can back into the discount rate by using DISC.

SYNTAX: *DISC(settlement,maturity,pr,redemption,basis)*

The DISC function returns the discount rate for a security. It takes the following arguments:

- *settlement*—This is the security's settlement date.
- *maturity*—This is the security's maturity date. The maturity date is the date when the security expires.
- *pr*—This is the security's price per $100 face value.
- *redemption*—This is the security's redemption value per $100 face value.
- *basis*—This is the day count basis. You use 0 for U.S. bonds.

*settlement*, *maturity*, and *basis* are truncated to integers. If *settlement* or *maturity* is not a valid date, DISC returns a #NUM! error. If *pr* is less than or equal to 0 or if *redemption* is less than or equal to 0, DISC returns a #NUM! error. If *basis* is less than 0 or if *basis* is greater than 4, DISC returns a #NUM! error. If *settlement* is greater than or equal to *maturity*, DISC returns a #NUM! error.

DISC calculates (Redemption value – Par value) / Par value and multiplies this by (Number of days in year / Days from settlement to maturity).

In Figure 25.20, Excel uses DISC to back into the discount rate.

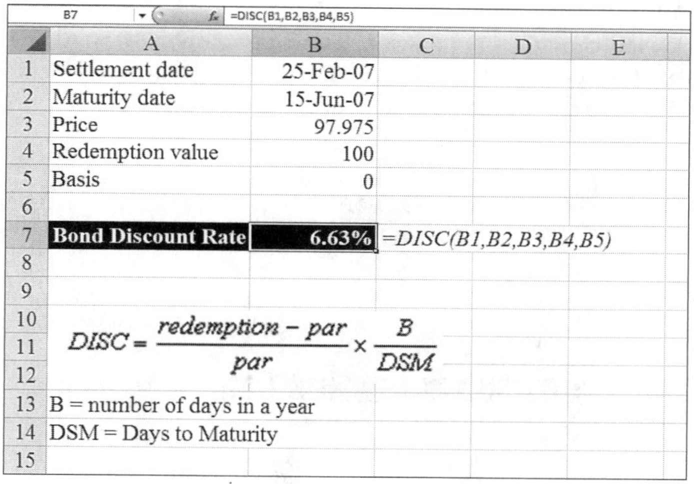

**Figure 25.20**
The DISC function can be used to derive the underlying discount rate for a bond.

HANDLING BONDS WITH AN ODD NUMBER OF DAYS IN THE FIRST OR LAST PERIOD

Excel provides four functions—ODDFPRICE, ODDFYIELD, ODDLPRICE, and ODDLYIELD—to handle the special case in which a bond has a short or long first or last period. This period has more or fewer days than all the other periods and is called an *odd period*. For an explanation of the arguments to these functions, see the information on the PRICE and YIELD functions, earlier in this chapter.

SYNTAX: ODDFPRICE(*settlement*,*maturity*,*issue*,*first_coupon*,*rate*,*yld*,*redemption*, *frequency*,*basis*) AND ODDFYIELD(*settlement*,*maturity*,*issue*,*first_coupon*,*rate*,*pr*, *redemption*,*frequency*,*basis*)

The ODDF functions handle cases in which the first period has an odd number of days. These are ODDFPRICE and ODDFYIELD. Each function has the extra argument *first_coupon*, which specifies the date for the odd first period.

SYNTAX: ODDLPRICE(*settlement,maturity,last_interest,rate,yld,redemption, frequency,basis*) AND ODDLYIELD(*settlement,maturity,last_interest,rate,pr, redemption,frequency,basis*)

The ODDL functions handle cases in which the last period has an odd number of days. These are ODDLPRICE and ODDLYIELD. These functions have the extra argument *last_interest*, which is the date of the final interest payment before maturity. Using this date, Excel can determine the length of the time for the last period.

## USING PRICEMAT AND YIELDMAT TO CALCULATE PRICE AND YIELD FOR ZERO-COUPON BONDS

A zero-coupon bond does not pay interest on the coupon dates. All interest is paid at maturity. Excel provides PRICEMAT and YIELDMAT to calculate price and yield for these securities. Figure 25.21 illustrates both of these functions.

**Figure 25.21**
YIELDMAT and PRICEMAT calculate bonds for which the interest is not paid until maturity.

| | B8 | ▼ | *fx* | =PRICEMAT(B1,B2,B3,B4,B5,B6) | | |
|---|---|---|---|---|---|---|
| | A | B | C | D | E | F |
| 1 | Settlement date | 15-Feb-08 | | | | |
| 2 | Maturity date | 13-Apr-08 | | | | |
| 3 | Issue date | 11-Nov-07 | | | | |
| 4 | Percent semiannual coupon | 6.10% | | | | |
| 5 | Percent yield | 6.10% | | | | |
| 6 | 30/360 basis | 0 | | | | |
| 7 | | | | | | |
| 8 | **PRICEMAT** | **99.9844989** | =PRICEMAT(B1,B2,B3,B4,B5,B6) | | | |
| 9 | | | | | | |
| 10 | Settlement date | 15-Feb-08 | | | | |
| 11 | Maturity date | 13-Apr-08 | | | | |
| 12 | Issue date | 11-Nov-07 | | | | |
| 13 | Percent semiannual coupon | 6.10% | | | | |
| 14 | Price | 100.0123 | | | | |
| 15 | 30/360 basis | 0 | | | | |
| 16 | | | | | | |
| 17 | **YIELDMAT** | **5.93%** | =YIELDMAT(B10,B11,B12,B13,B14,B15) | | | |
| 18 | | | | | | |

SYNTAX: PRICEMAT(*settlement_date,maturity_date,issue_date, rate_at_date_of_issue,annual_yield,day_basis*)

The PRICEMAT function returns the price per $100 face value of a security that pays interest at maturity.

SYNTAX: YIELDMAT(*settlement_date,maturity_date,issue_date, rate_at_date_of_issue,=price_per_$100_of_face_value,day_basis*)

The YIELDMAT function returns the annual yield of a security that pays interest at maturity.

## USING PRICEDISC AND YIELDDISC TO CALCULATE DISCOUNT BONDS

Excel provides PRICEDISC and YIELDDISC for calculating discounted bonds. Figure 25.22 illustrates these functions.

**Figure 25.22**
YIELDDISC and PRICEDISC calculate discounted bonds.

| | B8 | fx =PRICEDISC(B2,B3,B4,B5,B6) | |
|---|---|---|---|
| | A | B | C |
| 1 | **Description** | **Data** | |
| 2 | Settlement date | 16-Feb-08 | |
| 3 | Maturity date | 1-Mar-08 | |
| 4 | Percent discount rate | 5.25% | |
| 5 | Redemption value | $100 | |
| 6 | Day Basis | 0 | |
| 7 | | | |
| 8 | **Bond Price** | **99.78125** | =PRICEDISC(B2,B3,B4,B5,B6) |
| 9 | | | |
| 10 | Settlement date | 16-Feb-08 | |
| 11 | Maturity date | 1-Mar-08 | |
| 12 | Price | 99.78125 | |
| 13 | Redemption value | $100 | |
| 14 | Actual/360 basis | 0 | |
| 15 | | | |
| 16 | **YIELDDISC** | **5.26%** | =YIELDDISC(B10,B11,B12,B13,B14) |
| 17 | | | |

SYNTAX: PRICEDISC(*settlement_date,maturity_date,discount_rate, redemption_value_per_$100,day_basis*)

The PRICEDISC function returns the price per $100 face value of a discounted security.

SYNTAX: YIELDDISC(*settlement_date,maturity_date,price_per_$100_face_value, redemption_value_per_$100_of_face_value,day_basis*)

The YIELDDISC function returns the annual yield for a discounted security.

## CALCULATING T-BILLS

Treasury bills (T-bills) are a popular short-term investment. Backed by the U.S. government, they are considered one of the safest investments, although they offer a slightly lower interest rate than other types of investments.

The Federal Reserve uses a strange method for advertising the yield on T-bills: The Fed compares the total interest to the final value paid on maturity. This is backward from every other bond yield.

For example, say that you pay $98.7 for a T-bill that will pay $100 on maturity 13 weeks later. The Fed expresses the yield by comparing the $1.30 in interest to the $100 final value. Every other bond yield compares the $1.30 in interest to the $98.70 invested.

The Excel TBILL functions allow you to easily compare T-bills and regular bonds. Figure 25.23 illustrates the three T-bill functions.

**Figure 25.23**

TBILLEQ and the other TBILL functions deal with the irregularities of T-bill investing.

| | A | B | C | D |
|---|---|---|---|---|
| | B5 | ▾ | $f_x$ =TBILLEQ(B1,B2,B3) | |
| 1 | Settlement date | 31-Mar-08 | | |
| 2 | Maturity date | 1-Jun-08 | | |
| 3 | Percent discount rate | 9.14% | | |
| 4 | | | | |
| 5 | **Bond Equivalent Yield** | **9.42%** | =TBILLEQ(B1,B2,B3) | |
| 6 | | | | |
| 7 | Settlement date | 31-Mar-08 | | |
| 8 | Maturity date | 1-Jun-08 | | |
| 9 | Percent discount rate | 9% | | |
| 10 | | | | |
| 11 | **T-Bill Price** | **98.45** | =TBILLPRICE(B7,B8,B9) | |
| 12 | | | | |
| 13 | Settlement date | 31-Mar-08 | | |
| 14 | Maturity date | 1-Jun-08 | | |
| 15 | Price per $100 face value | 98.45 | | |
| 16 | | | | |
| 17 | **T-Bill Yield** | **9.14%** | =TBILLYIELD(B13,B14,B15) | |
| 18 | | | | |

SYNTAX: TBILLEQ(*settlement_date,maturity_date,discount_rate*)

The TBILLEQ function returns the bond-equivalent yield for a T-bill.

SYNTAX: TBILLPRICE(*settlement_date,maturity_date,discount_rate*)

The TBILLPRICE function returns the price per $100 face value for a T-bill.

SYNTAX: TBILLYIELD(*settlement_date,maturity_date,price_per_$100_face_value*)

The TBILLYIELD function returns the yield for a T-bill.

## USING ACCRINT OR ACCINTM TO CALCULATE ACCRUED INTEREST

If you are the original buyer of a bond and you buy that bond after the issue date, the bond will have earned some accrued interest during that gap. As the original buyer of the bond, you generally pay this interest back to the issuer when you take possession of the bond. This basically simplifies accounting for the issuer, which can issue identical payments at the next coupon date without having to worry about dozens of different settlement dates.

The ACCINT function calculates this accrued interest.

SYNTAX: ACCRINT(*issue,first_interest,settlement,rate,par,frequency,basis*)

The ACCRINT function returns the accrued interest for a security that pays periodic interest. This function takes the following arguments:

- *issue*—This is the security's issue date.
- *first_interest*—This is the security's first interest date.
- *settlement*—This is the security's settlement date. The security settlement date is the date after the issue date when the security is traded to the buyer. The ACCRINT function calculates the interest that would have been earned between the issue date and the settlement date.
- *rate*—This is the security's annual coupon rate.
- *par*—This is the security's par value. If you omit *par*, ACCRINT uses $1,000.
- *frequency*—This is the number of coupon payments per year.
- *basis*—This is the type of day count basis to use. You use 0 for U.S. bonds

If *issue* is greater than or equal to *settlement*, ACCRINT returns a #NUM! error.

Figure 25.24 demonstrates how the accrued interest changes when the gap between the issue date and settlement date extends.

**Figure 25.24**
As the original buyer of the bond, you owe the accrued interest to the issuer.

| | A | B | C | D | E | F |
|---|---|---|---|---|---|---|
| | B9 | | *fx* =ACCRINT(B1,B2,B3,B4,B5,B6,B7) | | | |
| 1 | Issue date | 1-Apr-08 | 1-Apr-08 | 1-Apr-08 | 1-Apr-08 | 1-Apr-08 |
| 2 | First interest date | 31-Aug-08 | 31-Aug-08 | 31-Aug-08 | 31-Aug-08 | 31-Aug-08 |
| 3 | Settlement date | 1-Jun-08 | 7-Apr-08 | 14-Apr-08 | 1-May-08 | 15-May-08 |
| 4 | Coupon rate | 6.00% | 6.00% | 6.00% | 6.00% | 6.00% |
| 5 | Par value | 1,000 | 1,000 | 1,000 | 1,000 | 1,000 |
| 6 | Frequency | 2 | 2 | 2 | 2 | 2 |
| 7 | 30/360 basis | 0 | 0 | 0 | 0 | 0 |
| 8 | | | | | | |
| 9 | **Accrued Interest** | **10.00** | 1.00 | 2.17 | 5.00 | 7.33 |
| 10 | | =ACCRINT(B1,B2,B3,B4,B5,B6,B7) | | | | |
| 11 | | | | | | |
| 12 | Issue date | 1-Apr-08 | | | | |
| 13 | Maturity date | 15-Jun-08 | | | | |
| 14 | Percent coupon | 6.00% | | | | |
| 15 | Par value | $1,000 | | | | |
| 16 | 30/360 basis | 0 | | | | |
| 17 | | | | | | |
| 18 | **Accrued Interest** | 12.33333 | =ACCRINTM(B12,B13,B14,B15,B16) | | | |
| 19 | | | | | | |

**NOTE**

The ACCINTM function calculates accrued interest for zero-coupon bonds (see Row 18 in Figure 25.24).

## USING DURATION TO UNDERSTAND PRICE VOLATILITY

*Duration* is a measurement, in years, of how long it takes for the price of a bond to be repaid by its cash flows. This measurement is not relevant for zero-coupon bonds because with a zero coupon bond, the duration is simultaneous with the maturity date.

Say that you have a 20-year bond with a 9% yield that pays interest twice a year. It might take about six years of interest payments before you earn back the original purchase price of the bond.

Duration is constantly changing. Immediately after a coupon date, the duration goes up slightly because the interest payment is no longer counted as a future cash flow. However, over the life of the bond, the duration gets progressively shorter, until the duration date corresponds with the maturity date. Duration is important because the higher the duration, the higher the price volatility for the security.

When Excel calculates a duration, using the DURATION function, it uses the method designed by Frederick Macaulay in the 1930s. This method multiplies the present value of each cash flow by the time it is received. Those values are summed and divided by the total price for the security.

Excel also has a modified duration function, MDURATION. This function calculates the duration if the yield would increase by 1% point. In Figure 25.25, the duration for the 9% yield is 5.99 years. The MDURATION return is 5.736 years. This is the duration if the yield would change from 9% to 10%. The difference between the duration and modified duration is an indicator of a bond price's volatility.

**Figure 25.25**
DURATION indicates how many years it will take to earn back the security's purchase price. MDURATION shows the change in duration if the yield were to increase by 1%.

| | B8 | ▾ | $f_x$ =DURATION(B1,B2,B3,B4,B5,B6) | |
|---|---|---|---|---|
| | A | | B | C |
| 1 | Settlement date | | 1-Jan-08 | |
| 2 | Maturity date | | 1-Jan-16 | |
| 3 | Percent coupon | | 8% | |
| 4 | Percent yield | | 9.00% | |
| 5 | Frequency | | 2 | |
| 6 | Actual basis | | 1 | |
| 7 | | | | |
| 8 | **DURATION** | | 5.994 | |
| 9 | **MDURATION** | | 5.736 | |
| 10 | | | | |

SYNTAX: DURATION(*settlement_date,maturity_date,coupon_rate,yield_rate, frequency,basis*)

The DURATION function returns the Macaulay duration for an assumed par value of $100. Duration is defined as the weighted average of the present value of the cash flows and is used as a measure of a bond price's response to changes in yield.

SYNTAX: MDURATION(*settlement_date*,*maturity_date*,*coupon_rate*,*yield_rate*, *frequency*,*basis*)

The MDURATION function returns the modified duration for a security with an assumed par value of $100.

# EXAMPLES OF MISCELLANEOUS FINANCIAL FUNCTIONS

Excel offers a few other financial functions that may be useful if you are dealing with ancient historical data. On April 9, 2001, all U.S. stock markets were forced to start trading securities in dollars and cents instead of dollars and fractions. The United States was the last nation using the fractional system, which was an 18th-century system.

In the fractional system, a stock price may have been reported in the newspaper as 5⅝, which is roughly equivalent to $5.63. However, a common system in brokerage houses was to record this as 5.5, with the .5 indicating ⅝. In an alternate system, prices were recorded in 16ths, with, for example, 1.03 meaning ³⁄₁₆.

Figure 25.26 shows an example of the functions Excel provides for converting between fractional numbers and decimal numbers.

**Figure 25.26**
You can convert old-style security fractional numbers to regular decimals and back by using DOLLARFR and DOLLARDE.

| | A | B | C | D | E | F | G |
|---|---|---|---|---|---|---|---|
| | C4 | ▼ | $f_x$ =DOLLARDE(A4,B4) | | | | |
| 1 | Fractions to Decimals | | | | Decimals to Fractions, in 16ths | | |
| 3 | Nomenclature | In | DollarDE | DollarFR | | | |
| 4 | 1.1 | 8 | **1.125** | **1.02** | =DOLLARFR(C4,16) | | |
| 5 | 1.2 | 8 | 1.25 | 1.04 | | | |
| 6 | 1.3 | 8 | 1.375 | 1.06 | | | |
| 7 | 1.4 | 8 | 1.5 | 1.08 | | | |
| 8 | 1.5 | 8 | 1.625 | 1.10 | | | |
| 9 | 1.6 | 8 | 1.75 | 1.12 | | | |
| 10 | 1.7 | 8 | 1.875 | 1.14 | | | |
| 11 | 1.01 | 16 | 1.0625 | 1.01 | | | |
| 12 | 1.02 | 16 | 1.125 | 1.02 | | | |
| 13 | 1.03 | 16 | 1.1875 | 1.03 | | | |
| 14 | 1.04 | 16 | 1.25 | 1.04 | | | |
| 15 | 1.05 | 16 | 1.3125 | 1.05 | | | |
| 16 | 1.06 | 16 | 1.375 | 1.06 | | | |
| 17 | 1.07 | 16 | 1.4375 | 1.07 | | | |
| 18 | 1.08 | 16 | 1.5 | 1.08 | | | |
| 19 | 1.09 | 16 | 1.5625 | 1.09 | | | |
| 20 | 1.10 | 16 | 1.625 | 1.10 | | | |
| 21 | 1.11 | 16 | 1.6875 | 1.11 | | | |
| 22 | 1.12 | 16 | 1.75 | 1.12 | | | |
| 23 | 1.13 | 16 | 1.8125 | 1.13 | | | |
| 24 | 1.14 | 16 | 1.875 | 1.14 | | | |
| 25 | 1.15 | 16 | 1.9375 | 1.15 | | | |

25

## USING DOLLARDE TO CONVERT TO DECIMALS

If you encounter an old worksheet that uses fractional prices, you can convert them to decimals by using DOLLARDE. You must specify the price in the nomenclature of the system and specify whether the number after the decimal point is in 8ths, 16ths, or 32nds.

SYNTAX: DOLLARDE(*fractional_dollar*,*fraction*)

The DOLLARDE function converts a dollar price expressed as a fraction into a dollar price expressed as a decimal number. You use DOLLARDE to convert fractional dollar numbers, such as securities prices, to decimal numbers.

- *fractional_dollar*—This is a number expressed as a fraction.
- *fraction*—This is the integer to use in the denominator of the fraction.

SYNTAX: DOLLARFR(decimal_dollar,fraction)

The DOLLARFR function converts a dollar price expressed as a decimal number into a dollar price expressed as a fraction.

## USING FVSCHEDULE TO CALCULATE THE FUTURE VALUE FOR A VARIABLE SCHEDULED INTEREST RATE

The FV function discussed at the beginning of this chapter assumes a constant interest rate. If you have a loan agreement that specifies a variable interest rate for future years, you can calculate the future value based on the scheduled interest rate. To do so, you use the FVSCHEDULE function.

SYNTAX: FVSCHEDULE(*principal*,*schedule*)

The FVSCHEDULE function returns the future value of an initial principal after applying a series of compound interest rates. You use FVSCHEDULE to calculate the future value of an investment with a variable or adjustable rate. This function takes the following arguments:

- *principal*—This is the present value.
- *schedule*—This is an array of interest rates to apply.

The values in *schedule* can be numbers or blank cells; any other value produces a #VALUE! error for FVSCHEDULE. Blank cells are taken as zeros (that is, no interest).

Figure 25.27 shows three examples of variable interest rates.

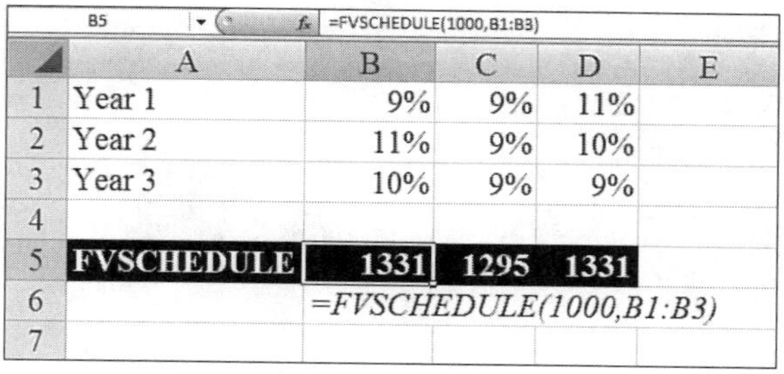

**Figure 25.27**
Calculating a future value for a series of scheduled future interest rates by using FVSCHEDULE.

# USING STATISTICAL FUNCTIONS

## In this chapter

Statistics in Excel fall into three broad categories:

- **Descriptive statistics that describe a dataset**—These include measures of central tendency and dispersion.
- **Regression tools**—These allow you to predict future values based on past values.
- **Inferential statistics**—This type of statistic allows you to predict the likelihood of an event happening, based on a sample of a population.

Table 26.1 provides an alphabetical list of all of Excel 2007's statistical functions. Detailed examples of the functions are provided in the remainder of the chapter.

### TABLE 26.1 ALPHABETICAL LIST OF STATISTICAL FUNCTIONS

| Function | Description |
|---|---|
| AVEDEV(*number1*,*number2*,...) | Returns the average of the absolute deviations of data points from their mean. AVEDEV is a measure of the variability in a dataset. |
| AVERAGE(*number1*,*number2*,...) | Returns the average (arithmetic mean) of the arguments. |
| AVERAGEA(*value1*,*value2*,...) | Calculates the average (arithmetic mean) of the values in the list of arguments. In addition to numbers, text and logical values such as TRUE and FALSE are included in the calculation. |
| BETADIST(*x*,*alpha*,*beta*,*A*,*B*) | Returns the cumulative beta probability density function. The cumulative beta probability density function is commonly used to study variation in the percentage of something across samples, such as the fraction of the day people spend watching television. |
| BETAINV(*probability*,*alpha*,*beta*,*A*,*B*) | Returns the inverse of the cumulative beta probability density function. That is, if *probability* is equal to BETADIST(*x*,...), then BETAINV(*probability*,...) is equal to *x*. The cumulative beta distribution can be used in project planning to model probable completion times, given an expected completion time and variability. |
| BINOMDIST(*number_s*,*trials*,*probability_s*,*cumulative*) | Returns the individual term binomial distribution probability. You use BINOMDIST in problems with a fixed number of tests or trials, when the outcomes of any trial are only success or failure, when trials are independent, and when the probability of success is constant throughout the experiment. For example, BINOMDIST can calculate the probability that two of the next three babies born will be male. |

| Function | Description |
|----------|-------------|
| CHIDIST(*x*,*degrees_freedom*) | Returns the one-tailed probability of the chi-squared distribution. The chi-squared distribution is associated with a chi-squared test. You use the chi-squared test to compare observed and expected values. For example, in a genetic experiment, you might hypothesize that the next generation of plants will exhibit a certain set of colors. By comparing the observed results with the expected ones, you can decide whether your original hypothesis is valid. |
| CHIINV(*probability*,*degrees_freedom*) | Returns the inverse of the one-tailed probability of the chi-squared distribution. If *probability* is equal to CHIDIST(*x*,...), then CHIINV(*probability*,...) is equal to *x*. You use this function to compare observed results with expected ones to decide whether your original hypothesis is valid. |
| CHITEST(*actual_range*,*expected_range*) | Returns the test for independence. CHITEST returns the value from the chi-squared distribution for the statistic and the appropriate degrees of freedom. You can use chi-squared tests to determine whether hypothesized results are verified by an experiment. |
| CONFIDENCE(*alpha*,*standard_dev*,*size*) | Returns the confidence interval for a population mean. The confidence interval is a range on either side of a sample mean. For example, if you order a product through the mail, you can determine, with a particular level of confidence, the earliest and latest the product will arrive. |
| CORREL(*array1*,*array2*) | Returns the correlation coefficient of the *array1* and *array2* cell ranges. You use the correlation coefficient to determine the relationship between two properties. For example, you can examine the relationship between a location's average temperature and the use of air conditioners. |
| COVAR(*array1*,*array2*) | Returns covariance, the average of the products of deviations for each data point pair. You use covariance to determine the relationship between two datasets. For example, you can examine whether greater income accompanies greater levels of education. |

*continues*

26

**TABLE 26.1 CONTINUED**

| Function | Description |
|---|---|
| CRITBINOM(*trials,probability_s,alpha*) | Returns the smallest value for which the cumulative binomial distribution is greater than or equal to a criterion value. You use this function for quality assurance applications. For example, you can use CRITBINOM to determine the greatest number of defective parts that are allowed to come off an assembly line run without having to reject the entire lot. |
| DEVSQ(*number1,number2,...*) | Returns the sum of squares of deviations of data points from their sample mean. |
| EXPONDIST(*x,lambda,cumulative*) | Returns the exponential distribution. You use EXPONDIST to model the time between events, such as how long a bank's automated teller machine takes to deliver cash. For example, you can use EXPONDIST to determine the probability that the process takes, at most, one minute. |
| FDIST(*x,degrees_freedom1,degrees_freedom2*) | Returns the $F$ probability distribution. You can use this function to determine whether two datasets have different degrees of diversity. For example, you can examine test scores given to men and women entering high school and determine whether the variability in the females is different from that found in the males. |
| FINV(*probability,degrees_freedom1, degrees_freedom2*) | Returns the inverse of the $F$ probability distribution. If *probability* is equal to FDIST(*x,...*), then FINV(*probability,...*) is equal to *x*. |
| FISHER(*x*) | Returns the Fisher transformation at *x*. This transformation produces a function that is approximately normally distributed rather than skewed. You use this function to perform hypothesis testing on the correlation coefficient. |
| FISHERINV(*y*) | Returns the inverse of the Fisher transformation. You use this transformation when analyzing correlations between ranges or arrays of data. If *y* is equal to FISHER(*x*), then FISHERINV(*y*) is equal to *x*. |

| Function | Description |
|---|---|
| FORECAST(*x*,*known_y's*,*known_x's*) | Calculates, or predicts, a future value by using existing values. The predicted value is a y value for a given x value. The known values are existing x values and y values, and the new value is predicted by using linear regression. You can use this function to predict future sales, inventory requirements, or consumer trends. |
| FREQUENCY(*data_array*,*bins_array*) | Calculates how often values occur within a range of values and returns a vertical array of numbers. For example, you can use FREQUENCY to count the number of test scores that fall within ranges of scores. Because FREQUENCY returns an array, it must be entered as an array formula. |
| FTEST(*array1*,*array2*) | Returns the result of an *F*-test. An *F*-test returns the one-tailed probability that the variances in *array1* and *array2* are not significantly different. You use this function to determine whether two samples have different variances. For example, given test scores from public and private schools, you can test whether those schools have different levels of diversity. |
| GAMMADIST(*x*,*alpha*,*beta*,*cumulative*) | Returns the gamma distribution. You can use this function to study variables that may have a skewed distribution. The gamma distribution is commonly used in queuing analysis. |
| GAMMAINV(*probability*,*alpha*,*beta*) | Returns the inverse of the gamma cumulative distribution. If *probability* is equal to GAMMADIST(*x*,...), then GAMMAINV(*probability*,...) is equal to *x*. |
| GAMMALN(*x*) | Returns the natural logarithm of the gamma function. |
| GEOMEAN(*number1*,*number2*,...) | Returns the geometric mean of an array or a range of positive data. For example, you can use GEOMEAN to calculate average growth rate given compound interest with variable rates. |
| GROWTH(*known_y's*,*known_x's*,*new_x's*,*const*) | Calculates predicted exponential growth by using existing data. GROWTH returns the y values for a series of new x values that you specify by using existing x values and y values. You can also use the GROWTH worksheet function to fit an exponential curve to existing x values and y values. |

26

*continues*

**TABLE 26.1    CONTINUED**

| Function | Description |
|---|---|
| HARMEAN(*number1*,*number2*,...) | Returns the harmonic mean of a dataset. The harmonic mean is the reciprocal of the arithmetic mean of reciprocals. |
| HYPGEOMDIST(*sample_s*,*number_sample*, *population_s*,*number_population*) | Returns the hypergeometric distribution. HYPGEOMDIST returns the probability of a given number of sample successes, given the sample size, population successes, and population size. You use HYPGEOMDIST for problems with a finite population, where each observation is either a success or a failure, and where each subset of a given size is chosen with equal likelihood. |
| INTERCEPT(*known_y's*,*known_x's*) | Calculates the point at which a line will intersect the y-axis by using existing x values and y values. The intercept point is based on a best-fit regression line plotted through the known x values and known y values. You use the intercept when you want to determine the value of the dependent variable when the independent variable is 0. For example, you can use the INTERCEPT function to predict a metal's electrical resistance at 0 degrees Celsius when your data points were taken at room temperature and higher. |
| KURT(*number1*,*number2*,...) | Returns the kurtosis of a dataset. Kurtosis characterizes the relative peakedness or flatness of a distribution compared with the normal distribution. Positive kurtosis indicates a relatively peaked distribution. Negative kurtosis indicates a relatively flat distribution. |
| LARGE(*array*,*k*) | Returns the *k*th largest value in a dataset. You can use this function to select a value based on its relative standing. For example, you can use LARGE to return a highest, runner-up, or third-place score. |
| LINEST(*known_y's*,*known_x's*,*const*,*stats*) | Calculates the statistics for a line by using the least-squares method to calculate a straight line that best fits the data and returns an array that describes the line. Because this function returns an array of values, it must be entered as an array formula. |

**26**

| Function | Description |
|---|---|
| LOGEST(*known_y's*,*known_x's*,*const*,*stats*) | In regression analysis, calculates an exponential curve that fits the data and returns an array of values that describes the curve. Because this function returns an array of values, it must be entered as an array formula. |
| LOGINV(*probability*,*mean*,*standard_dev*) | Returns the inverse of the lognormal cumulative distribution function of $x$, where LN($x$) is normally distributed with the parameters *mean* and *standard_dev*. If *probability* is equal to LOGNORMDIST($x$,...), LOGINV(*probability*,...) is equal to $x$. |
| LOGNORMDIST(*x*,*mean*,*standard_dev*) | Returns the cumulative lognormal distribution of $x$, where LN($x$) is normally distributed with the parameters *mean* and *standard_dev*. You use this function to analyze data that has been logarithmically transformed. |
| MAX(*number1*,*number2*,...) | Returns the largest value in a set of values. |
| MAXA(*value1*,*value2*,...) | Returns the largest value in a list of arguments. Text and logical values such as TRUE and FALSE are compared, as are numbers. |
| MEDIAN(*number1*,*number2*,...) | Returns the median of the given numbers. The median is the number in the middle of a set of numbers; that is, half the numbers have values that are greater than the median and half have values that are less. |
| MIN(*number1*,*number2*,...) | Returns the smallest number in a set of values. |
| MINA(*value1*,*value2*,...) | Returns the smallest value in a list of arguments. Text and logical values such as TRUE and FALSE are compared, as are numbers. |
| MODE(*number1*,*number2*,...) | Returns the most frequently occurring, or repetitive, value in an array or a range of data. Like MEDIAN, MODE is a location measure. |

26

*continues*

**TABLE 26.1   CONTINUED**

| Function | Description |
|---|---|
| NEGBINOMDIST(*number_f*,*number_s*, *probability_s*) | Returns the negative binomial distribution. NEGBINOMDIST returns the probability that there will be *number_f* failures before the *number_s*th success, when the constant probability of a success is *probability_s*. This function is similar to the binomial distribution function, except that the number of successes is fixed, and the number of trials is variable. As with the binomial distribution function, trials are assumed to be independent. |
| NORMDIST(*x*,*mean*,*standard_dev*,*cumulative*) | Returns the normal cumulative distribution for the specified mean and standard deviation. This function has a very wide range of applications in statistics, including hypothesis testing. |
| NORMINV(*probability*,*mean*,*standard_dev*) | Returns the inverse of the normal cumulative distribution for the specified mean and standard deviation. |
| NORMSDIST(*z*) | Returns the standard normal cumulative distribution function. The distribution has a mean of zero and a standard deviation of one. You use this function in place of a table of standard normal curve areas. |
| NORMSINV(*probability*) | Returns the inverse of the standard normal cumulative distribution. The distribution has a mean of zero and a standard deviation of one. |
| PEARSON(*array1*,*array2*) | Returns the Pearson product–moment correlation coefficient, $r$, a dimensionless index that ranges from $-1.0$ to $1.0$, inclusive, and reflects the extent of a linear relationship between two datasets. |
| PERCENTILE(*array*,*k*) | Returns the $k$th percentile of values in a range. You can use this function to establish a threshold of acceptance. For example, you can decide to examine candidates who score above the 90th percentile. |
| PERCENTRANK(*array*,*x*,*significance*) | Returns the rank of a value in a dataset as a percentage of the dataset. This function can be used to evaluate the relative standing of a value within a dataset. For example, you can use PERCENTRANK to evaluate the standing of an aptitude test score among all scores for the test. |

26

| Function | Description |
|---|---|
| PERMUT(*number*,*number_chosen*) | Returns the number of permutations for a given number of objects that can be selected from *number* objects. A permutation is any set or subset of objects or events where internal order is significant. Permutations are different from combinations, for which the internal order is not significant. You use this function for lottery-style probability calculations. |
| POISSON(*x*,*mean*,*cumulative*) | Returns the Poisson distribution. A common application of the Poisson distribution is predicting the number of events over a specific time, such as the number of cars arriving at a toll plaza in one minute. |
| PROB(*x_range*,*prob_range*,*lower_limit*, *upper_limit*) | Returns the probability that values in a range are between two limits. If *upper_limit* is not supplied, returns the probability that values in *x_range* are equal to *lower_limit*. |
| QUARTILE(*array*,*quart*) | Returns the quartile of a dataset. Quartiles are often used in sales and survey data to divide populations into groups. For example, you can use QUARTILE to find the top 25% of incomes in a population. |
| RANK(*number*,*ref*,*order*) | Returns the rank of a number in a list of numbers. The rank of a number is its size relative to other values in a list. (If you were to sort the list, the rank of the number would be its position.) |
| RSQ(*known_y's*,*known_x's*) | Returns the square of the Pearson product–moment correlation coefficient through data points in *known_y's* and *known_x's*. The $r$-squared value can be interpreted as the proportion of the variance in y attributable to the variance in x. |
| SKEW(*number1*,*number2*,...) | Returns the skewness of a distribution. Skewness characterizes the degree of asymmetry of a distribution around its mean. Positive skewness indicates a distribution with an asymmetric tail extending toward more positive values. Negative skewness indicates a distribution with an asymmetric tail extending toward more negative values. |

26

*continues*

**TABLE 26.1    CONTINUED**

| Function | Description |
|---|---|
| SLOPE(*known_y's*,*known_x's*) | Returns the slope of the linear regression line through data points in *known_y's* and *known_x's*. The slope is the vertical distance divided by the horizontal distance between any two points on the line, which is the rate of change along the regression line. |
| SMALL(*array*,*k*) | Returns the *k*th smallest value in a dataset. You use this function to return values with a particular relative standing in a dataset. |
| STANDARDIZE(*x*,*mean*,*standard_dev*) | Returns a normalized value from a distribution characterized by *mean* and *standard_dev*. |
| STDEV(*number1*,*number2*,...) | Estimates standard deviation based on a sample. The standard deviation is a measure of how widely values are dispersed from the average value (that is, the mean). |
| STDEVA(*value1*,*value2*,...) | Estimates standard deviation based on a sample. The standard deviation is a measure of how widely values are dispersed from the average value (that is, the mean). Text and logical values such as TRUE and FALSE are included in the calculation. |
| STDEVP(*number1*,*number2*,...) | Calculates standard deviation based on the entire population given as arguments. The standard deviation is a measure of how widely values are dispersed from the average value (that is, the mean). |
| STDEVPA(*value1*,*value2*,...) | Calculates standard deviation based on the entire population given as arguments, including text and logical values. The standard deviation is a measure of how widely values are dispersed from the average value (that is, the mean). |
| STEYX(*known_y's*,*known_x's*) | Returns the standard error of the predicted y value for each x in the regression. The standard error is a measure of the amount of error in the prediction of y for an individual x. |
| SUMSQ(*number1*,*number2*, ...) | Returns the sum of the squares of the arguments. |
| SUMX2MY2(*array_x*,*array_y*) | Returns the sum of the difference of squares of corresponding values in two arrays. |

26

| Function | Description |
|---|---|
| SUMX2PY2(*array_x*,*array_y*) | Returns the sum of the sum of squares of corresponding values in two arrays. The sum of the sum of squares is a common term in many statistical calculations. |
| SUMXMY2(*array_x*,*array_y*) | Returns the sum of squares of differences of corresponding values in two arrays. |
| TDIST(*x*,*degrees_freedom*,*tails*) | Returns the percentage points (that is, probability) for the Student $t$-distribution where a numeric value ($x$) is a calculated value of $t$ for which percentage points are to be computed. The $t$-distribution is used in the hypothesis testing of small sample datasets. You use this function in place of a table of critical values for the $t$-distribution. |
| TINV(*probability*,*degrees_freedom*) | Returns the t-value of the Student's $t$-distribution as a function of the probability and the degrees of freedom. |
| TREND(*known_y's*,*known_x's*,*new_x's*,*const*) | Returns values along a linear trend. Fits a straight line (using the method of least squares) to the arrays *known_y's* and *known_x's*. Returns the y values along that line for the array of *new_x's* that you specify. |
| TRIMMEAN(*array*,*percent*) | Returns the mean of the interior of a dataset. TRIMMEAN calculates the mean taken by excluding a percentage of data points from the top and bottom tails of a dataset. You can use this function when you want to exclude outlying data from your analysis. |
| TTEST(*array1*,*array2*,*tails*,*type*) | Returns the probability associated with a Student's $t$-test. You use TTEST to determine whether two samples are likely to have come from the same two underlying populations that have the same mean. |
| VAR(*number1*,*number2*,...) | Estimates variance based on a sample. |
| VARA(*value1*,*value2*,...) | Estimates variance based on a sample. In addition to numbers, text and logical values such as TRUE and FALSE are included in the calculation. |
| VARP(*number1*,*number2*,...) | Calculates variance based on the entire population. |

**26**

*continues*

**TABLE 26.1 CONTINUED**

| Function | Description |
|---|---|
| VARPA(*value1*,*value2*,...) | Calculates variance based on the entire population. In addition to numbers, text and logical values such as TRUE and FALSE are included in the calculation. |
| WEIBULL(*x*,*alpha*,*beta*,*cumulative*) | Returns the Weibull distribution. You use this distribution in reliability analysis, such as to calculate a device's mean time to failure. |
| ZTEST(*array*,*x*,*sigma*) | Returns the two-tailed *p* value of a *z*-test. The *z*-test generates a standard score for *x* with respect to the dataset, *array*, and returns the two-tailed probability for the normal distribution. You can use this function to assess the likelihood that a particular observation is drawn from a particular population. |

# EXAMPLES OF FUNCTIONS FOR DESCRIPTIVE STATISTICS

Descriptive statistics help describe a population of data. What is the largest? the smallest? the average? Are data points grouped to the left of the average or to the right of the average? How wide is the range of expected values? Do many members of the population have values in the middle, or are they evenly spread throughout the range? All these are measures of descriptive statistics.

Many situations in a business environment involve finding basic information about a dataset such as the largest or smallest values or the rank within a dataset.

## USING MIN OR MAX TO FIND THE SMALLEST OR LARGEST NUMERIC VALUE

If you have a large dataset and want to find the smallest or largest value in a column, rather than sort the dataset, you can use a function to find the value. To find the smallest numeric value, you use MIN. To find the largest numeric value, you use MAX.

Figure 26.1 shows a list of open receivables, by customer, for 59 customers. Even though the function references says that you can only find the MIN for 255 numbers, a single rectangular reference counts as one of the 255 arguments for the function. To find the smallest value in the range, you use =MIN(B2:B360). To find the largest value in the range, you use =MAX(B2:B360).

**SYNTAX:** =MIN(*number1*,*number2*,...)

The MIN function returns the smallest number in a set of values. The arguments *number1*, *number2*,... are 1 to 255 numbers for which you want to find the minimum value. You can specify arguments that are numbers, empty cells, logical values, or text representations of numbers. Arguments that are error values or text that cannot be translated into numbers cause errors. If an argument is an array or a reference, only numbers in that array or reference are used. Empty cells, logical values, or text in the array or reference are ignored. If logical values and text should not be ignored, you should use MINA instead. If the arguments contain no numbers, MIN returns 0.

**Figure 26.1**
You use MIN and MAX to find the smallest or largest receivables.

| | | | | |
|---|---|---|---|---|
| 54 | Paramount Clipboard Corporation | 10,419.12 | | |
| 55 | Compelling Treadmill Company | 8,912.83 | | |
| 56 | Steadfast Juicer Inc. | 7,555.98 | | |
| 57 | Secure Shingle Inc. | 10,535.76 | | |
| 58 | Paramount Scooter Corporation | 10,014.60 | | |
| 59 | Unsurpassed Sprayer Inc. | 10,069.74 | | |
| 60 | Secure Necktie Inc. | 8,800.63 | | |
| 61 | Total | 493,005.80 | | |
| 62 | | | | |
| 63 | Min | 3,572.80 | =MIN(B2:B60) | |
| 64 | Max | 13,560.43 | =MAX(B2:B60) | |
| 65 | Average | 8,356.03 | =AVERAGE(B2:B60) | |
| 66 | Median | 8,343.71 | =MEDIAN(B2:B60) | |
| 67 | | | | |

SYNTAX: =MAX(*number1,number2,...*)

The MAX function returns the largest value in a set of values. The arguments *number1, number2,...* are 1 to 255 numbers for which you want to find the maximum value. The remaining rules are similar to those for MIN, described in the preceding section.

NOTE

If you read the descriptions for MINA and MAXA, you might think that the functions can be used to find the smallest text value in a range. However, here is the Excel Help description for MAXA:

MAXA(*value1,value2*) returns the largest value in a list of arguments. Text and logical values such as TRUE and FALSE are compared as well as numbers.

The problem, however, is that text values are treated as the number 0 in the compare. It is a struggle to imagine a scenario where this would be mildly useful. If you have a series of positive numbers and want to know if any of them are text, you can use =MINA(A1:A99). If the result is 0, then you know that there is a text value in the range.

Similarly, if you have a range of negative numbers in A1:A99, you could use =MAXA(A1:A99). If any of the values are text, the result will return 0 instead of a negative number.

MINA and MAXA could be used to evaluate a series of TRUE/FALSE values. FALSE values are treated as 0. TRUE values are treated as 1.

26

## USING LARGE TO FIND THE TOP N VALUES IN A LIST OF VALUES

The MAX function discussed in the preceding section finds the single largest value in a list. Sometimes, it is interesting to find the top 10 values in a list. Say that with a list of customer receivables, someone in accounts receivable may want to call the top 10 receivables in an attempt to collect the accounts. The LARGE function can find the first, second, third, and so on largest values in a list.

SYNTAX: =LARGE(*array*,*k*)

The LARGE function returns the *k*th largest value in a dataset. You can use this function to select a value based on its relative standing. For example, you can use LARGE to return a highest, runner-up, or third-place score. This function takes the following arguments:

- *array*—This is the array or range of data for which you want to determine the *k*th largest value. If *array* is empty, LARGE returns a #NUM! error.

- *k*—This is the position (from the largest) in the array or cell range of data to return. If *k* is less than or equal to 0 or if *k* is greater than the number of data points, LARGE returns a #NUM! error.

You follow these steps to build a table of the five largest customer receivables:

1. Make the second argument of the function the numbers 1 through 5. Starting from the dataset shown in Figure 26.1, insert a new Column A to hold the values 1 through 5.

2. In A66:A70, enter the numbers 1 through 5.

3. In the column letters above the grid, grab the line between Columns A and B. Drag to the left to make this column narrower. It should be just wide enough to display the numbers in Column A.

4. In Column C, Row 66, enter =LARGE(. Use the mouse or arrow keys to highlight the range of data. After highlighting the data, press the F4 key to add dollar signs to the reference. This allows you to copy the reference to the next several rows while always pointing at the same range.

5. For the second argument, point to the 1 in Cell A66. Leave this reference as relative (that is, no dollar signs) so that it will change to A67, A68, and so on when copied. The first formula in Cell C66 indicates that the largest value is 13,560.43. So far, you've done a lot of work just to find out the same thing that the MAX function could have told you. However, the power comes in the next step.

6. Select Cell C66. Click the fill handle and drag down to Cell C70. You now have a list of the top five open receivables.

7. At this point, you know the amounts of the top receivables, but this immediately brings up the question of which customers have those receivables. Using lookup functions discussed in Chapter 24, "Using Financial Functions," you can retrieve the name associated with each receivable amount. Note that this method assumes that no two customers in the top five have exactly the same receivable.

8. Enter the following intermediate formula in Cell B66:s =MATCH(C66,$C$2:$C$60,0). This formula tells Excel to take the receivable value in Cell C66 and to find it in the list of open receivables. The MATCH function returns the row number within C2:C60 that has the matching value. For example, 13,560.43 is found in Cell C9. This is the eighth row in the range of C2:C60, so MATCH returns the number 8.

9. Finding out that the largest receivable in the eighth row of a range is not useful to a person trying to collect accounts receivables, so to return the name, ask for the eighth

value in the range of B2:B66. You can use the INDEX function to do this. =INDEX($B$2:$B$66,8) returns the customer with the largest receivable.

10. Combine the formulas from step 8 and step 9 into a single formula in Cell B66: =INDEX($B$2:$B$60,MATCH(C66,$C$2:$C$60,0)).

11. Copy the formula in Cell B66 down through Cell B70.

As shown in Figure 26.2, the result is a table in A66:A70 that shows the five largest customers. After receiving checks today, you can update the receivable amounts in C2:C60. If Best Raft sent in a check for $10,000, the formulas would automatically move Magnificent Electronics up to the fourth position and move the sixth customer up to the fifth spot.

**Figure 26.2**

The LARGE function in Column C allows this dynamic table to be built to show the five largest problems.

| | A | B | C | D | E | F |
|---|---|---|---|---|---|---|
| | | | C63 | | $f_x$ =MAX(C2:C60) | |
| 1 | | Customer | A/R | | | |
| 39 | | Top-Notch Gadget Corporation | 9,284.89 | | | |
| 40 | | Sure Lawn Traders | 8,343.71 | | | |
| 41 | | Astonishing Vegetable Inc. | 10,692.84 | | | |
| 42 | | Fashionable Thermostat Company | 9,600.82 | | | |
| 43 | | Tremendous Barometer Corporation | 9,474.56 | | | |
| 44 | | Distinctive Juicer Inc. | 7,984.78 | | | |
| 45 | | Fully Hardware Inc. | 6,757.70 | | | |
| 46 | | Unsurpassed Kettle Supply | 9,046.71 | | | |
| 47 | | Cool Gadget Traders | 10,247.22 | | | |
| 48 | | Fresh Instrument Inc. | 7,331.96 | | | |
| 49 | | Savory Hairpin Corporation | 5,584.69 | | | |
| 50 | | Vibrant Barometer Inc. | 9,956.00 | | | |
| 51 | | Best Doghouse Company | 6,594.83 | | | |
| 52 | | Easy Radio Company | 7,959.38 | | | |
| 53 | | Unusual Tripod Company | 6,900.10 | | | |
| 54 | | Paramount Clipboard Corporation | 10,419.12 | | | |
| 55 | | Compelling Treadmill Company | 8,912.83 | | | |
| 56 | | Steadfast Juicer Inc. | 7,555.98 | | | |
| 57 | | Secure Shingle Inc. | 10,535.76 | | | |
| 58 | | Paramount Scooter Corporation | 10,014.60 | | | |
| 59 | | Unsurpassed Sprayer Inc. | 10,069.74 | | | |
| 60 | | Secure Necktie Inc. | 8,800.63 | | | |
| 61 | | Total | 493,005.80 | | | |
| 62 | | | | | | |
| 63 | | Largest | 13,560.43 | =MAX(C2:C60) | | |
| 64 | | | | | | |
| 65 | | Largest Receivables | | | | |
| 66 | | 1 Fully Toothpick Company | 13,560.43 | =LARGE($C$2:$C$60,A66) | | |
| 67 | | 2 Savory Calculator Company | 12,493.41 | | | |
| 68 | | 3 Inventive Clipboard Corporation | 11,604.13 | | | |
| 69 | | 4 Best Raft Company | 11,582.61 | | | |
| 70 | | 5 Magnificent Electronics Partners | 11,087.71 | | | |
| 71 | | | | | | |
| 72 | | B66: =INDEX($B$2:$B$60,MATCH(C66,$C$2:$C$60,0)) | | | | |
| 73 | | | | | | |

## USING SMALL TO SEQUENCE A LIST IN DATE SEQUENCE

The MIN function finds the smallest value in a dataset. The SMALL function can find the $k$th smallest value. This can be great for finding not just the smallest value but the second-smallest, third-smallest, and so on. If $n$ is the number of data points in an array, SMALL(array,1) equals the smallest value, and SMALL(array,n) equals the largest value.

Syntax: `=SMALL(array,k)`

The `SMALL` function returns the *k*th smallest value in a dataset. You use this function to return values with a particular relative standing in a dataset. *array* is an array or a range of numeric data for which you want to determine the *k*th smallest value. If *array* is empty, `SMALL` returns a `#NUM!` error. *k* is the position (from the smallest) in the array or range of data to return. If *k* is less than or equal to 0 or if *k* exceeds the number of data points, `SMALL` returns a `#NUM!` error.

In Figure 26.3, range A2:B19 contains a list of book titles and their publication dates. To find the earliest dates for the books, you use `=SMALL()`.

This example contains a twist that makes the formula easier than in the example for `LARGE`. In the initial formula in Cell D2, the argument for *k* was generated using `ROW(A1)`. This function returns the number `1`. As the formula is copied from Cell D2 down to the remaining rows, the reference changes to `ROW(A2)` and so on. This allows each row in Column D to show a successively larger value from *array*.

The formula in Cell D2 is `=SMALL($B$2:$B$19,ROW(A1))`. After you have found the year in Column D, the formula in Cell E2 to return the title is `=INDEX($A$2:$A$19,MATCH (D2,$B$2:$B$19,0))`.

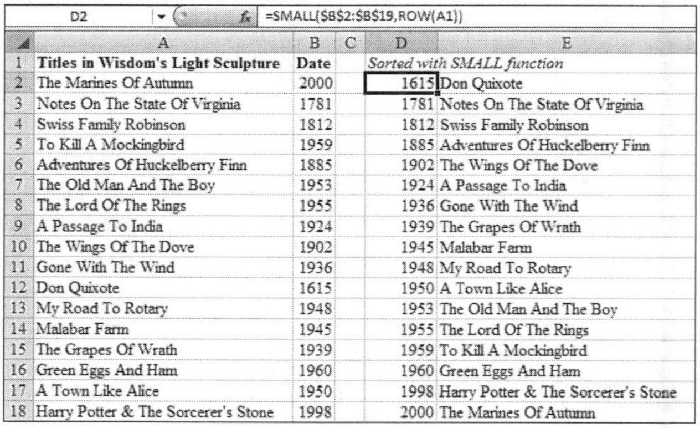

D2 =SMALL($B$2:$B$19,ROW(A1))

| | A | B | C | D | E |
|---|---|---|---|---|---|
| 1 | Titles in Wisdom's Light Sculpture | Date | | Sorted with SMALL function | |
| 2 | The Marines Of Autumn | 2000 | | 1615 | Don Quixote |
| 3 | Notes On The State Of Virginia | 1781 | | 1781 | Notes On The State Of Virginia |
| 4 | Swiss Family Robinson | 1812 | | 1812 | Swiss Family Robinson |
| 5 | To Kill A Mockingbird | 1959 | | 1885 | Adventures Of Huckelberry Finn |
| 6 | Adventures Of Huckelberry Finn | 1885 | | 1902 | The Wings Of The Dove |
| 7 | The Old Man And The Boy | 1953 | | 1924 | A Passage To India |
| 8 | The Lord Of The Rings | 1955 | | 1936 | Gone With The Wind |
| 9 | A Passage To India | 1924 | | 1939 | The Grapes Of Wrath |
| 10 | The Wings Of The Dove | 1902 | | 1945 | Malabar Farm |
| 11 | Gone With The Wind | 1936 | | 1948 | My Road To Rotary |
| 12 | Don Quixote | 1615 | | 1950 | A Town Like Alice |
| 13 | My Road To Rotary | 1948 | | 1953 | The Old Man And The Boy |
| 14 | Malabar Farm | 1945 | | 1955 | The Lord Of The Rings |
| 15 | The Grapes Of Wrath | 1939 | | 1959 | To Kill A Mockingbird |
| 16 | Green Eggs And Ham | 1960 | | 1960 | Green Eggs And Ham |
| 17 | A Town Like Alice | 1950 | | 1998 | Harry Potter & The Sorcerer's Stone |
| 18 | Harry Potter & The Sorcerer's Stone | 1998 | | 2000 | The Marines Of Autumn |

**Figure 26.3**
The `SMALL` function in Column D finds the earliest years in the list.

## Using `MEDIAN`, `MODE`, and `AVERAGE` to Find the Central Tendency of a Dataset

There are three popular measures to use when trying to find the middle scores in a range:

- **Mean**—The mean of a dataset is the mathematical average. It is calculated by adding all the values in the range and dividing by the number of values in the set. To calculate a mean in Excel, you use the `AVERAGE` function.

- **Median**—The median of a dataset is the value in the middle when the set is arranged from high to low. In the dataset, half the values are higher than the median and half the numbers are lower than the median. To calculate a median in Excel, you use the MEDIAN function.

- **Mode**—The mode of a dataset is the value that happens most often. To calculate a mode in Excel, you use the MODE function.

SYNTAX: =AVERAGE(*number1,number2,...*)

The AVERAGE function returns the average (that is, arithmetic mean) of the arguments. The arguments *number1, number2,...* are 1 to 255 numeric arguments for which you want the average. The arguments must be either numbers or names, arrays, or references that contain numbers. If an array or a reference argument contains text, logical values, or empty cells, those values are ignored; however, cells containing the value 0 are included.

CAUTION

> When averaging cells, keep in mind the difference between empty cells and those that contain the value 0. This can be particularly troubling if you have unchecked the Show a Zero in Cells That Have a Zero Value setting. You find this setting by clicking the Office icon and then selecting Excel Options, Advanced, Display Options for This Worksheet.

SYNTAX: =MEDIAN(*number1,number2,...*)

The MEDIAN function returns the median of the given numbers. The median is the number in the middle of a set of numbers; that is, half the numbers have values that are greater than the median and half have values that are less. If there is an even number of numbers in the set, then MEDIAN calculates the average of the two numbers in the middle.

The arguments *number1, number2,...* are 1 to 255 numbers for which you want the median. The arguments should be either numbers or names, arrays, or references that contain numbers. Microsoft Excel examines all the numbers in each reference or array argument. If an array or a reference argument contains text, logical values, or empty cells, those values are ignored; however, cells that contain the value 0 are included.

SYNTAX: =MODE(*number1,number2,...*)

The MODE function returns the most frequently occurring, or repetitive, value in an array or a range of data. Like MEDIAN, MODE is a location measure. In a set of values, the mode is the

26

most frequently occurring value; the median is the middle value; and the mean is the average value. No single measure of central tendency provides a complete picture of the data. Suppose data is clustered in three areas, half around a single low value, and half around two large values. Both `AVERAGE` and `MEDIAN` may return a value in the relatively empty middle, and `MODE` may return the dominant low value.

The arguments *`number1, number2,...`* are 1 to 255 arguments for which you want to calculate the mode. You can also use a single array or a reference to an array instead of arguments separated by commas. The arguments should be numbers, names, arrays, or references that contain numbers. If an array or reference argument contains text, logical values, or empty cells, those values are ignored; however, cells that contain the value `0` are included. If the dataset contains no duplicate data points, `MODE` returns a `#N/A` error.

Figure 26.4 shows examples of `AVERAGE`, `MEAN`, and `MODE`. Cell E2 calculates the arithmetic mean of the test scores in Column B: `80.55`. The median in Cell E3 is higher: `82`. This means that half the students scored above 82 and half scored below 82. The mode in Cell E4 is `88`. This is because 88 was the only score that appeared more than once in the class.

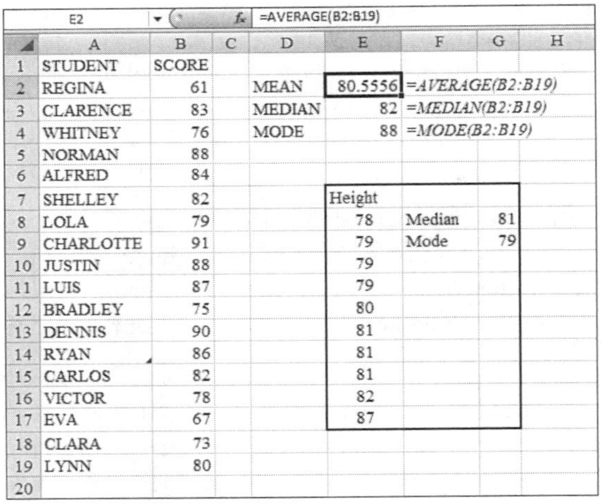

E2 | =AVERAGE(B2:B19)

| | A | B | C | D | E | F | G | H |
|---|---|---|---|---|---|---|---|---|
| 1 | STUDENT | SCORE | | | | | | |
| 2 | REGINA | 61 | | MEAN | 80.5556 | =AVERAGE(B2:B19) | | |
| 3 | CLARENCE | 83 | | MEDIAN | 82 | =MEDIAN(B2:B19) | | |
| 4 | WHITNEY | 76 | | MODE | 88 | =MODE(B2:B19) | | |
| 5 | NORMAN | 88 | | | | | | |
| 6 | ALFRED | 84 | | | | | | |
| 7 | SHELLEY | 82 | | | Height | | | |
| 8 | LOLA | 79 | | | 78 | Median | 81 | |
| 9 | CHARLOTTE | 91 | | | 79 | Mode | 79 | |
| 10 | JUSTIN | 88 | | | 79 | | | |
| 11 | LUIS | 87 | | | 79 | | | |
| 12 | BRADLEY | 75 | | | 80 | | | |
| 13 | DENNIS | 90 | | | 81 | | | |
| 14 | RYAN | 86 | | | 81 | | | |
| 15 | CARLOS | 82 | | | 81 | | | |
| 16 | VICTOR | 78 | | | 82 | | | |
| 17 | EVA | 67 | | | 87 | | | |
| 18 | CLARA | 73 | | | | | | |
| 19 | LYNN | 80 | | | | | | |
| 20 | | | | | | | | |

**Figure 26.4**
`AVERAGE`, `MEDIAN`, and `MODE` all describe the central tendencies of a dataset.

The range in E17:G17 demonstrates two anomalies with the median and mode. In this case, there are an even number of entries—10. It is impossible to figure out a median in this case, so Excel takes the average of the two values in the middle—80 and 81—to produce 80.5. This is the only situation in which the median is not a value from the table.

The table contains the height, in inches, of several members of the Cleveland Cavaliers. In this dataset, three players are 79 inches tall, and three players are 81 inches tall. Either answer qualifies as the value that happens most often. Thus, either answer could be the mode. In this case, `MODE` returns the first of these values it encounters in the dataset. If E7:E17 were sorted high to low, the `MODE` would report 81 inches.

## USING TRIMMEAN TO EXCLUDE OUTLIERS FROM THE MEAN

Sometimes a dataset includes a few outliers that radically skew the average. For example, say you have a list of gross margin percentages. Most percentages fall in the 45% to 50% range, but there was one deal where for customer satisfaction reasons, the product was given away at a loss. This one data point would skew the average unusually low.

The TRIMMEAN function takes the mean of data points but excludes the *n*% highest and lowest values. You have to use some care in expressing the *n*%.

### SYNTAX: =TRIMMEAN(*array*,*percent*)

The TRIMMEAN function returns the mean of the interior of a dataset. TRIMMEAN calculates the mean taken by excluding a percentage of data points from the top and bottom tails of a dataset. You can use this function when you want to exclude outlying data from your analysis. This function takes the following arguments:

- *array*—This is the array or range of values to trim and average.
- *percent*—This is the fractional number of data points to exclude from the calculation. For example, if *percent* is 0.2, 4 points are trimmed from a dataset of 20 points (that is, 20 × 0.2): 2 from the top and 2 from the bottom of the set.

If *percent* is less than 0 or *percent* is greater than 1, TRIMMEAN returns a #NUM! error. TRIMMEAN rounds the number of excluded data points down to the nearest multiple of 2. If *percent* equals 0.1, 10% of 30 data points equals 3 points. For symmetry, TRIMMEAN excludes a single value from the top and bottom of the dataset.

## USING GEOMEAN TO CALCULATE AVERAGE GROWTH RATE

Say that your 401(k) plan is invested in a stock market index fund. The stock market goes up 5%, 40%, and 15% in three successive years. Taking the average of these numbers might lead someone to believe that the average increase was 20% per year. This is not correct. The growth rates are all multiplied together to find an ending value of your investment. To find the average growth rate, you need to find a number that, when multiplied together three times, yields the same result as 105% × 140% × 115%. You can calculate this by using GEOMEAN.

To find the geometric mean of 10 numbers, you multiply the 10 numbers together and raise the sum to the 1/10 power. Excel lets you do this quickly with GEOMEAN.

### SYNTAX: =GEOMEAN(*number1*,*number2*,...)

The GEOMEAN function returns the geometric mean of an array or a range of positive data. For example, you can use GEOMEAN to calculate average growth rate, given compound interest with variable rates.

The arguments *number1*,*number2*,... are 1 to 255 arguments for which you want to calculate the mean. You can also use a single array or a reference to an array instead of arguments separated by commas.

26

The arguments must be either numbers or names, arrays, or references that contain numbers. If an array or a reference argument contains text, logical values, or empty cells, those values are ignored; however, cells that contain the value 0 are included. If any data point is less than or equal to 0, GEOMEAN returns a #NUM! error.

## USING HARMEAN TO FIND AVERAGE SPEEDS

The typical averaging function fails when you are measuring speeds over a period of time. Say that your exercise regimen is 5 minutes of walking at 2 mph, 25 minutes of running at 5 mph, and then 10 minutes of jogging at 3 mph. If you took the average of (2, 5, 5, 5, 5, 5, 3, 3), you would assume that you averaged 4.125 miles per hour.

The actual calculation for average speed would be to take the reciprocals of each speed, average those values, and then take the reciprocal of the result. In the exercise example, you would average ($\frac{1}{2}$, $\frac{1}{5}$, $\frac{1}{5}$, $\frac{1}{5}$, $\frac{1}{5}$, $\frac{1}{5}$, $\frac{1}{3}$, $\frac{1}{3}$) to obtain $\frac{13}{48}$. The you would take the reciprocal, $\frac{48}{13}$, to find the actual average speed of 3.69 mph.

SYNTAX: =HARMEAN(number1,number2,...)

The HARMEAN function returns the harmonic mean of a dataset. The harmonic mean is the reciprocal of the arithmetic mean of reciprocals. The arguments number1,number2,... are 1 to 255 arguments for which you want to calculate the mean. You can also use a single array or a reference to an array instead of arguments separated by commas.

The arguments must be either numbers or names, arrays, or references that contain numbers. If an array or a reference argument contains text, logical values, or empty cells, those values are ignored; however, cells that contain the value 0 are included. If any data point is less than or equal to 0, HARMEAN returns a #NUM! error. The harmonic mean is always less than the geometric mean, which is always less than the arithmetic mean.

## USING RANK TO CALCULATE THE POSITION WITHIN A LIST

There are times when you need to determine the order of values but you are not allowed to sort the data. The RANK function helps with this task. However, there is an anomaly with the function that you should understand.

Let's say five bowlers scored 187, 185, 185, 170, and 160. The traditional way to rank the players is that two players would have a rank of 2, and the next player would have a rank of 4. There would be no one ranked number 3. Although this is technically correct, it can cause problems if you have lookup values expecting to find a person ranked number 3. The example at the end of this section explains how to overcome such a situation.

SYNTAX: =RANK(number,ref,order)

The RANK function returns the rank of a number in a list of numbers. The rank of a number is its size relative to other values in a list. (If you were to sort the list, the rank of the number would be its position.) This function takes the following arguments:

- *number*—This is the number whose rank you want to find.
- *ref*—This is an array of, or a reference to, a list of numbers. Nonnumeric values in ref are ignored.
- *order*—This is a number that specifies how to rank *number*. For a value of 0 or if this argument is omitted, Excel ranks *number* as if ref were a list sorted in descending order. If order is any nonzero value, Excel ranks *number* as if ref were a list sorted in ascending order.

RANK gives duplicate numbers the same rank. However, the presence of duplicate numbers affects the ranks of subsequent numbers. For example, in a list of integers, if the number 10 appears twice and has a rank of 5, then 11 would have a rank of 7 (no number would have a rank of 6).

In Figure 26.5, Column B contains a list of scores. The formula for Cell C2 is =RANK(B2,$B$2:$B$13). Notice that the third argument is omitted, so the highest score will be ranked as number 1. Also notice that the second argument is marked as absolute so that the formula can be copied, and it will always point to the same *ref* range.

**Figure 26.5**

In this case, RANK works okay. Two students have a rank of 10, and no one is ranked 11.

| | A | B | C | D | E | F |
|---|---|---|---|---|---|---|
| | | C2 | | fx =RANK(B2,$B$2:$B$13) | | |
| 1 | NAME | COMPLETE | RANK | | | |
| 2 | YOLANDA HILL | 83 | 9 | =RANK(B2,$B$2:$B$13) | | |
| 3 | LEE DOUGLAS | 80 | 10 | | | |
| 4 | GREGORY BOWEN | 135 | 2 | | | |
| 5 | LOUIS MOLINA | 85 | 8 | | | |
| 6 | ANDREW HALL | 88 | 7 | | | |
| 7 | RANDY TRUJILLO | 117 | 4 | | | |
| 8 | MARTHA PHELPS | 80 | 10 | | | |
| 9 | CRAIG VAUGHAN | 70 | 12 | | | |
| 10 | SHARON COMPTON | 146 | 1 | | | |
| 11 | DOUGLAS BYERS | 104 | 5 | | | |
| 12 | LAURIE MEYER | 133 | 3 | | | |
| 13 | SONIA TRUJILLO | 93 | 6 | | | |
| 14 | | | | | | |

26

In Figure 26.6, the values in Column B are times in a cross-country race. In this case, the lowest rank should go to the fastest score. The formula in Cell C2 is =RANK(B2,$B$2:$B$8,1). Note that there is a third argument to specify that the lowest value should be ranked 1. In this case, however, there was a tie. The runners in Cells C6 and C7 both had the same time. The RANK function gives both of these values a rank of 2. This causes a problem in Row 13. This table is trying to identify the top three finishers by using lookup formulas. Because no one is ranked number 3, an error occurs.

The generally accepted solution is to use the RANK function and add the COUNTIF of how many times this value occurred previously in the list.

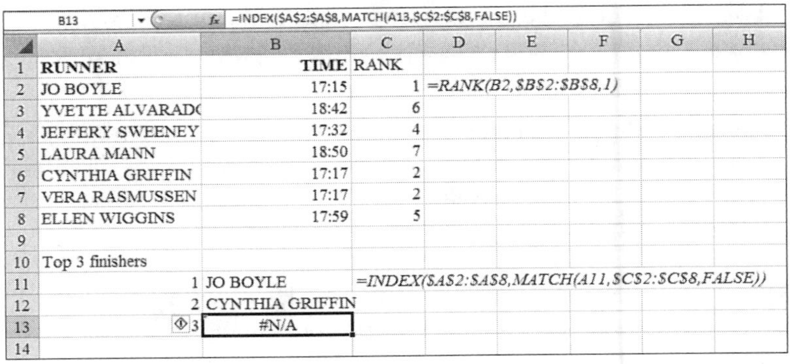

**Figure 26.6**
Two runners tied with the same score. This causes the lookup formulas in Row 13 to never find a match.

| | A | B | C | D | E | F | G | H |
|---|---|---|---|---|---|---|---|---|
| | B13 | | $f_x$ =INDEX($A$2:$A$8,MATCH(A13,$C$2:$C$8,FALSE)) | | | | | |
| 1 | RUNNER | | TIME | RANK | | | | |
| 2 | JO BOYLE | 17:15 | | 1 | =RANK(B2,$B$2:$B$8,1) | | | |
| 3 | YVETTE ALVARADO | 18:42 | | 6 | | | | |
| 4 | JEFFERY SWEENEY | 17:32 | | 4 | | | | |
| 5 | LAURA MANN | 18:50 | | 7 | | | | |
| 6 | CYNTHIA GRIFFIN | 17:17 | | 2 | | | | |
| 7 | VERA RASMUSSEN | 17:17 | | 2 | | | | |
| 8 | ELLEN WIGGINS | 17:59 | | 5 | | | | |
| 9 | | | | | | | | |
| 10 | Top 3 finishers | | | | | | | |
| 11 | | 1 | JO BOYLE | | =INDEX($A$2:$A$8,MATCH(A11,$C$2:$C$8,FALSE)) | | | |
| 12 | | 2 | CYNTHIA GRIFFIN | | | | | |
| 13 | | 3 | #N/A | | | | | |
| 14 | | | | | | | | |

In Figure 26.7, examine the formula in Cell C8. COUNTIF asks how many times the value in Cell B8 was found in B$2:B7. This final reference is an interesting reference. It tells Excel to count always from Row 2 down to the row above the current row. It is easier to build this formula in the final cell of the column and then copy it upwards.

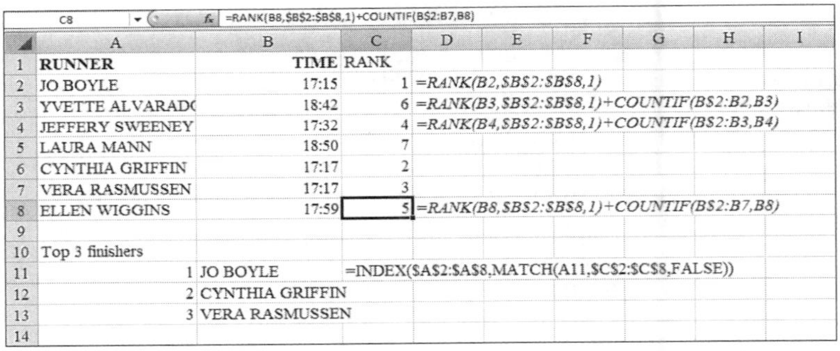

**Figure 26.7**
You use a COUNTIF to break ties.

| | A | B | C | D | E | F | G | H | I |
|---|---|---|---|---|---|---|---|---|---|
| | C8 | | $f_x$ =RANK(B8,$B$2:$B$8,1)+COUNTIF(B$2:B7,B8) | | | | | | |
| 1 | RUNNER | | TIME | RANK | | | | | |
| 2 | JO BOYLE | 17:15 | | 1 | =RANK(B2,$B$2:$B$8,1) | | | | |
| 3 | YVETTE ALVARADO | 18:42 | | 6 | =RANK(B3,$B$2:$B$8,1)+COUNTIF(B$2:B2,B3) | | | | |
| 4 | JEFFERY SWEENEY | 17:32 | | 4 | =RANK(B4,$B$2:$B$8,1)+COUNTIF(B$2:B3,B4) | | | | |
| 5 | LAURA MANN | 18:50 | | 7 | | | | | |
| 6 | CYNTHIA GRIFFIN | 17:17 | | 2 | | | | | |
| 7 | VERA RASMUSSEN | 17:17 | | 3 | | | | | |
| 8 | ELLEN WIGGINS | 17:59 | | 5 | =RANK(B8,$B$2:$B$8,1)+COUNTIF(B$2:B7,B8) | | | | |
| 9 | | | | | | | | | |
| 10 | Top 3 finishers | | | | | | | | |
| 11 | | 1 | JO BOYLE | | =INDEX($A$2:$A$8,MATCH(A11,$C$2:$C$8,FALSE)) | | | | |
| 12 | | 2 | CYNTHIA GRIFFIN | | | | | | |
| 13 | | 3 | VERA RASMUSSEN | | | | | | |
| 14 | | | | | | | | | |

## USING QUARTILE TO BREAK A DATASET INTO QUARTERS

Use QUARTILE to divide populations into groups.

**SYNTAX: =QUARTILE(array,quart)**

The QUARTILE function returns the quartile of a dataset. Quartiles are often used in sales and survey data to divide populations into groups. For example, you can use QUARTILE to find the top 25% of incomes in a population. This function takes the following arguments:

- *array*—This is the array or cell range of numeric values for which you want the quartile value. If *array* is empty, QUARTILE returns a #NUM! error.

- *quart*—This indicates which value to return. You use 0 for the minimum value, 1 for the first quartile (25th percentile), 2 for the median value (50th percentile), 3 for the third quartile (75th percentile), and 4 for the maximum value. If *quart* is not an integer, it is truncated. If *quart* is less than 0 or if quart is greater than 4, QUARTILE returns a #NUM! error.

NOTE

MIN, MEDIAN, and MAX return the same value as QUARTILE when *quart* is equal to 0, 2, and 4, respectively.

In Figure 26.8, the formulas in B20:C23 break out the limits for each quartile. The formula in Cell B20 is =QUARTILE($B$2:$B$17,0) to find the minimum value. The formula in Cells C20 and B21 is =QUARTILE($B$2:$B$17,1) to define the end of the first quartile and the start of the second quartile.

After the QUARTILE functions build the table in B20:C23, the VLOOKUP function returns the text in C2:C17. The formula in Cell C2 is =VLOOKUP(B2,$B$20:$D$23,3,TRUE).

**Figure 26.8**
The QUARTILE function can break up a dataset into four equal pieces.

| | A | B | C | D | E | F | G | H |
|---|---|---|---|---|---|---|---|---|
| 1 | Customer | Revenue | | | | | | |
| 2 | Distinctive Marble Supply | 600 | First Quartile | =VLOOKUP(B2,$B$20:$D$23,3,TRUE) | | | | |
| 3 | First-Rate Marble Inc. | 70000 | Fourth Quartile | | | | | |
| 4 | New Toothpick Inc. | 100 | First Quartile | | | | | |
| 5 | Refined Marble Inc. | 100000 | Fourth Quartile | | | | | |
| 6 | Powerful Shingle Corporation | 6000 | Second Quartile | | | | | |
| 7 | Bright Linen Inc. | 600 | First Quartile | | | | | |
| 8 | Stunning Vise Inc. | 40000 | Fourth Quartile | | | | | |
| 9 | Trendy Shovel Inc. | 10000 | Third Quartile | | | | | |
| 10 | Trouble-Free Toothpick Company | 10000 | Third Quartile | | | | | |
| 11 | Unique Tuner Corporation | 90000 | Fourth Quartile | | | | | |
| 12 | Tasty Chopstick Corporation | 1000 | Second Quartile | | | | | |
| 13 | Astonishing Bottle Corporation | 40000 | Fourth Quartile | | | | | |
| 14 | Easy Quilt Company | 10000 | Third Quartile | | | | | |
| 15 | Easy Furnace Supply | 300 | First Quartile | | | | | |
| 16 | Agile Freezer Corporation | 3000 | Second Quartile | | | | | |
| 17 | Wonderful Luggage Inc. | 7000 | Second Quartile | | | | | |
| 18 | | | | | | | | |
| 19 | | From | Thru | | =QUARTILE($B$2:$B$17,0) | | | |
| 20 | First Quartile | 100 | 900 First Quartile | | =QUARTILE($B$2:$B$17,1) | | | |
| 21 | Second Quartile | 900 | 8500 Second Quartile | | =QUARTILE($B$2:$B$17,2) | | | |
| 22 | Third Quartile | 8500 | 40000 Third Quartile | | =QUARTILE($B$2:$B$17,3) | | | |
| 23 | Fourth Quartile | 40000 | 100000 Fourth Quartile | | =QUARTILE($B$2:$B$17,4) | | | |
| 24 | | | | | | | | |

C23 • =QUARTILE($B$2:$B$17,4)

26

## USING PERCENTILE TO CALCULATE PERCENTILE

The QUARTILE function is fine if you are trying to find every record that is in the top 25% of a range. Sometimes, however, you need to find some other percentile. For example, all employees ranked above the 81st percentile may be eligible for a bonus this year. You can use the PERCENTILE function to determine the threshold for any percentile.

SYNTAX: =PERCENTILE(*array*,*k*)

The PERCENTILE function returns the *k*th percentile of values in a range. You can use this function to establish a threshold of acceptance. For example, you can decide to examine candidates who score above the 90th percentile. This function takes the following arguments:

■ *array*—This is the array or range of data that defines relative standing. If *array* is empty, PERCENTILE returns a #NUM! error.

- *k*—This is the percentile value in the range 0...1, inclusive. If *k* is nonnumeric, `PERCENTILE` returns a `#VALUE!` error. If *k* is less than 0 or if *k* is greater than 1, `PERCENTILE` returns a `#NUM!` error. If *k* is not a multiple of 1 / (*n* – 1), `PERCENTILE` interpolates to determine the value at the *k*th percentile.

In Figure 26.9, there are 33 employees in Column A. Their ratings on an annual review are shown in Column B. The formula in Cell F3, `=PERCENTILE(B2:B34,F2)`, calculates the level of the 81st percentile. After you determine the particular percentile, you can mark all the qualifying employees by using the formula `=B2>=$F$3` in cells C2:C33.

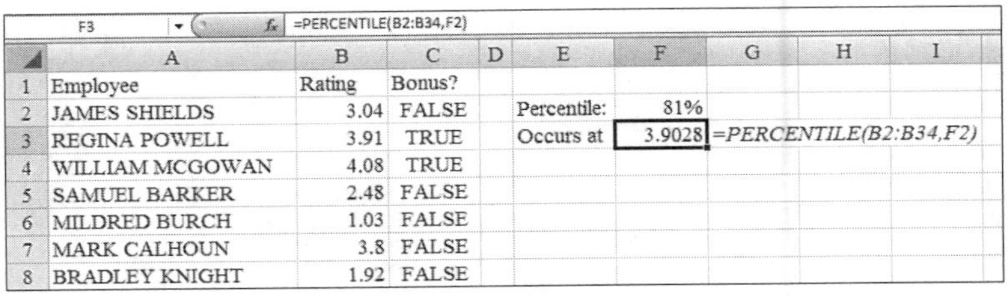

F3 =PERCENTILE(B2:B34,F2)

| | A | B | C | D | E | F | G | H | I |
|---|---|---|---|---|---|---|---|---|---|
| 1 | Employee | Rating | Bonus? | | | | | | |
| 2 | JAMES SHIELDS | 3.04 | FALSE | | Percentile: | 81% | | | |
| 3 | REGINA POWELL | 3.91 | TRUE | | Occurs at | 3.9028 | =PERCENTILE(B2:B34,F2) | | |
| 4 | WILLIAM MCGOWAN | 4.08 | TRUE | | | | | | |
| 5 | SAMUEL BARKER | 2.48 | FALSE | | | | | | |
| 6 | MILDRED BURCH | 1.03 | FALSE | | | | | | |
| 7 | MARK CALHOUN | 3.8 | FALSE | | | | | | |
| 8 | BRADLEY KNIGHT | 1.92 | FALSE | | | | | | |

**Figure 26.9**
Unlike `QUARTILE`, the `PERCENTILE` function can determine the breaking point for any particular percentile.

## USING PERCENTRANK TO ASSIGN A PERCENTILE TO EVERY RECORD

Say that you have a database of students in a graduating class. Each student has a certain grade point average. To determine each student's standing in the class, you use the `PERCENTRANK` function.



SYNTAX: `=PERCENTRANK(array,x,significance)`

The `PERCENTRANK` function returns the rank of a value in a dataset as a percentage of the dataset. This function can be used to evaluate the relative standing of a value within a dataset. For example, you can use `PERCENTRANK` to evaluate the standing of an aptitude test score among all scores for the test. This function takes the following arguments:

- *array*—This is the array or range of data with numeric values that defines relative standing. If *array* is empty, `PERCENTRANK` returns a `#NUM!` error.
- *x*—This is the value for which you want to know the rank. If *x* does not match one of the values in *array*, `PERCENTRANK` interpolates to return the correct percentage rank.
- *significance*—This is an optional value that identifies the number of significant digits for the returned percentage value. If it is omitted, `PERCENTRANK` uses three digits (that is, 0.xxx). If significance is less than 1, `PERCENTRANK` returns a `#NUM!` error.

This function is slightly different from `RANK`, so use caution. Typically, `RANK` and other functions would ask for *x* as the first argument and *array* as the second argument. If you use this function and everyone is assigned to the 100% level, you might have reversed the arguments. The Excel Help is a bit misleading with regard to significance. The Help topic indicates that a significance of 3 generates a value accurate to 0.xxx%. In fact, a significance of 3 returns xx.x%.

In Figure 26.10, the students' GPAs are in B2:B301. The rank for the first student is
=PERCENTRANK($B$2:$B$301,B2,3). Note that PERCENTRANK always starts with the lowest score
at the lowest percentile. To find the top students in the class, you use a conditional format
to highlight the students with percentiles above 90%.

**Figure 26.10**
The PERCENTRANK function assigns percentile values to an array of values.

| | A | B | C | D | E | F | G |
|---|---|---|---|---|---|---|---|
| 1 | Student | GPA | PercentRank | | | | |
| 2 | WHITNEY ABBOTT | 3.50 | 79.2% | =PERCENTRANK($B$2:$B$301,B2,3) | | |
| 3 | DOUGLAS ADKINS | 3.04 | 53.8% | | | | |
| 4 | ADAM ALBERT | 2.23 | 20.0% | | Significance | | |
| 5 | REGINA ALBERT | 3.58 | 81.9% | | 1 | 0.7 | |
| 6 | THELMA ALBERT | 3.09 | 57.5% | | 2 | 0.79 | |
| 7 | NORMAN ALVARADO | 2.86 | 46.1% | | 3 | 0.792 | |
| 8 | SHELLY ALVARADO | 2.57 | 33.7% | | 4 | 0.7926 | |
| 9 | KEVIN ARMSTRONG | 3.77 | 90.9% | | 5 | 0.79264 | |
| 10 | NAOMI ARMSTRONG | 3.61 | 82.9% | | | | |

Cell C2 = PERCENTRANK($B$2:$B$301,B2,3)

The table in E4:F9 shows the actual behavior of the *significance* argument. The values in
Column F show the PERCENTRANK of Cell B2 to the significance in Column E. You can see
that the student ranked at the 79.2th percentile is in the 70th percentile when the significance is 1. A significance of 1 would assign 30 records to be at the 70th percentile.

## USING AVEDEV, DEVSQ, VAR, AND STDEV TO CALCULATE DISPERSION

Functions such as AVERAGE tell you about the center of a range of data. Seeing the center is
not always the entire picture. The other key element of descriptive statistics is dispersion. If
you have a population, the average height might be $x$. If you look at dispersion, you can find
out if every member of the population is tightly grouped around the average or if there is
wide variability.

Here are several measures of dispersion:

- Average deviation is calculated by measuring the absolute difference of each data point
  from the mean and then averaging these values. Say the values in a population are 12,
  14, 16, 18, and 20. The mean is 16. Average deviation adds up 4, 2, 0, 2, and 4 and
  divides the total by 5 to yield 2.4. Excel offers AVEDEV to calculate this.

- Average deviation is not perfect. Say that you have another population of 11, 15, 16, 17,
  and 21. Again, the mean is 16. The average deviation averages 5, 1, 0, 1, and 5 to yield
  an average deviation of 2.4. If you want to measure how far from the mean the points
  range, you can add up the squares of each deviation. In this case, the square of 5 is 25,
  and it indicates more dispersion than the square of 4. Excel offers DEVSQ to calculate the
  squares of each deviation.

- Variance is a common measurement of dispersion. It averages the square deviations to
  come up with the variance of a dataset. Here is the one odd thing about variance: Say
  that you have 20 measurements, and they represent the entire population (for example,

**26**

the 20 fish in an aquarium). In this case, you divide DEVSQ by 20 to calculate the variance. You use VARP in Excel to do this. However, if your 20 values are a random sample, then variance is calculated by dividing DEVSQ by 20 – 1, or 19. You use VAR in Excel to calculate this.

- The measurement for variance is a square, right? You took all the deviations, squared them, and then averaged (or nearly averaged) them. The final popular measure of dispersion is calculated by taking the square root of the variance. This number is called standard deviation. Excel offers two functions for standard deviation. You use STDEVP if your dataset represents the entire population, and you use STDEV if your dataset represents only a sample of the population.

There are many theories about standard deviation. One rule of thumb says that 95% of a population will be located within two standard deviations of the mean. If you extend your range to within three standard deviations of the mean, that range should encompass 99.7% of the population.

Figure 26.11 shows the lengths of fish. Column A contains the lengths of all 20 fish in one particular tank at a science museum. Column E contains the lengths of 20 random fish observed while snorkeling at a coral reef. Both groups have a mean value of 18.58 inches, as shown in Cells C4 and G4.

The fish in the museum tank have an average deviation of 1.45 inches from the mean. Cells C6, C8, and C10 walk through the calculation of squares of deviation, variance, and standard deviation. The theory about standard deviation says that of the fish in the tank, 95% will occur between 15.08 inches and 22.07 inches.

The fish at the coral reef have an average deviation of 6.7 inches from the mean. Cells G6, G7, and G9 walk through the calculation of squares of deviation, variance, and standard deviation. The theory about standard deviation says that of the fish at the coral reef, 95% will be between 0.78 inches and 36.37 inches long.

Comparing these two results helps you to picture the likely populations of both locations. Although both have the same mean size, the variety of fish (that is, the measure of dispersion) at the coral reef is much higher than that at the aquarium.

SYNTAX: =AVEDEV(number1,number2,...)

The AVEDEV function returns the average of the absolute deviations of data points from their mean. AVEDEV is a measure of the variability in a dataset. AVEDEV is influenced by the unit of measurement in the input data.

SYNTAX: =DEVSQ(number1,number2,...)

The DEVSQ function returns the sum of squares of deviations of data points from their sample mean.

**Figure 26.11**
Although the averages are the same, the dispersion measurements paint a different picture of these populations.

| | G9 | | ▾ | $f_x$ | =STDEV(E4:E23) | | | |
|---|---|---|---|---|---|---|---|---|
| | A | B | C | D | E | F | G | H |
| 1 | Length of Fish | | | | | | | |
| 2 | | | | | | | | |
| 3 | Aquarium | | | | Coral Reef | | | |
| 4 | 15.6 | Mean | 18.58 | | 2 | Mean | 18.58 | |
| 5 | 15.8 | AveDev | 1.45 | | 8 | AveDev | 6.774 | |
| 6 | 16.6 | DevSq | 57.992 | | 9.7 | DevSq | 1503.45 | |
| 7 | 16.7 | Var | 3.05221 | | 10.3 | Var | 79.1291 | |
| 8 | 16.8 | VarP | 2.8996 | | 12 | VarP | 75.1726 | |
| 9 | 17.4 | Std Dev | 1.74706 | | 14 | Std Dev | 8.89545 | |
| 10 | 17.7 | Std DevP | 1.70282 | | 14.3 | Std DevP | 8.67021 | |
| 11 | 18.2 | | | | 16.2 | | | |
| 12 | 18.2 | 95% of population: | | | 16.7 | 95% of population: | | |
| 13 | 18.3 | From: | 15.0859 | | 16.9 | From: | 0.7891 | |
| 14 | 18.6 | Thru: | 22.0741 | | 17.7 | Thru: | 36.3709 | |
| 15 | 18.7 | | | | 18 | | | |
| 16 | 19.6 | | | | 18 | | | |
| 17 | 20 | | | | 22.3 | | | |
| 18 | 20.1 | | | | 25.8 | | | |
| 19 | 20.1 | | | | 24.3 | | | |
| 20 | 20.4 | | | | 25 | | | |
| 21 | 20.4 | | | | 28.1 | | | |
| 22 | 20.9 | | | | 32.6 | | | |
| 23 | 21.5 | | | | 39.7 | | | |
| 24 | | | | | | | | |

**SYNTAX:** =VAR(*number1*,*number2*,...)

The VAR function estimates variance based on a sample.

**SYNTAX:** =VARP(*number1*,*number2*,...)

The VARP function calculates variance based on the entire population.

**SYNTAX:** =STDEV(*number1*,*number2*,...)

The STDEV function estimates standard deviation based on a sample. The standard deviation is a measure of how widely values are dispersed from the average value (that is, the mean). The standard deviation is calculated using the "nonbiased" or "n – 1" method.

**SYNTAX:** =STDEVP(*number1*,*number2*,...)

The STDEVP function calculates standard deviation based on the entire population, given as arguments. The standard deviation is a measure of how widely values are dispersed from the average value (that is, the mean). STDEVP assumes that its arguments are the entire population. If your data represents a sample of the population, you can compute the standard deviation by using STDEV. For large sample sizes, STDEV and STDEVP return approximately equal values. The standard deviation is calculated using the "biased" or "n" method.

The arguments *number1*, *number2*,... are 1 to 255 arguments for which you want the average of the absolute deviations. You can also use a single array or a reference to an array instead of arguments separated by commas. The arguments must be either numbers or names, arrays, or references that contain numbers. If an array or a reference argument contains text, logical values, or empty cells, those values are ignored; however, cells that contain the value 0 are included.

26

CAUTION

> Logical values (TRUE/FALSE) are ignored in the STDDEV and STDDEVP calculations. There are some statistics for which you need to figure out how many people answered TRUE to a question. In order to count TRUE values as 1 and FALSE values as 0, you use VARA, VARPA, STDEVA, and STDEVPA versions of those four functions.

26

# EXAMPLES OF FUNCTIONS FOR REGRESSION AND FORECASTING

Regression analysis allows you to predict the future, based on past events. Say that you have observed total sales for the past several years. Regression analysis finds a line that best fits the past data points. You can then use the description of that line to predict results for the future data points.

Regression works by finding a line that can best be drawn through existing data points. In real-life data, the data points aren't arranged exactly in a line. Any line that the computer draws will have errors at any data point. Regression finds the line that minimizes the errors at each data point.

Consider the error in a regression line. The actual data point in Year 1 might by higher than the regression line by 2. In Year 2, the data might be lower by 1, and in Year 3 it might be lower by 1. If you added up these three errors, you would have an error of 0. This is a bad method. If you used this method to judge a line with errors of +400, –300, –100, it would also add up to an error of 0.

Instead, the regression engine sums the square of each error. In this case, the first line would have an error of $2^2 + -1^2 + -1^2$ or $4 + 1 + 1$, or 6. The second line would have an error of $400^2 + -300^2 + -100^2$ or $160{,}000 + 90{,}000 + 10{,}000$, or $260{,}000$. With this method, the error for the first line is clearly better than the error for the second line. This method is called the least-squares method.

You might wonder why regression doesn't add the absolute value of each error. Ideally, the errors around the regression line should be narrow. A line with errors of –4, +4, –4, +4 would results in a sum of squares of 64. A line with errors of –7, 1, 7, –1 would result in a sum of squares of 100. The sum of squares method would deem the earlier line to be better, while using absolute values would call them equal.

You need to consider one question before doing regression analysis. First, is the data series growing linearly or exponentially? Sales for a company might grow linearly. The number of bacteria cells in a Petri dish might grow exponentially. You use LINEST and TREND to predict sales that are growing linearly. You use LOGEST and GROWTH to predict bacteria that are growing exponentially.

In Figure 26.12, the chart on the left shows sales over time. These sales are growing linearly and could probably be predicted fairly well by a straight line. The dotted line in the chart is the straight-line regression for the dataset. Although each data point is either above or below the regression line, the error at any given data point is fairly small.

The chart on the right shows an exponential growth curve. In this chart, the dotted line shows the regression line plotted using LOGEST. Again, although the dotted line does not correlate exactly with the actual data points, it is fairly close.

**Figure 26.12**
These two datasets can be accurately predicted using regression.

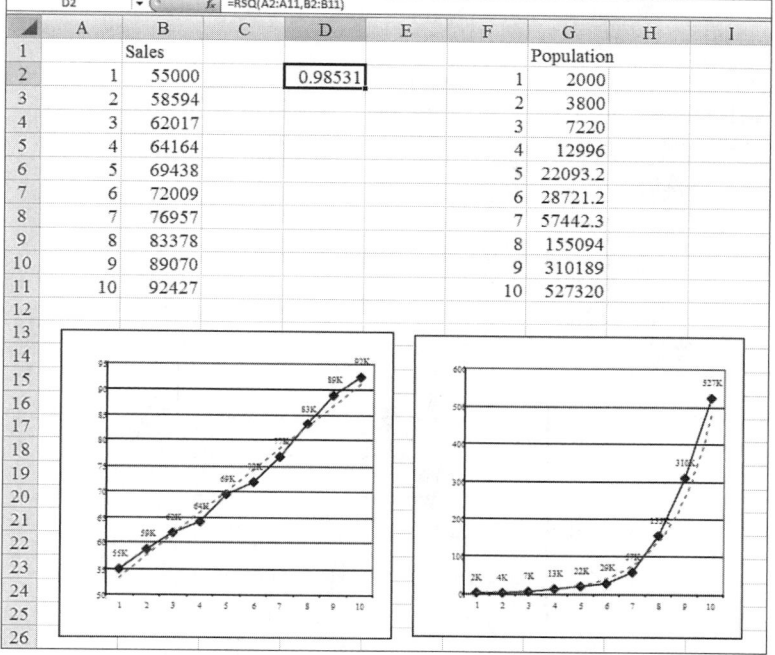

Here is the problem: Regression always finds a line to fit your dataset. In Figure 26.13, there is no apparent correlation between sales and time. Each year, the sales fluctuate wildly up or down. If you asked Excel to use regression, it would gladly predict the dotted line shown in the graph. The problem is that this line has no predictive ability. If you base your future sales on this line, you will get results that will vary greatly from the prediction.

Part of the results of regression analysis are statistics that tell how well the regression line fits the actual data. You should always check statistics such as $r$-squared or the standard error to see if the past data shows a relationship between the variables. The $r$-squared value is a value between 0 and 1. The closer that $r$-squared is to 1, the better the regression line. The $r$-squared for the left chart in Figure 26.12 is 0.985. The $r$-squared for the chart in Figure 26.13 is 0.000001, indicating that there is no correlation.

When you have data like the data in Figure 26.13, it does not mean that you cannot use regression analysis. It means that you need to think about the data to see if other factors could help describe the data. Let's say that the data represents sales of squares of roofing shingles in Florida. If you add data to the chart that describes the number of category 3+ hurricanes making landfall each year, the sales numbers begin to make sense. The $r$-squared

26

for predicting sales based on year is nearly 0. The *r*-squared for predicting sales based on hurricanes is 0.987. Since an *r*-squared of 1 means almost perfect correlation, you could base prediction of sales on a forecast of hurricanes.

**Figure 26.13**
This dataset has no correlation to time. LINEST happily predicts a line, but it is severely wrong most of the time.

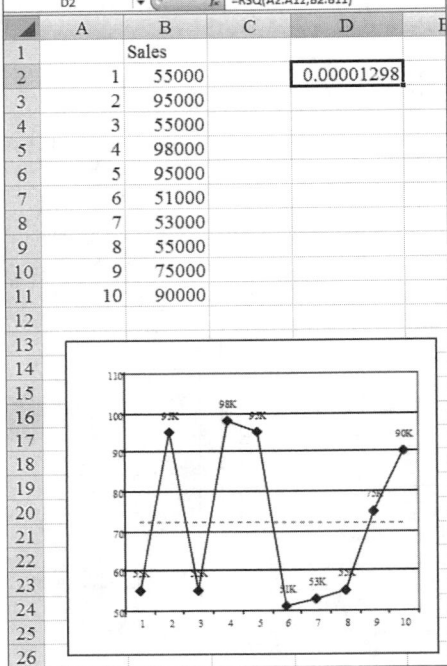

For all the following regression functions, the arguments list generally includes these two arguments (for brevity, they are described here once):

- *known_y's*—This is an array or a cell range of numeric dependent data points. This is the range of data that you want to predict. It might be the actual sales for the past several years or the population of bacteria for the past several hours.

- *known_x's*—This is the set of independent data points. These are the values that you think will lead to a prediction of the y values. For a simple time series, this might be a list of year numbers. It might be a list of other independent data points, such as the number of hurricanes making landfall each year.

The arguments must be either numbers or names, arrays, or references that contain numbers. If an array or a reference argument contains text, logical values, or empty cells, those values are ignored; however, cells that contain the value 0 are included. If known_y's and known_x's are empty or have a different number of data points, the function returns a #N/A error.

# FUNCTIONS FOR SIMPLE STRAIGHT-LINE REGRESSION: SLOPE AND INTERCEPT

With many things in Excel, there is a right way to do something. However, sometimes the powers-that-be decide that the right way is too difficult for Excel customers, so they offer alternative, easier ways to solve problems.

The LINEST function is powerful, and using it is the right way to calculate straight-line regression. However, because the LINEST function returns an array of values, it seemed too difficult, so Microsoft also offers the SLOPE and INTERCEPT functions to retrieve the key results from LINEST.

In mathematical terms, a line is described as y = mx + b:

- **y**—This is the value you are trying to predict. It could be sales for a given year.
- **b**—This is called the y-intercept. This is the base level of sales that you can count on year after year after year.
- **m**—This is the slope of the line. If your sales are going up by 1,000 per year, the slope is 1,000. If your sales are going up by 100,000 per year, the slope is 100,000.
- **x**—This is a point along the x-axis. In a problem where you are measuring sales over a span of several years, you can assign year numbers 1, 2, 3, and so on to each year. x then corresponds to a year number.

If you have a series of year numbers and sales for each year, you need to calculate both the SLOPE and INTERCEPT in order to describe the line.

### SYNTAX: =SLOPE(*known_y's,known_x's*)

The SLOPE function returns the slope of the linear regression line through data points in known_y's and known_x's. The slope is the vertical distance divided by the horizontal distance between any two points on the line; in other words, it is the rate of change along the regression line.

### SYNTAX: =INTERCEPT(*known_y's,known_x's*)

The INTERCEPT function calculates the point at which a line intersects the y-axis by using existing x values and y values. The intercept point is based on a best-fit regression line plotted through the known x values and known y values. You use the intercept when you want to determine the value of the dependent variable when the independent variable is 0.

In Figure 26.14, the sales in B2:B11 are the dependent variables. In the language of Excel, these are the known_y's. You are predicting that sales are increasing linearly over time. The year numbers in A2:A11 are the independent variables. In the language of Excel, these are the known_x's.

26

**Figure 26.14**
Using the `SLOPE` and `INTERCEPT` functions is a simple way to calculate a linear regression line.

E2 =INTERCEPT(B2:B11,A2:A11)

| | A | B | C | D | E | F | G | H |
|---|---|---|---|---|---|---|---|---|
| 1 | Year | Sales | | | | | | |
| 2 | 1 | 55000 | | Intercept: | 49,041 | =INTERCEPT(B2:B11,A2:A11) | | |
| 3 | 2 | 58594 | | Slope: | 4,230 | =SLOPE(B2:B11,A2:A11) | | |
| 4 | 3 | 62017 | | | | | | |
| 5 | 4 | 64164 | | | | | | |
| 6 | 5 | 69438 | | Prediction: | | | | |
| 7 | 6 | 72009 | | Year | Sales | | | |
| 8 | 7 | 76957 | | 11 | 95,570 | =$E$2+$E$3*D8 | | |
| 9 | 8 | 83378 | | 12 | 99,800 | | | |
| 10 | 9 | 89070 | | 13 | 104,029 | | | |
| 11 | 10 | 92427 | | 14 | 108,259 | | | |
| 12 | | | | 15 | 112,489 | | | |
| 13 | | | | | | | | |

The formula in Cell E2 calculates the intercept for the line by using `=INTERCEPT(B2:B11,A2:A11)`. The answer of `49,041` means that the model predicts that your sales in a hypothetical Year 0 would have been 49,041.

The formula in Cell E3 calculates the slope of the line by using `=SLOPE(B2:B11,A2:A11)`. The answer of `4,230` means that the model predicts that your sales are increasing by about 4,230 each year.

When you have the slope and y-intercept, you can build a new table to predict future sales. You enter year numbers 11 through 15 in D8:D12. The formula in Cell E8 needs to multiply the year number by the slope and add the intercept. That formula is `=$E$2+$E$3*D8`.

The values in Cells E8 through E12 are one prediction of future sales. This assumes that the past trends continue to work over the next five years.

## USING LINEST TO CALCULATE STRAIGHT-LINE REGRESSION WITH COMPLETE STATISTICS

Although `SLOPE` and `INTERCEPT` would do the job, the more powerful function is `LINEST`. Here is the difficulty: `LINEST` returns both the slope and the intercept. In addition, it returns a whole series of statistics. Anytime a function returns several values, you must enter the function by using Ctrl+Shift+Enter. You should also select a large enough range in advance before entering the formula. Figuring out the size of the range in advance is difficult because it varies, depending on the shape of the independent variables and also whether you ask for statistics.

However, `LINEST` is far more powerful than `SLOPE` and `INTERCEPT`. There are additional arguments available in `LINEST` that are not available in the easier functions.

SYNTAX: =LINEST(*known_y's,known_x's,const,stats*)

The LINEST function calculates the statistics for a line by using the least-squares method to calculate a straight line that best fits the data, and it returns an array that describes the line. Because this function returns an array of values, it must be entered as an array formula with Ctrl+Shift+Enter. The equation for the line is y = mx + b or y = m1x1 + m2x2 + ... + b (if there are multiple ranges of x values) where the dependent y value is a function of the independent x values. The m values are coefficients corresponding to each x value, and b is a constant value. Note that y, x, and m can be vectors. The array that LINEST returns is backward from what you would expect. The slope for the last independent variable appears first: {mn,mn-1,...,m1,b}. LINEST can also return additional regression statistics.

The LINEST function takes the following arguments:

- *known_y's*—This is the set of y values you already know in the relationship y = mx + b. If the array *known_y's* is in a single column, each column of *known_x's* is interpreted as a separate variable. If the array *known_y's* is in a single row, each row of *known_x's* is interpreted as a separate variable.

- *known_x's*—This is an optional set of x values that you may already know in the relationship y = mx + b. The array *known_x's* can include one or more sets of variables. If only one variable is used, *known_y's* and *known_x's* can be ranges of any shape, as long as they have equal dimensions. If more than one variable is used, *known_y's* must be a vector (that is, a range with a height of one row or a width of one column). If *known_x's* is omitted, it is assumed to be the array {1,2,3,...} that is the same size as *known_y's*.

- *const*—This is a logical value that specifies whether to force the constant b to equal 0. If *const* is TRUE or omitted, b is calculated normally. If *const* is FALSE, b is set equal to 0, and the m values are adjusted to fit y = mx.

- *stats*—This is a logical value that specifies whether to return additional regression statistics. If *stats* is TRUE, LINEST returns the additional regression statistics, so the returned array is {mn,mn-1,...,m1,b;sen,sen-1,...,se1,seb;r2,sey;F,df;ssreg,ssresid}. If *stats* is FALSE or omitted, LINEST returns only the m coefficients and the constant b. If you specify TRUE for *stats*, the additional regression statistics shown in Table 26.2 are possible return values.

**TABLE 26.2    ADDITIONAL REGRESSION STATISTICS FOR LINEST**

| Statistic | Description |
| --- | --- |
| se1,se2,...,sen | The standard errors for the coefficients m1,m2,...,mn. |
| Seb | The standard error for the constant b (seb = #N/A when *const* is FALSE). |

*continues*

**TABLE 26.2    CONTINUED**

| Statistic | Description |
|-----------|-------------|
| r2 | The coefficient of determination. You compare estimated and actual y values and ranges in value from 0 to 1. If it is 1, there is a perfect correlation in the sample—that is, there is no difference between the estimated y value and the actual y value. At the other extreme, if the coefficient of determination is 0, the regression equation is not helpful in predicting a y value. |
| Sey | The standard error for the y estimate. |
| F | The F statistic, or the F observed value. You use the F statistic to determine whether the observed relationship between the dependent and independent variables occurs by chance. |
| df | The degrees of freedom. You use the degrees of freedom to help you find F critical values in a statistical table. You compare the values you find in the table to the F statistic returned by LINEST to determine a confidence level for the model. |
| ssreg | The regression sum of squares. |
| ssresid | The residual sum of squares. |

Figure 26.16, later in this chapter, shows a visual map of the statistics being returned.

The accuracy of the line calculated by LINEST depends on the degree of scatter in the data. The more linear the data, the more accurate the LINEST model. LINEST uses the method of least squares for determining the best fit for the data.

The line- and curve-fitting functions LINEST and LOGEST can calculate the best straight line or exponential curve that fits the data. However, you have to decide which of the two results best fits the data. You can calculate TREND(known_y's,known_x's) for a straight line or GROWTH(known_y's, known_x's) for an exponential curve. These functions, without the known_x's argument, return an array of y values predicted along that line or curve at your actual data points. You can then compare the predicted values with the actual values. You might want to chart them both for a visual comparison.

In regression analysis, Microsoft Excel calculates for each point the squared difference between the y value estimated for that point and its actual y value. The sum of these squared differences is called the *residual sum of squares*. Microsoft Excel then calculates the sum of the squared differences between the actual y values and the average of the y values, which is called the *total sum of squares* (that is Regression sum of squares + Residual sum of squares). The smaller the residual sum of squares compared with the total sum of squares, the larger the value of the coefficient of determination, *r*-squared, which is an indicator of how well the equation resulting from the regression analysis explains the relationship among the variables.

Say that you rent a snowcone cart at a local amusement park. You create a table showing total snow cones sold for each day of last summer. In Figure 26.15, Column E shows the total snow cones sold by day. As you can see, the sales rise and fall sharply from day to day.

**Figure 26.15**
**The results of the `LINEST` function in G4:J8 are seemingly meaningless.**

G4 | {=LINEST(E4:E95,B4:D95,TRUE,TRUE)}

| | A | B | C | D | E | F | G | H | I | J |
|---|---|---|---|---|---|---|---|---|---|---|
| 2 | | | | | | | | | | |
| 3 | Date | Hi Temp | Weekend? | Rain? | Sales | | | | | |
| 4 | Fri 1-Jun | 74 | 0 | 0 | 112 | | -102.236 | 52.5182 | 2.61801 | -75.9629 |
| 5 | Sat 2-Jun | 75 | 1 | 0 | 173 | | 2.87963 | 2.73778 | 0.19978 | 16.0369 |
| 6 | Sun 3-Jun | 66 | 1 | 0 | 132 | | 0.95363 | 11.9556 | #N/A | #N/A |
| 7 | Mon 4-Jun | 72 | 0 | 0 | 106 | | 603.288 | 88 | #N/A | #N/A |
| 8 | Tue 5-Jun | 73 | 0 | 1 | 34 | | 258695 | 12578.4 | #N/A | #N/A |
| 9 | Wed 6-Jun | 64 | 0 | 1 | 25 | | | | | |

The previous manager of the cart had noticed certain trends in the data. Sales were better on the weekends than on weekdays. Sales were horrible when it rained. Sales improved as the weather became hotter in July and August.

Columns B:D in Figure 26.15 contain data related to temperature, weekends, and rain. Note that in Column C, the weekend data is binary data—either 0 or 1. In Column D, the manager could have kept information about the amount of rainfall each day but instead kept this as binary data as well. If the day was predominantly rainy, the manager recorded a 1 to indicate a rainout. If the day had just a spot of rain, the manager recorded it as a non-rainy day.

To perform regression on this data, you follow these steps:

1. Total the number of independent variables and add one. This is the number of columns the results of the regression will occupy. In the snow cone cart example, that is four columns.
2. Figure out how may rows the result of the regression will occupy. Because you plan on asking for statistics in the snow cone example, this is five rows.
3. Off to the side of the data, select a range that is four columns wide by five columns tall. This size is determined by the results of the first two steps.
4. Start to type the formula, `=LINEST(`.
5. For the *`known_y's`*, use the sales data in Column E; this would be E4:E95.
6. For the *`known_x's`*, use the values for temperature, weekend, and rain. This would be B4:D95. Note that the dates in Column A are not being used as an independent variable. The amusement park is an established park: There is nothing to indicate that attendance rises over the course of the season.
7. User `TRUE` for the next argument, which asks whether the intercept should be forced to be 0. This is not a requirement in the current situation. You want to allow the intercept to be calculated normally.
8. Use 1 or `TRUE` for the *`stats`* argument.

26

9. Although you have now typed the complete formula, =LINEST(E4:E95,B4:D95,TRUE,TRUE), do *not* press the Enter key. This is one formula that returns many results. You have to tell Excel to interpret the formula as an array formula. To do this, hold down Ctrl+Shift while pressing Enter. The function returns a seemingly meaningless range of numbers, as shown in Figure 26.15.

10. Start labeling the regression results in the upper-right corner. The value in the upper-right corner is the y-intercept. This is equivalent to the result of the INTERCEPT function.

11. Working in the top row from right to left, look at the slopes of the independent variables. These appear backward from how you originally specified them. Your independent variables were temperature, weekend, and rain. The slope for the last independent variable is in the top-left corner of the results. In Figure 26.16, Cell G4 is the slope associated with rain. Cell H4 is the slope associated with weekend. Cell H5 is the slope associated with temperature.

**Figure 26.16**

When you have the LINEST results, there are many more tests and charts that you can perform to test how good the regression model is.

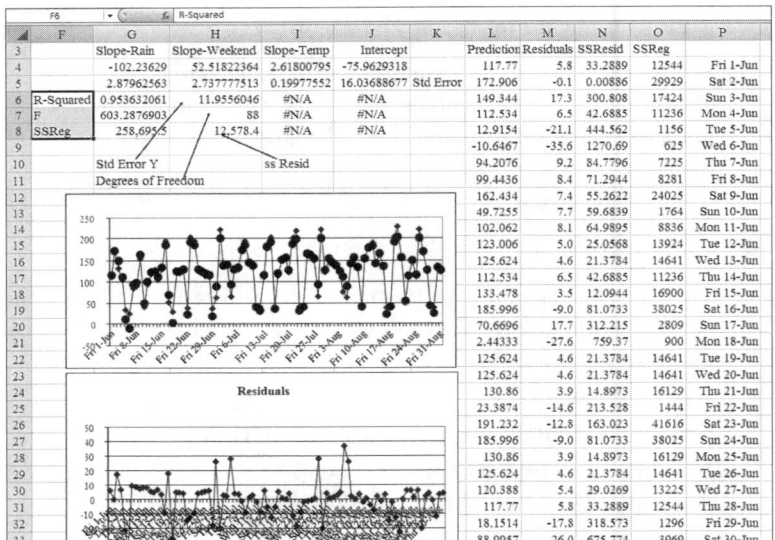

12. Take a look at these numbers for a second to see if they make sense. The intercept says you are going to sell –75 snow cones each day. This initially seems wrong. However, the value in Column I says that you will sell 2.6 snow cones for every degree of temperature. Because the lowest minimum high temperature for the summer would be about 60 degrees, the result suggests that you would sell a minimum of (60 × 2.6), or about 156 snow cones, due to temperature. Adding the –75 and 156 gets you to a minimum of 80 snow cones on a sunny day. Cell H4 suggests that you would sell about 52 extra snow cones on a weekend. Cell G4 suggests that you would sell 102 fewer snow cones on a rainy day.

13. Fill in the rest of the labels for statistics. The second row of the results shows the standard error for the number above it. The first column of the third row returns the

all-important *r*-squared value. If this value is close to 1, your model is doing a good job of predicting the data. The value of 0.95 shows that this model is fairly good. Row 3, Column 2 shows the standard error of Y. It is normal to have #N/A in any additional columns of Row 3. Row 4 contains the *F* statistic and degrees of freedom. Row 5 contains the sum of squares of the regression and the residual sum of squares. This is the number that Excel is trying to minimize when it fits the line using least squares.

14. In Column L, build a formula to predict sales with the results of the regression. This formula would be Intercept + Slope temp × Temp + Slope weekend × Weekend + Slope rain × Rain. The formula in Cell L4 is therefore =$J$4+$I$4*B4+$H$4*C4+$G$4*D4.

15. To visually compare the data, plot the actuals in Column E and the prediction in Column L on a chart. The chart in rows 12:22 shows that the prediction is tracking fairly well with the actual. There was a cold, rainy weekday near the beginning where the model predicted –10 sales versus an actual of 25.

16. For another interesting test, calculate the residual or error for each day. The data in Column M is the difference of Column L minus Column E. Plot this data. You should see many small positive and negative values. The values should swing from positive to negative frequently. The amount of scatter should not vary over time. You should not see many clusters of points that are either positive or negative. The chart in rows 24:34 shows that there are many positive residuals early in the summer, and there are fewer later in the summer. This might mean that the model is less successful at lower June temperatures than at higher August temperatures. Perhaps only real snow cone fans buy the product at temperatures of 60 to 80. Above 80 degrees, more people might buy the product.

## TROUBLESHOOTING LINEST

Remember that LINEST returns an array of values. In addition, you need to select a large enough range before entering the function, and you need to use Ctrl+Shift+Enter to enter the formula.

If you forget to use Ctrl+Shift+Enter, Excel returns just the top-left cell from the result set. In the dataset in Figure 26.15, this would just be the slope for the final independent variable (–102.236). If you enter LINEST and receive just one value, you should follow these steps:

1. Select a range starting with the LINEST formula in the upper-left corner. The range should be five rows tall. It should be at least two columns wide for models with one *known_x* column. Add additional columns for additional *known_x* series.

2. Press the F2 key to edit the current LINEST formula.

3. Hold down Ctrl+Shift+Enter to reenter the formula as an array.

Alternatively, you can use the INDEX function to pluck one particular value out of the LINEST function. For example, if you wanted to retrieve the *F* statistic from Row 4, Column 1, you could use =INDEX(LINEST(E4:E95,B4:D95,TRUE,TRUE),4,1).

26

In the simpler situation when you have only one independent x variable, you can obtain the slope and y-intercept values directly by using the following formula for slope:

`INDEX(LINEST(known_y's,known_x's),1)`

You use the following formula for the y-intercept:

`INDEX(LINEST(known_y's,known_x's),2)`

## Using FORECAST to Calculate Prediction for Any One Data Point

When you understand straight-line regression, you can use the FORECAST function to return a prediction for any point in the future.

**Syntax:** `=FORECAST(x,known_y's,known_x's)`

The FORECAST function calculates, or predicts, a future value by using existing values. The predicted value is a y value for a given x value. The known values are existing x values and y values, and the new value is predicted by using linear regression. You can use this function to predict future sales, inventory requirements, or consumer trends.

The FORECAST function takes the following arguments:

- *x*—This is the data point for which you want to predict a value. If *x* is nonnumeric, FORECAST returns a #VALUE! error.
- *known_y's*—This is the dependent array or range of data.
- *known_x's*—This is the independent array or range of data.

If known_y's and known_x's are empty or contain a different number of data points, FORECAST returns a #N/A error. If the variance of known_x's equals 0, then FORECAST returns a #DIV/0! error.

Figure 26.17 shows actual sales data for the past decade. Years are in Column A, and sales are in Column C. The sales data in C2:C12 is the range of known_y's. The years in A2:A12 is the range of known_x's.

To predict sales for future periods, you follow these steps:

1. Enter future years in A13:A2011.
2. In Column B, enter Actual or Forecast for each row so that the person reading the table understands that the new values are a forecast.
3. To predict sales for 2007, enter this formula in Cell C13:
   `=FORECAST(A13,$C$2:$C$12,$A$2:$A$12)`.
4. Copy the formula from Cell C13 down to C14:C17.

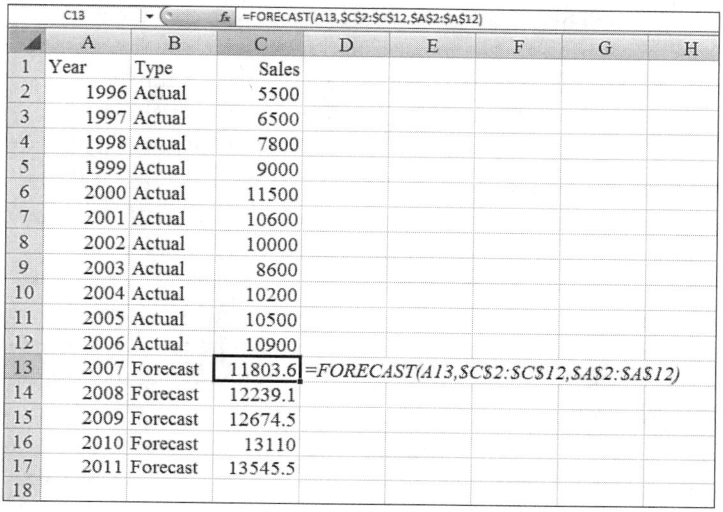

**Figure 26.17**
You use the
FORECAST function
to find the data point
for one future time
period.

| | A | B | C | D | E | F | G | H |
|---|---|---|---|---|---|---|---|---|
| | Year | Type | Sales | | | | | |
| 1 | Year | Type | Sales | | | | | |
| 2 | 1996 | Actual | 5500 | | | | | |
| 3 | 1997 | Actual | 6500 | | | | | |
| 4 | 1998 | Actual | 7800 | | | | | |
| 5 | 1999 | Actual | 9000 | | | | | |
| 6 | 2000 | Actual | 11500 | | | | | |
| 7 | 2001 | Actual | 10600 | | | | | |
| 8 | 2002 | Actual | 10000 | | | | | |
| 9 | 2003 | Actual | 8600 | | | | | |
| 10 | 2004 | Actual | 10200 | | | | | |
| 11 | 2005 | Actual | 10500 | | | | | |
| 12 | 2006 | Actual | 10900 | | | | | |
| 13 | 2007 | Forecast | 11803.6 | =FORECAST(A13,$C$2:$C$12,$A$2:$A$12) | | | | |
| 14 | 2008 | Forecast | 12239.1 | | | | | |
| 15 | 2009 | Forecast | 12674.5 | | | | | |
| 16 | 2010 | Forecast | 13110 | | | | | |
| 17 | 2011 | Forecast | 13545.5 | | | | | |
| 18 | | | | | | | | |

C13 — fx =FORECAST(A13,$C$2:$C$12,$A$2:$A$12)

**NOTE**

Note that FORECAST works only for straight-line regression. It also does not offer the ability to force the intercept to be 0. If you need this ability, you have to use LINEST and then build a prediction formula as in step 14 of the previous section or the TREND function as discussed in the next section.

## USING TREND TO CALCULATE MANY FUTURE DATA POINTS AT ONCE

The TREND function is another array function. This means that it can return many values from a single formula. If you think about the previous use of FORECAST in Figure 26.17, you realize that Excel really had to perform the linear regression multiple times—once for each of the cells in C13:C17. It would be better if you could perform the regression once and have Excel calculate all the values from that regression. The TREND function helps you do this.

SYNTAX: =TREND(known_y's,known_x's,new_x's,const)

The TREND function returns values along a linear trend. It fits a straight line (using the least-squares method) to the arrays known_y's and known_x's. It returns the y values along that line for the array of new_x's that you specify.

The TREND function takes the following arguments:

- known_y's—This is the set of y values you already know in the relationship y = mx + b. If the array known_y's is in a single column, each column of known_x's is interpreted as a separate variable. If the array known_y's is in a single row, each row of known_x's is interpreted as a separate variable.

- *known_x's*—This is an optional set of x values that you may already know in the relationship y = mx + b. The array *known_x's* can include one or more sets of variables. If only one variable is used, *known_y's* and *known_x's* can be ranges of any shape, as long as they have equal dimensions. If more than one variable is used, *known_y's* must be a vector (that is, a range with a height of one row or a width of one column). If *known_x's* is omitted, it is assumed to be the array {1,2,3,...} that is the same size as *known_y's*.

- *new_x's*—These are new x values for which you want TREND to return corresponding y values. *new_x's* must include a column (or row) for each independent variable, just as *known_x's* does. So, if *known_y's* is in a single column, *known_x's* and *new_x's* must have the same number of columns. If *known_y's* is in a single row, *known_x's* and *new_x's* must have the same number of rows. If you omit *new_x's*, it is assumed to be the same as *known_x's*. If you omit both *known_x's* and *new_x's*, they are assumed to be the array {1,2,3,...} that is the same size as *known_y's*.

- *const*—This is a logical value that specifies whether to force the constant b to equal 0. If *const* is TRUE or omitted, b is calculated normally. If *const* is FALSE, b is set equal to 0, and the m values are adjusted so that y = mx.

Formulas that return arrays must be entered as array formulas. This means that after entering the formula, you need to hold down Ctrl+Shift while pressing Enter.

Say that you are responsible for forecasting the material needs for a company that supplies roofing material. You have historical trends of usage by year. You've included past hurricane data because those events caused extraordinary demand. Your job is to predict how much roofing material you will sell, assuming that there are no hurricanes, but how much you might want to have lined up in case there are one, two, or three hurricanes. Here's what you do:

1. As in the worksheet shown in Figure 26.18, enter the actual data in A4:C17. Make the sales in Column C the *known_y's*.

2. Make the years and hurricane data in Columns A and B the *known_x's*.

3. Enter a new table in A22:B29. You want to find the forecasted requirements for 2007 and 2008 for the possibility that there are zero, one, two, or three hurricanes. The year and hurricane columns must be in the same format as the *known_x's* in step 2.

4. Keep in mind that because the TREND function is an array function, it can return several answers from one formula. Select the range C22:C29. With that range selected, start to type the formula =TREND(.

5. Enter C5:C19 for *known_y's*, which are past sales. Enter A5:A19 for *known_x's*. The new x values are the data in A22:B29.

6. Ensure that your formula is now =TREND(C5:C19,A5:B19,A22:B29). To finish the formula, hold down Ctrl+Shift while pressing Enter.

**26**

**Figure 26.18**
The TREND function is an array formula that can do one regression and return many future data points.

| | A | B | C | D | E | F |
|---|---|---|---|---|---|---|
| | C22 | ▾ | $f_x$ {=TREND(C5:C19,A5:B19,A22:B29)} | | | |
| 2 | | | | | | |
| 3 | Actual Demand | | | | | |
| 4 | Year | Hurricanes | Sales | | | |
| 5 | 1991 | 0 | 51000 | | | |
| 6 | 1992 | 1 | 81650 | | | |
| 7 | 1993 | 0 | 61800 | | | |
| 8 | 1994 | 0 | 63050 | | | |
| 9 | 1995 | 0 | 67900 | | | |
| 10 | 1996 | 0 | 72750 | | | |
| 11 | 1997 | 0 | 78400 | | | |
| 12 | 1998 | 0 | 85850 | | | |
| 13 | 1999 | 0 | 92700 | | | |
| 14 | 2000 | 0 | 96900 | | | |
| 15 | 2001 | 0 | 100000 | | | |
| 16 | 2002 | 0 | 107100 | | | |
| 17 | 2003 | 0 | 107800 | | | |
| 18 | 2004 | 2 | 168450 | | | |
| 19 | 2005 | 2 | 170000 | | | |
| 20 | | | | | | |
| 21 | Forecast Demand | | | | | |
| 22 | 2007 | 0 | 130069 | | | |
| 23 | 2007 | 1 | 155986 | | | |
| 24 | 2007 | 2 | 181903 | | | |
| 25 | 2007 | 3 | 207821 | | | |
| 26 | 2008 | 0 | 135071 | | | |
| 27 | 2008 | 1 | 160988 | | | |
| 28 | 2008 | 2 | 186905 | | | |
| 29 | 2008 | 3 | 212823 | | | |
| 30 | | | | | | |

The result is shown in C22:C29. The TREND function predicts that you will need a base level of 130 thousand in 2007 with no hurricanes. With two hurricanes in 2007, demand would rise to 182 thousand.

## USING LOGEST TO PERFORM EXPONENTIAL REGRESSION

Some patterns in business follow a linear regression. However, other items are not linear at all. If you are a scientist monitoring the growth of bacteria in a Petri jar, you will see exponential growth in the generations.

If you try to fit an exponential growth to a straight line, you have a large error. If the $r$-squared from linear regression is too low, you can try using exponential regression to see if the pattern of data matches exponential regression better. For exponential regression, you use the LOGEST function, which is similar to the LINEST function.

SYNTAX: =LOGEST(*known_y's,known_x's,const,stats*)

In regression analysis, the LOGEST function calculates an exponential curve that fits the data and returns an array of values that describes the curve. Because this function returns an array of values, it must be entered as an array formula. The equation for the curve is $y = b*m^x$ or $y = (b*(m1^{x1})*(m2^{x2})*\_)$ (if there are multiple x values), where the dependent y value is a function of the independent x values. The m values are bases that correspond to each exponent x value, and b is a constant value.

26

The LOGEST function takes the following arguments:

- *known_y's*—This is the set of y values you already know in the relationship y = b × m^x. If the array *known_y's* is in a single column, each column of *known_x's* is interpreted as a separate variable. If the array *known_y's* is in a single row, each row of *known_x's* is interpreted as a separate variable.

- *known_x's*—This is an optional set of x values you may already know in the relationship y = b × m^x. The array *known_x's* can include one or more sets of variables. If only one variable is used, *known_y's* and *known_x's* can be ranges of any shape, as long as they have equal dimensions. If more than one variable is used, *known_y's* must be a range of cells with a height of one row or a width of one column (which is also known as a vector). If *known_x's* is omitted, it is assumed to be the array {1,2,3,...} that is the same size as *known_y's*.

- *const*—This is a logical value that specifies whether to force the constant b to equal 1. If *const* is TRUE or omitted, b is calculated normally. If *const* is FALSE, b is set equal to 1, and the m values are fitted to y = m^x.

- *stats*—This is a logical value that specifies whether to return additional regression statistics. If *stats* is TRUE, LOGEST returns the additional regression statistics (refer to Figure 26.16), so the returned array is {mn,mn-1,...,m1,b;sen,sen-1,...,se1,seb;r2,sey; F,df;ssreg,ssresid}. If *stats* is FALSE or omitted, LOGEST returns only the m coefficients and the constant b.

The more a plot of data resembles an exponential curve, the better the calculated line fits the data. Like LINEST, LOGEST returns an array of values that describes a relationship among the values, but LINEST fits a straight line to the data; LOGEST fits an exponential curve.

Figure 26.19 shows an estimated population in Column B and the generation in Column A. To perform a exponential regression, you follow these steps:

1. Because there is one independent variable, the results from the regression occupy two columns, so find a blank range of the spreadsheet and select a range that is two columns wide by five rows tall, such as E2:F6.

2. Enter the beginning of the formula: =LOGEST(. Enter the *known_y's* as B2:B9 and the *known_x's* as A2:A9. Leave the *const* value blank. Specify TRUE for *statistics*. The formula should be =LOGEST(B2:B9,A2:A9,,TRUE).

3. Do not press Enter for the formula. Instead, hold down Ctrl+Shift while pressing Enter to tell Excel to interpret the result as an array formula and to return a table of values from LOGEST.

4. Add some labels to help interpret the statistics. The labels shown in Column D and G are examples.

5. To use the results of the regression in a prediction calculation, enter a different formula than with LINEST. The formula is Intercept × Slope^X. In Figure 26.19, to predict population values for a given generation in Cell I2, use =$F$2*$E$2^I2. Alternatively, you can use the GROWTH function, discussed in the next section.

**Figure 26.19**
When data is growing at an exponential rate, you use LOGEST to perform a regression analysis.

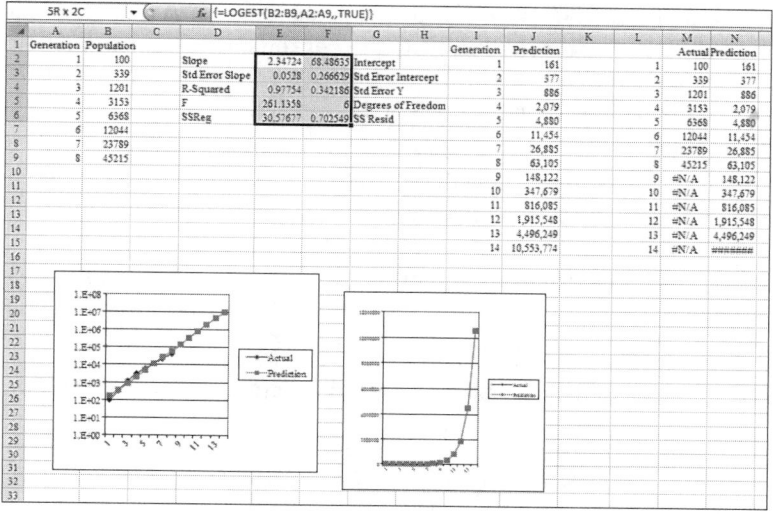

## USIGN GROWTH TO PREDICT MANY DATA POINTS FROM AN EXPONENTIAL REGRESSION

As the TREND function is able to extrapolate points from a linear regression, the GROWTH function is able to extrapolate points from an exponential regression.

SYNTAX: =GROWTH(*known_y's,known_x's,new_x's,const*)

The GROWTH function calculates predicted exponential growth by using existing data. GROWTH returns the y values for a series of new x values that you specify by using existing x values and y values. You can also use the GROWTH worksheet function to fit an exponential curve to existing x values and y values. This function takes the following arguments:

- *known_y's*—This is the set of y values you already know in the relationship $y = b \times m^x$. If the array *known_y's* is in a single column, each column of *known_x's* is interpreted as a separate variable. If the array *known_y's* is in a single row, each row of *known_x's* is interpreted as a separate variable. If any of the numbers in *known_y's* is 0 or negative, GROWTH returns a #NUM! error.

- *known_x's*—This is an optional set of x values that you may already know in the relationship $y = b \times m^x$. The array *known_x's* can include one or more sets of variables. If only one variable is used, *known_y's* and *known_x's* can be ranges of any shape, as long as they have equal dimensions. If more than one variable is used, *known_y's* must be a vector (that is, a range with a height of one row or a width of one column). If *known_x's* is omitted, it is assumed to be the array {1,2,3,...} that is the same size as *known_y's*.

- *new_x's*—These are new x values for which you want GROWTH to return corresponding y values. *new_x's* must include a column (or row) for each independent variable, just as *known_x's* does. So, if *known_y's* is in a single column, *known_x's* and *new_x's* must

26

have the same number of columns. If *known_y*'s is in a single row, *known_x*'s and *new_x*'s must have the same number of rows. If *new_x*'s is omitted, it is assumed to be the same as *known_x*'s. If both *known_x*'s and *new_x*'s are omitted, they are assumed to be the array {1,2,3,...} that is the same size as *known_y*'s.

- *const*—This is a logical value that specifies whether to force the constant b to equal 1. If *const* is TRUE or omitted, b is calculated normally. If *const* is FALSE, b is set equal to 1, and the m values are adjusted so that y = m^x.

When you have formulas that return arrays, you must enter them as array formulas after selecting the correct number of cells. To specify an array formula, you hold down Ctrl+Shift while pressing Enter.

In Figure 26.20, the original data is the population for the first 10 generations in A2:B11.

**Figure 26.20**

GROWTH performs an exponential regression and extrapolates the results in one step.

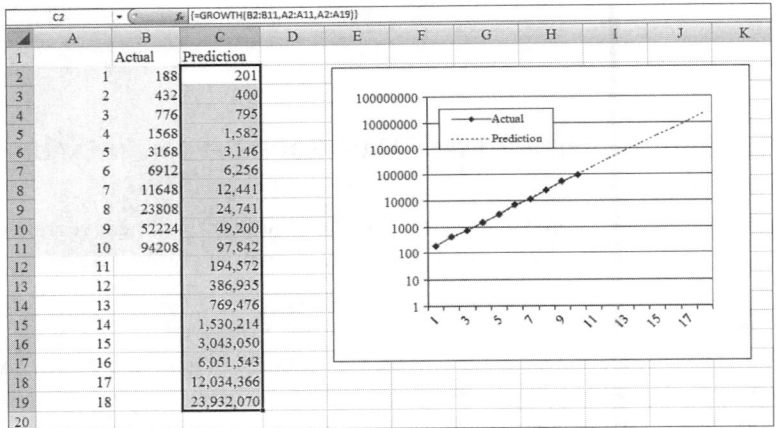

It would be interesting to run an exponential regression and see the prediction for future generations but also for the known generations as well. This would allow you to see how well the prediction tracks with current values. To do this, you follow these steps:

1. Add new generation numbers in A12:A18. The GROWTH function will use these numbers and return an array of values.

2. Select the entire range C2:C19 for the results before entering the formula.

3. Put the *known_y*'s in B2:B11. The *known_x*'s are in A2:A11. Put the *new_x*'s in A2:A19. The formula is =GROWTH(B2:B11,A2:A11,A2:A19).

4. After typing the formula, hold down Ctrl+Shift while pressing Enter. This should cause the formula to return values in each cell in C2:C19.

5. To visualize the original data and the prediction, plot A1:C19 on a line chart. Numbers at the end of the progression (24 million) make the scale of the chart so large that you cannot see the detail of the first 12 generations.

6. Right-click the numbers along the y-axis and choose Format Axis. On the Scale tab, choose Logarithmic Scale. The resulting chart allows you to examine both the smaller and larger numbers in the chart.

## USING PEARSON TO DETERMINE WHETHER A LINEAR RELATIONSHIP EXISTS

Remember that Excel blindly fits a regression line to any dataset. The fact that Excel returns a regression line does not mean that you should use it to make any predictions. The initial question to ask yourself is Does a linear relationship exist in this data?

The Pearson product–moment correlation coefficient, named after Karl Pearson, returns a value from –1.0 to +1.0. The calculation could make your head spin, but the important thing to know is that a PEARSON value closer to 1 or –1 means that a linear relationship exists. A value of 0 indicates no correlation between the independent and dependent variables.

**NOTE**

I am somewhat jealous that Microsoft has named an obscure function after fellow Excel consultant Chip Pearson. I am lobbying Microsoft for the inclusion of a JELEN function, possibly used to measure the degree of laid-backness caused by the gel in your shoe insoles. Seriously, Chip Pearson's website is one of the best established sources of articles on the Web about Excel. To peruse the articles, visit www.cpearson.com.

SYNTAX: =PEARSON(*array1*,*array2*)

The PEARSON function returns the Pearson product–moment correlation coefficient, $r$, a dimensionless index that ranges from –1.0 to 1.0, inclusive, and reflects the extent of a linear relationship between two datasets.

The PEARSON function takes the following arguments:

- *array1*—This is a set of independent values.
- *array2*—This is a set of dependent values.

The arguments must be either numbers or names, array constants, or references that contain numbers. If an array or a reference argument contains text, logical values, or empty cells, those values are ignored; however, cells that contain the value 0 are included. If *array1* and *array2* are empty or have a different number of data points, PEARSON returns a #N/A error.

The result of PEARSON is also sometimes known as $r$. Multiplying PEARSON by itself leads to the more famous $r$-squared test.

## USING RSQ TO DETERMINE THE STRENGTH OF A LINEAR RELATIONSHIP

$r$-squared is a popular measure of how well a regression line explains the variability in the y values. It is popular because the values range from 0 to 1. Numbers close to 1 mean that the regression line does a great job of predicting the values. Numbers close to 0 mean that the regression result can't predict the values at all.

*r*-squared is the statistic in the third row, first column of a LINEST function. It is also the square of the PEARSON function. You could use =INDEX(LINEST(),3,1) or =PEARSON()^2. But instead, Excel provides the easy-to-remember RSQ function.

**SYNTAX:** =RSQ(*known_y's*,*known_x's*)

The RSQ function returns the square of the Pearson product–moment correlation coefficient through data points in known_y's and known_x's. (For more information, see the section on the PEARSON function, earlier in this chapter.) The *r*-squared value can be interpreted as the proportion of the variance in y that is attributable to the variance in x.

The RSQ function takes the following arguments:

- *known_y's*—This is an array or a range of data points.
- *known_x's*—This is an array or a range of data points.

The arguments must be either numbers or names, arrays, or references that contain numbers. If an array or a reference argument contains text, logical values, or empty cells, those values are ignored; however, cells that contain the value 0 are included. If known_y's and known_x's are empty or have a different number of data points, RSQ returns a #N/A error.

Figure 26.21 shows four datasets and their associated *r*-squared values:

**Figure 26.21**
As *r*-squared approaches 1.0, the predictive ability of the regression line improves.

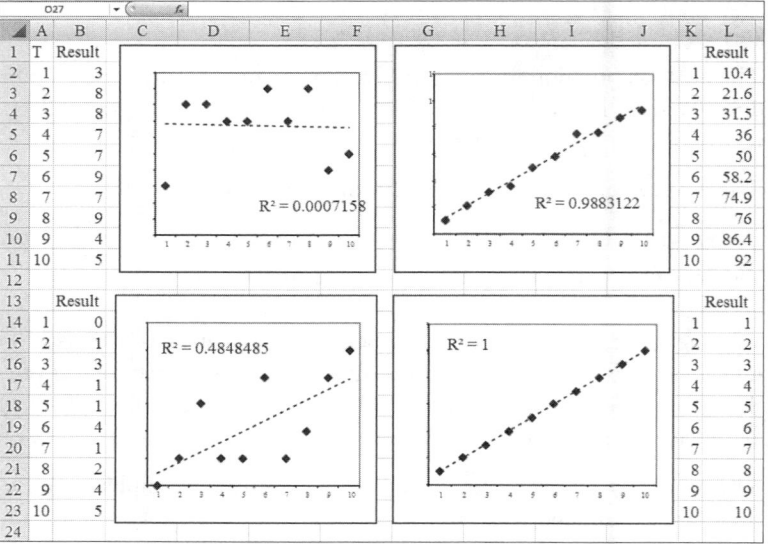

26

- The chart in the top-left corner has an *r*-squared near 0. There is little predictive ability in this regression line. In fact, the regression line is practically a horizontal line drawn through the mean of the data points.

- The chart in the lower-left corner has an *r*-squared of 0.48. There is a lot of variability in the dots, but they do seem to trend up. There are huge relative errors on certain data points (for example, the value of y = 1 when x = 7).

- The chart in the upper-right corner shows a nearly perfect correlation. The *r*-squared is appropriately high, at 0.988. This means that most of the variability in y is explained by x. There are some tiny minor variations above or below the line, but the regression is doing a great job.

- The final chart, in the lower right, illustrates a perfect correlation and an *r*-squared of 1.0. Every occurrence of y falls exactly on the regression line.

## Using STEYX to Calculate Standard Regression Error

Standard error is a measure of the quality of a regression line. In rough terms, the standard error is the size of an error that you might encounter for any particular point on the line. Smaller errors are better, and larger errors are worse. Standard error can also be used to calculate a confidence interval for any point.

Syntax: =STEYX(*known_y's*,*known_x's*)

The STEYX function returns the standard error of the predicted y value for each x in the regression. The standard error is a measure of the amount of error in the prediction of y for an individual x.

The STEYX function takes the following arguments:

- *known_y's*—This is an array or a range of dependent data points.
- *known_x's*—This is an array or a range of independent data points.

The arguments must be either numbers or names, arrays, or references that contain numbers. If an array or a reference argument contains text, logical values, or empty cells, those values are ignored; however, cells that contain the value 0 are included. If known_y's and known_x's are empty or have a different number of data points, STEYX returns a #N/A error.

To calculate standard error, you square all the residuals and add them together. Then you divide by the number of points, excluding the starting and ending points. Finally, you take the square root of that result to calculate standard error.

In general, a lower standard error is better than a higher one. A standard error of 2,000 when you are trying to predict the price of a $30,000 car isn't too bad. A standard error of 2,000 when you are trying to predict the price of a $3 jar of pickles is horrible. You need to compare the standard error to the size of the value you are predicting.

In Figure 26.22, two regressions attempt to predict the price of a car based on either mileage or age. The standard error for the mileage method is a little less than the standard error for the age method.

**Figure 26.22**
Standard error is another measure of the quality of a regression line.

| | B | C | D | E | F | G | H | I |
|---|---|---|---|---|---|---|---|---|
| | | | | | | G6 =STEYX(D5:D48,B5:B48) | | |
| 1 | Used Land Rover Discovery for Sale | | | | | | | |
| 2 | Within 50 miles of 44685 | | | | | | | |
| 3 | | | | | | | | |
| 4 | Age | Mileage | Price | | | | | |
| 5 | 3 | 35846 | 29995 | | | Age | Mileage | |
| 6 | 2 | 28000 | 29250 | | Std Error | 3673.486 | 3259.68 | |
| 7 | 3 | 21495 | 28890 | | | | | |
| 8 | 2 | 34357 | 25980 | | | | | |
| 9 | 4 | 35571 | 24900 | | | | | |

## USING COVAR TO DETERMINE WHETHER TWO VARIABLES VARY TOGETHER

Covariance is a measure of how greatly two variables vary together. If the value is 0, the variables do not appear to be related. For positive values, covariance indicates that as x increases, y also increases. For negative values, covariance indicates that as x increases, y decreases.

SYNTAX: =COVAR(array1,array2)

The COVAR function returns covariance, the average of the products of deviations for each data point pair. You use covariance to determine the relationship between two datasets. For example, you can examine whether greater income accompanies greater levels of education.

The COVAR function takes the following arguments:

- *array1*—This is the first cell range of integers.
- *array2*—This is the second cell range of integers.

The arguments must be either numbers or names, arrays, or references that contain numbers. If an array or a reference argument contains text, logical values, or empty cells, those values are ignored; however, cells that contain the value 0 are included. If array1 and array2 have different numbers of data points, COVAR returns a #N/A error. If either array1 or array2 is empty, COVAR returns a #DIV/0! error.

Covariances can become incredibly large. The unit of measurement is on the order of x times y. For a dimensionless measurement of correlation, you use CORREL instead of COVAR.

In Figure 26.23, the CORREL function measures the covariance between mileage and price. As mileage increases, price decreases.

## USING CORREL TO CALCULATE POSITIVE OR NEGATIVE CORRELATION

Instead of using covariance, you can calculate a correlation coefficient for two arrays. Let's use the mileage and price comparison from Figure 26.23. The two values would have a strong positive correlation if price went up as mileage went up. A perfect positive correlation would result in a correlation coefficient of 1.0.

**Figure 26.23**
COVAR shows that price and mileage are inversely correlated.

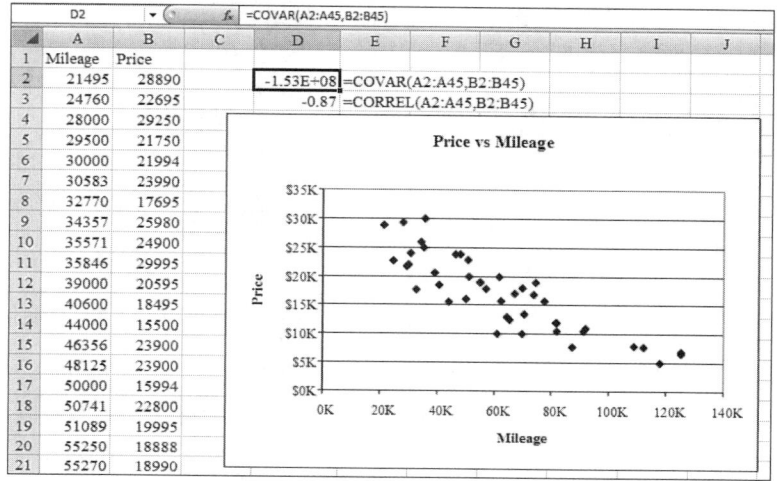

It is also possible (as in the mileage–price comparison case) for values to have an inverse correlation. As mileage increases, the price tends to decrease. If mileage were the only factor in the price of a car, the correlation coefficient would be –1.0 to indicate a perfect inverse correlation.

A correlation coefficient of 0 indicates that there is no correlation between the values.

SYNTAX: =CORREL(*array1*,*array2*)

The CORREL function returns the correlation coefficient of the array1 and array2 cell ranges. You use the correlation coefficient to determine the relationship between two properties. For example, you can examine the relationship between a location's average temperature and the use of air conditioners.

The CORREL function takes the following arguments:

- *array1*—This is a cell range of values.
- *array2*—This is a second cell range of values.

The arguments must be numbers or names, arrays, or references that contain numbers. If an array or reference argument contains text, logical values, or empty cells, those values are ignored; however, cells that contain the value 0 are included. If array1 and array2 have a different number of data points, CORREL returns a #N/A error. If either array1 or array2 is empty, or if s (the standard deviation) of their values equals 0, CORREL returns a #DIV/0! error.

In Figure 26.24, price and mileage have a correlation coefficient of 0.87. This indicates a fairly strong inverse correlation. As mileage increases, price decreases. The bottom-left chart shows two series with no correlation at all; the correlation coefficient is very close to 0. The bottom-right chart shows two series with perfect positive correlation of 1.0.

26

**Figure 26.24**
The CORREL function returns values from −1.0 to 1.0. Values near 0 indicate no correlation.

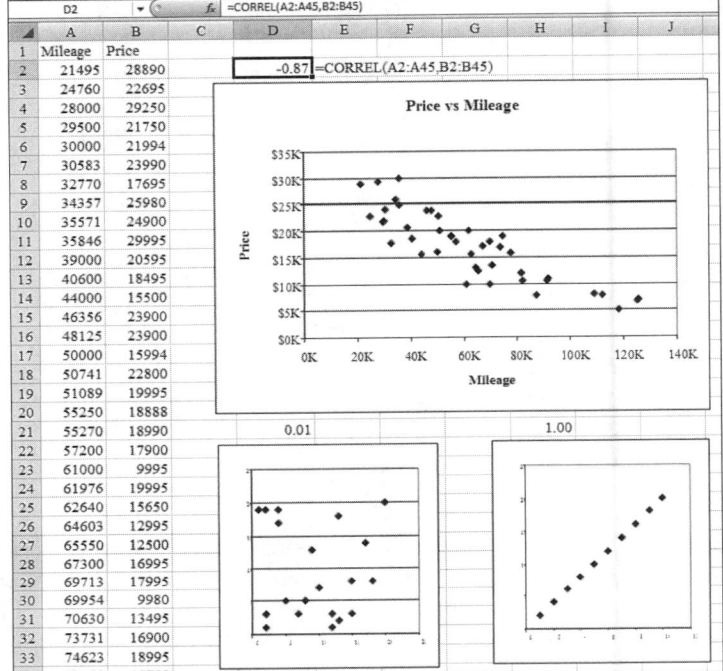

## USING FISHER TO PERFORM HYPOTHESIS TESTING ON CORRELATIONS

The Pearson value does not have a normal distribution. The graph of expected *r* values skews heavily toward 1. A statistician named Fisher found a formula that would transform the skewed *r* value into a normal distribution. You use the FISHER function to convert an *r* value. To take a FISHER value and return it to an r value, you use FISHERINV.

SYNTAX: =FISHER(x)

The FISHER function returns the Fisher transformation at *x*. This transformation produces a function that is approximately normally distributed rather than skewed. You use this function to perform hypothesis testing on the correlation coefficient.

The argument *x* is a numeric value for which you want the transformation. If *x* is nonnumeric, FISHER returns a #VALUE! error. If *x* is less than or equal to −1 or if *x* is greater than or equal to 1, FISHER returns a #NUM! error.

SYNTAX: =FISHERINV(y)

The FISHERINV function returns the inverse of the Fisher transformation. You use this transformation when analyzing correlations between ranges or arrays of data. If *y* is equal to FISHER(x), then FISHERINV(y) is equal to *x*.

The argument $y$ is the value for which you want to perform the inverse of the transformation. If $y$ is nonnumeric, FISHERINV returns a #VALUE! error.

## USING SKEW AND KURTOSIS

Two final statistics are used to describe a population:

- **Skew**—Skew is an indicator of symmetry. Actually, it is a measure of lack of symmetry. A skew value of 0 indicates that the population is perfectly symmetrical around the mean. Negative values indicate that the data is skewed to the left of the mean. Positive values indicate that the data is skewed to the right of the mean. You can use Excel's SKEW function to calculate skew.

- **Kurtosis**—Kurtosis indicates whether the distribution contains a spiky peak or is relatively flat. This measure compares a population to the standard normal distribution. If the kurtosis is less than 0, the population is flatter than the normal distribution. If the kurtosis is greater than 0, then the population is spikier than the normal distribution. You use Excel's KURT function to calculate kurtosis.

In Figure 26.25, there are two populations. The population in Column A contains one large spike of 19 data points at 2.36 inches and a single data point at 60.25 inches. You can think of this as a tank with 1 shark and 19 goldfish. The average size is 5.25 inches. The tail of the distribution is a very long tail to the right of the 5.25 inches mean, indicating a positive skew. The 19 goldfish cause a very spiky data point, causing a high kurtosis.

In Column E, the data points are uniformly distributed around the mean. The data is perfectly symmetrical, leading to a skew of 0.00. No data point has more than one member, causing the data to be extremely flat, with a negative kurtosis.

**Figure 26.25**
Skew and kurtosis return information about the symmetry and spikiness of a dataset.

| ▲ | A | B | C | D | E | F | G | H | I | J | K |
|---|---|---|---|---|---|---|---|---|---|---|---|
| 1 | | | | | | | | | | | |
| 2 | Tank 1 | | | | Tank 2 | | | | Tank 3 | | |
| 3 | 2.36 | Mean | 5.25 | | 0.5 | Mean | 5.25 | | 2.5 | Mean | 5.25 |
| 4 | 2.36 | Skew | 4.47 | | 1 | Skew | 0.00 | | 2.5 | Skew | -0.23 |
| 5 | 2.36 | Kurtosis | 20.00 | | 1.5 | Kurtosis | -1.20 | | 2.5 | Kurtosis | -1.28 |
| 6 | 2.36 | | | | 2 | | | | 2.5 | | |

SYNTAX: =SKEW(*number1,number2,...*)

The SKEW function returns the skewness of a distribution. Skewness characterizes the degree of asymmetry of a distribution around its mean. Positive skewness indicates a distribution with an asymmetric tail extending toward more positive values. Negative skewness indicates a distribution with an asymmetric tail extending toward more negative values.

The arguments *number1,number2...* are 1 to 255 arguments for which you want to calculate skewness. You can also use a single array or a reference to an array instead of arguments separated by commas. The arguments must be either numbers or names, arrays, or references that contain numbers. If an array or a reference argument contains text, logical values, or empty cells, those values are ignored; however, cells that contain the value 0 are included. If there are fewer than three data points, or if the sample standard deviation is 0, SKEW returns a #DIV/0! error.

**SYNTAX:** =KURT(*number1,number2, ...*)

The KURT function returns the kurtosis of a dataset. Kurtosis characterizes the relative peakedness or flatness of a distribution compared with the normal distribution. Positive kurtosis indicates a relatively peaked distribution. Negative kurtosis indicates a relatively flat distribution.

The arguments *number1,number2,...* are 1 to 255 arguments for which you want to calculate kurtosis. You can also use a single array or a reference to an array instead of arguments separated by commas. The arguments must be either numbers or names, arrays, or references that contain numbers. If an array or a reference argument contains text, logical values, or empty cells, those values are ignored; however, cells that contain the value 0 are included. If there are fewer than four data points, or if the standard deviation of the sample equals zero, KURT returns a #DIV/0! error.

# EXAMPLES OF FUNCTIONS FOR INFERENTIAL STATISTICS

Inferential statistics is the really powerful side of statistics. With descriptive statistics, you are able to describe a dataset. Describing a dataset might allow you to better understand the dataset. With regression, you use past trends to predict future results. With inferential statistics, you extrapolate information about a sample of the population to make predictions about the entire population.

## USING BINOMDIST TO DETERMINE PROBABILITY

A binomial test is a situation in which there are only two possible outcomes: Either an event happens or it does not happen.

For example, say that you have determined that on several nights of the week, someone has been sneaking in and eating leftovers from the department fridge. You don't know if it is the night security guard or the cleaning crew or even just Bob who works later than everyone else. After tracking this behavior for a month, you determine that food has been missing 27% of the time. How many days next week will food be missing? The BINOMDIST function can answer this question.

**SYNTAX:** =BINOMDIST(*number_s,trials,probability_s,cumulative*)

The BINOMDIST function returns the individual term binomial distribution probability. You use BINOMDIST in problems with a fixed number of tests or trials, when the outcomes of any trial are only success or failure, when trials are independent, and when the probability of success is constant throughout the experiment. For example, BINOMDIST can calculate the probability that two of the next three babies born will be male.

26

The `BINOMDIST` function takes the following arguments:

- *`number_s`*—This is the number of successes in trials.
- *`trials`*—This is the number of independent trials.
- *`probability_s`*—This is the probability of success on each trial.
- *`cumulative`*—This is a logical value that determines the form of the function. If *`cumulative`* is `TRUE`, then `BINOMDIST` returns the cumulative distribution function, which is the probability that there are at most *`number_s`* successes; if *`cumulative`* is `FALSE`, `BINOMDIST` returns the probability mass function, which is the probability that there are *`number_s`* successes.

`number_s` and *`trials`* are truncated to integers. If `number_s`, *`trials`*, or `probability_s` is non-numeric, `BINOMDIST` returns a `#VALUE!` error. If `number_s` is less than 0 or `number_s` is greater than trials, `BINOMDIST` returns a `#NUM!` error. If `probability_s` is less than 0 or `probability_s` is greater than 1, `BINOMDIST` returns a `#NUM!` error.

In Figure 26.26, range B5:B10 calculates the probability that food will be missing x days next week. In each case, *`trials`* is `5` because there are five workdays next week. The `probability_s` is `0.27`.

B5 =BINOMDIST(A5,$B$2,$B$1,FALSE)

| | A | B | C |
|---|---|---|---|
| 1 | Mean | 27% | - 27% of workdays, food is missing |
| 2 | Trials | 5 | There are five workdays next week |
| 3 | | | |
| 4 | # Days | Prob. | |
| 5 | 0 | 21% | 21% of the weeks, no food would be missing |
| 6 | 1 | 38% | 38% of the weeks, food is missing exactly one day |
| 7 | 2 | 28% | 28% of the weeks, food is missing exactly two days |
| 8 | 3 | 10% | 10% of the weeks, food is missing exactly three days |
| 9 | 4 | 2% | 2% of the weeks, food is missing exactly four days |
| 10 | 5 | 0% | You would never expect food to be missing five days in a row |
| 11 | | | |
| 12 | | | |
| 13 | # Days | Cumulative Probability | |
| 14 | 0 | 21% | *=BINOMDIST(A14,$B$2,$B$1,TRUE)* |
| 15 | 1 | 59% | |
| 16 | 2 | 87% | |
| 17 | 3 | 98% | |
| 18 | 4 | 100% | |
| 19 | 5 | 100% | |
| 20 | | | |
| 21 | What are the chances food will be missing 3 or more days next week? | | |
| 22 | 2 | 13% | *=1-BINOMDIST(A22,$B$2,$B$1,TRUE)* |
| 23 | | | |

**Figure 26.26**
For tests that are either `TRUE` or `FALSE`, the BINOMDIST function can calculate the probability of events.

Cell B15 calculates the cumulative probability that 0 or 1 successes will be encountered next week.

Note that BINOMDIST always calculates the probability starting from the left side of the curve. If you wanted to calculate the probability of three or more successes next week, you would have to use one minus the probability of two or fewer successes, as shown in Cell B22.

## USING CRITBINOM TO COVER MOST OF THE POSSIBLE BINOMIAL EVENTS

Many tests are binomial, as described in the preceding section. Say that you are exhibiting at a trade show. You expect 2,000 attendees at the trade show. Based on data from past trade shows, you predict that there is a 17% chance that an attendee will visit your booth and take a catalog. Your goal is to have enough catalogs so that you will be 95% sure to have enough catalogs for everyone. You can use the CRITBINOM function to predict how many catalogs you need.

SYNTAX: =CRITBINOM(*trials*,*probability_s*,*alpha*)

The CRTIBINOM function returns the smallest value for which the cumulative binomial distribution is greater than or equal to a criterion value. You use this function for quality assurance applications. For example, you can use CRITBINOM to determine the greatest number of defective parts you can allow to come off an assembly line run without needing to reject the entire lot.

The CRTIBINOM function takes the following arguments:

- *trials*—This is the number of Bernoulli trials.
- *probability_s*—This is the probability of a success on each trial.
- *alpha*—This is the criterion value.

If any argument is nonnumeric, CRITBINOM returns a #VALUE! error. If *trials* is not an integer, it is truncated. If *trials* is less than 0, CRITBINOM returns a #NUM! error. If probability_s is less than 0 or if probability_s is greater than 1, CRITBINOM returns a #NUM! error. If *alpha* is less than 0 or if *alpha* is greater than 1, CRITBINOM returns a #NUM! error.

In the trade show example, the number of trials is 2,000: Each attendee has a chance of picking up a catalog. The probability_s is 17%, and *alpha* is 0.95, although it would be interesting to see how many catalogs could be required at each level. Using this information, you follow these steps to determine how many catalogs you need:

1. Build a range with different values for *alpha* in Column A.
2. End the formula =CRITBINOM($B$2,$B$1,A8) in Cell B8.
3. Copy the formula from Cell B8 to the other cells in Column B.

As shown in Figure 26.27, you need to have 368 catalogs for the trade show.

## USING NEGBINOMDIST TO CALCULATE PROBABILITY

It is a fact that LeBron James has a career free throw percentage of 0.746. What are the odds that James would miss three free throws before he makes one free throw? You can use Excel's NEGBINOMDIST function to figure this out.

**Figure 26.27**
Based on response rates at last year's trade show, you can use CRITBINOM to predict how many catalogs to print.

| | A | B | C | D | E | F | G | H |
|---|---|---|---|---|---|---|---|---|
| | | | | | =CRITBINOM($B$2,$B$1,A5) | | | |
| 1 | Mean | 17% | - percent chance of any one attendee taking a catalog | | | | | |
| 2 | Trials | 2000 | Number of attendees expected | | | | | |
| 3 | | | | | | | | |
| 4 | Confidence | # catalogs | | | | | | |
| 5 | 70% | 349 | =CRITBINOM($B$2,$B$1,A5) | | | | | |
| 6 | 80% | 354 | | | | | | |
| 7 | 90% | 362 | | | | | | |
| 8 | 95% | 368 | | | | | | |
| 9 | 99% | 380 | | | | | | |
| 10 | | | | | | | | |

SYNTAX: =NEGBINOMDIST(*number_f*,*number_s*,*probability_s*)

The NEGBINOMDIST function returns the negative binomial distribution. It returns the probability that there will be *number_f* failures before the number_sth success, when the constant probability of a success is probability_s. This function is similar to the binomial distribution function, except that the number of successes is fixed, and the number of trials is variable. As with the binomial distribution function, trials are assumed to be independent. For example, you need to find 10 people who have excellent reflexes, and you know the probability that a candidate has these qualifications is 0.3. NEGBINOMDIST calculates the probability that you will interview a certain number of unqualified candidates before finding all 10 qualified candidates.

The NEGBINOMDIST function takes the following arguments:

- *number_f*—This is the number of failures.
- *number_s*—This is the threshold number of successes.
- *probability_s*—This is the probability of a success.

*number_f* and number_s are truncated to integers. If any argument is nonnumeric, NEGBINOMDIST returns a #VALUE! error. If probability_s is less than 0 or if *probability* is greater than 1, NEGBINOMDIST returns a #NUM! error. If (*number_f* + number_s − 1) is less than or equal to 0, NEGBINOMDIST returns a #NUM! error.

To solve the LeBron James problem, you use =NEGBINOMDIST(3,1,0.746). The answer is a 1.22% probability.

## USING POISSON TO PREDICT A NUMBER OF DISCRETE EVENTS OVER TIME

Say that you have to predict the number of discrete events that will happen over a certain period of time. This might be the number of customers who walk into a bank in an hour. It might be the number of lightning strikes on the Sears Tower in a year. (It can also be discrete events that occur in a certain distance or area or any other measurement.)

Unlike the binomial distribution, in which an event either happens or does not happen, the Poisson distribution can be zero, one, two, three, and so on events in the period. The nature of the Poisson distribution is that before the third customer can walk into the bank, the second customer has to walk into the bank. In theory, if you had a run on the bank, the upper limit would be the number of total account holders, but in practice, there is probably some logical upper limit to how many customers walk in, such as the number that walk in during a Friday payday lunch hour.

If you measure the average number of customers per hour over the several weeks, you can use this number to predict the likelihood that a particular number of customers will enter the bank in any hour by using the POISSON function.

SYNTAX: =POISSON(*x*,*mean*,*cumulative*)

The POISSON function returns the Poisson distribution. A common application of the Poisson distribution is predicting the number of events over a specific time, such as the number of cars arriving at a toll plaza in one minute. This function takes the following arguments:

- *x*—This is the number of events.
- *mean*—This is the expected numeric value.
- *cumulative*—This is a logical value that determines the form of the probability distribution returned.

If *x* is not an integer, it is truncated. If *x* or *mean* is nonnumeric, POISSON returns a #VALUE! error. If *x* is less than or equal to U, POISSON returns a #NUM! error. If *mean* is less than or equal to 0, POISSON returns a #NUM! error. If *cumulative* is TRUE, POISSON returns the cumulative Poisson probability that the number of random events occurring will be between 0 and *x*, inclusive; if *cumulative* is FALSE, it returns the Poisson probability mass function that the number of events occurring will be exactly *x*.

To solve the bank customer example, you follow these steps:

1. Calculate the mean number of customers entering the bank per hour over several weeks. Enter this in Cell B1 of the worksheet.
2. In A4:A24, enter the numbers from 0 to 20.
3. In Column B, calculate the probability that exactly *n* customers will enter the bank. In Cell B4, enter the formula =POISSON($A4,$B$1,FALSE).
4. In Column C, calculate the probability that 0 to *n* customers will enter the bank. In Cell C4, enter the formula =POISSON($A4,$B$1,TRUE).

In Figure 26.28, you can see that 84% of the time, your number of customers is expected to be between 0 and 11 customers per hour. If you staff up to handle 11 customers per hour, you should be covered 85% of the time.

## USING FREQUENCY TO CATEGORIZE CONTINUOUS DATA

The past few examples count whole numbers. It would be fairly difficult to have 0.3 persons walk into a bank. The outcome from the Poisson distribution would therefore have to be a whole number.

**Figure 26.28**
You can figure the number of customers per hour by using POISSON.

| | C4 | | $f_x$ =POISSON($A4,$B$1,TRUE) | | | | |
|---|---|---|---|---|---|---|---|
| | A | B | C | D | E | F | G |
| 1 | Mean | | 8.5 Average number of customers per hour at the bank | | | | |
| 2 | | | | | | | |
| 3 | Customers | Individual Probability | Cumulative Probability | | | | |
| 4 | 0 | 0.02% | 0.02% | | | | |
| 5 | 1 | 0.17% | 0.19% | | | | |
| 6 | 2 | 0.74% | 0.93% | | | | |
| 7 | 3 | 2.08% | 3.01% | | | | |
| 8 | 4 | 4.43% | 7.44% | | | | |
| 9 | 5 | 7.52% | 14.96% | | | | |
| 10 | 6 | 10.66% | 25.62% | | | | |
| 11 | 7 | 12.94% | 38.56% | | | | |
| 12 | 8 | 13.75% | 52.31% | | | | |
| 13 | 9 | 12.99% | 65.30% | | | | |
| 14 | 10 | 11.04% | 76.34% | | | | |
| 15 | 11 | 8.53% | 84.87% | | | | |
| 16 | 12 | 6.04% | 90.91% | | | | |
| 17 | 13 | 3.95% | 94.86% | | | | |
| 18 | 14 | 2.40% | 97.26% | | | | |
| 19 | 15 | 1.36% | 98.62% | | | | |
| 20 | 16 | 0.72% | 99.34% | | | | |
| 21 | 17 | 0.36% | 99.70% | | | | |
| 22 | 18 | 0.17% | 99.87% | | | | |
| 23 | 19 | 0.08% | 99.95% | | | | |
| 24 | 20 | 0.03% | 99.98% | | | | |
| 25 | | | | | | | |

Other measurements are continuous. The speed of a car passing a checkpoint is an example. Depending on the accuracy of the radar unit, a car could be determined to be going 55.1, 55.2, 55.3, 55.4 and so on miles per hour. It would not make sense to try to predict how many cars will be going exactly 55.0123 miles per hour; if you did, you would be lucky to have a height of 2 for any point along the continuous scale. Typically, the prediction question would be What percentage of cars are likely to be going between 65 and 70 miles per hour?

When you are working with a continuous range of measurements, the normal procedure is to group the measurements into ranges. Statisticians call each range a *bin*.

In Figure 26.29, the left chart shows the frequency curve for the speed of 2,000 cars passing a highway checkpoint. The recording unit measured speeds to the accuracy of 0.1 mile. The curve is incredibly noisy, with intense variation from point to point.

26

The middle chart shows the frequency curve after the data has been fit into bins of 1 mph each. There is still some noise in the distribution. For some reason, fewer people happened to be going 56 mph.

The right chart shows the frequency curve after the data has been fit into bins of 5 mph each. This curve is very smooth and shows that the data points seem to follow the normal bell curve.

**Figure 26.29**
With continuous variables, you can group the observed values into bins to see the underlying distribution curve emerge.

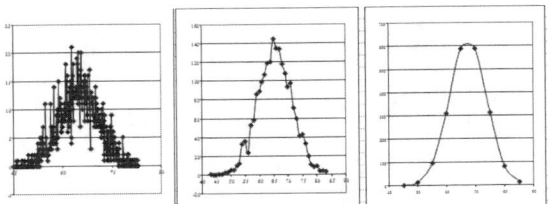

The process of grouping data into bins is handled with another array function: the FREQUENCY function.

SYNTAX: =FREQUENCY(*data_array*,*bins_array*)

The FREQUENCY function calculates how often values occur within a range of values, and it returns a vertical array of numbers. For example, you can use FREQUENCY to count the number of test scores that fall within ranges of scores. Because FREQUENCY returns an array, it must be entered as an array formula.

The FREQUENCY function takes the following arguments:

- *data_array*—This is an array of or a reference to a set of values for which you want to count frequencies. If *data_array* contains no values, FREQUENCY returns an array of zeros.
- *bins_array*—This is an array of or a reference to intervals into which you want to group the values in *data_array*. If *bins_array* contains no values, FREQUENCY returns the number of elements in *data_array*.

You enter FREQUENCY as an array formula after you select a range of adjacent cells into which you want the returned distribution to appear.

The number of elements in the returned array is one more than the number of elements in *bins_array*. The extra element in the returned array returns the count of any values above the highest interval. For example, when counting three ranges of values (intervals) that are entered into three cells, you need to be sure to enter FREQUENCY into four cells for the results. The extra cell returns the number of values in data_array that are greater than the third interval value. FREQUENCY ignores blank cells and text.

To use the FREQUENCY function, you follow these steps:

1. Figure out the expected range of values in the original dataset. You can do this by sorting the dataset or by using the MIN and MAX functions.

2. Decide on your bin sizes. Each bin should be roughly the same size. Use enough bins to get an accurate picture but not so many bins that the data becomes spiky and noisy. In Figure 26.30, the goal was bins of 5 mph each.

**Figure 26.30**
The tedious process of grouping values into ranges is handled easily with the FREQUENCY function.

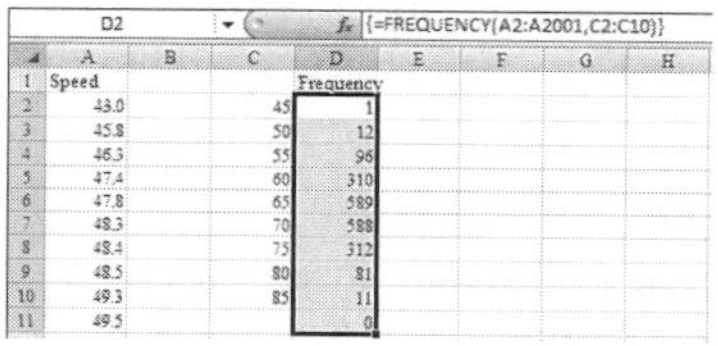

3. Enter the bins. This process is a bit tricky. If you want a bin for 40–45 mph, enter the number 45. For the bin of 45–50 mph, enter the number 50. In C2–C10, the numbers represent bins starting with 40–45 and ending with 80–85.

4. Select the range where the values will be returned. (The FREQUENCY function returns several values at once.) In Figure 26.30, select Cells D2:D11. Notice that this selection is one cell larger than your range of bins. The function returns one extra value in case there are any speeds faster than your top bin speed.

5. With D2:D11 selected, type the formula =FREQUENCY(A2:A2001,C2:C10). Do not press Enter at the end. You have to tell Excel to evaluate the formula as an array formula, so hold down Ctrl+Shift and then press Enter. Excel automatically groups the 2,000 individual data points into the 10 bins. You can then chart or analyze this range.

## USING NORMDIST TO CALCULATE THE PROBABILITY IN A NORMAL DISTRIBUTION

In Figure 26.31, the observed speeds along a highway seem to be following a normal distribution. A normal distribution is sometimes referred to as a *bell curve*. When you have a normal distribution, the curve can be described mathematically using only the average and standard deviation of the data.

**Figure 26.31**
If your data is normally distributed, you can predict the future by using NORMDIST.

| | F5 | | ▾ | | *fx* | =NORMDIST(65,$D$1,$D$2,TRUE) | | | | |
|---|---|---|---|---|---|---|---|---|---|---|
| ◢ | A | B | C | D | E | F | G | H | I | J |
| 1 | Speed | | Mean | | 65.0 | =AVERAGE(A2:A2001) | | | | |
| 2 | 43.0 | | Std Dev | | 5.97951 | =STDEV(A2:A2001) | | | | |
| 3 | 45.8 | | | | | | | | | |
| 4 | 46.3 | | Probability car going 75 or less: | | | 95.3% | =NORMDIST(75,$D$1,$D$2,TRUE) | | | |
| 5 | 47.4 | | Probability car going 65 or less: | | | 50.2% | =NORMDIST(65,$D$1,$D$2,TRUE) | | | |
| 6 | 47.8 | Probability car going between 65 and 75: | | | | 45.1% | =F4-F5 | | | |
| 7 | 48.3 | | | | | | | | | |

The NORMDIST function has a strange twist: It always returns the probability that a car will be going less than or equal to a value *x*. If you want to know the probability that the next car will be traveling between 65 and 75 mph, you have to figure out the cumulative probability of the car going less than 75 miles per hour and then subtract the cumulative probability of the car going less than 65 miles per hour. This requires two calls to the NORMDIST function.

SYNTAX: =NORMDIST(*x*,*mean*,*standard_dev*,*cumulative*)

The NORMDIST function returns the normal cumulative distribution for the specified mean and standard deviation. This function has a very wide range of applications in statistics, including hypothesis testing. This function takes the following arguments:

- *x*—This is the value for which you want the distribution.
- *mean*—This is the arithmetic mean of the distribution.
- *standard_dev*—This is the standard deviation of the distribution.
- *cumulative*—This is a logical value that determines the form of the function. If *cumulative* is TRUE, NORMDIST returns the cumulative distribution function; if *cumulative* is FALSE, NORMDIST returns the probability mass function.

If *mean* or standard_dev is nonnumeric, NORMDIST returns a #VALUE! error. If standard_dev is less than or equal to 0, NORMDIST returns a #NUM! error. If *mean* is 0 and standard_dev is 1, NORMDIST returns the standard normal distribution.

In Figure 26.31, the range of observed values is in A2:A2001. Formulas in Cells D1 and D2 calculate the average and standard deviation of the dataset. The goal is to find the probability of any car going between 65 and 75 mph. The formula in Cell F4 is =NORMDIST(75,$D$1,$D$2,TRUE); it predicts the likelihood of a car going 75 mph or less at 95.3%. The formula in Cell F5 is =NORMDIST(65,$D$1,$D$2,TRUE). This predicts the probability of a car going 65 mph or less at 50.2%.

You can back into the probability that the car will be going between 65 and 75 mph by subtracting 50.2% from 95.3%. The answer to your problem is 45.1% that the next car passing the checkpoint will be going between 65 and 75 mph.

## USING NORMINV TO CALCULATE THE VALUE FOR A CERTAIN PROBABILITY

In the preceding section, you used NORMDIST to find the probability that a car was going less than 75 mph. Sometimes, you might want to find the speed associated with a certain probability. For example, say you need to design a billboard that can be read by 80% of the drivers. If you know the mean and standard deviation of the speeds on the highway, you can use the NORMINV function to ask Excel to tell you that 80% of the drivers will be driving at X miles per hour or less.

SYNTAX: =NORMINV(*probability*,*mean*,*standard_dev*)

The NORMINV function returns the inverse of the normal cumulative distribution for the specified mean and standard deviation. This function takes the following arguments:

- *probability*—This is a probability corresponding to the normal distribution.
- *mean*—This is the arithmetic mean of the distribution.
- *standard_dev*—This is the standard deviation of the distribution.

If any argument is nonnumeric, NORMINV returns a #VALUE! error. If *probability* is less than 0 or if *probability* is greater than 1, NORMINV returns a #NUM! error. If standard_dev is less than or equal to 0, NORMINV returns a #NUM! error.

NORMINV uses an iterative technique for calculating the function. Given a probability value, NORMINV iterates until the result is accurate to within $\pm 3 \times 10^{-7}$. If NORMINV does not converge after 100 iterations, the function returns a #N/A error.

In Figure 26.32, a sample of speeds is listed in Column A. The formulas in Cells D2 and D3 calculate the mean and standard deviation. If you assume that the speeds follow a normal distribution, then 80% of the cars will be traveling 70 mph or less along this stretch of highway. The formula in Cell E6 is =NORMINV(D6,D$1,D$2).

**Figure 26.32**
Rather than use Goal Seek with the NORMDIST function, you can let Excel handle the iterations to back into an answer using NORMINV.

| | A | B | C | D | E | F | G | H |
|---|---|---|---|---|---|---|---|---|
| 1 | Speed | | Mean | 65.0 | =AVERAGE(A2:A2001) | | | |
| 2 | 43.0 | | Std Dev | 5.97951 | =STDEV(A2:A2001) | | | |
| 3 | 45.8 | | | | | | | |
| 4 | 46.3 | | | | | | | |
| 5 | 47.4 | | | Probability | Speed | | | |
| 6 | 47.8 | | | 80% | 70.00 | =NORMINV(D9,D1,D2) | | |
| 7 | 48.3 | | | 85% | 71.16 | | | |
| 8 | 48.4 | | | 90% | 72.63 | | | |
| 9 | 48.5 | | | 95% | 74.80 | | | |
| 10 | 49.3 | | | | | | | |

## USING NORMSDIST TO CALCULATE PROBABILITY

Before the days of spreadsheets, most statistics textbooks had tables of probabilities. In such a textbook, the basic problem states, for example, that the mean is 57.1 and the standard deviation is 8.2. To calculate the probability that a member of the population would have a value of 64 or less, your first step is to calculate a $z$ value. $z$ is simply the number of standard deviations away from the mean. In this case, 64 is 6.9 units above the mean. The standard deviation is 8.2. Your $z$ score is 6.9 / 8.4, or 0.841. Thus, you need to find the probability that any value is at 0.841 standard deviations above the mean or less. You then turn to a large appendix in the back of the textbook that lists many different z scores and the probability associated with each one. The table would look somewhat like Figure 26.33.

**Figure 26.33**
The NORMSDIST formula in Cell C17 makes tables of probabilities in statistics textbooks (like the one displayed in A2:K14) obsolete.

| | A | B | C | D | E | F | G | H | I | J | K |
|---|---|---|---|---|---|---|---|---|---|---|---|
| | | | | | | $f_x$ =NORMSDIST($A4+B$3) | | | | | |
| 1 | | | | | | | | | | | |
| 2 | | Second Digit of Z ----> | | | | | | | | | |
| 3 | z | 0.00 | 0.01 | 0.02 | 0.03 | 0.04 | 0.05 | 0.06 | 0.07 | 0.08 | 0.09 |
| 4 | 0.0 | 0.5000 | 0.5040 | 0.5080 | 0.5120 | 0.5160 | 0.5199 | 0.5239 | 0.5279 | 0.5319 | 0.5359 |
| 5 | 0.1 | 0.5398 | 0.5438 | 0.5478 | 0.5517 | 0.5557 | 0.5596 | 0.5636 | 0.5675 | 0.5714 | 0.5753 |
| 6 | 0.2 | 0.5793 | 0.5832 | 0.5871 | 0.5910 | 0.5948 | 0.5987 | 0.6026 | 0.6064 | 0.6103 | 0.6141 |
| 7 | 0.3 | 0.6179 | 0.6217 | 0.6255 | 0.6293 | 0.6331 | 0.6368 | 0.6406 | 0.6443 | 0.6480 | 0.6517 |
| 8 | 0.4 | 0.6554 | 0.6591 | 0.6628 | 0.6664 | 0.6700 | 0.6736 | 0.6772 | 0.6808 | 0.6844 | 0.6879 |
| 9 | 0.5 | 0.6915 | 0.6950 | 0.6985 | 0.7019 | 0.7054 | 0.7088 | 0.7123 | 0.7157 | 0.7190 | 0.7224 |
| 10 | 0.6 | 0.7257 | 0.7291 | 0.7324 | 0.7357 | 0.7389 | 0.7422 | 0.7454 | 0.7486 | 0.7517 | 0.7549 |
| 11 | 0.7 | 0.7580 | 0.7611 | 0.7642 | 0.7673 | 0.7704 | 0.7734 | 0.7764 | 0.7794 | 0.7823 | 0.7852 |
| 12 | 0.8 | 0.7881 | 0.7910 | 0.7939 | 0.7967 | 0.7995 | 0.8023 | 0.8051 | 0.8078 | 0.8106 | 0.8133 |
| 13 | 0.9 | 0.8159 | 0.8186 | 0.8212 | 0.8238 | 0.8264 | 0.8289 | 0.8315 | 0.8340 | 0.8365 | 0.8389 |
| 14 | 1 | 0.8413 | 0.8438 | 0.8461 | 0.8485 | 0.8508 | 0.8531 | 0.8554 | 0.8577 | 0.8599 | 0.8621 |
| 15 | | | | | | | | | | | |
| 16 | | 0.840 | 0.7995 | =NORMSDIST(B16) | | | | | | | |
| 17 | | 0.841 | 0.7998 | =NORMSDIST(B17) | | | | | | | |
| 18 | | | | | | | | | | | |

Depending on the accuracy of the table, you could find the probability associated with the z score. In Figure 26.33, you would go down the left column to the 0.8 row and across the table to the 0.04 column to find a value of 0.7995. This means that there is a 0.7995 probability that any random member will be at 0.84 standard deviations above the mean or below it.

The NORMSDIST function makes this table obsolete. (In fact, I created the table in the figure by using NORMSDIST). While the typical statistics textbook would show the approximate probability for z = 0.84 as 0.7995, Excel can now calculate the exact probability for z = 0.841 as 0.7998.

SYNTAX: =NORMSDIST(z)

The NORMSDIST function returns the standard normal cumulative distribution function. The distribution has a mean of 0 and a standard deviation of 1. You use this function in place of a table of standard normal curve areas.

The argument z is the value for which you want the distribution. If z is nonnumeric, NORMSDIST returns a #VALUE! error.

## USING NORMSINV TO CALCULATE A z SCORE FOR A GIVEN PROBABILITY

To calculate a z score for a given probability, you use the NORMSINV function. In Figure 26.34, the z score for 15% is –1.036. This means that in a normally distributed population, 15% of the population exists at the value of the mean minus 1.036 standard deviations.

**Figure 26.34**
You can back into a z score from a probability by using NORMSINV. You can then take the z score multiplied by a standard deviation to figure out the distance that your value lies from the mean.

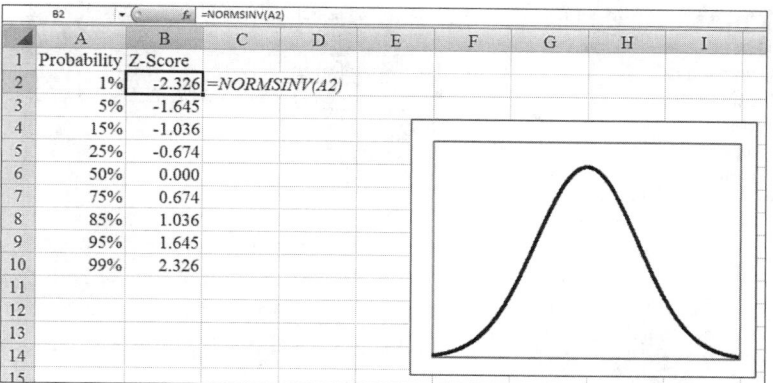

SYNTAX: =NORMSINV(*probability*)

The NORMSINV function returns the inverse of the standard normal cumulative distribution. The distribution has a mean of 0 and a standard deviation of 1.

The argument *probability* is a probability that corresponds to the normal distribution. If *probability* is nonnumeric, NORMSINV returns a #VALUE! error. If *probability* is less than 0 or if *probability* is greater than 1, NORMSINV returns a #NUM! error.

NORMSINV uses an iterative technique for calculating the function. Given a *probability* value, NORMSINV iterates until the result is accurate to within $\pm 3 \times 10^{-7}$. If NORMSINV does not converge after 100 iterations, the function returns an #N/A error.

The z score refers to a number of standard deviations away from the mean. If the z score is negative, the value lies to the left of the mean. if the z score is positive, the value lies to the right of the mean.

## USING STANDARDIZE TO CALCULATE THE DISTANCE FROM THE MEAN

To calculate the distance from a mean, you use the STANDARDIZE function. This function returns the positive or negative distance from the mean, expressed as the number of standard deviations.

SYNTAX: =STANDARDIZE(*x*,*mean*,*standard_dev*)

The STANDARDIZE function returns a normalized value from a distribution characterized by *mean* and standard_dev. This function takes the following arguments:

- *x*—This is the value you want to normalize.
- *mean*—This is the arithmetic mean of the distribution.
- *standard_dev*—This is the standard deviation of the distribution.

If standard_dev is less than or equal to 0, STANDARDIZE returns a #NUM! error. In Figure 26.35, a population has a mean of 65 and a standard deviation of 5. The normalized value of 75 is 2, indicating that 75 is 2 standard deviations away from the mean of 65.

26

**Figure 26.35**
STANDARDIZE does the basic math to calculate the distance from the mean, expressed as a number of standard deviations.

| | A | B | C | D | E | F | G |
|---|---|---|---|---|---|---|---|
| | | | | D2 ▾ | fx =STANDARDIZE(A2,B2,C2) | | |
| 1 | X | Mean | StDev | Standardize | | | |
| 2 | 50 | 65 | 5 | -3 | =STANDARDIZE(A2,B2,C2) | | |
| 3 | 55 | 65 | 5 | -2 | | | |
| 4 | 60 | 65 | 5 | -1 | | | |
| 5 | 65 | 65 | 5 | 0 | | | |
| 6 | 70 | 65 | 5 | 1 | | | |
| 7 | 75 | 65 | 5 | 2 | | | |
| 8 | 80 | 65 | 5 | 3 | | | |
| 9 | 85 | 65 | 5 | 4 | | | |
| 10 | 90 | 65 | 5 | 5 | | | |
| 11 | | | | | | | |

## USING STUDENT'S *T*-DISTRIBUTION FOR SMALL SAMPLE SIZES

All the previous examples using a normal distribution assume that the sample size is 30 or more. If you are using a small sample size—even as small as three members—you should use the Student's *t*-distribution.

> **NOTE**
>
> The unique assumption with the Student's *t*-distribution is that the underlying population is normally distributed.

An important concept in the Student's *t*-distribution is the degrees of freedom. If you know the mean of the sample but not the standard deviation of the population, the degrees of freedom is the sample size minus 1. When the degrees of freedom is 29 or above, the Student's *t*-distribution is nearly identical with the normal distribution. However, as the degrees of freedom drops, the distribution becomes flatter and wider.

SYNTAX: =TDIST(*x*,*degrees_freedom*,*tails*)

The TDIST function returns the percentage points (that is, probability) for the Student's *t*-distribution, where a numeric value (*x*) is a calculated value of *t* for which the percentage points are to be computed. The *t*-distribution is used in the hypothesis testing of small sample datasets. You use this function in place of a table of critical values for the *t*-distribution.

The TDIST function takes the following arguments:

- *x*—This is the numeric value at which to evaluate the distribution.
- *degrees_freedom*—This is an integer that indicates the number of degrees of freedom.
- *tails*—This specifies the number of distribution tails to return. If *tails* is 1, TDIST returns a one-tailed distribution. If *tails* is 2, TDIST returns a two-tailed distribution.

If any argument is nonnumeric, TDIST returns a #VALUE! error. If degrees_freedom is less than 1, TDIST returns a #NUM! error. The degrees_freedom and *tails* arguments are truncated to integers. If *tails* is any value other than 1 or 2, TDIST returns a #NUM! error.

SYNTAX: =TINV(*probability*,*degrees_freedom*)

The TINV function returns the *t*-value of the Student's *t*-distribution as a function of the probability and the degrees of freedom. This function takes the following arguments:

- *probability*—This is the probability associated with the two-tailed Student's *t*-distribution.

- *degrees_freedom*—This is the number of degrees of freedom to characterize the distribution.

If either argument is nonnumeric, TINV returns a #VALUE! error. If *probability* is less than 0 or if *probability* is greater than 1, TINV returns a #NUM! error. If degrees_freedom is not an integer, it is truncated. If degrees_freedom is less than 1, TINV returns a #NUM! error. TINV is calculated as TINV = p( t<X ), where X is a random variable that follows the *t*-distribution.

A one-tailed *t* value can be returned by replacing *probability* with 2*probability. For a probability of 0.05 and degrees of freedom of 10, the two-tailed value is calculated with TINV(0.05,10), which returns 2.28139. The one-tailed value for the same probability and degrees of freedom can be calculated with TINV(2*0.05,10), which returns 1.812462.

TINV uses an iterative technique for calculating the function. Given a probability value, TINV iterates until the result is accurate to within $\pm 3 \times 10^{-7}$. If TINV does not converge after 100 iterations, the function returns an #N/A error.

SYNTAX: =TTEST(*array1*,*array2*,*tails*,*type*)

Excel can also calculate the *t*-test to predict whether two samples come from populations with the same mean. For this, you use the TTEST function. The TTEST function returns the probability associated with a Student's *t*-test. You use TTEST to determine whether two samples are likely to have come from the same two underlying populations that have the same mean.

The TTEST function takes the following arguments:

- *array1*—This is the first dataset.
- *array2*—This is the second dataset.
- *tails*—This specifies the number of distribution tails. If *tails* is 1, TTEST uses the one-tailed distribution. If *tails* is 2, TTEST uses the two-tailed distribution.
- *type*—This is the kind of *t*-test to perform. See Table 26.3 for more information.

**TABLE 26.3    TYPES OF *T*-TESTS AVAILABLE WITH THE TTEST FUNCTION**

| If type Equals | This Test Is Performed |
| --- | --- |
| 1 | Paired |
| 2 | Two-sample equal variance (homoscedastic) |
| 3 | Two-sample unequal variance (heteroscedastic) |

26

If array1 and array2 have a different number of data points, and if *type* is 1 (paired), TTEST returns an #N/A error. The *tails* and *type* arguments are truncated to integers. If *tails* or *type* is nonnumeric, TTEST returns a #VALUE! error. If *tails* is any value other than 1 or 2, TTEST returns a #NUM! error.

In Figure 26.36, the means of the two samples are different: 11.15 versus 13.5. However, in Cell F2, TTEST returns 0.1577. Because this is greater than the typical alpha of 0.05, the difference in means may not be statistically significant. It is possible that these two samples were taken from the same population.

**Figure 26.36**
TTEST provides a formulaic equivalent to the key result from the Analysis Toolpak's T-Test feature.

| | E2 | | fx | =TTEST($A$2:$A$14,$B$2:$B$14,E$1,$G2) | | | |
|---|---|---|---|---|---|---|---|
| | A | B | C | D | E | F | G |
| 1 | Sample 1 | Sample 2 | | | 1 | 2 | |
| 2 | 9.96243 | 14.7336 | | 1 - Paired Samples | 0.07887199 | 0.15774397 | 1 |
| 3 | 10.9836 | 15.2397 | | 2 - Two-sample equal variance | 0.03895041 | 0.07790081 | 2 |
| 4 | 15.2866 | 7.78481 | | 3 - Two-sample unequal variance | 0.03968814 | 0.07937628 | 3 |
| 5 | 13.0246 | 8.08039 | | | | | |
| 6 | 8.80691 | 15.3099 | | t-Test: Paired Two Sample for Means | | | |
| 7 | 10.1553 | 12.9992 | | | | | |
| 8 | 16.1482 | 8.15473 | | | Variable 1 | Variable 2 | |
| 9 | 10.2348 | 14.6154 | | Mean | 11.1500653 | 13.5482847 | |
| 10 | 8.59473 | 17.1387 | | Variance | 7.22510765 | 14.8168691 | |
| 11 | 12.7652 | 18.0217 | | Observations | 13 | 13 | |
| 12 | 7.52736 | 17.2393 | | Pearson Correlation | -0.5263725 | | |
| 13 | 12.9356 | 17.2922 | | Hypothesized Mean Difference | 0 | | |
| 14 | 8.52547 | 9.51795 | | df | 12 | | |
| 15 | | | | t Stat | -1.5067315 | | |
| 16 | | | | P(T<=t) one-tail | 0.07887199 | | |
| 17 | | | | t Critical one-tail | 1.78228755 | | |
| 18 | | | | P(T<=t) two-tail | 0.15774397 | | |
| 19 | | | | t Critical two-tail | 2.17881283 | | |
| 20 | | | | | | | |

**NOTE**

The results in D6:F19 in Figure 26.36 are a snapshot produced by the Analysis Toolpak's T-Test feature. The formula in Cell F2 is a live version of the T-Test feature's result in Cell E16.

## USING CHITEST TO PERFORM GOODNESS-OF-FIT TESTING

A chi-squared test compares expected frequencies with observed frequencies. The CHITEST function performs the chi-square test for independence.

CHIINV is used to find the critical chi value for a certain probability and degrees of freedom. CHIDIST is used to determine the probability for a chi value and certain degrees of freedom.

SYNTAX: =CHITEST(*actual_range*,*expected_range*)

The CHITEST function returns the test for independence. CHITEST returns the value from the chi-squared distribution for the statistic and the appropriate degrees of freedom. You can use chi-squared tests to determine whether hypothesized results are verified by an experiment.

The CHITEST function takes the following arguments:

- *actual_range*—This is the range of data that contains observations to test against expected values.
- *expected_range*—This is the range of data that contains the ratio of the product of row totals and column totals to the grand total.

If actual_range and expected_range have different numbers of data points, CHITEST returns an #N/A error.

The chi-squared test first calculates a chi-squared statistic and then sums the differences of actual values from the expected values. CHITEST returns the probability for a chi-squared statistic and degrees of freedom, df, where df = $(r - 1)(c - 1)$.

SYNTAX: =CHIDIST(*x*,*degrees_freedom*)

The CHIDIST function returns the one-tailed probability of the chi-squared distribution. The chi-squared distribution is associated with a chi-squared test. You use the chi-squared test to compare observed and expected values. For example, a genetic experiment might hypothesize that the next generation of plants will exhibit a certain set of colors. By comparing the observed results with the expected ones, you can decide whether your original hypothesis is valid.

The CHIDIST function takes the following arguments:

- *x*—This is the value at which you want to evaluate the distribution.
- *degrees_freedom*—This is the number of degrees of freedom.

If either argument is nonnumeric, CHIDIST returns a #VALUE! error. If *x* is negative, CHIDIST returns a #NUM! error. If degrees_freedom is not an integer, it is truncated. If degrees_freedom is less than 1 or if degrees_freedom is greater than or equal to $10^{10}$, CHIDIST returns a #NUM! error.

SYNTAX: =CHIINV(*probability*,*degrees_freedom*)

The CHIINV function returns the inverse of the one-tailed probability of the chi-squared distribution. If *probability* equals CHIDIST(*x*,...), CHIINV(*probability*,...) equals *x*. You use the CHIINV function to compare observed results with expected ones to decide whether your original hypothesis is valid.

The CHIINV function takes the following arguments:

- *probability*—This is a probability associated with the chi-squared distribution.
- *degrees_freedom*—This is the number of degrees of freedom.

If either argument is nonnumeric, CHIINV returns a #VALUE! error. If *probability* is less than 0 or *probability* is greater than 1, CHIINV returns a #NUM! error. If degrees_freedom is not an integer, it is truncated. If degrees_freedom is less than 1 or if degrees_freedom is greater than or equal to $10^{10}$, CHIINV returns a #NUM! error.

CHIINV uses an iterative technique for calculating the function. Given a *probability* value, CHIINV iterates until the result is accurate to within $\pm 3 \times 10^{-7}$. If CHIINV does not converge after 100 iterations, the function returns an #N/A error.

**Figure 26.37**
You can calculate chi-squared testing with CHITEST.

| | B10 | | $f_x$ | =CHITEST(E4:E8,D4:D8) | |
|---|---|---|---|---|---|
| | A | B | C | D | E |
| 1 | How often do you use pivot tables? | | | | |
| 2 | | | | | |
| 3 | | Expected | Sample Size | Expected Frequency | Actual Frequency |
| 4 | Every day | 20% | 191 | 38 | 24 |
| 5 | Once a Week | 21% | 191 | 40 | 36 |
| 6 | Once a month | 10% | 191 | 19 | 74 |
| 7 | Once a year | 5% | 191 | 10 | 27 |
| 8 | What is a pivot table? | 44% | 191 | 84 | 30 |
| 9 | | | | | |
| 10 | CHITEST | 2.9427E-48 | =CHITEST(E4:E8,D4:D8) | | |
| 11 | | | | | |
| 12 | | Right-tail areas --------> | | | |
| 13 | Degrees of Freedom | 0.3 | 0.2 | 0.1 | 0.05 |
| 14 | 1 | 1.074 | 1.642 | 2.706 | 3.841 |
| 15 | 2 | 2.408 | 3.219 | 4.605 | 5.991 |
| 16 | 3 | 3.665 | 4.642 | 6.251 | 7.815 |
| 17 | 4 | 4.878 | 5.989 | 7.779 | 9.488 |
| 18 | 5 | 6.064 | 7.289 | 9.236 | 11.070 |
| 19 | | | | | |

## THE SUM OF SQUARES FUNCTIONS

Excel offers four functions with confusingly similar names. The hardest part of using these functions is figuring out which function does what. The first three functions require two identically sized arrays, named x and y. These are Excel's four sum of squares functions:

- SumX2MY2—For each pair of x and y, Excel calculates $x^2 - y^2$ and then sums these values. In this case, the M in the function name indicates *minus*.

- SumX2PY2—For each pair of x and y, Excel calculates $x^2 + y^2$ and then sums these values. In this case, the P in the function name indicates *plus*.

- SumXMY2—For each pair of x and y, Excel calculates $(x - y)^2$ and then sums these values. Again, the M indicates *minus*, and the lack of a 2 after the X indicates that it is the difference that is squared.

- SumSQ—Returns the sum of the squares of the arguments.

In Figure 26.38, the x array is in A2:A5, and the y array is in B2:B5. The formulas in D2:D5 calculate x – y for each pair. The formulas in E2:E5 square that difference for each pair. The formula in Cell E6 totals the sum of the squares. You could replace the five formulas in Column E with a single formula in Cell D6: =SUMSQ(D2:D5). Alternately, you could replace all the formulas in Columns D and E with a single use of SumXMY2 in Cell B9.

## Sum of the Sum of the Squares

Some statistical processes ask you to calculate the sum of the sum of the squares. However, a casual survey of several mathematicians could not find one concrete example of when this would be useful. In fact, the formula for SUMX2PY2(A2:A5,B2:B5) is mathematically equivalent to SUMSQ(A2:B5). Further, the formula for SUMX2MY2(A2:A5,B2:B5) is the same as SUMSQ(A2:A5)-SUMSQ(B2:B5). My theory on this is that some early spreadsheets included these functions in an effort to claim that they had more functions than a competitor. All future spreadsheets have included the functions just because some other competitor included them.

SYNTAX: =SUMSQ(*number1*,*number2*,...)

The SUMSQ function returns the sum of the squares of the arguments. The arguments *number1*,*number2*,... are 1 to 255 arguments for which you want the sum of the squares. You can also use a single array or a reference to an array instead of arguments separated by commas.

SYNTAX: =SUMXMY2(*array_x*,*array_y*)

The SUMXMY2 function returns the sum of squares of differences of corresponding values in two arrays. It takes the following arguments:

- *array_x*—This is the first array or range of values.
- *array_y*—This is the second array or range of values.

The arguments should be either numbers or names, arrays, or references that contain numbers. If an array or reference argument contains text, logical values, or empty cells, those values are ignored; however, cells that contain the value 0 are included. If array_x and array_y have a different number of values, SUMXMY2 returns an #N/A error.

**Figure 26.38**
Without doing any regression, you use SUMXMY2 to calculate the sum of the squares of the difference of two arrays.

| | A | B | C | D | E | F |
|---|---|---|---|---|---|---|
| | B9 | | fx | =SUMXMY2(A2:A5,B2:B5) | | |
| 1 | x | y | | x-y | (x-y)^2 | |
| 2 | 1 | 2 | | -1 | 1 | |
| 3 | 2 | 4 | | -2 | 4 | |
| 4 | 3 | 6 | | -3 | 9 | |
| 5 | 4 | 8 | | -4 | 16 | |
| 6 | | | SumSQ: | 30 | 30 | |
| 7 | | | | =SUMSQ(D2:D5) | | |
| 8 | | | | | | |
| 9 | SumXMY2 | 30 | =SUMXMY2(A2:A5,B2:B5) | | | |
| 10 | | | | | | |

SYNTAX: =SUMX2MY2(*array_x*,*array_y*)

The SUMX2MY2 function returns the sum of the difference of squares of corresponding values in two arrays. This function takes the following arguments:

- *array_x*—This is the first array or range of values.
- *array_y*—This is the second array or range of values.

The arguments should be either numbers or names, arrays, or references that contain numbers. If an array or a reference argument contains text, logical values, or empty cells, those values are ignored; however, cells that contain the value 0 are included. If array_x and array_y have a different number of values, SUMX2MY2 returns an #N/A error.

SYNTAX: =SUMX2PY2(*array_x,array_y*)

The SUMX2PY2 function returns the sum of the sum of squares of corresponding values in two arrays. The sum of the sum of squares is a common term in many statistical calculations. This function takes the following arguments:

■ *array_x*—This is the first array or range of values.

■ *array_y*—This is the second array or range of values.

The arguments should be either numbers or names, arrays, or references that contain numbers. If an array or reference argument contains text, logical values, or empty cells, those values are ignored; however, cells that contain the value 0 are included. If array_x and array_y have a different number of values, SUMX2PY2 returns an #N/A error.

In Figure 26.39, the one SUMX2PY2 formula in Cell B9 is much simpler than the five formulas in Column D, but if you really wanted to do this calculation, you could simply use SUMSQ, as shown in Cell B12.

I will go out on a limb and propose that none of the 400 million people using Excel actually use SUMX2PY2.

**Figure 26.39**
Microsoft won't say that these two functions are useful in statistics. I don't think they are useful anywhere.

## TESTING PROBABILITY ON LOGARITHMIC DISTRIBUTIONS

In the life sciences, a number of populations have logarithmic distributions. In the population shown in Figure 26.40, the values in the sample range from under 2 to over 38,000. The data clearly does not follow a normal distribution.

**Figure 26.40**
The LOGNORMDIST and LOGINV functions can make sense of a population where the natural logarithm of the population is normally distributed.

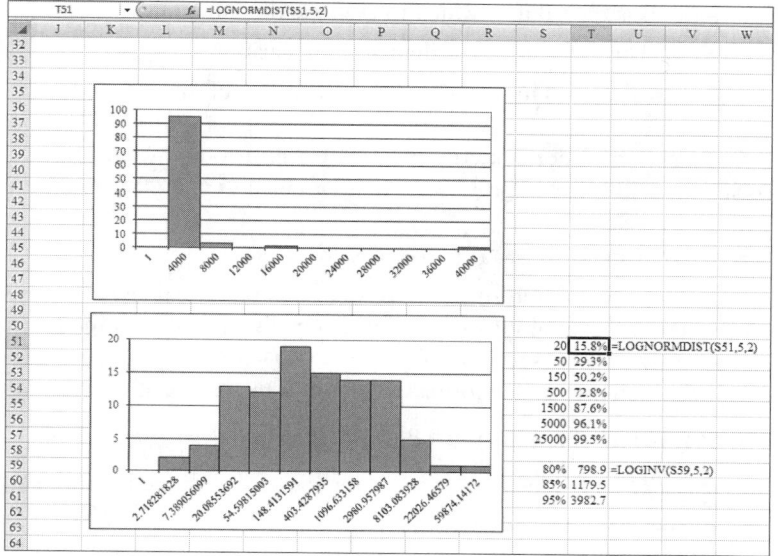

However, if you took the natural logarithm of each data point, the LN(x) of the members does follow a normal distribution. The mean of the natural logarithms is 5, with a standard deviation of 2.

Populations where the natural logarithm is normally distributed are called *lognormal distributions*. An example of a population with a lognormal distribution is the length of time that bacteria live in a disinfectant.

In the example where the mean of the natural logarithm values is 5 and the standard deviation is 2, take a look at what this really means: You use EXP(5) to see that the mean of 5 translates to 148. You would expect 65% of the population to be within 1 standard deviation of the mean. This range from EXP(3) to EXP(7) is from 20 to 1,096. The range for two standard deviations from the mean is EXP(1) and EXP(9), or 2.7 and 8,103.

Given a lognormal distribution where the mean of the natural logarithm of the population is 5 and the standard deviation is 2, you can predict what percentage of the population will be at a number *x* or below by using LOGNORMDIST. To find the value of *x* associated with a certain probability, you use LOGINV.

SYNTAX: =LOGNORMDIST(*x*,*mean*,*standard_dev*)

The LOGNORMDIST function returns the cumulative lognormal distribution of *x*, where the natural logarithm is normally distributed with the parameters *mean* and standard_dev. You use this function to analyze data that has been logarithmically transformed. This function takes the following arguments:

- *x*—This is the value at which to evaluate the function.
- *mean*—This is the mean of the natural logarithm.
- *standard_dev*—This is the standard deviation of the natural logarithm.

If any argument is nonnumeric, LOGNORMDIST returns a #VALUE! error. If *x* is less than or equal to 0 or if standard_dev is less than or equal to 0, LOGNORMDIST returns a #NUM! error.

**SYNTAX:** =LOGINV(*probability*,*mean*,*standard_dev*)

The LOGINV function returns the inverse of the lognormal cumulative distribution function of *x*, where the natural logarithm is normally distributed with the parameters *mean* and standard_dev. If *probability* is equal to LOGNORMDIST(*x*,...), LOGINV(*probability*,...) is equal to *x*. You use the lognormal distribution to analyze logarithmically transformed data.

The LOGINV function takes the following arguments:

- *probability*—This is a probability associated with the lognormal distribution.
- *mean*—This is the mean of the natural logarithm.
- *standard_dev*—This is the standard deviation of the natural logarithm.

If any argument is nonnumeric, LOGINV returns a #VALUE! error. If *probability* is less than 0 or if *probability* is greater than 1, LOGINV returns a #NUM! error. If standard_dev is less than or equal to 0, LOGINV returns a #NUM! error.

In Figure 26.40, the population varies from 1.7 to 38,577, but the LOGNORMDIST function predicts that 72.8% of the population is under 500, 87.6% is under 1,500, and 96.1% is under 5,000.

In Cell T60, the LOGINV function reveals that 95% of the population should be under 3,983.

## USING GAMMADIST AND GAMMAINV TO ANALYZE QUEUING TIMES

Earlier in this chapter, we discussed how to use a Poisson distribution to analyze how many customers might walk into a bank during any given hour. However, if the time between customers is relevant, you need to use the gamma distribution. The gamma distribution is described by two variables, alpha and beta. For a gamma distribution described by alpha and beta, you can find the probability that a value of *x* or less will occur with GAMMADIST. To find the value of *x* for a certain probability, you use GAMMAINV. The other remaining gamma-related function is GAMMALN.

**SYNTAX:** =GAMMADIST(*x*,*alpha*,*beta*,*cumulative*)

The GAMMADIST function returns the gamma distribution. You can use this function to study variables that may have a skewed distribution. The gamma distribution is commonly used in queuing analysis. This function takes the following arguments:

- *x*—This is the value at which you want to evaluate the distribution.
- *alpha*—This is a parameter to the distribution.

- *beta*—This is a parameter to the distribution.

- *cumulative*—This is a logical value that determines the form of the function. If *cumulative* is TRUE, GAMMADIST returns the cumulative distribution function; if *cumulative* is FALSE, GAMMADIST returns the probability mass function.

If *beta* is 1, GAMMADIST returns the standard gamma distribution. If *x*, *alpha*, or *beta* is non-numeric, GAMMADIST returns a #VALUE! error. If *x* is less than 0, GAMMADIST returns a #NUM! error. If *alpha* is less than or equal to 0 or if *beta* is less than or equal to 0, GAMMADIST returns a #NUM! error. When *alpha* is a positive integer, GAMMADIST is also known as the Erlang distribution.

### SYNTAX: =GAMMAINV(*probability*,*alpha*,*beta*)

The GAMMAINV function returns the inverse of the gamma cumulative distribution. If *probability* is equal to GAMMADIST(*x*,...), then GAMMAINV(*probability*,...) is equal to *x*. You can use this function to study a variable whose distribution may be skewed. This function takes the following arguments:

- *probability*—This is the probability associated with the gamma distribution.

- *alpha*—This is a parameter to the distribution.

- *beta*—This is a parameter to the distribution. If *beta* is 1, GAMMAINV returns the standard gamma distribution.

If any argument is nonnumeric, GAMMAINV returns a #VALUE! error. If *probability* is less than 0 or *probability* is greater than 1, GAMMAINV returns a #NUM! error. If *alpha* is less than or equal to 0 or if *beta* is less than or equal to 0, GAMMAINV returns the #NUM! error. If *beta* is less than or equal to 0, GAMMAINV returns a #NUM! error.

GAMMAINV uses an iterative technique to do its calculation. Given a probability value, GAMMAINV iterates until the result is accurate to within $\pm 3 \times 10^{-7}$. If GAMMAINV does not converge after 100 iterations, the function returns an #N/A error.

### SYNTAX: =GAMMALN(*x*)

The GAMMALN function returns the natural logarithm of the gamma function, $\Gamma(x)$. The argument *x* is the value for which you want to calculate GAMMALN.

If *x* is nonnumeric, GAMMALN returns a #VALUE! error. If *x* is less than or equal to 0, GAMMALN returns a #NUM! error. The number e raised to the GAMMALN(*i*) power, where *i* is an integer, returns the same result as $(i - 1)!$.

## CALCULATING PROBABILITY OF BETA DISTRIBUTIONS

A beta distribution is used to describe the variability of the percentage of something across samples, such as the percentage of the day people spend sleeping.

A beta distribution curve is described by two parameters, alpha and beta. For any given distribution, you can predict the likelihood that a value will be less than or equal to *x* by using BETADIST. To find the value of *x* associated with a certain probability, you use BETAINV.

SYNTAX: =BETADIST(*x*,*alpha*,*beta*,*A*,*B*)

The BETADIST function returns the cumulative beta probability density function. The cumulative beta probability density function is commonly used to study variation in the percentage of something across samples, such as the fraction of the day people spend watching television. This function takes the following arguments:

- *x*—This is the value between *a* and *b* at which to evaluate the function.
- *alpha*—This is a parameter to the distribution.
- *beta*—This is a parameter to the distribution.
- *a*—This is an optional lower bound to the interval of *x*.
- *b*—This is an optional upper bound to the interval of *x*.

If any argument is nonnumeric, BETADIST returns a #VALUE! error. If *alpha* is less than or equal to 0 or *beta* is less than or equal to 0, BETADIST returns a #NUM! error. If *x* is less than *a*, *x* is greater than *b*, or *a* equals *b*, BETADIST returns a #NUM! error. If you omit values for *a* and *b*, BETADIST uses the standard cumulative beta distribution, so that *a* equals 0 and *b* equals 1.

SYNTAX: =BETAINV(*probability*,*alpha*,*beta*,*A*,*B*)

The BETAINV function returns the inverse of the cumulative beta probability density function. That is, if *probability* is equal to BETADIST(*x*,...), then BETAINV(*probability*,...) is equal to *x*. The cumulative beta distribution can be used in project planning to model probable completion times, given an expected completion time and variability.

The BETAINV function takes the following arguments:

- *probability*—This is a probability associated with the beta distribution.
- *alpha*—This is a parameter to the distribution.
- *beta*—This is a parameter to the distribution.
- *a*—This is an optional lower bound to the interval of *x*.
- *b*—This is an optional upper bound to the interval of *x*.

If any argument is nonnumeric, BETAINV returns a #VALUE! error. If *alpha* is less than or equal to 0 or if *beta* is less than or equal to 0, BETAINV returns a #NUM! error. If *probability* is less than or equal to 0 or *probability* is greater than 1, BETAINV returns a #NUM! error. If you omit values for *a* and *b*, BETAINV uses the standard cumulative beta distribution, so that *a* equals 0 and *b* equals 1.

BETAINV uses an iterative technique for calculating the function. Given a *probability* value, BETAINV iterates until the result is accurate to within $\pm 3 \times 10 - 7$. If BETAINV does not converge after 100 iterations, the function returns an #N/A error.

## Using FTEST to Measure Differences in Variability

There are three functions for measuring variability among two populations. Say that you need to compare test results from males and test results from females. To determine whether one population has more variability than the other, you use FTEST. The FDIST function determines the probability that a value will be less than or equal to $X$. The FINV function returns the $X$ value associated with a certain probability.

**SYNTAX:** =FTEST(*array1,array2*)

The FTEST function returns the result of an *F*-test. An *F*-test returns the one-tailed probability that the variances in array1 and array2 are not significantly different. You use this function to determine whether two samples have different variances. For example, given test scores from public and private schools, you can test whether these schools have different levels of diversity.

The FTEST function takes the following arguments:

- *array1*—This is the first array or range of data.
- *array2*—This is the second array or range of data.

The arguments must be either numbers or names, arrays, or references that contain numbers. If an array or a reference argument contains text, logical values, or empty cells, those values are ignored; however, cells that contain the value 0 are included. If the number of data points in array1 or array2 is less than 2, or if the variance of array1 or array2 is 0, FTEST returns a #DIV/0! error.

**SYNTAX:** =FDIST(*x,degrees_freedom1,degrees_freedom2*)

The FDIST function returns the *F* probability distribution. You can use this function to determine whether two datasets have different degrees of diversity. For example, you can examine test scores given to men and women entering high school and determine whether the variability in the females is different from that found in the males.

The FDIST function takes the following arguments:

- *x*—This is the value at which to evaluate the function.
- *degrees_freedom1*—This is the numerator degrees of freedom.
- *degrees_freedom2*—This is the denominator degrees of freedom.

If any argument is nonnumeric, FDIST returns a #VALUE! error. If *x* is negative, FDIST returns a #NUM! error. If degrees_freedom1 or degrees_freedom2 is not an integer, it is truncated. If degrees_freedom1 is less than 1 or degrees_freedom1 is greater than or equal to 10^10, FDIST returns a #NUM! error. If degrees_freedom2 is less than 1 or degrees_freedom2 is greater than or equal to 10^10, FDIST returns a #NUM! error. FDIST is calculated as FDIST=P( F<x ), where F is a random variable that has an *F* distribution.

26

SYNTAX: =FINV(*probability*,*degrees_freedom1*,*degrees_freedom2*)

The FINV function returns the inverse of the *F* probability distribution. If *probability* is equal to FDIST(*x*,...), then FINV(*probability*,...) is equal to *x*. The *F* distribution can be used in an *F*-test that compares the degree of variability in two datasets. For example, you can analyze income distributions in the United States and Canada to determine whether the two countries have a similar degree of diversity.

This function takes the following arguments:

- *probability*—This is a probability associated with the *F* cumulative distribution.
- *degrees_freedom1*—This is the numerator degrees of freedom.
- *degrees_freedom2*—This is the denominator degrees of freedom.

If any argument is nonnumeric, FINV returns a #VALUE! error. If *probability* is less than 0 or *probability* is greater than 1, FINV returns a #NUM! error. If degrees_freedom1 or degrees_freedom2 is not an integer, it is truncated. If degrees_freedom1 is less than 1 or degrees_freedom1 is greater than or equal to 10^10, FINV returns a #NUM! error. If degrees_freedom2 is less than 1 or degrees_freedom2 is greater than or equal to 10^10, FINV returns a #NUM! error.

FINV can be used to return critical values from the *F* distribution. For example, the output of an ANOVA calculation often includes data for the *F* statistic, *F* probability, and *F* critical value at the 0.05 significance level. To return the critical value of *F*, you use the significance level as the probability argument to FINV.

FINV uses an iterative technique for calculating the function. Given a probability value, FINV iterates until the result is accurate to within $\pm 3 \times 10^{-7}$. If FINV does not converge after 100 iterations, the function returns an #N/A error.

## OTHER DISTRIBUTIONS: EXPONENTIAL, HYPERGEOMETRIC, AND WEIBULL

A few remaining probability distributions are available in Excel: exponential, hypergeometric, and Weibull.

SYNTAX: =EXPONDIST(*x*,*lambda*,*cumulative*)

The EXPONDIST function returns the exponential distribution. You use EXPONDIST to model the time between events, such as how long a bank's automated teller machine takes to deliver cash. For example, you can use EXPONDIST to determine the probability that the process takes, at most, one minute.

The EXPONDIST function takes the following arguments:

- *x*—This is the value of the function.
- *lambda*—This is the parameter value.
- *cumulative*—This is a logical value that indicates which form of the exponential function to provide. If *cumulative* is TRUE, EXPONDIST returns the cumulative distribution function; if *cumulative* is FALSE, EXPONDIST returns the probability density function.

If *x* or *lambda* is nonnumeric, EXPONDIST returns a #VALUE! error. If *x* is less than 0, EXPONDIST returns a #NUM! error. If *lambda* is less than or equal to 0, EXPONDIST returns a #NUM! error.

**Syntax: =HYPGEOMDIST(*sample_s*,*number_sample*,*population_s*,*number_population*)**

The HYPGEOMDIST function returns the hypergeometric distribution. HYPGEOMDIST returns the probability of a given number of sample successes, given the sample size, population successes, and population size. You use HYPGEOMDIST for a problem that has a finite population, where each observation is either a success or a failure, and where each subset of a given size is chosen with equal likelihood.

The HYPGEOMDIST function takes the following arguments:

- *sample_s*—This is the number of successes in the sample.
- *number_sample*—This is the size of the sample.
- *population_s*—This is the number of successes in the population.
- *number_population*—This is the population size.

All arguments are truncated to integers. If any argument is nonnumeric, HYPGEOMDIST returns a #VALUE! error. If sample_s is less than 0 or sample_s is greater than the lesser of number_sample or population_s, HYPGEOMDIST returns a #NUM! error. If sample_s is less than the larger of 0 or (number_sample – number_population + population_s), HYPGEOMDIST returns a #NUM! error. If number_sample is less than 0 or number_sample is greater than number_population, HYPGEOMDIST returns a #NUM! error. If population_s is less than 0 or population_s is greater than number_population, HYPGEOMDIST returns a #NUM! error. If number_population is less than 0, HYPGEOMDIST returns a #NUM! error. HYPGEOMDIST is used in sampling without replacement from a finite population.

**Syntax: =WEIBULL(*x*,*alpha*,*beta*,*cumulative*)**

The WEIBULL function returns the Weibull distribution. You use this distribution in reliability analysis, such as for calculating a device's mean time to failure. This function takes the following arguments:

- *x*—This is the value at which to evaluate the function.
- *alpha*—This is a parameter to the distribution.
- *beta*—This is a parameter to the distribution.
- *cumulative*—This determines the form of the function.

If *x*, *alpha*, or *beta* is nonnumeric, WEIBULL returns a #VALUE! error. If *x* is less than 0, WEIBULL returns a #NUM! error. If *alpha* is less than or equal to 0 or if *beta* is less than or equal to 0, WEIBULL returns a #NUM! error.

26

### Using PROB to Calculate Probability for a Population That Fits No Distribution Curve

In some cases, you might have a dataset that does not appear to follow any standard probability distribution curve. However, you may have sufficient past data to figure the probability of each outcome. In such a case, you can build a table of the possible outcomes and the probability of each outcome. You use the `PROB` function to figure out the chances that a value *X* will fall between an upper and a lower limit.

Syntax: `=PROB(x_range,prob_range,lower_limit,upper_limit)`

The `PROB` function returns the probability that values in a range are between two limits. If `upper_limit` is not supplied, `PROB` returns the probability that values in `x_range` are equal to `lower_limit`. This function takes the following arguments:

- *`x_range`*—This is the range of numeric values of `x` with which there are associated probabilities.
- *`prob_range`*—This is a set of probabilities associated with values in *`x_range`*.
- *`lower_limit`*—This is the lower bound on the value for which you want a probability.
- *`upper_limit`*—This is the optional upper bound on the value for which you want a probability.

If any value in `prob_range` is less than or equal to `0` or if any value in `prob_range` is greater than 1, `PROB` returns a `#NUM!` error. If the sum of the values in `prob_range` is greater than 1, `PROB` returns a `#NUM!` error. If `upper_limit` is omitted, `PROB` returns the probability of being equal to `lower_limit`. If `x_range` and `prob_range` contain a different number of data points, `PROB` returns an `#N/A` error.

In Figure 26.41, the table in A2:B9 shows the probability of achieving a particular score on a seven-point quiz. The range of possible scores in A2:A9 is used as the first argument. The range of probabilities in B2:B9 is used as the second argument. Various formulas in Column G find the probability of any given test falling between two values.

**Figure 26.41**
This may not fall into any known distribution curve, but the `PROB` function can calculate probabilities, nonetheless.

F3 =PROB($A$2:$A$9,$B$2:$B$9,D3,E3)

| | A | B | C | D | E | F | G | H | I | J |
|---|---|---|---|---|---|---|---|---|---|---|
| 1 | Result | Probability | | | | | | | | |
| 2 | 0 | 0.50% | | Between | and | Probability | | | | |
| 3 | 1 | 1% | | 0 | 2 | 3.0% | *=PROB($A$2:$A$9,$B$2:$B$9,D3,E3)* | | | |
| 4 | 2 | 1.50% | | 0 | 3 | 6.0% | | | | |
| 5 | 3 | 3% | | 3 | 5 | 33.0% | | | | |
| 6 | 4 | 12% | | 4 | 5 | 30.0% | | | | |
| 7 | 5 | 18% | | 6 | 7 | 64.0% | | | | |
| 8 | 6 | 52% | | | | | | | | |
| 9 | 7 | 12% | | | | | | | | |
| 10 | | | | | | | | | | |

## Using ZTEST and CONFIDENCE to Calculate Confidence Intervals

Confidence testing is one of the most confusing topics in statistics. Say that you have a very large population, such as the 400 million people who use Microsoft Excel. You would like to find out how many minutes per month people use pivot tables. It would be difficult to survey the 400 million people.

Instead, you find a way to survey 30 people. The mean of those 30 answers is 155 minutes per month. Think about the standard deviation of the entire population. There has to be wide variability because more than half the people using Excel never use pivot tables, and their answer would be zero. Somehow, you miraculously figure out that the standard deviation of the entire population is 220.

You can use the CONFIDENCE function to ask for the 90% confidence interval about this statistic. The formula =CONFIDENCE(0.10,220,30) returns a confidence interval of 66. This means that for any sample of 30 people using Excel, the mean of that sample will be within 66 of the true population mean 90% of the time.

In Figure 26.42, a confidence interval is drawn around the sample mean of 11 samples. The 90% confidence level is saying that in 90% of the samples, the confidence level drawn on the chart will include the true mean of the population.

**Figure 26.42**
The CONFIDENCE function does not give me a lot of confidence that I can predict the activities of 400 million people using Excel based on a survey of 10 people.

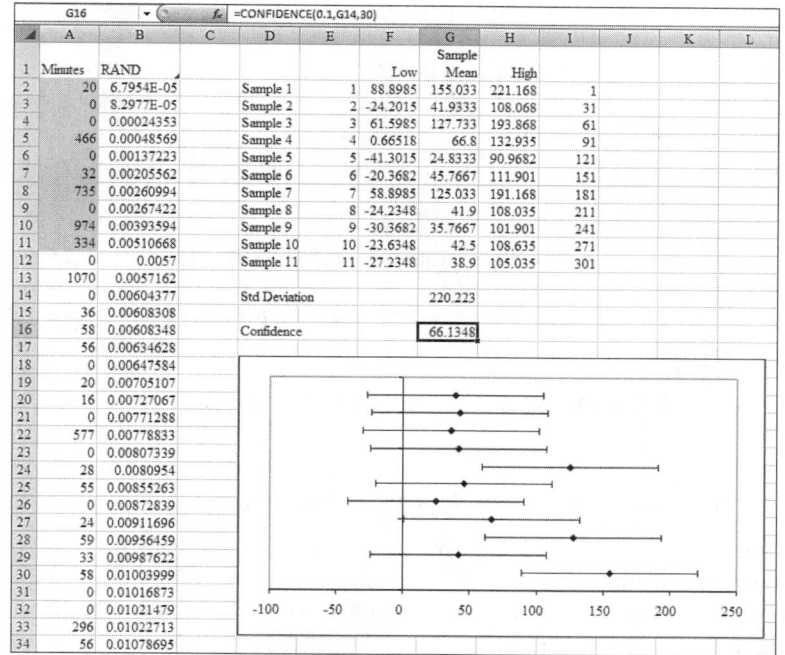

**CAUTION**

It is tempting to interpret the CONFIDENCE result to say that 90% of the population is within the error bars. This is wrong. Reread the last paragraph: If you use the sample mean plus or minus the confidence interval, you will include the true mean 9 out of 10 times.

Although the data in Figure 26.42 is fictitious, the actual mean of that entire population is 78. Of the 11 series drawn on the chart, 10 of the 11 happen to encompass the true mean of 78. Note, however, that the first sample mean of 156 is the one that does not include the true mean.

SYNTAX: =CONFIDENCE(*alpha*,*standard_dev*,*size*)

The CONFIDENCE function returns the confidence interval for a population mean. The confidence interval is a range on either side of a sample mean. For example, if you order a product through the mail, you can determine, with a particular level of confidence, the earliest and latest the product will arrive. This function takes the following arguments:

- *alpha*—This is the significance level used to compute the confidence level. The confidence level equals $100 \times (1 - alpha)\%$ or, in other words, an *alpha* of 0.05 indicates a 95% confidence level.

- *standard_dev*—This is the population standard deviation for the data range and is assumed to be known.

- *size*—This is the sample size.

If any argument is nonnumeric, CONFIDENCE returns a #VALUE! error. If *alpha* is less than or equal to 0 or *alpha* greater than or equal to 1, CONFIDENCE returns a #NUM! error. If standard_dev is less than or equal to 0, CONFIDENCE returns a #NUM! error. If *size* is not an integer, it is truncated. If *size* is less than 1, CONFIDENCE returns a #NUM! error.

> **NOTE**
> A slight problem with the confidence interval function is that the CONFIDENCE function expects that you know with certainty the standard deviation of the entire population. In real life, if you don't know the mean of the 400 million people using Excel, how would you ever calculate the standard deviation? In reality, when you don't know the population standard deviation, you often substitute the sample standard deviation, but this causes you to have to use the *t* distribution instead of CONFIDENCE.

**26**

## USING ZTEST TO ACCEPT OR REJECT A HYPOTHESIS

You use the ZTEST function for hypothesis testing. Say that I make a claim that you will be more confident using pivot tables after attending one of my Power Excel seminars. One month after one of my seminars, I randomly select 30 students from the class and ask them how many minutes during the month they used pivot tables. The sample mean comes back at 156 minutes. This mean is higher than most sample means. But is it high enough to be statistically valid? Could I have achieved a sample mean of 156 just randomly?

SYNTAX: =ZTEST(*array*,*x*,*sigma*)

The ZTEST function returns the two-tailed *p* value of a z-test. The z-test generates a standard score for *x* with respect to the dataset, *array*, and returns the two-tailed probability for the normal distribution. You can use this function to assess the likelihood that a particular observation is drawn from a particular population. This function takes the following arguments:

- *array*—This is the array or range of data against which to test *x*.
- *x*—This is the value to test.
- *sigma*—This is the population (known) standard deviation. If this argument is omitted, the sample standard deviation is used.

If *array* is empty, ZTEST returns an #N/A error.

## USING PERMUT TO CALCULATE THE NUMBER OF POSSIBLE ARRANGEMENTS

Say your company has 40 products in its catalog. You must choose four items to be featured in an upcoming SkyMall issue. The sequence in which the products appear in the ad is relevant. You would like to test the possible ads with a test audience. How many different possible ads could you generate? You use the PERMUT function to solve this problem.

SYNTAX: =PERMUT(*number*,*number_chosen*)

The PERMUT function returns the number of permutations for a given number of objects that can be selected from number objects. A permutation is any set or subset of objects or events in which internal order is significant. Permutations are different from combinations, for which the internal order is not significant. You use this function for lottery-style probability calculations.

The PERMUT function takes the following arguments:

- *number*—This is an integer that describes the number of objects.
- *number_chosen*—This is an integer that describes the number of objects in each permutation.

Both arguments are truncated to integers. If *number* or number_chosen is nonnumeric, PERMUT returns a #VALUE! error. If *number* is less than or equal to 0 or if number_chosen is less than 0, PERMUT returns a #NUM! error. If *number* is less than number_chosen, PERMUT returns a #NUM! error.

The formula to solve the SkyMall problem is =PERMUT(40,4). The result is that there are 2,193,360 possible permutations of products to appear in a one-page ad in the catalog. That is a lot of possibilities!

# USING THE ANALYSIS TOOLPAK TO PERFORM STATISTICAL ANALYSIS

The functions discussed in this chapter are wonderful for doing statistical analysis. If you can use a function to perform some analysis, the function offers a live result. You can change some assumptions, and the results automatically update.

However, many statisticians instead rely on the data tools available in the Analysis Toolpak. The Analysis Toolpak can provide beautiful snapshot-type reports that analyze a dataset. While these reports provide more information than a typical function, they have the downside that they do not automatically recalculate. If you change one of the assumptions in the dataset, you will have to rerun the analysis.

Excel offers many options for performing statistical analysis. Using functions in Excel provides real-time, live results of the data.

The Data Analysis tools in the Analysis Toolpak vary greatly. Some of them are poorly implemented and provide such narrow functionality that it would almost always be better to use your own functions rather than those tools.

On the other hand, some of the tools, such as Regression, provide additional statistics that run circles around the equivalent functions in Excel. In this case, it would be advantageous to use the Analysis Toolpak.

Remember, however, that when you use the Data Analysis tools from the Analysis Toolpak, they create static snapshots of the results. If you change the underlying data, you have to rerun the analysis.

## INSTALLING THE ANALYSIS TOOLPAK IN EXCEL 2007

In previous versions of Excel, many people would install the Analysis Toolpack because they needed it to enable the 89 functions it contained. When you enabled the Analysis Toolpak in order to access the additional functions, Excel silently added a new Data Analysis item to the Tools menu.

However, in Excel 2007, you have to enable the Analysis Toolpak in order to access the Data Analysis Menu Commands group. To do so, you follow these steps:

1. Click the Office icon to the left of the Home ribbon.
2. At the bottom of the menu, click Excel Options.
3. From the left list, choose Add-Ins. You see a long list of active and inactive add-ins.
4. From the very bottom of the window, select the Manage drop-down box and then choose Excel Add-ins, Click Go. You are taken back to the Excel 2003 Add-Ins dialog.
5. In the Add-Ins dialog, choose the Analysis Toolpak check box. Click OK.

If this process is successful, you get a new Analysis group on the Data ribbon. The group has a single button called Data Analysis, as shown in Figure 26.43. Note that this item is rather finicky. You must click Data Analysis in order to invoke the Data Analysis dialog box.

**Figure 26.43**
After you successfully install the Analysis Toolpak, a new group on the Data ribbon offers access to the Data Analysis dialog box.

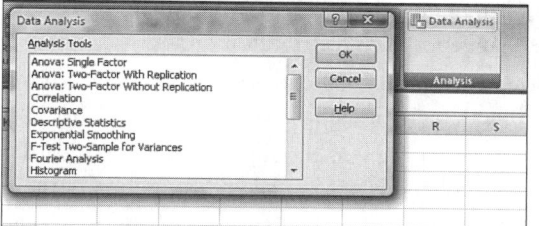

## GENERATING RANDOM NUMBERS BASED ON VARIOUS DISTRIBUTIONS

Whereas the RAND and RANDBETWEEN functions generate random numbers, the Random Number Generation choice in the Data Analysis dialog box allows you to create more sophisticated random number populations. Here's how you use it:

1. Make sure the Analysis Toolpak is installed.

2. From the Data ribbon, choose Data Analysis.

3. Scroll down and select Random Number Generation and click OK. The Random Number Generation dialog appears (see Figure 26.44).

**Figure 26.44**
You can generate random numbers by using the Random Number Generation dialog.

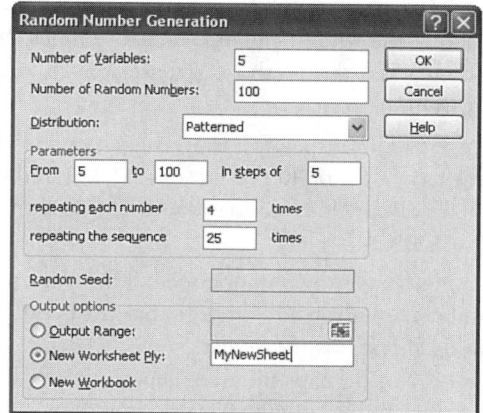

4. In the Random Number Generation dialog, choose the number of columns that you would like to fill with random numbers. If you want three columns of random numbers, enter 3 in the Number of Variables text box.

5. Choose the number of rows that you would like to fill with random numbers. If you want 100 rows of random numbers, fill in 100 in the Number of Random Numbers text box.

6. Select one of the seven options in the Distribution drop-down. The questions in the Parameters frame change for each distribution option:

- For a uniform distribution, you choose upper and lower limits in the Parameters frame. This functionality is similar to using the RAND worksheet function.

- For a normal distribution, you choose a mean and standard deviation. This functionality is very cool and is not available through the normal Excel functions.

- For a Bernoulli distribution, you choose a probability of success on each trial. Bernoulli random variables have a value of 0 or 1. If you want to model LeBron James's ability to make free throws, you use a Bernoulli distribution with a probability of success of 79.4%

- For a binomial distribution, you specify a p value and the number of trials. For example, you can generate number-of-trials Bernoulli random variables, the sum of which is a binomial random variable.

- For a Poisson distribution, you specify a value, *lambda*, that is equal to 1 / Mean. Poisson distributions are often used to characterize the number of events that occur per unit of time (for example, the average rate at which cars arrive at a toll plaza).

- For a patterned distribution, you specify five parameters. You specify a lower and upper limit in steps of a certain value. You can also specify that each number repeats *n* times and that the whole sequence repeats *y* times. Note that there is really nothing random about this method. You are actually simply creating numbers that follow a certain pattern.

- For a discrete distribution, you specify a range of values and their probabilities. In this case, you might have a list of 40 products in A2:A41 and then their probabilities of being selected in B2:B41. Note that the sum of the values in the probability column must add to 100%.

7. In the Random Seed text box, enter any numeric seed. This concept is a little bizarre. In a computer, random numbers are not really random. Scientists call them *pseudo-random*. If you leave the Random Seed text box, Excel uses some strange number (perhaps the number of seconds since 1900 or perhaps the free memory in the stack) as a seed. This ensures that you get different random numbers every time. However, if you enter your own seed, say 123, and then come back a month later with the same seed, Excel generates exactly the same list of random numbers.

8. For the output range, you can either choose an output range, a new worksheet, or a new workbook. For some unknown reason, this dialog box refers to a new worksheet as New Worksheet Ply.

## GENERATING A HISTOGRAM

Consider a set of 100 observations. If the possible values are from a continuous series, it is likely that you won't have any two values that are exactly the same. The chart of this data will show a lot of noise, as shown in Figure 26.45.

**Figure 26.45**
Plotting the individual points of a sample does not tell you a lot about the sample.

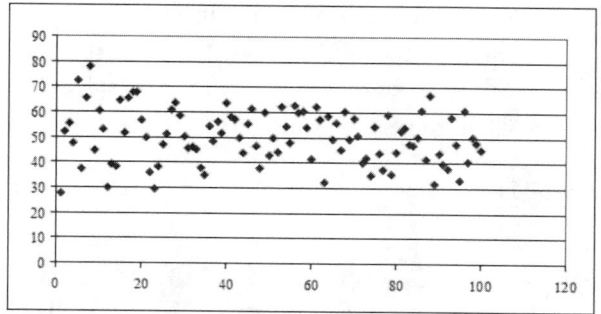

Statisticians instead prefer to group those values into similar categories. Perhaps logical categories for this dataset are 24–34, 35–44, 45–54, and so on The technical term for these groups is *bins*.

The Histogram tool takes a set of observations and groups them into bins, similarly to the way that the FREQUENCY function normally does. However, the histogram function goes further, offering the cumulative percentage of each bin, and then it re-sorts the bins into a Pareto analysis. Excel also offers to create a chart based on the output.

To use the Histogram tool, you follow these steps:

1. Make sure the Analysis Toolpak is installed.

2. Think about some groupings for your data and enter these in a new column in the worksheet. The first bin should be less than the minimum value in your dataset. If your bin range contains 25, 35, 45, then the first bin will include from 25 up through values just less than 35.

3. From the Data ribbon, choose Data Analysis. Then select Histogram and click OK. The Histogram dialog appears.

4. In the Histogram dialog, specify the range that contains your observations as the input range. This range does not need to be sorted. You may include a one-cell heading as part of the range. If you do, you must also include a one-cell heading for the bin range and also check the Labels option in step 6.

5. Specify your range from step 2 as the bin range. If you leave this blank, Excel chooses equal-size values between the minimum and maximum of your data. This rarely comes out to nice, neat bins, so feel free to use your own instead.

6. If your input and bin ranges contain one-cell headings, check the Labels box.

26

7. For the output, specify the upper-left corner of a blank spot on the current worksheet, or specify a new worksheet or a new workbook.

8. Check the Pareto box. Excel produces the histogram and then produces a second histogram. In the second histogram, the most popular bin is sorted to the top of the list.

9. Check the Cumulative box. Excel reports the cumulative percentage accounted for by values from the bottom of the list through the current bin.

10. Check the Chart Output box to ask for a chart. Note that this default chart is fairly plain looking and needs some customization to be acceptable.

11. Click OK to create the histogram.

Figure 26.46 shows the Histogram dialog box, along with the results of the histogram.

**Figure 26.46**
Using input area of Column A and the bins in Column C, Excel produces a histogram in E:J. This is significantly easier than using the FREQUENCY array formula.

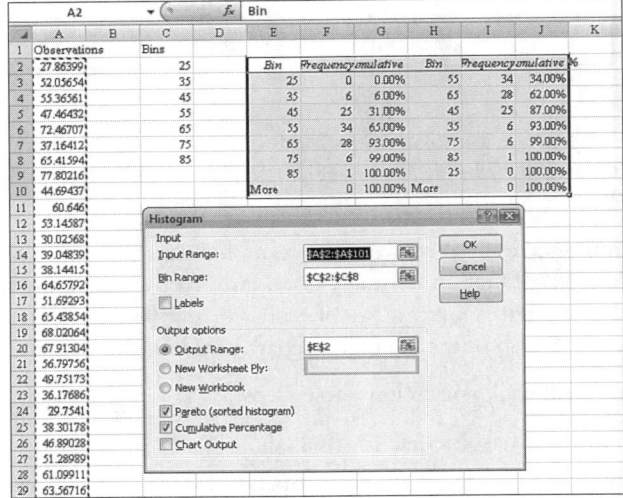

## GENERATING DESCRIPTIVE STATISTICS OF A POPULATION

Excel provides a large number of functions to describe datasets. Earlier in this chapter, you learned about functions to calculate the mean, median, mode, skew, and so on of your data. By using the Data Analysis tools, you can generate all these statistics in a single command. To do so, you follow these steps:

1. Make sure the Analysis Toolpak is installed.

2. From the Data ribbon, choose Data Analysis. Then select Descriptive Statistics and click OK. The Descriptive Statistics dialog appears.

3. In the Descriptive Statistics dialog, choose the input range for your dataset.

4. If the range in step 3 contains a heading in the first row, choose the Labels check box.

5. Set the output as a new range, a new worksheet, or a new workbook.

6. Choose Summary Statistics. Excel provides values for mean, standard error (of the mean), median, mode, standard deviation, variance, kurtosis, skewness, range, minimum, maximum, sum, count, largest (#), smallest (#), and confidence level.

7. Check the Confidence Level for Mean check box and specify the confidence level you want to use. For example, a confidence level of 95% calculates the confidence level of the mean at a significance of 5%.

8. If you would like row(s) in the output for the $k$th largest and/or smallest values, choose the appropriate check boxes and fill in the value for $k$. For example, if you ask for the $k$th largest with a value of 3, Excel report the third-largest value in the dataset.

9. Click OK. Results similar to those shown in Figure 26.47 are generated.

**Figure 26.47**
Excel can generate every descriptive statistic for a dataset with a single command. The output range in C3:D20 is generated from the dialog box shown.

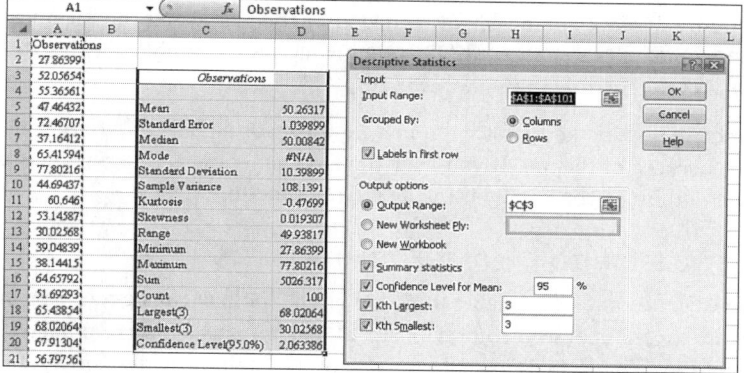

## RANKING RESULTS

The Excel RANK function has an inherent problem when two results in the dataset are tied. While the RANK function provides a workaround for this problem, the Rank and Percentile feature cannot overcome this limitation. If you are worried about the possibility of a tie in your dataset, you should use the RANK function instead of this command.

To assign a rank and percentage to a dataset, you follow these steps:

1. Make sure the Analysis Toolpak is installed. Then scroll down and select Rank and Percentile and click OK. The Rank and Percentile dialog appears.

2. From the Data ribbon, choose Data Analysis.

3. In the Rank and Percentile dialog, choose the input range for your dataset. The input range may contain a single-cell heading at the top of the data, but it may not contain any other nonnumeric data. In Figure 26.48, it would be nice if Excel could accept the names associated with each data point, but it cannot. You have to add them back later.

4. If your input range has a heading in the first row, check the Labels in First Row check box.

5. Choose an output range for the dataset. Excel returns the statistics shown in D1:G16 in Figure 26.48. Notice that the data points have been sorted in high-to-low sequence. In Column D, Excel refers to each cell as being at Point 1, Point 2, Point 3, and so on.

26

**Figure 26.48**
The rank and percentile function will sort the data, calculate a rank and a percentile function. It cannot resolve ties, however.

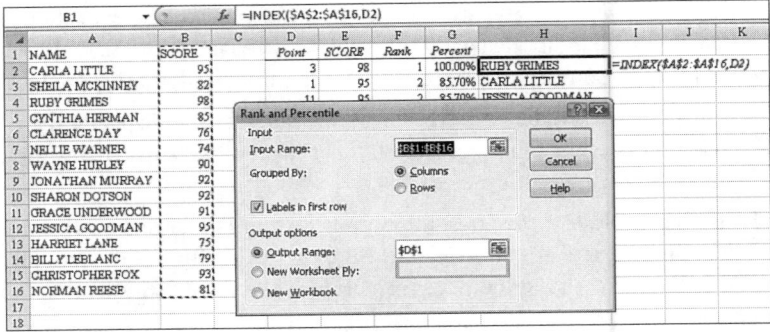

In Figure 26.48, Column H was added after the fact, using the formula =INDEX($A$2:$A$16,D2). Cell D2 contains the point number for this row. Basically, this function asks for the third value in A2:A16.

Notice that Carla and Jessica are in a tie for second place. No one in this dataset is ranked third because of this tie. If you used the RANK function as described earlier in this chapter, you could break the ties by using a COUNTIF function.

## USING REGRESSION TO PREDICT FUTURE RESULTS

The Regression tool available in the Analysis Toolpak runs circles around the LINEST function in Excel. As described previously, LINEST returns a bizarre unlabeled set of results for a regression. The Regression tool, on the other hand, provides a myriad of well-labeled statistics, analysis, and charts as the output.

To perform a regression analysis using the Regression tool, you follow these steps:

1. Make sure the Analysis Toolpak is installed.

2. Ensure that your data includes one independent variable, such as sales per day. It can also contain one or more dependent variables—items that might explain the variability in sales. (In this example, dependent variables include outside temperature, if it rained, and if it was a weekend.)

3. From the Data ribbon, choose Data Analysis. Then scroll down and select Regression and click OK. The Regression dialog appears.

4. In the Regression dialog, the Input Y range must be a single column of data. In this example, it is the range containing sales for each day. Be sure to include a cell at the top of the column that describes the data.

5. In the Input X Range text box, use a range that is the same height as the Y range. The X range can contain one column for each independent variable. In this example, the X range contains columns for temperature, rain, and weekend. For best results, include a cell at the top of each column, with the name of the variable.

6. If your ranges in steps 4 and 5 include headings, check the Labels check box.

7. If you want to force the y-intercept to be 0, check the Constant Is Zero check box.

8. The Confidence Level box is interesting. The program always gives statistics for a 95% confidence level. If you enter a different percentage in this box, you get two confidence levels: one for the default 95%, and one for the other value you enter.

9. Specify the output range as the top-left cell of a range. In this example, the regression output occupies from G2 to O119, so make sure that you have a really large area set aside for the results.

10. Fill in the remaining options in the Regression dialog to add sections to the report:

- **Residuals**—Select this to include residuals in the residuals output table.

- **Standardized Residuals**—Select this to include standardized residuals in the residuals output table.

- **Residual Plots**—Select this to generate a chart for each independent variable versus the residual.

- **Line Fit Plots**—Select this to generate a chart for predicted values versus the observed values.

- **Normal Probability Plots**—Select this to generate a chart that plots normal probability.

When you are done, the dialog box should look roughly as shown in Figure 26.49.

**Figure 26.49**
The hardest part of specifying a regression is remembering that the y range is the value you are trying to predict.

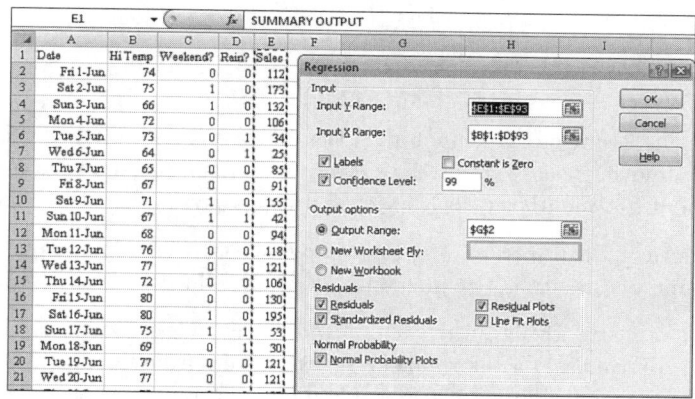

After you run the regression, Excel provides the following sections of the report (see Figure 26.50):

- Regression statistics such as *r*-squared are provided in the top section.

- An ANOVA analysis is provided.

- The actual regression results are provided in Column 2 of the third section. In this example, the prediction for sales comes from H18:H21. The formula would be that sales for any day will be –75 + 2.6 × High temperature + 52 if it is a weekend. If it is raining, you subtract 102 from this prediction. Remaining columns in this section return the standard error, *t* statistic, *p* value, and confidence limits for each variable.

26

**Figure 26.50**
The regression report from the Analysis Toolpak is fantastic. It provides a more comprehensive view than the LINEST function.

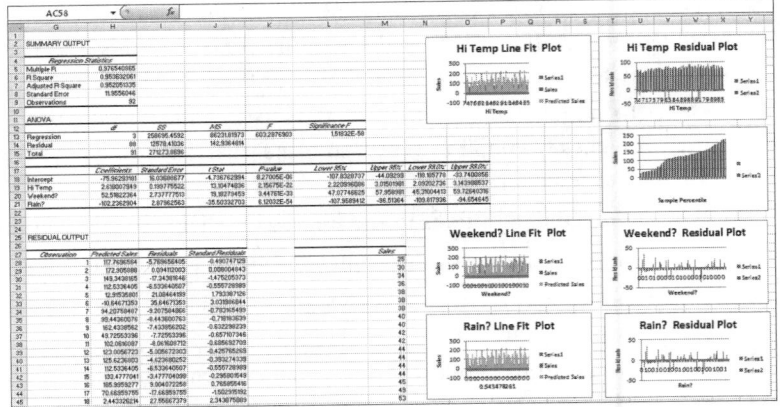

- The next section goes way beyond the LINEST function. Excel uses the regression results to predict sales for each day in the dataset. The predicted sales are in Column 2 of the dataset. The comparison of predicted sales to actual sales is shown in the Residuals column.

- Finally, Excel provides a probability table. The table explains that on the worst 12.5% of days, you might sell $44 or less.

## USING A MOVING AVERAGE TO FORECAST SALES

The Moving Average command in the Data Analysis tools is disappointing. The technique of using a moving average to produce future forecasts is based on the concept that variability in the month-to-month actuals is lessened if you always average three months.

After choosing Data Analysis, Moving Average, you can specify an input range that contains one column of sales data. The interval value of 3 produces a three-month moving average.

After you use the Moving Average command, Excel adds one column with a series of simple =AVERAGE() formulas. Each formula averages the sales from the previous month, this month, and the next month. In theory, you would then use this column as input to the forecasting methods to produce a future forecast.

In Figure 26.51, Column C is the new moving average column. Column D is the standard error column. This command is really a lot of hassle when you could easily add your own =AVERAGE formula in Column C.

## USING EXPONENTIAL SMOOTHING TO FORECAST SALES

The Exponential Smoothing feature in the Data Analysis tools allows you to set up a forecasting formula that uses exponential smoothing.

This method of forecasting requires only two points: the forecast for the previous month and the actual for the current month. The forecast for the next month is created by adding together 75% of the most recent actuals and 25% of the prior forecast.

**Figure 26.51**
The Moving Average feature of the Data Analysis tools is a long route to adding a simple formula.

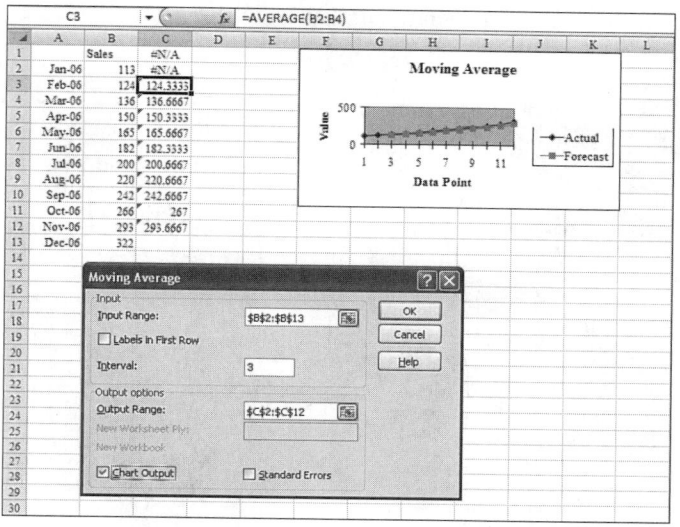

In this example, the 25% is called a *damping factor*. You can assign any damping factor that you want, but values in the 20% to 30% range are recommended.

To set up an exponential smoothing forecast, you follow these steps:

1. Make sure the Analysis Toolpak is installed.

2. Ensure that your data includes one column of sales data, such as sales per month.

3. From the Data ribbon, choose Data Analysis. Then select Exponential Smoothing and click OK. The Exponential Smoothing dialog appears.

4. In the Exponential Smoothing dialog, the Input range should be your single column of sales data. If you include a heading cell, check the Labels check box.

5. Ensure that the damping factor is between 0.20 and 0.30. With a damping factor of 0.30, the current forecast is based 70% on the most recent actuals and 30% on all the past forecasts.

6. Limit the output range to a cell on the current worksheet. Ideally, this range starts in the same row as your input range, in an adjacent column.

7. To create a chart comparing forecast and actuals, select the Chart Output check box.

8. Choose the Standard Errors check box. The output contains a second column with a standard error calculation. This calculation analyzes the current period and last three periods. In Row 5, enter the standard error formula =SQRT(SUMXMY2(B3:B5,C2:C4)/3). This formula subtracts the forecast from the actual for the last three months, squares the differences, adds them, divides to find an average, and then takes the square root of the average.

9. Click OK to produce the analysis.

Figure 26.52 shows the Exponential Smoothing dialog and the subsequent results of the analysis.

**Figure 26.52**
Exponential smoothing provides a forecast that is heavily weighted toward recent actuals.

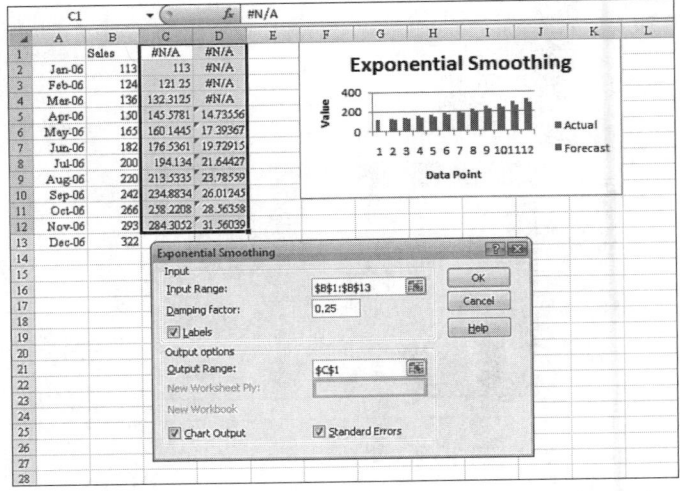

**NOTE**

Note that a bug prevents Excel from entering the label Sales Forecast in the top row of the output. You have to manually change the headings Excel generates.

Because the standard error column must analyze four months of forecasts and actuals, the first three data points in the standard error column are always #N/A!.

## USING CORRELATION OR COVARIANCE TO CALCULATE THE RELATIONSHIP BETWEEN MANY VARIABLES

Both covariance and correlation are measures of the extent to which two measurement variables vary together. I prefer the correlation coefficient because it is independent of the units involved.

Say that you are comparing height in inches or centimeters to weight in pounds or kilograms. The correlation coefficient returns a value from 1 to –1. Correlation coefficient values close to 0 indicate that there is little or no correlation between the measures. A value close to 1 indicates a strong positive correlation: As one variable increases, the other is likely to increase. A value close to –1 indicates a strong negative correlation: The value of one variable is likely to decrease as the value of the other variable increases.

You could calculate these values manually by using the CORREL or PEARSON functions in Excel, but the Data Analysis version is particularly well suited to datasets that have many measurements for each member of a population. In this case, the Correlation tool generates a correlation coefficient for every possible combination of the measurement statistics.

Figure 26.53 shows a database of body statistics for a sample of 125 people. For each person, the clinician measured 13 key measurements, such as height, weight, and so on. It would be interesting to see if height is a good predictor of weight or if some other measurement is appropriate.

**Figure 26.53**

In a collection of key measurement stats for 125 members of a population, which measurements are most related?

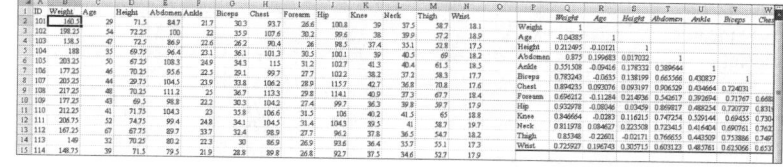

To build a matrix of correlation coefficients (or covariances), you follow these steps:

1. Make sure the Analysis Toolpak is installed.

2. Ensure that your data includes several columns of measurements for a population. Each row should represent another member of the population. Try to avoid missing values. If one measurement is missing for a population member, that member is thrown out of the entire calculation.

3. From the Data ribbon, choose Data Analysis. Then select Correlation (or Covariance) and click OK. The Correlation dialog appears.

4. In the Correlation dialog, ensure that the input range includes your row of headings and all the measurements. If you have an ID field, do not include it in the input range.

5. If your data has labels as the first row or column of the input range, check the Labels check box. If you don't include the labels, Excel has to make up labels, such as Column 1, Column 2, and so on.

6. Select the upper-left corner of the output range. If your input range has $n$ columns, the size of the output range will be $(n + 1) \times (n + 1)$.

7. Click OK to create the correlation matrix.

Figure 26.54 shows the Correlation dialog box and the resulting correlation matrix. In this particular example, height and weight have a weak correlation coefficient of 0.21. You can compare this to the correlation coefficient for hip and weight, which has a positive correlation of 0.93.

The covariance feature works the same as the correlation feature, except the output table is not scaled to provide answers between −1 and 1.

## USING SAMPLING TO CREATE RANDOM SAMPLES

Earlier in this chapter, in the section on the RAND function, you learned about a way to collect a random sample. You can also allow the Data Analysis tools to produce a random sample for you.

26

**Figure 26.54**
The correlation coefficient matrix produces results from –1 to 1. Values further away from 0 indicate a strong correlation between the measurement variables.

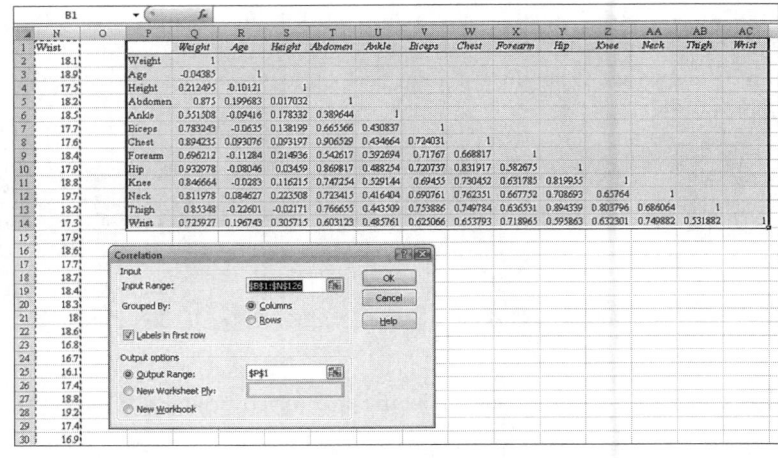

CAUTION

Perplexingly, the Random Sampling feature works only if your data is completely numeric. This function does not work if you need to select a sample of customers or products.

The Random Sampling feature offers two interesting ways to collect a sample. Excel can either randomly select *n* members of the population, or you can specify that Excel should select every *k*th member of the population.

You follow these steps to select a random sample:

1. Make sure the Analysis Toolpak is installed.

2. Ensure that your data is completely numeric. This feature works best on a single column of data, so ensure that you are selecting just a single column. If you have multiple columns of data, Excel randomly selects cells from the entire range; for example, the random sample might include Cells B2, A5, C7, D10, B2. Ensure that you do not include column headings if your data spans multiple columns.

3. From the Data ribbon, choose Data Analysis. Then scroll down and select Sampling and click OK. The Sampling dialog appears.

4. In the Sampling dialog, ensure that the input range includes your data range. If your data includes a single column, and you have headings in the first cell, select the Labels check box. Do not include labels if your population spans multiple columns.

5. For random sampling, ask for a specific number of samples. The other option is to specify periodic sampling, which provides every *n*th value in the dataset.

6. Specify the top-left cell of the output range and click OK.

In Figure 26.55, Excel has produced a random sample of 10 from a rectangular range of data.

**Figure 26.55**
A random sample from the Sampling dialog might include duplicates.

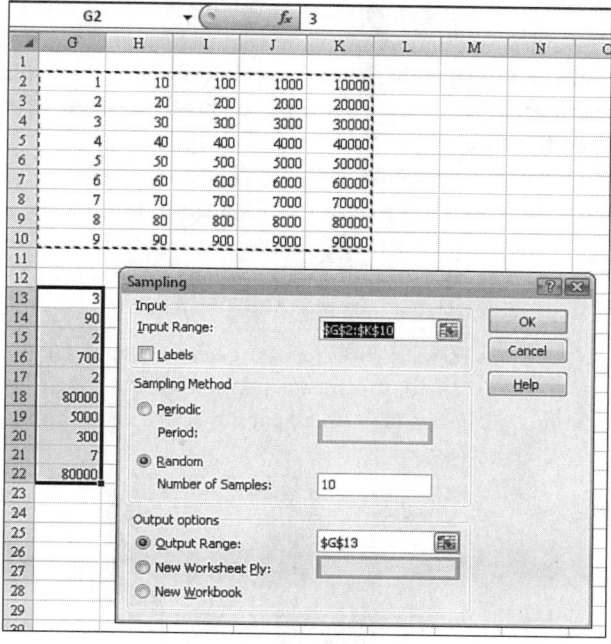

**NOTE**

> The Random Sampling feature allows for duplicates within the same sample. If you need to make sure that any given sample contains no duplicates, you should use the RAND function instead.

**NOTE**

> If you ask for a periodic sample, Excel traverses each column from left to right. Selecting every fourth value from G2:K10 in Figure 26.55 would select 4, 8 from the first column, and then 30, 70 from the second column. From 70, Excel would skip the next three values of 80, 90, and 100, and it would return 200 as the next periodic member of the sample.

## USING ANOVA TO PERFORM ANALYSIS OF VARIANCE TESTING

ANOVA stands for analysis of variance. The Data Analysis tools offer three forms of ANOVA testing:

- **Single-factor ANOVA**—This is for measuring variance for two or more samples with a single variable. For example, say that you have 18 farm fields. All are planted with the same variety of wheat. Six are treated with Nutrient A, six are treated with Nutrient B, and six are treated with Nutrient C. Single-variable ANOVA would analyze whether the variances in the populations were simply random or due to the fertilizers.

- **Two-factor ANOVA without replication**—This is for use when your data can be classified along two different dimensions. For example, say that half of the farm fields were downwind from an interstate highway that is heavily traveled by diesel trucks. You could analyze the variance caused by the fertilizer versus the variance caused by the carbon monoxide from the highway.

- **Two-factor ANOVA with replication**—If you have enough samples so that every combination of {fertilizer, highway} has multiple samples, you can perform two-factor ANOVA with replication. Otherwise, you use two-factor ANOVA without replication.

You follow these steps to perform a one-way ANOVA test:

1. If your data is set up as records with data for each field, arrange the data in columns for each variable. In Figure 26.56, this means taking the data from Column B and arranging it in three columns, E, F, and G, with a heading above each column.

**Figure 26.56**
The difference in the sample means is statistically significant.

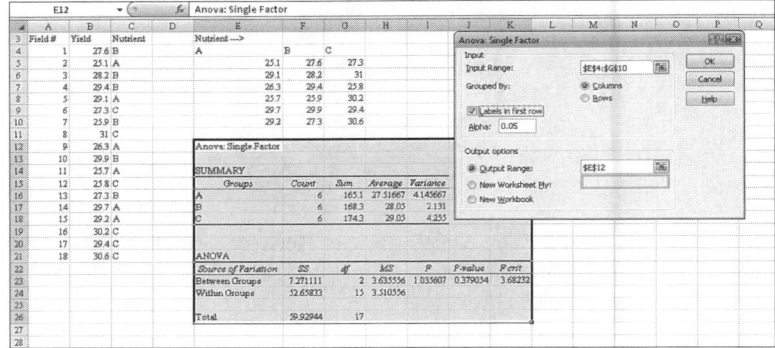

2. Choose a null hypothesis. For example, your null hypothesis might be that all the nutrients produce a similar mean. If you can reject the null hypothesis, then your hypothesis is that the selection nutrient has an impact on yield.

3. Choose a significance level, alpha, of 0.05. If the statistics from the ANOVA output show a *p* value greater than the alpha, then you can reject the null hypothesis and assume that the nutrient has an impact on yield.

4. Make sure the Analysis Toolpak is installed.

5. From the Data ribbon, choose Data Analysis. Then select ANOVA: Single Factor and click OK. The ANOVA: Single Factor dialog appears.

6. In the ANOVA: Single Factor dialog, ensure that the input range includes your columns of means.

7. If your input range includes a heading above each column, choose the Labels in First Row check box.

8. In the Alpha box, enter the level at which you want to evaluate critical values for the *F* statistic. The alpha level is a significance level related to the probability of having a type I error (that is, rejecting a true hypothesis).

9. Choose the top-left corner for the output range.

10. Click OK to produce the result.

In Figure 26.56, the important statistic is the $p$ value in Cell J23. Because this number is larger than alpha, you can reject the null hypothesis and assume that the nutrients had an impact on the yield.

You follow these steps to perform a two-way ANOVA test with replication:

1. Arrange your data so that one dimension is spread across the columns. (This can be tricky.)

2. Ensure that you have equal numbers of samples along the second dimension. In Figure 26.57, there were three rows of yields from fields downwind from a highway. These rows must be arranged together. For convenience, have a row label in Cell A7 to identify this block of data.

**Figure 26.57**
Setting up the input range in equal size rows is the key to successful use of Two-Factor ANOVA analysis.

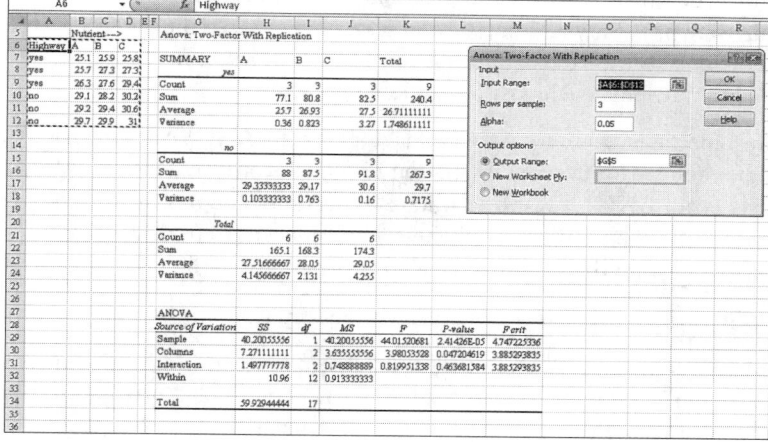

3. Because you had three rows of sample yields for fields adjacent to highways, you also have to find three rows of sample yields for fields away from highways. This block of three rows must immediately follow the other data. Again, for convenience, make sure there is a heading in the first column and first row of this block to identify the value along the second dimension.

4. Make sure the Analysis Toolpak is installed.

5. From the Data ribbon, choose Data Analysis. Then select ANOVA: Two-Factor with Replication and click OK. The ANOVA: Two-Factor with Replication dialog appears.

6. In the ANOVA: Two-Factor with Replication dialog, ensure that the input range includes sample values as well as an additional row above to identify the first-dimension variables and an additional column to the left to identify the second-dimension variable.

26

7. In the Rows per Sample text box, enter the number of rows in each block of data. In this present example, there are 3 rows of yields for highway fields and 3 rows for non-highway fields, so enter 3.

8. In the Alpha box, enter the level at which you want to evaluate critical values for the $F$ statistic. The alpha level is a significance level related to the probability of having a type I error (that is, rejecting a true hypothesis).

9. For the output range, select the top-left corner of a large blank area. The ANOVA results will take up 30 rows by 7 columns.

10. Click OK to perform the analysis.

In the results from this analysis, watch for the values in italics in the first column of the output range. The first block of data in the output range describes the first block of three rows in the input range, with a value of "yes" to the highway question.

The final block of the analysis shows the $p$ values for each dimension and the two dimensions combined. In this particular analysis, it appears that much of the variability is due to highway proximity and does not necessarily have that much to do with the nutrients. The $p$ value of 0.047 for the columns is not enough to reject the null hypothesis that the variability due to nutrients could just be random.

In some cases, you may have two factors for the ANOVA testing, but you may not have multiple samples for every combination of {dimension1, dimension2}. In this case, you can run two-factor ANOVA testing without replication. The results from this test contain less analysis than do the results from the test with replication. In this test, Excel does not predict if factors beyond the two dimensions are causing variability.

To perform a two-factor ANOVA without replication, you follow these steps:

1. Arrange your data in a crosstab fashion. Have values from Dimension 1 going across the top row of the data. Have values from Dimension 2 going down the left column of the data. Enter the sample value in each intersection.

2. Make sure the Analysis Toolpak is installed.

3. From the Data ribbon, choose Data Analysis. Then select ANOVA: Two-Factor Without Replication and click OK. The ANOVA: Two-Factor Without Replication dialog appears.

4. In the ANOVA: Two-Factor Without Replication dialog, ensure that the input range includes sample values as well as an additional row above to identify the first-dimension variables and an additional column to the left to identify the second-dimension variables.

5. Check the Labels box so that Excel can get the headings for the Dimension 1 and Dimension 2 values from the worksheet.

6. In the Alpha box, enter the level at which you want to evaluate critical values for the $F$ statistic. The alpha level is a significance level related to the probability of having a type I error (that is, rejecting a true hypothesis).

7. Click OK to run the analysis.

Excel analyzes the variance based on the rows and columns, as shown in Figure 26.58.

**Figure 26.58**
In this particular sample, the column drives variability more than the rows.

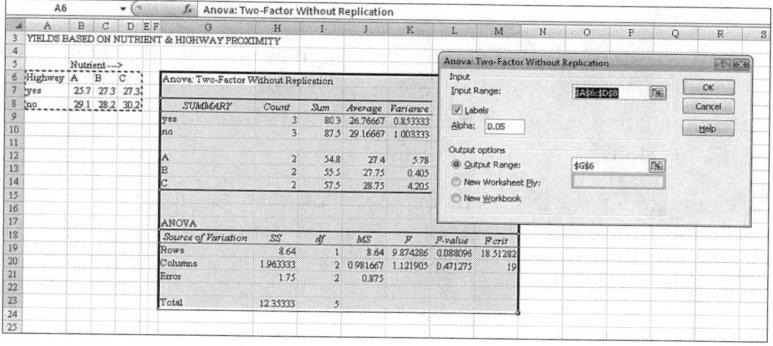

## USING THE *F*-TEST TO MEASURE VARIABILITY BETWEEN METHODS

If you want to compare two methods, it is helpful to know if the variances the two methods are roughly the same. The *F*-test was designed by statistician R. A. Fisher. (The *F* here stands for Fisher and nothing intuitive.) The *F*-test compares two variances, V1 / V2, to produce an *F* statistic. Values close to 1 indicate that the variances are similar.

To run an *F*-test, you follow these steps:

1. Set up two ranges with samples from each population. These samples do not have to have the same number of members.

2. Make sure the Analysis Toolpak is installed.

3. From the Data ribbon, choose Data Analysis. Then select F-Test Two-Sample for Variances. The F-Test Two Sample for Variances dialog appears.

4. In the F-Test Two Sample for Variances dialog, choose the range for both of your sample ranges.

5. In the Alpha box, enter the level at which you want to evaluate critical values for the F statistic. The alpha level is a significance level related to the probability of having a type I error (that is, rejecting a true hypothesis).

6. Select the top-left cell of an output range.

7. Click OK to produce the analysis.

The F-Test tool provides the result of a test of the null hypothesis that these two samples come from distributions with equal variances against the alternative that the variances are not equal in the underlying distributions.

The F-Test tool calculates the value of an *F* statistic. A value of *F* close to 1 provides evidence that the underlying population variances are equal.

There is a tricky element to the output table. If the *F* value is less than 1, you need to look to the next row, which has the label "P(F <= f) one-tail." It gives the probability of observing

26

a value of the $F$ statistic less than f when population variances are equal. The next row, labeled "F Critical one-tail," gives the critical value less than 1 for the chosen significance level, alpha.

If the $F$ statistic is greater than 1, the meanings of these rows are reversed. The row labeled "P(F <= f) one-tail" gives the probability of observing a value of the $F$ statistic greater than f when population variances are equal, and "F Critical one-tail" gives the critical value greater than 1 for alpha.

In Figure 26.59, the $F$ statistic of 0.88 is less than 1. This means that the null hypothesis is that the variances are unequal. The $F$ critical value is 0.35, meaning that you can reject the null hypothesis.

**Figure 26.59**
The $F$-test indicates whether two populations have an equal variance.

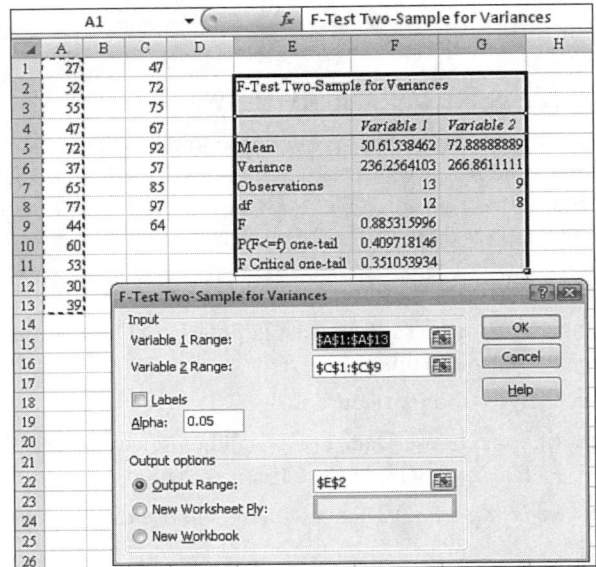

## PERFORMING A Z-TEST TO DETERMINE WHETHER TWO SAMPLES HAVE EQUAL MEANS

You use the Z-Test tool to test the null hypothesis that there is no difference between two population means against either one-sided or two-sided alternative hypotheses. z-tests are appropriate when the sample sizes are greater than 30. For sample sizes smaller than 30, you use $t$-tests, as described in the following section.

**NOTE**  If variances are not known, the worksheet function ZTEST should be used instead.

To run a z-test, you follow these steps:

1. Set up two ranges with data from each sample. Calculate the standard deviation of each population.

2. Make sure the Analysis Toolpak is installed.

3. From the Data ribbon, choose Data Analysis. Then Scroll down and select z-Test: Two-Sample for Means. The z-Test: Two Sample for Means dialog appears.

4. For Variable 1 Range, select the range of data for your first sample. If you choose a heading cell in this range, be sure to choose a heading cell in step 5.

5. For Variable 2 Range, select the range of data for your second sample.

6. For Hypothesized Mean Difference, if you have a reason to believe that there is a shift from one population to the other caused by an external event, note it here. For example, if you measured the height of every kid in the classroom, and the next day you measured the height of every kid while they were standing on a 6-inch bench, the 6 inches would be an explainable shift in the means.

7. For the variances, enter the standard deviations for both populations. As mentioned previously, if you don't know these, you should use the ZTEST worksheet function instead of this tool.

8. In the Alpha box, enter the confidence level for the test. This value must be in the range 0…1. The alpha level is a significance level related to the probability of having a type I error (that is, rejecting a true hypothesis).

9. Select the top-left cell of an output range.

10. Click OK to produce the analysis.

The results of a z-test are shown in Figure 26.60.

When analyzing the results, you should be careful to understand the output:

- "P(Z <= z) one-tail" is really P(Z >= ABS(z)), the probability of a z value further from 0 in the same direction as the observed z value when there is no difference between the population means.

- "P(Z <= z) two-tail" is really P(Z >= ABS(z) or Z <= -ABS(z)), the probability of a z value further from 0 in either direction than the observed z value when there is no difference between the population means. The two-tailed result is just the one-tailed result multiplied by 2.

## PERFORMING STUDENT'S T-TESTING TO TEST POPULATION MEANS

The two-sample T-Test tool tests for equality of the population means underlying each sample. There are three varieties of this test, based on assumptions:

- **t-Test: Paired Two Sample for Means**—If the two samples came from the same population, one before a treatment and one after the treatment, you use this test.

- **t-Test: Two-Sample Assuming Equal Variances**—If you believe that the variances of each population are equal, you use this test.

**Figure 26.60**
This z-test indicates that the samples came from different populations.

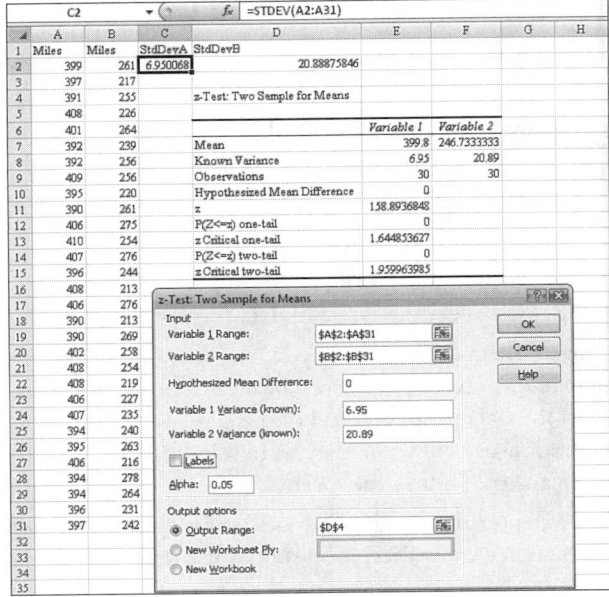

■ **t-Test: Two Sample Assuming Unequal Variances**—If you believe that the variances of the two populations are unequal, you use this test.

All three varieties produce a *t* statistic. The *t* statistic can be negative or nonnegative. Under the assumption of equal underlying population means, if *t* is less than 0, "P(T <= t) one-tail" gives the probability that a value of the *t* statistic would be observed that is more negative than *t*. If *t* is greater than or equal to 0, "P(T <= t) one-tail" gives the probability that a value of the *t* statistic would be observed that is more positive than *t*. "t Critical one-tail" gives the cutoff value so that the probability of observing a value of the *t* statistic greater than or equal to "t Critical one-tail" is alpha.

"P(T <= t) two-tail" gives the probability that a value of the *t* statistic would be observed that is larger in absolute value than *t*. "P Critical two-tail" gives the cutoff value so that the probability of an observed *t* statistic larger in absolute value than "P Critical two-tail" is alpha.

To perform a *t*-test, you follow these steps:

1. Set up two ranges with data from each sample.

2. Make sure the Analysis Toolpak is installed.

3. From the Data ribbon, choose Data Analysis. Then scroll down and select t-Test: Two-Sample Assuming Equal Variance. The t-Test dialog appears.

4. For Variable 1 Range, select the range of data for your first sample. If you choose a heading cell in this range, be sure to choose a heading cell in step 5.

5. For Variable 2 Range, select the range of data for your second sample.

6. For Hypothesized Mean Difference, if you have a reason to believe that there is a shift from one population to the other caused by an external event, note it here.

7. In the Alpha box, enter the confidence level for the test. This value must be in the range 0…1. The alpha level is a significance level related to the probability of having a type I error (that is, rejecting a true hypothesis).

8. Select the top-left cell of an output range.

9. Click OK to produce the analysis.

The results of a *t*-test are shown in Figure 26.61.

**Figure 26.61**
Based on a *t* statistic close to 0, you cannot assume that these came from different populations.

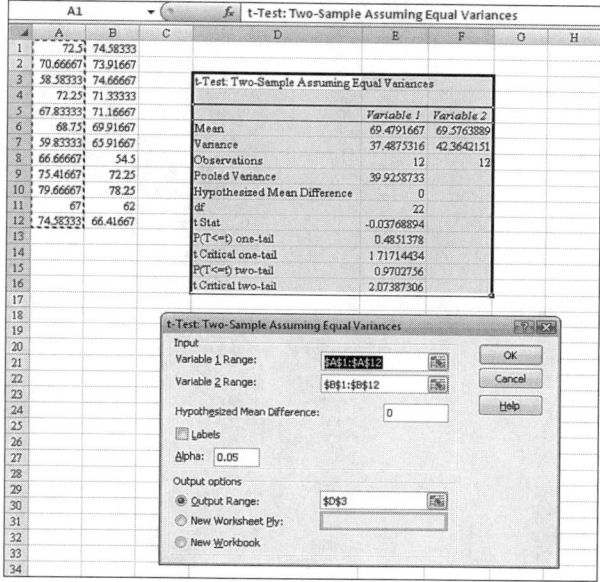

## USING FUNCTIONS VERSUS USING THE ANALYSIS TOOLPAK TOOLS

Excel offers many options for performing statistical analysis. Using functions in Excel provides real-time, live results of the data.

The Data Analysis tools in the Analysis Toolpak vary greatly. Some of them are poorly implemented and provide such narrow functionality that it would almost always be better to use your own functions rather than those tools.

On the other hand, some of the tools, such as Regression, provide additional statistics that run circles around the equivalent functions in Excel. In this case, it would be advantageous to use the Analysis Toolpak.

Remember, however, that when you use the Data Analysis tools from the Analysis Toolpak, they create static snapshots of the results. If you change the underlying data, you have to rerun the analysis.

26

# CHAPTER 27

# USING TRIG, MATRIX, AND ENGINEERING FUNCTIONS

## In this chapter

Scientists, mathematicians, and engineers, as well as high school mathematics students, will get the broadest use out of the functions in this chapter.

Even though many of the trigonometry functions might seem intimidating, I have tried to provide practical household examples for many of the functions. Anyone who has to lean a ladder up against a house can find a use for the trig functions.

The imaginary number functions might only be useful to electrical engineers, but any business analyst could make use of the techniques for solving linear equations.

Table 27.1 provides an alphabetical list of all of Excel 2007's trig functions. Detailed examples of the functions are provided later in the chapter.

**TABLE 27.1   ALPHABETICAL LIST OF TRIG FUNCTIONS**

| Function | Description |
|---|---|
| ACOS(*number*) | Returns the arccosine of a number. The arccosine is the angle whose cosine is *number*. The returned angle is given in radians in the range 0 to Π. |
| ACOSH(*number*) | Returns the inverse hyperbolic cosine of a number. *number* must be greater than or equal to 1. The inverse hyperbolic cosine is the value whose hyperbolic cosine is *number*, so ACOSH(COSH(*number*)) equals *number*. |
| ASIN(*number*) | Returns the arcsine of a number. The arcsine is the angle whose sine is *number*. The returned angle is given in radians in the range –Π / 2 to Π / 2. |
| ASINH(*number*) | Returns the inverse hyperbolic sine of a number. The inverse hyperbolic sine is the value whose hyperbolic sine is *number*, so ASINH(SINH(*number*)) equals *number*. |
| ATAN(*number*) | Returns the arctangent of a number. The arctangent is the angle whose tangent is *number*. The returned angle is given in radians in the range –Π / 2 to Π / 2. |
| ATAN2(*x_num*,*y_num*) | Returns the arctangent of the specified x- and y-coordinates. The arctangent is the angle from the x-axis to a line containing the origin (0, 0) and a point with coordinates (*x_num*, *y_num*). The angle is given in radians between –Π and Π, excluding –Π. |
| ATANH(*number*) | Returns the inverse hyperbolic tangent of a number. *number* must be between –1 and 1 (excluding –1 and 1). The inverse hyperbolic tangent is the value whose hyperbolic tangent is *number*, so ATANH(TANH(*number*)) equals *number*. |
| COS(*number*) | Returns the cosine of the given angle. |
| COSH(*number*) | Returns the hyperbolic cosine of a number. |
| DEGREES(*angle*) | Converts radians into degrees. |

27

| Function | Description |
|---|---|
| LN(*number*) | Returns the natural logarithm of *number*. Natural logarithms are based on the constant e (that is, 2.71828182845904). |
| LOG(*number*,*base*) | Returns the logarithm of *number* to the specified *base*. |
| LOG10(*number*) | Returns the base-10 logarithm of *number*. |
| RADIANS(*angle*) | Converts degrees to radians. |
| SIN(*number*) | Returns the sine of the given angle. |
| SINH(*number*) | Returns the hyperbolic sine of *number*. |
| TAN(*number*) | Returns the tangent of the given angle. |
| TANH(*number*) | Returns the hyperbolic tangent of *number*. |

Table 27.2 provides an alphabetical list of all of Excel 2007's matrix functions. Detailed examples of the functions are provided later in the chapter.

**TABLE 27.2    ALPHABETICAL LIST OF MATRIX FUNCTIONS**

| Function | Description |
|---|---|
| MDETERM(*array*) | Returns the matrix determinant of an array. |
| MINVERSE(*array*) | Returns the inverse matrix for the matrix stored in an array. |
| MMULT(*array1*,*array2*) | Returns the matrix product of two arrays. The result is an array with the same number of rows as *array1* and the same number of columns as *array2*. |
| SERIESSUM(*x*,*n*,*m*,*coefficients*) | Returns the sum of a power series based on the formula SERIES(*x*,*n*,*m*,*a*) ? $a_1x^n + a_2x^{(n+m)} + a_3x^{(n+2m)} + \ldots + a_ix^{(n+(i-1)m)}$ |
| SUMPRODUCT(*array1*,*array2*,*array3*,...) | Multiplies corresponding components in the given arrays and returns the sum of those products. |

Table 27.3 provides an alphabetical list of all of Excel 2007's engineering functions. Detailed examples of the functions are provided later in the chapter.

**TABLE 27.3    ALPHABETICAL LIST OF ENGINEERING FUNCTIONS**

| Function | Description |
|---|---|
| BESSELI(*x*,*n*) | Returns the modified Bessel function, which is equivalent to the BESSELJ function evaluated for purely imaginary arguments. |
| BESSELJ(*x*,*n*) | Returns the Bessel function of the first kind. |

*continues*

27

**TABLE 27.3  CONTINUED**

| Function | Description |
|---|---|
| BESSELK(*x*,*n*) | Returns the modified Bessel function of the second kind, which is equivalent to the BESSELY functions evaluated for purely imaginary arguments. |
| BESSELY(*x*,*n*) | Returns the Bessel function of the second kind. This is the most commonly used form of the Bessel functions. This function provides solutions of the Bessel differential equation and are infinite at x=0. This function is sometimes called the Neumann function. |
| BIN2DEC(*number*) | Converts a binary number to decimal. |
| BIN2HEX(*number*,*places*) | Converts a binary number to hexadecimal. |
| BIN2OCT(*number*,*places*) | Converts a binary number to octal. |
| COMPLEX(*real_num*,*i_num*,*suffix*) | Converts real and imaginary coefficients into a complex number in the form x + y*i* or x + y*j*. |
| CONVERT(*number*,*from_unit*,*to_unit*) | Converts a number from one measurement system to another. For example, CONVERT can translate a table of distances in miles to a table of distances in kilometers. |
| DEC2BIN(*number*,*places*) | Converts a decimal number to binary. |
| DEC2HEX(*number*,*places*) | Converts a decimal number to hexadecimal. |
| DEC2OCT(*number*,*places*) | Converts a decimal number to octal. |
| DELTA(*number1*,*number2*) | Tests whether two values are equal. Returns 1 if *number1* = *number2*; returns 0 otherwise. You use this function to filter a set of values. For example, by summing several DELTA functions, you can calculate the count of equal pairs. This function is also known as the Kronecker Delta function. |
| ERF(*lower_limit*,*upper_limit*) | Returns the ERROR function integrated between *lower_limit* and *upper_limit*. |
| ERFC(*x*) | Returns the complementary ERF function integrated between x and infinity. |
| GESTEP(*number*,*step*) | Returns 1 if *number* is greater than or equal to *step*; returns 0 otherwise. You use this function to filter a set of values. For example, by summing several GESTEP functions, you can calculate the count of values that exceed a threshold. |
| HEX2BIN(*number*,*places*) | Converts a hexadecimal number to binary. |
| HEX2DEC(*number*) | Converts a hexadecimal number to decimal. |
| HEX2OCT(*number*,*places*) | Converts a hexadecimal number to octal. |

| Function | Description |
|---|---|
| IMABS(*inumber*) | Returns the absolute value (modulus) of a complex number in x + y$i$ or x + y$j$ text format. |
| IMAGINARY(*inumber*) | Returns the imaginary coefficient of a complex number in x + y$i$ or x + y$j$ text format. |
| IMARGUMENT(*inumber*) | Returns the argument $\theta$ (theta), an angle expressed in radians, such that $x + yi = \lvert x + yi \rvert \times e^{i\theta} = \lvert x + yi \rvert (\cos\theta + i \sin\theta)$ |
| IMCONJUGATE(*inumber*) | Returns the complex conjugate of a complex number in x + y$i$ or x + y$j$ text format. |
| IMCOS(*inumber*) | Returns the cosine of a complex number in x + y$i$ or x + y$j$ text format. |
| IMDIV(*inumber1*,*inumber2*) | Returns the quotient of two complex numbers in x + y$i$ or x + y$j$ text format. |
| IMEXP(*inumber*) | Returns the exponential of a complex number in x + yi or x + yj text format. |
| IMLN(*inumber*) | Returns the natural logarithm of a complex number in x + y$i$ or x + y$j$ text format. |
| IMLOG10(*inumber*) | Returns the common logarithm (base-10) of a complex number in x + y$i$ or x + y$j$ text format. |
| IMLOG2(*inumber*) | Returns the base-2 logarithm of a complex number in x + y$i$ or x + y$j$ text format. |
| IMPOWER(*inumber*,*number*) | Returns a complex number in x + y$i$ or x + y$j$ text format raised to a power. |
| IMPRODUCT(*inumber1*,*inumber2*,...) | Returns the product of 2 to 29 complex numbers in x + y$i$ or x + y$j$ text format. |
| IMREAL(*inumber*) | Returns the real coefficient of a complex number in x + y$i$ or x + y$j$ text format. |
| IMSIN(*inumber*) | Returns the sine of a complex number in x + y$i$ or x + y$j$ text format. |
| IMSQRT(*inumber*) | Returns the square root of a complex number in x + y$i$ or x + y$j$ text format. |
| IMSUB(*inumber1*,*inumber2*) | Returns the difference of two complex numbers in x + y$i$ or x + y$j$ text format. |
| IMSUM(*inumber1*,*inumber2*,...) | Returns the sum of two or more complex numbers in x + y$i$ or x + y$j$ text format. |
| OCT2BIN(*number*,*places*) | Converts an octal number to binary. |
| OCT2DEC(*number*) | Converts an octal number to decimal. |
| OCT2HEX(*number*,*places*) | Converts an octal number to hexadecimal. |

27

# A BRIEF REVIEW OF TRIGONOMETRY BASICS

There are numerous real-life examples of situations in which trigonometry can be used. In case trigonometry is just a distant nightmare for you, the following sections review some of the basics.

## RADIANS VERSUS DEGREES

Nonmathemeticians discuss angles in terms of *degrees*. Most corners of a room are at a 90-degree angle. Mathematicians discuss angles in a different measurement, called *radians*.

While a circle is composed of 360 degrees, it is also composed of about 6.28 radians. Each radian is equal to about 57.3 degrees. The exact relationship of degrees to radians requires you to use the mathematical constant pi (Π), which is about 3.14159. There are $2 \times \Pi$ radians in a circle.

Because the trig functions were written with mathematicians in mind, they always expect the arguments to be expressed in radians.

The formula to convert degrees to radians is to multiply the degrees by PI() and divide by 180. To use this method, you would have to write formulas as shown in Cell C16 of Figure 27.1. Luckily, Excel provides the functions RADIANS and DEGREES to easily convert from one measurement to another.

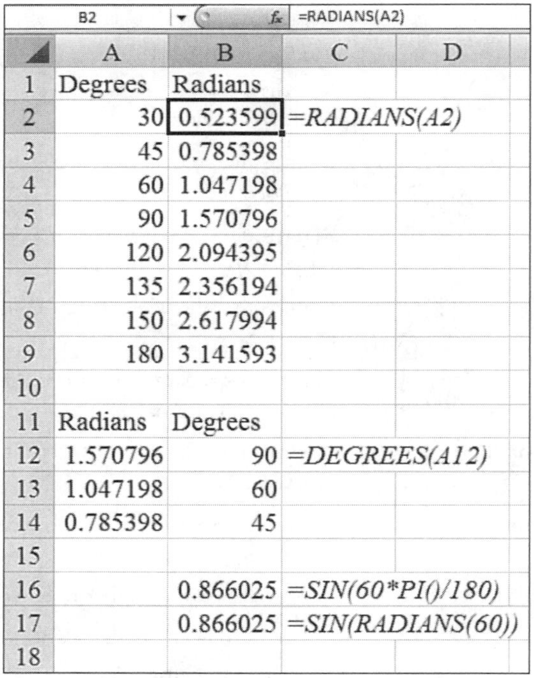

**Figure 27.1**
The trig functions in Excel expect degrees to be in radians. These two functions convert back and forth from radians to degrees.

| | B2 | | $f_x$ | =RADIANS(A2) | |
|---|---|---|---|---|---|
| | A | B | C | D | |
| 1 | Degrees | Radians | | | |
| 2 | 30 | 0.523599 | =RADIANS(A2) | | |
| 3 | 45 | 0.785398 | | | |
| 4 | 60 | 1.047198 | | | |
| 5 | 90 | 1.570796 | | | |
| 6 | 120 | 2.094395 | | | |
| 7 | 135 | 2.356194 | | | |
| 8 | 150 | 2.617994 | | | |
| 9 | 180 | 3.141593 | | | |
| 10 | | | | | |
| 11 | Radians | Degrees | | | |
| 12 | 1.570796 | 90 | =DEGREES(A12) | | |
| 13 | 1.047198 | 60 | | | |
| 14 | 0.785398 | 45 | | | |
| 15 | | | | | |
| 16 | | | 0.866025 | =SIN(60*PI()/180) | |
| 17 | | | 0.866025 | =SIN(RADIANS(60)) | |
| 18 | | | | | |

SYNTAX: DEGREES(*angle*)

The DEGREES function converts radians into degrees. The argument *angle* is the angle, in radians, that you want to convert.

SYNTAX: RADIANS(*angle*)

The RADIANS function converts degrees to radians. The argument *angle* is an angle, in degrees, that you want to convert.

In Figure 27.1, B2:B9 converts degrees to radians. The range B12:B14 converts radians back to degrees. The formulas in Rows 16 and 17 contrast using PI() / 180 with the RADIANS function.

## PYTHAGORAS AND RIGHT TRIANGLES

Trigonometry relies on triangles. Figure 27.2 shows a right triangle, which is a triangle that has one 90-degree angle. In a right triangle, the side opposite the right angle is known as the *hypotenuse*. In a right triangle, the square of the hypotenuse is equal to the sum of the squares of the two other sides. This is frequently expressed as c^2 = a^2 + b^2.

**Figure 27.2**
The Pythagorean theorem allows you to figure out the length of one leg of a right triangle if you know the length of the other two legs.

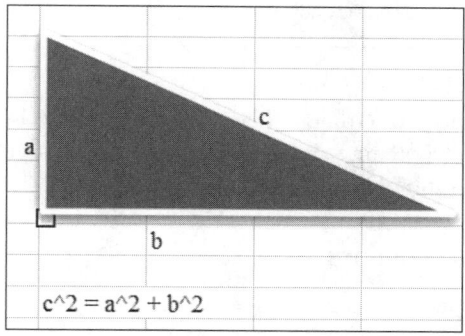

c^2 = a^2 + b^2

If you know that the two shorter legs of a right triangle measure 3 feet and 4 feet, then you know the following:

c^2 = 3^2 + 4^2

c^2 = 9 + 16

c^2 = 25

c = SQRT(25)

c = 5

Although this formula was discovered a thousand years before Pythagoras was alive, he certainly popularized it, and it is known as the Pythagorean theorem.

27

## ONE SIDE PLUS ONE ANGLE = TRIGONOMETRY

There are three classic functions in trigonometry: sine, cosine, and tangent. These functions describe the ratio of two sides of a triangle when you know the angles of the triangle.

Consider Figure 27.3. One angle is a right angle, which is 90 degrees. If you can figure out one of the other angles and the length of one leg of the triangle, you can figure out the length of all three sides of the triangle by using Excel.

**Figure 27.3**
If you know one angle and the length of one side of a right triangle, you can calculate all the sides of the triangle by using trigonometry.

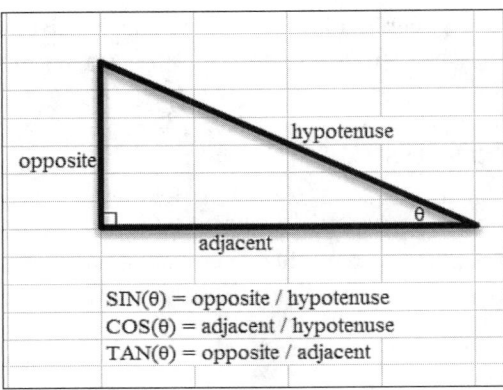

In Figure 27.3, one angle is marked θ (theta). The side across from θ is known as the *opposite* side. The side that is not the hypotenuse and is part of the angle θ is the *adjacent* side. Three classic functions describe the ratio of any two sides:

**TABLE 27.4    GUIDE TO TRIG FUNCTIONS**

| | |
|---|---|
| SIN(θ) | = Opposite / Hypotenuse |
| COS(θ) | = Adjacent / Hypotenuse |
| TAN(θ) | = Opposite / Adjacent |

Excel offers three trig functions that allow you to find various angles or lengths of a right triangle when you know various combinations of the other angles and/or sides. The examples in this section provide some real-world examples of using trigonometry.

## USING TAN TO FIND THE HEIGHT OF A TALL BUILDING FROM THE GROUND

Suppose you would like to measure the height of a tall building from the ground. The tangent function can find the height of a right triangle if you know the length of the base and the angle to the top of the triangle. To calculate the height of a building, you could follow these steps:

1. Starting from the building, measure out 35 feet along level ground. Sight to the top of the building and determine the angle from that point on the ground to the top of the building (for example, 69 degrees). The 35-feet figure is the length of the adjacent side of the triangle. You would like to solve for the opposite side of the triangle. The TAN function describes the ratio of the opposite side to the adjacent side.

2. In a cell in Excel, enter =TAN(RADIANS(69)). This tells you that the ratio of the height of the building to the 35 feet is 2.605.

3. Because 2.605 = Opposite / Adjacent, plug in 35 for the adjacent side, to get 2.605 = Opposite / 35.

4. To solve this equation, multiply both sides by 35. The answer, as shown in Cell E8 in Figure 27.4, is that the building is more than 91 feet tall.

**Figure 27.4**
You can use the TAN function to find the height of this building.

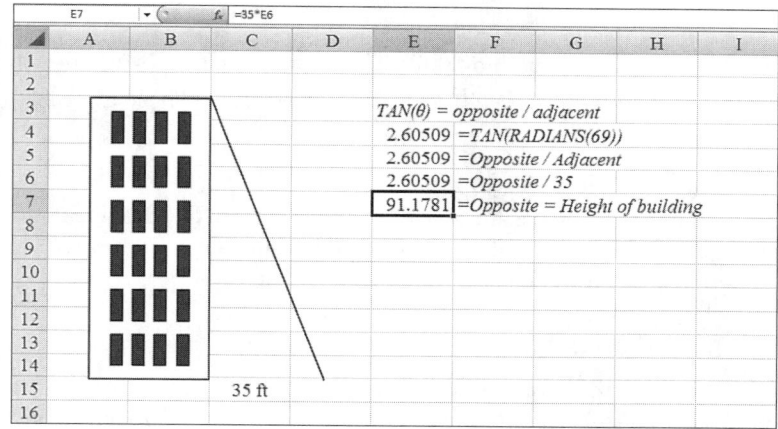

SYNTAX: TAN(number)

The TAN function returns the tangent of the given angle. The argument *number* is the angle, in radians, for which you want the tangent. If your argument is in degrees, you convert it to radians by using RADIANS(degrees) or multiply it by PI() / 180.

## USING SIN TO FIND THE HEIGHT OF A KITE IN A TREE

Suppose your children are flying a kite. They have let out all 150 feet of string. The kite gets caught at the top of a faraway tree, as shown in Figure 27.5.

To find the height of this tree, you follow these steps:

1. Sight the angle from the end of the string to the top of the tree. It measures 29 degrees.

2. Refer to Table 27.4 earlier in this chapter. Because you know the hypotenuse and want to find the opposite side, use the SIN function.

3. In a cell in Excel, enter =SIN(RADIANS(29)). The result is 0.484.

4. Because the sine is the ratio of the opposite side to the hypotenuse, create the formula 0.484 = Opposite / 150.

27

**Figure 27.5**
The SIN function can find the height of this tree when you know the length of the string.

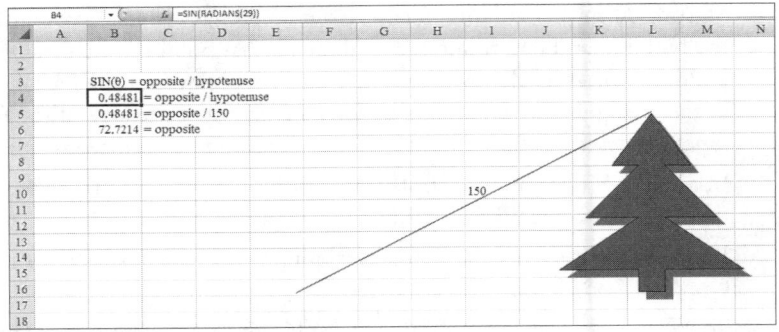

5. To solve for the opposite side, multiply both sides of the equation by 150. You find that the tree is over 72 feet tall.

6. Assess your tree-climbing skills. If you don't currently work for Davey Tree Experts, perhaps you should decide to buy the kids a new kite.

SYNTAX: SIN(*number*)

The SIN function returns the sine of the given angle. The argument *number* is the angle, in radians, for which you want the sine. If your argument is in degrees, you multiply it by PI() / 180 to convert it to radians.

## USING COS TO FIGURE OUT A LADDER'S LENGTH

Every year, my wife, Mary Ellen, hires Kevin the landscaper to hang a huge holiday wreath on the second story of our house. The holidays come and go, and I find that Kevin is wintering in Florida. The ladder that I own is not long enough to reach the wreath. Much to the humor of my neighbors, I stand next to the house, with my too-short ladder, and asses the situation. Figure 27.6 shows that I am 10 feet from the house, and the angle to the wreath hanger is 55 degrees. How long of a ladder do I need to borrow from the neighbors?

**Figure 27.6**
The COS function can find the length of the ladder needed to reach the objective.

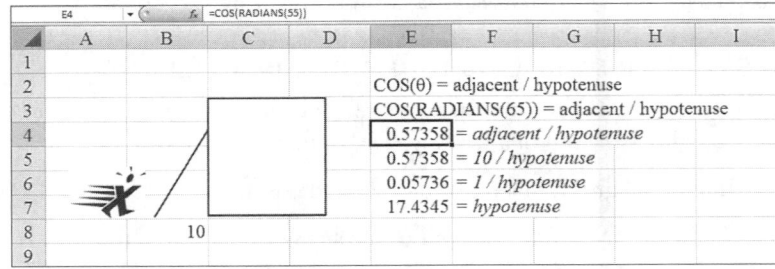

Table 27.4 (earlier in this chapter) shows that the COS function determines the relationship between the adjacent side and the hypotenuse. To find the length of the ladder, you follow these steps:

1. In Excel, enter =COS(RADIANS(55)). The result is 0.574.

2. Create the equation Adjacent / Hypotenuse = 0.574.

3. Divide both sides of the equation by 10. This tells you that the 1 / Hypotenuse is 17.43.

4. Divide both sides of the equation into 1. The result tells you that the hypotenuse is almost 17.5 feet.

I better visit Dick, the neighbor with the 18-foot ladder.

SYNTAX: COS(*number*)

The COS function returns the cosine of the given angle. The argument *number* is the angle, in radians, for which you want the cosine. If the angle is in degrees, you multiply it by PI() / 180 to convert it to radians.

**NOTE**

> The COS function requires extra steps because the initial pass produces a number for 1 / Hypotenuse. In real life, trigonometry offers a reciprocal of cosine called a *secant*. This measure is equal to Hypotenuse / Adjacent. Unfortunately, Excel does not offer functions for the secant, cosecant, or cotangent. These three functions are reciprocals of cosine, sine, and tangent.

### Excel in Practice: Measuring the Distance Across a Canyon

Have you ever seen a pair of surveyors working in your neighborhood? One of the pair is holding a tall pole, and the other person is looking through a sighting device. The surveyor can use trigonometry to measure distances or the angle of decline of a piece of land.

To try your surveying skills, you can measure the distance across a canyon. You start by standing on one side of the canyon with a sighting tool. Have your friend stand on the other side of the canyon, holding a 6-foot pole. The angle from the sighting device to the bottom of the 6-foot pole will be ridiculously small but measurable. You find that the angle comes out to 0.006 degrees. If you know the height of the opposite side is 6 feet and the angle is 0.006 degrees, you can find the distance across that portion of the canyon by using trigonometry.

Table 27.4 defines the tangent as the length of Opposite / Adjacent. Now that you have this information, you can follow these steps to find the distance across the canyon:

1. To convert 0.006 degrees to a tangent, use =TAN(RADIANS(0.006)). The result, 0.000105, is 6 / Adjacent.

2. Multiply both sides of the equation by Adjacent. Divide both sides of the equation by 0.000105.

3. In Cell F16 in Figure 27.7, the formula =6/0.000105 indicates that the canyon is 57,142 feet across.

4. In Cell F17, divide F16 by 5,280 to find that the canyon is 10.82 miles across at that point. Even if you are Evil Knievel, you probably don't want to attempt to jump across in your rocket-powered motorcycle.

27

**Figure 27.7**
You can calculate distances across a lake or canyon by using trigonometry.

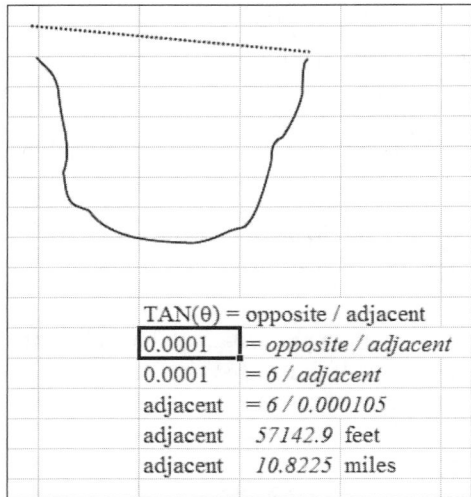

| | | |
|---|---|---|
| TAN(θ) = | opposite / adjacent | |
| 0.0001 | = opposite / adjacent | |
| 0.0001 | = 6 / adjacent | |
| adjacent | = 6 / 0.000105 | |
| adjacent | 57142.9 | feet |
| adjacent | 10.8225 | miles |

## USING THE ARC FUNCTIONS TO FIND THE MEASURE OF AN ANGLE

If you know the lengths of two sides of a right triangle, you can determine the angles of the triangle by using trigonometry.

The ARC function converts a sine value to an angle, in radians. Say that you know the opposite side of a triangle has a length of 3 and the hypotenuse has a length of 5. The sine value is Opposite / Hypotenuse, or 0.6. You use =ASIN(0.6) to convert the sine back to the measure of the angle.

**NOTE**

> The result of ASIN(0.6) produces the size of the angle, in radians. To convert from radians to degrees, you use =DEGREES(ASIN(0.6)).

Excel provides functions to reverse all three of the basic trig functions. You use ACOS to reverse COS, ASIN to reverse SIN, and ATAN to reverse TAN.

Figure 27.8 demonstrates how to use ACOS, ASIN, and ATAN to find the angle size of a right triangle. Keep in mind that the three angles in a triangle always add up to 180. Because you know that the right angle is 90 degrees, and Figure 27.8 calculates the second angle as 37 degrees, the third angle must be 53 degrees.

SYNTAX: ACOS(*number*)

The ACOS function returns the arccosine of a number. The arccosine is the angle whose cosine is *number*. The returned angle is given in radians, in the range 0 to Π. The argument *number* is the cosine of the angle you want and must be from –1 to 1. If you want to convert the result from radians to degrees, you multiply it by 180 / PI() or use the DEGREES function.

**Figure 27.8**
The ARC functions will find an angle from the ratio of two sides of the triangle.

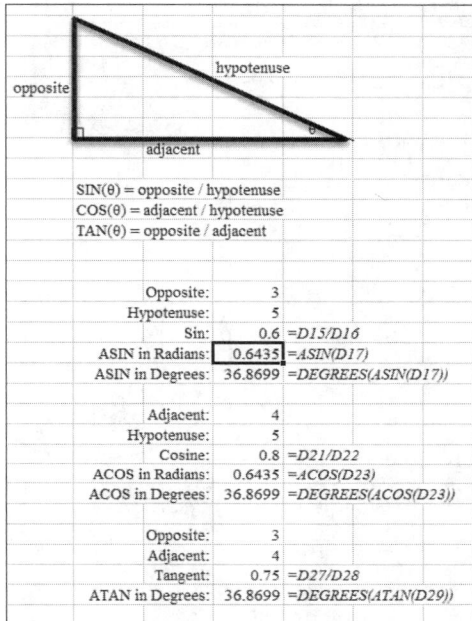

$SIN(\theta) = opposite / hypotenuse$
$COS(\theta) = adjacent / hypotenuse$
$TAN(\theta) = opposite / adjacent$

| | | |
|---|---|---|
| Opposite: | 3 | |
| Hypotenuse: | 5 | |
| Sin: | 0.6 | =D15/D16 |
| ASIN in Radians: | 0.6435 | =ASIN(D17) |
| ASIN in Degrees: | 36.8699 | =DEGREES(ASIN(D17)) |
| | | |
| Adjacent: | 4 | |
| Hypotenuse: | 5 | |
| Cosine: | 0.8 | =D21/D22 |
| ACOS in Radians: | 0.6435 | =ACOS(D23) |
| ACOS in Degrees: | 36.8699 | =DEGREES(ACOS(D23)) |
| | | |
| Opposite: | 3 | |
| Adjacent: | 4 | |
| Tangent: | 0.75 | =D27/D28 |
| ATAN in Degrees: | 36.8699 | =DEGREES(ATAN(D29)) |

SYNTAX: ASIN(*number*)

The ASIN function returns the arcsine of a number. The arcsine is the angle whose sine is *number*. The returned angle is given in radians, in the range –Π / 2 to Π /2. The argument *number* is the sine of the angle you want and must be from –1 to 1. To express the arcsine in degrees, you multiply the result by 180 / PI().

SYNTAX: ATAN(*number*)

The ATAN function returns the arctangent of a number. The arctangent is the angle whose tangent is *number*. The returned angle is given in radians, in the range –Π / 2 to Π / 2. The argument *number* is the tangent of the angle you want. To express the arctangent in degrees, you multiply the result by 180 / PI().

## USING ATAN2 TO CALCULATE ANGLES IN A CIRCLE

Figure 27.9 shows a unit circle. This is a circle with a radius of 1, plotted on a Cartesian grid. The point on the right side of the circle has a value of x = 1 and y = 0. This is defined as the *angle at zero degrees*.

The point at the top of the circle has a value of y = 1 and x = 0. This is defined as the *angle at 90 degrees*.

Given the coordinates of any two points on the circle (actually, of any two points anywhere), you can calculate the angle by using the ATAN2 function.

27

**Figure 27.9**
You use ATAN2 to find the angle from the x-axis to any point in Cartesian coordinates.

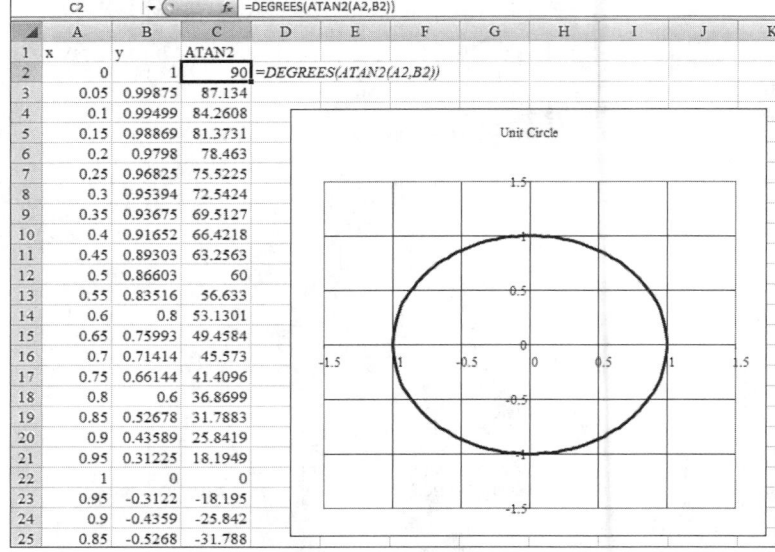

| | A | B | C | D |
|---|---|---|---|---|
| 1 | x | y | ATAN2 | |
| 2 | 0 | 1 | 90 | =DEGREES(ATAN2(A2,B2)) |
| 3 | 0.05 | 0.99875 | 87.134 | |
| 4 | 0.1 | 0.99499 | 84.2608 | |
| 5 | 0.15 | 0.98869 | 81.3731 | |
| 6 | 0.2 | 0.9798 | 78.463 | |
| 7 | 0.25 | 0.96825 | 75.5225 | |
| 8 | 0.3 | 0.95394 | 72.5424 | |
| 9 | 0.35 | 0.93675 | 69.5127 | |
| 10 | 0.4 | 0.91652 | 66.4218 | |
| 11 | 0.45 | 0.89303 | 63.2563 | |
| 12 | 0.5 | 0.86603 | 60 | |
| 13 | 0.55 | 0.83516 | 56.633 | |
| 14 | 0.6 | 0.8 | 53.1301 | |
| 15 | 0.65 | 0.75993 | 49.4584 | |
| 16 | 0.7 | 0.71414 | 45.573 | |
| 17 | 0.75 | 0.66144 | 41.4096 | |
| 18 | 0.8 | 0.6 | 36.8699 | |
| 19 | 0.85 | 0.52678 | 31.7883 | |
| 20 | 0.9 | 0.43589 | 25.8419 | |
| 21 | 0.95 | 0.31225 | 18.1949 | |
| 22 | 1 | 0 | 0 | |
| 23 | 0.95 | -0.3122 | -18.195 | |
| 24 | 0.9 | -0.4359 | -25.842 | |
| 25 | 0.85 | -0.5268 | -31.788 | |

SYNTAX: ATAN2(*x_num*,*y_num*)

The ATAN2 function returns the arctangent of the specified x- and y-coordinates. The arctangent is the angle from the x-axis to a line containing the origin (0, 0) and a point with coordinates (*x_num*, *y_num*). The angle is given in radians, between –Π and Π, excluding –Π. A positive result represents a counterclockwise angle from the x-axis; a negative result represents a clockwise angle.

This function takes the following arguments:

- *x_num*—This is the x-coordinate of the point.
- *y_num*—This is the y-coordinate of the point.

ATAN2(*a*,*b*) equals ATAN(*b*/*a*), except that *a* can equal 0 in ATAN2.

If both *x_num* and *y_num* are 0, ATAN2 returns a #DIV/0! error. To express the arctangent in degrees, you multiply the result by 180 / PI() or use the DEGREES function.

The formulas in Column C of Figure 27.9 find the ATAN2 of the points in Columns A and B. The result must be converted to degrees by using =DEGREES(ATAN2(A2,B2)).

## EMULATING GRAVITY USING HYPERBOLIC TRIGONOMETRY FUNCTIONS

You could apply the trigonometry functions shown so far in this chapter to solve problems in your environment. The hyperbolic trigonometry functions, which we examine next, are far more complex. As shown in Figure 27.10, the hyperbolic cosine function, COSH, is effective at graphing the arc of a rope hung between two points.

**Figure 27.10**
This shape defined by
COSH is also known
as a *catenary*.

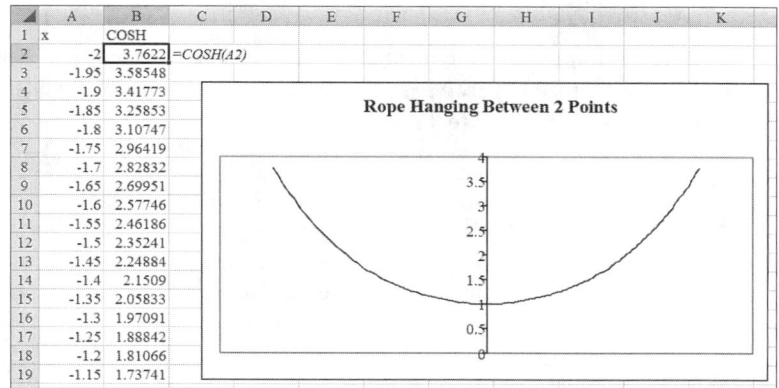

| | A | B | C | D | E | F | G | H | I | J | K |
|---|---|---|---|---|---|---|---|---|---|---|---|
| 1 | x | COSH | | | | | | | | | |
| 2 | -2 | 3.7622 | =COSH(A2) | | | | | | | | |
| 3 | -1.95 | 3.58548 | | | | | | | | | |
| 4 | -1.9 | 3.41773 | | | | | | | | | |
| 5 | -1.85 | 3.25853 | | | | | | | | | |
| 6 | -1.8 | 3.10747 | | | | | | | | | |
| 7 | -1.75 | 2.96419 | | | | | | | | | |
| 8 | -1.7 | 2.82832 | | | | | | | | | |
| 9 | -1.65 | 2.69951 | | | | | | | | | |
| 10 | -1.6 | 2.57746 | | | | | | | | | |
| 11 | -1.55 | 2.46186 | | | | | | | | | |
| 12 | -1.5 | 2.35241 | | | | | | | | | |
| 13 | -1.45 | 2.24884 | | | | | | | | | |
| 14 | -1.4 | 2.1509 | | | | | | | | | |
| 15 | -1.35 | 2.05833 | | | | | | | | | |
| 16 | -1.3 | 1.97091 | | | | | | | | | |
| 17 | -1.25 | 1.88842 | | | | | | | | | |
| 18 | -1.2 | 1.81066 | | | | | | | | | |
| 19 | -1.15 | 1.73741 | | | | | | | | | |

According to MathWorld.com, other uses for hyperbolic trigonometry include the following:

- Calculating the gravitational potential of a cylinder
- Calculating the rapidity of special relativity
- Calculating the profile of a laminar jet
- Calculating the Schwarzschild metric, using external isotropic Kruskal coordinates
- Emulating a uniform gravity field by a uniform acceleration, in general relativity

These are complex tasks and I won't fill you in on the details here. If you actually need to calculate the profile of a laminar jet, head to MathWorld.com for details.

Excel offers the hyperbolic functions SINH, COSH, and TANH, as well as the reverse functions ASINH, ACOSH, and ATANH.

SYNTAX: SINH(*number*)

The SINH function returns the hyperbolic sine of a number. The argument *number* is any real number.

SYNTAX: COSH(*number*)

The COSH function returns the hyperbolic cosine of a number. The argument *number* is any real number for which you want to find the hyperbolic cosine.

In Figure 27.10, the COSH function is used in Column B to calculate the path of a rope hanging between two points.

SYNTAX: TANH(*number*)

The TANH function returns the hyperbolic tangent of a number. The argument *number* is any real number.

27

SYNTAX: ASINH(*number*)

The ASINH function returns the inverse hyperbolic sine of a number. The inverse hyperbolic sine is the value whose hyperbolic sine is *number*, so ASINH(SINH(*number*)) equals *number*. The argument *number* is any real number.

SYNTAX: ACOSH(*number*)

The ACOSH function returns the inverse hyperbolic cosine of a number. *number* must be greater than or equal to 1. The inverse hyperbolic cosine is the value whose hyperbolic cosine is *number*, so ACOSH(COSH(*number*)) equals *number*. The argument *number* is any real number equal to or greater than 1.

SYNTAX: ATANH(*number*)

The ATANH function returns the inverse hyperbolic tangent of a number. *number* must be between –1 and 1 (excluding –1 and 1). The inverse hyperbolic tangent is the value whose hyperbolic tangent is *number*, so ATANH(TANH(*number*)) equals *number*. The argument *number* is any real number between 1 and –1.

# EXAMPLES OF LOGARITHM FUNCTIONS

If you've read many of my books, you know that I used to have a day job involving forecasting and operations planning. I was constantly battling with the sales force to provide accurate sales forecasts. At the end of each month, we produced a chart to show the forecasted demand and the actual demand. If the forecast and actual were within 15% of each other, this was considered a tolerable error, and no discussion was necessary. However, for any points outside the 15% tolerance, a team would figure out why we missed the forecast and how to prevent a similar miss in future months.

The initial charts looked horrible. There were 20 products being forecasted, and the monthly demand fell by anywhere from 50 units a month to 10,000 units a month. There were only a few products above the 5,000-unit level, but those few products made it impossible to see any detail for the 17 smaller products, as shown in Figure 27.11.

Rather than produce several different charts, our solution involved giving the y-axis of the chart a logarithmic scale.

## COMMON LOGARITHMS ON A BASE-10 SCALE

In a logarithmic scale, the distance from 1 to 10 on the scale is the same as the distance from 10 to 100 and the same as the distance from 100 to 1,000 and the same as the distance from 1,000 to 10,000. Each gridline basically appears at 10^1, 10^2, 10^3, 10^4, and so on.

The resulting chart allows you to see detail for the items selling 100 units as well as the items selling 8,000 units. Figure 27.12 shows the result of converting the chart in Figure 27.11 to a chart with a logarithmic y-axis.

**Figure 27.11**
No one can make out any detail for the smaller values on this chart. The scale of the two or three large products ruins the view of the smaller products.

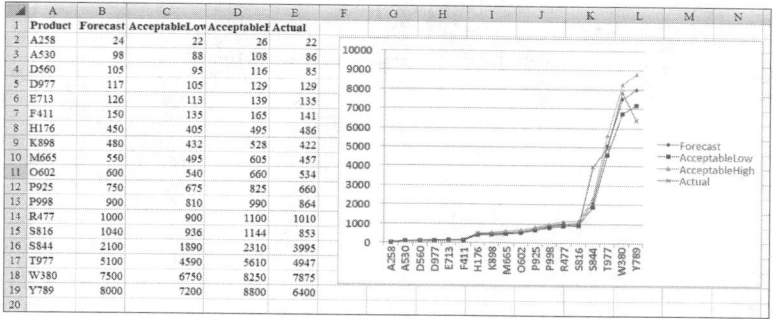

**Figure 27.12**
You can change the y-axis to show a logarithmic scale, and the detail of the smaller quantities becomes clear.

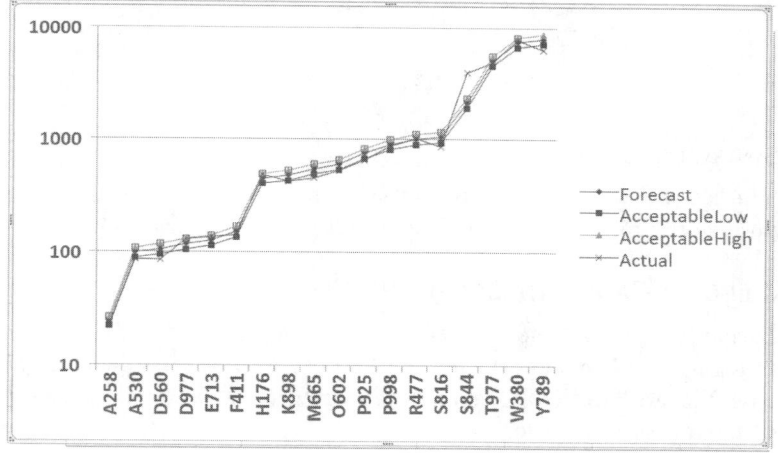

Basically, a logarithm raises a number—the base—to a certain power. In the case of the chart in Figure 27.12, each plot on the chart is located at a certain power of 10. In Figure 27.13, Columns B:E show the original numbers for the table. Columns G:J show the base-10 logarithm for the number.

10^1 is 10. 10^2 is 100. The number in Cell B3 is 98. This logarithm is going to be between 1 and 2, and probably much closer to 2. The formula in Cell G3 reveals that if 10 is raised to the 1.99126th power, you get 198.

As another example, 10^2 is 100, and 10^3 is 1,000. Cell B17 contains 5,100. The logarithm for 5,100 is somewhere between 2 and 3. The formula in Cell G17, =LOG10(B17), shows that 10^3.707 results in 5,100.

Excel offers four functions for dealing with logarithms. LOG10 calculates the logarithms based on raising 10 to a certain power. LOG can calculate the logarithm for any base. LN and EXP deal with a special logarithm.

27

**Figure 27.13**
The table in G:J is the base-10 logarithm of the numbers in B:E.

| | A | B | C | D | E | F | G | H | I | J |
|---|---|---|---|---|---|---|---|---|---|---|
| 1 | Product | Forecast | AcceptableLow | AcceptableHigh | Actual | | LOG10 | LOG10 | LOG10 | LOG10 |
| 2 | A258 | 24 | 20 | 28 | 22 | | 1.38021 | 1.30103 | 1.44716 | 1.34242 |
| 3 | A530 | 98 | 83 | 113 | 86 | | 1.99123 | 1.91908 | 2.05308 | 1.9345 |
| 4 | D560 | 105 | 89 | 121 | 85 | | 2.02119 | 1.94939 | 2.08279 | 1.92942 |
| 5 | D977 | 117 | 99 | 135 | 129 | | 2.06819 | 1.99564 | 2.13033 | 2.11059 |
| 6 | E713 | 126 | 107 | 145 | 135 | | 2.10037 | 2.02938 | 2.16137 | 2.13033 |
| 7 | F411 | 150 | 128 | 173 | 141 | | 2.17609 | 2.10721 | 2.23805 | 2.14922 |
| 8 | H176 | 450 | 383 | 518 | 486 | | 2.65321 | 2.5832 | 2.71433 | 2.68664 |
| 9 | K898 | 480 | 408 | 552 | 422 | | 2.68124 | 2.61066 | 2.74194 | 2.62531 |
| 10 | M665 | 550 | 468 | 633 | 457 | | 2.74036 | 2.67025 | 2.8014 | 2.65992 |
| 11 | O602 | 600 | 510 | 690 | 534 | | 2.77815 | 2.70757 | 2.83885 | 2.72754 |
| 12 | P925 | 750 | 638 | 863 | 660 | | 2.87506 | 2.80482 | 2.93601 | 2.81954 |
| 13 | P998 | 900 | 765 | 1035 | 864 | | 2.95424 | 2.88366 | 3.01494 | 2.93651 |
| 14 | R477 | 1000 | 850 | 1150 | 1010 | | 3 | 2.92942 | 3.0607 | 3.00432 |
| 15 | S816 | 1040 | 884 | 1196 | 853 | | 3.01703 | 2.94645 | 3.07773 | 2.93095 |
| 16 | S844 | 2100 | 1785 | 2415 | 3995 | | 3.32222 | 3.25164 | 3.38292 | 3.60152 |
| 17 | T977 | 5100 | 4335 | 5865 | 4947 | | 3.70757 | 3.63699 | 3.76827 | 3.69434 |
| 18 | W380 | 7500 | 6375 | 8625 | 7875 | | 3.87506 | 3.80448 | 3.93576 | 3.89625 |
| 19 | Y789 | 8000 | 6800 | 9200 | 6400 | | 3.90309 | 3.83251 | 3.96379 | 3.80618 |

*(Cell G2 contains the formula =LOG10(B2))*

**SYNTAX:** LOG10(*number*)

The LOG10 function returns the base-10 logarithm of a number. The argument *number* is the positive real number for which you want the base-10 logarithm.

## Using LOG to Calculate Logarithms for Any Base

Excel makes it simple to calculate the logarithm for any base, using the LOG function. Cell B2 of Figure 27.14 contains the formula =LOG(A2,2) to express the number in Column A as a base-2 logarithm. Cell E2 contains the formula =LOG(E2,2) to express the number in Column E as a base-5 logarithm.

**Figure 27.14**
The LOG function can calculate a logarithm with any base.

| | A | B | C | D | E | F | G | H | I | J | K | L |
|---|---|---|---|---|---|---|---|---|---|---|---|---|
| 1 | Number | LOG(A2,2) | | Number | Log(D2,5) | | Number | LOG(G2,12) | | 123456 | =LOG($J$1,J2) | |
| 2 | 2 | 1 | | 5 | 1 | | 12 | 1 | | 2 | 16.9136 | |
| 3 | 4 | 2 | | 25 | 2 | | 144 | 2 | | 3 | 10.6713 | |
| 4 | 8 | 3 | | 125 | 3 | | 1728 | 3 | | 4 | 8.45682 | |
| 5 | 16 | 4 | | 625 | 4 | | 20736 | 4 | | 5 | 7.28431 | |
| 6 | 32 | 5 | | 3125 | 5 | | 248832 | 5 | | 6 | 6.54309 | |
| 7 | 64 | 6 | | 15625 | 6 | | | | | 7 | 6.02476 | |
| 8 | 128 | 7 | | 15630 | 6.0002 | | | | | 8 | 5.63788 | |
| 9 | 256 | 8 | | 1250 | 4.43068 | | | | | 9 | 5.33566 | |
| 10 | 512 | 9 | | 15630 | 6.0002 | | | | | 10 | 5.09151 | |
| 11 | 1024 | 10 | | 3750 | 5.11328 | | | | | 11 | 4.88914 | |
| 12 | 2048 | 11 | | 15750 | 6.00495 | | | | | 12 | 4.71794 | |
| 13 | 4096 | 12 | | | | | | | | | | |
| 14 | 2080 | 11.02237 | | | | | | | | | | |
| 15 | | | | | | | | | | | | |

*(Cell K2 contains the formula =LOG($J$1,J2))*

**SYNTAX:** LOG(*number*,*base*)

The LOG function returns the logarithm of a number to the specified base. It takes the following arguments:

- *number*—This is the positive real number for which you want the logarithm.
- *base*—This is the base of the logarithm. If *base* is omitted, it is assumed to be 10.

---

### Little TwelveToes

Here is a simple test to see if you attended the same Saturday morning school that I did. Fill in this phrase: "Conjunction Junction, _____ _____ _____?"

If you instinctively sang, "What's My Function?" then you are a fellow alumnus of the school of Tom Yohe and David McCall. From 1973 until 1985, ABC snuck in educational cartoons in the middle of its other Saturday morning fare. Known collectively as *School House Rock*, these segments taught children multiplication tables, grammar, science facts, and American history.

Perhaps the most ambitious segment was the "Multiplication Rock" segment, about an alien planet where everyone had 12 toes. In this system, there would be new digits after 9: "dek, el, do. And his 12–do–would be written 1-0. Get it?" This little 60-second cartoon and jingle introduced a generation of children to the concept of a base-12 numbering system in a way that made perfect sense.

Column H of Figure 27.13 uses =LOG(x,12) to express logarithms in a base-12 system.

---

## Using LN and EXP to Calculate Natural Logarithms

In science, only two logarithms are used frequently. The first is the base-10 logarithm discussed previously. The second is a natural logarithm where numbers are expressed as a power of the number e. e is a special number. You can calculate e by adding up all the numbers in the series of $1 + [1 / (1!)] + [1 / (2!)] + [1 / (3!)] + [1 / (4!)] + [1(5!)] + [1 / (7!)] + [1(8!)] + [1 / (9!)] + [1 / (10!)] + \ldots$.

Luckily, 10! is 3.7 million, so 1 / (10!) is a very small number: 0.000000275573. After about 1 / (17!), the numbers are small enough that they are beyond Excel's 15-digit precision.

This infinite series converges toward a number around 2.718281. This number is known as the *transcendental number* and is abbreviated as e. Logarithms for base e are known as *natural logarithms*. You can calculate e in Excel by using a range such as the one shown in A4:C22 in Figure 27.15, or you can simply use =EXP(1), as shown in Cell C24.

Natural logarithms are very popular in science because anything with a constant rate of growth follows a curve described by natural logarithms. Radioactive isotopes, for example, decay along a curve described by natural logarithms.

While common logarithms with base 10 are called *logs*, natural logarithms with base e are written as *ln* (often pronounced *lon*). You calculate natural logarithms by using the LN function.

### Syntax: LN(*number*)

The LN function returns the natural logarithm of a number. Natural logarithms are based on the constant e (that is, 2.71828182845904). The argument *number* is the positive real number for which you want a natural logarithm.

27

**Figure 27.15**
The calculation of e is fairly complex, as shown in A4:C22. Instead, you can use =EXP(1).

| | C24 | ▾ | $f_x$ =EXP(1) | |
|---|---|---|---|---|
| ◢ | A | B | | C |
| 1 | e = 1 + (1/1!) + (1/2!) + (1/3!) + (1/4!) + (1/5!) + ... | | | |
| 2 | | | | |
| 3 | x | | FACT(x) | 1/Fact(x) |
| 4 | 0 | | 1 | 1.00000000000000000000 |
| 5 | 1 | | 1 | 1.00000000000000000000 |
| 6 | 2 | | 2 | 0.50000000000000000000 |
| 7 | 3 | | 6 | 0.16666666666666700000 |
| 8 | 4 | | 24 | 0.04166666666666670000 |
| 9 | 5 | | 120 | 0.00833333333333333000 |
| 10 | 6 | | 720 | 0.00138888888888889000 |
| 11 | 7 | | 5040 | 0.00019841269841269800 |
| 12 | 8 | | 40320 | 0.00002480158730158730 |
| 13 | 9 | | 362880 | 0.00000275573192239859 |
| 14 | 10 | | 3628800 | 0.00000027557319223986 |
| 15 | 11 | | 39916800 | 0.00000002505210838544 |
| 16 | 12 | | 479001600 | 0.00000000208767569879 |
| 17 | 13 | | 6227020800 | 0.00000000016059043837 |
| 18 | 14 | | 87178291200 | 0.00000000001147074560 |
| 19 | 15 | | 1,307,674,368,000 | 0.00000000000076471637 |
| 20 | 16 | | 20,922,789,888,000 | 0.00000000000004779477 |
| 21 | 17 | | 355,687,428,096,000 | 0.00000000000000281146 |
| 22 | | | Total: | 2.71828182845905000000 |
| 23 | | | | |
| 24 | | | =EXP(1): | 2.718281828 |
| 25 | | | | |

With common logarithms, you can easily convert the logarithm back to the original number by using =10^x. However, it is fairly difficult to write 2.71828182845904^x. Therefore, Excel provides the function EXP to raise e to any power.

SYNTAX: EXP(*number*)

The EXP function returns e raised to the power of *number*. The constant e equals 2.71828182845904, the base of the natural logarithm. The argument *number* is the exponent applied to the base e.

To calculate powers of other bases, you use the exponentiation operator (^). EXP is the inverse of LN, the natural logarithm of number.

To convert the logarithms in Column B in Figure 27.16, you use EXP(B2), as shown in Column C.

27

**Figure 27.16**
To reverse the
LN function, you
use EXP.

| | G8 | | $f_x$ | =+F8*E8 | | | |
|---|---|---|---|---|---|---|---|
| | A | B | C | D | E | F | G | H |
| 1 | x | LN(x) | EXP(b) | | | | |
| 2 | 2 | 0.69315 | 2 | | Question: What is 4.215 * 7.643? | | |
| 3 | 4 | 1.38629 | 4 | | Number | LN | |
| 4 | 5 | 1.60944 | 5 | | 4.215 | 1.43865 | =LN(E4) |
| 5 | 8 | 2.07944 | 8 | | 7.643 | 2.03379 | =LN(E5) |
| 6 | 9 | 2.19722 | 9 | | Total | 3.47244 | 32.2152 | =EXP(F6) |
| 7 | 10 | 2.30259 | 10 | | | | |
| 8 | 13 | 2.56495 | 13 | | 4.215 | 7.643 | 32.2152 | =F8*E8 |
| 9 | 14 | 2.63906 | 14 | | | | |
| 10 | 19 | 2.94444 | 19 | | Question: What is 27.453 / 4.873? | | |
| 11 | | | | | Number | LN | |
| 12 | | 9 | | | 27.453 | 3.31248 | =LN(E12) |
| 13 | | 2.19722 | =LOG(B12,EXP(1)) | | 4.873 | 1.58371 | =LN(E13) |
| 14 | | 2.19722 | =LN(B12) | | Difference | 1.72877 | =F12-F13 |
| 15 | | 9 | =EXP(1)^B14 | | EXP(F14) | 5.6337 | =EXP(F14) |
| 16 | | | | | | | |
| 17 | | | | | | 27.453 | |
| 18 | | | | | | 4.873 | |
| 19 | | | | | Check | 5.6337 | =F17/F18 |
| 20 | | | | | | | |

## Multiplying and Dividing by Adding and Subtracting

Think about the problem $3^4 \times 3^7$. In this problem, both of the base numbers are the same. The result is $3^{(7+4)}$, or $3^{11}$.

Similarly, if you want to divide $7^{21}$ by $7^5$, you can find the solution by subtracting: $7^{(21-5)}$, or $7^{16}$.

In Figure 27.16, E2:H9 walks through a long-winding way of multiplying using only LN and addition. To multiply $4.215 \times 7.643$, you take the LN of each number in Cells F4 and F5. You can then add these numbers in Cell F6. The formula in Cell G6 uses EXP to find the actual answer of 32.21525. Now, I realize that this all seems ridiculous because if you are doing this, you obviously have Excel and can just do the multiplication directly, as shown in Cell G8. However, this is an interesting property of logarithms.

The decay of radioactive isotopes follows a natural logarithmic curve. The basic formula is as follows:

Number of atoms after time T = Original number of atoms $\times e^{(T \times Constant)}$.

For Radium 226, the constant is –0.000436. The table in Figure 27.17 shows how to raise e to a certain power by using a table of years. You can see that about half the original sample will have decayed after 1,500 years!

**27**

**Figure 27.17**
For constant growth or decay problems, you can use EXP to raise e to a power.

| | B4 | ▾ | $f_x$ =EXP(-0.000436*A4) | | |
|---|---|---|---|---|---|
| ◢ | A | B | C | D | E |
| 1 | Decay of Radium 226 | | | | |
| 2 | | | | | |
| 3 | Years | % Left | | | |
| 4 | 500 | 80.4% | =EXP(-0.000436*A4) | | |
| 5 | 1000 | 64.7% | | | |
| 6 | 1500 | 52.0% | | | |
| 7 | 2000 | 41.8% | | | |
| 8 | 2500 | 33.6% | | | |
| 9 | 3000 | 27.0% | | | |
| 10 | 3500 | 21.7% | | | |
| 11 | 4000 | 17.5% | | | |
| 12 | 4500 | 14.1% | | | |
| 13 | 5000 | 11.3% | | | |
| 14 | 5500 | 9.1% | | | |
| 15 | 6000 | 7.3% | | | |
| 16 | 6500 | 5.9% | | | |
| 17 | 7000 | 4.7% | | | |
| 18 | 7500 | 3.8% | | | |
| 19 | 8000 | 3.1% | | | |

# WORKING WITH IMAGINARY NUMBERS

Multiply the number 2 by itself: =2^2 is 4. The square root of 4 is 2. Multiply the number –2 by itself: =-2^2 is also 4. Excel says =SQRT(4) is 2, but clearly it could also be -2 as well.

So, what is the square root of –4? There is no real number that produces –4 when multiplied by itself. Excel says that =SQRT(-4) is #NUM!.

To deal with theoretical numbers where the square root is a negative number, mathematicians invented the concept of the imaginary number, *i*. This number is the square root of –1. At first, no one was sure if this was relevant, so these numbers were given the name *imaginary numbers*. Since their invention, imaginary numbers have been discovered to have real-world applications. They are used extensively in the physics of electrical circuits. The name *imaginary* continues to stick.

In the parlance of imaginary numbers, the square root of –4 is 2*i*.

Often, the answer to a problem appears as an expression such as $a + b \times i$. In this case, both *a* and *b* are real numbers. This expression is a complex number. You can plot complex numbers on a coordinate graph (plotting *a* along the x-axis and *b* along the y axis) and do trigonometry with imaginary numbers.

Excel offers nine functions that deal with imaginary, or complex, numbers: COMPLEX, IMREAL, IMAGINARY, IMSUM, IMPRODUCT, IMDIV, IMABS, IMARGUMENT, and IMCONJUGATE.

## USING COMPLEX TO CONVERT *A* AND *B* INTO A COMPLEX NUMBER

It is hard to deal with complex numbers in Excel because they are basically text. Think about how you can store 5 + 2*i* in a cell; it would be difficult to do.

You can easily create a large range of complex numbers in the form *a* + *bi* if you have ranges of values for *a* and *b*. In Figure 27.18, pairs of *a* and *b* values are stored in the first two columns of a worksheet. The COMPLEX function in Column C converts these numbers to complex numbers.

**Figure 27.18**
The COMPLEX function builds text results in Column C. The eight IM functions can do math on these text values.

| | C2 | ▼ | *fx* | =COMPLEX(A2,B2) | | |
|---|---|---|---|---|---|---|
| | A | B | C | D | E | |
| 1 | a | b | Complex | | | |
| 2 | 15 | 15 | 15+15i | =COMPLEX(A2,B2) | | |
| 3 | 5 | 10 | 5+10i | | | |
| 4 | 9 | 15 | 9+15i | | | |
| 5 | 18 | 5 | 18+5i | | | |
| 6 | 15 | 13 | 15+13i | | | |
| 7 | 3 | 7 | 3+7i | | | |
| 8 | 10 | 6 | 10+6i | | | |
| 9 | 3 | 15 | 3+15i | | | |
| 10 | 5 | 17 | 5+17i | | | |
| 11 | 6 | 4 | 6+4i | | | |
| 12 | 2 | 12 | 2+12i | | | |
| 13 | 3 | 6 | 3+6i | | | |
| 14 | | | | | | |

SYNTAX: COMPLEX(*real_num*,*i_num*,*suffix*)

The COMPLEX function converts real and imaginary coefficients into a complex number in the form x + y*i* or x + y*j*. This function takes the following arguments:

- *real_num*—This is the real coefficient of the complex number.
- *i_num*—This is the imaginary coefficient of the complex number.
- *suffix*—This is the suffix for the imaginary component of the complex number. If omitted, *suffix* is assumed to be i.

**NOTE**

All complex number functions accept i and j for *suffix*, but they accept neither I nor J. Using uppercase results in a #VALUE! error. All functions that accept two or more complex numbers require that all suffixes match.

27

If *real_num* is nonnumeric, COMPLEX returns a #VALUE! error. If *i_num* is nonnumeric, COMPLEX returns a #VALUE! error. If *suffix* is neither i nor j, COMPLEX returns a #VALUE! error.

## USING IMREAL AND IMAGINARY TO BREAK APART COMPLEX NUMBERS

Complex numbers are in the form *a* + *bi*, where *i* is the imaginary square root of –1. Excel stores all complex numbers as text. If you use any of the IM functions to generate new complex numbers, you can extract the numbers *a* and *b* by using IMREAL and IMAGINARY.

In Figure 27.19, Column A contains a range of complex numbers. The formulas in Column B extract the real number portion of the complex number. The formulas in Column C extract the value that is multiplied by $i$ in the complex number.

**Figure 27.19**

IMREAL and IMAGINARY break a complex number expression in the form $a + bi$ into the numbers for $a$ and $b$.

| | A | B | C | D | E | F |
|---|---|---|---|---|---|---|
| | | | $f_x$ =IMREAL(A2) | | | |
| 1 | a+bi | a | b | | | |
| 2 | 14-10i | 14 | -10 | B2: | =IMREAL(A2) | |
| 3 | 2-2i | 2 | -2 | C2: | =IMAGINARY(A2) | |
| 4 | 7-13i | 7 | -13 | | | |
| 5 | 8+13i | 8 | 13 | | | |
| 6 | 10+15i | 10 | 15 | | | |
| 7 | 13-18i | 13 | -18 | | | |
| 8 | 11+19i | 11 | 19 | | | |
| 9 | 13-13i | 13 | -13 | | | |
| 10 | 11-10i | 11 | -10 | | | |
| 11 | 8-8i | 8 | -8 | | | |
| 12 | | | | | | |

**SYNTAX: IMREAL(inumber)**

The IMREAL function returns the real coefficient of a complex number in x + yi or x + yj text format. The argument inumber is a complex number for which you want the real coefficient.

If inumber is not in the form x + yi or x + yj, IMREAL returns a #NUM! error.

**SYNTAX: IMAGINARY(inumber)**

The IMAGINARY function returns the imaginary coefficient of a complex number in x + yi or x + yj text format. The argument inumber is a complex number for which you want the imaginary coefficient.

If inumber is not in the form x + yi or x + yj, IMAGINARY returns a #NUM! error.

## USING IMSUM TO ADD COMPLEX NUMBERS

Figure 27.20 shows two columns of complex numbers. A complex number is in the form $a + bi$. Both $a$ and $b$ are real numbers. The letter $i$ is the imaginary square root of $-1$.

Note that all of the "numbers" stored in Columns A and B are stored as text.

To add $(a + bi) + (c + di)$, you use the formula $(a + b) + (c + d)\ i$. You use IMSUM to calculate this.

**SYNTAX: IMSUM(inumber1,inumber2,...)**

The IMSUM function returns the sum of two or more complex numbers in x + yi or x + yj text format. The arguments inumber1,inumber2,... are 1 to 255 complex numbers to add.

If any argument is not in the form x + yi or x + yj, IMSUM returns a #NUM! error.

**Figure 27.20**
Even though all the complex numbers in Columns A and B are text, the IMSUM function adds them with ease.

| | A | B | C | D | E |
|---|---|---|---|---|---|
| | | | C2 ▾ $f_x$ =IMSUM(A2,B2) | | |
| 1 | | | IMSUM | | |
| 2 | 13+15i | 11+9i | 24+24i | =IMSUM(A2,B2) | |
| 3 | 14+19i | 10+18i | 24+37i | | |
| 4 | 17+4i | 19+14i | 36+18i | | |
| 5 | 18+17i | 7+7i | 25+24i | | |
| 6 | 19-20i | 5-9i | 24-29i | | |
| 7 | 6+3i | 8+9i | 14+12i | | |
| 8 | 6+9i | 4+19i | 10+28i | | |
| 9 | 5+2i | 15+11i | 20+13i | | |
| 10 | 20+16i | 5+12i | 25+28i | | |
| 11 | 15+11i | 6-12i | 21-i | | |
| 12 | 6+12i | 19+16i | 25+28i | | |
| 13 | 3+11i | 6+8i | 9+19i | | |
| 14 | 3+18i | 15+3i | 18+21i | | |
| 15 | 12+6i | 15+17i | 27+23i | | |
| 16 | 20-13i | 9+11i | 29-2i | | |
| 17 | | Total: | 331+243i | =IMSUM(C2:C16) | |
| 18 | | | | | |

## USING IMSUB, IMPRODUCT, AND IMDIV TO PERFORM BASIC MATH ON COMPLEX NUMBERS

As with the IMSUM function, there are similar rules for subtracting, multiplying, and dividing complex numbers. These are numbers stored as text in the form $a + bi$, where the constant $i$ is an imaginary number representing the square root of $-1$. These are the rules for the IMSUB, IMPRODUCT, and IMDIV functions:

- To subtract complex numbers, you use IMSUB. The formula for $(a + bi) - (c + di)$ is $(a - c) + (b - d) i$.
- To multiply complex numbers, you use IMPRODUCT. The formula for $(a + bi) \times (c + di)$ is $(ac - bd) + (ad + bc) i$.
- To divide complex numbers, you use IMDIV. The formula for $(a + bi) / (c + di)$ is $[(ac + bd) + (bc - ad) i] / (c^2 + d^2)$.

Figure 27.21 shows the results of the basic math functions for complex numbers.

SYNTAX: IMSUB(*inumber1*,*inumber2*)

The IMSUB function returns the difference between two complex numbers in x + y$i$ or x + y$j$ text format. This function takes the following arguments:

- *inumber1*—This is the complex number from which to subtract *inumber2*.
- *inumber2*—This is the complex number to subtract from *inumber1*.

If either number is not in the form x + y$i$ or x + y$j$, IMSUB returns a #NUM! error.

27

**Figure 27.21**
You can perform basic math with complex numbers.

| C2 | ▾ | $f_x$ =IMSUB(A2,B2) | | |
|---|---|---|---|---|
| | A | B | C | D | E |
| 1 | | | IMSUB | IMPRODUCT | IMDIV |
| 2 | 19-18i | 12+11i | 7-29i | 426-7i | 0.113207547169811-1.60377358490566i |
| 3 | 9+2i | 17+5i | -8-3i | 143+79i | 0.519108280254777-0.035031847133758i |
| 4 | 5-15i | 5-9i | -6i | -110-120i | 1.50943396226415-0.283018867924528i |
| 5 | 14+20i | 13-13i | 1+33i | 442+78i | -0.230769230769231+1.30769230769231i |
| 6 | 17+4i | 2+3i | 15+i | 22+59i | 3.53846153846154-3.30769230769231i |
| 7 | 18-18i | 17+16i | 1-34i | 594-18i | 0.0330275229357798-1.08990825688073i |
| 8 | 13+1i | 19+5i | -6-4i | 242+84i | 0.652849740932643-0.119170984455959i |
| 9 | 20-9i | 18+5i | 2-14i | 405-62i | 0.902578796561605-0.750716332378223i |
| 10 | 18+7i | 11+7i | 7 | 149+203i | 1.45294117647059-0.288235294117647i |
| 11 | 20+8i | 12+10i | 8-2i | 160+296i | 1.31147540983607-0.426229508196721i |
| 12 | | | | | |

SYNTAX: IMPRODUCT(*inumber1*,*inumber2*,...)

The IMPRODUCT function returns the product of 2 to 255 complex numbers in x + y*i* or x + y*j* text format. The arguments *inumber1*, *inumber2*,... are 1 to 255 complex numbers to multiply.

If *inumber1* or *inumber2* is not in the form x + y*i* or x + y*j*, IMPRODUCT returns a #NUM! error.

SYNTAX: IMDIV(*inumber1*,*inumber2*)

The IMDIV function returns the quotient of two complex numbers in x + y*i* or x + y*j* text format. This function takes the following arguments:

- *inumber1*—This is the complex numerator or dividend.
- *inumber2*—This is the complex denominator or divisor.

If *inumber1* or *inumber2* is not in the form x + y*i* or x + y*j*, IMDIV returns a #NUM! error.

## USING IMABS TO FIND THE DISTANCE FROM THE ORIGIN TO A COMPLEX NUMBER

A complex number is in the form *a* + *bi*, where *i* is an imaginary number representing the square root of –1. To plot complex numbers on a Cartesian grid, you use *a* for the x-axis and *b* for the y-axis.

The IMABS function calculates the distance from the (0, 0) origin in the grid. If you have a complex number in the form *a* + *bi*, the formula for an absolute value is =SQRT(a^2+b^2). This results in a real number.

SYNTAX: IMABS(*inumber*)

The IMABS function returns the absolute value (modulus) of a complex number in x + y*i* or x + y*j* text format. The argument *inumber* is a complex number for which you want the absolute value.

If *inumber* is not in the form x + y*i* or x + y*j*, IMABS returns a #NUM! error.

Figure 27.22 shows IMABS functions for several complex numbers. Note that the result of IMABS(a+bi) is equal to IMABS(b+ai).

**Figure 27.22**
Taking the absolute value of a complex number results in a real number.

| | A | B | C | D | E | F | G | H | I | J | K |
|---|---|---|---|---|---|---|---|---|---|---|---|
| | | B4 | ▾ | fx =IMABS(A4) | | | | | | | |
| 1 | | IMABS | | | | | | | | | |
| 2 | 3+4i | 5 | =IMABS(A2) | | IMABS(3+4i) = SQRT(3^2+4^2) = SQRT(9+16) = SQRT(25) = 5 | | | | | | |
| 3 | 4+3i | 5 | | | | | | | | | |
| 4 | 7+19i | 20.2485 | | | | | | | | | |
| 5 | 11+14i | 17.8045 | | | | | | | | | |
| 6 | 19+13i | 23.0217 | | | | | | | | | |
| 7 | 20+4i | 20.3961 | | | | | | | | | |
| 8 | 2+4i | 4.47214 | | | | | | | | | |
| 9 | 19+14i | 23.6008 | | | | | | | | | |
| 10 | 13+6i | 14.3178 | | | | | | | | | |
| 11 | 1+12i | 12.0416 | | | | | | | | | |
| 12 | | | | | | | | | | | |
| 13 | | Radians | Degrees | | | | | | | | |
| 14 | 3+4i | 0.9273 | 53.1301 | | | | | | | | |
| 15 | 4+3i | 0.6435 | 36.8699 | | | | | | | | |
| 16 | 7+19i | 1.21781 | 69.7751 | | | | | | | | |
| 17 | 11-14i | -0.9048 | -51.843 | | | | | | | | |
| 18 | 19+13i | 0.60005 | 34.3803 | | | | | | | | |
| 19 | 20+4i | 0.1974 | 11.3099 | | | | | | | | |
| 20 | -2+4i | 2.03444 | 116.565 | | | | | | | | |
| 21 | -19-14i | -2.5066 | -143.62 | | | | | | | | |
| 22 | 13+6i | 0.43241 | 24.7751 | | | | | | | | |
| 23 | 1+12i | 1.48766 | 85.2364 | | | | | | | | |
| 24 | | | | | | | | | | | |

## USING IMARGUMENT TO CALCULATE THE ANGLE TO A COMPLEX NUMBER

A complex number is in the form $a + bi$, where $i$ is an imaginary number representing the square root of –1. To plot complex numbers on a Cartesian grid, you use $a$ for the x-axis and $b$ for the y-axis.

The angle to a complex number assumes that the x-axis is 0 and rotates counter-clockwise. To find the angle, in radians, to any complex number plotted on a grid, you use IMARGUMENT.

B14:B23 in Figure 27.22 shows the angle for several complex numbers.

SYNTAX: IMARGUMENT(*inumber*)

The IMARGUMENT function returns the angle (θ) for an imaginary number. *inumber* is a complex number for which you want to calculate theta.

If *inumber* is not in the form x + yi or x + yj, IMARGUMENT returns a #NUM! error.

## USING IMCONJUGATE TO REVERSE THE SIGN OF AN IMAGINARY COMPONENT

A complex number is in the form $a + bi$, where $i$ is an imaginary number representing the square root of –1. To plot complex numbers on a Cartesian grid, you use $a$ for the x-axis and $b$ for the y-axis.

The IMCONJUGATE function creates a mirror image of a point, flipped across the x-axis. Put another way, the function changes the sign of the imaginary component. For example, 10 + 3*i* becomes 10 – 3*i*, and 10 – 3*i* becomes 10 + 3*i*.

27

SYNTAX: IMCONJUGATE(*inumber*)

The IMCONJUGATE function returns the complex conjugate of a complex number in x + y*i* or x + y*j* text format. The argument *inumber* is a complex number for which you want the conjugate.

If *inumber* is not in the form x + y*i* or x + y*j*, IMCONJUGATE returns a #NUM! error.

Figure 27.23 shows the results of several IMCONJUGATE formulas.

**Figure 27.23**
You can reverse the sign of the imaginary component of a complex number with IMCONJUGATE.

| | B2 | | | fx =IMCONJUGATE(A2) | |
|---|---|---|---|---|---|
| | A | B | C | D | E |
| 1 | | IMCONJUGATE | | | |
| 2 | 17+7i | 17-7i | =IMCONJUGATE(A2) | | |
| 3 | 14+3i | 14-3i | | | |
| 4 | 13+15i | 13-15i | | | |
| 5 | 9-16i | 9+16i | | | |
| 6 | 20-9i | 20+9i | | | |
| 7 | 17+2i | 17-2i | | | |
| 8 | 1+5i | 1-5i | | | |
| 9 | 2+1i | 2-i | | | |
| 10 | 20-6i | 20+6i | | | |
| 11 | 14+7i | 14-7i | | | |
| 12 | | | | | |

## CALCULATING POWERS, LOGARITHMS, AND TRIGONOMETRY FUNCTIONS WITH COMPLEX NUMBERS

The remaining eight IM functions calculate powers, exponents, logs, and trig functions from complex numbers:

- IMSQRT—This function calculates the square root of a complex number.
- IMPOWER—This function raises a complex number to a certain power.
- IMLOG10—This function calculates the base-10 logarithm or common logarithm of a complex number.
- IMLOG2—This function calculates the base-2 logarithm of a complex number.
- IMEXP—This function raises the constant e to a complex number. For more information, see the information on EXP, earlier in this chapter.
- IMLN—This function calculates the natural log of a complex number.
- IMSIN—This function calculates the sine of a complex number.
- IMCOS—This function calculates the cosine of a complex number.

Figure 27.24 shows the results of these functions for a complex number.

**Figure 27.24**
These functions calculate powers, logs, and trig functions, using text-based complex numbers.

| | A | B | C |
|---|---|---|---|
| | | B2 ▾ ⊙ *fx* =IMSQRT(B1) | |
| 1 | | 10+3i | |
| 2 | IMSQRT(B1) | 3.19689744196702+0.469204917339189i | |
| 3 | IMPOWER(B1,3) | 730+873i | |
| 4 | IMLOG10(B1) | 1.01871324897031+0.126578077554948i | |
| 5 | IMLOG2(B1) | 3.38409216264892+0.420483272058975i | |
| 6 | IMEXP(B1) | -21806.035863485+3108.375030493551i | |
| 7 | IMLN(B1) | 2.34567394111457+0.291456794477867i | |
| 8 | IMSIN(B1) | -5.47702066300171-8.40571363343848i | |
| 9 | IMCOS(B1) | -8.44748854502214+5.4499354467603i | |
| 10 | IMARGUMENT(B1) | 0.291456794 | |
| 11 | | | |

# SOLVING SIMULTANEOUS LINEAR EQUATIONS WITH MATRIX FUNCTIONS

You can use the Solver add-in to solve simultaneous equations, but Excel also offers three matrix functions that you can use to solve them. While the math involved in this is beyond the scope of this book, the steps in producing an answer are fairly straightforward.

The following is a problem taken from a math textbook in the Han Dynasty. The solution can easily be derived by using matrix functions in Excel.

There are three types of grain. Three bundles of the first, two of the second, and one of the third make 39 bushels. Two of the first, three of the second, and one of the third make 34 bushels. One of the first, two of the second, and three of the third make 26 bushels. How many bushels are in the bundles of each type of grain? To solve this problem, you follow these steps:

1. Convert the problem's words into algebraic equations. Assuming that the first type of grain is $a$, the second is $b$, and the third is $c$, you have these three equations:

   $3a + 2b + 1c = 39$

   $2a + 3b + 1c = 34$

   $1a + 2b + 3c = 26$

2. In Excel, set up three columns with headings a, b, and c. In the three rows below these columns, enter the coefficients from each equation. For example, the first row would contain 3, 2, and 1. The second row would contain 2, 3, and 1. The third row would contain 1, 2, and 3. In Figure 27.25, the range C5:E7 contains the matrix of coefficients.

3. In another range, enter a matrix of the answers for each equation. This range should be one column wide by three rows tall. The cells should contain 39, 34, and 26. In Figure 27.25, this range is in G5:G7.

27

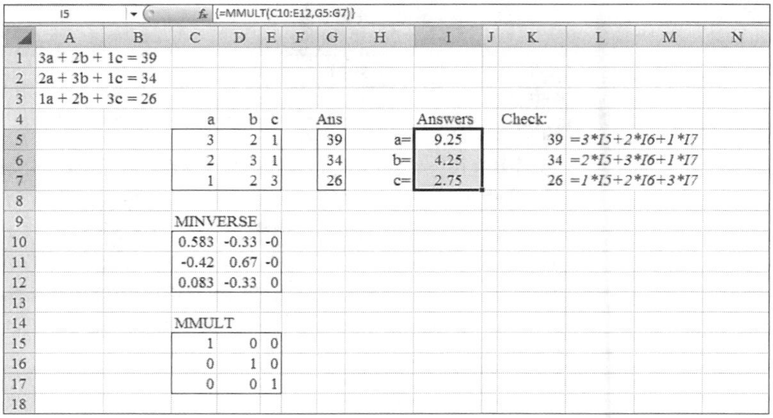

**Figure 27.25**
Amazingly, Excel can solve simultaneous equations by using a pair of matrix functions.

4. Select a new range that is the same size as the range in step 2. This range will hold an intermediate step with the inverse matrix. In the new range, type the formula =MINVERSE(C5:E7). Do not press Enter. Instead, hold down Ctrl+Shift while you press Enter. This key combination tells Excel to calculate an array and enter the results in all the selected cells. (See range C10:E12 in Figure 27.25.)

   The inverse of an array is an array that, when multiplied by the original array, produces a new array with 1s along the diagonal and 0s everywhere else. In Figure 27.25, the range C15:E17 contains the array formula =MMULT(C5:E7,C10:E12). As you can see in Figure 27.25, the result of the MMULT operation is indeed a matrix with a 1 along the diagonal and 0s everywhere else.

5. Select a range that is three cells high and one column wide. In this column, enter a MMULT function that multiplies the MINVERSE array from step 4 by the answers in step 3. In Figure 27.25, the formula in I5:I7 is =MMULT(C10:E12,G5:G7). Again, you must select all three cells before entering this formula, and you must hold down Ctrl+Shift+Enter to enter the formula. The results in Cells I5, I6, and I7 stand for the values of a, b, and c, respectively.

6. To make sure that everything worked, set up test formulas in column K. For example, the test formula in K5 checks to see if 3a+2b+c equals 39.

This entire process is fairly amazing. All the formulas are live formulas. If you change one of the input variables in any of the ranges, all the matrix functions instantly recalculate to solve the three simultaneous equations.

**SYNTAX:** MINVERSE(*array*)

The MINVERSE function returns the inverse matrix for the matrix stored in an array. The argument *array* is a numeric array with an equal number of rows and columns. *array* can be given as a cell range, such as A1:C3; as an array constant, such as {1,2,3;4,5,6;7,8,9}; or as a name for either of these.

If any cells in *array* are empty or contain text, MINVERSE returns a #VALUE! error. MINVERSE also returns a #VALUE! error if *array* does not have an equal number of rows and columns.

Formulas that return arrays must be entered as array formulas.

Inverse matrices, like determinants, are generally used for solving systems of mathematical equations that involve several variables. The product of a matrix and its inverse is the identity matrix—the square array in which the diagonal values equal 1 and all other values equal 0.

As an example of how a two-row, two-column matrix is calculated, suppose that the range A1:B2 contains the letters a, b, c, and d, which represent any four numbers. Table 27.5 shows the inverse of the matrix A1:B2.

**TABLE 27.5   INVERSE OF THE MATRIX SHOWN IN A1:B2 (SEE FIGURE 27.26)**

|  | Column A | Column B |
|---|---|---|
| Row 1 | d/(a*d-b*c) | b/(b*c-a*d) |
| Row 2 | c/(b*c-a*d) | a/(a*d-b*c) |

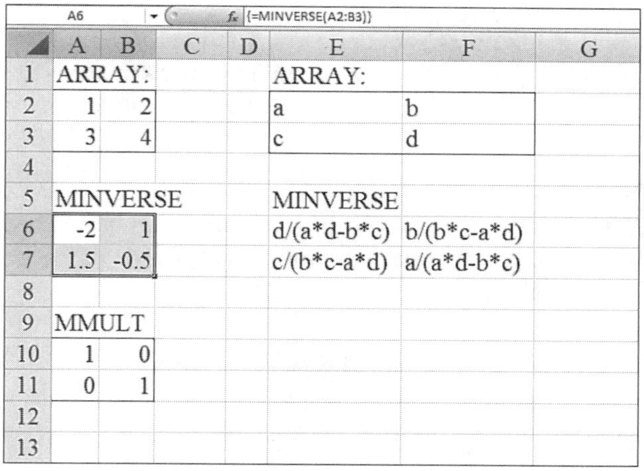

**Figure 27.26**
Range A6:B7 contains the MINVERSE of the original array. When you multiply an array and its MINVERSE array, the resulting array in A10:B11 contains 1s along the diagonal.

MINVERSE is calculated to an accuracy of approximately 16 digits, which may lead to a small numeric error when the cancellation is not complete. Thus, when you use MMULT on this array with the original array, you might find 0.000000000000001 instead of 0 in some cells.

Some square matrices cannot be inverted and return a #NUM! error with MINVERSE. The determinant for a noninvertable matrix is 0.

The MMULT function multiplies two arrays. The basic logic is that the top-left cell of the resulting array is the sum of multiplying the first row of Array 1 by the first column of Array 2. Figure 27.27 shows the rest of the rules for a 2 × 2 matrix.

**Figure 27.27**
The MMULT function performs matrix multiplication.

| | A | B | C | D | E | F | G |
|---|---|---|---|---|---|---|---|
| 1 | ARRAY A | | | | | | |
| 2 | 1 | 2 | | M(1,1) = A(1,1)*B(1,1) + A(1,2)*B(2,1) | | | |
| 3 | 3 | 4 | | M(1,2) = A(1,1)*B(1,2) + A(1,2)*B(2,2) | | | |
| 4 | | | | M(2,1) = A(2,1)*B(1,1) + A(2,2)*B(2,1) | | | |
| 5 | ARRAY B | | | M(2,2) = A(2,1)*B(1,2) + A(2,2)*B(2,2) | | | |
| 6 | 5 | 6 | | | | | |
| 7 | 7 | 8 | | | | | |
| 8 | | | | | | | |
| 9 | MMULT | | | | | | |
| 10 | 19 | 22 | | A10 = 1*5 + 2*7 = 19 | | | |
| 11 | 43 | 50 | | B10 = 1*6 + 2*8 = 22 | | | |
| 12 | | | | A11 = 3*5 + 4 * 7 = 43 | | | |
| 13 | | | | B11 = 3*6 + 4*8 = 50 | | | |
| 14 | | | | | | | |

A10   $\{=+MMULT(A2:B3,A6:B7)\}$

**SYNTAX:** MMULT(*array1*,*array2*)

The MMULT function returns the matrix product of two arrays. The result is an array with the same number of rows as *array1* and the same number of columns as *array2*.

The arguments *array1* and *array2* are the arrays you want to multiply. The number of columns in *array1* must be the same as the number of rows in *array2*, and both arrays must contain only numbers. *array1* and *array2* can be given as cell ranges, array constants, or references. If any cells are empty or contain text, or if the number of columns in *array1* is different from the number of rows in *array2*, MMULT returns a #VALUE! error.

In Figure 27.27, A2:B3 contains Array A. A6:B7 contains Array B. The result of the MMULT formula, Array M, is in A10:B11. The rules for the calculation of each cell in M are shown in D2:D5. The actual formulas are shown in D10:D13.

## USING MDETERM TO DETERMINE WHETHER A SIMULTANEOUS EQUATION HAS A SOLUTION

If your matrix of simultaneous equations is square, Excel can calculate a determinant of the array by using MDETERM. The determinant returns a single number, so this function does not need to be entered as an array. If the determinant of an array is nonzero, the simultaneous equation has a solution.

Figure 27.28 shows the calculation for the determinant of a 2 × 2 matrix.

**SYNTAX:** MDETERM(*array*)

The MDETERM function returns the matrix determinant of an array. The argument *array* is a numeric array with an equal number of rows and columns. *array* can be given as a cell range, such as A1:C3; as an array constant, such as {1,2,3;4,5,6;7,8,9}; or as a name to either of these. If any cells in *array* are empty or contain text, MDETERM returns a #VALUE! error. MDETERM also returns #VALUE! if *array* does not have an equal number of rows and columns.

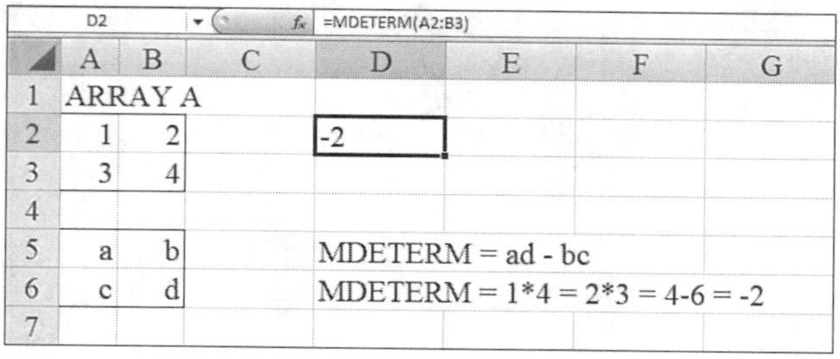

**Figure 27.28**

MDETERM returns the determinant of any square array. Determinants that are nonzero indicate that the simultaneous equations have a solution.

| D2 | ▾ | $f_x$ =MDETERM(A2:B3) | | | | |
|---|---|---|---|---|---|---|
| | A | B | C | D | E | F | G |
| 1 | ARRAY A | | | | | | |
| 2 | 1 | 2 | | -2 | | | |
| 3 | 3 | 4 | | | | | |
| 4 | | | | | | | |
| 5 | a | b | | MDETERM = ad - bc | | | |
| 6 | c | d | | MDETERM = 1*4 = 2*3 = 4-6 = -2 | | | |
| 7 | | | | | | | |

The matrix determinant is a number derived from the values in *array*. For a three-row, three-column array, A1:C3, the determinant is defined as follows:

```
MDETERM(A1:C3) = A1*(B2*C3-B3*C2) + A2*(B3*C1-B1*C3) + A3*(B1*C2-B2*C1)
```

Matrix determinants are generally used for solving systems of mathematical equations that involve several variables.

MDETERM is calculated with an accuracy of approximately 16 digits, which may lead to a small numeric error when the calculation is not complete. For example, the determinant of a singular matrix may differ from zero by 1E – 16.

Figure 27.28 shows a MDETERM calculation for a 2×2 array.

## USING SERIESSUM TO APPROXIMATE A FUNCTION WITH A POWER SERIES

There are situations in mathematics in which a value can be approximated by summing many factors in a series. If the series gets progressively smaller (for example, ½, ⅓, ¼, ⅕, ⅙, ⅐) the numbers eventually become smaller than Excel's 15-digit significance limit. This is referred to as a *power series*. In a power series, the exponent of each term is progressively changed. An example of a power series is $=a_1x^1 + a_2x^3 + a_3x^5 + a_4x^7 + a_5x^9$.

Figure 27.29 shows a very long, complex calculation. The coefficients in Column D are found by dividing factorials of even number digits into the number 1 and then multiplying every other value by –1. The value of *x* is 60 degrees, or PI() / 3. The exponents shown in Column E increase from 0 to 16 by 2s. In Column F, you raise X to the power in Column E. In Column G, you multiply Column D by Column F. Finally, you add up all the values in Column G to arrive at 0.5, which is a really good approximation of the cosine of 60 degrees.

This example is rather trivial because Excel actually offers a COS function. However, other functions use a power series to approximate a function. For example, one SERIESSUM function in B17 replaces all the calculations in Columns E, F, and G. The function needs the list of coefficients in Column D. In fact, the number of coefficients tells Excel how far to extend the series.

SYNTAX: SERIESSUM(*x,n,m,coefficients*)

The SERIESSUM function returns the sum of a power series. Many functions can be approximated by a power series expansion. This function takes the following arguments:

27

**Figure 27.29**
The SERIESSUM function can calculate a power series, given a value X, a pattern for the exponents, and a list of coefficients.

| | A | B | C | D | E | F | G | H |
|---|---|---|---|---|---|---|---|---|
| | B16 | | $f_x$ =SERIESSUM(B1,E4,E5,D4:D12) | | | | | |
| 1 | X: | 1.04719755 | =PI()/3 | | | | | |
| 2 | | | | | | | | |
| 3 | Even #s | Pos/Neg | 1/A! | B*C | Exponent | X^E | D*F | |
| 4 | 0 | 1 | 1.000000000000000 | 1.000000000000000 | 0 | 1 | 1.000000000000000 | |
| 5 | 2 | -1 | 0.500000000000000 | -0.500000000000000 | 2 | 1.096622711 | -0.548311355616075 | |
| 6 | 4 | 1 | 0.041666666666667 | 0.041666666666667 | 4 | 1.202581371 | 0.050107557116256 | |
| 7 | 6 | -1 | 0.001388888888889 | -0.001388888888889 | 6 | 1.318778043 | -0.001831636171268 | |
| 8 | 8 | 1 | 0.000024801587302 | 0.000024801587302 | 8 | 1.446201953 | 0.000035868104002 | |
| 9 | 10 | -1 | 0.000000275573192 | -0.000000275573192 | 10 | 1.585937907 | -0.000000437041972 | |
| 10 | 12 | 1 | 0.000000002087676 | 0.000000002087676 | 12 | 1.739175528 | 0.000000003630834 | |
| 11 | 14 | -1 | 0.000000000011471 | -0.000000000011471 | 14 | 1.907219382 | -0.000000000021877 | |
| 12 | 16 | 1 | 0.000000000000048 | 0.000000000000048 | 16 | 2.09150009 | 0.000000000000100 | |
| 13 | | | | | | | 0.500000000000000 | |
| 14 | | | | | | | | |
| 15 | | | =SeriesSum(x,n,m,a,a,a,a) = a1x^n + a2x^(n+m) + a3x^(n+2m)... | | | | | |
| 16 | | 0.5 | =SERIESSUM(B1,E4,E5,D4:D12) | | | | | |
| 17 | | | | | | | | |

- *x*—This is the input value to the power series.
- *n*—This is the initial power to which you want to raise *x*.
- *m*—This is the step by which to increase *n* for each term in the series.
- *coefficients*—This is a set of coefficients by which each successive power of *x* is multiplied. The number of values in *coefficients* determines the number of terms in the power series. For example, if there are three values in *coefficients*, there will be three terms in the power series.

If any argument is nonnumeric, SERIESSUM returns a #VALUE! error.

## USING SQRTPI TO FIND THE SQUARE ROOT OF A NUMBER MULTIPLIED BY PI

The SQRTPI function multiplies a number by Π and then takes the square root of the result. Because my exposure to Π is usually based on figuring out which pizza is the best deal, I've never had the occasion to multiply a number by Π and take the square root of the result. However, if your job requires you to take the square root of a number multiplied by Π, the SQRTPI function is just waiting for you to use it.

**TIP FROM**

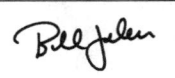

> If you are on this page because your job actually does require you to take the square root of Π multiplied by a number, drop me a line at MrExcel.com. I'll buy a real pizza for the first five readers who really have a legitimate need for this function.

SYNTAX: SQRTPI(*number*)

The SQRTPI function returns the square root of (*number* × Π). The argument *number* is the number by which Π is multiplied. If *number* is less than 0, SQRTPI returns a #NUM! error.

=SQRTPI(5) calculates 5*PI() as 15.7 and then takes the square root of 15.7, to return 3.96.

## USING SUMPRODUCT TO SUM BASED ON MULTIPLE CONDITIONS

The use of SUMPRODUCT will be dropping dramatically in Excel 2007. Until this point, SUMPRODUCT was one of the favorite methods for solving a particular limitation with SUMIF. However, since Microsoft added the SUMIFS function to Excel 2007, there will be less need for SUMPRODUCT.

In case you need to share your workbooks with people using prior versions of Excel, you can work through this example to solve the problem of conditionally summing a range based on two conditions. Say that you are starting with the data in column A:C of Figure 27.30. This simple dataset has fields for region, product, and sales.

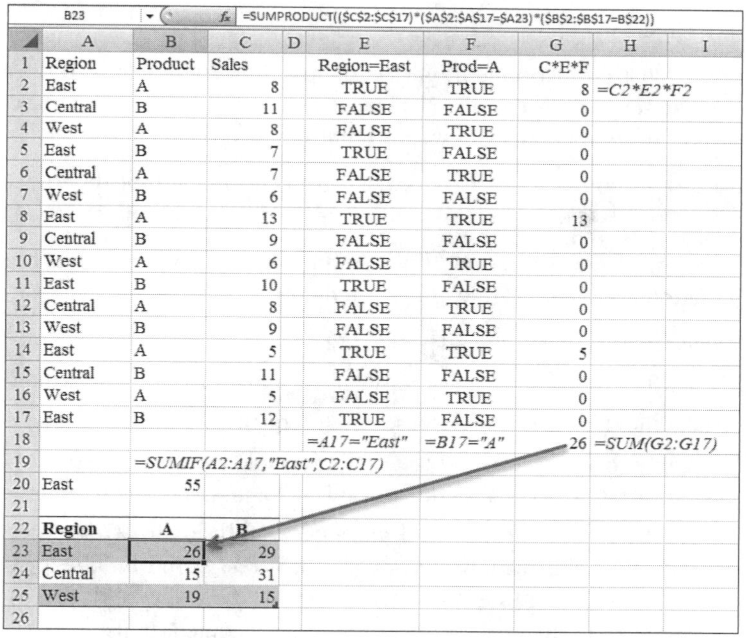

B23 | =SUMPRODUCT(($C$2:$C$17)*($A$2:$A$17=$A23)*($B$2:$B$17=B$22))

| | A | B | C | D | E | F | G | H | I |
|---|---|---|---|---|---|---|---|---|---|
| 1 | Region | Product | Sales | | Region=East | Prod=A | C*E*F | | |
| 2 | East | A | 8 | | TRUE | TRUE | 8 | =C2*E2*F2 | |
| 3 | Central | B | 11 | | FALSE | FALSE | 0 | | |
| 4 | West | A | 8 | | FALSE | TRUE | 0 | | |
| 5 | East | B | 7 | | TRUE | FALSE | 0 | | |
| 6 | Central | A | 7 | | FALSE | TRUE | 0 | | |
| 7 | West | B | 6 | | FALSE | FALSE | 0 | | |
| 8 | East | A | 13 | | TRUE | TRUE | 13 | | |
| 9 | Central | B | 9 | | FALSE | FALSE | 0 | | |
| 10 | West | A | 6 | | FALSE | TRUE | 0 | | |
| 11 | East | B | 10 | | TRUE | FALSE | 0 | | |
| 12 | Central | A | 8 | | FALSE | TRUE | 0 | | |
| 13 | West | B | 9 | | FALSE | FALSE | 0 | | |
| 14 | East | A | 5 | | TRUE | TRUE | 5 | | |
| 15 | Central | B | 11 | | FALSE | FALSE | 0 | | |
| 16 | West | A | 5 | | FALSE | TRUE | 0 | | |
| 17 | East | B | 12 | | TRUE | FALSE | 0 | | |
| 18 | | | | | =A17="East" | =B17="A" | 26 | =SUM(G2:G17) | |
| 19 | | =SUMIF(A2:A17,"East",C2:C17) | | | | | | | |
| 20 | East | 55 | | | | | | | |
| 21 | | | | | | | | | |
| 22 | **Region** | **A** | **B** | | | | | | |
| 23 | East | 26 | 29 | | | | | | |
| 24 | Central | 15 | 31 | | | | | | |
| 25 | West | 19 | 15 | | | | | | |
| 26 | | | | | | | | | |

**Figure 27.30**
The rather long and winding calculations in E2:G18 answer how many units meet two conditions. A single formula in B23 replaces all these steps.

The SUMIF command could easily add up all the sales that occurred in the east: =SUMIF(A2:A17,"East",C2:C17). But there is no way to use SUMIF to find the sum of all records that are in the east and for Product A. Using SUMPRODUCT to solve this problem requires you to think about a couple virtual arrays. I've actually entered these arrays as intermediate steps in Figure 27.30 so that you can picture them:

- In Column E, the formula tests whether the cell in Column A is equal to East.
- In Column F, the formula tests whether the cell in Column B is equal to A.
- Column G contains an interesting formula. Cell G2 multiplies the sales in Cell C2 by the TRUE/FALSE value in Cell E2 and then multiplies that by the TRUE/FALSE value in Cell G2. In Excel's treatment of TRUE/FALSE values, a TRUE is calculated as a 1, and a FALSE is

27

calculated as a 0. Thus, in Cell G2, the 8 × TRUE × TRUE is like multiplying $8 \times 1 \times 1$, which results in 8.

- If either cell in Column E or Column F is FALSE, Excel treats the value as a zero. Because zero times anything is zero, the result in Column G shows up as zero if the corresponding value in either Column E or Column F is FALSE.
- In Cell G18, a SUM function totals the products from Column G in order to answer how many sales of Product A were made in the east.

The SUMPRODUCT function does all the steps from Columns E, F, and G in a single function, as shown in Cell B23 in Figure 27.30.

SYNTAX: SUMPRODUCT(*array1*,*array2*,*array3*,...)

The SUMPRODUCT function multiplies corresponding components in the given arrays and returns the sum of those products. The arguments *array1*, *array2*, *array3*,... are 2 to 255 arrays whose components you want to multiply and then add together.

The *array* arguments must have the same dimensions. If they do not, SUMPRODUCT returns a #VALUE! error. SUMPRODUCT treats array entries that are not numeric as if they were zeros.

To solve a problem that has multiple conditions, you have to create three virtual arrays in the function arguments. Here's how you do it:

1. Make the first array the sales in C2:C17.
2. Make the second array a test to see if A is equal to East. This would be (A2:A17="East").
3. Make the third array a test to see if B is equal to A. This would be (B2:B17="A").
4. Multiply these three arrays to get the formula =SUMPRODUCT((C2:C17)*(A2:A17="East")* (B2:B17="A")). This provides a result of 26, just as in the previous example.
5. Make the function from step 4 more generic. In Figure 27.30, a summary table in A19:C22 has the headings East, Central, West, A, and B. The formula in B20 is =SUMPRODUCT(($C$2:$C$17)*($A$2:$A$17=$A20)*($B$2:$B$17=B$19)). This formula adds dollar signs so that the formula can be easily copied. It also replaces "East" with $A20 and "A" with B$19.
6. Copy this formula to the rest of the table. You now have an efficient conditional total that sums records based on two criteria.

# EXAMPLES OF ENGINEERING FUNCTIONS

There are not many true engineering functions in Excel. You will notice that I reclassified most of the IM functions into the previous section on imaginary numbers. All the BIN2, DEC2, HEX2, and OCT2 functions are, at best, interesting to software engineers.

The CONVERT function is interesting to everyone and is truly the one engineering function that could have been shown in Chapter 23, "Using Everyday Functions: Math, Date and Time, and Text Functions."

So there are just a handful of true engineering functions: The various BESSEL functions, ERF, DELTA, and the GESTEP functions are of use exclusively to engineers.

## CONVERTING FROM DECIMAL TO HEXADECIMAL AND BACK

A long time ago, I held a summer internship writing COBOL programs for a company. Whenever one of my programs crashed in the middle of the night, I was supposed to show up and read through a hexadecimal printout of the computer memory to figure out what went wrong.

In the hexadecimal numbering system, there are 16 digits. The digits, in order, are 0, 1, 2, 3, 4, 5, 6, 7, 8, 9, A, B, C, D, E, and F. The number that you and I know as 10 would be written as A in hexadecimal. The number 15 would be written as F in hexadecimal. After F comes the hexadecimal number 10, which is equivalent to 16 in decimal.

Hexadecimal numbers can get rather large. For example, the hex number C2 means $12 \times 16 + 2$ (remember that C is equivalent to a decimal 12). The hex number 1111 means $1 \times 16^3 + 1 \times 16^2 + 1 \times 16 + 1$, or 4,369.

There are actually calculators that let you add a number such as A52B with C2D4 to come up with the answer 167FF.

In Excel, you can easily convert numbers in the base-10 system to hexadecimal by using DEC2HEX. Similarly, you can convert hex numbers to a base-10 numbering system by using HEX2DEC.

### SYNTAX: DEC2HEX(*number*,*places*)

The DEC2HEX function converts a decimal number to hexadecimal. This function takes the following arguments:

- *number*—This is the decimal integer you want to convert. If *number* is negative, *places* is ignored, and DEC2HEX returns a 10-character (that is, 40-bit) hexadecimal number in which the most significant bit is the sign bit. The remaining 39 bits are magnitude bits. Negative numbers are represented using two's-complement notation.

- *places*—This is the number of characters to use. If *places* is omitted, DEC2HEX uses the minimum number of characters necessary. *places* is useful for padding the return value with leading 0s.

If *number* is less than –549,755,813,888 or if *number* is greater than 549,755,813,887, DEC2HEX returns a #NUM! error. If *number* is nonnumeric, DEC2HEX returns a #VALUE! error. If DEC2HEX requires more than *places* characters, it returns a #NUM! error.

If *places* is not an integer, it is truncated. If *places* is nonnumeric, DEC2HEX returns a #VALUE! error. If *places* is negative, DEC2HEX returns a #NUM! error.

27

Syntax: `HEX2DEC(number)`

The `HEX2DEC` function converts a hexadecimal number to decimal. The argument *`number`* is the hexadecimal number you want to convert. *`number`* cannot contain more than 10 characters (that is, 40 bits). The most significant bit of *`number`* is the sign bit. The remaining 39 bits are magnitude bits. Negative numbers are represented using two's-complement notation.

If *`number`* is not a valid hexadecimal number, `HEX2DEC` returns a `#NUM!` error.

Figure 27.31 shows a conversion from decimal to hexadecimal and back. Note that Cell B2 uses the *places* argument to specify that leading zeros should be added to generate a number that is 4 digits long.

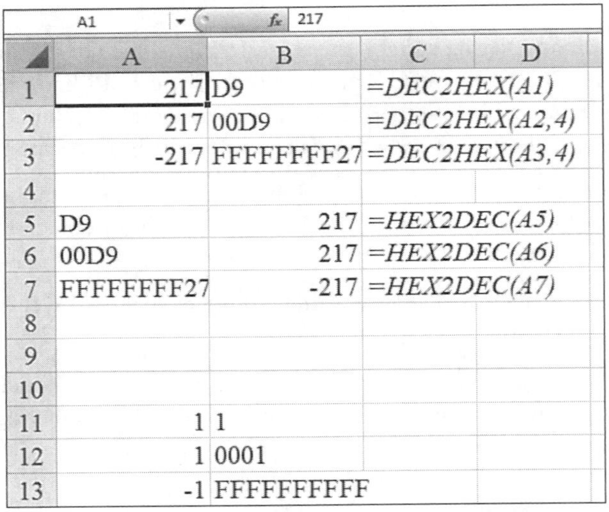

A1 fx 217

| | A | B | C | D |
|---|---|---|---|---|
| 1 | 217 | D9 | =DEC2HEX(A1) | |
| 2 | 217 | 00D9 | =DEC2HEX(A2,4) | |
| 3 | -217 | FFFFFFFF27 | =DEC2HEX(A3,4) | |
| 4 | | | | |
| 5 | D9 | 217 | =HEX2DEC(A5) | |
| 6 | 00D9 | 217 | =HEX2DEC(A6) | |
| 7 | FFFFFFFF27 | -217 | =HEX2DEC(A7) | |
| 8 | | | | |
| 9 | | | | |
| 10 | | | | |
| 11 | 1 | 1 | | |
| 12 | 1 | 0001 | | |
| 13 | -1 | FFFFFFFFFF | | |

**Figure 27.31**
Converting from decimal to hexadecimal and back.

## Converting from Decimal to Octal and Back

The octal numbering system is a base-8 numbering system. In this system, there are only eight digits, from 0 through 7. The decimal number 8 is represented in octal as 10.

Each numeric place in an octal number represents an additional power of 8. The octal number 1111 represents 1 × 8^3 + 1 × 8^2 + 1^8 + 1, or 512 + 64 + 8 + 1, or 585 in decimal.

You use `DEC2OCT` to convert from decimal to octal and `OCT2DEC` to convert from octal to decimal.

Syntax: `DEC2OCT(number,places)`

The `DEC2OCT` function converts a decimal number to octal. This function takes the following arguments:

- *`number`*—This is the decimal integer you want to convert. If *`number`* is negative, *`places`* is ignored, and `DEC2OCT` returns a 10-character (that is, 30-bit) octal number in which the most significant bit is the sign bit. The remaining 29 bits are magnitude bits. Negative numbers are represented using two's-complement notation.

■ *places*—This is the number of characters to use. If *places* is omitted, DEC2OCT uses the minimum number of characters necessary. *places* is useful for padding the return value with leading 0s.

If *number* is less than –536,870,912 or if *number* is greater than 536,870,911, DEC2OCT returns a #NUM! error. If *number* is nonnumeric, DEC2OCT returns a #VALUE! error. If DEC2OCT requires more than *places* characters, it returns a #NUM! error. If *places* is not an integer, it is truncated. If *places* is nonnumeric, DEC2OCT returns a #VALUE! error. If *places* is negative, DEC2OCT returns a #NUM! error.

SYNTAX: OCT2DEC(*number*)

The OCT2DEC function converts an octal number to decimal. The argument *number* is the octal number you want to convert. *number* cannot contain more than 10 octal characters (that is, 30 bits). The most significant bit of *number* is the sign bit. The remaining 29 bits are magnitude bits. Negative numbers are represented using two's-complement notation.

If *number* is not a valid octal number, OCT2DEC returns a #NUM! error.

Figure 27.32 shows a conversion from decimal to octal and back.

**Figure 27.32**
The *places* argument in Cell B2 controls the leading zeroes.

| | A | B | C | D |
|---|---|---|---|---|
| 1 | 18 | 22 | =DEC2OCT(A1) | |
| 2 | 640 | 00001200 | =DEC2OCT(A2,8) | |
| 3 | -512 | 7777777000 | =DEC2OCT(A3) | |
| 4 | | | | |
| 5 | 1200 | 640 | =OCT2DEC(A5) | |
| 6 | 00001200 | 640 | =OCT2DEC(A6) | |
| 7 | 7777777000 | -512 | =OCT2DEC(A7) | |
| 8 | | | | |

## CONVERTING FROM DECIMAL TO BINARY AND BACK

Although hexadecimal and octal numbering systems are seldom encountered anymore, many people still encounter binary number systems. Binary number systems are the language of computers because every circuit has a state of either 1 (meaning that electricity is present) or 0 (meaning that electricity is not present). Thus, the binary number system has only 2 digits, 0 and 1:

■ The rightmost digit in a binary number means 0 or 1.

■ The next rightmost digit represents $2^1$, or 2.

■ The next digit represents $2^2$, or 4.

- The next digit represents 2^3, or 8.
- The next digit represents 2^4, or 16.
- The next digit represents 2^5, or 32.
- The next digit represents 2^6, or 64.

For example, the binary number 1010101 means 64 + 16 + 4 + 1, or 85 in decimal. You use `DEC2BIN` to convert from decimal to binary and `BIN2DEC` to convert from binary to decimal. Note that `DEC2BIN` only works with the numbers 512 and lower.

SYNTAX: `DEC2BIN(`*`number`*`,`*`places`*`)`

The `DEC2BIN` function converts a decimal number to binary. This function takes the following arguments:

- *`number`*—This is the decimal integer you want to convert. If *`number`* is negative, *`places`* is ignored, and `DEC2BIN` returns a 10-character (that is, 10-bit) binary number in which the most significant bit is the sign bit. The remaining 9 bits are magnitude bits. Negative numbers are represented using two's-complement notation.
- *`places`*—This is the number of characters to use. If *`places`* is omitted, `DEC2BIN` uses the minimum number of characters necessary. *`places`* is useful for padding the return value with leading 0s.

If *`number`* is less than –512 or if *`number`* is greater than 511, `DEC2BIN` returns a `#NUM!` error. If *`number`* is nonnumeric, `DEC2BIN` returns a `#VALUE!` error. If `DEC2BIN` requires more than *`places`* characters, it returns the `#NUM!` error. If *`places`* is not an integer, it is truncated. If *`places`* is nonnumeric, `DEC2BIN` returns a `#VALUE!` error. If *`places`* is negative, `DEC2BIN` returns a `#NUM!` error.

**Figure 27.33**
Converting from decimal to binary and back.

B5 fx =BIN2DEC(A5)

| | A | B | C | D |
|---|---|---|---|---|
| 1 | 255 | 11111111 | =DEC2BIN(A1) | |
| 2 | 511 | 111111111 | =DEC2BIN(A2,8) | |
| 3 | -512 | 1000000000 | =DEC2BIN(A3) | |
| 4 | | | | |
| 5 | 101010101 | 341 | =BIN2DEC(A5) | |
| 6 | 1100 | 12 | =BIN2DEC(A6) | |
| 7 | 11111 | 31 | =BIN2DEC(A7) | |
| 8 | 1000000000 | -512 | =BIN2DEC(A7) | |
| 9 | | | | |

SYNTAX: `BIN2DEC(`*`number`*`)`

The `BIN2DEC` function converts a binary number to decimal. The argument *`number`* is the binary number you want to convert. *`number`* cannot contain more than 10 characters (that is, 10 bits). The most significant bit of *`number`* is the sign bit. The remaining 9 bits are magnitude bits. Negative numbers are represented using two's-complement notation.

If *number* is not a valid binary number, or if *number* contains more than 10 characters (that is, 10 bits), BIN2DEC returns a #NUM! error.

The formulas in Figure 27.33 convert from decimal to binary and from binary to decimal.

## Explaining the Two's Complement for Negative Numbers

In all the previous examples, the hex, octal, and binary numbers look bizarre for negative numbers. This is a special notation called *two's complement*. In Excel, we have to agree that a negative number occupies 10 characters. For example, Cell A1 in Figure 27.34 contains the number five in binary.

**Figure 27.34**
Negative numbers in two's complement are initially unnerving, until you understand the steps for converting them.

| | A | B | C | D | E | F | G | H |
|---|---|---|---|---|---|---|---|---|
| | | | | | A1 | | fx | '00 0000 0101 |
| 1 | 00 0000 0101 | Original Number in Binary (5) | | | | | | |
| 2 | 11 1111 1010 | Switch 0 and 1 to move to ones complement | | | | | | |
| 3 | 11 1111 1011 | Add 1 to convert to twos complement (-5) | | | | | | |
| 4 | | | | | | | | |
| 5 | 00 0000 0000 | Zero in Binary | | | | | | |
| 6 | 11 1111 1111 | Switch 0 and 1 to move to ones complement | | | | | | |
| 7 | 00 0000 0000 | Add 1 to convert to twos complement (ignoring the overflow digit) | | | | | | |
| 8 | | | | | | | | |
| 9 | 00 0000 0001 | One in binary | | | | | | |
| 10 | 11 1111 1110 | Ones complement | | | | | | |
| 11 | 11 1111 1111 | Add one to create twos complement | | | | | | |
| 12 | | | | | | | | |
| 13 | 11 1111 1011 | -5 in two's complement | | | | | | |
| 14 | 00 0000 0100 | Switch 0 and 1 | | | | | | |
| 15 | 00 0000 0101 | Add 1 to produce positive five in binary | | | | | | |
| 16 | | | | | | | | |

If the leftmost bit is a 1, then the number is assumed to be negative, and Excel assumes that the number is in two's-complement notation. There are two simple steps to convert a positive number to a negative number in two's complement:

1. Change every 0 to a 1 and every 1 to a 0. This produces a number in one's complement, as shown in Cell A2 in Figure 27.34.

2. Add 1 to the result from step 1 to convert to two's complement, as shown in Cell A3 in Figure 27.34.

27

Note that the leftmost bit is always set to a 1 for a negative number. This prevents Excel from representing 512 in binary. The binary representation of 512—1000000000—has a 1 in the leftmost digit, so no numbers over 511 can be represented in binary in Excel.

Converting from negative to positive in two's complement follows exactly the same method. Cell A13 in Figure 27.34 contains –5 in two's complement. In Cell A14, you switch all the 0s and 1s. In Cell A15, you add 1 to produce the original result in binary.

## CONVERTING FROM BINARY TO HEX TO OCTAL AND BACK

Excel offers six additional functions that can convert directly from octal to hexadecimal to binary. The major limitation of these functions is that Excel can represent as binary only numbers up to 511 in decimal. This is a significant limitation; anything larger than 1FF in hex or larger than 777 in octal returns an error if you try to convert it to binary.

These are the additional conversion functions:

- BIN2HEX(*number*,*places*)—This converts a binary number to hexadecimal.
- BIN2OCT(*number*,*places*)—This converts a binary number to octal.
- HEX2BIN(*number*,*places*)—This converts a hexadecimal number to binary.
- HEX2OCT(*number*,*places*)—This converts a hexadecimal number to octal.
- OCT2BIN(*number*,*places*)—This converts an octal number to binary.
- OCT2HEX(*number*,*places*)—This converts an octal number to hexadecimal.

Figure 27.35 demonstrates these conversion functions.

**Figure 27.35**
You can convert between hex, octal, and binary by using these six functions.

| | A | B | C | D | E |
|---|---|---|---|---|---|
| | A2 | ▾ (  | *fx* | =DEC2OCT(A$1) | |
| 1 | 511 | Decimal | | D2 | Hex |
| 2 | 777 | DEC2OCT | | 322 | HEX2OCT |
| 3 | 11111111 | DEC2BIN | | 11010010 | HEX2BIN |
| 4 | 1FF | DEC2HEX | | 210 | HEX2DEC |
| 5 | | | | | |
| 6 | 331 | Octal | | 1010011 | Binary |
| 7 | 11011001 | OCT2BIN | | 123 | BIN2OCT |
| 8 | D9 | OCT2HEX | | 53 | BIN2HEX |
| 9 | 217 | OCT2DEC | | 83 | BIN2DEC |
| 10 | | | | | |

## USING CONVERT TO CONVERT ENGLISH TO METRIC

The CONVERT function is an incredibly versatile function. It can convert measures in the following areas:

- Weight and mass
- Distance
- Time
- Pressure
- Force
- Energy
- Power
- Magnetism

27

- Temperature
- Liquid measure

**CAUTION**

At press time, a bug in Excel 2007 is causing most metric calculations in the CONVERT function to fail with a #N/A error. While I expect Microsoft to address this problem, I suspect that it will not be fixed until the first service pack. This section documents how the function is supposed to work, although many metric calculations may return #N/A errors in the initial release of Excel 2007.

SYNTAX: CONVERT(*number*,*from_unit*,*to_unit*)

The CONVERT function converts a number from one measurement system to another. For example, CONVERT can translate a table of distances in miles to a table of distances in kilometers. This function takes the following arguments:

- *number*—This is the value in *from_units* to convert.
- *from_unit*—This is the units for number.
- *to_unit*—This is the units for the result.

Tables 27.6 through 27.15 list the text values that CONVERT accepts for *from_unit* and *to_unit*.

If the input data types are incorrect, CONVERT returns a #VALUE! error. If the unit does not exist, CONVERT returns an #N/A error.

If the unit does not support an abbreviated unit prefix, CONVERT returns an #N/A error.

If the units are in different groups, CONVERT returns an #N/A error.

The unit abbreviations to use in CONVERT are case-sensitive.

Table 27.6 shows conversions possible for weights.

**TABLE 27.6    UNITS OF WEIGHT AND MASS**

| Unit of Weight | Abbreviation to Use in CONVERT |
|----------------|--------------------------------|
| Gram | g |
| Slug | sg |
| Pound mass | lbm |
| Atomic unit | u |
| Ounce mass | ozm |
| Exagram | Eg |
| Petagram | Pg |

*continues*

**Table 27.6 Continued**

| Unit of Weight | Abbreviation to Use in CONVERT |
|---|---|
| Teragram | Tg |
| Gigagram | Gg |
| Megagram | Mg |
| Kilogram | kg |
| Hectogram | hg |
| Dekaogram | eg |
| Decigram | dg |
| Centigram | cg |
| Milligram | mg |
| Microgram | ug |
| Nanogram | ng |
| Pictogram | pg |
| Femtogram | Fg |
| Attogram | Ag |

Figure 27.36 shows a conversion of weights and masses.

E28 =CONVERT(1,"sg","u")

| | A | B | C | D | E | F | G | H |
|---|---|---|---|---|---|---|---|---|
| 3 | | | | TO----> | | | | |
| 4 | | | | Gram | Slug | Pound Mass | Atomic Unit | Ounce Mass |
| 5 | | | | g | sg | lbm | u | ozm |
| 6 | FROM | Gram | g | 1 | 6.85221E-05 | 0.002205 | 6.02E+23 | 0.035274 |
| 7 | | Slug | sg | 14593.84 | 1 | 32.17392 | 8.79E+27 | 514.7828 |
| 8 | | Pound Mass | lbm | 453.5923 | 0.031081075 | 1 | 2.73E+26 | 16 |
| 9 | | Atomic Unit | u | 1.66E-24 | 1.13783E-28 | 3.66E-27 | 1 | 5.86E-26 |
| 10 | | Ounce Mass | ozm | 28.34952 | 0.001942567 | 0.0625 | 1.71E+25 | 1 |
| 11 | | exagram | Eg | 1E+18 | 6.85221E+13 | 2.2E+15 | 6.02E+41 | 3.53E+16 |
| 12 | | petagram | Pg | 1E+15 | 68522050005 | 2.2E+12 | 6.02E+38 | 3.53E+13 |
| 13 | | teragram | Tg | 1E+12 | 68522050.01 | 2.2E+09 | 6.02E+35 | 3.53E+10 |
| 14 | | gigagram | Gg | 1E+09 | 68522.05001 | 2204623 | 6.02E+32 | 35273972 |
| 15 | | megagram | Mg | 1000000 | 68.52205001 | 2204.623 | 6.02E+29 | 35273.97 |
| 16 | | kilogram | kg | 1000 | 0.06852205 | 2.204623 | 6.02E+26 | 35.27397 |
| 17 | | hectogram | hg | 100 | 0.006852205 | 0.220462 | 6.02E+25 | 3.527397 |
| 18 | | dekaogram | eg | 10 | 0.000685221 | 0.022046 | 6.02E+24 | 0.35274 |
| 19 | | decigram | dg | 0.1 | 6.85221E-06 | 0.00022 | 6.02E+22 | 0.003527 |
| 20 | | centigram | cg | 0.01 | 6.85221E-07 | 2.2E-05 | 6.02E+21 | 0.000353 |
| 21 | | milligram | mg | 0.001 | 6.85221E-08 | 2.2E-06 | 6.02E+20 | 3.53E-05 |
| 22 | | microgram | ug | 0.000001 | 6.85221E-11 | 2.2E-09 | 6.02E+17 | 3.53E-08 |
| 23 | | nanogram | ng | 1E-09 | 6.85221E-14 | 2.2E-12 | 6.02E+14 | 3.53E-11 |
| 24 | | picogram | pg | 1E-12 | 6.85221E-17 | 2.2E-15 | 6.02E+11 | 3.53E-14 |
| 25 | | femtogram | fg | 1E-15 | 6.85221E-20 | 2.2E-18 | 6.02E+08 | 3.53E-17 |
| 26 | | attogram | ag | 1E-18 | 6.85221E-23 | 2.2E-21 | 602217 | 3.53E-20 |
| 27 | | | | | | | | |
| 28 | | Atomic Units in a slug? | | | 8.78866E+27 | | | |
| 29 | | | | | | | | |

**Figure 27.36**
This table converts between the mass units in the left column and the various units along the top row.

27

Table 27.7 shows conversion units for distance.

**TABLE 27.7  UNITS OF DISTANCE**

| Unit of Distance | Abbreviation to Use in CONVERT |
| --- | --- |
| Statute mile | Mi |
| Nautical mile | Nmi |
| Inch | In |
| Foot | Ft |
| Yard | Yd |
| Angstrom | Ang |
| Pica (1/72 in.) | Pica |
| Meter | M |
| Exameter | Em |
| Petameter | Pm |
| Terameter | Tm |
| Gigameter | Gm |
| Megameter | Mm |
| Kilometer | Km |
| Hectometer | Hm |
| Dekaometer | Em |
| Decimeter | Dm |
| Centimeter | Cm |
| Millimeter | Mm |
| Micrometer | Um |
| Nanometer | Nm |

Figure 27.37 shows a conversion of distances.

Table 27.8 shows conversion abbreviations for measures of time.

**TABLE 27.8  UNITS OF TIME**

| Unit of Time | Abbreviation to Use in CONVERT |
| --- | --- |
| Year | Yr |
| Day | Day |
| Hour | Hr |
| Minute | Mn |
| Second | Sec |

27

**Figure 27.37**
This table converts between the distance units in the left column and the various units along the top row.

D31 | =CONVERT(1,"mi","Pica")

| | A | B | C | D | E | F | G | H | I | J | K |
|---|---|---|---|---|---|---|---|---|---|---|---|
| 3 | | **Distances** | | TO----> | | | | | | | |
| 4 | | | | **Statute mile** | **Nautical mile** | **Inch** | **Foot** | **Yard** | **Angstrom** | **Pica (1/72 in.)** | **Meter** |
| 5 | | | | mi | Nmi | in | ft | yd | ang | Pica | m |
| 6 | FROM | **Statute mile** | mi | 1 | 0.86897624 | 63360 | 5280 | 1760 | 1.6093E+13 | 4561920 | 1609.344 |
| 7 | | **Nautical mile** | Nmi | 1.15077945 | 1 | 72913.3858 | 6076.11549 | 2025.37183 | 1.852E+13 | 5249763.78 | 1852 |
| 8 | | **Inch** | in | 1.5783E-05 | 1.3715E-05 | 1 | 0.08333333 | 0.02777778 | 254000000 | 72 | 0.0254 |
| 9 | | **Foot** | ft | 0.00018939 | 0.00016458 | 12 | 1 | 0.33333333 | 3048000000 | 864 | 0.3048 |
| 10 | | **Yard** | yd | 0.00056818 | 0.00049374 | 36 | 3 | 1 | 9144000003 | 2592 | 0.9144 |
| 11 | | **Angstrom** | ang | 6.2137E-14 | 5.3996E-14 | 3.937E-09 | 3.2808E-10 | 1.0936E-10 | 1 | 2.8346E-07 | 1E-10 |
| 12 | | **Pica (1/72 in.)** | Pica | 2.1921E-07 | 1.9048E-07 | 0.01388889 | 0.00115741 | 0.0003858 | 3527777.78 | 1 | 0.00035278 |
| 13 | | **Meter** | m | 0.00062137 | 0.00053996 | 39.3700787 | 3.2808399 | 1.0936133 | 1E+10 | 2834.64567 | 1 |
| 14 | | **exameter** | Em | 6.2137E+14 | 5.3996E+14 | 3.937E+19 | 3.2808E+18 | 1.0936E+18 | 1E+28 | 2.8346E+21 | 1E+18 |
| 15 | | **petameter** | Pm | 6.2137E+11 | 5.3996E+11 | 3.937E+16 | 3.2808E+15 | 1.0936E+15 | 1E+25 | 2.8346E+18 | 1E+15 |
| 16 | | **terameter** | Tm | 621371192 | 539956803 | 3.937E+13 | 3.2808E+12 | 1.0936E+12 | 1E+22 | 2.8346E+15 | 1E+12 |
| 17 | | **gigameter** | Gm | 621371.192 | 539956.803 | 3.937E+10 | 3280839895 | 1093613298 | 1E+19 | 2.8346E+12 | 1000000000 |
| 18 | | **megameter** | Mm | 621.371192 | 539.956803 | 39370078.7 | 3280839.9 | 1093613.3 | 1E+16 | 2834645669 | 1000000 |
| 19 | | **kilometer** | km | 0.62137119 | 0.5399568 | 39370.0787 | 3280.8399 | 1093.6133 | 1E+13 | 2834645.67 | 1000 |
| 20 | | **hectometer** | hm | 0.06213712 | 0.05399568 | 3937.00787 | 328.08399 | 109.36133 | 1E+12 | 283464.567 | 100 |
| 21 | | **dekaometer** | em | 0.00621371 | 0.00539957 | 393.700787 | 32.808399 | 10.936133 | 1E+11 | 28346.4567 | 10 |
| 22 | | **decimeter** | dm | 6.2137E-05 | 5.3996E-05 | 3.93700787 | 0.32808399 | 0.10936133 | 1000000000 | 283.464567 | 0.1 |
| 23 | | **centimeter** | cm | 6.2137E-06 | 5.3996E-06 | 0.39370079 | 0.0328084 | 0.01093613 | 100000000 | 28.3464567 | 0.01 |
| 24 | | **millimeter** | mm | 6.2137E-07 | 5.3996E-07 | 0.03937008 | 0.00328084 | 0.00109361 | 10000000 | 2.83464567 | 0.001 |
| 25 | | **micrometer** | um | 6.2137E-10 | 5.3996E-10 | 3.937E-05 | 3.2808E-06 | 1.0936E-06 | 10000 | 0.00283465 | 0.000001 |
| 26 | | **nanometer** | nm | 6.2137E-13 | 5.3996E-13 | 3.937E-08 | 3.2808E-09 | 1.0936E-09 | 10 | 2.8346E-06 | 1E-09 |
| 27 | | **picometer** | pm | 6.2137E-16 | 5.3996E-16 | 3.937E-11 | 3.2808E-12 | 1.0936E-12 | 0.01 | 2.8346E-09 | 1E-12 |
| 28 | | **femtometer** | fm | 6.2137E-19 | 5.3996E-19 | 3.937E-14 | 3.2808E-15 | 1.0936E-15 | 0.00001 | 2.8346E-12 | 1E-15 |
| 29 | | **attometer** | am | 6.2137E-22 | 5.3996E-22 | 3.937E-17 | 3.2808E-18 | 1.0936E-18 | 0.0000001 | 2.8346E-15 | 1E-18 |
| 30 | | | | | | | | | | | |
| 31 | | **Picas in a mile?** | | 4561920 | | | | | | | |

Figure 27.38 shows a conversion of times.

**Figure 27.38**
This table converts between the time units in the left column and the various units along the top row.

D12 | =CONVERT(1,"day","sec")

| | A | B | C | D | E | F | G | H |
|---|---|---|---|---|---|---|---|---|
| 1 | | | | | | | | |
| 2 | | | | | | | | |
| 3 | | **Time** | | TO----> | | | | |
| 4 | | | | Year | Day | Hour | Minute | Second |
| 5 | | | | yr | day | hr | mn | sec |
| 6 | FROM | Year | yr | 1 | 365.25 | 8766 | 525960 | 31557600 |
| 7 | | Day | day | 0.002737851 | 1 | 24 | 1440 | 86400 |
| 8 | | Hour | hr | 0.000114077 | 0.041666667 | 1 | 60 | 3600 |
| 9 | | Minute | mn | 1.90129E-06 | 0.000694444 | 0.016666667 | 1 | 60 |
| 10 | | Second | sec | 3.16881E-08 | 1.15741E-05 | 0.000277778 | 0.016666667 | 1 |
| 11 | | | | | | | | |
| 12 | | **Seconds in a day?** | | 86400 | | | | |

Table 27.9 shows conversion values for units of pressure.

### Table 27.9 Units of Pressure

| Unit of Pressure | Abbreviation to Use in CONVERT |
|---|---|
| Pascal | `Pa` |
| Atmosphere | `atm` |
| mm of Mercury | `mmHg` |
| Exaatmosphere | `Eatm` |
| Petaatmosphere | `Patm` |
| Teraatmosphere | `Tatm` |

27

| Unit of Pressure | Abbreviation to Use in CONVERT |
|---|---|
| Gigaatmosphere | Gatm |
| Megaatmosphere | Matm |
| Kiloatmosphere | katm |
| Hectoatmosphere | hatm |
| Dekaoatmosphere | eatm |
| Deciatmosphere | datm |
| Centiatmosphere | catm |
| Milliatmosphere | matm |
| Microatmosphere | uatm |
| Nanoatmosphere | natm |
| Picoatmosphere | patm |
| Femtoatmosphere | fatm |
| Attoatmosphere | aatm |

Figure 27.39 shows a conversion of pressures.

**Figure 27.39**
This table converts between the pressure units in the left column and the various units along the top row.

| | | | | | D6 | | $f_x$ | =CONVERT(1,$C6,D$5) | | |
|---|---|---|---|---|---|---|---|---|---|---|

| | A | B | C | D | E | F |
|---|---|---|---|---|---|---|
| 3 | | Pressure | | TO----> | | |
| 4 | | | | Pascal | Atmosphere | mm of Mercury |
| 5 | | | Pa | atm | mmHg | |
| 6 | FROM | Pascal | Pa | 1 | 9.8692E-06 | 0.00750062 |
| 7 | | Atmosphere | atm | 101324.997 | 1 | 760 |
| 8 | | mm of Mercury | mmHg | 133.322364 | 0.00131579 | 1 |
| 9 | | exaatmosphere | Eatm | 1.0132E+23 | 1E+18 | 7.6E+20 |
| 10 | | petaatmosphere | Patm | 1.0132E+20 | 1E+15 | 7.6E+17 |
| 11 | | teraatmosphere | Tatm | 1.0132E+17 | 1E+12 | 7.6E+14 |
| 12 | | gigaatmosphere | Gatm | 1.0132E+14 | 1000000000 | 7.6E+11 |
| 13 | | megaatmosphere | Matm | 1.0132E+11 | 1000000 | 760000000 |
| 14 | | kiloatmosphere | katm | 101324997 | 1000 | 760000 |
| 15 | | hectoatmosphere | hatm | 10132499.7 | 100 | 76000 |
| 16 | | dekaoatmosphere | eatm | 1013249.97 | 10 | 7600 |
| 17 | | deciatmosphere | datm | 10132.4997 | 0.1 | 76 |
| 18 | | centiatmosphere | catm | 1013.24997 | 0.01 | 7.6 |
| 19 | | milliatmosphere | matm | 101.324997 | 0.001 | 0.76 |
| 20 | | microatmosphere | uatm | 0.101325 | 0.000001 | 0.00076 |
| 21 | | nanoatmosphere | natm | 0.00010132 | 1E-09 | 0.00000076 |
| 22 | | picoatmosphere | patm | 1.0132E-07 | 1E-12 | 7.6E-10 |
| 23 | | femtoatmosphere | fatm | 1.0132E-10 | 1E-15 | 7.6E-13 |
| 24 | | attoatmosphere | aatm | 1.0132E-13 | 1E-18 | 7.6E-16 |
| 25 | | | | | | |

27

Table 27.10 shows conversion values for units of force.

**TABLE 27.10    UNITS OF FORCE**

| Unit of Force | Abbreviation to Use in CONVERT |
| --- | --- |
| Newton | N |
| Dyne | dyn |
| Pound force | lbf |
| Exanewton | EN |
| Petanewton | PN |
| Teranewton | TN |
| Giganewton | GN |
| Meganewton | MN |
| Kilonewton | kN |
| Hectonewton | hN |
| Dekaonewton | eN |
| Decinewton | dN |
| Centinewton | cN |
| Millinewton | mN |
| Micronewton | uN |
| Nanonewton | nN |
| Piconewton | pN |
| Femtonewton | fN |
| Attonewton | aN |
| Exadyne | Edyn |
| Petadyne | Pdyn |
| Teradyne | Tdyn |
| Gigadyne | Gdyn |
| Megadyne | Mdyn |
| Kilodyne | kdyn |
| Hectodyne | hdyn |
| Dekaodyne | edyn |
| Decidyne | ddyn |
| Centidyne | cdyn |
| Millidyne | mdyn |
| Microdyne | udyn |

| Unit of Force | Abbreviation to Use in CONVERT |
|---|---|
| Nanodyne | ndyn |
| Picodyne | pdyn |
| Femtodyne | fdyn |
| Attodyne | adyn |

Figure 27.40 shows a conversion of forces.

**Figure 27.40**
This table converts between the force units in the left column and the various units along the top row.

D6 =CONVERT(1,$C6,D$5)

| | A | B | C | D | E | F |
|---|---|---|---|---|---|---|
| 4 | | | | Newton | Dyne | Pound force |
| 5 | | | | N | dyn | lbf |
| 6 | FROM | Newton | N | 1 | 100000 | 0.224808924 |
| 7 | | Dyne | dyn | 0.00001 | 1 | 2.24809E-06 |
| 8 | | Pound force | lbf | 4.448222 | 444822.2 | 1 |
| 9 | | exanewton | EN | 1E+18 | 1E+23 | 2.24809E+17 |
| 10 | | petanewton | PN | 1E+15 | 1E+20 | 2.24809E+14 |
| 11 | | teranewton | TN | 1E+12 | 1E+17 | 2.24809E+11 |
| 12 | | giganewton | GN | 1000000000 | 1E+14 | 224808923.7 |
| 13 | | meganewton | MN | 1000000 | 1E+11 | 224808.9237 |
| 14 | | kilonewton | kN | 1000 | 100000000 | 224.8089237 |
| 15 | | hectonewton | hN | 100 | 10000000 | 22.48089237 |
| 16 | | dekaonewton | eN | 10 | 1000000 | 2.248089237 |
| 17 | | decinewton | dN | 0.1 | 10000 | 0.022480892 |
| 18 | | centinewton | cN | 0.01 | 1000 | 0.002248089 |
| 19 | | millinewton | mN | 0.001 | 100 | 0.000224809 |
| 20 | | micronewton | uN | 0.000001 | 0.1 | 2.24809E-07 |
| 21 | | nanonewton | nN | 0.000000001 | 0.0001 | 2.24809E-10 |
| 22 | | piconewton | pN | 1E-12 | 0.0000001 | 2.24809E-13 |
| 23 | | femtonewton | fN | 1E-15 | 1E-10 | 2.24809E-16 |
| 24 | | attonewton | aN | 1E-18 | 1E-13 | 2.24809E-19 |
| 25 | | exadyne | Edyn | 1E+13 | 1E+18 | 2.24809E+12 |
| 26 | | petadyne | Pdyn | 10000000000 | 1E+15 | 2248089237 |
| 27 | | teradyne | Tdyn | 10000000 | 1E+12 | 2248089.237 |
| 28 | | gigadyne | Gdyn | 10000 | 1000000000 | 2248.089237 |
| 29 | | megadyne | Mdyn | 10 | 1000000 | 2.248089237 |
| 30 | | kilodyne | kdyn | 0.01 | 1000 | 0.002248089 |
| 31 | | hectodyne | hdyn | 0.001 | 100 | 0.000224809 |
| 32 | | dekaodyne | edyn | 0.0001 | 10 | 2.24809E-05 |
| 33 | | decidyne | ddyn | 0.000001 | 0.1 | 2.24809E-07 |
| 34 | | centidyne | cdyn | 0.0000001 | 0.01 | 2.24809E-08 |
| 35 | | millidyne | mdyn | 0.00000001 | 0.001 | 2.24809E-09 |
| 36 | | microdyne | udyn | 1E-11 | 0.000001 | 2.24809E-12 |
| 37 | | nanodyne | ndyn | 1E-14 | 0.000000001 | 2.24809E-15 |
| 38 | | picodyne | pdyn | 1E-17 | 1E-12 | 2.24809E-18 |
| 39 | | femtodyne | fdyn | 1E-20 | 1E-15 | 2.24809E-21 |
| 40 | | attodyne | adyn | 1E-23 | 1E-18 | 2.24809E-24 |
| 41 | | | | | | |

Table 27.11 shows conversions available for energy.

**Table 27.11 Units of Energy***

| Unit of Energy | Abbreviation to Use in CONVERT |
|---|---|
| Joule | J |
| Erg | e |
| Thermodynamic calorie | c |
| IT calorie | cal |
| Electron volt | eV |

*continues*

27

## TABLE 27.11 CONTINUED

| Unit of Energy | Abbreviation to Use in CONVERT |
| --- | --- |
| Horsepower-hour | HPh |
| Watt-hour | Wh |
| Foot-pound | flb |
| BTU | BTU |
| Exajoule | EJ |
| Petajoule | PJ |
| Terajoule | TJ |
| Gigajoule | GJ |
| Megajoule | MJ |
| Kilojoule | kJ |
| Hectojoule | hJ |
| Dekaojoule | eJ |
| Decijoule | dJ |
| Centijoule | cJ |
| Millijoule | mJ |
| Microjoule | uJ |
| Nanojoule | nJ |
| Picojoule | pJ |
| Femtojoule | fJ |
| Attojoule | aJ |

*This table shows the complete metric prefixes for joules. Similar metric prefixes can also be applied to ergs, thermodynamic calories, IT calories, electron volts, and Watt-hours. This adds 80 additional measurements available in the CONVERT function for Energy.*

Figure 27.41 shows a conversion of energies.

27

**Figure 27.41**
This table converts between the energy units in the left column and the various units along the top row.

D7 ▼ _fx_ =CONVERT(1,$C7,D$5)

|  |  |  | Joule | Erg | Thermodynamic calorie | IT calorie | Electron volt | Horsepower-hour | Watt-hour | Foot-pound | BTU |
|---|---|---|---|---|---|---|---|---|---|---|---|
|  |  |  | J | e | c | cal | eV | HPh | Wh | flb | BTU |
| FROM | Joule | J | 1 | 9999995.193 | 0.239006249 | 0.238846 | 6.24E+18 | 3.72506E-07 | 0.000278 | 23.73042 | 0.000948 |
|  | Erg | e | 1E-07 | 1 | 2.39006E-08 | 2.39E-08 | 6.24E+11 | 3.72507E-14 | 2.78E-11 | 2.37E-06 | 9.48E-11 |
|  | Thermodynamic calorie | c | 4.183991014 | 41839890.03 | 1 | 0.99933 | 2.61E+19 | 1.55856E-06 | 0.001162 | 99.28787 | 0.003966 |
|  | IT calorie | cal | 4.186794846 | 41867928.34 | 1.000670133 | 1 | 2.61E+19 | 1.55961E-06 | 0.001163 | 99.35441 | 0.003968 |
|  | Electron volt | eV | 1.60219E-19 | 1.60219E-12 | 3.82933E-20 | 3.83E-20 | 1 | 5.96826E-26 | 4.45E-23 | 3.8E-18 | 1.52E-22 |
|  | Horsepower-hour | HPh | 2684517.413 | 2.68452E+13 | 641616.4386 | 641186.8 | 1.68E+25 | 1 | 745.6997 | 63704732 | 2544.426 |
|  | Watt-hour | Wh | 3599.998206 | 35999964752 | 860.4220692 | 859.8459 | 2.25E+22 | 0.001341022 | 1 | 85429.48 | 3.412133 |
|  | Foot-pound | flb | 0.04214 | 421399.8007 | 0.010071723 | 0.010065 | 2.63E+17 | 1.56974E-08 | 1.17E-05 | 1 | 3.99E-05 |
|  | BTU | BTU | 1055.058138 | 10550576307 | 252.1654885 | 251.9966 | 6.59E+21 | 0.000393016 | 0.293072 | 25036.98 | 1 |
|  | exajoule | EJ | 1E+18 | 1E+25 | 2.39006E+17 | 2.39E+17 | 6.24E+36 | 3.72506E+11 | 2.78E+14 | 2.37E+19 | 9.48E+14 |
|  | petajoule | PJ | 1E+15 | 1E+22 | 2.39006E+14 | 2.39E+14 | 6.24E+33 | 372506430.8 | 2.78E+11 | 2.37E+16 | 9.48E+11 |
|  | terajoule | TJ | 1E+12 | 1E+19 | 2.39006E+11 | 2.39E+11 | 6.24E+30 | 372506.4308 | 2.78E+08 | 2.37E+13 | 9.48E+08 |
|  | gigajoule | GJ | 1000000000 | 1E+16 | 239006249.5 | 2.39E+08 | 6.24E+27 | 372.5064308 | 277777.9 | 2.37E+10 | 947815.1 |
|  | megajoule | MJ | 1000000 | 1E+13 | 239006.2495 | 238846.2 | 6.24E+24 | 0.372506431 | 277.7779 | 23730422 | 947.8151 |
|  | kilojoule | kJ | 1000 | 9999995193 | 239.0062495 | 238.8462 | 6.24E+21 | 0.000372506 | 0.277778 | 23730.42 | 0.947815 |
|  | hectojoule | hJ | 100 | 999999519.3 | 23.90062495 | 23.88462 | 6.24E+20 | 3.72506E-05 | 0.027778 | 2373.042 | 0.094782 |
|  | dekaojoule | eJ | 10 | 99999951.93 | 2.390062495 | 2.388462 | 6.24E+19 | 3.72506E-06 | 0.002778 | 237.3042 | 0.009478 |
|  | decijoule | dJ | 0.1 | 999999.5193 | 0.023900625 | 0.023885 | 6.24E+17 | 3.72506E-08 | 2.78E-05 | 2.373042 | 9.48E-05 |
|  | centijoule | cJ | 0.01 | 99999.95193 | 0.002390062 | 0.002388 | 6.24E+16 | 3.72506E-09 | 2.78E-06 | 0.237304 | 9.48E-06 |
|  | millijoule | mJ | 0.001 | 9999.995193 | 0.000239006 | 0.000239 | 6.24E+15 | 3.72506E-10 | 2.78E-07 | 0.023730 | 9.48E-07 |
|  | microjoule | uJ | 0.000001 | 9.999995193 | 2.39006E-07 | 2.39E-07 | 6.24E+12 | 3.72506E-13 | 2.78E-10 | 2.37E-05 | 9.48E-10 |
|  | nanojoule | nJ | 0.000000001 | 0.009999995 | 2.39006E-10 | 2.39E-10 | 6.24E+09 | 3.72506E-16 | 2.78E-13 | 2.37E-08 | 9.48E-13 |
|  | picojoule | pJ | 1E-12 | 1E-05 | 2.39006E-13 | 2.39E-13 | 6241457 | 3.72506E-19 | 2.78E-16 | 2.37E-11 | 9.48E-16 |
|  | femtojoule | fJ | 1E-15 | 1E-08 | 2.39006E-16 | 2.39E-16 | 6241.457 | 3.72506E-22 | 2.78E-19 | 2.37E-14 | 9.48E-19 |
|  | attojoule | aJ | 1E-18 | 1E-11 | 2.39006E-19 | 2.39E-19 | 6.241457 | 3.72506E-25 | 2.78E-22 | 2.37E-17 | 9.48E-22 |
|  | The metric prefixes also apply to e, c, cal, eV, Wh |  |  |  |  |  |  |  |  |  |  |

Table 27.12 shows conversions available for power.

## TABLE 27.12 UNITS OF POWER

| Unit of Power | Abbreviation to Use in CONVERT |
|---|---|
| Horsepower | HP |
| Watt | W |
| Exawatt | EW |
| Petawatt | PW |
| Terawatt | TW |
| Gigawatt | GW |
| Megawatt | MW |
| Kilowatt | kW |
| Hectowatt | hW |
| Dekaowatt | eW |
| Deciwatt | dW |
| Centiwatt | cW |

27

_continues_

## TABLE 27.12 CONTINUED

| Unit of Power | Abbreviation to Use in CONVERT |
|---|---|
| Milliwatt | mW |
| Microwatt | uW |
| Nanowatt | nW |
| Picowatt | pW |
| Femtowatt | fW |
| Attowatt | aW |

Figure 27.42 shows a conversion of powers.

**Figure 27.42**
This table converts between the power units in the left column and the various units along the top row.

| | | | D6 | ▼ | fx | =CONVERT(1,$C6,D$5) | |
|---|---|---|---|---|---|---|---|
| | A | B | C | D | E | | |
| 3 | | **Power** | | TO----> | | | |
| 4 | | | | Horsepower | Watt | | |
| 5 | | | | **HP** | **W** | | |
| 6 | FROM | Horsepower | HP | 1 | 745.701 | | |
| 7 | | Watt | W | 0.00134102 | 1 | | |
| 8 | | exawatt | EW | 1.341E+15 | 1E+18 | | |
| 9 | | petawatt | PW | 1.341E+12 | 1E+15 | | |
| 10 | | terawatt | TW | 1341020060 | 1E+12 | | |
| 11 | | gigawatt | GW | 1341020.06 | 1000000000 | | |
| 12 | | megawatt | MW | 1341.02006 | 1000000 | | |
| 13 | | kilowatt | kW | 1.34102006 | 1000 | | |
| 14 | | hectowatt | hW | 0.13410201 | 100 | | |
| 15 | | dekaowatt | eW | 0.0134102 | 10 | | |
| 16 | | deciwatt | dW | 0.0001341 | 0.1 | | |
| 17 | | centiwatt | cW | 1.341E-05 | 0.01 | | |
| 18 | | milliwatt | mW | 1.341E-06 | 0.001 | | |
| 19 | | microwatt | uW | 1.341E-09 | 0.000001 | | |
| 20 | | nanowatt | nW | 1.341E-12 | 1E-09 | | |
| 21 | | picowatt | pW | 1.341E-15 | 1E-12 | | |
| 22 | | femtowatt | fW | 1.341E-18 | 1E-15 | | |
| 23 | | attowatt | aW | 1.341E-21 | 1E-18 | | |
| 24 | | | | | | | |

Table 27.13 shows conversions available for units of magnetism.

## TABLE 27.13 UNITS OF MAGNETISM

| Unit of Magnetism | Abbreviation to Use in CONVERT |
|---|---|
| Tesla | T |
| Gauss | Ga |

| Unit of Magnetism | Abbreviation to Use in CONVERT |
|---|---|
| Exatesla | ET |
| Petatesla | PT |
| Teratesla | TT |
| Gigatesla | GT |
| Megatesla | MT |
| Kilotesla | kT |
| Hectotesla | hT |
| Dekaotesla | eT |
| Decitesla | dT |
| Centitesla | cT |
| Millitesla | mT |
| Microtesla | uT |
| Nanotesla | nT |
| Picotesla | pT |
| Femtotesla | fT |
| Attotesla | aT |
| Exagauss | Ega |
| Petagauss | Pga |
| Teragauss | Tga |
| Gigagauss | Gga |
| Megagauss | Mga |
| Kilogauss | kga |
| Hectogauss | hga |
| Dekaogauss | ega |
| Decigauss | dga |
| Centigauss | cga |
| Milligauss | mga |
| Microgauss | uga |
| Nanogauss | nga |
| Picogauss | pga |
| Femtogauss | fga |
| Attogauss | aga |

27

Figure 27.43 shows a conversion of magnetisms.

**Figure 27.43**
This table converts between the magnetism units in the left column and the various units along the top row.

D6 =CONVERT(1,$C6,D$5)

| | A | B | C | D | E |
|---|---|---|---|---|---|
| 3 | | **Magnetism** | | TO----> | |
| 4 | | | | Tesla | Gauss |
| 5 | | | | T | ga |
| 6 | FROM | Tesla | T | 1 | 10000 |
| 7 | | Gauss | ga | 0.0001 | 1 |
| 8 | | exatesla | ET | 1E+18 | 1E+22 |
| 9 | | petatesla | PT | 1E+15 | 1E+19 |
| 10 | | teratesla | TT | 1E+12 | 1E+16 |
| 11 | | gigatesla | GT | 1000000000 | 1E+13 |
| 12 | | megatesla | MT | 1000000 | 10000000000 |
| 13 | | kilotesla | kT | 1000 | 10000000 |
| 14 | | hectotesla | hT | 100 | 1000000 |
| 15 | | dekaotesla | eT | 10 | 100000 |
| 16 | | decitesla | dT | 0.1 | 1000 |
| 17 | | centitesla | cT | 0.01 | 100 |
| 18 | | millitesla | mT | 0.001 | 10 |
| 19 | | microtesla | uT | 0.000001 | 0.01 |
| 20 | | nanotesla | nT | 0.000000001 | 0.00001 |
| 21 | | picotesla | pT | 1E-12 | 0.00000001 |
| 22 | | femtotesla | fT | 1E-15 | 1E-11 |
| 23 | | attotesla | aT | 1E-18 | 1E-14 |
| 24 | | exagauss | Ega | 1E+14 | 1E+18 |
| 25 | | petagauss | Pga | 1E+11 | 1E+15 |
| 26 | | teragauss | Tga | 100000000 | 1E+12 |
| 27 | | gigagauss | Gga | 100000 | 1000000000 |
| 28 | | megagauss | Mga | 100 | 1000000 |
| 29 | | kilogauss | kga | 0.1 | 1000 |
| 30 | | hectogauss | hga | 0.01 | 100 |
| 31 | | dekaogauss | ega | 0.001 | 10 |
| 32 | | decigauss | dga | 0.00001 | 0.1 |
| 33 | | centigauss | cga | 0.000001 | 0.01 |
| 34 | | milligauss | mga | 0.0000001 | 0.001 |
| 35 | | microgauss | uga | 1E-10 | 0.000001 |
| 36 | | nanogauss | nga | 1E-13 | 0.000000001 |
| 37 | | picogauss | pga | 1E-16 | 1E-12 |
| 38 | | femtogauss | fga | 1E-19 | 1E-15 |
| 39 | | attogauss | aga | 1E-22 | 1E-18 |
| 40 | | | | | |

Table 27.14 shows conversion factors available for temperature systems.

**Table 27.14 Units of Temperature**

| Unit of Temperature | Abbreviation to Use in CONVERT |
|---|---|
| Degree Celsius | C |
| Degree Fahrenheit | F |
| Degree Kelvin | K |

Figure 27.44 shows a conversion of temperature systems.

**Figure 27.44**
This table converts between the temperature scales in the left column and the various scales along the top row.

D7 =CONVERT(1,$C7,D$5)

| | A | B | C | D | E | F | G |
|---|---|---|---|---|---|---|---|
| 3 | | **Temperature** | | TO----> | | | |
| 4 | | | | Degree Celsius | Degree Fahrenheit | Degree Kelvin | |
| 5 | | | | C | F | K | |
| 6 | FROM | Degree Celsius | C | 1 | 33.8 | 274.15 | |
| 7 | | Degree Fahrenheit | F | -17.2222222 | 1 | 255.928 | |
| 8 | | Degree Kelvin | K | -272.15 | -457.87 | 1 | |
| 9 | | | | | | | |

Table 27.15 shows conversion units available for liquid measurements.

**TABLE 27.15   UNITS OF LIQUID MEASURE**

| Unit of Liquid Measure | Abbreviation to Use in CONVERT |
| --- | --- |
| Teaspoon | tsp |
| Tablespoon | tbs |
| Fluid ounce | oz |
| Cup | cup |
| U.S. pint | pt |
| U.K. pint | uk_pt |
| Quart | qt |
| Gallon | gal |
| Liter | l |
| Exaliter | El |
| Petaliter | Pl |
| Teraliter | Tl |
| Gigaliter | Gl |
| Megaliter | Ml |
| Kiloliter | kl |
| Hectoliter | hl |
| Dekaoliter | el |
| Deciliter | dl |
| Centiliter | cl |
| Milliliter | ml |
| Microliter | ul |
| Nanoliter | nl |
| Picoliter | pl |
| Femtoliter | fl |
| Attoliter | al |

27

Figure 27.45 shows a conversion of liquid measures.

**Figure 27.45**
This table converts between the liquid measurement units in the left column and the various units along the top row.

D7 =CONVERT(1,$C7,D$5)

| | A | B | C | D | E | F | G | H | I | J | K | L |
|---|---|---|---|---|---|---|---|---|---|---|---|---|
| 3 | | **Liquid Measure** | | TO---> | | | | | | | | |
| 4 | | | | Teaspoon | Tablespoon | Fluid ounce | Cup | U.S. pint | U.K. pint | Quart | Gallon | Liter |
| 5 | | | | tsp | tbs | oz | cup | pt | uk_pt | qt | gal | l |
| 6 | FROM | Teaspoon | tsp | 1 | 0.33333333 | 0.166666667 | 0.02083 | 0.01042 | 0.008675585 | 0.00521 | 0.0013 | 0.00493 |
| 7 | | Tablespoon | tbs | 3 | 1 | 0.5 | 0.0625 | 0.03125 | 0.026026756 | 0.01563 | 0.00391 | 0.01479 |
| 8 | | Fluid ounce | oz | 6 | 2 | 1 | 0.125 | 0.0625 | 0.052053511 | 0.03125 | 0.00781 | 0.02958 |
| 9 | | Cup | cup | 48 | 16 | 8 | 1 | 0.5 | 0.416428088 | 0.25 | 0.0625 | 0.23664 |
| 10 | | U.S. pint | pt | 96 | 32 | 16 | 2 | 1 | 0.832856176 | 0.5 | 0.125 | 0.47328 |
| 11 | | U.K. pint | uk_pt | 115.266 | 38.422 | 19.211 | 2.40138 | 1.20069 | 1 | 0.60034 | 0.15009 | 0.56826 |
| 12 | | Quart | qt | 192 | 64 | 32 | 4 | 2 | 1.665712352 | 1 | 0.25 | 0.94656 |
| 13 | | Gallon | gal | 768 | 256 | 128 | 16 | 8 | 6.662849409 | 4 | 1 | 3.78624 |
| 14 | | Liter | l | 202.84 | 67.6133333 | 33.80666667 | 4.22583 | 2.11292 | 1.759755696 | 1.05646 | 0.26411 | 1 |
| 15 | | exaliter | El | 2.0284E+20 | 6.7613E+19 | 3.38067E+19 | 4.2E+18 | 2.1E+18 | 1.75976E+18 | 1.1E+18 | 2.6E+17 | 1E+18 |
| 16 | | petaliter | Pl | 2.0284E+17 | 6.7613E+16 | 3.38067E+16 | 4.2E+15 | 2.1E+15 | 1.75976E+15 | 1.1E+15 | 2.6E+14 | 1E+15 |
| 17 | | teraliter | Tl | 2.0284E+14 | 6.7613E+13 | 3.38067E+13 | 4.2E+12 | 2.1E+12 | 1.75976E+12 | 1.1E+12 | 2.6E+11 | 1E+12 |
| 18 | | gigaliter | Gl | 2.0284E+11 | 6.7613E+10 | 33806666667 | 4.2E+09 | 2.1E+09 | 1759755696 | 1.1E+09 | 2.6E+08 | 1E+09 |
| 19 | | megaliter | Ml | 202840000 | 67613333.3 | 33806666.67 | 4225833 | 2112917 | 1759755.696 | 1056458 | 264115 | 1000000 |
| 20 | | kiloliter | kl | 202840 | 67613.3333 | 33806.66667 | 4225.83 | 2112.92 | 1759.755696 | 1056.46 | 264.115 | 1000 |
| 21 | | hectoliter | hl | 20284 | 6761.33333 | 3380.666667 | 422.583 | 211.292 | 175.9755696 | 105.646 | 26.4115 | 100 |
| 22 | | dekaoliter | el | 2028.4 | 676.133333 | 338.0666667 | 42.2583 | 21.1292 | 17.59755696 | 10.5646 | 2.64115 | 10 |
| 23 | | deciliter | dl | 20.284 | 6.76133333 | 3.380666667 | 0.42258 | 0.21129 | 0.17597557 | 0.10565 | 0.02641 | 0.1 |
| 24 | | centiliter | cl | 2.0284 | 0.67613333 | 0.338066667 | 0.04226 | 0.02113 | 0.017597557 | 0.01056 | 0.00264 | 0.01 |
| 25 | | milliliter | ml | 0.20284 | 0.06761333 | 0.033806667 | 0.00423 | 0.00211 | 0.001759756 | 0.00106 | 0.00026 | 0.001 |
| 26 | | microliter | ul | 0.00020284 | 6.7613E-05 | 3.38067E-05 | 4.2E-06 | 2.1E-06 | 1.75976E-06 | 1.1E-06 | 2.6E-07 | 1E-06 |
| 27 | | nanoliter | nl | 2.0284E-07 | 6.7613E-08 | 3.38067E-08 | 4.2E-09 | 2.1E-09 | 1.75976E-09 | 1.1E-09 | 2.6E-10 | 1E-09 |
| 28 | | picoliter | pl | 2.0284E-10 | 6.7613E-11 | 3.38067E-11 | 4.2E-12 | 2.1E-12 | 1.75976E-12 | 1.1E-12 | 2.6E-13 | 1E-12 |
| 29 | | femtoliter | fl | 2.0284E-13 | 6.7613E-14 | 3.38067E-14 | 4.2E-15 | 2.1E-15 | 1.75976E-15 | 1.1E-15 | 2.6E-16 | 1E-15 |
| 30 | | attoliter | al | 2.0284E-16 | 6.7613E-17 | 3.38067E-17 | 4.2E-18 | 2.1E-18 | 1.75976E-18 | 1.1E-18 | 2.6E-19 | 1E-18 |
| 31 | | | | | | | | | | | | |

## Using DELTA or GESTEP to Filter a Set of Values

The functions `DELTA` and `GESTEP` are left over from a long-ago era. In the `SUMPRODUCT` function, you can see that Excel can now evaluate `TRUE*100` as `100` and `FALSE*100` as `0`. In early spreadsheet programs, you needed to explicitly convert TRUE to 1 and FALSE to 0. These two functions explicitly return `1` when a condition is true and `0` when a condition is false, allowing you to multiply the original number by the function in order to get conditional sums.

`DELTA` tests whether two values are equal. `GESTEP` tests whether a value is greater than or equal to a threshold value.

### Syntax: `DELTA(`*`number1`*`,`*`number2`*`)`

The `DELTA` function tests whether two values are equal. It returns `1` if *`number1`* equals *`number2`*; it returns `0` otherwise. You use this function to filter a set of values. For example, by summing several `DELTA` functions, you can calculate the count of equal pairs. This function is also known as the Kronecker Delta function. This function takes the following arguments:

27

- *`number1`*—This is the first number.
- *`number2`*—This is the second number. If omitted, *`number2`* is assumed to be `0`.

If either *`number1`* or *`number2`* is nonnumeric, `DELTA` returns a `#VALUE!` error.

Figure 27.46 shows a list of students and their test scores in Columns A and B. A large matrix of `DELTA` functions in C:W counts how many students achieved each score. Excel has many newer, better functions, such as `COUNTIF`, that can also achieve this result.

**Figure 27.46**
The DELTA functions in C2:W24 check whether the score in Column B is the same as the score in Row 1. Totals in row 25 complete the analysis.

C2 =DELTA($B2,C$1)

| | A STUDENT | B SCORE | C 80 | D 81 | E 82 | F 83 | G 84 | H 85 | I 86 | J 87 | K 88 | L 89 | M 90 | N 91 | O 92 | P 93 | Q 94 | R 95 | S 96 | T 97 | U 98 | V 99 | W 100 |
|---|---|---|---|---|---|---|---|---|---|---|---|---|---|---|---|---|---|---|---|---|---|---|---|
| 2 | RAYMOND | 81 | 0 | 1 | 0 | 0 | 0 | 0 | 0 | 0 | 0 | 0 | 0 | 0 | 0 | 0 | 0 | 0 | 0 | 0 | 0 | 0 | 0 |
| 3 | SEAN | 100 | 0 | 0 | 0 | 0 | 0 | 0 | 0 | 0 | 0 | 0 | 0 | 0 | 0 | 0 | 0 | 0 | 0 | 0 | 0 | 0 | 1 |
| 4 | ERIN | 100 | 0 | 0 | 0 | 0 | 0 | 0 | 0 | 0 | 0 | 0 | 0 | 0 | 0 | 0 | 0 | 0 | 0 | 0 | 0 | 0 | 1 |
| 5 | JACK | 90 | 0 | 0 | 0 | 0 | 0 | 0 | 0 | 0 | 0 | 0 | 1 | 0 | 0 | 0 | 0 | 0 | 0 | 0 | 0 | 0 | 0 |
| 6 | BRYAN | 90 | 0 | 0 | 0 | 0 | 0 | 0 | 0 | 0 | 0 | 0 | 1 | 0 | 0 | 0 | 0 | 0 | 0 | 0 | 0 | 0 | 0 |
| 7 | RANDY | 85 | 0 | 0 | 0 | 0 | 0 | 1 | 0 | 0 | 0 | 0 | 0 | 0 | 0 | 0 | 0 | 0 | 0 | 0 | 0 | 0 | 0 |
| 8 | HOWARD | 92 | 0 | 0 | 0 | 0 | 0 | 0 | 0 | 0 | 0 | 0 | 0 | 0 | 1 | 0 | 0 | 0 | 0 | 0 | 0 | 0 | 0 |
| 9 | TERESA | 90 | 0 | 0 | 0 | 0 | 0 | 0 | 0 | 0 | 0 | 0 | 1 | 0 | 0 | 0 | 0 | 0 | 0 | 0 | 0 | 0 | 0 |
| 10 | ELLA | 89 | 0 | 0 | 0 | 0 | 0 | 0 | 0 | 0 | 0 | 1 | 0 | 0 | 0 | 0 | 0 | 0 | 0 | 0 | 0 | 0 | 0 |
| 11 | BETTY | 83 | 0 | 0 | 0 | 1 | 0 | 0 | 0 | 0 | 0 | 0 | 0 | 0 | 0 | 0 | 0 | 0 | 0 | 0 | 0 | 0 | 0 |
| 12 | LUZ | 89 | 0 | 0 | 0 | 0 | 0 | 0 | 0 | 0 | 0 | 1 | 0 | 0 | 0 | 0 | 0 | 0 | 0 | 0 | 0 | 0 | 0 |
| 13 | ALICIA | 97 | 0 | 0 | 0 | 0 | 0 | 0 | 0 | 0 | 0 | 0 | 0 | 0 | 0 | 0 | 0 | 0 | 0 | 1 | 0 | 0 | 0 |
| 14 | CHARLENE | 100 | 0 | 0 | 0 | 0 | 0 | 0 | 0 | 0 | 0 | 0 | 0 | 0 | 0 | 0 | 0 | 0 | 0 | 0 | 0 | 0 | 1 |
| 15 | VICTORIA | 83 | 0 | 0 | 0 | 1 | 0 | 0 | 0 | 0 | 0 | 0 | 0 | 0 | 0 | 0 | 0 | 0 | 0 | 0 | 0 | 0 | 0 |
| 16 | LAUREN | 87 | 0 | 0 | 0 | 0 | 0 | 0 | 0 | 1 | 0 | 0 | 0 | 0 | 0 | 0 | 0 | 0 | 0 | 0 | 0 | 0 | 0 |
| 17 | TRACEY | 97 | 0 | 0 | 0 | 0 | 0 | 0 | 0 | 0 | 0 | 0 | 0 | 0 | 0 | 0 | 0 | 0 | 0 | 1 | 0 | 0 | 0 |
| 18 | KYLE | 83 | 0 | 0 | 0 | 1 | 0 | 0 | 0 | 0 | 0 | 0 | 0 | 0 | 0 | 0 | 0 | 0 | 0 | 0 | 0 | 0 | 0 |
| 19 | WILMA | 100 | 0 | 0 | 0 | 0 | 0 | 0 | 0 | 0 | 0 | 0 | 0 | 0 | 0 | 0 | 0 | 0 | 0 | 0 | 0 | 0 | 1 |
| 20 | MARCIA | 89 | 0 | 0 | 0 | 0 | 0 | 0 | 0 | 0 | 0 | 1 | 0 | 0 | 0 | 0 | 0 | 0 | 0 | 0 | 0 | 0 | 0 |
| 21 | WILLIE | 98 | 0 | 0 | 0 | 0 | 0 | 0 | 0 | 0 | 0 | 0 | 0 | 0 | 0 | 0 | 0 | 0 | 0 | 0 | 1 | 0 | 0 |
| 22 | EUGENE | 83 | 0 | 0 | 0 | 1 | 0 | 0 | 0 | 0 | 0 | 0 | 0 | 0 | 0 | 0 | 0 | 0 | 0 | 0 | 0 | 0 | 0 |
| 23 | LEAH | 90 | 0 | 0 | 0 | 0 | 0 | 0 | 0 | 0 | 0 | 0 | 1 | 0 | 0 | 0 | 0 | 0 | 0 | 0 | 0 | 0 | 0 |
| 24 | LORI | 86 | 0 | 0 | 0 | 0 | 0 | 0 | 1 | 0 | 0 | 0 | 0 | 0 | 0 | 0 | 0 | 0 | 0 | 0 | 0 | 0 | 0 |
| 25 | Total | | 0 | 1 | 0 | 4 | 0 | 1 | 1 | 1 | 0 | 3 | 4 | 0 | 1 | 0 | 0 | 0 | 0 | 2 | 1 | 0 | 4 |

**SYNTAX:** GESTEP(*number*,*step*)

The GESTEP function returns 1 if *number* is greater than or equal to *step*; it returns 0 otherwise. You use this function to filter a set of values. For example, by summing several GESTEP functions, you can calculate the count of values that exceed a threshold. This function takes the following arguments:

- *number*—This is the value to test against *step*.
- *step*—This is the threshold value. If you omit a value for *step*, GESTEP uses 0.

If any argument is nonnumeric, GESTEP returns a #VALUE! error.

## USING ERF AND ERFC TO CALCULATE THE ERROR FUNCTION AND ITS COMPLEMENT

An error function is designed to make it easier to represent integrals in the form $x^n \times e$ $(-ax^2)\ dx$. All such integrals can be written in terms of the integral $e^{(-u^2)}\ du$. If you integrate this from 0 to infinity, it converges to SQRT(PI)/2. The ERF function, then, is defined so that ERF converges to 1 at infinity.

The ERF function is ERF(x) = 2/SQRT(PI()) times the integral of $e^{(-u^2)}du$ integrated from 0 to x. The result of ERF is a value between 0 and 1.

Contrary to what Excel Help says, there are two syntax options available in Excel for ERF:

- ERF(*x*)—The common use of ERF is with a single argument. In this case, the function returns the ERF function. In the preceding formula, the integral is evaluated from 0 to x. For example, ERF(0.1) is 0.112463.
- ERF(*lower_limit*,*upper_limit*)—The second syntax for ERF provides a lower and an upper limit. In this case, Excel integrates from x to y.

27

NOTE

> Although ERF is defined for negative values, Excel does not calculate ERF for less than 0.
> If you need to do this, you have to turn to more comprehensive calculation engines, such
> as Mathematica.

The ERFC function provides the complement to ERF. In all cases, ERFC(x) is equal to
1-ERF(x).

Figure 27.47 charts the ERF and ERFC functions.

**Figure 27.47**

ERF quickly con-
verges very close to 1
for values of 3 or
above. ERFC is simply
1 – ERF.

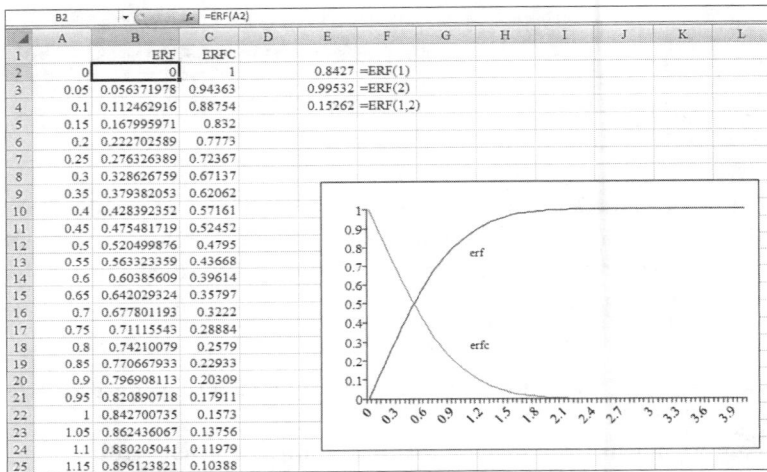

SYNTAX: ERF(x)

In this first syntax, the ERF function returns the error function for x.

SYNTAX: ERF(lower_limit,upper_limit)

In this second syntax, the ERF function returns the error function integrated between
lower_limit and upper_limit. This function takes the following arguments:

- lower_limit—This is the lower bound for integrating ERF.
- upper_limit—This is the upper bound for integrating ERF. If any argument is nonnumeric, ERF returns a #VALUE! error. If any argument is negative, ERF returns a #NUM!
  error.

27

## SYNTAX: ERFC(x)

The ERFC function returns the complementary ERF function integrated between $x$ and infinity. The argument $x$ is the lower bound for integrating ERF. If $x$ is nonnumeric, ERFC returns a #VALUE! error. If $x$ is negative, ERFC returns a #NUM! error.

## CALCULATING THE BESSEL FUNCTIONS

The BESSEL function is useful in many physics applications that involve solving classical partial differential equations in cylindrical coordinates. Excel offers four versions of the BESSEL function:

- BESSELJ—This solves the BESSEL function of the first kind. You use this function to solve BESSEL differential equations that are nonsingular at the origin.

- BESSELY—This solves the BESSEL functions of the second kind. You use this function to solve BESSEL differential equations that are singular at the origin. The BESSEL functions of the second kind are sometimes called Weber or Neumann functions.

- BESSELI—This solves the modified BESSEL differential equation. It is closely related to BESSELJ.

- BESSELK—This solves the modified BESSEL function of the second kind. This function is also known as the Basset function, Macdonald functions, or BESSEL functions of the third kind.

Each Bessel function takes two required arguments:

- $x$—This is the value at which to evaluate the function.
- $n$—This is the order of the BESSEL function. If $n$ is not an integer, it is truncated.

If $x$ is nonnumeric, BESSELI returns a #VALUE! error. If $n$ is nonnumeric, BESSELI returns a #VALUE! error. If $n$ is less than 0, BESSELI returns a #NUM! error.

Figure 27.48 shows the BESSELJ and BESSELY functions for orders of $n$ from 0 through 4.

**Figure 27.48**
This chart shows the BESSELJ and BESSELY functions.

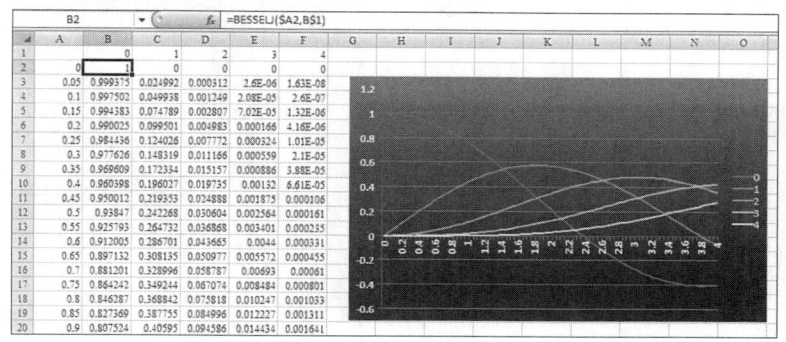

27

# USING THE ANALYSIS TOOLPACK TO PERFORM FAST FOURIER TRANSFORMS (FFTs)

Many of the engineering functions have been promoted from the Analysis Toolpack to the regular version of Excel. However, one feature is left orphaned in the Analysis Toolpack. If you need to perform Fourier analysis, you should install the Analysis Toolpack.

→ **See** "Installing the Analysis Toolpack in Excel 2007," **page 712**, in Chapter 26.

Fourier transforms are used to evaluate the output of an analog-to-digital conversion (ADC). To perform a Fourier Transform, you follow these steps:

1. Import your ADC data into Excel. The ADC record should contain a specific number of records that are powers of 2, up to 4,096 (for example, 2, 4, 8, 16, 32, 64, 128, 256, 512, 1,024, 2,048, or 4,096).

2. Make sure the Analysis Toolpack is installed.

3. From the Data ribbon, choose Data Analysis.

4. Select Fourier Analysis and click OK. The Fourier Analysis dialog appears.

5. In the Fourier Analysis dialog, select your ADC data as the input range. If your input range includes a heading, check the Labels in First Row box. In this case, your data must be $(n^2) + 1$ records long.

6. Choose the top-left cell of the output range.

7. Leave the Inverse check box unchecked. (It is used to convert FFT numbers in imaginary format back to the ADC format).

8. Click OK to perform the transformation.

In Figure 27.49, the original data is in Column A, and the transformed data is in Column C.

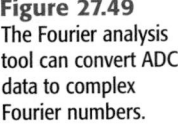

**Figure 27.49**
The Fourier analysis tool can convert ADC data to complex Fourier numbers.

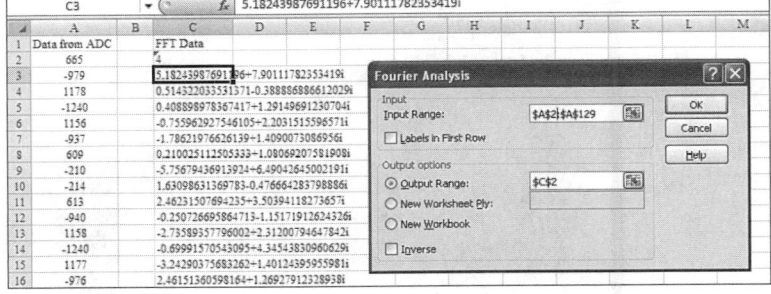

**Excel Troubleshooting: Sharing Workbooks with Legacy Versions**

A total of 89 functions that are part of the core set of functions in Excel 2007 were not included in the core functions of Excel 2003 and earlier.

In prior versions of Excel, the product was shipped with an add-in called the Analysis Toolpack. Hard-core Excel users, such as scientists, engineers, and finance professionals, often turned on the Analysis Toolpack. If you share your Excel 2007 workbook with a person who only occasionally uses Excel, it is possible that he or she has not enabled the Analysis Toolpack.

On a computer that does not have the Analysis Toolpack enabled, any reference to the following functions would automatically return the NAME error:

ACCRINT, ACCRINTM, AMORDEGRC, AMORLINC, BESSELI, BESSELJ, BESSELK, BESSELY, BIN2DEC, BIN2HEX, BIN2OCT, COMPLEX, CONVERT, COUPDAYBS, COUPDAYS, COUPDAYSNC, COUPNCD, COUPNUM, COUPPCD, CUMIPMT, CUMPRINC, DEC2BIN, DEC2HEX, DEC2OCT, DELTA, DISC, DOLLARDE, DOLLARFR, DURATION, EDATE, EFFECT, EOMONTH, ERF, ERFC, FACTDOUBLE, FVSCHEDULE, GCD, GESTEP, HEX2BIN, HEX2DEC, HEX2OCT, IMABS, IMAGINARY, IMARGUMENT, IMCONJUGATE, IMCOS, IMDIV, IMEXP, IMLN, IMLOG10, IMLOG2, IMPOWER, IMREAL, IMSIN, IMSQRT, IMSUB, INTRATE, ISEVEN, ISODD, LCM, MDURATION, MROUND, MULTINOMIAL, NETWORKDAYS, NOMINAL, OCT2BIN, OCT2DEC, OCT2HEX, ODDFPRICE, ODDFYIELD, ODDLPRICE, ODDLYIELD, PRICE, PRICEMAT, QUOTIENT, RANDBETWEEN, RECEIVED, SERIESSUM, SQRTPI, TBILLEQ, TBILLPRICE, TBILLYIELD, WEEKNUM, WORKDAY, XIRR, XNPV, YEARFRAC, YIELD, YIELDDISC, and YIELDMAT.

If you are sharing workbooks that use these function with people using Excel 2003 or earlier, you should remind them that they need to visit Tools, Add-Ins and make sure that the Analysis Toolpack option is checked before they open your workbooks.

27

# CHAPTER 28

# CONNECTING WORKSHEETS, WORKBOOKS, AND EXTERNAL DATA

## In this chapter

In Chapters 20, "Understanding Formulas," and 21, "Controlling Formulas," you learned how to set up formulas that calculate based on values within one worksheet. It is also very easy to connect a worksheet to several other worksheets or to connect various workbooks. Excel 2007 offers easier-than-ever ways to connect a worksheet to data from the Web, data from text files, or data from databases such as Access.

In this chapter, you'll learn how to do the following:

- Connect two worksheets
- Connect two workbooks
- Manage links between workbooks
- Connect to Web data
- Connect to text data
- Connect to Access data
- Manage connections

## CONNECTING TWO WORKSHEETS

Although Excel 2007 offer 17 billion cells on every worksheet, it is fairly common to separate any model onto several different worksheets. You might choose to have one worksheet for each month in a year or to have one worksheet for each functional area of a business. For example, Figure 28.1 shows a workbook with worksheets for revenue and expenses. Because different departments might be responsible for the functional areas, it makes sense to separate them into different worksheets. Eventually, though, you will want to pull information from the various worksheets into a single summary worksheet.

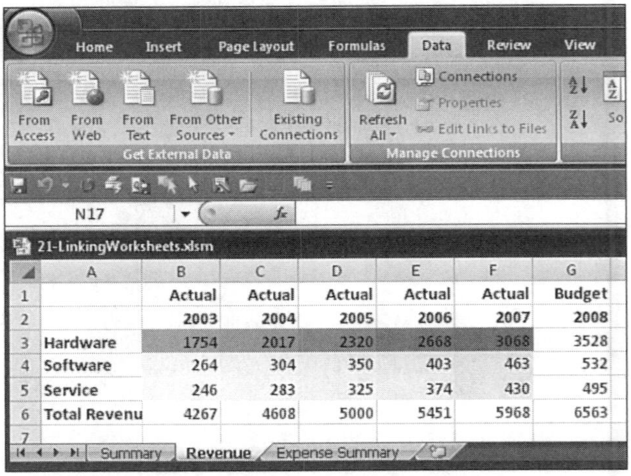

**Figure 28.1**
Different functional areas need to work on budgets for revenue and expenses, so revenue and expenses are kept on separate worksheets.

To create a formula that pulls data from another worksheet, you enter an equals sign to begin the formula, as shown in Figure 28.2.

Rather than try to remember the exact syntax, you can simply point to the correct cell. So after you type the equals sign, click the desired worksheet tab. Using the mouse, click on a cell to get the value from that cell. In Figure 28.3, Excel builds the formula =Revenue!F6 in the formula bar. Excel waits for you to either press the Enter key to accept the formula or press another operator key in order to add other cells to the formula.

When you press the Enter key to accept the formula, Excel jumps back to the starting worksheet. The desired figure is carried through to the worksheet.

**Figure 28.2**
To link to a cell on another worksheet, you start with an equals sign.

| | A | B | C |
|---|---|---|---|
| 1 | XYZ CO | | |
| 2 | BUDGET FOR 2008 | | |
| 3 | | | |
| 4 | | 2007 | 2008 |
| 5 | Revenue | = | |
| 6 | COGS | | |
| 7 | Gross Profit | | |
| 8 | | | |
| 9 | Expenses | | |
| 10 | Net Income | | |
| 11 | | | |
| 12 | 17179869184 | | |

SUM ▾ X ✓ fx =

**Figure 28.3**
Excel builds the syntax for you.

SUM ▾ X ✓ fx =Revenue!F6

| | A | B | C | D | E | F | G |
|---|---|---|---|---|---|---|---|
| 1 | | Actual | Actual | Actual | Actual | Actual | Budget |
| 2 | | 2003 | 2004 | 2005 | 2006 | 2007 | 2008 |
| 3 | Hardware | 1754 | 2017 | 2320 | 2668 | 3068 | 3528 |
| 4 | Software | 264 | 304 | 350 | 403 | 463 | 532 |
| 5 | Service | 246 | 283 | 325 | 374 | 430 | 495 |
| 6 | Total Revenue | 4267 | 4608 | 5000 | 5451 | 5968 | 6563 |

NOTE

The formula that Excel builds is a relative formula. You can easily copy B5 to B6 in order to retrieve the 2008 budget for revenue.

You continue this process until you have built a formula for each cell on the Summary worksheet. Note that it is okay to include an external cell as the argument for a function. Figure 28.4 shows the formula for each cell on the Summary worksheet.

**Figure 28.4**
A variety of formulas can link to various worksheets.

C9 ▾ fx =SUM(Expenses!G4:G7)

| | A | B | C |
|---|---|---|---|
| 1 | XYZ CO | | |
| 2 | BUDGET FOR 2008 | | |
| 3 | | | |
| 4 | | 2007 | 2008 |
| 5 | Revenue | =Revenue!F6 | =Revenue!G6 |
| 6 | COGS | =Expenses!F3 | =Expenses!G3 |
| 7 | Gross Profit | =B5-B6 | =C5-C6 |
| 8 | | | |
| 9 | Expenses | =SUM(Expenses!F4:F7) | =SUM(Expenses!G4:G7) |
| 10 | Net Income | =B7-B9 | =C7-C9 |

28

## SYNTAX DIFFERENCES WHEN A WORKSHEET NAME CONTAINS SPACES

In the examples in the previous section, the syntax is as follows:

```
=sheetname!celladdress
```

This syntax changes when one of the worksheet names contains a space. In this case, you must surround the worksheet name in apostrophes, like this (see Figure 28.5):

```
='sheet name'!celladdress
```

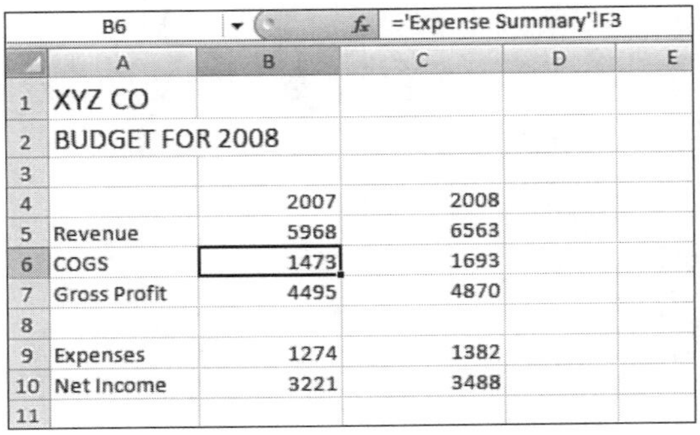

**Figure 28.5**
If a worksheet name contains a space, you must surround the name with apostrophes.

| | A | B | C | D | E |
|---|---|---|---|---|---|
| 1 | XYZ CO | | | | |
| 2 | BUDGET FOR 2008 | | | | |
| 3 | | | | | |
| 4 | | 2007 | 2008 | | |
| 5 | Revenue | 5968 | 6563 | | |
| 6 | COGS | 1473 | 1693 | | |
| 7 | Gross Profit | 4495 | 4870 | | |
| 8 | | | | | |
| 9 | Expenses | 1274 | 1382 | | |
| 10 | Net Income | 3221 | 3488 | | |
| 11 | | | | | |

B6    $f_x$ ='Expense Summary'!F3

# CONNECTING TO A WORKSHEET IN ANOTHER WORKBOOK

It is possible to set up links from a worksheet in one workbook to a worksheet in another workbook. Excel does an excellent job of managing these links and is even able to update values in the destination workbook when the source workbook is closed. It is easiest to create these links while both workbooks are open.

Say that a co-worker in another department maintains a workbook. You need to pull the sum of a few numbers from that workbook into your workbook. Your co-worker's workbook is referred to as the source workbook and your workbook is referred to as the destination workbook. To set up a formula in the destination workbook, which pulls data from the source workbook, follow these steps:

1. Open the destination workbook and leave it open in the background. In Figure 28.6, the destination workbook is the RegionTotals workbook.

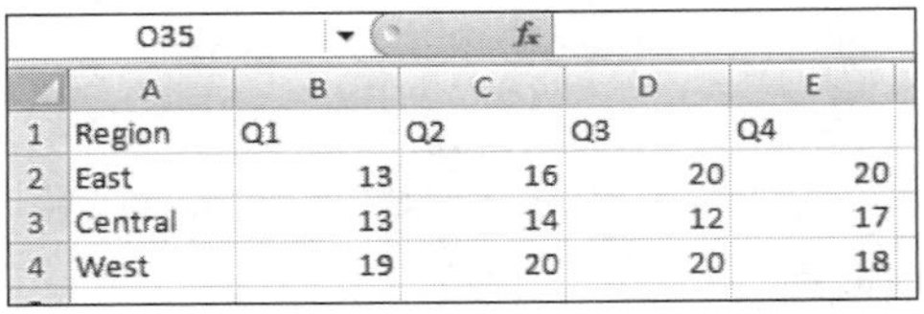

**Figure 28.6**
To pull values from this workbook into another workbook, it is easiest to have this workbook open in the background.

| | A | B | C | D | E |
|---|---|---|---|---|---|
| 1 | Region | Q1 | Q2 | Q3 | Q4 |
| 2 | East | 13 | 16 | 20 | 20 |
| 3 | Central | 13 | 14 | 12 | 17 |
| 4 | West | 19 | 20 | 20 | 18 |

O35    $f_x$

2. Open the destination workbook. In the destination workbook, add a formula. Start by typing **=SUM(** in that cell (see Figure 28.7).

28

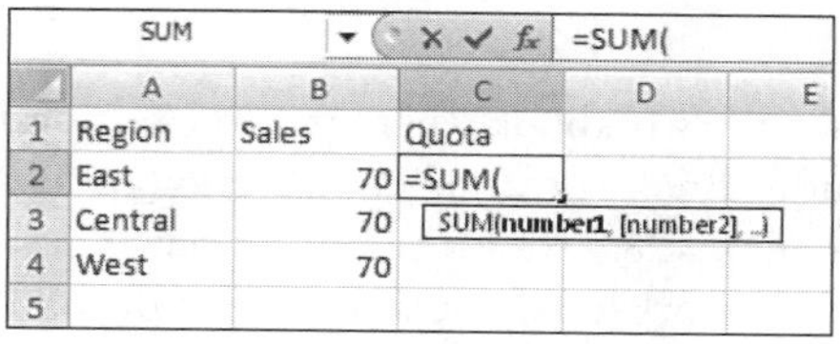

**Figure 28.7**
Rather than typing the reference at this point, it is easier to point to the cell.

| | A | B | C | D | E |
|---|---|---|---|---|---|
| | | | SUM | =SUM( | |
| 1 | Region | Sales | Quota | | |
| 2 | East | | 70 | =SUM( | |
| 3 | Central | | 70 | SUM(number1, [number2], ...) | |
| 4 | West | | 70 | | |
| 5 | | | | | |

3. In the Windows taskbar, click the icon for the source workbook. Using the mouse, click and drag to select the target cells. In the example in the figure, Excel shows that the provisional formula is =SUM([RegionTotals.xlsm]Quota!$B$2:EE$2.

**NOTE**

When you build a link from one worksheet to another worksheet in the same workbook, Excel defaults to using a relative reference for the cell. In Figure 28.8, note that Excel defaults to entering an absolute reference when the selected reference is in another workbook. At the point shown in the figure, you can press F4 three times to return to a relative reference.

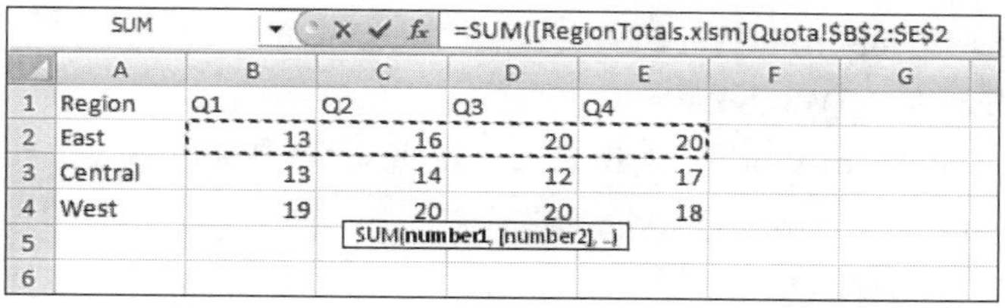

**Figure 28.8**
After you select the cells in another workbook, Excel defaults to an absolute reference.

SUM =SUM([RegionTotals.xlsm]Quota!$B$2:$E$2

| | A | B | C | D | E | F | G |
|---|---|---|---|---|---|---|---|
| 1 | Region | Q1 | Q2 | Q3 | Q4 | | |
| 2 | East | 13 | 16 | 20 | 20 | | |
| 3 | Central | 13 | 14 | 12 | 17 | | |
| 4 | West | 19 | 20 | 20 | 18 | | |
| 5 | | | SUM(number1, [number2], ...) | | | | |
| 6 | | | | | | | |

4. To complete the formula, type the closing parenthesis and then press Enter. You can now copy the formula to other cells in your target workbook.

## SYNTAX VARIATIONS WHEN CREATING LINKS

There are some key syntax variations you must understand when creating links between worksheets and/or workbooks:

- When the worksheet name contains a space, Excel automatically adds apostrophes around the workbook name and sheet name. An example is =SUM('[RegionTotals.xlsm]Forecast Quota'!B4:E4).
- Excel also adds apostrophes when the filename contains a space. An example is =SUM(' [Region Totals.xlsm]ForecastQuota'!B4:E4).
- When Excel refers to a file such as [RegionTotals.xlsm], you can assume that the file is currently open. When you close the linked file, Excel updates the formula in the linking workbook to include the complete pathname. For example, =SUM('C:\[Region Totals.xlsm]Quota'!$B$2:$E$2).
- When you save the linking file, Excel notes the current location of all the linked workbooks. Excel has a problem noting the location if you've linked to a workbook that is not yet saved.

## CREATING LINKS TO UNSAVED WORKBOOKS

Build a formula that links to a source workbook where the source workbook has not been saved. This formula might point to Book1 or Book3 or a workbook such as that. Attempt to save the destination workbook. Figure 28.9 shows a link to a new Book3 workbook. When you attempt to save the destination workbook, Excel presents a dialog that asks Is It OK to Save with References to Unsaved Documents? In general, you should cancel the save, switch to the unsaved source workbook, and then select File, Save As to save the file with a permanent name. Then you can come back to save the linking workbook.

**Figure 28.9**
A link to an unsaved
workbook.

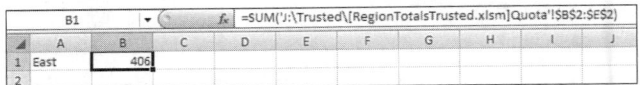

## USING THE LINKS TAB ON THE TRUST CENTER

By default, Excel applies security settings that frustrate your attempts to pull values from closed workbooks. Consider the following scenario using two workbooks labeled Workbook A and Workbook B:

1. Establish a link from Workbook A to Workbook B.
2. Save and close Workbook A.
3. Make changes to Workbook B. Save and close Workbook B.
4. On a future day, open Workbook B.
5. Open Workbook A.
6. In this case, the new values in Workbook B automatically flow through to Workbook A. However, if you attempt to later open Workbook A before opening Workbook B, you see a message below the ribbon and above the formula bar, as shown in Figure 28.10: Security Warning. Due to Your Security Settings, Automatic Update of Links Has Been Disabled. You can click either Enable Content or Trust Center.

**Figure 28.10**
New in Excel 2007,
linked files are
untrusted by default.

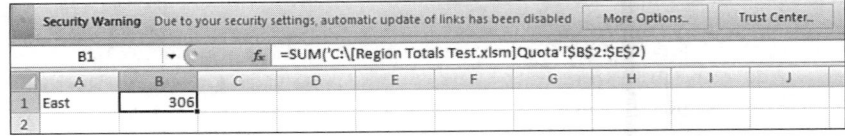

If you click Enable Content, a new Trust in Office dialog box offers you the security options to either leave the content disabled or to enable the content. It is a little unclear how updating the link to an external cell can make your document unsecure. If you want to see the current values from the closed workbook, you have no choice other than to enable this content, as shown in Figure 28.11.

Even more annoying, choosing Enable This Content is a temporary setting. The next time you open the workbook, Excel will again disable the automatic update of links.

To permanently allow the updating of links, you need to click the Trust Center button, choose the External Content section, and then select Enable All Workbooks Links, as shown in Figure 28.12.

**CAUTION**

If you choose to disable all links, Excel does not even warn you that you are seeing the wrong numbers. In Microsoft's attempt to prevent some obscure chance of a virus, these new settings will cause enough inadvertent errors to cause a Sarbanes-Oxley auditor to sweat.

**Figure 28.11**
You have to overlook this ominous warning from Microsoft to have Excel get a linked value from a closed workbook.

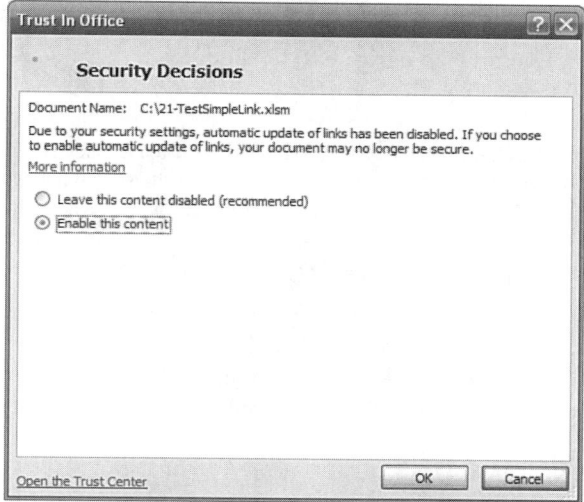

**Figure 28.12**
To permanently allow links, choose Enable All Workbook Links in this dialog.

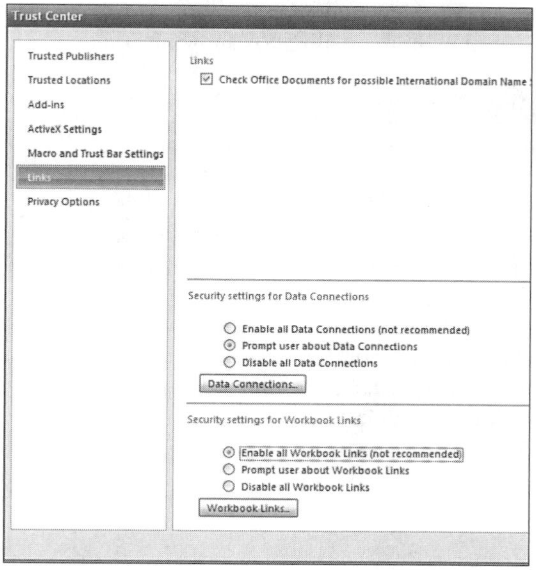

## OVERCOMING THE TRUST CENTER BY USING A TRUSTED LOCATION

There is a simple way to prevent the Trust Center from getting in your way. For example, if you generally store the budget documents in a c:\Budget\ folder on your hard drive, you can add this entire folder to your trusted locations. When the linking file is stored in a trusted location, the links automatically update, no matter what settings you have in the Links section of the Trust Center.

To add a folder to your trusted locations, you follow these steps:

1. Choose File, Excel Options, Trust Center.
2. Click Advanced Trust Center Settings, followed by Trusted Locations and Add New Location.
3. Click the Browse button and navigate to C:\Budget\.

NOTE

Curiously, having the linking workbook in a trusted location is sufficient. Even if this workbook is linking to a file in a nontrusted location, Excel happily updates the links.

## OPENING WORKBOOKS WITH LINKS TO CLOSED WORKBOOKS

Say that you have saved and closed the linking workbook. You update numbers in the linked workbook. You save and close the linked workbook. Later, when you open the linking workbook, Excel asks if you want to update the links to the other workbook. If you created both workbooks and you have possession of both workbooks, it is fine to allow the workbooks to update.

## DEALING WITH MISSING LINKED WORKBOOKS

If you received a linking workbook via email and do not have access to the linked workbooks, Excel alerts you that the workbook contains one or more links that cannot be updated. In this case, you should click Continue in the dialog box shown in Figure 28.13.

**Figure 28.13**
This message means that the linked workbook cannot be found. It shows up most often when someone mails you only the linking workbook.

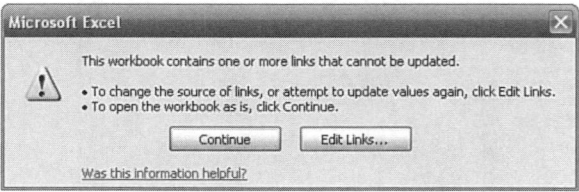

You also get this message if the linked workbook was renamed, moved, or deleted. In that case, you should click the Edit Links button to display the Edit Links dialog (see Figure 28.14). Then you should click the Change Source button to tell Excel that the linked workbook has a new name or location. Finally, you need to click the Break Link button to change all linked formulas to their current values.

28

**Figure 28.14**
You can manage or
change links by using
this dialog.

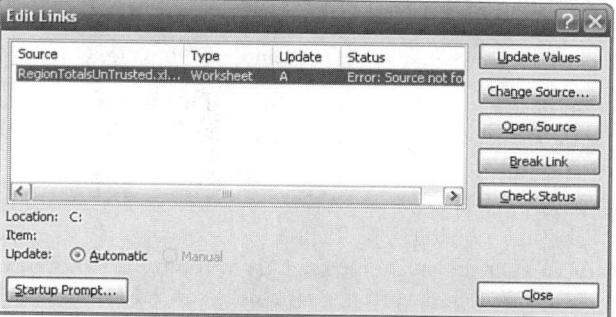

## PREVENTING THE UPDATE LINKS DIALOG FROM APPEARING

Say that you need to send a linking workbook to a co-worker. You want your co-worker to see the current values of the linking formulas without having the linked workbook. In this case, you want the co-worker to click Continue in Figure 28.13. However, some newer Excel customers think that every warning box is a disaster, so you might prefer to suppress that box for your co-worker. To do so, you follow these steps:

1. On the Data tab, in the Manage Connections group, choose Edit Links to Files.

2. In the lower-left corner of the dialog that appears, click the Startup Prompt button. The Startup Prompt dialog appears.

3. Select Don't Display the Alert and Don't Update Automatic Links (see Figure 28.15).

**Figure 28.15**
You can prevent
others from seeing the
Update Links message.

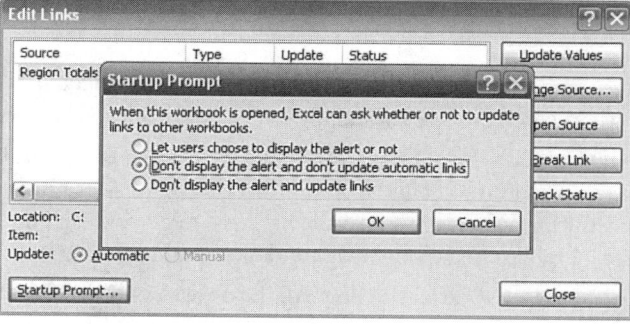

Of course, after emailing the workbook to your co-worker, you need to redisplay the Startup Prompt dialog and change it back so that you will get the updated links.

# CONNECTING TO DATA ON A WEB PAGE

Many Web pages comprise many tables of data. Any time you see columns of numbers or columns of data, it is very likely that you are seeing the results of a table. Usually the only things not in a table are paragraphs of body copy. And usually, there would be no need to update this information on a daily basis. Excel 2007 makes it even easier than past versions of Excel to link your Excel worksheet to a table on any Web page.

## SETTING UP A CONNECTION TO A WEB PAGE

To set up a connection between a worksheet and a Web page, you follow these steps:

1. Find a section of the worksheet that has several blank rows and blank columns. (Depending on the size of the selected sections of the Web page, you could return many rows or columns of data.)

2. On the Data ribbon, choose From Web from the Get External Data group. Excel opens the New Web Query dialog. This dialog looks remarkably like a mini Web browser, and it even opens to your default home page from Internet Explorer. However, as shown in Figure 28.16, the rendered Web page includes several yellow boxes with black arrows. These arrows indicate the tops of various tables on the page.

**Figure 28.16**
Notice the arrows indicating available tables on the Web page.

3. Using the search bar or the address bar, navigate to the selected Web page. For example, to retrieve stock quotes, you might use http://finance.yahoo.com.

4. If the Web page has a form, enter any values needed by the form. In this example, you would enter your desired ticker symbols into the Yahoo Get Quotes box and then press Go. The resulting Web page will probably have many tables. The Yahoo quotes page has at least 14 tables, many of which are tables that display advertisements.

5. Hover the mouse over various yellow and black arrows. Excel highlights the entire range of each table, as shown in Figure 28.17.

6. When you find the table that contains the information that you want, click that arrow. The arrow changes to a green checkmark, as shown in Figure 28.17.

7. In the upper-right corner of the New Web Query dialog, click the Options button. The Web Query Options dialog appears (see Figure 28.18).

8. Select whether the data from the Web page should be retrieved as text only or whether to have full HTML formatting in the results. Then click OK.

**Figure 28.17**
You select the table that contains the data for the worksheet.

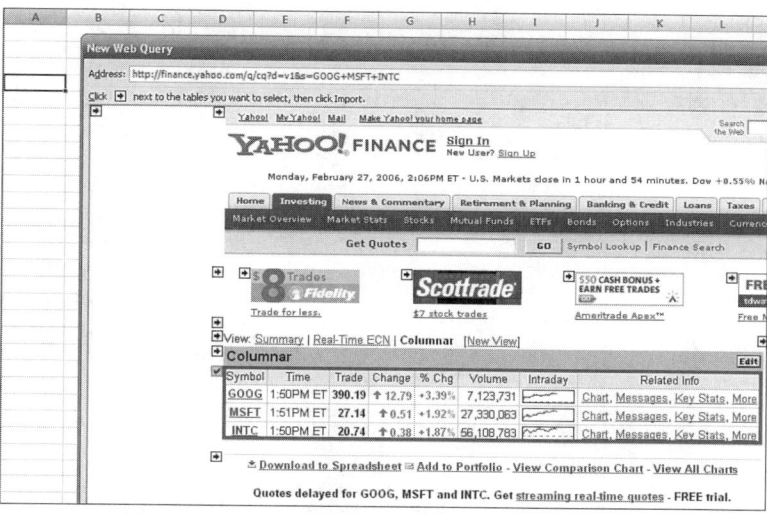

**Figure 28.18**
Most of the time, you want unformatted text.

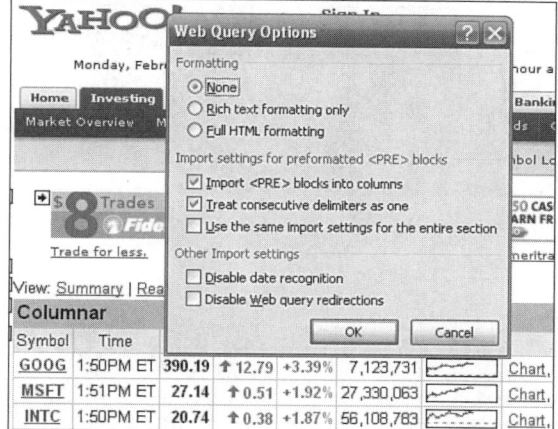

9. Click the Import button in the lower-right corner of the New Web Query dialog. Excel displays the Import Data dialog, which allows you to confirm the output location for the data from the Web query. If desired, click the Properties button to set up automatic refreshing of the Web data. The Connection Properties dialog appears (see Figure 28.19).

10. Use the Connection Properties dialog to set refresh options. For example, you can have the Web query refreshed every so many minutes, and you can also have the Web data refreshed when a file opens. This way, you can retrieve new data each day when you open the file. When you are done selecting options on this dialog, click OK. You will briefly see a bit of Web query code appear in the worksheet at your destination location. If your Internet connection is working, this is soon replaced by the data from the Web page, as shown in Figure 28.20.

28

**Figure 28.19**
You control the
refresh rate for the
Web query on this
dialog.

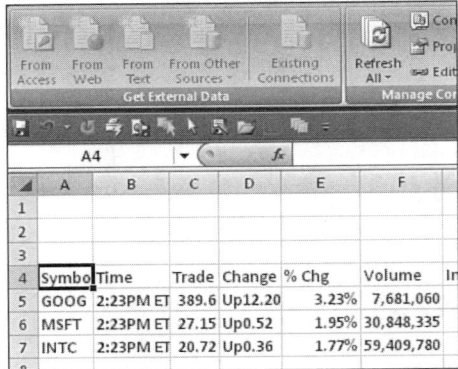

**Figure 28.20**
The results of the Web
query are imported to
your workbook.

Note in Figure 28.20 that all the Get External Data options in the ribbon are disabled. This happens when your cell pointer is located in external data. To set up a new Web query on the same worksheet, you simply move the cell pointer to a cell outside the retrieved data; for example, Cell A9 would be safe in the worksheet shown in Figure 28.20.

## MANAGING CELL PROPERTIES FOR WEB QUERIES

After you have retrieved a Web query, you can select a single cell in the query and choose Properties from the Manage Connections group on the Data ribbon. The External Data Range Properties dialog appears. As shown in Figure 28.21, this legacy dialog box includes additional properties for the query. In the Data Formatting and Layout section, you can choose options to preserve cell formatting and adjust column widths. Most importantly, you can specify that if the query returns more rows tomorrow, any formulas adjacent to the Web query should be expanded.

**Figure 28.21**
This dialog box
includes formatting
and formula
properties.

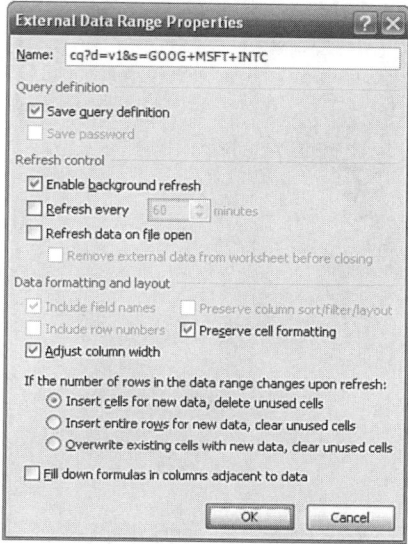

# SETTING UP A CONNECTION TO A TEXT FILE

It is possible to load data from a text file into Excel using the connection group. Follow
these steps:

1. On the Data ribbon, choose the From Text icon in the Get External Data group. The
   Import Text File dialog appears.

2. Browse to and select your text file. Excel launches the familiar Text Import Wizard –
   Step 1 of 3, where you can specify that the text is either delimited or fixed width.
   (Delimited text is text in which each column is separated by a character such as a
   comma or a tab. Fixed-width data is where each field is neatly lined up when viewed in
   a monospace font such as Courier New.)

3. Choose Delimited, as shown in Figure 28.22, and then click Next.

4. In step 2 of the wizard, change the Excel default Tab character between fields to a
   comma, as shown in Figure 28.23. (You may occasionally encounter files with a
   delimiter such as a pipe (|) or some other character. You can specify such a delimiter by
   choosing the Other check box and then specifying the character.)

5. In step 3, specify the field type for each field and whether certain fields should be skipped.

6. If you have a column of numbers where a leading zero needs to be preserved (for example, the zip code of Fort Kent, Maine, needs to stay as 04743 instead of being converted
   to 4743), choose Text as the field type for the zip code field.

7. Click the Advanced button to specify the characters used for thousands and decimal separators (see Figure 28.24). You can also specify that the minus appears after the number.

8. Click Finish. The Import Data dialog appears.

28

**Figure 28.22**
You navigate through the Text Import Wizard to set up a connection to a text file.

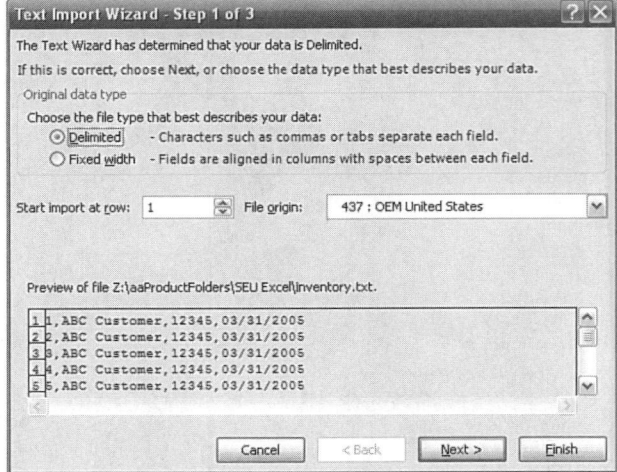

**Figure 28.23**
You specify the delimiter character in step 2.

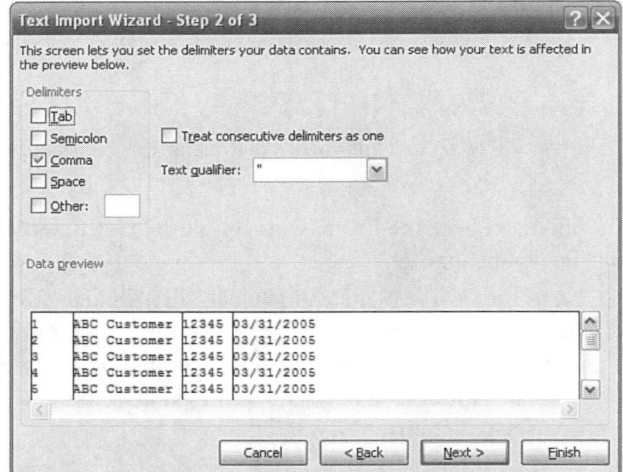

**Figure 28.24**
You select field types in step 3.

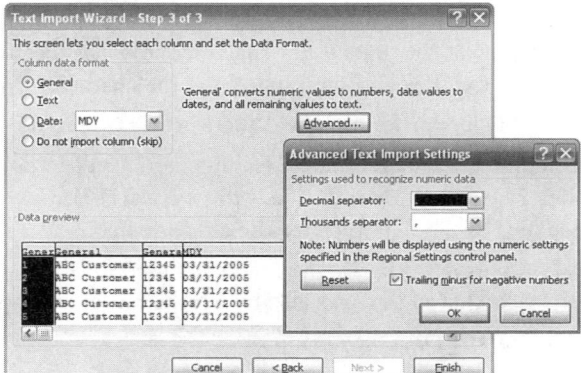

9. Specify a starting cell for the data, as shown in Figure 28.25.

**Figure 28.25**
In addition to specifying a starting cell, click the Properties button.

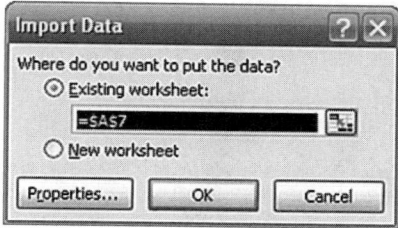

10. Click the Properties button. The Properties dialog appears.

11. Determine whether to have Excel ask you for the filename each day or if you should use the same file name each day. If your IT department is putting out an inventory.txt file every day, you will always want to connect to inventory.txt. Instead, your IT department might be exporting inv070217.txt today and inv070218.txt tomorrow. In that case, you would want Excel to ask you for a filename during every refresh. As shown in Figure 28.26, Excel defaults to Prompt for File Name on Refresh. If your filename will be the same and in the same folder every day, uncheck this default setting.

**Figure 28.26**
By default, Excel asks you for the filename during every refresh from a text connection. Turn this off if your file will be in a consistent location with the same name.

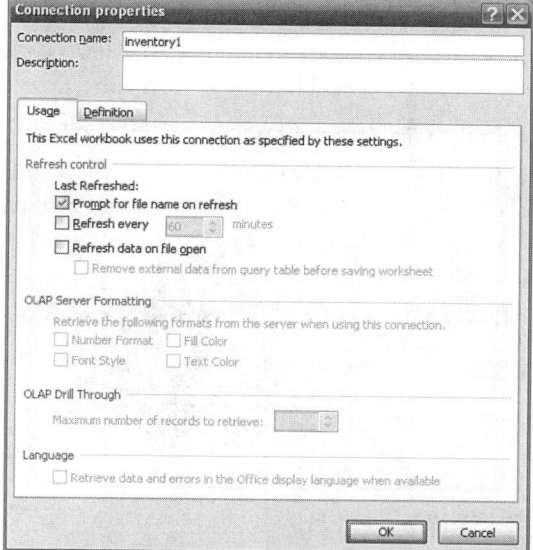

12. Accept the location for the import. Excel brings in all the records from the text file.

13. Click the Properties icon under Manage Connections on the Data tab in order to access additional properties for the query. In particular, you can control how Excel will handle new records each day and ask that any formulas in adjacent cells be extended as needed. The options for column sort/filter/layout are disabled for a text file. Figure 28.27 shows the External Data Range Properties dialog.

28

**Figure 28.27**
You can choose refresh options for the text connection.

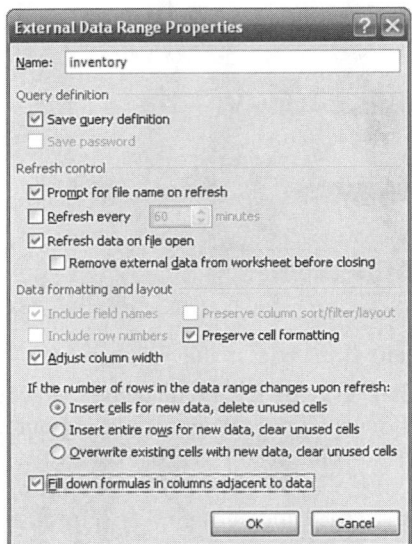

# SETTING UP A CONNECTION TO AN ACCESS DATABASE

Although Excel can now handle 1.1 million rows, you might encounter larger datasets that need to be stored in Access. You can connect to these larger datasets. You can create a connection to any table in an Access database. Here's what you do:

1. On the Data ribbon, in the Get External Data group, choose From Access.

2. Browse to select the .mdb file to which you want to link. You are then given an opportunity to choose any one table or query from the database. Each query is listed in the Type column as VIEW, as shown in Figure 28.28.

**Figure 28.28**
Using an Access connection, you can import a table or a predefined query.

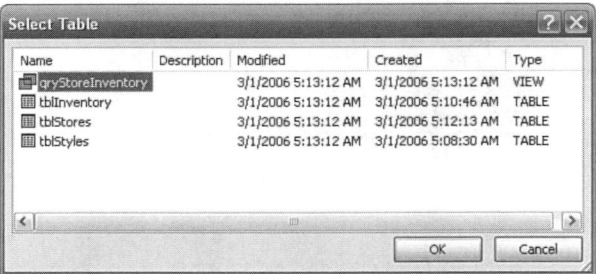

3. Choose whether your data should be imported as a table or used in a pivot table. With the Access connection, there is an additional option as shown in Figure 28.29. You can have the table imported to a regular table, or you can ask for the data to be used as the data source for a pivot table report. When the Access data is delivered to Excel, it is automatically set up as an Excel table with default formatting, as shown in Figure 28.30.

**Figure 28.29**
Access connections can be returned as a table or used as the source in a pivot table report.

**Figure 28.30**
By default, Excel treats the data with Excel 2007's table formatting and features.

| | A | B | C | D | E |
|---|---|---|---|---|---|
| 1 | Style | Store | StoreName | DESCRIPTION | Inventory |
| 2 | **14708 | 340004 | TUCSON | | 1 |
| 3 | 0189L | 340028 | SALT LAKE | 1 1/2CHOC COW W/BKL & BILLET | 1 |
| 4 | 1011 | 340015 | TOPANGA | | 1 |
| 5 | 1021 | 340045 | STANFORD | | 1 |
| 6 | 1021 | 340012 | BELLEVUE | | 1 |
| 7 | 1022 | 340006 | MISSION VIEJO | | 1 |
| 8 | 1031 | 340005 | ROSEVILLE | | 1 |
| 9 | 10403 | 340062 | PHIPPS PLAZA | 1 1/4 BLK DEVONSHIRE GOLF | 1 |
| 10 | 10403 | 340026 | CHANDLER | 1 1/4 BLK DEVONSHIRE GOLF | 2 |
| 11 | 10403 | 340028 | SALT LAKE | 1 1/4 BLK DEVONSHIRE GOLF | 3 |
| 12 | 10403 | 340030 | SEATTLE | 1 1/4 BLK DEVONSHIRE GOLF | 2 |
| 13 | 10403 | 340032 | FORT WAYNE | 1 1/4 BLK DEVONSHIRE GOLF | 5 |

**NOTE**

Note that if you select a query in Access, there might be a delay as the query is calculated. Excel displays a Getting Data… message in the table while the calculation is in process.

→ To learn more about pivot tables, **see** Chapter 11, "Formatting Pivot Table," **page 215**.

# SETTING UP SQL SERVER, XML, OLE DB, AND ODBC CONNECTIONS

Although Excel 2007 offers icons for Access, Web, and text connections, you can actually connect to a wide variety of other data sources. You access all these sources by clicking the From Other Sources icon on the Data ribbon. When you choose this option, you are presented with five choices, as shown in Figure 28.31.

SQL Server is Microsoft's structured query language database. Typically, when applications get too big to run smoothly in Microsoft Access, they will be migrated to the more robust SQL Server platform. Because SQL Server is a Microsoft product, connecting to SQL Server is easy. To connect, you will need the Server name, a userid, and a password.

Analysis Services is Microsoft's cube functionality, currently marketed as SQL Server Analysis Services. A cube database represents data along three or more dimensions. To connect, you will need the Server name, a userid, and a password.

28

**Figure 28.31**

Excel can connect to SQL Server, Analysis Services, XML, OLE DB data sources, or ODBC through Microsoft Query.

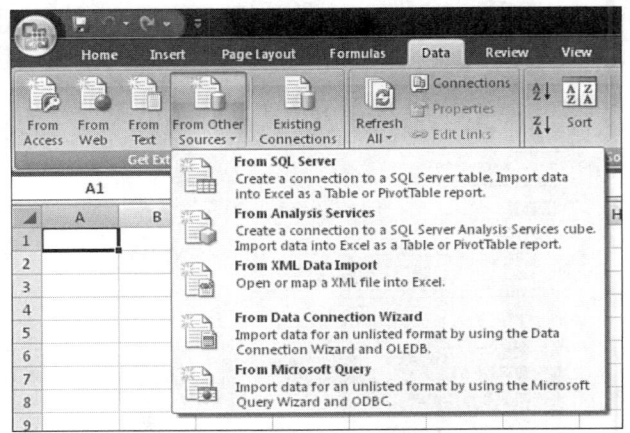

XML stands for Extensible Markup Language. This is a simple text file that includes both data and tags used to identify the data. An example illustrating a connection to XML data is shown in the next section.

OLE-DB stands for Object Linking and Embedding for Databases. This is a Microsoft interface written in the COM environment that allows Windows-based applications to access a wide variety of database types. Consult your database administer for required settings to connect through OLE-DB. Microsoft Query is an older technology that uses Open Database Connectivity (ODBC). If your company has implemented a non-Microsoft platform, ODBC is the interface that allows other programs such as Excel to connect to the database. Typically, the administrator of the system will be able to provide you with a *connect string* that you will use to access the other system's data. Microsoft Query also provides a method for Excel to build SQL queries against Access databases. For an example, see "Connecting Using Microsoft Query" later in the chapter.

## CONNECTING TO XML DATA

In the future, you will find more and more datasets based on XML. In reality, XML is like a CSV (comma-separated value) file on steroids. You can create or edit XML files by using Notepad. The difference between a CSV file and an XML file is that each field in XML contains a field identifier. This allows you to intelligently import only certain fields into a spreadsheet. Figure 28.32 shows a simple XML file that has two records.

In addition to the actual XML file, it is possible to have a definition document known as an XSD file or a database schema. You may also have one or more XSL files that are used to transform the data. But as long as you have at least one XML file, Excel will be happy to infer a schema, as shown in Figure 28.33.

As you can see in Figure 28.34, the data is then imported as an Excel table. This is pretty basic functionality. By using a trick in the VBA Editor, however, you can actually retrieve the schema and save it to allow Excel to do more XML tricks.

28

**Figure 28.32**
In this XML file seen in Notepad, note that each field starts and ends with `<fieldname>` and `</fieldname>` tags.

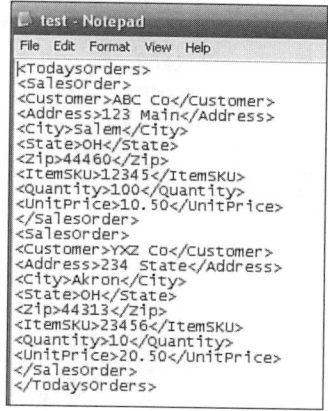

**Figure 28.33**
Without a schema file, Excel is limited to importing the data as a table. Luckily, Excel creates a schema file for you.

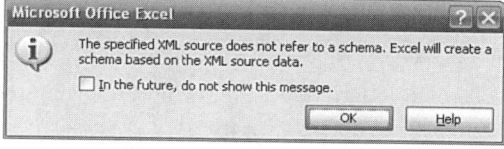

**Figure 28.34**
The data from Figure 28.32 after being imported to Excel.

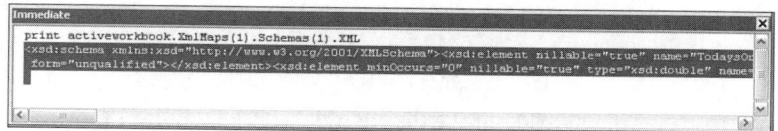

After Excel has imported the data, you can retrieve the schema by using the VBA Editor. To do so, you follow these steps:

1. Press Alt+F11 or click the VBA Editor icon on the Developer ribbon. The VBA Editor appears.

2. In the VBA Editor, press Ctrl+G to display the Immediate pane.

3. In the Immediate pane, type this line:

```
print activeworkbook.XmlMaps(1).Schemas(1).XML
```

Then press Enter. Excel responds by printing the entire schema for the XML file, as shown in Figure 28.35.

**Figure 28.35**
Excel will reply with the Schema.

4. Copy this text into a blank Notepad file and save as test.xsd in the same directory as the XML file.

Figure 28.36 shows the complete schema in Notepad, with WordWrap turned on.

**Figure 28.36**
You save the schema to enable additional XML features in Excel.

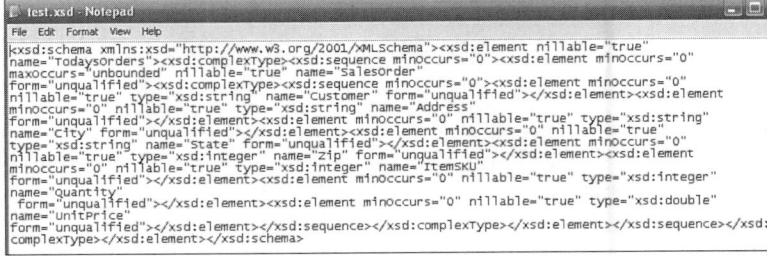

## CONNECTING USING MICROSOFT QUERY

The From Access icon on the Data ribbon allows you to retrieve all fields from any Access table or predefined query. There may be times when you want to join Access tables, filter records, or select only a subset of fields from a query. Excel 2007 offers the old Microsoft Query product for building such connections.

To build a new query against a table in an Access database, follow these steps:

1. In Excel 2007, choose Data, Get External Data, From Other Sources, From Microsoft Query. The Choose Data Source dialog appears.

2. Select MS Access Database, as shown in Figure 28.37. Click OK. The Select Database dialog will appear. (Note: The Choose Data Source dialog differentiates between Access and Access 2007 databases. If your data is in an Access 2007 database, choose MS Access 12.0 Databases instead.)

**Figure 28.37**
Choose MS Access Database in the Choose Data Source dialog.

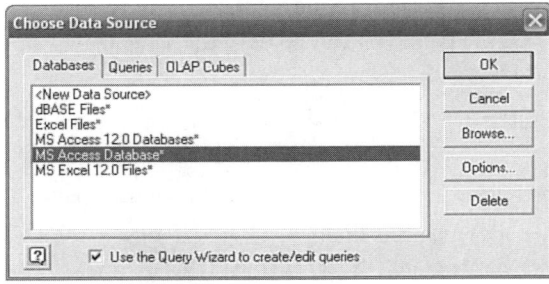

3. In the Select Database dialog, choose the Access database, as shown in Figure 28.38. (Although Office 2007 was supposed to be a complete rewrite, it is apparent that no one has updated this Windows 3.1–style dialog box in many years.) The Query Wizard dialog appears.

4. Choose to include particular fields from any table or query in the database. You Choose fields on the left side of the dialog and click the > button to move them to the right side of the dialog, as shown in Figure 28.39.

5. In the next step of the Query Wizard, set up filters for the query. In Figure 28.40, the filter is defined as only items where the inventory is greater than five.

**Figure 28.38**
You select the Access database.

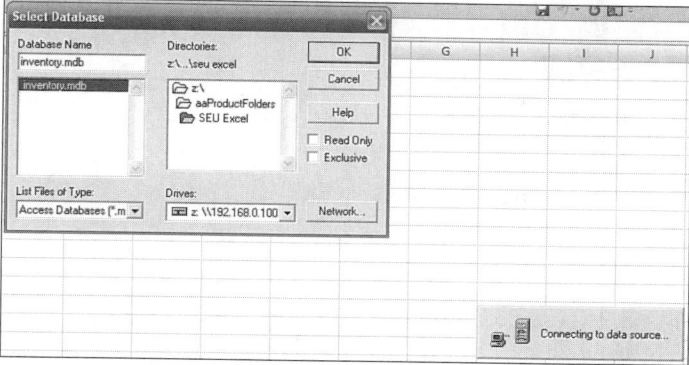

**Figure 28.39**
You select fields to be included in the query.

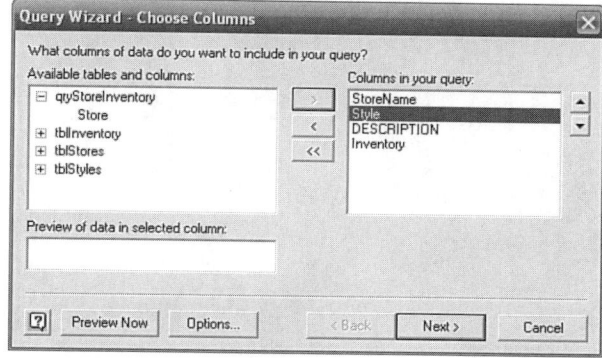

**Figure 28.40**
You define filters for the query.

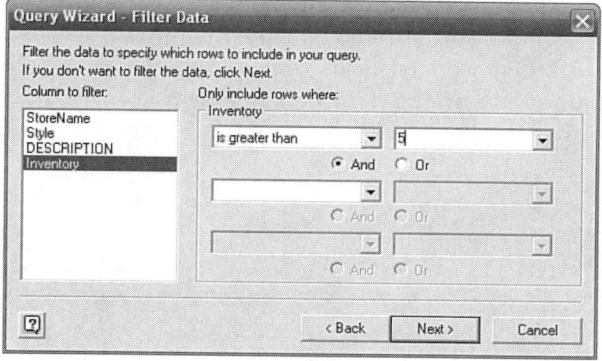

6. In the next step of the Query Wizard, specify up to three sort fields for the query, as shown in Figure 28.41.

7. In the final step of the Query Wizard, specify that you want to return the data to Microsoft Office Excel, as shown in Figure 28.42. You will are presented with an Import dialog that is similar to the one shown earlier.

28

**Figure 28.41**
You specify sort criteria.

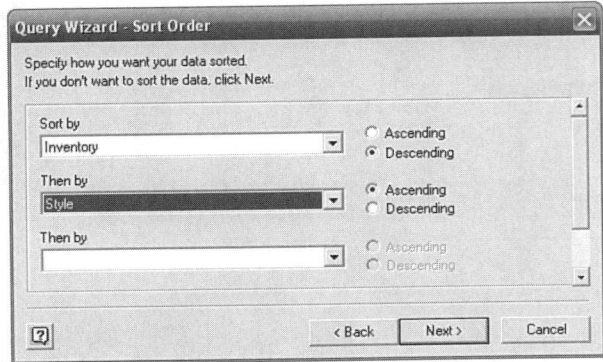

**Figure 28.42**
You return the data to Excel.

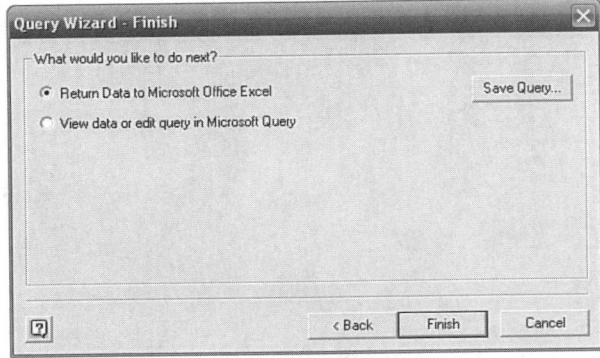

Contrast the current example with the previous example in "Setting Up a Connection to an Access Database." Although the previous example and this example use the same query from Access, the Microsoft Query option enables you to retrieve only the records with more than five items in inventory. The overhead involved in returning few records causes the query to run significantly faster. As shown in Figure 28.43, the data is returned in a sorted manner.

**Figure 28.43**
The final results from the MS Query connection.

| | A | B | C | D |
|---|---|---|---|---|
| 1 | Style | DESCRIPTION | StoreName | Inventory |
| 2 | D28016 | | WELLINGTON | 1100 |
| 3 | D28016 | | ST LOUIS | 1069 |
| 4 | 30090 | 1 1/8 BLK/PNT CROCO REVRSBLE | SOUTH WINDSOR | 882 |
| 5 | D28016 | | IRVINE SPECTRUM | 620 |
| 6 | D28016 | | WOODFIELD | 595 |
| 7 | D28016 | | KING OF PRUSSIA | 568 |
| 8 | D28099 | | MISSION VIEJO | 550 |
| 9 | D28099 | | SOMERSET | 492 |

# MANAGING CONNECTIONS

The Data ribbon includes a group called Manage Connections. As shown in Figure 28.44, this group includes an option to refresh all connections. Although the icon says Refresh All, there is a drop-down available where you can choose to refresh only the current query or to view properties for a connection.

**Figure 28.44**
You have one-click access to refreshing all connections.

Clicking the Connections icon brings up a summary of all the Web, text, Access, or ODBC connections in your workbook. This is a fantastic improvement in Excel 2007. As shown in Figure 28.45, you can click any connection in the top and then follow the hyperlink Click Here to See Where the Selected Connections Are Used in order to jump to the worksheet range that houses the results of the connection.

**Figure 28.45**
The new Workbook Connections dialog provides one stop to see all connections in the workbook.

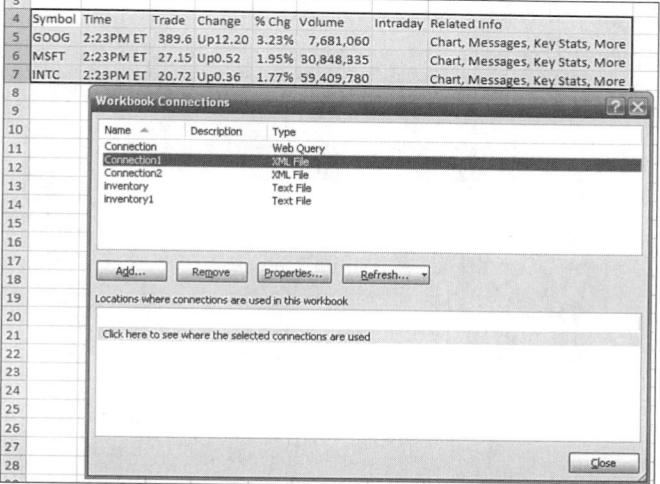

While this new dialog is very nearly a one-stop source for all external links, you might be disappointed to learn that links to other workbooks are not included in this dialog. You have to select Edit Links to Files from the Manage Connections group in order to display the Edit Links dialog, where you can check the status of any workbook links as well as maintain the link location, break the links, or adjust the startup prompt.

Excel offers fantastic connections. Although users have been able to link to Access databases for several versions, Excel 2007's improved support for SQL Server, XML, ODBC, text, Web, and Access data is unparalleled. The following Excel in Practice sidebar talks about setting up a connection to one of the newest data stores: an Excel 2007 workbook with half a million records.

28

**Figure 28.46**
Use Edit Links to manage formula links between workbooks.

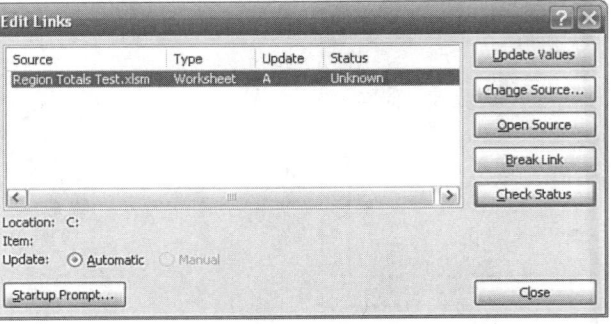

## Excel in Practice: Defining a Connection to a Separate Closed Workbook

While you can write formulas that link to external closed workbooks, those formulas cannot reference more than 10,000 cells. This is a serious limitation now that you can have more than a million rows in the external worksheet.

Rather than using simple linking via a formula, you can treat the other Excel file as a database file and connect to it using the Connection Manager! This technique will allow you to run queries against millions of cells in the external workbook.

For example, Figure 28.47 shows an Excel worksheet with more than 748,000 records. Link formulas would not be able to access more than 2% of the rows in this workbook. Using a connection will overcome this limitation.

**Figure 28.47**
With 20 columns, this worksheet contains 15 million cells.

| STORE # | STYLE | CLASS | SUB-CLASS | DESCRIPTION |
|---|---|---|---|---|
| 748838 | 340124 Z056Y | 91 | 98 | PAIGE BLK CALF/ |
| 748839 | 340124 Z056Z | 91 | 98 | PAIGE BLK CALF/ |
| 748840 | 340124 Z057K | 91 | 95 | COLETT BLK CALF |
| 748841 | 340124 Z057P | 91 | 98 | TEMPE BLK CALF |
| 748842 | 340124 Z057Q | 91 | 98 | TEMPE BLK CALF |
| 748843 | 340124 Z057S | 91 | 98 | TEMPE BLK CALF |
| 748844 | 340124 Z057T | 91 | 98 | TEMPE BLK CALF |
| 748845 | 340124 Z057W | 91 | 94 | TAOS BLK CALF V |
| 748846 | 340124 Z0582 | 91 | 98 | FIONA CHO NUB |
| 748847 | 340124 Z0585 | 91 | 95 | FRAN BLK SLIM \ |
| 748848 | 340124 Z058H | 91 | 94 | TOBY BLK GRAN( |
| 748849 | 340124 Z058V | 91 | 98 | TYNAN CHO MAI |
| 748850 | 340124 Z058W | 91 | 98 | TYNAN CHO MAI |
| 748851 | 340124 Z058Y | 91 | 98 | TYNAN BLK MAD |
| 748852 | 340124 Z058Z | 91 | 98 | TYNAN BLK MAD |
| 748853 | 340124 Z0592 | 91 | 95 | ERICA BLK PATEN |

To create a connection to the external workbook, follow these steps.:

1. From a blank workbook, choose Data, Get External Data, From Other Sources, From Microsoft Query. In the Choose Data Source dialog that appears, choose Excel 2007 Connection (also known as MS Excel 12.0 Files).
2. In the Select Workbook dialog, choose the Excel file and click OK.
3. In the next three Query Wizard dialogs, select your fields, the filter, and the sort.
4. In the final step, choose the option to view the query in Microsoft Query. The Microsoft Query dialog appears.
5. In the Microsoft Query dialog, choose View, Query Properties. The Query Properties dialog appears (see Figure 28.48)

6. Choose the Group Records check box and click OK. This will tell the query to return a summary dataset, totaling numeric fields for each unique combination of key fields. You will specify which fields to group and sum in the next two steps.

7. Select the Sum of Quantity heading in the lower half of the screen. Click the Sigma button in the toolbar to toggle through Sum, Min, Max, and Normal. Choose Sum as shown in Figure 28.49.

8. Choose File, Return Data to Microsoft Excel, as shown in Figure 28.50.

You now have a refreshable data connection to an external Excel workbook that has 750,000 records.

**Figure 28.48**
Grouping records will return one record per Region and Product.

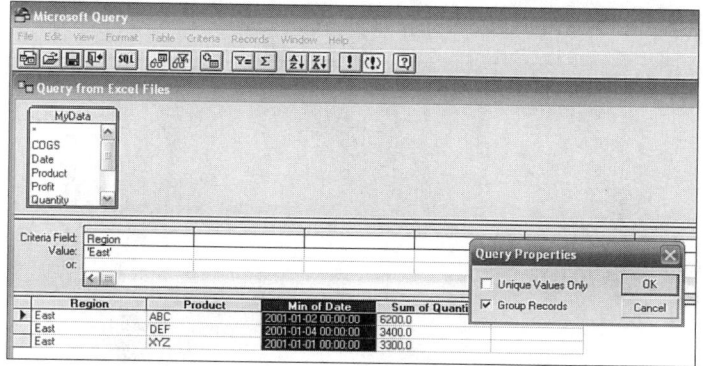

**Figure 28.49**
You select a sum property for each column.

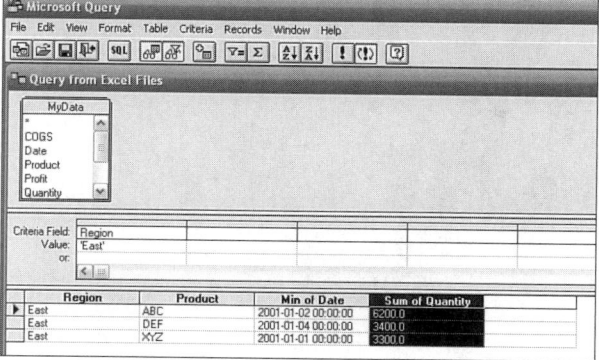

**Figure 28.50**
You close Microsoft Query and return the data.

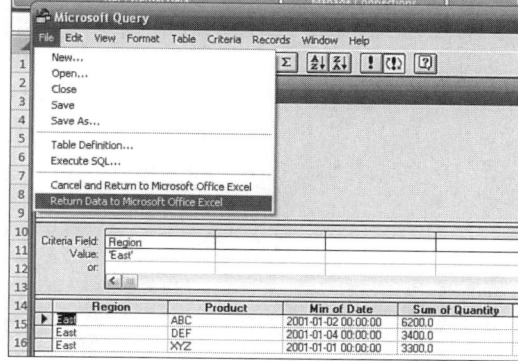

28

**Figure 28.51**
This is a three-line summary from the 750,000-record external workbook.

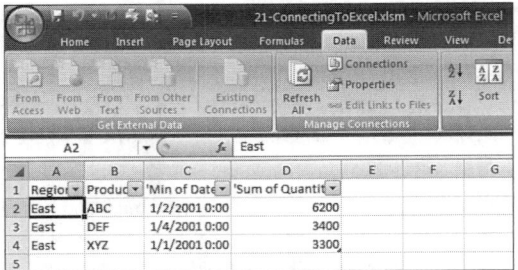

CHAPTER **29**

# USING SUPER FORMULAS IN EXCEL

## In this chapter

Excel offers an amazing variety of formulas. This chapter covers some of the unorthodox formulas that you can build in Excel. In this chapter, you will learn about the following:

- Using a formula to add the same cell across many sheets
- Using a formula to reference the previous sheet
- Editing multiple formulas into one
- Assigning a formula to a name
- Letting data determine the cell reference to use with the INDIRECT function
- Using a dynamic range with an offset
- Transposing relative column references to rows
- Using Row() or Column() to return an array of numbers
- Replacing thousands of formulas with one Ctrl+Shift+Enter (CSE) formula
- Using one formula to return a whole range of answers
- Doing conditional sums based on two or more conditions

# USING 3D FORMULAS TO SPEAR THROUGH MANY WORKSHEETS

It is common to have a workbook composed of identical worksheets for each month or quarter of the year. Every worksheet needs to have the same arrangement of rows.

If you want to total a particular cell across all of the worksheets, you might try to write a formula with one term for each sheet; for example, =Sheet1!A1+Sheet2!A1+Sheet3!A1.... However, Excel supports a special type of formula that will spear through several worksheets to add a particular cell from each worksheet. The syntax of the formula is =SUM(Sheet1:Sheet*n*!A1).

As shown in Figure 29.1, Net Income is in Row 22 on the January worksheet and is in the same row on the December worksheet. You cannot see this in Figure 29.1, but the arrangement of rows is identical on every worksheet.

When creating a worksheet, you might be tempted to write a formula like the one in Figure 29.2 that adds up each of the 12 worksheets, but doing so would be rather tedious.

Instead, you can write a formula that totals Cell B4 from each worksheet, Jan through Dec. The syntax of the formula is =SUM(Jan:Dec!B4). After you enter this formula in Cell B4, you can easily copy it to all the other relevant cells in the worksheet, as shown in Figure 29.3.

## REFERRING TO THE PREVIOUS WORKSHEET

When you have an arrangement of several sequential worksheets, you might wish to keep a running total. This total would be calculated as the total on this sheet plus the running total from the previous sheet.

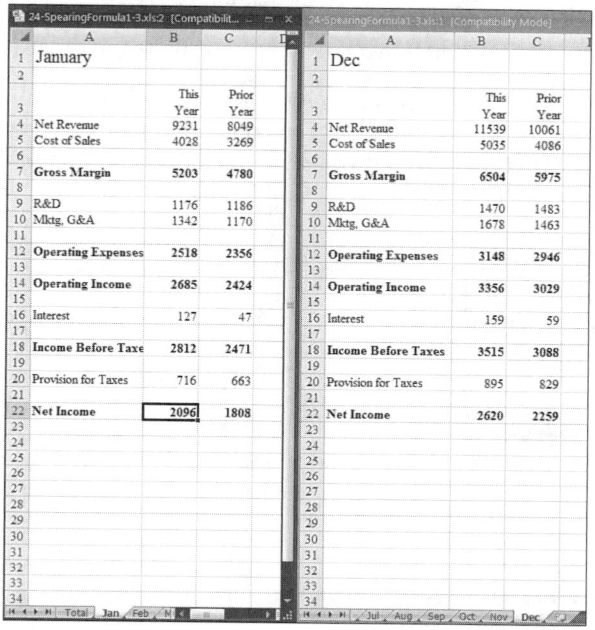

24-SpearingFormula1-3.xls:2 [Compatibilit...

| | A | B | C |
|---|---|---|---|
| 1 | January | | |
| 2 | | | |
| 3 | | This Year | Prior Year |
| 4 | Net Revenue | 9231 | 8049 |
| 5 | Cost of Sales | 4028 | 3269 |
| 6 | | | |
| 7 | **Gross Margin** | **5203** | **4780** |
| 8 | | | |
| 9 | R&D | 1176 | 1186 |
| 10 | Mktg, G&A | 1342 | 1170 |
| 11 | | | |
| 12 | **Operating Expenses** | **2518** | **2356** |
| 13 | | | |
| 14 | **Operating Income** | **2685** | **2424** |
| 15 | | | |
| 16 | Interest | 127 | 47 |
| 17 | | | |
| 18 | **Income Before Taxe** | **2812** | **2471** |
| 19 | | | |
| 20 | Provision for Taxes | 716 | 663 |
| 21 | | | |
| 22 | **Net Income** | **2096** | **1808** |

Total / Jan / Feb / M

24-SpearingFormula1-3.xls:1 [Compatibility Mode]

| | A | B | C |
|---|---|---|---|
| 1 | Dec | | |
| 2 | | | |
| 3 | | This Year | Prior Year |
| 4 | Net Revenue | 11539 | 10061 |
| 5 | Cost of Sales | 5035 | 4086 |
| 6 | | | |
| 7 | **Gross Margin** | **6504** | **5975** |
| 8 | | | |
| 9 | R&D | 1470 | 1483 |
| 10 | Mktg, G&A | 1678 | 1463 |
| 11 | | | |
| 12 | **Operating Expenses** | **3148** | **2946** |
| 13 | | | |
| 14 | **Operating Income** | **3356** | **3029** |
| 15 | | | |
| 16 | Interest | 159 | 59 |
| 17 | | | |
| 18 | **Income Before Taxes** | **3515** | **3088** |
| 19 | | | |
| 20 | Provision for Taxes | 895 | 829 |
| 21 | | | |
| 22 | **Net Income** | **2620** | **2259** |

Jul / Aug / Sep / Oct / Nov / Dec

**Figure 29.1**
The 12 workbooks, Jan through Dec, contain an identical arrangement of rows and columns.

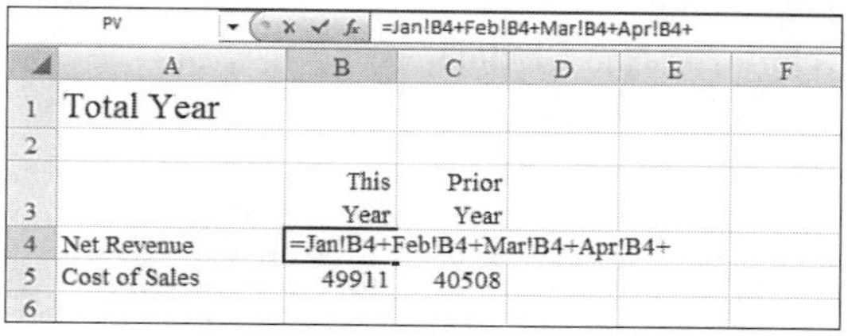

PV =Jan!B4+Feb!B4+Mar!B4+Apr!B4+

| | A | B | C | D | E | F |
|---|---|---|---|---|---|---|
| 1 | Total Year | | | | | |
| 2 | | | | | | |
| 3 | | This Year | Prior Year | | | |
| 4 | Net Revenue | =Jan!B4+Feb!B4+Mar!B4+Apr!B4+ | | | | |
| 5 | Cost of Sales | 49911 | 40508 | | | |
| 6 | | | | | | |

**Figure 29.2**
Writing a formula to point to all 12 worksheets would be tedious.

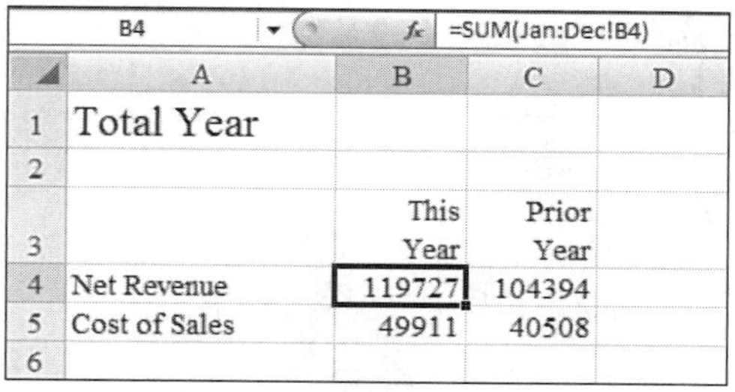

B4 =SUM(Jan:Dec!B4)

| | A | B | C | D |
|---|---|---|---|---|
| 1 | Total Year | | | |
| 2 | | | | |
| 3 | | This Year | Prior Year | |
| 4 | Net Revenue | 119727 | 104394 | |
| 5 | Cost of Sales | 49911 | 40508 | |
| 6 | | | | |

**Figure 29.3**
This formula spears through 12 worksheets to total Cell B4 from each worksheet from Jan through Dec.

It is somewhat difficult to build a formula that will always point to the previous sheet. Many try this wrong approach: build a formula on Sheet2 that points to Sheet1. When you make copies of Sheet2, to Sheet3, Sheet4, and so on, the formula continues to always point back to Sheet1. This is rarely what you want.

The solution involves a tiny user-defined function that can be written in Excel's macro editor.

This specific example shows you how to build a general purpose function that will return a value from a previous worksheet. This function can work in any situation.

Figure 29.4 shows a formula that returns the value from the previous month. On the Feb worksheet, this would refer to =Jan!B4. You could easily copy this formula to other cells within the Feb worksheet. However, if you copy the formula to Mar or Apr, the formula still points to the Jan worksheet, which is not what you want.

**Figure 29.4**
You need to rewrite this formula for each of the 11 other months.

| PV | ▼ ⊙ X ✔ ƒx | =Jan!B4 | | | | |
|---|---|---|---|---|---|---|
| | A | B | C | D | E | F |
| 1 | February | | | | | |
| 2 | | | | | | |
| 3 | | This Year | Prior Year | | Prior Month | |
| 4 | Net Revenue | 9416 | 8210 | | =Jan!B4 | |
| 5 | Cost of Sales | 4109 | 3335 | | | |
| 6 | | | | | | |

Excel offers a very cool solution to this problem. The solution requires a few lines of VBA macro code. Don't be afraid. I will get you there and back without any problems. Here's what you do:

1. Press Alt+F11 to launch the VBA editor.

2. In the VBA editor, choose Insert, Module.

3. Type these lines in the blank module:

```
Function PrevSheet(ByVal MyCell As Range)
    Application.Volatile
    On Error Resume Next
    PrevSheet = MyCell.Worksheet.Parent.Worksheets(MyCell.Worksheet.Index _
        - 1).Range(MyCell.Address).Value
End Function
```

Your screen should look similar to Figure 29.5.

**Figure 29.5**
The VBA editor screen should look like this.

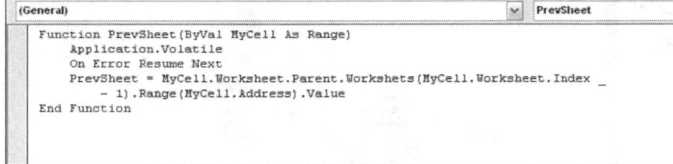

4. Choose File, Close to return to Excel.

To realize the power of this function, you can put the workbook in Group mode and enter the function in 11 worksheets at once:

1. Select the Feb worksheet.

2. Hold down the Shift key while clicking on the Dec worksheet tab. This highlights all 11 worksheets. Although you are seeing the Feb worksheet, anything you do will also happen to all 11 selected worksheets.

3. In Cell E4, enter =PrevSheet(B4), as shown in Figure 29.6.

**Figure 29.6**
Although you see the Feb worksheet, this formula is also entered on all 10 other sheets in the group.

| PV | | | | =PrevSheet(B4) | |
|---|---|---|---|---|---|
| | A | B | C | D E | F |
| 1 | February | | | | |
| 2 | | | | | |
| 3 | | This Year | Prior Year | Prior Month | |
| 4 | Net Revenue | 9416 | 8210 | =PrevSheet(B4) | |
| 5 | Cost of Sales | 4109 | 3335 | 4028 | |
| 6 | | | | | |

4. Press Enter to accept the formula. The Feb worksheet picks up the value from Jan, but each additional worksheet picks up the value from the previous sheet, as shown in Figure 29.7.

**Figure 29.7**
One formula using the custom function PrevSheet solves the prior month problem seamlessly across all the worksheets.

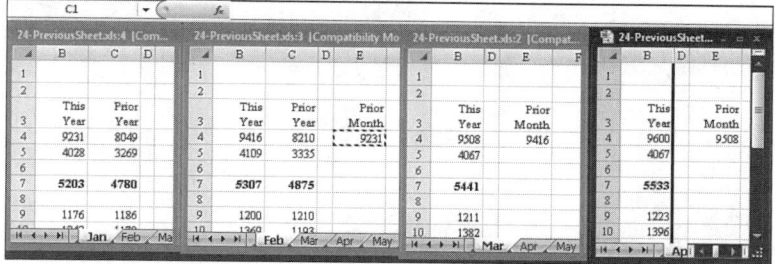

**TIP FROM**

To examine worksheets from the same workbook, select View, Window, New Window to create a second window of the workbook. Then select View, Window, Arrange, Vertical, OK to arrange the windows vertically. You now have two views of the same workbook, and you can change the right pane to be a different worksheet. The screenshot in Figure 29.7 reflects four new window commands before the windows are arranged vertically.

5. With the worksheets still in Group mode, copy Cell B4 from the Feb worksheet to Cells B5, B7, and so on.

6. Right-click any sheet tab and choose ungroup.

# COMBINING MULTIPLE FORMULAS INTO ONE FORMULA

With more than 350 functions available in Excel, it is possible to perform just about any calculation. Many times, however, it is easier to break the task down into many subformulas as you are trying to solve the problem.

For example, fellow Excel MVP and guru Bob Umlas once taught me that I could use the Substitute function to locate the last space in a word. This is handy for finding the last word in a sentence or name. However, unlike Bob, I always need to build this formula over the course of several columns. It takes me seven columns to do a trick that Bob can do in one. Figure 29.8 shows all the formulas used to replicate the trick.

**Figure 29.8**
It takes me seven formulas to isolate the last name.

| | A | B | C | D | E | F | G | H |
|---|---|---|---|---|---|---|---|---|
| 1 | NAME | No Spaces | Len A | Len B | # Spaces | Replace Last Space | Find ! | MID |
| 2 | ALLISON GILMORE | ALLISONGILMORE | 15 | 14 | 1 | ALLISON!GILMORE | 8 | GILMORE |
| 3 | MARY ELLEN JELEN | MARYELLENJELEN | 16 | 14 | 2 | MARY ELLEN!JELEN | 11 | JELEN |
| 4 | FANNIE PERRY | FANNIEPERRY | 12 | 11 | 1 | FANNIE!PERRY | 7 | PERRY |
| 5 | JOE BOB BRIGGS | JOEBOBBRIGGS | 14 | 12 | 2 | JOE BOB!BRIGGS | 8 | BRIGGS |
| 6 | JOSEPH HOWE | JOSEPHHOWE | 11 | 10 | 1 | JOSEPH!HOWE | 7 | HOWE |
| 7 | BILLIE JOE SPEARS | BILLIEJOESPEARS | 17 | 15 | 2 | BILLIE JOE!SPEARS | 11 | SPEARS |
| 8 | INEZ CERVANTES | INEZCERVANTES | 14 | 13 | 1 | INEZ!CERVANTES | 5 | CERVANTES |
| 9 | BILLY JOE JIM BOB | BILLYJOEJIMBOB | 17 | 14 | 3 | BILLY JOE JIM!BOB | 14 | BOB |
| 10 | JOE FRANKS | JOEFRANKS | 10 | 9 | 1 | JOE!FRANKS | 4 | FRANKS |
| 11 | MARY BETH SAMPSON | MARYBETHSAMPSON | 17 | 15 | 2 | MARY BETH!SAMPSON | 10 | SAMPSON |
| 12 | VERONICA MCKENZIE | VERONICAMCKENZIE | 17 | 16 | 1 | VERONICA!MCKENZIE | 9 | MCKENZIE |
| 13 | KATHLEEN BLACK | KATHLEENBLACK | 14 | 13 | 1 | KATHLEEN!BLACK | 9 | BLACK |
| 14 | BRANDI NGUYEN | BRANDINGUYEN | 13 | 12 | 1 | BRANDI!NGUYEN | 7 | NGUYEN |
| 15 | VELMA COCHRAN | VELMACOCHRAN | 13 | 12 | 1 | VELMA!COCHRAN | 6 | COCHRAN |
| 16 | | | | | | | | |
| 17 | Formulas used in Row 2: | | | | | | | |
| 18 | | B2: =SUBSTITUTE(A2," ","") | | | | | | |
| 19 | | C2: =LEN(A2) | | | | | | |
| 20 | | D2: =LEN(B2) | | | | | | |
| 21 | | E2: =C2-D2 | | | | | | |
| 22 | | F2: =SUBSTITUTE(A2," ","!",E2) | | | | | | |
| 23 | | G2: =FIND("!",F2) | | | | | | |
| 24 | | H2: =MID(A2,G2+1,C2-G2) | | | | | | |
| 25 | | | | | | | | |

After you have puzzled out a complicated set of interrelated functions to achieve a result, you can begin consolidating the formulas into one monster formula.

There is an easier way to combine many formulas into one formula. In general, follow these steps:

1. Examine the final formula. It will reference cells that contain one or more subformulas. Let's say that one of the subformulas is a cell such as ZZ123.

2. Move the cell pointer to the subformula in ZZ123.

3. Press F2 to put the formula in edit mode.

4. With the mouse, highlight the formula in the formula bar, but do not highlight the equals sign in the subformula.

5. Press Ctrl+C to copy this portion of the subformula to the clipboard.

6. Go back to the final formula. Press F2 to put the formula in edit mode.

7. In the formula bar, using the mouse, highlight the characters that point to the subformula. In this case, it is cell ZZ123.

8. Press Ctrl+V to paste the subformula in place of the ZZ123 reference.

9. Press Enter to accept this intermediate formula.

10. If there are additional references to a cell with a subformula in the final formula, repeat steps 1-10 for the next reference.

I realize this may be difficult to follow in the abstract. If you would like to follow along with a real example, follow these steps:

1. In Cell H2, the formula has a reference to Cell G2, as shown in Figure 29.9.

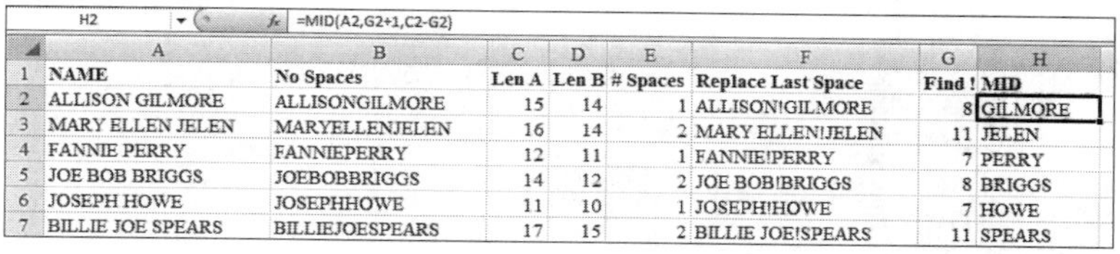

**Figure 29.9**
The goal is to replace G2 in this formula.

2. Move the cell pointer to G2.

3. In the formula bar, click and drag with the mouse to select all the characters in this formula except the equals sign, as shown in Figure 29.10.

4. Press Ctrl+C to copy the selected characters to the Clipboard.

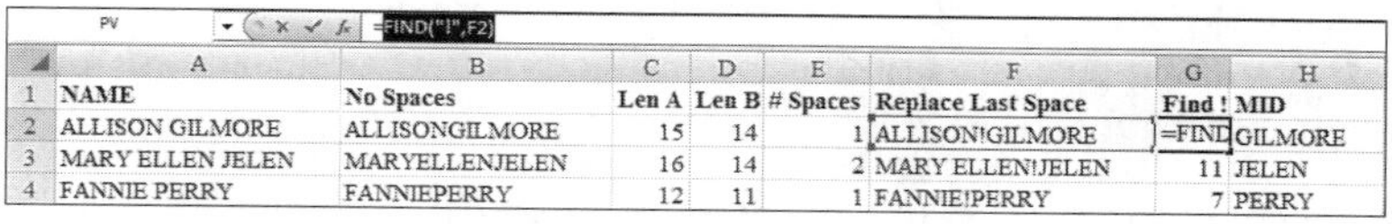

**Figure 29.10**
Copying characters from the formula bar is different from copying a cell.

5. Press Esc to exit Edit mode.

6. Move the cell pointer back to Cell H2 and highlight the characters G2 in the formula bar, as shown in Figure 29.11.

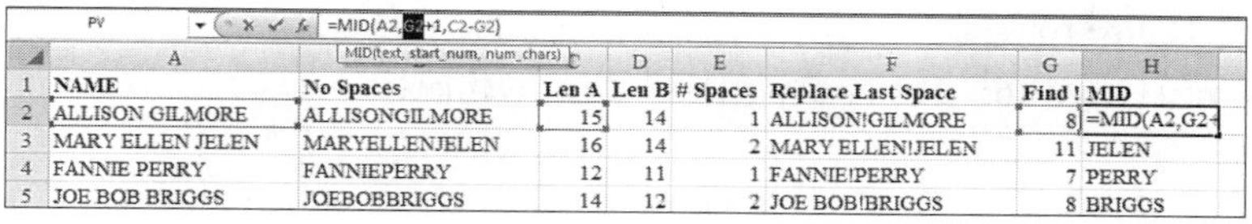

**Figure 29.11**
With the formula from Cell G2 on the clipboard, you select G2 in the final formula.

7. Press Ctrl+V to replace G2 with the formula from Cell G2, as shown in Figure 29.12

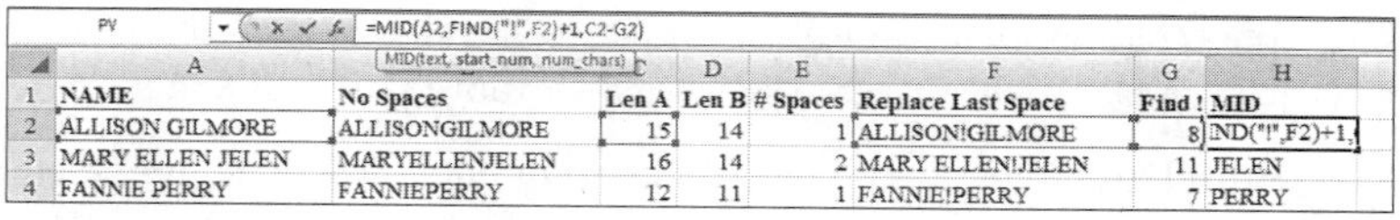

**Figure 29.12**
You can press Ctrl+V to paste the characters from the Cell G2 formula instead of the reference to Cell G2.

29

8. Repeat this process to replace the other G2 and C2 in the Cell H2 formula. Note that pasting the formula from Cell G2 introduces references to Cell F2.

9. Continue to replace any reference to a column other than Column A. After doing several copy and paste operations in the formula bar, you eventually end up with one monster formula.

10. Delete Columns B through G. People will be impressed with how you were able to write such an amazing formula (see Figure 29.13). In fact, someone might even say to you, "Wow! You are as smart as Bob Umlas!"

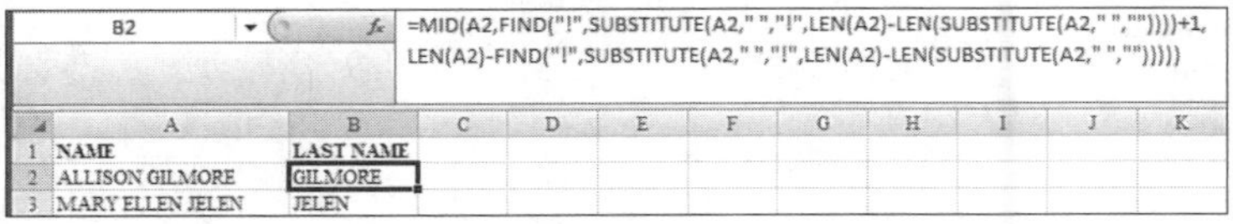

**Figure 29.13**
After several iterations of replacing references in the formula, you end up with one monster formula to replace the six subformulas.

## CALCULATING A CELL REFERENCE IN THE FORMULA BY USING THE INDIRECT FUNCTION

Usually a formula points to a particular cell or range of cells. Sometimes, though, you want a formula to point to a different cell as the result of a calculation. You can do this by using the INDIRECT function.

In general, this process involves writing a text-based formula that evaluates to a cell address. Although your particular situation will certainly be different, here are some examples of formulas that evaluate to a cell address:

- =CHAR(64+COLUMN(B275)&ROW(ZZ999)—evaluates to B999.
- ="Sheet"&ROW(A1)&"!C2" —evaluates to Sheet1!C2 in the current row, but to Sheet2!C2 when copied down one row, and to Sheet3!C2 when copied down to a third row.
- =CHAR(65+MONTH(A1))&"19"—evaluates to row B19 in January, C19 in February, and so on.

After you have a formula that evaluates to text that looks like a cell reference, you can use that formula as the argument to the INDIRECT() function. Excel will return the value in the cell indicated by the text formula.

One concrete example: if cell Z99 contains the value 1, then the formula of =INDIRECT("Z99") will return a value of 1. A more practical concrete example follows.

Say that in Figure 29.14, you would like to build a table to copy the current-month totals from each worksheet to a summary table on the Total worksheet. Without the INDIRECT function, you would have to separately enter 12 different formulas in Row 4—one for each month (for example, =Jan!$B4 for January, =Feb!$B4 for February, and so on).

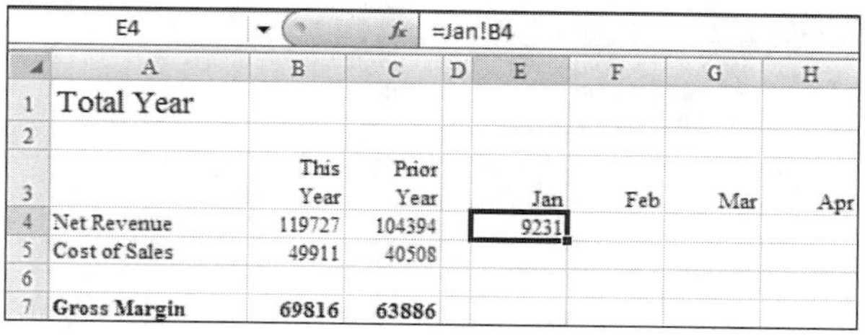

E4 =Jan!B4

| | A | B | C | D | E | F | G | H |
|---|---|---|---|---|---|---|---|---|
| 1 | Total Year | | | | | | | |
| 2 | | | | | | | | |
| 3 | | This Year | Prior Year | | Jan | Feb | Mar | Apr |
| 4 | Net Revenue | 119727 | 104394 | | 9231 | | | |
| 5 | Cost of Sales | 49911 | 40508 | | | | | |
| 6 | | | | | | | | |
| 7 | Gross Margin | 69816 | 63886 | | | | | |

**Figure 29.14** The first of 12 different formulas required in E4:P4.

You can solve this problem with a single formula that you can copy to the entire total worksheet. Follow these steps:

1. You will want to design a text formula in Cell E4 to point to the correct sheet and cell.
2. The worksheet has month headings in Row 3, so you can start to build a formula as `=E$3&"!"`. Note that the `$` before the `3` ensures that as the formula is copied to lower rows in the summary table; it will always point to the month heading in Row 3.
3. The next trick is finding a function that will return the address of Column B for Row 3. To do this, you can use the versatile function called `CELL`. The `CELL` function can return many bits of information about a reference, including the address of the cell. For example, `=CELL("address",$B4)` returns the text `$B$4`.
4. Figure 29.15 shows the intermediate result of entering `=E$3&"!"&CELL("Address",$B4)` into the table.

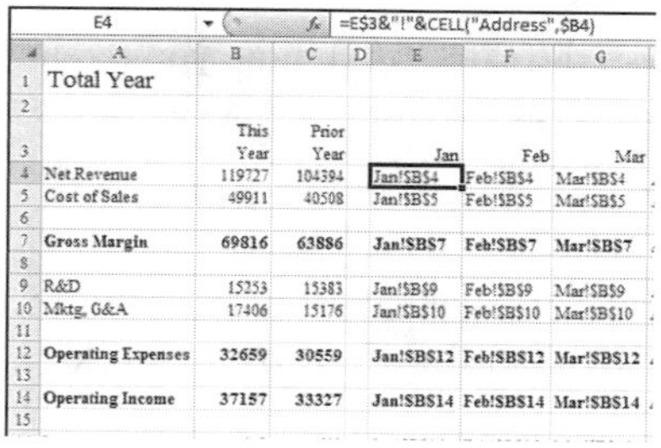

E4 =E$3&"!"&CELL("Address",$B4)

| | A | B | C | D | E | F | G |
|---|---|---|---|---|---|---|---|
| 1 | Total Year | | | | | | |
| 2 | | | | | | | |
| 3 | | This Year | Prior Year | | Jan | Feb | Mar |
| 4 | Net Revenue | 119727 | 104394 | | Jan!$B$4 | Feb!$B$4 | Mar!$B$4 |
| 5 | Cost of Sales | 49911 | 40508 | | Jan!$B$5 | Feb!$B$5 | Mar!$B$5 |
| 6 | | | | | | | |
| 7 | Gross Margin | 69816 | 63886 | | Jan!$B$7 | Feb!$B$7 | Mar!$B$7 |
| 8 | | | | | | | |
| 9 | R&D | 15253 | 15383 | | Jan!$B$9 | Feb!$B$9 | Mar!$B$9 |
| 10 | Mktg, G&A | 17406 | 15176 | | Jan!$B$10 | Feb!$B$10 | Mar!$B$10 |
| 11 | | | | | | | |
| 12 | Operating Expenses | 32659 | 30559 | | Jan!$B$12 | Feb!$B$12 | Mar!$B$12 |
| 13 | | | | | | | |
| 14 | Operating Income | 37157 | 33327 | | Jan!$B$14 | Feb!$B$14 | Mar!$B$14 |
| 15 | | | | | | | |

**Figure 29.15** All the formulas in E4:P22 are identical, but they return the reference to the cell from which the result should be copied.

The last step is to wrap the `INDIRECT` function around the formula in Cell E4. This tells Excel to evaluate the function inside `INDIRECT` to learn that Excel should return the value from Cell B4 on the Jan worksheet.

The whole trick to being efficient in Excel is being able to write one formula that can be copied to an entire range. Rather than going through the tedium of entering 12 different formulas in Row 4, you can use the `INDIRECT` function to enter just one formula everywhere in the range (see Figure 29.16).

**Figure 29.16**

You can wrap the formulas in the `INDIRECT` function to allow one formula to fill the entire table.

| | E4 | ▾ | | fx | =INDIRECT(E$3&"|"&CELL("Address",$B4)) | | | | | | | | | | | | |
|---|---|---|---|---|---|---|---|---|---|---|---|---|---|---|---|---|---|
| | A | B | C | D | E | F | G | H | I | J | K | L | M | N | O | P | Q |
| 1 | Total Year | | | | | | | | | | | | | | | | |
| 2 | | | | | | | | | | | | | | | | | |
| 3 | | This Year | Prior Year | | Jan | Feb | Mar | Apr | May | Jun | Jul | Aug | Sep | Oct | Nov | Dec | |
| 4 | Net Revenue | 119727 | 104394 | | 9231 | 9416 | 9508 | 9600 | 9693 | 9785 | 9877 | 9969 | 10154 | 10339 | 10616 | 11539 | |
| 5 | Cost of Sales | 49911 | 40508 | | 4028 | 4109 | 4067 | 4067 | 4067 | 4066 | 4066 | 4066 | 4103 | 4101 | 4136 | 5035 | |
| 6 | | | | | | | | | | | | | | | | | |
| 7 | Gross Margin | 69816 | 63886 | | 5203 | 5307 | 5441 | 5533 | 5626 | 5719 | 5811 | 5903 | 6051 | 6238 | 6480 | 6504 | |
| 8 | | | | | | | | | | | | | | | | | |

**NOTE**

Excel gurus will point out another benefit of the INDIRECT function. If you have a formula such as =SUM(A1:A10), and you insert a new Row 5, the formula normally expands to =SUM(A1:A11). However, there might be a time when you really want to sum only the first 10 records on the sheet. In this case, you can use the formula =SUM(INDIRECT("A1:A10")) to always point to Rows 1 through 10, no matter what rows are inserted or deleted.

**CAUTION**

There is an important limitation with INDIRECT functions. If you build an INDIRECT function that points to an external workbook, the formula works only when the external workbook is open.

## USING OFFSET TO REFER TO A RANGE THAT DYNAMICALLY RESIZES

When you first read the Help topic on the OFFSET function, you might wonder what would be the point of such a function. The OFFSET function allows you to describe a range by specifying five parameters:

- Any cell from which to start.
- The number of rows to move from the original cell in order to get to the upper-left corner of the reference. Positive numbers move down the worksheet, and negative number move up the spreadsheet.
- The number of columns to move from the original cell in order to get to the upper-left corner of the reference. Positive numbers move to the right from the original cell, and negative numbers move to the left.
- The number of rows in the reference.
- The number of columns in the reference.

It would be difficult to imagine why you would ever use =OFFSET(A1,2,3,4,5) to refer to the range D3:H6. However, when you consider that these arguments can be functions that calculate the size of a range, it starts to make sense.

Say that you start entering invoice amounts in Cell B2 and proceed down Column B. In order to write a sum formula that can expand to include any number of entries in Column B, you could count the number of numeric entries in Column B by using =COUNT(B:B). If you then use the COUNT function as the fourth argument in the OFFSET function, you have set up a dynamic formula that will always expand as new items are entered, as shown in Figure 29.17.

**Figure 29.17**
The `OFFSET` function allows you to describe a rectangular range that starts a calculated number of rows and columns from a starting point.

E1 | =SUM(OFFSET(B2,0,0,COUNT(B:B),1))

| | A | B | C | D | E | F | G |
|---|---|---|---|---|---|---|---|
| 1 | Invoice | Amount | | Total: | $2,527 | | |
| 2 | 1010 | $101 | | | | | |
| 3 | 1011 | $150 | | | | | |
| 4 | 1012 | $199 | | | | | |
| 5 | 1013 | $166 | | | | | |
| 6 | 1014 | $131 | | | | | |
| 7 | 1015 | $121 | | | | | |
| 8 | 1016 | $113 | | | | | |
| 9 | 1017 | $139 | | | | | |
| 10 | 1018 | $130 | | | | | |
| 11 | 1019 | $134 | | | | | |
| 12 | 1020 | $122 | | | | | |
| 13 | 1021 | $115 | | | | | |
| 14 | 1022 | $146 | | | | | |
| 15 | 1023 | $194 | | | | | |
| 16 | 1024 | $110 | | | | | |
| 17 | 1025 | $138 | | | | | |
| 18 | 1026 | $196 | | | | | |
| 19 | 1027 | $122 | | | | | |
| 20 | | | | | | | |

# Assigning a Formula to a Name

When you set up a named range, the Names box shows that the name has a value like `=Sheet1!A1`. Because this value contains an equals sign, you know that this value is actually a formula.

It is possible to assign a very complex formula to a name. Say that you have a workbook with 100 worksheets, with 20 columns of X and Y data in each worksheet, as shown in Figure 29.18. You want to continually update a transformation formula used on all the X and Y points. Every time the formula changes, you have to copy the new formula to all 20 columns on the 20 worksheets.

The technique involves writing a relative formula that will carry out the same transformation as your original formula. Assign this formula to a name. In each of the cells, use =*NamedFormula* instead of the formula.

The advantage is that you can now edit the formula in the Edit Name box and the new formula will be used throughout the workbook.

The following specific examples walk through the steps for one particular formula.

**Figure 29.18**
Every time the formula changes, you must copy it to 400 non-adjacent columns.

C2 | =COS(A2)/SIN(B2)

| | A | B | C | D | E | F | G |
|---|---|---|---|---|---|---|---|
| 1 | X | Y | Formula | | X | Y | Formula |
| 2 | 0.639523 | 0.477897 | 1.744636 | | 0.811692 | 0.239272 | 2.904152 |
| 3 | 0.966707 | 0.194101 | 2.944834 | | 0.621389 | 0.706054 | 1.253122 |
| 4 | 0.238926 | 0.150594 | 6.47619 | | 0.850939 | 0.36347 | 1.854406 |
| 5 | 0.703421 | 0.129919 | 5.886595 | | 0.372584 | 0.791509 | 1.309208 |
| 6 | 0.509818 | 0.155577 | 5.633007 | | 0.253356 | 0.77192 | 1.387899 |
| 7 | 0.131213 | 0.607468 | 1.736897 | | 0.549832 | 0.92877 | 1.064589 |

NOTE

While you usually write formulas in A1 notation made popular by VisiCalc and Lotus 1-2-3, Microsoft still supports the old R1C1 notation that was used in Microsoft Multimate back in 1982. In the R1C1 notation, a cell such as E2 is referenced as R2C5, meaning Row 2, Column 5. The following tip makes use of R1C1 notation.

You can use an R1C1 version of the INDIRECT function to create a formula to take the cosine of a cell two cells to the left of the formula cell and divide it by the sine of the cell to the left of the formula cell. To do so, you follow these steps:

→ For a complete discussion of R1C1 style references, **see** "Using R1C1 Style Formulas," **page 987**, in Chapter 36.

1. To take the cosine of a cell two cells to the left of the current cell, use =COS(SUM (INDIRECT("RC[-2]",False))).

2. To take the sin of the cell to the left of the formula cell, use =SIN(SUM(INDIRECT ("RC[-1]",False))).

3. Use Formulas, Named Cells, Name Manager to open the Name Manager dialog box.

4. Use the Name Manager dialog to assign the formula =COS(SUM(INDIRECT ("rc[-2]",FALSE)))/SIN(SUM(INDIRECT("rc[-1]",FALSE))) to a name such as MyFormula, as shown in Figure 29.19.

**Figure 29.19**
You can assign a name to a formula.

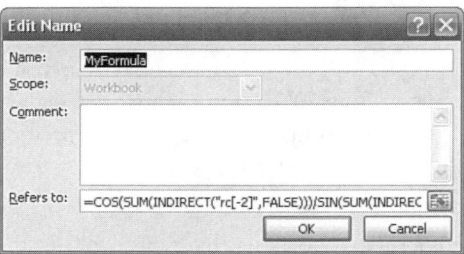

5. In each worksheet, replace the current formula with =MyFormula, as shown in Figure 29.20.

**Figure 29.20**
One last time, you copy the formula name to all 400 non-adjacent columns.

| | B | C | D | E | F | |
|---|---|---|---|---|---|---|
| | Y | Formula | | X | Y | F |
| | 0.477897 | 1.744636 | | 0.811692 | 0.239272 | |
| | 0.194101 | 2.944834 | | 0.621389 | 0.706054 | |
| | 0.150594 | 6.47619 | | 0.850939 | 0.36347 | |
| | 0.129919 | 5.886595 | | 0.372584 | 0.791509 | |

*fx* =MyFormula

6. Change the formula in the Edit Name dialog box and have the new calculation carried out in all 400 non-adjacent columns.

## TURNING A RANGE OF FORMULAS ON ITS SIDE

The Transpose option in the Paste Special dialog is great for changing values that span across several columns into values that go down a column. Here's an example:

1. In Figure 29.21, you select B1:M1 and then press Ctrl+C.

**Figure 29.21**
You can copy a range that spans several columns.

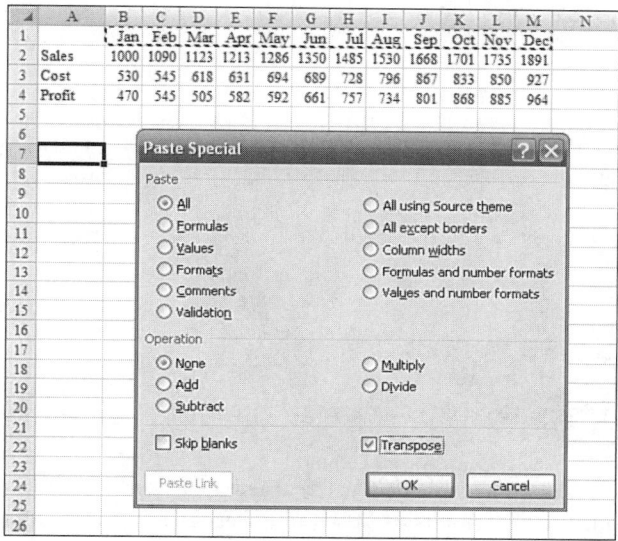

2. Select the top left cell where the range should be copied. In this example, select cell A7.
3. Select Home, Clipboard, Paste, Paste Special to open the Paste Special dialog.
4. Select Transpose in the Paste Special dialog.
5. Click OK. The month names now go down the row, as shown in Figure 29.22.

**Figure 29.22**
You can use the Paste Special dialog to turn a range on its side.

|  | A | B | C | D | E | F | G | H | I | J | K | L | M |
|---|---|---|---|---|---|---|---|---|---|---|---|---|---|
| 1 |  | Jan | Feb | Mar | Apr | May | Jun | Jul | Aug | Sep | Oct | Nov | Dec |
| 2 | Sales | 1000 | 1090 | 1123 | 1213 | 1286 | 1350 | 1485 | 1530 | 1668 | 1701 | 1735 | 1891 |
| 3 | Cost | 530 | 545 | 618 | 631 | 694 | 689 | 728 | 796 | 867 | 833 | 850 | 927 |
| 4 | Profit | 470 | 545 | 505 | 582 | 592 | 661 | 757 | 734 | 801 | 868 | 885 | 964 |
| 5 |  |  |  |  |  |  |  |  |  |  |  |  |  |
| 6 |  |  |  |  |  |  |  |  |  |  |  |  |  |
| 7 | Jan |  |  |  |  |  |  |  |  |  |  |  |  |
| 8 | Feb |  |  |  |  |  |  |  |  |  |  |  |  |
| 9 | Mar |  |  |  |  |  |  |  |  |  |  |  |  |
| 10 | Apr |  |  |  |  |  |  |  |  |  |  |  |  |
| 11 | May |  |  |  |  |  |  |  |  |  |  |  |  |
| 12 | Jun |  |  |  |  |  |  |  |  |  |  |  |  |
| 13 | Jul |  |  |  |  |  |  |  |  |  |  |  |  |
| 14 | Aug |  |  |  |  |  |  |  |  |  |  |  |  |
| 15 | Sep |  |  |  |  |  |  |  |  |  |  |  |  |
| 16 | Oct |  |  |  |  |  |  |  |  |  |  |  |  |
| 17 | Nov |  |  |  |  |  |  |  |  |  |  |  |  |
| 18 | Dec |  |  |  |  |  |  |  |  |  |  |  |  |
| 19 |  |  |  |  |  |  |  |  |  |  |  |  |  |  |
| 20 |  |  |  |  |  |  |  |  |  |  |  |  |  |  |

However, there is not a good way to copy the calculation for profit from Row 4 to the new table. You normally have to enter 12 different formulas in the range B7:B17 as shown in Figure 29.23.

**Figure 29.23**
Transposing with a formula requires a different formula in each cell.

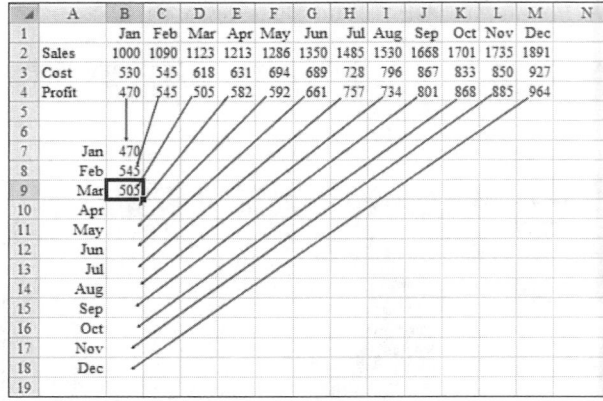

But there are two ways to easily enter a single formula that will turn those results on their side.

First, you can use the OFFSET function you learned about earlier in this chapter. You can set up an OFFSET function that points to $A$4 and offsets by an additional column as you copy the formula down the rows. Try it:

1. In Cell B7, enter =ROW(A1). The result is the number 1.

2. Copy the formula from Cell B7 down to B7:B18. The result returns a string of integers from 1 through 12, as shown in Figure 29.24

**Figure 29.24**
You can copy the =ROW(A1) formula down a column to create a sequence of integers.

| ◢ | A | B | C | D | E | F | G | H | I | J | K | L | M | N |
|---|---|---|---|---|---|---|---|---|---|---|---|---|---|---|
| 1 | | Jan | Feb | Mar | Apr | May | Jun | Jul | Aug | Sep | Oct | Nov | Dec | |
| 2 | Sales | 1000 | 1090 | 1123 | 1213 | 1286 | 1350 | 1485 | 1530 | 1668 | 1701 | 1735 | 1891 | |
| 3 | Cost | 530 | 545 | 618 | 631 | 694 | 689 | 728 | 796 | 867 | 833 | 850 | 927 | |
| 4 | Profit | 470 | 545 | 505 | 582 | 592 | 661 | 757 | 734 | 801 | 868 | 885 | 964 | |
| 5 | | | | | | | | | | | | | | |
| 6 | | | | | | | | | | | | | | |
| 7 | Jan | 1 | | | | | | | | | | | | |
| 8 | Feb | 2 | | | | | | | | | | | | |
| 9 | Mar | 3 | | | | | | | | | | | | |
| 10 | Apr | 4 | | | | | | | | | | | | |
| 11 | May | 5 | | | | | | | | | | | | |
| 12 | Jun | 6 | | | | | | | | | | | | |
| 13 | Jul | 7 | | | | | | | | | | | | |
| 14 | Aug | 8 | | | | | | | | | | | | |
| 15 | Sep | 9 | | | | | | | | | | | | |
| 16 | Oct | 10 | | | | | | | | | | | | |
| 17 | Nov | 11 | | | | | | | | | | | | |
| 18 | Dec | 12 | | | | | | | | | | | | |
| 19 | | | | | | | | | | | | | | |

3. Use the formula =ROW(A1) as the third argument in the OFFSET function. A formula of =OFFSET($A$4,0,ROW(A1)) will achieve the perfect result, as shown in Figure 29.25.

**Figure 29.25**
You can use the
ROW(A1) trick as the
Column Offset param-
eter in the OFFSET
function to turn a
range on its side.

| | B7 | | | | $f_x$ | =OFFSET($A$4,0,ROW(A1)) | | | | | | |
|---|---|---|---|---|---|---|---|---|---|---|---|---|
| | A | B | C | D | E | F | G | H | I | J | K | L | M |
| 1 | | Jan | Feb | Mar | Apr | May | Jun | Jul | Aug | Sep | Oct | Nov | Dec |
| 2 | Sales | 1000 | 1090 | 1123 | 1213 | 1286 | 1350 | 1485 | 1530 | 1668 | 1701 | 1735 | 1891 |
| 3 | Cost | 530 | 545 | 618 | 631 | 694 | 689 | 728 | 796 | 867 | 833 | 850 | 927 |
| 4 | Profit | 470 | 545 | 505 | 582 | 592 | 661 | 757 | 734 | 801 | 868 | 885 | 964 |
| 5 | | | | | | | | | | | | | |
| 6 | | | | | | | | | | | | | |
| 7 | Jan | 470 | | | | | | | | | | | |
| 8 | Feb | 545 | | | | | | | | | | | |
| 9 | Mar | 505 | | | | | | | | | | | |
| 10 | Apr | 582 | | | | | | | | | | | |
| 11 | May | 592 | | | | | | | | | | | |
| 12 | Jun | 661 | | | | | | | | | | | |
| 13 | Jul | 757 | | | | | | | | | | | |
| 14 | Aug | 734 | | | | | | | | | | | |
| 15 | Sep | 801 | | | | | | | | | | | |
| 16 | Oct | 868 | | | | | | | | | | | |
| 17 | Nov | 885 | | | | | | | | | | | |
| 18 | Dec | 964 | | | | | | | | | | | |

One danger exists with just about every method described in this chapter: They produce results that the average person does not understand. So if you want to end up with straight-forward formulas in B7:B18, you can use the following method:

1. Enter a formula such as =B4 in Cell B5.

2. Copy the first formula across Row 5 for each month.

3. Highlight the formulas in B5:M5.

4. Use Home, Editing, Find & Select, Replace to display the Find and Replace dialog. In the Find What box, enter an equals sign. In the Replace With box, enter an exclamation point. Click Replace All to change every occurrence of = to !. This converts the formulas to text, as shown in Figure 29.26.

**Figure 29.26**
Converting the formu-
las to text allows them
to be transposed.

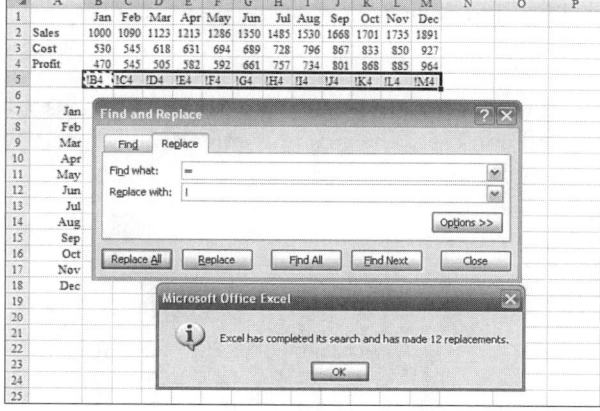

5. Copy the range and highlight a new cell (in this example, Cell B7).

6. Choose Home, Clipboard, Paste, Paste Special to open the Paste Special dialog and then select Transpose. Because the cells are all text, they transpose perfectly, as shown in Figure 29.27.

**Figure 29.27**
You change ! back to = to change to formulas.

| | A | B | C | D | E | F | G | H | I | J | K | L | M |
|---|---|---|---|---|---|---|---|---|---|---|---|---|---|
| 1 | | Jan | Feb | Mar | Apr | May | Jun | Jul | Aug | Sep | Oct | Nov | Dec |
| 2 | Sales | 1000 | 1090 | 1123 | 1213 | 1286 | 1350 | 1485 | 1530 | 1668 | 1701 | 1735 | 1891 |
| 3 | Cost | 530 | 545 | 618 | 631 | 694 | 689 | 728 | 796 | 867 | 833 | 850 | 927 |
| 4 | Profit | 470 | 545 | 505 | 582 | 592 | 661 | 757 | 734 | 801 | 868 | 885 | 964 |
| 5 | | !B4 | !C4 | !D4 | !E4 | !F4 | !G4 | !H4 | !I4 | !J4 | !K4 | !L4 | !M4 |
| 6 | | | | | | | | | | | | | |
| 7 | Jan | !B4 | | | | | | | | | | | |
| 8 | Feb | !C4 | | | | | | | | | | | |
| 9 | Mar | !D4 | | | | | | | | | | | |
| 10 | Apr | !E4 | | | | | | | | | | | |
| 11 | May | !F4 | | | | | | | | | | | |
| 12 | Jun | !G4 | | | | | | | | | | | |
| 13 | Jul | !H4 | | | | | | | | | | | |
| 14 | Aug | !I4 | | | | | | | | | | | |
| 15 | Sep | !J4 | | | | | | | | | | | |
| 16 | Oct | !K4 | | | | | | | | | | | |
| 17 | Nov | !L4 | | | | | | | | | | | |
| 18 | Dec | !M4 | | | | | | | | | | | |
| 19 | | | | | | | | | | | | | |

7. Use Home, Editing, Find & Select, Replace to display the Find and Replace dialog. Type an exclamation point in Find What and an equals sign in Replace With. Click Replace All to change every ! back to =. It now looks as if you actually typed all 12 formulas individually.

# Replacing Multiple Formulas with One Array Formula

There exists a wildly powerful type of formula that most Excel users have never experienced. This formula can do thousands of calculations in a single formula.

The formula is known as an array formula. You must use Ctrl+Shift+Enter when entering an array formula to tell Excel to evaluate the formula as an array.

Here is an example of the power of an array formula.

Consider the dataset shown in Figure 29.28. This database has transactional data showing quantity, unit price, and unit cost. The goal is to enter a single formula that will multiply each quantity by each price and sum the result.

**Figure 29.28**
The goal is to find the result of multiplying quantity by price for all records.

E2 | fx 379.75

| | A | B | C | D | E | F |
|---|---|---|---|---|---|---|
| 1 | Customer | Item | Qty | Price | Cost | |
| 2 | Different Umbrella Traders | C253 | 220 | 775 | 379.75 | |
| 3 | Agile Washer Traders | E710 | 605 | 347 | 188.65 | |
| 4 | Fashionable Shoe Company | C253 | 343 | 775 | 379.75 | |
| 5 | Fashionable Shoe Company | C253 | 247 | 775 | 379.75 | |
| 6 | Powerful Calculator Corporati | C253 | 63 | 775 | 379.75 | |
| 7 | Powerful Calculator Corporati | B722 | 107 | 645 | 316.05 | |
| 8 | Tasty Oven Inc. | C924 | 97 | 115 | 55.2 | |
| 9 | Different Umbrella Traders | A182 | 794 | 122 | 67.5 | |
| 10 | Powerful Calculator Corporati | B128 | 161 | 185 | 90.65 | |
| 11 | Honest Necktie Corporation | C670 | 491 | 395 | 201.45 | |
| 12 | Different Umbrella Traders | C924 | 195 | 115 | 55.2 | |
| 13 | Different Umbrella Traders | B722 | 753 | 581 | 316.05 | |
| 14 | Flexible Sandal Corporation | C924 | 15 | 115 | 55.2 | |

Most people would add a new column with formulas to multiply quantity times price as shown in Figure 29.29. This is easy to do. However, it adds 5,000 new formula cells to your worksheet.

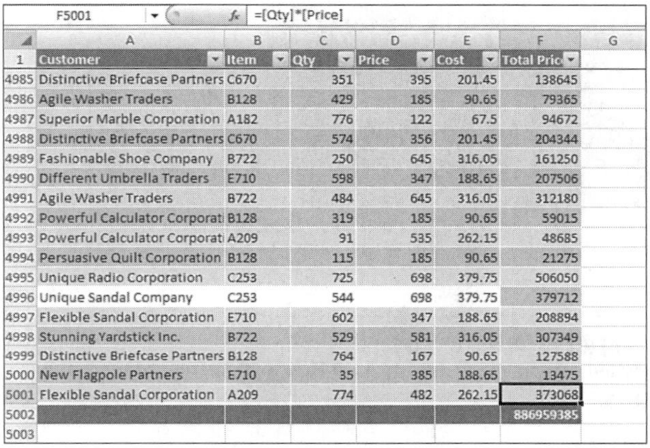

**Figure 29.29**
The typical approach to summing 5,000 calculations is to add a new column with the calculations and total that column.

It is possible to enter a calculation in one cell that will do the 5,000 calculations and total them. With tables in Excel 2007, you have two choices for writing this formula:

- =SUM(C2:C5000*D2:D5000) is an example of a formula for a range that has not been converted to a table.

- =SUM(Table1[Qty]*Table1[Price]) is an example of a formula for a range that has been converted to a table

Follow these steps:

1. Select a blank cell in the worksheet.

2. Type either formula previously shown.

3. Hold down Ctrl+Shift+Enter.

As shown in Figure 29.30, Excel will correctly calculate the result.

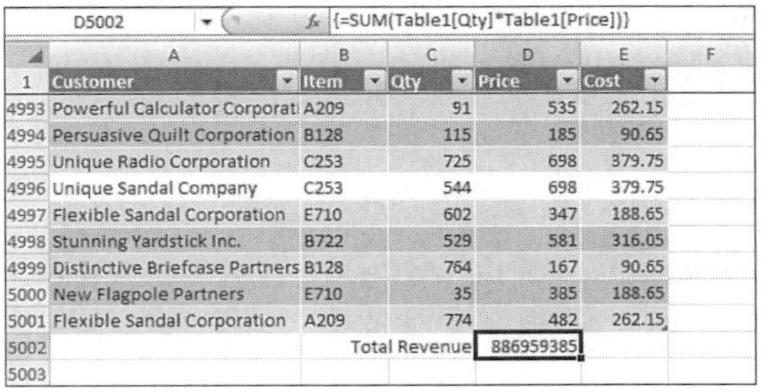

**Figure 29.30**
When you press Ctrl+Shift+Enter, Excel understands that this is not a typical formula.

If you fail to use Ctrl+Shift+Enter, Excel will return a #VALUE error, as shown in Figure 29.31.

**Figure 29.31**
If you don't press Ctrl+Shift+Enter, the formula returns a #VALUE! error.

| | D5002 | | *fx* =SUM(Table1[Qty]*Table1[Price]) | | | |
|---|---|---|---|---|---|---|
| | A | B | C | D | E | F |
| 1 | Customer | Item | Qty | Price | Cost | |
| 4993 | Powerful Calculator Corporat | A209 | 91 | 535 | 262.15 | |
| 4994 | Persuasive Quilt Corporation | B128 | 115 | 185 | 90.65 | |
| 4995 | Unique Radio Corporation | C253 | 725 | 698 | 379.75 | |
| 4996 | Unique Sandal Company | C253 | 544 | 698 | 379.75 | |
| 4997 | Flexible Sandal Corporation | E710 | 602 | 347 | 188.65 | |
| 4998 | Stunning Yardstick Inc. | B722 | 529 | 581 | 316.05 | |
| 4999 | Distinctive Briefcase Partners | B128 | 764 | 167 | 90.65 | |
| 5000 | New Flagpole Partners | E710 | 35 | 385 | 188.65 | |
| 5001 | Flexible Sandal Corporation | A209 | 774 | 482 | 262.15 | |
| 5002 | | | Total Revenue | #VALUE! | | |
| 5003 | | | | | | |

### Excel in Practice: Copying Array Formulas

There is a difficulty when copying array formulas. In Figure 29.32, the array formula in B5006 needs to be copied to B5006:K5025.

**Figure 29.32**
You want to copy this formula to the rest of the summary table.

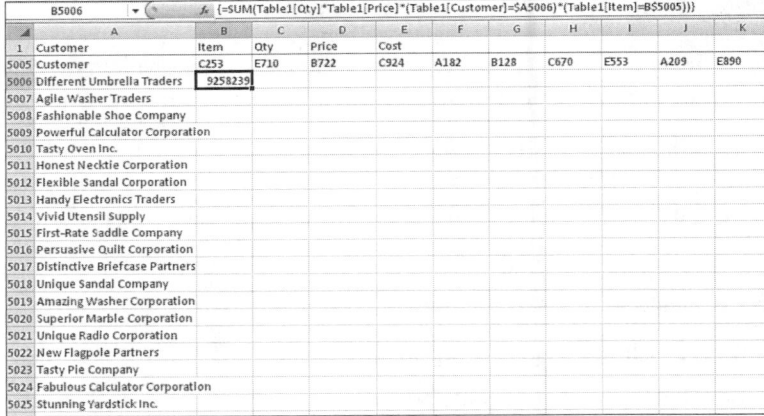

Normally, you would copy Cell B5006 and then paste to Cells B5006:K5025. With array formulas, this leads to an error. If you attempt to do this copy, you are told that you cannot move or change part of an array. The solution is to do the copy in two pieces:

1. Copy Cell B5006 to B5007:B5025.
2. Copy B5006:B5025 and paste it to C5006:K5006.

## FINDING CONDITIONAL SUMS BY USING SUMPRODUCT

It is possible to convert the previous array formula to a SUMPRODUCT formula:

```
=SUMPRODUCT((Table1[Qty])*(Table1[Price])*(Table1[Customer]=$A5006)*(Table1
[Item]=B$5005))
```

You can then enter this as a regular formula instead of an array.

# Using Names in Excel

## In this chapter

Long before Microsoft introduced tables and formulas like =Revenue-Cost, spreadsheets have offered the ability to assign a name to a cell, to a range of cells, or to a formula. The theory is that using a name for a range would be easier to understand when used in a formula. =SUM(MyExpenses) would make formulas more self-documenting than =SUM(Sheet5!AB2:AB99).

With Excel 2007, Microsoft added a new Name Manager interface to allow you to assign and use names effectively.

# DEFINING A NAME FOR A CELL BY USING THE NAME BOX

There are a variety of uses for names in a workbook. A name can be applied to any cell or range. Names are also useful for the following:

- Making formulas easier to understand
- Quick navigation
- Improving Solver's report results
- Storing a value that will be used over and over but that might occasionally need to change, such as a sales tax rate
- Storing formulas
- Defining a dynamic range

**NOTE**

Excel 2007 offers the new Table functionality (described in Chapter 8, "Fabulous Table Intelligence"). Although that feature allows you to create formulas using column names, the individual column names and the table name are not considered named ranges.

There are various ways to name a cell. The easiest way to define a name for a cell is to use the Name box. To do so, you select any cell in your worksheet. To the left of the formula bar is a box with the address of that cell. This box is known as the Name box. The quick way to assign a name is to click inside the Name box and type a name, such as **Revenue**. Figure 30.1 shows the Name box.

When you press Enter, Excel centers the name in the Name box, which indicates that the name has been assigned. This is your only indication that the name is valid and has been accepted.

The following are some basic rules for valid names:

- Names can be up to 255 characters long.
- Names cannot contain spaces. However, you can use an underscore or a period in a name. For example, the names Gross_Profit and Gross.Profit are valid.
- Names cannot look like cell addresses.
- Names cannot contain operator characters such as these: +-*/()^&<>=%.
- Names cannot contain special characters, such as these : !"#$',;:@[]{}` | ~.

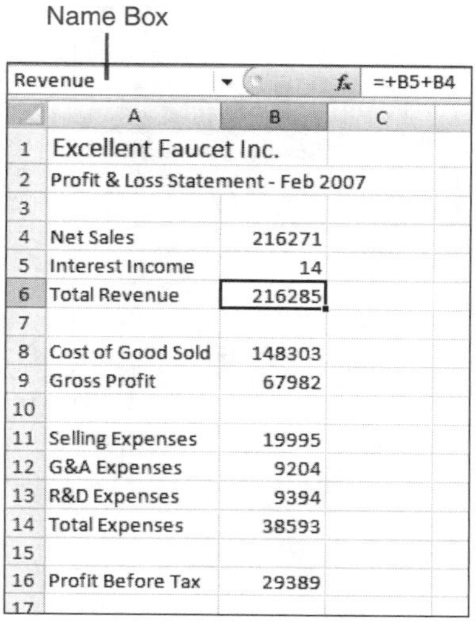

Name Box

**Figure 30.1**
The Name box is
to the left of the
formula bar.

Table 30.1 provides some examples of valid and invalid names.

| TABLE 30.1 | EXAMPLES OF VALID AND INVALID NAMES |
|---|---|
| **Valid Names** | **Invalid Names (why)** |
| SalesTax | Sales Tax (includes a space) |
| Sales_Tax | XFD123 (valid cell address) |
| Sales.Tax | Tax2007 (valid cell address) |
| SalesTax2007 | MyResults! (invalid special character) |

# NAMING A CELL BY USING THE NEW NAME DIALOG

The Formulas ribbon contains a group called Named Cells. The following example introduces the New Name dialog:

1. Select a cell that you would like to name. Click the Name a Range icon from the Formulas ribbon. The New Name dialog box appears. In Figure 30.2, cell B8 is being assigned a name.

2. The New Name box uses IntelliSense to propose a name. Notice that in this particular example, Excel's IntelliSense was able to ascertain that this cell contains the text Cost of Good Sold. Because that is not a valid name, Excel instead proposed naming the cell Cost_of_Good_Sold. You can either keep that name or override it with a name that you prefer. In this case, override that name with the name COGS.

As you can see in Figure 30.3, the name was applied because the Name box now shows COGS instead of B8.

**Figure 30.2**
You select a cell to be named and choose Name a Range from the Formulas ribbon.

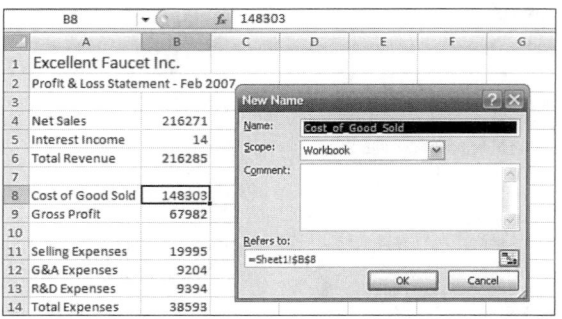

**Figure 30.3**
After you assign a name, the Name box reflects the new name.

# USING THE NAME BOX FOR QUICK NAVIGATION

One advantage of using names is that you can use the dropdown in the Name box to quickly jump to any named cell. This includes cells that might be in distant sections of the worksheet or even on other sheets in the workbook.

If you plan to use the Name box for navigation, assign a name to the upper-left corner of each section of your workbook. The Name box dropdown will then provide a mini-table of contents and people can use the Name box to quickly jump to any section of the workbook.

To illustrate this concept, follow these steps:

1. Click the New Sheet icon to add a new sheet to the workbook.
2. On the new sheet, go to a far-off cell. Give that cell a name such as SectionTwo. Return to the original sheet in the workbook.
3. Click the Name box's drop-down arrow to access a list of all names in the workbook, as shown in Figure 30.4.
4. Choose a name from the list to quickly navigate to that cell, even if it is on another worksheet.

As you can see, named ranges are a great tool for quickly navigating a workbook. Note that names are presented in the Name box alphabetically. If you want the names to appear in the Name box sequentially, you can add names such as Section1, Section2, Section3, and so on. Or prefix the section names with letters, such as A-Income, B-Costs, C-Expense, D-Tax, E-

Income. Then, you can quickly jump to a section by choosing it from the alphabetical list in the Name box. When used in this way, names in Excel are almost like bookmarks in Word.

**Figure 30.4**
The Name Box drop-down contains a list of all names in the workbook.

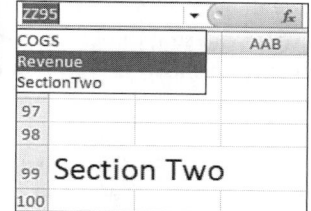

# USING SCOPE TO ALLOW DUPLICATE NAMES IN A WORKBOOK

Ideally, you would keep the names unique throughout a workbook. Although it is technically legal to add a name such as SectionOne to both Sheet1 and Sheet2, it is not a good idea. When you define the name on the first sheet, it is defined as a name with workbook-level scope. This means that you can easily navigate to SectionOne from any sheet in the workbook. If you attempt to set up the same name on a second worksheet, that name will have to be set up with worksheet-level scope. Names with worksheet-level scope override the workbook-level scope only on the sheets on which they are defined. For example, say you have a workbook with Sheet1, Sheet2, Sheet3, Sheet4, and Sheet5:

- On Sheet1, you use the Name box to assign the name SectionOne to Cell A9.
- On Sheet3, you use the New Name dialog to assign the name SectionOne to Cell A21. In the New Name dialog, you have to change the Scope setting from Workbook to Sheet3, as shown in Figure 30.5

**Figure 30.5**
You change the scope of the duplicate name to apply only on Sheet3.

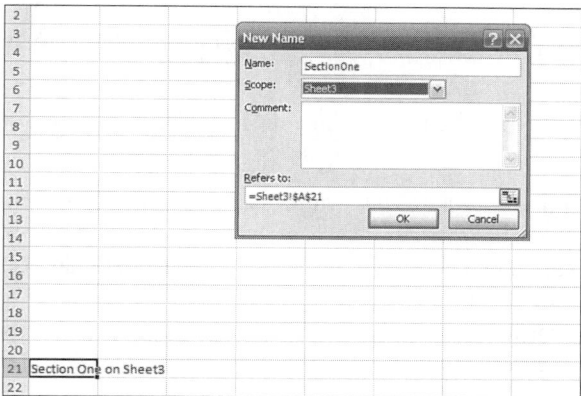

- If you are on Sheet3 and use the Name box to navigate to SectionOne, you will jump to Cell A21 on Sheet3.

■ If you are on any other sheet in the workbook and use the Name box to navigate to SectionOne, you will jump to Cell A9 on Sheet1.

You can see that this is fairly confusing. In general, you should stick with unique names that can have workbook-level scope. You should switch to using duplicate names with worksheet-level scope only when you have many nearly identical sheets in a workbook.

**30**

---

**Inadvertently Creating Worksheet-Level Scope**

It is easy to accidentally set up worksheet-level scope. Say that you set up a worksheet for January. You assign five workbook-level names on the worksheet. You then make a copy of this worksheet for February. All the names continue to exist on the February worksheet, but they have their scope set to only the February worksheet.

To avoid this problem, make copies of the worksheets before assigning names.

---

# USING NAMED RANGES TO SIMPLIFY FORMULAS

As introduced at the start of this chapter, the original reason for having named ranges was to simplify formulas. In theory, it is easier to understand a formula such as =(Revenue-Cost)/Revenue.

Be sure to define the names before entering formulas that refer to those cells. When you create a formula using the mouse or arrow key methods, Excel will automatically use the names in the formula.

In the following example, the worksheet in Figure 30.6 has a name of "Revenue" assigned to A6 and a name of "Cost" assigned to A8. Rather than typing =A6-A8 in cell A9, follow these steps to have Excel create a formula using names.

1. Select the cell where the formula should go. In this example, it is cell A9.
2. Type =.
3. Using the mouse, click the first cell in your formula. In this case, it is cell A6.
4. Type -.
5. Using the mouse, click the next cell in your formula. In this case, it is cell A8.
6. Press Enter.
7. Move the cell pointer back to the formula cell and look in the formula bar. You can see that Excel has built the formula =Revenues-COGS, as shown in Figure 30.6. In theory, this formula is self-documenting and easier to understand than =C6-C8.

You can also type a formula that uses names directly in a cell. For example, Figure 30.7 shows =Revenue*1.1 entered in Cell E6. When you press Enter, Excel recognizes this formula and multiplies Cell A6 by 1.1.

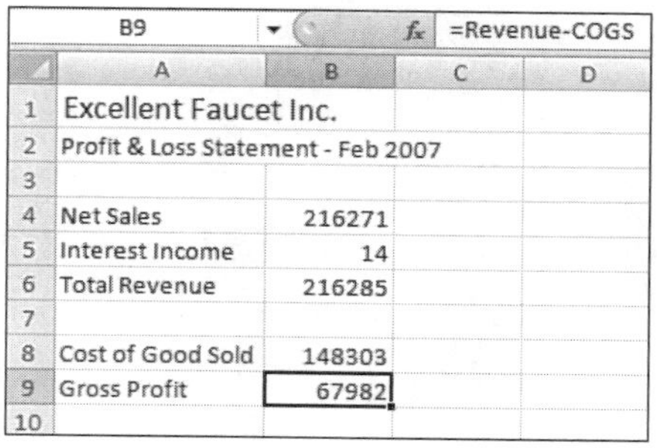

**Figure 30.6**
New formulas created after names have been assigned reflect the cell names in the formula.

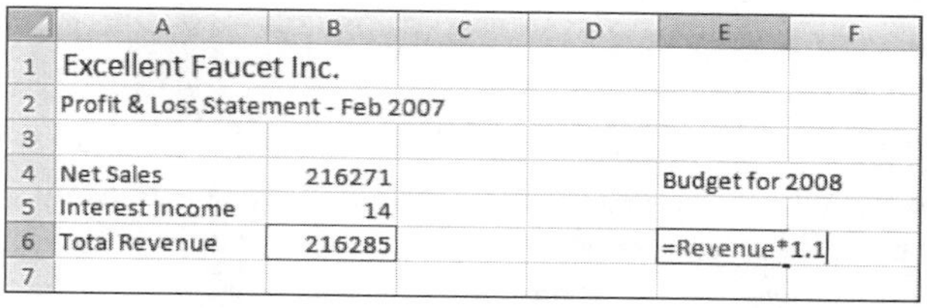

| | B9 | ▼ | | $f_x$ =Revenue-COGS | |
|---|---|---|---|---|---|
| | A | B | C | D | |
| 1 | Excellent Faucet Inc. | | | | |
| 2 | Profit & Loss Statement - Feb 2007 | | | | |
| 3 | | | | | |
| 4 | Net Sales | 216271 | | | |
| 5 | Interest Income | 14 | | | |
| 6 | Total Revenue | 216285 | | | |
| 7 | | | | | |
| 8 | Cost of Good Sold | 148303 | | | |
| 9 | Gross Profit | 67982 | | | |
| 10 | | | | | |

**Figure 30.7**
You can type formulas to reference existing cell names.

| | A | B | C | D | E | F |
|---|---|---|---|---|---|---|
| 1 | Excellent Faucet Inc. | | | | | |
| 2 | Profit & Loss Statement - Feb 2007 | | | | | |
| 3 | | | | | | |
| 4 | Net Sales | 216271 | | | Budget for 2008 | |
| 5 | Interest Income | 14 | | | | |
| 6 | Total Revenue | 216285 | | | =Revenue*1.1 | |
| 7 | | | | | | |

However, a problem crops up when one of the cells in the formula contains a name—especially if that name is defined strictly for navigational purposes. In this case, Excel will create an absolute reference to that cell. When you copy a formula that contains a name, the copied formula always points to the name. This can lead to unhappy results.

Here is an example to show how easily this can happen.

Figure 30.8 shows Cell A2 named SectionThree so that the name can be used as a bookmark.

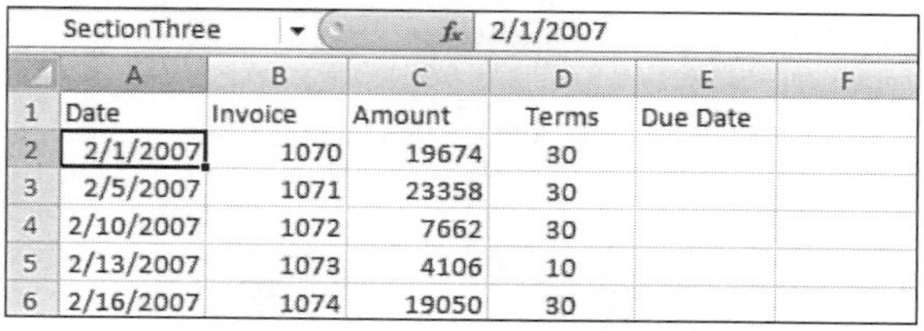

**Figure 30.8**
Cell A2 is named SectionThree to aid navigation.

| | SectionThree | ▼ | | $f_x$ 2/1/2007 | | |
|---|---|---|---|---|---|---|
| | A | B | C | D | E | F |
| 1 | Date | Invoice | Amount | Terms | Due Date | |
| 2 | 2/1/2007 | 1070 | 19674 | 30 | | |
| 3 | 2/5/2007 | 1071 | 23358 | 30 | | |
| 4 | 2/10/2007 | 1072 | 7662 | 30 | | |
| 5 | 2/13/2007 | 1073 | 4106 | 10 | | |
| 6 | 2/16/2007 | 1074 | 19050 | 30 | | |

In Cell E2 you enter a formula to calculate a due date. Using the mouse method, you type =, touch Cell A2 with the mouse, type +, and then touch Cell D2 with the mouse. Instead of entering the formula =A2+D2, you end up with the formula =SectionThree+D2.

Select Cell E2 and double-click the fill handle to copy the formula down to all rows. Examine the formula in Cell E5. As shown in Figure 30.9, although Cell D2 was correctly changed to Cell D5 in the copied formula, this cell and all the remaining cells in Column E are incorrectly pointing to Cell A2 because it was previously defined as a named range.

30

**Figure 30.9**
When you copy this formula, every cell points at Cell A2 because that cell previously had a defined name.

| | E5 | | | $f_x$ | =SectionThree+D5 | |
|---|---|---|---|---|---|---|
| | A | B | C | D | E | |
| 1 | Date | Invoice | Amount | Terms | Due Date | |
| 2 | 2/1/2007 | 1070 | 19674 | 30 | 3/3/2007 | |
| 3 | 2/5/2007 | 1071 | 23358 | 30 | 3/3/2007 | |
| 4 | 2/10/2007 | 1072 | 7662 | 30 | 3/3/2007 | |
| 5 | 2/13/2007 | 1073 | 4106 | 10 | 2/11/2007 | |
| 6 | 2/16/2007 | 1074 | 19050 | 30 | 3/3/2007 | |
| 7 | 2/21/2007 | 1075 | 25537 | 15 | 2/16/2007 | |

To overcome this problem, you need to use care when entering the original formula: You need to type =, type **A2+**, and then touch Cell D2. This override Excel's default behavior of automatically converting relative reference names to preexisting range names.

## RETROACTIVELY APPLYING NAMES TO FORMULAS

When you learn the trick discussed in "Using Named Ranges to Simplify Formulas," you might start naming all the input cells in your workbook, hoping that all the preexisting formulas will take on the new names. Unfortunately, this does not automatically work.

In Figure 30.10, the formula in B16 was entered first. Later, cells B9 and B14 were given the names GrossProfit and TotalExpenses, respectively. However, the preexisting formula in B16 continues to reflect the cell addresses instead of the names.

**Figure 30.10**
The legacy formula in Cell B16 does not reflect the new named ranges. You use Name a Range, Apply in order to display this dialog.

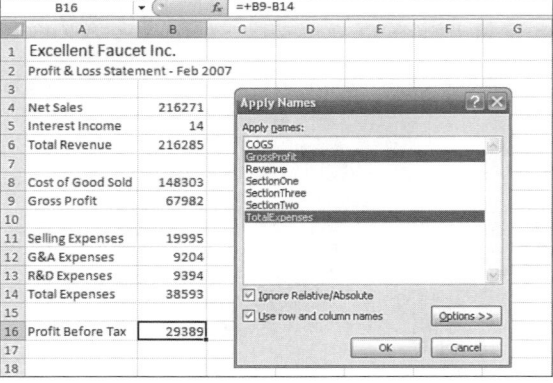

In order to make the names become part of existing formulas, you have to use the Apply command. Here is what you do:

1. On the Formulas ribbon, select the drop-down next to Name a Range and choose Apply. The Apply Names dialog appears, as shown in Figure 30.10.
2. Select as many names as you want in the Apply Names box. In this example, you would select at least GrossProfit and TotalExpenses and then click OK. Any existing formulas that point to these named cells change to include the cell names in the formula, as shown in Figure 30.11.

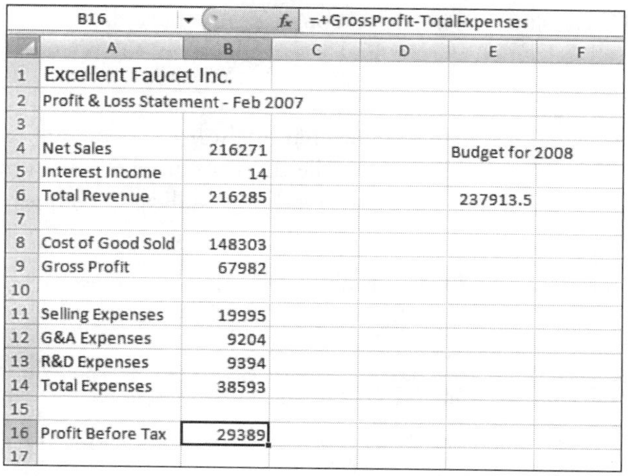

**Figure 30.11**
After you apply names, existing formulas are rewritten.

## USING NAMES TO REFER TO MULTIPLE-CELL RANGES

It is possible to define a name that refers to a larger range of cells. For example, you could select C11:C13 in Figure 30.12 and type a name, such as Expenses, in the Name box.

**Figure 30.12**
A name can refer to a rectangular range.

If you later select Expenses from the Name box, your cursor moves to Cell C11, and the entire range is selected. Having a name apply to a range allows formulas such as =Sum(Expenses).

## DEALING WITH INVALID LEGACY NAMING

To prevent confusion, a valid cell address may not be used as a name. In prior versions of Excel, this eliminated names from A1 through IV65536.

Excel 2007 now has columns named A through Z, AA through ZZ, and AAA through XFD. The same rule applied to Excel 2007 now invalidates names that start with IW through ZZ and AAA through XFD.

You can think of many three-letter names that might have been common in Excel 2003—names like Tax2007, ROI5, and so on. While those are perfectly legal in Excel 2003, they are no longer valid in Excel 2007 because they duplicate existing cell addresses in Excel 2007.

Figure 30.13 shows an Excel 2003 workbook that contains names such as Tax2004, Tax2005, and so on.

**Figure 30.13**
In Excel 2003, a range named Tax2004 for Cell B4 was perfectly legal because with only 256 columns, there was not a column called Tax.

| | C7 | | | $f_x$ =ROUND(CHOOSE(YEAR(A7)-2003,Tax2004,Tax2005,Tax2006,Tax2007)*B7,2) | | | | | | |
|---|---|---|---|---|---|---|---|---|---|---|
| | A | B | C | D | E | F | G | H | I | J | K |
| 1 | | | | | | | | | | |
| 2 | | | | | | | | | | |
| 3 | | | 2004 | 2005 | 2006 | 2007 | | | | |
| 4 | Tax Rates | 7% | 6.50% | 6.75% | 6.25% | | | | | |
| 5 | | | | | | | | | | |
| 6 | Date | Amount | Tax | | | | | | | |
| 7 | 6/19/2004 | 502.99 | 35.21 | | | | | | | |
| 8 | 1/3/2006 | 312.64 | 21.1 | | | | | | | |
| 9 | 4/16/2004 | 642.39 | 44.97 | | | | | | | |
| 10 | 5/24/2006 | 110.13 | 7.43 | | | | | | | |

You can open this workbook in Excel 2007. The workbook initially opens in legacy mode, with columns only through IV. When you attempt to save the file as an Excel 2007 workbook, Excel warns you that there are defined names that are now equivalent to valid cell addresses in Excel 2007, as shown in Figure 30.14.

**Figure 30.14**
When you try to save the Excel 2003 workbook as an Excel 2007 file, the established names must be changed.

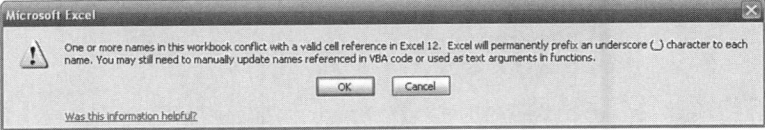

Microsoft Excel

One or more names in this workbook conflict with a valid cell reference in Excel 12.  Excel will permanently prefix an underscore (_) character to each name. You may still need to manually update names referenced in VBA code or used as text arguments in functions.

OK    Cancel

Was this information helpful?

After you close the message box in Figure 30.14, Excel attempts to warn you about every existing name. The first message box warns that Tax2004 will become _Tax2004. You can either click OK to each message or skip them by clicking OK to All.

Excel does a great job of updating the names and the formulas that use invalid names. Figure 30.15 shows the Excel 2003 worksheet after it is converted to Excel 2007. Each name now has an underscore at the beginning.

**Figure 30.15**
Excel correctly updated these references.

| | PV | | X ✓ $f_x$ =ROUND(CHOOSE(YEAR(A7)-2003,_Tax2004,_Tax2005,_Tax2006,_Tax2007)*B7,2) | | | | | | | | |
|---|---|---|---|---|---|---|---|---|---|---|---|
| | A | B | C | D | E | F | G | H | I | J | K | L |
| 1 | | | | | | | | | | | |
| 2 | | | | | | | | | | | |
| 3 | | | 2004 | 2005 | 2006 | 2007 | | | | | |
| 4 | Tax Rates | 7% | 6.50% | 6.75% | 6.25% | | | | | | |
| 5 | | | | | | | | | | | |
| 6 | Date | Amount | Tax | | | | | | | | |
| 7 | 6/19/2004 | 502.99 | =ROUND(CHOOSE(YEAR(A7)-2003,_Tax2004,_Tax2005,_Tax2006,_Tax2007)*B7,2) | | | | | | | | |
| 8 | 1/3/2006 | 312.64 | 21.1 | | | | | | | | |
| 9 | 4/16/2004 | 642.39 | 44.97 | | | | | | | | |

**CAUTION**

There are some formulas that Excel is not able to update. It would be efficient to rewrite the formula in Figure 30.13 as =B7*INDIRECT("TAX"&YEAR(A7)). Although this works perfectly in Excel 2003, as shown in Figure 30.16, Excel 2007 is not able to detect this type of name.

**Figure 30.16**
This formula builds a text reference to the name.

| | A | B | C | D | E | F | G |
|---|---|---|---|---|---|---|---|
| | | | C7 | | fx =B7*INDIRECT("TAX"&YEAR(A7)) | | |
| 1 | | | | | | | |
| 2 | | | | | | | |
| 3 | | | 2004 | 2005 | 2006 | 2007 | |
| 4 | Tax Rates | | 7% | 6.50% | 6.75% | 6.25% | |
| 5 | | | | | | | |
| 6 | Date | Amount | Tax | | | | |
| 7 | 6/19/2004 | 502.99 | 35.2093 | | | | |
| 8 | 1/3/2006 | 312.64 | 21.1032 | | | | |
| 9 | 4/16/2004 | 642.39 | 44.9673 | | | | |
| 10 | 5/24/2006 | 110.13 | 7.433775 | | | | |

When you save the Excel 2003 workbook as an Excel 2007 workbook, each name changes so that it begins with an underscore character (for example, from Tax2004 to _Tax2004). When you do the first recalculation, all the formulas from Cell C7 down fail, as shown in Figure 30.17. You have to edit the formula to manually add the underscore before TAX: =B7* INDIRECT("_TAX"&YEAR(A7)).

**Figure 30.17**
All these formulas fail when Excel 2007 renames the cells. This problem is limited to formulas where the cell address is passed as text.

| | A | B | C | D | E | F | G |
|---|---|---|---|---|---|---|---|
| | | | C7 | | fx =B7*INDIRECT("TAX"&YEAR(A7)) | | |
| 1 | | | | | | | |
| 2 | | | | | | | |
| 3 | | | 2004 | 2005 | 2006 | 2007 | |
| 4 | Tax Rates | | 7% | 6.50% | 6.75% | 6.25% | |
| 5 | | | | | | | |
| 6 | Date | Amount | Tax | | | | |
| 7 | 6/19/2004 | 502.99 | 0 | | | | |
| 8 | 1/3/2006 | 312.64 | 0 | | | | |
| 9 | 4/16/2004 | 642.39 | 0 | | | | |
| 10 | 5/24/2006 | 110.13 | 0 | | | | |
| 11 | 3/20/2005 | 520.24 | 0 | | | | |
| 12 | 11/12/2005 | 993.83 | 0 | | | | |
| 13 | 1/11/2005 | 619.84 | 0 | | | | |

## ADDING MANY NAMES AT ONCE FROM EXISTING LABELS AND HEADINGS

With Excel 2007 you can add many names in a single command, particularly if the names exist as labels or headings adjacent to the cells.

Say you have a worksheet with a series of labels in Column A and values in Column B. One example is shown in Figure 30.18. To do a wholesale assignment of names to the cells in Column B, you follow these steps:

1. Select the range of labels and the cells to which they refer. In this example, this would be A4:B16.

2. Select Formulas, Named Cells, Create from Selection. Excel displays the Create Names from Selected Range dialog.

3. Because the row labels are in the left column of the selected range, choose Left Column and then click OK, as shown in Figure 30.18.

**Figure 30.18**
When you make this selection, Excel uses the text values in the left column to assign names to all the non-blank cells in Column B of this range.

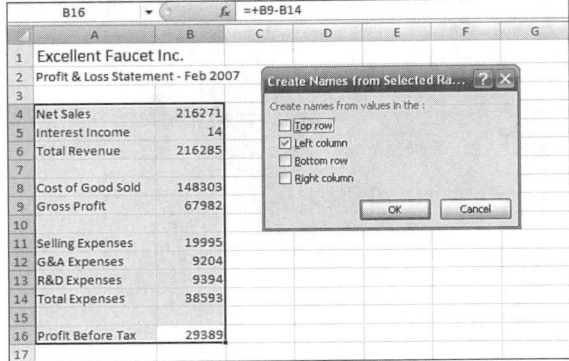

Excel does a fairly good job of assigning the names. Spaces are replaced with underscores to make the names valid. In this example, cell B4 is assigned the name Net_Sales. Cell C8 is assigned the name Cost_of_Good_Sold. In Row 12, where the label contains an ampersand (&), Excel replaces the ampersand with an underscore, to form the name G_A_Expenses. Although this is not as meaningful as it could be if you wrote the name yourself, it is still pretty good.

**CAUTION**

If Cell A12 were G & A Expenses, then Excel would replace every space and ampersand with an underscore, creating the name G___A_Expenses.

Excel uses the labels to the left of the selected cells to apply names.

In Excel 2007, you can apply names by using both the row labels and column headings at the same time. In Figure 30.19, the selections in the Create Names from Selected Ranges dialog mean that six new names will be added to the workbook. For example, Jan will refer to B2:B4.

The Create Names from Selected Range dialog is so flexible that it will even let you choose all four options at once. If you select all the check boxes in the Create Names from Selected Range dialog and then click OK, as shown in Figure 30.20, 12 new names will be added to the workbook.

In this example, the name Mar will refer to D2:D4. The name Month3 will also refer to D2:D4. If you select Month3 from the drop-down, Excel selects D2:D4, as shown in Figure 30.21. However, the name in the Name box reflects Mar because that is the first name, alphabetically, that applies to that range.

**Figure 30.19**
In Excel 2007 can create names based on the row labels and column headers at the same time.

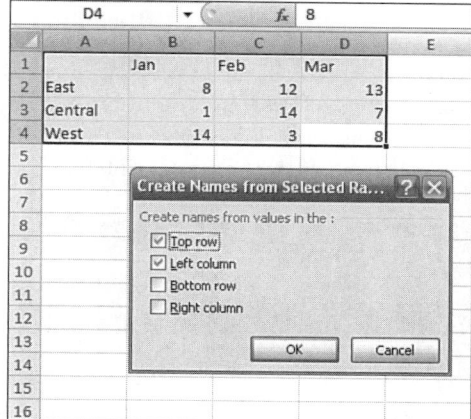

**Figure 30.20**
It is difficult to imagine a scenario in which you would want to, but you could even create names based on labels on all four edges of a range.

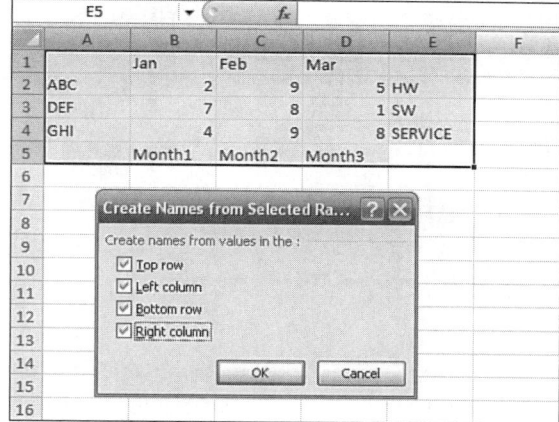

**Figure 30.21**
You can create two names for each three-cell range.

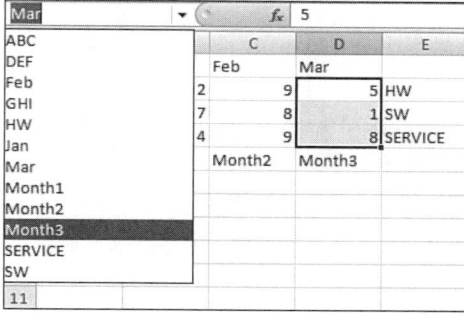

30

## MANAGING NAMES

Excel 2007 is a great improvement over previous Excel versions in terms of managing names. Whereas the previous six versions of Excel use the Insert Names dialog to manage names, Excel now offers the Name Manager dialog, shown in Figure 30.22. To open this dialog, you click the Name Manager icon on the Formulas ribbon.

**Figure 30.22**
You click Name Manager to display the vastly improved Manage Names dialog.

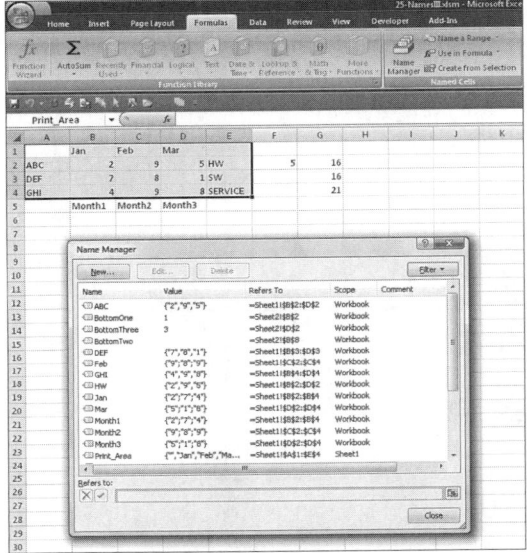

The Name Manager dialog shows the five fields for each name. Initially, certain columns may not be wide enough to show all the text in each column. You can resize the entire dialog by using the triangle in the lower-right corner. You can also resize columns by dragging the vertical bars between the column headings.

These are the columns in the Name Manager dialog:

- **Name**—Shows the current name.
- **Value**—Shows the current value. If the Name column refers to a rectangular range, each value in the range is shown in the Value column.
- **Refers To**—Shows the formula defined for the name. This might be a reference to a cell address, a constant value, or a formula.

- **Scope**—Indicates whether the name applies to the whole workbook or just to a certain worksheet.

- **Comment**—Shows any comments you might have typed when you originally defined a name.

Working with the Name Manager dialog is simple:

- To create a new name, you click the New Name button.

- To delete a name, you highlight the name and click Delete Name. You should do this with caution, however. If the name is in use, all the formulas that point to that name change to #REF! errors.

- To view the cells represented by a certain name, you choose the name from the Name column of the dialog and then click at the end of the Refers To box. Excel shows you that section of the worksheet behind the dialog.

- To reassign a name to a different set of cells, you choose the name from the Name column of the dialog and then click in the Refers To box. On the worksheet, you point to the new location for the name. After you select a new location, click the green checkbox to accept the new location. Click the red x button to revert to the original location.

- If you click a name from the Name column of the dialog and then click Edit Name, you have an opportunity to add or change the comment to the name or to change the scope.

- When you modify an existing name in the Name column of the dialog, any formulas that specifically reference that name are updated to point to the new cell.

## FILTERING THE NAME MANAGER DIALOG

In the upper-right corner of the Name Manager dialog is a button labeled Filter. You can click this button to access many powerful options. If you have defined names that have scope only to a worksheet, you can select Names Scoped to Worksheet in order to limit the Manages Names dialog to only those names, as shown in Figure 30.23.

**Figure 30.23**
The Filter button allows you to quickly narrow down to certain names.

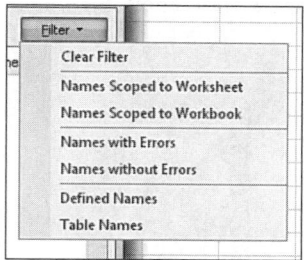

These are the options in the Filter drop-down:

- **Clear Filter**—Restores the list to the complete list.

- **Names Scoped to Worksheet** —Shows all worksheet-level names for the active worksheet and other worksheets.

- **Names Scoped to Workbook**—Shows all the global names that are scoped to a workbook.

- **Names with Errors**—Finds all names where the value is a cell error. Often, stray names left behind after copying a worksheet to a new workbook have #REF! errors. You can use the Names with Errors filter to find those names.

- **Names Without Errors**—Hides any invalid names.

- **Defined Names**—Specifies the names defined using the techniques described in this chapter. This option removes names defined as a result of creating pivot tables or formatting ranges as tables.

- **Table Names**—Shows only the values of table names. When you define a range as a table, the entire table is given a name such as Table1.

# USING A NAME TO HOLD A VALUE

So far all the names defined in this chapter have referred to a cell or a range of cells. It is possible to assign a constant value to a name by using the New Name dialog. You might do this to hold a value that could possibly change, but would likely rarely change. One example might be a sales tax rate.

To use a name to hold a value, follow these steps:

1. Either click the Name a Range icon or the Name Manager icon and then click Add Names. (Both of these icons are located in the Named Cells group on the Formulas ribbon.) The New Name dialog appears.

2. In the Name field of the New Name dialog, type a name, such as **Sales_Tax**.

3. In the Refers To box, remove any existing cell reference and type the new value (**=6%**, as shown in Figure 30.24).

**Figure 30.24**
In the New Name dialog, you can assign a constant value to a name.

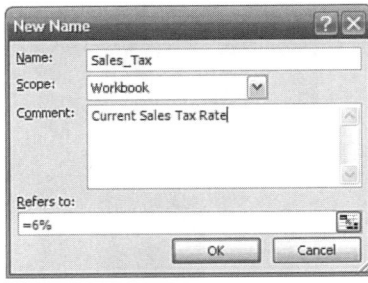

4. Write formulas that refer to the new name (for example, **Sales_Tax**). The formula might be something like `=C2*Sales_Tax`. In Figure 30.25, the range has been defined as a table. Thus, the formula of `=[MerchAmt]*Sales_Tax` uses both a table name in square brackets and the defined name `Sales_Tax`.

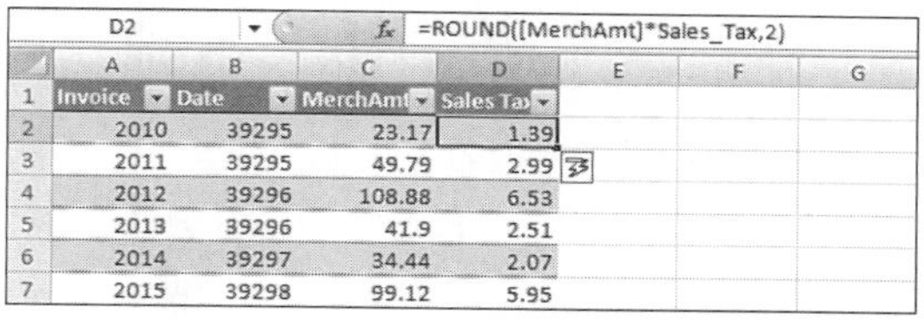

D2 | =ROUND([MerchAmt]*Sales_Tax,2)

| | A | B | C | D | E | F | G |
|---|---|---|---|---|---|---|---|
| 1 | Invoice | Date | MerchAmt | Sales Tax | | | |
| 2 | 2010 | 39295 | 23.17 | 1.39 | | | |
| 3 | 2011 | 39295 | 49.79 | 2.99 | | | |
| 4 | 2012 | 39296 | 108.88 | 6.53 | | | |
| 5 | 2013 | 39296 | 41.9 | 2.51 | | | |
| 6 | 2014 | 39297 | 34.44 | 2.07 | | | |
| 7 | 2015 | 39298 | 99.12 | 5.95 | | | |

**Figure 30.25**
MerchAmt, in square brackets, is a field name in the table. Sales_Tax is a defined name.

30

**CAUTION**

Use care when viewing potentially ambiguous references such as Sales_Tax and [Sales Tax] as shown in Figure 30.26. Remember, the name in square brackets is a table name assigned automatically by Excel.

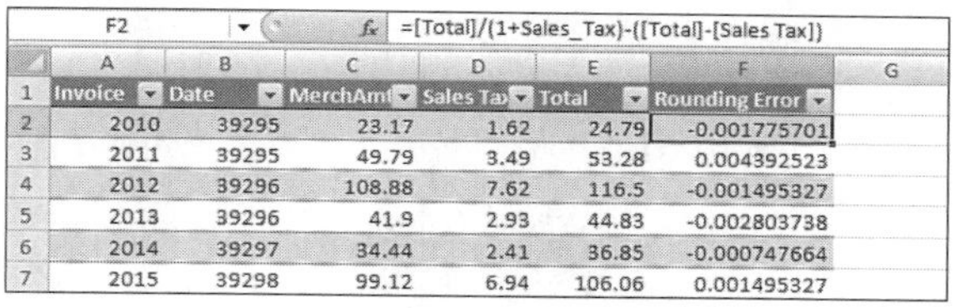

F2 | =[Total]/(1+Sales_Tax)-([Total]-[Sales Tax])

| | A | B | C | D | E | F | G |
|---|---|---|---|---|---|---|---|
| 1 | Invoice | Date | MerchAmt | Sales Tax | Total | Rounding Error | |
| 2 | 2010 | 39295 | 23.17 | 1.62 | 24.79 | -0.001775701 | |
| 3 | 2011 | 39295 | 49.79 | 3.49 | 53.28 | 0.004392523 | |
| 4 | 2012 | 39296 | 108.88 | 7.62 | 116.5 | -0.001495327 | |
| 5 | 2013 | 39296 | 41.9 | 2.93 | 44.83 | -0.002803738 | |
| 6 | 2014 | 39297 | 34.44 | 2.41 | 36.85 | -0.000747664 | |
| 7 | 2015 | 39298 | 99.12 | 6.94 | 106.06 | 0.001495327 | |

**Figure 30.26**
With defined names and table column names floating around, ambiguous formulas like this can turn up.

The advantage of using a name to refer to a constant is that if your tax rate changes, you can simply edit the value defined in the name, and all the formulas in the workbook will recalculate. To edit an existing name, you can click the Name Manager, click on the name, and choose Edit Name.

# ASSIGNING A FORMULA TO A NAME

While names are traditionally used to refer to cells or constant values, an interesting use is to use a name to refer to a formula.

Notice the Refers To box in Figure 30.27. Although the value there is a standard name that refers to a single cell, the Refers To box contains an = at the beginning, which means this named range is actually a formula.

As described in the following sections, there are a variety of situations in which assigning a formula to a name can be useful.

## USING BASIC NAMED FORMULAS

A named formula can allow you to replace a complicated formula with an easy to remember name. In this basic case, the formula contains no cell references.

**Figure 30.27**
Even a simple named range can be a formula assigned to a name.

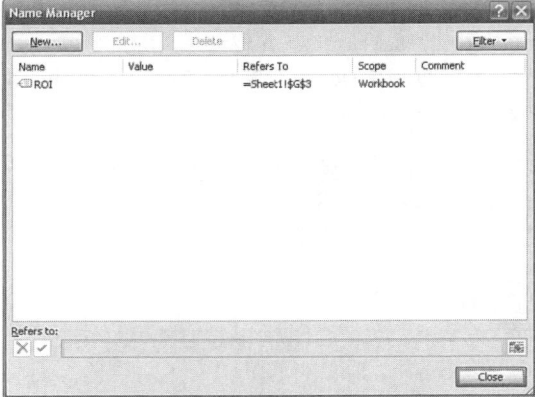

For example, let's say you have discovered a fairly complex formula that would be difficult to remember as shown in Figue 30.28

**Figure 30.28**
You can assign a complicated formula to a simpler name.

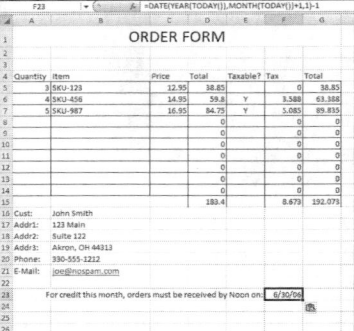

In this case, you could assign the formula =Date(Year(Today()),Month(Today())+1,1)-1 to a name such as MonthEnd, as shown in Figure 30.29

**Figure 30.29**
After a formula has been assigned to a name, you can use it as you would a constant.

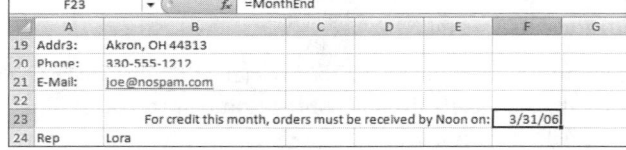

You could then use =MonthEnd in any cell to calculate the end of the current month.

## USING DYNAMIC NAMED FORMULAS

One cool example of a named formula is a reference that dynamically expands as more data is filled down a column.

Say that you have a list of valid sales reps on a hidden Sheet2 to be used as the list for a data validation drop-down. The list might extend from A1:A10 today, but as new sales reps are hired, the list may expand to A11, A12, A13, and so on.

The OFFSET() function has a parameter which specifies that a range should extend for X rows. If you use CountA(A:A) to return the number of rows, you can create a formula to dynamically expand or contract as cells are filled in or deleted. In theory, you would set up a formula to point to this range: =OFFSET(Sheet2!A1,0,0,CountA(Sheet2!A:A),0). However, use absolute references in the definition. In Figure 30.30, for example, the formula assigned to RepList is =OFFSET(Sheet2!$A$1,0,0,COUNTA(Sheet2!$A:$A),1).

30

**Figure 30.30**
This formula can expand to include the number of entries in Column A.

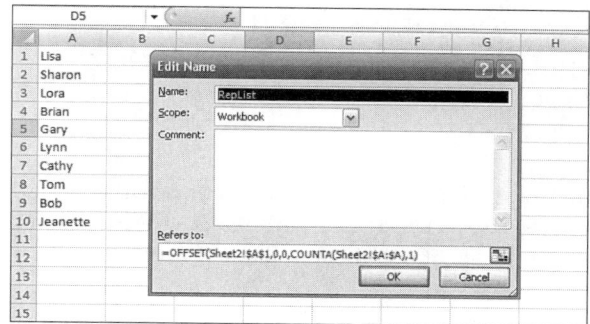

The name will automatically expand as new entries are added. To make use of this name in an in-cell dropdown, follow these steps:

Choose Data, Data Validation.

Change the Allow dropdown to List

In the source box, type **=RepList**.

Leave the In-cell dropdown box checked.

The completed dialog box is shown in Figure 30.31.

**Figure 30.31**
You can set up data validation to use a dynamic name.

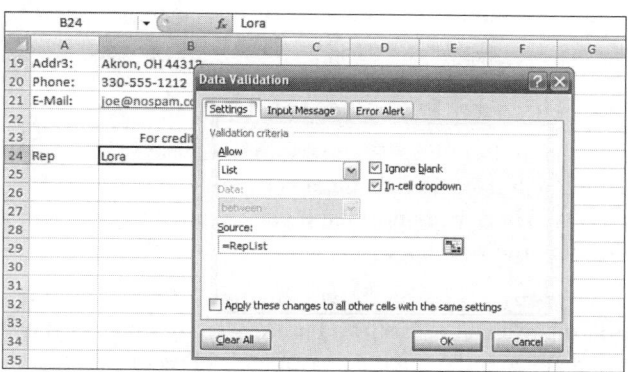

Initially, the cell with validation offers a drop-down that lists the 10 current reps, as shown in Figure 30.32.

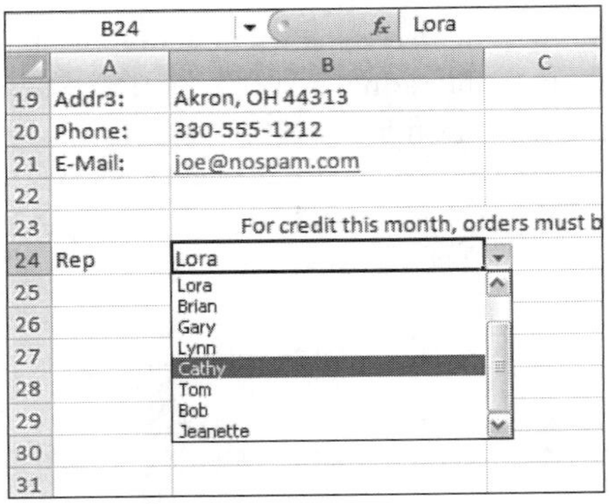

**Figure 30.32**
The result of adding data validation to a cell.

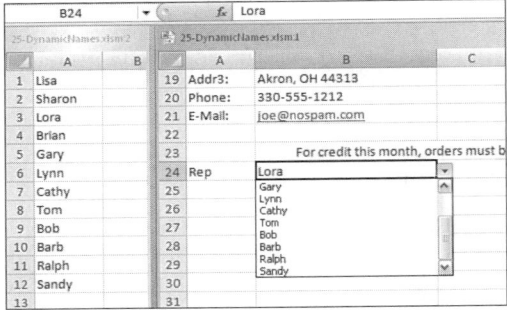

When the list on Sheet2 is edited, the drop-down in Sheet1 is automatically updated. In Figure 30.33, for example, you can see that Barb replaced Jeanette, and two new reps were added. The window on the left shows the new list on Sheet2, and the window on the right shows the current drop-down list.

**Figure 30.33**
As the list on Sheet2 changes, the dynamic formula expands to include the new cells in the list.

You can use a similar technique to make a chart series expand as new months are added.

→ For details on charting, **see** Chapter 16, "Using Excel Charts," **page 299**.

## USING A NAMED FORMULA TO POINT TO THE CELL ABOVE

In the example shown in Figure 30.30, it was important to make sure that all references were absolute. Although it seems strange, it is possible to make use of a relative reference in a named formula, as long as you understand one slightly buggy gotcha and two cautions if you use VBA or share the workbook with someone using Excel 97.

■ The gotcha happens in workbooks with multiple worksheets. A relative formula will work fine on the original worksheet, but incorrectly when used on another worksheet. A workaround that starts the reference with an ! solves this problem.

- The first caution is that this method fails if you are using VBA macros and the macro causes the worksheet to calculate.

- The second caution is that this method will crash Excel if the workbook is opened in Excel 97.

In Figure 30.34, the cell pointer is on Sheet1 in Cell A3. The name AboveMe is being defined as pointing to Cell A2. However, in the Refers To box, you need to press F4 three times to remove all the dollar signs from the reference.

**Figure 30.34**
Defining a relative reference in a named formula.

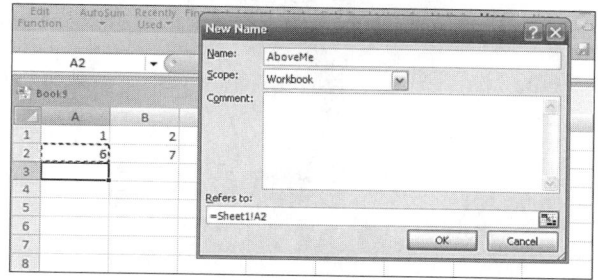

This relative formula initially appears to work perfectly. Cells A3:E3 in Figure 30.35 all contain the formula =AboveMe.

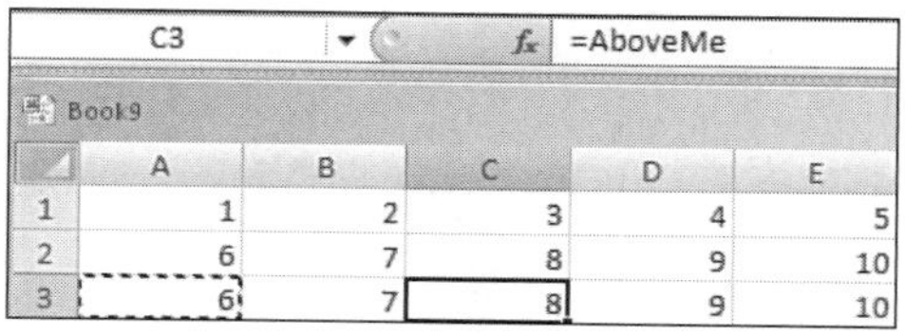

**Figure 30.35**
In this example, the relative reference in the named formula is working fine.

However, if you go to Sheet2 and enter the formula =AboveMe in Cell A3, the formula returns the value from Cell A2, but from Sheet1 instead of Sheet2. Figure 30.36 shows the answer 6 where you would expect 106.

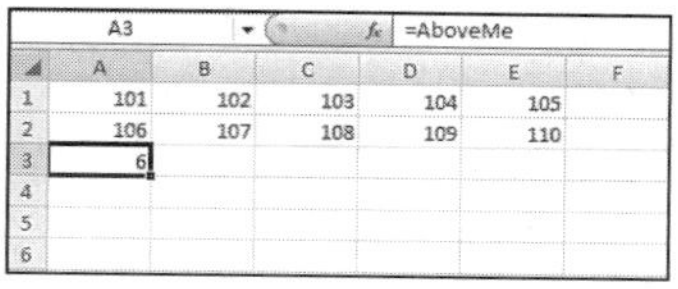

**Figure 30.36**
The relative reference in the named formula fails on another sheet.

The solution is to edit the name. To do so, you remove the reference to Sheet1, leaving a definition of =!A2, as shown in Figure 30.37.

**Figure 30.37**
Edit the formula to point to =!A2.

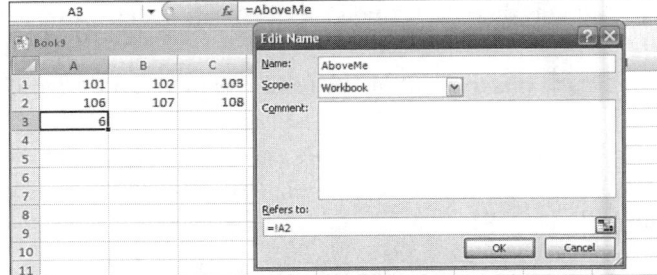

Now, when you close the Name Manager dialog and press F9 to recalculate, the formulas work as expected, as shown in Figure 30.38.

**Figure 30.38**
The relative reference of = !A2 now works as expected.

| | A | B | C | D | E | F |
|---|---|---|---|---|---|---|
| 1 | 101 | 102 | 103 | 104 | 105 | |
| 2 | 106 | 107 | 108 | 109 | 110 | |
| 3 | 106 | | | | | |
| 4 | | | | | | |

A3    fx =AboveMe

Book9

# CHAPTER 31

# USING WHAT IF, SCENARIO MANAGER, GOAL SEEK, AND SOLVER

**I**n this chapter

When Dan Bricklin invented VisiCalc in 1979, he was trying to come up with a tool that would let him recalculate his MBA school case studies quickly. Almost three decades later, spreadsheets are still used for the same functionality.

Newer spreadsheet tools such as Goal Seek and Solver allow you to back directly into the assumptions that lead to a solution. This chapter discusses some of Excel 2007's feaures that are helpful when you are tying to find a specific answer.

# USING WHAT-IF

Once you have set up a model in Excel, it is very easy to make copies of the model side by side and then change the various input variables to test their impact on the final result. Because this type of analysis answers the question of what happens if a change is made, it is known generically as what-if changes.

What-if analyses are the least formal method in this chapter. You simply copy the input variables and formulas multiple times. You can then vary the input variables until you reach a suitable solution.

For example, Figure 31.1 shows a worksheet to calculate the monthly payment on a new car purchase. In Cells E1, E2, and E3 are the known values: the price, term, and interest rate. Cell E4 calculates the monthly payment, using the =PMT() function.

**Figure 31.1**
You may not like the answer in Cell E4, but Excel makes the answer easy to find.

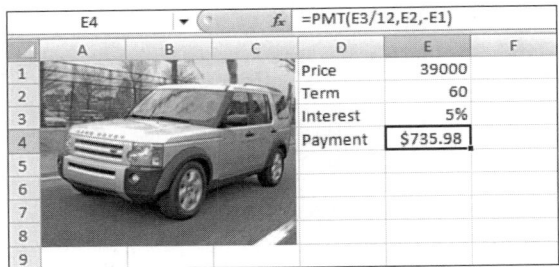

| | E4 | | | $f_x$ =PMT(E3/12,E2,-E1) | |
|---|---|---|---|---|---|
| | A | B | C | D | E | F |
| 1 | | | | Price | 39000 | |
| 2 | | | | Term | 60 | |
| 3 | | | | Interest | 5% | |
| 4 | | | | Payment | $735.98 | |
| 5 | | | | | | |
| 6 | | | | | | |
| 7 | | | | | | |
| 8 | | | | | | |
| 9 | | | | | | |

Cells E1:E4 are a self-contained mini-model. You can easily copy these cells several times over and perform what-if analysis on the car payment model.

Figure 31.2 shows a basic what-if worksheet. You can use this worksheet to manually plug in different numbers. Columns F and G show the effects of changing the number of months. Columns H:J factor in a lower interest rate. Columns K:M show the effects of finding a lower price. Based on a number of options, Column N starts to hone in on a scenario to get to the $695 target payment: Use 63 months, 5% interest, and a price of $38,500.

**Figure 31.2**
By making multiple copies of the table, you can create a simple What-If model.

| =PMT(N3/12,N2,-N1) | | | | | | | | | | | |
|---|---|---|---|---|---|---|---|---|---|---|---|
| D | E | F | G | H | I | J | K | L | M | N | O |
| Price | 39000 | 39000 | 39000 | 39000 | 39000 | 39000 | 38500 | 38500 | 38500 | 38500 | |
| Term | 60 | 66 | 72 | 60 | 66 | 72 | 60 | 66 | 72 | 63 | |
| Interest | 5% | 5% | 5% | 4.5% | 4.5% | 4.5% | 5% | 5% | 5% | 5% | |
| Payment | $735.98 | $677.10 | $628.09 | $727.08 | $668.15 | $619.09 | $726.54 | $668.42 | $620.04 | $696.09 | |

There is nothing magic about what-if analyses. There are no ribbon commands involved. You simply copy the model and plug in a few different numbers. The remaining topics in this chapter are more structured with better features.

## CREATING A TWO-VARIABLE WHAT-IF TABLE

The analysis in Figure 31.2 is fairly ad hoc. It basically enables you to try various combinations until you find one that is close to your target payment. If you have two variables to manipulate, you can use Excel's fairly powerful Data Table command. To use a data table, follow these steps:

1. Enter a formula in the upper-left corner of the table. This formula should point to at least two variable cells.

2. Along the left column of the table, enter various values for one of the input values.

3. Along the top row of the table, enter various values for the other input variable.

4. Select the entire table.

5. From the Data ribbon, select Data Tools, What-If Analysis, Data Table.

6. In the Data Table dialog box, enter a row input cell and a column input cell.

7. Click OK to complete the table.

For example, you can use the Data Table command to try to negotiate on price and term of the loan by following these steps:

1. Use the formula in Cell E4 as the formula in the top-left corner of your table.

2. From E5:E17, fill in various possible values for purchase price.

3. From F5:K5, fill in various possible values for the term of the loan.

4. Select the entire table, E4:K17, as shown in Figure 31.3.

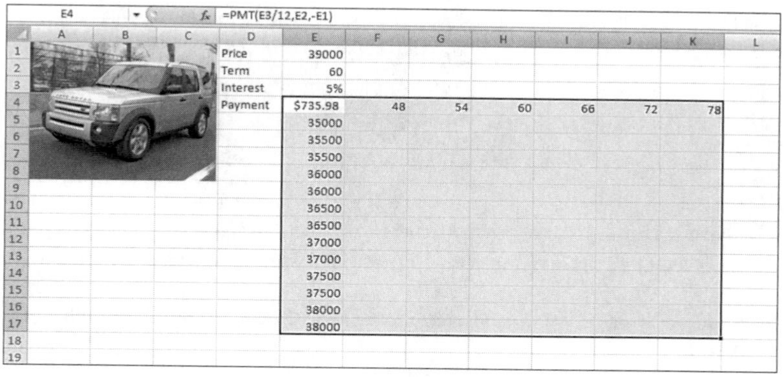

**Figure 31.3**
Preparing for a two-variable what-if analysis.

5. Select Data Table from the Data ribbon to display the Data Table dialog box, as shown in Figure 31.4. The dialog box asks you for a row input cell and a column input cell. The Row Input Cell field offers to take each value from the top row of the table and plug it into a particular cell.

6. Because the values in F5:K5 are loan terms, specify E2 for the row input cell.

7. Similarly, the Column Input Field offers to take each value from the left column and replace that value in a particular cell. Because these cells contain vehicle prices, choose E1 as the column input cell.

**Figure 31.4**
Setting up the Table dialog.

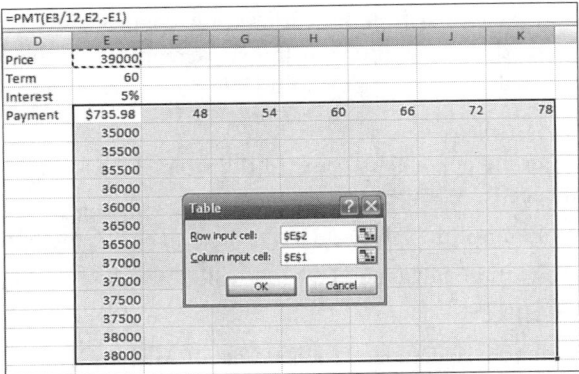

8. Click OK. Excel fills in the intersection of each row and column with the monthly payment, based on the price in the left column combined with the loan term in the top row. Figure 31.5 shows the resulting table.

**Figure 31.5**
Excel performs 78 what-if analyses in one command.

| =PMT(E3/12,E2,-E1) | | | | | | | |
|---|---|---|---|---|---|---|---|
| D | E | F | G | H | I | J | K | L |
| Price | 39000 | | | | | | |
| Term | 60 | | | | | | |
| Interest | 5% | | | | | | |
| Payment | $735.98 | 48 | 54 | 60 | 66 | 72 | 78 |
| | 35000 | 806.0253 | 725.1406 | 660.4932 | 607.6546 | 563.6726 | 526.5034 |
| | 35500 | 817.5399 | 735.4997 | 669.9288 | 616.3354 | 571.7251 | 534.0248 |
| | 35500 | 817.5399 | 735.4997 | 669.9288 | 616.3354 | 571.7251 | 534.0248 |
| | 36000 | 829.0546 | 745.8589 | 679.3644 | 625.0162 | 579.7776 | 541.5463 |
| | 36000 | 829.0546 | 745.8589 | 679.3644 | 625.0162 | 579.7776 | 541.5463 |
| | 36500 | 840.5692 | 756.218 | 688.8 | 633.697 | 587.83 | 549.0678 |
| | 36500 | 840.5692 | 756.218 | 688.8 | 633.697 | 587.83 | 549.0678 |
| | 37000 | 852.0839 | 766.5772 | 698.2356 | 642.3777 | 595.8825 | 556.5893 |
| | 37000 | 852.0839 | 766.5772 | 698.2356 | 642.3777 | 595.8825 | 556.5893 |
| | 37500 | 863.5985 | 776.9363 | 707.6713 | 651.0585 | 603.935 | 564.1107 |
| | 37500 | 863.5985 | 776.9363 | 707.6713 | 651.0585 | 603.935 | 564.1107 |
| | 38000 | 875.1132 | 787.2955 | 717.1069 | 659.7393 | 611.9874 | 571.6322 |
| | 38000 | 875.1132 | 787.2955 | 717.1069 | 659.7393 | 611.9874 | 571.6322 |

9. Reselect just the interior of the table. You can see that Excel represents the table with the TABLE() array function. Figure 31.6 shows the table with a heat map applied.

→ For more information on data visualizations, **see** "Creating Heat Maps with Color Scales," **page 158** in Chapter 9.

**NOTE**

Note that the values calculated in the table are live formula values. If you change the numbers along the edge of the table, the TABLE() array formula recalculates new loan payment amounts.

**Figure 31.6**
The values in the table are calculated by a single TABLE() array formula.

`{=TABLE(E2,E1)}`

| D | E | F | G | H | I | J | K | L |
|---|---|---|---|---|---|---|---|---|
| Price | 39000 | | | | | | | |
| Term | 60 | | | | | | | |
| Interest | 5% | | | | | | | |
| Payment | $735.98 | 48 | 51 | 54 | 57 | 60 | 63 | |
| | 35000 | 806.0253 | 763.1951 | 725.1406 | 691.1077 | 660.4932 | 632.8087 | |
| | 35500 | 817.5399 | 774.0979 | 735.4997 | 700.9807 | 669.9288 | 641.8488 | |
| | 36000 | 829.0546 | 785.0007 | 745.8589 | 710.8536 | 679.3644 | 650.8889 | |
| | 36500 | 840.5692 | 795.9035 | 756.218 | 720.7266 | 688.8 | 659.929 | |
| | 37000 | 852.0839 | 806.8062 | 766.5772 | 730.5996 | 698.2356 | 668.9692 | |
| | 37500 | 863.5985 | 817.709 | 776.9363 | 740.4725 | 707.6713 | 678.0093 | |
| | 38000 | 875.1132 | 828.6118 | 787.2955 | 750.3455 | 717.1069 | 687.0494 | |
| | 38500 | 886.6278 | 839.5146 | 797.6547 | 760.2185 | 726.5425 | 696.0895 | |
| | 39000 | 898.1424 | 850.4174 | 808.0138 | 770.0914 | 735.9781 | 705.1297 | |
| | 39500 | 909.6571 | 861.3202 | 818.373 | 779.9644 | 745.4137 | 714.1698 | |
| | 40000 | 921.1717 | 872.223 | 828.7321 | 789.8374 | 754.8493 | 723.2099 | |
| | 40500 | 932.6864 | 883.1258 | 839.0913 | 799.7103 | 764.285 | 732.25 | |
| | 41000 | 944.201 | 894.0285 | 849.4504 | 809.5833 | 773.7206 | 741.2902 | |

# USING SCENARIO MANAGER

The Data Table command is great for models with two variables that can change. Sometimes, however, you have models with far more variables that can change. In such a case, you should use the Scenario Manager, which allows you to create multiple scenarios, each changing up to 32 variables.

With up to 32 variables changing, it is best to use named ranges for all the input variables before you define your first scenario. One of the results of the Scenario Manager is a summary report. Using named ranges for all the input cells makes the report far easier to understand.

→ To learn how to use named ranges to your advantage, **see** "Using Named Ranges to Simplify Formulas," **page 846**, in Chapter 30.

Generally, Scenario Manager allows you to set up named scenarios such as "Best Case," "Worst Case," and "Most likely." In each scenario you can specify values for up to 32 variables.

You would then have a model that calculates results based on the 32 input variables. For example, you might have a business plan that projects sales for the next 120 months using growth rates in the input variable section of the spreadsheet. The important distinction is that while you may only have 32 input variables, you might base millions of formulas on these 32 input variables.

Use the Scenario Manager dialog box to quickly switch to a different set of input variables. The worksheet can quickly be calculated using Best Case and Worst Case scenarios.

For a specific example, Figure 31.7 shows a sales forecasting model. All the highlighted cells are variables that can change. The model calculates a total forecast in Cell B16 and a ratio in Cell B18. To set up and use scenarios, follow these steps:

1. Select Data, Data Tools, What-If Analysis, Scenario Manager to display the Scenario Manager dialog. Initially, the Scenario Manager indicates that there are no scenarios defined, as shown in Figure 31.8.

**Figure 31.7**
This forecast model is
based on nine variable
cells.

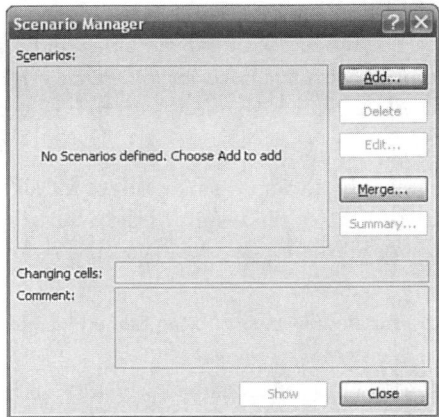

| | A | B | C | D | E |
|---|---|---|---|---|---|
| 1 | Sales Forecasting Model | | | | |
| 2 | | Total | 2006 | 2007 | 2008 |
| 3 | Existing Market Size | 400,000,000 | 400,000,000 | 400,000,000 | 400,000,000 |
| 4 | % Upgrading | | 7% | 24% | 9% |
| 5 | Total Upgraders | | 28,000,000 | 96,000,000 | 36,000,000 |
| 6 | % Upgraders buying book | | 15% | 12% | 2% |
| 7 | Upgrade Books | | 4,200,000 | 11,520,000 | 720,000 |
| 8 | Market Growth | 1% | 4,000,000 | 4,000,000 | 4,000,000 |
| 9 | % New Buying Book | | 15% | 15% | 15% |
| 10 | Growth Books | | 600,000 | 600,000 | 600,000 |
| 11 | Total Books | | 4,800,000 | 12,120,000 | 1,320,000 |
| 12 | OurCo Market Share | 12% | | | |
| 13 | Competitor A | 10% | | | |
| 14 | Competitor B | 11% | | | |
| 15 | All Others | 67% | | | |
| 16 | OurCo Book Sales | 2,188,800 | 576,000 | 1,454,400 | 158,400 |
| 17 | Office Sales | 172,000,000 | 32,000,000 | 100,000,000 | 40,000,000 |
| 18 | Conversion Rate | 1.3% | | | |

**Figure 31.8**
The Scenario Manager
dialog before you add
the first scenario.

2. Click the Add button to add the first scenario. The Edit Scenario dialog appears.

**TIP FROM**

It is best to add one scenario that represents your starting assumptions. Otherwise, those
numbers will be lost.

3. In the Edit Scenario dialog, choose which cells will be changing. Because the variable
   cells are not adjacent, select the first contiguous range and then Ctrl+click to add additional ranges, as shown in Figure 31.9.

   As shown in Figure 31.10, the Scenario Values dialog box appears, in which you can edit
   the values for each starting cell. It is a little annoying that this dialog can show only five
   values at a time. If your model contains the maximum of 32 values that can change, you
   have to scroll several times to see all the values in this dialog.

4. Edit any values in the Scenario Values dialog. If you have additional scenarios to add,
   click the Add button. When you are done assigning scenarios, click OK.

**Figure 31.9**
You Ctrl+click to select all the changing cells.

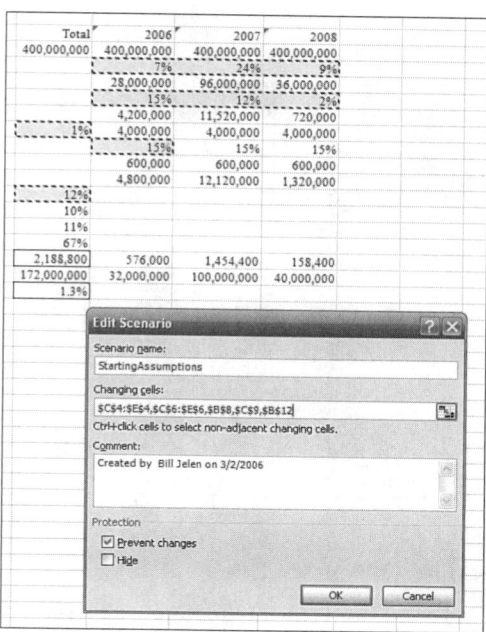

**Figure 31.10**
You use the Scenario Values dialog to edit values for a scenario.

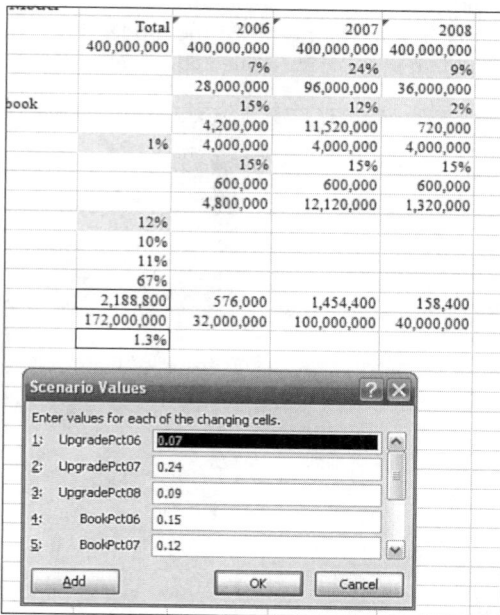

5. Try switching between scenarios in the Scenario Manager by either double-clicking a scenario or clicking the scenario and clicking Show, as shown in Figure 31.11. If you are going to add a new scenario similar to one existing scenario, show that scenario before clicking Add.

**Figure 31.11**
The new scenario is shown behind the dialog box after you double-click a scenario name.

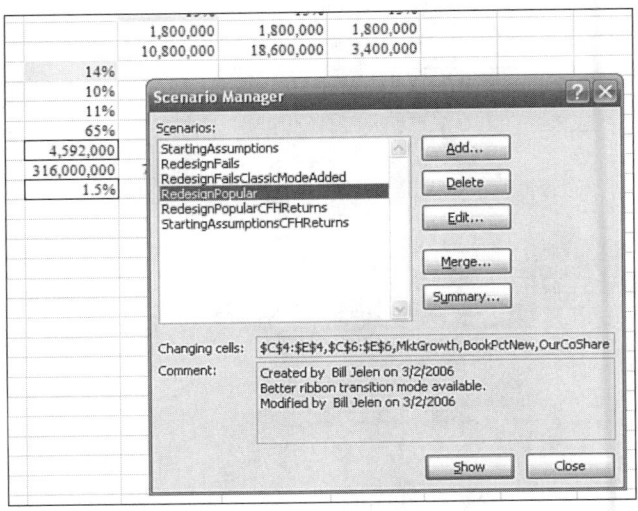

## CREATING A SCENARIO SUMMARY REPORT

One powerful feature of Excel scenarios is the ability to create a scenario summary report. When you click the Summary button on the Scenario Manager dialog, Excel allows you to choose either a scenario summary report or a pivot table report. In either case, you should select one or more cells that represent the results of the model. For example, Figure 31.12 shows OurCo Book Sales and Conversion Rate selected.

**Figure 31.12**
You can hold down Ctrl to select more than one result cell.

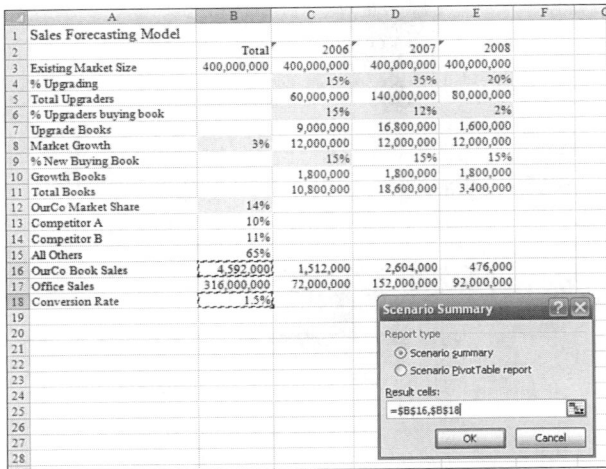

After specifying the results cells, the scenario summary report is added on a new worksheet in the workbook. This is an amazingly useful report that has a number of useful features.

After the initial creation, the summary is as shown in Figure 31.13. Notice that there are group and outline buttons along both the rows and the columns of the report. The plus sign next to Cell A3 indicates that the comments in Row 4 are currently hidden.

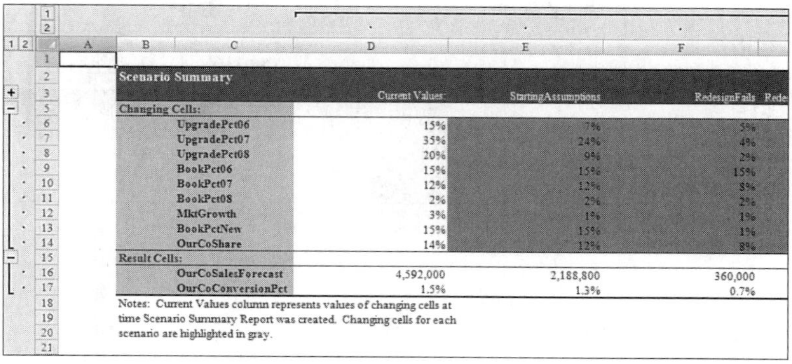

**Figure 31.13**
The default scenario summary report.

You can use word wrapping in a summary report. For example, Figure 31.13 shows that word wrapping was used to make the headings in Row 3 appear on two lines and that the column widths were adjusted. You will probably always have to make these adjustments to make your summary reports look better.

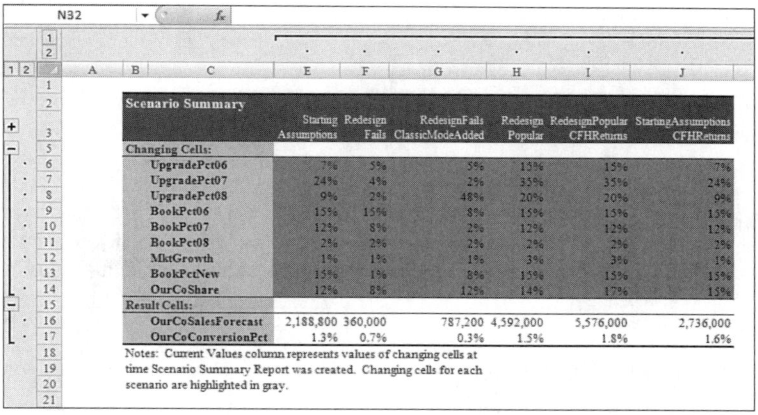

**Figure 31.14**
You can adjust word wrapping and column widths.

**TIP FROM**

*Bill Jelen*

To force word wrapping in the middle of a cell, you position your mouse cursor at the break point and press Alt+Enter.

If you click the minus sign next to Row 5, you can hide the assumption cells and just show the results, as shown in Figure 31.15.

As you create each scenario, the Scenario Manager adds a comment with your name and the date and time. You can also add your own comments. As shown in Figure 31.16, you can click the plus sign next to Row 3 to reveal the comments in the report.

**Figure 31.15**
If your manager's eyes glaze over with a table of numbers, you can show just the results.

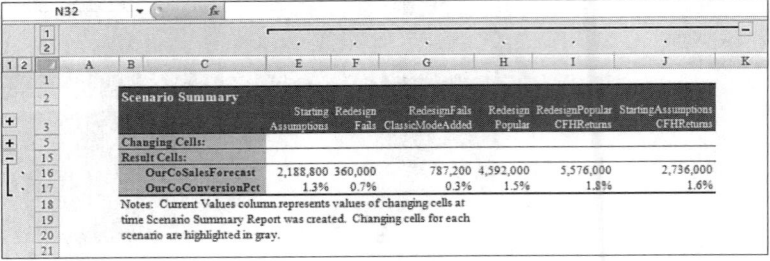

**Figure 31.16**
You can show comments in a report.

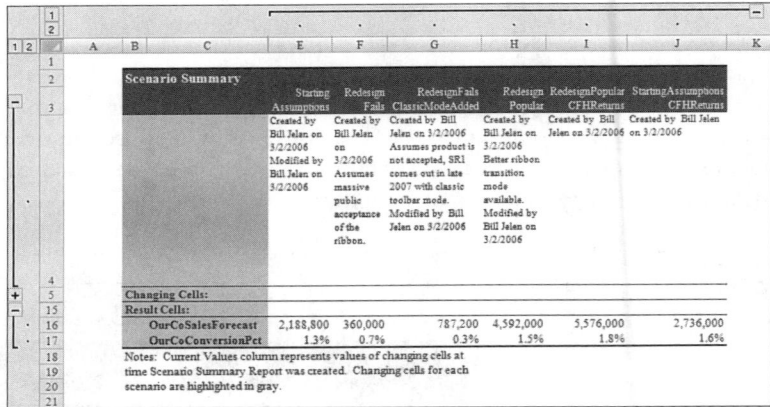

**CAUTION**

> The scenario summary report is a snapshot in time. If you later change scenarios or add new scenarios, you have to re-create (and re-format) the scenario summary report.

## ADDING MULTIPLE SCENARIOS

You might want to share a workbook with others and have them add their own scenarios so that you can get opinions from people in other areas of your company, such as sales, marketing, engineering, and manufacturing. To do this, follow these steps:

1. Save the workbook with just the starting scenario.

2. Route the workbook to each person. In a hidden field, Excel keeps track of who adds each scenario.

3. When you get the routed workbook back, open both the original workbook and the routed workbook.

4. Display the Scenario Manager in the original workbook.

5. Click the Merge button in order to display the Merge Scenarios dialog, as shown in Figure 31.17.

**Figure 31.17**
Merging scenarios from a workbook routed to others.

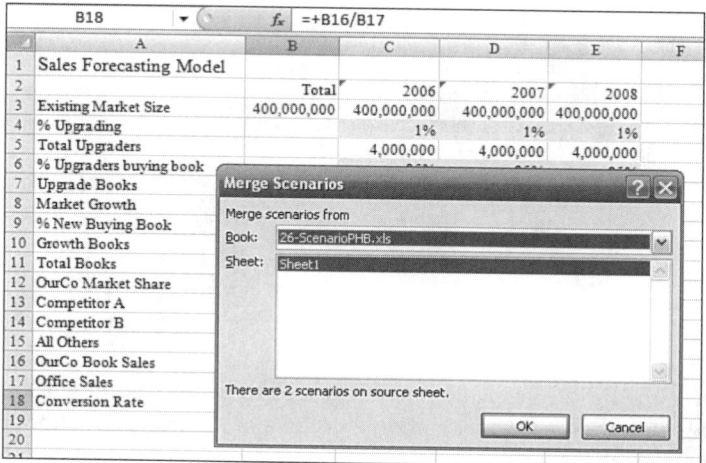

6. In the Book drop-down, choose the name of the routed workbook. In Figure 31.17, the dialog shows that two scenarios are available on Sheet 1.

7. Excel usually encounters identically named scenarios in the merge process. It differentiates any scenarios with identical names by adding a date or name to the incoming scenarios as shown in Figure 31.18. If these scenarios are truly identical to the scenario that you originally sent out, delete those scenarios.

**Figure 31.18**
Merged scenarios are added to the bottom of the list.

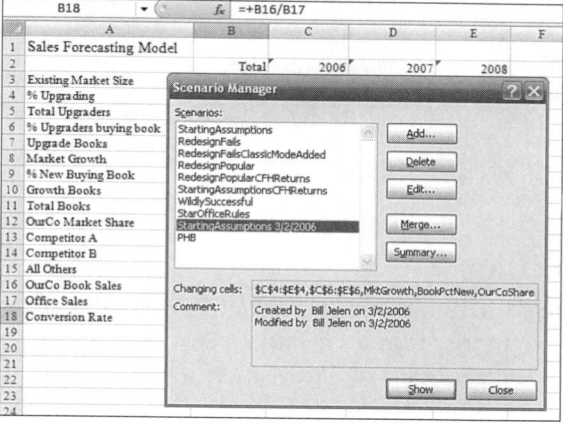

8. In the Scenario Manager, click Summary. The Scenario Summary dialog appears.

9. In the Scenario Summary dialog, click Scenario PivotTable report. The initial pivot table appears, as shown in Figure 31.19.

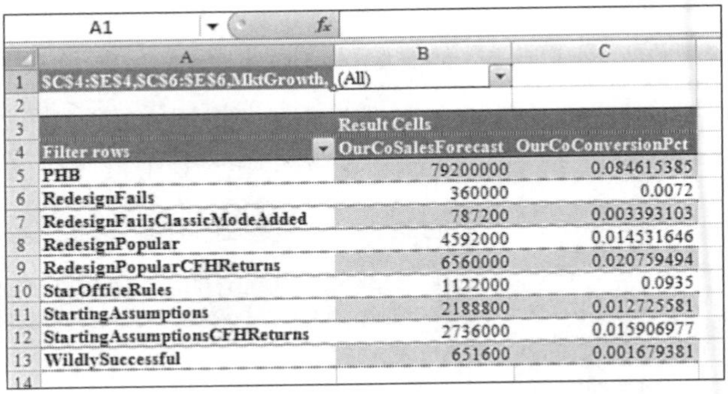

| | A | B | C |
|---|---|---|---|
| 1 | $C$4:$E$4,$C$6:$E$6,MktGrowth, | (All) | |
| 2 | | | |
| 3 | | Result Cells | |
| 4 | Filter rows | OurCoSalesForecast | OurCoConversionPct |
| 5 | PHB | 79200000 | 0.084615385 |
| 6 | RedesignFails | 360000 | 0.0072 |
| 7 | RedesignFailsClassicModeAdded | 787200 | 0.003393103 |
| 8 | RedesignPopular | 4592000 | 0.014531646 |
| 9 | RedesignPopularCFHReturns | 6560000 | 0.020759494 |
| 10 | StarOfficeRules | 1122000 | 0.0935 |
| 11 | StartingAssumptions | 2188800 | 0.012725581 |
| 12 | StartingAssumptionsCFHReturns | 2736000 | 0.015906977 |
| 13 | WildlySuccessful | 651600 | 0.001679381 |
| 14 | | | |

**Figure 31.19**
The default pivot table shows scenarios from all people on the routing list.

10. Drag the field from the Report Filter area to be the first Row Labels field. You can now see scenarios grouped by author. As shown in Figure 31.20, although this is an interesting view, there is not a good way to see the assumptions that each author used to arrive at his or her results.

31

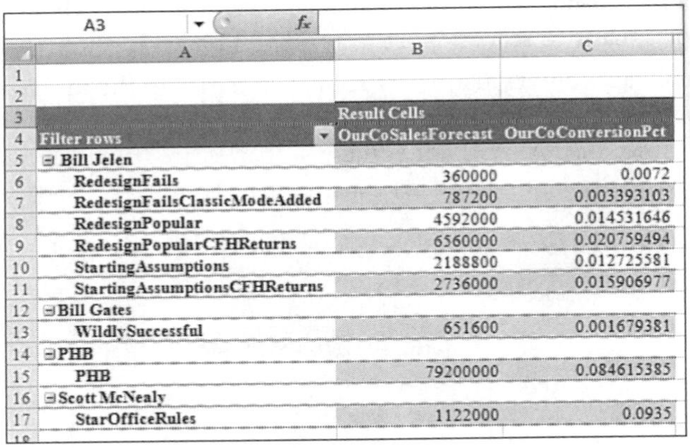

| | A | B | C |
|---|---|---|---|
| 1 | | | |
| 2 | | | |
| 3 | | Result Cells | |
| 4 | Filter rows | OurCoSalesForecast | OurCoConversionPct |
| 5 | ⊟ Bill Jelen | | |
| 6 | RedesignFails | 360000 | 0.0072 |
| 7 | RedesignFailsClassicModeAdded | 787200 | 0.003393103 |
| 8 | RedesignPopular | 4592000 | 0.014531646 |
| 9 | RedesignPopularCFHReturns | 6560000 | 0.020759494 |
| 10 | StartingAssumptions | 2188800 | 0.012725581 |
| 11 | StartingAssumptionsCFHReturns | 2736000 | 0.015906977 |
| 12 | ⊟ Bill Gates | | |
| 13 | WildlySuccessful | 651600 | 0.001679381 |
| 14 | ⊟ PHB | | |
| 15 | PHB | 79200000 | 0.084615385 |
| 16 | ⊟ Scott McNealy | | |
| 17 | StarOfficeRules | 1122000 | 0.0935 |

**Figure 31.20**
You can move the field from the Report Filter to the first row label in order to compare scenarios by person.

# Using Goal Seek

Have you seen the television show *The Price Is Right*? One of the games on the show is the Hi Lo game. A contestant tries to guess the price of an item, and Bob Barker tells the player that the actual price is higher or lower. The process of honing in on a price of $1.67 might involve guesses of $2, $1, $1.50, $1.75, $1.63, $1.69, $1.66, $1.68, and $1.67. Using the techniques described so far in this chapter, you might find yourself playing this game with Excel to try to narrow in on an answer.

You might have an Excel worksheet set up that calculates a final value using several input variables. How can you solve the formula in reverse? You want to find input variables that will generate a certain answer.

One difficult option is to determine if there is another Excel function that reverses the calculation. For example, =ARCSIN() performs the opposite of =SIN().

Another difficult option is to use algebra to attempt to solve for one of the input variables.

Mostly, though, I find people will simply play the "Hi-Lo" game, successively plugging in higher and lower answers to the input cell until they narrow in to an input variable that produces the desired result.

If you've ever found yourself playing the Hi-Lo game, check out the Goal Seek command. This command will, in effect, play the Hi-Lo game at hyperspeed, arriving at an answer within a second.

Consider the car payment example at the beginning of the chapter. You want to find a price that yields a $695 monthly payment. If you do some research, you might find the =PV() function that can solve this. Most people will simply plug in successively higher or lower values for the price in Cell E1 (refer to Figure 31.21).

Excel has an option that allows you to quickly hone in on a value. It is called Goal Seek. To use Goal Seek, follow these steps:

1. Select the answer cell. In this example, it would be the payment in Cell E4.
2. From the Data Tools group of the Data ribbon, select the What If Analysis drop-down and then choose Goal Seek. The Goal Seek dialog appears, as shown in Figure 31.21.

**Figure 31.21**
Goal Seek lets you find one value by changing one other cell.

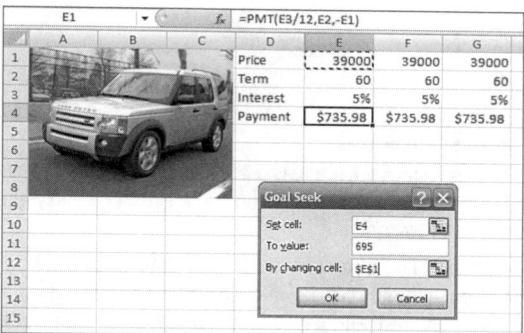

3. In the Goal Seek dialog, indicate that you want to set the answer cell to a particular value by changing a particular input cell. In this example, you want to set cell E4 to the value of $695 by changing Cell E1. Excel quickly tries to hone in on a value. When Excel gets to within a penny of the value, the Goal Seek Status dialog appears, as shown in Figure 31.22. This dialog reports that it was trying to reach a target value of $695 and was able to reach that value. Behind the dialog, the worksheet shows the proposed price of $36,828.54 in the worksheet.
4. Either accept this value by clicking OK or revert to the original value by clicking Cancel.

Goal Seek is great for quick calculations. Figure 31.23 shows an example in which two additional Goal Seek operations have been done. One operation set Cell F4 to $695 by changing the term in Cell F2. The next operation set Cell G4 to $695 by changing the interest rate in Cell G3.

**Figure 31.22**
You can choose to accept the proposed solution or revert to the previous numbers.

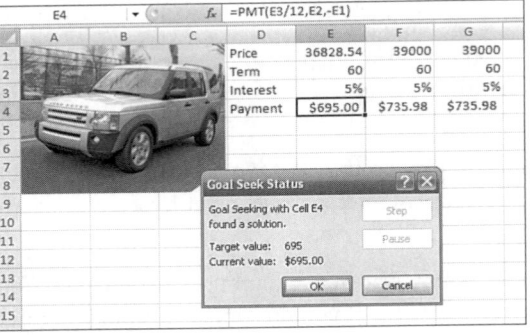

**Figure 31.23**
Three different Goal Seek commands find how to yield a $695 payment by changing either the price, term, or rate.

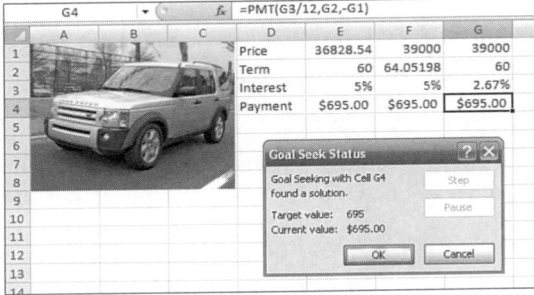

## Is It Cheating to Use Brute Force to Think Less?

Most of the time when you could use Goal Seek, there is a brainier solution. If you have a complex series of formulas set up using just the +, -, *, /, and ^ operators, you could almost certainly get out a pencil and do the algebra required to derive the formula you need.

In the preceding text, Figure 31.23 shows how you can use Goal Seek to figure out how to achieve a certain monthly payment by changing three different cells. Besides Goal Seek, Excel provides a function that can correctly find the term for a given price, interest, and payment: the NPER() function. For example, as shown in Figure 31.24, you can use the NPER() function in Cell G11 to calculate a more exact version than Goal Seek is able to discover. Similarly, in Cell E11 you can use =PV(E9/E12,E8,-E10) to discover the present value (that is, the vehicle price) of a loan. In Cell I11 you can use =RATE(I9,-I10,18)*12 to discover the rate needed to generate a monthly payment of $695 for a certain price and term.

**Figure 31.24**
Goal Seek prevents you from having to learn functions such as NPER().

| | | | | | | | | |
|---|---|---|---|---|---|---|---|---|
| | | | Price | 36828.541 | | 39000 | | 39000 |
| | | | Term | 60 | | 64.05198 | | 60 |
| | | | Interest | 5% | | 5% | | 2.67% |
| | | | Payment | $695.00 | | $695.00 | | $695.00 |
| | | | | | | | | |
| | | | | | | | | |
| | | | | | | | | |
| | | | Term | 60 | Price | 39000 | Price | 39000 |
| | | | Interest | 5% | Interest | 5% | Term | 60 |
| | | | Payment | 695 | Payment | 695 | Payment | 695 |
| | | | Price | $36,828.54 | Term | 64.05202 | Rate | 2.67% |

Excel might have to go through 100 iterations of a lightning-fast Bob Barker–style Hi Lo game in order to find the solution, but it usually finds that solution within a second or two. This is definitely faster than using paper and pencil to do the algebra or pulling out this book to learn about the NPER() function. If you are a loan officer at a bank, it might be worthwhile for you to learn how to use the NPER() function. However, if you are using this worksheet once every four years to figure out your next car purchase, it is perfectly fine to let Excel sweat through the brute-force calculations with Goal Seek.

## Troubleshooting Tip: When Goal Seek Won't Work

Some problems are not well suited to using Goal Seek. Goal Seek needs a clear mathematical relationship between the starting and ending cells. For example, the model in Figure 31.25 is set up to choose from among 20 different package plans. Each package offers a different number of tickets, meals, and vouchers. Cell E1 chooses a particular plan, and Cell E2 uses the INDEX() function to calculate the number of tickets associated with the plan. Because there is no mathematical sequence to the number of tickets in each plan, Goal Seek will have little chance of succeeding in this situation.

**Figure 31.25**
Because there is no mathematical order to the number of tickets offered in each plan, Goal Seek has little chance of finding a solution in this case.

| | E2 | | | $f_x$ | =INDEX(B7:B26,ROUND(E1,0)) | | | |
|---|---|---|---|---|---|---|---|---|
| | A | B | C | D | E | F | G | H |
| 1 | | | | Plan | 19 | | | |
| 2 | | | | Tickets | 2 | | | |
| 3 | | | | Value | 695 | | | |
| 4 | | | | Total | 1390 | | | |
| 5 | | | | | | | | |
| 6 | Plans: | Tickets | Meals | Vouchers | | | | |
| 7 | A | 4 | 15 | 6 | | | | |
| 8 | B | 12 | 4 | 9 | | | | |
| 9 | C | 13 | 11 | 1 | | | | |
| 10 | D | 5 | 18 | 2 | | | | |
| 11 | E | 6 | 11 | 8 | | | | |
| 12 | F | 20 | 1 | 4 | | | | |
| 13 | G | 10 | 6 | 9 | | | | |
| 14 | H | 7 | 14 | 4 | | | | |
| 15 | I | 8 | 7 | 10 | | | | |
| 16 | J | 15 | 2 | 8 | | | | |
| 17 | K | 16 | 6 | 3 | | | | |
| 18 | L | 11 | 0 | 14 | | | | |
| 19 | M | 18 | 0 | 7 | | | | |
| 20 | N | 17 | 5 | 3 | | | | |
| 21 | O | 3 | 15 | 7 | | | | |
| 22 | P | 9 | 8 | 8 | | | | |
| 23 | Q | 14 | 8 | 3 | | | | |
| 24 | R | 19 | 0 | 6 | | | | |
| 25 | S | 2 | 1 | 22 | | | | |
| 26 | T | 1 | 8 | 16 | | | | |
| 27 | | | | | | | | |

Say that you want to set the Total value in Cell E4 equal to 6950. A quick scan through the list of plans shows that Plan G offers 10 tickets, which would be worth exactly $6,950. However, Excel will have no chance of figuring this out using Goal Seek.

The following steps illustrate how you can watch the Goal Seek process in slow motion to see if Excel is getting closer:

1. Start Goal Seek. An answer is not immediately found.

2. Click the Pause button on the Goal Seek Status dialog. As shown in Figure 31.26, Excel is on its 33rd attempt at finding a value. In this pass, Excel is trying 18.24 in Cell E1. This is producing a value of 13205 instead of the desired value of 6950.

**Figure 31.26**
You can click Pause to examine how Excel is trying to solve the problem.

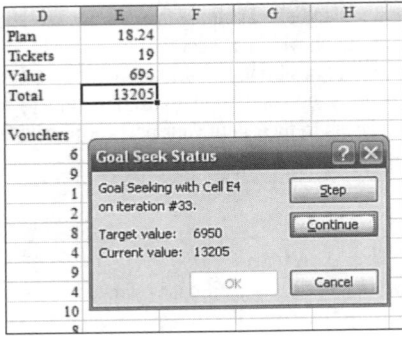

3, Click the Step button to proceed to the next guess. On the 34th iteration, Excel tries a plan of 13500743, which produces a #REF! error. Excel successively tries higher and higher values until, on step 64, it goes back to trying 18.24. Eventually, after 100 iterations, Excel gives up and reports that it cannot find a solution, as shown in Figure 31.27.

**Figure 31.27**
Goal Seek gives up after 100 iterations.

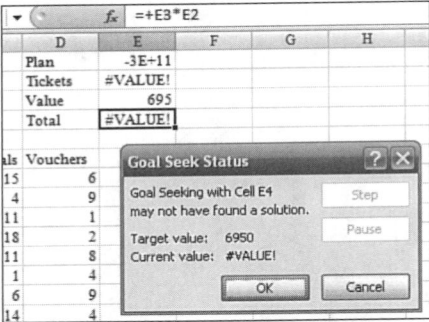

## USING GOAL SEEK IN A CHART

Excel provides an odd entry point for Goal Seek you can use when you are displaying a chart that contains series that are the result of a calculation.

You might be in a staff meeting and find that the senior manager does not like your projection for revenue. When the manager starts complaining, you can simply drag the chart data point to a new location, and Excel will display the Goal Seek dialog.

Here is how you use it:

1. In the chart, click on one data point to select the entire series.

2. Click on the data point a second time to select just that data point, as shown in Figure 31.28.

**Figure 31.28**
Selecting a single data
point in a chart.

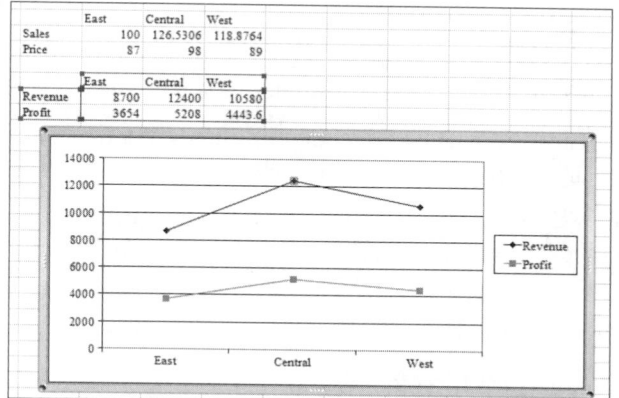

3. Using the mouse, drag the data point to a new location—around the 10,500 level. Excel displays the Goal Seek dialog, which indicates that you want to change Cell E8 to 10500 and asks which cell should be changed.

# USING SOLVER

It is possible to design problems that are far too complex for Goal Seek. These problems may have dozens of independent variables and various constraints. In such a case, you can use the Excel Solver add-in.

Using Solver is a bit tricky. With Solver, you specify a range of cells that can be changed. You are allowed to specify certain constraints on the solution. Finally, you indicate that you want one particular formula cell to either be maximized, minimized, or set to a particular value.

The Solver add-in, which is free with Excel, was written by Frontline Systems. Solver cannot solve some complex modeling systems. In such a case, you can purchase a premium version of Solver that can handle up to 2,000 input variables. To learn more about the premium version of Solver, visit Frontline Systems, at www.Solver.com.

## INSTALLING SOLVER

To install Solver, follow these steps:

1. Choose the Windows Icon menu, and then click Excel Options. The Options dialog appears.
2. Choose Add-Ins from the menu on the left of the Options dialog.
3. At the bottom of the Add-Ins page that appears, choose Excel Add-ins from the Manage drop-down. The Add-Ins dialog appears.
4. Click Go.
5. In the Add-Ins dialog, make sure that Solver is checked.

## SOLVING A MODEL USING SOLVER

To use Solver, your worksheet should contain one or more input variables. The worksheet should contain one or more formulas that result in a solution within a single cell.

For each input variable, there might be certain constraints. For example, you might want to assume that a certain variable must be positive or that it should be in a certain range of values.

When using Solver, you will identify the input range, the output cell, and the constraints. You can ask Solver to minimize or maximize the input cell. Or, you can ask Solver to set the output cell to a particular value.

Solver will rapidly loop through many different input variables, trying to find a combination that meets your goal.

This might be easier to understand with a concrete example. Figure 31.29 shows a worksheet used to model production of widgets. For the sake of this example, say you have a factory that is capable of making widgets. Cell B23 indicates that each worker can make five widgets per hour. Workers who work evenings, nights, or weekends are paid a shift differential. You can choose to keep your factory running for anywhere from 5 shifts a week (Monday through Friday, first shift) up to 21 shifts per week. You can basically sell as many widgets as you produce, provided that the overall cost is less than $2 per widget. You have a skilled workforce of 100 workers available for first shift, 82 workers for second shift, and 75 workers for third shift. How many shifts should the plant be open in order to maximize production? Solver runs circles around Goal Seek in situations that deal with multiple constraints. To find the answer, use Solver as follows:

**Figure 31.29**
A worksheet to model widget production.

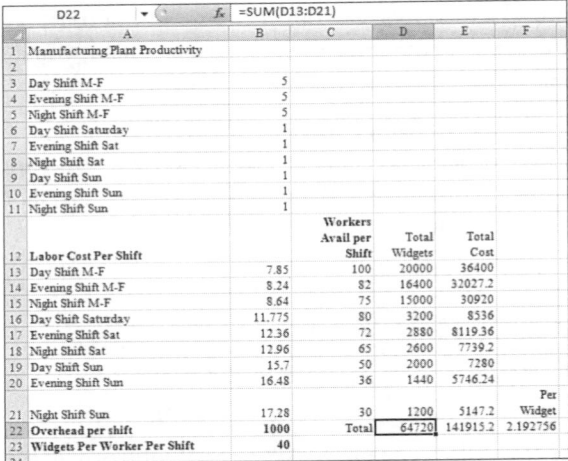

1. Note that Cells B3 through B11 define how many shifts the factory will be open. All the remaining cells in the model calculate the total number of widgets produced and the average cost per widget.

2. As with Goal Seek, you start out by telling Solver that you want to set a target cell equal to a maximum, minimum, or certain value by changing other cells. For example, the Solver Parameters dialog shown in Figure 31.30 indicates that the goal is to maximize widget production by altering the number of shifts.

**Figure 31.30**
Maximizing widget production.

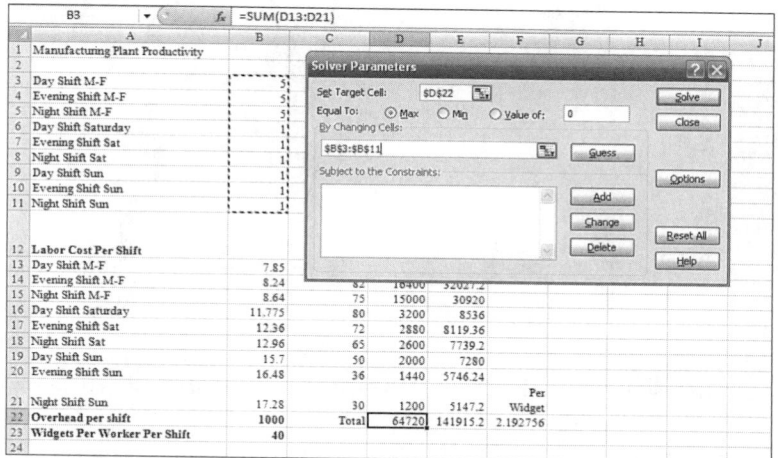

3. Enter the first constraint, that the market will only bear a manufacturing cost of $2 per widget. To specify this constraint, click the Add button in the Solver Parameters dialog.

4. As shown in Figure 31.31, tell Solver that the manufacturing cost must be less than or equal to $2 per widget.

**Figure 31.31**
Building the cost constraint.

5. Tell Solver that there cannot be a negative number of shifts. To do so, you need to add a constraint to indicate for each shift that the shift count must be greater than or equal to zero, as shown in Figure 31.32.

**Figure 31.32**
Although it is obvious
to you, Solver must be
told that it cannot
have negative num-
bers of shifts.

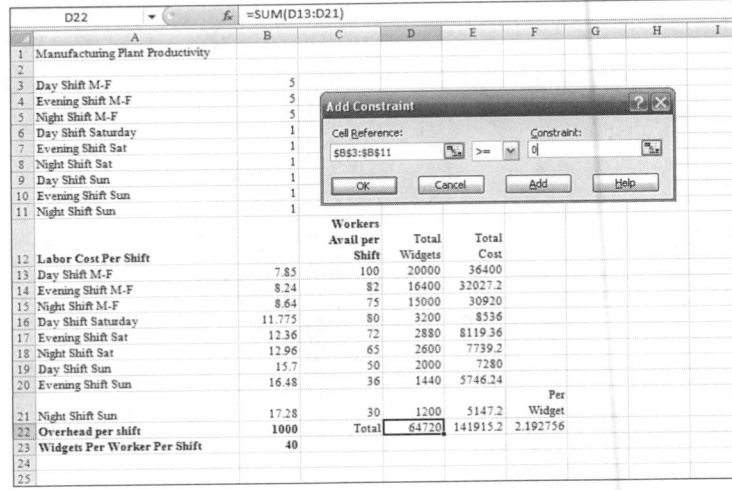

6. Specify that Cells B3:B5 must be less than or equal to five because you can have only five of each shift during the week.

7. In this model, it is not valid to work 0.32 shifts; only integer values can be used in a given range. Therefore, select the value int for the comparison operator to tell Solver that a certain range can accept only integers (see Figure 31.33).

**Figure 31.33**
You use the integer
constraint to prevent
fractional answers.

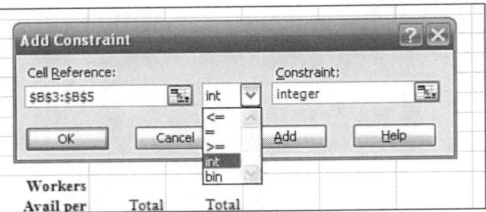

8. In this case, the Saturday and Sunday shifts are a special case: The company is either open or not. The only two possible values for each cell is 0 or 1. This is a special constraint called a binary constraint. Select the bin value in the comparison operator to specify that Cells B6 through B11 are limited to binary values.

9. After you have entered all the constraints, click OK to return to the Solver Parameters dialog.

10. Click the Options button on the Solver Parameters dialog to open the Solver Options dialog. Figure 31.34 shows that by default, Solver works for no more than 100 seconds. This is designed to prevent Solver from trying for a long time to find a solution.

11. When you have entered all the constraints and parameters, click OK to close the Solver Options dialog and return to the Solver Parameters dialog.

12. Click the Solve Model button on the Solver Parameters dialog. Solver begins to iterate through possible solutions. If Solver finds a result, it reports success, as shown in Figure 31.35.

**Figure 31.34**
You use the Solver Options dialog to fine-tune the processes used.

**Figure 31.35**
Solver reports success.

| | Manufacturing Plant Productivity | | | | |
|---|---|---|---|---|---|
| 3 | Day Shift M-F | 5 | | | |
| 4 | Evening Shift M-F | 5 | | | |
| 5 | Night Shift M-F | 5 | | | |
| 6 | Day Shift Saturday | 1 | | | |
| 7 | Evening Shift Sat | 0.558119 | | | |
| 8 | Night Shift Sat | 0 | | | |
| 9 | Day Shift Sun | 0 | | | |
| 10 | Evening Shift Sun | 0 | | | |
| 11 | Night Shift Sun | 0 | | | |

| | | Workers Avail per Shift | Total Widgets | Total Cost | |
|---|---|---|---|---|---|
| 12 | **Labor Cost Per Shift** | | | | |
| 13 | Day Shift M-F | 7.85 | 100 | 20000 | 36400 |
| 14 | Evening Shift M-F | 8.24 | 82 | 16400 | 32027.2 |
| 15 | Night Shift M-F | 8.64 | 75 | 15000 | 30920 |
| 16 | Day Shift Saturday | 11.775 | 80 | 3200 | 8536 |
| 17 | Evening Shift Sat | 12.36 | 72 | 1607.384 | 4531.572 |
| 18 | Night Shift Sat | 12.96 | 65 | 0 | 0 |
| 19 | Day Shift Sun | 15.7 | 50 | 0 | 0 |
| 20 | Evening Shift Sun | 16.48 | 36 | 0 | 0 |
| 21 | Night Shift Sun | 17.28 | 30 | 0 | 0 Per Widget |
| 22 | **Overhead per shift** | 1000 | Total | 56207.38 | 112414.8 | 2 |
| 23 | **Widgets Per Worker Per Shift** | 40 | | | |

Solver Results: Solver found a solution. All constraints and optimality conditions are satisfied.
○ Keep Solver Solution
○ Restore Original Values
Reports: Answer, Sensitivity, Limits

13. In the Solver Results dialog, choose the Answer to have Excel provide a new worksheet that compares the original and final values. As shown in Figure 31.36, the answer report is added as a new worksheet. In the answer report, Solver tells you that you can produce 54,600 widgets by operating five of each shift during the week and one Saturday shift. The remaining shifts are not cost-effective to keep the cost per widget in Cell F22 under $2. With this current solution, the cost per widget is $1.97.

You can save each Solver solution as a scenario. All these scenarios later show up in the Scenario Manager.

**Figure 31.36**
The day shift workers will be picking up some overtime on Saturdays, thanks to Solver.

| | A | B | C | D | E | F |
|---|---|---|---|---|---|---|
| | | | | Microsoft Excel 11.0 Answer Report | | |
| 6 | Target Cell (Max) | | | | | |
| 7 | | Cell | Name | Original Value | Final Value | |
| 8 | | $D$22 | Total Total Widgets | 57480 | 54600 | |
| 9 | | | | | | |
| 10 | | | | | | |
| 11 | Adjustable Cells | | | | | |
| 12 | | Cell | Name | Original Value | Final Value | |
| 13 | | $B$3 | Day Shift M-F | 5 | 5 | |
| 14 | | $B$4 | Evening Shift M-F | 5 | 5 | |
| 15 | | $B$5 | Night Shift M-F | 5 | 5 | |
| 16 | | $B$6 | Day Shift Saturday | 1 | 1 | |
| 17 | | $B$7 | Evening Shift Sat | 1 | 0 | |
| 18 | | $B$8 | Night Shift Sat | 0 | 0 | |
| 19 | | $B$9 | Day Shift Sun | 0 | 0 | |
| 20 | | $B$10 | Evening Shift Sun | 0 | 0 | |
| 21 | | $B$11 | Night Shift Sun | 0 | 0 | |
| 22 | | | | | | |
| 23 | | | | | | |
| 24 | Constraints | | | | | |
| 25 | | Cell | Name | Cell Value | Formula | Status |
| 26 | | $F$22 | Total Per Widget | 1.975882784 | $F$22<=2 | Not Binding |
| 27 | | $B$3 | Day Shift M-F | 5 | $B$3<=5 | Binding |
| 28 | | $B$4 | Evening Shift M-F | 5 | $B$4<=5 | Binding |

## Excel in Practice: Emergency Room Staffing

During flu season, the hospital emergency room (ER) has an overflow of patients. Here is a line of questioning about the problem.

**Q:** What is the basic flow when a patient is taken to the ER?

**A:** The patient is assessed by a nurse. The resident sees the patient. The resident then bounces the plans off an attending.

**Q:** How long does the resident spend on each patient, total?

**A:** 15 minutes with the patient, plus 5 minutes of paperwork

**Q:** How long does the attending spend per patient?

**A:** 5 minutes with the patient, plus 5 minutes of consultation with the resident

**Q:** How long does the nurse spend per patient?

**A:** About 30 minutes

**Q:** How long is the typical patient in the ER?

**A:** 1 hour

**Q:** How many treatment rooms does the ER have?

**A:** 20 rooms

**Q:** What is the current staffing per shift?

**A:** 2 attendings, 10 nurses, and 6 residents

Given all this information, you need to build a Solver model to find a way to get more patients through the ER. To do so, here is how the model works:

- Rows 2 through 4 of the model contain the current staffing levels for residents, attendings, and nurses. These will be the input cells for Solver.

- Row 5 contains a critical constraint: There are 20 treatment rooms. Therefore, no matter how many people you staff, there cannot be more than 20 patients being seen at once.

- Rows 6 through 10 state how many minutes each resource will spend with the patient. These values are fixed in the model. You are not trying to make the doctors spend less time with the patients.

- As shown in Figure 31.37, Row 12 calculates how many minutes of nursing time are available in an 8-hour shift. The formula calculates Cell B2 × 8 hours × 60 minutes per hour. Similar formulas in Rows 13 through 15 calculate how many minutes of each other resource are available per shift.

**Figure 31.37**
This formula in Cell B12 calculates the number of available nursing minutes per shift.

| | B12 | ▼ | $f_x$ =B2*8*60 | |
|---|---|---|---|---|
| | A | | B | C |
| 1 | **County General Emergency Room Planning** | | | |
| 2 | Number of Nurses | | 10 | |
| 3 | Number of Residents | | 6 | |
| 4 | Number of Attendings | | 2 | |
| 5 | Number of Rooms (Fixed) | | 20 | |
| 6 | **Each patient will use:** | | | |
| 7 | Minutes of Nursing time | | 30 | |
| 8 | Minutes of Resident time | | 20 | |
| 9 | Minutes of Attending time | | 10 | |
| 10 | Minutes in the room | | 60 | |
| 11 | **Person-Minutes in 8 hour shift** | | | |
| 12 | Nursing | | 4800 | |
| 13 | Resident | | 2880 | |
| 14 | Attending | | 960 | |
| 15 | Waiting/Procedure | | 9600 | |
| 16 | **Patients in 8 hour shift** | | | |
| 17 | Nursing | | 160 | |
| 18 | Resident | | 144 | |
| 19 | Attending | | 96 | |
| 20 | Waiting/Procedure | | 160 | |
| 21 | Total Number of Patients Through | | 96 | |
| 22 | Revenue per Patient | | 225 | |
| 23 | **Total Revenue** | | **21600** | |
| 24 | Cost for Nursing | | 1840 | |
| 25 | Cost for Residents | | 1440 | |
| 26 | Cost for Attendings | | 960 | |
| 27 | **Total Labor Cost** | | **4240** | |
| 28 | **Maximize Profit** | | **17360** | |
| 29 | | | | |
| 30 | | | | |

- In Row 17, if a nurse spends 30 minutes per patient, and the 10 nurses have 4,800 minutes available per shift, this means that they could potentially serve 160 patients in one shift. The formula in Cell B17 is B12/7. Similar formulas in Rows 18 through 20 calculate the process capacity for residents, attendings, and the room.

- Row 21 takes the minimum of Rows 17:20. If there is a bottleneck because of staffing, it will slow down all the other areas. At this point, the model is still trying to solve two problems: It is trying to maximize the number of patients seen while trying to make sure that there is not extra staff standing around. On the one hand, you want to maximize throughput and on the other hand, you want to minimize cost. The model takes a radical turn here, in an effort to come down to one number to represent both of these goals.

- Row 22 estimates some amount of revenue per patient.

- Row 23 calculates the total revenue.

- Rows 24 through 26 express the cost per resource per shift. Nursing costs $23 per hour, so you multiply that by 8 hours per shift and by the number of nurses in Cell B2.

- Row 27 calculates the total of the labor cost.

- Cell B28 calculates a hypothetical profit figure by subtracting labor cost from revenue. Even if these numbers aren't exact, the model can ask Solver to maximize profit. The act of maximizing profit will seek both to get the most patients through subject to constraints and also keep the staff to a minimum.

31

After converting all of those words to formulas, you can have Solver try to find the optimal staffing. To do so, follow these steps:

1. Start Solver.

2. Ask Solver to produce the maximum value in Cell B28 by changing the staffing levels in B2:B4. There are certain constraints. For example, you can't have half a doctor cover a shift, so cells B2:B4 must be integers and must be greater than zero. (See Figure 31.38.)

**Figure 31.38**
Asking Solver to maximize profit while adjusting staffing levels.

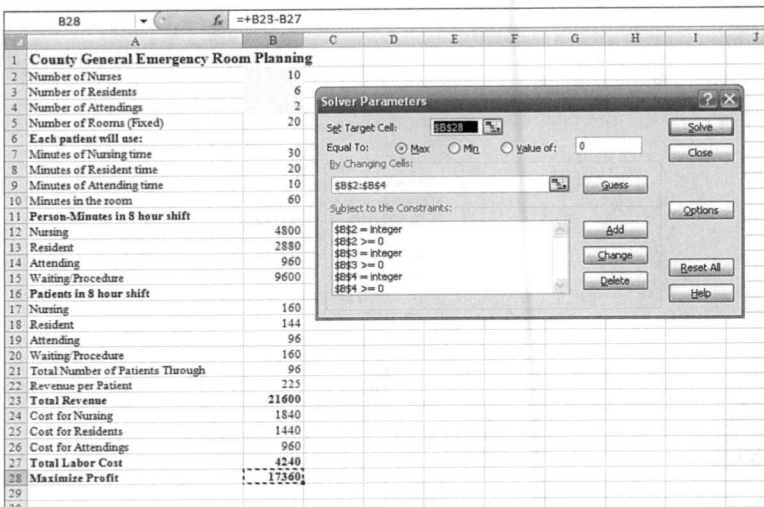

In a few seconds, Solver proposes a solution. The answer report suggests that you should increase staffing by adding 1 resident and 2 attendings, as shown in Figure 31.39.

**Figure 31.39**
The answer report shows the optimal staffing level.

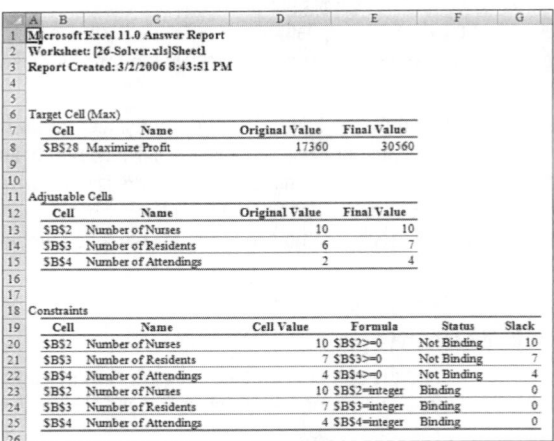

The answer report doesn't indicate any impact on patients, but if you examine the new answers in the original sheet, as shown in Figure 31.40, you see that the patient throughput has gone from 96 to 160. The model is suggesting that the attendings, and to a lesser degree, the residents, are the bottleneck in the process. Unless you build a new wing, you can't increase from the 20 existing treatment rooms. However, by adding staff, you can increase throughput in the existing rooms.

**Figure 31.40**
Patient throughput increases from 96 to 160 in the new model.

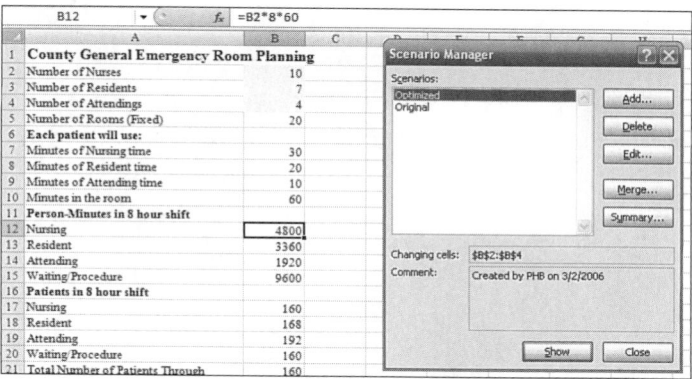

# FORMATTING AND SHARING INFORMATION

# FORMATTING WORKSHEETS

Formatting adds interest and readability to documents. If you have taken time to create a spreadsheet, you should also take the time to make sure that it is eye catching and readable.

You can format documents in Excel 2007 with any of these three methods:

- **Use tables styles**—As described in Chapter 8, "Fabulous Table Intelligence," you can use table styles to quickly format a table with banded rows, accents for totals, and so on.

- **Use cell styles**—You can use cell styles to identify titles, headings, and accent cells. The advantage of using cell styles is that you can quickly apply new themes to change the look and feel of a document.

- **Use formatting commands**—You can use traditional formatting commands to change the font, borders, fill, numeric formatting, columns widths, and row heights. The usual formatting icons are now found on the Home ribbon as well as in the Format Cells dialog box.

## WHY FORMAT WORKSHEETS?

You could easily open a blank worksheet and fill it with data without ever touching any of Excel's formatting commands. The result would be functional but not necessarily readable or eye catching.

Figure 32.1 contains an unformatted report in Excel.

**Figure 32.1**
After typing data into a spreadsheet, you have an unformatted report.

| | A | B | C | D | E | F | G |
|---|---|---|---|---|---|---|---|
| 1 | Astonishing Treadmill Inc. | | | | | | |
| 2 | Sales Forecast | | | | | | |
| 3 | 2008 | | | | | | |
| 4 | | | | | | | |
| 5 | Line | Product | Jan | Feb | Mar | Q1 | Apr |
| 6 | Consumer | A451 | 278.00 | 285.00 | 271.00 | 834.00 | 291.00 |
| 7 | | A636 | 357.00 | 334.00 | 387.00 | 1078.00 | 456.00 |
| 8 | | A686 | 161.00 | 144.00 | 244.00 | 549.00 | 165.00 |
| 9 | | B416 | 428.00 | 443.00 | 425.00 | 1296.00 | 448.00 |
| 10 | | B519 | 711.00 | 706.00 | 764.00 | 2181.00 | 697.00 |
| 11 | | D553 | 128.00 | 116.00 | 104.00 | 348.00 | 147.00 |
| 12 | | D555 | 376.00 | 405.00 | 378.00 | 1159.00 | 471.00 |
| 13 | | D801 | 353.00 | 352.00 | 377.00 | 1082.00 | 366.00 |
| 14 | | D914 | 296.00 | 274.00 | 279.00 | 849.00 | 394.00 |
| 15 | | E196 | 625.00 | 611.00 | 724.00 | 1960.00 | 700.00 |
| 16 | | E476 | 458.00 | 471.00 | 479.00 | 1408.00 | 484.00 |
| 17 | | Subtotal | 4171.00 | 4141.00 | 4432.00 | 12744.00 | 4619.00 |
| 18 | Profession | K121 | 174.00 | 244.00 | 149.00 | 567.00 | 193.00 |
| 19 | | K658 | 245.00 | 321.00 | 272.00 | 838.00 | 225.00 |
| 20 | | N713 | 301.00 | 368.00 | 325.00 | 994.00 | 289.00 |
| 21 | | O855 | 720.00 | 739.00 | 715.00 | 2174.00 | 789.00 |
| 22 | | O980 | 222.00 | 302.00 | 218.00 | 742.00 | 220.00 |
| 23 | | P450 | 388.00 | 412.00 | 363.00 | 1163.00 | 405.00 |
| 24 | | R737 | 360.00 | 342.00 | 380.00 | 1082.00 | 355.00 |
| 25 | | S484 | 104.00 | 175.00 | 83.00 | 362.00 | 107.00 |
| 26 | | T676 | 683.00 | 733.00 | 782.00 | 2198.00 | 713.00 |
| 27 | | X388 | 281.00 | 283.00 | 294.00 | 858.00 | 283.00 |
| 28 | | X862 | 367.00 | 451.00 | 423.00 | 1241.00 | 373.00 |
| 29 | | Z353 | 272.00 | 281.00 | 292.00 | 845.00 | 284.00 |
| 30 | | Subtotal | 4117.00 | 4651.00 | 4296.00 | 13064.00 | 4236.00 |
| 31 | | Total | 8288.00 | 8792.00 | 8728.00 | 25808.00 | 8855.00 |
| 32 | | | | | | | |

Figure 32.2 contains exactly the same data but with formatting applied. The formatted report is more interesting than the unformatted one. The reader can instantly focus on the totals for each line. Headings are aligned with the data. Borders break the data into sections. Accent colors highlight the subtotals and totals. The title is prominent, in a larger font and headline typeface. Numeric formatting has removed the extra decimal places and added thousands separators. The column widths are adjusted properly. A short row adds a visual break between the product lines. Headings for each product line are rotated, merged, and centered.

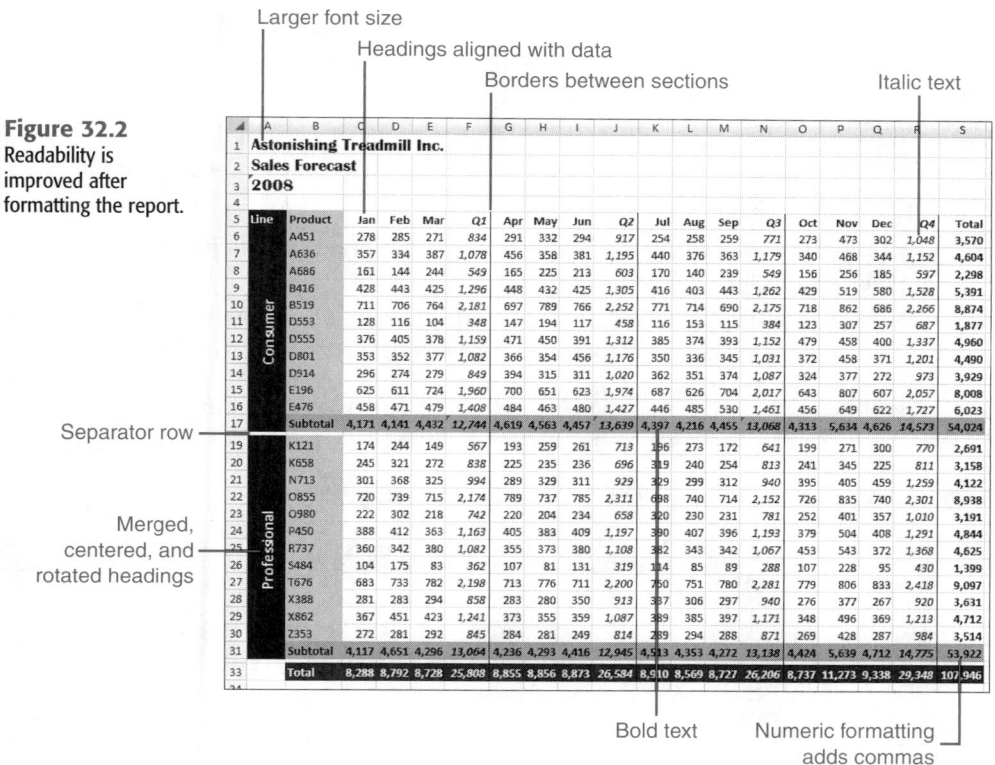

**Figure 32.2**
Readability is improved after formatting the report.

The formatting applied to Figure 32.2 takes a few extra minutes, but it dramatically increases the readability of the report. You've taken the time to put the worksheet together, and it is worth a couple minutes to help the consumer of the worksheet easily read it.

# USING TRADITIONAL FORMATTING

Formatting is typically carried out in the Format Cells dialog box or using the formatting icons located on the Home ribbon.

In Excel 2007, Microsoft took the icons formerly on the Formatting toolbar and arranged them in the Font, Alignment, and Number groups on the Home ribbon, as shown in Figure 32.3. Additional column- and row-formatting commands are available in the Format drop-down in the Cells group on the Home ribbon.

**Figure 32.3**
Most icons from the former Formatting toolbar are in the Font, Alignment, and Number tabs on the Home ribbon.

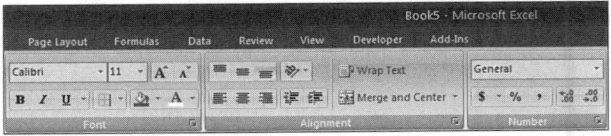

While analyzing SQM data from Microsoft Excel 2003, the Excel 2007 development team decided to promote some settings from the Format Cells dialog to the Home ribbon. Icons for wrapping text, vertical alignment, and text rotation have therefore been added to the icons formerly on the Formatting toolbar.

If your favorite setting is not on the Home ribbon, you can take one of the four entry paths to the Format Cells dialog, which provides access to additional settings, such as Shrink to Fit, Strikethrough, and more border settings:

- Press Ctrl+1 (that is Ctrl and the number 1). You can press Ctrl+Shift+F to display the Font tab on the same dialog.
- Click the double-diagonal arrow icons in the lower-right corner of the Font, Alignment, or Number groups. Each icon opens the dialog, with the focus on a different tab.
- Right-click any cell and choose Format Cells.
- On the Home ribbon, select Cells, Format, Format Cells.

As shown in Figure 32.4, the Format Cells dialog includes six tabs:

**Figure 32.4**
The Format Cells dialog offers complete control over cell formatting. You can visit this dialog when the icons on the ribbon don't provide enough detail.

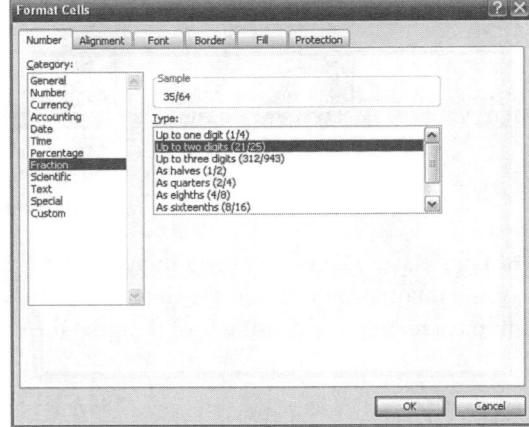

- **Number**—The Number tab gives you absolute control over numeric formatting. You can choose from 96,885 built-in formats or use the Custom category to create your own.
- **Alignment**—The Alignment tab offers settings for horizontal alignment, vertical alignment, rotation, wrap, merge, and shrinking to fit.

- **Font**—The Font tab controls font, size, style, underline, color, strikethrough, super-script, and subscript.

- **Border**—The Border tab controls line style and color for each of the four borders and the diagonals on each cell.

- **Fill**—The Fill tab offers 16 million fill colors, patterns, and now, for Excel 2007, cell gradients.

- **Protection**—You can use the Protection tab to lock or unlock certain cells. See Chapter 34, "Sharing Workbooks with Others," for more information.

## CHANGING NUMERIC FORMATS BY USING THE HOME RIBBON

Do you ever go shopping for hardware at a general-purpose store? I am amazed at their ability to have almost what I need but to never actually have what I need. I usually end up cursing my decision to stop at the general-purpose retailer and drive another mile down the road to Home Depot or Lowe's, where they always have exactly what I need.

Using the Number group on the Home ribbon is like shopping at a general-purpose retailer. It has a lot of settings for numeric formatting, but most of the time, they are not exactly what you need, and you end up visiting the Number tab on the Format Cells dialog.

To start, there are three icons, for currency, percentage, and comma style. The Percentage icon is useful. Unfortunately, the Currency and Comma icons both apply an Accounting style to a cell, and the Accounting style is inappropriate for everyone except accountants. Furthermore, these three icons are not toggle buttons. When you use one of them, there is not an icon to quickly go back to a general style (other than Undo).

The Increase and Decrease Decimal icons are useful. Each click of one of these buttons forces Excel to show one more or one fewer decimal place. If you have numbers showing two decimal places in all cells, a couple clicks on the Decrease Decimal icon solves the problem.

Figure 32.5 shows the Currency, Percentage, Comma, Increase Decimal, and Decrease Decimal buttons in the Number group of the Home ribbon.

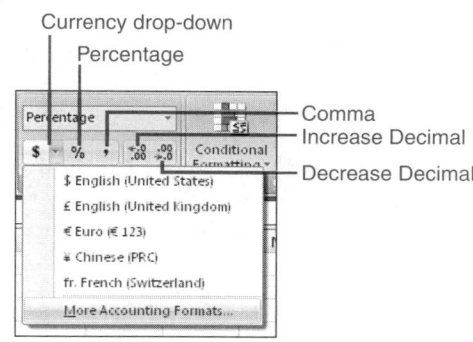

**Figure 32.5**
The Currency and Comma icons both use an Accounting style. This is wonderful for accountants, but others should resist using them.

Currency drop-down
Percentage
Comma
Increase Decimal
Decrease Decimal

32

Above the five buttons in the Number group is a new drop-down that has a dozen popular number styles. Figure 32.6 shows the styles in the drop-down. The range A2:F12 shows these styles applied to four different numbers.

**Figure 32.6**
Excel 2007 offers 12 popular number styles in this drop-down.

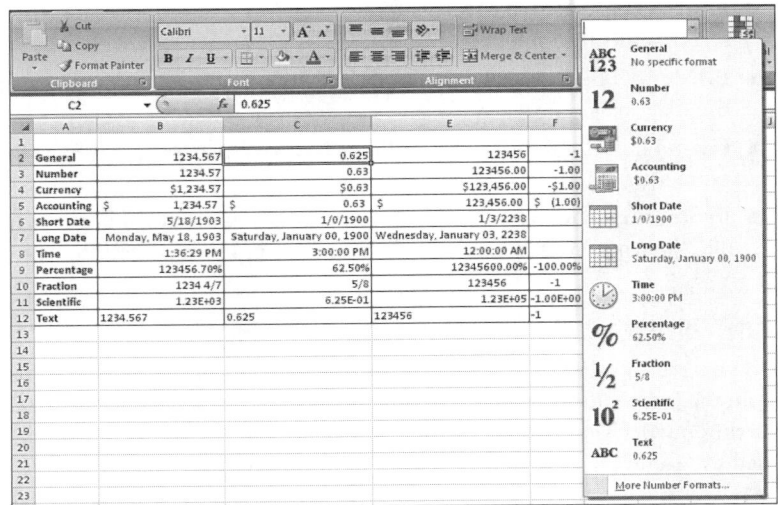

Here are some comments and cautions about using the number styles from the drop-down in the Home ribbon:

- General Format is a number format. Decimal places are shown if needed. No thousands separator is used. A negative number is shown with a minus sign before the number.

- Number does not use a thousands separator. It forces two decimal places, even with numbers that don't need decimal places, such as in Cell E3.

- Currency is a useful format for everyone. The currency symbol is shown immediately before the number. All numbers are expressed with two decimal places. Negatives are shown with a hyphen before the number.

- Accounting is great for financial statements and annoying for everything else. Negative numbers are shown in parentheses. Currency symbols are left-aligned with the edge of the cell. Positive numbers appear one character from the right edge of the cell to allow them to line up with negative numbers.

- Percentage uses two decimal places when selected from the drop-down. This is one format for which it is actually better to use the icon on the ribbon than the Format Cells dialog.

- Fraction defaults to showing a fraction with a one-digit divisor. If you have a number such as 0.925, some Excel number formats would correctly show this as 15/16. Unfortunately, the Fraction setting in this drop-down rounds it to 1.

## CHANGING NUMERIC FORMATS BY USING BUILT-IN FORMATS IN THE FORMAT CELLS DIALOG

The Format Cells dialog offers far more number formats than the Home ribbon. My favorite number format can only be accessed through the Format Cells dialog. I find that I avoid the buttons in the Number group in the Home ribbon and go directly to the Format Cells dialog.

You display the Format Cells dialog by clicking the double-diagonal arrow icon in the lower-right corner of the Number group of the Home ribbon. When you open the Format Cells dialog this way, the Number tab is the active tab.

There are 12 categories on the left side of the Number tab. The General and Text categories each have a single setting. The Custom category allows you to use formatting codes to build any number format. The remaining nine categories each offer a collection of controls to customize the numeric format.

### USING NUMERIC FORMATTING WITH THOUSANDS SEPARATORS

Using numeric formatting with thousands separators is my favorite format. The thousands of separators make the number easy to read. You can easily suppress the cents from the numbers. Microsoft does not offer buttons on the Home ribbon to select this format. The comma button would be a perfect place for it, but instead, Microsoft assigns that to the accounting format.

To format cells in numeric format, you follow these steps:

1. Press Ctrl+1 to display the Format Cells dialog.
2. Choose the Number category from the Number tab.
3. Check the box Use 1000 Separator.
4. Optionally, adjust the Decimal Places spin button to 0.
5. Optionally, select a method for displaying negative numbers.

Figure 32.7 shows the Number category of the Format Cells dialog.

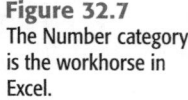

**Figure 32.7**
The Number category is the workhorse in Excel.

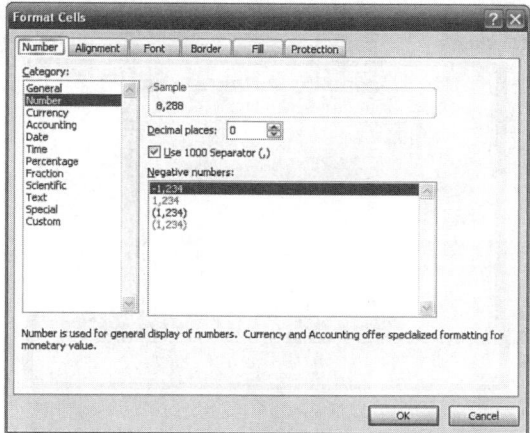

## DISPLAYING CURRENCY

There are two categories for currency. The Currency category is identical to the Number category shown in Figure 32.7, with the addition of a currency symbol drop-down. This drop-down offers 390 different currencies from around the world.

The second category, Accounting, always shows negative numbers in parentheses. With this category, the currency symbol is always left-aligned in the cell. The last digit of positive numbers appears one character from the right edge of the cell so that positive and negative numbers line up.

## DISPLAYING DATES AND TIMES

The Date category offers 17 built-in formats for displaying dates. The Time category offers nine built-in formats for displaying time. Each category has two formats that display both date and time.

The date formats vary from short dates, such as 3/14, to long dates, such as Wednesday, March 14, 2001. You should pay particular attention to the Date formats and the Sample box. Some formats show only the month and the day. Other formats show the month and the year. The values in the Type box are for March 14, 2001. Types such as March-01 display *month-year*. Types such as 14-Mar are displaying *day-month*.

An interesting format near the bottom of the list is the M type. This displays month names in JFMAMJJASOND style, as shown in Figure 32.8. Readers of the *Wall Street Journal*'s financial charts will instantly recognize that in this style, each month is represented by the first letter of the month. It works great when used as the labels along the x-axis of a chart.

**Figure 32.8**
A variety of date and time formats are available.

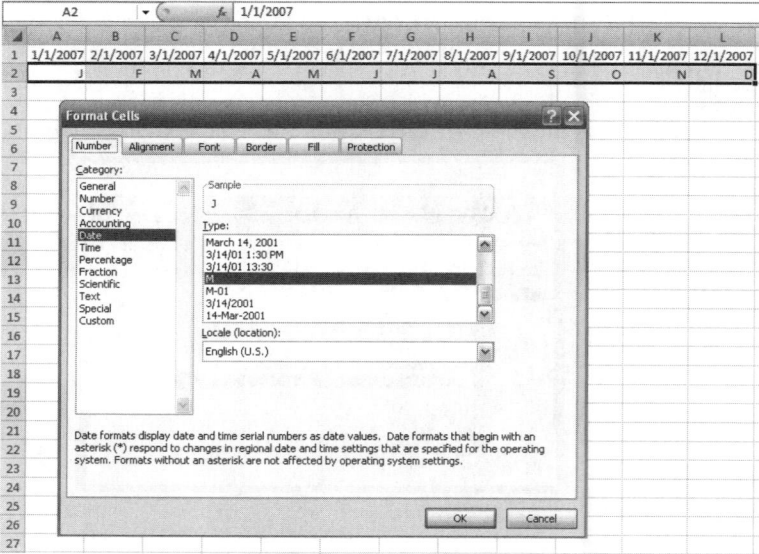

In the Time category, you should pay attention to an important distinction between the 1:30 PM, 13:30, and 37:30:55 types. The first type displays times from 12:00 AM through 11:59 PM. The second type displays military time. In this system, midnight is 0:00, and 11:59 PM is 23:59. Neither of these types displays hours in excess of 24 hours. If you are working on a weekly timesheet or any application where you need to display hours that total to more than 24 hours, you need to use the 37:30:55 type in the Time category. This format is one of few that displays hours in excess of 24.

## DISPLAYING FRACTIONS

The Fractions category rounds a decimal number to the nearest fraction. Types include fractions in halves, quarters, eighths, sixteenths, tenths, and hundredths. In addition, the first three types specify that the decimal should be reduced to the nearest fraction with up to one, two, or three digits in the denominator.

Figure 32.9 shows a variety of decimals formatted with five different fractional types. In Row 14, notice that this random number can appear as 1/2, 49/92, or 473/888 when using the Up To n Digit types. Excel rounds the number to the closest fraction.

In Column E, note that if you ask Excel to show the number in eighths, Excel uses 4/8 and 2/8 instead of 1/2 or 1/4.

**Figure 32.9**
Excel can display decimals as fractions in a variety of formats.

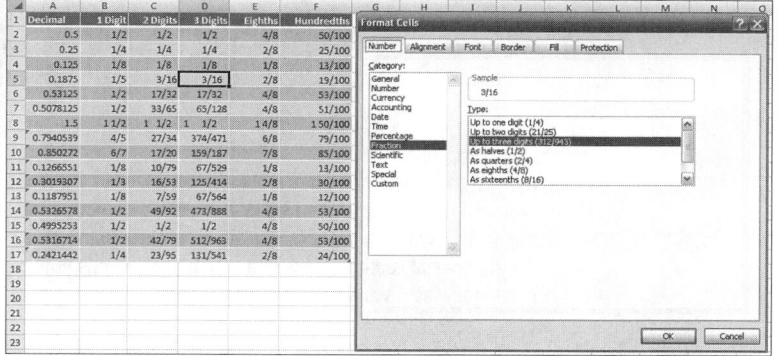

I am sure that I spent way too much time in junior high math learning how to reduce fractions. The first three fraction types of number formatting in Excel eliminate the need for manually reducing fractions.

## DISPLAYING ZIP CODES, TELEPHONE NUMBERS, AND SOCIAL SECURITY NUMBERS

Spreadsheets were invented in Cambridge, Massachusetts. If you enter the zip code for Cambridge (02138) in a cell, Excel does not display the zip code correctly. It truncates the leading zero, giving you a zip code of 2138.

To combat this problem, Excel provides four special formatting types, all of which are U.S. centric:

- The Zip Code and Zip Code + 4 styles ensure that east coast cities do not lose the leading zeros in their zip codes.

- The Phone Number type formats a telephone number with parentheses around the area code and a hyphen after the exchange.

- The Social Security Number type groups the digits into groups of three, two, and four numbers, separated by hyphens.

Figure 32.10 shows cells formatted with the four types, which are available in the Special category.

**Figure 32.10**
U.S. customers will appreciate the Special category in the Format Cells dialog.

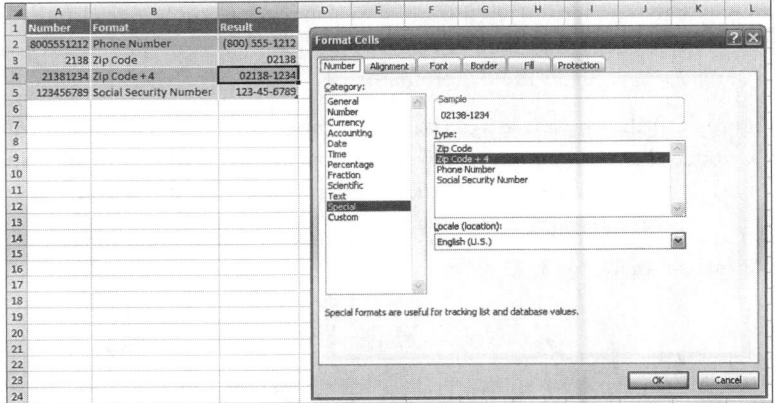

> **NOTE**
>
> If you happen to live in one of the other 191 countries in the world besides the United States, you will undoubtedly need other formatting for your postal codes, telephone numbers, or national ID numbers. You can create number formats such as the ones shown in the Special category as well as the other formats you might need by using the Custom category, as discussed in the next section.

## CHANGING NUMERIC FORMATS USING CUSTOM FORMATS

Custom number formats provide incredible power and flexibility. Although you don't need to know the complete set of rules for them, you will probably find a couple custom number formats that work perfectly for you and be able to make use of them.

To use a custom number format, you follow these steps:

1. Select the cells to be highlighted.
2. Display the Format Cells dialog by pressing Ctrl+1
3. Choose the Number tab.
4. Choose the Custom category.

5. Type the formatting codes in the Type box. Excel shows you a sample of the active cell formatted with this format in the Sample box.

6. Make sure this format looks correct and then click OK to accept it.

### USING THE FOUR ZONES OF A CUSTOM NUMBER FORMAT

A custom number format can contain up to four different formats, each separated by a semi-colon. The semicolons divide the format into up to four zones. Excel allows different formatting, depending on whether a cell contains a positive number, negative number, zero, or text. You need to keep in mind the following:

- Separate formatting codes for zones by using semicolons.
- If you type only one number format, it applies to all numbers.
- If you type only two formats, the first format applies to positive and zero. The second format is used for negative.
- If all four formats are used, they refer to positive, negative, zero, and text values, respectively.

In Figure 32.11, a custom number format uses all four zones. The table in Rows 11:14 shows how various numbers are displayed in this format. (Cell B14 appears in red type.)

**Figure 32.11**
The four zones of a custom number format can cause positive, negative, zero, and text values to display differently.

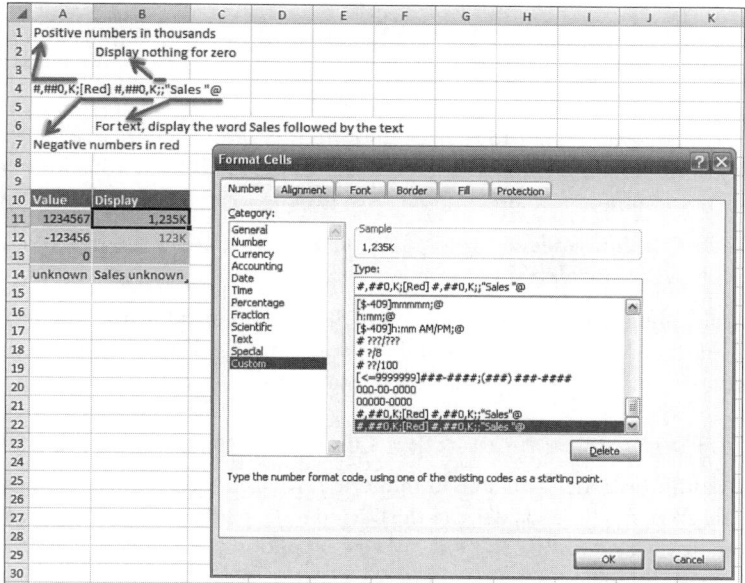

### CONTROLLING TEXT AND SPACING IN A CUSTOM NUMBER FORMAT

You can display a mix of text and numbers in a numeric cell. To do so, you simply include the text in double quotation marks. For example, `"The total is "$#,##0` precedes the number with the text shown in quotes.

If you need a single character, you can omit the quotation marks and precede the character with a backslash (\). For example, the code $#,##0,,\M displays numbers in millions and adds an M indicator after the number.

Some characters require neither a backslash nor quotation marks. These special characters are $ - + / ( ) : ! ^ & ' ~ { } = < > and the space character.

To add a specific amount of space to a format, you enter an underscore followed by a character. Excel then includes enough space to include that particular character. One frequent use for this is to include _) at the end of a positive number to leave enough space for a closing parenthesis. The positive numbers then line up with the negative numbers shown in parentheses.

To fill the space in a cell with a repeating character, you use an asterisk followed by the character. For example, the format **0 fills the leading space in a cell with asterisks. The format 0*- fills the trailing space in a cell with hyphens.

If you are expecting numbers but think you might occasionally have text in the cell, you can use the fourth zone of the format. You use the @ character to represent the text in the cell. For example, 0;0;0;"Unexpected entry of "@ highlights the text cells with a note.

### Controlling Decimal Places in a Custom Number Format

You use a zero as a placeholder when you want to force the place to be included. For example, 0.000 formats all numbers with three decimal places. If the number has more than three places, it will be rounded to three decimal places.

You use a pound sign (#) as a placeholder to display significant digits but not insignificant zeros. For example, 0.### displays up to three decimal places, if needed, but can display 1. for a whole number.

You use a question mark to replace insignificant zeros on either size of the decimal point with enough space to represent a digit in a fixed-width font. This format was designed to allow decimal points to line up, but with proportional fonts, it may not always work.

To include a thousands separator, you include a comma to the left of the decimal point. For example, #,##0 displays a thousands separator.

To scale a number by thousands, you include a comma after the numeric portion of the format. Each comma divides the number by a thousand. For example, 0, displays numbers in thousands, and 0,, displays numbers in millions.

### Using Conditions and Color in a Custom Number Format

The condition codes available in numeric formatting predate conditional formatting by a decade. You should consider the flexible conditional formatting features (see Chapter 9, "Visualizing Data in Excel") for any new conditions, but in case you encounter an old worksheet with these codes, it is valid to use eight colors in the format: red, blue, green, yellow, cyan, black, white and magenta. You include the color in square brackets. It should be the first element of any numeric formatting zone.

You can include a condition in square brackets after the color but before the numeric formatting. For example, [Red][<=100];[Blue][>100] displays numbers under 100 in red and other numbers in blue. The U.S. telephone special format uses this custom condition [<=9999999]###-####;(###) ###-####.

## USING DATES AND TIMES IN A CUSTOM NUMBER FORMAT

Although many of these settings are arcane, I still regularly use many of the date and time formats shown in Table 32.1. The various m and d codes allow flexibility in expressing dates.

**TABLE 32.1    DATE AND TIME FORMATS**

| To Display This | Use This Code |
| --- | --- |
| Months as 1–12 | m |
| Months as 01–12 | mm |
| Months as Jan–Dec | mmm |
| Months as January–December | mmmm |
| Months as the first letter of the month | mmmmm |
| Days as 1–31 | d |
| Days as 01–31 | dd |
| Days as Sun–Sat | ddd |
| Days as Sunday–Saturday | dddd |
| Years as 00–99 | yy |
| Years as 1900–9999 | yyyy |
| Hours as 0–23 | h |
| Hours as 00–23 | hh |
| Minutes as 0–59 | m |
| Minutes as 00–59 | mm |
| Seconds as 0–59 | s |
| Seconds as 00–59 | ss |
| Hours as 4 AM | h AM/PM |
| Time as 4:36 PM | h:mm AM/PM |
| Time as 4:36:03 P | h:mm:ss A/P |
| Elapsed time in hours (for example, 25:02) | [h]:mm |
| Elapsed time in minutes (for example, 63:46) | [mm]:ss |
| Elapsed time in seconds | [ss] |
| Fractions of a second | h:mm:ss.00 |

The custom number format m/d/yy displays the month and day numbers as one digit if possible. For example, dates formatted with this code would display as 1/9/08, 1/31/08, 9/9/09, and 12/31/08.

A custom number format of mm/dd/yy always uses two digits to display the month and day. Examples are 01/09/08 and 01/31/08.

The remaining date and time codes can display months as Jan, January, or J and days as 1, 01, Fri, or Friday.

NOTE

> Note that the letter m can be used as either a month or as a minute. If the m is preceded by an h or followed by an s, Excel assumes that you are referring to minutes. Otherwise, the month is displayed instead.

### DISPLAYING SCIENTIFIC NOTATION IN CUSTOM NUMBER FORMATS

To display numbers in scientific format, you use E-, or E+ exponent codes in a zone.

If a format contains a zero (0) or pound sign (#) to the right of an exponent code, Excel displays the number in scientific format and inserts an E. The number of zeros or pound signs to the right of a code determines the number of digits in the exponent. E- or e- places a minus sign by negative exponents. E+ or e+ places a minus sign by negative exponents and a plus sign by positive exponents.

Take the following, for example:

- 1450 formatted with 0.00E+00 would display as 1.45E+03
- 1450 formatted with 0.00E-00 would display as 1.45E03
- 0.00145 formatted with either code would display 1.45E-03

## ALIGNING CELLS

Worksheets look best when the headings above a column are aligned with the data in the column. Excel's default behavior is to left-align text and to right-align values and dates.

On the left side of Figure 32.12, the month headings in Row 5 are left-aligned, and the numeric values starting in Row 6 are right-aligned. This makes the worksheet look haphazard. To solve the problem, you can right-align the headings cells. The right side of Figure 32.12 shows the headings right-aligned.

To right-align cells, you select the cells and click the Right Align icon in the Alignment group of the Home ribbon.

NOTE

> The Alignment tab of the Format Cells dialog offers additional alignment choices, such as justified, distributed, and indented.

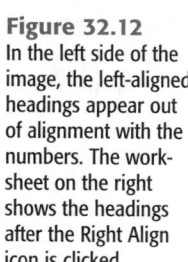

**Figure 32.12**
In the left side of the image, the left-aligned headings appear out of alignment with the numbers. The worksheet on the right shows the headings after the Right Align icon is clicked.

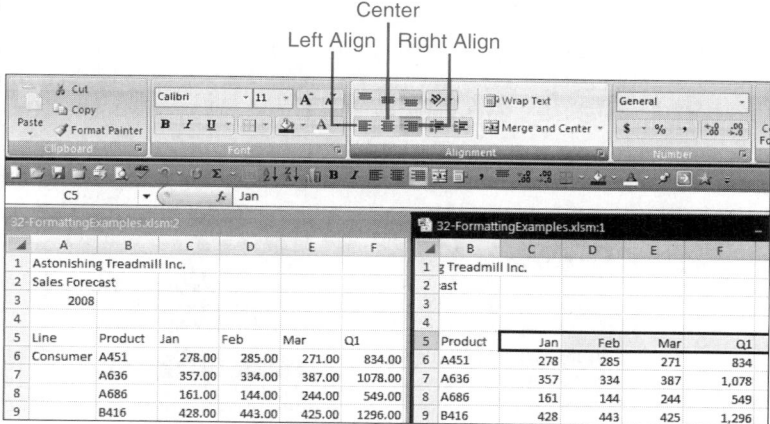

## CHANGING FONT SIZE

There are three icons in the Font group of the Home ribbon for changing font size:

- The Increase Font Size (A^) icon increases the font size in the selected cells to the next larger setting.

- The Decrease Font Size (A˅) icon decreases the font size in the selected cells to the next smaller setting.

- The Font Size drop-down offers a complete list of font sizes. You can hover over any font size to see the Live Preview of that size in the selected cells of the worksheet (see Figure 32.13).

**Figure 32.13**
When you use the Font Size drop-down, Live Preview shows you the effect of an increased font before you select the font.

**NOTE**

By using the Font tab of the Format Cells dialog, you can type an intermediate font size, such as 13.

## CHANGING FONT TYPEFACE

Changing the font typeface is vastly improved in Excel 2007. For a couple versions, the Font drop-down has been able to show the font names in the style of each font. Now, in Excel 2007, as you hover over the font, Live Preview shows you how the font will look in the selected cells in your worksheet, as shown in Figure 32.14. The Font name drop-down is in the Font group of the Home ribbon.

**Figure 32.14**
The Font drop-down in the Home ribbon now shows you the look of each font, and Live Preview shows you how your individual cells will look with the font applied.

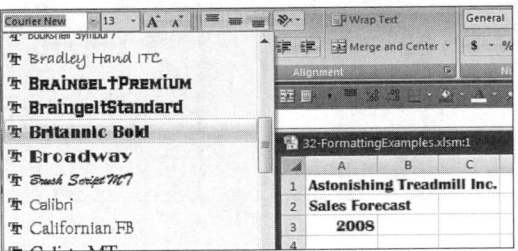

## APPLYING BOLD, ITALIC, AND UNDERLINE

Three icons in the Font group in the Home ribbon allow you to change the font to apply bold, italic, and underline. Unlike the icons in the Number group, these icons behave properly, toggling the property on and off. The Bold icon is a bold letter **B**. The Italic icon is an italic letter *I*. The Underline icon is either an underlined U or a double-underlined D. The Underline icon is actually a drop-down. As shown in Figure 32.15, you can choose the drop-down to change from Single Underline to Double Underline.

The underline style underlines the characters in the cell. If you have a cell that contains 123, the underline is 3 characters wide. If you have a cell with 1,234,567.89, the underline is 12 characters wide. If you need an underline to extend the entire width of a cell, you can select Single Accounting Underline or Double Accounting Underline on the Font tab of the Format Cells dialog. Or you can use a bottom border in the cell.

**Figure 32.15**
Bold, Italic, and Underline icons toggle the style on and off for the selected cells.

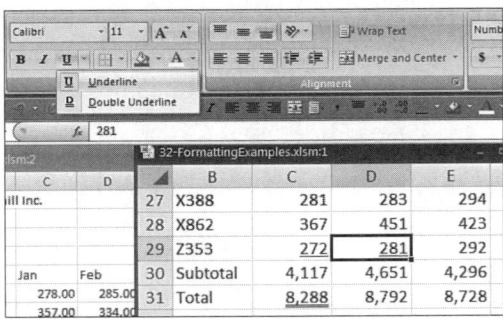

**NOTE**

By using the Font tab of the Format Cells dialog, you can also apply strikethrough, superscript, and subscript.

## USING BORDERS

There are 1.7 billion unique combinations of borders for any four-cell range. The Borders drop-down in the Font group of the Home ribbon offers 13 of the most popular options, as shown in Figure 32.16.

**Figure 32.16**
The Borders drop-down offers 13 of the most popular border choices.

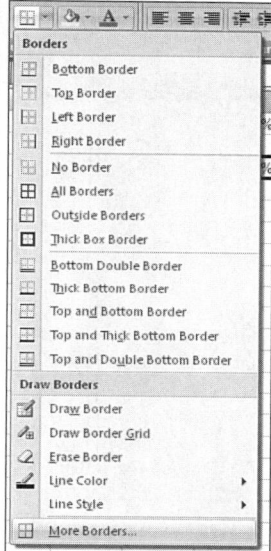

To apply borders to a range, you follow these steps:

1. Select the range.
2. On the Home ribbon, in the Font group, open the Borders drop-down.
3. Select one of the 13 presets from the drop-down. Live Preview does not work with borders, so you have to select a border before you see the effects.
4. If the presets do not present the combination you need, select More Borders from the drop-down to display the Borders tab of the Format Cells dialog.
5. In the Format Cells dialog, choose a line style from the Line section of the Borders tab.
6. Choose a color from the Color drop-down.
7. Draw borders by using one of the 11 preset buttons in the drop-down or click in and around the Text Text Text Text box.
8. If you need to mix colors in the range (for example, a blue top border and a red bottom border), repeat steps 5 through 7 for the other color or line style.
9. Click OK to apply the border.

There is an important concept to understand when applying borders to a range. Say that you select 20 rows by 20 columns (for example, cells A1:T20). If you apply a top border by using the drop-down, only the top row of cells A1:T1 have the border. Often, this is not what you were expecting. You might have wanted a border on the top of all 400 cells. In the

Format Cells dialog box, there is a representation of a 2×2 cell range, as shown in Figure 32.17. The border style drawn in the top edge of this box affects only the top edge of the range. The border style drawn in the middle horizontal line of the box affects all the horizontal borders on the inside of the selected range.

The fastest way to select all horizontal and vertical borders in the range is to click the Outline button and then the Inside button in the Presets section of the dialog.

**Figure 32.17**
If you need to change the color or the line style of the borders, you use the Format Cells dialog.

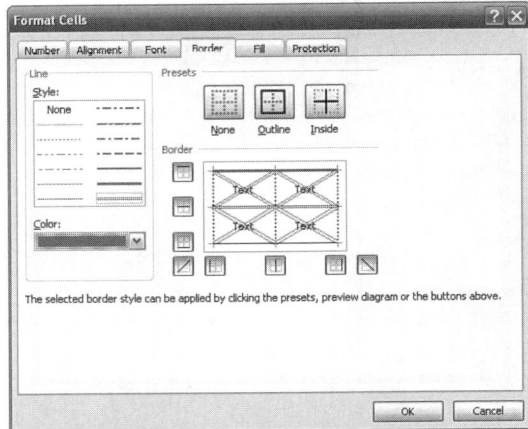

## COLORING CELLS

Excel 2007 adds the ability to use a gradient to fill a cell. This can provide an interesting look for a title cell. Gradient formatting is available only in the Format Cells dialog.

The Font group on the Home ribbon offers a paint bucket drop-down and an A drop-down. The paint bucket is a color chooser for the background fill of the cell. The A drop-down is a color chooser for the font color in the cell. Both drop-downs offer 6 shades of the 10 theme colors, 10 standard colors, and the option More Colors. The paint bucket drop-down also offers the menu choice No Fill, as shown in Figure 32.18.

The More Colors drop-down offers the two-tabbed Colors dialog. You can either choose a color from the Standard tab or enter an RGB value on the Custom tab.

The two-color gradient in a cell is a new feature in Excel 2007. To activate this feature, you follow these steps:

1. Select one or more cells. If you select a range of cells, Excel repeats the gradient for each cell in the range.
2. Press Ctrl+1 to display the Format Cells dialog.
3. Choose the Fill tab.
4. Click the Fill Effects button.
5. In the Color 1 and Color 2 drop-downs, choose two colors or choose one color and white.
6. In the Shading Styles section, choose a shading style.

**Figure 32.18**
The color drop-down offers theme colors, 10 standard colors, and the link More Colors.

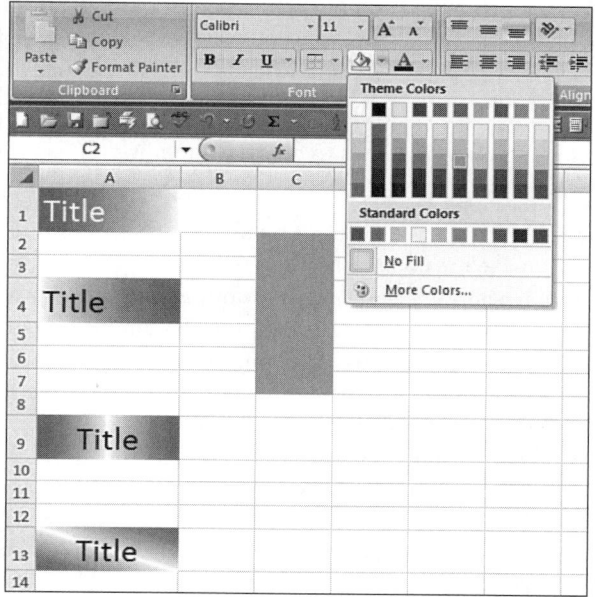

7. In the Variants section, choose one of the three variations. A sample is shown in the Sample box.

8. Click OK to close the Fill Effects dialog.

9. Click OK to close the Format Cells dialog.

Figure 32.19 shows the Fill Effects dialog. Cell A1 contains a vertical shading, from left to right. Cell A4 shows the opposite variant of vertical shading. Cell A9 shows the from-the-center variant of the vertical shading. Cell A13 shows a diagonal-down shading style.

**Figure 32.19**
In Excel 2007, you can add gradients as the fill within cells.

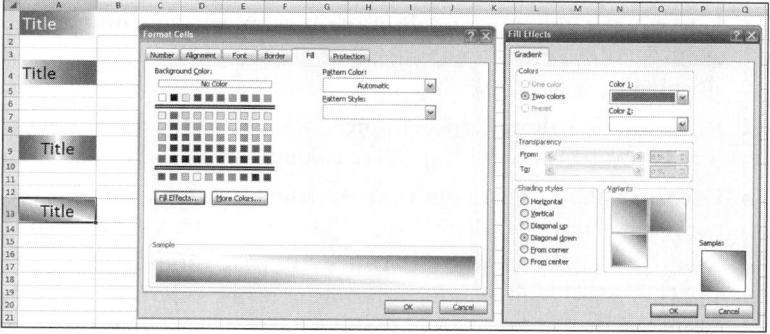

## ADJUSTING COLUMN WIDTHS AND ROW HEIGHTS

You can adjust the width of every column in a worksheet. In many cases, narrowing the columns to reduce wasted space can allow a report to fit on one page.

I always say that there are three or more ways to accomplish most tasks in Excel. In most cases, I have a favorite method to do any task and use that method exclusively. However, setting column widths and row heights is a task where I actively use many different methods, depending on the circumstances.

You can use the following seven methods to adjust column width. Every one of them applies equally well to adjusting row heights:

- **Click the border between the column headings**—As shown in Figure 32.20, you can drag to the left to make the column narrow. You can drag to the right to make the column wide. A ToolTip appears, showing the width in points and pixels. The advantage of this method is that you can simply drag until the column feels like it is the right width. The disadvantage is that this method fixes one column at a time.

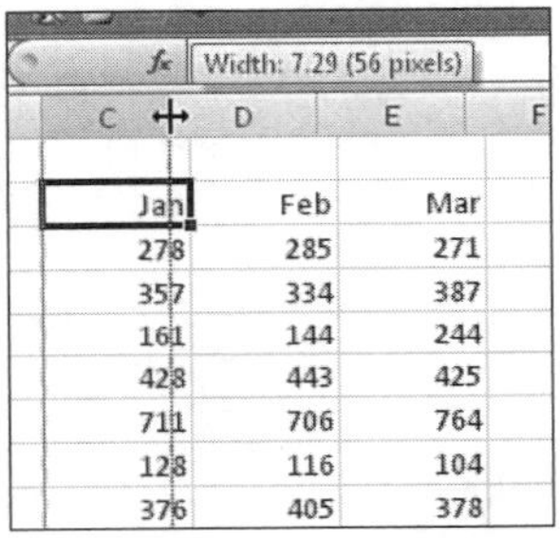

**Figure 32.20**
The right border between one cell letter and the next is the key to adjusting column widths.

- **Double-click the border between column headings**—Excel automatically adjusts the left column to fit the widest value in the column. The advantage of this method is that the column is exactly wide enough for the contents. The disadvantage is that a very long title in Cell A1 makes this method ineffective. You might have been planning on allowing the title in Cell A1 to spill over to B1, C1, and D1. However, the double-click method makes the column wide enough for the long title. (In this case, you want to use the final method in this list.)

- **Select many columns and drag the border for one column**—When you do this, the width for all columns is adjusted. The advantage of this method is that you can adjust all columns at once, and they are all a uniform width.

- **Select many columns and double-click one of the borders between column letters**—When you do this, all the columns adjust to fit their widest value.

- **Use the ribbon**—Select one or more columns. From the Cells group of the Home ribbon, select Format, Column Width. Then you enter a width in characters and click OK.

- **Apply one column's width to other columns**—If there is one column that is a suitable width, and you want all other columns to be the same width, you should use this method. You select the column with the correct width. Then you press Ctrl+C to copy. Next, you select the columns to be adjusted. Next, you choose the Clipboard section of the Home ribbon and select Paste, Paste Special, Column Widths. Finally, you click OK.

- **Autofit a column to all the data below the title rows**—If you have a long title in the first few rows and need to autofit the column to all the data below the title rows, you use this method. You click the first cell in the data range. Then you press the End key. Next, you hold down the Shift key while pressing the Down Arrow key. This selects a contiguous range from the starting cell downward. Now, you select the Cells section of the Home ribbon and then select Format, AutoFit Selection, as shown in Figure 32.21. If you were a power user in Excel 2003 or before, you might remember this method as Alt+O+C+A. This legacy keyboard shortcut still works.

**Figure 32.21**
The traditional column width command can be found in the Format drop-down in the Cells group of the Home ribbon.

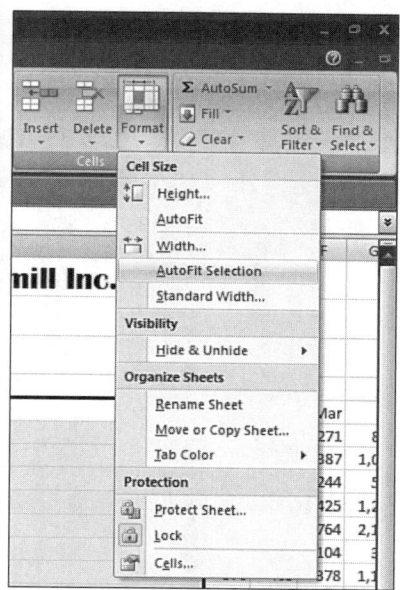

## USING MERGE AND CENTER

In general, merged cells are bad. If you have a merged cell in the middle of a data table, you will be unable to sort the data. You will be unable to cut and paste data unless the same cells are merged. However, it is okay to use merged cells as a title to group several columns together.

In Figure 32.22, the Consumer and Professional headings correspond to the columns B:F and G:K, respectively. It would be appropriate to center each heading above its columns.

**Figure 32.22**
Because the Row 2 categories are not part of the data table and would never need to be sorted, it is okay to merge and center those cells.

| | A | B | C | D | E | F | G | H | I | J | K |
|---|---|---|---|---|---|---|---|---|---|---|---|
| 1 | | | | | | | | | | | |
| 2 | | Consumer | | | | | Professional | | | | |
| 3 | Month | A451 | A636 | A686 | B416 | B519 | K121 | K658 | N713 | O855 | O980 |
| 4 | Jan | 167 | 198 | 168 | 139 | 153 | 145 | 144 | 198 | 195 | 168 |
| 5 | Feb | 166 | 132 | 135 | 150 | 183 | 170 | 198 | 103 | 195 | 194 |
| 6 | Mar | 191 | 103 | 112 | 190 | 136 | 124 | 151 | 108 | 167 | 182 |
| 7 | Apr | 125 | 147 | 175 | 150 | 190 | 182 | 154 | 140 | 173 | 178 |
| 8 | May | 121 | 160 | 147 | 169 | 170 | 183 | 147 | 138 | 196 | 181 |
| 9 | Jun | 131 | 166 | 185 | 179 | 196 | 165 | 140 | 177 | 191 | 177 |
| 10 | Jul | 182 | 118 | 144 | 116 | 172 | 171 | 158 | 141 | 149 | 170 |
| 11 | Aug | 137 | 129 | 183 | 163 | 105 | 188 | 103 | 116 | 195 | 102 |
| 12 | Sep | 130 | 108 | 124 | 177 | 170 | 108 | 168 | 168 | 142 | 138 |
| 13 | Oct | 146 | 197 | 180 | 177 | 143 | 180 | 152 | 177 | 188 | 123 |
| 14 | Nov | 154 | 153 | 180 | 158 | 129 | 110 | 118 | 179 | 151 | 155 |
| 15 | Dec | 107 | 162 | 151 | 145 | 158 | 178 | 180 | 159 | 129 | 188 |

To merge and center cells, you follow these steps:

1. Click in the cell that contains the value to be centered and drag to select the entire range to be merged. In this example, you would click in Cell B2 and drag to Cell F2. The result is that B2 is the active cell, and B2:F2 is selected.

2. From the Home ribbon, select Alignment, Merge and Center and then select Merge and Center again, as shown in Figure 32.23.

3. Repeat steps 1 and 2 for any other column headings.

4. Optionally, apply an outline border around the merged cells.

**Figure 32.23**
Select Merge and Center from the drop-down.

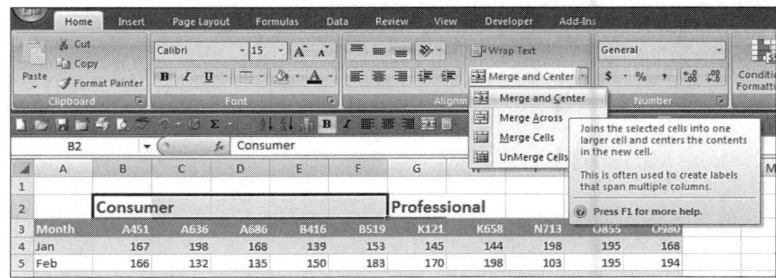

Note that after you merge the cells, the entire range becomes one cell. In Figure 32.24, the word *Consumer* is in an ultra-large Cell B2. In this worksheet, cells C2, D2, E2, and F2 no longer exist.

**Figure 32.24**
Columns are visually grouped into product lines by the merged cells.

| | A | B | C | D | E | F | G | H | I | J | K |
|---|---|---|---|---|---|---|---|---|---|---|---|
| 1 | | | | | | | | | | | |
| 2 | | | | Consumer | | | | Professional | | | |
| 3 | Month | A451 | A636 | A686 | B416 | B519 | K121 | K658 | N713 | O855 | O980 |
| 4 | Jan | 167 | 198 | 168 | 139 | 153 | 145 | 144 | 198 | 195 | 168 |
| 5 | Feb | 166 | 132 | 135 | 150 | 183 | 170 | 198 | 103 | 195 | 194 |
| 6 | Mar | 191 | 103 | 112 | 190 | 136 | 124 | 151 | 108 | 167 | 182 |
| 7 | Apr | 125 | 147 | 175 | 150 | 190 | 182 | 154 | 140 | 173 | 178 |

**NOTE**

The Merge Across selection in the drop-down merges the cells but does not center the value in the merged cell across the cells below.

## ROTATING TEXT

Vertical text is difficult to read. However, there are times when space considerations make it advantageous to use vertical text. In Figure 32.25, for example, the names in Row 5 are much wider than the values in the rest of the table. If you use Format, Autofit Selection, the report is too wide.

**Figure 32.25**
The headings are much wider than the data. Vertical text could solve the problem.

Astonishing Treadmill Inc.
Sales Forecast by Sales Representative
2008

| Product | Blankenship | Cunningham | Fitzpatrick | Hamilton | Henderson | Montgomery | Richardson | Stephenson | Strickland | Valenzuela | Vincent | Washington | Total |
|---|---|---|---|---|---|---|---|---|---|---|---|---|---|
| A451 | 339 | 258 | 293 | 316 | 252 | 304 | 339 | 322 | 310 | 258 | 293 | 287 | 3,571 |
| A696 | 438 | 332 | 377 | 408 | 325 | 392 | 438 | 415 | 400 | 332 | 377 | 370 | 4,604 |
| A686 | 218 | 166 | 188 | 203 | 162 | 196 | 218 | 207 | 200 | 166 | 188 | 185 | 2,297 |
| B416 | 513 | 389 | 442 | 477 | 380 | 460 | 513 | 486 | 468 | 389 | 442 | 433 | 5,392 |
| B519 | 844 | 640 | 727 | 786 | 626 | 756 | 844 | 800 | 771 | 640 | 727 | 713 | 8,874 |
| D553 | 178 | 135 | 154 | 166 | 132 | 160 | 178 | 169 | 163 | 135 | 154 | 151 | 1,875 |
| D555 | 472 | 358 | 407 | 439 | 350 | 423 | 472 | 447 | 431 | 358 | 407 | 398 | 4,962 |
| D801 | 427 | 324 | 368 | 397 | 317 | 383 | 427 | 405 | 390 | 324 | 368 | 361 | 4,491 |
| D914 | 374 | 283 | 322 | 348 | 277 | 335 | 374 | 354 | 341 | 283 | 322 | 316 | 3,929 |
| E196 | 761 | 578 | 656 | 709 | 564 | 683 | 761 | 722 | 696 | 578 | 656 | 643 | 8,007 |
| E476 | 573 | 434 | 494 | 533 | 425 | 513 | 573 | 543 | 523 | 434 | 494 | 484 | 6,023 |
| Subtotal | 5,137 | 3,897 | 4,428 | 4,782 | 3,810 | 4,605 | 5,137 | 4,870 | 4,693 | 3,897 | 4,428 | 4,341 | 54,025 |

(Column A contains a "Consumer" grouping label.)

In the Alignment tab of the Home group, an Orientation drop-down offers five variations of vertical text. Figure 32.26 compares the five available options. Although the Angle options look great, they only reduce the column width by 12%. Vertical Text reduces the column width by 75% but takes far more vertical space. The option Rotate Text Up reduces the column width by 73% and takes up less than half the vertical space of the Vertical Text option.

**Figure 32.26**
Of the five options, the Rotate Text options take up the least space.

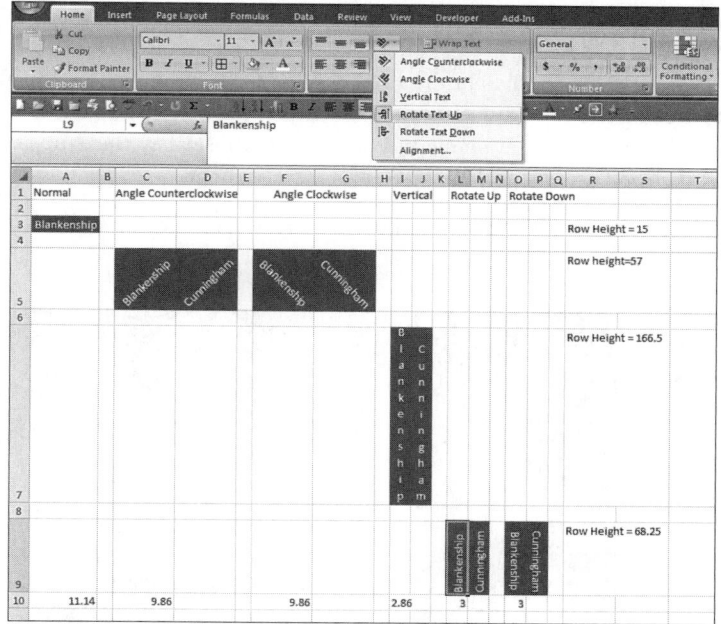

32

NOTE

After you rotate the text, select the Cells section of the Home ribbon and then select Format, AutoFit Selection again to narrow the columns.

If you need more control over the text orientation, you can select the Alignment option in the drop-down to display the Alignment tab of the Format Cells dialog. This tab allows rotation from 90 degrees to -90 degrees, in 1 degree increments, as shown in Figure 32.27.

**Figure 32.27**
The Alignment option allows 182 different orientation settings.

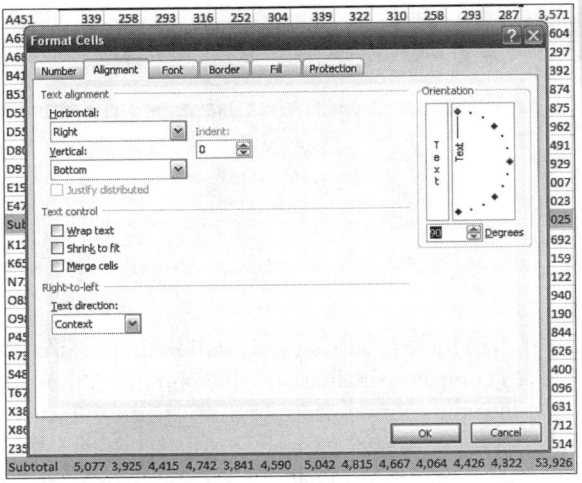

# FORMATTING WITH STYLES

Instead of using the settings in the Font group of the Home ribbon, you could format a report by using the built-in cell styles. Cell styles have been popular in Word for over a decade. They have been available in Excel, but because they were not given a spot on the Formatting toolbar, few people took advantage of them.

Figure 32.28 shows the styles available when you select Styles, Cell Styles in the Home ribbon.

**Figure 32.28**
The Cell Styles gallery offers various built-in cell styles.

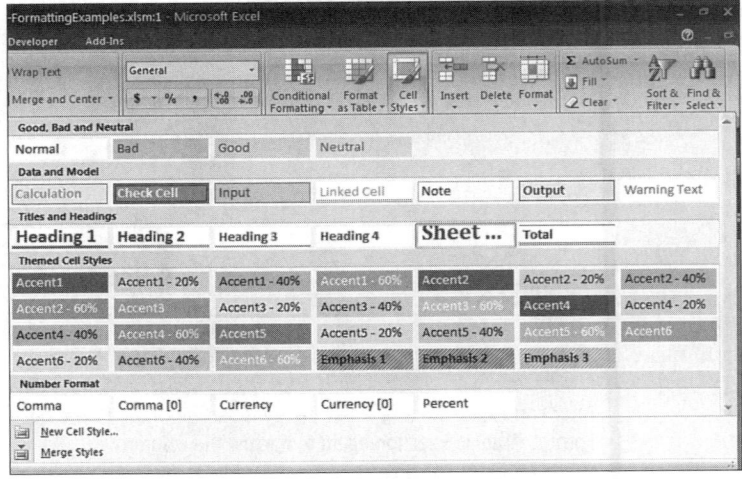

An advantage to using cell styles is that you can quickly convert the look and feel of a report by choosing from the themes on the Page Layout ribbon. Figure 32.29 shows 1 of the 20 available themes applied to the report.

**Figure 32.29**
When you choose a new theme, a report formatted with cell styles takes on a new look.

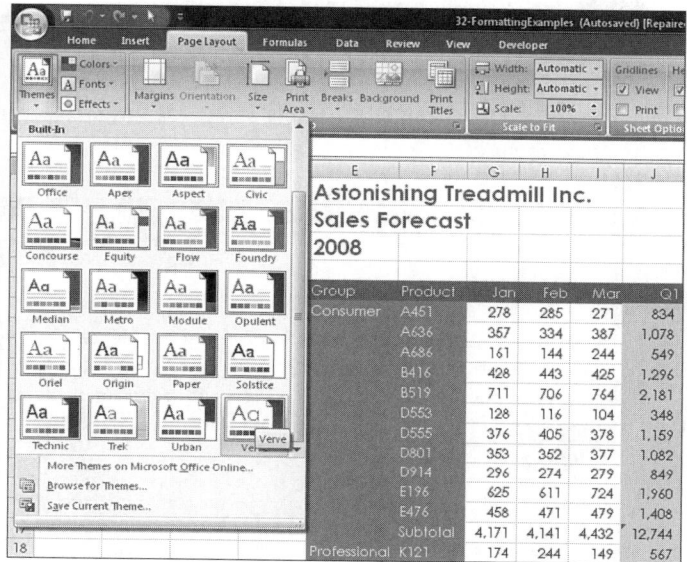

The Cell Styles gallery offers a menu item to add additional styles to a workbook. Using cell styles provides an interesting alternative to the traditional method of formatting.

# OTHER FORMATTING TECHNIQUES

You have the basics for formatting cells and worksheets. The rest of this chapter provides an overview of various formatting tips and tricks. These techniques discuss how to mix formatting within a single cell, wrap text in several cells, and use cell comments.

## FORMATTING INDIVIDUAL CHARACTERS

Occasionally, you might find yourself entering a short memo on a worksheet. This might occur as an introduction or as instructions to a lengthy workbook. Although Excel is not a full-featured word processor, it can do a few word processing tricks.

One trick is to highlight individual characters in a cell in order to add emphasis or to make them stand out. You can do this to any cell that does not contain a formula. In Figure 32.30, for example, text has been typed in Column A and allowed to extend over the edge of the column into Columns A:J. One word in Row 4 is in a bold, underlined, red font.

To format individual characters, you follow these steps:

1. Display the Home ribbon.
2. Select the cell that contains the characters to be formatted.
3. Press the F2 key to edit the cell
4. Using the mouse, highlight the characters in the formula bar.

5. Although most of the ribbon is grayed out, the options for font size, color, underline, bold, italics, and font name are available in the Font group of the Home ribbon. Apply any formatting, as desired, from this group.

6. If the changes are not visible in the formula bar, press Enter to accept the changes in order to preview them.

**Figure 32.30**
You can change the formatting for individual characters in a cell by selecting those characters in the formula bar.

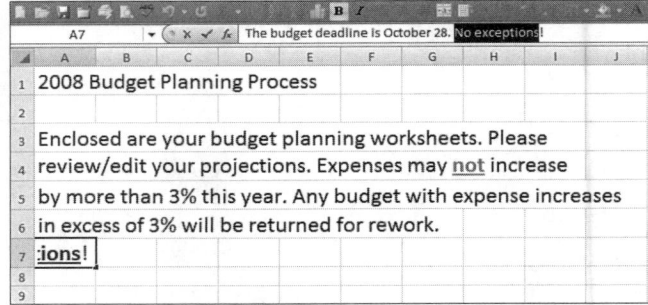

**CAUTION**

Using the technique described later in this chapter, in the section "Justifying Text in a Range," to justify text in a range wipes out the individual character formatting. Be sure to use that trick before doing a lot of formatting with the tricks described here.

## CHANGING THE DEFAULT FONT

Excel offers a default font setting to be used for all new workbooks. With the Excel 2007 paradigm of themes, the default font for new workbooks is initially the generic value of BODY FONT. This is not an actual font; it instead refers to the main font used by the current theme.

**NOTE**

If you like the concept of using themes to change the look and feel of a document, you should leave the default font setting as BODY FONT and change the font used in the theme. (For more information on customizing themes, see Chapter 5, "Galleries, Live Preview, and Themes.")

To change your default font for all new workbooks, you follow these steps:

1. The menu for changing the default font does not offer Live Preview of the fonts. Therefore, go to the Font section of the Home ribbon and select the Font drop-down to inspect the available fonts in their actual styles. Find the name of the font you want to use.

2. From the Office icon menu, choose Excel Options. The Excel Options dialog appears.

3. Click the Popular category in the left margin.

4. In the second section, When Creating New Workbooks, choose the Use This Font drop-down. Select the font name you chose in step 1.

5. Click OK to close the Excel Options dialog.

6. Close and restart Microsoft Excel for the changes to take effect.

The default font setting only has an effect in new workbooks. It does not affect workbooks previously created.

## WRAPPING TEXT IN A CELL

You might have one column in a table that contains long, descriptive text. If the text contains several sentences, it would be impractical to make the column wide enough to include the longest value in the column. Excel offers the capability to wrap text on a cell-by-cell basis to solve this problem.

When you wrap text, one annoying feature of Excel becomes evident. All cells in Excel are initially set to have their cell contents aligned with the bottom of the cell. You probably don't notice this because most cells in Excel are the same height. When you wrap text, however, the cell heights double or more, and it becomes very evident that the bottom alignment looks strange in this situation. To correct this problem, you follow these steps:

1. Decide on a reasonable column width for the column that contains the descriptive text. If you try to wrap text in a column that is only 8 points wide, you will be lucky to fit one word per line. If you have the space, a width of at least 24 will allow suitable results for the text wrapping.

2. From the Cells section of the Home ribbon, select Format, Column Width. Choose a width of 24 or higher.

3. Select the cells in the column to be wrapped.

4. From the Home ribbon, select Alignment, Wrap Text.

5. If the rows are too tall, you will have a tendency to grab the right edge of the column and drag it outward to make the description column wider. A long-standing bug causes Excel to not automatically resize the row heights after this step. You must select the Cells section of the Home ribbon and then select Format, Autofit to resize the row height after adjusting the column width.

6. Select all cells in the table.

7. From the Home ribbon, select Alignment, Top Align. The values in the other columns now align with the top of the descriptive text.

Figure 32.31 shows a table where the descriptions in Column B have had their text wrapped and all the cells are top-aligned.

32

**Figure 32.31**
After wrapping text in a column, you should top-align all columns.

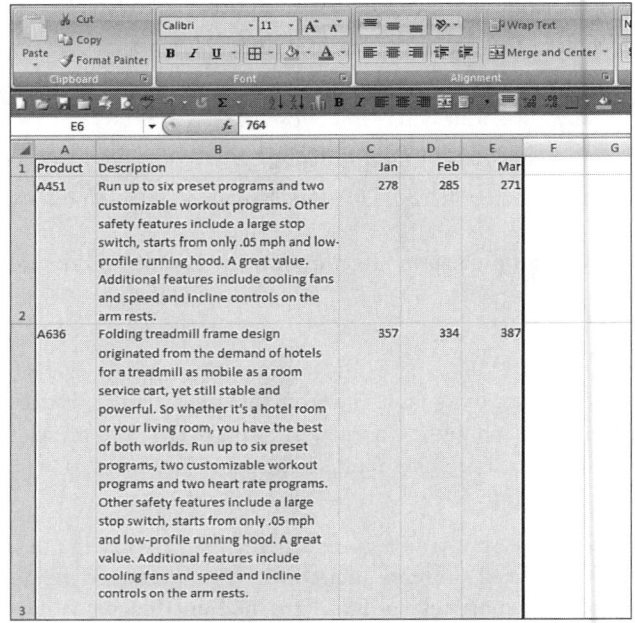

## JUSTIFYING TEXT IN A RANGE

When using Excel as a word processor to include a paragraph of explanatory body copy in a worksheet, you usually have to decide where to manually break each line.

Excel offers a command that reflows the text in a paragraph in order to fit a certain number of columns.

You need to do some careful preselection work before invoking the command. You follow these steps:

1. Ensure that your text is composed of one column of cells that contain body copy. It is fine if the sentences extend beyond one column, but the text should be arranged so that the left column contains text and the remaining columns are blank.

2. Ensure that the upper-left cell of your selection starts with the first line of text.

3. Ensure that the selection range is as wide as you want the finished text to be.

4. If your sentences currently extend beyond the desired width, Excel requires more rows in order to wrap the text. Include several extra rows in the selection rectangle. Figure 32.32 shows a suitable-sized selection range.

5. From the Home ribbon, select Editing, Fill, Justify. Excel flows the text so that each line is shorter than the selection range. Figure 32.33 shows the result.

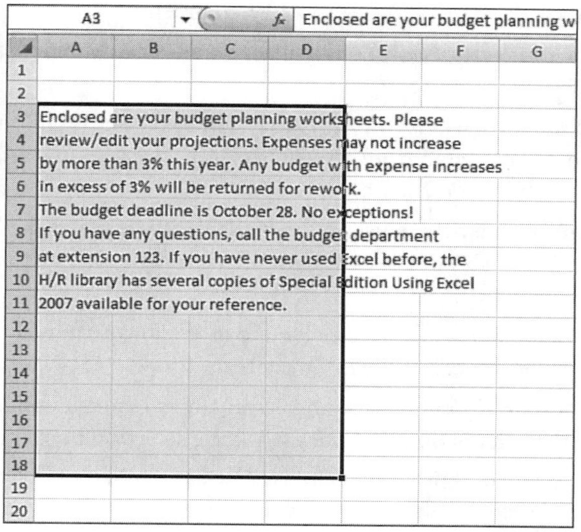

**Figure 32.32**
You need to select more rows than necessary. The number of columns selected determines the width of the final text.

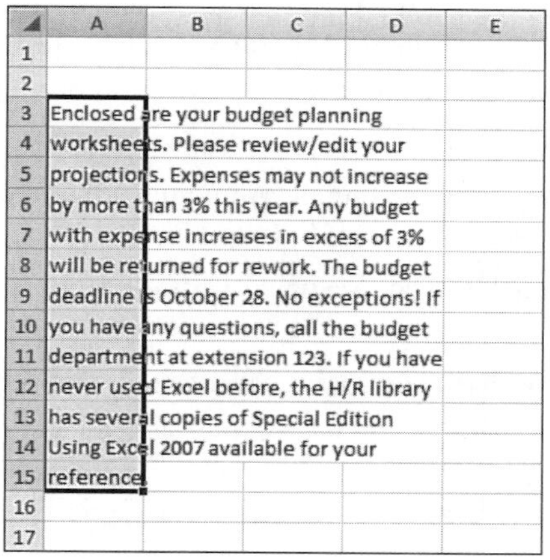

**Figure 32.33**
Excel flows the text to fit the width of the original selection.

## ADDING CELL COMMENTS

Cell comments can contain a few sentences or paragraphs to explain a cell. Although the default is for all comments to use a yellow sticky-note format, you can customize comments with colors, fonts, or even pictures.

In the default case, a comment causes a red triangle to appear in a cell. If you hover over the triangle, the comment appears. Alternatively, you can request that comments be displayed all the time. This creates an easy way to add instructions to a worksheet.

You follow these steps to insert a comment, format it, and cause it to be displayed continuously:

1. Select a cell to which you would like to add a comment.

2. Select Review, Comments, New Comment or right-click the cell and choose New Comment.

3. The default comment starts with your name in bold on line 1 and the insertion point on line 2. To remove your name from the comment, backspace through your name and then press Ctrl+B to turn off the bold.

4. Type instructions to the person using the worksheet. You can make the instructions longer than the initial size of the comment. (A comment can contain more than 2,000 words of body copy.)

5. After entering the text, click the resize handle in the lower-right corner of the comment. Drag to allow the comment to fit the text.

6. The selection border around the comment can either be made of diagonal lines or dots. If your selection border is diagonal lines, click the selection border to change it to dots.

7. Right-click the selection border and choose Format Comment. The Format Comment dialog appears.

8. In the Format Comment dialog, change the font, alignment, colors, and so on as desired. The Transparency setting on the Colors and Lines tab allows the underlying spreadsheet to show through the comment. If you choose the Fill Color drop-down, you can select Fill Effects and insert a picture as the background in the comment.

9. Click OK to return to the comment.

10. Right-click in the cell and choose Show/Hide Comments. This causes the comment to be permanently displayed on the worksheet.

11. To reposition the comment, click the comment. Drag the selection border to a new location.

Figure 32.34 shows a comment that has been formatted, resized, and set to be displayed.

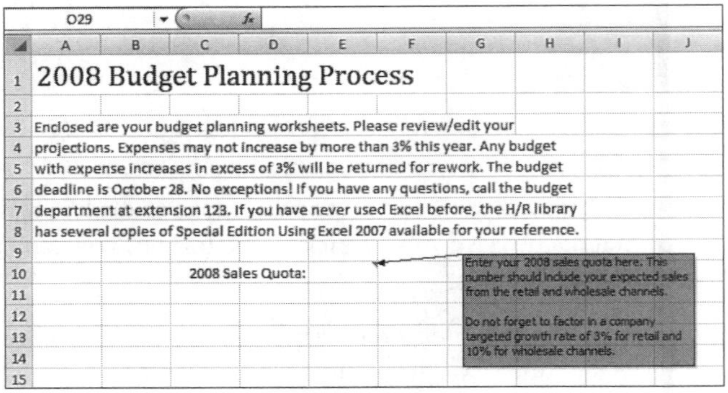

**Figure 32.34**
Cell comments can provide instructions or tips for people who use your spreadsheet.

# COPYING FORMATS

Excel worksheets tend to have many similar sections of data. After you've taken the time to format the first section, it would be great to be able to copy the formats from one section to another section. Excel 2007 offers two methods for doing this: pasting formats and using the Format Painter icon.

## PASTING FORMATS

An option on the Paste Special dialog allows you to paste only the formats from the Clipboard. The rules for copying and pasting formats are as follows:

- If your original selection is one cell, you can paste the formats to as many cells as you want.

- If your original selection is one row tall and multiple cells wide, you can paste the formats to multiple rows, and the final paste area will be as wide as the original copied range.

- If your original selection is one column wide and multiple cells tall, you can paste the formats to multiple columns, and the final paste area will be as tall as the original copied range.

- If your original selection is multiple rows tall and multiple columns wide, you can only paste the formats to an identically sized range. You select the upper-left corner of the range before pasting. Excel expands the selection to match the original size.

You follow these steps to copy formats:

1. Select a formatted section of a report. This might be one cell, one row of cells, or a rectangular range of cells.

2. Press Ctrl+C to copy the selected section to the Clipboard.

3. Select an unformatted section of your worksheet. If your selection in step 1 is a rectangular range, you can select just the top-left cell of the destination range.

4. From the Home ribbon, select Clipboard, Paste, Paste Special. The Paste Special dialog appears.

5. In the Paste section of the dialog, choose Formats, as shown in Figure 32.35.

6. Click OK. The formats from the original section are pasted to the new section. None of the values or formulas in the destination range are changed.

7. If you have multiple target destinations to format, repeat steps 3 through 6 as needed.

The disadvantage of using the Paste Special Formats method is that it does not change column widths. After the formats are copied from B:F to H:L in Figure 32.36, notice that Columns I:K did not pick up the narrower column widths from the source columns. This problem can be solved by using the Format Painter tool, described in the next section.

32

**Figure 32.35**
The Formats option in the Paste Special dialog copies cell formatting without affecting values or formulas.

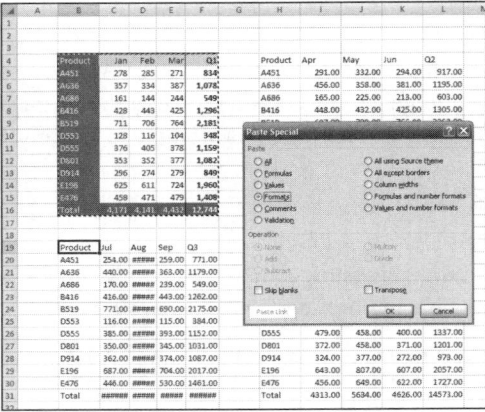

**Figure 32.36**
Pasting formats copies formats but does not resize columns.

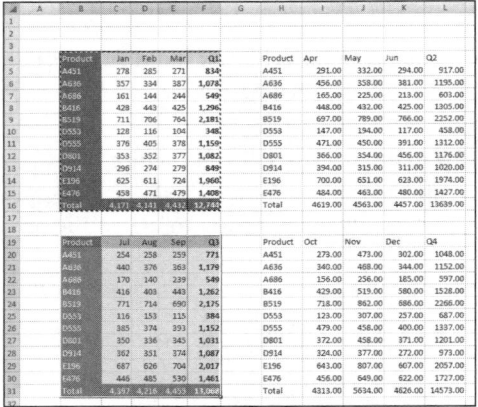

## USING THE FORMAT PAINTER

The Format Painter icon appears in the Clipboard group of the Home ribbon. The prominent location of the icon might encourage you to attempt to use this feature. The Format Painter is still tricky to use.

To copy a format from a source range to a destination range, you follow these steps:

1. Select the source range. If you want to copy column widths, the source range must include complete columns.

2. Click the Format Painter icon once in the Clipboard group of the Home ribbon. The mouse icon changes to a plus and a paintbrush.

3. Immediately use the mouse to click and drag to select a destination range. If the source range was five columns wide, the destination range should also be five columns wide.

4. If you accidentally click somewhere else or click the wrong size range, undo and start over.

The new ToolTip for the Format Painter icon advertises a little-known feature of the Format Painter: You can copy a format to many different ranges. To do this, you follow these steps:

1. Select the source range.
2. Double-click the Format Painter icon.
3. Click a new destination range. The format is copied.
4. Repeat step 3 as many times as you want.
5. When you are done formatting ranges, press Esc or single-click the Format Painter icon to turn off the feature.

## COPYING FORMATS TO A NEW WORKSHEET

There is an easy way to make a copy of a worksheet. This method is better than creating a new worksheet and copying formats from the original sheet to the new sheet. Among its advantages are the fact that column widths and row heights are copied and page setup settings are copied.

To copy a worksheet within the current workbook, you follow these steps:

1. Activate the worksheet to be copied.
2. Hold down the Ctrl key. Click the worksheet tab and drag it to a new location. A new sheet is created with a strange name, such as Sheet3 (2).
3. Right-click the sheet tab and choose Rename. The cursor moves to the tab, which is now editable.
4. Type a new name and press Enter. The tab has a new name.

To copy a worksheet to a new workbook, you follow these steps:

1. Activate the worksheet to be copied.
2. Right-click the sheet tab. Choose Move or Copy to display the Move or Copy dialog.
3. In the To Book drop-down, choose (new book).
4. Click Create a Copy.
5. Click OK. The single worksheet is copied to a new workbook.

---

**Excel in Practice: Elbow Formatting**

A slick effect for the upper-left corner of a table is to include two headings: a heading for the column labels and a heading for the row labels. Figure 32.37 shows an example. Although it requires a little trial and error, you can achieve this effect by using these steps:

1. Select the top-left cell in a table.
2. Press the spacebar four or five times.
3. Type the heading for the column labels.
4. Press Alt+Enter twice.

32

5. Type the heading for the row labels.

6. Press Ctrl+Enter to finish entering the cell and to keep the cell pointer in the top-left cell.

7. From the Home ribbon, select Font, Borders, More Borders.

8. In the Format Cells dialog, on the Border tab, click the lower-right icon in the Border section. This icon is for a diagonal that goes from the top-left to the bottom right.

9. Click OK to close the Format Cells dialog.

10. If the top word hits the diagonal line in the cell, edit the cell and add a space or two before the top word.

**Figure 32.37**
The elbow effect is used in Cell A1.

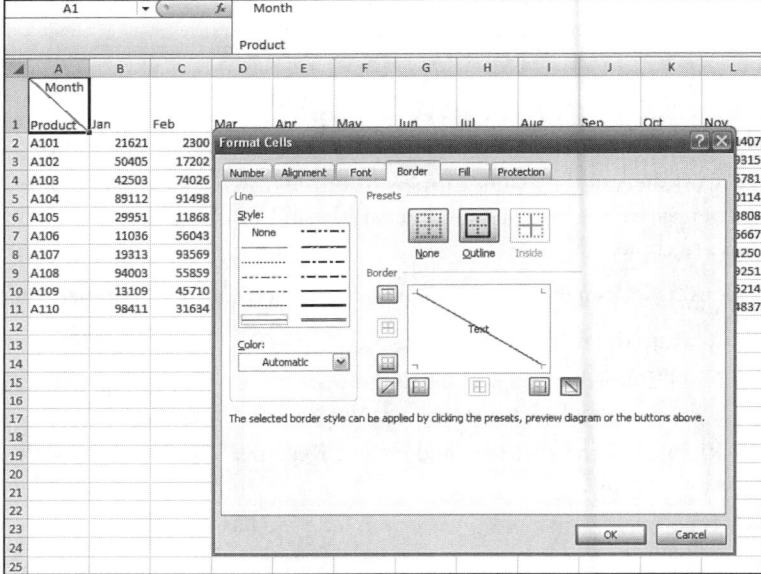

## Excel Troubleshooting: Unmerging Cells in Data Pasted from Web

Web designers use invisible tables as the underlying structure for almost every webpage. In an obsessive attempt to control spacing, the author of the HTML for a page will often define that certain values should span two columns or multiple rows. Unfortunately, when you copy and paste this data from the Web to Excel, the spanning of columns or rows causes Microsoft to turn on merged cells in the data. Although merged cells are fine for headings, they should not be used in the middle of data.

To turn off merged cells in data pasted from a webpage, you follow these steps:

1. Select the pasted data.

2. Display the Format Cells dialog by pressing Ctrl+1.

3. Select the Alignment tab.

4. The Merge Cell icon has a square in the check box to indicate that the selection has a mixture of merged and unmerged cells. Click the box once to produce a check mark in the box. Click the box a second time to clear the Merge Cells check box.

5. Click OK. The merged cells are converted to individual cells. You can now sort and copy the data as usual.

# PRINTING

## In this chapter

Excel 2007 offers a new Page Layout view, which is light-years ahead of the Page Break Preview mode offered in prior versions of Excel. This new view allows you to type and edit headers and footers right on the worksheet. Excel now offers support for different headers and footers on odd and even pages, and it even allows you to use a different header for the first page than for the rest of the document. Excel 2007 supports the use of color, images, and more in headers and footers.

For those who share a printer, one minor change will be major. In prior versions of Excel, if you printed 20 copies of a one-page document, Excel would send 20 print jobs to the printer. This was a huge problem if your printer sent a banner page before each print job. Finally, in Excel 2007, the software will spool all 20 pages into a single print job, eliminating the 19 extra banner pages.

Most of the major print options for controlling printing are arranged in two groups on the Page Layout ribbon. There is also a new Header & Footer Tools Design ribbon dedicated to editing headers and footers in Page Layout view.

## USING PAGE LAYOUT VIEW

When you open Excel, the default view is called Normal view. In prior versions of Excel, your only choices were Normal view and Page Break Preview mode. Microsoft has added the new Page Layout view, which is perfect when you are preparing a document for printing.

In Excel 2007, the three views are available either on the Workbook Views group of the View ribbon or on the right side of the status bar, as shown in Figure 33.1.

**Figure 33.1**
Buttons in the status bar make Page Layout view always available.

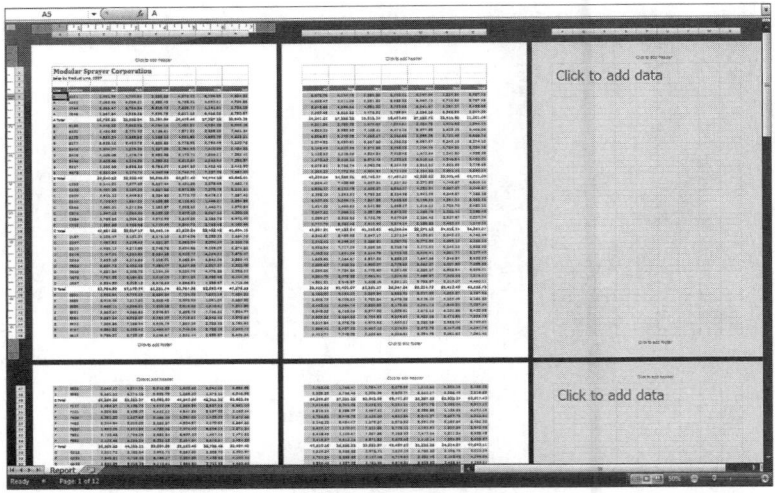

**33**

NOTE

The worksheet in the figure has been zoomed to 50% in order to show multiple pages. This does not automatically happen when you enter Page Layout view.

In Page Layout view, you have a fully functioning worksheet. The formula bar works. You can scroll around the worksheet as usual. However, these are the differences you'll find when you use Page Layout view compared to using Normal view:

- Whitespace appears to show the margins on each page. You have a clear view of any page breaks between columns or rows.

- A ruler appears below the formula bar. You can change margins by dragging the gray areas of the ruler.

- Areas are marked Click to Add Header and Click to Add Footer. Whereas headers and footers are buried in previous versions of Excel, the fact that headers and footers are available is obvious in Page Layout view.

- Areas outside the data area of a worksheet are marked with Click to Add Data. One of the problems with Page Break Preview mode is that areas outside the data area were grayed out. The new Click to Add Data labels invite you to continue adding pages to your worksheet.

- The only disadvantage to Page Layout view is that Excel turns off your Freeze Panes settings in Page Layout view. Excel needs to do this in order to emphasize that Print Titles is different from Freeze Panes. It is a bit disappointing that Excel doesn't remember the Freeze Panes settings and turn them back on when you return to Normal view. This feature will probably be added to the next version of Excel.

All in all, Page Layout view is an excellent improvement over Page Break Preview mode. It practically makes the ubiquitous Print Preview icon obsolete. Page Break Preview is still available (it is discussed later in this chapter, in the section "Working with Page Breaks"). I recommend that you try out Page Layout view when you are preparing to print.

# USING THE IMPROVED HEADERS AND FOOTERS

In Page Layout view, Click to Add Header appears above each page. To access the new Header & Footer Tools Design ribbon, you follow these steps:

1. Select View, Workbook Views, Page Layout View.

2. Click the words Click to Add Header above Row 1. You should see the new Header & Footer Tools Design ribbon. Note that the insertion cursor appears in a box in the center of the header area, as shown in Figure 33.2. There are extremely faint light blue boxes around the left and right sections of the header area. You can click in any of these three boxes to add a header to the left, center, or right section of the header area.

3. Add either an auto header or a custom header. Details on both methods are described in the following sections.

4. To format a header, you can use all the Font formatting options in the Home ribbon. You should use these formatting tools while the header is displayed.

4. To exit Header/Footer mode, click in any cell of the worksheet.

**TIP FROM**

> To directly edit the left or right header, click to the left or right of the words Click to Add Header. When you hover over this section, a gray box appears, encouraging you to click directly in a particular section of the header.

**Figure 33.2**
There are three faint sections in the header: left, center, and right.

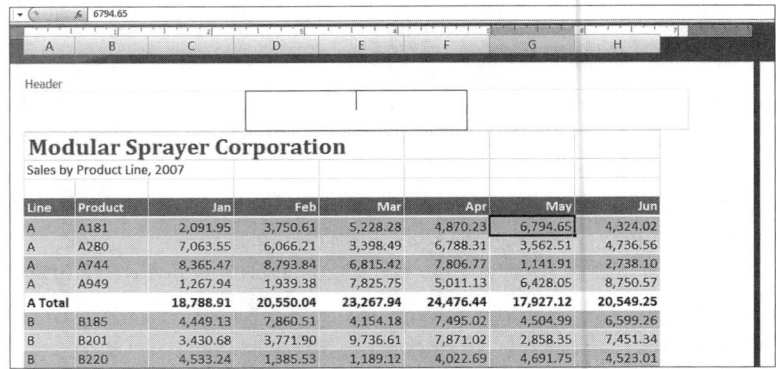

**NOTE**

> The process for adding footers is identical to the process for adding headers. Throughout the rest of this chapter, many sections describe headers. The identical instructions apply to footers.

## ADDING AN AUTO HEADER

For a quick header or footer, you can click the Auto Header or Auto Footer drop-down in the Header & Footer Tools Design ribbon. The drop-down offers 16 different automatic headers, including various page numbering styles, the system date, your name, the sheet name, and the file path and filename.

As shown in Figure 33.3, some of the Auto Header entries include values separated by commas. These entries put header values into the left, center, and right header sections.

**TIP FROM**

> Although you cannot add to the Auto Header list, you can select an automatic header that is close to what you want and then customize it.

## ADDING A CUSTOM HEADER

You can type any text you want in the three header and footer areas. One of the automatic headers says "Confidential," but you can customize this in any way dictated by your company. No matter what type of header you need, you can type it in the header. You click in any header area and type the text that needs to be there. To start a new line, you press Enter.

To include an ampersand in the header or footer, you must use the code &&. For example, to add the header Profit & Loss, you type **Profit && Loss**.

Excel enables you to add several fields to a header or a footer. These fields automatically update: If you add the current date and time, the header then reflects the date and time whenever the worksheet is printed.

**Figure 33.3**
To quickly add a header, you can choose from the Auto Header list.

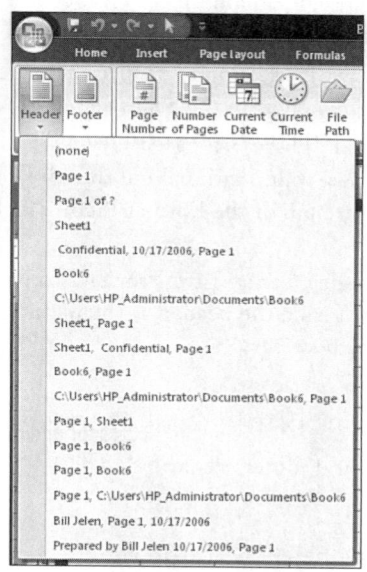

Icons for each field are located in the Header & Footer Elements group of the Header & Footer Tools Design ribbon. To add an element, you click in a header or footer area, position the cursor in the proper place, and click the appropriate icon in the ribbon. As long as the insertion cursor is in the header area, the screen displays the code for that field (for example, &[Date] or &[Time]). When you click in another header section, you see the current value of the autotext field.

## INSERTING A PICTURE IN A HEADER

You can add a picture to a header or footer. It can either be a small picture that prints in the header area or a large picture that extends below the header area and acts as a watermark behind the worksheet.

To add a picture to a header, you follow these steps:

1. Select View, Page Layout View.
2. Click in the header area of the document.
3. From the Header & Footer Tools Design ribbon, select Header & Footer Elements, Picture. Excel displays the Insert Picture dialog.

4. Browse to the proper folder. Select a picture and click Insert. Excel adds the text &[Picture] to the header. You can't actually see how large the picture will be until you click outside the header.

5. Click in the spreadsheet.

6. If you discover that the picture is too large, click in the header area.

7. From the Header & Footer Tools Design ribbon, select Header & Footer Elements, Format Picture. The Format Picture dialog appears.

8. In the Format Picture dialog, use the Size section to reduce the scale of the picture. If you use the spin button to change the height in the Scale section, the width is automatically changed as well, in order to keep the scale proportional.

9. If you want your picture to appear as a watermark behind the spreadsheet, you lighten the picture. To do so, click the Picture tab of the Format Picture dialog. Change the Color drop-down to Washout.

10. None of the picture items in the header feature Live Preview. To preview your picture, close the dialog box and then click outside the header. If the picture is not the way you want it, repeat steps 6 through 10 as necessary.

## USING DIFFERENT HEADERS AND FOOTERS IN THE SAME DOCUMENT

Excel 2007 allows four different header and footer scenarios:

- The same header/footer on all pages
- One header/footer on page 1 and a different header/footer on all other pages
- One header/footer on all odd pages and a different header/footer on all even pages.
- One header/footer on page 1, a second header footer on even pages, and a third header/footer on all odd pages from 3 on

Excel manages these scenarios by storing three headers for each worksheet. The first header is variously called the odd page header or the header. As you check and uncheck the options check boxes, the contents of each header remain constant, even though they might be used on different pages. Table 33.1 shows the details of each header option.

**TABLE 33.1  HEADER OPTIONS**

| Different First Page | Different Odd & Even Pages | Odd Page Header | Even Page Header | First Page Header |
| --- | --- | --- | --- | --- |
| Unchecked | Unchecked | Called the header and used on all pages | Not used | Not used |
| Unchecked | Checked | Called the odd page header and used for pages 1, 3, 5, and so on | Called the even page header and used for pages 2, 4, 6, and so on | Not used |
| Checked | Unchecked | Called the header and used on pages 2, 3, 4, and so on | Not used | Called the first page header and used for page 1 |

| Different First Page | Different Odd & Even Pages | Odd Page Header | Even Page Header | First Page Header |
|---|---|---|---|---|
| Checked | Checked | Called the odd page header and used for pages 3, 5, 7, and so on | Called the even page header and used for pages 2, 4, 6, and so on | Called the first page header and used for page 1 |

If you simply add a header in Page Layout view, it is known as the odd page header. In the default configuration, Excel displays the odd page header on all pages of the printout.

Excel has two other sets of headers that are initially hidden. One set is called the first page header. If you select Different First Page from the Options group on the Header & Footer Tools Design ribbon, Excel displays the first page header above page 1 and uses the odd page header everywhere else.

To minimize confusion, it is best to check the Options section check boxes Different First Page and Different Odd & Even before entering headers.

## SCALING HEADERS AND FOOTERS

Settings in the Page Layout ribbon allow you to force a worksheet to fit a certain number of pages. If the scaling options require a 75% scale on Sheet1 and a 95% scale on Sheet2, your headings are scaled as well. This causes your page numbers to appear at a different point size in various sections of the report.

Excel offers an option to force all headers and footers to print at 100% scale, regardless of the zoom for the sheet. To select this option, from the Header & Footer Tools Design ribbon, you select Options and uncheck Scale with Document.

33

# USING THE PAGE SETUP AND SHEET OPTIONS

Most of the page setup options are now in the Page Layout ribbon. The Page Setup, Scale to Fit, and Sheet Options groups reflect most of the items that used to be in the Page Setup dialog in prior versions of Excel.

**Figure 33.4**
Page setup options are controlled from the Page Layout ribbon.

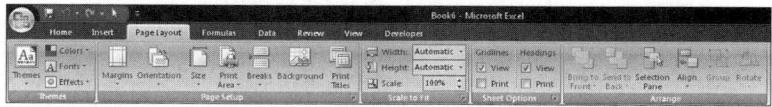

CAUTION

The Background icon is out of place in the Page Setup group of the Page Layout ribbon. While every other setting in this group affects the printed page, the Background icon is only for the background on the displayed page. If you want to have a printed watermark appear behind your spreadsheet, you should use a large picture in the header, as described in the section "Inserting a Picture in a Header," earlier in this chapter.

## ADJUSTING WORKSHEET MARGINS

There are three methods for adjusting worksheet margins:

- **Choose Page Layout, Margins**—This drop-down offers three settings: Normal, Wide, and Narrow. To apply one of these standard setups, you simply choose from the Margins drop-down, as shown in Figure 33.5.

**Figure 33.5**
New in Excel 2007, you can choose a quick setting for margins.

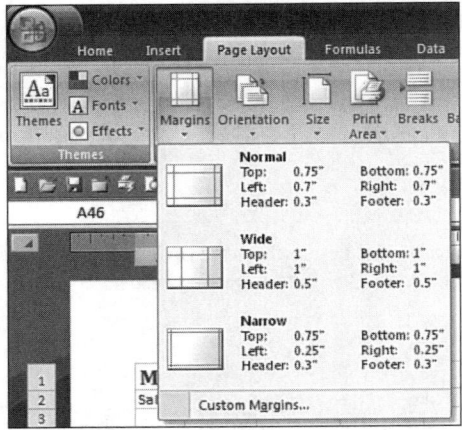

- **Choose Page Layout, Page Setup, Margins, Custom Margins**—You can now adjust the margins at the top, left, right, and bottom, as well as the margins for the footer and header. As shown in Figure 33.6, the dialog you use for this is the same as in legacy versions of Excel.

**Figure 33.6**
For control over each margin, you use the Margins tab of the Page Setup dialog.

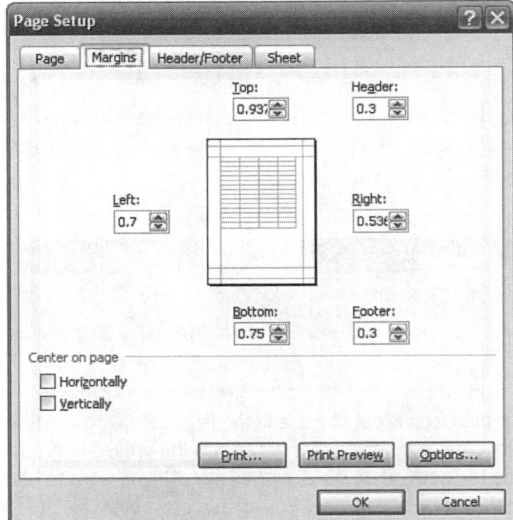

■ **Choose View, Workbook Views, Page Layout View**—When you do this, gray margins appear on each edge of the ruler. You can drag the gray margins in or out to decrease/increase the margins.

## ADJUSTING WORKSHEET ORIENTATION

Changing a report to print sideways (that is, landscape) now takes just a couple mouse clicks. From the Page Layout ribbon, you can select Page Setup to see the Orientation drop-down, which offers Portrait and Landscape options, as shown in Figure 33.7.

**Figure 33.7**
You can make a report print sideways by choosing Landscape.

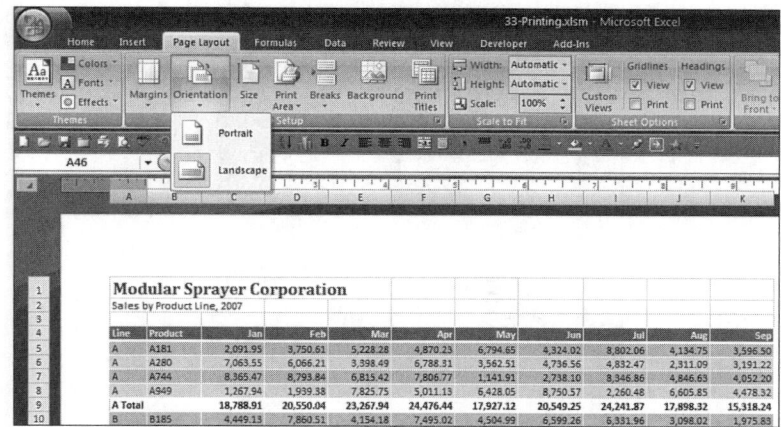

## SETTING WORKSHEET PAPER SIZE

A multitude of standard paper sizes are now available from the Size drop-down in the Page Layout ribbon, as shown in Figure 33.8. You can choose one of the standard sizes or select the More menu option to specify a new size.

**TIP FROM**

> Some paper sizes, such as 11"×17", are available only if your selected printer offers that size. If your default printer cannot print large-format paper, you should change the printer selection in the Print dialog and then return to the Page Setup dialog to select the larger-format paper.

## SETTING THE PRINT AREA

By default, Excel does print all the nonblank cells on a worksheet. Sometimes, you have a nicely formatted table of data to print, with some work cells in an out-of-the way location. To prevent the work cells from being printed, you follow these steps:

33

**Figure 33.8**
You can select a built-in paper size or click More to specify a custom size.

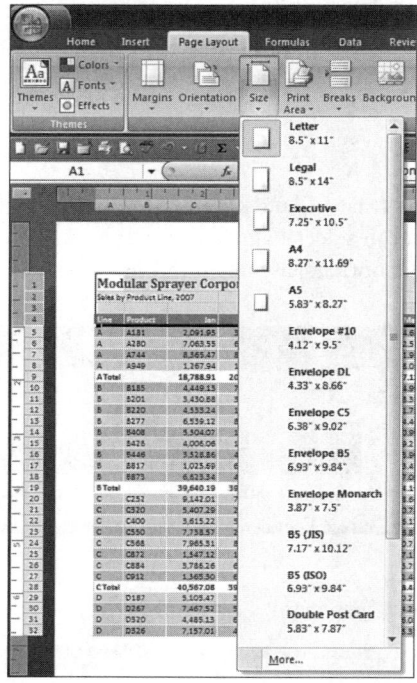

1.  Select the range of cells to be included in the print range. This might be a range of cells such as A1:Z99, or you might want to print everything in certain columns. In the latter case, your selection might be columns C:X.

2.  From the Page Layout ribbon, select Page Setup, Print Area, Set Print Area.

To later clear the print area and print everything on the worksheet, you can use the Clear Print Area option from the Set Print Area drop-down.

Occasionally, you will want to ignore the print areas and print everything on the worksheet. In this case, you can use the Print icon and check the box Ignore Print Areas, as shown in Figure 33.9.

## ADDING PRINT TITLES

For reports that will span more than one page, you may want the headings from the report to print at the top of each page. Although the Print Titles icon has been promoted to a large icon on the Page Layout ribbon, this command leads back to the somewhat confusing Page Layout dialog. In Figure 33.10, for example, the report is two pages wide and several pages tall. When you get to the printed page 2, there the printed report has no title or column headings. You would probably want to have the titles and column headings repeat at the top of each row.

**Figure 33.9**
To override the print area, you can choose Ignore Print Areas.

Ignore Print Area ——

**Figure 33.10**
You can use the Page Setup dialog to specify print titles to repeat on each page.

Also in Figure 33.10, the product line information from Columns A and B is considered row labels. It would be ideal if the row labels could repeat at the left side of the pages. To assign print titles, you follow these steps:

1. From the Page Layout ribbon, select Page Setup, Print Titles. The Page Setup dialog appears, open to the Sheet tab.

2. In the Rows to Repeat at Top box, enter the rows that should print at the top of the page. You can specify either a single row (for example, 1:1, 2:2) or a range of rows (for example, 1:4, 2:5).

33

3. If you want columns to print at the left side of each page, enter columns in the Columns to Repeat at Left box. You can specify either a single column (for example, A:A, B:B) or multiple columns (for example, A:C, C:D).

4. Click OK to return to the worksheet.

## SCALING OPTIONS

You will often have worksheets in Excel that are just a few columns too wide or a few rows too long to fit on a page. Excel has had scaling options for a long time, but it is not clear on the Page Layout ribbon how the scaling options work.

The Scale to Fit group on the Page Layout ribbon provides options for width, height, and a percentage scale. In most cases, you will either change height, width, or both to achieve the desired effect.

If your worksheet is a few columns too wide, you change the Width drop-down to specify that the worksheet should fit on one page. If you have a report that is just a bit too tall, you change the Height drop-down to specify that the worksheet should be one page tall. As shown in Figure 33.11, when you select either of these options, the Scale option is grayed out, but it still shows the scaling percentage used to make the report fit.

**Figure 33.11**
After you choose Scale to Fit 1 Page wide, the Scale option is grayed out but shows the actual percentage scaling used.

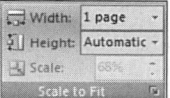

**33**

If you plan on printing multiple worksheets in order to produce a printed report, you should pay attention to the scaling percentage. If Sheet1 is scaled to 77% and Sheet2 is scaled to 82%, the characters on some pages of your report will appear larger than others. You can manually set Sheet2 to 82% scaling in order to match the other worksheet.

## PRINTING GRIDLINES AND HEADINGS

To print the gridlines on a worksheet, from the Page Layout ribbon, you select Sheet Options, Gridlines, Print.

You can also print the A-B-C column headings and 1-2-3 row headings. To do this, from the Page Layout ribbon, you select Sheet Options, Headings, Print. This option is great when you are printing formulas and you need to see the cell address of each cell.

# WORKING WITH PAGE BREAKS

There are two varieties of page breaks: automatic and manual.

An automatic page break occurs when Excel reaches the bottom or right margin of a physical page. These page breaks automatically change as you add rows, delete rows, or even change the height of certain rows on the page.

Initially, automatic page breaks are not shown in the worksheet. After you go to Print Preview and return to Normal view, automatic page breaks are shown in the document, using a thin dashed line. Automatic page breaks are also evident in Page Layout view and Page Break Preview mode.

**TIP FROM**

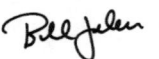

Print Preview is practically obsolete now that the Page Layout view has been added. To access the old Print Preview, you click the Office icon and then choose Print, Print Preview.

You can manually insert page breaks at rows or columns where you want to start a new page. You might want to insert a manual page break, for example, at the start of a new section in a report. A manual page break does not automatically change in response to changes in the worksheet rows.

## MANUALLY ADDING PAGE BREAKS

To manually add a page break at a certain row, you follow these steps:

1. Select an entire row by clicking the row number that should be the first row on the new page. Alternatively, select Cell A in that row.
2. From the Page Layout ribbon, select Page Setup, Breaks, Insert Page Break.

To manually add a page break at a certain column, you follow these steps:

1. Select an entire column by clicking the number above the column that should be the first column on the new page. Alternatively, select Row 1 in that column.
2. From the Page Layout ribbon, select Page Setup, Breaks, Insert Page Break.

**CAUTION**

If you insert a page break while the cell pointer is outside Row 1 or Column A, Excel simultaneously inserts a row page break and a column page break. This is rarely what you want. Make sure to select a cell in column A to insert a row break or to select a cell in row 1 to insert a column break.

## MANUAL VERSUS AUTOMATIC PAGE BREAKS

In Normal view, there is a subtle visual difference between manual and automatic page breaks. For example, in Figure 33.12, an automatic page break occurs after Row 145, and a

33

manual page break has been inserted after Row 151. The dashed line used to indicate a manual page break is more pronounced than the line used to indicate an automatic page break.

**Figure 33.12**
In Normal view, the page break indicator is bolder for manual page breaks.

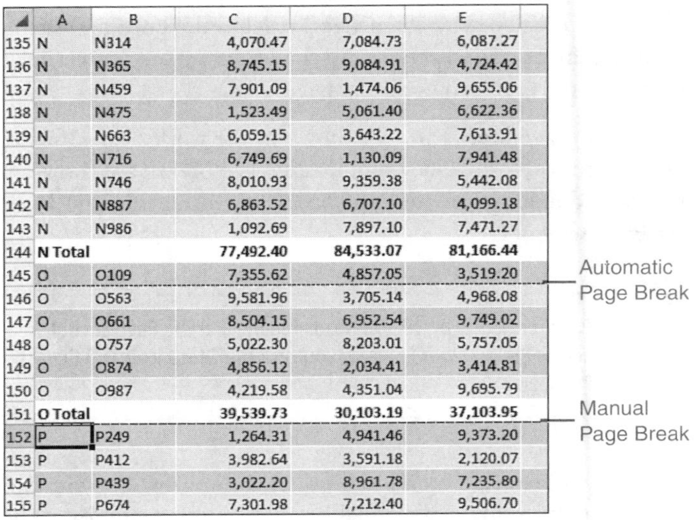

| | A | B | C | D | E |
|---|---|---|---|---|---|
| 135 | N | N314 | 4,070.47 | 7,084.73 | 6,087.27 |
| 136 | N | N365 | 8,745.15 | 9,084.91 | 4,724.42 |
| 137 | N | N459 | 7,901.09 | 1,474.06 | 9,655.06 |
| 138 | N | N475 | 1,523.49 | 5,061.40 | 6,622.36 |
| 139 | N | N663 | 6,059.15 | 3,643.22 | 7,613.91 |
| 140 | N | N716 | 6,749.69 | 1,130.09 | 7,941.48 |
| 141 | N | N746 | 8,010.93 | 9,359.38 | 5,442.08 |
| 142 | N | N887 | 6,863.52 | 6,707.10 | 4,099.18 |
| 143 | N | N986 | 1,092.69 | 7,897.10 | 7,471.27 |
| 144 | N Total | | 77,492.40 | 84,533.07 | 81,166.44 |
| 145 | O | O109 | 7,355.62 | 4,857.05 | 3,519.20 |
| 146 | O | O563 | 9,581.96 | 3,705.14 | 4,968.08 |
| 147 | O | O661 | 8,504.15 | 6,952.54 | 9,749.02 |
| 148 | O | O757 | 5,022.30 | 8,203.01 | 5,757.05 |
| 149 | O | O874 | 4,856.12 | 2,034.41 | 3,414.81 |
| 150 | O | O987 | 4,219.58 | 4,351.04 | 9,695.79 |
| 151 | O Total | | 39,539.73 | 30,103.19 | 37,103.95 |
| 152 | P | P249 | 1,264.31 | 4,941.46 | 9,373.20 |
| 153 | P | P412 | 3,982.64 | 3,591.18 | 2,120.07 |
| 154 | P | P439 | 3,022.20 | 8,961.78 | 7,235.80 |
| 155 | P | P674 | 7,301.98 | 7,212.40 | 9,506.70 |

Automatic Page Break

Manual Page Break

To see a better view of page breaks, you can select View, Page Break Preview to switch to Page Break Preview mode, as shown in Figure 33.13. In this mode, automatic page breaks are shown as dotted blue lines. Manual page breaks are shown as solid lines.

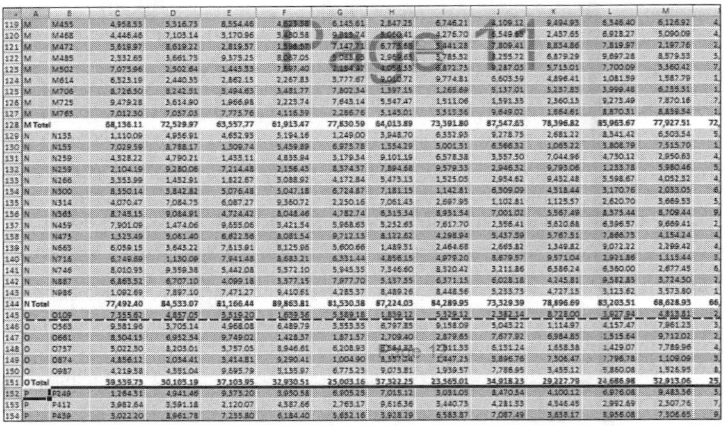

**Figure 33.13**
In Page Break Preview mode, automatic page breaks are shown using a dotted line and manual page breaks using a solid line.

## USING PAGE BREAK PREVIEW TO MAKE CHANGES

An advantage of Page Break Preview mode is that while you are in this mode, you can move a page break by dragging the line associated with the page break. If you drag an automatic page break to expand the number of rows or columns on a page, Excel automatically changes the Scale percentage for all pages.

## REMOVING MANUAL PAGE BREAKS

To remove a manual page break for a row, you follow these steps:

1. Position the cursor in the row below the page break.
2. From the Page Layout ribbon, select Page Setup, Breaks, Remove Page Break.

To remove a manual page break for a column, you follow these steps:

1. Position the cursor in the column to the right of the page break.
2. From the Page Layout ribbon, select Page Setup, Breaks, Remove Page Break.

To remove all manual page breaks, from the Page Layout ribbon, you select Page Setup, Breaks, Reset All Page Breaks.

# PRINTING

There are two methods for printing. You can click the Quick Print icon to send one copy of the active sheet to the currently selected printer. For additional control over the printer, number of copies, or the worksheet to print, you can use the Print dialog box.

## CHOOSING QUICK PRINT

To send a copy of the worksheet to the active printer, you can click the Office icon and then choose Print, Quick Print. The Quick Print icon is usually available in your Quick Access toolbar, unless someone has customized the toolbar and removed the icon. See Chapter 2 for information on customizing the toolbar.

## CONTROLLING PRINT OPTIONS BY USING THE PRINT DIALOG BOX

To access additional printing options, you can use the Print dialog box, shown in Figure 33.14. To open this dialog, you select the Office icon and then choose Print.

**Figure 33.14**
Additional printing options can be controlled in the Print dialog.

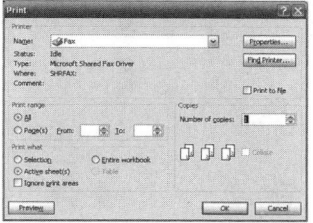

In the Print dialog, the Name drop-down lists all the available printers. To print to a different printer, you select a printer from this drop-down.

By default, Excel prints the entire print range. To print specific pages, you use the From and To spin buttons. To print more than one copy of the document, you can change the

Copies spin button. If you select more than one copy, you can select the Collate check box. If Collate is turned on, Excel prints pages 1, 2, 3, 1, 2, 3, 1, 2, 3, and so on. If Collate is turned off, Excel prints pages 1, 1, 1, 2, 2, 2, 3, 3, 3, and so on.

The Print What section of the Print dialog offers five choices:

- **Selection**—You should choose this option to override the print area and print only the selected range of data.
- **Active Sheet**(s)—This is the default. When it is selected, Excel prints the print area on each selected sheet.
- **Entire Workbook**—When this option is selected, Excel prints the print area on all visible sheets in the workbook.
- **Table**—When this option is selected, Excel prints the current table.
- **Ignore Print Areas**—This check box works in conjunction with Active Sheet(s) and Entire Workbook. If your print area is set up to define a subset of the worksheet as the print area, choosing Ignore Print Area causes the entire workbook to be printed.

## CONTROLLING PRINTER OPTIONS

Depending on your printer model, there may be additional print settings available. Although Excel does not control these values, there is a button that allows you to access your printer's options panel. To use this button, you follow these steps:

1. Select the Office icon and then choose Print. The Print dialog appears.
2. In the Print dialog, near the Printer Name drop-down, click choose the Properties button. The Printer Options dialog for your particular printer appears. This dialog varies, depending on your printer. Its available settings might include color adjustments, toner usage, and more.

33

# SHARING WORKBOOKS WITH OTHERS

## In this chapter

The common method of sharing a workbook is to email the workbook. You can easily do this from within Excel. Microsoft increasingly realizes that you might be using Excel as the preferred tool for business intelligence, and that you might be distributing the output of your worksheet in non-Excel platforms.

Although the interactivity feature has been depreciated, Excel 2007 continues to offer support for publishing a worksheet to a Static Web page. Office 2007 also adds support for distributing files as PDFs or distributing workbooks via a new server product available through SharePoint. Due to legal wranglings in Europe, Microsoft agreed to remove the PDF functionality from the shipping version of Office 2007 and instead make it an add-in downloadable from Office Online.

# SENDING A WORKBOOK VIA EMAIL

The fastest way to send a workbook via email is to send it directly from Excel. If Outlook is your default email client, this is easy to do. To do so, you follow these steps:

1. Open the workbook you want to send.

2. Arrange the window so that it appears as you would like it to appear for your email recipient. This might mean scrolling explanatory notes into view or making some other adjustments.

3. From the Office icon menu, select Send, Email. You now see a window that looks identical to the Outlook Send Mail window (see Figure 34.1).

4. Click in the To box and type an email address or select email recipients.

5. If desired, change the subject line to something different than the filename.

6. Type any message.

7. Click the Send button to send the message and return to Microsoft Excel.

**Figure 34.1**
This Outlook dialog box is actually part of Excel.

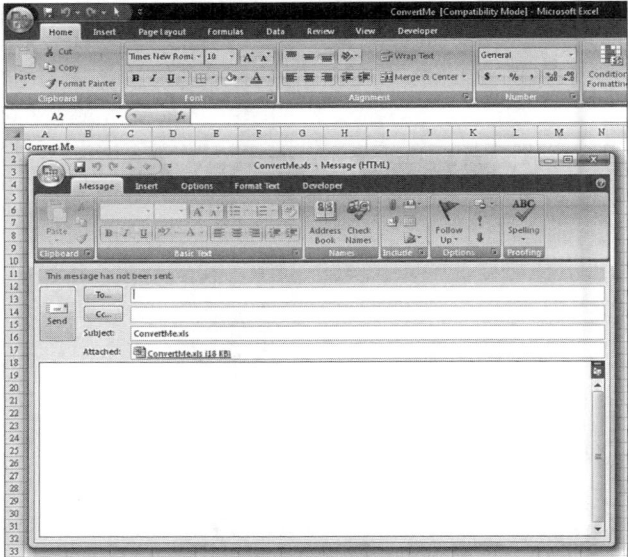

# CREATING A PDF FROM A WORKSHEET

With much fanfare, Microsoft announced that it would be including the ability to create PDF files with Office 2007. This would be a cool feature because sending workbooks via PDF would allow you to send read-only versions of documents to people who may or may not have Excel.

Through all the beta versions of Office, you could click the Office icon and then select Save As, PDF or XPS, as shown in Figure 34.2.

**Figure 34.2**
In beta versions of Excel, saving to PDF was built in.

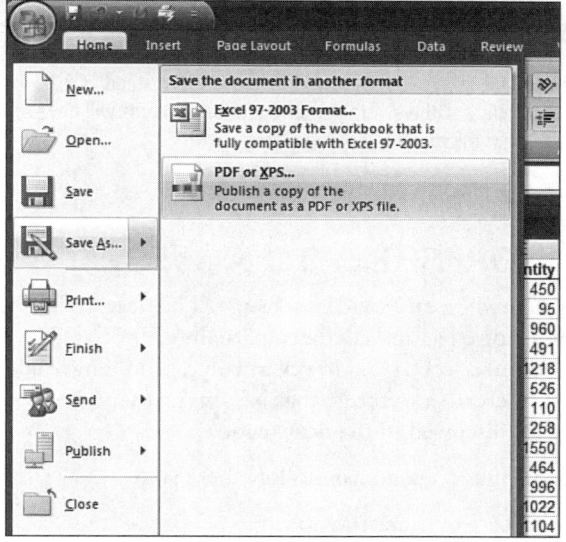

NOTE

The ability to save as a PDF file was an important "catch-up" feature for Microsoft. Sun Microsystems Star Office has supported creating PDF files for several years.

As this book goes to press, the status of this feature is uncertain. Adobe has filed suit in a European court, claiming that this feature violates its rights. (Adobe created the PDF file format and created the original PDF reader, Acrobat.) This is unusual. Adobe did not complain when Star Office or any of dozens of other packages offered ways to create PDF files. At this time, Microsoft has removed the feature from Office 2007. You can re-install the feature by downloading a free add-in from Office Online. Visit Office Online (http://office.microsoft. com) for information on the current state of the feature.

Assuming that the feature is added back via an add-in, the dialog box is shown in Figure 34.3. You have the option to save the file in a high-resolution format suitable for printing or a low-resolution format that is suitable for viewing on the screen.

**Figure 34.3**
Choose PDF or XPS, and then high or low resolution.

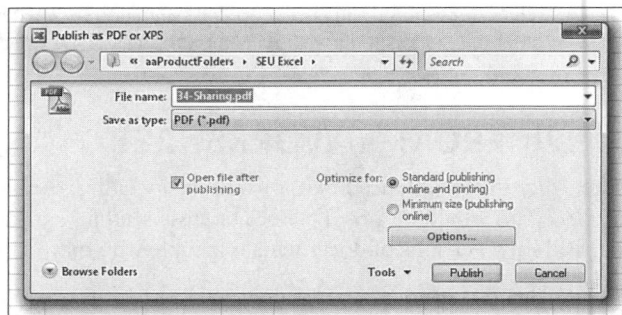

TIP FROM

*Bill Jelen*

Although Adobe's PDF format is ubiquitous, you might consider starting to use Microsoft's new XPS file format. This format will compete with PDF. To save as XPS, you use the Save as Type drop-down to choose XPS instead of PDF. An XPS reader ships with Microsoft Vista. Others with earlier operating systems will have to download a free reader from Microsoft to open the files.

# PUBLISHING A WORKSHEET TO A WEBPAGE

Excel data can be presented on an HTML webpage. This feature has been available for several versions, and the feature has actually been partially depreciated in Excel 2007. You can still publish a workbook to a webpage. However, you can no longer add interactivity to the webpage. If you want to create a webpage that has interactivity, you now have to use Excel Services for SharePoint, discussed in the next section.

To publish a static view of a webpage, you follow these steps:

1. Activate the worksheet you want to publish.
2. Select the range you want to publish.
3. From the Office icon menu, select Save As, Save As Type drop-down, Web Page. The Save As dialog appears.
4. In the Save As dialog, choose to publish either the selection or the entire workbook.
5. Click Change Title to add a title to the webpage. The title appears both in the blue title bar of the browser and as a heading above the data.
6. Click the Publish button to display the Publish as Web Page dialog, as shown in Figure 34.4. Specify the output filename for the HTML file.

7. If you want to always publish this file every time the workbook is saved, choose the AutoRepublish check box.

8. If you want to immediately preview the webpage, choose the Open Published Web Page in Browser check box.

9. Click the Publish button.

**Figure 34.4**
When publishing as a webpage, you specify the range to be published and the output filename.

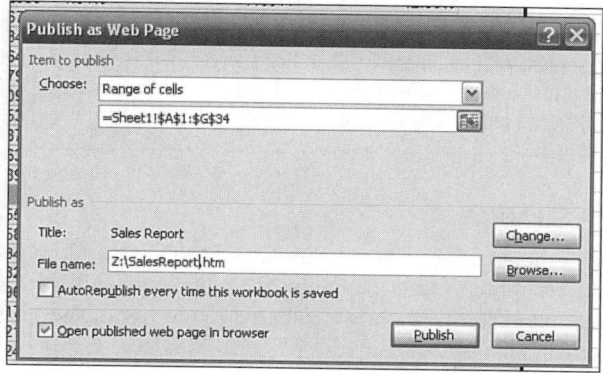

The published webpage includes all the data in the range, font colors, background colors, and numeric formatting. It does not include newer features, such as icon sets. Figure 34.5 compares the original and web versions of the worksheet.

**Figure 34.5**
The final webpage includes a static view of the worksheet.

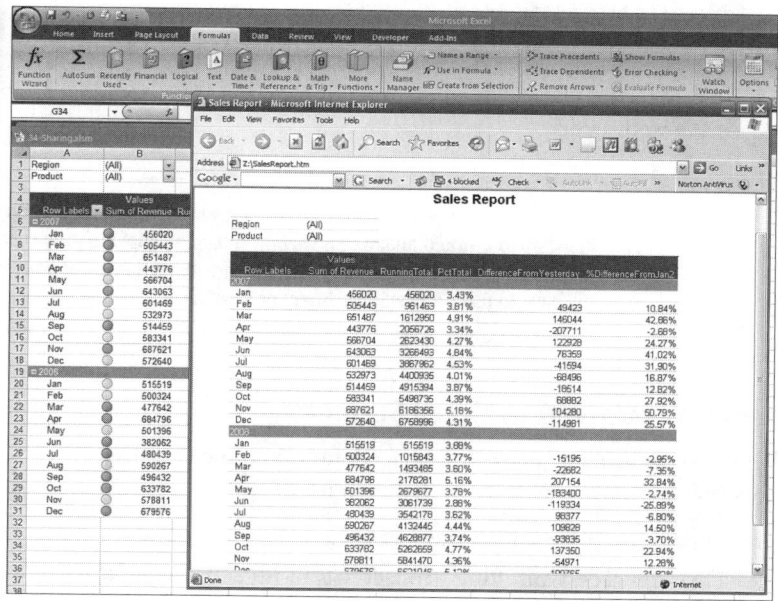

If you need to have interactivity on a webpage, you need to use either Excel Services for SharePoint, as discussed in the next section, or a third-party tool, such as the one available from www.SpreadsheetConverter.com.

# PUBLISHING TO A SERVER

Instead of the limited interactivity available in Excel 2003's Save as Web Page feature, Microsoft has invested heavily in a new component of Excel to allow you to share HTML on a corporate intranet.

**CAUTION**

> Although this feature is new, unique, and interesting, you will have to work in an environment with an Enterprise SharePoint server in order to make use of the functionality. Because only a tiny segment of the Excel community has access to Enterprise SharePoint servers, I only briefly touch on the functionality here.

## EXCEL SERVICES AT A GLANCE

Say that someone authors a spreadsheet using Excel 2007. This file is then saved to a SharePoint document library. Other people in the company could click on the document in SharePoint. The person then sees a browser-based rendering of the spreadsheet that is somewhat interactive. This is the basic idea of Excel Services.

Behind the scenes, Excel Services actually opens the original spreadsheet. It refreshes any external data. It then builds a DHTML view of the spreadsheet that can be displayed in any modern browser.

Microsoft envisions that people will use Excel Services for three basic scenarios:

- Sharing spreadsheets through a browser
- Populating key indicator sections of executive dashboards
- Reusing logic encapsulated in Excel spreadsheets as a back end to any language that can speak web services

**NOTE**

> Excel Services is not a spreadsheet authoring tool. When many people heard the name, they hoped it would finally be a way for multiple people to truly collaborate on a spreadsheet on a server. Unfortunately, it is not. If you need to collaborate on a spreadsheet, you still have to use Google Spreadsheet or WikiCalc to do what Excel cannot manage to do.

## DEFINING INTERACTIVITY IN EXCEL SERVICES

People viewing a spreadsheet in SharePoint do not need to have Excel 2007 installed. In the browser, they have access to limited interactivity:

- They can scroll through the spreadsheet.
- They can access autofilter drop-downs to filter the data.
- They can access page field drop-downs in pivot tables.
- They can change certain cells that the author of the spreadsheet defined as workbook parameters.

The author of the spreadsheet must define parameters when saving the file to SharePoint. In addition, each parameter must be in a named cell.

## SAVING A WORKBOOK TO EXCEL SERVICES

To save a file to Excel Services, you follow these steps:

1. Identify any cells that you want to be changeable parameters in the browser.
2. For each parameter cell, select Formulas, Name Manager, New and assign a name.
3. From the Office icon menu, select Publish, Excel Services.
4. Type a name for the workbook.
5. Click the Excel Services Options button. The Excel Services Options dialog appears.
6. On the Show tab, choose whether the entire workbook or only a portion is visible.
7. Click the Parameters tab. Click the Add button to display the Add Parameters dialog, as shown in Figure 34.6.
8. For each named cell that you want to be a parameter, click to create a check mark next to the name.
9. Click OK to close the Add Parameters dialog.
10. Click OK to close the Excel Services Options dialog.
11. Click Save to save the workbook.

**Figure 34.6**
You define which named cells should be parameters in the SharePoint browser view of the workbook.

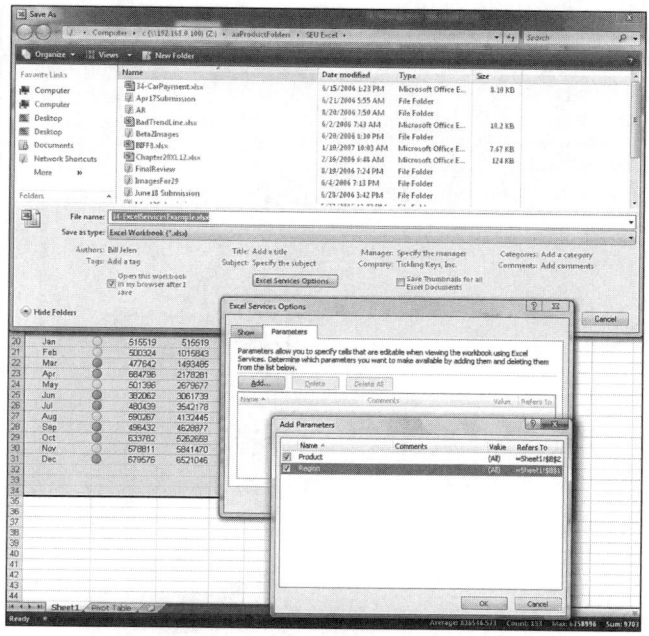

When this file is viewed in the browser, the Excel file provides support for new Excel 2007 features, such as data bars, conditional formatting, and data visualizations.

# CHAPTER 35

# MORE TIPS AND TRICKS FOR EXCEL 2007

**In this chapter**

This book is full of tips and tricks throughout the chapters. This particular chapter is a catch-all for some of the tips that did not find a home elsewhere in the book.

A few of the features discussed in this chapter—such as multithreaded calculation, digital signatures, the document inspector, and translations—are new to Excel 2007. Others, such as automatic subtotals, have been around for a decade but are overlooked by most people who use Excel.

**TIP FROM**

*Bill Jelen*

If you like the tips in this chapter, check out *Learn Excel from MrExcel: 277 Excel Mysteries Solved* at www.mrexcel.com/learn-excel.html. It is filled with 277 quick tips like these. You can also download four or five tips every week—absolutely free—by signing up at the website.

# SPEEDING UP CALCULATION BY USING MULTITHREADED CALCULATION

For the first time, Excel 2007 is written to take advantage of dual-core machines (that is, machines with two CPUs). Multithreaded calculation allows Excel to spot formulas that can be calculated concurrently and then run those formulas on multiple processors simultaneously.

The first time you calculate a spreadsheet in Excel 2007 on a dual-core machine, Excel has to examine the formula dependency table and then perform the calculation. The process of deciding which formulas can be calculated concurrently causes the first calculation to take as long as normal. The time required for the next calculation dramatically decreases. In a perfect example, a workbook with Monte Carlo simulation, the reduction is linear: A workbook calculates in half the time. In other workbooks, the reduction is significant but not linear.

To enable multithreaded calculation, you follow these steps:

1. Select the Office icon and then choose Excel Options. The Excel Options dialog appears.

2. Choose the Advanced category and then select Formulas.

3. Choose Enable Multi-threaded Calculation, as shown in Figure 35.1.

4. Unless you are using XLL add-ins, choose the Use all Processors setting. If you are using XLL add-ins, see the following note.

**NOTE**

It is possible to set the calculation threads to a number higher than the number of processors. This is beneficial if your workbook is making calls to XLL user-defined functions on a server. If each function requires 15 seconds and you have a dozen such functions, Excel must wait for each function to finish before calling the next function, requiring 3 minutes to calculate. If you set the number of threads to 12, Excel could call all 12 XLL functions simultaneously, reducing calculation time to less than 30 seconds.

**Figure 35.1**
The multithreaded calculation option is buried in the Advanced category of the Excel Options dialog.

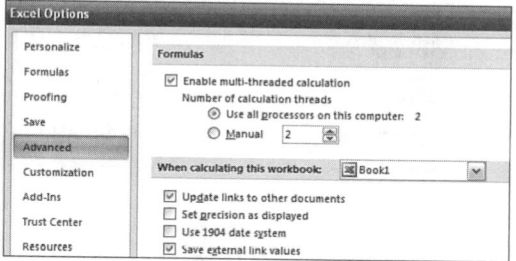

# WATCHING THE RESULTS OF A FAR-OFF CELL

Sometimes you need to keep an eye on a single result on a worksheet other than the one you're currently in. For example, you might have a workbook in which assumptions on multiple worksheets produce a final ROI. As you change the assumptions, it would be good to know the impact on ROI.

It can be time-consuming to constantly switch back and forth to the results worksheet after every change. Instead, you can set up a watch to show you the current value of the far-off cell(s). People developing VBA macros in Excel have had a Watch Window dialog available in VBA for over a decade. Microsoft finally added a Watch Window dialog to Excel 2003.

To set up a watch, you follow these steps:

1. Choose Formulas, Formula Auditing, Watch Window in order to display the floating Watch Window dialog over the worksheet.
2. Click Add Watch in the Watch Window dialog.
3. In the Add Watch dialog, click the RefEdit button and then click on cells that you want to watch.
4. Click Add to add the cell(s) to the Watch Window dialog.
5. Repeat steps 2–4 as necessary.
6. Position the Watch Window dialog in an out-of-the-way location above your worksheet so that you can continue to work.

Every time you make a change to the worksheet, the Watch Window dialog shows you the current value of the watched cells, as shown in Figure 35.2.

**Figure 35.2**
The Watch Window dialog shows you the results of key cells that you define. These cells can be in far-off cells or on other worksheets.

| | D5 | | | ƒₓ | =+C5*2 | | | | | | |
|---|---|---|---|---|---|---|---|---|---|---|---|
| | A | B | D | E | F | G | H | I | J | K | L |
| 1 | Section 1: Historical Trends (Per Month) | | | | | | | | | | |
| 2 | | | | | | | | | | | |
| 3 | | Store Type | Rent | Sales | Profit | Labor | Net | | | | |
| 4 | | Regular | 2200 | 12456 | 6228 | 6480 | -2452 | | | | |
| 5 | | BigBox | 5200 | 36500 | 18250 | 8640 | 4410 | | | | |
| 6 | | | | | | | | | | | |
| 7 | Section 2: Number of Stores | | | | | | | | | | |
| 8 | | | | | | | | | | | |
| 9 | | Regular | | | | | | | | | |
| 10 | | BigBox | | | | | | | | | |
| 11 | | | | | | | | | | | |
| 12 | Section 3: Analysis of Profitability of Current Store Mix | | | | | | | | | | |
| 13 | | | Net Profit | NP% | | | | | | | |
| 14 | | Total Chain | 7353936 | 7.9% | | | | | | | |
| 15 | | Regular | -2383344 | -19.7% | | | | | | | |
| 16 | | Big Box | 9737280 | 12.1% | | | | | | | |

Watch Window

Add Watch... | Delete Watch

| Book | Sheet | Name | Cell | Value | Formula |
|---|---|---|---|---|---|
| Watch... | Sheet2 | | F10 | 473.324 | =0.482*F9 |
| Watch... | Sheet1 | | W842 | 5,754,185.62 | =+V842*1.01 |

35

When the watch is defined, you can toggle the Watch Window dialog by using the Watch Window icon in the Formulas ribbon.

**TIP FROM**

> You can double-click any entry in the Watch Window dialog to scroll to that cell.

The Watch Window dialog is better than the old Camera tool feature because the Watch Window dialog can stay in view as you move to other worksheets. However, you can still use the Camera tool feature. To do so, you copy some cells, select a new range, and choose Paste, Paste Picture Link from the Home ribbon. Excel pastes a picture of the far-off range in a new location. The Camera tool is often used to build a dashboard view. You can paste a picture of key indicators from several worksheets onto a single overview workbook. The picture is more like a webcam than a picture; it constantly shows the current values of the selected range.

# LOOKING FOR HIDDEN DATA IN A WORKBOOK

There have been some embarrassing government snafus recently in which a government agency issued a whitepaper on a certain topic. Office gurus then looked in certain fields in the Word or Excel document and proved that the document actually came from a lobbying firm.

Microsoft has added a document inspector feature to allow anyone to discover what hidden information might be in a document. The document inspector can find items that may not be visible in the grid but can still be discovered by anyone who is familiar with Office.

To inspect a document, you follow these steps:

1. Save the workbook.
2. Select the Office icon and then choose Prepare, Document Inspector. The Document Inspector dialog appears, showing all the items that will be searched, as shown in Figure 35.3.

**Figure 35.3**
The document inspector searches for data that is stored with the workbook but not visible in the grid.

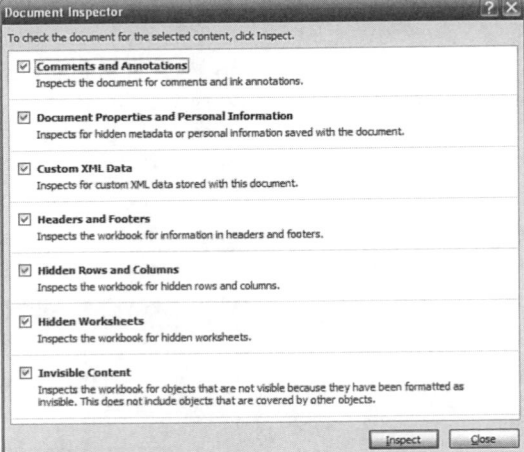

35

3. Click Inspect. The Document Inspector indicates any items that are found.

4. Click Remove All in any section to remove those items.

5. Use Save As to save the file with a new name.

**CAUTION**

It is relatively destructive to simply remove all hidden worksheets in a workbook. If you do, you will likely find items that no longer calculate correctly.

# MARKING A DOCUMENT AS FINAL TO PREVENT CHANGES

You can set the read-only property of a document to true to mark a document as final to prevent changes. For some reason, this also prevents the document from being emailed from within Excel.

To set a document as read-only, you choose the Office icon and then select Finish, Mark as Final. If someone gives you a document with this setting turned on, you can choose the Office icon and then select Finish, Mark as Final to turn off the feature. You are then able to send and save the workbook.

# OPENING THE SAME FILES EVERYDAY

In some jobs, you might have to open the same workbooks at the same time to perform a certain recurring task. For example, perhaps you spend an hour every morning recording new accounts receivable balances while processing the morning postal mail. This task might require you to open the AR.xlsm file, the Customer.xlsm file, and the BankDeposit.xlsm file. If these three files are stored in different folders, it can be slightly tedious to open each document one at a time.

After opening the files manually, you can specify that the files belong to a workspace. Then, when you open that workspace, Excel will open all the documents associated with the workspace.

To set up a workspace, you follow these steps:

1. Close all open workbooks.

2. Open each workbook associated with the task.

3. From the View ribbon, choose Window, Save Workspace. The Save Workspace dialog appears.

4. Browse to a location to save the workspace. Give the workspace a name. Click Save. Note that the file is saved with an .xlw extension.

The next time you need to open those files, you select File, Open and choose the XLW file.

> **NOTE**
>
> Saving a workspace does not embed the files or save the files themselves. The XLW file is actually just a list of the pathnames and filenames of the documents to be saved.

If you later rename one of the files or move one of them to a new location, you have to re-create and resave the workspace.

# DOWNLOADING COOL SPREADSHEETS FROM OFFICE ONLINE

There are dozens of free spreadsheets available in the New Workbook dialog. These spreadsheet templates come from Office Online. They are designed to solve many of the day-to-day tasks you might need to track in Excel.

As shown in Figure 35.4, the available templates are varied, from a mortgage amortization schedule to a pivot table showing the NFL schedule week-by-week.

**Figure 35.4**
Dozens of workbook templates in 17 categories are available for free from Office Online.

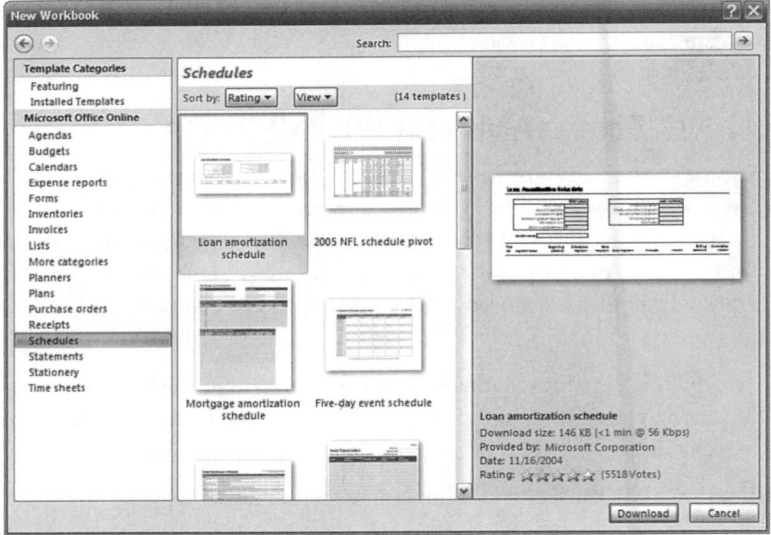

To access the documents, you follow these steps:

1. Ensure that you are connected to the Internet.

2. From the Office icon menu, choose New. The New Workbook dialog appears.

3. On the left side of the New Workbook dialog, choose one of the 17 categories. The center of the dialog shows the available templates.

35

4. Click any template in the center of the dialog to see a preview of the document on the right. The preview indicates the size of the file, the provider, the date, and rating by others.

5. To download and open the file in Excel, click the Download button.

6. Open the file and then select File, Save As to save the file on your computer.

> **NOTE**
>
> The More Categories item in the category list in the New Workbook dialog contains templates for address books, balance sheets, calculators, charts, estimates, evaluations, forecasts, games, ID cards, itineraries, journals, ledgers, logs, quotes, records, reports, scorecards, surveys, NCAA tournament bracket sheets, trackers, and more.

# ADDING VISUAL INTEREST BY USING A BACKGROUND PICTURE

You can replace the boring white background for a spreadsheet with any picture to add visual interest. Doing this might not be a good idea for a table full of numbers, but it can make a great introductory menu worksheet with links to other sheets in the document, as shown in Figure 35.5.

**Figure 35.5**
You can add a picture as the background for a worksheet.

Each worksheet can have one background picture that is tiled to fill the worksheet. You specify the background by selecting Page Layout, Page Setup, Background.

NOTE

> The background appears only on the computer display. It does not print.

# COMPARING DOCUMENTS SIDE-BY-SIDE WITH SYNCHRONOUS SCROLLING

Say that you have two documents that should be nearly identical. Perhaps you started with a workbook and then routed the workbook to a coworker. You have your original workbook and the new workbook, and you want to visually compare them.

A feature introduced in Excel 2003 lets you scroll both windows at the same time. You can arrange the windows so that they are both visible. As you scroll the active document, the other document scrolls at the same rate. This can allow you to visibly compare the documents.

To compare two documents side-by-side in this manner, you follow these steps:

1. Close all other documents.
2. Open the first workbook.
3. Open the second workbook.
4. Select View, Window, View Side by Side.
5. If you have more than two workbooks open, you have to choose just one of the other workbooks to be used for the comparison. The two workbooks appear together.
6. If the windows are split horizontally, one above the other, select View, Window, Arrange, Vertical to have the worksheets appear side-by-side.
7. Begin scrolling through the data using the scrollbar or the wheel on your scroll mouse.

Synchronous scrolling does not work well if someone deleted or inserted extra rows in one workbook. To solve this problem, you follow these steps:

1. If one worksheet has extra rows and is out of sync with the other worksheet, click View, Window, Synchronous Scrolling to temporarily turn off this feature.
2. Use the arrow keys or scrollbar to line up the worksheets. Scroll one worksheet so that both worksheets have the same record as the top row in the window.
3. Click View, Window, Synchronous Scrolling again to turn the feature back on. You can now continue scrolling the rows below the mismatched rows.

For example, someone inserted five blank rows in the right document in Figure 35.6. To fix this problem, you would turn off Synchronous Scrolling, line up Row 20 on the left with Row 15 on the right, and turn scrolling back on.

**Figure 35.6**
Use View Side by Side with Synchronous Scrolling to visually compare two workbooks.

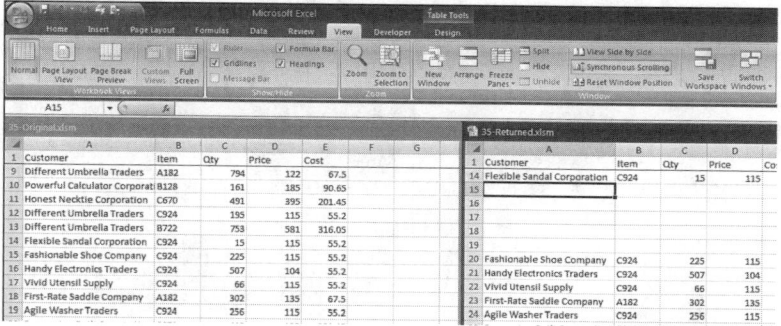

To compare two worksheets of the same workbook, you use View, Window, New Window to create a virtual second instance of a single workbook. Then you display the second sheet in the second instance and then follow steps 4 through 6 above. To remove the second virtual instance of the workbook, you click the X in the upper-right corner of the second instance.

# CALCULATING A FORMULA IN SLOW MOTION

If you have a particularly complicated formula, you can watch how Excel calculates the formula in slow motion. This can help you locate any logic errors in the worksheet.

To evaluate a formula in slow motion, you follow these steps:

1. Select the cell that contains the formula.

2. Select Formulas, Formula Auditing, Evaluate Formula. The Evaluate Formula dialog box appears, showing the formula. One element of the formula is underlined, indicating that this element will be calculated next.

3. To immediately see the value of the underlined element, click Evaluate.

4. If you want to see how that element is calculated, instead of clicking Evaluate, click Step In. Excel shows the formula for that element.

5. Eventually, the final level is evaluated to a number. Click Step Out to return one level up the dialog.

6. Continue clicking Evaluate until you arrive at the answer shown in the cell.

35

Figure 35.7 shows an Evaluate Formula dialog, after Step In was clicked twice.

**Figure 35.7**
The Evaluate Formula dialog allows you to watch the formula calculation in slow motion.

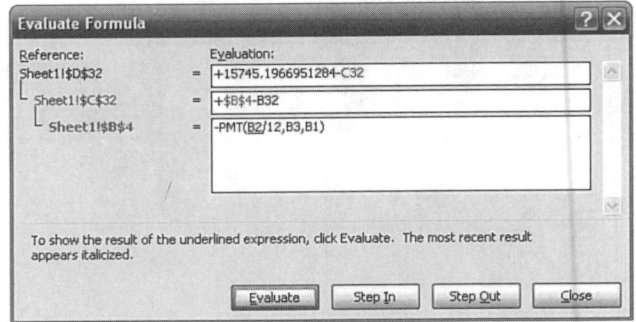

**TIP FROM**

Watch for the underlined portion of the formula because that is the element to be calculated next. Using the Evaluate Formula dialog allows you to verify the order of operations that Excel uses.

# INSERTING A SYMBOL IN A CELL

Obscure key combinations are available to insert many symbols. However, you do not have to learn any of them. Instead, you can use Insert, Text, Symbol to display the Symbol dialog box.

In the Symbol dialog, you scroll through many subsets of the current font. When you find the desired symbol, you select it and click the Insert button, as shown in Figure 35.8.

**Figure 35.8**
Instead of memorizing arcane key combinations, you can use Insert Symbol to add symbols to a workbook.

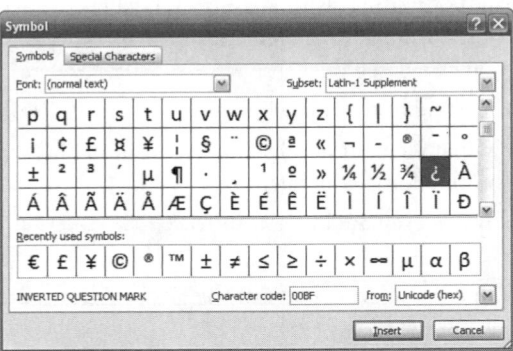

# ADDING A DIGITAL SIGNATURE LINE TO A WORKBOOK

You've probably encountered webpages where the authenticity of the web owner is verified with a digital certificate. Most likely, you notice this when the person's certificate has expired.

35

Microsoft has added a similar concept to Microsoft Excel 2007 and Microsoft Word 2007. When you attach a digital signature to a document, you are authenticating that you are really you. This process will help to prevent others from altering your work. After you sign a document, it is converted to read-only to ensure that no one changes the document after you sign it.

Digital signatures are provided by a third-party certifying authority. There is a fee for this service. To purchase a digital signature, you select Insert, Text, Signature Line, Add Signature Services. This leads to a list of approved digital certificate providers. Choose a provider and follow the steps on their website to purchase and install the signature.

To add a digital signature to a file, you open the file and then select Insert, Text, Digital Signature. Then you right-click the signature and choose Signature Setup to access the dialog box shown in Figure 35.9.

**Figure 35.9**
After adding a signature, you right-click to access the Signature Setup dialog.

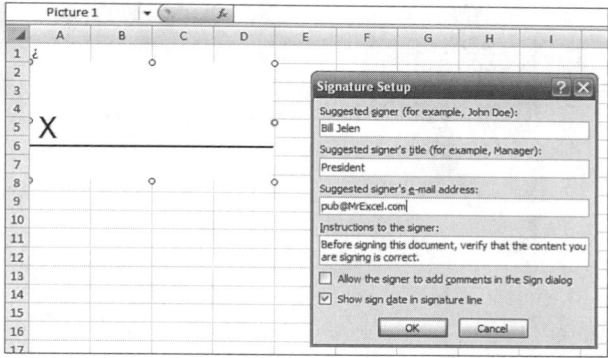

To sign a signature line, you follow these steps:

1. Double-click the signature line in the document. The Sign dialog appears.

2. In the Sign dialog, do one of the following:

   - Type your name in the box next to the X to add a printed version of your signature.

   - Click Select Image and choose a graphics file of your signature.

   - On a tablet PC, sign your name in the box by using the inking feature.

Your document is now electronically signed.

# PROTECTING A WORKSHEET

If you have many formulas in a worksheet, you might want to prevent others from changing them. In a typical scenario, your worksheet might have some input variables at the top. You may want to allow those items to be changed, but you may not want your formulas to be changed.

To protect a worksheet, you follow these steps:

1. Select the input cells in your worksheet. These are the cells that you want to allow someone to change.

2. Press Ctrl+1 or go to the Cells group of the Home ribbon and select Format, Format Cells. The Format Cells dialog appears.

3. On the Protection tab of the Format Cells dialog, uncheck the Locked check box, as shown in Figure 35.10. Click OK.

**Figure 35.10**
By default, all cells have their locked property set to TRUE.

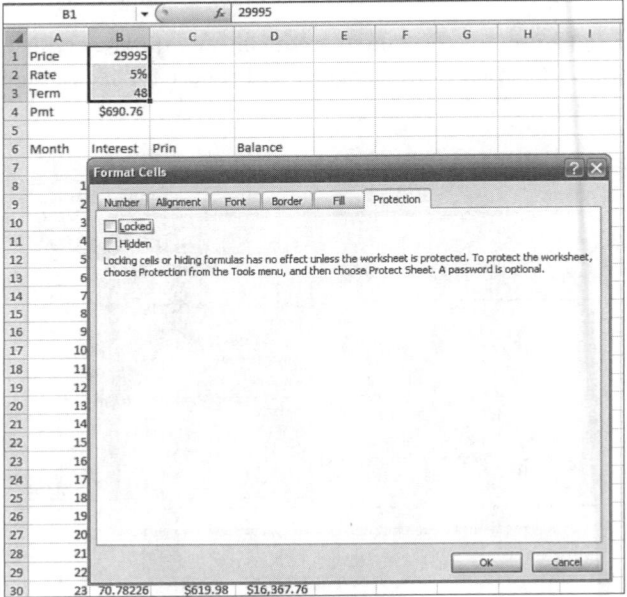

4. Choose Home, Cells, Protection, Protect Sheet. The Protect Sheet dialog appears. As shown in Figure 35.11, Excel offers to require a password for unprotecting the sheet. These passwords are easy to break using utilities freely available on the Internet. Don't rely on this password to keep anyone out of the document.

5. Optionally, change what is allowed to happen in the protected workbook.

6. Click OK to apply the protection.

**Figure 35.11**
Do not rely on this password for security, as it can easily be broken.

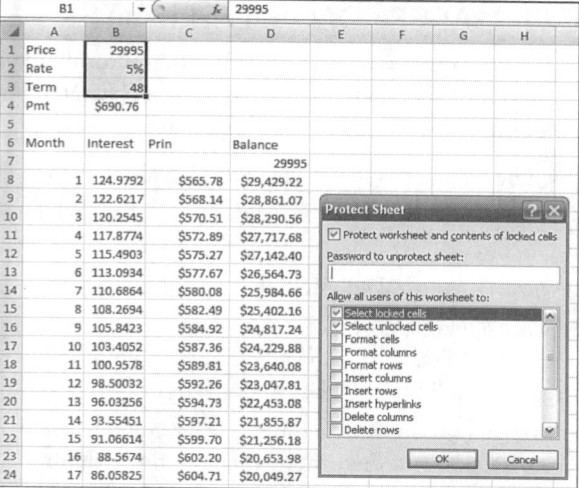

# SHARING A WORKBOOK

Excel is not a collaborative program. Multiple people cannot access a workbook at the same time. Excel offers a Share Workbook icon under Review, Changes, Share Workbook. After you share a workbook, it becomes so limited, it is practically unusable.

Shared workbooks cannot have tables. You cannot insert blocks of cells in them. You cannot delete their worksheets. You cannot merge cells, add conditional formats, add validation, add charts, add pictures, add or change pivot tables, insert hyperlinks, use scenarios, use subtotals, write macros, or edit array formulas in shared workbooks. Basically, all but the simplest spreadsheets are unsharable.

**TIP FROM**

> If you need to have two people edit an Excel file at the same time, you can upload the workbook to Google Spreadsheet. For more information, visit spreadsheets.google.com.

You can find one new feature in Excel 2007 regarding sharing by selecting the Office icon and then Publish, Create Document Workspace. With the Create Document Workspace feature, you can save a workbook to a server and require others to check the file out before editing. This prevents multiple people from simultaneously editing the workbook.

35

# SEPARATING TEXT BASED ON A DELIMITER

Depending on the source of your data, you might find that information is loaded into Excel with many fields in one cell. If the fields are separated by a character, you can separate the data into multiple columns. To do so, you follow these steps:

1. Select the one-column range that contains multiple values in each cell.

2. Select Data, Data Tools, Convert Text to Table. Excel displays the Convert Text to Columns Wizard dialog.

3. In Step 1 of the wizard, choose Delimited and click Next.

4. In Step 2 of the wizard, choose your delimiter. Excel offers check boxes for Tab, Semicolon, Comma, and Space. If your delimiter is something different, choose the Other box and type the delimiter. Click Next.

5. In Step 3 of the wizard, indicate whether any of your columns are dates. Click the column in the Data Preview section and then choose Date in the Column Data Format section.

6. By default, Excel replaces the selected column and uses adjacent blank columns. To write the results to a different output area, enter a destination in Step 3 of the wizard, as shown in Figure 35.12.

7. Click Finish to parse the column.

8. Excel does not automatically make the columns wide enough, so select the Cells section of the Home ribbon and then select Format, Width, AutoFit to make the output columns wide enough for the contents.

**Figure 35.12**
You specify field types and an output range in Step 3 of the wizard.

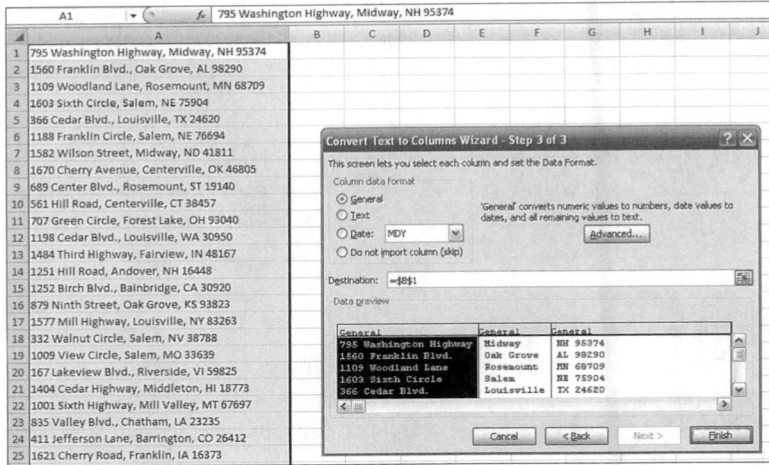

# ADDING AUTOMATIC SUBTOTALS

When you have a database of detailed data, you might want to add subtotals to each group of records. If your data has one field that identifies the groups, you can use the Subtotals command to quickly add the subtotals. Figure 35.13 shows a dataset that is suitable for this.

**Figure 35.13**
After sorting, you can
quickly add subtotals
to this dataset.

| | A | B | C | D | E | F | G |
|---|---|---|---|---|---|---|---|
| 1 | Invoice | Date | Customer | Hardware | Software | Shipping | Total |
| 2 | 1101 | 1/2/2007 | Steadfast Freezer Company | 752 | 15 | 9.95 | 776.95 |
| 3 | 1102 | 1/3/2007 | Ideal Shoe Traders | 1329 | 135 | 10.95 | 1474.95 |
| 4 | 1103 | 1/4/2007 | Steadfast Freezer Company | 746 | 235 | 11.95 | 992.95 |
| 5 | 1104 | 1/4/2007 | Handy Sandal Corporation | 1137 | 168 | 12.95 | 1317.95 |
| 6 | 1105 | 1/5/2007 | Brilliant Umbrella Company | 993 | 231 | 13.95 | 1237.95 |
| 7 | 1106 | 1/5/2007 | Steadfast Freezer Company | 1328 | 265 | 14.95 | 1607.95 |
| 8 | 1107 | 1/6/2007 | Mouthwatering Chopstick Corporation | 932 | 8 | 15.95 | 955.95 |
| 9 | 1108 | 1/7/2007 | Remarkable Bottle Corporation | 504 | 40 | 16.95 | 560.95 |
| 10 | 1109 | 1/7/2007 | Remarkable Bottle Corporation | 1076 | 47 | 17.95 | 1140.95 |
| 11 | 1110 | 1/7/2007 | Steadfast Freezer Company | 1316 | 169 | 18.95 | 1503.95 |
| 12 | 1111 | 1/8/2007 | Handy Sandal Corporation | 890 | 37 | 19.95 | 946.95 |
| 13 | 1112 | 1/9/2007 | Rare Scooter Inc. | 1223 | 171 | 20.95 | 1414.95 |
| 14 | 1113 | 1/10/2007 | Well-Suited Adhesive Inc. | 1014 | 209 | 21.95 | 1244.95 |
| 15 | 1114 | 1/10/2007 | Flexible Opener Inc. | 798 | 160 | 22.95 | 980.95 |

You follow these steps to add subtotals to a dataset:

1. Sort the dataset by your group field. Select one cell in that column and choose Data, Sort & Filter, AZ.

2. Select one cell in your dataset.

3. Choose Data, Outline, Subtotal. Excel displays the Subtotal dialog box.

4. In the Subtotal dialog, change the At Each Change In drop-down to reflect your group field.

5. Ensure that Use Function is set to Sum.

6. For each field that you want totaled, check the field in the Add Subtotal To list, as shown in Figure 35.14.

**Figure 35.14**
You specify the fields
to be totaled in the
Subtotal dialog.

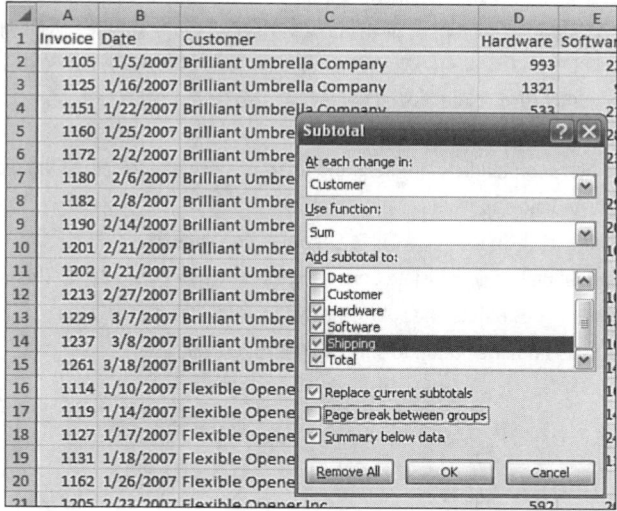

7. If you want a page break after each group, choose Page Break Between Groups.

8. Click OK to add subtotals. Excel adds a subtotal between each group, as shown in Figure 35.15.

**Figure 35.15**
Excel inserts extra rows between groups and adds subtotals.

| | | Invoice | Date | Customer | Hardware | Software | Shipping | Total |
|---|---|---|---|---|---|---|---|---|
| · | 146 | 1214 | 2/27/2007 | Steadfast Freezer Company | 1253 | 196 | 122.95 | 1571.95 |
| · | 147 | 1215 | 2/28/2007 | Steadfast Freezer Company | 685 | 110 | 123.95 | 918.95 |
| · | 148 | 1220 | 3/1/2007 | Steadfast Freezer Company | 523 | 70 | 128.95 | 721.95 |
| · | 149 | 1234 | 3/8/2007 | Steadfast Freezer Company | 861 | 288 | 142.95 | 1291.95 |
| · | 150 | 1247 | 3/12/2007 | Steadfast Freezer Company | 1114 | 48 | 155.95 | 1317.95 |
| · | 151 | 1254 | 3/15/2007 | Steadfast Freezer Company | 616 | 105 | 162.95 | 883.95 |
| · | 152 | 1257 | 3/17/2007 | Steadfast Freezer Company | 841 | 35 | 165.95 | 1041.95 |
| | 153 | | | **Steadfast Freezer Company Total** | 14109 | 2402 | 1466.2 | 17977.2 |
| · | 154 | 1126 | 1/17/2007 | Trendy Raft Corporation | 1313 | 204 | 34.95 | 1551.95 |
| · | 155 | 1142 | 1/18/2007 | Trendy Raft Corporation | 1124 | 109 | 50.95 | 1283.95 |
| · | 156 | 1145 | 1/20/2007 | Trendy Raft Corporation | 785 | 299 | 53.95 | 1137.95 |
| · | 157 | 1156 | 1/23/2007 | Trendy Raft Corporation | 595 | 284 | 64.95 | 943.95 |
| · | 158 | 1163 | 1/27/2007 | Trendy Raft Corporation | 881 | 114 | 71.95 | 1066.95 |
| · | 159 | 1173 | 2/3/2007 | Trendy Raft Corporation | 892 | 208 | 81.95 | 1181.95 |
| · | 160 | 1177 | 2/5/2007 | Trendy Raft Corporation | 883 | 290 | 85.95 | 1258.95 |
| · | 161 | 1183 | 2/9/2007 | Trendy Raft Corporation | 1074 | 248 | 91.95 | 1413.95 |
| · | 162 | 1207 | 2/23/2007 | Trendy Raft Corporation | 1317 | 99 | 115.95 | 1531.95 |
| · | 163 | 1253 | 3/15/2007 | Trendy Raft Corporation | 956 | 153 | 161.95 | 1270.95 |
| · | 164 | 1259 | 3/17/2007 | Trendy Raft Corporation | 705 | 254 | 167.95 | 1126.95 |
| | 165 | | | **Trendy Raft Corporation Total** | 10525 | 2262 | 982.45 | 13769.5 |
| · | 166 | 1113 | 1/10/2007 | Well-Suited Adhesive Inc. | 1014 | 209 | 21.95 | 1244.95 |
| · | 167 | 1115 | 1/11/2007 | Well-Suited Adhesive Inc. | 650 | 117 | 23.95 | 790.95 |
| · | 168 | 1120 | 1/14/2007 | Well-Suited Adhesive Inc. | 1264 | 139 | 28.95 | 1431.95 |
| · | 169 | 1122 | 1/15/2007 | Well-Suited Adhesive Inc. | 1325 | 168 | 30.95 | 1523.95 |
| · | 170 | 1140 | 1/18/2007 | Well-Suited Adhesive Inc. | 513 | 73 | 48.95 | 634.95 |
| · | 171 | 1148 | 1/21/2007 | Well-Suited Adhesive Inc. | 735 | 9 | 56.95 | 800.95 |
| · | 172 | 1168 | 1/31/2007 | Well-Suited Adhesive Inc. | 1207 | 258 | 76.95 | 1541.95 |
| · | 173 | 1186 | 2/12/2007 | Well-Suited Adhesive Inc. | 936 | 18 | 94.95 | 1048.95 |
| · | 174 | 1194 | 2/17/2007 | Well-Suited Adhesive Inc. | 851 | 277 | 102.95 | 1230.95 |
| | 175 | | | **Well-Suited Adhesive Inc. Total** | 8495 | 1268 | 486.55 | 10249.6 |
| | 176 | | | **Grand Total** | 154648 | 23894 | 14652.9 | 193195 |

## Excel in Practice: Formatting the Subtotal Rows

When it adds subtotals, Excel adds three group and outline buttons to the left of Cell A1. If you click the 2 group and outline button, Excel hides rows so that you see only the subtotal rows.

Many people try to copy the subtotal rows or to apply formatting to the subtotal rows when the data is collapsed. This does not work because Excel copies or formats the hidden rows as well.

To format only the subtotal rows, you follow these steps:

1. Click the 2 group and outline button.

2. Select from the first subtotal down to the grand total. This actually selects all the hidden rows as well.

3. Press F5. The GoTo dialog appears.

4. In the Go To dialog, click Special. The Go To Special dialog appears.

5. In the Go To Special dialog, click Visible Cells Only, as shown in Figure 35.16. Then click OK.

6. Apply any formatting desired for the subtotal rows.

7. Click the 3 group and outline button to show all the rows again.

35

**Figure 35.16**
The Go To Special dialog allows you to select only the subtotal lines.

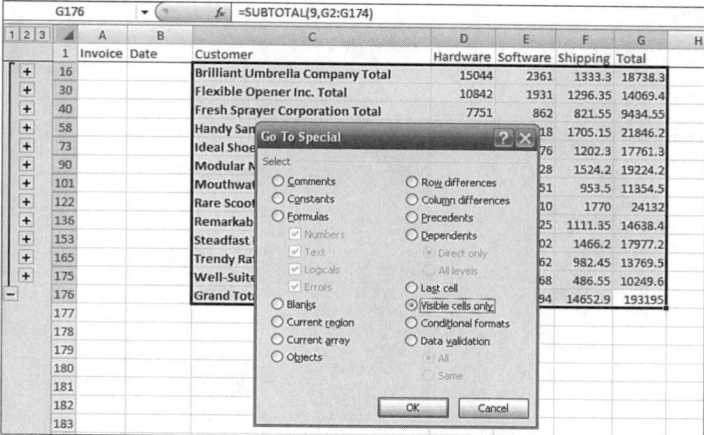

# TRANSLATING TEXT

If you are a fan of AltaVista's Babel Fish Translation Web site, you can now perform a similar translation inside your Excel documents. The Babel Fish project is not a professional translator. The translations produced are often very rough and sometimes humorous.

However, if someone has sent you a document in a foreign language, you can convert the text from the foreign language to a form of broken English so that you can often get the basic meaning of the text.

Instead of using Babel Fish, the Excel 2007 translation service uses a lesser-known service: WorldLingo.com.

The Excel 2007 service can only translate a single cell at a time. To use the service, follow these steps:

1. Select the cell containing text that you want to translate.

2. On the Review ribbon, click Translate.

3. In the Research task pane, choose a From and To language. The Research pane will show you the translation from WordLingo, as shown in Figure 35.17.

4. Select the translated text by dragging over it with the mouse. Press Ctrl+C to copy the translation to the clipboard.

5. Click in a cell in your Excel worksheet and press Ctrl+V to paste.

**35**

This feature would be far more powerful if you could translate entire blocks of cells and automatically return the translations in an adjacent column.

**Figure 35.17**
The translation service is not leaving me the wild one.

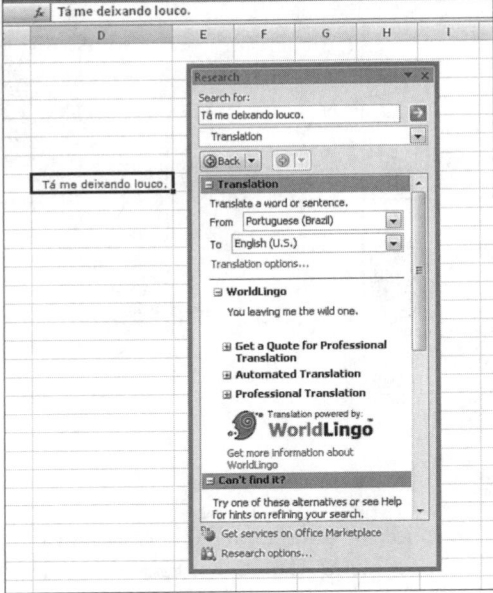

TIP FROM

For more tips, subscribe to the free daily MrExcel iTunes podcast. See www.mrexcel.com/podcast.shtml for details.

35

# MORE POWER

# CHAPTER 36

# Automating Repetitive Functions Using VBA Macros

**36**

Every copy of Excel shipped since 1995 has included the powerful Visual Basic for Applications (VBA) lurking behind the grid. With VBA, you can do anything that you can do in the regular interface, and you can do it much faster. VBA shines when you have many repetitive tasks to undertake.

Learning to use macros is a good news/bad news proposition.

The good news is that Microsoft Office provides a macro recorder that can write a macro as you work. The bads news is that it is not easy to record a macro that will work consistently with any dataset. To really unleash the power of macros, you need to understand how to edit recorded macro code. You can then record a macro that is close to what you want and then edit that macro to create something that will run the way you want it to work.

# CHECKING SECURITY SETTINGS BEFORE USING MACROS

On March 26, 1999, a hacker named Kwyjibo launched the Melissa virus. This particular virus used VBA macros in Word to propagate itself. Microsoft took a lot of heat over the fact that macros were able to run without the knowledge of the person running the computer. In response, Microsoft has made it more difficult to run macros in subsequent versions of Excel. At one point, there was even some concern that Microsoft would remove support for VBA macros, but Microsoft has committed to support VBA macros for another 10 to 15 years.

Before you can use macros, you have to take some positive steps to affirm that you want to record or run a macro.

---

**Triple Word Score**

The original Melissa virus macro spread via email as a Word document. The document would arrive with the message subject "Here is the document that you asked for." When a user opened the document in Word, the virus would attach itself to the Normal.dot file and attempt to email itself to others in the user's address book. This propagation method is what attracted the attention.

The point of the Melissa virus was to check the system clock every time the user opened a document. If the user happened to open the document when the minute, day, and month all matched, the virus would perform its dirty work. So, for example, if you opened the document on October 10 at 8:10 a.m. or perhaps on June 6 at 6:06 p.m., the virus would kick in. Assuming an 8-hour work day, there are 96 minutes throughout the year when opening the Word document would triggered the virus. That works out to about a 7 in 1,000 chance that a user who opened the email attachment would be struck by the virus.

In a tip of the hat to the old board game Scrabble, the hacker had an insidious plan: if the user opened the document at the moment when the month, day, and minute matched on the system clock, the program would insert the following text in the Word document: "Twenty-two points, plus triple-word-score, plus fifty points for using all my letters. Game's over. I'm outta here."

Thanks to this silly virus, VBA programmers now have to jump through hoops in order to use macros.

---

## ENABLING VBA SECURITY

To enable VBA security, follow these steps:

1. Select File, Excel Options to open the Excel Settings dialog.

2. Choose the Personalize category, In the first section—Top Options for Working With Excel—choose Show Developer Tab in the Ribbon.

3. Click OK to exit the Excel Settings dialog. You now have a Developer tab on the ribbon.

4. On the Developer tab, click Macro Security in the Code group. The Security dialog appears.

5. In the Security dialog, change the Macro Settings to Disable All Macros with Notification. With this setting, Excel alerts you whenever you are opening a workbook that has macros attached.

6. When you open a document and get the warning that the document has macros attached, if this is a document that you wrote and you expect macros to be there, click Enable to enable the macros.

# RECORDING A MACRO

Before you start recording a macro, you need to think about how to break the task into easily repeatable steps. The macro recorder is great at recording navigation done using arrow keys. Therefore, you want to use only the keyboard for navigation while using the macro recorder.

Plan out your macro before recording it. Think about the steps you need to perform. If you need to fix many items in a worksheet, you might want to select the first item first. This way, the macro can perform an action on cells relative to the original selection.

To record a macro, follow these steps:

1. On the Developer ribbon, choose Record Macro.

2. In the Record Macro dialog box, type a name for the macro. The name can not contain spaces (for example, instead of `Macro Name`, use `MacroName`).

3. Choose if you want to store the macro in the current workbook, a new workbook, or a special Personal Macro Workbook. The personal macro workbook is a special workbook designed to hold general purpose macros that might apply to any workbook. If you are unsure, choose to store the recorded macro in the current workbook.

4. Assign a shortcut key for the macro. Ctrl+J is a safe key, because nothing is currently assigned to Ctrl+J. This shortcut key will allow you to run the macro again.

5. Click OK to close the Record Macro dialog.

6. Turn on relative recording by clicking the Use Relative References icon in the Code group of the Developer ribbon. Relative recording will record the action of moving a certain numbers of cells from the active cell.

**CAUTION**

> The alternative is an absolute recording. This method is extremely literal. The action of moving down three cells from A1 will be recorded as "Select cell A4." That action is extremely limited—it would only work when the macro is played back with the active cell in A1.

7. Perform the actions you want to store in the macro.

8. Click the red Stop Recording button in the left side of the status bar.

9. Save the workbook before testing the macro.

10. Test the macro playback by typing the shortcut key assigned in step 4.

# CASE STUDY: MACRO FOR FORMATTING FOR A MAIL MERGE

A co-worker has some names and addresses in Excel. She needs to do a mail merge in Word. Rather than teach her how to do a mail merge, you offer to do the mail merge for her. In theory, this should take you a couple minutes. However, when the list of names arrives in the Excel worksheet, you realize that the data is in the wrong format. In the Excel worksheet, the names are going down Column A, as shown in Figure 36.1.

**Figure 36.1**
A simple task such as doing a mail merge is incredibly difficult when the data is in the wrong format.

In order to successfully do a mail merge, the Excel worksheet should have fields for name, street address, and city+state+zip code, as shown in Figure 36.2.

Before you start recording a macro, you need to think about how to break the task into easily repeatable steps. The macro recorder is great at recording navigation done using arrow keys. Therefore, ideally, you want to use only the keyboard for navigation while using the macro recorder.

It would be good to record a macro that can fix one name in the list. Assume that you start with the cell pointer on a person's name at the beginning of the macro, as shown in Figure 36.3. The macro would need to perform these steps to fix one record and end up on the name of the second person in the list:

**Figure 36.2**
The goal is to produce data with fields in columns.

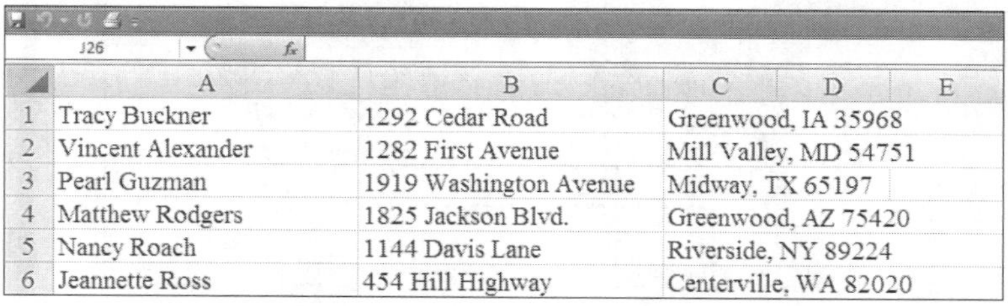

| | A | B | C | D | E |
|---|---|---|---|---|---|
| 1 | Tracy Buckner | 1292 Cedar Road | Greenwood, IA 35968 | | |
| 2 | Vincent Alexander | 1282 First Avenue | Mill Valley, MD 54751 | | |
| 3 | Pearl Guzman | 1919 Washington Avenue | Midway, TX 65197 | | |
| 4 | Matthew Rodgers | 1825 Jackson Blvd. | Greenwood, AZ 75420 | | |
| 5 | Nancy Roach | 1144 Davis Lane | Riverside, NY 89224 | | |
| 6 | Jeannette Ross | 454 Hill Highway | Centerville, WA 82020 | | |

**Figure 36.3**
You start with a name selected.

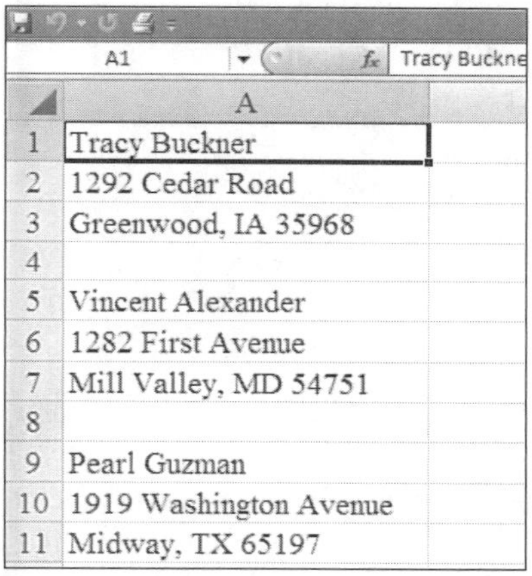

A1 Tracy Buckne

| | A |
|---|---|
| 1 | Tracy Buckner |
| 2 | 1292 Cedar Road |
| 3 | Greenwood, IA 35968 |
| 4 | |
| 5 | Vincent Alexander |
| 6 | 1282 First Avenue |
| 7 | Mill Valley, MD 54751 |
| 8 | |
| 9 | Pearl Guzman |
| 10 | 1919 Washington Avenue |
| 11 | Midway, TX 65197 |

1. Press the Down Arrow key to move to the address cell.
2. Press Ctrl+X to cut the address.
3. Press the Up Arrow key and then the Right Arrow key to move next to the name.
4. Press Ctrl+V to paste the address, as shown in Figure 36.4.

**Figure 36.4**
You cut and paste the address.

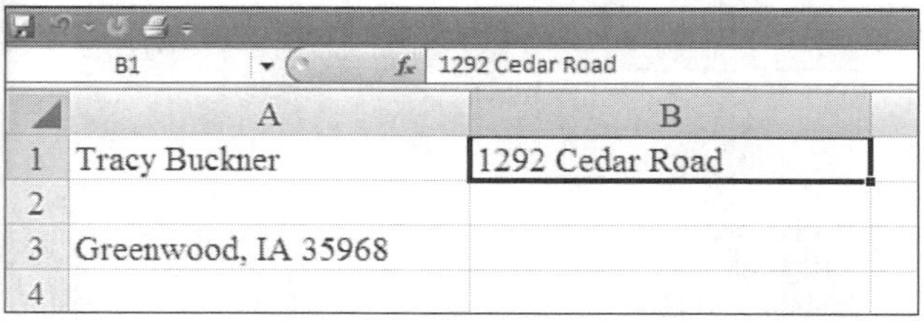

B1 1292 Cedar Road

| | A | B |
|---|---|---|
| 1 | Tracy Buckner | 1292 Cedar Road |
| 2 | | |
| 3 | Greenwood, IA 35968 | |
| 4 | | |

5. Press the Left Arrow key once and the Down Arrow key twice to move to the cell for city, state, and zip code.
6. Press Ctrl+X to cut the city, as shown in Figure 36.5.
7. Press the Up Arrow key twice and the Right Arrow key twice to move to the right of the street cell.
8. Press Ctrl+V to paste the city.
9. Press the Left Arrow key twice and the Down Arrow key once to move to the now blank row just below the name.

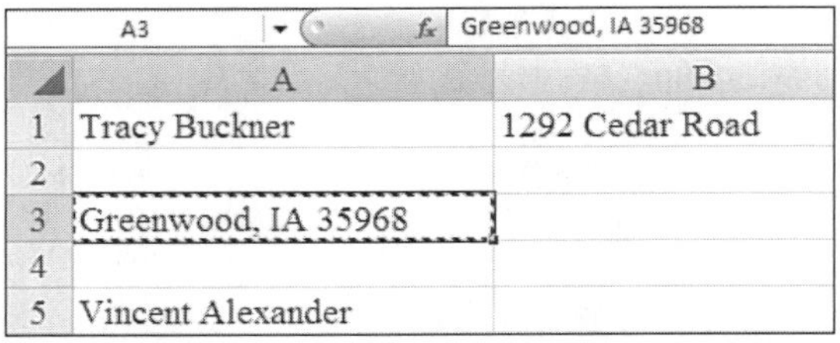

**Figure 36.5**
You cut the city.

| | A | B |
|---|---|---|
| 1 | Tracy Buckner | 1292 Cedar Road |
| 2 | | |
| 3 | Greenwood, IA 35968 | |
| 4 | | |
| 5 | Vincent Alexander | |

A3 — fx Greenwood, IA 35968

**10.** Hold down the Shift key while pressing the Down Arrow key twice in order to select the three blank rows, as shown in Figure 36.6.

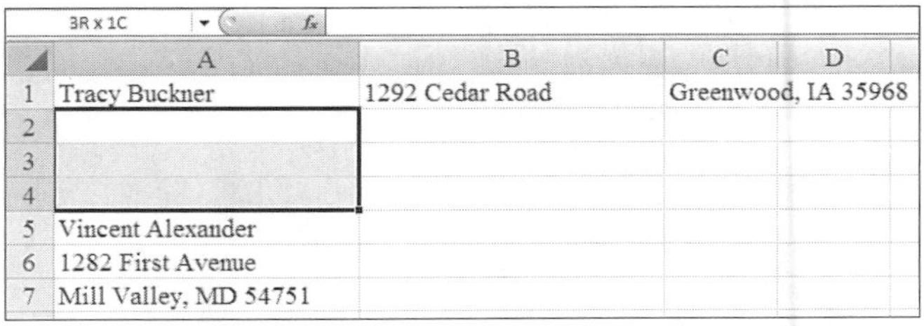

**Figure 36.6**
You select three blank rows prior to deleting.

3R x 1C — fx

| | A | B | C | D |
|---|---|---|---|---|
| 1 | Tracy Buckner | 1292 Cedar Road | Greenwood, IA 35968 | |
| 2 | | | | |
| 3 | | | | |
| 4 | | | | |
| 5 | Vincent Alexander | | | |
| 6 | 1282 First Avenue | | | |
| 7 | Mill Valley, MD 54751 | | | |

**11.** Press Ctrl+- to invoke the delete command. Press R+Enter to delete the row.

When you run a macro that goes through these steps, Excel deletes the three blank rows, but the selection now contains the three cells that encompass the next record, as shown in Figure 36.7. Ideally, the macro should end with only the name selected. Therefore, the macro now needs to press the Up Arrow key and the Down Arrow key. Moving the cell pointer up a cell and then back to the name causes only a single cell to be selected, as shown in Figure 36.8.

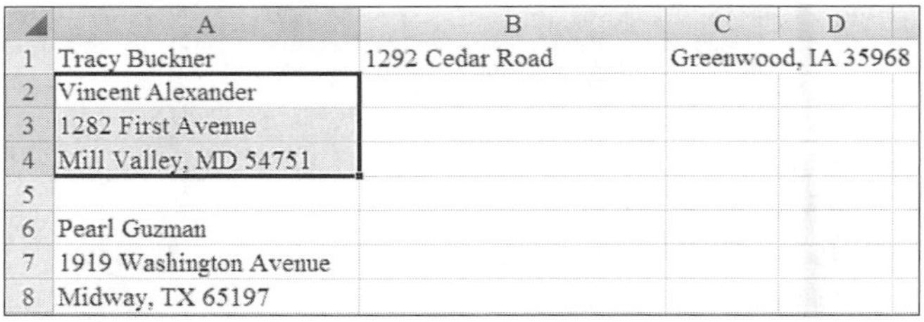

**Figure 36.7**
You need only one cell selected instead of three.

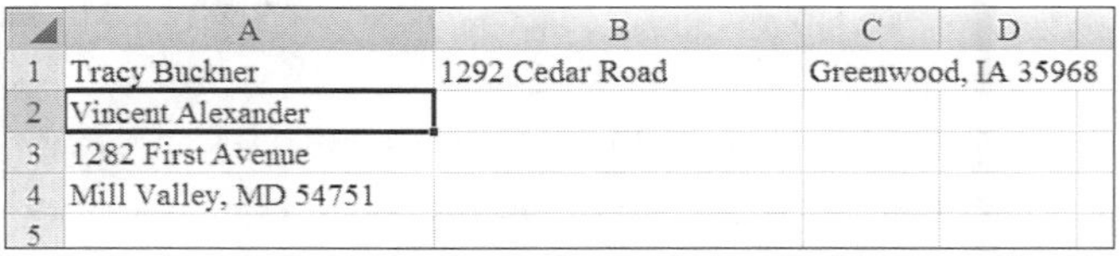

| | A | B | C | D |
|---|---|---|---|---|
| 1 | Tracy Buckner | 1292 Cedar Road | Greenwood, IA 35968 | |
| 2 | Vincent Alexander | | | |
| 3 | 1282 First Avenue | | | |
| 4 | Mill Valley, MD 54751 | | | |
| 5 | | | | |
| 6 | Pearl Guzman | | | |
| 7 | 1919 Washington Avenue | | | |
| 8 | Midway, TX 65197 | | | |

**Figure 36.8**
You finish the macro with the cell pointer on the next name.

| | A | B | C | D |
|---|---|---|---|---|
| 1 | Tracy Buckner | 1292 Cedar Road | Greenwood, IA 35968 | |
| 2 | Vincent Alexander | | | |
| 3 | 1282 First Avenue | | | |
| 4 | Mill Valley, MD 54751 | | | |
| 5 | | | | |

If the macro correctly performs all these steps, the first name and address are properly formatted. The blank rows left between the first and second names are deleted.

By making sure that the macro starts on a name and ends up on the next name, you allow the macro to be run repeatedly. If you assign this macro to the keyboard shortcut Ctrl+J, you can then hold down Ctrl+J and quickly fix records, one after the other.

## HOW NOT TO RECORD A MACRO: THE DEFAULT STATE OF THE MACRO RECORDER

The default state of the macro recorder is a very stupid state. If you recorded the preceding steps in the macro recorder, the macro recorder would take your actions very literally. The English pseudocode for recording these steps would say this:

1. Move to Cell A2.
2. Cut Cell A2 and paste to Cell B1.
3. Move to Cell A3.
4. Cut Cell A3 and paste to Cell C1.
5. Delete Rows 2 through 4.
6. Select Cell A2.

This macro will work, but it will only work for one record. After you recorded this macro, your worksheet would look like the one shown in Figure 36.9.

**Figure 36.9**
After recording the macro in default mode, the first record is fixed, and you might think you are ready to run the macro to fix the second record.

| | A | B | C | D |
|---|---|---|---|---|
| 1 | Tracy Buckner | 1292 Cedar Road | Greenwood, IA 35968 | |
| 2 | Vincent Alexander | | | |
| 3 | 1282 First Avenue | | | |
| 4 | Mill Valley, MD 54751 | | | |
| 5 | | | | |
| 6 | Pearl Guzman | | | |
| 7 | 1919 Washington Avenue | | | |
| 8 | Midway, TX 65197 | | | |
| 9 | | | | |

When the default macro runs, it moves the name Vincent Alexander from Cell A2 and pastes it on top of the address in Cell B1. It then takes the address in Cell A3 and pastes it on top of the city in Cell C1. It then deletes Rows 2, 3, and 4, removing the city and state. As shown in Figure 36.10, the macro provides the wrong result.

**Figure 36.10**
When the default macro runs, it ruins two records.

| | A | B | C | D |
|---|---|---|---|---|
| 1 | Tracy Buckner | Vincent Alexander | 1282 First Avenue | |
| 2 | | | | |
| 3 | Pearl Guzman | | | |
| 4 | 1919 Washington Avenue | | | |
| 5 | Midway, TX 65197 | | | |
| 6 | | | | |
| 7 | Matthew Rodgers | | | |

If you blindly ran this macro 100 times to convert 100 addresses, the macro would happily "eat" all 100 records, leaving you with just one record (and not even a correct record), as shown in Figure 36.11.

**36**

**Figure 36.11**
Run the default macro 100 times, and it destroys your entire dataset. Luckily, there is a different mode available for recording relative macros, as described in the next section.

| ◢ | A | B |
|---|---|---|
| 1 | Tracy Buckner | Rosemount, NY 93801 |
| 2 | | |
| 3 | | |
| 4 | | |

To overcome this problem, use relative references as discussed in the next section.

## RELATIVE REFERENCES IN MACRO RECORDING

There is an icon in the Code group on the Developer tab on the ribbon called Use Relative References. The key to recording useful macros is to judiciously turn on and off the relative recording setting. If you performed the steps described in the preceding section in relative recording mode, Excel would write code that does this:

1. Move down one cell.
2. Cut that cell.
3. Move up and over one cell and paste.
4. Move left and down two cells.
5. Cut that cell.
6. Move up and over two cells and paste.
7. Move left two cells, move down one cell, and delete three rows.
8. Move up and down one cell in order to select a single cell.

These steps are far more generic than those recorded using the default state of the macro recorder and would work for any record, provided that you started the macro with the cell pointer on the first cell that contains a name.

For this example, you need to record the entire macro with relative recording turned on.

## STARTING THE MACRO RECORDER

At this point, you have rehearsed the steps needed for a macro that puts data records into a format that will be usable for a mail merge. After you make sure that the cell pointer is starting on the name in Cell A1, you are ready to turn on the macro recorder.

You shouldn't be nervous, but you really want to perform the steps correctly. If you move the cell pointer in the wrong direction, the macro recorder will happily record that for you and play it back. It would be annoying to watch the macro recorder play back your mistakes 100 times a day for the next five years, so follow these steps to correctly create the macro:

1. On the Developer tab of the ribbon, click the Record Macro icon from the Code group. The Record Macro dialog appears.

2. Excel suggests giving this macro the unimaginative name Macro1. You can use any name you want, up to 20 characters, and without spaces. For this example, name the macro FixOneRecord.

3. Choose a shortcut key for the macro. The shortcut key is very important. In the present example, you will have to run this macro once for each record, so you might choose something like Ctrl+A, which is easy to press. However, note that assigning a macro to Ctrl+A will overwrite the usual action of that keystroke (selecting all cells). If you are writing a macro that will be used all day every day, you should use a shortcut key that is not assigned to any existing shortcuts, such as Ctrl+J or Ctrl+K.

4. Make a selection from the Store Macro In drop-down. You have the option of storing the macro in this workbook, in a new workbook, or in the personal macro workbook. If this is a general-purpose macro that you will use everyday on every file, it would make sense to store the macro in the personal macro workbook. However, because this macro is going to be used just to solve a current problem, store it in the current workbook.

5. Fill in a description if you think you will be using this macro long enough to forget what it does. When you are done making selections on the Record Macro dialog (see Figure 36.12), click OK. The Record Macro icon changes to a Stop Recording icon.

**Figure 36.12**
After making the needed selections, click OK to begin recording.

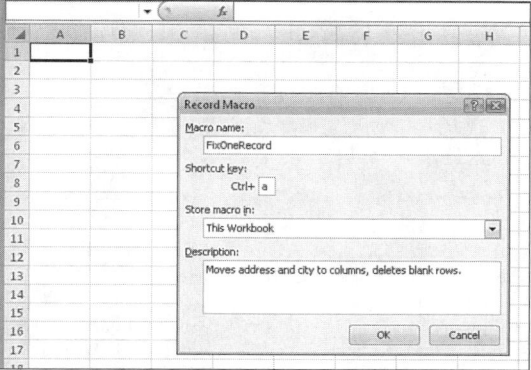

6. Click the Use Relative References icon in the Developer ribbon. The icon becomes highlighted.

7. Press the Down Arrow key to move to the address cell.

8. Press Ctrl+X to cut the address.

9. Press the Up Arrow key and then the Right Arrow key to move next to the name.

10. Press Ctrl+V to paste the address.

11. Press the Left Arrow key once and the Down Arrow key twice to move to the cell for city, state, and zip code.

12. Press Ctrl+X to cut the city

13. Press the Up Arrow key twice and the Right Arrow key twice to move to the right of the street cell.

14. Press Ctrl+V to paste the city.

15. Press the Left Arrow key twice and the Down Arrow key once to move to the now blank row just below the name.

16. Hold down the Shift key while pressing the Down Arrow key twice in order to select the three blank rows.

17. Press Ctrl+- to invoke the delete command. Press R+Enter to delete the row.

18. Press the Up Arrow key and the Down Arrow key. Moving the cell pointer up a cell and then back to the name will cause only a single cell to be selected.

19. When you are done, click the Stop Recording button.

This macro will successfully fix any record in the database, provided the cellpointer is on the cell containing the name when you run the macro. Try playing back the macro by pressing Ctrl+A to fix one record. To fix all records, hold down Ctrl+A until all records are fixed.

## RUNNING A MACRO

To run a macro, you follow these steps:

1. Click the green triangle on the Code group of the Developer tab. The Macro dialog appears, as shown in Figure 36.13.

**Figure 36.13**
Playing back a macro by using the Macro dialog.

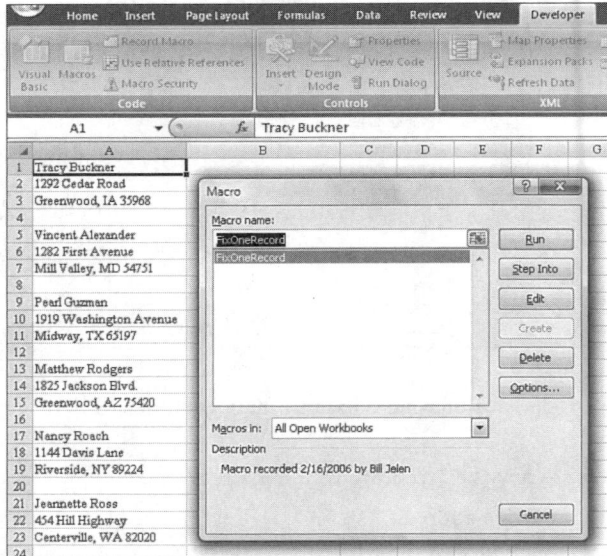

2. Select your macro and click the Run button. The macro fixes the first record.

**CAUTION**

When you run a macro, there is no undo. Therefore, you should save a file before running a new macro on it. It is easy to have accidentally recorded the macro in default mode instead of relative mode. You need to save the macro so that you can easily go back to the current state in case something doesn't work right.

3. Press Ctrl+A to run the FixOneRecord macro. As shown in Figure 36.14, the second record is fixed.

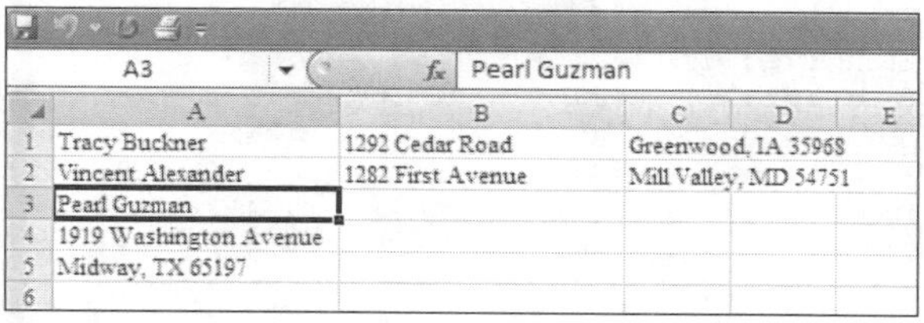

**Figure 36.14**
Results of a successful macro.

4. Hold down Ctrl+A to repeatedly run the macro. In a matter of seconds, all 100 names are in a format that is ready to use in a mail merge.

This first example represents an ideal use of a one-time macro. Someone gave you data that was in a bad format. The process to fix the data involved mindless repetition. If there had just been four records, you could have easily mindlessly fixed the records. But because there were 100 records in this example, it made sense to quickly record a macro and then run the macro repeatedly to solve the problem. You recorded the entire macro in relative mode, and you did not have to edit the macro at all. You probably run into a few situations a week where a quick one-time-use macro would make your job easier.

# EVERYDAY-USE MACRO EXAMPLE: FORMATTING AN INVOICE REGISTER

The macro recorder does not solve all tasks perfectly, however. Many times, you need to record a macro and then edit the recorded code to make the macro a bit more general. This example demonstrates how to do that.

In this example, a system writes out a file every day. This file contains a list of invoices generated on the previous day. The file predictably contains six columns—NAME, DATE, INVOICE, REVENUE, SALES TAX, and TOTAL—as shown in Figure 36.15. The file also looks horrible: The columns are the wrong width, there is no title, there is not a total row at the bottom. You would like a macro that would open this file, make the columns wider, add a total row, add a title, make the headings bold, and save the file with a new name. The following sections describe how to create this macro.

## USING THE END KEY TO HANDLE A VARIABLE NUMBER OF ROWS

One of the inherent problems with this example is that your file will have a different number of rows every day. If you record a macro for this today to add totals in Row 16, it will not work tomorrow, when you might have 22 invoices. The solution is to use the End key to navigate to the last row of your data.

You use the End key to move to the edge of a contiguous range of data. In Figure 36.15, if you press the End key and then the Down Arrow key, you would move to Cell A15. If you press the End key and then the Up Arrow key, you move back to Cell A1. You can press the End key followed by the Right Arrow key to move to Cell F1.

**Figure 36.15**
You can create a
macro to format this
file every day.

| | A | B | C | D | E | F |
|---|---|---|---|---|---|---|
| 1 | NAME | DATE | INVOICE | REVENUE | SALES TAX | TOTAL |
| 2 | TERRI D( | 2/17/2007 | 10217 | 252.11 | 15.13 | 267.24 |
| 3 | ELSIE H( | 2/17/2007 | 10218 | 68.67 | 4.12 | 72.79 |
| 4 | HAROLD | 2/17/2007 | 10219 | 111.4 | 6.68 | 118.08 |
| 5 | SHAWN ( | 2/17/2007 | 10220 | 151.47 | 9.09 | 160.56 |
| 6 | KRISTIN | 2/17/2007 | 10221 | 131.71 | 7.9 | 139.61 |
| 7 | DAVID A | 2/17/2007 | 10222 | 221.62 | 13.3 | 234.92 |
| 8 | ROSA PR | 2/17/2007 | 10223 | 225.02 | 13.5 | 238.52 |
| 9 | NORA SF | 2/17/2007 | 10224 | 261.84 | 15.71 | 277.55 |
| 10 | CRAIG B | 2/17/2007 | 10225 | 195.08 | 11.7 | 206.78 |
| 11 | BILLIE Cl | 2/17/2007 | 10226 | 72.31 | 4.34 | 76.65 |
| 12 | ADAM W | 2/17/2007 | 10227 | 168.12 | 10.09 | 178.21 |
| 13 | ANDREW | 2/17/2007 | 10228 | 79.54 | 4.77 | 84.31 |
| 14 | BRANDI | 2/17/2007 | 10229 | 258.73 | 15.52 | 274.25 |
| 15 | LAURIE I | 2/17/2007 | 10230 | 248.44 | 14.91 | 263.35 |

You can also use the End key to jump over an abyss of empty cells. If you are currently at the edge of a range—for example, Cell F1—and press End followed by the Right Arrow key, Excel jumps over all the blank cells and stops either at the next nonblank cell in Row 1 or at the right edge of the worksheet, Cell XFD1.

You might be tempted to start in Cell A1, press End, press the Down Arrow key, and then press the Down Arrow key again to move to the first blank row in the data. However, that is the wrong thing to do. This data file is coming from another system. One day, I guarantee that some crazy cashier will find a way to enter an order without a customer name. She will happen upon the accidental keystroke combination that causes the cash register to allow an order without a customer name. On that day, the End+Down Arrow key combination will stop at the wrong row and add totals in the middle of your dataset. To prevent this problem, you should have the macro go through these steps:

1. Open the file.
2. Turn on absolute recording.
3. Press the F5 key to display the GoTo dialog.
4. Go to Cell A1048576 (the last cell in the worksheet).
5. Turn on relative recording.
6. Type End+Up Arrow to move to the last row that contains data.
7. Type the Down Arrow key to move to the blank row.
8. Type the word **Total**.
9. Move right three cells.
10. Hold down the Shift key while moving right two cells.
11. Click the AutoSum button.
12. Select all cells.
13. Choose Format, Column, AutoFit.
14. Turn on absolute recording.

15. Select Row 1.

16. Press Ctrl+B to apply bold.

17. Insert two rows.

18. Move to Cell A1.

19. Enter the formula `="Invoices for "&TEXT(B4,"mmmm d, yyyy")`.

20. Use Save As to save the file with a new name to reflect today's date.

21. Click the Stop Recording button.

Before recording this macro, you need to open a blank Excel workbook and save it with the name MacroToImportInvoices.xlsm.

In this macro example, you use a mix of relative and absolute recording to produce a macro that handles any number of rows of data. The macro will be fairly useful, with two annoying limitations:

- If you saved the file as 2006-Feb-17Invoices.xls, the macro will attempt to overwrite that file everyday.

- The macro will always want to open the same file. This is great if your cash register system always produces a file with the same name in the same folder. However, you might want the option to browse for a different file each day.

Both of these changes require you to edit the recorded macro, as described in the next section.

## Editing a Macro

To edit a macro, follow these steps:

1. Go to the Developer tab, and in the Code group, click the Macros button. The Macro dialog appears.

2. In the Macro dialog, select your macro and click Edit (see Figure 36.16). The Visual Basic Editor (VBE) is launched.

**Figure 36.16**

Launching the VBE through the Macro dialog is an easy way to make sure you find the proper code.

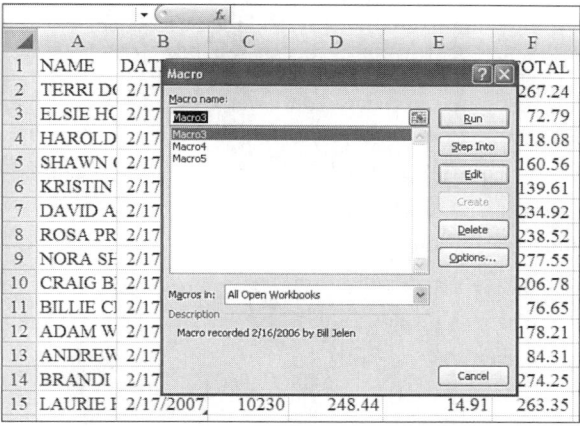

36

A number of panes are available in the VBE, but it is common to have three particular panes displayed, as shown in Figure 36.17:

- **Code pane**—The actual lines of the macro code are in the Code pane, which is usually on the right side of the screen.

- **Project pane**—This pane, in the upper left, shows every open workbook. Within the workbooks you can see objects for each worksheet, an object for this workbook, and one or more code modules. If you cannot see the Project pane, you press use Ctrl+R or select View, Project Explorer to open it.

- **Properties pane**—This pane, in the lower left, is very useful if you are designing custom dialog boxes. You can Press F4 to display the Properties pane.

Project Pane          Code Pane

**Figure 36.17**
The VBE allows editing of recorded macro code.

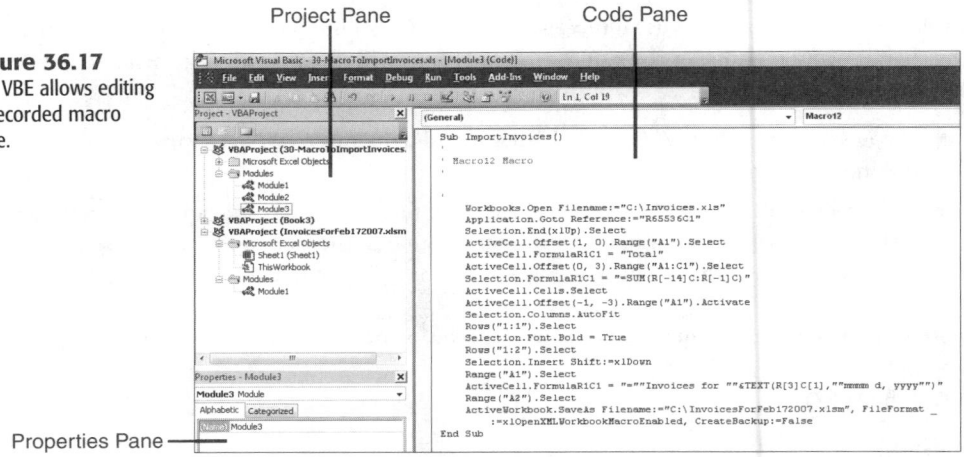

Properties Pane

# UNDERSTANDING VBA CODE—AN ANALOGY

In the 1980s and early 1990s, many people going through school were exposed to an introductory class in a programming language called BASIC. Although Excel macros are written in Visual Basic for Applications, the fact that both languages contain the word *basic* does not mean that BASIC and VBA are the same or even similar. BASIC is a procedural language. VBA is an object-oriented language. In VBA, the focus is on objects. This can make VBA confusing to someone who has learned to program in BASIC.

The syntax of VBA is made up of objects, methods, collections, arguments, and properties. If you have never programmed in an object-oriented language, these terms, and the VBA code itself, might seem foreign to you. The following sections compare these five elements to parts of speech:

- An object is similar to a noun
- A method is similar to a verb
- A collection is similar to a plural noun
- An argument is similar to an adverb
- A property is similar to an adjective

Each of the following sections describe the similarity between the VBA element and a part of speech. It also describes how to recognize the various elements when you examine VBA Code.

## COMPARING OBJECT.METHOD TO NOUNS AND VERBS

As an object-oriented language, the objects in VBA are of primary importance. Think of an object as any noun in Excel. Examples of objects are a cell, a row, a column, a worksheet, and a workbook.

A method is any action that you can peform on an object. This is similar to a verb. You can add a worksheet. You can delete a row. You can clear a cell. In Excel VBA, words like "Add," "Delete," and "Clear," are methods.

Objects and methods are joined together by a period, although in VBA, people pronounce the period as a dot. The object is first, followed by a dot, followed by the method. For example, object.method is pronounced "object-dot-method" and indicates that the method performs on the object. This is confusing because it is backward from how English is spoken. If we all spoke VBA instead of English, our day would be filled with sentences like "car.drive" and "dinner.eat." When you see a period in VBA, it usually means that the word after the period is acting upon the word to the left of the period.

## COMPARING COLLECTIONS TO PLURAL NOUNS

In an Excel workbook, there is not a single cell but a collection of many cells. Many workbooks will contain several worksheets. Anytime you have multiple instances of a certain object, VBA refers to this as a collection.

The "s" at the end of an object may seem subtle, but it indicates you are dealing with a collection instead of a single object. While ThisWorkbook refers to a single workbook, Workbooks refers to a collection of all of the open workbooks. This is a very important distinction to understand.

There are two main ways to refer to a single worksheet in a collection of worksheets: You can refer to a worksheet by its number or by its name. For example, Worksheets(1) and Worksheets("Jan") might refer to the same worksheet.

## COMPARING PARAMETERS TO ADVERBS

When you invoke a command such as the Save As command, a dialog box pops up, and you have the opportunity to specify several options that change how the command will be carried out. If the Save As command is a method, then the options for it are parameters. Just like an adverb modifies a verb, a parameter modifies a method.

Most of the time, parameters are recorded by using the syntax
*ParameterName:=ParameterValue.*

One of the reasons that recorded code gets to be so long is that the macro recorder makes note of every option on the dialog box, whether you select it or not.

Consider this line of code for `SaveAs`:

```
ActiveWorkbook.SaveAs Filename:="C:\Something.xls", _
FileFormat:=xlOpenXMLWorkbookMacroEnabled, _
CreateBackup:=False
```

In this recorded macro for `SaveAs`, the recorder noted parameter values for `Filename`, `FileFormat`, and `CreateBackup`. Figure 36.18 shows the Save As dialog box. `Filename` and `FileFormat` are clearly evident on the form, but where are the rest of those options?

**Figure 36.18**
It seems like the macro recorder is making up options that are not on the dialog box.

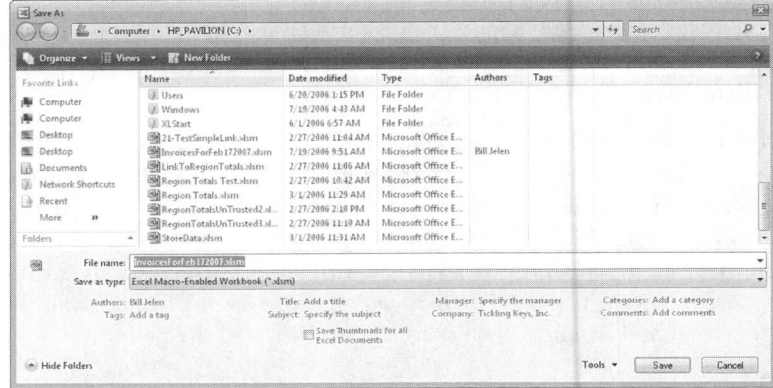

In the bottom corner of the dialog is a Tools drop-down. If you choose Tools and then General Options, you see a dialog box with four additional options, as shown in Figure 36.19. Even though you did not touch this Save Options dialog, Excel recorded the values in it for you.

**Figure 36.19**
Even though you did not touch the Save Options dialog box, the macro recorder recorded the values from it.

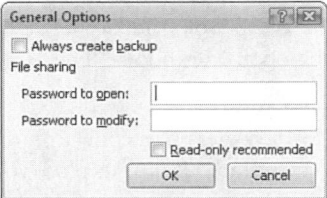

Parameters have some potentially confusing aspects. Most of the time, there is a space following the method and then a list of one or more *ParameterName*:=*ParameterValue* constructs, separated by a comma and a space. However, there are a couple exceptions:

- If the result of the method is acted upon by another method, the list of parameters is enclosed in parentheses, and there is no space after the method name. This commonly happens when you add a chart to a worksheet and then Excel selects the chart.

- When you use the parameter name, you can specify the parameters in any sequence you like. The Help topic for the method reveals the official default order for the parameters. If you specify the parameters in the exact sequence specified in Help, you are allowed to leave off the parameter names. However, this is a poor coding practice. Even if you've memorized the default order for the parameters, you can not assume that everyone else reading your code will know the default order. The problem is that sometimes the macro recorder will record code in this style. For example, here is a line of code that was recorded when I added WordArt to a worksheet:

```
ActiveSheet.Shapes.AddTextEffect(msoTextEffect2, "Test", _
    "Arial Black", 36#, msoFalse, msoFalse, 323.25, 142.5).Select
```

It would be very difficult to figure out this line of code without looking at the help topic. To access Help, you can click anywhere in the method of AddTextEffect. The help topic reveals that the correct parameter order is the one shown in Figure 36.20.

**Figure 36.20**
The Help topic for each method helps decode the default order of the parameters.

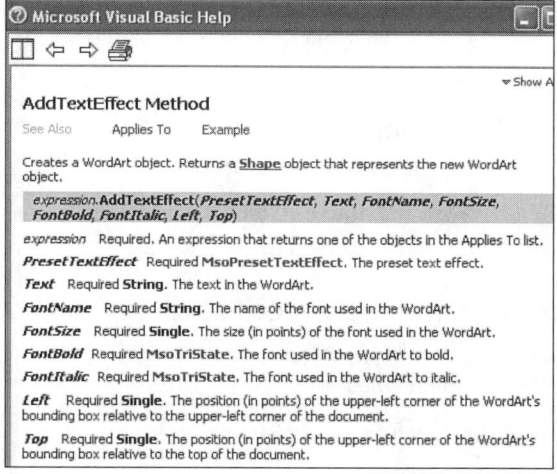

Again, parameters are like adverbs. They generally appear with a *ParameterName:=* *ParameterValue* construct, but there are times when the macro recorder lists the parameter values in their default order, without the parameter names or the :=.

---

**Accessing VBA Help**

If you are going to be recording and editing macros, you need to have the VBA Help file installed on the computer. Frustratingly, it is not installed by default. If Help is not installed on your machine, it is worth your time to find the installation disc and reinstall Excel with the VBA Help option selected.

When VBA Help is installed, you can click on any object, method, argument, or parameter in VBA and press the F1 key to display a complete description of the item. The Help topic lists the valid properties associated with the object and the valid methods that can be used on the object. Often, the Help topic will include an example as well. To use the code in the example, you can highlight the code, press Ctrl+C to copy, and then paste this code directly into the Code pane of the VBE.

---

## COMPARING ADJECTIVES

The final construct in VBA is the adjective used to describe an object. In VBA, adjectives are called *properties*. Think about a cell in Excel with a formula in it. The cell has many properties. These are some of the most popular properties:

- Value (the value shown in the cell)
- Formula (the formula used to calculate Value)
- Font Name
- Font Size
- Font Color
- Cell Interior Color

In VBA, you can either check on the value of a property or you can set the property to a new value. To change several cells to be bold, for example, you would change their Bold property to true:

```
Selection.Font.Bold = True
```

You could also check to see if a property equals a certain value.

```
If Selection.Value = 100 then Selection.Font.Bold = True
```

Properties are generally used with the dot construct, and they are almost always followed by = (as contrasted with the := used with parameters). For example, PropertyName = value.

## USING THE ANALOGY WHILE EXAMINING RECORDED CODE

When you understand that a period generally separates an object from a method, you can start to make sense of the recorded code.

For example, the following line performs the Open method:

```
Workbooks.Open Filename:="C:\Invoices.xls"
```
In this example, the Filename parameter is shown with := after the parameter name.

This first line in the following example performs the Select method on one particular member of the Rows collection:

```
Rows("1:1").Select
Selection.Font.Bold = True
```

The second line then sets the Bold property of the Font property of the selection to true. Using these two lines of code is equivalent to selecting Row 1 and clicking the Bold icon.

**TIP FROM**

In the Excel user interface, you generally have to select a cell before you can change something in it. In a macro, there is no need to select something first. For example, you can replace the two lines in the preceding example with this single line of code:

```
Rows("1:1").Font.Bold = True
```

The advantage of this method is that the macro will run even faster than before.

# USING SIMPLE VARIABLES AND OBJECT VARIABLES

The macro recorder never records a variable, but you can add variables to a macro when you edit the code. Let's say that you need to do a number of operations to the row where the totals will be located. Rather than repeatedly going to the last row in the spreadsheet and pressing the End+Up Arrow, you could assign the row number to a variable:

```
FinalRow = Range("A1048576").End(xlup).Row
TotalRow = FinalRow + 1
```

The words FinalRow and TotalRow are variables that each hold a single value. If you have data in Rows 2 through 25 today, FinalRow will hold the value 25, and TotalRow will hold the value of 26. This allows you to use efficient code such as the following:

```
Range("A" & TotalRow).Value = "Total"
Range("C" & TotalRow).Formula = "=SUM(C2:C"& TotalRow & ")"
Range("D" & TotalRow).Formula = "=SUM(D2:E"& TotalRow & ")"
Range("E" & TotalRow).Formula = "=SUM(E2:E"& TotalRow & ")"
```

VBA also offers a powerful variable called an *object variable*. An object variable can be used to represent any object, such as a worksheet, a chart, or a cell. Whereas a simple variable holds one value, an object variable holds values for every property associated with the object.

Object variables are declared using the Dim statement and then assigned using the Set statement:

```
Dim WSD as worksheet
Set WSD = Worksheets("Sheet1")
```

Using object variables offers several advantages. First, it is easier to refer to WSD than to ActiveWorkbook.Worksheets("Sheet1"). Second, if you define the object variable with a DIM statement at the beginning of the macro, as you type new lines of code, the VBE's AutoComplete feature shows a list of valid methods and properties for the object, as shown in Figure 36.21.

**Figure 36.21**
Object variables hold many properties instead of a single value.

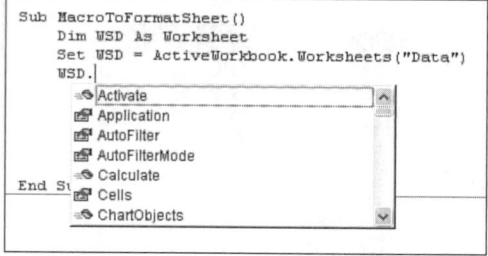

# USING R1C1-STYLE FORMULAS

If you are a history buff, you might know that VisiCalc was the first spreadsheet program for PCs. When Dan Bricklin and Bob Frankston invented VisiCalc, they used the A1 style for naming cells. In those early days, VisiCalc had competitors such as SuperCalc and a Microsoft program called MultiPlan. This early Microsoft spreadsheet used the notation of R1C1 to refer to Cell A1. The cell that we know today as E17 would have been called R17C5, for Row 17, Column 5.

In 1985, Microsoft launched Excel version 1.0 for the Macintosh. Excel originally continued to use the R1C1 style of notation. During the next 10 years, Excel and Lotus 1-2-3 were

36

locked in a bitter battle for market share. Lotus was the early leader, and it had adopted the A1 notation style familiar to VisiCalc customers. To capture more market share, Microsoft allowed Excel to use either A1-style notation or R1C1-style notation. Even today, in Excel 2007, you can turn on R1C1 style notation (by choosing Office Icon, Excel Options, Formulas, R1C1 Reference Style). Hardly anyone actually uses R1C1 reference style; however, the macro recorder always records formulas in R1C1 style.

Figure 36.22 shows the familiar formula =SUM(D$2:D15). When entered in Cell D16, this formula adds up everything from Row 2 to the row just above the current cell.

**Figure 36.22**
This familiar formula
is in A1-style notation.

| | A | B | C | D | E | F |
|---|---|---|---|---|---|---|
| | | | | fx | =SUM(D$2:D15) | |
| 1 | NAME | DATE | INVOICE | REVENUE | S TAX | TOTAL |
| 2 | TERRI DONOVAN | 2/17/2007 | 10217 | 252.11 | 15.13 | 267.24 |
| 3 | ELSIE HOUSTON | 2/17/2007 | 10218 | 68.67 | 4.12 | 72.79 |
| 4 | HAROLD HARTMAN | 2/17/2007 | 10219 | 111.4 | 6.68 | 118.08 |
| 5 | SHAWN GREER | 2/17/2007 | 10220 | 151.47 | 9.09 | 160.56 |
| 6 | KRISTIN ATKINS | 2/17/2007 | 10221 | 131.71 | 7.9 | 139.61 |
| 7 | DAVID ALLEN | 2/17/2007 | 10222 | 221.62 | 13.3 | 234.92 |
| 8 | ROSA PRATT | 2/17/2007 | 10223 | 225.02 | 13.5 | 238.52 |
| 9 | NORA SHEPHERD | 2/17/2007 | 10224 | 261.84 | 15.71 | 277.55 |
| 10 | CRAIG BERNARD | 2/17/2007 | 10225 | 195.08 | 11.7 | 206.78 |
| 11 | BILLIE CRAWFORD | 2/17/2007 | 10226 | 72.31 | 4.34 | 76.65 |
| 12 | ADAM WINTERS | 2/17/2007 | 10227 | 168.12 | 10.09 | 178.21 |
| 13 | ANDREW DODSON | 2/17/2007 | 10228 | 79.54 | 4.77 | 84.31 |
| 14 | BRANDI SHAW | 2/17/2007 | 10229 | 258.73 | 15.52 | 274.25 |
| 15 | LAURIE HOWARD | 2/17/2007 | 10230 | 248.44 | 14.91 | 263.35 |
| 16 | Total | | | 2446.06 | 146.76 | 2592.82 |
| 17 | | | | | | |

*(Cell reference box: D16)*

If you now turn on R1C1 style in this worksheet, the formula changes to =SUM(R2C:R[-1]C), as shown in Figure 36.23.

**Figure 36.23**
The formula in R1C1
notation would be
confusing to most
spreadsheet users.

| | 1 | 2 | 3 | 4 | 5 | 6 |
|---|---|---|---|---|---|---|
| | | | | fx | =SUM(R2C:R[-1]C) | |
| 1 | NAME | DATE | INVOICE | REVENUE | S TAX | TOTAL |
| 2 | TERRI DONOVAN | 2/17/2007 | 10217 | 252.11 | 15.13 | 267.24 |
| 3 | ELSIE HOUSTON | 2/17/2007 | 10218 | 68.67 | 4.12 | 72.79 |
| 4 | HAROLD HARTMAN | 2/17/2007 | 10219 | 111.4 | 6.68 | 118.08 |
| 5 | SHAWN GREER | 2/17/2007 | 10220 | 151.47 | 9.09 | 160.56 |
| 6 | KRISTIN ATKINS | 2/17/2007 | 10221 | 131.71 | 7.9 | 139.61 |
| 7 | DAVID ALLEN | 2/17/2007 | 10222 | 221.62 | 13.3 | 234.92 |
| 8 | ROSA PRATT | 2/17/2007 | 10223 | 225.02 | 13.5 | 238.52 |
| 9 | NORA SHEPHERD | 2/17/2007 | 10224 | 261.84 | 15.71 | 277.55 |
| 10 | CRAIG BERNARD | 2/17/2007 | 10225 | 195.08 | 11.7 | 206.78 |
| 11 | BILLIE CRAWFORD | 2/17/2007 | 10226 | 72.31 | 4.34 | 76.65 |
| 12 | ADAM WINTERS | 2/17/2007 | 10227 | 168.12 | 10.09 | 178.21 |
| 13 | ANDREW DODSON | 2/17/2007 | 10228 | 79.54 | 4.77 | 84.31 |
| 14 | BRANDI SHAW | 2/17/2007 | 10229 | 258.73 | 15.52 | 274.25 |
| 15 | LAURIE HOWARD | 2/17/2007 | 10230 | 248.44 | 14.91 | 263.35 |
| 16 | Total | | | 2446.06 | 146.76 | 2592.82 |
| 17 | | | | | | |

*(Cell reference box: R16C4)*

In R1C1 notation, the reference RC refers to the current cell. You can modify RC by adding a particular row number or column number. For example, R2C refers to the cell in Row 2 of the current column. RC1 refers to the cell in this row that is in Column 1.

If you put a row number or column number in square brackets, it refers to a relative number of cells from the current cell. If you have a formula in Cell D16 and use the reference

R[1]C[-2], you are referring to the cell one row below D16 and two columns to the left of D16, which would be cell B17.

You are probably wondering why the macro recorder uses this arcane notation style when recording formulas. It turns out that this style is fantastic for formulas. For example, take a look at the formulas in Column F of the worksheet, as shown in Figure 36.24. Every formula is a little different. When you copy F2 to F3, Excel has to change the references of E2 and D2 to be E3 and D3.

**Figure 36.24**
In A1 style, every formula in F2:F15 is different.

| D | E | F |
|---|---|---|
| **REVENUE** | **SALES TAX** | **TOTAL** |
| 252.11 | =ROUND(0.06*D2,2) | =+E2+D2 |
| 68.67 | =ROUND(0.06*D3,2) | =+E3+D3 |
| 111.4 | =ROUND(0.06*D4,2) | =+E4+D4 |
| 151.47 | =ROUND(0.06*D5,2) | =+E5+D5 |
| 131.71 | =ROUND(0.06*D6,2) | =+E6+D6 |
| 221.62 | =ROUND(0.06*D7,2) | =+E7+D7 |
| 225.02 | =ROUND(0.06*D8,2) | =+E8+D8 |
| 261.84 | =ROUND(0.06*D9,2) | =+E9+D9 |
| 195.08 | =ROUND(0.06*D10,2) | =+E10+D10 |
| 72.31 | =ROUND(0.06*D11,2) | =+E11+D11 |
| 168.12 | =ROUND(0.06*D12,2) | =+E12+D12 |
| 79.54 | =ROUND(0.06*D13,2) | =+E13+D13 |
| 258.73 | =ROUND(0.06*D14,2) | =+E14+D14 |
| 248.44 | =ROUND(0.06*D15,2) | =+E15+D15 |
| =SUM(D$2:D15) | =SUM(E2:E15) | =SUM(F2:F15) |

Now, look at these same formulas in R1C1 style, as shown in Figure 36.25. Every formula in that range is exactly identical. This makes sense: The formula is actually saying, "Add the sales tax one cell to the left of me to the merchandise amount that is two cells to the left of me."

**Figure 36.25**
In R1C1 style, every formula in F2:F15 is identical.

| 4 | 5 | 6 |
|---|---|---|
| **REVENUE** | **SALES TAX** | **TOTAL** |
| 252.11 | =ROUND(0.06*RC[-1],2) | =+RC[-1]+RC[-2] |
| 68.67 | =ROUND(0.06*RC[-1],2) | =+RC[-1]+RC[-2] |
| 111.4 | =ROUND(0.06*RC[-1],2) | =+RC[-1]+RC[-2] |
| 151.47 | =ROUND(0.06*RC[-1],2) | =+RC[-1]+RC[-2] |
| 131.71 | =ROUND(0.06*RC[-1],2) | =+RC[-1]+RC[-2] |
| 221.62 | =ROUND(0.06*RC[-1],2) | =+RC[-1]+RC[-2] |
| 225.02 | =ROUND(0.06*RC[-1],2) | =+RC[-1]+RC[-2] |
| 261.84 | =ROUND(0.06*RC[-1],2) | =+RC[-1]+RC[-2] |
| 195.08 | =ROUND(0.06*RC[-1],2) | =+RC[-1]+RC[-2] |
| 72.31 | =ROUND(0.06*RC[-1],2) | =+RC[-1]+RC[-2] |
| 168.12 | =ROUND(0.06*RC[-1],2) | =+RC[-1]+RC[-2] |
| 79.54 | =ROUND(0.06*RC[-1],2) | =+RC[-1]+RC[-2] |
| 258.73 | =ROUND(0.06*RC[-1],2) | =+RC[-1]+RC[-2] |
| 248.44 | =ROUND(0.06*RC[-1],2) | =+RC[-1]+RC[-2] |
| =SUM(R2C:R[-1]C) | =SUM(R[-14]C:R[-1]C) | =SUM(R[-14]C:R[ |

If you were forced to use A1-style formulas in a macro, you might have to enter the formula in Cell F2 and then copy the formula from F2 to the remaining cells:

```
Range("F2").Formula = "=D2+E2"
Range("F2").Copy Destination:=Range("F3:F15")
```

Instead, using R1C1 style formulas, you can enter all the formulas in one line of code:

```
Range("F2:F15").FormulaR1C1 = "=RC[-2]+RC[-1]"
```

If you are not yet convinced to learn how to use R1C1-style formulas, the final straw is that you have to use R1C1-style formulas when setting up conditional formatting in VBA.

## FIXING CALCULATION ERRORS IN MACROS

Probably the most important reason to understand R1C1 formulas is to make sure that the macro recorder recorded the proper formula. Remember that when you recorded the macro described in the section "Using the End Key to Handle a Variable Number of Rows" earlier in this chapter, you had selected cells D16:F16 and clicked the AutoSum button. Excel recorded the following line of code:

```
Selection.FormulaR1C1 = "=SUM(R[-14]C:R[-1]C)"
```

This formula adds up a range from 14 rows above the selection to the cell just above the selection. This works only on days on which you have exactly 14 rows of data. This is one of the most annoying bugs in a macro. Although many times, a macro will return an error if you try to do something wrong, if you run this macro on tomorrow's invoice file and there are 20 invoices, the macro will happily total only the last 14 invoices instead of all 20 invoices. You could easily distribute this report with a wrong total for several days before someone realizes that something is amiss.

It is easy to correct the formula. You know that you have headings in Row 1 and the first invoice will appear in Row 2. You need the macro to sum from Row 2 to the row just above the current cell. Therefore, you need to change the formula to this:

```
Selection.FormulaR1C1 = "=SUM(R2C:R[-1]C)"
```

# CUSTOMIZING THE EVERYDAY-USE MACRO EXAMPLE: GetOpenFileName AND GetSaveAsFileName

The everyday-use macro you recorded earlier in this chapter (for formatting an invoice register) is hard-coded to always open the same file and to always save with the same filename. To make the macro more general, you might like to allow the person running the macro to browse for the file each morning and then to specify a new filename during the Save As. Excel offers a very easy way to display the File Open or File Save As dialog. Here is the code you need to use:

```
FileToOpen = Application.GetOpenFileName( _
    FileFilter:="Excel Files,*.xlsm", _
    Title:="Select Today's Invoice File")
```

Note that this code displays the File Open dialog and allows a file to be selected. When you click Open, the dialog assigns the filename to the variable. It does not actually open the file. You then need to open the file specified in the variable:

```
Workbooks.Open Filename:=FileToOpen
```

When you want to ask for the filename to use in saving the file, use this code:

```
    NewFileName = Application.GetSaveAsFilename( _
        Title:="Select File Name for Today")
    ActiveWorkbook.SaveAs Filename:=NewFileName, _
        FileFormat:=xlOpenXMLWorkbookMacroEnabled
```

The following macro is the final macro to use each day:

```
Sub ImportInvoicesFixed()
' ImportInvoices Macro
' With Changes
    FileToOpen = Application.GetOpenFileName( _
        FileFilter:= _
        "Excel files (*.xls;*.xlsb;*.xlsx;*.xlsm)" & _
        ",*.xls;*.xlsb;*.xlsx;*.xlsb)",
        Title:="Select Today's Invoice File")
    Workbooks.Open Filename:=FileToOpen
    Application.Goto Reference:="R1048576C1"
    Selection.End(xlUp).Select
    ActiveCell.Offset(1, 0).Range("A1").Select
    ActiveCell.FormulaR1C1 = "'Total"
    ActiveCell.Offset(0, 3).Range("A1:C1").Select
    Selection.FormulaR1C1 = "=SUM(R[-14]C:R[-1]C)"
    Selection.Columns.AutoFit
    Rows("1:1").Select
    Selection.Font.Bold = True
    Cells.Select
    Range("A1").Select
    Selection.EntireRow.Insert
    Selection.EntireRow.Insert
    ActiveCell.FormulaR1C1 = _
        "=""Invoices for ""&TEXT(R[3]C[1],""mmmm d, yyyy"")"
    Range("A2").Select
    NewFileName = Application.GetSaveAsFilename( _
        Title:="Select File Name for Today")
    ActiveWorkbook.SaveAs Filename:=NewFileName, _
        FileFormat:=xlOpenXMLWorkbookMacroEnabled
End Sub
```

Out of the 19 lines in the macro, you needed to correct 1 line—the total formula. In order to add functionality, you added two lines and changed two other lines. This is fairly typical: Perhaps 10% to 20% of a recorded macro generally needs to be adjusted.

# FROM-SCRATCH MACRO EXAMPLE: LOOPS, FLOW CONTROL, AND REFERRING TO RANGES

Say you work for a company that sells printers and scanners to commercial accounts. When you sell a piece of hardware, you also try to sell a service plan for that hardware. Customers in your state are taxed. Your accounting software provides a daily download that looks like Columns A:D in Figure 36.26.

You want to create a macro that examines each row in the dataset and carries out a different action, based on the value in Column D. This is a macro that you will probably want to write from scratch. The following sections describe how you do it.

## LOOPING THROUGH ALL ROWS

The loop most commonly used in VBA is a For-Next loop. This is identical to the loop that you might have learned about in a BASIC class.

36

**Figure 36.26**
Your accounting software groups all hardware, service, and tax amounts into a single column.

A31 | 1018

| | A | B | C | D |
|---|---|---|---|---|
| 1 | **Invoice** | **Customer** | **Product** | **Revenue** |
| 2 | 1010 | Supreme Toothpick Company | Printer | 262 |
| 3 | 1010 | Supreme Toothpick Company | Scanner | 454 |
| 4 | 1010 | Supreme Toothpick Company | Service Plan | 107 |
| 5 | 1010 | Supreme Toothpick Company | Sales Tax | 49.38 |
| 6 | 1011 | Fashionable Necktie Company | Printer | 127 |
| 7 | 1011 | Fashionable Necktie Company | Scanner | 994 |
| 8 | 1011 | Fashionable Necktie Company | Sales Tax | 67.26 |
| 9 | 1012 | Top-Notch Juicer Inc. | Printer | 985 |
| 10 | 1012 | Top-Notch Juicer Inc. | Service Plan | 148 |
| 11 | 1012 | Top-Notch Juicer Inc. | Sales Tax | 67.98 |
| 12 | 1013 | Unusual Aquarium Traders | Printer | 290 |
| 13 | 1013 | Unusual Aquarium Traders | Scanner | 655 |
| 14 | 1013 | Unusual Aquarium Traders | Sales Tax | 56.7 |

In this example, the loop starts with a `For` statement. You specify that on each pass through the loop, a certain variable will change from a low value to a high value. This simple macro will run through the loop 10 times. On the first pass through the loop, the variable `x` will be equal to `1`. The two lines inside the loop will assign the value `1` to Cells A1 and B1. When the macro encounters the `Next x` line, it will return to the start of the loop, increment `x` by `1`, and run through the loop again. The next time through the loop, the value of `x` will be `2`. Cell A2 will be assigned the number `2`, and cell B2 will show `4` (which is the square of 2). Eventually, `x` will be equal to `10`. At the `Next x` line, the macro will allow the loop to finish. The following is the code for this `macro`:

```
Sub WriteSquares()
    For x = 1 To 10
        Range("A" & x).Value = x
        Range("B" & x).Value = x * x
    Next x
End Sub
```

After you run this macro, you have a simple table that shows the numbers 1 through 10 and their squares, as shown in Figure 36.27

**Figure 36.27**
This simple loop fills in 10 rows.

R26C12

| | 1 | 2 |
|---|---|---|
| 2 | 2 | 4 |
| 3 | 3 | 9 |
| 4 | 4 | 16 |
| 5 | 5 | 25 |
| 6 | 6 | 36 |
| 7 | 7 | 49 |
| 8 | 8 | 64 |
| 9 | 9 | 81 |
| 10 | 10 | 100 |

After a loop is written, it is easy to adjust it. If you want a table showing all the squares from 1 to 100, you would simply adjust the `For x = 1 to 10` line to be `For x = 1 to 100`.

There is an optional clause in the `For` statement called the *step value*. If no step value is shown, the program moves through the loop by incrementing the variable by 1 each time through the loop. If you wanted to check only the even-numbered rows, you could change the loop to be `For x = 2 to 100 Step 2`.

If you are going to be optionally deleting rows from a range of data, it is important to start at the bottom and proceed to the top of the range. You would use `-1` as the step value:

```
For x = 100 to 1 step -1
```

## REFERRING TO RANGES

The macro recorder uses the `Range` property to refer to a particular range. You might see the macro recorder refer to ranges such as `Range("B3")` or `Range("W1:Z100")`.

The loop code shown in the preceding section emulates this style of referring to ranges. On the third time through the loop, this line of code would refer to Cell B3:

```
Range("B" & x).value = x * x
```

But what if you wanted to loop through each column? How would you handle that? If you wanted to continue using the `Range` property, you would have to jump through some hoops to figure out the letter that is associated with Column 5:

```
For y = 1 to 26
    ThisCol = Char(64+y)
    Range(ThisCol & 1).value = ThisCol
Next y
```

This method works fine if you are using only 26 or fewer columns. But if you needed to loop through all the columns out to Column XFD, you would spend all day trying to write the logic to assign the column label WMJ to Column 15896.

Instead of using the `Range` property, you can use the `Cells` property. `Cells` requires that you specify a numeric row number and a numeric column number. For example, Cell B3 would be specified as follows:

```
Cells(3, 2)
```

If you need to refer to a rectangular range, you can use the `Resize` property. `Resize` requires you to specify the number of rows and the number of columns. To refer to W1:Z100, for example, you would use this:

```
Cells(1, 23).Resize(100, 3)
```

It is certainly difficult to figure out that this refers to W1:Z100, but it allows you to easily loop through rows or columns.

You could use the following code to make every other column bold:

```
For y = 1 to 100 step 2
    Cells(1, y).Resize(200, 1).Font.Bold = True
Next y
```

36

## COMBINING A LOOP WITH FinalRow

Earlier in this chapter, you learned how to use the End key to find the final row in a dataset. After finding the final row in the dataset and assigning it to a variable, you can specify that the loop should run through FinalRow:

```
FinalRow = Cells(1048576, 1).End(xlUp).row
For x = 2 to FinalRow
    ' Perform some action
Next x
```

# MAKING DECISIONS BY USING FLOW CONTROL

*Flow control* is the ability to make decisions within a macro. As described in the following sections, two commonly used flow control constructs are If-End If and Select Case.

### USING THE IF-END IF CONSTRUCT

Say that you need a macro to delete any records that say Sales Tax. You could accomplish this with a simple If-End If construct:

```
If Cells(x, 4).Value = "Sales Tax" Then
    Cells(x, 1).EntireRow.Delete
End If
```

This construct always starts with the word If, followed by a logical test, followed by the word Then. Every line between the first line and the End If line is executed only if the logical test is true.

Now say that you want to enhance the macro so that any other amounts that contain service plan revenue are moved to Column F. To do this, you use the ElseIf line to enter a second condition and block of lines to be used in that condition:

```
If Cells(x, 4).Value = "Sales Tax" Then
    Cells(x, 1).EntireRow.Delete
ElseIf Cells(x, 4).Value = "Service Plan" Then
    Cells(x, 5).Cut Destination:=Cells(x, 6)
End If
```

You could continue adding ElseIf statements to handle other situations. Eventually, just before the End If, you could add an Else block to handle any other condition that you haven't thought about.

### USING THE Select Case CONSTRUCT

If you reach a point where you have many ElseIf statements all testing the same value, it might make sense to switch to a Select Case construct. To illustrate, say that you want to loop through all the records, examining the product in Column C. If Column C contains a printer, you want to move the amount in Column D to a new Column E. Scanner revenue should go to a new Column F. Service plans go to a new Column H. Sales tax goes to a new Column I. You should also handle the situation where something is sold and contains none of those products. In that case, you would move the revenue to a new Column G.

The construct begins with Select Case and then the value to check. The construct ends with End Select, which is similar to End If.

Each subblock of code starts with the word Case and one or more possible values. If you needed to check for Printer or Printers, you would enclose each in quotes and separate them with a comma.

After checking for all the possible values you can think of, you might add a Case Else subblock to handle any other stray values that might be entered in Column C.

The following code checks to see what product is in column C. Depending on the product, the program copies the revenue from column D to a specific column.

```
Select Case Cells(x, 3).Value
    Case "Printer", "Printers"
        Cells(x, 4).Copy Destination:=Cells(x, 5)
    Case "Scanner", "Scanners"
        Cells(x, 4).Copy Destination:=Cells(x, 6)
    Case "Service Plan"
        Cells(x, 4).Copy Destination:=Cells(x, 8)
    Case "Sales Tax"
        Cells(x, 4).Copy Destination:=Cells(x, 9)
    Case Else
        ' Something unexpected was sold
        Cells(x, 4).Copy Destination:=Cells(x, 7)
End Select
```

## Putting Together the From-Scratch Example: Testing Each Record in a Loop

Using the building blocks described in the preceding sections, you can now write the code for a macro that finds the last row, loops through the records, and copies the total revenue to the appropriate column. Now you need to add new headings for the additional columns, as shown in Figure 3.28.

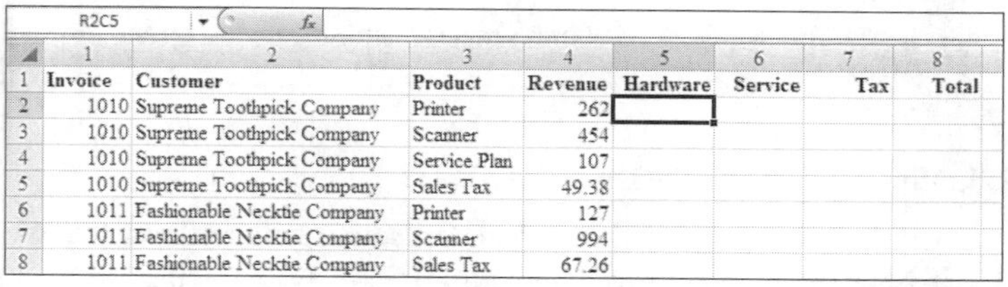

**Figure 36.28**
Adding new headings before running the macro.

| | 1 | 2 | 3 | 4 | 5 | 6 | 7 | 8 |
|---|---|---|---|---|---|---|---|---|
| 1 | Invoice | Customer | Product | Revenue | Hardware | Service | Tax | Total |
| 2 | 1010 | Supreme Toothpick Company | Printer | 262 | | | | |
| 3 | 1010 | Supreme Toothpick Company | Scanner | 454 | | | | |
| 4 | 1010 | Supreme Toothpick Company | Service Plan | 107 | | | | |
| 5 | 1010 | Supreme Toothpick Company | Sales Tax | 49.38 | | | | |
| 6 | 1011 | Fashionable Necktie Company | Printer | 127 | | | | |
| 7 | 1011 | Fashionable Necktie Company | Scanner | 994 | | | | |
| 8 | 1011 | Fashionable Necktie Company | Sales Tax | 67.26 | | | | |

The macro should use the End property to locate the final row. It should also prefill Columns E through I with 0s. Next, it should loop from Row 2 down to the final row. For each record, the revenue column should be moved to one of the columns. At the end of the loop, the program alerts you that the program is complete, using a MsgBox command. The following is the complete code of this macro:

```
Sub MoveRevenue2()
    FinalRow = Cells(65536, 1).End(xlUp).Row
    Range("E2", Cells(FinalRow, 9)).Value = 0
    For x = FinalRow To 2 Step -1
```

```
        Select Case Cells(x, 3).Value
            Case "Printer", "Printers"
                Cells(x, 4).Copy Destination:=Cells(x, 5)
            Case "Scanner", "Scanners"
                Cells(x, 4).Copy Destination:=Cells(x, 6)
            Case "Service Plan"
                Cells(x, 4).Copy Destination:=Cells(x, 8)
            Case "Sales Tax"
                Cells(x, 4).Copy Destination:=Cells(x, 9)
            Case Else
                ' Something unexpected was sold
                Cells(x, 4).Copy Destination:=Cells(x, 7)
        End Select
    Next x
    MsgBox "Macro complete"
End Sub
```

After you run this macro, you see that the revenue amounts have been copied to the appropriate columns, as shown in Figure 36.29.

**Figure 36.29**
After running the macro, you have a breakout of revenue by product.

| | 1 | 2 | 3 | 4 | 5 | 6 | 7 | 8 | 9 |
|---|---|---|---|---|---|---|---|---|---|
| 1 | Invoice | Customer | Product | Revenue | Printer | Scanner | Accessory | Service | Tax |
| 2 | 1010 | Supreme Toothpick Company | Printer | 262 | 262 | 0 | 0 | 0 | 0 |
| 3 | 1010 | Supreme Toothpick Company | Scanner | 454 | 0 | 454 | 0 | 0 | 0 |
| 4 | 1010 | Supreme Toothpick Company | Service Plan | 107 | 0 | 0 | 0 | 107 | 0 |
| 5 | 1010 | Supreme Toothpick Company | Sales Tax | 49.38 | 0 | 0 | 0 | 0 | 49.38 |
| 6 | 1011 | Fashionable Necktie Company | Printer | 127 | 127 | 0 | 0 | 0 | 0 |
| 7 | 1011 | Fashionable Necktie Company | Scanner | 994 | 0 | 994 | 0 | 0 | 0 |
| 8 | 1011 | Fashionable Necktie Company | Sales Tax | 67.26 | 0 | 0 | 0 | 0 | 67.26 |

TIP FROM

An alternative syntax of the `Range` property is to specify the top-left and bottom-right cells in the range, separated by a comma. In the macro described here, for example, you know you want to fill from Cell E2 to the last row in Column I. You can describe this range as follows:

```
Range("E2", Cells(FinalRow, 9))
```

This syntax is sometimes simpler than using `Cells()` and `Resize()`.

## A SPECIAL CASE: DELETING SOME RECORDS

If a loop will be conditionally deleting records, you will run into trouble if it is a typical For-Next loop. Let's say you want to delete all the sales tax records, as follows:

```
Sub ThisWontWork()
    FinalRow = Cells(65536, 1).End(xlUp).Row
    For x = 2 To FinalRow
        If Cells(x, 3).Value = "Sales Tax" Then
            Cells(x, 1).EntireRow.Delete
        Else
            Cells(x, 5).Value = "Checked"
        End If
    Next x
End Sub
```

Consider the data in Figure 36.30.

**Figure 36.30**
A forward-running loop encounters problems.

The first time through the loop, x is equal to 2. Cell C2 does not contain tax, so Cell E2 has the word checked. A similar result occurs for Rows 3 and 4. The fourth time through the loop, Cell C5 contains tax. The macro deletes the tax in Row 5. However, Excel then moves the old Row 6 up to Row 5, as shown in Figure 36.31. The next time through the loop, the program inspects Row 6, and the data that is now in Row 5 will never be checked.

**Figure 36.31**
The old Row 6 data moves up to occupy the deleted Row 5. This row will never be checked.

The macro succeeds in deleting tax, but several rows were never checked, and several extra blank rows at the bottom were needlessly checked, as shown in Figure 36.32.

**Figure 36.32**
Several rows went unchecked in this loop.

The solution is to have the loop run backward. You need to start at the final row and proceed up through the sheet to Row 2. When the macro deletes tax in Row 31, it can then proceed to checking Row 30, knowing that nothing has been destroyed (yet) in Row 30 and above.

To reverse the flow of the loop, you have to tell the loop to start at the final row, but you also have to tell the loop to use a step value of -1. The start of the loop would use this line of code:

```
For x = FinalRow to 2 Step -1
```

The macro needed here represents a fairly common task: looping through all the records in order to conditionally do something to each record.

The following macro correctly deletes all the sales tax records:

```
Sub DeleteTaxOK()
    FinalRow = Cells(65536, 1).End(xlUp).Row
    For x = FinalRow To 2 Step -1
        If Cells(x, 3).Value = "Sales Tax" Then
            Cells(x, 1).EntireRow.Delete
        Else
            Cells(x, 5).Value = "Checked"
        End If
    Next x
End Sub
```

For the example described here, the macro recorder would be almost no help. You would have to write this simple macro from scratch. However, it is a powerful macro that can simplify tasks when you have hundreds of thousands of rows of data.

> **NOTE**
>
> It is common to indent each line of code with four spaces. Any lines of code inside an If-EndIf block or inside a For-Next loop are indented an additional four spaces. If you have typed a line of code that is indented eight spaces and press Enter at the end of the line of code, the VBE will automatically indent the next line to eight spaces. Each press of the Tab key will indent by an additional four spaces. Pressing Shift+Tab will remove four spaces of indentation.

# COMBINATION MACRO EXAMPLE: CREATING A REPORT FOR EACH CUSTOMER

Many real-life scenarios require you to use a combination of recorded code and code written from scratch. For example, Figure 36.33 shows a dataset with all your invoices for the year. In this case, say you would like to produce a workbook for each customer that you can mail to the customer.

One way to handle this task would be to use an advanced filter to get a list of all unique customers in Column A. You would then loop through these customers, applying an AutoFilter to the dataset in order to see only the customers that match the selected customer. After the dataset is filtered, you could select the visible cells only and copy them to a new workbook. Then you could save the workbook with the name of the customer and then return to the original workbook.

**Figure 36.33**
The goal is to provide a subset of this data to each customer.

R17C12

| | 1 | 2 | 3 | 4 | 5 | 6 |
|---|---|---|---|---|---|---|
| 1 | **Customer** | **Invoice** | **Date** | **Purchases** | **Paid** | **Open Balance** |
| 2 | Hip Lawn Corporation | 1001 | 1/2/07 | 8846 | 8846 | 0 |
| 3 | Vivid Chopstick Traders | 1002 | 1/2/07 | 1688 | 1688 | 0 |
| 4 | Unusual Doorbell Company | 1003 | 1/2/07 | 8415 | 8415 | 0 |
| 5 | Excellent Utensil Corporation | 1004 | 1/2/07 | 2619 | 2619 | 0 |
| 6 | Hip Lawn Corporation | 1005 | 1/3/07 | 11476 | 11476 | 0 |
| 7 | Fascinating Oven Supply | 1006 | 1/3/07 | 4958 | 0 | 4958 |
| 8 | Savory Glass Inc. | 1007 | 1/3/07 | 11243 | 11243 | 0 |
| 9 | Superior Bobsled Corporation | 1008 | 1/3/07 | 4419 | 4419 | 0 |
| 10 | Hip Lawn Corporation | 1009 | 1/3/07 | 12562 | 12562 | 0 |
| 11 | Savory Glass Inc. | 1010 | 1/3/07 | 7409 | 7409 | 0 |
| 12 | Fascinating Oven Supply | 1011 | 1/4/07 | 8141 | 0 | 8141 |
| 13 | Steadfast Meter Inc. | 1012 | 1/4/07 | 2744 | 2744 | 0 |
| 14 | Hip Lawn Corporation | 1013 | 1/4/07 | 4876 | 4876 | 0 |

You could start by creating a blank procedure with comments to spell out the steps in the preceding paragraphs. Then you would add in code for the loop and other simple tasks, such as copying the selection to a new workbook. Whenever you encounter a step that you've never written code for, you could just leave a comment with question marks. This would allow you to go back and record parts of the process in order to finish the macro.

Your first pass at a well-commented macro might look like this:

```
Sub ProduceReportForEachCustomer()
    ' Define object variables for new workbook
    Dim WBN As Workbook
    Dim WSN As Worksheet
    ' Define object variables for the current workbook
    Dim WBO As Workbook
    Dim WSO As Worksheet
    Set WBO = ActiveWorkbook
    Set WSO = ActiveSheet

    ' Find the FinalRow in today's dataset
    FinalRow = Range("A60000").End(xlUp).Row

    ' Use an Advanced filter to copy unique customers
    ' from column A to column H
    ' ???

    'Find the final customer in column H
    FinalCust = Range("H1").End(xlDown).Row

    ' Loop through each customer
    For x = 2 To FinalCust
        ' Turn on the AutoFilter for this customer
        ' ???

        ' Create a new workbook
        Set WBN = Workbooks.Add
        Set WSN = WBN.Worksheets(1)


        ' In the original workbook, select visible cells
        ' ???

        ' Copy the selection to the new workbook
```

```
        Selection.Copy Destination:=WSN.Cells(3, 1)

        ' AutoFit columns in the new workbook
        WSN.Columns.AutoFit

        ' Add a title to the new workbook
        WSN.Range("A1").Value = _
            "Recap of Purchases for " & WSN.Cells(4, 1).Value

        ' Save the new book
        WBN.SaveAs Filename:="C:\" & WSN.Cells(4, 1).Value & ".xls"
        WBN.Close SaveChanges:=False

        'Return to the original workbook
        WBO.Activate
        WBN.Select
    Next x

End Sub
```

As described in the following sections, to create this macro, you need to figure out how to code the advanced filter to copy a unique list of customers to Column H. You then need to figure out how to apply a filter to Column A. Finally, you need to figure out how to select only the visible cells from the filter.

## Using the Advanced Filter for Unique Records

You need to figure out how to use an advanced filter to finish the following section of code:

```
' Find the FinalRow in today's dataset
FinalRow = Range("A60000").End(xlUp).Row

' Use an Advanced filter to copy unique customers
' from column A to column H
' ???
```

To use an advanced filter on this section of code, follow these steps:

1. Turn on the macro recorder.

2. On the Data tab, in the Sort & Filter group, click the Advanced icon to open the Advanced Filter dialog.

3. Choose the option Copy to Another Location.

4. Adjust the list range to refer only to Column A. The copy-to range will be Cell H1.

5. Check the Unique Records Only box.

6. When the dialog looks as shown in Figure 36.34, click OK. The result is a new range of data in Column H, with each customer listed just once, as shown in Figure 36.35.

7. On the Developer tab, click Stop Recording.

8. Use the Macros button to choose Macro1 and then select Edit.

**Figure 36.34**
Using an advanced filter to get a unique list of customers.

| | B | C | D | E | F | G | H |
|---|---|---|---|---|---|---|---|
| | Invoice | Date | Purchases | | Paid | Open Balance | Customer |
| | 1001 | 1/2/07 | 8846 | 8846 | 0 | | |
| | 1002 | 1/2/07 | 1688 | 1688 | 0 | | |
| | | | 415 | 8415 | 0 | | |
| | | | 19 | 2619 | 0 | | |
| | | | 76 | 11476 | 0 | | |
| | | | 58 | 0 | 4958 | | |
| | | | 43 | 11243 | 0 | | |
| | | | 19 | 4419 | 0 | | |
| | | | 62 | 12562 | 0 | | |
| | | | 09 | 7409 | 0 | | |
| | | | 41 | 0 | 8141 | | |
| | | | 44 | 2744 | 0 | | |
| | | | 76 | 4876 | 0 | | |
| | 1014 | 1/4/07 | 7613 | 7613 | 0 | | |

**Advanced Filter**

Action
- ○ Filter the list, in-place
- ● Copy to another location

List range: $A$1:$F$1001
Criteria range:
Copy to: $H$1
☑ Unique records only

[ OK ] [ Cancel ]

**Figure 36.35**
The advanced filter produces a list of customers for the macro to loop through.

| Customer | |
|---|---|
| Hip Lawn Corporation | |
| Vivid Chopstick Traders | |
| Unusual Doorbell Company | |
| Excellent Utensil Corporation | |
| Fascinating Oven Supply | |
| Savory Glass Inc. | |
| Superior Bobsled Corporation | |
| Steadfast Meter Inc. | |
| Sure Yardstick Corporation | |
| Magnificent Linen Partners | |
| Brilliant Chopstick Company | |
| Different Scooter Supply | |
| Mouthwatering Clipboard Corporation | |
| New Gadget Company | |
| Appealing Opener Partners | |
| Trouble-Free Bottle Inc. | |
| Wonderful Opener Supply | |
| Modular Tuner Corporation | |
| Magnificent Doghouse Inc. | |
| Stunning Freezer Inc. | |

**TIP FROM**

> Even though you have an existing Module1 with your code, Excel chooses to record the new macro into a new module. You therefore need to copy recorded code from Module2 and then use the Project Explorer to switch to Module1 to paste the code into your macro.

Even though the Advanced Filter dialog is still one of the most complicated facets of Excel 2007, the recorded macro is remarkably simple:

```
Sub Macro1()
'
' Macro1 Macro
'

'
    Range("A1:A1001").AdvancedFilter Action:=xlFilterCopy, CopyToRange:=Range( _
        "H1"), Unique:=True
    Range("H1").Select
End Sub
```

In your macro, there is no reason to select Cell H1, so you can delete that line of code. The remaining problem is that the macro recorder hard-coded that today's dataset contains 1,000 rows. You might want to generalize this to handle any number of rows. The follow code reflects these changes:

```
FinalRow = Range("A65536").End(xlUp).Row
Range("A1:A" & FinalRow) .AdvancedFilter Action:=xlFilterCopy, _
    CopyToRange:=Range("H1"), Unique:=True
```

## USING AUTOFILTER

When you have a list of customers, the macro will loop through each customer. The goal is to use an AutoFilter to display only the records for each particular customer. You now need to finish this section of code:

```
' Loop through each customer
For x = 2 To FinalCust
    ' Turn on the AutoFilter for this customer
    ' ???
```

To apply an AutoFilter to this section of code, follow these steps:

1. On the Developer tab, choose Record Macro.
2. On the Home tab, choose the icon Sort & Filter – Filter. Drop-down arrows are turned on for each field.
3. In the drop-down in Cell A1, uncheck Select All and then check Hip Lawn Corporation.
4. Back on the Developer tab, stop recording the macro.
5. Use the Macros button to locate and edit Macro2 as follows:

```
Sub Macro2()
'
' Macro2 Macro
'

'
    Range("A2").Select
    Application.CutCopyMode = False
    Selection.AutoFilter
    Selection.AutoFilter Field:=1, Criteria1:="Hip Lawn Corporation"
End Sub
```

The macro recorder always does too much selecting. You rarely have to select something before you can operate on it. You can theorize that the only line of this macro that matters is the `Selection.AutoFilter` line. Because you will always be looking at the AutoFilter drop-down in Cell A1, you can replace `Selection` with `Range("A1")`. Rather than continually ask for one specific customer, you can replace the end of the line with a reference to a cell in Column H:

```
Range("A1").AutoFilter Field:=1, Criteria1:=Cells(x, 8).Value
```

## SELECTING VISIBLE CELLS ONLY

After you use the AutoFilter in the macro, you see only records for one customer. However, as you can see in Figure 36.36, the other records are still there; they are just hidden. If you copied the range to a new worksheet, all the hidden rows would come along, and you would end up with 20 copies of your entire dataset.

**Figure 36.36**
If you copy this range
to a new worksheet,
the hidden rows copy
as well.

| ◢ | A | B |
|---|---|---|
| 1 | **Customer** | 🔽 **Invoi** 🔽 |
| 2 | Hip Lawn Corporation | 1001 |
| 6 | Hip Lawn Corporation | 1005 |
| 10 | Hip Lawn Corporation | 1009 |
| 14 | Hip Lawn Corporation | 1013 |
| 60 | Hip Lawn Corporation | 1059 |

The long way to select visible cells only is to press F5 to display the GoTo dialog. In the GoTo dialog, you click the Special button and then click Visible Cells Only. The shortcut, however, is to simply press Alt+;.

In order to learn how to select visible cells only in VBA, record the macro by following these steps:

1. Select the data in Columns A through F.

2. Turn on the macro recorder and press Alt+;.

3. Stop the macro recorder. You should see that the recorded macro has just one line of code:

```
Sub Macro5()
'
' Macro5 Macro
'


    Selection.SpecialCells(xlCellTypeVisible).Select
End Sub
```

In your original outline of the macro, you had contemplated selecting visible cells only and then doing the copy in another statement, like this:

```
' In the original workbook, select visible cells
' ???

' Copy the selection to the new workbook
Selection.Copy Destination:=WSN.Cells(3, 1)
```

Instead, simply copy the visible cells in one statement:

```
' In the original workbook, select visible cells
WSO.Range("A1:F" & FinalRow).SpecialCells(xlCellTypeVisible).Copy _
    Destination:=WSN.Cells(3, 1)
```

## THE COMBINATION MACRO EXAMPLE: PUTTING IT ALL TOGETHER

The following macro started as a bunch of comments and a skeleton of a loop:

```
Sub ProduceReportForEachCustomerFinished()
    ' Define object variables for new workbook
    Dim WBN As Workbook
    Dim WSN As Worksheet
    ' Define object variables for the current workbook
    Dim WBO As Workbook
    Dim WSO As Worksheet
    Set WBO = ActiveWorkbook
    Set WSO = ActiveSheet

    ' Find the FinalRow in today's dataset
```

```
        FinalRow = Range("A60000").End(xlUp).Row

        ' Use an Advanced filter to copy unique customers
        ' from column A to column H
        Range("A1:A" & FinalRow).AdvancedFilter Action:=xlFilterCopy, _
            CopyToRange:=Range("H1"), Unique:=True

        'Find the final customer in column H
        FinalCust = Range("H1").End(xlDown).Row

        ' Loop through each customer
        For x = 2 To FinalCust
            ' Turn on the AutoFilter for this customer
            Range("A1").AutoFilter Field:=1, Criteria1:=Cells(x, 8).Value

            ' Create a new workbook
            Set WBN = Workbooks.Add
            Set WSN = WBN.Worksheets(1)

            ' In the original workbook, select visible cells
            WSO.Range("A1:F" & FinalRow).SpecialCells(xlCellTypeVisible).Copy _
                Destination:=WSN.Cells(3, 1)

            ' AutoFit columns in the new workbook
            WSN.Columns.AutoFit

            ' Add a title to the new workbook
            WSN.Range("A1").Value = "Recap of Purchases for " & WSN.Cells(4, 1).Value

            ' Save the new book
            WBN.SaveAs Filename:="C:\" & WSN.Cells(4, 1).Value & ".xls"
            WBN.Close SaveChanges:=False

            'Return to the original workbook
            WBO.Activate
            WBN.Select
        Next x


End Sub
```

After doing three small tests with the macro recorder, you were able to fill in the sections to actually copy the customer records to a new workbook. After running this macro, you should have a new workbook for each customer on your hard drive, ready to be distributed via email.

# CONCLUSION

VBA macros open up a wide possibility of automation for Excel worksheets. Any time that you are faced with a daunting, mindless task, you can turn it into a challenging exercise by trying to design a macro to do the task instead. It usually takes less time to design a macro than it does to complete the task. You should save every macro you write. Soon you will have a library of macros that handle many common tasks, and they will allow you to develop macros faster. The next time you need to perform a similar task, you can roll out the macro and perform the steps in seconds instead of hours.

# CHAPTER 37

# INTERACTING WITH OTHER OFFICE APPLICATIONS

## In this chapter

After authoring a worksheet in Excel, you might need to include its information in a PowerPoint presentation or a Word document. Or you might want to add portions of your spreadsheet in your OneNote workbook (assuming that your version came with OneNote). The collaborative nature of Office 2007 applications allow you to do this with ease.

Although the core Office 2007 applications offer themes and the new ribbon interface, they still do not play perfectly well together. The Microsoft marketing machine would have you believe that themes are designed to make all your documents, from Excel to Word to PowerPoint, look similar. However, after data is been pasted from Excel to another application, changes to the theme do not carry through. I would expect this will be one of the areas that Microsoft works on for Office 14.

In certain cases, you can utilize Excel data without ever opening the Excel file. If you have a list of addresses in Excel, you can access that list when doing a mail merge in Microsoft Word 2007. Excel can receive data from other Office applications. For example, you might author body copy in Word and then copy it to a text box in Excel. Data from Access can also be used as the source data for an external query in Excel or even for a pivot table.

# PASTING EXCEL DATA TO MICROSOFT ONENOTE

Microsoft OneNote 2007 is being bundled as part of Microsoft Office 2007 for the Student and Home editions. This product was introduced in Office 2003 but was never bundled with any version of Office. It is a fantastic product but a product that not many people were willing to spend $99 to buy. Now that OneNote is bundled with some versions of Office, it will finally get the exposure needed to allow more people to gravitate toward its ability to organize notes in one place.

In the initial release of OneNote, the ability to present tabular data was dismal. OneNote 2007 finally does an adequate job of presenting tabular data from Excel. OneNote offers several formatting options to choose from after pasting Excel data to OneNote. These options are contrasted here.

Figure 37.1 shows a region in an Excel worksheet that has been formatted with various built-in styles.

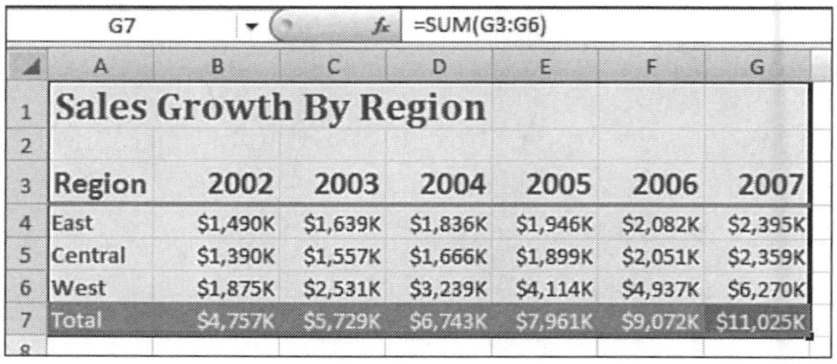

**Figure 37.1**
You select a region of the worksheet that you would like to copy to OneNote.

| | G7 | | $f_x$ | =SUM(G3:G6) | | |
| --- | --- | --- | --- | --- | --- | --- |
| | A | B | C | D | E | F | G |
| 1 | Sales Growth By Region | | | | | | |
| 2 | | | | | | | |
| 3 | Region | 2002 | 2003 | 2004 | 2005 | 2006 | 2007 |
| 4 | East | $1,490K | $1,639K | $1,836K | $1,946K | $2,082K | $2,395K |
| 5 | Central | $1,390K | $1,557K | $1,666K | $1,899K | $2,051K | $2,359K |
| 6 | West | $1,875K | $2,531K | $3,239K | $4,114K | $4,937K | $6,270K |
| 7 | Total | $4,757K | $5,729K | $6,743K | $7,961K | $9,072K | $11,025K |

To copy an Excel region to OneNote, you follow these steps:

1. Select the range in Excel.
2. Press Ctrl+C to copy the selected range to the Clipboard.
3. Switch to Microsoft OneNote 2007.
4. Click in the approximate location where you would like the data to be pasted.
5. Use Edit, Paste or Ctrl+V to paste the data. A Paste Options drop-down appears to the right of the pasted range.
6. Click the arrow next to the Paste Options drop-down. The choices follow:
   - **Keep Source Formatting:** This option is shown in Figure 37.2. The color fills are not present, and the word wrap from the former Cell A1 is a little bizarre, but you still see the basic look and feel of the worksheet.
   - **Match Destination Formatting:** Figure 37.3 shows the results of choosing Match Destination Formatting from the Paste Options drop-down. All the fonts are pasted at the same size and color.
   - **Keep Text Only:** This option generally looks horrible with data from Excel. It should be avoided.
   - **Paste as Picture:** This option keeps the exact look of the document from Excel, including the color fills, as shown in Figure 37.4. The only problem with this format is that you cannot use the clipboard to copy numbers from the picture.
7. Choose one of the options from the drop-down to complete the paste.

**Figure 37.2**
When Keep Source Formatting is selected, the text colors and sizes are pasted from Excel.

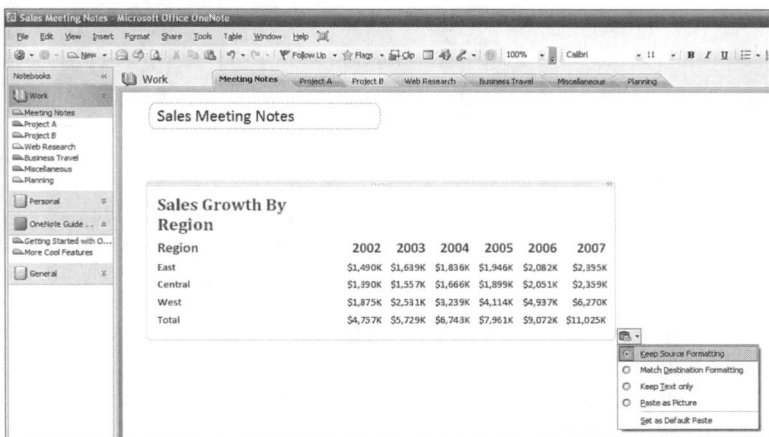

37

**Figure 37.3**
When Match Destination Formatting is selected, the text colors are kept, but the sizes are made uniform to match the current font size.

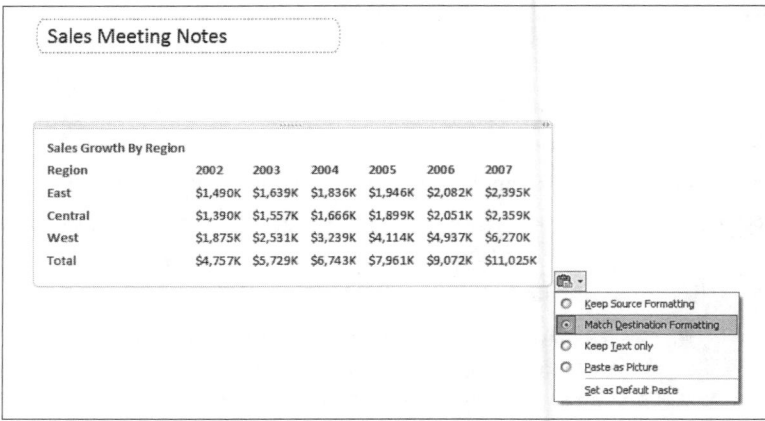

**Figure 37.4**
Convert the pasted selection to a table to produce an exact representation of the formatting from Excel.

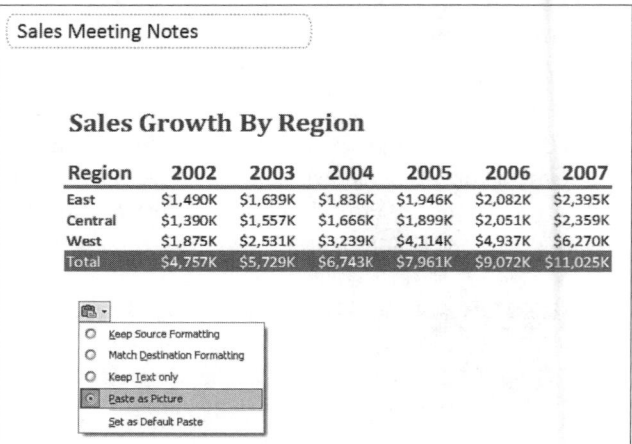

The final option in OneNote is to create a screen clipping to be pasted to OneNote. This option produces an exact screen capture of a region of the worksheet. To do this, you follow these steps:

1. In Excel, arrange the window so that you can see all the data and elements that need to be copied to OneNote.

2. Switch to OneNote. (Do not stop at any other applications first because the screen clipping utility goes to the last application window active before the command.) Position the cursor at a point where you would like the screen clipping to be pasted.

3. Select Insert, Screen Clipping. The OneNote window is hidden, and you see a grayed-out rendering of the last active application.

4. Using your mouse, drag a rectangle around the area you want to copy. As you drag, the rectangular area switches from grayed out to color, as shown in Figure 37.5.

5. When you release the mouse, the screen clipping is transferred to OneNote. OneNote adds a footer indicating the date and time of the clipping.

**Figure 37.5**
After invoking screen clipping from OneNote, you draw a rectangle to indicate the area to be copied.

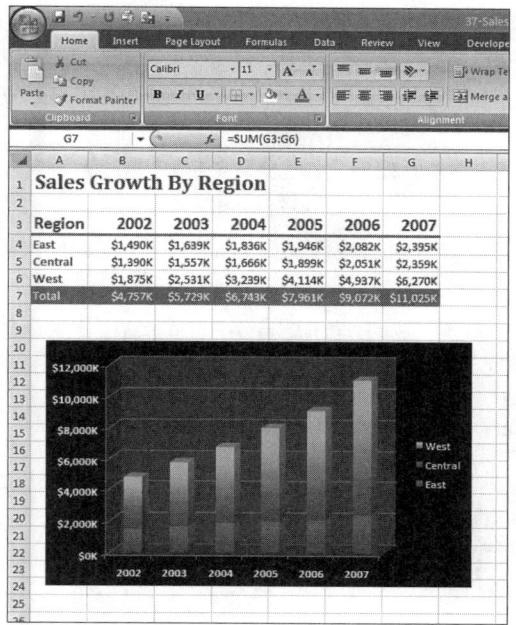

Support for tables has dramatically improved in OneNote 2007. Whereas pasting Excel tables to OneNote 2003 was disappointing, there are now three viable options for pasting Excel data to OneNote.

# PASTING EXCEL DATA TO POWERPOINT

The process of copying data from Excel to PowerPoint is simpler in Excel 2007 than in previous versions.

By default, if you copy a range and paste to PowerPoint, the range is pasted in HTML format. This means that none of the formulas are live.

In prior versions of Office, Excel data was pasted to PowerPoint as an Excel object. This meant that even if you pasted 20 cells, the entire workbook was lurking behind the 20 cells and accessible to anyone who could open the PowerPoint file.

## USING EXCEL TABLES IN POWERPOINT

To copy data from Excel to PowerPoint, you follow these steps:

1. Prepare a blank slide in PowerPoint that is ready to accept the data from Excel.
2. Open the desired Excel workbook.
3. Select the range to be copied.
4. Press Ctrl+C to copy the selected range.
5. Switch back to PowerPoint.

6. From the Home ribbon, choose Paste.

7. If some columns are not wide enough after the paste (see Figure 37.6), resize the table to be slightly larger and drag the column borders to allow the contents to fit.

**Figure 37.6**
Tables might need to be resized after being pasted to PowerPoint.

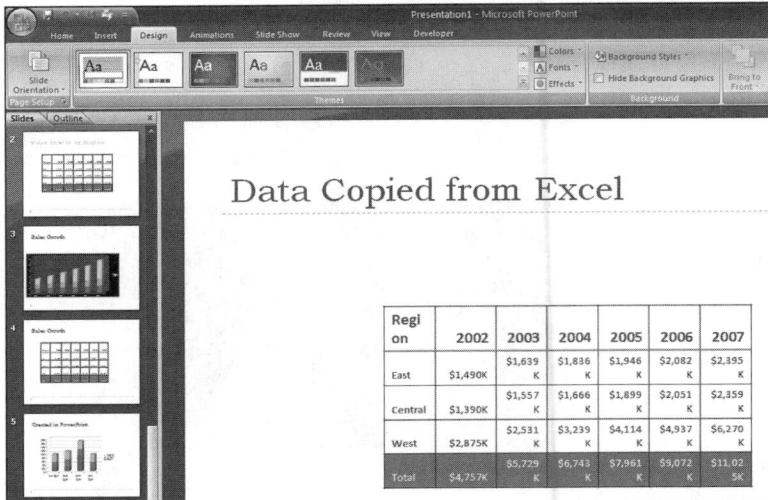

This method uses the default paste method, which is now Paste as HTML. If you instead prefer to go back to the old method, you choose Paste, Paste Special, Microsoft Office Excel Worksheet Object.

CAUTION

The data in a table is not affected by changes to the theme on the Design tab in PowerPoint. This seems to be a massive oversight on Microsoft's part.

## USING EXCEL CHARTS IN POWERPOINT

The process of copying charts from Excel to PowerPoint works much better than the process of copying tables from Excel. The resulting chart is completely editable in PowerPoint. In addition, changes to the slide theme change the look and feel of the chart.

To copy a chart to PowerPoint, you follow these steps:

1. Prepare a blank slide in PowerPoint that is ready to accept the data from Excel.

2. Open the desired Excel workbook.

3. Select the chart to be copied.

4. Press Ctrl+C to copy the selected chart.

5. Switch back to PowerPoint.

6. From the Home ribbon, choose Paste.

As shown in Figure 37.7, the chart is pasted to the slide. You can resize the chart to fill the area on the slide.

**Figure 37.7**
Charts pasted into PowerPoint have the same look and feel as in Excel, as well as the same user interface tabs on the ribbon.

37

When the chart is selected in PowerPoint, three new ribbon tabs offer the same chart experience as is available in Excel.

# CREATING TABLES IN EXCEL AND PASTING TO WORD

Microsoft Word is excellent for typing body text. When you need to start creating tables in Word, however, the program is a bit confusing. If you are more comfortable with Excel than Word, it makes sense to switch to Excel, create and format a table, and then paste the table back to the Word document. This gives you better control over column widths, plus the possibility to provide formulas for calculating some of the content of the table.

To create a table for Word, using Excel, you follow these steps:

1. Position the insertion cursor in Word at a point where the table should go.
2. Switch to Excel and open a blank document.
3. Type the data in columns in Excel.
4. If you use formulas to build rows of the table, it is best to convert the formulas to values before copying to Word. To do so, select the formulas and press Ctrl+C to copy. Then select Home, Paste, Paste Values.
5. If you have chosen a theme in Word, choose the identical theme in Excel.
6. Select the table and then select the Cells section of the Home ribbon and choose Format, Width, AutoFit Selection.

7. Optionally, apply a table format as shown in Chapter 8.

8. Select the table in Excel and then press Ctrl+C to copy.

9. Switch to Word.

10. From the Home ribbon, choose Paste. An HTML representation of the table is pasted into Word. The column widths, alignment, font, font color, and fill copy perfectly from Excel, as shown in Figure 37.8.

**Figure 37.8**
An Excel range copied to Word builds a perfect table, with all the right column widths.

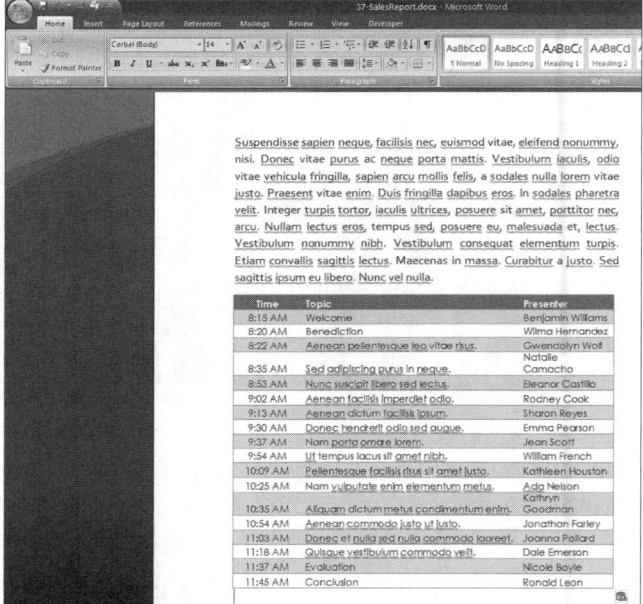

# PASTING WORD DATA TO AN EXCEL TEXT BOX

Although Excel is great at handling tables of numbers, it does not have the editing tools needed to make it easy to handle body copy as well as in Word. If you want to be able to type paragraphs of text without needing to judge the length of each line, you should use Word to prepare the text and then paste it to a text box in Excel. You can follow these steps to build a section of body copy for use in Excel:

1. Switch to Microsoft Word and open a blank document.

2. Type the text. Use any formatting you like, such as underlining, bold, italics, font size, font changes, and so on.

3. Select the text in Word.

4. Press Ctrl+C to copy the selected text.

5. Switch to Excel.

6. On the Insert ribbon, choose Text, Text Box.

7. Drag in the worksheet to define the shape of the text box.

8. When you release the mouse, the insertion point is at the start of the text box. Press Ctrl+V to paste.

9. By default, text boxes have a visible border. To remove the border, select Drawing Tools Format, Shape Styles, Shape Outline, No Outline.

10. If you need to resize or further format the text, select the text in the text box. The mini toolbar appears. If desired, change font size, style, and so on.

If you need to fine-tune the text box, follow these steps:

1. Click outside the text box.

2. Right-click the text box and choose Format Shape. The Format Shape dialog appears.

3. In the Format Shape dialog, select the Text Box category.

4. Select an internal margin, select text alignment, add columns, or resize the shape to fit the text, as shown in Figure 37.9.

**Figure 37.9**
After copying Word text to a text box, you can use the formatting tools to fine-tune the text box.

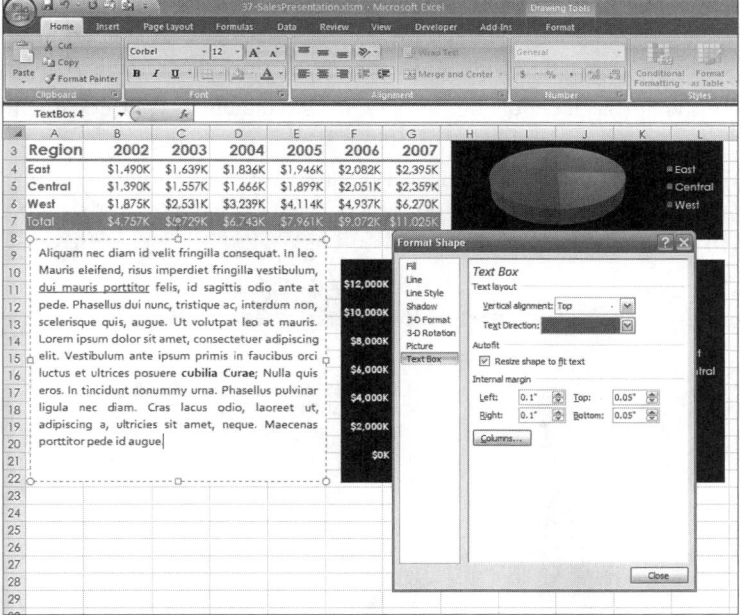

# USING EXCEL DATA IN A WORD MAIL MERGE

Word's mail merge tools allow you to create a printed form letter that is customized to each person in an Excel list of names. For the best results, your Excel table should include columns for first name, last name, address line 1, address line 2, city, state or province, and zip or postal code.

You follow these steps to perform a mail merge in Word using Excel data:

1. Prepare your data in Excel. Include headings for each column. Do not include any blank columns or entirely blank rows.

2. To simplify the mail merge, select the range and press Ctrl+T to convert the range to a table. Be sure to specify that the table has headers.

3. Save and close the Excel workbook.

4. Open Microsoft Word.

5. Leave a few blank lines at the top for the address block and greeting.

6. Type the rest of the letter.

7. Choose Mailings, Start Mail Merge, Start Mail Merge, Step by Step Mail Merge. A Mail Merge task pane appears on the right side of the screen.

8. By default, Step 1 of the task pane indicates that you are producing a letter. At the bottom of the task pane, click the hyperlink for Next.

9. In Step 2 of the task pane, choose to use the current document. Click Next.

10. In Step 3 of the task pane, choose Use an Existing List and then choose Select List. The Select Data Source dialog appears.

11. Browse to your Excel file and click Open. The Select Table dialog appears.

12. In the Select Table dialog, Word selects the table in your document. Click OK to confirm. Word displays the Mail Merge Recipients dialog.

13. If desired, choose to filter or sort the list, as shown in Figure 37.10. Click OK to continue.

**Figure 37.10**
You preview the records from Excel in this dialog.

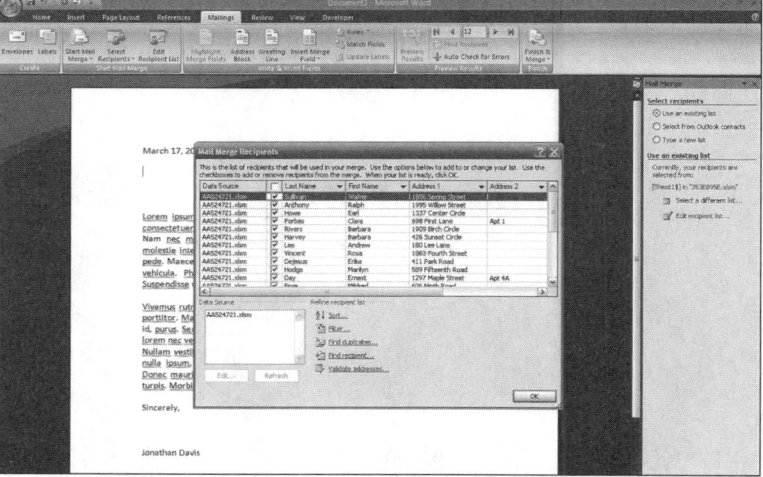

14. In the Mail Merge taskbar, click Next.

15. In Step 4 of the task pane, the instructions say to write your letter. This is the step where you insert placeholders from the Excel file. In the Mailings ribbon, choose Write & Insert Fields, Match Fields. The Match Fields dialog appears.

16. Depending on your headings, the IntelliSense might match your headings to the proper fields. Browse through the fields to make sure all your fields have been matched. If you know that there is a field in your Excel file that does not appear on the right side of the Match Fields dialog, use the drop-down to map the Excel column to the proper field in Word, as shown in Figure 37.11. Word has categories for items that you might not have included in your data. It is okay if you don't have a match for every possible Word field. However, make sure that Word knows about every field in your data.

**Figure 37.11**
Before attempting to insert fields, make sure that Word has correctly identified any name or address fields in your data.

17. Position the insertion cursor where the address block should go. In the Mailings ribbon, click Address Block. Excel displays the Insert Address Block dialog. You can preview the various addresses here. If there are problems, use the Match Fields dialog to rematch the fields.

18. Click OK to close the Insert Address Block dialog. Words adds a field code to your document that looks like <<AddressBlock>>. The insertion point remains on the same line as the address block, so press Enter to move to the next line.

19. From the Mailings ribbon, choose Greeting Line. In the Insert Greeting Line dialog that appears, build your greeting line. The three drop-downs allow you to specify "Dear" or "To," various forms of the person's name, and a comma or a colon. Click OK.

20. If desired, include fields from the Excel file in the body of your letter. For example, a marketing letter might refer to the person's city in the body of the letter. Position the cursor at the appropriate place in the letter. From the ribbon, choose the Insert Merge Field drop-down. From the list, select the appropriate field from the Excel file.

21. In the Mail Merge task pane, select Next to proceed to Step 5 of the task pane.

22. In Step 5 of the task pane, Word previews the letter for the first recipient. You can format the address block at this point. You can also use the >> button on the taskbar to browse through the names.

**23.** In the task pane, click Next.

**24.** In Step 6 of the task pane, choose to print or edit individual letters, if needed. If you choose Print, Word sends one letter to the printer for each row in your Excel list. If you choose Edit Individual Letters, Excel creates a new document with a new page for each document.

Using Mail Merge in Word is a quick way to send customized letters to many recipients at once. The Mailings toolbar has options for creating envelopes and mailing labels as well. The steps for both of these document types are similar to those just provided for mail merges.

# BUILDING A PIVOT TABLE FROM ACCESS QUERIES

Microsoft Access is the database component of Microsoft Office. It is included in the Professional versions of Office 2007 but not with the Home edition of Microsoft Office.

Before Excel 2007, many people occasionally encountered Access when they had more than 65,536 rows of data. Now that Excel can handle 1.1 million rows, there will be less casual use of Access.

Access is a relational database. This means that relationships can be defined between multiple tables, and these tables can be joined together in a query. In Figure 37.12, a query is defined in Access to join two tables together. Calculated fields can calculate values from fields in each table.

**Figure 37.12**
This query joins
multiple Access tables.

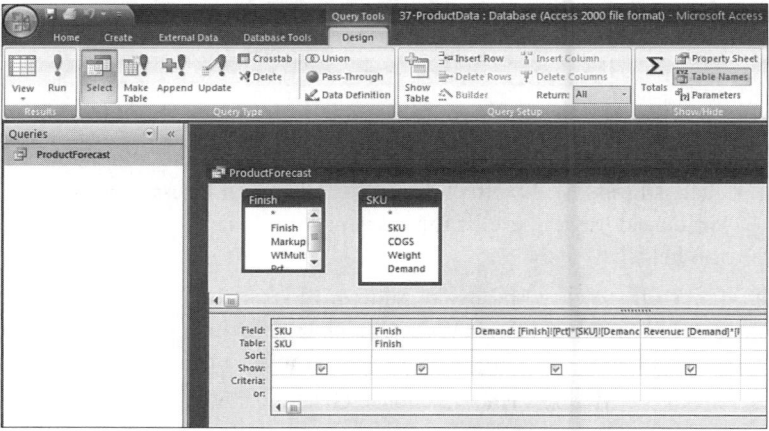

To use this data in an Excel pivot table, you follow these steps:

**1.** Ensure that the Access database is saved in a trusted location. If you are unsure of trusted locations, choose the Office icon and then select Excel Options, Trust Center, Trust Center Settings, Trusted Locations. If the location of the Access database is not in the list of trusted locations, choose Add New Location.

**2.** In Excel, choose Insert, Tables, PivotTable. The Create Pivot Table dialog appears.

**3.** In the Create Pivot Table dialog, choose Use an External Data Source.

**4.** Click the Choose Connection button. The Existing Connections dialog appears.

5. In the Existing Connections dialog, click Browse for More.

6. Browse to and select your database. Click Open. The Select Table dialog appears.

7. As shown in Figure 37.13, the Select Table dialog offers all the available tables and views in the Access database. Note that queries in Access are shown as views. Click the desired view and click OK.

**Figure 37.13**
Excel shows a list of available tables and queries.

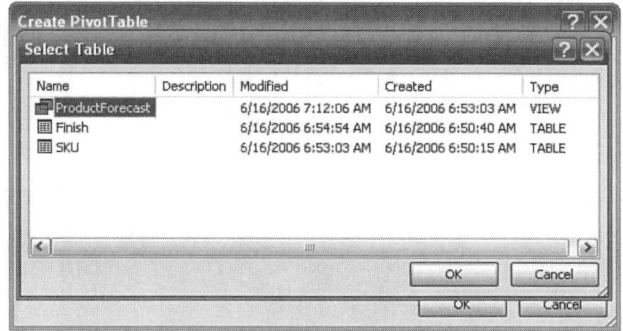

8. Click OK to create the pivot table. The Access data is now available for querying. You can choose pivot table fields as described in Chapter 10, "Using Pivot Tables to Analyze Data."

The advantage of this method is that the data never has to be copied to Excel. In this case, two relatively small Access tables are joined into a larger query result. As shown in Figure 37.14, the pivot table presents results from the query without having to store the detailed data in Excel.

**Figure 37.14**
This pivot table creates a summary from thousands of virtual rows of data in Access without ever storing that data in the workbook.

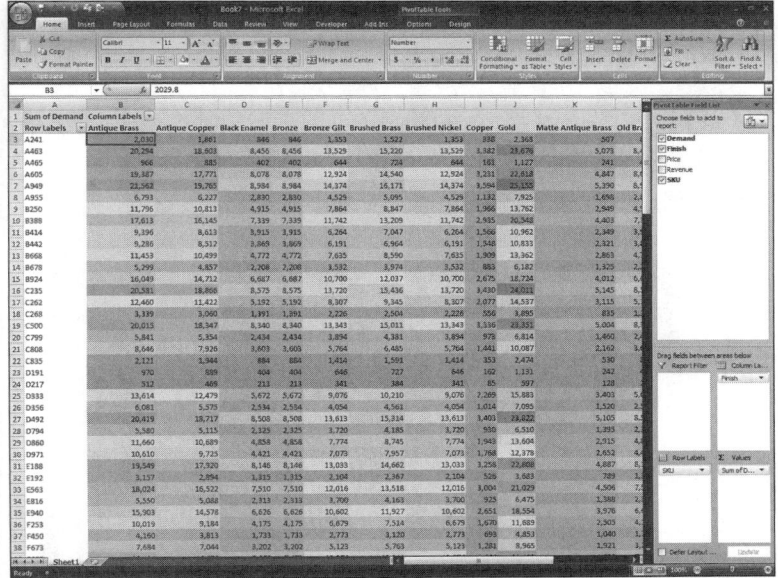

# CHAPTER 38

# A Tour of the Best Add-Ins for Excel

## In this chapter

Although Excel can do amazing things, it cannot do everything. There are plenty of niche industries that need more functions or more specialized operations than what is available in Excel.

Sometimes, someone recognizes a common need. After seeing dozens of questions in Excel newsgroups about converting uppercase to lowercase, for example, a developer might offer an add-in to make that task easier than the current five-step process.

Literally thousands of add-ins are available for Excel. Many are being rewritten to be compliant with Excel 2007. This chapter is by no means a comprehensive list of add-ins available, but it contains some of my favorites.

## CUSTOMIZING THE RIBBON BY USING CUSTOMIZERIBBON

Whereas it was extremely easy to customize the menus in Excel 2003, it is nearly impossible to do so in Excel 2007. You have to be a developer who can work with Ribbon XML in order to customize the ribbons.

Patrick Schmid wrote the must-have solution for any normal person who wants to customize the ribbons. His COM add-in adds a CustomizeRibbon icon to the View tab. You can then use CustomizeRibbon to add new groups to any ribbon tab or even add a new tab to the ribbon (see Figure 38.1).

**Figure 38.1**
You can customize Excel's ribbons by using Patrick Schmid's CustomizeRibbon add-in.

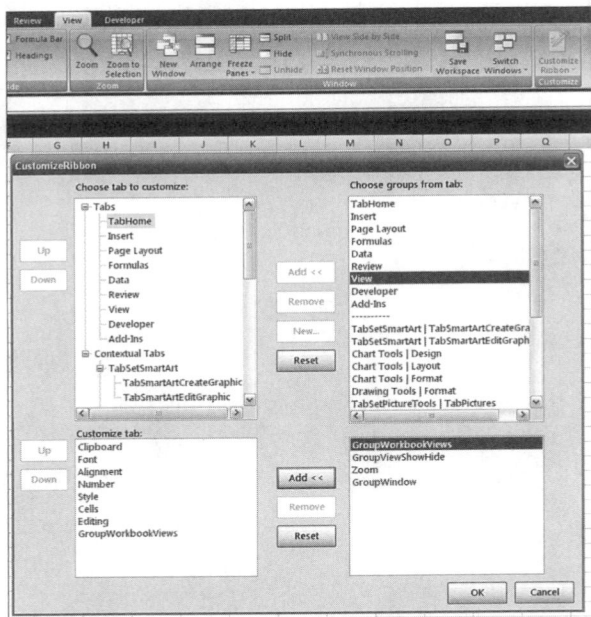

Patrick plans to offer a limited freeware version and a more powerful version for sale. You can download or purchase Patrick's add-in from http://pschmid.net.

# LOADING PDF DATA TO EXCEL BY USING ABLE2EXTRACT

People love sending data in PDF files. Now that Microsoft is providing a PDF creation utility, more and more documents will be emailed via PDF.

The authors of PDF documents often use PDF format to ensure that the data cannot be altered. Other times, the authors want to make sure that someone who does not have Excel can still view the data. Although these are fine ideas, getting data back out of PDF and into Excel is very difficult.

Data copied and pasted from PDF to Excel usually loses its columnar format. Able2Extract solves this problem. You simply open a PDF file in Able2Extract, and you can convert the contained data to Excel with one click. Or, if you need absolute control, you can specify regions so that, for example, titles and headers beyond page 1 are not imported.

There are some PDF files out there where the entire document is a scanned image of the original file. The Professional version of Able2Extract can even deal with these.

You can download a free trial version of Able2Extract from www.investintech.com/able2extract.html.

# DOING ACCESS WITH EXCEL BY USING DIGDB

The most amazing add-in for Excel is DigDB from Data Instrument Group. Data Instrument has taken all the difficult database operations you might ever want to do and made them possible in Excel. Now that you might be dealing with 1.1 million rows in Excel 2007, these functions will be especially important.

DigDB offers more than 40 new functions in Excel. The following is a partial list:

- Use Access-like queries, joins, and aggregates in Excel
- Perform roll-ups, which are better than pivot tables, including the Median function
- Match tables, including a fuzzy match
- Count/extract unique values in a range
- Combine columns
- Insert, delete, and copy select by row intervals
- Fill blank cells in a range by interpolating
- Extract valid emails from a range
- Transpose a cross table to a list

You can download a free trial of DigDB from www.digdb.com.

38

# CREATING DASHBOARDS BY USING SPEEDOMETER CHART CREATOR

When executive dashboards became the rage, many people wanted to take the term literally and offer a series of speedometer charts on their dashboards. The circular chart shown in Figure 38.2, created using Speedometer Chart Creator from Mala Singh, has various colors around the perimeter of the speedometer. A pointer indicates today's value, and an alternate pointer shows yesterday's value, so you can see whether there has been improvement.

**Figure 38.2**
You can create dashboards by using the Speedometer Chart Creator from Mala Singh.

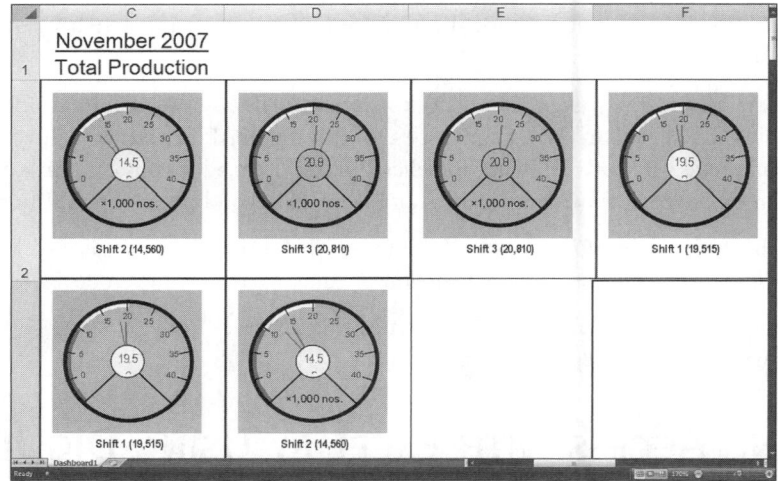

To purchase the speedometer chart creator, visit www.mrexcel.com/speedometer.html.

# ACCESSING MORE FUNCTIONS BY USING MoreFunc.dll

MVP Laurent Longre offers a free Excel add-in that has 66 new functions. Although some of the functions are specialized, there are great functions of use to many people using Excel. The following are just some of the new functions:

- LastRow—This function finds the last filled row in any column.
- PageNum—This function finds the page number of any cell.
- SheetName—This function finds the name of the current sheet.
- WordCount—This function finds the number of words in text.
- NBText—This function spells out a number as text in any of 13 languages.
- ISO.Weeknum—This function finds the ISO-compliant week number of a day.
- CountIf.3D—This function is the same as Countif but for 3-D references.

You can download the MoreFunc.dll for free from http://xcell05.free.fr/.

# Using Add-ins from AddIns.com

Bob Flanagan of Macro Systems has dozens of add-ins available at Add-Ins.com. The most famous of these add-in is Spreadsheet Assistant. This single add-in provides the ability to simplify dozens of tasks, including the following:

- Perform any math action on a range of cells.
- Adjust text with the Paragraph Fixer feature.
- Toggle AutoComplete on or off.
- Fill blanks with the entry above.
- Copy a sum to the Clipboard.
- Insert a sticky note.
- Change letter case.
- Freeze panes on multiple sheets.
- Use many new functions, such as `GrowthRate`, `LookForText`, `NumberToCurrency`, `DateInMonth`, `RemoveAllSpaces`, and `TrimLeft`.

In addition to Spreadsheet Assistant, Bob offers numerous other time-saving and specialty functions. Visit www.add-ins.com for more information.

38

# INDEX

## Symbols

######, 414

#DIV?0!, 414

#N/A!, 414

#REF!, 414

#VALUE!, 414

+ (plus sign), 397

## A

Able2Extract, loading PDF files to Excel, 1021

ABS(), 178, 452
figuring out magnitude of ERROR, 474-475

absolute cell references, 389-390

absolute reference formulas, preventing inadvertent creation of, 847-848

absolute references, 390

accepting hypothesis, 710-711

Access, building pivot tables from Access queries, 1016-1017

Access databases, connecting to, 812-813

accessing VBA Help, 985

ACCINTM, 624

ACCRINT, 624-625

ACOS, 736, 746

ACOSH, 736, 750

active fields, collapsing and expanding in pivot tables, 216-217

ad hoc reporting tools, filtering pivot tables, 251-252

Add Watch dialog, 427

add-ins
Able2Extract, 1021
CustomizeRibbon, 1020
DigDB, 1021
MoreFunc.dll, 1022-1023
Speedometer Chart Creator, 1022

Add-Ins ribbon, 30

adding
automatic subtotals, 962-964
AVERAGEIF() to conditional formulas, 444
background pictures, 955
blank rows to pivot tables, 222-223
borders to pictures, 356
cell comments, 919-920
clip art to worksheets, 360
columns, automatically, 139
commands to Quick Access toolbar, 43-45
comments to formulas (N), 542-543
complex numbers, 758
custom headers, 928-929
data, 315-316
data fields to value section (pivot tables), 224-227
digital signatures to workbooks, 958-959
drop lines to surface charts, 316-317
effects to pictures, 356-358
fields to pivot tables, 208-209
using formulas, 252-254
formulas to tables, 139-140
hyperlinks with HYPERLINK, 574-575
icons based on value, icon sets, 161-162
images to SmartArt, 338-339
items along dimensions (pivot tables), 255
calculated items, 256-257
grouping, 257-258

many names at once from existing labels and headings, 851-852
multiple scenarios, Scenario Manager, 872-874
numbers with status bar, 60-61
rows, automatically, 138-139
total rows to tables, 137-138
values when combining duplicates, 274-275
worksheets with New Sheet icon, 63

AddIns.com, 1023

addition, order of operations, 411-412

ADDRESS, 571

adjectives, comparing (VBA), 985-986

adjusting
column widths and row heights, 909-911
worksheet margins, 932-933
worksheet orientation, 933

Advanced Filter command, 284-285
formulas, 285-286
troubleshooting, 285

advanced filters, using for unique records, 1000-1002

adverbs, comparing to parameters (VBA), 983-985

Alert the User When a Potentially Time-Consuming Operation Occurs, 107

Align Right, 42

aligning cells, custom number format, 904-905

Alt shortcut, Excel 2003, 77

alternate calendar systems, 497

ampersand (&) operator, joining text, 505-506

# THIS BOOK IS SAFARI ENABLED

## INCLUDES FREE 45-DAY ACCESS TO THE ONLINE EDITION

The Safari® Enabled icon on the cover of your favorite technology book means the book is available through Safari Bookshelf. When you buy this book, you get free access to the online edition for 45 days.

Safari Bookshelf is an electronic reference library that lets you easily search thousands of technical books, find code samples, download chapters, and access technical information whenever and wherever you need it.

**TO GAIN 45-DAY SAFARI ENABLED ACCESS TO THIS BOOK:**

- Go to **http://www.quepublishing.com/safarienabled**
- Complete the brief registration form
- Enter the coupon code found in the front of this book on the "Copyright" page

If you have difficulty registering on Safari Bookshelf or accessing the online edition, please e-mail customer-service@safaribooksonline.com.

 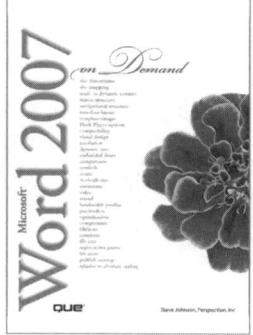